A HANDBOOK OF TRANSPORT ECONOMICS

T0330049

A Céline et Matthieu, mes deux enfants chéris

To Laura and Amanda

To Camille and to my children and grandchildren

To Chris and my growing family

A Handbook of
Transport Economics

Edited by

André de Palma

Ecole Normale Supérieure de Cachan, France

Robin Lindsey

University of British Columbia, Canada

Emile Quinet

Paris School of Economics, ENPC, Paris, France

Roger Vickerman

University of Kent, UK

Edward Elgar
Cheltenham, UK • Northampton, MA, USA

Published by
Edward Elgar Publishing Limited
The Lypiatts
15 Lansdown Road
Cheltenham
Glos GL50 2JA
UK

Edward Elgar Publishing, Inc.
William Pratt House
9 Dewey Court
Northampton
Massachusetts 01060
USA

A catalogue record for this book
is available from the British Library

Library of Congress Control Number: 2009941004

ISBN 978 1 84720 203 1 (cased)
ISBN 978 1 78347 285 7 (paperback)

Typeset by Servis Filmsetting Ltd, Stockport, Cheshire

Contents

PART IV   OPTIMAL PUBLIC DECISIONS

PART V   COMPETITION AND REGULATION

Editors and contributors

EDITORS

André de Palma
Ecole Normale Supérieure, Cachan, France
andre.depalma@ens-cachan.fr

Robin Lindsey
Sauder School of Business
The University of British Columbia, Canada
Robin.Lindsey@sauder.ubc.ca

Emile Quinet
Ecole des Ponts ParisTech and Paris School of Economics, France
quinet@enpc.fr

Roger Vickerman
The University of Kent, UK
R.W.Vickerman@kent.ac.uk

CONTRIBUTORS

Simon P. Anderson
University of Virginia, USA
sa9w@virginia.edu

Henrik Andersson
Toulouse School of Economics (UT1, CNRS, LERNA), France
henrik.andersson@tse-fr.eu

Richard Arnott
Department of Economics
University of California, Riverside, USA
richard.arnott@ucr.edu

Bekir Bartin
Department of Civil and Environmental Engineering
Rutgers University, USA
bbartin@rci.rutgers.edu

Leonardo J. Basso
Civil Engineering Department
Universidad de Chile, Chile
lbasso@ing.uchile.cl

Alberto Behar
Department of Economics
University of Oxford, UK
alberto.behar@economics.ox.ac.uk

Moshe Ben-Akiva
Civil and Environmental Engineering
Massachusetts Institute of Technology, USA
mba@mit.edu

Yossi Berechman
Department of Economics
The City College
The City University of New York, USA
jberechman@ccny.cuny.edu

Michel Beuthe
Group Transport & Mobility (GTM)
Louvain School of Management,
Catholic University of Mons (FUCAM), Belgium
michel.beuthe@fucam.ac.be

Chandra R. Bhat
Department of Civil, Architectural and Environmental Engineering
The University of Texas at Austin, USA
bhat@mail.utexas.edu

Johannes Bröcker
Institute for Regional Research
Kiel University, Germany
broecker@economics.uni-kiel.de

Mary R. Brooks
Dalhousie University, Canada
m.brooks@dal.ca

Kenneth Button
George Mason University, USA
kbutton@gmu.edu

Caspar G. Chorus
Section of Transport and Logistics
Delft University of Technology, The Netherlands
c.g.chorus@tudelft.nl

Joseph A. Clougherty
College of Business
University of Illinois at Urbana-Champaign, USA
jaclough@illinois.edu

Mark Delucchi
Institute of Transportation Studies
University of California, Davis, USA
madelucchi@ucdavis.edu

Antonio Estache
Universite Libre de Bruxelles and the European Center for Advanced Research in
  Economics and Statistics (ECARES), Belgium
aestache@ulb.ac.be

Mogens Fosgerau
Danish Institute for Transport Research, Denmark
mf@transport.dtu.dk

Rainer Friedrich
IER University of Stuttgart, Germany
rf@ier.uni-stuttgart.de

Philippe Gagnepain
Paris School of Economics-Université Paris 1, France
philippe.gagnepain@univ-paris1.fr

Jonathan L. Gifford
School of Public Policy
George Mason University, USA
jgifford@gmu.edu

David Gillen
Centre for Transportation Studies
Sauder School of Business
The University of British Columbia, Canada
david.gillen@sauder.ubc.ca

Daniel Graham
Department of Civil and Environmental Engineering
Imperial College, UK
d.j.graham@imperial.ac.uk

David A. Hensher
Institute of Transport and Logistics Studies, Faculty of Economics and Business
The University of Sydney, Australia
david.hensher@sydney.edu.au

Elisabetta Iossa
Brunel University, UK, and University of Tor Vergata, CMPO and EIEF, Italy
Elisabetta.Iossa@brunel.ac.uk

Marc Ivaldi
Toulouse School of Economics
University of Toulouse, France
Marc.ivaldi@tse-fr.eu

Sergio R. Jara-Díaz
Civil Engineering Department
Universidad de Chile, Chile
jaradiaz@ing.uchile.cl

Ellis Juan
Mexico Country Representative
Inter-American Development Bank, USA
ellisj@iadb.org

Yoshitsugu Kanemoto
Graduate School of Public Policy and Graduate School of Economics
University of Tokyo, Japan
kanemoto@e.u-tokyo.ac.jp

Miren Lafourcade
Université Paris-Sud 11 (ADIS) and Paris School of Economics, France
lafourcade@pse.ens.fr

James Laird
Institute for Transport Studies
University of Leeds, UK
j.j.laird@its.leeds.ac.uk

Don McCubbin
Institute of Transportation Studies
University of California, Davis, USA
dmccubbi@yahoo.com

Peter Mackie
Institute for Transport Studies
University of Leeds, UK
p.j.mackie@its.leeds.ac.uk

David Martimort
Paris School of Economics, France
martimor@cict.fr

Hilde Meersman
Department of Transport and Regional Economics
University of Antwerp, Belgium
hilde.meersman@ua.ac.be

Jean Mercenier
ERMES, Université Panthéon-Assas (Paris 2), France
Jean.Mercenier@u-paris2.fr

Catherine Muller-Vibes
Institut d'Economie Industrielle, Toulouse, France
catherinevibes@hotmail.com

Chris Nash
Institute for Transport Studies
University of Leeds, UK
c.a.nash@its.leeds.ac.uk

Tae Hoon Oum
Sauder School of Business, Vancouver, Canada
tae.oum@sauder.ubc.ca

Kaan Ozbay
Department of Civil and Environmental Engineering
Rutgers University, USA
kaan@rci.rutgers.edu

Abdul Rawoof Pinjari
Department of Civil and Environmental Engineering
University of South Florida, USA
Email: apinjari@usf.edu

Marco Ponti
Politecnico di Milano University, Italy
marco.ponti@polimi.it.

Stef Proost
Center for Economic Studies
KULeuven (B), Belgium
stef.proost@econ.kuleuven.be

Régis Renault
Université de Cergy Pontoise, France
Regis.renault@eco.u-cergy.fr

Piet Rietveld
Faculty of Economics
VU University, Amsterdam, The Netherlands
prietveld@feweb.vu.nl

Georgina Santos
School of City and Regional Planning
Cardiff University, UK
SantosG@Cardiff.ac.uk

Takatoshi Tabuchi
Department of Economics
University of Tokyo, Japan
ttabuchi@e.u-tokyo.ac.jp

Jacques-François Thisse
CORE, Université catholique de Louvain, Belgium, Ecole Nationale des Ponts et
    Chaussées, France and CEPR, UK
jacques.thisse@uclouvain.be

Harry J.P. Timmermans
Urban Planning Group
Eindhoven University of Technology, The Netherlands
h.j.p.timmermans@bwk.tue.nl

Alain Trannoy
EHESS, GREQAM-IDEP, France
Alain.trannoy@univmed.fr

Nicolas Treich
Toulouse School of Economics (INRA, LERNA)
Université Toulouse 1 Capitole, France
nicolas.treich@tse-fr.eu

Lourdes Trujillo
Universidad de Las Palmas de Gran Canaria, Spain
ltrujillo@daea.ulpgc.es

Eddy Van de Voorde
Department of Transport and Regional Economics
University of Antwerp, Belgium
eddy.vandevoorde@ua.ac.be

Thierry Vanelslander
Department of Transport and Regional Economics
University of Antwerp, Belgium
thierry.vanelslander@ua.ac.be

Anthony J. Venables
Department of Economics
University of Oxford, UK
tony.venables@economics.ox.ac.uk

Erik Verhoef
Department of Spatial Economics
VU University, Amsterdam, The Netherlands
everhoef@feweb.vu.nl

Joan L. Walker
Civil and Environmental Engineering
Global Metropolitan Studies
University of California at Berkeley, USA
joanwalker@berkeley.edu

William G. Waters II
Centre for Transportation Studies
Sauder School of Business
The University of British Columbia, Canada
william.waters@sauder.ubc.ca

Michael Wegener
Spiekermann & Wegener Urban and Regional Research (S&W), Germany
mw@spiekermann-wegener.de

Katsuhiro Yamaguchi
Graduate School of Public Policy
The University of Tokyo, Japan
yamaguchi@pp.u-tokyo.ac.jp

Ozlem Yanmaz-Tuzel
Department of Civil and Environmental Engineering
Rutgers University, USA
yanmaz@rci.rutgers.edu

Yuichiro Yoshida
National Graduate Institute for Policy Studies
Tokyo, Japan
yoshida@grips.ac.jp

Anming Zhang
Sauder School of Business
The University of British Columbia, Canada
anming.zhang@sauder.ubc.ca

Yimin Zhang
China Europe International Business School
Shanghai, China
zyimin@ceibs.edu

Foreword
Daniel McFadden

This *Handbook*, edited by de Palma, Lindsey, Quinet and Vickerman, is welcome for its novelty and originality. It is not the first handbook on transport; there are other excellent volumes that focus on the transport sector or on sub-sectors within transport. These handbooks tend to provide a synthesis of the subject from the different viewpoints of a range of disciplines including operational research, political science, engineering and management as well as economics. There are also handbooks which focus on particular branches of economics such as public economics, development economics and regional and urban economics. But no previous handbook has focussed so deliberately on the transport sector, through the lens of one discipline, economics. What justifies such an approach? One obvious, albeit rather simple, reason is that transport is a sector that presents a range of economic problems and has therefore been studied in great detail through economic analysis, as the editors stress in their introductory chapter.

However, two questions remain:

- First, is it possible to talk about an 'economics of transport' without considering the contribution of other disciplines?
- Second, is there a 'specific economics of transport' which lends itself to such particular attention?

The answer to the first question is relatively easy. In order to understand the application of economics to the transport sector, it is necessary to have a basic knowledge of the specific conditions which underlie activity in the sector. A simple expression of this is given through the knowledge that we all have as users of transport. For example, we know the distinction between infrastructure and operations, we know that most airports are located outside cities because land is cheaper there, noise is less of a nuisance and so on. In order to understand these functions and the problems they pose, the editors appropriately recommend that readers start with their own textbook '*Principles of Transport Economics*' to which this *Handbook* represents a logical extension.

My opinion, which is shared implicitly by the editors, is that the economics of transport are fundamentally problems of economics, but applied to a particular sector which has some very specific characteristics. From where does that specificity arise? It can be identified in terms of the numerical values of parameters such as the incidence of scale economies, or the environmental costs imposed by different modes of transport, or the incidence of a particular form of organization such as the oligopoly structures found in airline competition or the public–private partnerships often found for the provision of infrastructure. Transport does not require a unique economics based on paradigms and mechanisms that differ from other sectors of the economy. But transport is characterized by certain specific features.

The first of these specific characteristics is the role of space. Transport is necessary because activities are spatially separated and this separation affects the economic analysis: it creates variable rents for land, it changes the laws of competition and it generates spatial inequalities. The role of transport in the structuring of space is an important issue in policy towards land use. Progress has been made in recent years in understanding the links between transport and land use, notably through the 'new economic geography' following the pathbreaking work of Paul Krugman. The *Handbook* deals with these new advances in detail and explains their significance. But this area still remains tentative and incomplete, particularly in terms of its dynamics, the time lags involved, and the importance of public policy decisions affecting it. All of these combine to create new problems for us to solve.

The second specific characteristic is time. First, spatial separation implies that time is needed to travel. The use of time was first modeled in detail by Gary Becker. Becker treated time as an attribute of all consumption, not just transport, but transport is a sector where time has a particularly important role especially when reliability and comfort are considered. Second, since transport is consumed as it is produced, the choice of when to travel is a key factor in the use of transport. Following the initial work of William Vickrey, there has been considerable research on modeling trip-timing decisions, including work by the editors of this *Handbook*, which contributes to the literature on dynamic models. Third, time, and especially long periods of time counted in years or decades, arises because of the durability of transport infrastructure and the mobile plant which uses it. These long time periods complicate investment decisions. A fourth aspect related to time is the problem of scheduling and pricing of transport services by suppliers. This encompasses not only commonplace tasks such as designing bus timetables but also the use of ITS technology such as yield management software which is routinely used to allocate seats on planes and trains, but can also be used to allocate hotel rooms, hospital beds and facilities in other sectors of the economy.

The third characteristic of transport economics is the multiplicity of decisions that have to be made: choice of destination, transport mode, departure time and route, as well as long-run decisions such as residential location, workplace and vehicle ownership. Most of these choices are discrete. The theory of discrete choice, which I developed in my own research, has become a workhorse not only in transportation but also in many other areas such as industrial organization and marketing. This theory is particularly useful for taking into account the fact that decisions relating to transport are part of a much wider set of decisions relating to the choices between a range of activities, or to the sequential decisions determined by experience or memory, all filtered by psychological attitudes. The diagram below suggests a structure for analysis of these decisions which provides a basis for the way research is developing. It suggests how the development of discrete choice models has led researchers to explore types of behavior which are omitted from the traditional theory of rational behavior under perfect information. The decision maker in our models is far from being fully rational and responds to stimuli usually studied by psychologists. Curiously enough, a parallel development has occurred in the study of risk, which has abandoned the use of models based on expected utility in favor of models which allow for perception bias and the asymmetry of gains and losses. Moreover, there are further parallels with the theory of behavior in an imperfect world originating with the work of Maurice Allais and continued by Daniel Kahneman's Nobel-prize-winning work on prospect theory; developments which were influenced by Herbert Simon's work

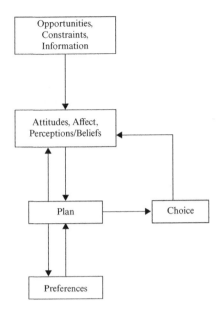

Figure 0.1   The process of decision making (adapted from McFadden 1999)

on bounded rationality. Such models are applicable to many decision situations, both individual and group. Using an integrated view that draws on economics and psychology they are particularly well suited to transport. Valuably, the *Handbook* includes a specific chapter devoted to the psychology of decisions.

The final characteristic I want to emphasize is the relationship between the public and private sectors in the provision and management of transport. Once again, this is not a problem solely related to transport; it can be found in many instances relating to public utilities, including for example, energy and water. However, it is in transport where it has been developed furthest. There are two main explanations for this. The first relates to the importance and nature of externalities, in particular congestion externalities which are endemic to transport. It is thus the role of the regulator or state to take measures to control the undesirable effects. Such measures can include policies on prices or quantities, changes of legislation, and the use of new information and communication technologies such as flexible pricing based on current or forecast levels of aggregate usage. The second explanation arises from the fact that for several reasons, both institutional and technical, public authorities are deeply involved in the supply of transport services. From this has arisen the development of public–private partnerships as well as the need to consider imperfect competition, indirect taxation, contracts and regulation under asymmetric information along the lines developed by James Mirrlees and Eric Maskin.

These four characteristics underpin the structure of the *Handbook* and the selection of topics in each of the five parts. Each topic is addressed by one of the best specialists in the area. The contributors have been chosen for their ability and reputation; some are transport specialists, but others work mainly in other fields. However, each is an expert who is recognised as having contributed to the economics of transport. The *Handbook* does not deal with every topic, but it includes most of the important topics, particularly those which identify important future developments in the nature and study of transport. I want to thank the editors for bringing this project to fruition and compiling in one volume contributions which will interest both transport specialists and economists. Engineers and management experts will benefit from the summaries, and rigorous analysis, of recent advances in economic research applied to their fields of interest. Researchers and students in economics will see how economic theory can be applied in a specific context to enrich the study of one sector, transport. In this way, the *Handbook* contributes to the cross-fertilisation of different areas of knowledge and constitutes an important development in the advancement of that knowledge.

REFERENCE

McFadden, D., 1999, Rationality for economists, *Journal of Risk and Uncertainty*, **19**, 73–105.

1 Introduction

André de Palma, Robin Lindsey, Emile Quinet and
Roger Vickerman

The transport sector holds a special place in economics for a number of reasons. First, several basic concepts that are widely used in economic analysis originated from the study of developments and policy issues in transport. Jules Dupuit (1844) established the foundations of surplus theory and welfare economics while he was grappling with the social value of transport infrastructure. The seminal theory of discrete choice developed by Daniel McFadden (1974) and others was motivated by a desire to understand and predict individual choices of transport mode. William Vickrey's (1963) well-known work on transport congestion and queuing has been applied well beyond the transport sector. And the self-financing theorem due to Herbert Mohring and Mitchell Harwitz (1962) arose from the question of whether efficient traffic congestion charges suffice to pay for the construction of an optimally sized road.

Second, the costs of transport are central to economic activity as Adam Smith (1776) recognized in his famous observation on how the scale of production is limited by the extent of the market. Indeed, transport costs play a special role in several fields of economics. In spatial economics transport costs underlie land rent (Johann Heinrich von Thünen), location choices of firms (Alfred Weber) and the existence of location and price equilibrium in competitive markets (Harold Hotelling, 1929). Transport costs are also central in the new economic geography (Paul Krugman, 1991) which seeks to explain the extent of agglomeration in human activity over space and disparities in regional development.

Conversely, due to many facets of transport markets, economic theory is widely applied to the transport sector. In some parts of the transport sector – notably infrastructure – public management is preeminent, and issues arise in which welfare economics and social choice theories can be brought to bear. This is also true where redistribution and equity are concerns as is often the case for regional transport. The private sector dominates in other parts of transport, such as operations, and industrial organization economics comes to the fore. With increasing frequency transport infrastructure and services are provided by a mix of public and private institutions, often via concessions and public–private partnership (PPP) arrangements. Private finance has been introduced in fields which used to be the realm of public management and funding, and here the theories of contracts and regulation are an indispensable tool. Transport is also a major source of externalities, both negative (for example, pollution) and positive (for example, agglomeration externalities and economics of traffic density), and theories of corrective taxation and subsidies pioneered by Arthur Pigou (1924) can be applied. Last but not least, economic analysis has enlightened the links between transport and economic development. Transport is a kind of kaleidoscope of the various aspects of economic analysis.

Another feature of transport economics is that the issues relate very much to the real world and scholars are devoted to answering practical questions. The path from theory to application is often shorter in transport economics than in other fields of economics. New concepts and theoretical developments are quickly adapted towards application, and combined with expert advice and field experience into policy recommendations for decision makers.

Transport is an exciting and rapidly evolving field. The main drivers of change are technological progress and societal evolution. In recent years new technologies of information and communication have emerged that are leading to major innovations in applications such as traveler information services and pricing of infrastructure usage. These technologies have also profoundly transformed logistics for firms, and they are beginning to have noticeable impacts on the daily activity and travel patterns of households. The volume of travel is affected by two opposing forces: economic growth, on the one hand, which tends to boost mobility, and concerns about the environment and energy supply which tend to dampen it.

The structure of transport markets has also changed a lot. The trend is towards more competition, but generally imperfect oligopolistic or monopolistically competitive competition. Competition takes various forms entailing not only classical price competition, but also competition in frequency and other dimensions of service quality with widespread use of price discrimination and other practices for market segmentation. The governance of the transport sector is itself changing with opposing trends towards both more and less regulation depending on the country and mode of transport. Governments and other institutions are also grappling with how to address the effects of transport on local environments and global climate change.

These various developments in the transport sector are influencing transport research. We are seeing renewed interest from researchers in the way transport interacts with the wider economy. There have been important developments in the economic analysis of markets and regulation, and in the economics of information. There is growing appreciation for the importance of network structure in applications ranging from congestion pricing of road traffic to competition in airline markets. And increasingly sophisticated econometric methods are being brought to bear in such diverse applications as transport demand, price discrimination, economies of scale and scope, and the importance of travel time reliability.

The various aspects and developments in transport and transport economics reveal both the value of a *Handbook in Transport Economics* and the challenges in preparing one. The value is clear since a handbook allows scholars, students, consultants and decision makers to learn and master in one volume the main themes, issues and methods in the economics of transport. The challenges arise because of the sheer diversity in the nature of transport across modes, countries and time, as well as the diversity of regulatory frameworks and economic methods used in the study of the field.

The chapters of the *Handbook* have been written by acknowledged experts in their fields. Each chapter provides a state-of-the-art review of the latest research and scholarly thinking from the author's or authors' distinctive viewpoint. Many authors also discuss how their findings can be used by decision makers in the public and private sectors for the general purpose of improving transport policy objectives and the means of achieving them.

The *Handbook* has been structured to complement the organization of the textbook by two of the editors, Emile Quinet and Roger Vickerman's *Principles of Transport Economics* (Edward Elgar, 2004). There are two reasons for doing so. First, it will enable the reader to move from the basic introduction of principles in the textbook to a more detailed and advanced elaboration of key issues here. Second, the textbook is divided into parts that provide a logical sequence for study of the transport system.

Although each chapter in the *Handbook* is designed to be read on its own as a self-contained treatment of one topic in transport economics, many of the topics are so interconnected that a piecemeal reading will fail to provide a full picture of the linkages and challenges facing the transport sector as a whole. For instance, pricing, investment and regulation are closely interrelated and require an appreciation of the economics of transport demand, the structure and determinants of costs and the wider economy which transport serves. Readers are therefore encouraged to progress systematically through the *Handbook* from Part I through Part V.

Part I sets the transport sector within the framework of overall economic activity, mainly through the concepts and mechanisms of spatial economics. The tools are general equilibrium models, urban modeling and analyses of urban growth.

Next, as it is normal for the study of any economic sector, the demand for and costs of transport are analyzed in Parts II and III. Transport demand has a number of idiosyncratic features that require specific attention and models. Among the more recent models are improved discrete choice models, choice of departure time models and activity-based programs. Collectively, these models constitute a major improvement on traditional four-step models that are still widely used by both researchers and practitioners.

More so than for most other economic sectors, infrastructure and external costs account for large fractions of the costs of transport. Scale economies can be significant for infrastructure and under the conditions of the self-financing theorem efficient user charges do not fully pay for the costs of construction. A need for subsidy then arises. External costs create another type of market failure that calls either for additional user charges or some other means of intervention.

With the basics of transport demand and costs in hand it is possible to study how transport services should be procured. This analysis can be conducted at two levels. The first, which is the more theoretical and normative, is founded on surplus theory, draws on the lessons of welfare economics and can be thought of as providing recommendations to a benevolent planner. This social choice perspective is developed in Part IV of the *Handbook* on 'Optimal public decisions'. Another point of view, closer to the paradigm of public choice theory and positive analysis, examines the process of 'Competition and regulation' dealt with in Part V. The reference paradigms here are principal–agent analysis, the theories of contracts and incentives and industrial organization theory.

We now summarize the main contributions of the chapters in each of Parts I–V.

PART I: TRANSPORT AND SPATIAL ECONOMY

Although transport planning has traditionally involved the modeling of interactions with the economy, the relationship between transport and the rest of the economy has acquired a greater emphasis through the development of the New Economic Geography.

Although links with local urban and regional economies feature in land-use transport interaction (LUTI) models, the new economic geography (NEG) offers a more formal economic modeling of these relationships. This has also linked to a renewed interest in the role of transport costs in determining the magnitude and patterns of international trade. Both the traditional and new lines of research are included in this first section of the *Handbook* with an emphasis on spatial economics.

Part I begins with a thorough review of two classical and related but contrasting approaches to the traditional modeling of urban and regional systems. Johannes Bröcker and Jean Mercenier (General equilibrium models for transportation economics) present a general equilibrium approach. General equilibrium (GE) models build on rigorous modeling of the way microeconomic agents respond to market signals when maximizing their own objectives. From the interaction between the resulting supply and demand decisions, and conditional on the organizational structure of each market, new signals emerge that feed back on the optimal decisions of all agents. The computation of a GE consists in determining a system of signals and an allocation of resources between individuals, sectors of activities, regions and time periods, such that all agents are at their optimum subject to their respective budget, technological and other constraints. The set of transactions conducted in each market leaves each agent simultaneously in equilibrium such that there is no incentive to change behavior. Chapter 2 concludes by reviewing how GE models can be used in transport economics, particularly in evaluation and appraisal, while recognizing the restrictive assumptions which need to be made and the effort required to obtain the required information.

Michael Wegener (Transport in spatial models of economic development) describes the more traditional but still widely used set of LUTI models. His chapter offers a valuable comparison of different types of models, detailing their particular strengths and weaknesses. The first part deals with multiregional economic models which are not based on individual firm or household behavior, but on regional aggregates such as gross domestic product or employment, possibly classified by economic sector. Some of these models explicitly specify trade flows between regions and some do not. The second part of the chapter deals with models which focus on the intraregional location of firms with various degrees of spatial and sectoral resolution. The most recent development is fully microscopic models of firm life cycles ('firmography') and firm location within metropolitan regions that use stochastic Monte Carlo simulation. These models typically work with high-resolution grid cells as spatial units. The chapter concludes by assessing how well the models deal with the new challenges of energy scarcity and climate protection.

The remaining chapters of Part I deal with more detailed spatial analysis based on mechanisms of the NEG. Miren Lafourcade and Jacques-François Thisse (New economic geography: The role of transport costs) provide the background to transport–economy interactions in their review of the NEG and its contribution to economics. Economic geography explains why human activity is concentrated in a large variety of economic agglomerations rather than distributed uniformly over space. At the core of the NEG approach is the trade-off between increasing returns and transport costs. The chapter presents historical data to show that falling transport costs may contribute to rising spatial income inequalities over very long time periods. It then provides an overview of the main explanations proposed by NEG for the emergence of a core-periphery structure in a world of falling transport costs. The theory also indicates that, once obstacles to trade are sufficiently low, spatial inequalities might well vanish. Hence, evidence is found to show that spatial inequalities would first rise and then fall. Next, the chapter shows how transport costs can be modeled and measured, and describes the results from the few empirical attempts to test the predictions of NEG models. The chapter concludes with some implications of NEG for transport economics and policy.

In the following chapter (Transport costs and international trade), Alberto Behar and Tony Venables investigate the effect of transport costs on international trade. They begin by examining the relationship between transport costs and the volume and nature of international trade and then explore why trade costs vary across space and time, showing that trade costs have not fallen as much as is commonly believed. The core of their chapter is a detailed analysis drawing on the empirical literature of the impact of transport costs on trade and the determinants of those costs. The chapter concludes with a more detailed look at the estimation problems encountered in such empirical work.

In the final chapter of Part I, Takatoshi Tabuchi (City formation and transport costs) applies the models and mechanisms of NEG to the development of cities. He focuses on the heterogeneity of space and the effect of externalities that reinforce the advantages of locations. Changes in spatial structures both within and between cities may be explained by the decrease in transport costs. A simple general equilibrium model is used in order to examine how perfect competition is inconsistent with the existence of transport costs. A typical urban economic theory of a monocentric city in heterogeneous space is briefly sketched and then extended with technological externalities. The assumption of perfect competition is replaced by monopolistic competition with pecuniary externalities in an NEG model, which is then combined with urban economics. The chapter shows how some of the stylized facts of urban economies can be explained by the trade-offs between commuting cost, face-to-face communication cost and intercity trade cost leading to the negative gradients of rent and population density and the suburbanization of households. Together the models of urban economics and NEG can explain the existence of polycentric cities. Thus, it is shown that distance is a significant factor in economic theory as well as in the real world, despite all the developments in transport technologies.

PART II: THE DEMAND FOR TRANSPORT

While Part I of the Handbook sets the scene by describing the role of transport in the economy, the following two parts deal with the core of transport economics – demand and costs. The five chapters relating to demand cover approaches to modeling demand as well as the key element in the evaluation of demand – the value of time savings. These chapters do not attempt to review all aspects of transport demand modeling. Practice in this field is well known, and good summaries are found elsewhere. The focus here is on the main recent developments.

One of these developments concerns the value of time – a core element in the evaluation of transport demand. The nature of the demand for transport is that it involves an input of time by the individual for personal transport or by the shipper in the case of freight. The value of this time varies between individuals (or shipments), and indeed between different journey purposes for the same individual, and is not reflected accurately in any price paid for transport. Travel time savings constitute the most important user benefit from transport improvements. David Hensher (Valuation of travel time savings) provides a comprehensive review of value of travel time savings (VTTS) with attention to both theory and application. His chapter begins with an overview of the major theoretical approaches and empirical paradigms that have evolved to value time savings, especially the progress in how revealed (or market) preference and stated choice data is being used to estimate models. Mixed logit models and stated choice methods have now become the state of the art (and to some extent practice) in deriving estimates of VTTS. Drawing on these models and methods, the author presents empirical evidence to illustrate the range of useful measures for components of travel time in passenger and freight contexts, some of which are handled using the Hensher formula which combines information from marginal productivity and utility maximization conditions.

One of the main contributions of transport studies to wider economic applications is the development of discrete choice models. Joan Walker and Moshe Ben-Akiva (Advances in discrete choice: mixture models) explain how recent advances in discrete choice models have been driven by the growth in computer power and use of simulation, which have allowed for unprecedented flexibility in model form. Their chapter provides a brief review of the foundations of discrete choice analysis and the classic model forms of probit and the generalized extreme value (GEV) family (for example, logit, nested logit and cross-nested logit) before moving on to mixture models which are being used in a wide array of statistical modeling procedures as a way to relax restrictive assumptions and generalize model forms. It concludes by presenting empirical results from a land-use and transportation study, which is used to demonstrate the various discrete choice model formulations.

Another advance in traffic modeling is the dynamic modeling framework, pioneered by the work of Vickrey, and subsequently Arnott, de Palma and Lindsey. Recent advances in this field are reviewed by André de Palma and Mogens Fosgerau (Dynamic traffic modeling). They begin by providing an overview of the conventional static equilibrium approach which combines demand (for mobility) and supply (road capacity). In the static model, both the flow of trips and congestion delay are assumed to be constant. A drawback of the static model is that the time interval during which travel occurs is not specified so that the model cannot describe changes in the duration of congestion that result from changes in demand or capacity. This limitation is overcome in the Vickrey bottleneck model which combines congestion in the form of queuing behind a bottleneck with users' trip-timing preferences and departure time decisions. de Palma and Fosgerau derive the user equilibrium and social optimum for the basic bottleneck model, and explain how the optimum can be decentralized using a time-varying toll. They then review some extensions of the basic model that encompass elastic demand, user heterogeneity, stochastic demand and capacity and small networks. They conclude by identifying some unresolved modelling issues that apply not only to the bottleneck model but to trip-timing preferences and congestion dynamics in general.

A contrasting approach that is gaining interest is reviewed in the following chapter by Abdul Rawoof Pinjari and Chandra Bhat who discuss activity models (Activity-based travel demand analysis) for passenger transport. The interest in analyzing the potential of travel demand management policies to manage travel demand has led to a shift in the focus of travel demand modeling from the statistical prediction of aggregate-level, long-term, travel demand to understanding disaggregate-level (that is individual-level) behavioral responses to short-term demand management policies such as ridesharing incentives, congestion pricing and employer-based demand management schemes (alternate work schedules, telecommuting and so forth). Since individuals respond in complex ways to such changes in travel conditions, traditional trip-based travel models may be limited in their usefulness and activity-based methods have been developed in response. Pinjari and Bhat discuss the salient aspects of the activity-based approach by presenting a theoretical and policy-oriented comparison of the trip-based and activity-based approaches. They review the emerging developments and future research directions along three important dimensions of activity participation and travel: inter-personal interactions, time and space. They then examine ways in which activity-based travel forecasting systems can be integrated with other modeling systems (such as land-use models and dynamic traffic assignment models) to build larger and more comprehensive urban modeling systems.

Although much of the work on transport demand has been developed for personal transport, many of the principles can be transferred to freight transport demand. There are however some crucial differences that justify devoting a separate chapter to freight transport in the context of the overall treatment of logistics and supply chain management. Logistics has changed a lot in recent decades, leading to an increasing integration between transport and the management of firms. Logistics draws on a number of disciplines in which pure economic analysis holds a minor role. Michel Beuthe (Economics of transport logistics) redresses this imbalance by using economic principles to address the fundamental question of the total logistic costs of activities. Costs are incurred in transportation and inventory management, and are affected by choice of route and consignment size. Michel Beuthe demonstrates the importance of these processes and offers lessons which have an immediate application in a number of areas (see, for example, the discussion of maritime shipping by Mary Brooks).

PART III: THE COST OF TRANSPORT

The demand for transport establishes the benefits from transport infrastructure and the services provided with it to transport people and freight. Part III deals with the costs of building the infrastructure and operating the services. The costs of transport include both the direct costs of transport operators and infrastructure managers and the external costs which transport imposes both on other users, for example, through congestion and accidents, and on non-users through energy consumption, local air pollution and greenhouse gas emissions. Part III of the *Handbook* addresses some approaches for internalizing these external effects. We delay a full discussion of congestion until the following section, where it is dealt with in the context of congestion pricing.

The costs of transport operators are analyzed by Leonardo Basso, Sergio Jara-Diaz and Bill Waters (Cost functions for transport firms). Operator costs are shaped by the fact that the costs of the various services produced on a transport network are interdependent through network effects. The emphasis in their chapter is less on mode-specific issues than on the nature of a transport cost function, and the challenges and methods of estimating the function. They cover a range of theoretical topics including the economics of multiple-output production and costs, and economies of scale, scope and traffic

density on transport networks. They then review the empirical evidence on these economies. Traditional methods of estimating cost functions have had rather limited success
in predicting firm behavior. Various methodological advances to improve predictive
accuracy have been developed in the last 15 years, and these are reviewed in the chapter.

Much of the innovation in transport has been concerned with enhancing productivity.
Tae Oum, Katsuhiro Yamaguchi and Yuichiro Yoshida (Efficiency measurement theory
and its application to airport benchmarking) review the theory of efficiency measurement
and illustrate it with an application to airports. Efficiency measurement and benchmarking are useful both for comparing the efficiency of a firm relative to its peers/competitors
and for investigating the effects of a public policy or regulation. They are also useful
to a firm seeking to improve its efficiency performance relative to a benchmark unit.
Efficiency measurement is critical for industries where firms do not face strong competition since the market cannot be relied on to discipline firms effectively. Prominent
examples in transportation are firms that provide infrastructure for airports, seaports,
highways and urban transit systems. Airports are an important and challenging example.
The fact that airports produce multiple outputs using a common set of inputs calls for a
delicate and sophisticated treatment in measuring their efficiencies. The chapter presents
the conventional methodologies of efficiency measurement such as data envelopment
analysis, stochastic frontier analysis, productivity indexes and some recent developments
in efficiency measurement literature. It then provides a literature review of results on
airport efficiency measurement, recent advances on airport efficiency measurement and
some recent empirical estimates of the effects of ownership forms and governance structures on airport efficiency.

Transport is distinguished from many other economic sectors by the importance –
both absolute and relative – of external costs. There is a significant and rapidly growing
body of literature within transport economics on the estimation of these costs. Another
branch of literature deals with how to control externalities following the theoretical
guidelines established by Arthur Pigou and Paul Samuelson.

Stef Proost sets the scene in a complete guide to the concept and use of external costs
in transport economics (Theory of external costs). The chapter addresses some basic
questions: what are external costs, why do they arise in market economies, is there any
difference between external costs generated by producers and consumers, how do external costs interact with other market failures and what does this imply in terms of policy
instruments? A theoretical general equilibrium model is used to define the concept of
external cost and how the marginal external cost is related to the efficiency properties
of the standard competitive equilibrium. Since the general equilibrium model is rather
cumbersome, the use of the external cost concept for policy analysis is shown with the
help of two simple illustrations: the optimal pollution model and the partial equilibrium
model. The principal external costs encountered in transport are briefly discussed and
the properties of different policy instruments are analyzed. Finally the chapter considers
the use of external cost concepts and policy instruments in a second-best context where
more than one market failure is present.

America and Europe differ substantially in terms of levels of external costs, approaches
to evaluating external costs and policies toward controlling external costs. Accordingly,
two chapters provide separate treatments for the two sides of the Atlantic. The US
approach is discussed by Mark Delucchi and Don McCubbin (External costs of trans-

port in the United States). Their chapter provides a comprehensive coverage of road, rail, air and water transport; passenger transport and freight transport; and congestion, accident, air pollution, climate change, noise, water pollution and energy-security costs. A separate section of the chapter is devoted to each of the main types of external cost. Each section first reviews methods and issues in the estimation of the costs associated with that externality, and then presents estimates of those costs. Wide variations in estimation methods, data and assumptions confound the comparison of estimates across modes. Delucchi and McCubbin conclude that external safety and congestion costs will remain significant until major changes in transportation activity occur. The mitigation of energy-security costs and climate-change costs depends on the pace of introduction of non-petroleum fuels, which is difficult to predict. Air pollution costs are likely to be of diminishing importance.

The European approach to external transport costs is summarized by Rainer Friedrich and Emile Quinet (External costs of transport in Europe). Internalization of external costs is one of the priorities of the European Commission. This is reflected in the large number of European studies which have been concerned not only with evaluating external costs, but also with the means of implementing their findings in terms of pricing and charges, in estimating the potential gain which would be derived from their implementation and in featuring what could be the use of the corresponding revenues. The majority of the European studies are designed to be integrated directly into project evaluation or transport pricing. By contrast, American studies have been largely the product of independent research centers, typically without direct translation into practical applications. Methodologically, the approaches used in Europe and the US are similar, but the emphasis is often on different goals. The costs of energy security are a higher priority in the United States than Europe, whereas environmental costs and the positive externalities from transport such as those embodied in the Mohring effect play a larger role in European studies. The ranking of external costs by importance is generally the same in the two continents: the largest cost is congestion followed by accidents, air pollution and noise. Climate change costs are the smallest. Whilst the estimation of the polluting and climate change effects of transport involve both difficult issues of scientific measurement and difficult monetary evaluation problems which have been the subject of much debate and controversy there remain two issues where transport interacts with more developed surrogate markets.

The following two chapters in Part III are devoted to these interactions. Henrik Andersson and Nicolas Treich (The value of a statistical life) are concerned with the value of human life. This has been a controversial topic on both philosophical and technical grounds, but the fact remains that transport accidents are a major cause of deaths and there is a need to place a value on reducing this toll. The value of human life can be estimated both directly through productivity and labor markets and indirectly through insurance. The authors take care to distinguish between the value of a *statistical* life (VSL) and the amount that individuals are willing to pay to save an identified life. It is the VSL that is of interest for public policy. The chapter focuses on the willingness to pay (WTP) approach to estimating the VSL. It surveys some classical theoretical and empirical findings on the VSL, but also attempts to clarify some of the issues often raised by the application of the WTP approach to the study of mortality risks. Procedures for eliciting preferences for safety have advanced considerably, but new questions continue to arise. The decision problem of a social planner who must select optimal public safety expenditures is contrasted with the situation in which individuals make their own decisions that may have social consequences. The estimates presented in the chapter depend, however, on some key assumptions, in particular on the utility derived from bequests. To date we have little sense of the properties of bequest utility, and how it should vary across the population and time.

Besides safety issues, the relationships between transport and energy markets are of critical and growing importance. Ken Button (Transport and energy) discusses the links between the two markets. Energy is a major input for transport and it is also significant for its strategic implications. The chapter describes how historical developments in energy and transport have evolved in parallel. The emergence of developing countries has changed the picture in terms of current and future world consumption patterns. Distortions in the energy market have consequences for transport that arise from several factors: non-renewability of oil reserves; the oligopolistic and cartelized nature of oil supply; environmental effects of energy consumption; and the conflict with policy towards the oil industry and the market imperfections which arise from the diverging objectives of different countries. Various policy options and instruments are considered which can modify consumption patterns: taxes and subsidies, vehicle fuel-efficiency standards, controls on vehicle use and the development of alternative technologies. In Button's opinion, some combination of all of these instruments is likely to be needed to support efficient usage of energy for transport.

Concluding Part III, and as an application of the concepts described in earlier chapters, Yossi Berechman, Bekir Bartin, Ozlem Yanmaz-Tuzel and Kaan Ozbay (The full marginal costs of highway travel: Methods and empirical estimation for North America) analyze the full marginal costs (FMC) of highway travel. FMC is defined as the overall costs incurred by society from an additional unit of transportation output. It is composed of direct costs to users and indirect costs to society from non-internalized externalities. The chapter begins by characterizing the optimal price and capacity level for a transport link and deriving a formula for the extent to which user charges cover the costs of infrastructure. Empirical evidence on scale economies in capacity provision is presented. Empirical estimates are then reviewed for the FMC of highway travel inclusive of vehicle operating costs, travel time costs, accident costs, environmental costs and infrastructure costs. The chapter concludes with an application concerning three major roadway widening projects on the Northern New Jersey highway network. The application illustrates the importance of conducting full-cost analysis at the network level in order to account for the effects of expanding individual links on equilibrium traffic flows on links, and between origin-destination pairs, over whole road networks.

PART IV: OPTIMAL PUBLIC DECISIONS

For many years the public sector has been involved in transport as both direct provider and regulator. This relationship has been changing recently in response to pressure on public budgets and a belief in the effectiveness of introducing competition. Parts IV and V of the *Handbook* explore the basis of policy towards transport. Part IV deals with optimal collective decisions from a welfare economics perspective, while Part V deals with competition and regulation from a point of view more akin to public choice theory.

Part IV begins with an introduction to surplus theory which underlies any discussion of the wider value of transport. Yoshi Kanemoto (Surplus theory) shows how the concept of consumer's surplus lies at the heart of cost–benefit analysis (CBA). Starting from the original concept developed by Jules Dupuit, the practical application of CBA spread to a variety of public infrastructure projects during the first half of the twentieth century. This chapter reviews the theoretical foundation of CBA using the money-metric utility function as a basis for consumer's surplus and examines compensating variation, equivalent variation and Marshallian consumer's surplus. The chapter shows how this approach differs from a financial appraisal, with the main difference arising from the use of shadow prices. It then describes how the distribution of benefits can be analyzed within a general equilibrium framework. Finally, consideration is given to consumer's surplus measures in random utility discrete choice models that are widely used in transport demand models.

Peter Mackie, Dan Graham and James Laird (The direct and wider impacts of transport projects: a review) review the state of the art in applying cost–benefit analysis to the practical appraisal of projects. They emphasize two aspects of project appraisal for which recent advances have been made. One is how appraisal can incorporate the wider economic impacts of transport projects – a topic that links back to Part I of the *Handbook*. The other is how to address issues relating to the values of time and human life as discussed in Part III. The chapter reflects on both the relative importance of the various aspects of wider impacts and the extent to which the outcomes vary from project to project. The authors conclude that it is difficult to develop general rules about the magnitude of the wider impacts.

The next two chapters deal with the important issue of pricing. Simon Anderson and Régis Renault (Price discrimination) deal with price discrimination which is widely employed in transport markets as well as other sectors of the economy. Anderson and Renault discuss the rationale for price discrimination and how discriminatory prices compare with welfare-maximizing pricing. Price discrimination arises when a firm sells different units of the same good at different prices. Examples include special tariffs for certain customer groups (for example, students or senior citizens), varying prices with the number of units purchased and varying prices by time of day, week or season. The chapter examines the basis for each form of pricing, and discusses the extent to which price discrimination depends on the market power of the firm and the possibility of arbitrage between consumers. It also reviews empirical evidence on the incidence of such pricing practices under different market structures.

Georgina Santos and Erik Verhoef (Road congestion pricing) focus on congestion pricing of roads which is becoming an increasingly popular subject as proposals for various forms of road pricing surface around the world. The authors return to the use of pricing for internalizing transport externalities, discussed in Part III, and provide an in-depth review of the theory and practice of road pricing. The chapter begins by presenting the simple textbook theory of the optimal congestion charge. It then describes complications to the theory such as the dynamics of traffic flows, and second-best pricing when other markets are distorted (for example, other transport modes are not optimally priced) or when there are constraints on what roads can be tolled or on how tolls can be differentiated by type of traveler. Since congestion pricing is rather limited in practice there is relatively little evidence on how well it can work. The chapter reviews four operational schemes that are working well: High Occupancy Toll lanes in the US, Singapore's electronic road pricing system, London's congestion charging scheme, and Stockholm's congestion tax. Interestingly, none of these schemes were designed on the basis of first-best or second-best theoretical guidelines, but rather for ease of comprehension and use. The chapter concludes by discussing welfare-distributional and acceptability issues that continue to impede widespread implementation of road pricing.

The following two chapters in Part IV deal with the role of information in transport, which is growing in importance with the development of new technologies of information and communication. Piet Rietveld (The economics of information in transport) discusses some economic aspects of information in transport. If travelers lack complete information on the travel alternatives available to them they could make suboptimal choices and hence could benefit from acquiring more information. This chapter analyzes the costs and benefits of two primary modes of information acquisition: information search – for example by means of Advanced Traveler Information Systems (ATIS) – and information acquisition via trial and error. Given rapid advances in ATIS technology it seems likely that ATIS will gain importance as a source of information although situations will remain in which trial and error is more cost-effective. In some contexts, such as transport on congested road networks, better information conveys benefits not only directly to travelers who receive it, but also indirectly through changes in the decisions of informed travelers to uninformed travelers as well. This implies that, in the absence of direct corrective mechanisms such as congestion pricing, there are positive externalities in the information market which makes a case for subsidies to users or providers of information services.

The second chapter on information and transport by Caspar Chorus and Harry Timmermans (Personal intelligent travel assistants) describes how rapid technological developments in mobile communications and satellite technology are leading toward what can be called a Personal Intelligent Travel Assistant (PITA). PITAs go beyond existing ATIS in providing information that is: dynamic or predictive personalized (that is, based on a traveler's preferences, location and current circumstances); and multimodal. PITAs can provide travelers with three types of service: information about the attributes of a known alternative, information about an unknown alternative, or advice on what option to choose. Given the large investments required for the successful development and deployment of PITA services, a clear understanding of their benefits is needed. This chapter provides models of the value of information from PITA services. After reviewing the value of information from a generic conceptual perspective, it develops specific formalizations of information value for the three types of PITA service.

Any means of allocation has distributive implications. In his chapter (Equity dimensions of transport policy), Alain Trannoy argues that equity has been a much less central concept in transport than in other fields such as education, health or housing. He reviews the equity dimensions arising in the design of transport infrastructure, and discusses the relevance and implications of criteria such as maximum or minimum average distance. He advocates the use of Nash bargaining solutions, shows the paradoxes which may arise from equity solutions when growth is taken into account and suggests a new criterion taking into account growth, welfare and migration in situations where regions have strong cultural identities. The equity dimensions of classical CBA are examined and the equity issues which arise in the cost sharing of infrastructures. Trannoy then reviews the equity issues in transport operations, such as transfers in kind (for example, free transport for old people), compensating commuters and the equity issues of congestion. Finally, he considers the potential for defining indicators of equity which encompass both transport infrastructure and operations, stressing the importance of equality of opportunities of mobility, and hence providing a means of judging the transport policies of various countries.

The final chapter in Part IV by Jonathan Gifford (Psychology and rationality in user behavior: the case of scarcity) examines some of the non-economic factors which may affect the way transport capacity is used. Gifford focuses on non-conventional aspects of managing scarcity in transportation resources. He provides an overview of the relevant theoretical perspectives from the behavioral literature – an interdisciplinary approach including psychology, sociology and economics – and examines how its concepts apply to transportation decisions and transport policy. The chapter briefly touches upon the transportation demand management (TDM) literature as it relates to the management of scarcity before concluding with a summary of the challenges in designing effective TDM tools, and identifying opportunities for future research.

PART V: COMPETITION AND REGULATION

This final part of the *Handbook* considers various issues related to how the mix of competitive forces and regulatory constraints affects transport markets. The discussion draws on the theories of asymmetric information, uncertainty, incentives and contracts.

An overview of the issues is provided by Marco Ponti (Competition, regulation and public service obligations), who presents both a theoretical overview and the experience of a former regulator in the transport sector. The chapter outlines both the rationale and the means for public intervention, and shows how the principles of service provision can be satisfied in very different ways through concessions, private finance, tariff regulation and competition. Several key issues for transport regulation are developed: congestion and the regulation of access; problems of price-cap regulation; the regulation of investment and of quality of service; and the specific problem of the number of tills (that is, whether to regulate provision in a particular sector in its totality or separately for each element). The analysis shows how effectively regulation can influence policy towards transport in terms of efficiency, innovation and investment. Finally, the way in which regulation can accommodate the exercise of public service obligations and distributional issues is demonstrated. The chapter concludes that Demsetz-style competition can be compatible with social objectives, and that liberalization does not necessarily undermine the role of the state but rather requires reinforcement of regulations and control of market failures.

The following two chapters consider issues relating to infrastructure provision, and in particular the use of PPPs. Elisabetta Iossa and David Martimort (The theory of incentives applied to the transport sector) underline the potential problems arising from the implementation of PPPs in transport and their incentive properties. These include the optimism embodied in forecasts and the frequency of renegotiation resulting from such optimism, but it is also recognized that PPPs can be a great success. Because of this diversity of outcomes the authors see it necessary to revisit the theoretical basis of PPPs to establish whether and how mechanisms for successful PPPs can be established. Four principal determining factors are analyzed: the degree of integration of functions (planning, construction, operation); the transfer of risk from public to private sector; the duration of contracts and the use of private finance. Starting with a simple model of incentives the authors present a series of results which have as common elements the degree of integration of functions, the role of the regulator (providing a link with Marco Ponti's chapter) and the length of contracts.

To complement this theoretical analysis Antonio Estache, Ellis Juan and Lourdes Trujillo (Public–private partnerships in transport) provide a general survey of experiences with PPPs in transport. They provide a historical account of the development of PPPs and their increasingly important role in recent decades. Many PPPs have failed, and yet enthusiasm for PPPs has continued undiminished. The main issues which arise are examined: the financial aspects as the main driving force for the growth of PPPs and the increasing sophistication of the financial arrangements. Using historical examples, it is shown that risk lies at the core of problems with PPPs in terms of their consequences and management. Finally the chapter considers the role of the public sector, not least in providing an overall structure for the system – providing a link with the discussion of regulation of previous chapters. The authors consider that the recent financial crisis has not reduced the appetite for PPPs, but has reinforced the need to consider the means of implementation and the contracts which accompany such partnerships.

The remaining chapters deal with a range of issues arising in individual modes. Richard Arnott (Parking economics) considers parking: an aspect of private car usage which is frequently overlooked. Much infrastructure and space is devoted to parking, and the deadweight loss due to inefficient parking policy may be as large as that due to the underpricing of urban automobile congestion. Yet much less work has been done on the economics of parking than on the economics of traffic congestion. Arnott reviews the nascent literature on the economics of parking with particular attention to downtown parking. The economics of parking are complicated by a number of market distortions. Most shopping center parking and employer-provided parking is free to users, and most on-street parking is underpriced. However, parking garages and parking lots derive market power from their unique locations, and set parking fees above marginal cost. A further consideration is that the demand for parking is derived from the demand for automobile travel which is generally underpriced. As a result of these and other complications, existing parking policies can be difficult to assess, and new policies can be difficult to formulate and optimize. Nevertheless, with improvements in the parking models used by transportation planners and growing acceptance of pricing policies, there is reason to hope that parking pricing and other practices will become more economically efficient in the foreseeable future.

Philippe Gagnepain, Marc Ivaldi and Catherine Muller-Vibes (The industrial organization of competition in local bus services) provide an overall review of the local bus service industry. Drawing on a broad literature survey they first examine the major characteristics of demand and costs for local bus service and how they can be estimated. They then describe the characteristics of competition which appears to play out mainly with respect to service frequency rather than fares. Both theory and empirical evidence overwhelmingly suggest that the industry is not contestable. Local operators usually have monopoly power and can earn high profits. Various factors militate against contestability: entry barriers; sunk costs; the advantages of incumbents in terms of economies of experience, scale, traffic density and scope; the use of practices that raise rivals' costs and the ability of incumbents to changes fares and timetables rapidly.

Chris Nash (Competition and regulation in rail transport) looks at the rail sector. This has undergone enormous changes in the UK in the past two decades from a sector which was dominated by large state-owned vertically integrated monopolies to one where the vertical integration has been largely unbundled and competition introduced. Competition occurs both for franchised local monopolies (that is, competition for the market) and in some cases on-track between competing operators (that is, competition within the market). The chapter reviews the wide variety of organizational and regulatory structures for the rail industry to provide evidence on what approaches to competition and regulation work best and in what circumstances. It then considers research on the specific issues of vertical separation, open access competition for freight and passenger traffic, franchising for freight and passenger traffic, and regulation and infrastructure charges. The chapter concludes that most railway reforms have had some beneficial effects, but that all such reforms are a compromise between introducing competition and minimizing transactions costs and loss of economies of scale, density and scope. It appears that different solutions work best in different circumstances, but it is difficult to provide definitive evidence or recommendations on what type of regulation and form of competition should be implemented in a given market.

The next two chapters deal with aviation. David Gillen (Airport governance and regulation: three decades of aviation system reform) examines the evolution of airport governance and the various forms it takes, and assesses the case for privatization. He describes the different types of economic regulation that have accompanied this evolution which range from tight rate-of-return regulation to liberalized light-handed implicit regulation. He also reviews arguments that have been made both for and against economic regulation. Several policy-relevant conclusions are drawn. First, airports are not hybrid corporations that must choose between serving customers or shareholders. Second, if regulation is deemed necessary, light-handed regulation seems superior even to dual till rate-of-return regulation. Third, airline deregulation has shifted the balance of power away from airports and toward airlines. Fourth, dynamic efficiency (that is, innovation in terms of new types of aviation service or ways to manage airports such as congestion pricing) has been underemphasized in the debate over privatization. Gillen argues that regulators should take the 'long view' and foster the competitive process rather than emulating the competitive outcome.

Anming Zhang, Yimin Zhang and Joseph Clougherty (Competition and regulation in air transport) look at changes in competition and regulation in the airline industry. Following US airline deregulation in the late 1970s there has been a worldwide move away from government regulation towards liberalization of air services and 'open skies'. The unleashing of airline competition has induced airlines to take a number of strategic actions including: mergers and consolidation; competition over service frequency, flight scheduling and fares; hub-and-spoke network formation; and international alliance agreements. This chapter provides a review of research into the reasons behind, and welfare implications of, these strategic actions. It departs from previous reviews of the topic in employing game-theoretic analysis, by systematically examining the international dimensions to air transport competition, and by focusing on recent developments such as rapid growth of the cargo sector which carries nearly 40 per cent of world trade by value.

Similar to the treatment of airports and airlines, two chapters in Part V look at maritime transport by dealing separately with seaports and shipping companies. Eddy Van de Voorde, Hilde Meersman and Thierry Vanelslander (Competition and regulation in seaports) examine changes in the port sector. The port sector has been subject to privatization and deregulation with consequences for competition within as well as outside the sector. At the same time, increased cooperation and merger activities have been driven by the search for scale economies and control over the logistics chain. The authors show how the resulting concentration may lead to abuses of market power that undermine the advantages of deregulation. The chapter starts by defining the key concepts of a seaport, port activities, port players and port competition. It then focuses on two major forces which impact the port sector: changes in organizational structures of the ports as a consequence of privatization and deregulation, and efforts by shipping companies to gain control over the logistics chain. Finally, it discusses some changes that are likely to affect port competition in the near future.

Mary Brooks (Competition and regulation in maritime transport) reviews the changing competitive environment in the market for maritime transport services. She begins with a general summary of maritime freight transport, and then provides separate in-depth descriptions of the market structure and regulation of tanker and dry bulk markets (called tramp markets), and liner markets. Tramp markets have been treated in a relatively laissez-faire fashion with only limited regulation from a competition perspective. By contrast, competition authorities have heavily regulated the liner market and Brooks explores the reasons for this very different approach.

*   *   *

We have attempted in this *Handbook* to provide a comprehensive account of the major areas of interest in transport economics and many of the big changes in both analysis and empirical evidence. Nevertheless, some topics have not been covered. One reason is that for some topics, such as transport demand elasticities, CBA and transport demand modeling, there are good, recent reviews or manuals to which little could be added. Another reason is that the sheer number of subjects that could be included would greatly exceed the feasible length of the *Handbook*.

Nevertheless, it is possible from the contents of the *Handbook* to highlight a number of subjects and policy issues deserving further attention. We mention just a few here. As the chapters in Part I demonstrate, our understanding of the relationship between transport and the spatial economy has changed fundamentally in the past two decades and the topic is wide open for more theoretical and empirical research. For example, only recently has reliable empirical evidence become available on the magnitude of the economy-wide impacts of transport projects and further work could confirm that these effects should be incorporated into standard project evaluation practice. Another priority is to develop further the activity modeling approach which seeks to explain transport demand from consistent utility-theoretic principles in terms of the underlying demand to undertake activities at different locations at different times. The advent of ATIS and other technological developments in information and communication will have wide-ranging implications for passenger and freight transport that deserve attention. Encouragingly, the theory of regulation is gaining influence with regulatory policy makers as well as becoming better at predicting outcomes, and with further advances it can be hoped that a better balance between competition and appropriate forms of regulation can be achieved. It is clear from this non-exhaustive review that transport economics is an evolving field and that the state-of-the art developed in this *Handbook* will have to be updated in due course.

Finally we must pay tribute to the the *Direction de la recherche et de l'innovation* of the French Ministry in charge of Environment, to the University of Kent and to the Ecole Normale Supérieure de Cachan for financial support, and more especially to Nicolas Coulombel who took on the responsibility for ensuring consistency in the presentation of the final manuscript, but also reviewed the overall coherency of the book and provided valuable advice on the contents of the individual chapters. We also acknowledge the contribution to this volume made by Bill Waters who died suddenly during the final stages of completion. He made a huge contribution to many areas of transport economics and will be greatly missed.

REFERENCES

Dupuit, J.A., 1844, De la mesure de l'utilité des travaux publics. *Annales des Ponts et Chaussées,* **8**.

Hotelling, H., 1929, Stability in competition. *Economic Journal,* **39**, 41–57.

Krugman, P.R., 1991, Increasing returns to scale and economic geography. *Journal of Political Economy,* **99**, 483–499.

McFadden, D., 1974, Conditional logit analysis of qualitative choice behavior. In P. Zarembka, ed., *Frontiers of Econometrics,* London: Academic Press, pp. 105–142.

Mohring, H. and M. Harwitz, 1962, *Highway Benefits: An Analytical Framework.* Evanston, IL: Transportation Center, Northwestern University.

Pigou, A.C., 1924, *The Economics of Welfare.* London: Macmillan.

Smith, A., 1776, *An Inquiry into the Nature and Causes of the Wealth of Nations.* London: W. Strahan and T. Cadell.

Thünen, J.H. von, 1826, *Der Isolierte Staat in Beziehung auf Landscaft und Nationalökonomie.* Transl. by C. M. Wartenburg, 1966, *von Thünen's Isolated State.* Oxford: Pergamon Press.

Vickrey, W.S., 1963, Pricing urban and suburban transport. *American Economic Review,* **59**, 452–465.

Weber, A., 1909, *Über den Standort der Industrien.* Transl. by C. J. Friedrich, 1929, *Alfred Weber's Theory of the Location of Industries.* Chicago, IL: University of Chicago Press.

PART I

TRANSPORT AND SPATIAL ECONOMY

2 General equilibrium models for transportation economics

Johannes Bröcker and Jean Mercenier

INTRODUCTION

Applied – or computable – general equilibrium models (AGE or CGE) build on rigorous modelling of microeconomic agents' behaviours (households, firms and so forth). These agents are exposed to signals (in prices, quantities and so forth) provided by markets (for goods, assets, production factors and so forth). Agents make decisions by explicit maximization of their own criterion (utility, profits, portfolio returns and so forth). These choices determine their positions on each market. From the interaction between these supply and demand decisions, and conditional on the form of organization that prevails on each market (perfect competition, monopolistic or oligopolistic competition and so forth), new signals emerge that feed back on the optimal decisions of all agents. The general equilibrium (GE) typically describes a stable state of consistency between these individual decisions: when the signals that condition individual choices coincide with those emitted by markets so that there is no incentive for anyone to change position. The computation of a GE therefore consists in determining a system of signals and an allocation between individuals, sectors of activities, regions, possibly time periods and so forth, such that all agents are at their optimum yet satisfying their respective constraints (budget, technological and so forth) and that the set of transactions conducted on each market corresponds to the desired set of transactions by all agents simultaneously.

Governments of course have the ability to influence both directly (by taxes, transfers and so forth) and indirectly (by their own demand and supply decisions on individual markets and so forth) the environment that agents face and therefore their behaviours and the resulting resource allocation. It should be clear from what precedes that, in principle at least, any kind of microeconomic behaviour and any degree of disaggregation of agents can be built in an applied GE, and it will always be possible to evaluate and compare equilibria in terms of individual welfare. For this reason AGE models are now indispensable tools of policy analysis. See Shoven and Whalley (1984) for an introduction and Ginsburgh and Keyzer (1997) for an advanced textbook presentation; see Srinivasan and Whalley (1986), Mercenier and Srinivasan (1994) and Fossati and Wiegard (2002) for illustrative applications. Bröcker (2004) provides an alternative introduction to CGE applications to transport problems. For solution software, computer codes and illustrative applications, see www.gams.com.

There is no free lunch, however: computations can be extremely costly. For this reason transportation economics has, until recently, mainly relied on the restrictive cost–benefit approach. The traditional cost–benefit evaluation of a new road, for example, measures the benefit by the consumers' surplus of users generated by reducing generalized costs, and subtracts building costs in market values as well as the net increase of technological external costs caused by existing and induced traffic. For this approach to be valid the following three conditions must hold: (1) markets are perfectly competitive and cleared by fully flexible prices; (2) welfare distribution is not an issue, that is, each euro counts equally, irrespective of who gets it; and (3) technological externalities outside the transport sector are negligible. None of these conditions are particularly appealing to modern economists and policy makers so that with the spectacular development of computing possibilities, the CGE approach is becoming increasingly popular in transportation economics. A typical transport economics application is to study quantitative impacts of transport initiatives like infrastructure investments or pricing policies on economic variables.

It is the aim of this chapter to provide an introduction to the use of the CGE approach in transportation policy evaluation. For this, we start – in the following section – with a short tutorial on the CGE methodology, and introduce what constitutes the core elements of most – if not all – CGE models. Having set the stage, we then discuss how transport is introduced in applied GE models. The chapter closes with a brief conclusion.

A SHORT INTRODUCTION TO CGE MODELLING

Any AGE model builds on a data matrix that accounts for all the transactions in the economy during a base period: we therefore begin this section with a short description of how these transaction data are organized. We then describe how preferences and technologies are specified and calibrated so that, in the absence of shocks, the model replicates the base-year data set. For this, we first assume perfect competition prevails in a closed economy setting. The basic model is then extended (1) to acknowledge the possible existence of increasing returns to scale technologies and imperfect competition between firms; (2) to multicountry/region models with trade.

The Base Year Data Set

Consider a closed economy comprising producers, households and a government. Producers are grouped into industries or sectors indexed s,t according to the type of goods they produce; households are grouped according to some characteristic – such as income class – indexed h.[1] During a specified period of time, all these agents simultaneously operate on different markets where they make transactions. Table 2.1 provides a symbolic representation of all these transactions organized in a meaningful way. Incomes (appearing with a negative sign) and expenditures of all agents are displayed so as to make explicit the consistency constraints imposed by the general equilibrium of the economy.[2] It is useful to explore this table in some detail.

Column (a) details the cost structure of sector s (there is one such column for each sector) with line (1) reporting payments to industry t (there is one such line for each industry) for material inputs bought in quantities X_{ts} at market prices $(1 + \tau_t^Z)p_t^Z$, where p_t^Z denotes the producer price and $\tau_t^Z p_t^Z$ a unit *ad valorem* tax levied on the producer's output. Total material input costs are reported in line (2) where we have introduced an aggregate price index for material inputs, p_s^X, and $X_{\cdot s}$ the number of units of the corresponding aggregate bundle of intermediates, so that $\Sigma_t(1 + \tau_t^Z)p_t^Z X_{ts} = p_s^X X_{\cdot s}$. (The way

Table 2.1 Organizing all the economy's transactions

	(a)	(b)	(c)	(d)	(e)
(1)	$(1 + \tau_t^Z)p_t^Z X_{ts}$	$(1 + \tau_t^Z)p_t^Z C_{ht}$	$(1 + \tau_t^Z)p_t^Z G_t$	$(1 + \tau_t^Z)p_t^Z I_t$	Total demand for good t at market prices: $(1 + \tau_s^Z)p_s^Z\left[\sum_s X_{ts} + \sum_h C_{ht} + G_t + I_t\right]$
(2) $= \sum_t (1)$	$p_s^X X_{ss}$	$p_h^{Con}Con_h$	$p^{Gov}Gov$	$p^{Inv}Inv$	
(3)	$w_f F_{fs}^{dem}$	$- w_f \overline{F_{fh}^{sup}}$			Balance of factor market f
(4) $= \sum_f (3)$	$p_s^Q Q_s$				
(5) $= (2) + (4)$	$p_s^Z Z_s$				
(6)	$\tau_s^Z p_s^Z Z_s$		$- \tau_s^Z p_s^Z Z_s$		
(7)		$\tau^{Inc}\sum_f w_f \overline{F_{fh}^{sup}}$	$- \tau^{Inc}\sum_{fh} w_f \overline{F_{fh}^{sup}}$		
(8)		Sav_h	Sav^{Gov}	$-p^{Inv} Inv$	Investment – saving balance
(9)	Total supply of good s at market prices: $(1 + \tau_s^Z)p_s^Z Z_s$	Balance of household h budget constraint	Balance of Government budget constraint	Balance of investors budget constraint	

the latter two aggregate variables are related to the others will be detailed later.) Sector s also rents production factors indexed f at unit prices w_f in quantities F_{fs}^{dem} as reported in line (3) – with one such line for each f. Summing over factors provides the sector's value added at factor costs, reported in line (4), where again we introduce an aggregate price index p_s^Q and the corresponding quantities Q_s so that we have: $\Sigma_f w_f F_{fs}^{dem} = p_s^Q Q_s$. Summing total expenditures on both material and factor inputs defines (reported in line (5)) the sector's output value with Z_s the number of goods supplied at unit price p_s^Z. The good is taxed at *ad valorem* rate τ_s^Z (line (6) reports the amount of taxes levied on the sector's output) so that the market value of output s is $(1 + \tau_s^Z)p_s^Z Z_s$ reported in line (9).

Column (b) reports all ingredients of the household h budget constraint (there is one such column for each h). Income is earned by supplying factor services to firms (line (3)), and shared between taxes (line (7)), savings (line (8)) and consumption of goods (line (1)). Summing line (1) over all t defines h's aggregate consumption expenditure (line (2)), where a consumption basket with unit price p_h^{Con} has been implicitly defined. Line (9) reports the household's balance between accounted incomes and expenditures, which we know should always be null. Column (c) similarly reports all ingredients of the government budget constraint. Column (d) is associated with a fictitious investor that 'spends' the economy's total saving (line (8), the investor's 'income') on market goods (line (1)), combining them into investment composites with unit price p^{Inv} such that $\Sigma_t(1 + \tau_t^Z)p_t^Z I_t = p^{Inv} Inv$ (line (2)). The investor's budget balances to zero (line (9)). Now, adding cells (a) to (d) from line (1) defines total expenditures on each industry's good – reported in cell (1,e) – which, by construction, equals the total supplied value of that good – displayed in cell (9,a).[3]

Observe that, by construction, factor markets balance (cell (3,e) reports the line sum that is null), investment-spending equals the economy's supply of saving (cell (8,e) reports the line sum that is null) and all agents satisfy their budget constraints (cells (9,b), (9,c), and (9,d)).

Specification and Calibration

The economy underlying Table 2.1 is populated by agents that take into account signals provided by markets and make rational choices by optimizing some criterion subject to their technological and/or budget constraints. Our task as applied GE modellers is then to make assumptions on market structures prevailing at base year, to postulate functional forms for preferences and technologies, solve each agent's optimization problem and set parameter values such that, in absence of shock, each decision maker replicates its base year transaction flows as reported by the data matrix.

To illustrate this, assume that all markets are perfectly competitive and technologies have constant returns to scale. Producer s will naturally seek to minimize its production cost conditional on some output target. For example, with a Cobb-Douglas technology, the firm solves, holding Z_s fixed,

$$\underset{\{X_{ts}, F_{fs}^{dem}\}}{\text{Min}} \ \Sigma_t(1 + \tau_t^Z)p_t^Z X_{ts} + \Sigma_f w_f F_{fs}^{dem}$$

$$\text{s.t.} \ \ln Z_s = \alpha_{0s}^Z + \Sigma_t \alpha_{ts}^X \ln X_{ts} + \Sigma_f \alpha_{fs}^F \ln F_{fs}^{dem} \quad \Sigma_t \alpha_{ts}^X + \Sigma_f \alpha_{fs}^F = 1 \quad (2.1)$$

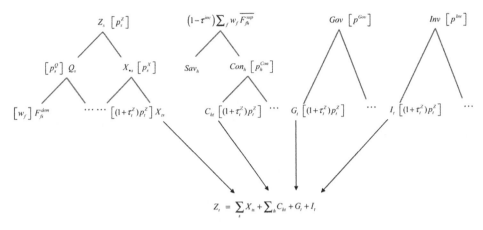

Figure 2.1   A schematic representation of agents' preferences or technologies

where all the symbols have been previously introduced (and appear in column (a) of Table 2.1) except the α-coefficients which denote parameters (elasticities and a scale). Most industry observers would however advocate for a less restrictive technology than one that imposes identical substitution elasticities between any pair of inputs. A more realistic alternative consists to group similar inputs into bundles, and to characterize substitutability differently within each bundle. Assume for instance that in industry s, it is known that substitution is easy between capital and labour, but that complementarity prevails between material inputs, yet that both input bundles account for a constant share of total cost. We could model this by nesting technologies: primary factors would be combined using a constant elasticity of substitution (CES) production function to yield an aggregate factor service called 'value added'; material inputs would enter a Leontief-type sub-technology to produce an aggregate 'intermediate mix', which would then be combined with value added using a Cobb-Douglas to produce the final good. Endowed with such a technology – illustrated in the left part of Figure 2.1 – the producer's decision problem looks much more complicated, but we know from Gorman (1959) that it can be decomposed into small and easy to handle sub-optimization problems because all sub-technologies are additively separable. We now show how such a technology can be calibrated to fit the data in Table 2.1.

We start with primary factors: the sector s producer's sub-problem consists of choosing the mix of factor services that minimizes costs of producing some specified level Q_s of value added, given market prices for factors and a CES technology. Formally,

$$\underset{\{F_{fs}^{dem}\}}{\text{Min}} \ \sum_f w_f F_{fs}^{dem}$$

$$\text{s.t.} \ Q_s = \left\{ \sum_f \alpha_{fs}^F [F_{fs}^{dem}]^{-\rho_s^Q} \right\}^{-\frac{1}{\rho_s^Q}} \quad -1 < \rho_s^Q < \infty \tag{2.2}$$

(for a given level of Q_s) where α_{fs}^F and ρ_s^Q are parameters; $\sigma_s^Q = 1/(1 + \rho_s^Q)$ is the elasticity of substitution between factors. The first-order conditions of this problem are immediately derived as:

$$\begin{cases} w_f F_{fs}^{dem} = [\alpha_{fs}^F]^{\sigma_s^Q} \left[\dfrac{p_s^Q}{w_f} \right]^{\sigma_s^Q - 1} p_s^Q Q_s \quad \forall f \\ [p_s^Q]^{1 - \sigma_s^Q} = \sum_f [\alpha_{fs}^F]^{\sigma_s^Q} [w_f]^{1 - \sigma_s^Q} \end{cases} \tag{2.3}$$

where the second equation, obtained by substitution of optimal factor demands into the constraint, relates the Lagrange multiplier to the factor prices w_f in a way that completely accounts for the technology. It is easily checked that p_s^Q necessarily satisfies

$$p_s^Q Q_s = \sum_f w_f F_{fs}^{dem} \tag{2.4}$$

(as stated in Table 2.1, cell (4,a)) and can be interpreted as the sector's value added price index. Normalizing this price to unity only affects measurement units of value added and is therefore innocuous; for the same reason, factor prices can in general be set to unity at base year. It is then straightforward to calibrate factor demands to fit the data in Table 2.1:

$$[\alpha_{fs}^F]^{\sigma_s^Q} = \frac{w_f F_{fs}^{dem}}{p_s^Q Q_s} \quad \forall f = \frac{\text{cell } (3, a)}{\text{cell } (4, a)} \tag{2.5}$$

This completes the calibration of factor demands even though we are unable to identify σ_s^Q from the share-parameters α_{fs}^F: values for substitution elasticities have to be provided from outside information.

We next turn to intermediate goods that are combined, assuming complementarity, into an aggregate material input mix. Optimal demands for intermediate goods X_{ts} are derived, for given levels of $X_{\cdot s}$, from cost-minimization taking prices as given using Leontief technologies:

$$\underset{\{X_{ts}\}}{\text{Min}} \sum_t (1 + \tau_t^Z) p_t^Z X_{ts}$$

$$\text{s.t. } X_{\cdot s} = \frac{X_{ts}}{\alpha_{ts}^X} \quad \forall t \tag{2.6}$$

where α_{ts}^X is now the amount of good from industry t necessary for sector s to produce one unit of aggregate intermediate input. Optimal demands immediately follow as:

$$X_{ts} = \alpha_{ts}^X X_{\cdot s} \quad \forall t \tag{2.7}$$

and the aggregate intermediate price p_s^X satisfies

$$p_s^X X_{\cdot s} = \sum_t (1 + \tau_t^Z) p_t^Z X_{ts} \tag{2.8}$$

from which we get

$$p_s^X = \sum_t (1 + \tau_t^Z) p_t^Z \alpha_{ts}^X \tag{2.9}$$

where again it is innocuous to choose units of the intermediate bundle so that $p_s^X = 1$. Calibration of the α_{ts}^X is straightforward: from Table 2.1, we know the amount paid to industry t as a share of total expenses on intermediate goods:

$$\frac{(1 + \tau_t^Z)p_t^Z X_{ts}}{p_s^X X_{\cdot s}} = \frac{\text{cell } (1, a)}{\text{cell } (2, a)};$$

(2.10)

eliminating X_{ts} using optimal demands and p_s^X thanks to normalization, the left-hand side becomes $(1 + \tau_t^Z)p_t^Z \alpha_{ts}^X$. We easily get the base-year tax rate τ_t^Z as:

$$\tau_t^Z = \frac{\text{cell } (6, a)}{\text{cell } (5, a)};$$

(2.11)

set $p_t^Z = 1 \ \forall t$ at base year (as will be justified soon), it immediately follows that

$$\alpha_{ts}^X = \frac{1}{(1 + \tau_t^Z)} \cdot \frac{\text{cell } (1, a)}{\text{cell } (2, a)}.$$

(2.12)

We finally turn to the upper-level of the technology, where value added and the aggregate bundle of intermediate goods are combined knowing that expenditure shares are thought to be constant so that the sub-technology is a Cobb-Douglas and the optimization sub-problem writes as:

$$\underset{\{Q_s, X_{\cdot s}\}}{\text{Min }} p_s^Q Q_s + p_s^X X_{\cdot s}$$

$$\text{s.t. } \ln Z_s = \alpha_{0s}^Z + \alpha_s^Q \ln Q_s + \alpha_s^X \ln X_{\cdot s}$$

(2.13)

with given prices and output level Z_s. The solution is:

$$\begin{cases} p_s^Q Q_s = \alpha_s^Q p_s^Z Z_s \\ p_s^X X_{\cdot s} = \alpha_s^X p_s^Z Z_s \\ \ln p_s^Z = \alpha_s^Q \ln p_s^Q + \alpha_s^X \ln p_s^X \end{cases}$$

(2.14)

with

$$p_s^Z Z_s = p_s^Q Q_s + p_s^X X_{\cdot s}$$

(2.15)

and the shares are immediately calibrated from the data:

$$\alpha_s^Q = \frac{\text{cell } (4, a)}{\text{cell } (5, a)}$$

(2.16)

$$\alpha_s^X = \frac{\text{cell } (2, a)}{\text{cell } (5, a)}$$

(2.16)

Observe once again that the data provide information on equilibrium values of flows at base-year: we are therefore free to normalize output prices p_s^Z to unity and to define output volumes consistently. Collecting the terms for sector s, we get the producer part of Table 2.2.

Table 2.2   A simple CGE model of a closed perfectly competitive economy

- Producer s

$$\begin{cases} X_{ts} = \alpha_{ts}^X X_{\bullet s} \quad \forall t \\ p_s^X = \sum_t (1 + \tau_t^Z) p_t^Z \alpha_{ts}^X \end{cases}$$

$$\begin{cases} w_f F_{fs}^{dem} = [\alpha_{fs}^F]^{\sigma_s^Q} \left[\dfrac{p_s^Q}{w_f}\right]^{\sigma_s^Q - 1} p_s^Q Q_s \quad \forall f \\ [p_s^Q]^{1 - \sigma_s^Q} = \sum_f [\alpha_{fs}^F]^{\sigma_s^Q} [w_f]^{1 - \sigma_s^Q} \end{cases}$$

$$\begin{cases} p_s^Q Q_s = \alpha_s^Q p_s^Z Z_s \\ p_s^X X_{\bullet s} = \alpha_s^X p_s^Z Z_s \\ \ln p_s^Z = \alpha_s^Q \ln p_s^Q + \alpha_{\bullet s}^X \ln p_s^X \end{cases}$$

- Household h

$$Sav_h = \mu(1 - \tau^{Inc}) \sum_f w_f \overline{F_{fh}^{sup}}$$

$$p_h^{Con} Con_h = (1 - \mu)(1 - \tau^{Inc}) \sum_f w_f \overline{F_{fh}^{sup}}$$

$$\begin{cases} (1 + \tau_t^Z) p_t^Z C_{ht} = [\alpha_{ht}^C]^{\sigma_h^C} \left[\dfrac{p_h^{Con}}{(1 + \tau_t^Z) p_t^Z}\right]^{\sigma_h^C - 1} p_h^{Con} Con_h \quad \forall t \\ [p_h^{Con}]^{1 - \sigma_h^C} = \sum_t [\alpha_{ht}^C]^{\sigma_h^C} [(1 + \tau_t^Z) p_t^Z]^{1 - \sigma_h^C} \end{cases}$$

- Government

$$p^{Gov} \overline{Gov} + Sav^{Gov} = \sum_s \tau_s^Z p_s^Z Z_s + \tau^{Inc} \sum_{fh} w_f \overline{F_{fh}^{sup}}$$

$$\begin{cases} G_t = \alpha_t^{Gov} \overline{Gov} \quad \forall t \\ p^{Gov} = \sum_t (1 + \tau_t^Z) p_t^Z \alpha_t^{Gov} \end{cases}$$

- Investor

$$p^{Inv} Inv = \sum_h Sav_h + Sav^{Gov}$$

$$\begin{cases} (1 + \tau_t^Z) p_t^Z I_t = [\alpha_t^{Inv}]^{\sigma_{Inv}} \left[\dfrac{p^{Inv}}{(1 + \tau_t^Z) p_t^Z}\right]^{\sigma_{Inv} - 1} p^{Inv} Inv \quad \forall t \\ [p^{Inv}]^{1 - \sigma_{Inv}} = \sum_t [\alpha_t^{Inv}]^{\sigma_{Inv}} [(1 + \tau_t^Z) p_t^Z]^{1 - \sigma_{Inv}} \end{cases}$$

- Equilibrium conditions

$$Z_t = \sum_s X_{ts} + \sum_h C_{ht} + G_t + I_t \quad \forall t$$

$$\sum_h \overline{F_{fh}^{sup}} = \sum_s F_{fs}^{dem} \quad \forall f$$

We should proceed in a similar way for each of the other agents in this economy (see Figure 2.1) but, for space-saving reasons, we leave this as an exercise for the reader. The model is then completed by adding equilibrium conditions to each market. Table 2.2 displays a complete illustrative CGE system. We have there assumed constant factor supplies $(\overline{F_{fh}^{sup}})$ and CES preferences for each household h, and parameterized the saving (μ) and income tax rates (τ^{Inc}); h's budget constraint therefore determines its aggregate consumption level Con_h. For the Government, we have assumed Leontief preferences and exogenous real aggregate consumption $(\overline{Gov})$; given that tax rates have been parameterized, it is the deficit/surplus that will have to adjust to satisfy the budget constraint of the public sector with this specification. Investors are assumed to use CES technologies to combine final goods into a capital aggregate in amount *Inv* consistent with the economy's supply of savings.[4]

The reader should observe that:

- All coefficients in this economy of Table 2.2 have been calibrated on the base year data set, except substitution elasticities for which we rely on outside information: econometric estimates should in principle be used, but this could be extremely tedious if, as is usually the case, there are many sectors, households and factors. Also, results often tend to be quite robust to small changes of these substitution elasticity values. For this reason, CGE models often rely (arguably excessively so) on 'guestimates' (meaning: an educated guess) and favour *ex post* sensitivity analyses (see below).

- All agents are, by construction, on their budget constraints in this economy; by Walras' law, one market equilibrium condition is redundant and could be dropped from the system. Therefore, only relative prices are determined, not absolute price levels: a numéraire good has to be arbitrarily chosen, and all values are expressed in units of that good.

- A general equilibrium of this economy is an allocation (quantities produced, consumed and so forth) supported by a vector of prices that solves a square non-linear system of equations. By construction, with unchanged levels of exogenous variables $(\overline{F_{fh}^{sup}}, \overline{Gov})$ and policy parameters (τ_t^Z, τ^{Inc}), the computed equilibrium will replicate the base year data. (It should be clear that numerous different model specifications can be made consistent with the same base year data by calibration. Calibration is therefore only a convenient way to force consistency on a specific model choice, it does not validate nor provide a selection mechanism.) To analyze the impact of a policy change, the model can be simulated by altering the relevant policy parameter/variable and computing the new equilibrium. Results are then reported as per-cent deviations from initial equilibrium values.

- *Ex post* sensitivity analysis consists in calibrating the model and performing the same policy experiment for alternative values of some (in particular guestimated) parameters within a reasonable range, and check whether the policy conclusions remain qualitatively unchanged. If this is not the case, then additional statistical work is presumably called for to identify a most accurate value for that parameter.

- Rarely mentioned by CGE modelers, a problem arises from the possibility that equilibriums may not be unique (see Kehoe, 1991). Obviously, the whole benchmarking-calibration exercise is on a different logical level in a world with multiple equilibriums, and it is not clear what the comparative statics policy exercises really mean in such circumstances: which is the 'relevant' equilibrium to pick among the set of possible solutions? It is remarkable that no case of multiple solutions has been reported to be encountered in calibrated applied GE models of competitive economies, so that, to date, whether or not non-uniqueness of equilibriums is more than a theoretically possible occurrence remains an open question.

Introducing Increasing Returns to Scale and Imperfect Competition

In many sectors, increasing returns to scale technologies and imperfect competition cannot be assumed away. We show how this complication can be dealt with in an applied GE model.

The individual firm's increasing returns technology

With increasing returns to scale technologies, output scale matters and we need to distinguish between individual firms and sector aggregates: we identify firm related variables by lower-case letters, while upper-case letters refer as before to industry aggregates (though for notation ease the sector index is dropped).

The most convenient method is to introduce a distinction between variable inputs and fixed inputs. Variable inputs will typically include all of the intermediate inputs and some of the factor inputs, even though, to simplify the exposition, we shall neglect material inputs in what follows. Fixed quantities of some primary inputs are required to operate the firm at any positive level of output. Therefore, the total demand for a factor f by an individual firm can be expressed as: $f_f^{dem} = f_f^v + \overline{f_f^F}$, where superscripts v and F refer respectively to 'variable' and 'fixed' factors. The individual technology is then written as

$$z = F(\ldots, f_f^{dem} - \overline{f_f^F}, \ldots), f_f^{dem} \geq \overline{f_f^F} \quad \forall f \tag{2.17}$$

where z is the firm's real output, and $F(\ldots)$ is linearly homogenous. The individual firm's problem is then to minimize costs of producing a specified target output level z:

$$\underset{\{k^v, l^v\}}{\text{Min}} \sum_f w_f f_f^v + fx \quad \text{s.t. } z = F(\cdots, f_f^v, \cdots)$$

$$\text{s.t. } fx = \sum_f w_f \overline{f_f^F} \tag{2.18}$$

where fx denotes the total fixed cost; this immediately yields the optimal input mix of variable inputs:

$$\frac{\partial F(\cdots, f_f^v, \cdots)}{\partial f_f^v} = \frac{w_f}{v}$$

$$vz = \sum_f w_f f_f^v \tag{2.19}$$

where v denotes the marginal (or variable-unit) cost which differs from the average (or total unit) cost due to the presence of fixed inputs by firms.

Imperfect competition and prices

Imperfect competition can take many different forms. Within a sector, goods may be assumed homogeneous or differentiated; this will bare consequences on the type of competition that can prevail in that industry. Firms will always be assumed to maximize profits, but the optimal price-cost margins will depend on whether the firm's strategic variable is assumed to be its selling price or its production scale (a firm cannot, of course, choose both). Also important is whether the firm is assumed to expect, and therefore to take into account when making its optimal decisions, a strategic reaction by competitors to changes in its own behaviour. In all cases, industry concentration will matter: the equilibrium outcome of an oligopoly game will, in general, differ significantly from the one to emerge from a large group assumption. In applications, firms will most generally – if not always – be assumed symmetric within a sector, that is, they will share the same technology and have the same size, so that they charge the same price albeit for possibly differentiated products. This is quite convenient because Herfindahl industry concentration indices are supplied by most statistical agencies, and can be shown to be the inverse of the number of firms under the symmetry assumption. Hence, using this outside information, it is possible to calibrate variables related to the individual firm from data on industry aggregates.

It is clearly beyond the scope of this chapter to detail the entire possible alternative modelling strategies of imperfectly competitive markets. For illustrative purpose, let us assume that products are homogeneous within the sector and that the competitive game is 'Nash in output' (or *Cournot–Nash*), that is, firms choose the level of their production scale to maximize profits, expecting no reaction from their competitors (a reasonable assumption if the number of competitors is large enough). Formally, the individual producer seeks to

$$\operatorname*{Max}_{z} prof(z) = p^{z}(Z)z - (vz + fx). \qquad (2.20)$$

where $prof(z)$ is the firm's profits and $p^{z}(Z)$ is the *equilibrium market price*. Observe that the former depends on the firm's output z and the latter on the aggregate supply Z in that industry. Solving the maximization problem with respect to z yields the famous Lerner pricing rule:

$$\frac{p^{z} - v}{p^{z}} = -\frac{d \ln p^{z}(Z)}{d \ln z}$$

$$= -\varepsilon^{C}(z, p^{z}(Z)) \qquad (2.21)$$

where $\varepsilon^{C}(z, p^{z}(Z))$ measures the market *equilibrium price* elasticity with respect to the individual firm's output z: except in extremely simplified cases, this elasticity is a complicated object. It will typically depend on preference parameters underlying demand functions (that is, substitution elasticities) as well as on market shares for which data are available at base year; $\varepsilon^{C}(z, p^{z}(Z))$ can therefore be calibrated. Assuming zero profits to prevail at base year between a known (from base-year Herfindahl indices) number of symmetric firms, and normalizing $p^{z}(Z)$ to unity, the variable unit cost v can be determined using the Lerner equation; the level of fixed costs fx follows then immediately. See Mercenier (1995a, 2002) for elaborations on this. In the simulations, firms within a sector will often be allowed to respond to changes in profitability by (costlessly) entering/exiting the market: the equilibrium number of competitors is determined by imposing zero supra-normal profits (the output price then equals the average production cost).

At this stage, it should be mentioned that non-convexities in production technologies generically imply that the equilibrium will not be unique. Mercenier (1995b) presents a numerical example of multiplicity in a large-scale applied GE model calibrated on real world data. It seems therefore that in this generation of CGE models, non-uniqueness of equilibriums is not a theoretical *curiosum*, but a potentially serious problem. Disregarding this could lead to dramatically wrong policy appraisals.

Multi-Country/Region Model with Trade

Our previous model lacks realism in that it assumes no trade with other countries or regions. Depending on the focus of the analysis, trade can be introduced either by setting a number of single-country models together and letting them interact, or by assuming that the country under consideration is so small that it does not affect equilibrium in the rest of the world: foreign prices and incomes are then treated as exogenous. In both cases, the modeller has to decide whether goods in an industrial category produced in different countries are identical from the customers' viewpoint.

One of the most popular assumptions (known as the Armington, 1969, assumption) is that goods from the same sector are differentiated in demand by countries of origin. The main justification for this specification is that, because of data restrictions and/or to simplify computations, the modeller works with highly aggregated sectors of activity; even if products are identical across countries at a very fine level of industry disaggregation, the composition of the aggregate basket of goods is unlikely to be identical across regions. The specification is attractive because it accounts for the large amount of cross-hauling (that is, two-way trade in identical goods) observed in the data, and given that even at fine levels of activity disaggregation, most countries produce goods in all product categories.

The simplest way to implement an Armington system is by assuming that all domestic agents buy units of a common composite basket composed of goods from all geographic origins. The composition and the price of this Armington good result as usual from cost minimization. To see how this is done, let i, j index countries or regions, and let E_{ijs} be the flow of sector s goods exported from i to j at prices $p_{is}^E = (1 + \tau_{is}^Z)p_{is}^{Z}$.[5] Assuming a CES aggregator, import demands by region j result from:

$$\operatorname*{Min}_{\{E_{ijs}\}} \sum_i p_{is}^E E_{ijs} \quad \text{s.t.} \quad E_{\cdot js} = \left\{ \sum_i \alpha_{ijs}^E [E_{ijs}]^{-\rho_{js}^E} \right\}^{-\frac{1}{\rho_{js}^E}} \quad -1 < \rho_{js}^E < \infty \qquad (2.22)$$

for given export prices and aggregate demand levels $E_{\cdot js}$; this yields:

$$
\begin{cases}
p_{is}^E E_{ijs} = [\alpha_{ijs}^E]^{\sigma_{js}^E} \left[\dfrac{p_{js}^{Arm}}{p_{is}^E} \right]^{\sigma_{js}^E - 1} p_{js}^{Arm} E_{\cdot js} \\[4mm]
[p_{js}^{Arm}]^{1 - \sigma_{js}^E} = \sum_i [\alpha_{ijs}^E]^{\sigma_{js}^E} [p_{is}^E]^{1 - \sigma_{js}^E}
\end{cases}
\qquad (2.23)
$$

with $\sigma_{js}^E = 1/(1 + \rho_{js}^E)$ the substitution elasticity, p_{js}^{Arm} the unit-price of the Armington aggregate and $E_{\cdot js}$ is the amount of the sector s Armington good demanded by country j:

$$E_{\cdot js} = \sum_t X_{jst} + \sum_h C_{jhs} + G_{js} + I_{js}. \tag{2.24}$$

The market equilibrium condition for good t in our model of Table 2.2 then becomes:

$$Z_{jt} = \sum_i E_{jit} \; \forall t. \tag{2.25}$$

Given the base-year bilateral trade data-matrix, we know the expenditure flows $(p_{is}^E E_{ijs})$, as well as $(p_{js}^{Arm} E_{\cdot js}) = \sum_i (p_{is}^E E_{ijs})$; set $p_{js}^{Arm} = 1$ at base year, and pick values of the substitution elasticities σ_{js}^E from outside trade-econometric evidence. The bilateral trade share-parameters can then immediately be calibrated as:

$$[\alpha_{ijs}^E]^{\sigma_{js}^E} = [p_{is}^E]^{\sigma_{js}^E - 1} \cdot \frac{(p_{is}^E E_{ijs})}{(p_{js}^{Arm} E_{\cdot js})}. \tag{2.26}$$

Observe that with the above specification, even the smallest country faces endogenous terms of trade and enjoys some market power, though perfect competition can prevail among producers (and indeed implicitly prevails in our exposition as implied by our reference to Table 2.2) so that firms do not take advantage of this market power. In many sectors where production involves fixed costs, firms tend to choose specific product varieties and to specialize, taking advantage of their market power on the chosen niche. The previous framework can easily be extended to account for this possibility, as we now show.

Let N_{is} be the number of firms producing differentiated varieties of good s in country i; assume that firms operating within the same country and sector are symmetric (same technology and same market shares, hence, same price) and let e_{ijs}^f be an individual i firm's sales to market j. As in the Armington case, this demand e_{ijs}^f can be derived from utility maximization in region j provided preferences are amended to acknowledge the existence of product varieties as follows:

$$E_{\cdot js} = \left\{ \sum_i \sum_{f=1}^{N_{is}} [e_{ijs}^f]^{-\rho_{js}^E} \right\}^{-\frac{1}{\rho_{js}^E}}$$

$$= \left\{ \sum_i N_{is} [e_{ijs}]^{-\rho_{js}^E} \right\}^{-\frac{1}{\rho_{js}^E}} \tag{2.27}$$

where the second equality takes account of the symmetry assumption between firms.[6] Cost minimization then yields:

$$\begin{cases} p_{is}^E e_{ijs} = \left[\dfrac{p_{js}^{DS}}{p_{is}^E} \right]^{\sigma_{js}^E - 1} p_{js}^{DS} E_{\cdot js} \\[4mm] [p_{js}^{DS}]^{1 - \sigma_{js}^E} = \sum_i N_{is} [p_{is}^E]^{1 - \sigma_{js}^E} \end{cases} \tag{2.28}$$

where p_{js}^{DS} is the (Dixit–Stiglitz) price aggregator. Though this expression may look very similar to system (2.1) it is actually quite different: with entry/exit of firms into the industry due to zero supra-normal equilibrium profits, N_{is} will be an endogenous variable.

INTRODUCING TRANSPORT IN CGE MODELS

Transport in Single-region Models

So far, nothing has been said about transport. How does it enter the scene? At a first sight, transport is just one or a subset of commodities, produced by one or a subset of industries, consumed by households and used as an input by firms. These transport related sectors can be differentiated by transport object (passengers versus freight, bulk versus container), by distance class (short versus long), by mode and other characteristics. Typically, demand would be specified by some form of nesting as illustrated in Figure 2.1. A household could, for example, choose between consumption of travel services and consumption of other goods, and then, conditional on having chosen travel, how much of his private car and of public transportation to use. Thus, apparently, nothing has to be added to what has been explained so far.

At least three aspects of transport need however a special treatment:

- Transport demand and benefits generated by transport do not only depend on monetary cost, but also on time needed for travel or freight.
- Transport generates negative externalities within the transport sector itself – congestion – as well as outside the transport sector.
- Transport is in most cases not utility generating by itself, but it is instrumental for other activities such as working, shopping, tourism, visiting friends or events and so forth. Similarly, transport is not directly an input of firms, but instrumental for buying, selling or exchanging information.

We first introduce transport demand of households depending on monetary cost as well as on travel time. Transport is then just a consumer good like other goods, and we disregard it being possibly instrumental for other purposes. We then introduce commuting as a means to labour income earning. We deal afterwards with transport demand of firms and finally with transport related externalities.

Travel demand of households

An average UK citizen spends 87 minutes per day travelling and 14 percent of his or her total expenditure on transport (UK National Statistics Online, figures for 2005). If an hour travel time is valued at the hourly wage, time costs and monetary costs of travelling are of a similar magnitude, and the former can obviously not be neglected. Also, many transport policy measures mainly affect travel time, not monetary cost, and thus the time component is essential for policy evaluation. The household's allocation of time between work and leisure should now be modelled, and its labour supply therefore endogenized. See Jara-Diaz (2000) and chapter by David Hensher for a review on allocation and valuation of travel time.

Let production factor $f = L$ be labour so that F_{Lh}^{sup} is the amount of labour the household decides to supply; T_h^l and $\overline{T}_h$ are respectively demand for leisure time and total time endowment. Finally, denote $t_{hs} \geq 0$ as the travel time associated with each unit of the consumption of good s. $t_{hs} = 0$, unless good s is travel. Sticking to the assumption in Table 2.2 of CES preferences and a fixed saving rate, the household's decision results from

$$\underset{\{C_{hs}, T_h^l\}}{\text{Max}} \left\{ \beta_h [T_h^l]^{-\rho_h^C} + \sum_s \alpha_{hs}^C [C_{hs}]^{-\rho_h^C} \right\}^{-\frac{1}{\rho_h^C}} \tag{2.29}$$

subject to the budget constraint

$$\sum_s (1 + \tau_s^Z) p_s^Z C_{hs} = (1 - \mu)(1 - \tau^{Inc}) \left[w_L F_{Lh}^{sup} + \sum_{f \neq L} w_f \overline{F_{fh}^{sup}} \right] \tag{2.30}$$

and the time constraint

$$T_h^l + F_{Lh}^{sup} + \sum_s t_{hs} C_{hs} = \overline{T}_h. \tag{2.31}$$

Using the latter constraint to substitute out F_{Lh}^{sup} from the budget equation, we get:

$$\sum_s (1 + \tau_s^Z) p_s^Z C_{hs} = (1 - \mu)(1 - \tau^{Inc}) \left(-w_L T_h^l - w_L \sum_s t_{hs} C_{hs} + w_L \overline{T}_h + \sum_{f \neq L} w_f \overline{F_{fh}^{sup}} \right). \tag{2.32}$$

This can be rewritten as

$$\omega T_h^l + \sum_s \pi_{hs} C_{hs} = (1 - \mu)(1 - \tau^{Inc}) \left(w_L \overline{T}_h + \sum_{f \neq L} w_f \overline{F_{fh}^{sup}} \right) \tag{2.33}$$

where the net wage (net of saving and taxes) $\omega = (1 - \mu)(1 - \tau^{Inc}) w_L$ is the consumer's valuation of leisure time and $\pi_{hs} = (1 + \tau_s^Z) p_s^Z + \omega t_{hs}$ is the cost to consumer per unit of consumption good s. If s denotes travel, this is usually referred to by transport economists as the 'generalized cost per unit of travel'. Solving the maximization problem yields:

$$p_h^{Con} Con_h = (1 - \mu)(1 - \tau^{Inc}) \left[w_L \overline{T}_h + \sum_{f \neq L} w_f \overline{F_{fh}^{sup}} \right]$$

$$\pi_{hs} C_{hs} = [\alpha_{hs}^C]^{\sigma_h^C} \left[\frac{p_h^{Con}}{\pi_{hs}} \right]^{\sigma_h^C - 1} p_h^{Con} Con_h \quad \forall s$$

$$\omega T_h^l = [\beta_h]^{\sigma_h^C} \left[\frac{p_h^{Con}}{\omega} \right]^{\sigma_h^C - 1} p_h^{Con} Con_h$$

$$[p_h^{Con}]^{1 - \sigma_h^C} = [\beta_h]^{\sigma_h^C} \omega^{1 - \sigma_h^C} + \sum_s [\alpha_{hs}^C]^{\sigma_h^C} \pi_{hs}^{1 - \sigma_h^C} \tag{2.34}$$

Labour supply F_{Lh}^{sup} is then determined using the time constraint. The share parameters α_{hs}^C and β_h can be calibrated from base-year data as before, provided information is available on the household's time endowment, leisure and travel time.

Though straightforward, this approach has two drawbacks. The first is that, in its valuation of travel time, the household takes into account only that part of lost labour income that goes into consumption, neglecting the one that goes into saving. This is due to our restrictive assumption of a constant savings rate. To relax this assumption would require an intertemporal approach beyond the scope of this chapter. The second drawback is that econometric estimates of valuations of travel time savings (VTTS) are typically considerably smaller than the wage rate, even if corrected for income taxes and the saving rate. Furthermore, VTTS vary significantly over travel purposes, being smaller for leisure trips than for commuting. This is indirect evidence that people prefer spending time travelling over spending time working (see chapter by David Hensher). The simplest way to take this into account is by adding a preference term $\Sigma_s \gamma_{hs} t_{hs} C_{hs}$ to the household's objective function, with γ_{hs} denoting the utility per unit of time spent on travel item s. The household's demand system becomes:

$$C_{hs} = \zeta_h [\alpha_{hs}^C]^{\sigma_h^C} [\lambda_h \tilde{\pi}_{hs}]^{-\sigma_h^C}$$

$$T_h^l = \zeta_h [\beta_h]^{\sigma_h^C} [\lambda_h \omega]^{-\sigma_h^C} \tag{2.35}$$

with

$$\tilde{\pi}_{hs} = \pi_{hs} - (\gamma_{hs}/\lambda_h) t_{hs} = (1 + \tau_s^Z) p_s^Z + \tilde{\omega}_{hs} t_{hs}$$

$$\tilde{\omega}_{hs} = \omega - \gamma_{hs}/\lambda_h. \tag{2.36}$$

The two new unknowns ζ_h and λ_h are obtained by the budget constraint and the restriction

$$1 = [\beta_h]^{\sigma_h^C} [\lambda_h \omega]^{1 - \sigma_h^C} + \sum_s [\alpha_h^C]^{\sigma_h^C} [\lambda_h \tilde{\pi}_{hs}]^{1 - \sigma_h^C} \tag{2.37}$$

where λ_h is the Lagrange multiplier associated with the budget constraint, i.e. marginal utility of income. If s denotes travel, $\tilde{\pi}_{hs}$ is now the generalised cost per unit of travel, with VTTS $\tilde{\omega}_{hs}$. The VTTS is the net wage, corrected for the preference term γ_{hs}/λ_h representing the marginal utility of spending time with travel type s, translated into monetary units by the term $1/\lambda_h$. Note that the VTTS now not only depends on the wage rate, but also on all prices, travel time, income and the time endowment. The larger γ_{hs} is, the more the VTTS is reduced compared to the specification without travel time in the utility function. As before, all parameters except the elasticity of substitution can be calibrated from observed benchmark data. The additional information needed is the VTTS for each item of travel demand necessary for the calibration of γ_{hs}. In what precedes, we have specified all preferences as one-level CES: obviously, everything can be extended to nested CES or other functional forms.

Commuting

An interesting application of CGE models in transport is to look at the interaction between commuting costs and the labour market. In many countries commuting costs are deducted from the tax base. This reduces distortions in job choice, but may distort residential location choices (Wrede, 2003). In order to quantify these distortions an explicit modelling of commuting costs is needed.

Assume commuters do not care whether they spend time working or travelling to their job. They will choose commuting modes so as to maximise hourly wage, net of commuting cost, where an hour covers working plus commuting time. Let m index travel modes and assume for simplicity that industry disaggregation is such that each travel mode is a specific sector. Then, C_{hm} is demand by h of a specific commodity with market price $(1 + \tau_m^Z)p_m^Z$. Denote unit travel time-cost by t_{hm} and let T_h^W be gross working time, including commuting time. The household wants to maximize the net wage w_{Lh}^{net} per hour worked, subject to a 'commuting production function' that combines travel quantities by modes as inputs to produce an aggregate 'travel to work' service. The household thus obtains the net wage from solving

$$T_h^W w_{Lh}^{net} = \underset{\{C_{hm}\}}{\text{Max}}\{w_L(T_h^W - \sum_m t_{hm}C_{hm}) - \sum_m (1 + \tau_m^Z)p_m^Z C_{hm}\}$$

$$\text{s.t.} \left[\sum_m \delta_{hm} C_{hm}^{-\rho_h^M}\right]^{-\frac{1}{\rho_h^M}} = T_h^W \tag{2.38}$$

where we have assumed a CES commuting production function. (Any level of nesting could of course be introduced here.) Note that the amount of the travel service needed is assumed proportional to work time. This implies that work time is varied in terms of person-days per week, not time per day. Solving the problem is straightforward and left to the reader. As before, share parameters δ_{hm} can be calibrated from observed commuting data by mode, while substitution elasticities $\sigma_h^M = 1/(1 + \rho_h^M)$ have to be imported from econometric studies on responses of mode choice on generalised costs. In the household's decision problem we just have to replace F_{Lh}^{sup} in the time constraint with gross working time T_h^W, and w_L with the net wage w_{Lh}^{net}.

Firms
Firms buy transport services (for both passengers and freight) as a production input. In a multiregional model, firms' transport demands are explicitly related to the interregional flows of goods. In single region models they are treated just as any other input with one change: firms bear costs not only in money but also in time. Monetary costs for transport can be observed in a sufficiently detailed input–output table, while time costs have to be imputed using travel time information and VTTS estimates for firms. For producing the input 'freight services', say, one introduces a production function with a service as output and transport quantities by mode as inputs. A nested CES is again convenient here. To take account of time costs, a simple trick helps: the transport quantity by mode is itself regarded as a Leontief composite of a transport service (produced e.g. by the trucking industry) and a service called 'travel time' (that is, spending time with employees, equipment and goods 'on the road'). This service is simply introduced as another commodity, produced by an industry, that may, for example, only use labour (representing employee's time) and capital (representing capital costs of goods and equipment bound in transport).

Endogenous travel times and externalities
Travel times have been assumed fixed so far. Transport infrastructure is however a collective good with congestion, and thus travel times depend on both capacity and

aggregate demand. To model this, t_{hm} is usually related to the ratio of aggregate travel demand D_m to capacity K_m as follows:

$$t_{hm} = t_{hm}^0 + \alpha_{hm}^t (D_m/K_m)^{\varepsilon_m} \tag{2.39}$$

where t_{hm}^0 denotes free-flow travel time. Agents in the economy, either households or firms, are assumed too small to perceive any influence they could have on D_m so that t_{hm} remains fixed in their individual optimization problems. The elasticity ε_m is notoriously difficult to estimate, and its reliability is questionable because congestion varies a lot across different parts of the network, time of the day and day of the week and year. For welfare evaluations of policies affecting congestion such as road pricing, fuel taxes and infrastructure investment, endogenous travel times, even if imperfectly modelled, are nevertheless an indispensable model ingredient.

Another important element is externalities imposed by transport on the other parts of the economy. The least demanding way to take them into account is to neglect externalities on firms, and to assume separability for households meaning that no household decision is affected by externalities. Formally this means to specify household utility as a function of externalities and a sub-utility that only depends on the decision variables. In this case, the solution of the equilibrium can be done first, disregarding externalities, and the evaluation of the welfare impact is added afterwards. The main difficulty is to get a reliable parameterization of the welfare impact of externalities. This includes, first, a measure of how traffic emissions translate into immissions affecting the household's wellbeing, and second, a measure of the impact of the immissions on utility. Under additive separability one would subtract a linear function of damage indicators from the mentioned sub-utility. The coefficients of this linear expression are calibrated such that one reproduces the willingness to pay (WTP) for damage reductions in the benchmark equilibrium. The WTPs must be imported from econometric estimates using revealed or stated preference data.

Transport in Multi-region Models

Regions can have any scale from parts of the world (Asia, Europe and so forth) down to residential zones in an urban area. In a multi-location setting for an urban area, the focus is on shopping, commuting and other passenger trips, and on residential and commercial location choices. On a larger regional or national scale, the focus is on long distance passenger traffic and on freight. We here concentrate on the latter and briefly deal with urban models in a special subsection below.

Our introduction of trade in CGE models assumed that the price charged by a firm exporting is the same as the price paid by the cross-border customer. Realism requires that, upon destination, goods be priced to include 'trade margins' (freight cost, wholesaling, storing and so forth). Consider freight costs alone for expositional ease. The destination price p_{ijs}^M of good s exported by i to j is the mill price (possibly including local taxes though we neglect these hereafter) plus the freight cost f_{ijs}:

$$p_{ijs}^M = p_{is}^E + f_{ijs}. \tag{2.40}$$

f_{ijs} is of course paid to the industry producing the transport service from i to j. Industries producing a service driving a wedge between mill price and customer price are called margin industries. Wholesale and retail trade are other important margin industries. Transport policy affects the economy via its impact on f_{ijs}.

A Leontief technology is usually adopted to transform the good at the factory gate into the good at the location of the customer. Let θ_{ijs} denote transport service per unit of delivered good so that $\theta_{ijs}E_{ijs}$ is demand for the transport service associated with trade flow E_{ijs}. This service may be supplied by a firm located in the exporting region, or in the destination region. In the latter case, $f_{ijs} = \theta_{ijs}p_{jt}^Z$ is the per unit transport margin with p_{jt}^Z the price of a unit transport service (sector t) in region j. Industries producing the transport service have monetary as well as time costs, which are taken into account in just the same way as explained for transport input of firms above.

Obviously, introducing margin industries makes complex multiregional models even more complex. A popular alternative is the 'iceberg' approach. Here, no transport service is produced: the exported good melts on its way from origin to destination, so that the exported quantities E_{ijs} differ from those that reach destination, denoted M_{ijs}. Let $0 < \psi_{ijs} < 1$ be the melting factor, so that $M_{ijs} = \psi_{ijs}E_{ijs}$. Assuming that transport is a competitive zero profit activity, the destination price is $p_{ijs}^M = p_{ijs}^E/\psi_{ijs}$, so that values at origin and destination are identical:

$$p_{ijs}^M M_{ijs} = p_{ijs}^E E_{ijs} \qquad (2.41)$$

The parameter ψ_{ijs} has to be calibrated so that transport costs are a per centage share in trade value for the benchmark. Transport policies affecting trade costs can be evaluated by changing this parameter. Obviously, ψ_{ijs} can account for both monetary and time costs; furthermore, it may be made to depend on endogenous travel times.

Applications

Single-region models
Typical applications of single-region models to transport issues are the studies of Conrad (1997) and Conrad and Heng (2002) and a series of papers by Mayeres and Proost (for example, 2001, 2004); see also the useful review by Munk (2003). Mayeres and Proost (2004) introduce a highly detailed structure of the transport market for passengers, distinguishing private versus business as well as different modes. They also introduce different types of households in order to identify distributional impacts of transport policies.

The applications all take account of congestion in some way. Conrad and Heng (2002) assume the effective stock of capital in the transport industry to be decreasing in capacity use. Their aim is to show whether a capacity increase in Germany is welfare improving. Given the calibration of the model, which is debatable regarding the congestion function, their answer is affirmative.

Models that cover private passenger flows take account of monetary as well as time costs that determine demand decision, much in the same way as described above. This leads to demand functions for transport with generalized costs substituted for prices. Most importantly, the VTTS becomes an endogenous variable that generally depends on all prices and income. Particularly, it depends on wages, thus introducing interdependence between transport and the labour market (Berg, 2007). This approach allows congestion to be taken into account in a more direct and less ad hoc way than in Conrad and Heng (2002). Relying on speed-flow relations from transport engineering one can make travel times depend on the volume of flows, given infrastructure capacities (as shown above). A policy affecting transport demand through taxes, fees or fuel prices, or a policy affecting capacity through infrastructure investment has a direct impact on travel times and possibly monetary travel costs; these in turn enter the demand decisions such that adjustments of congestion, travel times, prices, flows as well as transactions on all goods and factor markets eventually lead to a new equilibrium. In equilibrium, all agents make their optimal choices, given prices as well as travel times are determined by the equilibrium level of congestion. The most sophisticated brands of such models even take other externalities like noise, accident risks and air pollution into account (Mayeres and Proost, 2004). For the sake of simplicity preferences are usually assumed to be separable between utility from goods and travel on the one hand and environmental quality on the other, such that environmental externalities have an impact on utility, but not on decisions (Mayeres and Proost, 2004). It is thus neglected that people might, for example, travel more, if they move to the suburbs in order to escape from urban noise and air pollution.

Models of this brand seem to be an ideal framework for analyzing the impact of transport policies on a wide range of interesting variables such as transport quantities, congestion, incomes and prices. Even more important is their ability to assess welfare effects, for the aggregate economy and/or for different household types. They thus extend the classical welfare-theoretical cost–benefit analysis to a general equilibrium framework. There are, however, also drawbacks. One is the notorious uncertainty about elasticities, which is of course a general problem of CGE applications. The prior choice of functional forms that is usually left untouched in sensitivity analysis might even be more problematic. Another drawback is that the macro style of these models averages out a lot of details, which could be the decisive factor to reach policy conclusions. A case in point is the macroeconomic congestion function. Congestion greatly varies by region, time of day, day of the week and from link to link. For calibrating the macro congestion function one must fix a point on the macro speed-flow schedule for the whole economy, which must be understood as some kind of average. But obviously, speed as a function of average flow can be very different from average speed, when the average is taken over speeds as functions of flows under a lot of different conditions regarding link, time of day and so forth. One can of course try to differentiate to any degree, but the lack of spatial detail remains a problem.

Multi-region models

Multiregional models aim at quantifying regional effects of transport policy, particularly of infrastructure investment. Typically, they introduce trade costs that are reduced by investing into certain transport links. An early contribution starting this literature is Buckley (1992). His model is a standard perfect competition approach with three regions and five industries. Interregional trade follows an Armington approach. Cost and expenditure functions are nests of either Leontief or CD functions. Transport is a Leontief complement of interregional flows. It is assumed to be produced at the place of origin. Buckley's experiment is to increase labour productivity in one region's transport sector. The results show how the welfare gain is distributed across regions.

Venables and Gasiorek (1998) improve upon this idea by allowing for more regions and industries, more flexible functional forms and – most importantly – by applying the Dixit–Stiglitz approach to monopolistic competition in the production sector. This brings scale effects into the impact analysis, which are not existent in the traditional perfect competition framework. Cost reductions lead to expansion of output; this in turn makes producers move down the average cost curve. This gives rise to effects that the SACTRA report (Department for Transport, 1999) has called 'wider economic effects' of transport cost reductions. In a perfect competition framework without externalities such effects cannot exist: the welfare gain in monetary terms, generated by a marginal transport cost reduction, is just this marginal transport cost reduction, no less, no more. This is different with economies of scale: the marginal welfare gain tends to exceed the marginal cost reduction. The ratio of the former over the latter, called the 'total benefit multiplier', is in the order of 1.4 in the authors' numerical experiments. One should be aware that this multiplier may not only blow up gains, but possible losses as well: regions losing due to other regions moving closer to one another can lose more with increasing than with constant returns, because they move up rather than down the average cost curve.

In a series of research projects for the European Commission, Bröcker and co-authors (Bröcker et al., 2010) have applied a similar approach with a smaller number of industries (just one tradable and one non-tradable sector in most cases), but a very large number of regions, such that the spatial distribution of welfare effects generated, for example, by the commission's TEN-T infrastructure program can be monitored in much detail (see also Bröcker, 2001a, 2001b, 2002).

Kim and Hewings (2003) and Kim et al. (2004) follow a different line of argument for identifying regional impacts of transport infrastructure improvements. They let firms use transport infrastructure as a production input that is provided for free. The level of service of the transport infrastructure is measured as a Harris-type (Harris, 1954) potential indicator of accessibility. The authors find a positive network effect of infrastructure policy, meaning that the welfare gain of an entire network of new projects exceeds the sum of the effects, if all projects are evaluated separately.

Urban models

A more recent branch of CGE applications in transport looks at urban passenger transport, focusing on the transport–land use nexus. Anas and collaborators (Anas and Hyok-Joo, 2006; Anas and Kim, 1996; Anas and Liu, 2007; Anas and Xu, 1999) lead the field. These authors succeeded in modelling, in a general equilibrium framework, location decisions of households and firms, travel decisions for shopping and commuting, goods and services production decisions of firms, and goods and services consumption decisions of households. Households' consumption and travel decisions are micro based: households maximize utility subject to a budget as well as a time constraint. Travel times are obtained from a stochastic user equilibrium (Sheffi, 1985) in a congested network. In equilibrium, markets for land, labour, goods and services clear, and travel times are expected minimal times given equilibrium flows through the network. Due to the congestion externality the equilibrium allocation is not Pareto-efficient. In a recent extension there are also housing, construction and demolition sectors in order to model the dynamics of the housing stock.

An important methodological innovation in this work is merging the continuous demand approach of traditional CGE models with the discrete choice concept. If one took all households as homogenous, a rather unrealistic equilibrium pattern with strictly separated land use zones would emerge, and bang-bang type responses of households' location decisions to shocks would be observed.

The utility U_{ij} of a household residing at i and working at j is assumed to have three additive components, $U_{ij} = \tilde{U}_{ij} + A_{ij} + u_{ij}$:

- The systematic component $\tilde{U}_{ij}$ is a function of continuously measured quantities of goods and service consumption, as usual. It must be defined in a way that makes it dimensionless. For homothetic preferences, it is $\tilde{U}_{ij} = \ln V_{ij}$, if V_{ij} is a linear-homogeneous representation of preferences.
- A_{ij} is the inherent attractiveness of the residence–work place pair ij. It delivers the degree of freedom needed to reproduce any observed distribution of the population across such pairs in a benchmark data set.
- u_{ij} is an idiosyncratic component varying across individuals of the ij-population, which otherwise are taken to be identical. u_{ij} is assumed to be independent identically Gumbel distributed. This implies that the share of the total population choosing the ij-pair is described by a logit model.

This framework is about to replace the so-called LUTI models in urban simulation (Waddell, 2000; Wegener, 2004; see also chapter by Michael Wegener), that follow a tradition initiated by Lowry (1964). Models of the latter kind do a good job in simulating land-use implications of urban transport policies, but due to the lack of micro-foundation they are unable to quantify welfare effects. Furthermore, understating the price mechanism in these models leads to ad-hoc mechanisms equilibrating markets that are not very convincing. In both respects Anas and co-authors made a big step forward, offering a framework for simulating a wide range of policies such as infra-structure provision, subsidizing certain modes, road pricing, cordon pricing, supply of parking lots and more. For any such policy one can not only simulate price and quantity impacts, but also welfare impacts by residential zone, type of household and income group. These are the issues that debates about urban transport policies typically focus on.

CONCLUSIONS

During the last 20 years, computable general equilibrium (CGE) models have become standard tools of quantitative policy assessment. Their appeal has built on their rigorous grounding in economic theory: individual agent's decision-making behaviour is derived from explicit optimization under strictly specified technological or budget constraints, given market signals that ensure global consistency. These theoretical foundations have made CGE models appear particularly useful for ex-ante evaluations of policy reforms.

In this chapter, we have discussed how the standard CGE framework can be extended to include most – if not all – the elements that are the focus of transportation policy analysis.

Powerful as it is, the whole apparatus relies on the concept of 'representative agent' despite unclear aggregation procedures to link these aggregate optimizing decision makers to the numerous individual agents whose behaviour they are meant to capture. Yet, large and detailed micro data-sets on individual behaviour in their full heterogeneity are increasingly being made available, and for many issues, working with myriads of actual economic agents rather than with a few hypothetical ones is extremely appealing as it makes possible to precisely identify the winners and the losers of a reform – obviously a major concern to policy makers. One can therefore conjecture that in the future, CGE modelers will devise explicit aggregation procedures in order to be able to keep track, in their general equilibrium models, of the full heterogeneity in individual behaviours provided by the micro data-sets. See Magnani and Mercenier (2009) for an effort in that direction.

NOTES

1. How finely defined are these industries or household groups is arbitrary, and will depend on the type of analysis. The modeller clearly faces a trade-off here: a finer disaggregation might provide richer answers, but it will require more and possibly less reliable data, it will necessitate additional possibly more questionable assumptions, and it will make the model more difficult to solve and the predictions more difficult to interpret.
2. Though slightly different in presentation, this table is conceptually identical to what is known in the literature as a social accounting matrix (SAM).
3. Our presentation implicitly assumes that all industries are perfectly competitive. Assuming imperfect competition in some industries would only require mild reinterpretation of some variables, as shown later.
4. Other specifications are of course possible: clearly, which of the variables are left free to adjust and which are kept fixed will depend on the type of policy explored.
5. We could of course assume a specific *ad valorem* tax/subsidy rate on exports; this would, however, require amending the government budget constraint, without bringing any additional insight.
6. These preferences, associated with the name of Dixit–Stiglitz (1977), are also known as 'love-for-variety' preferences because they acknowledge increasing returns in utility with respect to the number of available varieties. Similar technologies can be used by firms to combine intermediate inputs with differentiated varieties to yield increasing returns to specialization. Such a technology, first introduced by Ethier (1982), is a key element in the 'new economic geography' and in many models of the endogenous growth literature.

REFERENCES

Anas, A. and R. Hyok-Joo, 2006, Curbing urban sprawl with congestion tolls and urban boundaries. *Regional Science and Urban Economics*, **36**, 510–541.

Anas, A. and I. Kim, 1996, General equilibrium models of polycentric urban land use with endogenous congestion and job agglomeration. *Journal of Urban Economics*, **40**, 232–256.

Anas, A. and Y. Liu, 2007, A regional economy, land use, and transportation model (RELU-TRAN): Formulation, algorithm design and testing. *Journal of Regional Science*, **47** (3), 415–455.

Anas, A. and R. Xu, 1999, Congestion, land use and job dispersion: A general equilibrium model. *Journal of Urban Economics*, **45**, 451–473.

Armington, P.S., 1969, Geographic pattern of trade and the effects of price changes. *IMF Staff Papers*, **16**, 176–199.

Berg, C., 2007, Household transport demand in a CGE-framework. *Environmental & Resource Economics*, **37**, 573–597.

Bröcker, J., 2001a, Spatial effects of transport infrastructure: The role of market structure. In J. Roy and W. Schulz, eds, *Theories of Regional Competition*, Baden-Baden: Nomos, pp. 181–193.

Bröcker, J., 2001b, Trans-European effects of 'Trans-European Networks'. In F. Bolle and M. Carlberg, eds, *Advances in Behavioral Economics: Essays in Honor of Horst Todt*. Heidelberg: Physica, pp. 141–157.

Bröcker, J., 2002, Spatial effects of European transport policy: a CGE approach. In G.J.D. Hewings, M. Sonis and D. Boyce, eds, *Trade, Networks and Hierachies: Modelling Regional and Interregional Economies*. Berlin, Heidelberg and New York: Springer, pp. 11–28.

Bröcker, J., 2004, Computable general equilibrium analysis in transportation economics. In D.A. Hensher, K.J. Button, K.E. Haynes and P.R. Stopher, eds, *Handbook of Transport Geography and Spatial Systems*. Amsterdam: Elsevier, pp. 269–289.

Bröcker, J., A. Korzhenevych and C. Schürmann, 2010, Assessing spatial equity and efficiency impacts of transport infrastructure projects. *Transportation Research Part B*, **44**, 795–811.

Buckley, P.H., 1992, A transportation-oriented interregional computable general equilibrium model of the United States. *The Annals of Regional Science*, **26**, 331–348.

Conrad K., 1997, Traffic, transportation, infrastructure and externalities: a theoretical framework for CGE-analysis. *The Annals of Regional Science*, **31**, 369–389.

Conrad, K. and S. Heng, 2002, Financing road infrastructure by savings in congestion costs: a CGE analysis. *The Annals of Regional Science*, **36**, 107–122.

Department for Transport, 1999, *Transport and the Economy*, Report by Standing Advisory Committee on Trunk Road Assessment (SACTRA). Available at www.dft.gov.uk/pgr/economics/sactra/

Dixit, A. and J. Stiglitz, 1977, Monopolistic competition and optimum product diversity. *American Economic Review*, **67** (3), 297–308.

Ethier W., 1982, National and international returns to scale in the modern theory of international trade. *American Economic Review*, **73**, 389–405.

Fossati A. and W. Wiegard, eds, 2002, *Policy Evaluation with Computable General Equilibrium Models*. London: Routledge.

Ginsburgh V. and M. Keyzer, 1997, *The Structure of Applied General Equilibrium Models*. Cambridge, MA: MIT Press.

Gorman W., 1959, Separable Utility and Aggregation, *Econometrica*, **27**, 469–481.

Harris, C., 1954, The market as a factor in the localization of industry in the United States. *Annals of the Association of American Geographers*, **64**, 315–348.

Jara-Diaz, S.R., 2000, Allocation and value of travel time savings. In D.A. Hensher and K.J. Button, eds, *Handbooks in Transport, Vol 1: Handbook of Transport Modelling*. Amsterdam: Pergamon-Elsevier, pp. 303–309.

Kehoe T., 1991, Computation and multiplicity of equilibria. In W. Hildenbrand and H. Sonnenschein, eds, *Handbook of Mathematical Economics Vol IV*. Amsterdam: North-Holland, pp. 2049–2143.

Kim, E. and G.J.D. Hewings, 2003, An application of integrated transport network – multiregional CGE framework II: calibration of network effects of highway. REAL Discussion Paper 03-T-24, Urbana, Illinois.

Kim, E., G.J.D. Hewings and C. Hong, 2004, An application of an integrated transport network-multiregional CGE model: a framework for the economic analysis of highway projects. *Economic Systems Research*, **16** (3), 235–258.

Lowry, I.S., 1964, A Model of Metropolis. Memorandum RM-4035-RC. Santa Monica: RAND Corporation.

Magnani R. and J. Mercenier, 2009, On linking microsimulation and computable GE by exact aggregation of heterogeneous discrete-choice making agents. *Economic Modelling*, **26** (3), 560–570.

Mayeres, I. and S. Proost, 2001, Marginal tax reform, externalities and income distribution. *Journal of Public Economics*, **79** (2), 343–363.

Mayeres, I. and S. Proost, 2004, Testing alternative transport pricing strategies: a CGE analysis for Belgium. Paper presented at the conference on 'Input–Output and General Equilibrium: Data, Modeling and Policy Analysis', Brussels, 2–4 September 2004.

Mercenier, J., 1995a, Can '1992' reduce unemployment in Europe? On welfare and employment effects of Europe's move to a single market. *Journal of Policy Modeling*, **17** (1), 1–37.

Mercenier J., 1995b, Nonuniqueness of solutions in applied general equilibrium models with scale economies and imperfect competition. *Economic Theory*, **6**, 161–177.

Mercenier J., 2002, An applied intertemporal general equilibrium model of trade and production with scale economies, product differentiation and imperfect competition. In A. Fossati and W. Wiegard, eds, *Policy Evaluation with Computable General Equilibrium Models*. London: Routledge, pp. 85–104.

Mercenier, J. and T.N. Srinivasan, eds, 1994, *Applied General Equilibrium and Economic Development : Present Achievements and Future Trends*. Ann Arbor, MI: The University of Michigan Press.

Munk, K.J., 2003, Computable general equilibrium models and their use for transport policy analysis. Danmarks TransportForskning (DTF), Rapport 4, Lyngby, Denmark.

Sheffi, Y., 1985, *Urban Transportation Networks: Equilibrium Analysis with Mathematical Programming Methods*. Englewood Cliffs, NJ: Prentice-Hall.

Shoven J.B. and Whalley J., 1984, Applied general equilibrium models of taxation and international trade: an introduction and survey. *Journal of Economic Literature*, **22**, 1007–1051.

Srinivasan T.N. and J. Whalley, eds, 1986, *General Equilibrium Trade Policy Modelling*. Cambridge, MA: MIT Press.

Venables, A.J. and M. Gasiorek, 1998, The welfare implications of transport improvements in the presence of market failure. Report to Standing Advisory Committee on Truck Road Assessment (SACTRA), Department of the Environment, Transport and the Regions, UK.

Waddell, P., 2000, UrbanSim: modeling urban development for land use, transportation and environmental planning. *Journal of the American Planning Association*, **68**, 297–314.

Wegener, M., 2004, Overview of land use and transport models. In D.A. Hensher, K.J. Button, K.E. Haynes and P.R. Stopher, eds, *Handbook of Transport Geography and Spatial Systems*. Amsterdam: Elsevier, pp. 127–146.

Wrede, M., 2003, Tax deductibility of commuting expenses and residential land use with more than one center. CESifo Working Papers 972.

3 Transport in spatial models of economic development
Michael Wegener

INTRODUCTION

This chapter gives an overview of the role of transport in spatial models of economic development. The term overview indicates that, unlike in the other chapters in this part of the *Handbook*, individual models are not presented in detail but instead a cross-cutting, comparative review of relevant current approaches to modeling the contribution of transport to economic development is given. The term spatial indicates that the analysis addresses all scales, from the global through the continental, national and regional to the local scale. The movement from global to local is accompanied by a change in spatial resolution from the macroeconomic level of whole countries or regions to the microeconomic level of individual firms. At each level different aspects of transport become relevant for location decisions, and different techniques need to be applied to model the impact of transport on economic development. The term economic development is used to focus the analysis on one specific type of forecasting distinct from others, such as forecasting demographic development, migration, residential location, transport flows or environmental impacts, notwithstanding the fact that many of the models examined forecast these as well.

The chapter is organized into two major parts. The first part deals with multiregional economic models. The size of their regions may differ, but all of them consider regional aggregates instead of individual firms, such as gross domestic product or employment, possibly classified by economic sector. Some of these models explicitly model trade flows between regions and some do not. The second part deals with intraregional location of firms. Here various degrees of resolution are found. Some models continue to model aggregate output or employment by industry in subregions of various size, usually synonymous with the travel analysis zones of a regional transport model, either with or without explicit modeling of flows of people and goods between subregions. The most recent development is fully microscopic models of firm life cycles ('firmography') and firm location within metropolitan regions using stochastic Monte Carlo simulation. These models typically work with high-resolution grid cells as spatial units.

In the Conclusions section, the models examined are assessed with respect to the new challenges of energy scarcity and climate protection, and their ability to appropriately deal with these challenges is analyzed.

MULTIREGIONAL ECONOMIC MODELS

The important role of transport infrastructure and quality of service for regional development is one of the fundamental principles of spatial economics. In its most simplified

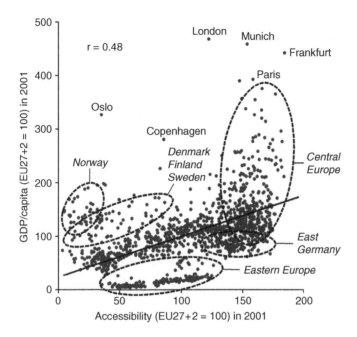

Source: S&W accessibility model

Figure 3.1 Accessibility and GDP per capita of NUTS-3 regions

form it implies that regions with better access to the locations of input materials and markets will, *ceteris paribus*, be more productive, more competitive and hence more successful than more remote and isolated regions.

However, the relationship between transport and economic development is more complex (Vickerman et, al., 1999). There are successful regions in the European core confirming the theoretical expectation that location matters. However, there are also centrally located regions suffering from industrial decline and high unemployment. On the other side of the spectrum the poorest regions, as theory would predict, are at the periphery, but there are also prosperous peripheral regions, such as the Nordic countries. To make things even more difficult, some of the economically fastest growing regions are among the most peripheral ones, such as some regions in the new EU member states in Eastern Europe (see Figure 3.1).

So, it is not surprising that it has been difficult to empirically verify the impact of transport infrastructure on regional development (Vickerman, 1994). There is a clear positive correlation between transport infrastructure endowment or the location in interregional networks and the levels of economic indicators such as GDP per capita (for example, Biehl, 1986, 1991; Keeble et al., 1982, 1988). However, this correlation may merely reflect historical agglomeration processes rather than causal relationships still effective today (cf. Bröcker and Peschel, 1988). Attempts to explain changes in economic indicators, that is, economic growth and decline, by transport investment have been much less successful. The reason for this failure may be that in countries with an already highly developed transport infrastructure further transport network improvements bring only marginal benefits (Bröcker et al., 2004). The conclusion is that transport improvements have strong impacts on regional development only where they result in removing a bottleneck (Blum, 1982; Biehl, 1986, 1991).

There is even disagreement on the direction of the impact and thus whether transport infrastructure contributes to regional polarization or decentralization (Vickerman, 1994). Some analysts argue that regional development policies based on the creation of infrastructure have not succeeded in reducing regional disparities, whereas others point out that it has yet to be ascertained that the reduction of barriers between regions has disadvantaged peripheral regions (Bröcker and Peschel, 1988). From a theoretical point of view, both effects can occur. A new motorway or high-speed rail connection between a peripheral and a central region makes it easier for producers in the peripheral region to market their products in the large cities, but may also expose the region to the competition of more advanced products from the center and so endanger formerly secure regional monopolies (Vickerman et al., 1999; Quinet and Vickerman, 2004).

There exists a broad spectrum of theoretical approaches to explain the impacts of transport infrastructure investments on regional socio-economic development. Originating from different scientific disciplines and intellectual traditions, these approaches presently coexist, even though they are partially in contradiction.

Historically, theories about the spatial economy started with von Thünen's (1826) isolated state in which economic location is a function of market access. Marshall (1890) added synergies between complementary industries as a location factor, and Weber (1909) access to suppliers and labor. Christaller's (1933) central place theory introduced economies of scale to explain the multilevel polycentric system of cities as a function of service areas of different size, and Lösch (1940) did the same for centers of production as a function of market areas. At the height of neoclassical theory, Ohlin (1933) proposed that under conditions of perfect competition and factor mobility and constant returns to scale interregional flows of capital, labor and trade will lead to equal prices of production factors and goods in all regions. The opposite position was taken by Perroux (1955) and Myrdal (1957) who proposed that because there *are* barriers to mobility and economies of scale, the presence of advanced industries will, in a process of 'cumulative circular causation', lead to spatial polarization between prospering and lagging regions.

A synthesis between the two opposing views was offered by the new economic geography (Krugman, 1991; Krugman and Venables, 1995; Fujita et al., 1999). The new economic geography explains regional economic development as the result of the interplay between agglomeration forces (economies of scale) and spatial interaction costs as illustrated by the vertical and horizontal dimensions of the diagram in Figure 3.2.

The theory suggests that the prevailing historical trend of increasing economies of scale and decreasing transport costs has led from isolated dispersed settlements to an ever more polarized spatial structure with a small number of dominant agglomerations (the white arrows in the diagram). If a more balanced polycentric spatial structure is a political objective, either the trend towards increasing economies of scale or the trend towards ever lower transport costs needs to be stopped or even reversed (the solid arrows in the diagram). One important conclusion of this is that not only vertical linkages are important but also horizontal linkages between cities with complementary economic specialization. The new economic geography has also overcome unrealistic assumptions

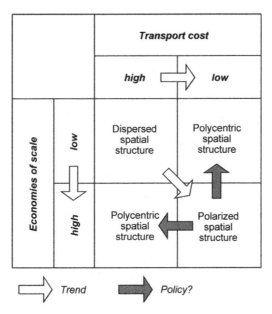

Figure 3.2   Economies of scale and transport cost

of neoclassical theory, such as the assumption of perfect competition, by adopting the concept of imperfect (monopolistic) competition.

Other contributions to the theory of regional economic development include institutional economics, which address the importance of property rights and transactions (Coase, 1960; Williamson, 1966), evolutionary economics linked to theories of synergy, self-organization and complexity in the spirit of Forrester (1968), and more recently theories about the role of global cities (Sassen, 1991), spatial clusters of complementary industries (Porter, 1990) and the growing importance of information technologies (Castells, 1989) and creative industries (Florida, 2004). However, only a few of these newer theoretical approaches have been used for applied quantitative models of regional economic development to date.

There are three types of regional economic development models: regional production function models, multiregional input–output models and spatial computable general equilibrium models.

Regional Production Function Models

Production function approaches model economic activity in a region as a function of production factors. The classical production factors are capital, labor and land. In modern production function approaches, among other location factors, infrastructure is added as a public input used by firms within the region (Jochimsen, 1966; Buhr, 1975; Aschauer, 1989; 1993). The assumption behind the expanded production function is that regions with higher levels of infrastructure provision will have higher output levels, and that in regions with cheap and abundant transport infrastructure more transport-intensive goods will be produced. The main problem of regional production functions is that their econometric estimation tends to confound rather than clarify the complex causal relationships and substitution effects between production factors. This holds equally for production function approaches including measures of regional transport infrastructure endowment. In addition the latter suffer from the fact that they disregard the network quality of transport infrastructure, that is, value a kilometer of motorway or railway the same everywhere, irrespective of where they lead to.

More recent production function approaches attempt to respond to the latter criticism by replacing the simple infrastructure endowment indicators in the regional production function by more complex accessibility indicators. Accessibility indicators in most cases are some form of population or economic potential based on the assumption that regions with better access to markets have a higher probability of being economically successful. Pioneering examples of empirical potential studies for Europe are Keeble et al. (1982, 1988). Today, approaches relying only on accessibility or potential measures have been replaced by hybrid approaches where accessibility is but one of several explanatory factors of regional economic growth, including soft location factors. Also the accessibility indicators used have become much more diversified by type, industry and mode (see Schürmann et al., 1997). The SASI, ASTRA and MASST models are models of this type incorporating accessibility among other explanatory variables.

- *SASI.* The SASI model developed at the Vienna University of Technology and the University of Dortmund is a recursive simulation model of socio-economic development of regions in Europe (Wegener and Bökemann, 1998; Wegener, 2008). Subject to exogenous assumptions about the economic and demographic development of the European Union as a whole, the model predicts the impacts of transport infrastructure investments and transport system improvements, in particular of the trans-European transport networks. It differs from other regional economic models by modeling not only production (the demand side of regional labor markets) but also population and migration (the supply side of regional labor markets). The sectoral production functions of SASI include production factors (some of them delayed) representing regional capital, labor market potential, economic structure, sector-specific accessibility indicators and soft location factors, such as research and development and quality of life. The SASI model has been applied in several EU projects, such as IASON, ESPON 1.1.3 and 2.1.1, and AlpenCorS, and STEPs and projects for national and regional authorities.
- *ASTRA.* The ASTRA model developed at the University of Karlsruhe is a recursive-dynamic model of the system-dynamics type designed to assess the likely impacts of transport policies on the regional economy and environment (Schade, 2005). Its macroeconomic submodel determines regional supply and demand and inter-industry linkages using national input–output tables. Regional supply is forecast by a Cobb–Douglas production function calculating potential output as a function of production factors, which are labor supply, capital stock, natural resources and technical progress in the form of total factor productivity depending on sectoral investment, freight transport time savings and labor productivity. The ASTRA model also contains submodels of passenger travel and freight transport, the size and composition of the vehicle fleet and environmental impacts of transport, such as emissions, noise, accidents and congestion. ASTRA has been applied

in several national projects, for example, Germany and Italy, and in EU projects, such as STEPs and iTREN-2030.

- *MASST*. The MASST (MAcroeconomic Sectoral, Social, Territorial) model was developed at the Politecnico di Milano to assess long-term scenarios of spatial development in Europe in the ESPON program (ESPON 3.2, 2006; Capello, 2007; Capello et al., 2008). MASST models national and regional GDP growth, population and migration based on alternative assumptions about macroeconomic tendencies and policy assumptions, such as interest, savings, exchange and inflation rates, public expenditures, geographical reorientation, foreign direct investment, trends in public debts, energy prices and migration policies, as well as new institutional arrangements, such as further integration of the European Union and European policies, such as structural and agricultural funds and transport infrastructure priorities. Accessibility of a region is calculated as its economic potential, that is, as the sum of the difference between the per-capita income of all other regions and that of the region divided by their distance to it.

Multiregional Input–Output Models

Multiregional input–output models represent interregional and inter-industry linkages using the Leontief (1966) multiregional input–output framework. These models estimate inter-industry and interregional trade flows as a function of technical inter-industry input–output coefficients and transport costs (Echenique, 2004). Final demand in each region is exogenous. Regional supply, however, is elastic, so that the models can be used to forecast regional economic development in response to changes in transport costs. If transport costs rise, industries and households tend to order more products from suppliers in nearby regions so that the exports of these regions grow and those of faraway regions decline. Examples of operational multiregional – models are MEPLAN, TRANUS, PECAS, DELTA and RUBMRIO.

- *MEPLAN*. The MEPLAN model was developed by Marcial Echenique at the University of Cambridge (Echenique et al., 1969, 1990). It models regional economic development and transport flows based on national input–output tables expanded by households of different types as consumers of goods and services and producers of labor. Interregional trade flows, that is, regional imports and exports, are predicted as a function of regional supply and demand by commodity type and production prices plus transport costs. The trade flows are converted to freight flows and passenger trips and assigned to a multimodal transport network. The flows in the network generate congestion which affects transport costs. The revised transport costs are fed back to the economic model until equilibrium is achieved. The model is made quasi-dynamic by computing an equilibrium for a series of time steps. The MEPLAN model has been applied to many regions, countries and Europe as a whole, for example, in the Channel Tunnel study to assess the likely economic impacts of the fixed link between the European continent and the United Kingdom (Rohr and Williams, 1994).
- *TRANUS*. The TRANUS model developed by Tomás de la Barra et al. at Modelistica in Venezuela is based on a random utility derivation of the spatial

input–output model (de la Barra, 1979, 1989). Like MEPLAN the model simulates the location of production and consumption at the level of regions as a function of production prices and transport costs thus generating flows of commodities and services which are then converted to freight and passenger trips. TRANUS interacts with its own transport model based on a multimodal logit assignment procedure particularly suited for multimodal transport networks with multiple choices and low levels of congestion. Logsum transport disutilities are fed back to the spatial input–output model and influence the flows of commodities and services there. The TRANUS model was applied to the state of Oregon, to Spain, to Venezuela and several other Latin American regions, and more recently to a highly detailed model of Chile.

- *PECAS.* The Production, Exchange and Consumption Allocation System (PECAS) developed at the University of Calgary extends the MEPLAN framework by 'make' and 'use' matrices to represent production and consumption and the transaction of goods and services from supplier to demander using 'exchanges' as submarkets with endogenous prices and elastic export and import functions (Hunt and Abraham, 2005). The PECAS model is being applied to a growing number of North American regions and US states.

- *DELTA.* The land-use/economic modeling package developed by David Simmonds and colleagues (Simmonds, 1999; Simmonds and Skinner, 2003) works at two spatial levels, though not in all applications. The higher spatial level incorporates a spatial input–output model in which trade flows are influenced by transport costs linked with a model of investment and a migration model. The higher-level version has been applied to Scotland and several areas in England and to the whole of Great Britain.

- *RUBMRIO.* A similar input–output based model of production and trade patterns was developed at the University of Texas at Austin for the 254 counties in Texas using nested logit models for inputs and transport mode choice (Zhao and Kockelman, 2004; Kockelman et al., 2005; Huang and Kockelman, 2008).

Spatial Computable General Equilibrium Models

Following the ideas of the new economic geography, more recent input–output based models of trade flows include economies of scale and imperfect (monopolistic) competition. Such multiregional input–output models are today called spatial computable general equilibrium (SCGE) models, although the term CGE originally had a broader meaning (see the chapter by Bröcker and Mercenier in this volume). The distinction between SCGE models and multiregional input–output models is becoming more and more blurred as the latter also determine a general equilibrium between transport and location and are designed for computers. Examples of SCGE models are CGEurope, RAEM and recent versions of the REMI model.

- *CGEurope.* The CGEurope model developed at the University of Kiel is a multiregional spatial computable general equilibrium model in which transport costs are expenditures of firms for transport and business travel (Bröcker, 1998; Bröcker et al., 2004, 2010). It assumes imperfect (monopolistic) competition of the Dixit–

Stiglitz (1977) type in each region for the markets of tradable goods and perfect competition for local goods and factor markets. Prices and quantities respond to changes in transport times and transport costs resulting in changes in income and welfare in each region. The CGEurope model predicts the spatial distribution of production factors in a target year in a comparative static equilibrium analysis, that is, by comparing cases with and without implementation of the policies leaving everything else unchanged. The main output of the model is the so-called Hick's measure of variation, that is, the monetary equivalent of the change of welfare of households. CGEurope has been applied in several EU projects, such as IASON, ESPON 2.1.1 and TEN-CONNECT.

- *RAEM.* The RAEM model developed at the University of Groningen and TNO Delft is a SCGE model of regional capital investment and stock and flow relationships of households and firms (Oosterhaven et al., 1998; Ivanova, 2007). Households maximize their utility of consumption of goods and services under budget constraints, and industries minimize their costs of labor, capital and inputs under technology constraints. Each sector consists of identical firms each producing a unique specification of a particular commodity, which gives them monopolistic power over their consumers. Households and domestic sectors consume transport services in their consumption and production activities. The latest version RAEM 3.0 includes international trade and interregional migration. The model determines equilibrium of supply and demand and interregional trade flows in each time period. RAEM was developed for the Netherlands and has been applied in a simplified version (RAEM-Light) in Hungary, Japan and South Korea.
- *REMI PI+.* The REMI model developed at the University of Massachusetts (Treyz, 1980; Treyz et al., 1992) originally was a multiregional input–output model with endogenous final demand. Its latest version, PI+ (Policy Insight), is a new economic geography extension of the original REMI framework with endogenous real estate prices, labor mobility and inter-industry purchases (Fan et al., 2000). It relaxes some of the restrictive assumptions of new economic geography in that workers are mobile between sectors and regions, real estate prices are explicit in consumption and production, and differentiated inputs are used in production. Agglomeration forces in the model are consumers' and producers' prices and wages, the centrifugal force in the model is the limited supply of land. Evolutionary equilibrium is determined taking account of different speeds of adjustment of different subsystems over time. Previous generations of the REMI model have been applied for policy analyses in over a hundred regional and state agencies in North America and Europe.

Comparison

The three types of model, regional production function models, multiregional input–output models and spatial computable general equilibrium models, have much in common with respect to the underlying theory (see Table 3.1). All three are aggregate models at the meso-scale of regions. All consider transport a production factor of great importance for regional economic development. There are no neoclassical models assuming perfect factor mobility in the set of models discussed here, as all of them model

Table 3.1   Comparison of multiregional economic models

Model type	Model	Trade flows	Imperfect competition	Networks	Demo-graphy	Migration	Dynamics
Regional production function	SASI	no	implicit	yes	yes	yes	yes
	ASTRA	output	implicit	no	yes	yes	yes
	MASST	no	implicit	no	yes	yes	yes
Multiregional input–output	MEPLAN	yes	no	yes	no	no	no
	TRANUS	yes	no	yes	no	no	no
	PECAS	yes	no	yes	no	no	partly
	DELTA	yes	implicit	external	no	yes	partly
	RUBMRIO	yes	no	external	no	yes	partly
SCGE	CGEurope	yes	yes	external	no	no	no
	RAEM	yes	yes	external	no	yes	yes
	REMI PI+	yes	yes	no	yes	yes	yes

spatial impedance in the form of transport costs and other forms of barriers, though with different detail. Markets with imperfect competition, increasing returns to scale and bounded rationality under uncertainty by economic agents are addressed in models of all three groups, either by the nonlinear specification of production factors in the extended production functions or by logit type utility functions in the multiregional input–output models or by the Dixit–Stiglitz model of monopolistic competition in the SCGE models.

However, there are also major differences. Multiregional input–output models and SCGE models explicitly model trade flows between regions based on product prices and transport costs and determine regional growth of industrial sectors from these flows. Production function models aggregate trade and travel flows into one complex variable, accessibility. Needless to say that the explicit modeling of purchases of firms from other regions based on comparison of product price, diversity and transport cost is superior to the econometric estimation of the aggregate impact of accessibility on regional economic development, in particular if not only trade volumes but also prices are endogenous as in SCGE and some multiregional input–output models.

More problematic are obvious omissions in some of the models. If in the ASTRA model accessibility is expressed only as freight transport time for distance bands or in the MASST model only by interregional distance or kilometers of roads in a region, these models are likely to underestimate the impact of network improvements, in particular of rail investments. The CGEurope model assumes that regional labor is constant and immobile and so fails to take account of the impacts of demographic change and inter-regional migration on regional labor markets. The SASI model presently treats regional sector productivity as exogenous instead of modeling improvement in productivity through better accessibility. However, all these deficiencies can be easily overcome by relatively minor model modifications.

Another relevant difference between the models is their treatment of dynamics. Multiregional input–output models and SCGE models assume that markets are in equi-librium, at the start and target year (CGEurope), at the end of each period (MEPLAN, TRANUS, PECAS, DELTA, RUBMRIO, RAEM) or after a number of periods (REMI

PI+, partly combined with dynamic components, such as investments or migrations). The production function models, however, are all recursively dynamic with different types of adjustment delays.

In particular, the latter difference, between equilibrium and dynamics, seems to affect the sensitivity of the models to transport cost changes. This is suggested by a comparison of the results of the CGEurope and SASI models. In the EU projects IASON (Bröcker et al., 2004) and ESPON 2.1.1 (Bröcker et al., 2005) the two models were applied to the same study area, the same regional and network data and the same policy scenarios. It turned out that the two models agreed with respect to the direction and spatial distribution of the effects of the policies and whether the policies contribute to greater cohesion or polarization between the regions in Europe, but differed with respect to the magnitude of the responses by a factor of up to ten, with the SASI model showing the stronger responses. Possible reasons for this divergence included differences in the specification of transport costs, in particular with respect to border impediments, the neglect of mobile capital in SASI and the neglect of mobile labor in CGEurope. Another hypothesis was that CGEurope as an equilibrium model primarily predicts short-term responses, whereas the quasi-dynamic SASI model shows self-reinforcing cumulative effects over time (Bröcker et al., 2004, 168-175). Further research will be necessary to test the two hypotheses.

MODELS OF INTRAREGIONAL INDUSTRY LOCATION

The location behavior of industries within urban areas differs from decisions to locate in a certain region by the location factors considered. Because the choice of a region has already been made, location factors are equal for all parts of the region and become irrelevant. Now other attributes, such as short-distance access to customers and suppliers, land use and environmental constraints, land availability and land price or rent, become important (Wegener and Fürst, 1999).

Like at the intraregional scale, there exists a broad spectrum of theoretical approaches to explain the impacts of transport policies on intraregional location of industries, and there is a similar coexistence of partly contradictory theoretical concepts originating from different scientific disciplines and intellectual traditions.

An assumption of urban economic theories is that land with good accessibility is more attractive and has a higher market value than peripheral locations. This assumption again goes back to von Thünen (1826) and has since been varied and refined in many ways. Economic location theories become more complex if location costs in the form of land prices are taken into account. Probably the most influential example is the theory of the urban land market by Alonso (1964). Firms look for the optimum constellation of size (economies of scale) and location (agglomeration economies) given their specific mix of products, production technology and pattern of suppliers and customers and choose that location at which their bid rent, that is the land price they are willing to pay to maximize their profits, equals the asking rent of the landlord, so that the land market is in equilibrium. A firm with higher added value per unit of land is therefore able to pay a higher price than a firm with less intensive land utilization, everything else being equal. Alonso's theory has been the point of departure for a multitude of urban economics approaches. In more advanced variations, restrictive assumptions such as perfect competition and complete information or the monocentric city have been relaxed (for example, Anas, 1982).

Other theories of urban industry location start from intersectoral and interregional factor and commodity flows. The physical analogy of the first spatial interaction model, the gravity model, was replaced by better founded formulations derived from statistical mechanics (Wilson, 1967) or information theory (Snickars and Weibull, 1976), yet even after these substitutions the spatial interaction model did not provide any explanation of spatial behavior. Only later did it become possible (Anas, 1983) to link it via random utility theory (Domencich and McFadden, 1975; McFadden, 1978) to psychological theories of human decision behavior (Luce, 1959).

As with multiregional input–output models, it is only a small step from the spatial interaction model to its application as a location model. If it is possible to make inferences from the distribution of human activities to the spatial interactions between them, it is also possible to identify the location of activities giving rise to a certain trip pattern. Already Reilly (1941) had postulated that shopping trips follow the 'law of retail gravitation'. Lowry's (1964) *Model of Metropolis* applied a shopping trip model to determine retail and service locations. The Huff (1964) and Lakshmanan–Hansen (1965) models predicted retail sales from shopping trips of households given competing retail facilities, and Harris and Wilson (1978) predicted the response by retailers to such sales. Time geography (Chapin, 1965; Chapin and Weiss, 1968; Hägerstrand, 1970) introduced time and cost budgets, within which individuals, according to their social role, income and level of technology (for example, car ownership) command *action spaces* of different size and duration. Only locations within these action spaces are considered.

Models of intraregional location of industries are typically embedded in integrated models of urban land use and transport (for reviews, see Wegener, 1994, 2004; Hunt et al., 2005). As with multiregional economic models, two major groups can be distinguished: models that predict locations and models that predict spatial interactions. Yet, different from multiregional economic models, the first integrated models of urban development were spatial interaction location models originating from the Lowry (1964) model.

Spatial Interaction Location Models

Spatial interaction location models reverse the rationale of the gravity model of mobility behavior by predicting the location of activities as origins or destinations of trips or commodity flows. Typically, the locations of basic, that is export-oriented industries, are taken as exogenous, as in the Lowry model. The locations of non-basic employment are a function of shopping and service trips from residential locations and land availability. An early model of this type was ITLUP (now METROPILUS). Other models of this type model locations as destinations of flows derived from an input–output table as in multiregional input–output models, only that now land availability and land price are taken into account. Examples are MEPLAN, TRANUS and PECAS.

- *ITLUP.* The Integrated Transportation and Land Use Package developed by Putman (1983, 1991, 1998) consists of a residential location model (DRAM) linked to an employment location model (EMPAL). EMPAL forecasts basic and non-basic employment as destinations of work and shopping trips, that is a function of access to labor and markets. ITLUP has been applied in a large number of metropolitan areas in the United States and other countries. Now embedded in a GIS shell, it is called METROPILUS (Putman and Shih-Liang, 2001). A slightly simpler version, TELUM, was distributed free to all metropolitan planning organizations in the United States.

- *MEPLAN*. There exist different versions of MEPLAN for multiregional and for intraregional applications (Echenique et al., 1969, 1990). The intraregional applications differ from the multiregional applications by the inclusion of land availability and land price as location factors. The intraregional application of MEPLAN has been applied to many metropolitan regions, such as Dortmund, Bilbao, Helsinki, Naples, Cambridgeshire and Greater London.

- *TRANUS*. The same software of TRANUS (de la Barra, 1979, 1989) is used for multi- and intraregional applications. For intraregional applications the spatial input–output framework adds elastic demand functions combined with logit choice and equilibrium prices. This allows the representation of real estate markets including different types of floorspace and land. The resulting model has been applied to over a hundred cities and metropolitan areas in Latin America, North America, Europe and Asia. The program code of TRANUS is available as Open Source.

- *PECAS*. As noted above, the PECAS model extends the multiregional input–output framework by transactions of goods and services via 'exchanges' as sub-markets (Hunt and Abraham, 2005). There exist different versions of PECAS for multiregional and for intraregional applications. The intraregional version is being applied to an increasing number of metropolitan areas in North America. These applications differ from the multiregional applications by the combination with a land development model taking account of accessibility, neighborhood and site attributes and land availability and land price as location factors as in the utility-based location models discussed below. The program code of PECAS is also available as Open Source.

Bid-rent Location Models

Bid-rent location models follow the theory of the urban land market by Alonso (1964) in which firms choose that location at which their bid rent equals the market rent. The bid rent of firms is the land price at which their profits are maximized given their cost structure, that is, sales price minus production and transport costs plus profit divided by size of land. Examples of bid-rent location models of firms are MUSSA and RURBAN.

- *MUSSA*. The 5-Stage Land-Use Transport Model was developed at the University of Chile by Martinez (1992). The latest version of MUSSA (Martinez and Donoso, 2001; Bravo et al., 2010) represents the urban real estate market as an auction on which supply (landowners and developers) and demand (households and firms) interact until the bid rent of households and firms (defined as the inverse of their utility function in rents) and the asking rents of landowners and developers are in equilibrium subject to constraints, such as zoning regulations, taxation or subsidies. The MUSSA model is linked to a transport model which provides it with accessibility indicators for the utility functions of each zone. MUSSA has been applied to Santiago de Chile and, under the name CUBE LAND, in combination with different transport models in several metropolitan areas in the United States and Asia.

- *RURBAN*. The Random Utility Rent-Bidding Analysis (RURBAN) model developed at Tohoku University in Sendai, Japan (Miyamoto and Udomsri, 1996; Miyamoto et al., 2007), is an integrated urban model based on random utility theory and rent-bidding analysis. The model presupposes that the general equilibrium of the land market is obtained under the condition that the demand for land derived from random utility theory and the supply of land derived from rent bidding analysis are equal. The employment location model of RURBAN simulates location behavior of firms as a bidding process between firms and land owners resulting in market clearing at equilibrium prices. RURBAN has been applied to the metropolitan areas of Sapporo and Sendai in Japan and of Bangkok in Thailand.

Utility-based Location Models

Utility-based approaches are similar to bid-rent approaches in that they model location behavior as choices between options of different attractiveness but avoid the monetization of location factors by converting them, including land price or rent, to a common utility scale similar to extended regional production functions. Typical location factors include accessibility indicators, neighborhood attributes, site or building attributes and land price or rent. The utility of a location is then a linear or log-linear combination of the utilities of these attributes, and the choice model typically is of the discrete choice or logit type. Examples of utility-based location models are IRPUD, UrbanSim, DELTA, MARS and TIGRIS XL.

- *IRPUD*. The land use transport model developed at the University of Dortmund (Wegener, 1982, 2001) is a simulation model of intraregional location and mobility decisions in a metropolitan area. Employment is located or relocated as a function of the capacity of vacant industrial or commercial buildings and their attractiveness in terms of land use type, neighborhood characteristics and price. New industrial or commercial buildings are allocated to available land as a function of its attractiveness in terms of land use type, neighborhood characteristics and price in relation to expected profit. Retail locations are determined including purchasing power potential as accessibility indicator in the attractiveness function. Land prices are updated after each simulation period responding to vacancy rates and reflecting demand and supply in the previous period. The IRPUD model has been applied to the urban region of Dortmund, Germany.
- *UrbanSim*. The UrbanSim model developed at the University of Washington by Waddell (1998, 2002) is a microeconomic model of location choice of households and firms. In the employment location model individual jobs are allocated to suitable locations from a randomly selected set of vacant buildings taking account of their attractiveness in terms of real estate characteristics (price, type of space,

density, age), neighborhood characteristics (average land values, land-use mix, employment in other sectors) and regional accessibility. Developers invest in new construction or redevelopment taking account of real estate characteristics (current development, policy constraints, land and improvement value), site location (proximity to highways, existing and recent development) and regional accessibility. Land prices are adjusted after each simulation period taking account of site and neighborhood characteristics, accessibility, vacancy rates and policy effects on land prices. UrbanSim has been applied in a growing number of metropolitan areas in the United States and Europe. The program code of UrbanSim is available as Open Source.

- *DELTA.* The lower level of the land-use/economic modeling package developed by David Simmonds and colleagues (Simmonds, 1999; Simmonds and Skinner, 2003) predicts spatial development at the regional/urban scale. Where the upper-level component of DELTA is implemented (see above), its economic forecasts drive the lower level which predicts employment. Employment is located/relocated to zones by logit models of floorspace supply, floorspace rent, floorspace quality, accessibility and environmental quality. Accessibility indicators are calculated using travel times and transport costs provided by a linked transport model. Floorspace rents are determined endogenously based on vacancy rates reflecting supply and demand. The DELTA model has been applied to Greater London, Greater Manchester, Scotland and several urban areas and regions in Britain as well as to Auckland, New Zealand.

- *MARS.* The MARS model developed at the University of Leeds and the Vienna University of Technology is a strategic land-use transport model based on the principles of systems dynamics (Pfaffenbichler, 2003; Pfaffenbichler et al., 2008). It includes a transport model without network based on exogenous interzonal distances, travel times and travel costs, with congestion approximated by a capacity constraint function. Work places are relocated between zones as a function of their accessibility, availability of land, the construction costs and average household income as a proxy for consumption potential and labor cost. Accessibility is calculated as potential to reach work places and shopping facilities with travel times and travel costs calculated in the transport model. The MARS model has been applied to ten European cities, including Leeds and Vienna, and several cities in Asia and America.

- *TIGRIS XL.* The TIGRIS XL model developed for government agencies in the Netherlands (RAND Europe, 2006; Zondag, 2007) is an integrated land-use transport model consisting of five modules representing specific markets, the land market, the housing market, the commercial real estate market and the labor market, and a sixth, demographic module. The labor market module predicts the location behavior of firms as a function of accessibility, land availability and other location factors of 1308 zones covering the whole of the Netherlands. TIGRIS XL interacts with the National Transport Model (LMS) of the Netherlands every five years to calculate various accessibility indicators, such as travel times, vehicle hours in congestion, number of jobs or other opportunities that can be reached within 45 minutes by car or public transport and utility-based logsum accessibility measures.

Table 3.2   Comparison of models of intraregional industry location

Model type	Model	Input–output	Labor market	Networks	Goods transport	Dynamics	Micro-simulation
Spatial interaction location	ITLUP	no	no	yes	no	no	no
	MEPLAN	yes	no	yes	yes	no	no
	TRANUS	yes	no	yes	yes	no	no
	PECAS	yes	yes	yes	yes	no	partly
Bid-rent location	MUSSA	no	yes	external	no	no	no
	RURBAN	no	no	yes	no	no	no
Utility-based location	IRPUD	no	yes	yes	no	yes	partly
	UrbanSim	no	yes	external	no	yes	yes
	DELTA	yes	yes	external	yes	yes	no
	MARS	no	no	no	no	yes	no
	TIGRIS XL	no	yes	external	no	yes	no

Comparison

The brief overview of current approaches to model intraregional industry location cannot do justice to the great advances in urban modeling made over the last several decades, in particular the linkages between urban economic development and the supply side of urban labor markets, demographic development, household formation and labor force participation. Compared to this progress, the differences between the models are not very significant (see Table 3.2).

All models referred to contain the necessary variables to respond to current transport policies, from transport infrastructure investment to travel demand management through taxation, road user charges or public transport fares. All models provide the information needed to assess the desirability of the effects of policies.

A difference between the models exists, as explained above, in the way they model location: spatial interaction models model location as origins or destinations with or without an input–output framework, whereas bid-rent and utility-based location models use logit functions with locational attributes similar to the production factors in extended production functions.

Another difference is whether transport is fully integrated into the model or whether the results of an existing transport model are used – this has implications for implementing the feedback between transport and location and the ability to model goods transport unless the integration between the land use and transport models is really tight.

A third difference is whether the models explicitly model demographics, household formation, labor force participation, the regional labor market and unemployment. Here bid-rent and utility-based models stand out, whereas in spatial-interaction location models labor supply is assumed to equal labor demand at the origins of trade flows.

A fourth difference of potential relevance is, just as with multiregional models, the treatment of dynamics. Bid-rent models, such as MUSSA and RURBAN, but also spatial interaction models, such as MEPLAN, TRANUS and PECAS achieve equilibrium of both land use and transport in each simulation period, sometimes combined with dynamic components, such as land development. The utility-based models IRPUD, UrbanSim, DELTA and MARS are quasi-dynamic based on the view that urban systems are open systems subject to external influences and both negative and positive feedback loops and are therefore not likely to ever achieve equilibrium, except perhaps in daily traffic.

That the issue of equilibrium or dynamics may be important was demonstrated by a recent project in which different models were applied to the same policy scenarios, though this time to different cities. In the EU project 'Transport Strategies under the Scarcity of Energy Supply' (STEPs) different scenarios of fuel price increases were assessed using different urban models, among them MEPLAN, TRANUS, IRPUD and MARS. As it turned out, MEPLAN and TRANUS, two equilibrium models, showed significantly lower fuel price elasticities in their results (much lower than the proverbial -0.3) than the dynamic IRPUD. This seems to corroborate the hypothesis that equilibrium models tend to model short-term elasticities and dynamic models long-term elasticities (Fiorello et al., 2006, pp. 137–150). The dynamic MARS model, however, showed even lower elasticities than MEPLAN and TRANUS. A possible reason for these differences in response could be that IRPUD takes account of household travel cost budgets, which can expand only a little if also other household expenditures become more expensive. Further research will be necessary to test these hypotheses.

A final difference is whether the models are aggregate or agent-based, that is apply microsimulation. Of the models examined here, PECAS, IRPUD and UrbanSim use microsimulation in some or all of their submodels. The most recent development in modeling intraregional location of industries are fully microscopic models of firm life cycles ('firmography') and firm location within metropolitan regions using stochastic Monte Carlo simulation. These models typically work with high-resolution parcels or grid cells as spatial units and individual firms and workers as agents. Recent examples of microscopic models of intraregional firm location are Moeckel (2007) and de Bok (2007). However, to date, these models are still experimental, and many methodological problems, such as indivisibility of large firms and the effects of stochastic variation, that is, that identical runs with different seeds of the random number generator lead to different results, have yet to be solved (Wegener, 2011).

CONCLUSIONS

The review of spatial models of economic development in this chapter has shown a broad range of approaches differing in spatial resolution, model design and treatment of dynamics.

The first distinction is between macroeconomic models at the interregional scale on the one hand and models at the intraregional or urban scale at the other. Multiregional models predict the location of industries in terms of employment or output in GDP for countries or regions within countries. For these models regional endowments, such as economic structure, human capital, infrastructure and long-distance accessibility are relevant production factors, and European or national policies with respect to taxation, public investment, freedom of movement of capital and labor and transport infrastructure relevant policy variables. For models at the urban or regional scale other variables, such as availability of land and access to local markets are relevant location factors, and both national policies, such as taxes and user fees, and local policies, such as transport investments and travel demand management, relevant policy variables. These differences suggest that no model is likely to be suitable for all spatial levels, but that multilevel systems of models of different spatial resolution are needed.

The second distinction is between location and spatial interaction models. From a conceptual point of view, explicit modeling of interregional trade is clearly superior. However, the added complexity of multiregional input–output models or SCGE models and the computational burden of bringing them to equilibrium still represents a major challenge for their practical application for several future years and a large number of policy scenarios.

This leads to the third distinction, the one between equilibrium and dynamic models. If, as it has been suggested, dynamic models have a better chance of predicting long-term behavioral responses, the aggregation of spatial interactions into accessibility indicators in production function models and to focus on adjustment processes over time instead of convergence to equilibrium may be a pragmatic compromise.

The possibility that long-term and short-term responses of economic location to changing transport costs may differ substantially, leads to a further and final question: how will current models of economic location cope with future challenges? Most experts agree that due to the depletion of finite fossil fuel resources and growing energy demand by fast growing developing countries like China and India and possible political instability in the oil producing countries, transport, despite all efforts towards more energy-efficient vehicles and alternative fuels, will become more expensive. In addition, the imperatives of climate protection, in particular the need to reduce CO_2 emission in the richest countries by 80 percent by 2050, will require government action to internalize the environmental external costs of fossil fuels by taxation or user fees if market prices continue to be too low to achieve the agreed reduction targets. Will the present generation of economic location models, which were calibrated in times of cheap energy, be able to adequately deal with non-marginal fuel price increases? There are doubts until contrary evidence. As it has been shown for multiregional and intraregional models, equilibrium models and models that do not consider transport budget constraints are likely to underestimate the long-term behavioral impacts of substantial transport cost increases.

This calls for a major new research effort to assess the methodology of state-of-the-art economic location models in the light of these new challenges.

ACKNOWLEDGMENTS

The author is grateful to the model developers who checked the information about their models in this review for correctness.

REFERENCES

Alonso, W., 1964, *Location and Land Use*. Cambridge, MA: Harvard University Press.
Anas, A., 1982, *Residential Location Models and Urban Transportation: Economic Theory, Econometrics, and Policy Analysis with Discrete Choice Models*. New York: Academic Press.

Anas, A., 1983, Discrete choice theory, information theory and the multinomial logit and gravity models. *Transportation Research Part B*, **17**, 13–23.

Aschauer, D.A., 1989, Is public expenditure productive? *Journal of Monetary Economics*, **23** (2), 177–200.

Aschauer, D.A., 1993, Public capital and economic growth. In The Jerome Levy Economic Institute, ed., *Public Policy Brief*. Annandale-on-Hudson, NY: Bard College, pp. 9–30.

Biehl, D., ed., 1986, The contribution of infrastructure to regional development. Final Report of the Infrastructure Studies Group to the Commission of the European Communities, Luxembourg: Office for Official Publications of the European Communities.

Biehl, D., 1991, The role of infrastructure in regional development. In R.W. Vickerman, ed., *Infrastructure and Regional Development*. London: Pion, pp. 9–35.

Blum, U., 1982, Effects of transportation investments on regional growth: a theoretical and empirical investigation, *Papers of the Regional Science Association*, **49**, 169–184.

Bravo, M., L. Briceño, R. Cominetti, C. Cortés, and F. Martinez, 2010, An integrated behavioral model of the land-use and transport systems with network congestion and location externalities. *Transport Research Part B*, **44**, 584–596.

Bröcker, J., 1998, Operational spatial computable general equilibrium modeling. *The Annals of Regional Science*, **32**, 367–387.

Bröcker, J., 2004, Computable general equilibrium analysis in transportation economics. In D.A. Hensher, and K.J. Button, eds, *Transport Geography and Spatial Systems*, Handbook 5 of Handbooks in Transport. Kidlington, UK: Pergamon/Elsevier Science, pp. 269–289.

Bröcker, J., R. Capello, L. Lundqvist, L. Meyer, J. Rouwendal, N. Schneekloth, A. Spairani, M. Spangenberg, K. Spiekermann, D. van Vuuren, R. Vickerman, and M. Wegener, 2005, Territorial Impact of EU Transport and TEN Policies. Final Report of ESPON 2.1.1. Kiel: Institute of Regional Research, Christian Albrechts University. Available at www.espon.eu/

Bröcker, J., A. Korzhenevych, and C. Schürmann, 2010, Assessing spatial equity and efficiency impacts of transport infrastructure projects. *Transportation Research Part B*, **44** (7), 795–811.

Bröcker, J., R. Meyer, N. Schneekloth, C. Schürmann, K. Spiekermann, and M. Wegener, 2004, Modelling the socio-economic and spatial impacts of EU transport policy. Deliverable D6 of IASON (Integrated Appraisal of Spatial Economic and Network Effects of Transport Investments and Policies). Kiel: Institute of Regional Research, Christian Albrechts University.

Bröcker, J. and K. Peschel, 1988, Trade. In W. Molle, and R. Cappelin, eds, *Regional Impact of Community Policies in Europe*. Aldershot, UK: Avebury.

Buhr, W., 1975, *Die Rolle der materiellen Infrastruktur im regionalen Wirtschaftswachstum*. Berlin: Duncker & Humblot.

Capello, R., 2007, A forecasting territorial model of regional growth: the MASST model. *Annals of Regional Science*, **41** (4), 753–787.

Capello, R., R. Camagni, U. Fratesi, and B. Chizzolini, 2008, *Modelling Regional Scenarios for an Enlarged Europe*. Berlin/Heidelberg: Springer.

Castells, M., 1989, *The Informational City*. Oxford: Basil Blackwell.

Chapin, F.S., 1965, *Urban Land Use Planning*. Urbana, IL: University of Illinois Press.

Chapin, F.S. and S.F. Weiss 1968, A probabilistic model for residential growth. *Transportation Research*, **2**, 375–390.

Christaller, W., 1933 (1968), *Die zentralen Orte in Süddeutschland*, Jena, new edition. Darmstadt: Wissenschaftliche Buchgesellschaft.

Coase, R.H., 1960, The problem of social cost. *Journal of Law and Economics*, **3** (1), 1–44.

de Bok, M., 2007, Infrastructure and firm dynamics. PhD Thesis, Delft: Delft University of Technology.

de la Barra, T., 1979, *Towards a framework for integrated land use and transport modelling*. PhD Dissertation, Cambridge: University of Cambridge.

de la Barra, T., 1989, *Integrated Land Use and Transport Modelling*. Cambridge: Cambridge University Press.

Dixit, A.K. and J.E. Stiglitz, 1977, Monopolistic competition and optimum product diversity. *American Economic Review*, **67**, 297–308.

Domencich, T.A. and D. McFadden, 1975, *Urban Travel Demand: a Behavioral Analysis*. Amsterdam: North Holland.

Echenique, M., 2004, Econometric models of land use and transportation. In D.A. Hensher, K.J. Button, eds, *Transport Geography and Spatial Systems*, Handbook 5 of Handbooks in Transport. Kidlington, UK: Pergamon/Elsevier Science, pp. 185–202.

Echenique, M.H., D. Crowther, and W. Lindsay, 1969, A spatial model for urban stock and activity. *Regional Studies*, **3**, 281–312.

Echenique, M.H., A.D.J. Flowerdew, J.D. Hunt, T.R. Mayo, I.J. Skidmore, and D.C. Simmonds, 1990, The MEPLAN models of Bilbao, Leeds and Dortmund. *Transport Reviews*, **10**, 309–322.

ESPON 3.2, 2006, Spatial scenarios and orientations in relation to the ESDP and EU cohesion policy (Final report). Brussels: IGEAT, Free University of Brussels. Available at www.espon.eu/

Fan, W., F. Treyz, and G. Treyz, 2000, An evolutionary new economic geography model, *Journal of Regional Science*, **40** (4), 671–695.

Fiorello, D., G. Huismans, E. López, C. Marques, T. Steenberghen, M. Wegener, and G. Zografos, 2006, *Transport Strategies under the Scarcity of Energy Supply*. A. Monzon and A. Nuijten, eds, STEPs Final Report. The Hague: Buck Consultants International. Available at www.steps-eu.com/reports.htm.

Florida, R., 2004, *The Rise of the Creative Class*. New York: Basic Books.

Forrester J.W., 1968, *Principles of Systems*. Waltham, MA: Pegasus Communications.

Fujita, M., P. Krugman, and A.J. Venables, 1999, *The Spatial Economy: Cities, Regions, and International Trade*. Cambridge, MA: MIT Press.

Hägerstrand, T., 1970, What about people in regional science? *Papers of the Regional Science Association*, **24**, 7–21.

Harris, B. and A.G. Wilson, 1978, Equilibrium values and dynamics of attractiveness terms in production-constrained spatial interaction models. *Environment and Planning A*, **10**, 371–388.

Huang, T. and K. Kockelman, 2008, The introduction of dynamic features in a random-utility-based multiregional input–output model of trade, production, and location choice. *Journal of the Transportation Research Forum*, **47** (1), 23–42.

Huff, D.L., 1964, Defining and estimating a trading area. *Journal of Marketing*, **28**, 34–38.

Hunt, J.D. and J.E. Abraham, 2005, Design and implementation of PECAS: a generalised system for the allocation of economic production, exchange and consumption quantities. In M.E.H. Lee-Gosselin, and S.T. Doherty, eds, *Integrated Land-Use and Transportation Models: Behavioural Foundations*. St. Louis, MO: Elsevier, pp. 253–274.

Hunt, J.D., E.J. Miller, and D.S. Kriger, 2005, Current operational urban land-use transport modeling frameworks. *Transport Reviews*, **25** (3), 329–376.

Ivanova, O., 2007, On the development of the new version of the RAEM model for the Netherlands, Paper presented at the Joint Congress of the European Regional Science Association and ASRDLF, Paris.

Jochimsen, R., 1966, *Theorie der Infrastruktur. Grundlagen der marktwirtschaftlichen Entwicklung*. Tübingen: Mohr.

Keeble, D., P.L. Owens, and C. Thompson, 1982, Regional accessibility and economic potential in the European Community. *Regional Studies*, **16**, 419–432.

Keeble, D., J. Offord, and S. Walker, 1988, *Peripheral Regions in a Community of Twelve Member States*. Luxembourg: Office for Official Publications of the European Communities.

Kockelman, K., L. Jin, Y. Zhao, and N. Ruiz-Juri, 2005, Tracking land use, transport and industrial production using random-utility based multizonal input–output models: applications for Texas trade. *Journal of Transport Geography*, **13** (3), 275–286.

Krugman, P., 1991, *Geography and Trade*. Leuven, Belgium: Leuven University Press.

Krugmann, P. and A. Venables, 1995, Globalisation and the inequality of nations. *Quarterly Journal of Economics*, **60** (4), 857–880.

Lakshmanan, T.R. and W.G. Hansen, 1965, A retail market potential model. *Journal of the American Institute of Planners*, **31**, 134–143.

Leontief, W., 1966, *Input–Output Economics*. Oxford: Oxford University Press.

Lowry, I.S., 1964, *A Model of Metropolis*. RM-4035-RC, Santa Monica, CA: Rand Corporation.

Lösch, A., 1940 (1962), *Die räumliche Ordnung der Wirtschaft*, Jena, new edition. Stuttgart: Fischer.

Luce, R.D., 1959, *Individual Choice Behavior*. New York: Wiley.

Marshall, A., 1890 (1966), *Principles of Economics*, Reprint of the 8th edition of 1920. London: Macmillan.

Martinez, F.J., 1992, The bid–choice land-use model: an integrated economic framework. *Environment and Planning A*, **24**, 871–885.

Martinez, F. and P. Donoso, 2001, Modeling land use planning effects: zone regulations and subsidies. In D. Hensher, ed., *Travel Behaviour Research, The Leading Edge*. Kidlington, UK: Pergamon/Elsevier Science, pp. 647–658.

McFadden, D., 1978, Modelling the choice of residential location. In A. Karlquist, et al., eds., *Spatial Interaction Theory and Residential Location*. Amsterdam: North Holland, pp. 75–96.

Miyamoto, K. and R. Udomsri, 1996, An analysis system for integrated policy measures regarding land use, transport and the environment in a metropolis. In Y. Hayashi, and J. Roy, eds, *Transport, Land Use and the Environment*. Dordrecht: Kluwer, pp. 259–280.

Miyamoto, K., V. Vichiensan, N. Sugiki, and K. Kitazume, 2007, Applications of RURBAN integrated with a transport model in detailed zone systems. *Selected Proceedings of the 11th World Conference on Transport Research*, Berkeley, CA.

Moeckel, R., 2007, *Business Location Decisions and Urban Sprawl. A Microsimulation of Business Relocation and Firmography*. Dortmund: Institute of Spatial Planning, University of Dortmund.

Myrdal, G., 1957, *Economic Theory and Underdeveloped Regions*. London: Duckworth.
Ohlin, B., 1933, *Interregional and International Trade*. Cambridge: Addison Wesley.
Oosterhaven, J., J.E. Sturm, and P. Zwaneveld, 1998, Naar een theoretische onderbouwde aanpak can voor-wartse economische effecten: Modelmatige definitie. Groningen/Delft: University of Groningen, TNO.
Perroux, F., 1955, Note sur la notion du pôle de croissance. *Economique Appliquée*, 307–320.
Pfaffenbichler, P., 2003, *The Strategic, Dynamic and Integrated Urban Land Use and Transport Model MARS*. Beiträge zu einer ökologisch und sozial verträglichen Verkehrsplanung 1/2003, Vienna: Vienna University of Technology.
Pfaffenbichler, P., G. Emberger, and S.P. Shepherd, 2008, The integrated dynamic land use and transport model MARS. *Networks and Spatial Economics*, **8** (2–3), 183–200.
Porter, M., 1990, *The Competitive Advantage of Nations*. New York: Free Press.
Putman, S.H., 1983, *Integrated Urban Models: Policy Analysis of Transportation and Land Use*. London: Pion.
Putman, S.H., 1991, *Integrated Urban Models 2, New Research and Applications of Optimization and Dynamics*. London: Pion.
Putman, S.H., 1998, Results from implementation of integrated transportation and land use models in metropolitan regions. In L. Lundqvist, L.-G. Mattsson, and T.J. Kim, eds, *Network Infrastructure and the Urban Environment: Recent Advances in Land-Use/Transportation Modelling*. Berlin/Heidelberg/New York: Springer, pp. 268–287.
Putman, S.H. and C. Shih-Liang, 2001, The METROPILUS planning support system: urban models and GIS. In R.K. Brail, and R.E. Klosterman, eds, *Planning Support Systems: Integrating Geographic Information Systems, Models and Visualization Tools*. Redland, CA: ESRI Press, pp. 99–128.
Quinet, E. and R. Vickerman, 2004, *Principles of Transport Economics*. Cheltenham, UK: Edward Elgar.
RAND Europe, 2006, *TIGRIS XL 1.0 – Documentatie*. Leiden, the Netherlands: RAND Europe.
Reilly, W., 1941, *The Law of Retail Gravitation*. New York: Pillsbury.
Rohr, C. and I.N. Williams, 1994, Modelling the regional economic impacts of the Channel Tunnel. *Environment and Planning B*, **21**, 555–568.
Sassen, S., 1991, *The Global City*. New York: Princeton University Press.
Schade, W., 2005, Strategic sustainability analysis: concept and application for the assessment of European transport policy. Karlsruhe Papers in Economic Policy Research, 17, Baden-Baden: Nomos.
Schürmann, C., Spiekermann, K., Wegener, M., 1997, *Accessibility Indicators*, Berichte aus dem Institut für Raumplanung 39, Dortmund: Institute of Spatial Planning, University of Dortmund.
Simmonds, D., 1999, The design of the DELTA land-use modelling package, *Environment and Planning B*, **26**, 665–684.
Simmonds, D.C. and A. Skinner, 2003, The South and West Yorkshire strategic land-use/transportation model. In G. Clarke, and J. Stillwell, eds, *Applied GIS and Spatial Analysis*. Chichester, UK: Wiley, 195–214.
Snickars, F., Weibull, J.W., 1976, A minimum information principle. *Regional Science and Urban Economics*, **7**, 137–168.
Treyz, G.I., 1980, Design of a multi-regional policy analysis model. *Journal of Regional Science*, **20**, 191–206.
Treyz, G.I., D.S. Rickman, and G. Shao, 1992, The REMI economic-demographic forecasting and simulation model. *International Regional Science Review*, **14** (3), 221–253.
Vickerman, R.W., 1994, Regional science and new transport infrastructure. In J. Cuadrado Rouro, P. Nijkamp, and P. Salva, eds, *Moving Frontiers: Economic Restructuring, Regional Development and Emerging Networks*. Aldershot: Avebury, pp. 151–165.
Vickerman, R., K. Spiekermann, and M. Wegener, 1999, Accessibility and economic development in Europe. *Regional Studies*, **33** (1), 1–15.
Von Thünen, J.H., 1826, *Der isolierte Staat in Beziehung auf Landwirtschaft und Nationalökonomie*, Hamburg.
Waddell, P., 1998, UrbanSim Overview. Available at www.urbansim.org.
Waddell, P., 2002, UrbanSim: modeling urban development for land use, transportation and environmental planning. *Journal of the American Planning Association*, **68**, 297–314.
Weber, A., 1909, *Über den Standort der Industrien*. Tübingen, Germany: Mohr.
Wegener, M., 1982, Modeling urban decline: a multilevel economic–demographic model for the Dortmund region. *International Regional Science Review*, **7**, 217–241.
Wegener, M., 1994, Operational urban models: state of the art. *Journal of the American Planning Association*, **60**, 17–29. Reprinted in A. Reggiani, K. Button, and P. Nijkamp, eds, 2006, *Planning Models. Classics in Planning 2*. Cheltenham, UK: Edward Elgar, pp. 72–84.
Wegener, M., 2001, *The IRPUD Model*. Dortmund: Institute of Spatial Planning, University of Dortmund. Available at www.spiekermann-wegener.de/mod/pdf/IRPUD_Model_2001.pdf.
Wegener, M., 2004, Overview of land-use transport models. In D.A. Hensher, and K. Button, eds, *Transport Geography and Spatial Systems*, Handbook 5 of Handbooks in Transport. Kidlington, UK: Pergamon/Elsevier Science, pp 127–146.

Wegener, M., 2008, SASI Model Description. Working Paper 08/01, Dortmund: Spiekermann & Wegener Urban and Regional Research. Available at www.spiekermann-wegener.de/mod/pdf/AP_0801.pdf.

Wegener, M., 2011, From macro to micro: how much micro is too much? *Transport Reviews*, **31** (2), 161–177

Wegener, M., Bökemann, D., 1998, *The SASI Model: Model Structure*, SASI Deliverable D8. *Berichte aus dem Institut für Raumplanung* 40. Dortmund: Institute of Spatial Planning, University of Dortmund. Available at www.raumplanung.tu-dortmund.de/irpud/pubdetails/viewpublication/Berichte/040/

Wegener, M., Fürst, F., 1999, *Land-Use Transport Interaction: State of the Art*, Berichte aus dem Institut für Raumplanung 46. Dortmund: Institute of Spatial Planning, University of Dortmund. Available at www.raumplanung.tu-dortmund.de/irpud/pubdetails/viewpublication/Berichte/046/

Williamson, O.E., 1966, *Markets and Hierarchies, Analysis and Antitrust Implications*. New York: Macmillan.

Wilson, A.G., 1967, A statistical theory of spatial distribution models. *Transportation Research*, **1**, 253–69.

Zhao, Y. and K. Kockelman, 2004, The random-utility-based multiregional input–output model: solution existence and uniqueness. *Transportation Research Part B*, **38** (9), 789–807.

Zondag, B., 2007, *Joint Modeling of Land-Use, Transport and Economy*. Delft, the Netherlands: TRAIL Research School, Delft University of Technology.

4 New economic geography: the role of transport costs
Miren Lafourcade and Jacques-François Thisse

INTRODUCTION

Just as matter in the solar system is concentrated in a small number of bodies (the planets and their satellites) economic life is concentrated in a fairly limited number of human settlements (cities and clusters). The main purpose of economic geography is to explain why human activity is unevenly distributed across places and formed a large variety of economic agglomerations. Although using 'agglomeration' as a generic term is convenient at a certain level of abstraction, it must be kept in mind that this concept refers to very distinct real world situations. At one extreme of the spectrum lies the North–South divide. At the other, restaurants, movie theaters or shops selling similar products are often clustered within the same neighborhood, not to say on the same street.

In the foregoing examples, what drives the location of firms and consumers is the *accessibility to spatially dispersed markets*, a fact that has been recognized for long both in spatial economics and regional science (Fujita and Thisse, 2002). Accessibility is itself measured by all the costs generated by the various types of spatial frictions that economic agents face in the exchange process. In the case of goods and services, such costs are called *trade costs*. Spulber (2007) refers to them as 'the four Ts': (a) *Transaction costs* that result from doing business at a distance due to differences in customs, business practices, as well as political and legal climates; (b) *Tariff and non-tariff costs* such as different anti-pollution standards, anti-dumping practices and the massive regulations that still restrict trade and investment; (c) *Transport costs* per se because goods have to reach their consumption place, while many services remain non-tradable; and (d) *Time costs* as, despite Internet and video-conferences, there are still communication impediments across dispersed distribution and manufacturing facilities that slow down reactions to changes in market conditions, while the time needed to ship certain types of goods has a high value. Because they stand for the costs of coordinating and connecting transactions between supplier and customer locations, trade costs are likely to stay on the center stage as they are crucial to the global firm. For example, trade and marketing costs account for 70 per cent of the retail price of a Barbie doll (Spulber, 2007). Regarding the purpose of this chapter, it should be clear that trade costs, being the inherent attribute of exchanges across locations, are also central to the development of economic geography and its various applications.[1]

All distance-related costs having dramatically decreased with technological advances in transportation and the development of the new communication technologies (see, for example, Bairoch, 1997), the following question suggests itself: *what is the impact of falling transport and communication costs on the location of economic activity?* Not surprisingly, but often forgotten, the answer depends on the spatial scale of analysis (Anas et al., 1998). New economic geography (henceforth NEG) is designed to operate at the regional level, thus implying that the focus is on interregional relationships.[2] Furthermore, once it is recognized that trading goods is costly, it must equally be acknowledged that spatial frictions matter to firms and workers. Accordingly, *NEG deals with situations in which the lack of mobility of goods and factors has equal relevance.* By changing the cost of trading goods across space, transport policies impact on the interregional distribution of activities through the location decisions made by firms and workers. We will thus see how NEG can shed new light on these policies' effects for the spatial organization of the economy.

Another fundamental ingredient of the space-economy is that production must display *increasing returns* to scale, meaning that a proportional increase of all inputs yields a more than proportional increase of output. Otherwise, it would always be preferable to subdivide firms up to the point where all consumption places would accommodate very small units producing only for the local customers. Firms and households would thus reduce trade and their transport expenditures to zero, a situation that may be referred to as *backyard capitalism*. However, once economic activities are not perfectly divisible, the transport of goods or people between some places becomes unavoidable because production arises only in a few places.

It has been recognized for long that *the trade-off between increasing returns and transport costs is central to the understanding of the geography of economic activities* (Koopmans, 1957; Krugman, 1995). As transport costs increase with distance, each plant supplies consumers located within a certain radius whose length depends on the relative level of freight costs and the intensity of increasing returns, whereas those located beyond this radius are supplied by other units. By modifying both transport costs and firms' technologies, the Industrial Revolution has deeply affected the terms of the above-mentioned trade-off in a way that is not easy to predict.

Even though it is true that economic activities are, at least to some extent, spatially concentrated because of natural features (think of rivers and harbors), it is reasonable to believe that these features explain only a fraction of the magnitude of regional disparities. This is why NEG has chosen to focus on pure economic mechanisms relying on the trade-off between increasing returns and different types of mobility costs. To achieve its goal, NEG borrows at will concepts and tools from microeconomics, trade theories and industrial organization. Although, as always in economics, everything depends on everything else, geographical economics adds a new element to this: *in all places, what is nearby has more influence than what is far away*. Such a postulate concurs with the gravity prediction, that is, the intensity of flows of people, goods and ideas between two places is positively affected by their respective size and negatively by the distance separating those places.

As will be seen, accounting for increasing returns yields a message that vastly differs from the standard neoclassical paradigm. Even though transport costs must be positive for space to matter, one should not infer from this observation that location matters less when transport costs decrease. Quite the opposite, by making them more footloose, NEG shows that *lower transport costs make firms more sensitive to minor differences between regions*. As a result, a tiny difference may have a big impact on the spatial distribution of economic activity.

Furthermore, by showing that *distance and borders remain major impediments to trade and interactions between spatially separated firms and consumers*, empirical applications of the gravity model also run against the idea that the tyranny of distance is disappearing (Head and Mayer, 2004). In the same vein, Anderson and van Wincoop (2004) provide a very detailed estimate of trade costs and conclude that they would reach a level approximately equal to 170 percent of the average mill price of manufactured goods (the variance across goods is high, however). This estimate can be broken down into 55 percent arising from internal costs and 74 percent from international costs (1.7 = 1.55 × 1.74 − 1). The international costs are broken down in turn into 21 percent arising from transport costs and 44 percent from costs connected with border effects (1.74 = 1.21 × 1.44). Tariff and non-tariff barriers account for 8 percent of the border effects (exceptionally 10 or 20 percent in the case of developing countries), language differences for 7 percent currency differences for 14 percent and other costs, including information, for 9 percent (all in all, 1.44 = 1.08 × 1.07 × 1.14 × 1.09). Hence, *the share of transport costs in the consumer price of manufactured goods remains high*. According to Disdier and Head (2008), distance would impede trade even more today than 50 years ago. Such a rather surprising result could stem from the fact that, once competition is unleashed, the value of time (the fourth T) is expected to rise inexorably due to the need for reliability and flexibility in goods' delivery. We will return to those issues later in this chapter.

The remainder of this chapter is organized as follows. The next section uses historical data to show that falling transport costs may be associated with rising spatial inequalities over very long periods. The following section provides an overview of the main explanations proposed by NEG to explain the emergence of a core–periphery structure in a world characterized by decreasing transport and communication costs. Specifically, we survey a large range of issues involving mobile physical capital or mobile human capital. The material presented in this section suggests that *falling transport costs foster the agglomeration of the mobile production factor in a small number of regions*. However, adding more relevant variables to the canonical core–periphery model leads us to qualify this conclusion. More precisely, we will see that, once obstacles to trade are sufficiently low, spatial inequalities might well vanish. Hence, falling transport and communication costs would be associated with *a bell-shaped curve of spatial development*: spatial inequalities would first rise and then fall. This is confirmed by the evolution of the spatial pattern of activities within France: taking 1860 as our benchmark, Combes et al. (2011) observe that manufacturing activities are more concentrated in 1930 and more dispersed in 2000 than in 1860. Several factors can explain why this could be so: (1) workers have different matches with regions, (2) non-traded goods, especially housing, have higher prices in big agglomerations, (3) firms belonging to the intermediate and final sectors compete for workers, and (4) firms fragment their activities across spatially separated units. The next section has two related purposes. It provides an overview on how transport costs are modeled and measured, and describes the results derived from the use of such measures in a few empirical attempts to validate NEG models. The last section discusses some implications of NEG for transport economics and policy.[3,4]

THE RISE OF SPATIAL INEQUALITIES IN PRE-WORLD WAR I EUROPE

What makes NEG relevant to economists, transport analysts and policy makers is the fact that *the process of economic development is spatially uneven*. To illustrate this phenomenon, it is worth looking at the estimates, provided by Bairoch (1997), of the GDP per capita over the period 1800–1913. This corresponds to a period of intense technological progress that preceded a long series of political disturbances; they are given in Table 4.1. Although caution must be taken when using these numbers, they still reveal clear tendencies.

First, in 1800, most countries, except the Netherlands and, to a lesser extent, the UK, had fairly similar incomes per capita. As the Industrial Revolution developed and spread across the continent, each country experienced growth: the average GDP increases from 200 dollars in 1800 to 550 dollars in 1913. However, the process of economic growth also affected countries in a very unequal way. This is shown by the rise of the coefficient of variation that rose from 0.12 to 0.42, which confirms the existence of strongly rising spatial inequalities.

Second, countries with the highest growth rates are those located close to the UK, which became the center of the global economy of the nineteenth century. This is readily

Table 4.1   Per capita GDP of European countries expressed in 1960 US dollars and prices

Countries	1800	1830	1850	1870	1890	1900	1913
Austria-Hungary	200	240	275	310	370	425	510
Belgium	200	240	335	450	55	650	815
Bulgaria	175	185	205	225	260	275	285
Denmark	205	225	280	365	525	655	885
Finland	180	190	230	300	370	430	525
France	205	275	345	450	525	610	670
Germany	200	240	305	425	540	645	790
Greece	190	195	220	255	300	310	335
Italy	220	240	260	300	315	345	455
Netherlands	270	320	385	470	570	610	740
Norway	185	225	285	340	430	475	615
Portugal	230	250	275	290	295	320	335
Romania	190	195	205	225	265	300	370
Russia	170	180	190	220	210	260	340
Serbia	185	200	215	235	260	270	300
Spain	210	250	295	315	325	365	400
Sweden	195	235	270	315	405	495	705
Switzerland	190	240	340	485	645	730	895
UK	240	355	470	650	815	915	1035
Mean	200	240	285	350	400	465	550
Coefficient of variation	0.12	0.18	0.23	0.31	0.38	0.39	0.42

verified by means of a regression of the logarithm of the GDP per capita on the logarithm of the distance to the UK, which shows that the impact of this variable is significantly negative. Moreover, the absolute value of this regression coefficient, which has the meaning of elasticity, rises from 0.090 in 1800 and reaches a peak equal to 0.426 in 1890 (and remains stable afterwards). Stated differently, before the Industrial Revolution, a decrease of 10 per cent in the distance to the UK is accompanied by an increase of the GDP per capita equal to 0.9 percent. By World War I, this elasticity had reached 4.4 percent, thus showing how far spatial inequalities had evolved during the nineteenth century.

Therefore, we may safely conclude that the process of economic growth is localized, while the relative rates of economic growth among nations have been strongly related to their distance to the center of the European economy. It is worth stressing here that the emergence of such a core-periphery structure arose while transport costs were falling at a historically unprecedented rate. For example, Bairoch (1997) estimates that, on the whole, between 1800 and 1910, the reduction in the real average prices of transportation was in the order of 10 to 1. Hence, while the European economy experienced a rapid growth, this phenomenal decrease in transport costs did not trigger a more or less even distribution of wealth across nations. We will see below how NEG can explain this seemingly paradoxical result.

DO LOWER TRANSPORT COSTS FOSTER MORE SPATIAL INEQUALITY?

Regional economics has long been dominated by the neoclassical model in which technologies display constant returns to scale and markets operate under perfect competition. In such a setting, regional wage differences push and pull workers until wages are equalized between regions. Simultaneously, capital flows from regions where it is abundant to regions where it is scarce. In equilibrium, the capital/labor ratio is equal across regions and both factors receive the same return in each region. This model is, therefore, unable to account for both the international discrepancies described above and the development of interregional trade, thus pointing to the need for an alternative approach.

There is a broad consensus among economists and geographers to consider the space-economy as the outcome of a process involving two types of opposing forces: *agglomeration forces* and *dispersion forces* (Papageorgiou and Smith, 1983). The resulting spatial distribution of economic activities is thus a complex balance between these forces that push and pull both consumers and firms.[5] What NEG intends to do is to determine the nature of these forces at the multi-regional level and the way in which they interact. This appears to be a difficult task since the cause often becomes the effect, and vice versa, thereby making the relationship of causality *circular* and the process of spatial development *cumulative*. This is precisely what Krugman (1991, p. 486) means when he writes 'manufactures production will tend to concentrate where there is a large market, but the market will be large where manufactures production is concentrated'.

In general, the intensity of agglomeration and dispersion forces decreases with transport costs. Although it is precisely their balance that determines the shape of the space-economy, there is no clear indication regarding the relative intensity of those forces as transport costs decrease. This is why the main questions that NEG addresses keep their relevance: when do we observe an agglomerated or a dispersed pattern of production at the interregional level, and what is the impact that decreasing transport and communication costs have on the intensity of the agglomeration and dispersion forces operating at that spatial scale. To this end, NEG uses a simple setting borrowed from modern trade theories, in which the impact of a wide range of agglomeration and dispersion forces may be discussed.

The Basic Framework

In this and the next section, our frame of reference involves two regions, two sectors, called agriculture and manufacturing, and two production factors.[6] The agricultural sector produces a homogeneous good under constant returns and perfect competition, whereas the manufacturing sector produces a differentiated good under increasing returns and monopolistic competition. There are several reasons for using monopolistic competition as a market structure. First, firms are endowed with monopoly power on the product market because they sell differentiated varieties. That firms choose to sell differentiated products reflects the fundamental fact that consumers have either a love for variety or different ideal products.[7] As a matter of fact, both economists and business analysts see product variety as one of the main gains of trade and economic integration (Spulber, 2007). Thanks to their market power, firms' operating profits allow them to cover their fixed production costs. Second, because there is a continuum of firms, each one is negligible to the market. This makes interactions among firms much easier to handle than in spatial competition theory, which is often plagued with the non-existence of equilibrium (d'Aspremont et al., 1979). When labor is homogeneous, firms have no market power on the labor market and are, therefore, wage-takers. This in turn allows for a general equilibrium analysis involving firms that produce under increasing returns and act on both the product and labor markets, something that is still out of reach when firms operate under oligopolistic competition. Last, the fact that firms located in the same region supply a range of differentiated products captures the idea that a big regional agglomeration makes a wide set of opportunities available to the consumers/ workers living in that region.[8]

The Mobility of Capital

As described above, NEG deals with the mobility of goods and factors. To start with, we consider the case of goods and capital because it is easier to handle. In contrast to standard trade theory, firms are now free to choose their locations and they set up where their profits are highest. However, consumers/workers continue to be immobile. Furthermore, the mobility of manufactured goods is constrained by positive transport costs. It is, therefore, tempting to conclude that the region with the larger market will always attract firms because this location minimizes transport costs borne by firms in supplying both markets. However, this argument ignores the fact that when more firms locate within the same region, local competition is intensified and profits are depressed. The spatial distribution of firms then arises from the balancing of two opposite forces: the agglomeration force is generated by each firm's desire for *market access*, whereas the dispersion force finds its origin in each firm's desire to *relax competition* by moving away from competitors.

When one region is larger in terms of population and purchasing power, the push and pull system reaches equilibrium when this region attracts *a more than proportional share of firms*, a property that has been coined the 'home market effect' (Combes et al., 2008b; Helpman and Krugman, 1985). Because of its comparative advantage in terms of size, it seems natural that this region should attract more firms. What is less expected is that the share of firms exceeds the relative size of this region, thus implying that the initial advantage is magnified.

As the large region is also the one that offers the wider array of varieties, it is a net exporter of the manufactured good and a net importer of the agricultural good. The two regions are, therefore, partially specialized: the large one in the production of the manufactured good and the small one in that of the agricultural good. This type of specialization owes nothing to a Ricardian comparative advantage, the nature of the forces at work here being totally different. Indeed, the equilibrium distribution of firms relies here on the interplay between the market-access and market-crowding forces, which are endogenous since their intensity varies with the way capital is allocated between regions.

The intensity of the home market effect varies with the level of transport costs: when economic integration gets deeper, the intensity of the agglomeration force increases, whereas the intensity of the dispersion force decreases. This result can be understood as follows. On the one hand, a higher degree of integration makes exports to the small market easier, which allows firms to exploit more intensively their scale economies; on the other hand, the deepening of integration reduces the advantages associated with geographical isolation in the small market where there is less competition. These two effects push toward more agglomeration of the manufacturing sector, thus implying that, as transport costs go down, the small region gets de-industrialized to the benefit of the large one.

Equally important are the implications of that result for people's wellbeing. Even though all consumers will benefit from lower transport costs, those in the larger region will achieve the greatest benefits from their direct access to a wider array of products. This has an unexpected implication, that is, *building new and more efficient transport infrastructure may exacerbate spatial inequalities*. Stated differently, lowering transport costs enhances the mobility of capital, rather than substitutes for it, and makes the two economies less similar. It also leads to over-agglomeration of the manufacturing sector in the large region (Ottaviano and van Ypersele, 2005). Hence, contrary to general belief, better transport infrastructure may exacerbate regional disparities. For example, the economic integration of Italy through the construction of national railway and highway systems had fostered the de-industrialization of the Mezzogiorno at the benefit of Northern Italy (Faini, 1983). We will return to this important issue later in this chapter.

The Mobility of Labor

While the movement of capital to a region brings with it the benefits of added production capability, the returns from this capital need not be spent in the same region. By contrast, when skilled workers move to a new region, they bring with them *both their production and consumption capabilities*. As a result, their movements simultaneously affect the *size* of labor and product markets in both the origin and the destination regions, expanding in the former and shrinking in the latter. This is likely the main difference between capital and labor mobility. It has a major implication, that is, the existence of multiple equilibria, meaning that the region where economic activity develops is a priori undetermined. In other words, considerations external to the model must be taken into account to select a particular equilibrium. The last difference to be stressed is that the mobility of capital is driven by differences in *nominal* returns, whereas workers move when there is a positive difference in *real* wages. This is because the gap in living costs matters to workers who consume in the region where they work, but not to capital-owners who consume their income in their region of residence, which need not be the region where their capital is invested.

This is the starting point for Krugman's 1991 paper. When some workers choose to migrate, their move affects the welfare of those who stay put. Indeed, as said above, their migrations change the relative attractiveness of both origin and destination regions. These effects have the nature of pecuniary externalities because workers do not take these effects into account in making their decision to migrate. Moreover, such externalities are of particular importance when markets are imperfectly competitive because market prices fail to reflect the true social value of individual decisions. This is why the effects of migration must be studied within a general equilibrium framework encapsulating the interactions between product and labor markets, but which must also account for the fact that individuals are both workers and consumers.

In Krugman's model, one factor (farmers) is spatially immobile and used as an input in the agricultural sector; the second factor (workers) is spatially mobile and used as an input in the manufacturing sector. In what has come to be known as the *core–periphery model*, two major effects are at work: one involves firms and the other workers. Assume that one region becomes slightly bigger than the other. First, this increase in market size leads to a higher demand for the manufactured good. Given what we have seen above, this increase in market size generates a more than proportionate increase in the share of firms, thus pushing nominal wages up. Second, the presence of more firms means a greater variety of local products and, therefore, a lower local price index – a cost-of-living effect. Accordingly, real wages should rise, and this region should attract a new flow of workers. The combination of these two effects should reinforce each of its components and lead to the eventual agglomeration of all firms and workers in a single region – the *core* of the economy, while the other regions form the *periphery*.

Even though this process seems to generate a 'snowball' effect, it is not obvious that it will always develop according to that prediction. Indeed, the foregoing argument has ignored several key impacts of migration on the labor market. On the one hand, the increased supply of labor in the region of destination will tend to push wages down. On the other hand, since new workers are also consumers, there may be an increase in local demand for the manufactured good that leads to a higher demand for labor. So the final impact on nominal wages is hard to predict. Likewise, there is increased competition in the product market, which makes the region less attractive to firms. The combination of all those effects may lead to a 'snowball meltdown', which results in the spatial dispersion of firms and workers.

Turning next to the specific conditions for agglomeration or dispersion to arise, Krugman and others have shown that *the level of transport costs is the key parameter*

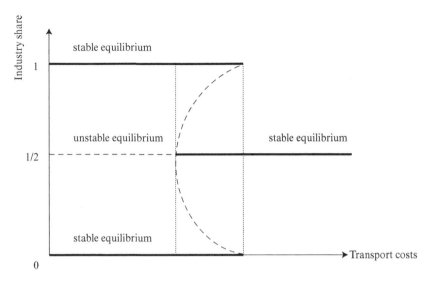

Figure 4.1   Transport costs and industry share when labor is mobile

(Combes et al., 2008b; Fujita et al., 1999; Krugman, 1991). On the one hand, if transport costs are sufficiently high, interregional shipments of goods are discouraged, which
strengthens the dispersion force. The economy then displays a symmetric regional
pattern of production in which firms focus mainly on local markets. Because the distribution of workers is the same within each region, spatial disparities vanish in that there
are no interregional price and wage differentials. As in new trade theories, there is intra-
industry trade. Integration has only positive effects provided that the spatial pattern
remains the same.

On the other hand, if transport costs are sufficiently low, then all manufacturing firms
will concentrate into the *core*, while the *periphery* supplies only the agricultural good. In
this way, firms are able to exploit increasing returns by selling more goods in the larger
market without losing much business in the smaller market. Typically, the core will be a
region with and the periphery a region without a major urban center. It is worth stressing here that the core–periphery structure emerges as the equilibrium balance of a system
of opposite forces. Spatial inequalities reflect here the uneven distribution of jobs across
regions and arise as the involuntary consequence of decisions made by a myriad of economic agents pursuing their own interests. The resulting pattern of trade now involves
intersectoral trade because one region has built a Ricardian comparative advantage in
producing the manufactured good. Let us stress, once more, the fact that this advantage
is not exogenous, as in standard trade theory.

As illustrated by Figure 4.1, high transport costs sustain a pattern in which activities
are equally split between the two regions, meaning that the share of the manufacturing
sector is half in each region (the thick lines describe the stable equilibria and the dashed
lines the unstable equilibria). At the other extreme of the spectrum, low transport costs
foster the agglomeration of activities within a single region, hence implying that the share
is either 0 or 1. For intermediate values, both configurations are stable equilibria, in
which case the actual spatial pattern heavily depends on history. Those spatial patterns

of production, as well as the conditions under which they emerge, provide a crude, but accurate, description of the general trends summarized in the previous section.

Thus, the mobility of labor exacerbates the general tendencies uncovered for the mobility of capital, the reason being that the size of local markets changes with labor migration. For such self-reinforcing changes to occur, it must be that trading between regions becomes sufficiently cheap. Putting all these results together shows that lowering transport costs first leaves the location of economic activity unchanged, and then gives rise to a snowball effect that stops only when an extreme form of economic agglomeration is obtained.

One important implication of the cumulative causation triggered by the interplay of agglomeration and dispersion forces is the emergence of what can be called *putty-clay geography*. Even though firms are a priori footloose, once the agglomeration process is set into motion, it keeps developing within the same region. Individual choices become more rigid because of the self-reinforcing nature of the agglomeration mechanism (the snowball effect mentioned above). In other words, the process of agglomeration sparks a *lock-in effect*. Hence, although firms and workers are (almost) freed from natural constraints, they are still connected through more complex networks of interactions, which are more difficult to unearth than the standard location factors related to the supply of natural resources.

A Welfare Analysis of the Core–periphery Model

Whether there is too much or too little agglomeration is an issue that has never been in short supply and it is fair to say that this is one of the main questions that policy makers would like to address. The core–periphery model shows that migration is not necessarily a force pushing for the equalization of standards of living. It may just as well reduce gaps in welfare levels as exacerbate regional disparities. Besides the standard inefficiencies generated by firms pricing above marginal costs, Krugman's model contains new sources of inefficiency stemming from agents' mobility. Firms and workers move without taking into account the benefits and losses they generate for both the host and departure regions. Accordingly, if it is reasonable to expect the market outcome to be inefficient, there is a priori no general indication as to the social desirability of agglomeration or dispersion.

Before proceeding, a warning is in order: both the planner seeking to maximize global efficiency and the market work with the same agglomeration and dispersion forces. Since the planning optimum and the market equilibrium depend on the fundamental characteristics of the economy, the agglomeration and dispersion forces discussed above are to be taken into account in both cases. What makes the two solutions different is the institutional mechanism used to solve the trade-off between these forces. Such a difference is often poorly understood, thus leading the public and some policy makers to believe that the socially optimal pattern of activities has nothing to do with what the free play of market forces yields. In particular, *agglomeration may be socially efficient*. This is so when transport costs are sufficiently low. The reason is simple to grasp: firms are able to take advantage of the larger market created by their concentration to exploit scale economies, while guaranteeing the inhabitants of the periphery a good access to their products.

Unfortunately, welfare analyses do not deliver a simple and unambiguous message about the equilibrium spatial pattern of economic activity in the core–periphery model. Neither of the two possible equilibria – agglomeration or dispersion – Pareto dominates the other, because farmers living in the periphery always prefer dispersion, whereas farmers and workers living in the core always prefer agglomeration. In order to compare these two market outcomes, Charlot et al. (2006) use compensation mechanisms put forward in public economics to evaluate the social desirability of a move, using market prices and equilibrium wages to compute the compensations to be paid either by those who gain from the move (Kaldor), or by those who would be hurt by the move (Hicks). They show that, once transport costs are sufficiently low, agglomeration is preferred to dispersion in that farmers and workers in the core can compensate farmers staying in the periphery. However, the latter are unable to compensate farmers and workers who would choose to form what becomes the core. This implies that none of the two configurations is preferred to the other with respect to the two criteria. Such indeterminacy may be viewed as the 'synthesis' of contrasted views prevailing in a domain crowded by hot debates.

This indeterminacy may be resolved by resorting to specific social welfare functions. Charlot et al. consider the CES family that encapsulates different attitudes toward inequality across individuals, and includes the utilitarian and Rawlsian criteria as polar cases. As expected, the relative merits of agglomeration then critically depend on societal values. If society does not care much about inequality across individuals, agglomeration (dispersion) is socially desirable once transport costs are below (above) some threshold, the value of which depends on the fundamental parameters of the economy. Even though these results are derived from social preferences defined on individualistic utilities, it is worth noting that they lead to policy recommendations that can be regarded as being region-based. This is because the market yields much contrasted distributions of income in the core–periphery structure, which correspond to equally contrasted distributions of skills between regions, as illustrated by Duranton and Monastiriotis (2002) for England, and by Combes et al. (2008a) for France.

When individual preferences are quasi-linear, one may go one step further because the total surplus is measured by the sum of individual utilities across regions and groups of workers. In this case, it is possible to determine some clear-cut and suggestive results (Ottaviano and Thisse, 2002). First, workers do not necessarily benefit from their concentration into a single region. Indeed, as said above, they do not account for the impact of their migration on their collective welfare, which typically differs from their individual welfare. This difference arises, on the one hand, because of the intensified competition that affects prices and wages and, on the other, because of the larger size of the regional markets for both products and labor. The net effect is, therefore, a priori undetermined. It has been shown, however, that the net effect is negative when transport costs take intermediate values. This is so because agglomeration leads to very low prices, whence very low wages, thus implying that the collective gains associated with agglomeration do not permit any compensation for the resulting social losses. By contrast, when transport costs are very low, both the market solution and the social optimum involve the agglomeration of the manufactured sector. This means that the total surplus is high enough for everyone in the core and the periphery to be better off. Of course, for this to arise, inter-regional transfers from the core to the periphery are to be implemented.

This is not the end of the story, however. Once local interactions and knowledge spillovers among firms are taken into account, the market outcome is likely to exhibit under-agglomeration for a wider range of transport cost values (Belleflamme et al., 2000).[9] Although the process of interaction goes both ways, firms worry only about their role as 'receivers' but tend to neglect the fact that they are also 'transmitters' to others. Furthermore, at the optimum, prices are set at the marginal cost level, while locations are chosen so as to maximize the difference between the benefits of agglomeration and total transport costs. By contrast, at the market outcome, firms take advantage of their spatial separation to relax price competition and, whence, to make higher profits. These interactions yield *clusters that are too small from the social point of view*. In a setting involving a housing market, this result is confirmed by Pflüger and Südekum (2008) who show that there is under-agglomeration for low trade costs (see also Helpman, 1998).

A Growth Approach to Regional Disparities

One may wonder what the implications of the core–periphery model become once we allow the manufacturing sector to expand through the entry of new firms and a larger number of varieties. The main question is now to figure out how growth and location affect each other. More precisely, do regional discrepancies widen or fall over time, and what are the main reasons for such an evolution? To answer these questions, the core-periphery model is grafted onto an endogenous growth model involving an R&D sector, such as those developed in Grossman and Helpman (1991).

The R&D sector uses workers as its sole input to produce patents that manufacturing firms must buy to enter the product market. The price of a patent is the equivalent of the firms' fixed production cost in the core–periphery model. Hence, the number of manufacturing firms is now variable. Farmers can work indifferently in the agricultural or manufacturing sectors, where they are paid the same wage. Although the frame of reference remains very much the same as in the core–periphery model, new issues arise because workers are free to move back and forth between regions over time, thus changing the location of the R&D sector.

Fujita and Thisse (2002) show that, at the steady-state, the spatial distribution of the R&D sector remains the same over time while the total number of patents/varieties/firms grows at a constant rate. The growth rate is measured by the variation in the number of varieties and changes with the spatial distribution of workers. In other words, *the growth of the global economy depends on its spatial organization*. When patents can be used indifferently in either region, the market outcome is such that the entire R&D activity is always concentrated into a single region. Furthermore, the manufacturing sector is fully or partially agglomerated in the same region as the R&D sector, depending on the level of transport costs. Thus, the existence of a R&D sector is a strong agglomeration force, which magnifies the circular causation pinned down in the core–periphery model.

This result gives credence to the existence of a trade-off between growth and spatial equity. However, in contrast to what the analysis of the core–periphery model suggests, the welfare analysis performed by Fujita and Thisse supports the idea that the additional growth spurred by agglomeration may lead to a Pareto-dominant outcome. Specifically, when the economy moves from dispersion to agglomeration, innovation follows a faster pace. As a consequence, even those who stay put in the periphery are better off than under dispersion, provided that the growth effect triggered by agglomeration is strong enough. It is worth stressing here that *this Pareto-dominance property does not require any interregional transfers*: it is a pure effect of market interaction.

Clearly, the farmers living in the core of the economy enjoy a higher level of welfare than those in the periphery. Yet, even though agglomeration generates more growth and makes everybody better off, the gap enlarges between the core and the periphery. Hence, agglomeration gives rise to regressive effects in terms of spatial equity, one region being much richer than the other. Such widening welfare gaps may call for corrective policies, but such policies might in turn hurt growth and, thus, individual welfare. Note, finally, that regional income discrepancies again reflect the spatial distribution of jobs and skills. Core and periphery welfares diverge because faster growth generates additional gains that the R&D sector is able to spur by being agglomerated.

THE BELL-SHAPED CURVE OF SPATIAL DEVELOPMENT

Imperfect Labor Mobility

In the foregoing section, workers are assumed to have the same preferences. Although this assumption is not uncommon in economic modeling, it is highly implausible that all potentially mobile individuals will react in the same way to a given 'economic gap' between regions. Some people show a high degree of attachment to the region where they are born; they will stay put even though they may guarantee themselves higher living standards in another region. In the same spirit, lifetime considerations such as marriage, divorce and the like play an important role in the decision to migrate (Greenwood, 1997). Note, finally, that regions are not similar and exhibit different natural and cultural features, whereas people value differently local and cultural amenities. Typically, individuals exhibit idiosyncratic tastes about such attributes, so that non-economic considerations matter to potentially mobile workers when they make their decision to move or not. In particular, as argued in hedonic models of migration, once individual welfare levels get sufficiently high through the steady increase of income, workers tend to pay more attention to the non-market attributes of their environment (Knapp and Graves, 1989).

Although individual motivations are difficult to model because they are many and often non-observable, it turns out to be possible to identify their aggregate impact on the spatial distribution of economic activities by using discrete choice theory, which aims at predicting the aggregate behavior of individuals facing mutually exclusive choices (Anderson et al., 1992; Train, 2003). In other words, a discrete choice model can be used to capture the aggregate matching between individuals and regions.[10] Building on this idea, Tabuchi and Thisse (2002) have combined the core–periphery model previously sketched with the logit model of discrete choice theory in order to assess the impact of heterogeneity in migration behavior. In such a context, interregional migrations become sluggish, which in turn generates a very different global pattern: *the industry displays a smooth bell-shaped curve of spatial development*.

As transport costs steadily decline, more and more firms get agglomerated in one region for the reasons explained above, but the agglomeration process is now gradual and smooth. However, full agglomeration never arises because some workers have a

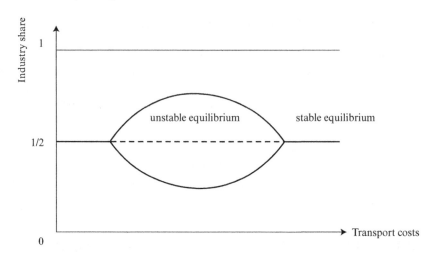

Figure 4.2   Transport costs and industry share when labor is imperfectly mobile

very good match with their region of origin and choose not to migrate. After having reached a peak, the manufacturing sector gradually gets re-dispersed. This is because *the non-economic factors that drive the choice of a residential location become predominant and take over the economic forces stressed by NEG*, the intensity of which decreases with falling transport costs. As a result, the relationship between the degree of spatial concentration and the level of transport costs is bell-shaped (see Figure 4.2 for an illustration). Furthermore, the domain over which this curve develops shrinks as the population becomes more heterogeneous, confirming once more the importance of the type of labor mobility. Therefore, idiosyncratic factors in migration decisions act as a strong dispersion force and change the global pattern of location decisions into a bell-shaped curve.

The Role of Non-tradable Goods

Tradable goods do not account for a very large fraction of the GDP of developed countries. On the contrary, many consumption goods and services are produced locally and not traded between regions. The forces pushing toward factor price equalization within every region thus lead to additional costs generated by the agglomeration of firms and workers within the same region. This in turn increases the cost of living in the large region and may induce some workers to change place. A natural way to capture this phenomenon is to focus on the land market where competition gets tougher, hence the land rent rises, as more people establish themselves in the same area. Indeed, as argued in urban economics, a growing flow of workers makes commuting and housing costs higher in the city that accommodates the new comers (Fujita, 1989).

When firms set up within a central business district, workers distribute themselves around this center and commute on a daily basis. Competition for land generates a land rent whose value decreases as the distance to the employment center rises. This implies that, both the land rent and the average commuting cost are shifted upward when more workers reside in the city. Eventually, as the population keeps rising, the costs borne by workers within the agglomeration become too high to be compensated by a better access to the array of tradable goods. Therefore, dispersion arises once shipping costs have reached a sufficiently low level by comparison with commuting costs (Ottaviano et al., 2002; Tabuchi, 1998). Lower urban costs in the periphery more than offset the additional transport costs to be paid for consuming the varieties produced in the other region. Consequently, as transport costs fall, the economy involves dispersion, agglomeration and re-dispersion. This is strikingly similar to what we have seen in the sub-section above about imperfect labor mobility, but what triggers the re-dispersion of workers is now the crowding of the land market.[11]

Two final comments are in order. First, the redispersion process across regions depends on the efficiency of urban transport infrastructures, thus showing why *urban and interregional transport policies should be coordinated*. If commuting costs are low (high), the agglomeration will remain the equilibrium outcome for a wider (narrower) range of transport cost values, as illustrated by the emergence of large polycentric metropolises in the United States (Anas et al., 1998). The relocation of manufactured activities away from large metropolitan areas toward medium-sized cities provides an example of the impact that high commuting costs may have on firms' locations (Henderson, 1997). Second, the burden of urban costs may be alleviated when *secondary employment centers are created*. Such a morphological change in the urban structure, which makes the city polycentric, slows down the re-dispersion process and allows the agglomeration to maintain, at least to a large extent, its supremacy (Cavailhès et al., 2007). This draws attention to two facts that transport analysts often neglect: on the one hand, the local mobility of people (i.e. commuting) may affect the global organization of the economy and, on the other hand, the global mobility of commodities is likely to have an impact on the local organization of production and employment.

Vertical Linkages

So far in the analysis, agglomeration is driven by the endogeneity of the size of local markets caused by the mobility of consumers/workers. When labor is immobile across regions but mobile between sectors, the cumulative causation falls short and the symmetric equilibrium is the only stable outcome. However, another reason for the market size to be endogenous is the presence of input–output linkages between firms: *what is an output for one firm is an input for another*. Intermediate production represents a big share of the industrial output. For example, in the United States, intermediate consumption of goods accounted for almost 69 per cent of the total production manufactured in 1997. Besides the standard competition effect, the entry of a new firm in a region also increases the market size of upstream firms-suppliers (market size effect) and decreases the costs of downstream firms-customers (cost effect). In such a context, the agglomeration of the final and intermediate sectors in a particular region may occur because firms want to be close to their customers or suppliers.

This alternative setting allows one to shed light on two new forces that are likely to play a major role in the evolution of the space-economy (Krugman and Venables, 1995). When more firms are concentrated in a region where the supply of labor is totally inelastic, they will end up paying higher wages to their workers if the size of the two industrial sectors becomes large. This has two opposing effects for the core region. On the one hand, the final demand in this region increases because consumers enjoy higher incomes there. We find again a force of agglomeration linked to final demand, as in Krugman. However, this is no longer triggered by an increase in the size of the population, but by an increase in individual incomes. On the other hand, the same phenomenon generates a force of dispersion, which feeds the fear of de-industrialization, that is, the high labor costs that prevail in the core. If wages are much lower in the periphery, beyond some level of integration, *firms will find it profitable to relocate there*, even if the demand for their product is lower than in the core. In doing so, they have the possibility to produce at lower costs while keeping a very good access to the core region.[12]

Thus, if the impact of economic integration highlighted previously – namely, the strengthening of regional inequalities – continues to appear up to a certain level of integration, the inverse process is set in motion beyond this level, thus showing that the pursuit of economic integration contributes to a decrease in regional inequalities. We therefore find a re-industrialization of the periphery and even a possible, and simultaneous, de-industrialization of the core. This new phenomenon of regional convergence, which arises here for very high degrees of integration, concurs with the prediction that re-equilibrating forces in favor of peripheral zones come into play once transport costs have reached a sufficiently low level. The relocation of some activities in the new Member States of the European Union seems to confirm the plausibility of such an evolution (Brülhart, 2006).

The Spatial Fragmentation of Firms

A growing number of firms choose to break down their production process into various stages spread across different regions. Specifically, the modern firm organizes and performs discrete activities in distinct locations, which altogether form a *supply chain* starting at the conception of the product and ending at its delivery. This spatial fragmentation of production aims at taking advantage of differences in technologies, factor endowments, or factor prices across places (Feenstra, 1998; Spulber, 2007). The most commonly observed pattern is such that firms re-locate their production activities in low-wage regions or countries, while keeping their strategic functions (for example, management, R&D, marketing and finance) concentrated in a few affluent urban regions where the high-skilled workers they need are available.

In such a context, the development of new communication technologies is a major force that should be accounted for. It goes hand in hand with the growing role of transportation firms in the global logistics. With this in mind, two types of spatial costs must then be considered, namely communication costs and transport costs. Low transport costs allow firms producing overseas to sell their output on their home market at a low price. Equally important, but perhaps less recognized, is the fact that coordinating activities within a firm is more costly when headquarters and plant are physically separated because the transmission of information remains incomplete and imperfect (Leamer and Storper, 2001). However, lower communication costs make coordination easier and, therefore, facilitate the process of fragmentation. More precisely, in order to make low-wage areas more attractive for the establishment of their production, firms need both the development of new communication technologies and substantial decreases in transport costs.

Assume that each firm has two units, one headquarters and one plant. All head-quarters are located in the same region and use skilled labor, whereas plants use headquarter-services together with unskilled labor. A firm is free to decentralize its production overseas by choosing distinct locations for its plant and headquarters. Apart from this change, the framework used is the same as earlier in the chapter. Two main scenarios are to be distinguished as they lead to very different patterns (Fujita and Thisse, 2006). When communication costs are sufficiently high, all firms are national and established in the core region. Once communication costs steadily decrease, the industry moves toward a configuration in which some firms become multinational whereas others remain national. Eventually, when these costs have reached a sufficiently low level, the economy ends up with a de-industrialized core that retains only firms' strategic functions.

A fall in transport costs may lead to fairly contrasted patterns of production. In particular, two scenarios are to be considered. When communication costs are high, reducing transport costs leads to a growing agglomeration of plants within the core, very much as in the core–periphery model. However, the agglomeration process here is gradual instead of exhibiting a bang-bang behavior. Things are totally different when communication costs are low. For high transport costs, most plants are still located within the core region. However, once these costs fall below some threshold, the re-location process unfolds over a small range of transport cost values. This could explain why the process of de-industrialization of some developed regions seems, first, to be slow and, then, to proceed quickly, yielding a space-economy very different from the initial one.[13]

In a related context, Robert-Nicoud (2008) stresses a different aspect of the fragmentation process, which allows firms to simultaneously reap the benefit of agglomeration economies in the core regions and of low wages in the periphery. Specifically, the reduction of employment in some routine tasks in rich regions helps sustain and reinforce employment in the core competencies of firms in such regions. Consequently, the loss of some (unskilled) jobs permits to retain firms' 'core competencies' in the core regions as well as the corresponding (skilled) jobs. By contrast, preventing firms from outsourcing their routine tasks abroad is likely to induce them to relocate their entire activities in the periphery, thus destroying *all* jobs in what was the core.

Thus, by facilitating the vertical disintegration of firms, lower communication costs are likely to have a deep impact on the structure of employment in developed countries. It should be clear that the interaction between communication costs and transport costs has become a critical issue for the future of the space-economy.

HOW TO MEASURE TRANSPORT COSTS AND THEIR IMPACT ON THE DISTRIBUTION OF ACTIVITIES?

In NEG models, the transport sector is a *silent* sector. To a large extent, this is because economists have a fairly simplistic view of transport costs, which leads them to disregard several important dimensions stressed by transportation economists (Rietveld and Vickerman, 2004). Yet, such measures are crucial when we come to the evaluation of the impact of lowering transport costs on the spatial distribution of activities in real-world economies.

The Measurement of Transport Costs

Most NEG models build on the standard iceberg formulation of transport costs. Albeit popularized by Samuelson (1954), the iceberg frame goes back to von Thünen (1826) who argued that transport costs would be given by the amount of grains consumed by horses pulling the loaded carriages. In line with this metaphor, most NEG models rest on the assumption that moving commodities incurs the loss of a given share of the load. Modeling transport costs as if goods were truly 'melting' en route is a convenient analytical device that circumvents the need to consider the transport sector per se and its related interactions with other markets. To be precise, the iceberg formulation implies that transport costs are multiplicative to the 'free-on-board' (FOB) price of products, so that any increase in this price raises freight charges proportionally. Conversely, any increase in the iceberg cost translates into a larger delivered or 'cost–insurance–freight' (CIF) price. Denoting by p the FOB price and by p^* the CIF price, the freight rate is equal to $(p^*/p) - 1$.

In that spirit, the first generation of NEG empirics uses two series of transport cost proxies. The first one is the share of GDP spent in transport activities. In the United States, Glaeser and Kohlhase (2004) report that this share has fallen from about 10 per cent in late nineteenth century to about 3 percent nowadays. Adding logistic and transport activities yields a larger share of 9.5 percent (Wilson, 2006).

However, the share of transport and logistic expenditures in GDP provides only a lower bound for actual transport costs because it neglects two major features. First, national accounts exclude in-house transport, which may account for up to 15 percent of transport activities in a country such as France. Second, a large share of GDP is not shipped across locations. Hence, the above data provides at best very crude approximations of actual transport expenditures on traded goods. It seems therefore preferable to evaluate transport costs from other sources.

Based on customs data, transport costs may be computed as the ratio between the CIF value of a traded flow reported by the importing country, which is inclusive of freight charges, and the related FOB value reported by the exporting country, which is exclusive of these charges. The CIF/FOB *transport margin* is commodity-specific and varies with the origin–destination route. Unfortunately, for many countries, especially developing ones, this technique yields large inconsistencies that are mostly due to discrepancies in trade reporting techniques (Hummels and Lugovskyy, 2006).

In a few importing nations, such as New Zealand, the United States or Latin American countries (Argentina, Chile, Brazil, Paraguay and Uruguay), freight expenditures are directly reported in import customs declarations. For these countries, the ratio of freight charges to import values yields a transport cost that is purged from the aforementioned inconsistencies. Building on this method, Hummels (2001) reports *considerable variation in freight rates across importers, exporting routes and goods.* The United States is shown to have the lowest transport costs with a 3.8 percent margin, which is around four-fold that of a land-locked country such as Paraguay (13.3 percent). Hummels (2007) evaluates that, even for the median US good shipped, the related freight rate was nine times larger than the corresponding tariff duty in 2004. Along the same line, the Global Trade Analysis Project (GTAP), which provides one of the most disaggregated databases on import customs declarations, reports average transport margins that would range, for the United States, between 0.4 per cent (cobalt ores) and 136 per cent (grapefruit).[14] The variability across routes is also very large, the lower and upper bounds being for, respectively, the countries close to the United States (Canada and Mexico) and distant trading partners such as Australia.

Nonetheless, a warning is in order regarding the use of transport margins computed from trade data. A major pitfall of this method is that freight expenditures might be low because trade strategies are designed by firms and carriers to reduce transport costs. If traders substitute away from goods or routes with relative high freight costs, the picture drawn from trade margins could be misleading, and the real average level of transport costs vastly underestimated. In addition, null flows, which remain mostly ignored in empirical analyses, probably mean that the transport costs of some goods are prohibitive. A well-known example is provided by the non-tradable goods whose share in households' and firms' consumption is large. One way to circumvent both the endogeneity of transport margins and its related trade composition effects is to identify the various factors that determine the absolute level of freight costs, a question to which we now move.

The cost of shipping commodities across regions depends on several variables. The most common functional form used in empirical works builds on the success story of the gravity model, which has been the workhorse of new trade theories (Feenstra, 2003). It is given by the following expression:

$$t_{ij} = \delta_0 Dist_{ij}^{-\delta_1} f(X_{ij}, X_i, X_j) \qquad (4.1)$$

where δ_0 is a parameter evaluating the overall efficiency of the transport sector, $Dist_{ij}$ is the distance between the region of origin i and the region of destination j,[15] δ_1 is a parameter measuring the distance-decay effect, while f is a separable function of three vectors of variables, namely the non-distance pair-specific (X_{ij}), the origin-specific (X_i) and the destination-specific (X_j) factors affecting transport costs. Typical variables and their impact are described below.

First, transport involves industry-specific costs, which depend on the nature and the quality of the commodity shipped. These costs are often approximated by the weight to value ratio of goods, which captures the scale effects generated by high trade volumes and the differences in both the transportability (bulk size) and the quality of goods (damage liabilities). Hummels (2001) estimates that the elasticity of the weight to value ratio is very similar to that of distance (close to 0.25), which means that doubling either the unit value of goods or the distance covered yields an increase in transport costs equal to $19\% = (2^{0.25} - 1) \times 100\%$.[16] However, these elasticities significantly vary across transport modes. For example, an additional mile is far more expensive for air (from 27 percent up to 43 percent) than for ocean freight (15 per cent), while a marginal increase in the unit value of goods has a lower impact on road transport costs than on air or rail freight rates (Hummels, 2007). Albeit important, the weight to value ratio is difficult to observe at the interregional level or within free-trade areas and, absent data, t_{ij} is often non-industry specific.

Second, whenever shipments have to cross borders, transit delays, custom inspections, changes in bulk standards or transport mode switching involve additional charges. Once again, absent data, such losses are often captured by a dummy equal to one if i and j are separated by a border and to zero otherwise. Conversely, trade may be facilitated by international agreements, technological progress, transit infrastructure, integrated transport networks (for instance between neighboring countries), or smooth geography. For instance, Limão and Venables (2001) consider adjacency (a dummy indicating whether i and j have a common border), landlockness (two dummies indicating whether i and j do not have access to the sea), insularity (two dummies indicating whether i and j are islands), and infrastructure density (both between and within i and j). According to their estimates, in comparison with a coastal country, a landlocked country would bear an additional transport cost of 50 percent, which could be overcome partially by improving onshore and transit infrastructure. By improving its infrastructure from the median to the top 25th percentile, a country would save about 13 percent in transport costs, which would be equivalent to make it 2358 km closer to its trading partners. Micco and Serebrisky (2006) find that improving airport accessibility and size from the first quartile (say Uzbekistan or Honduras) to the third quartile (say France) would reduce air transport costs by 10 percent. Along the same line, Clark et al. (2004) evaluate the role of seaport efficiency by combining both the effects of port infrastructure and quality in cargo handling services. Their results suggest that improving port efficiency from the 25th bottom percentile (say Ethiopia or Ecuador) to the 25th top percentile (say Singapore or Hong Kong) would reduce shipping costs by more than 12 percent, which amounts to a shrinking of the average distance by 500 miles.

In the same vein, the intensity of competition and the level of technological change in the transport sector are two other critical and interrelated determinants of transport cost variations. For example, commercial routes are less subject to monopoly power as competition pushes down mark-ups and induces carriers to partially absorb variations in transport costs, yielding incomplete pass-through (Hummels et al., 2009). In other words, restrictions imposed by strongly regulated transport regimes might contribute to increase transport fees. Fink et al. (2002) provide an illuminating example of how collusion influences the level of transport costs. They estimate that anti-competitive practices, such as maritime conferences that facilitate informal price agreements among liner companies, would add a premium of up to 25 percent to ocean transport costs. Consequently, transport deregulation could well lead to a large reduction in freight rates. For example, liberalizing port services would be equivalent to decreasing maritime transport costs by 9 percent (Fink et al., 2002), while moving the air transport competition regime to a system of Open Sky agreements would give rise to a similar decline in air cargo costs (Micco and Serebrisky, 2006). Innovation in the transport or logistic industry may either alleviate or strengthen competition. For example, in maritime transport containerization has triggered large freight cost reductions in cargo handling and increasing cargo transshipments, which in turn have favored international tramping and the hub-organization of maritime routes (Levinson, 2006; Mohammed and Williamson, 2004). Hummels (2007) also argues that improvements in avionics, wing design, materials, together with the adoption of jet engines, would have yielded a ten-fold decline in air shipping prices since the late 1950s.

Third, and last, notwithstanding the direct monetary cost of shipments, *time* becomes an increasingly relevant dimension in transport because firms and consumers have an increasing willingness to pay for fast delivery. For example, Hummels (2001) argues that manufacturing firms would be willing to pay 0.8 percent of the value of goods to save one day of ocean shipping. This is equivalent to a tariff of 16 percent for an average 20-day long trip. Furthermore, switching from slow to fast transport (for example, from maritime vessels to steamers or air shipping) would have been equivalent to a four-fold reduction in the tariffs on manufactured goods. Time is crucial for instance in the fashion business: the shorter the product cycle, the better a retailer can respond to changes in demand, reduce unsold inventory, and avoid shortage of popular items. Evans and Harrigan (2005) do observe that the sources of US apparel imports have actually shifted in a way such that products where timeliness matters could be delivered by nearby countries. Hence, even though fast transport is far more expensive, freight costs are pushed upward by the increasing desire for fast delivery.

In order to account for most of the aforementioned elements, Combes and Lafourcade (2005) use the concept of *generalized transport cost*, and combine both several distance and time monetary costs, which depend directly on competition, technology, infrastructure and energy prices.[17] Based on a shift-share analysis of these different components for road transport, they find out that the 38 percent average decline in freight costs that has occurred between 1978 and 1998 in France was mostly triggered by technological improvements and deregulation. By contrast, the infrastructure and fuel costs contributions were only marginal (about 3 percent). This highlights the fact that transport liberalization might be more effective in reducing freight rates than a larger supply of transport infrastructures, at least for developed countries. At this stage, it is worth noting that the 'ESPON programme' has developed a very detailed Geographic Information System (GIS) that computes generalized transport costs between European regions for road, rail and air transport networks.[18]

How Transport Costs Affect the Location of Activities: The Simulation of Large-scale Models

NEG empirics use transport cost functions such as Equation (4.1) to simulate the impact of decreasing transport costs between economies involving several regions/countries and industries. Applied NEG is still in its infancy, however, and very few studies have actually succeeded in testing NEG theoretical predictions in their *structural*, and not simply reduced, form.

A first example is provided by Forslid et al. (2002) who simulate the changes in the location of 14 industries following trade liberalization across four large European areas (north, east, west and south). To this end, they develop a large-scale computable general equilibrium model with vertical linkages, and experiment with successive variations in trade costs, among which tariffs and US-GTAP transport margins are extrapolated to Europe. The most abrupt changes in location patterns arise in three industries – textiles, leather and food products – which all move out from their initial location to agglomerate in the area endowed with the largest comparative advantage. Most of the other industries – metals, chemicals, transport equipment and machinery – exhibit a bell-shaped pattern of relocation, the gains of concentrating in the core being progressively offset as trade costs keep falling. Such results, therefore, corroborate the theoretical predictions of NEG models regarding the evolution of both location patterns and welfare levels.

In a recent paper, Bosker et al. (2010) calibrate the standard NEG model with vertical linkages on 194 NUTS2 European regions. They consider a special case of (4.1) and estimate the parameters of the expression:

$$t_{ij} = \delta_0 Dist_{ij}^{-\delta_1}(1 + \delta_2 X_{ij}) \tag{4.2}$$

where X_{ij} is a dummy indicating whether i and j are separated by a border. They proceed by simulating the changes in the spatial distribution of activities sparked by a decrease of δ_0. Two scenarios are considered. In the first one, labor is mobile: transport costs reductions strengthen the process of agglomeration, and may even yield a full agglomeration in the Parisian metropolitan area for very low values of δ_0. In the second one, labor is immobile: lowering transport costs now leads to a bell-shaped agglomeration pattern. These results thus confirm the main predictions of NEG. Bosker et al. (2010) also provide a numerical evaluation of δ_0 that would match the top of the bell-shaped curve. Interestingly, the corresponding pattern of activities fits a banana-shaped corridor, known as the 'Blue Banana', stretching from southern Britain down to northern Italy, passing through Brussels, Amsterdam, Frankfurt and Zurich. It covers one of the world's highest concentrations of people, wealth and industry. Note, however, that this corridor is not homogenous in that it contains quite a few 'holes', very much as an affluent city has poor neighbourhoods.

Combes and Lafourcade (2011) allow the function t_{ij} to be commodity-specific by assuming that freight charges incurred for each industry vary proportionally to the generalized transport cost discussed above. They estimate the proportion factor for ten different industries, using a NEG model with vertical linkages. Plugging these estimates into the equilibrium conditions, they observe that a 30 per cent drop in generalized transport costs would result in a more balanced distribution of employment across French regions, with different degrees of adjustment according to the sectors. By way of contrast, they find that the degree of spatial concentration increases within a large number of regions. Hence, there would be less polarization at the national level, but more at the local one.

Using the ESPON database, Bröcker (2005) assesses the spatial impact of four different scenarios of the EU transport policy and evaluates the resulting welfare variations for NUTS3 regions. The first two scenarios consist of implementing the list of Trans-European Networks priority projects, which aim to improve the accessibility of lagging EU regions. The third scenario analyses the effects of imposing a toll on the entire European road network. The last scenario is a mixture of infrastructure and price policies. Interestingly, infrastructure policies are shown to be pro-cohesive in that they favor a balanced and polycentric spatial development, whereas pricing policies have a clear anti-cohesive tendency harmful to the periphery.

The main limit of most existing empirical studies lies in the fact that firms are not allowed to relocate following changes in transport costs. Variations in spatial disparities and welfare are translated only through changes in existing firms' sizes and prices, as well as in transport modes. Dealing with the endogenous choice of locations is one of the main tasks on the research agenda.

WHAT ARE THE POLICY IMPLICATIONS AND WHERE SHOULD WE GO NOW?

Standard trade theories tell us indirectly how economic activities might be distributed across space. In Ricardian and Hecksher–Ohlin–Samuelson theories, regions specialize according to their comparative advantage in terms of their relative productivity levels or factor abundance. In contrast, NEG argues that the location of activity, hence the pattern of trade and the demand for transport services, is driven by the interaction between scale economies, market size and transport costs.

One of the main accomplishments of NEG is to show that policies aiming at reducing transport costs affect social welfare in new ways as firms and workers are to relocate in response to long-run changes in freight rates and consumer prices. When locations are fixed, freight-reducing policies affect trade flows as well as commodity prices. They are likely to reduce static dead-weight losses arising from market power in the manufacturing sector by making the market for these goods more integrated and, therefore, more competitive. However, once locations are endogenous, such policies may generate new dead-weight losses due to the possible sub-optimal redistribution of firms and workers across regions. For example, according to the core–periphery model, falling transport costs should lead to the agglomeration of firms and workers in a handful of affluent urban areas, whereas many regions would accommodate a low level of economic life.[19] If true, *the development of more efficient transport infrastructure would exacerbate regional disparities*, a result opposite to what transport authorities expect.[20] Furthermore, by making cheaper the transport of commodities in *both* directions, one must keep in mind that the construction of a new infrastructure facilitates an increase of imports to, just as well as an increase of exports from, the small region. As a result, the small region may pull out some of its firms. In particular, when firms have different efficiency levels, decreasing transport costs lead the more efficient firms to move to the core and the less efficient firms to move to the periphery (Baldwin and Okubo, 2006; Okubo et al., 2010).

NEG, therefore, sheds light on the fact that European regional policies fail to deliver their expected outcome because they do not rest on good assessments of the spatial impacts of new transport infrastructure (Midelfart-Knarvik and Overman, 2002; Vickerman et al., 1999). For the development of such infrastructure to attract new firms, the local market must be sufficiently large and/or endowed with some specific competitive advantage. Otherwise, a policy that systematically aims at improving the accessibility of a small region to the global economy runs the risk of being *ineffective in promoting the development of this region.* Such a policy, which is one of the main tools used by the European Commission to reduce regional disparities, must be supplemented by other instruments to boost regional development. It should also be noted that, once a core exists, all other regions aspire to be linked to it. One of the ironies of the transport investments made to help peripheral regions is that it ends up strengthening the core. Even worse, NEG suggests that being a land-locked or remote region could well be a comparative advantage that allows some regions to keep their manufacturing sector because firms are protected by the barrier of high transport costs (Ago et al., 2006; Behrens et al., 2006).

Though seemingly provocative, such considerations are not entirely new. In 1885, Wilhelm Launhardt, a civil engineer who worked on the construction of transport infrastructures in Germany, observed that 'the improvement of means of transport is dangerous for costly goods: these lose the most effective protection of all tariff protections, namely that provided by bad roads.' (Launhardt, 1885, p. 150 of the English translation). It should also be emphasized that the cumulative nature of the agglomeration process makes such a pattern particularly robust to various types of shocks, thus showing why it is hard to foster a more balanced pattern of activities. In other words, affluent regions enjoy the existence of agglomeration rents that single-minded policies cannot easily dissipate. Consequently, if the objective of the European Commission is to foster a more balanced distribution of economic activities across European regions, it should add more instruments to its policy portfolio.

However, we have also seen that the evolution of the space-economy depends on the interaction between several forces that are not taken into account by the core–periphery model. Adding new ingredients to this setting, such as the sluggish mobility of workers, the existence of non-tradable goods, the demand for intermediate goods, or the spatial fragmentation of firms, suggests the existence of a bell-shaped curve linking regional disparities and economic integration. Taking into account these new mechanisms leads us, therefore, to believe that a sufficiently extensive economic integration of the space-economy should favor the development of several large urban regions, which could be spread over the territory of the EU. Eventually, spatial inequalities at the interregional level would be (partially) reduced through the redispersion of the manufacturing sector, as in the United States where this sector is increasingly located within medium- or low-population density areas (Glaeser and Kohlhase, 2004).

If, from the economic policy viewpoint, there seems to be a trade-off between economic efficiency and spatial equity in the first stages of the integration process, more recent developments in NEG suggest that the pursuit of integration makes it possible to win on both fronts. In other words, the bad idea would be to fall between two stools, as partial integration does not capitalize on all the benefits of efficiency while generating regional inequalities. However, there are also dynamic benefits associated with the spatial concentration of the R&D sector, which can boost the growth of the global economy. We must bear in mind, therefore, that the reduction of spatial inequalities is probably not costless for the economy as a whole.

One of the main limitations of NEG is the almost systematic use of a two-region symmetric framework describing a featureless world. In particular, such a setting does not allow for the existence of different trade routes and eliminates geographical factors, such as the accessibility to the sea or the fact of being landlocked, whose importance for the development of economic activity has been stressed in the literature (see, for example Gallup et al., 1999). Extending the NEG framework to the case of an arbitrary number of regions appears to be a formidable task. The new fundamental ingredient that a multi-regional setting brings about is the existence of a fundamental geographical asymmetry, that is, *the accessibility to markets varies across regions*.[21] It is indeed reasonable to expect the *relative position* of regions within the transport space (and, more generally, within abstract spaces involving cultural, linguistic and political proximity) to affect the interregional distribution of firms. In this perspective, one of the most ambitious and interesting works is provided by Behrens et al. (2009b), who show that the home market effect can be extended to account for the relative position of markets, which is itself described by a matrix of transport costs. This model eliminates the various linkages effects stressed by

NEG to focus on size and distance effects only. This approach also makes it possible to study how lower transport costs, which affect the location choices made by firms, amplify or reduce the geographical advantage and disadvantage held by particular regions (Matsuyama, 1998).

Another distinctive feature of multi-regional settings is to integrate explicitly various specificities of real-world transport networks (Thomas, 2002). In this perspective, it is worth mentioning here that standard location theory has used partial equilibrium models to derive many results that are potentially interesting to transportation economists.[22] Therefore, once it is recognized that the design and structure of transport networks affect the spatial distribution of activities, it should be clear that combining those results with NEG should be a high priority in the research agenda. That said, the path-dependency uncovered by NEG has an important policy implication: the order in which individual transport development projects are carried out is likely to be important for the impact the whole program will have on the economic geography of a country as well as on the spatial distribution of the costs and benefits it generates (Peeters et al. 2000).

Along the same lines, empirical evidence suggests that the growing openness of national economies to trade has a significant impact on the location of economic activities *within* countries (Ades and Glaeser, 1995). The above-mentioned difficulty in characterizing the spatial distribution of economic activity across many locations, as well as a genuine distinction between regions and countries, has limited such investigations. Countries and regions are to be distinguished from each other in terms of both shipping costs and factor mobility. Specifically, shipping goods between regions is typically cheaper than shipping them between countries. Moreover, factor mobility is often much lower between than inside countries and trade is hampered by transport costs between regions and by trade costs between countries. Preliminary analysis suggests that lower intra-national transport costs foster regional agglomeration within countries when international trade costs are high; by contrast, low international trade costs push toward regional dispersion when intra-national transport costs are high (Behrens et al., 2009a; Martin and Rogers, 1995). In the same vein, we have seen that reductions in intra-national transport costs may trigger the interregional dispersion of activities together with their agglomeration at the infra-regional level (Combes and Lafourcade, 2011). Although much remains to be done, such results point to the need for coordinating national/regional transport policies and international agreements that affect the level of trade costs across countries.

It should also be emphasized that, despite the more and more precise measurement of (generalized) transport costs, NEG still fails to provide an explicit description of the interactions between the transport and manufacturing sectors as well as between carriers themselves. In particular, modeling explicitly the transport sector and the formation of freight rates through the strategic behavior of carriers, as well as competition between transport modes, should attract more attention (Behrens et al., 2009a). Furthermore, integrating variables specific to the transport sector, such as density economies, market segmentation in the supply of transport services, logistic features and scheduling considerations should also be addressed. All in all, it should be clear that a more realistic description of transport cost, which could offset or redirect some of the effects coming out of existing models, would make NEG more appealing and relevant to transportation economists. In particular, accounting for time-related variables is likely to push up freight rates in a globalizing world, thus inviting us to study the opposite thought experiment of NEG, that is: what are the consequences of *increasing* transport costs. This entire area is strongly under-analyzed and deserves much more attention in the future research agenda. Finally, NEG has totally neglected to account for the costs of infrastructure, being content to assume that transport costs go up or down exogenously. Yet, the trade-off is neat: either capital is invested in a larger number of goods, which are traded at higher costs, or capital is invested in transport infrastructure to facilitate the exchange of a smaller number of goods.

To conclude, we find it fair to say that NEG provides a broad conceptual framework to study the articulation between transport policies designed at the local and global levels. In particular, NEG allows one to understand *how different types of spatial frictions generated at different spatial scales*, such as commuting and shopping costs at the local level, interregional shipping costs and international trade costs at the global level, *interact to shape the whole economy* in ways that are not straightforward to figure out. This aspect of transport policy is often overlooked by decision makers who tend to focus on a single spatial scale, neglecting the various implications that their policy recommendations may have at other levels of analysis. More generally, because NEG raises questions directly related to several economic fields, it also highlights the importance for transport analysts to pay more attention to the implications of decisions made in domains that are at first sight far from their own interests.

Despite its many restrictive features, NEG has thus succeeded in throwing light on issues that had remained unexplained for a long time. However, it is true that more work is called for if the purpose is to make NEG operational to transport analysts. Specifically, there is a need for computable and calibrated general spatial equilibrium models coping with vertical linkages and including several sectors and regions connected through a network having a specific design. In this perspective, Bröcker (2005) and Bosker et al. (2010) are good places to start and see the chapter by Johannes Bröcker and Jean Mercenier.

ACKNOWLEDGMENTS

We gratefully acknowledge André de Palma, Robin Lindsey and Kenneth Small for insightful comments.

NOTES

1. Trade costs involve both additive and multiplicative terms with respect to the mill price of goods, as excise and *ad valorem* taxes. Behrens (2006) has shown that both specifications lead to similar results regarding the spatial distribution of the industry.
2. This choice of a macroscopic scale allows us to avoid looking closely at the goings-on inside agglomerations. Indeed, the very nature of local interactions implies that most of them can be overlooked on the interregional scale.
3. It should also be stressed that NEG is closely related to location theory and regional science. These links cannot be discussed here. The reader is referred to Ottaviano and Thisse (2005) for a detailed discussion of the relationships between these various branches of literature.
4. Throughout this chapter, we will focus on the nature and implications of the main findings of NEG for transportation economics.

5. Note that the acting forces need not be the same at different spatial scales, for example, a multi-regional system or a city.
6. Note that the interpretation of the two sectors and production factors used here is not crucial for the argument. It is made for expositional convenience, the critical point being that one factor is mobile and the other immobile. For example, the immobile factor could be land or non-tradable services.
7. See Anderson et al. (1992) for a detailed discussion of product differentiation issues relevant for NEG.
8. Spatial competition models allow for a richer description of market interactions among firms but remain confined to partial equilibrium settings that do not cope with the labor market. Interestingly, the conclusions drawn from such models concur with those derived from NEG (Fujita and Thisse, 2002).
9. Note, however, that the progressive decrease of communication costs is likely to spread the extent of spillovers, thus leading local interactions to become regional in nature.
10. It is worth mentioning that such a modeling strategy agrees with the rich body of literature, known as *spatial interaction theory*, which has been developed by geographers and transport analysts (Anas, 1983; Wilson, 1970). Indeed, besides workers' location choices, trade flows also obey a structure akin to this theory as they are generated by consumers who have a preference for variety. Thus, the kind of approach proposed here reconciles different approaches developed in economic geography within a unified framework.
11. Negative externalities arising in the urban agglomeration, such as transport congestion, pollution and a high crime rate, play a similar role and speed up the re-dispersion of activities toward less crowded regions.
12. See Puga (1999) for what remains after about ten years the best discussion of those various issues.
13. The re-dispersion of firms, which occurs through their fragmentation, rests on the existence of sufficiently strong interregional wage differentials. Any force that narrows down the wage gap thus thwarts the re-dispersion of firms and, consequently, contributes to maintain the core–periphery structure (Faini, 1999).
14. See www.gtap.agecon.purdue.edu/resources/download/135.pdf
15. At the level of macro-regions, it usually refers to the geodesic distance between the main cities of the origin and destination regions.
16. Note also that, quite unexpectedly, physical distance does not only matter for commodity flows. Blum and Goldfarb (2006) find that, for taste-dependent differentiated digital products (such as music or electronic games), a 1 per cent increase in distance reduces the number of websites visits by 3.25 per cent, once controlled for other key-determinants such as language or internet penetration.
17. For road transport, the distance-related costs include fuel, tires, and vehicle maintenance expenditures, while the time-related costs include drivers' wages, insurance costs and damage liabilities, vehicle depreciation, and the loading time.
18. See www.espon.eu/mmp/online/website/content/tools/127/index_EN.html.
19. In contrast to what anti-globalization activists believe, trade is not intrinsically responsible for the existence of regional disparities. Behrens (2004) has shown that prohibitive trade costs do not rule out the formation of a core–periphery structure.
20. Other results presented in the second part of Fujita et al. (1999) point in the same direction.
21. It is worth recalling, in passing, that the simplest firm location model accounts for the fact that the access to several markets is the key-issue faced by a firm making a location choice.
22. See Beckmann and Thisse (1986) for a survey of this literature, which is often ignored in NEG.

REFERENCES

Ades, A. and E. Glaeser, 1995, Trade and circuses: explaining urban giants. *Quarterly Journal of Economics*, **110**, 195–227.
Ago, A., I. Isono and T. Tabuchi, 2006, Locational disadvantage of the hub. *Annals of Regional Science*, **40**, 819–848.
Anas, A., 1983, Discrete choice theory, information theory, and the multinomial logit and gravity models. *Transportation Research Part B*, **17**, 13–23.
Anas, A., R. Arnott and K.A. Small, 1998, Urban spatial structure. *Journal of Economic Literature*, **36**, 1426–1464.
Anderson, J. and E. van Wincoop, 2004, Trade costs. *Journal of Economic Literature*, **42**, 691–751.
Anderson, S.P., A. de Palma and J.-F. Thisse, 1992, *Discrete Choice Theory of Product Differentiation*. Cambridge, MA: The MIT Press.
Bairoch, P., 1997, *Victoires et déboires. Histoire économique et sociale du monde du XVIe siècle à nos jours*. Paris: Editions Gallimard.

Baldwin, R.E. and T. Okubo, 2006, Heterogeneous firms, agglomeration and economic geography: spatial selection and sorting. *Journal of Economic Geography*, **6**, 323–346.

Beckmann, M.J. and J.-F. Thisse, 1986, The location of production activities. In P. Nijkamp, ed., *Handbook of Regional and Urban Economics, Volume I*. Amsterdam: North-Holland, pp. 21–95.

Behrens, K., 2004, Agglomeration without trade: how non-traded goods shape the space-economy. *Journal of Urban Economics*, **55**, 68–92.

Behrens, K., 2006, Do changes in transport costs and tariffs shape the space-economy in the same way? *Papers in Regional Science*, **85**, 379–399.

Behrens, K., C. Gaigné, G.I.P. Ottaviano and J.-F. Thisse, 2006, Is remoteness a locational disadvantage? *Journal of Economic Geography*, **6**, 347–368.

Behrens, K., C. Gaigné, G.I.P. Ottaviano and J.-F. Thisse, 2007, Countries, regions and trade: on the welfare impacts of integration. *European Economic Review*, **51**, 1277–1301.

Behrens, K., C. Gaigné and J.-F. Thisse, 2009a, Industry location and welfare when transport costs are endogenous. *Journal of Urban Economics*, **65**, 195–208.

Behrens, K., A. Lamorgese, G.I.P. Ottaviano and T. Tabuchi, 2009b, Beyond the home market effect: market size and specialization in a multi-country world. *Journal of International Economics*, **79**, 259–265.

Belleflamme, P., P. Picard and J.-F. Thisse, 2000, An economic theory of regional clusters. *Journal of Urban Economics*, **48**, 158–84.

Blum, B. and A. Goldfarb, 2006, Does the internet defy the law of gravity? *Journal of International Economics*, **70**, 384–405.

Bosker, M., S. Brakman, H. Garretsen and M. Schramm, 2010, Adding geography to the new economic geography. *Journal of Economic Geography*, **10**, 793–823.

Bröcker J. 2005, Spatial effects of european transport initiatives: an update. In Territorial impact of EU transport and TEN policies, ESPON project 2.1.1.

Brülhart, M., 2006, The fading attraction of central regions: an empirical note on core–periphery gradients in Western Europe. *Spatial Economic Analysis*, **1**, 227–235.

Cavailhès, J., C. Gaigné, T. Tabuchi and J.-F. Thisse, 2007, Trade and the structure of cities. *Journal of Urban Economics*, **62**, 383–404.

Charlot, S., C. Gaigné, F. Robert-Nicoud and J.-F. Thisse, 2006, Agglomeration and welfare: the core–periphery model in the light of Bentham, Kaldor, and Rawls. *Journal of Public Economics*, **90**, 325–347.

Clark, X., D. Dollar and A. Micco, 2004, Port efficiency, maritime transport costs, and bilateral trade. *Journal of Development Economics*, **75**, 417–450.

Combes, P.-P., G. Duranton and L. Gobillon, 2008a, Spatial wage disparities: sorting Matters! *Journal of Urban Economics*, **63**, 723–742.

Combes, P.-P. and M. Lafourcade, 2005, Transport costs: measures, determinants, and regional policy implications for France. *Journal of Economic Geography*, **5**, 319–349.

Combes, P.-P. and M. Lafourcade, 2011, Competition, market access and economic geography: structural estimations and predictions for France. *Regional Science and Urban Economics*, forthcoming.

Combes, P.P., M. Lafourcade, J.-F. Thisse and J.-C. Toutain, 2011, The rise and fall of spatial inequalities in France, a long run perspective. *Explanations in Economic History*, **48**, 243–271.

Combes, P.-P., T. Mayer and J.-F. Thisse, 2008b, *Economic Geography. The Integration of Regions and Nations*. Princeton, NJ: Princeton University Press.

d'Aspremont, C., J.J. Gabszewicz and J.-F. Thisse, 1979, On hotelling's stability in competition. *Econometrica*, **47**, 1045–1050.

Disdier, A.C. and K. Head, 2008, The puzzling persistence of the distance effect on bilateral trade. *Review of Economics and Statistics*, **90**, 37–48.

Duranton, G. and V. Monastiriotis, 2002, Mind the gaps: the evolution of regional earnings inequalities in the UK 1982–1997. *Journal of Regional Science*, **42**, 219–256.

Evans C. and J. Harrigan, 2005, Distance, time, and specialization: lean retailing in general equilibrium. *American Economic Review*, **95**, 292–313.

Faini, R., 1983, Cumulative processes of de-industrialisation in an open region: the case of Southern Italy, 1951–1973. *Journal of Development Economics*, **12**, 277–301.

Faini, R., 1999, Trade unions and regional development. *European Economic Review*, **43**, 457–474.

Feenstra, R.C., 1998, Integration of trade and disintegration of production in the global economy. *Journal of Economic Perspectives*, **12** (4), 31–50.

Feenstra, R.C., 2003, *Advanced International Trade*. Princeton, NJ: Princeton University Press.

Fink, C., A. Mattoo and I.C. Neagu, 2002, Trade in international maritime services: how much does policy matter? *World Bank Economic Review*, **16**, 81–108.

Forslid, R., J. Haaland and K.-H. Midelfart-Knarvik, 2002, A U-shaped Europe? A simulation study of industrial location. *Journal of International Economics*, **57**, 273–297.

Fujita, M., 1989, *Urban Economic Theory, Land Use and City Size*. Cambridge: Cambridge University Press.

Fujita, M., P. Krugman and A.J. Venables, 1999, *The Spatial Economy. Cities, Regions and International Trade*. Cambridge, MA: The MIT Press.
Fujita, M. and J.-F. Thisse, 2002, *Economics of Agglomeration. Cities, Industrial Location and Regional Growth*. Cambridge: Cambridge University Press.
Fujita, M. and J.-F. Thisse, 2006, Globalization and the evolution of the supply chain: who gains and who loses? *International Economic Review*, **47**, 811–836.
Gallup, J.L., J.D. Sachs and A. Mellinger, 1999, Geography and economic development. *International Regional Science Review*, **22**, 179–232.
Glaeser, E.L. and J.E. Kohlhase, 2004, Cities, regions and the decline of transport costs. *Papers in Regional Science*, **83**, 197–228.
Greenwood, M.L., 1997, Internal migration in developed countries. In M.R. Rosenzweig and O. Stark, eds, *Handbook of Population and Family Economics*. Amsterdam: North-Holland, pp. 648–719.
Grossman, G. and E. Helpman, E., 1991, *Innovation and Growth in the World Economy*. Cambridge, MA: The MIT Press.
Head, K. and T. Mayer, 2004, The empirics of agglomeration and trade. In J.V. Henderson and J.F. Thisse, eds, *Handbook of Regional ad Urban Economics, Volume IV*. Amsterdam: North-Holland, pp. 2609–2669.
Helpman, E., 1998, The size of regions. In D. Pines, E. Sadka and I. Zilcha, eds, *Topics in Public Economics, Theoretical and Empirical Analysis*. Cambridge: Cambridge University Press, pp. 33–54.
Helpman, E. and P.R. Krugman., 1985, *Market Structure and Foreign Trade*. Cambridge, MA: The MIT Press.
Henderson, J.V., 1997, Medium size cities. *Regional Science and Urban Economics*, **27**, 583–612.
Hummels, D., 2001, Time as a trade barrier. GTAP Working Papers No. 1152, Center for Global Trade Analysis, Department of Agricultural Economics, Purdue University.
Hummels, D., 2007, International transportation costs and trade in the second era of globalization. *Journal of Economic Perspectives*, **21** (3), 131–154.
Hummels, D. and V. Lugovskyy, 2006, Are matched partner trade statistics a usable measure of transportation costs? *Review of International Economics*, **14**, 69–86.
Hummels, D., V. Lugovskyy and A. Skiba, 2009, The trade reducing effects of market power in international shipping. *Journal of Development Economics* **89**, 84–97.
Knapp, T.A. and P.R. Graves, 1989, On the role of amenities in models of migration and regional development. *Journal of Regional Science*, **29**, 71–87.
Koopmans, T.C., 1957, *Three Essays on the State of Economic Science*. New York: McGraw-Hill.
Krugman, P.R., 1991, Increasing returns and economic geography. *Journal of Political Economy*, **99**, 483–499.
Krugman, P.R., 1995, *Development, Geography, and Economic Theory*. Cambridge, MA: The MIT Press.
Krugman, P.R. and Venables, A.J., 1995, Globalization and the inequality of nations. *Quarterly Journal of Economics*, **110**, 857–880.
Launhardt, W., 1885, *Mathematische Begründung der Volkswirtschaftslehre*. Leipzig: B.G. Teubner. English translation: *Mathematical Principles of Economics*. Aldershot, UK: Edward Elgar, 1993.
Leamer, E.E. and M. Storper, 2001, The economic geography of the internet age. *Journal of International Business Studies*, **32**, 641–655.
Levinson, M., 2006, *The Box: How the Shipping Container Made the World Smaller and the World Economy Bigger*. Princeton, NJ: Princeton University Press.
Limão, N. and A.J. Venables, 2001, Infrastructure, geographical disadvantage, transport costs and trade. *World Bank Economic Review*, **15**, 451–479.
Martin, Ph. and C.A. Rogers, 1995, Industrial location and public infrastructure. *Journal of International Economics*, **39**, 335–351.
Matsuyama, K., 1998, Geography of the world economy. Mimeo, Northwestern University. Available at http://faculty.wcas.northwestern.edu/~kmatsu/#research.
Micco, A. and T. Serebrisky, 2006, Competition regimes and air transport costs: the effects of open skies agreements. *Journal of International Economics*, **70**, 25–51.
Midelfart-Knarvik, K.H. and H.G. Overman, 2002, Delocation and European integration: is structural spending justified? *Economic Policy*, **35**, 321–359.
Mohammed, S.I. and J. Williamson, 2004, Freight rates and productivity gains in british tramp shipping 1869–1950. *Explorations in Economic History*, **41**, 172–203.
Okubo, T., P. Picard and J.-F. Thisse, 2010, The spatial selection of heterogeneous firms. Journal of International Economics, **82**, 230–237.
Ottaviano, G.I.P., T. Tabuchi and J.-F. Thisse, 2002, Agglomeration and trade revisited. *International Economic Review*, **43**, 409–436.
Ottaviano, G.I.P. and J.-F. Thisse, 2002, Integration, agglomeration and the political economics of factor mobility. *Journal of Public Economics*, **83**, 429–456.
Ottaviano, G.I.P. and J.-F. Thisse, 2005, New economic geography: what about the N? *Environment and Planning A*, **37**, 1707–1725.

Ottaviano, G.I.P. and T. van Ypersele, 2005, Market size and tax competition. *Journal of International Economics*, **67**, 25–46.

Papageorgiou, Y.Y. and T.R. Smith, 1983, Agglomeration as local instability of spatially uniform steady-states. *Econometrica*, **51**, 1109–1120.

Pflüger, M. and J. Südekum, 2008, Integration, agglomeration and welfare. *Journal of Urban Economics*, **63**, 544-566.

Peeters, D., J.-F. Thisse and I. Thomas, 2000, On high speed connections and the location of human activities. *Environment and Planning A*, **32**, 2097–2112.

Puga, D., 1999, The rise and fall of regional inequalities. *European Economic Review*, **43**, 303–334.

Rietveld, P. and R. Vickerman, 2004, Transport in regional science: the 'death of distance' is premature. *Papers in Regional Science*, **83**, 229–248.

Robert-Nicoud, F., 2008, Off-shoring of routine tasks and (de)industrialization: threat or opportunity – and for whom. *Journal of Urban Economics*, **63**, 517–535.

Samuelson, P.A., 1954, The transfer problem and transport cost, II: analysis of effects of trade impediments. *Economic Journal*, **64**, 264–289.

Spulber, D.F., 2007, *Global Competitive Strategy*. Cambridge: Cambridge University Press.

Tabuchi, T., 1998, Urban agglomeration and dispersion: a synthesis of Alonso and Krugman. *Journal of Urban Economics*, **44**, 333–351.

Tabuchi, T. and J.-F. Thisse, 2002, Taste heterogeneity, labor mobility and economic geography. *Journal of Development Economics*, **69**, 155–177.

Thomas, I., 2002, *Transportation Networks and the Optimal Location of Human Activities. A Numerical Geography Approach*. Cheltenham, UK: Edward Elgar.

Train, K. 2003, *Discrete Choice Methods with Simulation*. Cambridge: Cambridge University Press.

Vickerman, R., K. Spiekermann and M. Wegener, 1999, Accessibility and economic development in Europe. *Regional Studies*, **33**, 1–15.

von Thünen, J.H. 1826, *Der Isolierte Staat in Beziehung auf Landwirtschaft und Nationalökonomie*. Hamburg: Perthes. English translation: *The Isolated State*. Oxford: Pergamon Press, 1966.

Wilson, A.G., 1970, *Entropy in Regional and Urban Modelling*. London: Pion.

Wilson, R., 2006, 17th Annual State of Logistics Report. Available at www.loginstitute.ca/.

5 Transport costs and international trade
Alberto Behar and Anthony J. Venables

INTRODUCTION

International trade has grown substantially faster than world income through most of the post war period,[1] and at the same time the share of manufacturing in world trade has increased substantially (WTO, 2007). Globalization has transformed many economies, and some authors have heralded the age of 'Flat Earth' (Friedman 2005). Yet international economic interactions remain small relative to interactions that take place within national borders. Trade is choked off by distance, by borders and by a variety of political and cultural obstacles. Integration into the world economy is widely viewed as one of the key factors underlying the success of the fastest growing economies (Growth Commission, 2008) yet many countries remain isolated and have failed to achieve this integration. Transport costs are one, amongst many, of the factors that shape these trade patterns. This chapter investigates the impact of transport costs on international trade, looking both at the influence of transport costs on trade and at the determinants of international transport costs.

The first issue we study is the impact of transport costs on the volume and nature of international trade. To what extent has the rise in international trade been driven by changes in transport costs? Why is cross-country and cross-regional experience so different? Transport costs also influence modal choice, the commodity composition of trade and the organization of production, particularly as 'just-in-time' methods get extended to the global level. In turn, these new production methods are placing increasing demands on the transport system.

The second issue is the determinants of international transport costs. There is enormous cross-country variation in transport costs and in trade costs more generally. To what extent are these determined by geography, or by infrastructure investments or institutional barriers? Through time, the evidence is that transport costs have not fallen as much as many people might expect. We explore this paradox.

We take as organizing structure the following relationship, which embeds both our questions.

Trade = F{income, policy, cultural affinity, transport costs = f(distance,

geography, infrastructure, trade facilitation, technology, fuel costs)}   (5.1)

The relationship can be thought of as applying to any particular bilateral trade flow between a source country and a destination country and is written to reflect the different channels through which variables affect trade. Trade flows depend on characteristics of the source and destination countries, such as their economic size as reflected in income. It also depends on 'between country' characteristics such as their policy towards each other and their cultural affinity. The characteristics we are primarily interested in are transport costs, which manifest themselves as freight charges and non-pecuniary costs like speed and reliability. Transport costs shape trade, and are in turn determined by underlying variables such as distance and other features of geography, infrastructure quality, trade facilitation measures, fuel costs and transport technology.

The variables in Equation (5.1) are not exhaustive, but are indicative of the relationships that have been studied. The most frequently studied empirical part of the relationship is the gravity model of trade, which can be thought of as a reduced form that focuses on how underlying aspects of income, geography and other variables shape trade, but without specifying the precise channel. For example, distance is thought to impede trade by increasing freight costs and increasing the length of transit, but may also operate through other channels such as the costs of gathering information on market opportunities. A brief review of this approach is the subject of the next section of the chapter.

The third section of the chapter turns to the effects of transport costs on trade. It reviews the evidence of cross-country variation in transport costs and uses alternative sources of data to study the influence of freight rates on trade volumes. We also consider different modes of transport in the context of the trade-off between time-in-transit delays and freight charges.

We then move on to review literature on the determinants of transport costs. We organize this in two sections, looking first at cross-country variation, and then at the evolution of freight rates through time. This section of the chapter in particular draws heavily on the work of David Hummels and his recent survey (Hummels, 2007). It also explains how transport developments enabled new forms of international organization of production to develop and discusses the implications of such developments.

In the fifth section we discuss some technical issues involved in establishing findings in this area, particularly the estimation of gravity models. The final section draws on our findings to discuss some of the broader implications. Are the trade-related benefits worth the costs of improving transport? Do lower trade costs raise incomes?

GRAVITY: THE REDUCED FORM

One of the most robust – and extensively studied – relationships in economics is the gravity model of international trade. It can be thought of as a reduced form of Equation (5.1), in which the researcher is interested in how the underlying variables influence trade flows, but does not specify the mechanisms through which effects occur. A typical empirical gravity specification would take the form

$$\text{trade}_{ij} = \beta_1 \text{GDP}_i + \beta_2 \text{GDP}_j + \tau_1 \text{Distance}_{ij} + \tau_2 \text{Landlocked}_i$$

$$+ \tau_3 \text{Infrastructure}_i + \tau_4 \text{Trade facilitation}_i + u_{ij}, \qquad (5.2)$$

where trade is measured as exports from country i to country j. The equation is typically estimated in log linear form,[2] such that τ_1 can be interpreted as the elasticity of trade with respect to distance. Distance is a bilateral variable but many other variables – for example, the landlocked dummy, measures of infrastructure quality or trade facilitation – are country-specific.[3] Many empirical studies refer to the rigorous theoretical economic foundations underpinning gravity,[4] but often ignore the potential implications for the estimation of coefficients and their interpretation; we touch on some of these issues in a later section.

Numerous gravity studies are surveyed in Anderson and van Wincoop (2004) and the main findings are as follows. Income (GDP) of both countries enters with coefficients close to unity. The bilateral distance[5] between two countries is highly significant, and typically enters with a coefficient of $\tau_1 = -0.9$ (see Disdier and Head 2008 for a meta study of values of this coefficient). A puzzle that has attracted attention is that the absolute value of the distance coefficient appears to have increased through time. Disdier and Head (2008) find that studies on data prior to 1960 produce an average estimate of around -0.75 while using data for later periods changes the mean estimated value to -0.9. Consistent with this, Brun et al. (2005) estimate positive coefficients for the interaction between distance and time. Of course, these findings do not mean that long distance trade has declined, but simply that short distance trade has increased more than long distance. Carrere and Schiff (2004) show that the distance of the average trade flow declined steadily over the period 1962–2000. We discuss possible reasons for the continued importance of distance when we look at the determinants of transport costs.

GDP and distance typically account for 70 percent of the cross-country variation in trade, but other variables are also significant. Other geographical characteristics include having a common border (neighbors trade more) and country area (large countries trade less); islands trade more, but landlocked countries trade less. Limão and Venables (2001) calculate that landlocked countries trade about 60 percent less than their coastal counterparts with otherwise similar characteristics and Clarke, Dollar and Micco (2004) report a difference of approximately one third. Irwin and Terviö (2002) find that geographic characteristics explain about 30 to 40 percent of the variance of the log of the bilateral trade share of GDP.

Man-made characteristics also matter. An improvement in exporter's infrastructure from the 75th percentile to the median raises trade volumes by 28 percent and, for landlocked countries, the infrastructure of transit countries also matters (Limão and Venables, 2001). Nordås and Piermartini (2004) include separate infrastructure measures – rail, roads, telecommunications, ports and airports – and find that all measures are important but that ports have the biggest impact on trade.

In addition to physical infrastructure, trade facilitation is important. Wilson et al. (2005) evaluate four measures of trade facilitation: port facilities, customs handling, the regulatory environment and the availability of service sector infrastructure. Improvements in all four measures would have material impacts on both exports and imports. Behar (2009) negatively associates export volumes with export documentation, which suggests red tape can affect trade. The World Bank *Logistics Performance Index*[6] captures infrastructural and institutional contributors to transport costs and Behar et al. (2009) find that a one standard deviation improvement in logistics (which, for example, would put Rwanda on a par with Nigeria) would raise exports by about 46 per cent for an average-size developing country.

While the gravity model is the reduced form relationship between trade, income and

geography, the task in this chapter is to identify the role of transport costs in this relationship. How do transport costs affect trade, and what determines transport costs?

TRANSPORT COSTS AND TRADE

The next step is to identify the effect of the transport cost channel in the determination of trade flows. This involves obtaining data on transport costs and investigating a
form of Equation (5.1) which uses this information while excluding other variables that
are expected to affect trade volumes only via their effect on transport costs. Rewriting
Equation (5.1) as

$$\text{Trade} = F(\text{income, policy, cultural affinity, transport costs}), \qquad (5.3)$$

we are interested in the strength of the last argument in the function. This section starts
by reviewing the transport cost data that is available and proceeds to discuss the relationship between various transport costs measures and trade, looking across countries and
over time. Different modes of transport offer different quality of service – in particular
with respect to speed and reliability – in return for different freight charges, and we
examine this trade-off.

Measuring Transport Costs

There is wide dispersion of transport costs across countries. Table 5.1 gives the regional
averages of the costs for shipping a standard container, where the average is taken of the
cost of importing and exporting a container. It shows that clearing goods is twice as expensive in sub-Saharan Africa as in East Asia and the Pacific. Particular country examples
make the point more vividly; average freight costs for a 20 foot container are about $450 in
Singapore and Malaysia yet more than $5500 in Chad and the Central African Republic.
Table 5.1 also presents transport costs in terms of the time it takes to comply with all the
procedures necessary for import/export regulations, inland transportation and handling,

Table 5.1   Average costs and handling time for a 20 foot container

Region	Cost (dollars)	Time (days)
East Asia & Pacific	931	23.7
Eastern Europe & Central Asia	1678	27.6
Latin America & Caribbean	1362	19.75
Middle East & North Africa	1128	24.2
OECD	1118	10.75
South Asia	1437	32.3
Sub-Saharan Africa	2154	36.5

Source: World Bank (2011), *Doing Business* website; *2009 data* (average calculated using data for imports
and exports).

but excludes port-to-port shipping. OECD countries can clear goods quickly (but not necessarily cheaply). Within the regional averages there is wide dispersion of country performance. Singapore takes an average of 3 days to clear imports, Brazil takes 12 days, while neighboring Venezuela takes 49. Chad takes 100 and Iraq takes 101 days. Including shipping, transporting goods from Europe to Asia takes about 5 weeks (Hummels, 2007).

Data in Table 5.1 are provided by the World Bank, which uses the methodology in Djankov et al. (2006).[7] They cover about 180 countries, are based on surveys of freight forwarders in each country, and the data are updated annually. The data for the cost of importing and exporting a standardized container of goods include fees associated with completing the procedures to export or import the goods, such as costs for documents, administrative fees for customs clearance and technical control, customs broker fees, terminal handling charges and inland transport.

While the data are broad in composition, they only report averages for each country's trade with all its trading partners. Data on shipping quotes provide the bilateral dimension. Limão and Venables (2001) obtain quotes for shipping a standard container from Baltimore to various destinations. The quotes are for aggregate products and based only on one city of origin, although information on the route enables the journey to be broken into sea and overland stages. Portugal-Perez and Wilson (2009) report costs of shipping a container of textiles between selected city pairs. Clarke et al. (2004) use data from the US Import Waterborne Databank, which covers shipments to a number of US ports, and disaggregates commodities to the six-digit Harmonized System level. Freight rates for different modes of transport can also be found in trade journals (Hummels 2001b).

The data discussed above are derived from shipping quotes or surveys. An alternative source is national customs data, which allows extraction of very detailed product information. This has the advantage of being extremely disaggregated. For example, the US Census Bureau has, since 1974, made data available on US imports at the ten-digit product level by exporter country, mode of transport and district of entry. Imports are valued both inclusive and exclusive of freight and insurance charges and the discrepancy provides the measure of freight costs (see Hummels, 2001b). New Zealand has information from 1963–97 and more recent data (since the 1990s) is available for a number of Latin American and Caribbean countries (Hummels, 2007). However, data of this type is only available for a relatively small set of countries.

A further source of data is derived from the IMF Direction of Trade Statistics (DOT), which allows comparison of data reported by the exporting country 'free-on-board' (fob) with the corresponding import data reported by the importer inclusive of the costs of insurance and freight (cif). The cif/fob ratio is then taken as a measure of transport costs. On average, this ratio was 1.28 in 1990 (Limão and Venables, 2001). This data has the advantage of broad country coverage, covering up to 25 000 potential bilateral trade flows, and most countries have good information from the 1980s onwards. However, problems include the fact that it is an aggregate over all commodities and so depends on the composition of trade, and that a high proportion of observations are imputed.[8]

The Responsiveness of Trade to Transport Costs

We have demonstrated large cross-country variations in transport costs in terms of time and money, but do they contribute to variations in trade?

Empirical studies have regressed trade flows on various measures of transport costs. To avoid omitted variable bias such regressions include a number of control variables, although they should only be included if they are thought to affect trade through channels other than transport costs. Dealing with variables that may work through a number of channels may be difficult. For example, including distance in such a regression would, in principle, give evidence of a relationship other than through the transport cost channel. In practice, identification is seldom so neat in econometrics, so it would be hard to be confident that some of the effects of transport costs are not being picked up also by the distance variable.

Econometric studies suggest that freight costs have a statistically significant and quantitatively important impact on trade flows. Limão and Venables (2001) use both cif/fob measures and freight rates and find estimates of the elasticity of trade with respect to the freight cost factor[9] in the range −2 to −3.5. The quantitative importance of freight rates is indicated by their calculation that a move from the median value to the 75th percentile in their sample cuts trade volumes by two-thirds. With a similar methodology, Clarke et al. (2004) estimate an elasticity of about −1.3 for country-specific transport costs. Because shipping costs are quoted on a per unit basis, the *ad valorem* cost falls proportionately as the price of the good rises (or equivalently, as the weight falls), despite potentially higher handling or insurance costs. This has been used to argue that transport costs lead to the export of higher quality products (Hummels and Skiba, 2004).

The Contribution of Transport Costs to Trade Growth

The studies above were based primarily on using cross-section variation to identify the impact of freight costs on trade. How important have reductions in freight costs been in driving the growth of world trade through time? Baier and Bergstrand (2001) look at the determinants of the growth of trade in the period 1958–60 to 1986–88. They use data for 16 OECD countries to find an elasticity of trade with respect to the cif/fob ratio of −3, consistent with the cross-section findings of the previous sub-section. The main contribution of Baier and Bergstrand's paper is to estimate the relative contributions of income growth, trade liberalization, and changes in transport costs to the recorded growth of trade. Their estimates suggest that reductions in trade costs played a minor part in this growth. Income growth accounted for 66 per cent of the growth, trade liberalization for 26 per cent, and lower transport costs just 8 per cent. Combined, the 34 per cent attributed to trade costs (that is, transport costs plus trade policy restrictions) is consistent with Jacks et al. (2008), who attribute 31 per cent of the 1950–2000 trade expansion to trade costs[10] and calculate a much higher proportion (55 per cent) for the pre-World War I trade boom.

Despite estimating a similar elasticity, the results in Baier and Bergstrand (2001) suggest transport costs have a relatively minor role, yet those in Limão and Venables (2001) imply transport costs are very important. The reason for this apparent contradiction is that the cross-section variation in freight rates in the sample is large, consistent with Table 5.1, while transport costs did not fall very much over time. This is somewhat at odds with the popular belief that transport costs have fallen in recent times and the reasoning for this is elaborated later.

Transport Costs and Modal Choice

Transport costs shape not only the volume of trade, but also the modal choice. Most goods travel by ship, but a striking development in recent years has been the growing volume of goods shipped by air. Over the period 1975–2004, manufactured goods traded by air grew by 7.4 per cent per annum while goods traded across the ocean grew by 4.4 per cent per annum. Furthermore, planes tend to carry more valuable goods over longer distances. In volume terms, less than 1 per cent of goods now travel by air, but more than a third of the value of goods imported by the United States now arrives on planes.[11] In terms of ton-miles, the growth rate of air transport was even higher than that of other modes (Hummels, 2007).

The modal choice is primarily a trade-off between higher monetary transport costs and faster journey time. Reliability and a reduction in delivery uncertainty are particularly important for trade in intermediates or in products where demand may be transient (Harrigan and Venables, 2006). By comparing the freight costs of alternative transport modes with journey times, researchers have been able to come up with measures of the value of time saved in transit. For example, Hummels (2001a) matches shipments that are similar in all respects (commodity, country of origin, final destination) except mode of transport. If there are two matched shipments, that is two very similar trades going on, but one by sea and one by air, then it can be argued that shippers must be close to indifference between modes. Since the modes differ in cost and speed, shippers' choices give an implicit value of the time saved. This turns out to be extremely high, being worth as much as 0.5 per cent of the value of goods shipped, *per day*. Taking a mean ocean voyage of 20 days and assigning one day to air travel, Hummels computes a 9 per cent tax equivalent of time costs for the United States such that the transport cost factor associated with time delays in 1.09.

Hummels and Schaur (2009) estimate the value of time saving using US import data that report the price and quantity of air shipping relative to ocean shipping as well as time delays associated with ocean shipping. The idea is that a firm's willingness to pay for more expensive air shipping is increasing in the number of days saved with airplanes and decreasing in the premium paid to ship by air. Using this approach, Hummels et al. (2007) calculate tariff equivalent costs of time delays and produce these by geographic region and product. For example, they calculate that avoiding a day of delay would be worth 2 per cent of the value of a shipment of road vehicles, but only 0.2 per cent for footwear. How does delay impact the volume of trade? Djankov et al. (2006) calculate that the trade impediment of an additional day in transit reduces trade by more than 1 per cent. Given the variations seen in Table 5.1, handling delays are contributing substantially to variations in trade volumes. Djankov et al. calculate that, were Uganda to reduce its transit times from 58 days to the median of 27, this would be equivalent to reducing its distance from its trading partners by 2200 km.

In summary, we revealed the responsiveness of trade to transport costs is large. Delay costs are of the same order of magnitude as freight costs, affecting trade volumes and the mode of transport. Because of large variations across regions, transport costs are an important factor in explaining trade patterns, but they have not necessarily contributed greatly to recent increased trade volumes.

THE DETERMINANTS OF TRANSPORT COSTS

We now shift our attention from the implications of transport costs to their determinants. In terms of Equation (5.1), we are interested in establishing the effects of the arguments in the transport cost function, that is, looking in detail at the relationship:

Transport costs = f(distance, geography, infrastructure, trade facilitation,

technology, fuel costs, . . .)   (5.4)

Once again, evidence comes from both cross-section and time-series data and we look at each in turn.

Cross-section

As noted in Table 5.1, there is considerable dispersion of transport costs, together with wide variations in the natural and man-made barriers between countries. What factors determine the magnitude of these cost barriers?

Distance and geography
The review in Abe and Wilson (2009) concludes that the elasticity of transport cost per unit weight with respect to port-to-port distance is between 0.14 to 0.21. The elasticity is well below unity and indicates diminishing average costs with respect to distance. The measure does not allow for whether the distance is by land or by sea. Reduced-form gravity models do not account for this distinction, but some studies of costs do. Limão and Venables (2001) find that an extra 1000 km distance raises costs by seven times more if the distance is overland than if it is maritime. In Hummels (2001b), the elasticities of transport costs with respect to distance are 0.46 (air), 0.39 (rail), 0.275 (road) and 0.22 (sea). In later work, Hummels (2007) estimates that, although the distance elasticity of costs was higher by air than by sea, it has declined faster over time such that they had practically equal elasticities of 0.16 (air) and 0.15 (sea) in 2004. The summary in Abe and Wilson (2009) concludes the elasticity is higher by land than by sea, all of which suggest access to the coast is important.

Indeed, landlocked countries face a major cost disadvantage, which is important because more than a fifth of the world's countries are landlocked. According to World Bank data,[12] the world's ten highest freight costs are dominated by landlocked countries and even Switzerland ranks among the worst third of countries. Limão and Venables (2001) find that landlocked countries have transport costs that are 50 per cent higher than other comparable countries. Some regions are disproportionately landlocked; in particular, 40 per cent of sub-Saharan Africa's people live in landlocked countries (Ndulu et al., 2007). For these nations, it is especially important to be able to move across land cheaply and quickly. Thus, the quality of transport infrastructure and ease of transit can be important factors.

Infrastructure and trade facilitation
Infrastructure investment, while costly to undertake, has a major impact in reducing transport costs. The stock of infrastructure is frequently measured by an index of road,

rail and telecommunications capacity, as pioneered by Canning (1998). Updated data is produced in the *World Development Indicators* giving the per centage of paved roads in a country. The Global Competitiveness Report, published by the World Economic Forum, has information on telephone density. The *Logistics Performance Index* (LPI) from the World Bank combines objective measures and the subjective opinions of logistics professionals (Arvis et al., 2007).

To investigate the importance of infrastructure, Limão and Venables (2001) use an index based on Canning's work to calculate that variation in infrastructure accounts for 40 per cent of the variation in predicted transport costs in coastal countries and up to 60 per cent in landlocked countries. Improvements in road, rail and telephone infrastructure from the 25th to 75th percentile would overcome more than half the disadvantage of being landlocked.

Given that most goods travel by ship (Hummels, 2007), it is no surprise that many studies emphasize the importance of ports. Clarke et al. (2004) use port efficiency measures based on an index from the *Global Competitiveness Report,* which in turn is based on business surveys.[13] According to the report, Singapore has a score of 6.8 and Bosnia–Herzegovina has a score of 1.5 on a 1–7 scale. Namibia scores highly (5.4), yet Brazil, despite being more developed, ranks 127th out of 133 countries with a score of 2.6 (World Economic Forum, 2009). Clarke et al. (2004) estimate that a deterioration in port quality from the 75th to 25th percentile raises shipping costs 12 per cent and is like being 60 per cent further away from markets. Because the elasticity of costs with respect to distance is well below unity (as we saw earlier), they argue the remoteness disadvantage can be overcome with well-run ports.

Infrastructure may require a lot of investment while the ability to manage shipments efficiently may require technological and managerial improvements. Ports are in part a natural phenomenon but their effectiveness is also institutional. For example, Clarke et al. (2004) confirm ports are more efficient if there is less organized crime, but find a non-linear relationship between efficiency and regulation, with some being better than too much or none.

Hoekman and Nicita (2008) report the fees associated with procedures to import a 20-foot container average $1212 in low income countries compared to $814 in high income countries. At the same time, the LPI measure of customs clearance quality displays much greater satisfaction in rich countries than poor.[14] The LPI is based in part on perceptions but also on objective numbers like the rate of physical inspection – many countries choose to inspect 100 per cent of the goods physically while many others inspect only 1 per cent – and on the actual days procedures take, where the time taken between the submission of an accepted customs declaration and customs clearance is less than a day in many countries but ten days in Benin and Sierra Leone (Arvis et al., 2007). There can be many procedural impediments. For example, Djankov et al. (2006) note it takes 17 procedures to export a good from Burundi, which take more than two months to complete. Burundi is far from the coast and needs to cross borders, but Fiji does not have this problem. Why then do exporters in Fiji need 13 signatures[15] when the French need two? Thus, while geography is important and while clearing customs can require potentially expensive technology or know-how, red tape clearly plays a role.

Teravanithorn and Raballand (2008) document a negative simple correlation between the overall LPI and transport prices, which implies a one standard deviation improvement in logistics (two-thirds of a unit) would reduce the cost of truck transport by about 1 US cent per vehicle-km. Arvis et al. (2007) calculate that, on average, a one-point fall in the LPI corresponds to exports taking three more days to travel from the warehouse to port. Improving Ethiopian logistics half way to South African levels is equivalent to a 7.5 per cent tariff reduction on Ethiopian exports (Portugal-Perez and Wilson, 2009).

To summarize, transport costs are determined in part by the physical geography of distance and landlocked-ness, but also significantly by the fact that goods spend a lot of time moving slowly between borders or standing still at borders. Wilson (2003) calculates that the average time spent waiting at a border could have been used to travel 1600 km inland. This can be due to physical infrastructure deficiencies like ports but also because of procedural delays.

Market power

So far we have considered the prices paid by users of transport in terms of the costs of supplying those services, but price–cost mark-ups also matter. While tramp shipping is set on spot markets, much liner shipping is priced by conferences, which facilitate collusion and possible exploitation of market power. According to Hummels et al. (2009), one in six importer–exporter pairs worldwide was served by only one ship operating on that route. Over half were served by three or fewer ships, which in many cases were owned by a single carrier. Davies (1986) argues that, despite a market structure conducive to collusion, the general cargo market is sufficiently contestable to prevent it. In contrast, Fink et al. (2000) reveal that higher prices occur where there are price fixing agreements, but this may be endogenous. Thinking of transport services as a derived demand, Hummels et al. (2009) establish that transport prices are higher if there is a low elasticity of import demand and that having more shippers lowers the price and the impact of the elasticity. These two studies indicate the exercise of market power, which implies more competition would reduce transport charges.

It is not only ocean shipping that is subject to a lack of competition. In road transport, deregulation in France, Mexico and elsewhere has increased market entry and reduced prices (Teravanithorn and Raballand, 2008). In the United States, deregulation of freight meant most truck workers stopped being represented by the Teamsters union and lost bargaining power (Belzer, 1995). Lack of effective competition is widespread in Africa, and means that ground transport prices are relatively high even though costs are not. While prices range from 6 to 11 US cents/km in Africa, they are 5 cents/km in Western Europe. Yet costs are 1.87 and 1.33 cents/km in Central and East Africa compared to 1.52 (Spain) and 1.71 (Germany) cents/km in Western Europe. The wide margin of price over cost in Africa is not due to superior service because measures of transport quality are also inferior (Teravanithorn and Raballand, 2008).

Time Series

We have highlighted some factors that determine the variation in transport costs between countries and now turn to the factors that have caused them to change through time. As we saw earlier, there are puzzles to do with the relatively minor role of trade costs in driving the growth of trade volumes and the increase in the absolute magnitude of the distance coefficient in gravity equations. To explain these, we have to look in more detail at the evolution of transport costs.

The evolution of transport costs
The second half of the twentieth century saw continuing transport innovation. Technical innovation involved containerization and jet transport. Institutional innovation included open registry shipping (the practice of registering vessels under flags of convenience to circumvent higher regulatory and manning costs imposed by wealthier nations), open skies agreements, and other transport deregulation (Hummels, 2007). By facilitating the transfer of goods on and off ships, the costs of using a container ship are half those of a conventional ship per unit of freight, even after factoring in higher capital costs for container ships (Levinson, 2006).[16]

Did the cost of moving goods fall? Aircraft revenue per ton-km fell from 3.87 in 1955 to 0.30 in 2004 (measured in 2000 US dollars), with a particularly steep fall taking place after the introduction of the jet engine (Hummels, 2007). Micco and Serebrisky (2006) find that open skies agreements reduced air transport costs by 9 per cent . While there is evidence that the price of air transport declined, the same is not true for ships. Hummels (2007) tracks the trends of ocean shipping over time. For bulk cargo, he uses US data to show that, while the price of transport fell steadily in real dollars per ton, it did not fall relative to the value of goods shipped. Bulk cargo does not use containers, but liner shipping does. German data show that liner prices (deflated using the GDP deflator or a traded goods price index) rose in the 1970s and fell in the late 1980s onwards such that they have remained more or less unchanged in *ad valorem* terms over 50 years.

Given the dominance of shipping in trade volumes, the United States and German data imply that falls in overall transportation costs have been modest. This in turn informs why transport costs have been attributed a fairly small role in the post-World War II boom in trade (as seen earlier), but why did these technological changes not have a more dramatic effect?

The main reason appears to be input costs. Levinson (2006) reports that heavily unionized labor delayed the introduction of container shipping and reaped a share of the cost savings. For example, they negotiated additional unnecessary loading and unloading procedures to generate extra work. Workers' power diminished in the 1970s, just in time for the first oil price shock in 1973. Hummels (2007) argues the rising fuel costs had an upward effect on transport costs in the 1970s. Only after fuel costs began to moderate did transport costs fall.

This argument is supported by evidence on the contribution of fuel to costs. Fuel can comprise 40–63 per cent of operating costs depending on ship size.[17] UNCTAD (2009) calculates the elasticity of costs with respect to fuel prices is 0.19–0.36 for containerized vessels. Transporting oil is similar, but dry bulk costs are more fuel price elastic. They place their results in the context of a 'rule-of-thumb' elasticity of 0.4 for bulk goods and a bit less for containerized cargo.[18] Is it possible to isolate a contribution of containers in the absence of fuel costs? Industry reports cited in Levinson (2006) attribute big savings to the container. For example, by the late 1980s, freight rates from Asia to the United States were calculated to be 40–60 per cent lower. More generally, Clarke et al. (2004) find containerization is negatively associated with transport prices across countries, as do Abe and Wilson (2009).

Transport quality, the mode of production and distance

Many of the benefits of improved transport technology accrued through reduced journey times and better reliability, as well as through lower costs. This is evident for air travel and also applies to other modes. For example, one of the main benefits of the container manifested itself as time reductions associated with ease of transfer to land transport. Maritime shipping times have also fallen; Hummels (2001a) reports that the average shipping time for routes to the United States fell from 40 days to 10 days between 1950 and 1998.[19]

These changes have had important implications for the composition of trade, enabling previously non-traded goods to be traded, and allowing new production methods to be used. The clearest example of the benefits of faster shipping time has been in the growth of non-traditional agricultural exports, such as sub-Saharan Africa's exports of cut flowers and fresh vegetables.[20] It is not only agricultural goods that are time sensitive, as we saw in our discussion of the value of time in transit. It also applies to manufactures, and lower transport times are one of the factors driving the increasing share of manufactures in world trade (UNIDO, 2009).

These changes have enabled new forms of manufacturing to develop. Manufacturing processes are becoming increasingly fragmented, a phenomenon that has been labeled 'trade in tasks', 'value-chains' or 'off-shoring' (Grossman and Rossi-Hansberg 2008; UNIDO, 2009). Levinson (2006) argues this would not have been feasible without the standardized shipping container. Furthermore, the more widespread adoption of just-in-time concepts, for example the use of manufacturing's just-in-time principles in retailing (Nordås et al., 2006), has placed increased importance on the value of time and on the importance of distance.

These phenomena mean that the modest contribution of transport to the growth of world trade volumes found by Baier and Bergstrand (2001) underplays the impact of transport improvements on trade. Transport improvements have had a much more significant impact on trade – and the organization of production more widely – than is captured in their measure of trade costs.

They also explain the puzzle that trade has become more local. Time-sensitive products can now be traded internationally, but often this trade is with nearby countries to minimize both the length and the possible variance of journey times. Evans and Harrigan (2005) find that, if timely delivery is important, the goods will be produced near the source of final demand. For example, US apparel imports that are susceptible to fashion trends and whose popularity is unpredictable are being increasingly imported from nearby countries. Thus, the World Bank argues that lower transport costs are *increasing* the regionalization of trade so that distance is more important than before (2009).

METHODOLOGICAL ISSUES

The studies that we have discussed provide insights into the determinants of transport costs and their role in determining overall volumes of trade. However, there are numerous unsolved problems in the literature, some of them methodological. Gravity models have received particular study with, for example, Anderson and van Wincoop (2004) discussing empirical issues and Disdier and Head (2008) using meta analysis to investigate how they may impact the results. We discuss two of these issues.

Third Country Effects and Zeroes

Equation (5.2) models a bilateral trade flow between two countries. One set of issues in gravity modeling stems from the importance of third-country effects, on the one-hand, and from the large number of cases where there are no bilateral trade flows, on the other.

Properly grounded gravity models incorporate the fact that demand for a product depends on its price relative to that of other products. Therefore, the trade response to a reduction in transport costs between a pair of countries depends on changes in transport costs elsewhere. This is the intuition behind 'multilateral resistance', a term coined and modeled by Anderson and van Wincoop (2003, 2004). This work, which is frequently cited by empirical researchers, dictates that there should be terms controlling for these third country effects; in other words, there should be controls for transport costs other than in the importer–exporter pair. Despite frequent citation, two of the paper's key messages are often ignored. First, omitting such controls can lead to biased estimates, for example of the distance coefficient τ_1. The use of importer and exporter fixed effects can resolve the estimation issues. Second, even with τ_1 correctly estimated, the terms representing the third country effects are hidden in the fixed effects, so the trade response based only on τ_1 is still miscalculated. Dealing with these effects fully required solving a non-linear system of prices, which may be why almost no empirical studies did so. However, a recent contribution by Baier and Bergstrand (2009) allows one to take account of these effects using easily constructed controls such that one can continue to estimate a single gravity equation by OLS and conduct comparative statics including third country effects. We expect many future empirical gravity models to do so.

The gravity literature has also renewed its attention on the prevalence of zeros in international trade, which typically comprises half the world's bilateral trade pairs. One therefore needs to distinguish between effects which condition on countries already trading and effects which open new trade partnerships. Francois et al. (2007) investigate the latter. However, even if one is interested in estimating the former using a specification like Equation (5.2) the existence of zeros can be problematic due to sample selection issues (Coe and Hoffmaister, 1999; Santos Silva and Tenreyro, 2006).

A recent theoretical explanation for zeroes is based on the heterogeneous productivities of exporting firms. As noted in Bernard et al. (2007), a relatively small proportion of firms export. Helpman et al. (2008) develop a two-step method which accounts for zeros and firm heterogeneity using the argument that only the more productive firms will find it sufficiently profitable to cover the fixed costs of exporting to a destination. In the first step, they estimate a probit model for bilateral country-level exports, which they use to construct controls for zeros and for the proportion of firms selling from the exporter to the importer. They then add these controls to the otherwise standard gravity model. Behar and Nelson (2009) find that ignoring this factor leads to an underestimate of the effects of trade costs on trade for the average country.

Endogeneity and Non-linearities

A significant coefficient in Equation (5.2) is usually interpreted as a causal effect of, say, infrastructure on trade. Yet many explanatory variables can be endogenous. For example, increased trade can reduce the ease of transit and increase transport cost; as trade volumes surged in China, the average wait time at Shanghai's port expanded by 2 days in 2003 (Djankov et al., 2006). Abe and Wilson (2009) find evidence that congested ports indeed generate higher costs. In contrast, it may be that higher trade volumes stimulate the construction of new infrastructure and the introduction of more efficient clearance technologies: the marginal value of investments in trade facilitating measures may be higher if exports are high, while some aspects of the logistics technology are subject to scale economies and thus only worthwhile at very high volumes. Djankov et al. (2006) note that, as a result of the added congestion, Shanghai added 12 loading berths in 2004. Hummels and Skiba (2004) find evidence that trade affected the timing of containerization and Levinson (2006, pp. 233) quotes that 'If ever there was a business in which economies of scale mattered, container shipping was it.' From an empirical perspective, the congestion argument implies an underestimate of the gravity model coefficients while the increasing-returns argument implies an overestimate. A standard approach to dealing with endogeneity bias is the use of instrumental variables.[21] However, as in many applications, finding suitable instruments can be difficult.

Other important factors are potential trade-imbalances, which limit the scope for splitting fixed costs over two journeys but which may provide cheap prices to those exploiting spare capacity on the return journey. For example, US exporters to the Caribbean pay 83 per cent more than US importers because the ship is 72 per cent empty on the way to the United States (Furchsluger, 2000). Having a full ship on one or both legs reduces costs. Having a big ship also reduces costs. For example, access to Buenos Aires costs $70 per container for a 200 TEU vessel but only $14 for a 1000 TEU one (Clarke et al., 2004). However, the additional fixed cost of a bigger vessel only becomes worthwhile at a certain level of trade. Furthermore, the process of moving goods is inherently subject to non-linearities and bottlenecks. For example, a major road upgrading program will have a limited impact on costs and time if the port is full or the border is closed. Although one may try to approximate such features by interacting the variables, they may not accurately capture the inherent non-linearities.

This section has highlighted some issues that may impede the accurate estimation of the coefficients in the gravity model and may lead to incorrect calculation of the effects of transport costs on trade. Nonetheless, taking it as given that the coefficients have been accurately estimated and that the trade effects have been properly calculated, what are the broader implications?

Conclusions

Transport costs affect international trade and vice versa. Both are influenced by considerations of geography, technology, infrastructure, fuel costs and policy towards trade facilitation. Researchers have sought both to quantify reduced form relationships and to explore the channels through which they operate. Our synthesis of these relationships is given in Equation (5.1) and we return to it to pull results together. For example, consider the effect of distance on trade. Expressed in elasticity form, we could write

$$\frac{\Delta Trade}{\Delta Dist} \times \frac{Dist}{Trade} = \left(\frac{\partial Trade}{\partial Cost} \times \frac{Cost}{Trade}\right) \times \left(\frac{\Delta Cost}{\Delta Dist} \times \frac{Dist}{Cost}\right) + \frac{\partial Trade}{\partial Dist} \times \frac{Dist}{Trade}$$

$$-0.9 \qquad\qquad -3.0 \qquad\qquad 0.2 \qquad\qquad ? \qquad (5.5)$$

The left hand side gives the overall (or reduced form) effect of distance on trade, while the right hand side decomposes it into a part associated with freight costs and a residual. The gravity model estimates reviewed above indicate a consensus reduced-form elasticity of trade with respect to distance of -0.9. In the following section, we found that the elasticity of trade with respect to the freight cost factor is of the order -3. Estimates of the elasticity of freight costs with respect to distance vary greatly across modes, but a summary order of magnitude is 0.2. The relationship above suggests freight costs account for two thirds of the effect of distance ($0.2 \times -3 = -0.6$). The remaining third could be accounted for by delays – although the relationship between distance and time is highly non-linear due to its effect on modal choice – and the effect of distance through channels other than freight costs, such as cultural or language proximity.

Distance is not the only important geographical factor. Being landlocked increases trade costs by 50 per cent and reduces trade volumes by 30–60 per cent, numbers that are broadly consistent with the elasticity of trade with respect to costs given above. Geography is not the only determinant and the hard and soft infrastructure of transport can offset the geographical disadvantage faced by some countries. Over time, technical change and the price of fuel have influenced transport costs and trade volumes. In the case of fuel costs, it is reasonable to assume the effect on trade is exclusively through the freight cost channel. Therefore, we can use the rule-of-thumb relationship of -0.4 identified above to calculate an elasticity of trade with respect to fuel costs of $0.4 \times -3 = -1.2$.

While historical studies suggest that the contribution of falling trade costs to the growth of trade is smaller than might have been expected, the puzzle is resolved by the fact that the measured fall in trade costs is quite low. Looking back, there are several reasons for this. One is the continuing importance of fuel costs. A second is that it is the fall in trade costs relative to the value of goods shipped that is the key variable, and it is not obvious that technical advance in transport has been consistently more rapid that technical progress in other areas. Finally, much of the technical advance in transport has gone into improved quality (speed and reliability) rather than lower cost.

Some aspects of the change in quality of transport services have been widely researched. We saw that time in transit is valuable and that transport times have fallen. This has affected trade volumes, but the full impact of these changes is broader. Quicker transport has allowed new time-sensitive products to be traded internationally – be it agricultural goods from Africa or fashion sensitive goods from Asia. They are also transforming the patterns of world production as just-in-time and similar management techniques come to be operated on an international level through production networks.

Finally, what are the implications of transport costs for growth and development, and what policy messages follow? We have found evidence of measures that can reduce transport costs and hence stimulate trade. Does it naturally follow that such measures should be undertaken? The gains from trade have been extensively, if controversially, researched. Measures of openness have been used as a variable in cross-country growth regressions. For example, Frankel and Romer (1999) use a gravity model to instrument for trade flows and in turn use this to argue that trade has a large and robust, albeit moderately statistically significant, causal impact on growth.[22] A more structural approach is presented in Redding and Venables (2004), who emphasize the effect of remoteness and other trade costs on per capita income through the trade channel. Remote economies are disadvantaged through two mechanisms. One is that imports – including essential imports such as fuel and capital equipment – are relatively expensive. The other is that such locations face cost hurdles in exporting, and are consequently unattractive to investors looking for locations in which to produce and export. Redding and Venables formalize these ideas in the concepts of supplier access and market access and show these measures are important determinants of countries' levels of income.

On the other side of the policy choice, are the costs incurred in infrastructure or other investments. Cost–benefit analysis is widely used on a project by project basis. The wider – and more international – the project, the harder it is to make such calculations. An example is that of Buys et al. (2006), who calculate that a program of road network expansion in Africa would increase trade by $250 billion over 15 years and cost the project at $20 billion plus $1 billion per year. Trade does not map directly to benefits, but a bolder calculation is offered by Abe and Wilson (2009). They find that transport cost reductions from investments in East Asian port infrastructure would generate $8 million of consumer surplus per year and cost less than $3 million per year. In principle, regulatory reforms such as reducing the number of documents required to export should be cheap to implement and some suggest that trade facilitation of this sort is 'low hanging fruit' (Nordas et al., 2006). However, this naively ignores the political elements behind them; for example allocating someone a procedural post is a source of patronage. Furthermore, developing countries may lack the technical expertise required to implement new systems.[23]

Additionally there are, in the nature of international trade, cross-country externalities and complementarities. For example, we saw that landlocked countries' transport costs and trade volumes are highly dependent on their neighbors' policies. In the case of trade policy, the WTO exists to internalize such effects. For transport investments, arrangements are more ad hoc, falling to bilateral or plurilateral cooperation between countries supplemented by supra-national bodies such as the European Union, or the funding and technical assistance of the development banks. For example, the UN sponsored 'Almaty Program' is aimed at relieving some of the difficulties faced by landlocked countries. Goals include recognizing freedom of transit, developing regional transport infrastructure and fostering transnational co-operation (Arvis et al., 2007). The World Bank emphasizes the importance of regional infrastructure projects and broader trade facilitation measures (World Bank, 2009). The work surveyed in this chapter suggests such initiatives will help reduce transport costs and boost trade volumes for many countries and their neighbors.

NOTES

1. Between 1950 and 2007 international trade grew at 6 per cent per annum while GDP grew by 3.8 per cent.
2. For an example of a non-linear specification, see Coe and Hoffmaister (1999).
3. Our illustrative specification emphasises the country-specific features of the exporter, but could easily include importer-specific features as well.
4. For example, see Anderson (1979) and Bergstrand (1985).
5. The distance measure is the great circle distance, which is the shortest distance between any two points on the earth's surface measured along the surface of the earth. The two points are usually the capital or largest commercial cities of each country, although sometimes weighted measures based on multiple cities may be used.
6. The Logistics Performance Index is a new dataset produced by the World Bank. It is constructed using principal component analysis based on six measures, namely (a) the efficiency of the clearance process by customs and other border agencies, (b) transport and information technology infrastructure, (c) local logistics industry competence, (d) the ease and affordability of international shipments, (e) the facility to track and trace shipments and (f) the timeliness with which shipments reach their destination. It therefore captures a broad spectrum of factors which influence transport costs.
7. The data are readily available at http://www.doingbusiness.org/ExploreTopics/TradingAcrossBorders/.
8. See Hummels (2001b) and Hummels and Lugovskyy (2006) for a discussion.
9. The freight cost factor measures the impact of trade costs on the delivered price. Thus, if trade costs are 10% of the value of the product the trade cost factor is 1.1. It is natural to measure the elasticity of a trade flow with respect to this delivered cost, not the trade cost alone.
10. They derive their measure of trade costs by comparing international trade flows with internal flows in a way that is consistent with a large number of formal gravity models. The method does not permit a further decomposition into transport and non-transport costs.
11. The value of shipments by sea also far exceeds the value of shipments by land (Moreira, Volpe and Blyde, 2008).
12. Taken from their *Doing Business* website at www.doingbusiness.org
13. Wilson et al. (2005) combine this sea port measure with a measure of airport quality.
14. The data can be accessed at www.worldbank.org/lpi.
15. Bill of loading, cargo release order, certificate of origin, commercial invoice, consular invoice customs export declaration, terminal handling receipts, export license, foreign exchange authorization inspection report, packing list, tax certificate, technical standard/health certificate.
16. Containerized cargo forms 70 per cent of all trade and 90 per cent of liner trade from developed countries. Liners operate on fixed routes and schedules and are used for non-bulk cargo. Dry bulk cargo uses co-called tramp ships, which have irregular routes and schedules (Clarke et al., 2004; UNCTAD, 2009).
17. This clearly depends on fuel costs too. For example, fuel rose from a quarter of operating costs to one-half of operating costs between 1972 and 1974 (Levinson, 2006).
18. A simple comparison of changes in aviation fuel prices and airline operating costs implies an elasticity of 0.48 for air transport (Hummels, 2009).
19. However, high oil prices lead to the production of more fuel efficient but slower ships (Levinson, 2006).
20. Djankov et al. (2006) estimate that a day's delay reduces a country's relative exports of time-sensitive to time-insensitive agricultural goods by 6 per cent.
21. See for example Chapter 5 in Wooldridge (2002)
22. In many applications, the use of instruments leads to larger standard errors and hence lower significance levels.
23. For a further discussion, see Engman (2005).

REFERENCES

Abe, K. and J. Wilson, 2009, Weathering the Storm: Investing in Port Infrastructure to Lower Trade Costs in East Asia. World Bank Policy Research Working Paper 4911.

Anderson, J., 1979, A Theoretical Foundation for the Gravity Equation, *American Economic Review*, **69** (1), 106–116.

Anderson, J. and E. van Wincoop, 2003, Gravity with gravitas: a solution to the border puzzle, *American Economic Review*, **93** (1), 170–192.

Anderson, J. and E. van Wincoop, 2004, Trade costs. *Journal of Economic Literature*, **42** (3), 691–751.

Arvis, J., M. Mustra, J. Panzer, L. Ojala and T. Naula, 2007, Connecting to compete: trade logistics in the global economy. The World Bank, Washington.

Arvis, J.-F., G. Raballiland and J-F. Marteau, 2007, The cost of being landlocked: logistics costs and supply chain reliability. World Bank Policy Research Working Paper.

Baier, S. and J. Bergstrand, 2001, The growth of world trade: tariffs, transport costs, and income similarity. *Journal of International Economics*, **53**, 1–27.

Baier, S. and J. Bergstrand, 2009, Bonus Vetus OLS: a simple method for approximating international trade-cost effects using the gravity equation, *Journal of International Economics*, **77**, 77–85.

Behar, A., 2009, De 'Bonus Vetus OLS': approximating the international trade-cost effects of export documentation, FREIT Working Paper #37.

Behar, A., P. Manners and B. Nelson, 2009, Exports and logistics. Oxford Department of Economics Discussion Paper 439.

Belzer, M. 1995, Collective bargaining after deregulation: do the teamsters still count? *Industrial and Labor Relations Review*, **48** (4), 636–655.

Bergstrand, J., 1985, The gravity equation in international trade: some microeconomic foundations and empirical evidence. *The Review of Economics and Statistics*, **67** (3), 474–481.

Bernard, A., J. Jensen, S. Redding and P. Schott, 2007, Firms in international trade. *Journal of Economic Perspectives*, **21** (3), 105–130.

Brun, J., C. Carrerė, P. Guillaumont and J. de Melo, 2005, Has distance died? Evidence from a panel gravity model. *World Bank Economic Review*, **19**, 99–120.

Buys, P., U. Deichmann and D. Wheeler, 2006, Road network upgrading and overland trade expansion in Sub-Saharan Africa. World Bank Development Policy Research Group.

Canning, D., 1998, A database of world stocks of infrastructure, 1950–95. *World Bank Economic Review*, **3** (12), 529–547.

Carrere, C. and M. Schiff, On the geography of trade: distance is alive and well. *Revue Economique*, **56** (6), 1249–1274.

Clarke, X., D. Dollar and A. Micco, 2004, Port efficiency, maritime transport costs, and bilateral trade. *Journal of Development Economics*, **75**, 417–450.

Coe, D. and A. Hoffmaister, 1999, North–South trade: is Africa unusual? *Journal of African Economies*, **8** (2), 228–256.

Davies, J., 1986, *The Theory of Contestable Markets and its Application to the Liner Shipping Industry*. Ottawa, Canada: Canadian Transport Commission.

Disdier, A. and K. Head, 2008, The puzzling persistence of the distance effect on bilateral trade. *Review of Economics and Statistics*, **90** (1), 37–48.

Djankov, S., C. Freund and C. Pham, 2006, Trading on time. World Bank Policy Research Working Paper 3909.

Engman, M., 2005, The economic impact of trade facilitation. OECD Trade Policy Working Papers 21.

Evans, C. and J. Harrigan, 2005, Distance, time, and specialization: lean retailing in general equilibrium. *American Economic Review*, **95** (1), 292–313.

Fink, C., A. Mattoo and I. Neagu, 2000, Trade in international maritime services: how much does policy matter? *World Bank Economic Review*, **16** (1), 81–108.

Francois, J., K. Kepler and M. Manchin, 2007, Institutions, infrastructure, and trade. World Bank Policy Research Working Paper 4152.

Frankel, J. and D. Romer, 1999, Does trade cause growth? *American Economic Review*, **89** (3), 379–399.

Friedman, T., 2005, *The World is Flat: a Brief History of the Twenty-First Century*. London: Farrar, Straus and Giroux.

Furchsluger, J., 2000, Port and shipping services in the Caribbean: the vital link for integration. Mimeo.

Grossman, G.M. and E. Rossi-Hansberg, 2008, Trading tasks: a simple theory of offshoring. *American Economic Review*, **98** (5), 1978–1997.

Growth Commission, 2008, The Growth Report: Strategies for Sustained Growth and Inclusive Development. Washington DC: World Bank.

Harrigan, J. and A. Venables, 2006, Timeliness and agglomeration. *Journal of Urban Economics*, **59** (2), 300–316.

Helpman, E., M. Melitz and Y. Rubinstein, 2008, Estimating trade flows: trading partners and trading volumes. *Quarterly Journal of Economics*, **123** (2), 441–487.

Hoekman, B. and A. Nicita, 2008, Trade policy, trade costs, and developing country trade. World Bank Policy Research Working Paper 4797.

Hummels, D., 2001a, Time as a trade barrier. GTAP Working Paper.

Hummels, D., 2001b, Toward a geography of trade costs. Mimeo.

Hummels, D., 2007, Transportation costs and international trade in the second era of globalization. *Journal of Economic Perspectives*, **21** (3), 131–154.

Hummels, D., 2009, Globalization and freight transport costs in maritime shipping and aviation. International Transport Forum Working Paper 3.

Hummels, D. and V. Lugovskyy, 2006, Are matched partner trade statistics a usable measure of transportation costs? *Review of International Economics*, **14** (1), 69–86.

Hummels, D. and G. Schaur, 2009, Hedging price volatility using fast transport. NBER Working Paper 15154.

Hummels, D. and A. Skiba, 2004, Shipping the good apples out: an empirical confirmation of the Alchian–Allen conjecture. *Journal of Political Economy*, **112** (6), 1384–1402.

Hummels, D., V. Lugovskyy and A. Skiba, 2009, The trade reducing effects of market power in international shipping. *Journal of Development Economics*, **89**, 84–97.

Hummels, D., P. Minor, A. Reisman and E. Endean, 2007, Calculating tariff equivalents for time in trade. USAID/Nathan Associates.

Irwin, A. and M. Terviö, 2002, Does trade raise income? Evidence from the twentieth century. *Journal of International Economics*, **58**, 1–18.

Jacks, D., C. Meissner and D. Novy, 2008, Trade costs: 1870–2000. *American Economic Review Papers and Proceedings*, **98** (2), 529–534.

Levinson, M., 2006, *The Box: How the Shipping Container Made the World Smaller and the World Economy Bigger*. Princeton, NJ: Princeton University Press.

Limão, N. and A. Venables, 2001, Infrastructure, geographical disadvantage, transport costs and trade. *World Bank Economic Review*, **15** (3), 451–479.

Micco, A. and T. Serebrisky, 2006, Competition regimes and air transport costs: the effects of open skies agreements. *Journal of International Economics*, **70**, 25–51.

Moreira, M., C. Volpe and J. Blyde, 2008, Unclogging the veins of Latin America and the Caribbean: a report on the impact of transport costs on the region's trade. Inter-American Development Bank.

Ndulu, B., L. Chakraborty, L. Lijane, V. Ramachandran and J. Wolgin, 2007, Challenges of African Growth: Opportunities, Constraints and Strategic Directions. Washington DC: World Bank.

Nordås, H. and R. Piermartini, 2004, Infrastructure and trade. WTO Staff Working Paper.

Nordås, H., E. Pinali and M. Geloso Grosso, 2006, Logistics and time as a trade barrier. OECD Trade Policy Working Papers No. 35.

Portugal-Perez, A. and J. Wilson, 2009, Trade costs in Africa: barriers and opportunities for reform. World Bank Policy Research Paper 4619.

Radelet, S. and J. Sachs, 1998, Shipping costs, manufactured exports and economic growth. Report prepared for the World Bank. Available at: http://Inweb90.worldbank.org/ECA/Transport.nsf/ECADocByUnid/BAE7AB18A78A8BA985256B040057E4FA?Opendocument.

Redding, S. and A. Venables, 2004, Economic geography and international inequality. *Journal of International Economics*, **62**, 53–82.

Santos Silva, J. and S. Tenreyro, 2006, The log of gravity. *Review of Economics and Statistics*, **88**, 641–658.

Teravaninthorn, S. and G. Raballand, 2008, *Transport Prices and Costs in Africa: A Review of the Main International Corridors*. Washington DC: World Bank.

UNCTAD, 2009, Oil prices and maritime freight rates: An empirical investigation. Draft.

UNIDO, 2009, Industrial development report 2009. Breaking in and moving up: new industrial challenges for the bottom billion and the middle-income countries. Vienna: United Nations Industrial Development Organization.

Wilson, J., 2003, Trade facilitation: new issues in a development context, trade note No. 12. World Bank, Washington DC.

Wilson, J., C. Mann and T. Otsuki, 2005, Assessing the benefits of trade facilitation: a global Perspective. *The World Economy*, 841–871.

Wooldridge, J., 2002, *Econometric Analysis of Cross-Section and Panel Data*. Cambridge, MA: MIT Press.

World Bank, 2008, Safe, clean, and affordable transport for development: the World Bank Group's transport business strategy for 2008–2012.

World Bank, 2009, World development report: reshaping economic geography. The World Bank, Washington.

World Bank, 2011, Doing business. Available at www.doingbusiness.org.

World Economic Forum, 2009, The global competitiveness report 2009–10. The World Economic Forum, Geneva.

World Trade Organization, 2007, World trade report: trade in a globalizing world. WTO, Geneva.

6 City formation and transport costs
Takatoshi Tabuchi

INTRODUCTION

Most economic activities take place in cities, which are characterized by spatial externalities and heterogeneity. Apparently, they do not satisfy the postulates of the traditional economic theory, particularly general equilibrium theory under perfect competition. In fact, the presence of numerous large cities worldwide suggests that we need to reconsider the applications of traditional economic theory to urban economies, such as the agglomeration of firms and households.

There is no doubt that political power exerts a strong influence on agglomeration. According to Bairoch (1988), the population of Rome amounted to one million during the second century, while it fell to below 20 000 in the fourteenth century. Apart from the political and historical factors, the main factors pertaining to city formation are heterogeneity of space and externalities in space.

Heterogeneity of space is the rule in the real world. We often observe that cities are located at key junctions of trade routes such as harbors. This is Cronon's (1991) first nature (original, prehuman nature). Other things being equal, firms are attracted to locationally advantageous regions even though the advantages are but slight. The small concentration of firms would enable regions to finance social overhead capital, which is Cronon's (1991) second nature (artificial nature that people erect atop first nature). This would in turn reinforce the concentration of firms further. Moreover, they are bound to the location because of agglomeration economies under costly trade. This is the so-called lock-in effect. Heterogeneity of space is also found in the interregional/international differences in factor endowments. Regions and countries tend to specialize in producing goods according to the factors of production that are relatively abundant and thus carry out trade. This is Ricardian comparative advantage.

Externalities in space are also common across the globe. According to Scitovsky (1954), externalities are classified into technological externalities and pecuniary externalities. While the former are associated with non-market interactions, such as public hazards and knowledge spillovers, the latter involve market interactions through the trading of a variety of goods. We will be dealing with both externalities.

The changes in spatial structures both within and between cities may be explained by the decrease in transport costs due to the improvements in transport technologies according to new economic geography (NEG). In fact, the Industrial Revolution dramatically changed the spatial distribution of economic activities and led to the formation of large cities as observed in Table 6.1.

In addition to urbanization, we should consider the stylized facts of urban economies, such as the suburbanization of households, negative gradients of land rent and population density, agglomeration of economic activities, and polycentric configuration within large cities. For example, polycentric configurations of economic activities in Boston

Table 6.1   Urbanization in the world

Year	UK	France	USA	Japan
1800	23.0	12.0	5.0	14.0
1850	45.0	19.0	14.0	15.0
1910	75.0	38.0	42.0	18.0
1950	79.0	55.2	64.2	38.0
1960	78.4	61.9	70.0	63.9
1970	77.1	71.1	73.6	72.1
1980	87.9	73.3	73.7	76.2
1990	88.7	74.1	75.2	77.4
2000	89.4	75.8	79.1	78.7
2005	89.7	76.7	80.8	86.3

Source: Bairoch (1988), United Nations (2007)

metropolitan area are visualized by Kawabata (2002, Figure 5.3.1) and those in Tokyo metropolitan area are by Kawabata and Takahashi (2005, Figure 1). The purpose of this chapter is to elucidate the reasons underlying the stylized facts by focusing on the changes in transport costs, which involve commuting costs, face-to-face communication costs and trade costs.

In the next section, we begin with a simple general equilibrium model in order to examine how perfect competition is inconsistent with the existence of transport costs. Then, given spatial heterogeneity, a typical urban economic theory of a monocentric city is briefly sketched in a first section, while its extension with technological externalities is presented in a second section. The assumption of perfect competition is replaced by monopolistic competition with pecuniary externalities in NEG, which is described in the following section. In the penultimate section, NEG is combined with urban economics. A final section concludes the chapter.

SPATIAL IMPOSSIBILITY THEOREM

Samuelson (1952) revealed that interregional difference in the price of a good does not exceed the interregional transport cost. Stated differently, if the price difference is greater than the interregional shipping cost, trading firms would earn profits through interregional arbitrage. The spatial price equilibrium is so simple that increasing the number of goods and the number of regions does not complicate the analysis. As a result, transport costs as spatial frictions between regions have not been seriously taken into account in mainstream economic theory, particularly general equilibrium theory under perfect competition.

The importance of transport costs was recognized by Starrett (1978), who established the spatial impossibility theorem as follows: *there exists no competitive equilibrium*[1] *in the presence of transport costs when the production technology is constant or decreasing returns to scale under perfect competition.* This theorem can be understood through the following example. There are *n* locations, each of which is occupied by one of *n* individuals. There are *n* goods, which are consumed by each individual. If each individual produces a different good under indivisible production technology, then trade would take place between all of them. However, the individuals would produce all the goods by themselves in order to avoid transport costs. This constitutes the so-called backyard capitalism, which is not possible unless production by individuals is perfectly divisible. This is the reason why the spatial impossibility theorem holds: there is no competitive equilibrium in the presence of indivisibility in production together with transport costs.[2]

In the real world, people are not self-sufficient; rather, we produce a few goods and trade them in exchange for a variety of goods made in other regions. In order to describe such economic behavior, some of the existing assumptions should be altered, as will be seen in the subsequent sections. In the next section, we retain the standard assumption of perfect competition with constant returns to scale, but assume an exogenous central business district (CBD). Competitive equilibrium is ensured by heterogeneous space that is generated by the existence of a CBD, whereas it is precluded under homogeneous space. Homogeneity often yields bang-bang solutions like Bertrand's price competition. Since goods produced in the CBD are shipped to the rest of the world, the CBD also acts as a port, and hence, this is called a port city model. In the section following the next one, although we still assume perfect competition, we introduce technological externalities that do not involve market interactions in order to identify the economic activities that occur inside CBDs. Because CBDs are not predetermined, this is called a non-port city. On the other hand, in later sections we assume pecuniary externalities in transactions involving market interactions rather than technological externalities. To allow pecuniary externalities to arise, production technology is assumed to be increasing returns to scale, implying that the market is imperfectly competitive.

URBAN ECONOMICS AND TRANSPORT COST

Port city models can be traced back to the agricultural location theory pioneered by von Thünen (1826). He assumed a marketplace on a featureless plain, where various kinds of agricultural production take place according to the distance from the marketplace and the value of products per unit of land. For example, tomatoes are produced near the marketplace in order to avoid high transport costs, whereas rice is produced far away. This principle can be readily extended to manufacturing location by interpreting agricultural farms as manufacturing firms. Firms tend to locate themselves near the marketplace when the transport costs of goods and the productivity of the land are high. This is because they can avoid the high transport costs and afford the high land rent.

Port City Model

Replacing marketplace with CBD and agricultural and manufacturing land use with residential land use, Alonso (1964) established the theory of residential location, which is now a part of mainstream urban economics. In what follows, we present a simplified version of his model. Consider a linear space. It is homogeneous except for the existence of a CBD, which is approximated as a spaceless point. The remainder of the space is used for housing or agriculture. The city is small and open in that migration to and from the city is free. Since the migration equalizes the utilities between the city and the rest of the world, the number of people L in the city is endogenously determined.

Each individual has identical preferences with respect to the housing space $s(x)$ and the composite good $z(x)$, which excludes housing space, where x is the distance from the CBD. Individuals commute to the CBD and earn a fixed amount of income y.[3] That is, an individual located at x maximizes the utility

$$\max_{s(x),\, z(x),\, x} u(s(x), z(x))$$

subject to the income constraint

$$r(x)s(x) + z(x) + T(x) = y,$$

where $r(x)$ is the unit land rent, the price of the composite good is normalized to one, and $T(x)$ is the commuting cost to the CBD.[4] Computing the first-order conditions, we arrive at

$$r'(x) = -\frac{T'(x)}{s(x)}. \tag{6.1}$$

We know from Equation (6.1) that the land rent is monotonically decreasing in the distance from the CBD. We also know that by multiplying both sides of Equation (6.1) by $-s(x)$, the marginal decrease in the housing expenditure $-r'(x)s(x)$ is compensated for by the marginal increase in the commuting cost $T'(x)$ for any location x. That is, consumers are faced with a trade-off between commuting cost and land rent, that is, a trade-off between the composite good and residential space.

It is also evident from Equation (6.1) that $r'(x)$ decreases in magnitude in x, that is, the land rent is convex. This is because $T''(x)$ does not vary much across locations, whereas $s(x)$ increases in x. This implies that city residents avoid high land rent and spend more on the composite good near the CBD, while the opposite is true for suburban residents. Note that these results are obtained in a scenario with the assumption of costless relocation of residents, which guarantees equal utilities for any location in the city. This is called *intracity equilibrium*, or location equilibrium.[5]

Comparative Statics

In order to simplify the analysis, each individual is assumed to consume a fixed amount of space for housing $s(x) = \bar{s}$, and the commuting cost is assumed to be proportional to the distance $T(x) = Tx$ hereafter. Then, the total demand for residential space is given by $\bar{s}L$. Since the space is linear, the distance from the CBD to the city border is then given by $\bar{s}L/2$. Let r_a be the agricultural land rent, that is, the opportunity cost of land. Define the *bid rent* of an individual at location x as the highest price that an individual is willing to pay for housing space. Then, this is equal to the agricultural land rent at the city borders, that is, $r(\pm\bar{s}L/2) = r_a$. In this manner, land is allocated for a variety of activities through land rent.

Free migration equalizes the utility between the city and the rest of the world such that $u(\bar{s}, z(x)) = \bar{u}$, where $\bar{u}$ is the exogenous utility level in the rest of the world. This implies that

$$y - r(x)\bar{s} - Tx = z(x) = \bar{z}$$

is constant across locations. Hence, the equilibrium city size is determined as

$$L^* = \frac{2}{\bar{s}T}(y - r_a\bar{s} - \bar{z}).$$

Since the city size is inversely proportional to the unit commuting cost T, the city size is enlarged when the unit commuting cost decreases due to technological progress in the transport sector. As documented by Mills and Hamilton (1994), the progress in transport technology, particularly during the Industrial Revolution, substantially expanded the physical distance of commuting, which led to a sudden increase in city size of London, among others. Note that the technological progress in transport facilities has contributed not only to the ease of commuting but also to intercity trade. The latter impact will be examined in a later section.

The expansion of city borders due to the increase in city size agrees with the stylized fact of *suburbanization*. This can be described more precisely if the space for housing is variable, although it becomes complicated mathematically. When the unit commuting cost T decreases, while households located in the suburbs can avoid the commuting cost and rent a larger lot size for housing, there remain the same for the households located near the CBD. As a result, some households would relocate to the suburbs. Such suburbanization is often observed in large cities all over the world. So far, the lot size was assumed to be fixed. If the lot size is variable, then a negative gradient of population density with respect to distance from the CBD is expected. Furthermore, if housing is constructed not only by land, but also by capital, these production factors are substituted according to distance from the CBD. As a result, high-rise buildings, which require intensive capital, are built near the CBD in order to avoid a high land rent, whereas housing units, which require intensive land, are built in the suburbs.[6]

Relaxing some of the assumptions in the model further allows us to approximate the real cities. For example, if city residents receive different incomes, then they would be spatially segregated: low income people near the CBD with small lot size while high income people would aggregate in the suburbs in housing units with large lot size.[7] If land is not available for rent but rather for purchase and sale, and if replacing buildings is very costly, then the model yields a positive gradient of population density and urban sprawl (Harrison and Kain, 1974). Furthermore, if landowners are forward-looking, they may keep space vacant even near the CBD until time is ripe (Fujita, 1982). Although such dynamic considerations fits the reality, dynamic models are often analytically intractable. We therefore confine to static models throughout the chapter.

NON-PORT CITY AND TRANSPORT COST

Spatial externalities were hitherto absent. However, there is ample evidence of the existence of agglomeration economies that yield large cities. In this section, we focus on technological externalities between firms. For detailed explanations of the microfoundations of various agglomeration economies, see Fujita and Thisse (2002) and Duranton and Puga (2004).

Face-to-face Communication Cost

Contrary to the assumption in previous section, in reality, the CBD is spacious. There are many firms agglomerating in the CBD and paying high rent, especially in large cities. For example, consider the extremely high rent at the CBD in New York City. Firms can avoid the high rent by relocating to remote regions, which is, however, rarely done in the real world. This is evidence of the importance of being in proximity to the other firms located in the CBD, that is, technological externalities.

Firms are heterogenous in that they produce different goods and services by using different intermediate inputs. The intermediate inputs involve non-market interactions by communicating messages in addition to intermediate goods and materials. Non-market interactions include information services and knowledge transfers, which can be obtained by contacting or communicating with other firms.

Some of the information may be obtained by using telecommunication technologies, such as telephone and e-mail. However, important and informal information can be obtained only through face-to-face communications.[8] The same can be said for certain transactions between firms.

Since such contacts are invaluable and essential for firms, they necessarily locate themselves in the vicinity of other firms and form an agglomeration in the CBD. Access to other firms can be captured as the sum of the transport cost of visiting all firms:

$$\sum_{z} t(x - z)\, b(z), \qquad (6.2)$$

where $t(x - z)$ is the face-to-face communication cost of visiting other firms from locations x to z, and $b(z)$ is the distribution of firms at location z.[9] The face-to-face communication cost is the conveyance cost of information and communications, which increases with distance.

If the face-to-face communication cost is proportional to distance, firms will wish to choose the median location that minimizes the sum of the transport cost given by Equation (6.2). However, all firms cannot locate at the same location unless a towering building were constructed. It is land rent or office floor rent that plays a major role in allocating firms to different locations. It can be verified that market office rent is the highest at the median location and that it decreases according to the distance from the median location. Thus, since better access is compensated by higher rent, firms are indifferent to locations within the CBD. This is the intracity equilibrium in the CBD. In this manner, the distribution $b(x)$ of firms is endogenously determined, as depicted in Figure 6.1.

Firms in the CBD would not relocate to a remote region because of the high travel cost from a remote region to the CBD. However, what if a firm in the CBD were to relocate to a remote region? It would have to incur a high travel cost, which is considered as a private cost for the firm. There is more to it. All remaining firms in the CBD would be required to travel to the remote region solely for the purpose of communicating with the relocated firm. Although each travel cost is small for each firm, the sum is not negligible. Because the relocating firm does not take this situation into account in its

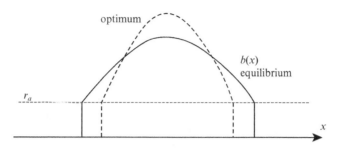

Figure 6.1   Equilibrium and optimum distributions of firms in the CBD

relocation decision, it constitutes a social cost that is borne by the remaining firms. This is a technological externality without market interactions, which leads to market failure. As a result, a market outcome does not coincide with an efficient distribution of firms. Since proximity is a positive externality, one can show that an equilibrium distribution of firms (solid curve) is more dispersed than the socially optimum one (dashed curve), as described in Figure 6.1. In order to attain a socially optimal allocation of firms, a Pigovian subsidy rather than a Pigovian tax is required so as to encourage firms to locate themselves closer to the center of the CBD.

This conclusion is contrasted to that under negative externalities, such as congestion and pollution caused by firms. In the presence of negative externalities, the opposite conclusion can be drawn: an equilibrium distribution of firms is excessively agglomerated as compared with the socially optimum one. In this case, a city government should levy a Pigovian tax on firms located near the center of the CBD. Alternatively, all commuting traffic or all emissions could be taxed while leaving location decisions up to firms.

Non-port City Model

Although the location of firms inside the CBD is analyzed in detail in the previous subsection, the residential location has not been taken into consideration. Ogawa and Fujita (1980), Imai (1982) and Fujita and Ogawa (1982) have developed general equilibrium models involving firm and residential locations, where both firms and households compete for urban land. The idea of bid rent is the same as that mentioned earlier: the agent who bids the highest rent for a plot of land occupies it in the land market. It is not a priori known as to which agents are located at the center of geographical space and how many CBDs emerge as an equilibrium outcome. That is, the locations and sizes of the CBDs are endogenously determined in the models, which is in stark contrast to Alonso's model explained above.

Firms maximize the net profits, which are defined as revenue minus land rent, the wage cost, and the face-to-face communication/transaction costs given by Equation (6.2). On the other hand, each worker maximizes their utility subject to the income constraint, as in the previous section. They choose not only where to live but also where to work. Once a residential location and a job site are chosen, commuting trips by workers are determined in the labor market.

For simplicity, assume that each firm occupies a fixed lot size and each worker consumes a fixed lot size for residence.[10] Given the distance decay face-to-face communication/

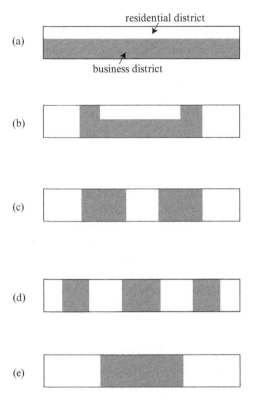

Figure 6.2   The spatial configurations in the non-port city model

transaction cost function and the linear commuting cost function, Fujita and Ogawa (1982) obtained equilibrium distributions of firms and workers as illustrated in Figure 6.2. The distributions in the figures are as follows: (a) a completely integrated configuration, (b) an incompletely integrated configuration, (c) a duocentric configuration, (d) a tricentric configuration and (e) a monocentric configuration, respectively.

These configurations are determined by the trade-off between face-to-face communication/transaction cost and commuting cost. One extreme case is (a), the completely integrated configuration. It emerges when the commuting cost is much higher than the transaction cost. This would best represent the situation of the old days, before the Industrial Revolution occurred. In these times, since there were no commuter railways and automobiles, workers had to commute by walking. In order to avoid the burden of prohibitive opportunity costs of time, they chose to live close to their workplaces.

Another extreme case is (e), the monocentric configuration, which appears when the commuting cost is much lower than the transaction cost. As this configuration is typical worldwide, it is inferred that the progress in commuting transport technology has substantially reduced the opportunity costs of commuting time. On the other hand, face-to-face transaction costs have greatly increased in recent times due to the rise in the opportunity costs of time, and hence, reflect the sky-high rent for office spaces, particularly in the CBDs of large cities.

Even more interesting are (c), the duocentric configuration and (d), the tricentric configuration, which occur with the intermediate commuting cost and the transaction cost. These polycentric configurations are generated endogenously, that is, the number and locations of business districts are not determined a priori. In (d), the tricentric configuration, the CBD is larger in size than the two peripheral business districts, and land rent has a peak in each business district. These results are precisely what we often observe in large polycentric cities.

NEW ECONOMIC GEOGRAPHY AND TRANSPORT COST

Thus far, we have been focusing on the impacts of transport costs of commuting and face-to-face communications on spatial structures of economic activities. However, we have neglected the impacts of transport costs after the production, that is, trade costs which involve shipping and shopping costs. In this section, we consider how people produce goods and trade them with others in the presence of increasing returns to scale in production. Due to the increasing returns to scale, each individual would produce only one variety in large quantities and convey it to a marketplace by incurring the transport cost, rather than being self-sufficient by producing many varieties in small quantities, which is the scenario in the backyard capitalism.

Hence, of importance is the proximity to a marketplace as well as the degree of increasing returns to scale in production. If the marketplace is far away, people would establish a new one nearby. However, if many marketplaces are created at many locations, then the number of varieties of goods available in each marketplace would be reduced. This is not desirable for consumers, who prefer a diverse range of goods. This suggests that there is a trade-off between transport costs (access to a market) and love for variety (number of goods). Economides and Siow (1988) showed that the equilibrium number of markets is determined by transport cost and love for variety and that there are too many or too few markets, depending on the degree of technological externalities. In what follows, we consider a general equilibrium model with costly trade and pecuniary externalities under monopolistic competition, where each individual produces a good, consumes varieties of goods, and chooses location to reside.

The Model and Short-run Equilibrium

NEG was established by Krugman (1980, 1991). Since Krugman's model is somewhat complicated, we describe the NEG model in Ottaviano et al. (2002) below.[11]

In this NEG model, there are farmers and manufacturing workers in the economy. Farmers can be considered as unskilled workers and manufacturing workers can be considered as skilled workers. Farmers are immobile and equally distributed across two cities $r = 1, 2$, while workers are immobile in the short-run but mobile between cities in the long-run. The masses of farmers and workers are A and L, respectively, which are sufficiently large.

There is a homogenous good and a horizontally differentiated good. The homogenous good is freely traded between cities and is chosen as the numéraire. On the other hand, transporting the differentiated good between cities requires τ units of the numéraire per unit. In NEG, τ refers to trade costs because transporting a good may involve not only distance-related costs but also distance-unrelated costs, such as tariff and non-tariff barriers. According to Anderson and van Wincoop (2004), the transport costs are less than half of the costs of barriers in international trade between industrialized countries.

The homogenous good is produced using the labor of farmers A under constant returns to scale, implying that perfect competition prevails. The differentiated good is produced using the labor of workers L under increasing returns to scale, and hence, imperfect competition prevails. The market is monopolistically competitive because the mass of workers is large and each firm produces a different variety of the good. Individual utility in city r is given by

$$U_r = \alpha \int_0^n q_r(i)\, di - \frac{\beta}{2} \int_0^n [q_r(i)]^2 di - \frac{\gamma}{2} \left[\int_0^n q_r(i)\, di \right]^2 + q_0, \qquad (6.3)$$

where n is the number of varieties, $q_r(i)$ is the quantity of variety i in city r, α, β, and γ are positive parameters, and q_0 is the quantity of the homogenous good, which is the numéraire. α expresses the intensity of preferences for the varieties, β means that consumers are biased toward a dispersed consumption of varieties, and γ implies a degree of substitutability between varieties. Individual budget constraint can be written as follows:

$$\int_0^n p_r(i)\, q_r(i)\, di + q_0 = y_r + \bar{q}_0,$$

where $p_r(i)$ is the consumer price of variety i in city r, y_r is the individual's labor income in city r, and $\bar{q}_0$ is the initial endowment of the numéraire. Solving the first-order conditions for $q_r(i)$ with the budget constraint, we have the linear demand for variety i:

$$q_r(i) = \frac{\alpha}{\beta + \gamma n} - \frac{1}{\beta} p_r(i) + \frac{\gamma}{\beta(\beta + \gamma n)} P_r, \qquad (6.4)$$

where $P_r \equiv \int_0^n p_r(i)\, di$ is the price index in city r. Because the varieties are symmetric, i is dropped hereafter.

Production technology in agriculture requires one unit of farmers A in order to produce one unit of the homogeneous good. Since this good is costlessly traded, the factor price equalization holds in this sector, that is, $w_1^A = w_2^A = 1$. Production technology in manufacturing requires φ units of workers L in order to produce any amount of a variety. Let n_r and L_r be the mass of firms and workers, respectively, in city r. Due to the increasing returns to scale in manufacturing production, n_r is also regarded as the number of varieties. Labor market clearing implies $n_r = L_r/\varphi$ so that the total mass of firms given by $n = L/\varphi$ is constant. The profits of a firm in city r are given by

$$\pi_r = p_{rr} q_r(p_{rr}) (A/2 + L_r) + (p_{rs} - \tau) q_s(p_{rs}) (A/2 + L_s) - \varphi w_r, \qquad (6.5)$$

where p_{rs} is the price quoted by a firm located in city r and selling in city s, $A/2$ is the number of farmers in each city, and w_r is the worker's wage in city r. Each firm price discriminates the two spatially separated markets under monopolistic competition. That is, each firm maximizes its profit Equation (6.5) with respect to p_{rr} and p_{rs} by neglecting its influence on the price indices P_r.[12] This yields a Nash equilibrium with a continuum of players in which prices are interdependent as follows:

$$p_{rr}^* = \frac{\alpha\beta + \gamma\tau(n - n_r)/2}{2\beta + \gamma n} \quad \text{and} \quad p_{sr}^* = p_{rr}^* + \frac{\tau}{2}. \tag{6.6}$$

This is the short-run price equilibrium in that the distribution of manufacturing firms is fixed. Observe the pro-competitive effect: the equilibrium price in city r is decreasing in the number of firms in city r. This effect is stronger when the trade cost τ is larger. The equilibrium prices given by (6) rise when the trade cost increases (large τ) and goods are bad substitutes (small γ). Note that no interregional arbitrage is profitable because the interregional price differential $\tau/2$ is less than the trade cost τ from the second equation in (6.6).

In order to guarantee a positive demand in Equation (6.4) regardless of the distribution of firms,

$$\tau < \tau_{trade} \equiv \frac{2\alpha\beta}{2\beta + \gamma n} \tag{6.7}$$

is assumed to hold. Consequently, there is intra-industry trade and reciprocal dumping.[13]

Assuming free entry of firms, the equilibrium wage w_r^* is obtained by plugging the equilibrium prices Equation (6.6) into the profit Equation (6.5) and setting it equal to zero. The demand Equation (6.4) is also obtained by plugging in prices Equation (6.6). Hence, the indirect utility V_r^* is expressed as a function of $\lambda \equiv L_1/L$ together with the parameters. It can be shown that V_1^* increases with λ for small τ and decreases with λ for large τ. The size effect can also be established, wherein the utility and wage in the larger city are always higher.

Long-run Equilibrium

Firms and workers migrate from low to high utility cities in the long-run until the utility differential disappears. An intercity equilibrium arises when no worker has a unilateral incentive to migrate from her city. Mathematically, such an equilibrium arises at $0 < \lambda^* < 1$ when the indirect utility differential is

$$\Delta V(\lambda^*) \equiv V_1 - V_2 = C\tau(\tau^* - \tau)(\lambda^* - 1/2) = 0, \tag{6.8}$$

or at $\lambda = 1$ when $\Delta V(1) \geq 0$, or at $\lambda^* = 0$ when $\Delta V(0) \leq 0$. Note that C and τ^* are positive and given by the collections of parameters except τ.

We know from Equation (6.8) that the symmetric configuration $\lambda^* = 1/2$ is always an equilibrium. In order to check its local stability, consider whether a marginal deviation of workers from the equilibrium brings the distribution of workers back to the original one. This can be examined by computing the sign of the derivative of Equation (6.8) at the symmetric equilibrium $\lambda^* = 1/2$. It is readily verified that the symmetric configuration $\lambda^* = 1/2$ is the only stable equilibrium if $\tau > \tau^*$. That is, manufacturing activities are dispersed and autarkic when the trade cost is sufficiently high.[14]

However, if the trade cost is low ($\tau < \tau^*$), then the symmetric equilibrium is unstable and workers agglomerate in one of the two cities ($\lambda^* = 0, 1$) and enjoy agglomeration benefits, such as a wide array of varieties and a high wage. Hence, the threshold τ^* is called the symmetry break point and the agglomeration sustain point. In summary, *falling trade costs leads to the agglomeration of manufacturing activities*, which is the main message of NEG. Examinations of the threshold τ^* reveal that the more likely is the agglomeration of the manufacturing activities, the stronger are the increasing returns ($d\tau^*/d\varphi > 0$) and love for variety ($d\tau^*/d\gamma < 0$).

Changes in the size of a city λ affect the indirect utilities through wages and price indices. These can be decomposed into the supply linkage (forward linkage), the demand linkage (backward linkage), and the competition effect. The supply linkage is the effect of market size on price indices, taking wages as given. Since the price indices decrease in the market size, a large city is preferable for consumers. Therefore, the supply linkage acts as an agglomeration force for workers. On the other hand, the demand linkage and the competition effect are the effects of market size on wages, taking price indices as given. The former is an agglomeration force for firms because the demand and profits increase with the expansion of market size. However, the latter is a dispersion force for firms because increases in market size implies more firms with keener price competition.

In sum, the spatial distribution of manufacturing activities is determined by the two agglomeration forces and the dispersion force. It can be verified that the agglomeration forces dominate the dispersion force when the trade cost τ is small, the fixed cost φ is large, the share of manufacturing labor L/A is large, and/or goods are sufficiently differentiated. In this case, higher profits/wages and lower price indices would attract more firms and workers, thus generating circular causation among locational decisions and fostering the agglomeration of manufacturing activities. It should be noted that falling trade costs due to technological progress in transport facilities does not necessarily lead to the agglomeration of firms if space for housing is taken into account, as will be seen in the next section.

Before doing so, it is of interest to compare NEG in this section with Hotelling's (1929) spatial competition. Spatial competition considers the consumption side of transport costs, rather than the production side of transporting costs. That is, spatial competition focuses on transport costs of shopping, while putting transport costs of intermediate goods, information exchange and commuting aside.

A typical model of spatial competition is as follows.[15] Consumers are uniformly distributed over a line segment, do not change their residence, and go shopping at a retail firm. Given the consumers' behavior, retail firms maximize their profits by choosing locations and prices of goods strategically. This is oligopolistic competition, whereas NEG deals with monopolistic competition. When consumers' preference for differentiated goods is represented by logit, de Palma et al. (1985) showed that firms agglomerate at the center of the line segment when the transport cost for shopping is small and/or goods are sufficiently differentiated between firms. It is worth noting that the centripetal and centrifugal forces at work in NEG are also found in spatial competition: the former force is the market access, which is the strongest at the center; and the latter is the price competition, which is related to the distances to other retail firms. Hence, we confirm that the transport cost as a distance friction is a significant factor of location decisions by economic agents in a broad spectrum of economic models.

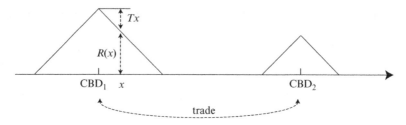

Figure 6.3   A model of NEG combined with urban economics

URBAN ECONOMICS AND NEW ECONOMIC GEOGRAPHY

Urban economics as elaborated at the beginning of this chapter considers only one city and focuses on the spatial structure within the one city. On the other hand, NEG as elaborated in the previous section takes multiple cities into account but neglects the spatial structures by confining cities to spaceless points. It would be worthwhile to combine the basic ingredients from urban economics and NEG by considering multiple cities with the spatial structures.

Following Section 7 in Ottaviano et al. (2002), assume two cities in a one-dimensional space, as illustrated in Figure 6.3. Each worker living at distance x from the CBD$_r$ in city r consumes one unit of land by paying the land rent and commutes to the CBD$_r$, which is approximated as a point. Manufacturing production in the CBD$_r$ and intercity trade is carried out in exactly the same as that in the NEG model described above. The agricultural good is produced in the suburbs of the cities.

The commuting cost is assumed to be linear in distance as before, that is, $T(x) = Tx$. Because each lot size is one, $L_r/2$ workers reside to the left and right of the CBD$_r$ uniformly. Because all workers reach the same utility level within each city in equilibrium, the land rent at distance x from the CBD$_r$ is given by

$$r^*(x) = T(L_r/2 - x),$$

where the opportunity cost of land r_a is normalized to zero. When the land rent goes to absentee landlords, the commuting cost plus land rent at any location in city r is given by $TL_r/2$ irrespective of location x. The utility differential is then redefined as

$$\Delta V_\theta(\lambda^*) \equiv \Delta V(\lambda^*) - TL(\lambda - 1/2).$$

Checking the stability as previously, one can show that there exist two thresholds of τ and that as trade costs continue decreasing, firms are first dispersed, then agglomerated and finally re-dispersed.[16]

The initial and final dispersions are due to different reasons. In the former, firms are dispersed in order to reduce the high trade cost to immobile farmers. In the latter, workers are dispersed in order to alleviate the high commuting cost and land rent. Thus, the agglomeration force is the strongest when the trade cost is intermediate. That is, there is a U-shaped relationship between the degree of agglomeration and the trade costs. This implies that spatial inequality in terms of nominal income is also U-shaped as shown in the chapter by Lafourcade and Thisse (this volume).

Finally, it should be noted that the urban structure may be different from re-dispersion in the last stage of development if the number and location of CBDs are not predetermined. We have seen above that the urban structure is monocentric when the commuting cost T is high relative to the face-to-face communication cost t, whereas it is polycentric when T is smaller than t. We have also seen that intercity configuration is agglomeration when the commuting cost T and the intercity trade cost τ are high. Considering this interplay between trade cost, commuting cost, and communication cost, Cavailhes et al. (2007) have shown that a high commuting cost yields dispersion to *polycentric cities*, where a large CBD and small subcenters are endogenously created.[17]

Despite many advantages accruing from the agglomeration of firms in CBDs, firms may choose to form edge cities or employment subcenters, which are concentrations of business, shopping, and entertainment in the suburbs. They are often observed in large cities where the commuting cost and land rent become sufficiently large. Although agglomeration benefits are not large in edge cities, workers do not have to pay high commuting costs and land rent.[18] In fact, in recent years, polycentric cities and edge cities are increasing in many countries (Garreau, 1991; MacMillen and Smith, 2003).

CONCLUDING REMARKS

Some of the stylized facts of urban economies can be explained by the trade-offs between commuting cost, face-to-face communication cost, and intercity trade cost. Alonso's (1964) urban economics discussed at the beginning of this chapter shows that the presence of the commuting cost leads to the negative gradients of rent and population density and the suburbanization of households. Fujita and Ogawa's (1982) non-port city model with technological externalities described after exhibits polycentricity in large cities by introducing the face-to-face communication/transaction cost. Krugman's (1991) NEG with pecuniary externalities presented in this chapter explains the urbanization and agglomeration of economic activities in recent years due to the decrease in the intercity trade cost. The combined model of urban economics and NEG also yields polycentric cities together with agglomeration. Thus, distance is a significant factor in economic theory as well as in the real world, despite all the developments in transport technologies.

The main message of NEG is the agglomeration of manufacturing activities due to falling transport costs. However, things do not seem to be quite that simple. We have seen that the effect of transport improvements on the concentration of economic activities is U-shaped in the presence of commuting cost and land rent. Such a U-shape is also analytically obtained by introducing somewhat different assumptions. Among others, it is obtained by Puga (1999), who assumes land for agriculture, by Tabuchi and Thisse (2002), who assume heterogeneous taste for regions, and by Picard and Zeng (2005), who assume agricultural transport costs. More comprehensive studies on the effect of transport developments on the agglomeration of economic activities are called for.

ACKNOWLEDGEMENT

I thank André de Palma and Robin Lindsey for helpful comments and suggestions.

NOTES

1. Competitive equilibrium is the existence of a price vector such that supply equals demand for each good and each individual maximizes its profit or utility.
2. See Chapter 2 in Fujita and Thisse (2002) for more general frameworks of the spatial impossibility theorem.
3. See Mills (1967) for the case wherein production with capital and labor in the CBD is explicitly taken into account.
4. The commuting cost $T(x)$ does not involve the congestion costs of car commuting during rush hour traffic. In order to ease congestion, a large share of land should be allocated near the CBD for roads (Solow and Vickrey, 1971), or congestion tolls should be levied (De Lara et al., 2008).
5. Since there is no externality in this model, the equilibrium is always efficient. See Kanemoto (1987) for urban economic models involving technological externalities.
6. See Wheaton (1974) for more details on a comparative static analysis of the spatial structure of a city.
7. This result may be upset when opportunity costs of commuting time are involved. If the income elasticity of value of commuting time exceeds that of demand for lot size, then high income people would reside near the CBD.
8. Information technologies are considered to be substitutes for face-to-face communications. However, they may be complements when telephone and e-mail are used for arranging face-to-face contacts (Gaspar and Glaeser, 1998).
9. There is a series of papers on modeling face-to-face contacts between firms, such as Beckmann (1976), Borukhov and Hochman (1977), Tabuchi (1986), Tauchen and Witte (1984) and Vaughan (1975).
10. Relaxing the assumptions on lot size, Lucas and Rossi-Hansberg (2002) obtained somewhat more generalized results.
11. See the chapter by Lafourcade and Thisse for more details on the basic framework of NEG. For various NEG models, see Baldwin et al. (2003).
12. That is why we consider a continuum of firms/varieties Equation (6.3).
13. If Equation (6.7) does not hold, there is inter-industry trade (one-way trade of manufacturing good) or autarky.
14. Multinational firms could build a plant in each region in order to circumvent a high transport cost if the cost of building plants is small (Markusen, 2002).
15. See Anderson et al. (1992) for various models of spatial competition.
16. This is also demonstrated by Tabuchi (1998). Helpman (1998) demonstrated that falling trade costs yields the dispersion of firms.
17. Polycentric cities are also modeled by Henderson and Mitra (1996) as edge cities whose locations are strategically determined by a city developer.
18. Another possibility is telecommuting, which is a displacement of the daily commute to the workplace by telecommunication links, such as videotelephony and e-mail systems, at home. However, the existing small share of telecommuting workers is a consequence of the current technological limitations of information and telecommunications.

REFERENCES

Alonso, W., 1964, *Location and Land Use*. Cambridge, MA: Harvard University Press.
Anderson, J.E. and E. van Wincoop, 2004, Trade costs. *Journal of Economic Literature*, **42**, 691–751.
Anderson, S.P., A. de Palma and J.-F. Thisse, 1992, *Discrete Choice Theory of Product Differentiation*. Cambridge, MA: MIT Press.
Bairoch, P., 1988, *Cities and Economic Development: From the Dawn of History to the Present*. Chicago: University of Chicago Press.
Baldwin, R.E., R. Forslid, Ph. Martin, G.I.P. Ottaviano and F. Robert-Nicoud, 2003, *Economic Geography and Public Policy*. Princeton, NJ: Princeton University Press.

Beckmann, M.J., 1976, Spatial equilibrium in the dispersed city. In G.J. Papageorgiou, ed., *Mathematical Land Use Theory*. Lanham, MD: Lexington Books.
Borukhov, E. and O. Hochman, 1977, Optimum and market equilibrium in a model of a city without a predetermined center. *Environment and Planning A*, **9**, 849–856.
Cavailhes, J., C. Gaigne, T. Tabuchi and J.-F. Thisse, 2007, Trade and the structure of cities. *Journal of Urban Economics*, **62** (3), 383–404.
Cronon, W., 1991, *Nature's Metropolis: Chicago and the Great West*. New York: Norton.
De Lara, M., A. de Palma, M. Kilani and S. Piperno, 2008, Congestion pricing and long term urban form: application to Île-de-France. Mimeo.
de Palma, A., V. Ginsburgh, Y.Y. Papageorgiou and J.-F. Thisse, 1985, The principle of minimum differentiation holds under sufficient heterogeneity. *Econometrica*, **53**, 767–781.
Duranton, G. and D. Puga, 2004, Micro-foundations of urban agglomeration economies. In J.V. Henderson and J. F. Thisse, eds, *Handbook of Regional and Urban Economics*, Volume 4. Amsterdam: Elsevier, pp. 2063–2117.
Economides, N. and A. Siow, 1988, The division of markets is limited by the extent of liquidity (spatial competition with externalities). *American Economic Review*, **78**, 108–121.
Fujita, M., 1982, Spatial patterns of residential development. *Journal of Urban Economics*, **12**, 22–52.
Fujita, M. and H. Ogawa, 1982, Multiple equilibria and structural transition of non-monocentric urban configurations. *Regional Science and Urban Economics*, **12**, 161–196.
Fujita, M. and J.-F. Thisse, 2002, *Economics of Agglomeration*. Cambridge: Cambridge University Press.
Garreau, J., 1991, *Edge City: Life on the New Frontier*. New York: Doubleday.
Gaspar, J. and E.L. Glaeser, 1998, Information technology and the future of cities. *Journal of Urban Economics*, **43**, 136–156.
Harrison, D. and J.F. Kain, 1974, Cumulative urban growth and urban density functions. *Journal of Urban Economics*, **1**, 61–98.
Helpman, E., 1998, The size of regions. In D. Pines, E. Sadka and I. Zilcha, eds, *Topics in Public Economics. Theoretical and Applied Analysis*. Cambridge: Cambridge University Press, pp. 33–54.
Henderson, V. and A. Mitra, 1996, The new urban landscape: developers and edge cities. *Regional Science and Urban Economics*, **26**, 613–643.
Hotelling, H., 1929, Stability in competition. *Economic Journal*, **39**, 41–57.
Imai, H., 1982, CBD hypothesis and economies of agglomeration. *Journal of Economic Theory*, **28**, 275–299.
Kanemoto, Y., 1987, Externalities in space. In J.J. Gabszewicz and J.F. Thisse, eds, *Fundamentals of Pure and Applied Economics*, **11**. Oxford: Harwood, pp. 43–103.
Kawabata, M., 2002, Access to jobs: transportation barriers faced by low-skilled autoless workers in US metropolitan areas. PhD Dissertation, Department of Urban Studies and Planning, Massachusetts Institute of Technology.
Kawabata, M. and A. Takahashi, 2005, Spatial dimensions of job accessibility by commuting time and mode in the Tokyo metropolitan area. *GIS—Riron to Ōyō*, **13**, 139–148.
Krugman, P., 1980, Scale economies, product differentiation and the pattern of trade. *American Economic Review*, **70**, 950–959.
Krugman, P., 1991, Increasing returns and economic geography. *Journal of Political Economy*, **99**, 483–499.
Lucas, R.E. and E. Rossi-Hansberg, 2002, On the internal structure of cities. *Econometrica*, **70**, 1445–1476.
MacMillen, D.P. and S.C. Smith, 2003, The number of subcenters in large urban areas. *Journal of Urban Economics*, **53**, 321–338.
Markusen, J.R., 2002, *Multinational Firms and the Theory of International Trade*. Cambridge, MA: MIT Press.
Mills, E.S., 1967, An aggregative model of resource allocation in a metropolitan area. *American Economic Review*, **57**, 197–210.
Mills, E.S. and B.W. Hamilton, 1994, *Urban Economics*, Fifth Edition. New York: Harper Collins.
Ogawa, H. and M. Fujita, 1980, Equilibrium land use patterns in a nonmonocentric city. *Journal of Regional Science*, **20**, 455–475.
Ottaviano, G.I.P., T. Tabuchi and J.-F. Thisse, 2002, Agglomeration and trade revisited. *International Economic Review*, **43**, 409–436.
Picard, P. and D.-Z. Zeng, 2005, Agricultural sector and industrial agglomeration. *Journal of Development Economics*, **77**, 75–106.
Puga, D., 1999, The rise and fall of regional inequalities. *European Economic Review*, **43**, 303–334.
Samuelson, P., 1952, Spatial price equilibrium and linear programming. *American Economic Review*, **42**, 283–303.
Scitovsky, T., 1954, Two concepts of external economies. *Journal of Political Economy*, **62**, 143–151.
Solow, R.M. and W.S. Vickrey, 1971, Land use in a long narrow city. *Journal of Economic Theory*, **3**, 430–447.
Starrett, D.A., 1978, Market allocations of location choice in a model with free mobility. *Journal of Economic Theory*, **17**, 21–37.

Tabuchi, T., 1986, Urban agglomeration economies in a linear city. *Regional Science and Urban Economics*, **16**, 421–436.

Tabuchi, T., 1998, Urban agglomeration and dispersion: a synthesis of Alonso and Krugman. *Journal of Urban Economics*, **44**, 333–351.

Tabuchi, T. and J.-F. Thisse, 2002, Taste heterogeneity, labor mobility and economic geography. *Journal of Development Economics*, **69**, 155–177.

Tauchen, H. and A.D. Witte, 1984, Socially optimal and equilibrium distributions of office activity: models with exogenous and endogenous contacts. *Journal of Urban Economics*, **15**, 66–86.

United Nations, 2007, *World Urbanization Prospect*. Available at http://esa.un.org/unup/.

Vaughan, R.J., 1975, 'Optimum' distribution of population within a linear city. *Transportation Research*, **9**, 25–29.

von Thünen, J.H., 1826, *Der Isolierte Staat in Beziehung auf Landwirtschaft und Nationalökonomie*. Hamburg: Perthes. English translation: *The Isolated State*. Oxford: Pergamon Press, 1966.

Wheaton, W.C., 1974, A comparative static analysis of urban spatial structure. *Journal of Economic Theory*, **9**, 223–237.

PART II

THE DEMAND FOR
TRANSPORT

7 Valuation of travel time savings
David A. Hensher

INTRODUCTION

The interest in valuing travel time savings (VTTS) continues unabated with a huge and growing theoretical and empirical literature. Time savings is still the most important user benefit in transportation studies in all of its manifestations. This includes trip time variability (or reliability), the heterogeneity of trip time such as free flow, slowed down and stop/start/crawl time for road-based modes; and walk, wait, transfer and in-vehicle standing/sitting time for public transport. In addition, many potential user benefits are correlates of travel time such as safety, ride quality and toll road payment mechanism, and can be expressed as equivalent VTTS in applications that use a generalized cost expression to evaluate the demand for competing options.

In this chapter, we focus on theory and application. The chapter begins with an overview of the major theoretical and empirical themes including the broad distinction between utility maximization and productivity theoretic frameworks, empirical paradigms that have evolved to value time savings, especially the progress in how revealed (or market) preference and stated choice (SC) data is being used to estimate models to calculate VTTS; adjustments required in behavioral VTTS to obtain resource and equity values for economic evaluation; and the growth in VTTS over time. Given the presence of preference heterogeneity for attributes that are traded to establish estimates of VTTS across a sampled population, we draw on mixed logit models and stated choice methods (for example, optimal designs) that have now become the state of the art (and to some extent practice) in deriving estimates of VTTS (mean and standard deviation) within the utility maximizing framework. We present existing empirical evidence to illustrate the range of useful empirical measures for components of travel time in passenger and freight contexts, some of which are handled using the Hensher formula which combines information from the marginal productivity and utility maximization settings.

THEORETICAL FRAMEWORKS

The development of empirical measures of VTTS is a derivative of theoretical anteced-ents in economics which recognize that the consumption of time and the time budget constraint play an important role in determining the amount of time that an individual allocates to specific activities, and how this time is traded with other resources to estab-lish a willingness to pay for heterogeneous units of time. The literature offers two theo-retical perspectives on VTTS – one associated with the behavioral rule that agents act as if they are utility maximizers, and the productivity model that suggests that the valua-tion of time savings is the sum of the opportunity cost of time and the relative marginal disutility of spending time in one activity compared to another activity. The opportunity cost is typically the expenses outlaid for which there is no financial return.

Strictly speaking, it is not possible to save time literally, but time can be reallocated. Reducing time spent in one activity enables that time to be put to other uses. There are theoretical links between wage rates and the VTTS, although this relationship has become less clear as models of consumer behavior and time allocation have become more sophisticated. A simple neoclassical model portrays the household's income–leisure trade-off in which leisure time must be sacrificed in order to work to generate income. The wages received are compensation for the loss of time. In a simple model where people are free to choose the number of hours worked, and ignoring any disutility of work, the wage rate would be a measure of the marginal value of time savings, whether spent working to increase income or retained as leisure.

But the world is not so simple. People do not necessarily control their hours of work, in which case the value of time savings could be above or below the wage (Moses and Williamson, 1963). There is disutility associated with (at least) the last increments of hours worked, therefore the wage is not just compensation for time sacrificed (for example, Johnson, 1966; Oort, 1969). More general formulations of the value of time savings recognize that time is an intimate part of consumption activity, along with money budget constraints (Becker, 1956; Evans, 1972) with constraints on the amounts of time required for various activities and on the ability to substitute time from one activity to another; that affect the marginal value of time saved (for example, Bruzelius, 1979; De Donnea, 1972; De Serpa, 1971, 1973; Jara Diaz, 2007; Train and McFadden, 1978; Truong and Hensher, 1985).

The net result is that theory provides us with warnings that simple relationships between wage rates and values of time savings are incomplete, and guidance for the type of constraints or relationships to look for in setting up empirical investigations of VTTS. But ultimately, determining a representative VTTS is a matter of empirical study rather than by derivation from theoretical principles alone.

Travel Time as a Commodity

The realization that time is a scarce resource which affects the demand for market goods and services, just like the allocation of scarce money resources, suggests that time is an important input in consumption activities. It is also a factor in production activity (that is, work). The use of time in 'non-productive' activities thus involves an opportunity cost that must be valued. Theories of time allocation form a natural framework within which to derive a theoretical measure of VTTS. Key ideas are presented below with more detail in many sources, especially recent contributions by Jara Diaz (1998, 2000, 2007).

Time can be viewed as a commodity because it can generate utility directly to the individual when 'consumed' in specific activities. But at the same time, it also acts as a *means for the consumption* of market goods and services, just as money is a means for the purchasing (and hence consumption) of these goods and services. In its role as a commodity, time in a specific activity i is not the same commodity as time in another activity j. Consider the following model in Equation (7.1) after DeSerpa (1971). The individual's utility function can be expressed as:

$$U = U(x_1, T_1; x_2, T_2, \ldots, x_n, T_n) \tag{7.1}$$

where $\{T_1, \ldots, T_n\}$ is the time spent in activities 1 to n, and $\{x_1, \ldots, x_n\}$ is market goods and services consumed jointly with time in the activities. 'Commodities' denote market goods and/or services and/or time inputs into activities, the latter defined in terms of inputs rather than 'output'. In its role as a means for the consumption of goods and services x_i's, time is subjected to a resource constraint:

$$\sum_{i=1}^{n} T_i \leq T_0 \tag{7.2}$$

Similarly, the means for purchasing the x_i's are also subject to a resource constraint:

$$\sum_{i=1}^{n} p_i x_i \leq M \tag{7.3}$$

Time consumption in many activities is not entirely a matter of an individual's own free will. So in addition to the time-resource constraint (7.2), there are time consumption constraints:

$$T_i \geq a_i x_i; i = 1, \ldots, n \tag{7.4}$$

These constraints include technological and institutional constraints. Examples of technological constraints are the available set of transport modes that have limits on the combinations of travel times and costs that can be offered. An example of an institutional constraint is the legal speed limit.

This model has the following characteristics. The level of utility is dependent on the consumption of all goods and on the time assigned to all activities including work, unlike Becker (1965); see also Evans (1972). There are time and income constraints, and the latter includes a variable work time that generates income through a wage rate; there are exogenous minimum time restrictions for travel and fixed work, and endogenous ones for all the other activities, that depend on goods consumption.

To establish the trade-off between time and price, we have to define the consumer's optimization problem as that of maximizing utility subject to the time and money resource constraints and the time consumption limit, as follows:

$$L = U(X, T) + \mu \left(T^\circ - \sum_i T_i \right) + \lambda \left(M - \sum_i p_i x_i \right) + \sum_i \kappa_i (T_i - a_i x_i) \tag{7.5}$$

We use a standard technique referred to as Lagrange multiplier where L is the Lagrangian and μ, λ and κ_i are Lagrange multipliers. Equation (7.5) specifies the objective function and the set of three budget and time consumption constraints. The theoretical interpretation of the Lagrange multipliers within the framework of non-linear programming, establishes that they correspond to the variation of the objective function evaluated at the optimum due to a marginal relaxation of the corresponding restriction. This way, the multiplier μ associated with the time restriction is the marginal utility of time representing by how much utility would increase if individual time available was increased by one unit. Equivalently, λ is the marginal utility of income and κ_i is the marginal utility of saving time in the ith activity.

The first order conditions for maximum utility are required to establish the marginal rate of substitution between time and money, noting that $\partial U/\partial z$ is the marginal utility of attribute z:

$$\frac{\partial U}{\partial x_i} = \lambda p_i + \kappa_i a_i$$

$$\frac{\partial U}{\partial T_i} = \mu - \kappa_i$$

$$\frac{\partial U}{\partial M} = \lambda$$

$$\kappa_i(T_i - a_i x_i) = 0 \tag{7.6}$$

To derive the value of travel time savings we divide the second condition by the third condition:

$$\frac{\partial U/\partial T_i}{\partial U/\partial M} = \frac{\mu - \kappa_i}{\lambda} \tag{7.7}$$

From the interpretation of the multipliers, three concepts of time value were defined by DeSerpa (1971): the value of time as a resource for the individual (μ/λ); the value of saving time in the ith activity (κ_i/λ); and the value of assigning time to the ith activity (($\partial U/\partial T_i)/\lambda$). The last two definitions are activity specific, while the first is not. Also, the value of assigning time to an activity is the money value of the direct marginal utility. Beyond these definitions, one can add the marginal price of assigning time to an activity which, in the case of work, would correspond to minus the marginal wage (Gronau, 1986). The value of saving time in the ith activity will be zero if the individual *voluntarily* assigns to it more time than the required minimum (which is how DeSerpa defined a leisure activity).[1] It will be positive otherwise. This means that the individual will be willing to pay to reduce the time assigned to a certain activity only if he is constrained to assign more time to it than desired.

To establish a relation between the different concepts of time value, the first order conditions above can be manipulated to obtain a result originally established by Oort (1969).

$$\frac{\kappa_i}{\lambda} = \frac{\mu}{\lambda} - \frac{\partial U/\partial T_i}{\lambda} = w + \frac{\partial U/\partial T_w}{\lambda} - \frac{\partial U/\partial T_i}{\lambda} \tag{7.8}$$

This expression shows that the value of saving time in the ith activity is equal to the value of doing something else minus the value of assigning time to that particular activity because it is being reduced. Equation (7.8) improves over Becker (1965), for whom time was valued at the wage rate, and over Johnson (1966), for whom the value of time was μ/λ. For those activities that are assigned more time than the minimum required ($\kappa_i = 0$, a leisure activity), the value of assigning time $(\partial U/\partial T_i)/\lambda$ is equal to μ/λ for all of them. This is the reason why DeSerpa called it the value of leisure. On the other hand, μ/λ is also equal to the total value of work, which has two components: the money reward (the wage rate) and the value of its marginal utility. Therefore, the value of saving time in a constrained activity is equal to the value of leisure (or work) minus its marginal utility value (presumably negative). Jara-Diaz (2000, 2008) presents the details.

If we consider the particular case of travel, it can be shown that the value of saving travel time, κ_i/λ, corresponds exactly to the ratio between the marginal utilities of time and cost that are estimated as part of the modal utility in a discrete travel choice model. This has been shown in different forms by various authors (Bates, 1987, after Truong and Hensher, 1985; Jara-Díaz 1998, 2007). Although empirical values for κ_i/λ can be estimated using the discrete travel choice framework, so far no methodology has been developed to estimate the different elements in Equation (7.8) from a model system. The only antecedent is Truong and Hensher's (1985) effort at obtaining μ/λ as part of the coefficient of travel time in mode choice models (which they claim was $\mu/\lambda - \kappa_i/\lambda$), which prompted Bates' (1987) identification of that coefficient as κ_i/λ only.

The Production Cost Approach

Hensher (1977) suggested an alternative (but related) approach to deriving the value of travel time savings for work-related travel than that commonly used for non-business travel activity, and applied it initially in the context of domestic and international air travel. The approach recognizes a number of components of opportunity cost and relative disutility. Traditionally, an alternative to the behavioural approach to travel time savings valuation in the work-travel context was the adoption of marginal productivity theory which states that an employer can be expected to employ labor up to the point at which the marginal costs of employment equate with the marginal value of production. The value of working travel time savings is then estimated as equal to the gross wage rate (including on-costs to the employer such as workers compensation tax, leave loadings, sick leave pay and superannuation contributions), plus a marginal wage increment to allow for any savings in overheads associated with a worker travelling in contrast to spending the equivalent time in the office. This traditional approach makes questionable assumptions about the transfer of travel time to other purposes, it neglects possible productive use of in-travel time (particularly at the marginal rate), and ignores the utility to the worker of time spent at work compared to travelling.

Hensher extended the productivity model as four main elements: a productivity effect, a relative disutility cost, a loss of leisure time and any compensation transfer between employer and worker. These components are combined into the following formula, known as the *Hensher formula*:

$$\text{VTTS} = (1 - r - pq)*MP + \frac{1-r}{1-t}*VW + \frac{r}{1-t}*VL + MPF \qquad (7.9)$$

where

r	=	proportion of travel time saved which is used for leisure
p	=	proportion of travel time saved at the expense of work done while travelling

q	$=$	relative productivity of work done while travelling compared with the equivalent time in the office
MP	$=$	the marginal product of labor
VL	$=$	the value to the worker of leisure relative to travel time
VW	$=$	the value to the worker of work time while in the office relative to travel time
MPF	$=$	the value of extra output generated due to reduced fatigue
t	$=$	worker's personal tax rate, the inflation of rVL and $(1 - r)VW$ reflecting compensation. An employer has to compensate a worker for travel, in terms of travel time savings rather than increased income, to allow for the fact that increases in the worker's utility are not subject to tax.

VL is the traditional behavioral VTTS associated with trading travel time with leisure (that is, non-work) time, obtained from Equation (7.11) below. The traditional category of business/commercial car travel is usually reserved for 'travel as part of work'. However a significant amount of work-related travel involves activities such as driving to the airport or to a client's office and being in a plane. Since a high percentage of the travel time associated with the latter activity occurs outside of *normal* working hours (that is, the person would not be travelling at this time during the normal period of work expected by the employer), there is a leisure time trade-off being made. The value of travel time savings in some work-related circumstances thus can be expected to be lower than the average gross wage rate, reflecting the mix of both employer time and non-work time.

The approach has been applied in many studies in Sweden, Norway, the Netherlands and the UK and is the preferred and accepted (official) method. The dominating components of Equation (7.9) are $(1 - r)MP$, rVL and $(1 - r)VW$. It is common in many applications to not differentiate the value of travel time savings to the employee by whether the time saved would be spent at work or on leisure, thus implicitly assuming that the private VTTS (VP) is the same in both cases, or that VW equals VL. Data on the other components such as p are also typically not available (with q set equal to 1.0 and the influence of t and MPF assumed to be negligible[2]), reducing the empirical formula to (7.10).

$$VBTT = (1 - r)MP + r\,VP \tag{7.10}$$

The UK Department of Transport Value of Time study revisited the problem in 1981 (Lowe, 1982), giving an equation similar to Equation (7.10). There was an added complexity in the form of the marginal wage increment, which was added to the gross wage rate to give what Equation (7.10) has as MP. This would be particularly relevant in times of full employment, where overtime working was endemic and the only way to get further hours of labour was to lengthen overtime working at premium payments. Given the other uncertainties, this complexity is probably one too many.

In applying this formula to business air travel, Hensher (1977) concluded that the value to the employer of saving an hour of travelling time is less than the full wage rate, and typically around 70 per cent of the average gross wage rate. Unpublished studies undertaken by the Hague Consulting Group in 1994 in the Netherlands, the UK and Sweden, using Hensher's formula provide supporting evidence for business values of travel time savings being significantly less than the gross wage rate. Overall, the value to the employer of savings in car travel times in the UK are approximately 50 per cent of the average gross wage rate, 61 per cent in the Netherlands and 32 per cent in Sweden. The lower Swedish value is attributable to greater productivity in the car (especially due to high growth in mobile phones). MVA et al. (1987) also apply the Hensher formula to business trips in the UK.

IDENTIFYING THE EMPIRICAL ELEMENTS OF THE VALUE OF TRAVEL TIME SAVINGS

The theoretical notion of the value of travel time savings has been shown to have two components: an opportunity cost component reflecting the economic value of the resources associated with the 'consumption' of time (referred to as the shadow price of time), and a relative (dis)utility component reflecting the alternative circumstances under which a unit of time is 'consumed'. For example, 20 minutes spent waiting at an airport engenders greater disutility to a traveller than 20 minutes in a plane or a car. The amount of time resource is the same and hence the opportunity cost is equivalent. This important distinction, linked back to the theoretical model has been translated into an appropriate empirical model of consumer (or traveller) behavior choice by Truong and Hensher (1985) and Bates (1987) of the form in (7.8).

$$V_i = \alpha_i - \lambda C_i - \kappa_i T_i \tag{7.11}$$

where V_i represents the (indirect) utility expression associated with mode i, α_i is a constant measuring the average influence of the unobserved influences on choice of mode i, C_i is the monetary cost of using mode i, and T_i is the travel time associated with mode *i*. Importantly the parameter λ associated with money cost is independent of mode *i*; in contrast the parameter κ_i associated with travel time is dependent on the particular mode. The latter reflects the different circumstances under which travel time is consumed in the use of each mode (for example, train versus plane versus car). The VTTS is given by κ_i/λ. If the shadow price of time (time being a scarce resource) and its actual value in a specific activity are the same, then κ_i/λ equals μ/λ. That is, the relative disutility of travel time is zero.

The important implication of this derivation of an empirical indirect utility expression (7.11) from economic theory as applied in a mode choice context is that it is not possible to identify the resource value of travel time unless we can assume that the relative disutility associated with spending time on alternative modes of transport is zero. What we can measure is the *value of transferring time* from activity *i* to some non-travel activity (as originally suggested by Truong and Hensher, 1985). To be able to separate out the resource price of time from the value of saving time, we would need to know a priori the resource price of time. Treating the differences in mode-specific values of transferring time (due to different parameter estimates for each mode) as zero (that is, by constraining the parameters to be identical across the modes) is not a mechanism for obtaining a resource value. This is only possible by imposing the strong assumption that the marginal (dis)utility of time spent travelling is zero, in contrast to it being constant for all modal alternatives.

The value of travel time savings presented above is strictly a behavioral value, derived from a trade-off of the relative importance of time and money to a representative

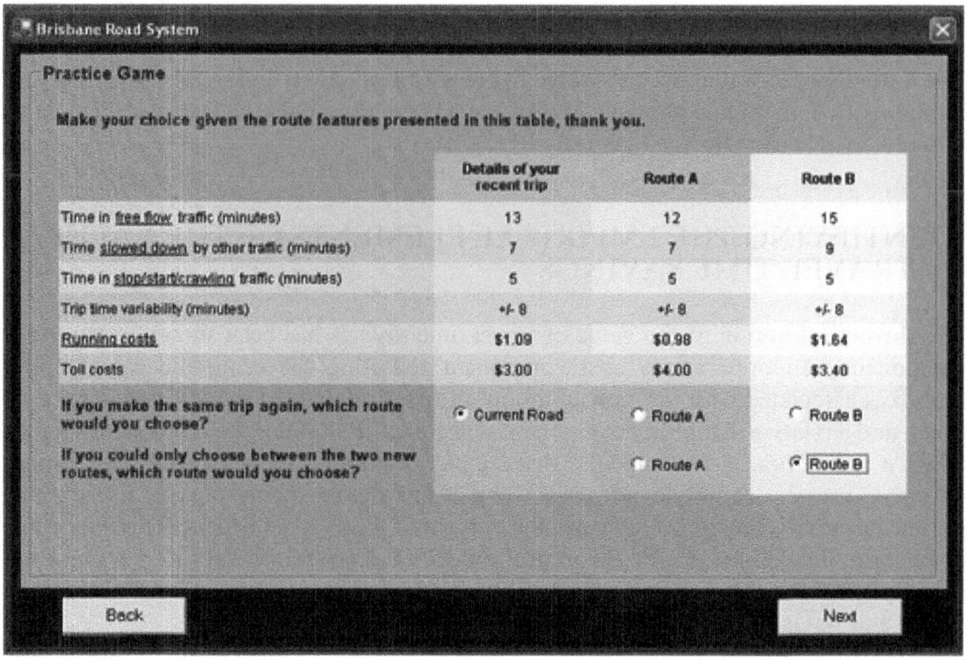

	Details of your recent trip	Route A	Route B
Time in free flow traffic (minutes)	13	12	15
Time slowed down by other traffic (minutes)	7	7	9
Time in stop/start/crawling traffic (minutes)	5	5	5
Trip time variability (minutes)	+/- 8	+/- 8	+/- 8
Running costs	$1.09	$0.98	$1.64
Toll costs	$3.00	$4.00	$3.40
If you make the same trip again, which route would you choose?	⦿ Current Road	○ Route A	○ Route B
If you could only choose between the two new routes, which route would you choose?		○ Route A	⦿ Route B

Figure 7.1   Stated choice screen

individual in a pre-defined market segment (for example, intercity business or non-business travelers). We can quantify λ and κ_i by collecting data from a sample of passenger activities of the components of travel time and cost associated with competing modes for a specific trip. By observing the mode that is chosen, which reveals a preference for a particular mode, we can estimate a travel choice model (such as a mixed logit model, see below) and hence derive the behavioral VTTS.

Alternatively we can design a stated choice experiment in which we offer different levels of a set of attributes associated with each available alternative (which can include modes and fare classes) and seek the sampled respondent's stated choice (or preference ranking). We can vary the levels of the attributes and repeat the empirical inquiry to reveal the preferences of individual for various combinations of levels of attributes. The use of stated choice (or stated preference (SP)) methods is increasingly popular in valuation studies because of the ability to study in more detail the trade-offs being made by individuals over a larger set of attribute mixes than is typically observed in real markets. Hensher et al. 1999, Louviere et al. (2000), Hensher et al. (2005) and Rose and Bliemer (2007) provide details of these methods which are used in most of the empirical studies reported below. An illustrative stated choice screen is shown in Figure 7.1 (above).

Adjusting Behavioral Values For Non-resource And Equity Impacts

To obtain values of the cost to society of time resources consumed in travel, we have to adjust the behavioral VTTS. Assuming that the opportunity cost associated with the time resource is measured by the (competitive) market price, and that market prices are often distorted true resource (shadow) prices due to the presence of a number of externalities, practice has involved some limited adjustments to allow for distortions created by taxation.

In deciding on a practical resource value we have to establish the nature of the alternative use activity and especially identify typical circumstances in which various trips involve time that is a mix of leisure and work time requiring that a weighted average of the appropriate work and non-work time values should be used. The criteria for determining whether a traveller in saving time is actually trading with leisure time (non-work time) or work time should be determined according to whether the transferred time is converted to an income generating activity which is subject to tax or not. One way of aiding the process is to focus on elasticities such as of hours worked with respect to the gross wage rate, and the response of hours worked and that taken in leisure as a result of savings in travel time. Forsyth (1980) discusses this issue.

The possibility of time savings for a work-related trip being associated with a mix of leisure and work time makes the use of the phrase 'value of *working* time savings' somewhat ambiguous. Current practice is adopted in part for convenience and in part due to the paucity of empirical evidence on the mix of alternative use of time between leisure and work time.

For all work-related activities (that is, travel taking place during time that is contributing to the productive output of a business), marginal productivity theory suggests that the value of output to an employer is its return net of any indirect tax, and the cost of labor to the employer is its price (including on-costs) inclusive of income tax. If the resource cost of labor is its price in employment before the removal of income tax, then it is traditionally valued before indirect taxation is added.

For non-working or 'leisure' time, the willingness to trade time for money approach assumes that the traded money would have been spent on goods that carry indirect taxation. The resources associated with the time trade are thus equal to the expenditure less the indirect taxation. Therefore, non-working time savings should be valued at the behavioral value adjusted by the inverse of (1 + the average rate of indirect taxation). The taxation adjustment is normally applied to an equity value of time savings; that is, a behavioral value which treats everyone as if they had the same mean income, although this is not an approach which should necessarily be recommended. Where the rate of indirect taxation differs widely between alternative use activities, then the application on an average rate will be grossly misleading. Some attention is required to the distribution of actual rates of indirect taxation to establish if this empirically really matters. If equity values are used, then the resource value for non-working time should be derived from this equity value.

Updating VTTS Over Time

The literature on how to treat changes in VTTS over time has existed for over 30 years. In the earlier years it was assumed that the mean VTTS was a function of the average gross personal income (or the average wage rate) and the percentage change over time in the average wage rate was used to adjust the mean VTTS. The adjustment used the exact same percentage for VTTS. In recent years research has been accumulating (primarily in the UK as part of a number of UK Value of Time Studies commissioned by the Department for Transport) on whether this assumption of proportionality is appropriate. There have been four strands of work.

Theoretically, it has been argued (notably in MVA et al., 1987) that there is no prior reason for a proportionality trend, or indeed any monotonic relationship. The reason for this is that the VTTS is shorthand for the ratio of two distinct quantities – the marginal utility of the time, and the marginal utility of money. There is a strong expectation that the marginal utility of money decreases as (disposable) income increases, but the corresponding statement for time would be an expectation that the marginal utility of time savings decreases as the availability of (disposable) time increases (Hensher and Goodwin, 2004). Both are confounded by changes in tastes, leisure activities, education and opportunities or choice set open to people of different incomes. Overall, there probably is a reason to expect that willingness to pay for time savings increases with income, largely because of the money effect, but this does not translate into utility, and need not be proportional.

Empirically, there is now available a large set of studies of the ratio of utilities (though not their separate variation), in which the resulting VTTS have been compared with income within the studies, or can be compared across studies. Both the MVA study and a subsequent one by Accent et al. (1999) came to a similar conclusion, using cross-sectional studies for 1985 and 1991, that there was evidence of an increasing relationship, but less than proportional as income increases. Their recommendations were to assume that values of time savings would grow over time, but at a rate less than the increase in income expected.

This comparison of VTTS results, and a further 1995 study in which VTTS was formulated as a function of gross personal income, produced a series of income elasticities to approximate the impact on the average VTTS of overall income changes over time. For car drivers (and passengers) they recommended income elasticities of 0.45 (business travel), 0.65 (commuting) and 0.35 (other travel) – in other words, VTTS would grow at about half the rate of income, for personal travel. There is less empirical support for similar effects for commercial vehicles (which include light commercials and heavy vehicles), and the same study recommended the use of real GDP growth per capita as a proxy for growth in spending power, and thus approximately in the long run for growth in the value of goods transported. The implication would be a secular growth in the weight afforded to goods travel in project evaluation over time, as compared with personal travel, for which there is little supporting evidence, and not a strong obvious rationale.

Similar evidence to support such elasticities is provided by Steer Davies Gleave in a recent study in Sydney (unpublished) where they plotted the relationship between mean VTTS (all in $US) and GDP per capita for 14 data points. The implied elasticity was reported as 0.5. Thus a 1 per cent increase in GDP per capita produces a 0.5 per cent increase in the mean VTTS (holding everything else constant).

A third approach has been developed by Wardman (1998a, b, 2001) applying formal meta-analysis techniques to around 1000 data points drawn from UK studies for urban and interurban travel choices. His early results suggested a 0.5 elasticity of VTTS with respect to income, and the later study noted a wide range of different influences depending on methodology, differences between time series and cross section studies and so forth. The range of results was large, and there was scope for considerable judgement in interpreting the results. Wardman concluded that a rather higher elasticity of 0.72 is appropriate with a 95 per cent confidence interval of ± 43 per cent.

The time-series based GDP elasticity in Wardman's 2001 study is greater than the large amount of cross-sectional evidence regarding the income elasticity. If, as is suggested by Gunn (2007), there has been a downward trend in the value of in-vehicle travel time savings independent of income, and given that real GDP per capita is sufficiently highly correlated with the time trend that it will discern any such effects, Wardman concluded that the real GDP per capita elasticity of 0.723 is consistent with a 'pure' income elasticity in excess of 0.723. The evidence on elasticities for growth adjustment suggests a range from 0.35 to 0.723.

A fourth strand of evidence relates to empirical work in a different tradition, the estimation of price elasticities mostly using econometric methods on aggregate data. There is an important connection with VTTS studies in this connection, both because the ratio of price and travel time elasticities reflect the ratios of the marginal utilities when using a generalized cost approach, and also because the price elasticity is an alternative, and directly relevant, approach to estimating revenues from tolls.

A common practice, in a number of countries, has been to assume VTTS proportional to income, and price and time combined within generalized cost. Taken together, this implied that, other things being equal, the price elasticity will tend to be inversely proportional to income, with a strong expectation for price elasticity to decline over time. The result being that it would be progressively easier over time to raise large revenues, but more difficult to influence traffic, from toll or other charging systems. However, a literature review and meta analysis of price elasticity results carried out by Hanly et al. (2002) shows a puzzling result – there is no sign of any systematic decline in price elasticities in studies over the last 30 years, nor from re-analysis of specific data series divided by time period. This applied to a wide range of different price elasticities, for example, fuel prices, vehicle prices, public transport fares, and so forth. Indeed, there were some signs of the elasticities increasing over time, though this was not well established. They argued that if the strong assumption for VTTS to increase with income, and price elasticity correspondingly to decline were well founded, than the effect should be big enough to be able to see some signs of it happening over the last 30 years, which was not the case.

In summary, the theory suggests that the utility of time savings is not necessarily related to income in any specific direction, but the willingness to pay for them should increase with income. Empirical VTTS studies suggest the willingness to pay has increased over time, but less than proportionally, somewhere between a quarter and three-quarters of the rate of income increase. Price elasticity studies do not show any sign of price elasticity declining over time in a way which would be expected if values of time increased with income.

Overall it seems reasonable to conclude that revenue calculations – especially where year-by-year[3] cash flow is of interest – will not be safely made by assuming VTTS will grow proportionally to income. The VTTS benefit will grow less than this,[4] and/or the resistance to price increases will decline less. Thus to assume that VTTS will increase in proportion to income is essentially to assume that the market for time savings is strongly buoyant over time, and even if the early revenues are risky, in future years revenue growth will be strong: this assumption will tend to be overoptimistic on revenue, and potentially underestimate behavioral response, that is, the same direction as the distribution issues discussed above, and therefore tending to reinforce the problem rather than offset it.

ISSUES IN VTTS ESTIMATION

Although the process of modelling to determine the preference weights for trading travel time with money in order to derive empirical measures of VTTS is relatively straight-forward, we have a number of discrete choice modelling methods available to use. The choice comes down to the amount of behavioural realism we wish to recognize in the component of the utility expression for each alternative that is not represented by the set of observed sources of relative utility.

To be more precise, although an analyst would have identified a set of attributes in a choice experiment or a revealed preference study, there will always be other influences on the choice response. These need to be accounted for and are included in the utility expression for each alternative as a composite 'attribute' known as the random component (or random error). It is random simply because we have no way of identifying its content and assigning the information to each sampled respondent.

The simplest way of treating this random component is to assume that it has the same properties across all alternatives (that is, it has a common variance) and that it is uncorrelated across the alternatives, and indeed across all choice sets where respondents are given multiple state choice scenarios to assess or a revealed preference panel data set is being used. The model associated with this strict assumption is known as the multinomial logit (MNL) model and is the most commonly used model form (see Chapter 4 of Hensher et al., 2005; Chapter 3 of Louviere et al., 2000; or Train 2003).

However, there is a burgeoning literature which shows the inherent limitations of the MNL model, especially for valuation of travel time savings (see, for example, Hensher, 2001a, b, c, 2006; Train, 2003). The main criticism is the inability to allow for differences (that is, heterogeneity) in preferences, and the failure to allow for correlation across the alternatives in each choice set in the presence of choice experiments of observations associated with the same person (for example, 16 choice sets per sampled respondent). To accommodate these important and realistic sources of potential influence on the derivation of VTTS, analysts routinely now use a more advanced discrete choice model known as the mixed logit model. The correlation between alternatives is handled nicely through a different specification of the parameter weights, introduced in the next paragraph.

The utility expression associated with an alternative in the mixed logit (ML) model is the same as that for the MNL model except that the analyst may nominate one or more attribute weights (including alternative-specific constants) to be treated as random parameters, with the variance estimated together with the mean. The use of random parameters enables us to derive distributions for VTTS. The selected random parameters can take a number of predefined distributions, such as normal, lognormal or triangular. The selection of the distribution assumption for each random parameter has behavioral implications. For example, the normal distribution has the potential to produce both positive and negative VTTS across the parameter distribution, whereas the lognormal limits the distribution to a positive sign, but typically produces a very thick tail that can be behaviorally implausible for valuation (Hensher, 2006). The triangular distribution has a density function that looks like a tent: a peak in the centre and dropping off linearly on both sides of the centre. Constrained distributions can be used to ensure that the VTTS is positive over the distribution as well as avoiding the long tail typically associated with a few very large (and unrealistic) VTTS.

Under the mixed logit form, the attributes with random parameters induce a distribution around the mean that provides a mechanism for revealing preference differences. This heterogeneity may be refined by making it a function of observed contextual influences such as trip length and household income. This is a way of revealing specific sources of systematic variation in unobserved heterogeneity across a sampled population such that VTTS can be allowed to vary over the range of trip length. We can also account for correlation between random parameter attributes.[5]

To establish the distribution of preferences for the range of attributes, modelers begin by assuming that sampled individuals $q = 1, \ldots, Q$ face a choice among J alternatives, denoted $j = 1, \ldots, J$ in each of T choice settings, $t = 1, \ldots, T$. The random utility model associates utility for individual q with each alternative in each choice situation.

$$U_{qjt} = \boldsymbol{\beta}'\mathbf{x}_{qt} + \varepsilon_{qjt} \tag{7.12}$$

Individual-specific heterogeneity is introduced into the utility function in Equation (7.12) through the parameter, $\boldsymbol{\beta}$. We allow the 'individual-specific' parameter vector to vary across individuals both randomly and systematically with observable variables, $\mathbf{z}_q$. In the simplest case, the (uncorrelated) random parameters are specified as (based on Hensher et al. 2005) Equation (7.13).

$$\boldsymbol{\beta}_q = \boldsymbol{\beta} + \boldsymbol{\Delta}\mathbf{z}_q + \boldsymbol{\Sigma}^{1/2}\mathbf{v}_q$$

$$= \boldsymbol{\beta} + \boldsymbol{\Delta}\mathbf{z}_q + \boldsymbol{\eta}_q.$$

$$\text{or } \beta_{qk} = \beta_k + \boldsymbol{\delta}_k'\mathbf{z}_q + \eta_{qk}, \tag{7.13}$$

where β_{qk} is the random coefficient for the kth attribute faced by individual q. $\boldsymbol{\beta} + \boldsymbol{\Delta}\mathbf{z}_q$ accommodates heterogeneity in the mean of the distribution of the random parameters. The random vector $\mathbf{v}_q$ endows the random parameter with its stochastic properties. For convenience, denote the matrix of known variances of the random draws as $\mathbf{W}$. The scale factors which provide the unknown standard deviations of the random parameters are arrayed on the diagonal of the diagonal variance matrix, $\boldsymbol{\Sigma}^{1/2}$.

The *mixed logit* class of models assumes a general distribution for β_{qk} and an IID extreme value type 1 distribution for ε_{qjt}. That is, β_{qk} can take on different distributional forms.[6] For a given value of $\boldsymbol{\beta}_q$, the *conditional* (on $\mathbf{z}_q$ and $\mathbf{v}_q$) probability for choice j in choice situation t is multinomial logit, since the remaining random term, ε_{qjt}, is IID extreme value:

$$P_{qjt}(\text{choice } j \mid \boldsymbol{\Omega}, \mathbf{X}_{qt}, \mathbf{z}_q, \mathbf{v}_q) = \exp(\boldsymbol{\beta}_q'\mathbf{x}_{qjt})/\Sigma_j\exp(\boldsymbol{\beta}_q'\mathbf{x}_{qjt}) \tag{7.14}$$

We label as the *unconditional* choice probability, the expected value of the logit probability over all the possible values of $\boldsymbol{\beta}_q$; that is, integrated over these values, weighted by the density of $\boldsymbol{\beta}_q$ which is conditioned on the observable individual-specific information $(\mathbf{z}_q)$, but not on the unobservable $\mathbf{v}_q$. This probability density is induced by the random component in the model for $\boldsymbol{\beta}_q$, namely $\mathbf{v}_q$. The unconditional choice probability is given as Equation (7.15):

$$\mathbf{P}_{qjt}(\text{choice } j \mid \boldsymbol{\Omega}, \mathbf{X}_{qt}, \mathbf{z}_q) = \int_{v_q} P_{qjt}(\boldsymbol{\beta}_q \mid \boldsymbol{\Omega}, \mathbf{X}_{qt}, \mathbf{z}_q, \mathbf{v}_q) f(\mathbf{v}_q \mid \mathbf{W}) dv_q \qquad (7.15)$$

where the elements of $\boldsymbol{\Omega}$ are the underlying parameters of the distribution of $\boldsymbol{\beta}_q$. Details on estimation of the parameters of the mixed logit model by maximum simulated likelihood may be found in Train (2003).

EMPIRICAL EVIDENCE

The empirical evidence on VTTS is extensive. The challenge is to identify evidence that is based on studies that use state of the practice (or state of the art) methods in terms of data design and estimation methods. We have chosen to be selective, drawing on evidence that we either have produced personally or have sourced from reputable studies, purely to illustrate the range of evidence, rather than to cover the global field. We distinguish urban and long-distance contexts.

Urban Empirical Evidence

We focus on VTTS examples that have been obtained in studies undertaken by Hensher and colleagues in Australia. The specific application is the assessment of the time savings benefits associated with the construction of toll roads in major metropolitan areas. Increasingly, such studies are being commissioned by consortia of banks, construction companies and toll road operators. The primary interest is in developing empirical measures of three components of overall VTTS for commuters and non-commuters: free flow time (FFT), slowed down time (SDT), and stop/start/crawl time (SSCT). Table 7.1 summarizes estimates of VTTS derived from mixed logit models with analytical distribution on travel times. As expected the mean VTTS for free flow time is lower than that for slowed down and stop-start time, suggesting that traveler's are willing, on average, to pay more to save a unit of time that is associated with congestion. The models from which the Australian estimates have been extracted also accounted for the variability in trip travel time and what is commonly referred to in tolling studies as the quality bonus that toll roads provide compared to non-tolled routes such as increased safety, nicer landscaping and no traffic lights. Accounting for additional influences means that any confoundment between VTTS and other effects has been minimized.

Symmetry Versus Asymmetry in VTTS[7]

In a linear model, the observed utility of alternative i is given by an equation like Equation (7.16).

Table 7.1   Illustrative VTTS for urban roads (including toll roads) ($ per person hour) in AUD2005

Attribute	Commuter		Non Commuter	
	Average	St. dev	Average	St. dev
Weighted average VTTS[a]	$18.23	$4.54	$14.53	$3.23
Free Flow	$12.84	$2.62	$11.97	$2.33
Slowed down	$18.03	$3.66	$15.21	$2.98
Stop Start Crawl	$24.70	$5.04	$18.43	$3.65
Trip Time Variability	$4.84	$0.98	$5.02	$0.96
Freeway quality bonus	–	–	$0.54	$0.26

Note: [a] VTTS for total time is a weighted average based on the mix of time components for the current trip.

$$V_i = \delta_i + \delta_{Toll(i)} + \delta_{FC(i)} + \beta_{FF}FF_i + \beta_{SDT}SDT_i + \beta_C C_i + \beta_T Toll_i \qquad (7.16)$$

where δi is a constant associated with alternative i (normalized to zero for one alternative[8]), and βFF, βSDT, βC and βT are the coefficients associated with free flow travel time (*FFT*), slowed-down travel time (*SDT*), running cost (*C*) and road tolls (*Toll*), respectively. Travel time attributes are expressed in minutes, while travel cost attributes are expressed in Australian dollars (AUD). The two additional parameters $\delta Toll(i)$ and $\delta FC(i)$ are only estimated in the case where a toll is charged for alternative i and in the case where alternative *i* includes no free flow time (that is, *FC* = fully congested).

The above specification can be adapted to work with differences in relation to a reference or RP (revealed preference) alternative, as opposed to using the absolute values presented to respondents in the SP experiments. The use of a referencing approach relates to prospect theory (Kahneman and Tversky, 1979), according to which, due to limitations on their ability to cognitively solve difficult problems, decision makers simplify the choice process by evaluating the gains or losses to be made by choosing a specific alternative, relative to a neutral or status quo point. For the reference alternative r, the utility function is rewritten to include only the three dummy variables δr (*ASC*), $\delta Toll(r)$ (toll road dummy) and $\delta FC(r)$ (fully congested dummy). For SP alternative *j* (where $j \neq r$), the observed utility function is given by:

$$V_{j,new} = \delta_j + \delta_{Toll(j)} + \delta_{FC(j)} + \beta_{FF(inc)}\max(FF_j - FF_r, 0) + \beta_{FF(dec)}\max(FF_r - FF_j, 0)$$

$$+ \beta_{SDT(inc)}\max(SDT_j - SDT_r, 0) + \beta_{SDT(dec)}\max(SDT_r - SDT_j, 0)$$

$$+ \beta_{C(inc)}\max(C_j - C_r, 0) + \beta_{C(dec)}\max(C_r - C_j, 0) + \beta_{Toll(inc)}\max(Toll_j - Toll_r, 0)$$

$$+ \beta_{Toll(dec)}\max(Toll_r - Toll_j, 0) \qquad (7.17)$$

This specification is obtained through taking differences for the four attributes relative to the reference alternative, where separate coefficients are estimated for increases (*inc*) and decreases (*dec*), hence allowing for asymmetrical responses. The resulting model structure is still very easy to estimate and also apply, which is crucial for practical large-scale modeling analyses.

A point that deserves some attention before describing the results of the modeling analysis is the way in which the models deal with the repeated choice nature of the data. Not accounting for the possible correlation between the behavior of a given respondent across the individual choice situations can potentially have a significant effect on model results, especially in terms of biased standard errors. In an analysis looking at differences between the response to gains and losses, issues with over- or underestimated standard errors can clearly lead to misleading conclusions.

Rather than relying on the use of a lagged response formulation (cf. Train, 2003) or a jackknife correction approach (cf. Cirillo et al., 2000), we can make use of an error components specification of the mixed logit (MMNL) model[9] to account for individual specific correlation. With $Vn,t,RP,base$, $Vn,t,SP1,base$ and $Vn,t,SP2,base$ giving the base utilities for the three alternatives[10] for respondent n and choice situation t, the final utility function (for respondent *n* and choice situation *t*) is given by Equation (7.18) for the reference alternative and two stated preference alternatives.

$$U_{n,t,RP} = V_{n,t,RP,base} + \theta\,\xi_{n,RP} + \varepsilon_{n,k,RP}$$

$$U_{n,t,SP,1} = V_{n,t,SP1,base} + \theta\,\xi_{n,SP1} + \varepsilon_{n,k,SP1}$$

$$U_{n,t,SP,2} = V_{n,t,SP2,base} + \theta\,\xi_{n,SP2} + \varepsilon_{n,k,SP2} \tag{7.18}$$

where $\varepsilon_{n,k,RP}$, $\varepsilon_{n,k,SP1}$ and $\varepsilon_{n,k,SP2}$ are the IID draws from a type I extreme value distribution, and $\xi_{n,RP}$, $\xi_{n,SP1}$ and $\xi_{n,SP2}$ are draws from three independent Normal variates with a zero mean and a standard deviation of 1. To allow for correlation across replications for the same individual, the integration over these latter three variates is carried out at the respondent level rather than the individual observation level. However, the fact that independent $N(0, 1)$ draws are used for different alternatives (that is, $\xi_{n,RP}$, $\xi_{n,SP1}$ and $\xi_{n,SP2}$) means that the correlation does not extend to correlation across alternatives but is restricted to correlation across replications for the same individual and a given alternative. Finally, the fact that the separate error components are distributed identically means that the model remains homoscedastic.

Letting jn, t refer to the alternative chosen by respondent n in choice situation t (with $t = 1, \ldots, T$), the contribution of respondent *n* to the log-likelihood function is then given by:

$$LL_n = \ln\left(\int_{\xi_n}\left(\prod_{t=1}^{T}P(j_{n,t}|V_{n,t,RP,base}, V_{n,t,SP1,base}, V_{n,t,SP2,base}, \xi_{n,RP}, \xi_{n,SP1}, \xi_{n,SP2}, \theta)\right)f(\xi_n)\,d\xi_n\right) \tag{7.19}$$

where ξ groups together $\xi_{n,RP}$, $\xi_{n,SP1}$ and $\xi_{n,SP2}$ and where $f(\xi_n)$ refers to the joint distribution of the elements in ξ, with a diagonal covariance matrix.

In Table 7.2 we summarize the trade-offs between the various estimated parameters, giving the monetary values of changes in travel time, as well as the willingness to pay a bonus in return for avoiding congestion and road tolls. These trade-offs were calculated separately for the travel cost and road toll coefficient, where the low level of differences

Table 7.2   Willingness to pay indicators for base models (AUD2005)

	versus β_C		versus β_{Toll}	
	Non-commuters	Commuters	Non-commuters	Commuters
β_{FF} ($/hour)	13.39	13.30	12.62	15.95
β_{SDT} ($/hour)	14.95	16.60	14.09	19.90
δ_{FC} ($)	4.89	-0.95^a	4.61	-1.14^a
δ_{Toll} ($)	0.74	1.14	0.70	1.37

Notes: ^{a} Numerator of trade-off not significant beyond 25 percent level of confidence.

Table 7.3   Willingness to pay indicators for asymmetrical models (AUD2005)

	versus β_C		versus β_{Toll}	
	Non-commuters	Commuters	Non-commuters	Commuters
β_{FF} ($/hour)	9.99	7.27	6.72	6.40
β_{SDT} ($/hour)	15.51	13.70	10.44	12.07
δ_{FC} ($)	-0.18^a	-2.01^b	-0.12^a	-1.77^b
δ_{Toll} ($)	1.82	1.45	1.22	1.28

Notes:
^{a} Numerator of trade-off not significant beyond 4 percent level of confidence.
^{b} Numerator of trade-off not significant beyond 93 percent level of confidence.

needs to be recognized when comparing the results. The main differences between the two sets of trade-offs and across the two population segments arise in the greater willingness by commuters to accept increases in road tolls, and the higher sensitivity to slowed down time for commuters.

In an asymmetrical model, the calculation is slightly different, as we now have separate coefficients for increases and decreases, suggesting different possible combinations of VTTS calculations. As an example, the willingness to accept increases in travel cost in return for reductions in free flow time would be given by $-\beta FF(dec)/\beta C(inc)$. This approach was used to calculate willingness to pay indicators for the two components of travel time with the two separate cost components, where trade-offs were also calculated for δFC and δT. The results of these calculations are summarized in Table 7.3.

In comparison with the results for the base model, there are some significant differences. The willingness to accept increases in travel cost in return for reductions in free flow time decreases by 25 per cent and 45 per cent for non-commuters and commuters respectively. Even more significant decreases (47 per cent and 60 per cent) are observed when looking at the willingness to accept (WTA) increases in road tolls. While the WTA increases in travel cost in return for reductions in slowed down time stays almost constant for non-commuters, it decreases by 17 per cent for commuters (when compared to the base model). When using road tolls instead of travel cost, there are decreases in both population segments, by 26 per cent and 39 per cent, respectively. These differences are yet another indication of the effects of allowing for asymmetrical response rates.

Table 7.4   Aggregate summary of VTTS

Trip purpose	Mode	USD 2000	USD 2000	Short	Medium	Long
		Mean in-vehicle time	Mean out of vehicle time	Mean in-vehicle time	Mean in-vehicle time	Mean in-vehicle time
business	air	37.55	64.33		30.60	52.31
business	car	34.67		60.87	33.42	22.12
business	all*	31.35			31.35	
non-business	air	23.76		27.77	21.30	30.85
non-business	car	8.29		8.08	7.78	9.75
non-business	train	14.54				
non-business	all	6.75			6.75	

Notes: 'all' means that the parameters used to calculate VTTS were generic. This is not a weighted average of the car and air values above. Short is typically trips up 100 km, medium is trips 100–300 km and long is trips over 300 km.

Non-urban Empirical Evidence

We reviewed a large number of empirical studies to establish a range of VTTS for non-business and business intercity travel. The key references are Algers et al. (1995), Bhat (1995), HCG (1990), Hensher (1978, 2001a), Hensher and Sullivan (2003), Hoffer et al. (1998), Kurri and Pursula (1995), Ramjerdi (1993) and Simonetti and de Dios Ortuzar (2001). We have synthesised the evidence and summarized it in Table 7.4. Some of the VTTS are averages across all trip lengths while some are trip length specific. Using exchange rates for the date of the empirical study data collection we have converted all VTTS to US dollars and then applied a consumer price index adjustment to express all USD into USD 2000. The VTTS reported are the set that we believe are based on credible empirical inquiry and represent the state of practice in the derivation of behavioural VTTS.

A range of VTTS can be derived from subsets of the values in Table 7.5. We provide overall mean estimates for business and non-business travel for the main modes (car, air, train) and in some cases values based on all modes. In addition trip length estimates are provided although this is rather tricky given the different cut-offs.

Furthermore, the aggregation across studies has tended to flatten out the distribution that one observes within studies that have allowed for trip length. The Norwegian evidence suggests that VTTS declines with trip length for car business, is U-shaped for air business, beginning high, decreasing and then increasing almost back to the highest value; is flat for air non-business and declines slightly for car non-business. For New Zealand car non-business trips, the VTTS increases as trip length increases, the opposite of Norway. Comparisons of averages across studies with problems in meaningfully grouping trip lengths are problematic and we promote a view that beyond the profile of the mean estimates aggregated and averaged across studies by mode and trip purpose, trip length effects are appropriately identified within specific study contexts. The only evidence we have is from Norway and New Zealand. From the synthesized evidence we identify a mean VTTS for air business travel of $37.55 per person hour in USD 2000 and $23.76 per person hour for air non-business in USD 2000.

Table 7.5   A synthesis of the empirical evidence on behavioral values of in vehicle travel time savings (standardized to USD 2000)

Country	Year	Geo-graphical Locn	Distance	Mode	Purpose	Per hr	To USD2000
Sweden	1994	various	> 50 km	air	business	141	18.682
Norway	1995	various	> 50 km	air	business	343	55.381
Norway	1995	various	100–300 km	air	business	258	41.657
Norway	1995	various	> 300 km	air	business	324	52.314
USA	1995	intercity	Nationwide	air	business	34.5	37.715
Australia	1999	Syd–Can	300 km	All	business	46.71	31.352
Finland	1995	intercity	varies	car	business	124.6	28.604
Norway	1996	intercity	< 50 km	car	business	253	40.850
Norway	1995	intercity	50–100 km	car	business	377	60.871
Norway	1995	intercity	100–300 km	car	business	207	33.423
Norway	1995	intercity	> 300 km	car	business	137	22.120
Sweden	1994	intercity	> 50 km	car	business	167	22.126
Sweden	1994	intercity	> 50 km	IC-Train	business	129	17.092
Sweden	1994	intercity	> 50 km	X2000-Train	business	134	17.754
Sweden	1994	various	> 50 km	air	non-business	88	11.659
Norway	1995	various	> 30 km	air	non-business	155	25.027
Norway	1995	various	50–100 km	air	non-business	172	27.771
Norway	1995	various	100–300 km	air	non-business	170	27.449
Norway	1995	various	> 300 km	air	non-business	151	24.381
USA	1995	intercity	Nationwide	air	non-business	19.5	21.317
Chile	1993	intercity	520 km	air	non-business	13312	37.311
Spain	1992	intercity	40 min	air	non-business	1360	15.158
Australia	1999	Syd–Can	300 km	All	non-business	10.05	6.746
Finland	1996	intercity	varies	car driver	non-business	16	3.673
Norway	1995	intercity	> 50 km	car driver	non-business	86	13.886
Norway	1995	intercity	50–100 km	car driver	non-business	101	16.308
Norway	1995	intercity	100–300 km	car driver	non-business	97	15.662
Norway	1995	intercity	> 300 km	car driver	non-business	77	12.433
Sweden	1994	intercity	> 50 km	car driver	non-business	81	10.732
New Zealand	1999	intercity	30–540 mins	car driver	non-business	7.86	4.588
New Zealand	1999	intercity	< 100 mins	car driver	non-business	6	3.503
New Zealand	1999	intercity	100–200 mins	car driver	non-business	7.6	4.437
New Zealand	1999	intercity	200–300 mins	car driver	non-business	9	5.254
New Zealand	1999	intercity	300–400 mins	car driver	non-business	10.5	6.129
New Zealand	1999	intercity	> 400 mins	car driver	non-business	12.1	7.063
New Zealand	2000	intercity	> 3 h	car driver	non-business	6.97	4.069
Sweden	1994	intercity	> 50 km	IC-Train	non-business	74	9.804
Sweden	1994	intercity	> 50 km	X2000-Train	non-business	102	13.514

Employer-business Travel in Australia: A Case Study

In this section we undertake an assessment of trips based on marginal productivity and consumer theory, in which we assume that the value of savings in business travel time (VBTTS) is divided into the employer component that trades travel with work, equal to the opportunity cost of time to the employer, plus the employee component that trades travel with leisure or work (equal to the value to the employee of leisure or work time relative to travel time). We draw on Australian data to illustrate the magnitude of such values.

Secondary data is required that provides the number of trips per given time period for employer-business vehicle drivers in each gross personal income class. In the Australian context, the mean gross personal income for the employer business segment employees is used to calculate the average hourly gross wage rate which in 2005/06 was $47.50 per person hour.

With salary on-cost averaging 40 per cent, and a marginal wage increment of 5 per cent (assuming that the marginal disutility of equivalent time travelling versus in the office = 0), the opportunity cost to the employer is approximately $69.82 per employee hour in 2005. The marginal wage increment of 5 per cent is an allowance commonly applied to allow for additional overheads that are saved as a result of the employee not spending the time in the office. These include, for example, electricity, average costs of meetings avoided that are paid for by the traveler's organization and phone calls.

This assumes that all travel time occurs during working hours. When we update this to 2006, based on a CPI increase of 3.97 per cent, the opportunity cost to the employer is $72.60. To identify the VBTTS we have to identify the incidence of employer-business travel that occurs in and outside of income-earning hours.

The results presented above for employer business assume that all travel time is occurring during work hours. At the other extreme we might assume that all travel occurs outside of working hours and can be calculated from car and taxi VTTS for employees travelling on business. These VTTS from standard discrete choice models on a sample of employees traveling on business are the source of the employees' VTTS for travel in non-work time.

The frequently missing ingredient is knowledge of the proportion of travel time that occurs in hours that are income-earning versus those that occur outside of these hours that are compensated or not by the employer, in financial terms. Hensher (1977) found that 60 per cent of such time is income-earning in Sydney. New surveys in 2005 in Australia suggest that the 60:40 rule should be revised to 72:28. The appropriate VTTS for employer-business trips is calculated from the formula:

$$\text{VBTTS} = (\text{proportion of travel time in income} - \text{earning hours}$$

$$* \text{ opportunity cost to the employer}) + (\text{proportion of travel in}$$

$$\text{non income-earning hours} * VTTS \text{ of employees}).$$

For example, if we assume that the VTTS is $30.78 per person hour, then given the evidence above,

$$\text{VBTTS} = (0.72 \times \$72.60 + 0.28 \times \$30.78) = \$60.89 \text{ per person hour.}$$

Empirical Evidence on Urban Freight Distribution

As part of a larger study detailed in Hensher et al. (2007) we studied the behavioral responses of transporters and shippers in the freight distribution chain to various trip

Table 7.6   VTTS measures (AUD 2005 per hour)

	Free-flow time	Slowed-down time
Mean	$42.48	$83.77
Standard Deviation	$22.95	$8.88

Table 7.7   VRG measures (AUD per percentage point)

	Transporters	Shippers – Freight Rate Only	Shippers – Freight Rate and Costs
Mean	$3.54	$10.32	$12.67
Standard Deviation	$0.46	$1.94	$2.87

profiles as defined by components of travel time, probability of arriving on time, running and toll costs and distance-based congestion charges. The data was collected using a computer aided personal survey instrument (CAPI) with a sample of transporters and shippers. The outputs of interest herein are summarized in Tables 7.6 and 7.7. The interest in VTTS is restricted to transporters; whereas the focus on VRG (value of reliability gains) applies to both transporters and shippers.

Transporters demonstrate a clear marginal disutility for travel in slowed-down conditions, with a mean VTTS for slowed-down time twice as high as the VTTS for free-flow time. Furthermore, heterogeneity in preferences with respect to slowed-down time is significantly lower across transporters than heterogeneity in preferences with respect to free-flow time; the ratio of the mean VTTS for slowed-down time to its standard deviation is only approximately one-fifth the corresponding ratio for free-flow time. The policy implications are clear. Specifically, in the context of a variable user charge, any reductions in travel in congested conditions would benefit most transporters at a rate that may frequently exceed the corresponding level of the charges. For example, considering a transporter at the mean of the VTTS distribution, a given trip alternative that offers a savings of 30 minutes of slowed-down time – worth $41.89 – would benefit from the utilization of that alternative as long as the variable charges did not exceed $0.41, $0.83 or $1.68 per kilometer for a trip of 100, 50 or 25 kilometers, respectively. Given the relatively small spread of VTTS values around the mean, the majority of transporters would experience similar opportunities.

Whilst transporters demonstrate a value of reliability gains of $3.54 per percentage point of improvement in on-time arrival, shippers place an even higher value on reliability. This is intuitive, as reliability may be a larger item of concern to shippers than travel time (that is, it is more beneficial to know that shipments are likely to arrive on-time than it is to know that shipments are expected to arrive within a given time frame whose reliability cannot be guaranteed). To illustrate how to interpret the values in Table 7.7, suppose the free route on average has trips arriving on time 91 per cent of the time and the toll route can deliver on time arrival 97 per cent of the time, then the value of trip time reliability, based on a 6 per cent point difference, is 6 × 3.54 = $21.24 per trip. This gets added in after calculating the trip time savings and converting to dollars using FF VTTS and SD/SS VTTS.

Using the shipper's only cost measure in the analysis (that is, the freight rate), the mean VRG for shippers is $10.32, or almost three times as large as the corresponding VRG for transporters. However, given shippers' significant disutility of costs faced by the transporter, coupled with a lack of precedent for such willingness-to-pay measures, it is plausible that one must include all costs in the calculation, whether they are borne directly by the respondent or are only as indirect sources of disutility (that is, through the perceived threat of an increased freight rate). Hence, we calculated a VRG for shippers based on a weighted average of the freight rate and the transporter's costs. This variant of VRG is somewhat higher than the VRG based solely on the freight rate; at $12.67 per percentage point, this VRG estimate implies that shippers are approximately three-and-a-half times more sensitive to the probability of on-time arrival than transporters. Again, this is intuitive, as shippers are impacted by arrival reliability through both the need to satisfy customers, as well as through time sensitivity in the production of items. That is, delays of incoming goods may adversely impact the production or provision of goods worth more than the incoming goods themselves. Transporters face similar concerns with respect to on-time arrival reliability; however the scope of these concerns may be limited to customer satisfaction.

CONCLUSION

This chapter has provided an overview of some of the main theoretical and empirical frameworks that are used to support the conceptualisation and estimation of willingness to pay (WTP) measures for travel time savings.

The literature is developing at a fast pace, especially the development of new methods to empirically estimate the parameters used in the derivation of VTTS. Most notably, the focus in recent years has been on the refinement of stated choice experiments (see Rose and Bliemer, 2007) to improve the behavioral and statistical efficiency of the designs and respondent assessment strategies, in order to capture the processes used to evaluate attribute packages in choice scenarios, as well as conditioning the derived estimates of VTTS.

As one example, the growing interest in the attribute processing strategies (APS) adopted by respondents has shown that failing to account for process rules tends to result in statistically higher mean estimates of values of travel time savings. Incorporating process heterogeneity in a joint choice model of process and outcome is a way of recognizing the range of ways in which information embedded in attributes such as travel time, comfort, reliability and cost is assessed by a sample of heterogeneous individuals. Hensher (2010) reviews the main ways in which individuals evaluate attributes such as travel time and cost, which we refer to as APSs. These include attribute non-attendance, aggregating attributes with a common metric (for example, walk time and wait time), and imposing thresholds on attributes that represent the range of relevance.

NOTES

1. The value of *saving* time in an activity is the willingness to pay to reduce that activity. If the individual assigns voluntarily more time than the minimum required, he is not willing to pay to reduce it precisely because the value of the marginal utility is positive (what De Serpa called the value of time assigned to

the activity). See (2.42) in Jara Diaz (2007) where the value of saving time is the expression on the left hand side, and the value of time assigned is the value of the marginal utility (far right term). Thus, if the individual assigns more time than needed, the multiplier κ_j is zero and the value of the marginal utility is μ/λ (positive and equal for all activities whose κ_j is nil). Discussions with Sergio Jara Diaz are appreciated.

2. The UK Department for Transport has recently commenced a review of the formulae in order to establish possible amendments to the empirical components in the context of rail travel.

3. All cash-flow calculations rely heavily on year-by-year build-up or decline of the market, but this issue is the least well treated of any issue in travel demand forecasting which nearly always focuses on end-states, not on paths over time. The main exception is price elasticity studies, which mostly show short run (one year) effects being rather less than half as great as long run (5–10 year) effects. Ignoring such demand effects will make a big hole in the early revenues, which may be practically more important than the other issues discussed in this chapter.

4. Ken Small (personal communication) raises a very important issue: if the elasticity is constant over long periods, travel time will become completely unimportant relative to other considerations in just another few decades of growth. Furthermore, if it has been constant for the last century, travel time must have been enormously important (relatively) a century ago, which does not appear to square with common observations.

5. The presence of additional terms as a representation of random tastes of each individual that do not vary across the repeated choice sets in an SC experiment can induce a correlation among the utility of different alternatives (Hensher and Greene, 2003; McFadden and Train, 2000). It is the mixture of an extreme value type 1 (EV1) distribution for the overall utility expression and embedded distribution of the taste weights across a sample which has led to the phrase 'mixed logit' (Train 2003). One can choose to treat the random effects as different across the alternatives but independent (that is, different standard deviations); or as different across alternatives and inter-alternative correlated. The correlated structure of data on choice sets that is drawn from the same individual (as in stated choice tasks) can also be handled within this framework.

6. The random parameters specification can accommodate correlation amongst the alternatives. Since b_q can contain alternative specific constants which may be correlated, this specification can induce correlation across alternatives. It follows that the model does not impose the IIA assumption. Restrictions can be imposed at numerous points in the model to produce a wide variety of specifications.

7. This section draws on material written by the author with Stephane Hess and John Rose (Hess et al., 2007).

8. The significance of an ASC related to an unlabeled alternative simply implies that after controlling for the effects of the modelled attributes, this alternative has been chosen more or less frequently than the base alternative. It is possible that this might be the case because the alternative is close to the reference alternative, or that culturally, those undertaking the experiment tend to read left to right. Failure to estimate an ASC would in this case correlate the alternative order effect into the other estimated parameters, possibly distorting the model results.

9. Our method differs from the commonly used approach of capturing serial correlation with a random coefficients formulation where tastes are assumed to vary across respondents but remain constant across observations for the same respondent. This approach not only makes the considerable assumption of an absence of inter-observational variation (cf. Hess and Rose, 2007), but the results are potentially also affected by confounding between serial correlation and random taste heterogeneity.

10. Independently of which specification is used, models based on Equation (7.16).

REFERENCES

Accent Marketing and Hague Consulting Group, 1999, The value of travel time on UK roads 1994. Report prepared for the Department of Transport, London.

Algers, S., J. Lindqvist Dillén and S. Widlert, 1995, The national Swedish value of time study. Proceedings of the 23rd European Transport Forum, PTRC, Transportation Planning Methods.

Bates, J., 1987, Measuring travel time values with a discrete choice model: a note. *The Economic Journal*, **97**, 493–498.

Becker, G., 1965, A theory of the allocation of time. *The Economic Journal*, **75**, 493–517.

Bhat, C., 1995, A heteroscedastic extreme value model of intercity travel mode choice. *Transportation Research Part B*, **29** (6), 471–483.

Bruzelius, N., 1979, *The Value of Travel Time*. London: Croom Helm.

Cirillo, C., K. Lindveld and A. Daly, 2000, Eliminating bias due to the repeated measurements problem in

SP data. In J. de D. Ortúzar, ed., *Stated Preference Modelling Techniques: PTRC Perspectives 4*. London: PTRC Education and Research Services Ltd.

De Donnea, F.X., 1972, Consumer behaviour, transport mode choice and value of time: some micro-economic models. *Regional and Urban Economics,* **1**, 355–382.

DeSerpa, A., 1971, A theory of the economics of time. *The Economic Journal,* **81**, 828–846.

DeSerpa, A.C., 1973, Microeconomic theory and the valuation of travel time: some clarification. *Regional and Urban Economics,* **2**, 401–410.

Evans, A.W., 1972, On the theory of the valuation and allocation of time. *Scottish Journal of Political Economy,* **19**, 1–17.

Forsyth, P., 1980, The value of time in an economy with taxation. *Journal of Transport Economics and Policy,* **14** (3), 337–362.

Gronau, R., 1986, Home production: a survey. In Y. Ashenfelter and R. Layard, eds, *Handbook of Labour Economics,* Vol. 1. Amsterdam: North Holland.

Gunn, H.F., 2007, An introduction to the valuation of travel-time savings and losses. In *Handbook of Transport Modelling*, 2nd edn, Vol. 1. D.A. Hensher and K.J. Button, eds. Amsterdam: Elsevier Science Ltd, pp. 433–448.

Hague Consulting Group, HCG, 1990, The Netherlands' value of time study: final report. Hague, the Netherlands: Haag.

Hanly, P., J. Dargay and P. Goodwin, 2002, Review of income and price elasticities in the demand for road traffic. Final Report to Department for Transport, ESRC Transport Studies Unit, University College London.

Hensher, D.A., 1977, *Value of Business Travel Time*. Oxford: Pergamon Press.

Hensher, D.A., 1978, Valuation of journey attributes: some existing empirical evidence. In D.A. Hensher and Q. Dalvi, eds, *Determinants of Travel Choice*. Farnborough: Saxon House, pp. 203–265.

Hensher, D.A., 2001a, Measurement of the valuation of travel time savings. *Journal of Transport Economics and Policy* (Special Issue in Honour of Michael Beesley), **35** (1), 71–98.

Hensher, D.A., 2001b, The valuation of commuter travel time savings for car drivers: evaluating alternative model specifications. *Transportation,* **28** (2), 101–118.

Hensher, D.A., 2001c, The sensitivity of the valuation of travel time savings to the specification of unobserved effects. *Transportation Research Part E* (Special Issue on Value of Travel Time Savings), **37** (2–3), 129–142.

Hensher, D.A., 2006, The signs of the times: imposing a globally signed condition on willingness to pay distributions. *Transportation,* **33** (3), 205–222.

Hensher, D.A., 2010, Attribute processing, heuristics and preference construction in choice analysis. In S. Hess and A. Daly, eds, *State-of-Art and State-of-Practice in Choice Modelling*. Bingley, UK: Emerald Press, pp. 35–70.

Hensher, D.A. and P.B. Goodwin, 2004, Implementation of values of time savings: the extended set of considerations in a tollroad context. *Transport Policy,* **11** (2), 171–181.

Hensher, D.A. and W.H. Greene, 2003, Mixed logit models: state of practice. *Transportation,* **30** (2), 133–176.

Hensher, D.A. and C. Sullivan, 2003, Willingness to pay for road curviness and road type. *Transportation Research Part D,* **8** (2), 139–155.

Hensher, D.A., J.J. Louviere and J. Swait, 1999, Combining sources of preference data. *Journal of Econometrics,* **89**, 197–221.

Hensher, D.A., S.M. Puckett and J. Rose, 2007, Agency decision making in freight distribution chains: establishing a parsimonious empirical strategy from alternative behavioural structures. *Transportation Research Part B,* **41** (9), 924–949.

Hensher, D.A., J.M. Rose and W.H. Greene, 2005, *Applied Choice Analysis: A Primer*. Cambridge: Cambridge University Press.

Hess, S. and J.M. Rose, 2007, Some lessons for working with repeated choice data. Paper presented at the World Conference of Transport Research, Berkeley, CA., August.

Hess, S., J. Rose and D.A. Hensher, 2007, Asymmetrical preference formation in willingness to pay estimates in discrete choice models. Institute of Transport and Logistics Studies, University of Sydney, February.

Hoffer, S., F. Berardino, J. Smith and S. Rubin, 1998, Economic values for evaluation of federal aviation administration investment and regulatory decisions. Federal Aviation Administration (FAA) Report (FAA-APO-98-8), June 1997. Available at http://api.hq.faa.gov/pubs.asp?Lev2=4.

Jara-Díaz, S.R., 1998, Time and income in travel choice: towards a microeconomic activity framework. In T. Garling, T. Laitia, K. Westin, eds, *Theoretical Foundations of Travel Choice Modelling*. Oxford: Pergamon, pp. 51–73.

Jara-Díaz, S.R., 2000, Allocation and valuation of travel time savings. In D. Hensher and K. Button, eds, *Handbook of Transport Modelling*. Oxford: Pergamon Press, pp. 303–319.

Jara-Díaz, S.R., 2007, *Transport Economics Theory*. Oxford: Elsevier Science.

Johnson, M., 1966, Travel time and the price of leisure. *Western Economic Journal,* **4**, 135–145.

Kahneman, D. and A. Tversky, 1979, Prospect theory: an analysis of decisions under risk. *Econometrica*, **47** (2), 263–291.

Kurri, J. and M. Pursula, 1995, Finnish preliminary value of time studies. *KFB & VTI forskning/research*, **14** (4), 50–70.

Louviere, J.J., D.A. Hensher and J.F. Swait, 2000, *Stated Choice Methods and Analysis*. Cambridge: Cambridge University Press.

Lowe, S.R., 1982, Theoretical considerations. Value of Time Working Paper 3, DoT, London.

McFadden, D. and K. Train, 2000, Mixed MNL models for discrete response. *Journal of Applied Econometrics*, **15**, 447–470.

Moses, L. and H. Williamson, 1963, Value of time, choice of mode and the subsidy issue in urban transportation. *Journal of Political Economy*, **71**, 247–264.

MVA Consultancy, Institute of Transport Studies University of Leeds and Transport Studies Unit University of Oxford, 1987, *The Value of Travel Time Savings*. London: Policy Journals.

Oort, O., 1969, The evaluation of travelling time. *Journal of Transport Economics and Policy*, **3**, 279–286.

Ramjerdi, F., 1993, Value of travel time savings: theories and empirical evidences. TØI Report 213/1993, Oslo, Norway.

Rose, J. and M. Bliemer, 2007, Stated preference experimental design strategies. In D.A. Hensher, and K.J. Button, eds, *Handbook of Transport Modelling*, 2nd edn, Oxford: Elsevier, pp. 151–180.

Simonetti, C. and J. de Dios Ortuzar, 2001, Modelling air travel and deriving values of time with the mixed data estimation method. Departamento de Ingeniería de Transporte, Pontificia Universidad Católica de Chile.

Train, K., 2003, *Discrete Choice Methods with Simulation*. Cambridge: Cambridge University Press.

Train, K. and D. McFadden, 1978, The goods/leisure tradeoff and disaggregate work trip mode choice models. *Transportation Research*, **12**, 349–353.

Truong, T. and D. Hensher, 1985, Measurement of travel time values and opportunity cost from a discrete-choice model, *Economic Journal*, **95**, 438–451.

Wardman, M., 1998a, The value of travel time: a review of British Evidence. *Journal of Transport Economics and Policy*, **32** (3), 285–316.

Wardman, M., 1998b, A review of British evidence on the valuations of time and service quality. Working Paper 525, Institute for Transport Studies, University of Leeds.

Wardman, M., 2001, UK value of time. Working Paper 4, Institute for Transport Studies, University of Leeds.

8 Advances in discrete choice: mixture models
Joan L. Walker and Moshe Ben-Akiva

INTRODUCTION

Recent advances in discrete choice models have been driven by the growth in computer power and use of simulation, which have allowed for unprecedented flexibility in model form. In this chapter, we review both the basic discrete choice models and the latest formulations. In particular, we focus on the concept of mixture models. Mixture models are currently being used in a wide array of statistical modeling procedures as a way to relax restrictive assumptions and generalize model forms. As mixing allows for any distributional form to be approximated, this represents a powerful and important advancement in discrete choice analysis.

We first briefly review the foundations of discrete choice analysis and the classic model forms of probit and the generalized extreme value family (or GEV), for example, logit, nested logit and cross-nested logit. Then we will move onto mixture models, beginning with basic formulations and then covering more advanced forms, including what we call *behavioral (or structural) mixture models*. The last section presents empirical results from a land use and transportation study, which we use to demonstrate the various choice model formulations.

FOUNDATIONS OF DISCRETE CHOICE ANALYSIS

We start by providing the foundations of choice analysis, including the choice modeling framework and the random utility model. This section is based on Ben-Akiva and Lerman (1985), where further details can be obtained.

Choice Modeling Framework

This section presents the basic elements that are used to model a decision maker's choice among a set of mutually exclusive and collectively exhaustive alternatives. The following elements of the choice problem must be defined:

Who (or what) is the decision maker? The decision making entity can be an individual person, group of persons, or an organization.

What are the characteristics of the decision maker? Individuals have different tastes, and therefore we must explicitly treat the differences in the decision-making processes among individuals. Therefore the characteristics of the decision maker (for example, gender, age, and firm size) become an important part of the problem.

What are the alternatives? The decision maker chooses from a finite and countable set of alternatives. The *universal set* consists of the entire feasible set of alternatives as defined by the choice environment. A decision maker may only consider a subset of this universal set, and this consideration set is termed a *choice set*.

What are the attributes of the alternatives? In discrete choice analysis, we characterize each alternative by its attributes, for example the travel time and travel cost of a mode. Decision makers evaluate the attractiveness of an alternative based on these attribute values. Attributes may be measured on a continuous scale (time, cost) or be categorical (make or model of automobile). Furthermore, categorical attributes can be ordinal (compact, mid-size, full size) or nominal (red, green, blue). Some may be more straightforward to measure (price, existence of air conditioning), whereas others may be more complex (comfort, reliability).

What is the decision rule that the decision maker uses to make a choice? The decision rule describes the process by which the decision maker evaluates the information available and arrives at a unique choice. There is a wide array of possible decision rules, including dominance, satisfaction, lexicographic, elimination by aspect, habitual, imitation, and utility. It is this latter class that is most often associated with discrete choice analysis due to its extensive use in the development of the predictive models of human behavior emphasized here. Utility theory derives from microeconomic consumer theory. A utility-based decision rule means that the attractiveness of an alternative is reducible to a scalar, and this scalar is denoted utility. Such a utility implies the notion that the decision maker makes trade-offs in comparing different attributes.

Extensions of Consumer Theory for Discrete Choice Analysis

While utility theory is not necessary for the behavioral models described in this chapter, microeconomic consumer theory does provide a helpful means of interpreting the framework, deriving choice models, and deriving measures of welfare change. Here we briefly discuss how economic consumer theory extends to discrete choice analysis. The seminal work linking discrete choice analysis with consumer theory is attributed to McFadden (1974). This section is based on Ben-Akiva and Lerman (1985) and Walker (2001).

Classic economic consumer theory assumes that consumers are rational decision makers. Consumers are faced with a set of possible consumption bundles, or collection of goods, where a single bundle can include a number of products, each of different quantities. Consumers are able to assign preferences to each of the various bundles and then choose the most preferred bundle. Under the assumptions of complete, transitive, and continuous preferences, there exists an ordinal utility function that expresses mathematically the consumer's preferences and associates a real number (or, more precisely, a cardinal realization) with each possible bundle such that it summarizes the preference orderings of the consumer. Consumer behavior is then an optimization problem in which the consumer selects the consumption bundle such that her utility is maximized subject to her budget constraint. The optimization is solved to obtain the demand functions in the form of quantities of goods demanded as a function of income and prices. The demand function can then be substituted back into the utility equation to derive the indirect utility function, defined as the maximum utility that is achievable under given prices and income. The indirect utility function (a function of prices and income, not quantities) is what is used in discrete choice analysis, and will be referred to simply as *utility* throughout this chapter.

There are several extensions to classic consumer theory that are important to discrete choice models.

First, classic consumer theory is concerned with continuous (that is, infinitely divisible) products, which is necessary for the calculus-based derivations of many of the key results. Discrete choice theory is concerned with a choice among a set of mutually exclusive alternatives, and therefore a different mathematical approach is necessary.

Second, classic consumer theory assumes homogeneous goods, and therefore the utility is a function of quantities only and not attributes. Lancaster (1966) proposed that it is the attributes (or, in his terminology, *characteristics*) of the goods that determine the utility they provide, and therefore utility can be expressed as a function of the attributes of the commodities (for example, a car has a make, model, and level of fuel efficiency).

Finally, classic consumer theory assumes deterministic behavior. Probabilistic choice models originated in psychology with Thurstone (1927), and were further developed by Luce (1959) and Marschak (1960). These introduced the concept that individual choice behavior is probabilistic as a way to explain observed intransitivity of preferences. Marschak (1960) provided a link to economics with the concept of random utility theory. McFadden (1974) then built the connection between econometric models of probabilistic choice and utility theory. Random utility theory attributes the source of the stochasticity to incomplete information of the analyst, and Manski (1977) identified four sources of uncertainty: unobserved alternative attributes, unobserved individual characteristics (or taste variations), measurement errors, and proxy (or instrumental) variables. More information can be obtained from Anderson et al. (1992), which discusses these issues at length. Therefore, utility is modeled as a random variable, consisting of an observable (that is, measurable) component and an unobservable (that is, random from the point of the modeler) component.

These modifications lead to the operational framework for discrete choice analysis that is described in the next section. That is, a framework that works for discrete choices among related commodities, makes use of a stochastic utility broken into systematic and random components, and is a function of attributes of the alternatives and characteristics of the decision maker.

Random Utility Model

Random utility theory, the origins of which were described above, is the most common theoretical basis of discrete choice models. The random utility model (or RUM) operationalizes this theory. In RUM, the utility is treated as a random variable. Specifically, the utility that individual n associates with alternative i in the choice set C_n is given by

$$U_{in} = V_{in} + \varepsilon_{in}. \tag{8.1}$$

V_{in} is the deterministic (or systematic) part of the utility, and is a function of the attributes of the alternative itself and the characteristics of the decision maker (together denoted as x_{in}). The term ε_{in} is the random component, capturing the unobservable portion of the utility. As we assume the alternative with the highest utility is chosen, the probability that alternative i is chosen by decision maker n from choice set C_n is

$$P(i|C_n) = P[U_{in} \geq U_{jn}, \forall j \in C_n] = P[U_{in} = \max_{j \in C_n} U_{jn}]. \tag{8.2}$$

Or, substituting in the deterministic and random components of the utility,

$$P(i|C_n) = P[V_{in} + \varepsilon_{in} \geq V_{jn} + \varepsilon_{jn}, \forall j \in C_n]$$

$$= P[\varepsilon_{jn} - \varepsilon_{in} \leq V_{in} - V_{jn}, \forall j \in C_n]. \tag{8.3}$$

This is a multivariate cumulative distribution function of a vector of epsilon differences (with respect to alternative *i*) evaluated for the vector of systematic utility differences (also with respect to alternative *i*).

The output of a random utility model is the probability of an individual selecting each alternative. These individual probabilities can be aggregated to produce forecasts for the population.

Simplifying assumptions are often made in order to maintain parsimonious and tractable discrete choice models. An assumption already highlighted above is that of utility maximization. Other simplifying assumptions include deterministic choice sets, the use of straightforward explanatory variables x_{in} (for example, relatively easy to measure characteristics of the decision maker and attributes of the alternative), and linearity in the unknown parameters β (that is, $V_{in} = \beta x_{in}$). Another key assumption is made on the distribution of the random component, ε, and this is addressed in the next section.

THE CLASSIC DISCRETE CHOICE MODELS

An operational discrete choice model requires calculation of the probability. To calculate the probability, one needs to specify the systematic portion of the utility (V) and the distribution of the random terms (ε). We described above how V is specified as a function of attributes. This section focuses on the distribution of the ε and how different distributional assumptions lead to different choice models. If we do not know very much about the distribution of ε (which is most often the case), the selection of an appropriate ε distribution becomes an issue of empirical exploration and mathematical convenience. While the assumptions employed in this section are relatively naïve, the point of the subsequent sections is to introduce more behavioral assumptions about the distribution of the random terms.

Here we present the most typical assumptions that are made regarding the distribution of ε, and we present the operational discrete choice model that result in each case. While such assumptions are made on the utilities in level form, the derivation of the model is based on the utility differences. The distribution of epsilon differences is derived from the assumed distribution of the epsilons in level form. The probability equation for the choice model is then simply the cumulative distribution function (cdf) of the epsilon differences evaluated at the differences of systematic utilities.

Probit

The name probit comes from *probability unit*. The probit model is based on the most obvious assumption to make, which is that the vector of random components

$\varepsilon_n = (\varepsilon_{1n}, \varepsilon_{2n}, \ldots, \varepsilon_{J_n n})'$ is multivariate normal distributed with a vector of means 0 and a $J_n \times J_n$ variance–covariance matrix Σ_ε, where J_n is the number of alternatives in C_n. For example, in the binomial case,

$$\begin{bmatrix} \varepsilon_{1n} \\ \varepsilon_{2n} \end{bmatrix} \sim N\left(\begin{bmatrix} 0 \\ 0 \end{bmatrix}, \begin{bmatrix} \sigma_1^2 & \sigma_{12} \\ \sigma_{12} & \sigma_2^2 \end{bmatrix} \right), \tag{8.4}$$

where σ_i^2 and σ_{ij} are the variance and covariance elements of Σ_ε. The difference in epsilons is

$$(\varepsilon_{2n} - \varepsilon_{1n}) \sim N(0, \sigma_1^2 + \sigma_2^2 - 2\sigma_{12}), \tag{8.5}$$

which we denote as $\Delta\varepsilon_n \sim N(0, \sigma^2)$.

The probability density function (pdf) is then

$$f(\Delta\varepsilon_n) = \frac{1}{\sigma\sqrt{2\pi}} e^{-\frac{1}{2}\left(\frac{\Delta\varepsilon}{\sigma}\right)^2}. \tag{8.6}$$

And the probit choice probability is the cumulative normal distribution, which is the integral over the pdf:

$$P(1|C_n) = \frac{1}{\sigma\sqrt{2\pi}} \int_{-\infty}^{V_n} e^{-\frac{1}{2}\left(\frac{q}{\sigma}\right)^2} dq = \Phi\left(\frac{V_n}{\sigma}\right), \tag{8.7}$$

where $V_n = V_{1n} - V_{2n}$ and $\Phi(\cdot)$ is the standard cumulative normal distribution.

For trinomial probit, where we have taken the utility differences with respect to the first alternative, the distribution of differenced epsilons is

$$\begin{bmatrix} \varepsilon_2 - \varepsilon_1 \\ \varepsilon_3 - \varepsilon_1 \end{bmatrix} \sim N\left(0, \Sigma_1 = \begin{bmatrix} \sigma_1^2 + \sigma_2^2 - 2\sigma_{12} & \sigma_1^2 + \sigma_{23} - \sigma_{12} - \sigma_{13} \\ \sigma_1^2 + \sigma_{23} - \sigma_{12} - \sigma_{13} & \sigma_1^2 + \sigma_3^2 - 2\sigma_{13} \end{bmatrix} \right). \tag{8.8}$$

Let $n(q; 0, \Sigma_1)$ denote the above bivariate density evaluated at the column vector $q = (q_1, q_2)'$, where Σ_1 is the variance–covariance matrix of epsilon differences taken with respect to alternative 1. The probability is then

$$P(1|C_n) = P(\varepsilon_{2n} - \varepsilon_{1n} \le V_{1n} - V_{2n} \text{ and } \varepsilon_{3n} - \varepsilon_{1n} \le V_{1n} - V_{3n}).$$

$$= \int_{-\infty}^{V_{1n}-V_{2n}} \int_{-\infty}^{V_{1n}-V_{3n}} n(q; 0, \Sigma_1) dq_1 dq_2. \tag{8.9}$$

More generally, a probit equation for a choice amongst J_n alternatives is based on the assumption that the random components of the utility functions are multivariate normal distributed with mean vector zero. The random component differences, $\Delta\varepsilon_1$, taken with respect to the first alternative is also multivariate normal distributed $\Delta\varepsilon_1 \sim MVN(0, \Sigma_1)$, with a distribution as follows:

$$f(\Delta\varepsilon_1) = (2\pi)^{-\frac{J_n-1}{2}}|\Sigma_1|^{-\frac{1}{2}}e^{-\frac{1}{2}(\Delta\varepsilon_1'\Sigma_1^{-1}\Delta\varepsilon_1)}. \tag{8.10}$$

Defining $n(q; 0, \Sigma_1)$ as the above multivariate density evaluated at the $(J_n - 1) \times 1$ column vector q, the probability of choosing alternative 1 is then

$$P(1|C_n) = \int_{-\infty}^{V_{1n}-V_{2n}} \int_{-\infty}^{V_{1n}-V_{3n}} \cdots \int_{-\infty}^{V_{1n}-V_{Jn}} n(q; 0, \Sigma_1)\, dq. \tag{8.11}$$

This model requires evaluation of a $J_n - 1$ integral to evaluate the choice probabilities. The main advantage of probit is its ability to capture all correlations among alternatives via the fully specified variance–covariance matrix Σ_1 of epsilon differences. However, it has no closed form expression and requires either numerical integration or simulation. Therefore, the closed form models presented next are attractive.

GEV Family: Logit, Nested Logit and Cross-nested Logit

The other set of classic discrete choice models are all members of the GEV family. (More recently GEV is being referred to as MEV or multivariate extreme value to be more consistent with the nomenclature for the statistical distribution employed.) This is a large family of models that include the logit and the nested-logit models. The logit model, the simplest of the GEV family, has been more popular than probit because of its tractability. However, it imposes restrictions on the covariance structure, which may be unrealistic in some contexts. The derivations of other models in the GEV family are aimed at relaxing restrictions, while maintaining tractability.

The term logit comes from *logistic probability unit*. The model was first introduced in the context of binomial choice. The binomial logit model arises from the assumption that $\varepsilon = \varepsilon_j - \varepsilon_i$ is logistically distributed (and ε_i, ε_j are iid extreme value), namely

$$F(\varepsilon) = \frac{1}{1 + e^{-\mu\varepsilon}} \text{ (the cdf) and}$$

$$f(\varepsilon) = \frac{\mu e^{-\mu\varepsilon}}{(1 + e^{-\mu\varepsilon})^2} \text{ (the pdf),} \tag{8.12}$$

where μ is a strictly positive scale parameter. Under the assumption that ε is logistically distributed, the cdf above is used to derive the choice probability for alternative i:

$$P_n(i) = P(U_{in} \geq U_{jn}) = \frac{1}{1 + e^{-\mu(V_{in}-V_{jn})}} = \frac{e^{\mu V_{in}}}{e^{\mu V_{in}} + e^{\mu V_{jn}}}. \tag{8.13}$$

More generally, a logit model with two or more alternatives is derived from the assumption that the random components of the utility functions are independent and identically extreme value distributed. That is, each ε_{in} for all i and n is distributed as

$$F(\varepsilon) = exp[-e^{-\mu(\varepsilon-\eta)}] \text{ (the cdf) and}$$

$$f(\varepsilon) = \mu e^{-\mu(\varepsilon-\eta)} exp[-e^{-\mu(\varepsilon-\eta)}] \text{ (the pdf)}, \tag{8.14}$$

where η is a location parameter (irrelevant as it cancels out) and μ is the same strictly positive scale parameter as in binomial logit above. As presented above, the difference of the two iid extreme value random variables has a logistic distribution and the choice probability is then the cdf of a logistic. While the derivation of the probability function for the multinomial case is not as transparent as the binomial logit (it requires further manipulation of the distributions above), the probability that a given individual n chooses alternative i within a choice set C_n is given by

$$P(i|C_n) = \frac{e^{\mu V_{in}}}{\Sigma_{j \in C_n} e^{\mu V_{jn}}}. \tag{8.15}$$

We don't show the derivation of this probability from the iid extreme value distributions; however, it is an intuitive extension from the binomial case where the denominator is now the sum of all J_n alternatives in the choice set C_n.

An important property of the logit model is independence from irrelevant alternatives (IIA). That is, the ratio of the probabilities of any two alternatives (i and j below) is independent of the choice set (C_1 and C_2 below) as follows:

$$\frac{P(i|C_1)}{P(j|C_1)} = \frac{P(i|C_2)}{P(j|C_2)} \forall i, j, C_1, C_2, \tag{8.16}$$

where $i, j \in C_1, i, j \in C_2, C_1 \subseteq C_n$ and $C_2 \subseteq C_n$.

This property is both a blessing and a curse. It is a blessing because (if valid), it simplifies the analysis, for example subsets of a choice set can be considered independently and alternatives can be added in forecasting. The property is also necessary to derive techniques that are commonly used in practice, for example sampling of alternatives. However, in many cases this property is inconsistent with behavior, and therefore logit cannot be used.

The core of the problem leading to logit's IIA property is the assumption that the random components are mutually independent. The nested logit model relaxes this assumption of logit, capturing some correlations among alternatives. It overcomes the IIA problem when utilities of alternatives are correlated (such as the red bus and blue bus problem) or when multidimensional choices are considered (such as departure time and route choice). It is based on the partitioning of the choice set C_n into M mutually exclusive and collectively exhaustive nests C_{mn}. Here we present the model in the case of two levels, although the model can be extended to any number of levels (see Ben-Akiva and Lerman, 1985). The probability that decision maker n chooses alternative i within nest C_{mn} is given by the product of a marginal probability (of choosing a particular nest C_{mn}) and a conditional probability (of choosing a particular alternative i within that nest) as follows:

$$P(i|C_n) = P(C_{mn}|C_n)P(i|C_{mn}), \tag{8.17}$$

where:

$$P(C_{mn}|C_n) = \frac{e^{\mu V_{C_{mn}}}}{\sum_{l=1}^{M} e^{\mu V_{C_{ln}}}},$$ (8.18a)

$$P(i|C_{mn}) = \frac{e^{\mu_m V_{in}}}{\sum_{j \in C_{mn}} e^{\mu_m V_{jn}}}, \text{ and}$$ (8.18b)

$$V_{C_{mn}} = \frac{1}{\mu_m} \ln \sum_{j \in C_{mn}} e^{\mu_m V_{jn}}.$$ (8.18c)

The first probability is the probability of choosing from within a particular nest C_{mn}. The second probability is probability of choosing alternative i in nest C_{mn} conditioned on choosing one of the alternatives from within nest C_{mn}. The last term $V_{C_{mn}}$ is the systematic part of the expected maximum utility of the alternatives in nest C_{mn}. It is also known as the logsum, inclusive value, or accessibility, and it is an attempt to describe an individual's utility of the *best* alternative *within* nest C_{mn}. As the random components for each individual are unknown, this value of the best alternative is an expected value. The formula of the expected value derives from the properties of the extreme value distribution (stated below as *result number 3* of the G-function).

Parameters μ and μ_m reflect the correlation among alternatives within the nest C_{mn}. The correlation between the utility of two alternatives is

$$Corr(U_{in}, U_{jn}) = \begin{cases} 1 - \dfrac{\mu^2}{\mu_m^2} & \text{if } i \text{ and } j \in C_{mn} \\ 0 & \text{otherwise} \end{cases},$$ (8.19)

where $0 < \mu/\mu_m \leq 1$ (see Ben-Akiva and Lerman, 1985). If $\mu = \mu_m$ for all m then $Corr(U_{in}, U_{jn}) = 0$ for all i not equal to j and the model reverts to logit. It is not possible to identify μ and all μ_m in the model, and one must be constrained (typically one of them is set to 1).

More generally, logit and nested logit are members of the GEV family of models, which were proposed by McFadden (1978). The GEV family is attractive because it allows for a multivariate distribution of the random components (that is, it relaxes the independence assumption) and yet retains a closed form expression for the choice probability.

A GEV model depends on a function G, which is a non-negative, differentiable function defined for positive arguments with the following properties (from Ben-Akiva and Lerman, 1985):

1. G is homogeneous of degree $\mu > 0$; that is $G(\alpha z_1, \ldots, \alpha z_i, \ldots \alpha z_{J_n}) = \alpha^\mu G(z_1, \ldots, z_i, \ldots z_{J_n})$.[1]

2. $\lim_{z_i \to \infty} G(z_1, \ldots, z_i, \ldots z_{J_n}) = \infty, \forall i = 1, \ldots, J_n$.

3. The kth partial derivative with respect to k distinct z_i is non-negative if k is odd, and non-positive if k is even.

A function G (called the *G-function*) that satisfies these conditions yields the following three results:

1. The cumulative distribution function is

$$F(\varepsilon_1, \ldots, \varepsilon_{J_n}) = e^{-G(e^{-\varepsilon_1}, \ldots, e^{-\varepsilon_{J_n}})}.$$

(8.20)

2. The choice model is

$$P(i|C_n) = \frac{e^{V_{in}} \dfrac{\partial G(e^{V_{1n}}, \ldots, e^{V_{J_n}})}{\partial e^{V_{in}}}}{\mu G(e^{V_{1n}}, \ldots, e^{V_{J_n}})},$$

(8.21)

or, denoting $G_i(e^{V_{1n}}, \ldots, e^{V_{J_n}}) = \dfrac{\partial G(e^{V_{1n}}, \ldots, e^{V_{J_n}})}{\partial e^{V_{in}}}$, we can write

$$P(i|C_n) = \frac{e^{V_{in}} G_i(e^{V_{1n}}, \ldots, e^{V_{J_n}})}{\mu G(e^{V_{1n}}, \ldots, e^{V_{J_n}})}.$$

(8.22)

McFadden (1978) shows that the choice model defined by this equation is consistent with random utility maximization. This probability can be rewritten in the form of a logit model (see Ben-Akiva and Lerman, 1985, for the derivation) as:

$$P(i|C_n) = \frac{e^{V_{in} + \ln G_i(\ldots)}}{\sum_{j=1}^{J_n} e^{V_{jn} + \ln G_j(\ldots)}}.$$

(8.23)

As described in Ben-Akiva and Lerman (1985), the 'extra twist' beyond logit is that 'the utilities of the alternatives are functions of not only their own attributes (through the V's) but also of the attributes of the competing alternatives (through the partial derivatives of the G-function)'. It is this additional portion of the utility that allows for a departure from IIA.

3. The expected maximum utility (V_C) of a set of alternatives $i = 1, \ldots, J_n$ is:

$$V_C = \frac{\ln G(e^{V_1}, \ldots, e^{V_{J_n}}) + \gamma}{\mu}, \text{ where } \gamma \text{ is Euler's constant } (\sim 0.577).$$

(8.24)

From the GEV theorem, the known family of logit models can be derived. The logit model is a GEV model with G-function

$$G(z) = \sum_{i=1}^{J_n} z_i^{\mu}.$$

(8.25)

Nested logit has a G-function of

$$G(z) = \sum_{m=1}^{M} \left(\sum_{i \in C_{mn}} z_i^{\mu_m} \right)^{\frac{\mu}{\mu_m}},$$

(8.26)

where M is defined (as above) as the number of nests.

The only other commonly used GEV form is the cross-nested logit model (and its variants, including paired combinatorial logit and generalized nested logit, see Koppelman and Sethi, 2000), which has a G-function of

$$G(z) = \sum_{m=1}^{M} \left(\sum_{j \in C_n} \alpha_{jm} z_i^{\mu_m} \right)^{\frac{\mu}{\mu_m}}.$$
(8.27)

While the GEV model does allow for multivariate random component distribution, it still has limitations. The mixture models described in the next section further relax the restrictions.

MIXTURE MODELS

There has been an evolving sophistication of choice models in which restrictions of earlier model forms are relaxed. The latest wave of advances has been in the area of mixture models. Mixtures have been used for a long time in mathematics as a way to generate flexible distributional forms.

To demonstrate the idea of mixtures and to motivate their usefulness, we take a step *away* from choice models and consider a simple mixture of normal distributions. (This is not probit and does not have to do with the random components of a choice model; here we present an example of a mixture with plain-vanilla random variables that have normal distributions.) Figure 8.1 demonstrates how a mixture of two normal distributions yields a bimodal distribution that could not otherwise be captured by a standard parametric distribution. The mixture shown is 40 per cent of a $N(mean = 2, standard deviation = 1)$ and 60 per cent of a $N(mean = 6, standard deviation = 2)$, which yields the binomial distribution denoted by the solid line. Mathematically, this resulting bimodal probability

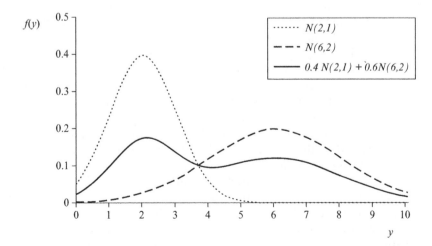

Figure 8.1   Discrete mixture of normal distributions

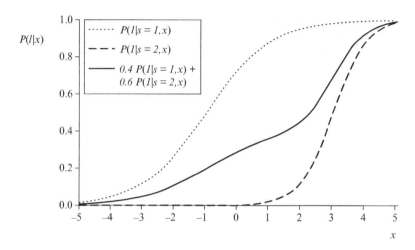

Figure 8.2   Discrete mixture of binomial logit probability distribution

density function can be written as a convex combination of the two underlying normal probability densities as follows:

$$h(y) = 0.4\, \phi\!\left(\frac{y - 2}{1}\right) + 0.6\, \phi\!\left(\frac{y - 6}{2}\right),$$ (8.28)

where $\phi(\cdot)$ is the standard normal density distribution with mean equal to 0 and variance equal to 1. To emphasize, the key with mixtures is that they are a straightforward way of taking relatively restrictive functions and generating more flexible functions.

Now we return to choice models and discuss mixtures within this context. As with the more general example above that mixed normal distributions, the motivation of mixing choice models is also to obtain more flexible models. The mixture model of interest for choice modeling is a *probability mixture model*, which is a probability distribution that is a convex combination of other probability distributions. A choice model analogy to Figure 8.1 is shown in Figure 8.2. This is a discrete probability mixture of two binomial logit probabilities. Each logit probability is explained by a constant and a continuous explanatory variable x (plotted along the x-axis). The vertical axis is the probability of choosing alternative 1. One of the binomial logits ($s = 1$) has an intercept of 1 and a coefficient of x of 1. The other binomial logit ($s = 2$) has an intercept of -6 and the coefficient of x is 2. These logit models result in probability functions that are S-curves. The coefficient of x impacts the steepness of the curve and so the second logit ($s = 2$) has a steeper incline than the first ($s = 1$). The inflection points of the S-curves are at probability 0.5, which is when the systematic utility is equal to 0. The systematic utility for the first logit is $1 + x$ and so the inflection point is at $x = -1$. The systematic utility of the second logit is $-6 + 2x$ and so the inflection point is at $x = 3$. While these logit functions lead to standard and inflexible S-curves, mixing the two can lead to more flexible functions. We show such a mixture in Figure 8.2 that mixes 40 per cent from the first logit with 60 per cent from the second. The resulting mixed probability distribution is then

$$P(i = 1|x) = 0.4P(i = 1|s = 1, x) + 0.6P(i = 1|s = 2, x)$$

$$= 0.4\frac{1}{1 + e^{-(1+x)}} + 0.6\frac{1}{1 + e^{-(-6+2x)}}. \tag{8.29}$$

As with the mixture of normals in Figure 8.1, the mixed probability (the solid line in Figure 8.2) is a far departure from the inflexible S-curve and has a shape that could otherwise not be captured by a standard discrete choice model. What we have shown here is a simple example to motivate mixtures in choice models. Note that this is an example of a *latent class choice model*, which will be discussed and generalized later in the chapter.

While these are both examples of mixtures with a discrete mixing distribution, the mixing distribution can also be continuous. For example, a choice model with a normally distributed random parameter has a continuous mixing distribution, namely, the normal density distribution.

Early exploration of mixture models in discrete choice arose through the quest for a smooth probability simulator to estimate a probit model (Bolduc and Ben-Akiva, 1991; McFadden, 1989; Stern, 1992; and described in Walker et al., 2007). From a behavioral perspective, an early motivation of mixture models in discrete choice was to capture heterogeneity of choice set. For example, the logit captivity model (Ben-Akiva, 1977; Gaudry and Dagenais, 1979) is a discrete mixture of a standard logit model and a 'captive' model in which the choice set is reduced to a single alternative. Another early motivation was to account for unobserved taste heterogeneity. Boyd and Mellman (1980) and Cardell and Dunbar (1980) employed mixture models of logit on market share data and Ben-Akiva et al. (1993) on individual-level data. Other motivations include allowing for flexible substitution patterns (for example, Brownstone and Train, 1999), to capture panel effects (for example, Erdem, 1996), and to account for unobserved effects (for example, Toledo, 2003). Further discussion of these variations, including additional references, is provided below.

Typology of Mixture Models

Probability mixture models are a broad class of model that can vary on a number of dimensions. The distribution being mixed can be any type of choice model (logit, GEV, probit and so forth, and dynamic or static). The mixing distribution can be continuous or discrete, and can be specified with covariates or without. The mixing distribution can be motivated by either statistical or behavioral principles. Further, behavioral specifications can be in regard to different aspects of the choice model such as decision rules and tastes. The models may employ only the choice response as an indicator of the preference (utility), or they may employ additional indicators specific to the mixing aspect and so on.

Variation along these dimensions lead to an endless number of mixture models that can, indeed, approximate any distributional form. McFadden and Train (2000) demonstrate, for example, that a mixed logit model can approximate any random utility model to any degree of accuracy. Mixture models are typically more complex to estimate than choice models without mixing. However increases in computational power, improvement in optimization techniques, and use of simulation and alternative estimators (such as Bayesian) have made such complex models possible and have lead to a proliferation of their use. Train (2009) provides discussion of such advances.

In the remainder of this chapter, we first review the most typical form of discrete and continuous mixtures found in the choice modeling literature. Following this review, we motivate and discuss *behavioral* mixture models.

Discrete Probability Mixtures

Recall that the simple example of a choice model mixture that was presented above (Figure 8.2) was a discrete mixture of choice probabilities. The general formulation of discrete probability mixtures takes the form

$$P(i|C_n, \gamma) = \sum_{s=1}^{s} \gamma_s P(i|C_{sn}, \theta_s) \tag{8.30}$$

where $P(i|C_n, \gamma)$ is the probability of interest, $s = 1, \ldots, S$ denotes distinct classes, the distributions being mixed are the class-specific choice probabilities, $P(i|C_{sn}, \theta_s)$ (with unknown class-specific coefficients θ_s), and the mixing distribution γ_s are the class membership probabilities (which must sum to 1). In the simple example presented above, $S = 2$ and the class-specific choice probabilities are both binomial logit. Discrete choice mixtures are employed when there is believed to be distinct, yet unknown, classes of behavior within the population. The most basic form is shown here in which the mixing distribution is not a function of covariates. This model has been popular in market research to do market segmentation. The covariate mixture model will be presented in the next section on behavioral mixture models, and further references will be provided. The primary advantages of discrete choice mixture models (versus the continuous probability mixtures presented next) are that the probability distribution does not require an integral (unless it is a mixture of choice models that require an integral) and it does not require a-priori specification of the distribution of the parameters.

Continuous Probability Mixtures

The continuous mixture choice model takes the form

$$P(i|C_n, \gamma) = \int_\theta P(i|C_n, \theta) g(\theta|\gamma) d\theta, \tag{8.31}$$

where $P(i|C_n, \gamma)$ is the probability of interest (and γ the unknown parameters), $P(i|C_n, \theta)$ is the choice probability distribution being mixed (with parameters θ) and $g(\theta|\gamma)$ is the mixing distribution. Note that if $g(\theta|\gamma)$ takes on discrete values, then this reduces to the discrete probability mixture described above. The continuous mixture form has been widely used for a variety of purposes. The most common use is to capture random taste variation as in random parameter logit (for example, Hess et al., 2005). Other uses include modeling alternative-specific variances (for example, Gönül and Srinivasan, 1993), flexible substitution patterns (for example, Bhat, 1998), correlations over multiple responses (for example, Revelt and Train, 1998), correlations over time (for example, Toledo, 2003), and correlations over space (for example, Vichiensan et al., 2005).

Various choice models have been used for $P(i|C_n, \theta)$, most typically logit but also other GEV forms such as nested logit (for example, Dugundji and Walker, 2005).

The primary specification issue of a continuous probability mixture is the specification of the mixing distribution. Various distributions have been used such as normal, lognormal, and triangular (see, for example, the discussion in Train, 2009) and these distributions can either be independent univariate distributions over the choice model parameters or be multivariate distributions. Typically, the mixing distribution is not a function of covariates, although it can include covariates (for example, Greene et al., 2006). The primary estimation issue is the costly computation of the integral, for which simulation techniques are primarily employed (see Train, 2009). Thus, it has the same disadvantages as the probit model. However, it is advantageous over probit because it allows for non-normal mixing distributions.

Limitations of Mixture Models

The mixture models thus described are powerful; the model forms can fit any distribution and significantly increase model fit. However, there are also issues that arise with such mixture approaches. First is that the sophisticated models of the covariance are a black box in that, while they may provide an excellent fit to the data, the cause or source of the distribution is not readily apparent. Difficulties arise from the explosion of parameters that are difficult to interpret, a tendency to overfit the data, and the lack of insight provided for policy and marketing analysis. Additionally, use of such mixture models for forecasting requires the assumption that the distributions have temporal stability, which is highly suspect.

BEHAVIORAL MIXTURE MODELS

The limitations just described lead to the direction of *behavioral (or structural) mixture models*. The concept of the behavioral mixture model is to provide a behavioral rationale to the mixture rather than an ad-hoc distribution. This is done by modeling the covariance structure via explicit latent variable constructs as the method to capture the source of behavioral heterogeneity. That is, treat the mixing distribution as an additional model – a mixing distribution of behavioral factors based on a-priori considerations that have meaning and its estimation results can be interpreted.

A framework for behavioral mixture models is shown in Figure 8.3, which was presented in Ben-Akiva et al. (2002b) in the context of incorporating attitudes and perceptions in choice models. Observable variables are shown in rectangles and unobservable or latent variables are shown in ellipses. Solid arrows represent structural equations (cause-and-effect relationships) and dashed arrows represent measurement equations (relationships between observable indicators and the underlying latent variables). The framework for a traditional choice model is shown within Figure 3 as those elements with a bold outline. In the traditional case, preferences (captured mathematically via utility functions) are the only latent variables. While the preferences are unobserved, revealed and stated preferences (which can be observed) are used to make inferences on preferences. Further, characteristics of the respondents and attributes of the alternatives

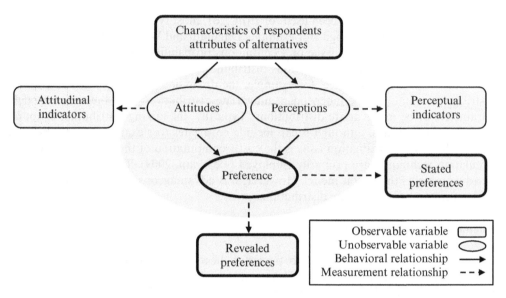

Source: Ben-Akiva et al. (2002b)

Figure 8.3   Conceptual framework for behavioral mixture models

(also observable) are assumed to be causal factors affecting preferences. The resulting models directly link the observed inputs to the observed output, thereby assuming that behavior is implicitly captured in the utility function.

The mixture models described above extend the traditional framework through less restrictive specifications of the distributions of the disturbance terms in the choice model's utility function. The idea behind the behavioral mixture model is to specify such mixtures with latent constructs to capture attitudes and perceptions. Further, these attitudes and perceptions may be explained by observable attributes of the alternatives and characteristics of the individual. Kahneman (1997) and other behavioral scientists have emphasized the importance of attitudes as the 'emotional core' driving many decision-making processes. Ajzen (2005) describes an attitude as 'a disposition to respond favorably or unfavorably to an object, person, institution, or event'. In the context of choice modeling, an attitude is a predisposition towards exhibiting a particular behavior. Attitudes are formed over time and are affected by social norms and past experience.

A more general way to interpret the latent variables in this framework is that the attitude latent variable is an unobserved characteristic of the respondent. The perception latent variable captures attributes of the alternatives as perceived by the decision maker. The key to the behavioral mixture is that these explicit and interpretable latent constructs define the mixing distributions. The fact that these latent constructs define the mixing distribution will become apparent when the mathematical formulations are presented in the following sections. Effectively what is done is that there are two models being combined: the choice model, which is a function of the latent variables, and the latent variables model. For example, choice may be a function of a factor such as environmental consciousness. To begin to model environmental consciousness, we

Environmental awareness
- *I am willing to pay more for travel if it would help the environment.*
- *Use of transit can help improve the environment.*

Sensitivity to schedules
- *I need to make trips to a wide variety of locations each week.*
- *I need the flexibility to make many trips during the day.*
- *I generally make the same types of trips at the same times.*

Urban form preferences
- *I am willing to travel longer to have a big house and a garden.*
- *I like to live within walking distance to shops and restaurants.*
- *I enjoy the hustle and bustle of the city.*

Responses are collected on a Likert scale. For example, the respondent is asked to state how much he/she agrees with each statement on a scale from 1 (do not agree at all) to 5 (completely agree).

Figure 8.4   Example of survey questions to obtain psychometric indicators for attitudes toward transportation and urban form

need to make assumptions about a distribution and corresponding unknown parameters (such as mean and variance), and explain these parameters in terms of covariates. We call this model of the latent variable a structural model (solid arrows in the figure) because it represents the behavior of interest. This model of environmental consciousness then becomes the mixing distribution over which the choice probability is mixed or integrated.

The framework also shows the use of indicators of the latent variables. Just as stated and revealed preferences are indicators of preferences, we may also have attitudinal and perceptual indicators to provide information on attitudes and perceptions. For example, the psychometric indicators shown in Figure 8.4 are indicators of latent constructs related to attitudes towards transportation and urban form. We refer to the relationships between the latent variables and such indicators measurement equations (dashed arrows), because they are additional measurements to help identify the parameters of the latent variable model and are not a part of the behavior of interest. Use of such indicators becomes important in order to estimate more complex behavioral structures.

Finally, the latent variables can be either discrete or continuous, and each form is taken in turn in the next two sections of the chapter and mathematical formulations are provided.

Discrete Behavioral Mixtures

In its simplest form, a discrete behavioral mixture is closely related to the discrete mixture model described above, with the addition that the class-membership model is parameterized with socio-economic and situational data. Such a specification provides a causal or behavioral structure to the heterogeneity. The model then takes the form

$$P(i|C_n, \gamma) = \sum_{s=1}^{s} Q_n(s|\gamma) P(i|C_{sn}, \theta_s), \tag{8.32}$$

where $P(i|C_n, \gamma)$ is the probability of interest, $s = 1, \ldots, S$ denotes distinct behavioral classes, the distributions being mixed $P(i|C_{sn}, \theta_s)$ are the class-specific choice probabilities, and the parameters of the mixing distribution $Q_n(s|\gamma)$ are class membership probabilities parameterized by coefficients γ and which must sum to 1. Such a model is behavioral on two fronts: the latent classes themselves have distinct behavioral meanings and the membership in these latent classes is explained by covariates. This form of the discrete behavioral mixture is particularly accessible as there are well-established estimation software programs to estimate such models (also known as latent class choice models). While we leave the introduction of the indicators (which add complexity to the model) to the next section on the *continuous* behavioral mixtures, the reader is referred to Gopinath (1995) for examples of discrete behavioral mixtures with indicators.

The discrete behavioral mixtures are used when there is believed to be distinct, yet unknown, classes of behavior within the population. The behavior can vary across classes in terms of the choice set considered (for example, Ben-Akiva and Boccara 1995; Manski, 1977; Swait and Ben-Akiva, 1987), decision protocol (for example, Gopinath, 1995), or taste parameters (for example, Greene and Hensher, 2003; Kamakura and Russell, 1989; and Walker and Li, 2007). Among other advantages, the insights on market segmentation derived from the discrete behavioral mixture model provide a powerful analysis tool. An example of such will be provided in the empirical results section.

Continuous Behavioral Mixtures

Continuous behavioral mixture models refer to cases in which the latent variables are continuous constructs. The framework and notation for continuous latent variable models with indicators is shown in Figure 8.5. This formulation and discussion are adapted from Ben-Akiva et al. (2002b). The motivation is to employ as the mixing distribution a multivariate distribution of behavioral factors with parameters that have interpretation. Here we note these behavioral factors as x^*, to distinguish them from the observable factors x. There are two models we have to specify: the choice model ($x, x^* \to U \to i$ in Figure 8.5) and the model for the latent behavioral factors ($x \to x^* \to I$ in Figure 8.5).

In terms of the choice model, the preferences are a function of both observed variables x and latent variables x^*. The choice probability of i is then conditioned on both on x and x^* as follows:

$$P(i|x, x^*; \theta), \tag{8.33}$$

where θ is a set of unknown parameters to be estimated. The probability can take on the form of any choice model. However, unlike a traditional choice model, the latent variables are unknown explanatory variables and must be integrated out. This brings us to the second model, the distribution of the latent behavioral factors.

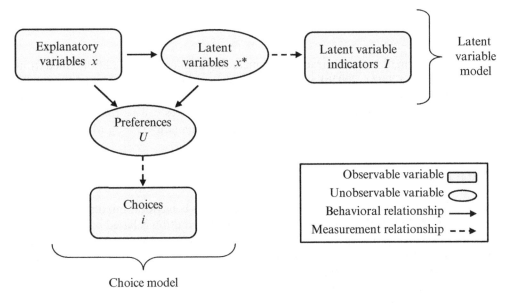

Source: Ben-Akiva et al. (2002b)

Figure 8.5   Behavioral mixture model framework

To develop the latent variable behavioral model, we need to make a-priori assumptions about the distribution of the latent factors and on the covariates x that explain their parameters. Further, this distribution has unknown parameters to be estimated γ. We denote this distribution as $f_s(x^*|x; \gamma)$. The subscript s is used to denote that this is a structural relationship, that is, it represents the behavior of interest. This is to distinguish it from the measurement equation that is described next. Combining the choice model above with the latent variable behavioral model, we have

$$P(i|x; \theta, \gamma) = \int_{x^*} P(i|x, x^*; \theta) f_s(x^*|x; \gamma) dx^*. \tag{8.34}$$

In this model, the latent variable model is the mixing function. As this model has an interpretation (for example an attitude such as environmental consciousness), we call this a behavioral mixture.

While it is possible to stop at the equation above, it is difficult to obtain identification of the unknown parameters related to the latent variables. Therefore, additional measurements in the form of psychometric indicators (e.g., Figure 8.4) are incorporated. To incorporate these measurements, we need an additional model, which we call a measurement model. The model requires assumptions about the conditional distribution of indicators as a function of the latent variables and a set of parameters α, or $f_m(I|x^*; \alpha)$. Here, the subscript m is used to denote that it is a measurement model rather than a structural model. Introducing this third component to the behavioral mixture above, the joint likelihood of the choice and the latent variable indicators becomes

$$P(i, I|x; \theta, \gamma, \alpha) = \int_{x^*} P(i|x, x^*; \theta) f_m(I|x^*; \alpha) f_s(x^*|x; \gamma) dx^*. \qquad (8.35)$$

Additional information on this framework, including applications, can be obtained from Ben-Akiva et al. (2002a, 2002b) and Walker and Ben-Akiva (2002). McFadden (1986) presented the methodological seed for introducing latent variables into choice models. Other early applications of continuous behavioral mixtures can be found in Ashok et al. (2002), Boersch-Supan et al. (1996), Cambridge Systematics (1986), Morikawa et al. (2002) and Train et al. (1987).

What is Behavioral?

Clearly there is a continuum as to how behavioral is a behavioral mixture model. The key idea of a behavioral mixture is that the mixing distribution is based on a behavioral hypothesis or theory that involves latent variables. This leads to an explicit and behavioral model of the mixing distribution, which may include both discrete and continuous latent variables as well as structural relationships among latent variables. Further, with survey data oriented to the inclusion of latent variables, the indicators will be heavily relied upon in order to better estimate the unknown parameters in the model.

EMPIRICAL APPLICATION

In this empirical application we demonstrate the various choice model formulations using a single dataset. The objective is simply to provide an example and is not intended as a test or competition between models to determine which one is the best from both theoretical and practical reasons. The application focuses on a central aspect of transportation, which is the interaction between transport and land use. The study investigates how choices of residential location are impacted by accessibility to work as well as to shopping, services, entertainment, and parks. Different modes are considered, including auto, bus, bike and walk. In addition to the transport-related factors, other factors that influence residential location are included such as housing price, crime and schools.

For this application, we make use of a stated preference survey of household residential location choice decisions conducted as part of a transport study in Portland, Oregon, in 1994. This survey is a small part of a large data collection effort conducted in Portland to improve their travel demand models. The effort included a rich household activity and travel survey that gathered household demographic data as well as revealed and stated preferences regarding a wide range of transport and land use behavior. The full effort as well as further detail on the piece used here is available in Cambridge Systematics (1996).

The objective of the stated preference survey we use here was to better understand the effect of urban design and transport policies on residential location decisions. Each survey question asked for a preference among five hypothetical housing options, with alternatives varying across price, size, community amenities, accessibility, and several other factors influencing residential choices. An example choice experiment is provided in Figure 8.6. Each choice experiment consisted of the five alternatives shown (buy single-family, buy multi-family, rent single-family, rent multi-family, and move out of the metro area)

	(Alternative 1)	(Alternative 2)	(Alternative 3)	(Alternative 4)	(Alternative 5)
	Buy Single Family	Buy Multi-Family	Rent Single Family	Rent Multi-Family	
Type of dwelling	*single house*	*apartment*	*duplex / row house*	*condominium*	Move out of the metro area
Residence size	*< 1000 sq. ft.*	*500–1,000 sq. ft.*	*1500 – 2000 sq. ft.*	*< 500 sq. ft.*	
Lot size	*< 5000 sq. ft.*	*n/a*	*5000 – 7500 sq. ft.*	*n/a*	
Parking	*street parking only*	*street parking only*	*driveway, no garage*	*reserved, uncovered*	
Price or monthly rents	*< $75K*	*$50K – $100K*	*> $1200*	*$300 – $600*	
Community type	*mixed use*	*mixed use*	*rural*	*urban*	
Housing mix	*mostly single family*	*mostly multi-family*	*mostly multi-family*	*mostly multi-family*	
Age of development	*10–15 years*	*0–5 years*	*10–15 years*	*0–5 years*	
Mix of residential ownership	*mostly own*	*mostly own*	*mostly rent*	*mostly own*	
Shops/services/entertainment	*community square*	*basic shops*	*community square*	*basic, specialty shops*	
Local parks	*none*	*yes*	*none*	*none*	
Bicycle paths	*none*	*yes*	*yes*	*yes*	
School quality	*very good*	*very good*	*fair*	*fair*	
Neighborhood safety	*average*	*average*	*average*	*average*	
Shopping prices relative to avg	*20% more*	*20% more*	*same*	*10% more*	
Walking time to shops	*20–30 minutes*	*20–30 minutes*	*< 10 minutes*	*10–20 minutes*	
Bus fare, travel time to shops	*$1.00, 15–20 minutes*	*$1.00, > 20 minutes*	*$0.50, 5–10 minutes*	*$0.50, < 5 minutes*	
Travel time to work by auto	*> 20 minutes*	*15–20 minutes*	*15–20 minutes*	*< 10 minutes*	
Travel time to work by transit	*> 45 minutes*	*30–45 minutes*	*30–45 minutes*	*15–30 minutes*	

Source: Adapted from Cambridge Systematics (1996)

Figure 8.6   Choice experiment example

and the list of attributes shown (type of dwelling, residence size and so forth). Note that almost half of the attributes are closely related to transport and accessibility, whereas the remaining attributes are important non-transport factors that influence residential choice. The fifth alternative of moving out of the metro area is a so-called 'opt-out' alternative.

Each individual was presented with eight different choice experiments of the format shown in Figure 8.6, and the values of the attributes that describe each alternative varied across each choice experiment. There were 16 different versions (blocks) of the questionnaire, that is 16 different sets of eight choice experiments, each appearing as in Figure 8.6 but with differing attributes selected based on the experimental design. The survey was administered to 611 individuals (we use a cleaned set of 507 individuals) and each survey respondent was assigned randomly to one of the 16 blocks.

Using these data, we estimate five different models:

1. Logit
2. Nested Logit
3. Logit mixture – error component
4. Logit mixture – random parameter
5. Behavioral logit mixture – latent class choice model

The estimation results are presented in Table 8.1.[2] Each model estimates the probability of choosing each of the five alternatives: buy single family, buy multiple family,

Table 8.1a Estimation results

Variable	Model 1 Logit		Model 2 Nested Logit		Model 3 Logit Mixture 1 Error Component	
	Coef	*t*-stat	Coef	*t*-stat	Coef	*t*-stat
Housing Attributes						
Monthly rent ($00) – low/middle income	−0.135	**−13.0**	−0.126	**−10.0**	−0.162	**−13.8**
Monthly rent ($00) – high income	−0.077	**−5.3**	−0.069	**−4.1**	−0.051	**−2.9**
Monthly rent ($00) – income not available	−0.136	**−7.7**	−0.128	**−6.8**	−0.160	**−6.6**
Purchase price ($000) – low income	−0.905	**−13.4**	−0.853	**−10.9**	−1.192	**−13.7**
Purchase price ($000) – middle income	−0.617	**−11.2**	−0.573	**−8.9**	−0.719	**−10.7**
Purchase price ($000) – high income	−0.307	**−4.7**	−0.272	**−3.9**	−0.249	**−3.0**
Purchase price ($000) – income not available	−0.582	**−7.2**	−0.537	**−6.1**	−0.644	**−5.7**
Single house (v. Duplex)	0.323	**5.9**	0.293	**4.9**	0.382	**6.3**
Condo (v. Apartment)	0.162	**2.3**	0.143	**2.1**	0.170	**2.3**
Residential size (square feet/1000)	0.380	**7.7**	0.352	**6.7**	0.440	**8.3**
Lot size (square feet/1000)	0.008	1.3	0.008	1.4	0.008	1.2
Neighborhood Attributes						
Mostly owners (v. mostly renters)	0.151	**3.4**	0.141	**3.4**	0.181	**3.8**
Mostly multi-family housing (v. mostly single family)	−0.026	−0.6	−0.027	−0.7	−0.041	−0.9
Schools – 75 percentile (v. below 60)	0.268	**5.0**	0.246	**4.6**	0.190	**2.8**
Schools – 60–75 percentile (v. below 60)	0.166	**2.7**	0.155	**2.6**	0.301	**5.1**
Above average safety (v. average)	0.103	**2.5**	0.102	**2.6**	0.127	**2.8**
Mixed use (v. rural)	0.057	0.9	0.054	1.0	0.073	1.1
Urban (v. rural)	0.013	0.2	0.020	0.3	0.040	0.6
Suburban (v. rural)	−0.075	−1.2	−0.066	−1.1	−0.062	−0.9
Local bike path (v. no local bike path)	0.079	1.8	0.069	1.7	0.083	1.8
Local park (v. no local park)	0.020	0.5	0.016	0.4	0.021	0.5
Local community square (v. no shops)	0.190	**3.2**	0.175	**3.1**	0.213	**3.3**
Basic plus specialty shops (v. no shops)	0.146	**2.4**	0.144	**2.5**	0.173	**2.6**
Basic shops (v. no shops)	0.129	**2.1**	0.116	**2.0**	0.153	**2.3**
Transport Attributes						
Walk time to local shops (minutes)	−0.007	**−3.7**	−0.007	**−3.7**	−0.009	**−4.0**
Travel time to work by auto (minutes)	−0.004	−0.9	−0.004	−0.9	−0.001	−0.2
Travel time to work by transit (minutes)	−0.006	**−2.6**	−0.005	**−2.5**	−0.006	**−2.6**
Off street parking available (v. no off street parking)	0.364	**6.3**	0.331	**5.3**	0.427	**6.9**
Correlation Terms						
Nesting parameter – Buy alternatives			1.150	1.0 v. 1		
Nesting parameter – Rent alternatives			1.130	0.8 v. 1		
Nesting parameter – Move out alternative			1.000	fixed		
Standard deviation – Buy alternatives					0.840	**7.0**
Standard deviation – Rent alternatives					1.182	**10.8**
Standard deviation – Move out alternative					2.178	**20.5**
Number of observations	4056		4056		4056	
Number of parameters	34		36		37	
Null Log-likelihood	−6527.88		−6527.88		−6527.88	
Final Log-likelihood	−5729.35		−5728.48		−5044.40	
Rho-square	0.122		0.122		0.227	
Adjusted rho-square	0.117		0.117		0.222	

Source: Model 1 and 5 from Walker and Li (2007)

| Model 4 Logit Mixture 2 Random Parameter | | | | Model 5 Behavioral Logit Mixture | | | | | | | |
| Mean | | Standard Dev. | | Class Independent | | Class 1 'Suburban' | | Class 2 'Transit' | | Class 3 'Urban' | |
Coef	t-stat	Coef	t-stat	Coef	t-stat	Coef	t-stat	Coef	t-stat	Coef	t-stat
-0.212	-11.4	0.107	6.0	-0.152	-11.5						
-0.122	-3.2	0.149	3.8	-0.079	-3.6						
-0.171	-5.4	0.021	0.5	-0.160	-5.0						
-1.520	-9.3	0.846	5.4	-1.007	-9.8						
-0.925	-11.2	0.380	6.1	-0.928	-11.2						
-0.310	-2.5	0.488	1.7	-0.534	-4.8						
-0.780	-4.9	0.582	4.8	-0.783	-4.4						
0.428	6.1					0.503	4.3	0.840	5.8	-0.318	-2.1
0.223	2.6					0.302	1.7	0.468	2.0	0.036	0.3
0.485	7.2	0.630	9.5			1.377	12.9	-0.335	-2.4	0.049	0.4
-0.001	-0.1	0.092	10.2			0.009	0.8	0.059	3.7	-0.052	-3.4
0.183	3.4					0.226	2.3	-0.070	-0.6	0.278	2.7
-0.056	-1.1					-0.179	-1.9	0.204	1.6	-0.126	-1.3
0.391	5.4					0.618	4.3	0.381	2.3	0.174	1.4
0.243	3.1					0.336	2.3	0.294	1.6	0.029	0.2
0.141	2.8					0.226	2.4	-0.235	-1.9	0.295	2.9
0.064	0.8					0.133	1.0	-0.160	-1.0	0.261	1.8
0.050	0.6					0.000	0.0	-0.271	-1.6	0.407	2.8
-0.091	-1.2					-0.199	-1.4	-0.128	-0.7	0.106	0.7
0.118	2.2					-0.100	-1.0	0.415	3.2	0.135	1.3
0.051	1.0					0.073	0.8	0.154	1.2	-0.110	-1.2
0.216	2.9					0.301	2.1	0.115	0.7	0.240	1.6
0.131	1.6					0.453	3.1	-0.540	-2.8	0.374	2.7
0.148	1.9					0.198	1.4	-0.170	-1.0	0.404	2.8
-0.011	-4.5	0.019	4.7			-0.010	-2.3	0.006	1.0	-0.019	-4.1
-0.005	-0.8	0.015	1.3			-0.015	-1.5	0.029	2.1	-0.014	-1.1
-0.006	-2.4	0.014	3.8			-0.003	-0.6	-0.021	-3.5	0.006	1.1
0.484	6.4					0.633	5.2	0.333	2.1	0.408	3.0
		0.519	3.7	0.932	6.4						
		1.200	9.4	1.251	9.3						
		2.740	16.3	2.166	16.5						
4056				4056							
49				115							
-6527.88				-6527.88							
-4917.74				-4796.64							
0.247				0.265							
0.239				0.248							

rent single family, rent multiple family, and move out of the metropolitan area. The alternatives are described by the variables listed in the left column of the table, which have been grouped into attributes related to the house, neighborhood, and accessibility. The household characteristic of income is interacted with the price variables (either purchase price for the two buy alternatives or monthly rent for the two rent alternatives).

The 'classic' models of logit and nested logit are presented first. The nested logit model is specified with the two buy alternatives in one nest, the two rent alternatives in a second nest, and the move out of the metro area in a third nest. In this case, the nested logit model is not significantly different from the logit model. (Other nesting structures also were not significant.) The logit model performs well in that a large proportion of this laundry list of attributes are significant, the signs are as expected, and relative magnitude of parameters make sense.

Next the logit mixture models are presented. First is the error component formulation, which is specified to be similar in concept to the nested logit. However, the key difference is that the error components capture the correlation across multiple responses from a single individual, which is ignored in nested logit. Further, nested logit has identical alternative specific variances, whereas the error component formulation allows for the variances of alternative utilities to differ. As the results show, these differences lead to a significant increase in fit in the error component model over the nested logit model.

Another major advantage of logit mixture model is the ability to capture heterogeneity through random parameters. The fourth model presents results of such a specification in which standard deviations are estimated for a subset of model parameters. Most parameters demonstrate unobserved heterogeneity and the fit of the model increases substantially. While the mixed logit estimation results thus far indicate substantial heterogeneity, the models are not particularly informative as to the behavioral drivers of the heterogeneity. It is the fifth model, our behavioral mixture model, which tries to address this.

Model five is a latent class choice model with three distinct behavioral classes. This model is explained in detail in Walker and Li (2007), and here described briefly to demonstrate the concept of behavioral mixtures. The behavioral driver of the model is that there are 'deep-rooted and embedded, prevalent attitudes towards different types of residential areas' (Aeroe, 2001). As Walker and Li (2007) describe, 'In this context of residential location choices, such lifestyle differences lead to differences in considerations, criterion, and preferences for location'. The behavioral mixture of interest is then of the discrete case where the mixture is over these lifestyle types.

The estimation results are shown in Table 8.1a and Table 8.1b. There are three lifestyle classes predicted by the model (that is, $S = 3$), where the number of classes was determined endogenously by estimating models with different number of classes. There are two sets of estimated coefficients (estimated simultaneously). First is the residential choice model conditional on lifestyle, which is shown in Table 8.1a. The coefficients of the class-specific residential choice probability vary across the three classes, which denote different trade-offs being made by the different lifestyle groups. The second set of coefficients is the class membership model, shown in Table 8.1b. It is a logit equation where the alternatives are the different lifestyle choices (the latent classes) and the explanatory

Table 8.1b Estimation results (continued)

Variable		Model 5 continued					
		Behavioral Logit Mixture - Class Membership					
		Class 1 (43%)		Class 2 (30%)		Class 3 (27%)	
		Affluent, more established families		Less affluent, younger families and non-families		Older, non-family, professionals	
		Coef	*t*-stat	Coef	*t*-stat	Coef	*t*-stat
	Intercept	−1.673	−1.9	1.513	1.6	0.161	0.2
Household Structure	Number of children under 5 years old	1.273	1.0	1.431	1.1	−2.704	−1.0
	Number of children from 5 to 11	*0.426*	*2.4*	*−0.117*	*−0.5*	*−0.309*	*−1.2*
	Number of children from 12 to 17	0.300	1.1	0.097	0.4	−0.398	−1.0
	Number of persons 18 and over	0.444	1.5	−0.163	−0.5	−0.282	−0.9
	Non-family dummy	−0.706	−1.7	0.124	0.3	0.582	1.7
Employment	Number of employed persons	−0.096	−0.5	−0.048	−0.2	0.145	0.5
	Number of retired persons	−0.480	−1.4	0.076	0.2	0.404	1.3
	Dummy if at least one "manager/professional"	*0.131*	*0.6*	*−0.571*	*−2.1*	*0.440*	*1.6*
	Maximum number of work hours	−0.002	−0.3	−0.004	−0.4	0.006	0.9
Age of the Head of Household	Piecewise linear age of HOH: age 20-35	−0.030	−0.6	0.040	0.9	−0.010	−0.2
	Piecewise linear age of HOH: age 36-60	*0.020*	*1.1*	*−0.058*	*−2.7*	*0.037*	*1.8*
	Piecewise linear age of HOH: age 60 plus	0.035	0.9	0.003	0.1	−0.038	−1.5
Resources	*Dummy for medium income*	*1.760*	*3.4*	*−0.904*	*−1.9*	*−0.855*	*−2.2*
	Dummy for high income	*1.607*	*4.4*	*−1.026*	*−3.7*	*−0.581*	*−1.9*
	Dummy for income not reported	*2.183*	*4.6*	*−2.151*	*−3.7*	*−0.032*	*−0.1*

Notes: Italics indicates parameters that vary significantly across classes (Wald statistic, 90% confidence).

variables include information on household structure, employment, the age of the head of household, and resources available to the household.

Summarizing from Walker and Li (2007), the estimation results suggests the following three lifestyle segments (where the description of the lifestyle is interpreted from the class-specific parameters in Table 8.1 and the character of members in the class is interpreted from Table 8.1b):

- Lifestyle 1: Households that are suburban, auto, and school oriented. These tend to be affluent, more established families.
- Lifestyle 2: Households that are transit oriented and also prefer a suburban setting. These tend to be less affluent, younger families and non-families.
- Lifestyle 3: Households that are urban and auto oriented. These tend to be older, non-family professionals.

While the socio-economic variables related to lifecycle are shown to have significant explanatory power, Walker and Li (2007) point out that 'there remained significant aspects of lifestyle preferences that could not be explained by such observable explanatory variables'. This is an indication that the behavioral mixture construct is critical; the variation in preferences cannot be captured systematically.

In this empirical demonstration, all three mixture models resulted in significant improvements of fit over the conventional logit and nested logit models. Further, the behavioral mixture model provides the best fit to the data. However, this is not always the case and, indeed, is not the most important advantage. (Note that these data could not support additional correlation parameters in the random parameter model beyond what is reported here.) A larger issue is that the covariance structures of the error component and random parameter models do not provide much insight into the behavior. On the other hand, the behavioral mixture provides a behavioral rationale for the mixture through the concept of latent lifestyles, and this rationale is supported by behavioral theory. This behavioral structure provides a better foundation for model development (for example, rationale to search for more parsimonious models), policy and marketing analysis (for example, how to influence the behavior of the different classes), and forecasting (for example, in dealing with issue of temporal stability).

While the behavioral mixture model presented here is farthest along the behavioral continuum of the five models presented, clearly the model could be made even more behavioral. First, the process we followed was exploratory in that we allowed the number of classes and the structure of the lifestyle groups to be inferred from the data. A stronger behavioral case could be made by using a confirmatory approach in which the lifestyle classes and their socio-economic drivers were based on behavioral theory regarding lifestyles and residential location choices. Further, the causal factors for lifestyle likely include other latent factors (attitudes) that should be explicitly captured in the model specification. In order to develop such a complex model, additional measurement indicators would likely be needed. Nonetheless, the behavioral mixture as presented here does provide evidence for improved statistical fit, easier interpretation, and greater policy relevance.

FUTURE DIRECTIONS

Enabled by computer processing power and use of simulation and mixture methods, discrete choice models have evolved considerably to where very complex formulations of the covariance structure can be captured. In this chapter, we describe this evolution from underlying behavioral principles, to basic IIA choice models, to probit and GEV, to mixture models. We conclude with the need to further pursue the concept of behavioral mixture models, which provide a behavioral rationale to the mixing structure through explicit latent variable constructs. Rather than just providing a better fit to the data, these models have potential to provide greater temporal stability and behavioral insight for policy and marketing analysis.

NOTES

1. McFadden's original formulation with $\mu = 1$ was generalized to $\mu > 0$ by Ben-Akiva and François (1983). The normalization of $\mu > 1$ is known as normalization from the root. The generalization allows for normalization to take place at other parts of the tree.
2. All estimated parameters are shown except the following six due to space: four alternative specific constants and two bias parameters capturing current renters choosing to rent and current single family dwellers choosing single family. 'Number of the parameters' at the bottom of the table shows the total number of estimated parameters for each model.

REFERENCES

Aeroe, T., 2001, Residential preferences, choice of housing, and lifestyle. Ph.D. Thesis (English Summary), Aalborg University.

Ajzen, I., 2005, *Attitudes, Personality, and Behavior*, 2nd edn. Milton-Keynes, England: Open University Press, McGraw-Hill.

Anderson, S.P., A. de Palma and J.-F. Thisse, 1992, *Discrete Choice Theory of Product Differentiation*. Cambridge, MA: MIT Press.

Ashok, K., W.R. Dillon and S. Yuan, 2002, Extending discrete choice models to incorporate attitudinal and other latent variables. *Journal of Marketing Research*, **39**, 31–46.

Ben-Akiva, M., 1977, Choice models with simple choice set generating processes. Working Paper, Department of Civil Engineering, Massachusetts Institute of Technology, Cambridge, MA.

Ben-Akiva, M.E. and B. Boccara, 1995, Discrete choice models with latent choice sets. *International Journal of Research in Marketing*, **12**, 9–24.

Ben-Akiva, M. and B. François, 1983, μ Homogeneous generalized extreme value model. Working paper, Department of Civil Engineering, Massachusetts Institute of Technology, Cambridge, MA.

Ben-Akiva, M.E. and S.R. Lerman, 1985, *Discrete Choice Analysis: Theory and Application to Travel Demand*. Cambridge, MA: MIT Press.

Ben-Akiva, M., D. Bolduc and M. Bradley, 1993, Estimation of travel mode choice models with randomly distributed values of time. *Transportation Research Record*, **1413**, 88–97.

Ben-Akiva, M., D. McFadden, K. Train, J. Walker, C. Bhat, M. Bierlaire, D. Bolduc, A. Boersch-Supan, D. Brownstone, D. Bunch, A. Daly, A. de Palma, D. Gopinath, A. Karlstrom and M. Munizaga, 2002a, Hybrid choice models: progress and challenges. *Marketing Letters*, **13** (3), 163–175.

Ben-Akiva, M., J. Walker, A. Bernardino, D. Gopinath, T. Morikawa and A. Polydoropoulou, 2002b, Integration of choice and latent variable models. In H. Mahmassani, ed., *In Perpetual Motion: Travel Behaviour Research Opportunities and Application Challenges*. Amsterdam: Elsevier Science, pp. 431–470.

Bhat, C.R., 1998, Accommodating flexible substitution patterns in multi-dimensional choice modeling: formulation and application to travel mode and departure time choice. *Transportation Research Part B*, **32** (7), 455–466.

Boersch-Supan, A., D.L. McFadden and R. Schnabel, 1996, Living arrangements: health and wealth effects. In D.A. Wise, ed., *Advances in the Economics of Aging*. Chicago, IL: The University of Chicago Press, pp. 193–216.

Bolduc, D. and M. Ben-Akiva, 1991, A multinomial probit formulation for large choice sets. *Proceedings of the Sixth International Conference on Travel Behavior*, **2**, 243–258.

Boyd, J. and J. Mellman, 1980, The effect of fuel economy standards on the US automotive market: a hedonic demand analysis. *Transportation Research Part A*, **14**, 367–378.

Brownstone, D. and K. Train, 1999, Forecasting new product penetration with flexible substitution patterns. *Journal of Econometrics*, **89**, 109–129.

Cambridge Systematics Inc., 1986, Customer preference and behavior project report. Prepared for the Electric Power Research Institute.

Cambridge Systematics Inc., 1996, Data collection in the Portland, Oregon metropolitan area, Travel Model Improvement Program. Track D Data Research Program, Prepared for the US Department of Transportation.

Cardell, S. and F. Dunbar, 1980, Measuring the societal impacts of automobile downsizing. *Transportation Research Part A*, **14**, 423–434.

Dugundji, E.R. and J.L. Walker, 2005, Discrete choice with social and spatial network interdependencies. *Transportation Research Record*, **1921**, 70–78.

Erdem, T., 1996, A dynamic analysis of market structure based on panel data. *Marketing Science*, **15**, 359–378.

Gaudry, M.J.I. and M.G. Dagenais, 1979, The Dogit Model. *Transportation Research Part B*, **13** (2), 105–112.

Gopinath, D.A., 1995, Modeling heterogeneity in discrete choice processes: application to travel demand. PhD Dissertation, Department of Civil and Environmental Engineering, Massachusetts Institute of Technology.

Gönül, F. and K. Srinivasan, 1993, Modeling multiple sources of heterogeneity in multinomial logit models: methodological and managerial issues. *Marketing Science*, **12** (3), 213–229.

Greene, W.H. and D.A. Hensher, 2003, A latent class model for discrete choice analysis: contrasts with mixed logit. *Transportation Research Part B*, **37**, 681–698.

Greene, W.H., D.A. Hensher and J. Rose, 2006, Accounting for heterogeneity in the variance of unobserved effects in mixed logit models. *Transportation Research Part B*, **40**, 75–92.

Hess, S., M. Bierlaire and J.W. Polak, 2005, Estimation of value of travel-time savings using mixed logit models. *Transportation Research Part A*, **39** (2–3), 221–236.

Kahneman, D., 1997, Economists have preferences, psychologists have attitudes. Presented at NSF Symposium on Preference Elicitation, UC Berkeley, Berkeley, CA.

Kamakura, W.A. and G.J. Russell, 1989, A probabilistic choice model for market segmentation and elasticity structure. *Journal of Marketing Research*, **25**, 379–390.

Koppelman, F.S. and V. Sethi, 2000, Closed-form discrete-choice models. In D.A. Hensher and K.J. Button, eds, *Handbook of Transport Modeling*. Bingley, UK: Emerald Group Publishing, pp. 211–227.

Lancaster, K., 1966, A new approach to consumer theory. *Journal of Political Economy*, **74**, 132–157.

Luce, R.D., 1959, *Individual Choice Behavior*. New York: Wiley.

Manski, C., 1977, The structure of random utility models. *Theory and Decision*, **8**, 229–254.

Marschak, J., 1960, Binary choice constraints on random utility indicators. In K. Arrow, ed., *Stanford Symposium on Mathematical Methods in the Social Sciences*. Stanford, CA: Stanford University Press.

McFadden, D., 1974, Conditional logit analysis of qualitative choice behavior. In P. Zarembka, ed., *Frontiers of Econometrics*. London: Academic Press, pp. 105–142.

McFadden, D., 1978, Modeling the choice of residential location. In A. Karlqvist, L. Lundqvist, F. Snickars and J. Weibull, eds, *Spatial Interaction Theory and Residential Location*. Amsterdam: North-Holland, pp. 75–96.

McFadden, D., 1986, The choice theory approach to marketing research. *Marketing Science*, **5** (4), 275–297.

McFadden, D., 1989, A method of simulated moments for estimation of discrete response models without numerical integration. *Econometrica*, **57** (5), 995–1026.

McFadden, D. and K. Train, 2000, Mixed MNL models of discrete response. *Journal of Applied Econometrics*, **15**, 447–470.

Morikawa, T., M. Ben-Akiva and D. McFadden, 2002, Discrete choice models incorporating revealed preferences and psychometric data. *Econometric Models in Marketing, Advances in Econometrics*, **16**, 29–55.

Revelt, D. and K. Train, 1998, Mixed logit with repeated choices: households' choice of appliance efficiency level. *Review of Economics and Statistics*, **80** (4), 647–657.

Stern, S., 1992, A method for smoothing simulated moments of discrete probabilities in multinomial probit models. *Econometrica*, **60** (4), 943–952.

Swait, J.D. and M. Ben-Akiva, 1987, Incorporating random constraints in discrete models of choice set generation. *Transportation Research Part B*, **21** (2), 91–102.

Thurstone, L., 1927, A law of comparative judgement, *Psychological Review*, **34**, 273–286.

Toledo, T., 2003, Integrating driver behavior modeling. PhD Dissertation, Department of Civil and Environmental Engineering, Massachusetts Institute of Technology.

Train, K., 2009, *Discrete Choice Methods with Simulation*, 2nd edn, Cambridge: Cambridge University Press.

Train, K., D. McFadden and A. Goett, 1987, Consumer attitudes and voluntary rate schedules for public utilities. *Review of Economics and Statistics*, **69**, 383–391.

Vichiensan, V., K. Miyamoto and Y. Tokunaga, 2005, Mixed logit modeling framework with structuralized spatial effects: a test of applicability with area unit systems in location choice analysis. *Journal of the Eastern Asian Society for Transportation Studies*, **6**, 3789–3802.

Walker, J.L., 2001, Extended discrete choice models: integrated framework, flexible error structures, and latent variables. PhD Dissertation, Department of Civil and Environmental Engineering, Massachusetts Institute of Technology.

Walker, J.L. and M. Ben-Akiva, 2002, Generalized random utility model. *Mathematical Social Sciences*, **43** (3), 303–343.

Walker, J.L. and J. Li, 2007, Latent lifestyle preferences and household location decisions. *Journal of Geographical Systems*, **9** (1), 77–101.

Walker, J.L., M. Ben-Akiva and D. Bolduc, 2007, Identification of parameters in normal error component logit-mixture (NECLM) models. *Journal of Applied Econometrics*, **22**, 1095–1125.

9 Dynamic traffic modeling
André de Palma and Mogens Fosgerau

INTRODUCTION

This chapter provides a brief introduction to dynamic congestion models, based on the Vickrey (1969) bottleneck model which has become the main workhorse model for economic analysis of situations involving congestion dynamics.

The word *dynamic* can have several possible meanings. One possibility is that it relates to the way traffic systems evolve and users learn from day to day. In the context of the bottleneck model, it relates to intra-day timing, that is, to the interdependencies between traffic congestion at different times within a given day.

We shall discuss dynamic approaches against the background of static models. Static models assume that congestion is constant over some given time period. A congestion law provides the travel time as a function of the entering flow. The time dimension is not explicitly involved: all quantities are computed as single figures specific to a time period.

The basic static model considers a network comprising nodes and links. The nodes are centroids of zones, associating trip ends within a zone with a point that is a node in the network. Links connect the nodes. A cost function describes the cost of using each link. Congestion means that the cost increases as the number of users of the link increases. The demand is given by the origin–destination (O–D) matrix, indicating the number of trips between pairs of nodes. The solution involves the choice of route within the network for each O–D pair. Traffic volume on each link, the travel cost of using each link, the cost of making each trip, and the total travel cost for all users all depend on these route-choice decisions.

Each user for each O–D pair is assumed to choose a route in the network that minimizes the sum of link costs for the trip. But users compete for the same space and the route choices of users in one O–D pair affect the costs experienced by other users through congestion. We can imagine a process where users keep revising their route choices in response to the route choices of other users. We seek an equilibrium in which no user can reduce his cost by choosing a different route. This equilibrium concept is due to Wardrop (1952). This problem was first given a mathematical formulation and solution for a general network by Beckmann et al. (1956). We will discuss the static model in more detail below in the context of simple networks.

The static model remains a basic tool for the mathematical description of congested networks. The static model does, however, omit important features of congestion. The static model is hence unsatisfactory for a number of purposes.

The main feature that the static model omits is that congestion varies over the day, with pronounced morning and afternoon peaks in most cities. Travel times can easily increase by a factor of two from the beginning to the height of the peak. To design and evaluate policies for tackling congestion it is necessary to recognize these variations.

There are a number of fundamental features of congested demand peaks that a model should take into account.

First, travelers choose not only a route, but also a departure time in response to how congestion varies over the course of a day. When a policy is implemented that affects peak congestion, travellers respond by changing departure time. The departure time changes are systematic on average and can be observed in the aggregate temporal shape of the peak. Think, for example, of car traffic entering the central business district (CBD) of some large city. The number of travellers reaching their workplaces per hour is fixed at the capacity rate during the morning peak. So if the number of workplaces in the CBD increases, the duration of the morning peak must increase too. Similarly, if capacity is increased, the duration of the peak will shrink. The duration of the peak thus depends on both demand and capacity. Such observations suggest that trip timing is endogenous and speak in favour of dynamic models.

Second, travelers incur more than just monetary costs and travel time costs when they make a trip. Travelers have preferences regarding the timing of trips and deviations from the preferred timing are costly. Such scheduling costs are comparable in magnitude to congestion-delay costs as a fraction of total user costs. These scheduling costs are by nature ignored in static models. This means that static models cannot reveal the effect of policies that affect scheduling costs.

Third, many relevant policies can only be described within a dynamic model. A congestion toll or parking fee that varies over time as congestion increases and decreases is an obvious example.

The basic dynamic model discussed in this chapter, the bottleneck model, starts directly from the above observations regarding within-day dynamics. It is therefore well suited to analyze policies that rely on these dynamics. It was introduced by William Vickrey (1969). Arnott et al. (1993a) revisited and extended this seminal but almost forgotten model. It is a tractable model and it leads to a number of important insights. The model features one O–D pair (let us say residence and workplace), one route and one bottleneck. The bottleneck represents any road segment that constitutes a binding capacity constraint. The bottleneck allows users to pass only at some fixed rate. There is a continuum of users and it takes some positive interval of time for them all to pass the bottleneck. Users are identical and they wish to arrive at the destination at the same ideal time t^*. Because of the bottleneck, all but one user must arrive either before or after t^*. Deviation from t^* represents a cost for users. They also incur a travel time cost, which includes free flow travel time and delays in the bottleneck. Individuals choose a departure time to minimize the sum of schedule delay and travel time costs.

To analyze this situation, we consider an equilibrium in which no traveler has incentive to change his departure time choice. This is an instance of a Nash equilibrium (Haurie and Marcotte, 1985), which is the natural generalization of Wardrop equilibrium. Individuals are identical and therefore they experience the same cost in equilibrium. One might wonder whether the Nash equilibrium concept has any counterpart in the real world. We see Nash equilibrium as a benchmark. Like anything else in our models, it is an idealization, describing a situation that we hope is not too far from reality. The appeal of Nash equilibrium is that it is a rest point for any dynamic mechanism whereby informed travellers revise their (departure time) choice, if they do not achieve the maximum utility available to them.

Travelers incur the same generalized travel cost in equilibrium, but they have different trips. Some depart early, experience only a short delay at the bottleneck, but arrive early at work. Others avoid queuing delay by departing late, but arrive also late at work. Those who arrive near the preferred arrival time will experience most congestion and have the longest travel time. In this way, the bottleneck model describes a congested demand peak with a queue that first builds up and then dissolves.

The endogenous choice of the departure time was independently studied by de Palma et al. (1983), who proposed a dynamic model incorporating a random utility departure time choice model and a generalized queuing model. In contrast to the Vickrey bottleneck model, where the capacity constraint is either active or not, the supply model of de Palma et al. shifts smoothly from the uncongested to the congested regime.

An area of economic literature has grown out of these two initial contributions, exploring a number of issues in the context of the basic bottleneck model: for example, equilibrium, social optimum, decentralization of the social optimum via pricing, second best pricing (including step tolls), elastic demand, heterogeneous individuals, small networks (routes in parallel and routes in series), stochastic capacity and demand, alternative treatments of congestion and pricing on large networks. The basic model has also been extended to include mode choice, parking congestion, modeling of the evening commute and non-commuting trips. The research stream initiated with M. Ben-Akiva had more focus on numerical computation, and it has led, amongst other development, to the METROPOLIS software for large networks, discussed below.

This chapter first reviews the simple static model of congestion, where time is not explicitly considered. This serves as a background for the dynamic model. We then introduce the basic bottleneck model and continue to discuss some of the extensions mentioned.

THE STATIC MODEL OF CONGESTION[1]

Static Networks

We begin with a simple example. Consider a fixed number $N > 0$ of travelers having two routes available. The travelers split with $n_1 > 0$ on the first route and $n_2 > 0$ on the second route, where $n_1 + n_2 = N$. The cost associated with each route is taken to be a linear function of traffic such that the average cost on route i is $C_i(n_i) = a_i + b_i n_i$. The cost is a so-called generalized cost, combining monetary cost and travel time in a single monetary equivalent. The Nash equilibrium occurs when no traveller wants to change route, which requires that $C_1(n_1) = C_2(n_2)$. Solving this equation leads to the equilibrium solution[2]

$$n_1^e = \frac{a_2 - a_1}{b_1 + b_2} + \frac{b_2}{b_1 + b_2}N, \; n_2^e = N - n_1^e.$$

The Nash equilibrium has every traveler minimize his/her own cost. We can alternatively consider social optimum where the total cost for all travelers is minimized. In general the social optimum is not a Nash equilibrium. The social optimum minimizes the total cost function

$$\min_{n_1,n_2} W(n_1, n_2) = n_1 C_1(n_1) + n_2 C_2(n_2).$$

The total cost associated with use of route i is $n_i C_i(n_i)$. The marginal cost of an additional user is

$$\frac{d[n_i C_i(n_i)]}{dn_i} = C_i(n_i) + b_i n_i.$$

In this expression, $C_i(n_i)$ is the cost paid by the marginal user. The remainder $b_i n_i$ is an externality: it is the part of the increase in the total cost that is not borne by the additional user. The first-order condition for social optimum requires equal marginal costs, or

$$C_1(n_1) + b_1 n_1 = C_2(n_2) + b_2 n_2. \tag{9.1}$$

The only difference between this and the first-order condition for the equilibrium is the terms representing the externalities of the two routes. The externalities are zero if $b_i = 0$, $i = 1, 2$, that is, if adding an additional user does not lead to increased average travel cost. In this case, the social optimum would be the same as the equilibrium.

The social optimum has

$$n_1^o = \frac{a_2 - a_1}{2b_1 + 2b_2} + \frac{2b_2}{2b_1 + 2b_2} N, \ n_2^o = N - n_1^o. \tag{9.2}$$

The solution is written in this way to emphasize the similarity to the Nash equilibrium. The only difference between the optimum and the equilibrium outcomes is that the marginal costs, the b_i, have been replaced by $2b_i$ in the expression for the optimum outcome. This indicates that the optimum can be achieved as an equilibrium outcome by setting a toll equal to $n_i b_i$ on each of the two routes. This has the effect of doubling the variable cost from the perspective of users and the expression in Equation (9.2) then becomes the equilibrium outcome.

Elastic Demand

The discussion so far has considered a fixed number of travelers N. We now allow demand to be elastic, limiting attention to just one route. Travelers on this route are identical, except for different willingness to pay to travel. Figure 9.1 shows a downward-sloping inverse demand curve $D(N)$ to reflect that demand decreases as the cost increases. The curve $C(N)$ is again an average cost curve expressing the cost that each traveller incurs. The curve $MC(N)$ is a marginal cost curve, expressing the marginal change in total cost following a marginal increase in the number of travellers; in other words[3]

$$MC(N) = C(N) + N \cdot C'(N).$$

When the cost curve is increasing, the marginal cost curve will lie above the cost curve.

The equilibrium occurs at the intersection of the demand curve with the average cost curve at the point b. The marginal traveler at this point is indifferent between traveling

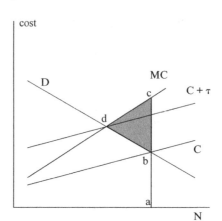

Figure 9.1   A static model

and not traveling, he faces a cost corresponding to the line segment a–b and a benefit of the same size. For travelers in aggregate, however, the cost of adding the marginal traveler is given by the MC curve. For the marginal traveler at point b, this cost corresponds to the line segment a–c. So the last traveler imposes a net loss corresponding to the line segment b–c on the group of all travelers. If usage was reduced to the point where the MC curve crosses the demand curve, then the corresponding loss is zero for the traveler at the point d. The total loss in market equilibrium is then represented by the shaded triangle b–c–d in Figure 9.1.

The optimal toll, labeled τ in Figure 9.1, implements the optimum at the point d, where the private benefit is equal to the marginal cost. The toll is required because drivers ignore the costs they impose on other drivers. The toll is just the difference, evaluated at the social optimum, between the marginal cost and the average cost, *i.e.* the externality.

THE BASIC BOTTLENECK MODEL

We now introduce the basic Vickrey bottleneck model in its simplest form. Consider a continuum of $N > 0$ identical travelers, who all make a trip. They have to pass a bottleneck, which is located d_1 time units from the trip origin and d_2 time units from the destination. Denote the time of arrival at the bottleneck of a traveler by t and the exit time from the bottleneck as a. The situation is illustrated in Figure 9.2. A traveler departs from the origin at time $t - d_1$ and arrives at the bottleneck at time t. There he/she is delayed until time $a \geq t$ at which time he/she exits from the bottleneck to arrive at the destination at time $a + d_2$.

Each traveler has a scheduling cost expressing his/her preferences concerning the timing of the trip. Travelers are assumed to have a preferred arrival time t^* and they dislike arriving earlier or later at the destination. Travelers also prefer the trip to be as quick as possible. For a trip that starts at time t_1 and ends at time t_2, consider then a cost of the form

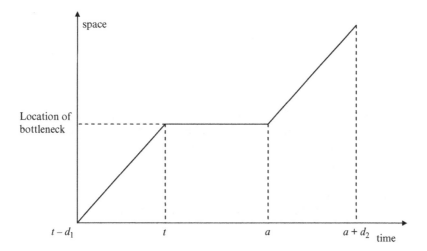

Figure 9.2   Trip timing

$$c(t_1, t_2) = \alpha \cdot (t_2 - t_1) + \beta \cdot \max(t^* - t_2, 0) + \gamma \cdot \max(t_2 - t^*, 0), \qquad (9.3)$$

where $0 < \beta, 0 < \gamma$ and $\beta < \alpha$. In this formulation, α is the marginal cost of travel time, β is the marginal cost of arriving earlier than the preferred arrival time, γ is the marginal cost of arriving later, and these values are constant. The deviation $t_2 - t^*$ between the actual arrival time and the preferred arrival time is called schedule delay and it is possible to speak of schedule delay early and schedule delay late, depending on the sign of the schedule delay.[4] This cost formulation has become colloquially known as $\alpha - \beta - \gamma$ preferences. Later, we shall consider scheduling cost of a general form.

The travel time d_1 between the origin and the bottleneck adds the same constant amount to the scheduling cost of all travelers and so it can be set to zero without affecting the behavior of travelers in the model. Similarly, the travel time d_2 between the bottleneck and the destination can be set to zero by redefining the preferred arrival time. So without loss of generality we may let $d_1 = d_2 = 0$. This means that the time of departure is the same as the time of arrival at the bottleneck and that the time of exit from the bottleneck is the same as the time of arrival at the destination.

Travelers depart from the origin according to an aggregate schedule, described in terms of the cumulative departure rate R, where $R(a)$ is the number of travellers who have departed before time a. So R is similar to a cumulative distribution function: it is proportional to the probability that a random traveller has departed before time a. R is increasing, since travelers never return. Moreover, $R(-\infty) = 0$ and $R(\infty) = N$. The departure rate $\rho(a) = R'(a)$, wherever R is differentiable.

The bottleneck can serve at most s travelers per time unit. Travelers who have not yet been served wait before the bottleneck. The bottleneck serves travellers in the sequence in which they arrived (first-in-first-out or FIFO). The bottleneck capacity is always used if there are travelers waiting before it.

Recall that Nash equilibrium is defined as a situation in which no traveler is able to decrease his cost by choosing a different departure time. Since travelers are identical, this definition reduces to the requirement that all travelers experience the same cost and that the cost would be higher for departure times that are not chosen by any travelers.

Denote the interval of departures and arrivals as $I = [a_0, a_1]$. Let us consider some properties of Nash equilibrium. First, there will be queue from the time the first traveler departs until the last traveler departs, since otherwise there would be a gap in the queue and somebody could move into the gap to decrease cost. Second, the queue will end at the time the last traveler departs, since otherwise he/she could wait until the queue was gone and reduce cost. This shows that the departure interval is just long enough for all travelers to pass the bottleneck. Third, as the cost of the first and the last travelers are equal and since they experience no queue, they must experience the same cost due to schedule delay. These insights are summarized in the following equations.

$$a_1 - a_0 = N/s, \tag{9.4}$$

$$\beta \cdot (t^* - a_0) = \gamma \cdot (a_1 - t^*). \tag{9.5}$$

Equation (9.4) ensures that arrivals take place during an interval that is just long enough that all travelers can pass the bottleneck. Equation (9.5) ensures that no traveler will want to depart at any time outside I.

Solving these two equations leads to

$$a_0 = t^* - \frac{\gamma}{\beta + \gamma} \frac{N}{s},$$

$$a_1 = t^* + \frac{\beta}{\beta + \gamma} \frac{N}{s}$$

and the equilibrium cost for every traveler is

$$\frac{\beta\gamma}{\beta + \gamma} \frac{N}{s} \equiv \delta \frac{N}{s}.$$

This is linear in the number of travelers and so the simple static model could be viewed as a reduced form of the dynamic model.

Equations (9.4) and (9.5) are extremely useful in that they determine the equilibrium cost of travelers as a function of the number of travelers and the bottleneck capacity. The total cost is then $\delta N^2/s$ with corresponding marginal cost $2\delta N/s$, of which half is internal cost to each traveller and the other half is external. The marginal change in total cost following a change in capacity s is $-\delta N^2/s^2$. Since there is no toll, price equals travel cost: $p^e = \delta N/s$, that is price is a function of N and s. The function is thus a reduced-form supply function, which is very useful, especially in analytical work, together with a trip demand function.

There is always a queue during the interval I. This means that the bottleneck capacity is fully utilized and hence that sd travelers pass the bottleneck during an interval of length d. At time a, a total of $R(a)$ travellers have entered the bottleneck, taking a total time of

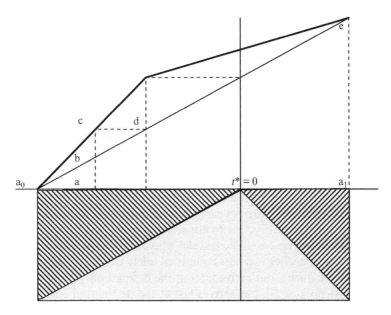

Figure 9.3   *Equilibrium departure schedule under* $\alpha - \beta - \gamma$ *preferences*

$R(a)/s$ to pass. The first traveler enters and exits the bottleneck at time a_0. Hence a traveler arriving at bottleneck at time a exits at time $a_0 + R(a)/s$. Travelers are identical so they incur the same scheduling cost in equilibrium. Normalising $t^* = 0$, it emerges that

$$\delta \frac{N}{s} = \alpha \cdot \frac{R(a)}{s} + \beta \cdot \max\left(-a_0 - \frac{R(a)}{s}, 0\right) + \gamma \cdot \max\left(a_0 + \frac{R(a)}{s}, 0\right).$$

Differentiating this expression leads to

$$\rho(a) = \begin{cases} s\dfrac{\alpha}{\alpha - \beta}, & a_0 + \dfrac{R(a)}{s} \leq 0 \\[2ex] s\dfrac{\alpha}{\alpha + \gamma}, & a_0 + \dfrac{R(a)}{s} > 0 \end{cases}$$

during interval *I*. A few observations are immediately available. Initially the departure rate is constant and higher than s (since $\beta < \alpha$). It is high until the traveler who arrives exactly on time. Later travellers depart at a constant rate which is lower than s.

Figure 9.3 shows the resulting departure schedule. The horizontal axis is time and the vertical axis is the number of departures, ranging from 0 to N. The thick kinked curve is the cumulative departure rate R. Departures begin at time a_0 and end at time a_1 with $R(a_1) = N$. The line segment connecting point a_0 to point e represents the number of travelers served by the bottleneck, it has slope s.

The first departures take place at a rate larger than capacity and queue builds up. For example, at time a, the number of travelers who have departed corresponds to the length of the segment $a - c$, while the number of travelers who have been served by the bottleneck corresponds to the length of the segment $a - b$. Thus the queue at that time has length corresponding to the segment $b - c$. The travellers in the queue at time a will all have been served by time d, which is then the time at which the traveller departing at time a is served by the bottleneck. The time spent in the bottleneck equals the length of the queue at the time of departure divided by the capacity.

The traveler departing at time d exits the bottleneck exactly at time a_*. Therefore the departure rate drops below capacity at this time and the queue begins to dissolve. It also follows that the queue reaches its maximum length at time d.

For the top half of the figure, the horizontal time axis refers both to the departure time from the origin and to the arrival time at the destination. For the bottom half of the figure, the time axis instead refers to the arrival time at the destination. The shaded areas on the bottom half of Figure 9.3 shows the composition of the scheduling cost throughout the peak. The first traveller arrives early and is not delayed in the bottleneck so his/her cost is $\beta \cdot (a_* - a_0)$. Later travelers do not arrive as early, but are delayed more in the queue and incur the same trip cost. The traveler who arrives at the preferred arrival time is the most delayed and his/her trip cost comprises solely travel time cost. Later arrivals are less delayed in the queue, but arrive later at the destination. The last traveler is not delayed in the bottleneck at all, but arrives last at the destination and incurs a cost of $\gamma \cdot (a_1 - a_*)$.

Optimal Tolling

The queue that arises in equilibrium in the bottleneck model is sheer waste. It generates no benefit at all. If travelers could be induced to depart at the capacity rate s during the equilibrium interval I, then there would be no queue. All travelers (except the very first and the very last) would gain from reduced travel time while arriving at the destination at exactly the same time as in equilibrium. A main insight of the bottleneck model is that it is possible to achieve this outcome through the application of a toll.

So consider a time varying toll $\tau(\cdot) \geq 0$ charged at the time of arrival at the bottleneck. We make the additional behavioral assumption that travelers choose departure time to minimize the sum of the toll and the trip cost. We restrict attention to tolls that have $\tau(a_0) = \tau(a_1) = 0$ and are zero outside the departure interval I. This means that Equations (9.4) and (9.5) still apply. If the toll is well-behaved, in ways to be explained below, then Nash equilibrium exists and departures still occur in the interval I. Therefore the equilibrium cost is the same as in the no-toll equilibrium discussed above.

Travelers do not lose, but somebody else may gain since revenue from the toll can be used for other purposes. The size of the toll revenue is

$$\int_{a_0}^{a_1} \tau(s)\,ds, \tag{9.6}$$

and this represents a net welfare gain.

Since the cost must be constant in equilibrium, we have

$$\tau(a) = \delta\frac{N}{s} - c\left(a, \frac{R(a)}{s} + a_0\right), \tag{9.7}$$

where R is now the departure rate that results when the toll is imposed. It is (intuitively) clear that maximal efficiency is attained when the toll revenue is as large as it can be without destroying the equilibrium. Increasing $\tau(a)$ in Equation (9.7) will reduce $R(a)$.[5] Moreover, the queue cannot be negative and so we must require that $R(a) \geq s(a - a_0)$. Therefore the maximal toll maintains zero queue and the least possible cumulative departure rate, that is, $R(a) = s \cdot (a - a_0)$. This corresponds to a constant departure rate $\rho(a) = s$. The optimal toll is

$$\tau(a) = \delta\frac{N}{s} - c(a, a) = \delta\frac{N}{s} - \beta \cdot \max(-a, 0) - \gamma \cdot \max(a, 0)$$

for $a \in I$ and zero otherwise. This toll is initially zero at time a_0. Then it increases at the rate β until it reaches a maximum of $\delta N/s$ at time 0. It then decreases at the rate γ until it is again zero at time a_1. The optimal toll corresponds to the gray shaded area in Figure 9.3. In a sense, it just replaces the cost of queueing by a toll. The efficiency gain is achieved because queueing is pure waste whereas the toll revenue is just a transfer.

Elastic Demand

The discussion of the bottleneck model so far has assumed demand to be inelastic. A natural extension is to assume that the number of travelers deciding to participate in the peak depends on the equilibrium cost (Arnott et al., 1993a). The trip cost

$$p = \tau(a) + c(a, a_0 + R(a)/s) \tag{9.8}$$

is the same for all travelers in equilibrium. This implies that the total toll payment is $N \cdot (p - \bar{c})$, where $\bar{c}$ is the average scheduling cost of travelers. Let $N(\cdot) > 0$, $N'(\cdot) < 0$ be a downward sloping demand function such that $N(p)$ is the realised demand.

This is a very convenient way to extend the model: conditional on any equilibrium number of travelers, the properties of equilibrium are exactly the same as in the inelastic case. The equilibrium number of travelers is uniquely determined since demand is decreasing as a function of the equilibrium cost of travelers while the equilibrium cost of travelers is increasing as a function of the number of travelers. This simplicity comes, however, at a cost as it requires separability between trip timing on the one hand and participation on the other.

The separability of trip timing and participation implies that the optimal toll with elastic demand is the same as in the case of inelastic demand. To see this, note first that the optimal toll is able to remove queuing, so the average cost of travellers remains equal to $\delta N/s$. Consider the following welfare function

$$W(p) = \int_p^\infty N(s)\,ds + N \cdot (p - \bar{c}),$$

that is the sum of consumer surplus and the total toll revenue. To find the welfare optimising toll, note that

$$\bar{c} = \frac{s}{N} \int_{a_0}^{a_1} c(a, a) \, da,$$

which can be shown to imply that

$$\frac{\partial \bar{c}}{\partial p} = \frac{N'(p)}{N(p)} (\delta N/s - \bar{c}).$$

Using this to evaluate the first-order condition for maximum of $W(p)$ leads to $p = \delta N/s$. That is, the optimal price should equal the equilibrium scheduling cost. Using Equation (9.8) shows that the optimal toll is $\tau(a) = \delta N/s - c(a, a)$, which is the same as in the case of inelastic demand.

Optimal Capacity and Self-financing

Consider now a situation in which the optimal toll applies while capacity s is supplied at cost $K(s) \geq 0$, with $K' > 0$. We extend the social welfare function with the cost of capacity provision

$$W(p,s) = \int_{p}^{\infty} N(r) \, dr + N \cdot (p - \bar{c}) - K(s).$$

For any given capacity s, the optimal value of $\tau(a) = \delta N/s - c(a, a)$ is as shown above. Note that

$$\frac{\partial \bar{c}}{\partial s} = \frac{1}{s} (\delta N/s - \bar{c}).$$

This can be used to show that capacity is optimal when $sK'(s) = N \cdot (p - \bar{c})$. That is, the revenue from the optimal toll is equal to $sK'(s)$.

This finding leads directly to the self-financing theorem for the bottleneck model. If capacity is produced at constant returns to scale, that is, if $K(s) = sK'(s)$ with $K'(s)$ constant, then the optimal toll exactly finances the optimal capacity $K(s) = N \cdot (p - \bar{c})$. If there are increasing returns to scale, then $K(s) > sK'(s)$, in which case the optimal toll cannot finance the optimal capacity.

The self-financing result is also called the cost recovery theorem. It is an instance of a general self-financing theorem by Mohring and Harwitz (1962), which assumes that travel cost is homogenous of degree zero in capacity and use. A number of results on self-financing are summarized by Verhoef and Mohring (2009).

The optimal capacity can be computed in the three regimes: no toll, coarse step toll and optimal fine toll. It can be shown that the optimal capacity is the lowest for the optimal fine toll, intermediary for the coarse toll and larger for the no toll regime (see Arnott et al., 1993a, for a proof). These results apply with inelastic as well as elastic demand.

SCHEDULING PREFERENCES

General Formulation

The $\alpha - \beta - \gamma$ formulation of scheduling cost used above is a special case of more general scheduling preferences, introduced in this section. Below we revisit the bottleneck model from the perspective of these general scheduling preferences.

In order to describe the traveler choice of trip timing in a more general way, we formulate scheduling preferences for a given trip in the form of scheduling utility $u(t_1, t_2)$, where t_1 is the departure time and t_2 is the arrival time,. We shall make minimal assumptions regarding the specification of u.

It is natural to require that $u_1 = du/dt_1 > 0$, such that it is always preferred to depart later, given t_2.[6] Similarly, requiring $u_2 = du/dt_2 < 0$ ensures that arriving earlier is always preferred, given t_1. An increase in travel time then always leads to a utility loss, since travellers will either have to depart earlier or arrive later. Define the function $v(a) = u(a, a)$ as the scheduling utility that a traveler would receive if travel was instantaneous. Assume that v is quasi-concave and attains maximum at $v(t^*)$. This assures that for any $d > 0$ there is a unique solution to the equation $v(a) = v(a + d)$. It also implies that v is increasing for $a < t^*$ and decreasing for $a > t^*$.

We incorporate monetary cost by considering utility to be $u - \tau$. In some cases it is more convenient to talk about cost, which will then be the negative of utility, that is, $\tau - u$. In either case, it is implied that there is separability between scheduling and monetary cost. That is, a constant cost does not affect the preferences regarding trip timing.

In some situations it is necessary to specify scheduling utility further by imposing a certain functional form. For example, the $\alpha - \beta - \gamma$ formulation specifies the scheduling cost completely up to a few parameters. Such restriction can be necessary for reasons of identification in econometric work, but in general it is preferable to specify as little as possible, since restricting the model entails the risk of introducing errors. In theoretical models it is similarly preferable to work with general formulations, since otherwise there is a risk that the results one may obtain depend on the specific formulation.

In some cases it may be considered acceptable to impose a separability condition, just as we have done in the case of monetary cost and trip timing. The timing of the trip is given by a departure time and an arrival time and we work under the assumption that these times are all that matter about trip timing. The travel time is the difference between the departure time and the arrival time. We could equivalently describe trip timing in terms of travel time and arrival time or in terms of travel time and departure time. From the perspective of general scheduling utility $u(t_1, t_2)$, this leads to three possibilities for introducing a separability condition.

$$u(t_1, t_2) = f(t_2 - t_2) + g(t_1)$$

$$u(t_1, t_2) = f(t_2 - t_1) + g(t_2)$$

$$u(t_1, t_2) = f(t_1) + g(t_2)$$

The first condition would say that scheduling utility is separable in travel time and departure time. The second condition would say instead that scheduling utility is separable in travel time and arrival time. The $\alpha - \beta - \gamma$ scheduling cost is a special case of this second possibility: Changing the travel time does not affect the traveler preferences regarding arrival time and vice versa. The third possible separability condition is used in the Vickrey (1973) formulation of scheduling preferences that we will consider in the next section. Here scheduling utility is separable in departure time and arrival time. That is, changing departure time, does not affect the preferences regarding arrival time and vice versa.

The concept of the preferred arrival time t^* was used to define the $\alpha - \beta - \gamma$ scheduling cost. It makes sense to talk about a preferred arrival time when there is separability in travel time and arrival time, since then the preferred arrival time is not affected by the travel time. Without this separability, there is no single preferred arrival time since the preferred time to arrive depends on the travel time. If instead scheduling utility is separable in departure time and travel time, then we would want to talk about a preferred departure time. In some contexts, for example the afternoon commute from work to home, this might be a more natural concept. In general, neither the concept of a preferred arrival time nor a preferred departure time may be relevant. We shall now discuss Vickrey (1973) scheduling preferences, which are separable in departure time and arrival time.

Vickrey (1973) Scheduling Preferences

Consider an individual travelling between two locations indexed by $i = 1,2$. He derives utility at the time dependent rate η_i at location i. Let us say he starts the day at time T_1 at location 1 and ends the day at time T_2 at location 2. If he departs from location 1 at time t_1 and arrives (later) at location 2 at time t_2, then he obtains scheduling utility

$$u(t_1, t_2) = \int_{T_1}^{t_1} \eta_1(s)\,ds + \int_{t_2}^{T_2} \eta_2(s)\,ds. \tag{9.9}$$

The formulation is illustrated in Figure 9.4.

Note that when T_1 and T_2 are fixed, these numbers can be replaced by arbitrary numbers in Equation (9.9) without affecting the implied preferences. Assume that $\eta_1 > 0$, $\eta'_1 < 0$, $\eta_2 > 0$, $\eta'_2 < 0$ and that there is a point in time, t^*, where $\eta_1(t^*) = \eta_2(t^*)$. Speaking in terms of the morning commute these conditions imply that a traveler prefers to be at home or at work to traveling, that his/her marginal utility of staying later at home is decreasing, that his/her marginal utility of arriving earlier at work is also decreasing, and that there is a time (t^*) when he/she would optimally transfer from home to work if instant travel was possible. Given a travel time of d, he/she would optimally depart at the time $t(d)$ depending on d when $\eta_1(t(d)) = \eta_2(t(d) + d)$. It is straightforward to derive that his/her value of time would be

$$-\frac{\partial u(t(d), t(d) + d)}{\partial d} = \eta_2(t(d) + d).$$

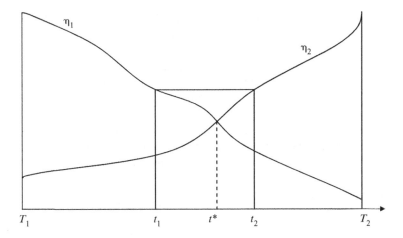

Figure 9.4   Vickrey (1973) scheduling preferences

This is strictly increasing as a function of *d*. Using survey data on stated choice, Tseng and Verhoef (2008) provide empirical estimates of time varying utility rates corresponding to the Vickrey (1973) model.

The Cost of Travel Time Variability

When travel time is random and travelers are risk averse, the random travel time variability leads to additional cost, the cost of travel time variability. Both Vickrey formulations of scheduling preferences are useful for deriving measures of the cost of travel time variability as well as of the scheduling impact of the headway of scheduled services. Such cost measures can be useful to incorporate elements of dynamic congestion in reduced form in static models. Consider a traveler who is about to undertake a given trip. The travel time for the trip is random from the perspective of the traveler. While he/she does not know the travel time outcome before making the trip, the traveler knows the travel time distribution. The travel time distribution is independent of the departure time of the traveler. The latter is a strong assumption but necessary for the results.

The traveler is assumed to choose his/her departure time optimally, so as to maximize his/her expected scheduling utility. That makes the expected scheduling utility a function just of the travel time distribution. Therefore it is possible in principle to evaluate how the expected scheduling utility depends on the travel time distribution. Simple expressions are available for the two Vickrey specifications of scheduling preferences.

In the case of $\alpha - \beta - \gamma$ preferences, Fosgerau and Karlstrom (2010) show that the expected trip cost with optimal departure time is

$$\alpha \cdot \mu + \sigma \cdot (\beta + \gamma) \int_{\gamma/(\beta+\gamma)}^{1} \Phi^{-1}(s)\,ds,$$

which is linear in the mean and in the standard deviation of travel time. This is a practical advantage in applications. The expression depends on the shape of the travel time distribution through the presence of Φ in the integral and so Φ must be taken into account if the marginal value of standard deviation of travel time is to be transferred from one setting to another. In the same vein, Fosgerau (2009) uses $\alpha - \beta - \gamma$ scheduling cost to derive simple expressions for the value of headway for scheduled services. In the case of Vickrey (1973) scheduling preferences with linear utility rates, Fosgerau and Engelson (2011) carry out a parallel exercise. They show that with random travel time and unconstrained choice of departure time, the expected scheduling cost with the optimal choice of departure time is a linear function of travel time, travel time squared and the variance of travel time. Parallel results are also provided for the value of headway for scheduled services. In contrast to the case of $\alpha - \beta - \gamma$ scheduling cost, it is possible also to derive a simple expression for the expected scheduling cost for the case of a scheduled service with random travel time.

The Bottleneck Model Revisited

The results discussed above for the basic bottleneck model survive in some form with more general scheduling preferences. The setup of the model is as before, the only change is that now travelers are assumed to have scheduling preferences of the general form discussed above. Without loss of generality we may again consider $d_1 = d_2 = 0$, since the exact form of scheduling preferences is not specified.

It is easy to argue, using the same argument as in the simple case, that Nash equilibrium requires departures in an interval $I = [a_0, a_1]$ satisfying

$$a_1 - a_0 = N/s, \tag{9.10}$$

$$v(a_0) = v(a_1). \tag{9.11}$$

This is illustrated in Figure 9.5. Moreover, the queue has length zero at time a_0 and a_1 but it is strictly positive at any time in the interior of this interval. The second condition (9.11) has a unique solution since v is quasiconcave and it ensures that no traveler will want to depart at any time outside I.

Equations (9.10) and (9.11) determine the equilibrium utility of travelers as a function of the number of travelers and the bottleneck capacity. It is then straightforward to derive the marginal external congestion cost and the marginal benefit of capacity expansion.

As in the basic model, there is always a queue during the interval I and a traveler arriving at the bottleneck at time a exits at time $a_0 + R(a)/s$. Travelers are identical so they achieve the same scheduling utility in equilibrium

$$v(a_0) = u\left(a, a_0 + \frac{R(a)}{s}\right).$$

Consider now a time varying toll $\tau(\cdot) \geq 0$ charged at the time of arrival at the bottleneck. We restrict attention to tolls that have $\tau(a_0) = \tau(a_1) = 0$ and are zero outside the departure interval I. This means that Equations (9.10) and (9.11) still apply. If the toll is not too large, then Nash equilibrium exists with departures still in the interval I.[7]

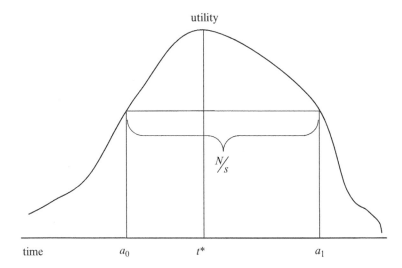

Figure 9.5   The function v and the equilibrium departure interval

Therefore the equilibrium utility $v(a_0)$ is the same as in the no-toll equilibrium. As in the basic model, the optimal toll maintains the departure rate at capacity. The optimal toll is then given by $\tau(a) = v(a) - v(a_0)$ for $a \in I$ and zero otherwise.

The conclusions regarding elastic demand extend to the case of general scheduling preferences. That is, the optimal toll is still $p = \tau - u$, which is the same as in the case of inelastic demand. The conclusions regarding optimal capacity and self-financing also carry over to the general case. That is, if capacity is supplied at constant cost and optimally chosen, then the optimal toll exactly finances the capacity cost.

EXTENSIONS OF THE BOTTLENECK MODEL

The bottleneck model is useful in many ways. It generates a number of insights concerning dynamic congestion, while being still relatively simple and tractable. The model is useful if the mechanisms it describes are representative of the real world. It is, however, a highly stylized description of actual congested networks. It is therefore of interest to extend the model by introducing more relevant features. Such an exercise has two main purposes. One is to gauge the robustness of the conclusions of the basic model. We can have greater confidence in conclusions that survive in more general versions of the model. The other main purpose is to generate new insights that were not available with the basic model. This section proceeds with a presentation of some of the extensions of the bottleneck model available in the literature.

Second Best Pricing

The optimal toll described above varies continuously over time. A real toll could do the same to any relevant degree of precision, but there remains the problem that travelers

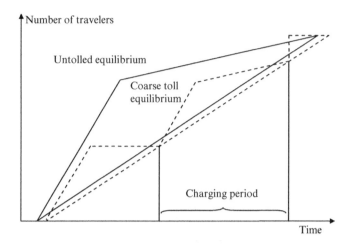

Figure 9.6   The optimal coarse toll

may not be able to understand such a complex pricing structure. Moreover, there may be technological reasons for varying tolls less frequently. Acceptability of road pricing is also a fundamental issue (see, for example, de Palma et al., 2007, on this issue).

Such considerations have led researchers to consider tolls that vary in steps. In the context of the bottleneck, Arnott et al. (1990) consider the simplest step toll, namely a toll that is positive and constant during some interval and zero otherwise. Such a toll has also been called a coarse toll.

The discrete jumps of such a toll generate some new properties of the resulting equilibrium. Three groups of travelers can be identified according to whether they travel before, during or after the tolling period. Figure 9.6 compares the cumulative departure curve in the step-toll equilibrium and compares it with the no-toll equilibrium. Consider first the time before the toll is turned on. The cost of the last traveler not to pay the toll should be the same as the cost of the first traveler to pay the toll. To achieve this equality, there must be a period with no departures between these two travelers. Early in the morning travelers depart at a high rate, they pay no toll and consequently depart at the same rate as they would in no-toll equilibrium. Just before the departure time at which travelers would begin to pay the toll, departures cease for a while and the queue dissipates gradually as travelers are served by the bottleneck.

Departures start again when the queue has diminished just enough for the toll payment to be compensated by lower queueing time. The optimal single step toll is timed such that the queue has just disappeared at the time the toll kicks in. Departures for the group of travelers paying the toll then continue following the pattern analyzed above. The toll is constant for these travelers and hence does not affect the departure rates. The departure rate is consequently high until the time at which a traveler arrives at the destination exactly on time, and then it drops to a lower level. The optimal single step toll is timed such that the queue has just disappeared at the time the toll lifts.

A new phenomenon emerges relating to the third and final group of travelers who do not pay the toll. As shown in Figure 9.6, there is no queue at the moment before they depart. But the first traveler to depart must have the same cost in equilibrium as the other travelers. This can only happen if there is a mass departure at this time. In a mass departure, travelers depart so closely together that their sequence in the queue is random. In this case, travelers are assumed to account for their expected trip cost.

It turns out that all the remaining travelers depart at once under the optimal coarse toll if $\alpha < \gamma$ as has been found in most empirical studies. On average they are better off than a traveler who waits until the queue has gone before departing. But all travelers must achieve the same expected cost in equilibrium. Therefore the first traveler departs later under the coarse toll than under no toll.

Arnott et al. (1990) carried out their analysis for the case of a single step coarse toll. Laih (1994, 2004) extended this analysis to the case of multistep tolls using a slightly modified queueing technology in which some travelers can wait in a separate queue for the toll to lift, while those paying the toll pass the bottleneck.[8] Laih then showed that at most $n/(n + 1)$ of the total queueing time can be eliminated with the optimal n-step toll. Daganzo and Garcia (2000) also consider a step toll with the modified queueing technology. They divide travelers into two groups. Travelers from the first group are not liable to pay any toll. Travelers from the second group are liable to pay a constant step toll if they pass the bottleneck during the tolling period, otherwise they do not have to pay any toll. If the toll is high enough then travelers from the tolled group will avoid the tolling period. The tolling period is timed such that it fits exactly with the equilibrium departure interval of the untolled group. As a consequence, travelers from the untolled group can find an equilibrium during the tolling period and be strictly better off than without the scheme. Travelers from the tolled group are not worse off, since they travel during the same interval as without the scheme and avoid paying any toll by traveling outside the toll period. The essential insight is that the equilibrium cost is determined by the first and last travelers (as in Equations (9.5) or (9.11)) as long as capacity is fully utilized during the departure interval.

The function of the toll in this example is to reserve the bottleneck capacity for a specific group of travelers during a specific interval of time. Shen and Zhang (2010) describe a mechanism that uses ramp metering to achieve a similar effect.

Random Capacity and Demand

Arnott et al. (1999) consider bottleneck congestion in a situation where capacity varies randomly from day to day. The ratio is fixed within a day and given the ratio the evolution of the queue is then deterministic. Travelers choose departure time without knowing the random ratio of the day. They are assumed to find equilibrium in expected utility given the information they have. Arnott et al. (1999) identify circumstances in which the static model is not consistent with a reduced form of the dynamic model. A perhaps surprising result is that providing more information can decrease welfare when demand is elastic and congestion is not efficiently tolled.

Lindsey (2009) considers self-financing in the bottleneck model with random capacity and demand. He finds that the Mohring–Harwitz self-financing theorem survives randomness as long as the information used to set the optimal toll is the same as the information that is available to travelers.

De Palma and Fosgerau (2009) include random travel time variability in a different way. They consider the bottleneck model with fixed capacity but where the FIFO property of the bottleneck model is replaced by random queue sorting, where all travellers in the queue at any given time have the same probability of exiting the queue at that moment. A range of intermediate regimes is also considered. Equations (9.10) and (9.11) still apply and the results that follow from these hence also apply.

Queues take time to dissipate. This physical property of queues has implications for how queues evolve over the course of a day. An empirical regularity of congested demand peaks is that the mean travel time peaks later than the variance of travel time. Fosgerau (2010) shows how this phenomenon arises in a dynamic model of congestion with the ratio of demand to capacity being random.

Heterogeneity

An extension to the basic bottleneck model which is clearly very important is to allow for heterogeneity. The basic model describes travelers as having identical scheduling preferences and identical preferred arrival time. This is very far from reality. For example, using survey data, Fosgerau (2006) estimates the distribution of the value of travel time, α. After conditioning on a number of controls, he finds that the remaining variation in the value of travel time has more than a factor of 50 between the 20th and 80th percentiles of the value of travel time distribution. There is every reason to think that preferences regarding earliness and lateness are similarly heterogeneous.

One of the first questions to ask when such heterogeneity is allowed in the bottleneck models is whether equilibrium still exists and whether it is unique. Analysis of the model would be severely complicated if this failed. This is the subject of Lindsey (2004), who presents general conditions under which equilibrium exists in the basic bottleneck model extended with heterogeneity in the form of a finite number of homogenous groups of travelers. Lindsey provides a review of previous literature regarding preference heterogeneity in the dynamic model.

Parking

Parking is costly in that it competes for urban space with other uses. Cruising for parking is a significant contributor to urban congestion. Arnott and co-authors have published a series of papers on this and related issues, a recent reference is Arnott and Rowse (2009).

There are a few papers on downtown parking in a dynamic framework in which parking occupies space and the attractiveness of a parking space decreases with the distance to the CBD. Arnott et al. (1991) use the bottleneck model to assess the relative efficiency of road tolls and parking fees. Without pricing, drivers occupy parking in order of increasing distance from the CBD. A time-varying toll can prevent queueing, but does not affect the order in which parking spots are taken. Optimal location-dependent parking fees may be superior; they do not eliminate queueing, but induce drivers to park in order of decreasing distance from the CBD, thereby concentrating arrival times closer to work start times. Zhang, Huang and Zhang (2008) integrate AM and PM commutes with parking in this framework.

Small Networks with Dynamic Congestion

This section considers some simple extensions from one link to small networks. Consider first two routes in parallel connecting an origin with a destination. There are $N > 0$

travellers with $\alpha - \beta - \gamma$ scheduling preferences. They each have to choose a route and a departure time. Each route has a certain fixed travel time and a bottleneck with fixed capacity. Denote the fixed travel times by T_i and the capacities by s_i, $i = 1, 2$. Denote also the number of travelers choosing route i as $n_i > 0$ where $N = n_1 + n_2$, since all travelers choose one and only one route. Moreover, let ρ_i denote the arrival rate at the bottleneck for each of the routes.

Consider first the choice of departure time conditional on the number of travelers on each route. From the previous analysis we know that in equilibrium they incur a trip cost of $\delta n_i/s_i$ on each route. There exists a unique equilibrium where

$$\alpha T_1 + \delta \frac{n_1}{s_1} = \alpha T_2 + \delta \frac{n_2}{s_2}.$$

This is equivalent to Equation (9.1) for the static model. It is straightforward to verify that the equilibrium number of travelers on route 1 is

$$n_1 = N \frac{s_1}{s_1 + s_2} + \frac{\alpha}{\delta} \frac{s_1 s_2}{s_1 + s_2} (T_2 - T_1),$$

and the equilibrium cost is

$$C = \alpha \frac{s_1 T_1 + s_2 T_2}{s_1 + s_2} + \delta \frac{N}{s_1 + s_2}.$$

This shows that two bottlenecks in parallel act just like a single bottleneck. The equivalent single bottleneck would have a fixed travel time that is a weighted average of the fixed travel times on the two routes and it would have a bottleneck capacity that is the sum of the capacities of the two routes. This result can be generalized to any number of parallel routes.

A toll may be set at each bottleneck just as if it was a single bottleneck with elastic demand. As we have seen, the optimal toll does not affect the cost of using each route. Hence, the split of travelers between routes is not affected by optimal tolling: the optimal toll does not reallocate between routes, but only across departure times. This is a very different conclusion than was reached in the static model, where the social optimum had a different allocation of travelers on routes than the equilibrium.

There is another situation in which several bottlenecks acts like a single bottleneck. This happens when bottlenecks are connected in a serial manner. In this case, the effective capacity is just the minimum of the bottleneck capacities. That is, the binding capacity constraint is that of the smallest bottleneck.

The property that parallel or serial bottlenecks can be reduced to a single equivalent bottleneck seems likely to survive if $\alpha - \beta - \gamma$ preferences are replaced by general preferences. The description of the equivalent bottleneck does become more complicated. The property that equilibrium usage of the parallel routes is optimal also survives.

Arnott et al. (1993b) analyze a Y-shaped network of bottlenecks to show that a Braess type paradox can arise: an increase in capacity can lead to increased cost. Analysis of more complicated networks is complicated and no general results on networks of bottlenecks seem to be available.

Large Networks

The extension of the dynamic model to large networks remains a difficult problem. So far, existence and uniqueness of equilibrium have not been established (in spite of many attempts). The dynamic traffic assignment problem (Merchant and Nemhauser, 1978) is the subject of a large literature spanning several disciplines. Heydecker and Addison (2005) and Zhang and Zhang (2010) derive some analytical results.

Otherwise, the literature mostly uses numerical methods. Dynamic traffic assignment models are also difficult to work with numerically due to the dimensionality of the problem, which quickly becomes extreme.

Consider a simulation model in which travelers choose the least-cost path through a network. Conditional on the actions of all other travelers, the problem of finding the least-cost path is feasible to solve using well-established algorithms (Dijkstra, 1959). These algorithms are quite efficient but nevertheless require nontrivial time to execute. The dynamic version of such a model is formulated in continuous time; we may want to approximate it using discrete time steps of one second. In, say, a four hour peak period there are 14 400 possible departure time choices. In order to simulate the choice of departure time, we have to find the least-cost path for each possible departure time. Consider a city which can be adequately represented by a zone system of 500 zones. Then the O–D-matrix, indicating the size of O–D flows is a 500 by 500 matrix with 25 000 entries. So the model will have to solve 3.6 billion shortest path problems through the network connecting the 500 zones. This will have to be done many times in order for such a simulation to identify an equilibrium in which no traveler will want to change his/her choice of departure time and route. The result is a huge computational problem and it is practically impossible to handle using a naïve approach.

This section describes one approach taken to this problem, used in the model METROPOLIS (de Palma et al., 1997). The basic idea for reducing the amount of computation is to drop the assumption that travelers can choose the shortest path considering the whole network at once. At each intersection, travelers are able to observe the travel cost on each downstream link. But they do not observe the travel cost on links further downstream. Instead they are able to form an expectation regarding the travel cost from the next downstream nodes until the destination. Travelers then choose the next link with the smallest expected total cost to reach the destination, that is, the smallest sum of the cost of the next link and the downstream expected cost. This portrays travelers as making dynamic discrete choices and these are readily formulated as a dynamic programming model using the Bellman principle.[9,10]

The simulation model looks for equilibrium using a process which can be interpreted as a day-to-day learning process. At the end of each day, the past outcomes for all travelers are pooled and this pool of information is common knowledge. During the next day, travelers have this information available when forming expectations. The idiosyncratic error terms are the same day after day (for departure time choice model). The choice of route can be either deterministic or stochastic (in such case, error terms are i.i.d. over space and time).

Other Congestion Functions

Henderson (1974) formulated a dynamic model of congestion using a similar setup to Vickrey (1969), but in which the travel time is determined by the flow at the time of departure and where flows departing at different times do not interact. Chu (1995) showed that the original Henderson formulation had problems due to nonexistence of equilibrium and proposed a reformulation in which travel time for a traveller is instead determined by the flow at the time of arrival at the destination. The Chu formulation has the Vickrey bottleneck as a limiting case.

CONCLUSIONS

This chapter has presented an overview of dynamic models of congestion, focusing on results derived from the Vickrey bottleneck model. This model combines in a compact way the essential features of congestion dynamics. We have also argued that some fundamental features of congestion are inherently dynamic, which makes dynamic models indispensable for many purposes. In particular, dynamic models can be used to study a variety of policies that cannot be studied with static models. These include road pricing with a time-varying component, flexible work hours, staggered work hours, dynamic access control and ramp metering used to differentiate capacity allocation. Pricing policies are much more effective when tolls depend on the time of the day, for stylized as well as for real networks (see Santos, 2004).

Research into congestion dynamics remains a very active area with many unresolved issues of high importance. We will mention a few here. Economic analyses using dynamic models of congestion are usually undertaken on the assumption that users are in Nash equilibrium. It would therefore be of interest to give general conditions under which Nash equilibrium exists (for general networks). It would further be of interest to specify learning mechanisms that would lead to Nash equilibrium. A learning mechanism is a rule that travelers use to update their choice of departure time and route in the presence of information concerning past outcomes. The existence of learning mechanisms leading to Nash equilibrium would support the presumption that the notion of Nash equilibrium is useful as a benchmark for actual congestion phenomena. Knowledge about learning mechanisms leading to Nash equilibrium may also be useful for the design of algorithms to find Nash equilibrium in simulation models.

Progress would also be desirable concerning the nature of scheduling preferences. The discussion in this chapter has taken for granted that travelers are equipped with scheduling preferences and that these can be regarded as exogenous from the point of view of our analysis. Our transportation perspective has led us to be concerned with the timing of trips and we view travelers simply as having preferences regarding timing such that they can respond to circumstances by changing their trip timing in sensible ways. These times are hardly the fundamental objects of preference and, strictly speaking, it only makes sense to formulate preferences in these terms when circumstances such as the activities before and after the trip can be regarded as exogenous. This is, however, not a very appealing position. If I know that my trip will take more time, then I will adjust my schedule for the day to take this into account. I care, for example, about not being late for appointments. But I make the appointments myself and so my scheduling preferences are a consequence of choice (see the chapter of Pinjara and Bhat on this issue).

It is natural to ask why commuters mostly prefer to arrive at work at the same time. Various contributions have answered this question by pointing to agglomeration forces at the workplace, whereby productivity and wages are affected by the degree of overlap in work times, see Hall (1989), Henderson (1981) and Wilson (1988). If this view is correct, then changes to the transport system will affect agglomeration, which in turn will affect commuter scheduling preferences. It remains to be seen how such mechanisms matter for our understanding of the effect of transport policies.

Endogeneity of scheduling preferences may also matter for the value of information. Consider a trip exposed to random travel time variability. At some point in time, I will learn the size of delay. If scheduling preferences are exogenous, then it only matters whether I learn about the size of the delay soon enough to adjust my departure time. If scheduling preferences are endogenous, then it also matters whether I learn about the size of the delay soon enough to adjust my schedule. Kreps and Porteus (1978) consider dynamic choice behavior under conditions of uncertainty, with emphasis on the timing of the resolution of uncertainty.

As discussed in this chapter, the current state of the topic of dynamic congestion modeling provides a range of general insights from small stylised models. Numerical simulation models exist to deal with the complexities of real size networks. In between, there is a large gap. Numerical simulation has the drawback that it must rely on particular assumptions, which may or may not provide good approximations to the object of interest. So a main motivation for continued theoretical research into dynamic models of congestion is the desire for increased generality. The fewer assumptions required for a conclusion, the more certain we can be that it applies. As this chapter has discussed, there are a number of directions in which we would like to extend our models so that they become better able to account for the facts that travelers are very heterogeneous, they make route and scheduling decisions based on limited information, they interact heavily in ways related to scheduling and they move about in complex networks that are subject to random shocks. The other main motivation for research into the area is the potential for providing a better empirical foundation for our models. One possibility that naturally comes to mind is to seek to utilize data sources such as GPS data to obtain a better understanding of actual trip scheduling behavior.

In conclusion, many exciting things have been done, giving us many important insights into congestion dynamics, and there are still many exciting things waiting to be done.

ACKNOWLEDGEMENT

We would like to thank Robin Lindsey for many useful comments, suggestions and references.

NOTES

1.   For a more detailed analysis of congestion in the static model, see the chapter by Santos and Verhoef.
2.   We assume the parameters are such that this equation leads to positive flows on each route.

3. C' denotes the derivative of C.
4. Small (1982) tested a range of formulations of scheduling preferences, including the $\alpha - \beta - \gamma$ preferences as a special case.
5. Since $c_2(t_1, t_2) < 0$. This follows since $\beta < \alpha$. We use subscripts to denote partial derivatives.
6. We use subscripts to denote partial derivatives.
7. Provided that the toll does not decrease too quickly. A quickly decreasing toll may induce travelers to avoid certain departure times, which leads to unused capacity.
8. Laih (1994) did not recognize that it was necessary to reformulate the queueing technology in order to obtain his results. This was rectified in Laih (2004).
9. The exact optimization procedure used in METROPOLIS was never published since it is commercial proprietary software.
10. Dynamic discrete choice models are surveyed in Aguirregabiria and Mira (2010).

REFERENCES

Aguirregabiria, V. and P. Mira, 2010, Dynamic discrete choice structural models: a survey. *Journal of Econometrics*, **156**, 38–67.

Arnott, R.A., A. de Palma, and R. Lindsey, 1990, Economics of a bottleneck. *Journal of Urban Economics*, **27**, 111–130.

Arnott, R.A., A. de Palma, and R. Lindsey, 1991, A temporal and spatial equilibrium analysis of commuter parking. *Journal of Public Economics*, **45**, 301–335.

Arnott, R.A., A. de Palma, and R. Lindsey, 1993a, A structural model of peak-period congestion: a traffic bottleneck with elastic demand. *American Economic Review*, **83**, 161–179.

Arnott, R.A., A. de Palma, and R. Lindsey 1993b, Properties of dynamic traffic equilibrium involving bottlenecks, including a paradox and metering. *Transportation Science*, **27**, 148–160.

Arnott, R.A., A. de Palma, and R. Lindsey, 1999, Information and time-of-usage decisions in the bottleneck model with stochastic capacity and demand. *European Economic Review*, **43**, 525–548.

Arnott, R. and J. Rowse, 2009, Downtown parking in auto city. *Regional Science and Urban Economics*, **39**, 1–14.

Beckmann, M.J., C.B. McGuire, and C.B. Winston, 1956, *Studies in the Economics of Transportation*. New Haven, CT: Yale University Press.

Chu, X., 1995, Alternative congestion pricing schedules. *Regional Science and Urban Economics*, **29**, 697–722.

Daganzo, C.F. and R.C. Garcia, 2000, A Pareto improving strategy for the time-dependent morning commute problem. *Transportation Science*, **34**, 303–311.

de Palma, A., M. Ben-Akiva, C. Lefèvre, and N. Litinas, 1983, Stochastic equilibrium model of peak period traffic congestion. *Transportation Science*, **17**, 430–453.

de Palma, A. and M. Fosgerau, 2009, Random queues and risk averse users. Working Paper, Ecole Polytechnique, France.

de Palma, A., R. Lindsey, and S. Proost, eds, 2007, Investment and the use of tax and toll revenues in the transport sector: the research agenda. In *Investment and the Use of Tax and Toll Revenues in the Transport Sector*, pp. 1–26.

de Palma, A., F. Marchal, and Y. Nesterov, 1997, METROPOLIS - modular system for dynamic traffic simulation. *Transportation Research Record*, **1607**, 178–184.

Dijkstra, E.W., 1959, A note on two problems in connection with graphs. *Numerische Mathematik*, **1**, 269–271.

Fosgerau, M., 2006, Investigating the distribution of the value of travel time savings. *Transportation Research Part B: Methodological*, **40**, 688–707.

Fosgerau, M., 2009, The marginal social cost of headway for a scheduled service. *Transportation Research Part B: Methodological*, **43**, 813–820.

Fosgerau, M., 2010, On the relation between the mean and variance of delay in dynamic queues with random capacity and demand. *Journal of Economic Dynamics and Control*, **34**, 598–603.

Fosgerau, M. and L. Engelson, 2011, The value of travel time variance. *Transportation Research Part B*, **45**(1), 1–8.

Fosgerau, M. and A. Karlstrom, 2010, The value of reliability. *Transportation Research Part B*, **44**, 38–49.

Hall, R.E., 1989, Temporal agglomeration. Working paper 3143, National Bureau of Economic Research.

Haurie, A. and P. Marcotte, 1985, On the relationship between Nash-Cournot and Wardrop equilibria. *Networks*, **15**, 295–308.

Henderson, J.V., 1974, Road congestion: a reconsideration of pricing theory. *Journal of Urban Economics*, **1**, 346–365.

Henderson, J.V., 1981, The economics of staggered work hours. *Journal of Urban Economics,* **9**, 349–364.

Heydecker, B.G. and J.D. Addison, 2005, Analysis of dynamic traffic equilibrium with departure time choice. *Transportation Science, 39*, 39–57.

Kreps, D.M. and E.L. Porteus, 1978, Temporal resolution of uncertainty and dynamic choice theory. *Econometrica, 46*, 185–200.

Laih, C.-H., 1994, Queueing at a bottleneck with single- and multi-step tolls. *Transportation Research Part A,* **28**, 197–208.

Laih, C.H., 2004, Effects of the optimal step toll scheme on equilibrium commuter behaviour. *Applied Economics,* **36**, 59–81.

Lindsey, R., 2004, Existence, uniqueness, and trip cost function properties of user equilibrium in the bottleneck model with multiple user classes. *Transportation Science,* **38**, 293–314.

Lindsey, R., 2009, Cost recovery from congestion tolls with random capacity and demand. *Journal of Urban Economics,* **66**, 16–24.

Merchant, D.K. and G.L. Nemhauser, 1978, A model and an algorithm for the dynamic traffic assignment problems. *Transportation Science,* **12**, 183–199.

Mohring, H. and M. Harwitz, 1962, *Highway Benefits: An Analytical Framework.* Evanston, IL: Northwestern University Press.

Santos, G., ed., 2004, Road pricing: theory and evidence, *Research in Transportation Economics,* **9**, XI–XIII.

Shen, W. and H.M. Zhang, 2010, Pareto-improving ramp metering strategies for reducing congestion in the morning commute. *Transportation Research Part A: Policy and Practice,* **44**, 676–696.

Small, K., 1982, The scheduling of consumer activities: work trips. *American Economic Review,* **72**, 467–479.

Tseng, Y.Y. and E.T. Verhoef, 2008, Value of time by time of day: a stated-preference study. *Transportation Research Part B: Methodological,* **42**, 607–618.

Verhoef, E.T. and H. Mohring, 2009, Self-financing roads. *International Journal of Sustainable Transportation,* **3**, 293–311.

Vickrey, W.S., 1969, Congestion theory and transport investment. *American Economic Review, 59*, 251–261.

Vickrey, W.S., 1973, Pricing, metering, and efficiently using urban transportation facilities. Highway Research Record, **476**, 36–48.

Wardrop, J.G., 1952, Some theoretical aspects of road traffic research. *Proceedings of the Institute of Civil Engineering,* **II**, 325–378.

Wilson, P.W., 1988, Wage variation resulting from staggered work hours. *Journal of Urban Economics,* **24**, 9–26.

Zhang, X. and H. Zhang, 2010, Simultaneous departure time/route choices in queuing networks and a novel paradox. *Networks and Spatial Economics,* **10**, 93–112.

Zhang, X., H.J. Huang and H.M. Zhang, 2008, Integrated daily commuting patterns and optimal road tolls and parking fees in a linear city. Transportation Research Part B, **42**(1), 35–56.

10 Activity-based travel demand analysis
Abdul Rawoof Pinjari and Chandra R. Bhat

INTRODUCTION

The primary focus of transportation planning, until the past three decades or so, was to meet long-term mobility needs by providing adequate transportation infrastructure supply. In such a supply-oriented planning process, the main role of travel demand models was to predict aggregate travel demand for long-term socio-economic scenarios, transport capacity characteristics and land-use configurations.

Over the past three decades, however, because of escalating capital costs of new infrastructure and increasing concerns regarding traffic congestion and air-quality deterioration, the supply-oriented focus of transportation planning has expanded to include the objective of addressing accessibility needs and problems by managing travel demand within the available transportation supply. Consequently, there has been an increasing interest in travel demand management strategies, such as congestion pricing, that attempt to change transport service characteristics to influence individual travel behavior and control aggregate travel demand.

The interest in analyzing the potential of travel demand management policies to manage travel demand, in turn, has led to a shift in the focus of travel demand modeling from the statistical prediction of aggregate-level long-term travel demand to understanding disaggregate-level (that is individual-level) behavioral responses to short-term demand management policies such as ridesharing incentives, congestion pricing and employer-based demand management schemes (alternate work schedules, telecommuting, and so forth). Individuals respond in complex ways to such changes in travel conditions. The limitation of the traditionally used *statistically oriented* trip-based travel modeling approach in capturing these complex individual responses has resulted in the development of *behaviorally oriented* activity-based approaches to modeling passenger travel demand.[1]

The origin of the activity-based approach dates back to the 1960s from Chapin's (Chapin, 1974) research on activity patterns of urban population. Chapin provided a motivational framework in which societal constraints and inherent individual motivations interact to shape activity participation patterns. This framework, however, ignored the spatial context (or geography of) activity participation and did not address the relationship between activities and travel. During the same time, the first explicit discussion in the literature on activity participation in the context of time and space appears to have been proposed by Hägerstrand (1970).[2] While Hägerstrand's work addressed the relationship between activity participation and time-space concepts, it was the seminal work by Jones (1979) that explicitly addressed the relationship between activities, travel and time and space. Specifically, Jones identified travel as derived from the need to participate in activities at different points in space and time. Subsequent to the research of Jones (1979) and a conference held in 1981 on 'Travel demand analysis: activity-based and other new approaches' (see Carpenter and Jones 1983 for the conference proceedings), the activity-based approach started gaining significant research attention in the 1980s.[3]

Parallel to the early research discussed above in the regional science field, microeconomic utility maximization-based consumption and home production theories of time allocation to activities (Becker, 1965; Evans, 1972) further added to the early theoretical foundations of activity-travel analysis. In addition, the random utility maximization-based consumer choice theory (McFadden, 1973) provided the most popular approach to activity-travel analysis to date.

In the 1990s, several factors provided further stimulus to move from the trip-based to activity based approach to modeling travel demand.[4] These factors included: (a) the increased information demands placed on travel demand models by public policy mandates (such as the ISTEA, TEA-21 and the CAAA), (b) the increasing need to evaluate the effectiveness of short-term travel demand management policies (Bhat and Koppelman, 1999) and (c) the increasing realization of the limitations of the trip-based approach from a behavioral validly stand point and a predictive accuracy stand point (see Axhausen and Gärling, 1992; Jones et al., 1993). Further, the improved analytical tools, modeling methodologies, computation capacity and power and data collection methods accelerated the research shift to an activity-based paradigm.

In recent years, activity-based methods have received much attention and seen considerable progress, as discussed in the remainder of this chapter. In the next section, we discuss the salient aspects of the activity-based approach by presenting a theoretical and policy-oriented comparison of the trip-based and activity-based approaches. The following section presents an overview of the various activity-travel forecasting systems in the literature. Then we discuss the emerging developments, and future research directions along three important dimensions of activity participation and travel: (a) inter-personal interactions, (b) time and (c) space. Another section focuses on the integration of activity-based travel forecasting systems with other modeling systems (such as land use models and dynamic traffic assignment models) to build larger and comprehensive urban modeling systems. The final section summarizes the chapter.

TRIP-BASED VERSUS ACTIVITY-BASED APPROACHES

The fundamental difference between the trip-based and activity-based approaches is that the former approach directly focuses on 'trips' without explicit recognition of the motivation or reason for the trips and travel. The activity-based approach, on the other hand, views travel as a demand derived from the need to pursue activities (see Bhat and Koppelman, 1999; Davidson et al., 2007; and Jones et al., 1990), and focuses on 'activity participation behavior'. The underlying philosophy is to better understand the behavioral basis for individual decisions regarding participation in activities in certain places at given times (and hence the resulting travel needs). This behavioral basis includes all the factors that influence the why, how, when and where of performed activities and resulting travel. Among these factors are the needs, preferences, prejudices and habits of individuals (and households), the cultural/social norms of the community and the travel service characteristics of the surrounding environment.

Another difference between the two approaches is in the way travel is represented. The trip-based approach represents travel as a mere collection of 'trips'. Each trip is considered as independent of other trips, without considering the inter relationship in the choice attributes (such as time, destination and mode) of different trips. Such a neglect of the temporal, spatial and modal linkages between the trips can lead to illogical trip chain predictions, and distorted evaluations of the impact of policy actions.[5] On the other hand, the activity-based approach precludes illogical mode-trip chains by using 'tours' as the basic elements to represent and model travel patterns. Tours are chains of trips beginning and ending at a same location, say, home or work. The tour-based representation helps maintain the consistency across, and capture the interdependency (and consistency) of the modeled choice attributes among, the trips of the same tour. In addition to the tour-based representation of travel, the activity-based approach focuses on sequences or patterns of activity participation and travel behavior (using the whole day or longer periods of time as the unit of analysis). Such an approach can address travel demand management issues through an examination of how people modify their activity participations (for example, will individuals substitute more out-of-home activities for in-home activities in the evening if they arrived early from work due to a work-schedule change?).

The third major difference between the trip-based and the activity-based approaches is in the way the time dimension of activities and travel is considered. In the trip-based approach, time is reduced to being simply a 'cost' of making a trip and a day is viewed as a combination of broadly defined peak and off-peak time periods. On the other hand, activity-based approach views individuals' activity-travel patterns are a result of their time-use decisions within a continuous time domain. Individuals have 24 hours in a day (or multiples of 24 hours for longer periods of time) and decide how to use that time among (or allocate that time to) activities and travel (and with whom) subject to their socio-demographic, spatial, temporal, transportation system and other contextual constraints. These decisions determine the generation and scheduling of trips. Hence, determining the impact of travel demand management policies on time-use behavior is an important precursor step to assessing the impact of such polices on individual travel behavior.

The fourth major difference between the two approaches relates to the level of aggregation. In the trip-based approach, most aspects of travel (number of trips, modal split and so forth) are analyzed at an aggregate level. The study area is divided into several spatial units labeled as traffic analysis zones (TAZ). Then, the total numbers of trip exchanges are estimated for each pair of TAZs by each travel mode and by each route, during each coarsely defined time of day. Consequently, trip-based methods accommodate the effect of socio-demographic attributes of households and individuals in a very limited fashion, which limits the ability of the method to evaluate travel impacts of long-term socio-demographic shifts. The activity-based models, on the other hand, have the ability to relatively easily accommodate virtually any number of decision factors related to the socio-demographic characteristics of the individuals who actually make the activity-travel choices, and the travel service characteristics of the surrounding environment. Thus the activity-based models are better equipped to forecast the longer-term changes in travel demand in response to the changes in the socio-demographic composition and the travel environment of urban areas. Further, using activity-based models, the impact of policies can be assessed by predicting individual-level behavioral responses instead of employing trip-based statistical averages that are aggregated over coarsely defined demographic segments.

Given the behavioral basis and conceptual advantages, the activity-based approach can potentially offer a better ability to evaluate a wide variety of transportation policy initiatives that cannot be either analyzed, or may not be accurately analyzed, using a traditional trip-based framework. For example, trip-based models have very limited ability to predict traveler responses to travel demand management strategies such as congestion pricing, because of the highly aggregate treatment of the time-of-day dimension, and the ignorance of temporal linkages across different trips. Activity-based models are better suited to model the impact of congestion pricing strategies because they capture individual responses to tolls including the potential mode shifts, departure timing shifts, and the potential substitution patterns among different dimensions of travel (mode, timing and so forth). In addition to the incorporation of temporal linkages among various trips (across the day) of an individual, the activity-based modeling approach facilitates the accommodation of the linkages across the activity participation decisions and travel patterns of different individuals in a household. Such an explicit modeling of inter-individual interactions and the resulting joint travel is essential in the context of occupancy-specific tolling strategies such as high occupancy vehicle (HOV) lanes and high occupancy toll (HOT) lanes (Davidson et al., 2007). Trip-based models, on the other hand, have no ability to incorporate joint travel patterns and cannot provide credible estimates of shared-ride travel for informing HOV/HOT lane policy making.

ACTIVITY-BASED TRAVEL DEMAND MODELING SYSTEMS

This section provides an overview of the activity-based travel forecasting systems in the literature. Most of the models developed to date can be classified into one of two modeling approaches: (1) utility maximization-based econometric model systems, and (2) rule-based computational process model systems. However, it is important to note that the above two approaches have been neither exclusive nor exhaustive. Several other approaches, including: (1) time-space prisms and constraints, (2) operations research/mathematical programming approaches, and (3) agent-based approaches have been employed, either in combination with the above approaches or separately, to develop activity-based model systems. The modeling approaches and the models within each approach are discussed below.

Utility Maximization-based Econometric Model Systems

The underlying theory behind utility maximization-based modeling systems comes from the economic theories of consumer choice (for example, Becker 1965) that individuals make their activity-travel decisions to maximize the utility derived from the choices they make. These model systems usually consist of a series of utility maximization-based discrete choice models (that is, multinomial logit and nested logit models) that are used to predict several components of individuals' activity-travel decisions. In addition to such utility maximization-based model components, several model systems employ other econometric structures, including hazard-based duration structures, and ordered response structures to model various activity-travel decisions. In all, these model systems employ econometric systems of equations (most of which are utility maximization-based) to capture relationships between individual-level socio-demographics and activity-travel environment attributes on the one hand and the observed activity-travel decision outcomes on the other.

The two main criticisms of this approach are that: (1) individuals are not necessarily fully rational utility maximizers (Timmermans et al., 2002) and (2) the approach does not explicitly model the underlying decision processes and behavioral mechanisms that lead to observed activity-travel decisions. Nonetheless, the approach is very amenable to the development of operational activity-based travel forecasting systems. In this section, we provide an overview of a representative sample of such travel forecasting systems that are either fully developed or under development for practical transportation planning purposes. The model systems include: (1) The models developed (or under development) for various planning agencies such as Portland METRO (Bradley et al., 1998), San Francisco SFCTA (Bradley et al., 2001), New York NYMTC (Vovsha et al., 2002), Columbus MORPC (PB Consult 2005), Sacramento SACOG (Bowman and Bradley, 2005–2006) and Atlanta ARC (PB et al., 2006) and (2) the models developed in the research community (CEMDAP and FAMOS).[6]

The first group of models can be categorized into (1) *full individual day pattern* modeling systems, and (2) *enhanced (or linked) full individual day pattern* modeling systems. The *full individual day pattern* modeling systems follow the concept of an over-arching daily activity-travel pattern proposed by Bowman and Ben-Akiva (2001). These systems are based on an underlying system of multinomial logit and nested logit models in a particular hierarchy, although with minor variations. The Portland, San Francisco, New York and Sacramento models belong to this category. We briefly describe the features of the Sacramento model as an example of a *full individual day pattern* model in the subsequent section. The *enhanced (or linked) full individual day pattern* modeling systems, on the other hand, are an enhancement of the *full individual day pattern* models to accommodate intra-household interactions in activity-travel engagement. That is, the full-day activity schedule approach of Bowman and Ben-Akiva (2001) is enhanced to explicitly recognize and model the linkages across the activity-travel patterns of individuals (for example, joint activity engagement and travel) in a household. The reader is referred to the documentation of the activity-based models developed for Columbus and Atlanta regions (PB Consult, 2005; PB et al., 2006) for details on such linked full individual day pattern model systems.

Activity-travel forecasting system of the Sacramento activity-based model
The activity-travel forecasting system in the Sacramento model, labeled as DaySim, belongs to the *full individual day pattern* modeling systems category in that it predicts each individual's full-day activity and travel schedule in the study area.

DaySim consists of an econometric micro-simulation system with a three-tier hierarchy of: (1) day-level activity pattern choice models (or, simply, pattern-level choice models), (2) tour-level choice models and (3) trip/stop-level choice models. Each of the models in this hierarchy consists of a series of econometric choice models, as outlined in Table 10.1. For all these individual model components, Table 10.1 lists the model name and the output of the model, the econometric structure, and the set of choice alternatives. As can be observed from the table, each of the activity-travel choices is modeled using either a multinomial logit or a nested logit structure. The reader will note here that

Table 10.1   Activity-travel forecasting system of the Sacramento activity-based model

Model ID	Model name and outcome	Model structure	Choice alternatives
Day-level activity-pattern choice models: Predict the number of home-based tours a person undertakes during a day for seven purposes, and the occurrence of additional stops during the day for the same seven purposes. Purposes: work, school, escort, personal business, shopping, meal and social/recreational, in that order of priority.			
1.1	Daily activity pattern model: jointly predicts whether or not a person participates in tours and extra stops for seven activity purposes in a day.	MNL (Multinomial logit)	Feasible alternatives of 2080 combinations of 0 or 1+ tours, and 0 or 1+ stops for seven activity purposes. Base alterative is *Stay at home*.
1.2	Number of tours for each of the seven activity purposes for which tour making is predicted from the above model.	MNL	1,2 or 3 tours for each purpose.
Tour-level models: Predict primary *destination*, mode and time-of-day, in that order, for all tours. A work-based tour generation model is also included.			
2.1	Parcel-level tour primary *destination* zone and parcel choice model (for each of the tours predicted in the above step). This model is applied for all tours in the order of their priority, with high priority tour-outcomes known at the low-priority tour models.	NL (Nested logit) for work-tour, and MNL for non-work and non-school tours	Sample of available parcels (parcel availability based on purpose-specific size and travel time). Work-tour model has usual work location in a nest.
2.2	Work-based tour generation model: predicts the number and purpose of work-based sub-tours that originate for each home-based work tour predicted by models 1.1, 1.2 and 2.1. These work-based subtours take priority after home-based work tours.	MNL model, applied repeatedly	One (more) subtour for any of seven purposes, or no (more) subtours. In application, the model is repeated until the third subtour purpose or *No (more) subtour* is predicted.
2.3	Tour-level main *mode* choice models (by purpose, for all tours): predict the tour-level mode choice.	NL	Drive transit walk, walk transit drive, walk transit walk, school bus, shared ride 3+, shared ride 2, drive alone, bike, walk.

2.4	Tour-level *time-of-day* choice models by purpose: predict half-hour time periods of arrival at and departure from primary destination.	MNL	Combinations of all feasible half-hour intervals of arrival and departure = $48 \times 49/2$.
2.5	Intermediate stop generation models (predicts the exact number and purpose of stops for the half-tours leading to and from the primary destination of the tour).	MNL model, applied repeatedly for all half-tours	One (more) stop for any of seven purposes, or no (more) stops. In application, model is repeated until the fifth stop purpose or *no (more) stops* is predicted.

Stop-level models: (Stops in half-tour before primary destination are modeled in the reverse chronological order. Location, mode, and 30-minute time period of arrival at location are modeled in that order, and departure time is derived from level-of-service tables. After the trip chain for the first half-tour is modeled, the trip chain for the second half-tour back to the tour origin is similarly modeled in regular chronological order).

3.1	Intermediate stop *location*: Predicts the destination zone and parcel of each intermediate stop, conditional on tour origin and primary destination, and location of previous stops.	MNL	Sample of available parcels drawn from an importance sampling procedure at three levels of geography (stratum, TAZ, and parcel). Parcel availability based on purpose-specific size and travel time.
3.2	Trip *mode* choice (conditional on main tour mode, the mode of previously modeled adjacent trip, and the specific origin–destination pair anchors).	MNL	Drive to transit, walk to transit, school bus, shared ride 3+ and 2, drive alone, bike, walk.
3.3	Trip *time-of-day* choice models by purpose: Predict arrival time (departure time) choice for stops in first (second) half tour, conditional on the time windows remaining from previous choices.	MNL	Feasible alternatives among the 48 half-hour time period alternatives.

219

the models are numbered hierarchically in the table to represent the sequence in which the activity-travel decisions are modeled in DaySim. The choice outcomes from models higher in the hierarchy (assumed to be of higher priority to the decision maker) are treated as known in the lower level models.

As can be observed from the table, the *pattern-level* models consist of models numbered 1.1 (the daily activity pattern model) and 1.2 (the number of tours model). These models predict: (1) the occurrence (and the number) of home-based tours (that is, tours that originate and end at home) specifically for each of the following seven activity purposes during a day: work, school, escort, personal business, shopping, meal and social/recreational, and (2) the occurrence of additional stops/trips that may occur (in other tours) for these seven purposes. The *tour-level* models (numbered 2.1, 2.3, 2.4 and 2.5 in the table) predict the primary destination (that is, the destination of the primary stop for which this tour is made), travel mode, time-of-day of travel (that is, time of arrival at, and time of departure from primary destination), and the number of additional stops by purpose (other than the primary stop) for all tours. Tour-level models also include a work-based tour (that is, a tour that originates and ends at work) generation model (numbered 2.2) that predicts the number (and purpose) of work-based tours for each home-based work tour predicted by models 1.1 and 1.2. The *stop-level* models predict the stop location (or destination), mode choice, and time-of-day of travel for each of the stops (other than the primary stops) generated in the previous steps.

Among the models listed in Table 10.1, models 1.1, 1.2, 2.2 and 2.5 together form the activity and travel *generation models*, which provide as outputs a list of all the activities, tours and trips generated for the person-day. These activities, tours and trips are scheduled using the other tour-level and trip-level models, which can also be labeled as the *scheduling models*. The scheduling models determine the when (time-of-day), where (destination) and how (mode) of the generated activities and travel.

The above-described activity-travel forecasting system is applied, in succession, to each (and every) individual in the study area to obtain the full-day activity and travel information of all individuals in the population.

CEMDAP

CEMDAP (Comprehensive Econometric Microsimulator for Activity-Travel Patterns; Bhat et al., 2004; and Pinjari et al., 2006) is a continuous time activity-travel forecasting system that is based on a range of discrete choice, hazard-based duration and regression-based econometric models. Similar to the aforementioned model systems, the activity-travel patterns in CEMDAP are represented in a hierarchy of pattern-level attributes, tour-level attributes and stop-level attributes. The difference, however, is that the attributes in CEMDAP characterize a continuous time activity-travel pattern built within the space-time constraints imposed by work and school activities. Hence separate representation frameworks and modeling sequences are adopted for workers (defined as adults who go to work or school and children who go to school on the day) and non-workers (non-working adults and non-school going children), while incorporating coupling dependencies due to inter-personal interactions (between parents and children).

Activity-travel representation frameworks for workers in CEMDAP (drawn from Bhat and Singh, 2000):   The daily pattern of workers is characterized by five different sub-

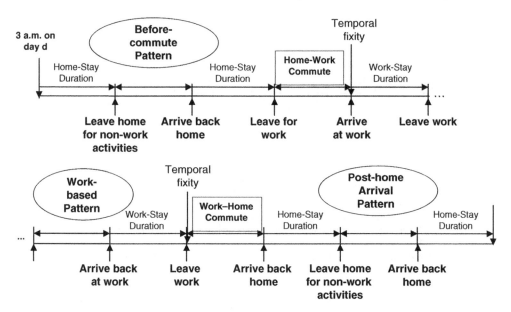

Figure 10.1   Diagrammatic representation of worker activity-travel pattern in CEMDAP

patterns: (1) before-work (BW) pattern, which represents the activity-travel undertaken before leaving home to work; (2) home–work commute (HW) pattern, which represents the activity-travel pursued during the home-to-work commute; (3) work-based (WB) pattern, which includes all activity and travel undertaken from work; (4) work–home commute (WH) pattern, which represents the activity-travel pursued during the work-to-home commute; and (5) the post home arrival pattern (referred to as after-work or AW pattern), which comprises the activity and travel behavior of individuals after arriving home at the end of the work-to-home commute. Within each of the BW, WB and AW patterns, there might be several tours. A tour is a circuit that begins and ends at home for the BW and AW patterns and is a circuit that begins and ends at work for WB pattern. Further, each tour within the BW, WB and AW patterns may comprise several activity stops. Similarly, the HW and WH commute patterns may also comprise several activity stops. Figure 10.1 provides a diagrammatic representation of the worker activity-travel pattern in terms of the overall pattern, the component tours and stops.

The characterization of the complete workday activity-travel pattern is accomplished by identifying a number of different attributes within the representation discussed above. These attributes may be classified based on the level of representation they are associated with: that is, whether they are associated with a pattern, a tour or a stop. Pattern-level attributes include the number of tours for the BW, WB and AW patterns, and the home-stay duration before the HW commute pattern. Tour-level attributes include the travel mode, number of stops, and home-stay duration before each tour in the BW and AW patterns, work-stay duration before each tour in the WB pattern and the sequence of tours in each pattern. Stop-level attributes include activity type, travel time from previous stop, location of stop, activity duration and the sequence of the stop in the tour.

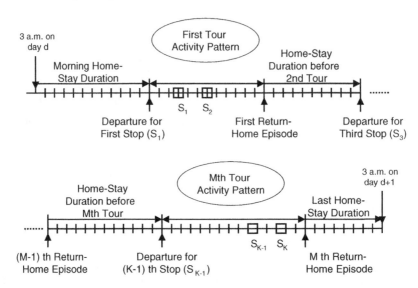

Figure 10.2   Diagrammatic representation of the activity-travel pattern of non-workers in CEMDAP

Activity-travel representation frameworks for non-workers in CEMDAP (drawn from Bhat and Misra, 2000):   In the case of non-workers, the activity-travel pattern is considered as a set of out-of-home activity episodes (or stops) of different types interspersed with in-home activity stays. The chain of stops between two in-home activity episodes is referred to as a tour. The pattern is represented diagrammatically in Figure 10.2. A non-worker's daily activity-travel pattern is characterized again by attributes associated with the entire daily pattern, a tour in the day and a stop. Pattern-level attributes include whether or not the individual makes any stops during the day, the number of stops of each activity type if the individual leaves home during the day, and the sequencing of all episodes (both stops and in-home episodes). The only tour-level attribute is the travel mode for the tour. Stop-level attributes include the activity duration, travel time to stop from previous episode (except for the first home-stay episode), and the location of out-of-home episodes (that is, stops).

The modeling of the activity-travel pattern of individuals entails the determination of each of the attributes that characterize the representation structure described above. Due to the large number of attributes and the large number of possible choice alternatives for each attribute, the joint modeling of all these attributes is infeasible. Consequently, a modeling framework that is feasible to implement from a practical standpoint is required. The framework adopted in CEMDAP is described below.

CEMDAP'S modeling and micro-simulation framework (drawn from Pinjari et al., 2006):   CEMDAP comprises a suite of econometric models, each model corresponding to the determination of one or more activity/travel choices of an individual or household. These models may be broadly grouped into two systems: (1) the generation-allocation model system and (2) the scheduling model system. The first system of models is focused on modeling the decision of individuals/households to undertake different types of activities (such as work, school, shopping and discretionary) during the day and the allocation of responsibilities among individuals (for example, determination of which parent would escort the child to and from school). Table 10.2 lists the precise econometric structure and the choice alternatives for each of the model components in this system. The second system (that is, the scheduling model system) determines how the generated activities are scheduled to form the complete activity-travel pattern for each individual in the household, accommodating the space-time constraints imposed by work, school and escorting children's activities. That is, these models determine the choices such as number of tours, mode and number of stops for each tour, and the activity-type, location, and duration for each stop in each tour. Table 10.3 lists the econometric structures and the set of choice alternatives for each model in this second system.

CEMDAP's micro-simulation prediction procedure is represented schematically in Figure 10.3. Each step in the figure involves the application of several models in a systematic fashion. This micro-simulation procedure is applied to each and every household and individual of an urban area to predict the overall activity-travel patterns in the area.

FAMOS
FAMOS (Florida Activity Mobility Simulator; Pendyala, 2004; Pendyala et al., 2005) is similar to CEMDAP in the explicit recognition of space-time constraints, and the continuous time nature of the modeling system. FAMOS consists of a prism-constrained activity travel simulator (PCATS) that simulates the activities and trips undertaken by an individual together with the locations, modes, times, durations and sequence of the activities and travel. The unique feature of this simulator is that Hägerstrand's space–time prisms[7] are utilized to represent and model the spatial and temporal constraints under which individuals undertake activities and trips (hence, the name prism-constrained activity-travel simulator). The boundaries (or frontiers) of these space–time prisms, within which the individual activity travel patterns must take place, are determined by using stochastic frontier models (see Pendyala et al., 2002). Subsequently, the activity-travel patterns are simulated within the boundaries of the space–time prisms.

Rule-based Computational Process Models

Rule-based computational process models (CPM) have been proposed as another approach to modeling activity-travel behavior. A CPM is basically a computer program implementation of a production system model, which is a set of rules in the form of condition-action (if-then) pairs that specify how a task is solved (Gärling et al., 1994). CPM researchers argue that complex human activity-travel behavior may not always be able to be represented as an outcome of utility maximization (Timmermans et al., 2002). Rather, the underlying principle of the CPMs is that individuals use context dependent choice heuristics to make decisions pertaining to activities and travel. These models attempt to mimic how individuals think when building schedules. The model systems can be viewed as an exhaustive set of rules in the form of condition-action pairs to specify how a task is solved.

A limitation of CPMs, however, is that there are still unresolved issues in the development of CPMs that make it difficult to determine the statistical significance of the factors

Table 10.2   The generation-allocation model system in CEMDAP

Model ID	Model name	Econometric structure	Choice alternatives	Comments
GA1	Children's decision to go to school	Binary logit	Yes, no	Applicable only to children who are students. The determination of whether or not a child is a student is made in the CEMSELTS module (see Eluru et al. 2008).
GA2	Children's school start time (time from 3 a.m.)	Hazard-duration	Continuous time	
GA3	Children's school end time (time from school start time)	Hazard-duration	Continuous time	
GA4	Decision to go to work	Binary logit	Yes, no	Applicable only to individuals above the age of 16 and who are workers. The determination of whether or not an individual is a worker is made in the CEMSELTS module.
GA5	Work start and end times	Multinomial logit	528 discrete time period combinations	
GA6	Decision to undertake work related activities	Binary logit	Yes, no	
GA7	Adult's decision to go to school	Binary logit	Yes, no	Applicable only to adults who are students, as determined in CEMSELTS.
GA8	Adult's school start time (time from 3 AM)	Regression	Continuous time	
GA9	Adult's school end time (time from school start time)	Regression	Continuous time	
GA10	Mode to school for children	Multinomial logit	Driven by parent, driven by other, school bus, walk/bike	Applicable only to children who go to school.
GA11	Mode from school for children	Multinomial logit	Driven by parent, driven by other, school bus, walk/bike	
GA12	Allocation of drop off episode to parent	Binary logit	Father, mother	Applicable only to non-single parent household with children who go to school.
GA13	Allocation of pick up episode to parent	Binary logit	Father, mother	

GA14	Decision of child to undertake discretionary activity jointly with parent	Binary logit	Yes, no	Second model in this row is applicable only to non-single parent households with children who go to school.
GA15	Allocation of the joint discretionary episodes to one of the parents	Binary logit	Father, mother	
GA16	Decision of child to undertake independent discretionary activity	Binary logit	Yes, no	
GA17	Decision of household to undertake grocery shopping	Binary logit	Yes, no	Second model in this row is applicable only if the household is determined (using the first model in this row) to undertake shopping.
GA18	Decision of an adult to undertake grocery shopping	Binary logit	Yes, no	
GA19	Decision of an adult to undertake household/personal business	Binary logit	Yes, no	
GA20	Decision of an adult to undertake social/recreational activities	Binary logit	Yes, no	
GA21	Decision of an adult to undertake eat out activities	Binary logit	Yes, no	
GA22	Decision of an adult to undertake other serve passenger activities	Binary logit	Yes, no	

Notes:
1. A child is an individual whose age is less than 16 years, and an adult is an individual whose age is 16 years or more.
2. CEMSELTS = Comprehensive Econometric Microsimulator for SocioEconomics, Land-use and Transportation Systems.
3. In the CEMDAP architecture, all individuals in the population have to be classified into one of the following three categories: (1) student (2) worker and (3) non-student, non-worker. CEMDAP, in its current form, does not accept the category of 'student and worker'.
4. GA1–GA9 model the work/school participation decisions, GA10–GA16 model the children's travel needs and allocation of escort responsibility, and GA17–GA22 model the individual-level activity participation choice.

Table 10.3   The scheduling model system in CEMDAP

Model ID	Model name	Econometric structure	Choice alternatives
WS1	Commute mode	Multinomial logit	Solo driver, driver with passenger, passenger, transit, walk/bike
WS2	Number of stops in work–home commute	Ordered probit	0,1,2
WS3	Number of stops in home–work commute	Ordered probit	0,1,2
WS4	Number of after-work tours	Ordered probit	0,1,2
WS5	Number of work-based tours	Ordered probit	0,1,2
WS6	Number of before-work tours	Ordered probit	0,1
WS7	Tour mode	Multinomial logit	Solo driver, driver with passenger, passenger, transit, walk/bike
WS8	Number of stops in a tour	Ordered probit	1,2,3,4,5
WS9	Home/work stay duration before a tour	Regression	Continuous time
WS10	Activity type at stop	Multinomial logit	Work-related, shopping, household/personal business, eat out, other serve passenger
WS11	Activity duration at stop	Linear regression	Continuous time
WS12	Travel time to stop	Linear regression	Continuous time
WS13	Stop location	Spatial location choice	Choice alternatives based on estimated travel time
NWS1	Number of independent tours	Ordered probit	1,2,3,4
NWS2	Decision to undertake an independent tour before pickup-up/joint discretionary tour	Binary logit	Yes, no
NWS3	Decision to undertake an independent tour after pickup-up/joint discretionary tour	Binary logit	Yes, no
NWS4	Tour Mode	Multinomial logit	Solo driver, driver with passenger, passenger, transit, walk/bike
NWS5	Number of stops in a tour	Ordered probit	1,2,3,4,5
NWS6	Number of stops following a pick-up/drop-off stop in a tour	Ordered probit	0,1
NWS7	Home stay duration before a tour	Regression	Continuous time
NWS8	Activity type at stop	Multinomial logit	Work-related, shopping, household/personal business, eat out, other serve passenger
NWS9	Activity duration at stop	Linear Regression	Continuous time

Table 10.3   (continued)

Model ID	Model name	Econometric structure	Choice alternatives
NWS10	Travel time to stop	Linear Regression	Continuous time
NWS11	Stop location	Spatial location choice	Choice alternatives based on estimated travel time
JS1	Departure time from home	Regression	Continuous time
JS2	Activity duration at stop	Regression	Continuous time
JS3	Travel time to stop	Regression	Continuous time
JS4	Location of stop	Spatial location choice	Continuous time
CS1	School-home commute time	Regression	Continuous time
CS2	Home-school commute time	Regression	Continuous time
CS3	Mode for independent discretionary tour	Multinomial logit	Drive by other, walk/bike
CS4	Departure time from home for independent discretionary tour	Regression	Continuous time
CS5	Activity duration at independent discretionary stop	Regression	Continuous time
CS6	Travel time to independent discretionary stop	Regression	Continuous time
CS7	Location of independent discretionary stop	Spatial location choice	Pre-determined subset of zones

that affect scheduling decisions. Also, most CPMs consider the generation of activity episodes (and one or more attributes of each episode) to be exogenous, and focus only on the scheduling or sequencing of activities. Even for activity scheduling and sequencing, it is difficult to enumerate all the decision rules underlying such a complex process. Nonetheless, this research is valuable in providing insights into activity-travel scheduling processes of individuals that can, at the least, be used to inform the development of operational travel demand models.

The important CPMs in the literature are listed and briefly discussed next.

CARLA (Clarke, 1986)
CARLA (for Combinatorial Algorithm for Rescheduling Lists of Activities) was one of the earliest rule-based activity scheduling models, developed by the Oxford University Transport Studies Unit (Clarke, 1986). This model uses an exogenously available activity program (list of activities to be scheduled, durations and timing) to generate all feasible activity pattern changes to proposed policies. The potential changes include retiming of activities, change of travel mode, or change in location. Since there can be a large number of resulting activity sequences, the feasibility of an activity sequence is dependent on a number of predefined rules including logical timing and location-related constraints and interpersonal coupling constraints and personal preferences. Subsequently, combinatorics and heuristics are used to choose one of the feasible activity sequences.

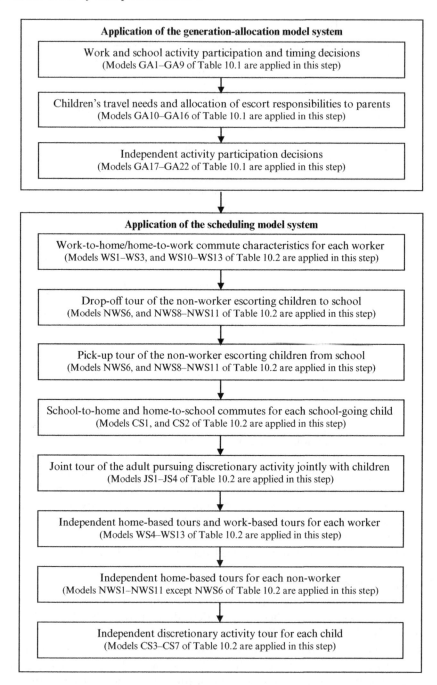

Figure 10.3   Micro-simulation framework in CEMDAP

STARCHILD (Recker et al., 1986a, 1986b)

STARCHILD (for Simulation of Travel/Activity Responses to Complex Household Interactive Logistic Decisions) works in two stages. In the first, pre-travel stage, the individual decides on a planned activity episode schedule based on an exogenously available directory of activities along with the duration, location, and time window for participation. In the second stage, the model identifies feasible alternatives (based on a detailed set of constraints, including timing, location, and household level coupling constraints), and groups the alternatives together into statistically similar categories. Subsequently, a logit model is used to establish pattern choice. Thus, STARCHILD extends the feasible activity pattern generation approach of CARLA by adding a logit choice model of actual choice.[8]

SCHEDULER (Gärling et al., 1989)

In SCHEDULER, a long term calendar (or a set of prior commitments, activity episodes, durations and timing details) is assumed to be present at the start of any time period. From this long term calendar, a small set of episodes with high priority (priority is defined based on prior commitments, preferences and constraints) are selected to be executed in the short term. The short-term activities are sequenced and their locations are determined based on a 'distance-minimizing' heuristic procedure.

AMOS (Kitamura et al., 1996)

AMOS (for Activity MObility Simulator) takes an observed daily activity-travel pattern of an individual (baseline pattern), identifies the set of associated constraints based on a set of rules, and synthesizes the possible adaptations (that is, changes in departure time to work, switch mode, and so forth) in the individual's activity-travel patterns due to the changes in the activity-travel environment. The adaptation possibilities are generated and prioritized in a response generator that is calibrated using neural networks and the stated responses of commuters to a variety of transport policies. Subsequently, an activity-travel pattern modifier identifies the most likely activity-travel pattern response option, and an evaluation routine serves to decide if the option is satisfactory. These adaptation steps are repeated until an acceptable adjustment (in the activity-travel patterns) is found.

SMASH (Ettema et al., 1993)

SMASH (for Simulation Model of Activity Scheduling Heuristics) assumes that the activity scheduling process is a sequential and step-wise process of decision making. Starting with an empty schedule (and a long-term activity calendar), at each step, depending on the current schedule and the available alternatives, the individual is assumed to adjust the existing schedule by adding, or deleting, or rescheduling or simply stopping the adjustment (and hence the scheduling) process. To make a decision on adding, deleting, rescheduling or stopping the scheduling process, a model calibrated using the nested logit approach is used.

ALBATROSS (Arentze and Timmermans, 2000, 2005)

ALBATROSS (for A learning-BAsed TRansportation Oriented Simulation System) is a comprehensive and advanced CPM-based activity-travel modeling system developed at the Eindhoven University in The Netherlands. The inputs to the system are (1) an activity diary describing the individuals' activity sequence, purpose, timing and duration, (2) a list of constraints, (3) individual and household characteristics, (4) zonal data and (5) transport system characteristics. The system uses the activity diary data to start with an initial skeleton-schedule (along with the start times and locations) of fixed activities of the day. Flexible activities are then added to the skeleton. At this point the activity participation profile (activity, with whom and duration) is known. Subsequently, a scheduling engine determines the timing, trip chaining patterns, mode choice and destinations. The scheduling engine may reschedule the previously scheduled flexible activities whenever a new flexible activity is scheduled.

A distinct feature of ALBATROSS, different from other rule-based models, is the use of observed data to endogenously derive decision-making heuristics, instead of using relatively ad-hoc rules. Further, the model incorporates learning mechanisms (see Arentze and Timmermans 2005; Gärling et al., 1994; Joh et al., 2006) in the development of decision-making heuristics.

TASHA (Miller and Roorda, 2003; Roorda and Miller, 2005)

TASHA (for Travel and Activity Scheduler for Household Agents) is another state-of-the art activity-travel scheduling model. In TASHA, activity scheduling occurs to carry out *projects*. Projects are defined as a set of coordinated activities performed to achieve a common goal. For example, activities such as shopping for food, preparing meals and having a dinner with guests are all tied together by a common goal, which is to hold a dinner party (Miller and Roorda, 2003). For each project, an *agenda* (list) of activity episodes is generated that can potentially be executed in the context of the project. The model recognizes and incorporates the idea that activity scheduling is a path-dependent process and the final outcome of the scheduling process depends on the order in which decisions are made. Thus the agenda is dynamically augmented with further details (such as add an activity, or delete an activity either because it is executed or canceled) until the project's purpose is fulfilled. Innovative and intuitive concepts such as *activity precedence* and *scheduling conflict resolution* are utilized to inform the development of path dependent (or dynamic) schedule planning and adjustment (or rescheduling) strategies and household-level interdependencies. A specifically tailored survey was conducted to observe the process (rather than outcomes, that are observed in the usual activity-travel surveys) of activity scheduling and inform the development of decision-making rules (see Doherty et al., 2004; Roorda and Miller, 2005).

Agent-based Modeling Systems

The agent-based modeling systems incorporate the complexity of human behavior using 'agents' that are *autonomous* and *interactive* in nature (see Odell, 2002). The autonomy and the interactive nature are based on behavioral rules that may evolve over time, with every new *experience*. While the use of behavioral *rules* is similar to the rule-based CPM approach, the agent-based approach allows the agents to learn, modify, and improve their interactions with the environment. Thus, the linkages between the choices made by individuals may evolve over time, as opposed to a fixed, and limited, pattern of linkages that are represented in traditional rule-based CPM models. Although the agent-based modeling approach is becoming increasingly popular in such fields as economics (Dosi et al., 1996), social sciences (Gilbert and Conte, 1995) and ecology (Grimm, 1999), it is only in the recent past that this approach has been utilized in the activity-travel behavior modeling arena (see Buliung and Kanaroglou, 2007, for a review). Examples of agent-based activity-travel model systems include ALBATROSS, TRANSIMS and MATSIM. The reader will note here that although ALBATROSS was discussed within the context of rule-based CPM models, the system is growing to incorporate the features of agent-based modeling approaches such as learning and adaptation (see Arentze and Timmermans 2005; Joh et al., 2006). TRANSIMS (LANL, 2007) and MATSIM (Balmer et al., 2005; MATSIM, 2007) represent advanced efforts of agent-based activity-travel scheduling coupled with dynamic traffic flow simulation.

DIMENSIONS OF ACTIVITY-TRAVEL BEHAVIOR: A RESEARCH SYNTHESIS

In this section, we provide a synthesis of the literature on various dimensions of activity-travel behavior that have received substantial attention in the past decade and/or that have started gaining increasing importance in recent years. These different dimensions include: (1) interpersonal interactions, (2) the time dimension of activity-travel behavior and (3) the space dimension of activity-travel behavior. Within each area, we also identify directions for future research.

Interpersonal Interactions

The recognition of the role of inter-individual interactions in travel decisions dates back to the 1970s when Hägerstrand (1970) identified coupling constraints that define the timing, location, and the duration of activities that are pursued with other individuals. Early studies in this area include, for example, Koppelman and Townsend (1987) who analyzed household-level time allocation patterns. Subsequently, several studies (for example, Pas 1985) further emphasized the need for the explicit recognition of inter-individual interactions in activity-based travel analysis, especially at the household level. Since the turn of the century, there has been an increasing recognition that interpersonal interactions play an important role in shaping individuals' activity-travel patterns (see, for example, Srinivasan and Bhat, 2008). In this section, we focus on three major sources of inter-personal interactions: (1) household members, (2) children[9] and (3) social networks.

Intra-household interactions

Very broadly, household-level interactions in an activity-travel context arise from inter-related decision processes associated with (1) the sharing and allocation of responsibilities (maintenance activities) and resources (vehicles), (2) the facilitation of the activity participation and travel needs of mobility-dependent household members (for example, children, the elderly and other mobility-constrained members) and (3) the joint activity engagement and travel. Recent empirical studies in this area focus on:

1. Activity/task allocation (see, for example, Ettema et al., 2004; Scott and Kanaroglou, 2002; Srinivasan and Bhat, 2005; Zhang et al., 2004);
2. Joint activity-travel engagement (see, for example, Gliebe and Koppelman, 2002; Scott and Kanaroglou, 2002; Zhang et al., 2004); and
3. Children's activity-travel arrangements (Sener and Bhat, 2007).

There are several research challenges remaining in the area of intra-household interactions. These include a better understanding of activity and vehicle allocation among members of a household, and the negotiation and altruistic processes among individuals leading up to observed activity-travel patterns. Such research efforts can be facilitated through the collection of data on task and resource allocation, and joint activity-travel engagement. Another important research need relates to the understanding of the impacts of children and other mobility-dependent individuals on adult activity-travel patterns (and the reverse impact of these adults' patterns on the activity-travel patterns of mobility-dependent individuals). The next section provides a detailed discussion on the importance of explicitly recognizing children and their activity-travel patterns in travel demand modeling.

Children's activity-travel behavior
The focus of analysis in existing activity-based research has almost exclusively been on the activity-travel patterns of adults. However, children's travel needs affect the travel patterns of other family members to a considerable extent. Children depend, to a large extent, on household adults or other adults to drive them to after-school activities. In addition to serve-passenger activities, children can also impact adults' activity-travel patterns in the form of joint activity participation in such activities as shopping, going to the park and other social–recreational activities. In addition, the consideration of children's activity-travel patterns is important in its own right. Specifically, children's activity-travel patterns contribute directly to travel by non-drive alone modes of transportation. Thus, it is important to consider the activity-travel patterns of children, and explicitly inter-link these with those of adults' activity-travel patterns.

Most previous research in the area of children's activity-travel patterns has been exploratory in nature (see, for example, Copperman and Bhat, 2007; McDonald, 2006). The studies that go beyond broad descriptive research have almost exclusively focused on the mode for children's trips to and from school. Only a few studies have begun to address joint travel between parents and children, but even these studies have limited their analysis to accompaniment decisions related to school travel (see Yarlagadda and Srinivasan, 2008). Future research should focus on addressing the factors that contribute to children's non-school mode choice, as well as the activity generation and scheduling decisions related to children's participation in activities during the weekday and weekend. In addition, joint travel and activity participation should address joint participations and accompaniment arrangement for children's non-school activities (see Sener and Bhat, 2007, for a study that addresses who children spend time with in out-of-home recreational activities).

Role of social networks
A recently emerging research area related to inter-personal interactions is the influence of social networks on activity-travel behavior (Arentze and Timmermans, 2007;

Axhausen, 2005; Carasco and Miller, 2006; Dugundgi and Walker, 2005; Hackney, 2005; Páez and Scott, 2007). The social network of an individual can influence several aspects of his/her activity-travel decisions, including the activity-travel generation, timing and scheduling of activities and trips, and route and destination choices (Arentze and Timmermans, 2007; Páez and Scott, 2007). Further, understanding the dynamics of social networks (that is, the formation of new social links and dissolution of old social links) can help forecast the dynamics of activity-travel patterns across time (Arentze and Timmermans, 2007). Besides, incorporating the role of social networks will add to the behavioral realism of activity-travel behavior models. Finally, and interestingly, a particular advantage of considering social networks lies in the decrease in computational time in the destination choice step due to the potential winnowing down of the number of feasible spatial location alternatives for activity participation (Hackney, 2005).

Although only recently emerging, the topic of social networks and its interactions with activity-travel behavior is likely to gain research attention in the coming years. The most limiting issue in the study of social networks today is the lack of information on the extent and nature of social networks in travel behavior survey data (Axhausen, 2006). Hence, the immediate research need is to design and administer surveys with an objective to capture social networks and their roles.

The Time Dimension of Activity-travel Behavior

The appropriate treatment of the time dimension of activity-travel behavior is perhaps the most important prerequisite to accurately forecasting activity-travel patterns. This is because time is the main backdrop/setting within which the entire activity-travel decision making takes place (see Kurani and Lee-Gosselin, 1996). Because of the treatment of time as a building block for activity-travel patterns, the following temporal aspects of activity-travel behavior have received significant attention: (1) time-use in activities, and (2) activity-travel timing and scheduling.

Time-use in activities
The subject of activity time use has gained substantial attention in the travel demand field in the past two decades, with several threads of research efforts. From a conceptual/ analytical standpoint, several studies use a resource allocation formulation based on classic economic theories of time allocation (Becker 1965; Evans 1972). Random utility maximization and related microeconomic theory-based approaches have been particularly popular approaches to modeling activity time allocation (see Bhat, 2005; and Jara-Diaz et al., 2007; Meloni et al., 2004, for recent examples).

Recent research in this area has begun to examine time-use in the context of such related dimensions of activity-travel behavior as: (1) inter-personal interdependencies, accompaniment and the social context (see, for example, Gliebe and Koppelman, 2002; Harvey and Taylor, 2000; Sener and Bhat, 2007; and Zhang et al., 2004), (2) multi-day/ weekly time-use behavior (see, for example, Lee and McNally, 2003; and Spissu et al., 2007), (3) substitution patterns between in-home and out-of-home time use (Kuppam and Pendyala, 2001; Meloni et al., 2004) and (4) the impact of information and communications technology (ICT) on time-use (de Graaff and Rietveld, 2007). A particular emphasis of recent time-use studies has been on discretionary activities, due to the extent of choice exercised in discretionary activities relative to non-discretionary activities.

It is interesting to note that most of the time-use studies focus only on the activity generation aspect of the activity-travel behavior. That is, the time-use studies to date focus on the types of activities undertaken by individuals within a given time frame. These studies ignore the settings (that is, the spatial, temporal, scheduling, sequencing and accompaniment contexts) within which the activities are carried out (with a few exceptions mentioned above, which examine the accompaniment and social contexts). The field would benefit from integrated analyses of time allocation and activity settings, including the spatial, temporal, scheduling, and sequencing contexts. Other areas for future research in the time-use area include: (1) the analysis of in-home activity time allocation and activity settings using data with detailed in-home activity type classification, and (2) the application of economic theory-based formulations for the empirical analyses of activity time allocation, monetary expenditures, consumption, and travel.

Activity-travel timing and scheduling
This section provides a discussion of recent research on individuals' activity-travel timing and scheduling behavior. Specifically, the discussion is oriented along three directions along which the research has progressed: (1) time-of-day forecasting, (2) activity-travel scheduling and (3) time-frame of analysis.

Time-of-day forecasting: An important objective of transportation planning is to analyze the temporal variations in transportation demand to identify the need for, and evaluate the potential effectiveness of, travel demand management policies (such as time varying congestion pricing) aimed at spreading the peak period travel into the non-peak periods of the day. Such an analysis requires an appropriate incorporation of the impact of time-varying travel level-of-service (LOS) conditions on activity-travel timing decisions. The importance of modeling time-of-day decisions in response to varying level of service conditions has long been recognized now, dating back to Vickrey's (1969) demand–supply equilibrium-based bottleneck formulation of urban traffic congestion, Small's (1982) discrete choice demand formulation of time-of-day choice with schedule delay considerations and Arnott et al.'s (1993) that combine the bottleneck supply-side formulation of Vickrey and the demand-side formulation of Small. Further, most practical travel modeling applications today adopt some type of travel demand and supply (that is, transportation level-of-service) equilibration process that helps in incorporating the impact of time-varying travel LOS conditions to a certain extent.

It is important to recognize, however, that high resolution (in time) forecasts are required to better understand the impact of time varying level-of-service on activity-travel behavior. The four-step models, because of their aggregate treatment of the time, are not well-equipped to provide such high resolution forecasts. Further, the trip-based methods that are at the core of four-step models ignore the temporal linkages of different trips. Recent developments toward overcoming these limitations include (1) continuous time modeling approaches and (2) tour based approaches. Continuous time modeling approaches allow the prediction of activity timing decisions and travel departure/arrival timing decisions in the continuous time domain (or as very finely categorized intervals of time domain; that is, almost continuous time domain) rather than in discrete time periods such as a.m./p.m. peak/off-peak periods. Examples of such applications include Bhat and Steed (2002), and Pinjari et al. (2007). These studies use either hazard-based duration or discrete choice modeling approaches to develop continuous time or almost continuous time models. The time of day models developed within the context of the tour-based approach jointly predict the tour departure time from home/work and either the arrival time back home/work or the tour duration. Such tour-based time-of-day models are at the heart of several comprehensive activity-based travel forecasting systems today. Nonetheless, more research is required to appropriately integrate these developments into a demand-supply equilibration framework (see subsection on Connecting long-term and short-term choices below for more discussion).

Activity-travel scheduling: Earlier research in the activity-travel timing area has largely focused on modeling individuals' travel timing (that is, trip/tour departure and/arrival time) decisions, by using either discrete time or continuous-time approaches. More recently, there has been an increasing recognition that observed activity-travel timing outcomes are a result of an underlying activity scheduling process that involves the planning and execution of activities over time (see Doherty et al., 2002). In view of this recognition, more research is warranted on the scheduling or sequencing of activities using detailed data on activity-travel scheduling (and rescheduling) processes and mechanisms (see, for example, Doherty et al., 2004; Lee and McNally, 2006, for recent attempts of such surveys).

Time-frame of activity-travel analysis: Most of the earlier activity-travel behavior studies have focused on a single day as the time period for analysis of activity-travel patterns. Such single day analyses make an implicit assumption of uniformity and behavioral independence in activity processes and decisions from one day to the next. Clearly, there may be substantial day-to-day dependence as well as variation in activity-travel patterns. Further, many activities (such as grocery shopping or recreational pursuits) are likely to have a longer cycle for participation. Thus, single day analyses cannot reflect multi-day shifts in activity-travel patterns in response to policy actions such as work-week compression.

The limitations of single day activity-travel behavior analysis have led to several multi-day and multi-week data collection efforts in the recent past (see, for example, Axhausen et al., 2002). Availability of multi-day and multi-week data has, in turn, resulted in an increasing number of multi-day/multi-week studies (Bhat et al., 2005; Buliung and Roorda 2006; Schlich and Axhausen, 2003; Spissu et al., 2008) focusing on understanding the temporal rhythms and variations in activity-travel behavior. However, a limited number of studies focus on determining the appropriate time frame of analysis (see, for example, Habib et al., 2008). While these studies provide preliminary evidence that discretionary activity participation may be characterized as being on a weekly rhythm (or perhaps longer time scale), more research is warranted to determine the appropriate time frame for different types of activities. More specifically, it is important to recognize that not all activities may be associated with time cycles of similar length. Another important and related issue is the time horizon of activity-travel planning and scheduling. Specifically, it is important to understand and model the complex interlacing of multiple time horizons that may be associated with the planning, scheduling, and execution of different activities and related travel over time (Doherty et al., 2002).

The Space Dimension of Activity-travel Behavior

Space in an activity-travel context refers to location choice behavior and the impact of spatial (or location-specific) elements on activity-travel patterns. Current research interests in spatial analysis include: (1) spatial dependencies, (2) spatial representation and perception and (3) space-time interactions and constraints.

Spatial dependencies

Spatial dependencies in an activity-travel context refer to the dependence of activity-travel behavior on spatial elements, and hence the variation of activity-travel behavior over space (Fotheringham et al., 2000). Spatial dependence leads to three spatial analytic issues in activity-travel behavior modeling: (1) spatial autocorrelation (that is behavioral similarities across spatially proximate individuals and households due to common unobserved spatial elements; see Franzese and Hays, 2008), (2) spatial heterogeneity (variability in the relationships between activity-travel patterns and exogenous determinants over space due to location-specific effects; see Páez, 2007) and (3) spatial heteroskedasticity (variation in the location-specific unobserved factors that affect activity-travel patterns; Páez, 2007). It is important to account for such spatial dependencies to avoid inconsistent parameter estimates.

Spatial representation and perception

An important space-related issue in the context of activity-based analysis is spatial representation. Since the 1950s, the spatial configuration of a region has been represented in the form of spatial units, known as TAZs, for the purpose of transportation modeling and planning. These TAZs were created for use in the trip-based approach to travel demand modeling. The shift from the trip-based approach to an activity-based approach to travel demand analysis has generally been accompanied by consideration of a finer spatial representation of areal units (such as parcels). Such a move to finer spatial configurations may be advantageous due to the potential improvement in the accuracy of predicted travel patterns obtained from the better representation of the land-use and transportation network. However, a danger of using very fine resolutions of space is that the geographical context of activity-travel decision-making may be lost (see Guo and Bhat, 2007b). Thus, while there seems to be a general consensus that the TAZ system used in trip-based methods is rather coarse and unable to accurately represent such network attributes as access to transit stops, it is not at all clear what the appropriate spatial resolution (and representation) should be to better capture activity-travel choices. Besides, it may be that different resolutions are needed for different types of activity-travel related decisions (for instance, residential choice versus activity location choice) and different demographic population groups.

Another important issue that is related to spatial representation is the Modifiable Area Unit Problem (MAUP). Specifically, MAUP is associated with the sensitivity of spatial analytic results to the way in which the spatial units are defined. (see Guo and Bhat, 2004; Páez and Scott, 2004). While there have been several studies showing the presence of the MAUP problem in several analytic contexts involving spatial elements, there have not been adequate attempts at controlling for the MAUP issue in activity-travel studies. This naturally leads to the following question: what is the best way to *represent* the spatial configuration and alleviate MAUP and other spatial representation-related problems in activity-based travel demand models? Guo and Bhat (2004) argue that the fundamental reason behind MAUP is the inconsistency between the *representation* of spatial configuration in analytic models and decision makers' *perception* of space, and that if the spatial characteristics are measured and represented in the same way as decision makers perceive and process spatial information, there would be less concern of MAUP.

A related issue is the scale at which individuals perceive space when making activity-travel decisions, both in terms of decision units (that is, the scale of the 'neighborhood' that is the unit of decision) as well as the extent of the effect of variables that impact the choice of decision unit (for example, do individuals consider crime rates or access to activities within a narrow 1-mile band or 5-mile bands around spatial units?).

In all, in the context of space perception, there has been very little research on understanding people's mental perceptions of the spatial attributes of the environments in which they live, work, and travel to and from. Taxonomies need to be developed for describing how different types of activity-travel decisions depend on individuals' mental representations of space. People generally do not possess complete knowledge of their surroundings, but are able to select (filter) useful spatial information. Examining this spatial cognition is important for understanding how people adapt through changes of their mental representation of static environments and to changes of the environments at different spatial and time scales (see Golledge and Gärling 2004; Kitchin and Blades, 2002, on spatial cognition and learning issues in travel behavior modeling).

Space-time interactions and constraints

It is now widely recognized that human activity and travel patterns are undertaken within time–space prisms, which are defined by spatial–temporal interactions that are influenced by transportation system characteristics (Hägerstrand, 1970). Thus these interactions must be incorporated into the analysis of human activity and travel patterns. Further, the nature of time–space interactions is closely tied to spatial cognition and perception (Pendyala et al., 2002). For example, the spatial perception of, and preference for, a certain kind of land-use mix and built environment in residential choice may be based on household desires to relax time constraints through increased accessibility to activities. Possible future lines of enquiry in this area include: (1) the recognition of the types of time–space interactions in an activity-travel context, (2) data collection for understanding time-space interactions, (3) trade-offs between temporal (activity timing and duration) and spatial (spatial location) decisions, (4) impact of information and communication technologies on time-space interactions, (5) variation of the time–space interactions based on activity type, time-of-day and activity-travel environment characteristics and (6) variation of the time–space interactions over longer periods of time (weeks, months and years).

In this context, recent developments in space–time geographic information system (GIS) methods (see for example, the 3D GIS approach by Kwan and Lee, 2004; the temporal GIS approach by Shaw and Xin, 2003; and the integrated spatio-temporal approach of Kang and Scott, 2006) offer very useful visualization, computation and analytical methods. It is expected that these methods will further advance our understanding of human activity-travel behavior in general, and space-time interactions and constraints in particular.

INTEGRATION WITH OTHER MODELS

This section focuses on the integration of activity-based travel forecasting models with other model systems of interest in urban transportation planning, with the objective of building comprehensive urban modeling systems.

The Need for Integration

Conventional wisdom has long indicated that socio-demographics, land use and transportation are intricately linked (Mitchell and Rapkin, 1954,). The recognition of the linkages among socio-demographics, land use and transportation is important for realistic forecasts of travel demand. Conventional methods, however, use aggregate exogenous forecasts of socio-demographics and land use to feed into travel models and, consequently, cannot capture the multitude of interactions that arise over space and time among the different decision makers. The shortcomings of the conventional approach have led researchers to develop approaches that capture socio-demographic, land-use and travel behavior processes in an integrated manner. Such behavioral approaches emphasize the interactions among population socioeconomic processes, the households' long-term choice behaviors and the employment, housing and transportation markets within which individuals and households act (Waddell et al., 2001). From an activity-travel forecasting perspective, these integrated urban modeling systems need to consider several important issues that are outlined in this section.

Generation of disaggregate socio-demographic inputs for forecast years

Activity-based travel forecasting systems require highly disaggregate socio-demographics as inputs, including data records of each and every individual and household in the study area. However, it is practically infeasible to collect the information for each and every household and individual in any study area. Hence, disaggregate population generation procedures are used to create synthetic records of each and every individual and household for activity-travel microsimulation purposes (see Bowman, 2004, for reviews of synthetic population generators). However, to be able to forecast the individual activity-travel patterns and aggregate transport demand at a future point in time, activity-based travel demand models require, as inputs, the disaggregate socio-demographics, and the land-use and transportation system characteristics of that point in time. While the above mentioned synthetic population generation procedures can generate the disaggregate socio-demographic inputs for the base year (that is, the year at which the activity-travel prediction starts and for which the aggregate demographic inputs and the survey data are available), other model systems are required to forecast the disaggregate socio-demographics at a future point in time.

Individuals and households evolve through a socio-demographic process over time. As the socio-demographic process unfolds, individuals may move onto different life-cycle stages such as begin/finish schooling, enter/exit the labor market and change jobs. Similarly, households may decide to own a house as opposed to rent, move to another location and acquire/dispose off a vehicle. Such socio-demographic processes need to be modeled explicitly to ensure that the distribution of population attributes (personal and household) and that of land-use characteristics are representative at each point of time and are sufficiently detailed to support the activity-travel forecasting models. There have been relatively limited attempts to build models of sociodemographic evolution for the purpose of travel forecasting. Examples in the transportation field include the Comprehensive Econometric Microsimulator for Socio-Economics, Land use and Transportation System (CEMSELTS) by Bhat and colleagues (Eluru et al., 2008), DEMOgraphic (Micro) Simulation (DEMOS) system by Sundararajan and Goulias (2003), and the Micro-analytic Integrated Demographic Accounting System (MIDAS) by Goulias and Kitamura, 1996. Examples from the non-transportation field include DYNACAN (Morrison, 1998) and LIFEPATHS (Gribble, 2000).

Connecting long-term and short-term choices
Most of the travel demand models treat the longer-term choices concerning the housing (such as residential tenure, housing type and residential location), vehicle ownership and employment choices (such as enter/exit labor market and employment type) as exogenous inputs. Consequently, the land-use (in and around which the individuals live, work and travel to) is treated as exogenous to travel demand models. In such cases, the possibility that households can adjust with combinations of short- and long-term behavioral responses to land-use and transportation policies is systematically ignored (Waddell, 2001). A significant increase in transport costs, for example, could result in a household adapting with any combination of daily activity and travel pattern changes, vehicle ownership changes, job location changes and residential location changes.

While most of the travel forecasting models treat the long-term choices and hence the land-use as exogenous to travel behavior, there have been recent attempts to model the longer-term and shorter-term choices in an integrated manner, including OPUS/Urbansim (Waddell et al., 2006), ILUTE (Salivini and Miller, 2005) and ILUMASS (Strauch et al., 2003). There have also been models studying the relationships between individual elements of land-use related choices and travel behavior choices. However, most of these models and model systems are trip-based. That is, although these studies attempt to study the land-use and travel behavior processes in an integrated manner, the travel behavior aspect of these studies is based on a trip-based approach. There have been a few attempts of integrated land-use and activity-travel behavior studies using the activity-based approach to activity-travel analysis (see Ben-Akiva and Bowman, 1998; Pinjari et al., 2007). Also, ILUTE and OPUS are recent prototype based systems of more comprehensive integrated land-use and activity-travel forecasting systems.

Demand–supply interactions
The end use of travel forecasting models is, in general, the prediction of traffic flow conditions under alternative socio-demographic, land use, and transportation level-of-service scenarios. The traffic flow conditions, which are usually predicted after a traffic assignment procedure, are a result of the interactions between the individual-level demand for travel, and the travel options and the level-of-service (or the capacity) supplied by the transportation system. It is important to consider such demand–supply interactions for accurate predictions of activity-travel behavior, and the resulting traffic flow conditions. Further, since the travel level-of-service (and hence the available transportation capacity) varies with the temporal variation in travel demand, and the demand for travel is, in-turn, dependent on the transportation level-of-service, the interactions

may be time-dependent and hence dynamic in nature. Thus, it is important to consider the dynamics of the interactions between travel demand and the supply of transportation capacity. See Lin et al. (2008) for a review of the literature on the integration of transportation demand and supply analysis, and for a development of an integrated activity-based travel forecasting and dynamic traffic assignment modeling system.

Similar to how transportation market processes (that is, the interactions between individual-level travel demand and the transportation supply) influence the individual-level activity-travel patterns, the housing and labor market processes influence the residential and employment choices of individuals. In fact, individuals act within the context of, and interact with, housing, labor and transportation markets to make their residential, employment and activity-travel choices. While the transportation market process may occur over shorter time frames (such as days or weeks), the employment and housing market processes are likely to occur over longer periods of time. That is, in the short-term, the daily activity-travel patterns are directly influenced by the dynamics of the interaction between travel demand and supply, while in the long-term the activity-travel behavior is indirectly affected by the impact of housing and labor market processes on the residential and employment choices, and also on the land-use and transportation system. If the activity-travel behavior of individuals and households is to be captured properly over a longer time frame, the interactions with, and the evolution over time of, all these markets should be explicitly considered, along with the socio-demographic processes and the long-term housing and employment choices.

An Integrated Urban Modeling System

In view of the preceding discussion, travel demand models should be integrated with other models that can forecast, over a multi-year time frame, the socio-demographic processes and the housing and employment market processes. The integrated model system should be able to capture the above discussed supply-demand interactions in the housing, employment, and transportation markets. A conceptual framework of such a system, labeled as the Comprehensive Econometric Microsimulator for Urban Systems (CEMUS), being developed at the University of Texas, is provided in Figure 10.4.

CEMUS places the focus on households and individuals, and businesses and developers that are the primary decision makers in an urban system. CEMUS takes as inputs the aggregate socioeconomics and the land-use and transportation system characteristics for the base year, as well as policy actions being considered for future years. The aggregate-level base year socio-economic data are first fed into a synthetic population generator (SPG) module to produce a disaggregate-level synthetic dataset describing a subset of the socio-economic characteristics of all the households and individuals residing in the study area (see Guo and Bhat, 2007a, for information on the SPG module). Additional base-year socio-economic attributes related to mobility, schooling, and employment at the individual level, and residential/vehicle ownership choices at the household level, that are difficult to synthesize (or cannot be synthesized) directly from the aggregate socioeconomic data for the base year are simulated by the CEMSELTS module. The base year socio-economic data, along with the land-use and transportation system attributes, are then run through the CEMDAP to obtain individual-level activity-travel patterns. The activity-travel patterns are subsequently passed through

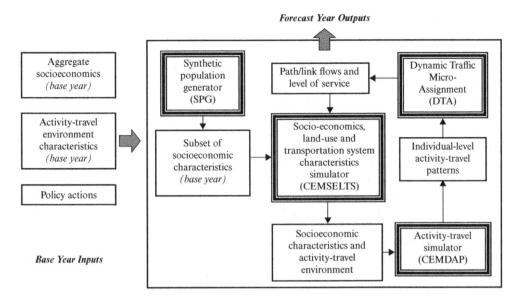

Figure 10.4 Schematic of the CEMUS Model System

a dynamic traffic micro-assignment scheme to determine path flows, link flows, and transportation system level-of-service by time of day (see Lin et al., 2008 for a discussion of recent efforts on integrating an activity-travel simulator and a dynamic traffic microsimulator). The resulting transportation system level-of-service characteristics are fed back to CEMSELTS to generate a revised set of activity-travel environment attributes, which is passed through CEMDAP along with the socioeconomic data to generate revised individual activity-travel patterns. This 'within-year' iteration is continued until base-year equilibrium is achieved. This completes the simulation for the base year.

The next phase, which takes the population one step forward in time (that is, one year), starts with CEMSELTS updating the population, urban-form and the land-use markets (note that SPG is used only to generate the disaggregate-level synthetic population for the base-year and is not used beyond the base year). An initial set of transportation system attributes is generated by CEMSELTS for this next time step based on (1) the population, urban form and land-use markets for the next time step, (2) the transportation system attributes from the previous year in the simulation and (3) the future year policy scenarios provided as input to CEMUS. The CEMSELTS outputs are then input into CEMDAP, which interfaces with a dynamic micro-assignment scheme in a series of equilibrium iterations for the next time step (just as for the base year) to obtain the 'one time step' outputs. The loop continues for several time steps forward until the socioeconomics, land-use, and transportation system path/link flows and transportation system level of service are obtained for the forecast year specified by the analyst. During this iterative process, the effects of the prescribed policy actions can be evaluated based on the simulated network flows and speeds for any intermediate year between the base year and the forecast year.

SUMMARY AND DISCUSSION

Over the past three decades, the activity-based approach has received significant attention and seen considerable progress. This chapter discusses the fundamentals of the activity-based approach to travel demand modeling, and presents an overview of various activity-based travel forecasting systems. Further, the chapter discusses the recent progress in understanding the time, space, and inter-personal interaction aspects of activity-travel behavior and identifies future research directions. Finally, the chapter emphasizes the need to integrate activity-travel forecasting systems with other systems to design comprehensive and integrated urban modeling systems.

It is worth noting here that several research directions identified in the chapter correspond to understanding the decision-making processes that lead to observed activity-travel patterns. For example, in the context of activity-travel timing outcomes, there has been an increasing recognition that observed activity-travel timing outcomes are a result of an underlying activity scheduling process that involves the planning and execution of activities over time (see Doherty et al., 2002). Similarly, in a spatial context, there is a need to understand individuals' perceptions of space when making activity-travel decisions. Further, in the context of inter-individual interactions, more work is needed to understand the negotiation and altruistic processes among individuals leading up to observed assignment of activity-travel tasks and allocation of vehicles. However, to date, the dominant approach to understanding activity-travel behavior is the analysis of the relationship between exogenous socio-demographics and activity-travel environment characteristics on the one hand, and the revealed activity-travel patterns on the other. This approach does not shed light on the underlying mental processes and behavioral decision-making mechanisms that lead to observed activity-travel patterns. Specifically, we lack a detailed understanding of (1) how households and individuals acquire and assimilate information about their environment, (2) how this information or perception is used to make activity-travel decisions, (3) what aspects of activity travel behavior (and to what extent) are pre-planned (subject to dynamic adjustment and re-adjustment) versus unplanned, (4) the order in which decisions are made and (5) how individuals interact with other individuals and their activity-travel environment when making activity-travel decisions. One contributing factor for the limited amount of research on decision processes is the lack of detailed data on decision-making mechanisms leading up to the revealed activity-travel patterns. Recent attempts to construct surveys designed to collect information on the activity scheduling process include, for example, Doherty et al. (2004), and Lee and McNally (2006), Mohammadian and Doherty (2006), and Roorda and Miller (2005). In addition to the need for such detailed data, theoretical developments are needed to understand the decision-making processes that lead up to observed activity-travel patterns. In this context, alternatives to the utility maximization approach, such as lexicographic ordering and satisfying decision-making rules, behavioral theories of bounded rationality, loss sensitivity and subordinateness, variety seeking and so forth may need to be explored. A related issue that must be addressed is heterogeneity in decision-making processes across decision-making agents.

ACKNOWLEDGMENTS

The authors would like to thank Rachel Copperman and Ipek Sener for their contributions to parts on Children's activity-travel behavior and Role of social networks, respectively. Thanks also to Naveen Eluru, Jessica Guo and Siva Srinivasan for their contribution to Pinjari et al. (2006) from which the CEMDAP description presented in this chapter is drawn.

NOTES

1. The reader will note here that the activity-based approach has emerged in the context of modeling passenger travel demand, not for freight travel modeling.
2. In his presidential address at a regional science association congress in 1969, Hägerstrand identified three types of constraints that shape individual activity patterns: (1) authoritative constraints, (2) capability constraints, and (3) coupling constraints. Authoritative constraints refer to the constraints imposed by the spatial and temporal opportunities of activity participation (These authoritative space-time constraints laid the foundation for what are now known as 'space-time prisms' and 'space-time paths'). Capability constraints refer to constraints imposed by biological needs (such as eating and sleeping) and/or resources (income, availability of cars and so forth) to undertake activities. Coupling constraints define where, when, and the duration of planned activities that are to be pursued with other individuals.
3. For a detailed review of the research on activity-based travel behavior analysis and modeling in the 1980s, the reader is referred to Kitamura (1988).
4. For an overview of the research on activity-based travel analysis in the 1990s, the reader is referred to Bhat and Koppelman (1999).
5. Take, for example, an individual who drives alone to work and makes a shopping stop on the way back home from work. The mode choices for the home-work and work-home trips in this scenario are not independent. So in the face of transit improvements, the person may not switch to transit because the evening commute shopping stop may be more conveniently pursued by driving. However, the trip-based approach can over-predict the shift to transit due to ignoring the linkage between the trips identified above.
6. For a comparative review of the design features of each of these models, the reader is referred to Bradley and Bowman (2006).
7. Hägerstrand's space-time prism is a conceptual framework to capture spatial and temporal constraints on individual's activity-travel patterns. Space–time prisms can be constructed by considering a three-dimensional (3D) space, with a two-dimensional horizontal plane representing the geographical space with different activity locations, and a vertical axis representing the time dimension. Within such a 3D space, the space–time coordinates defined by the spatial and temporal constraints of a person (for example, she/he can leave home no earlier than time t_0 and she/he must be at work no later than t_1) form the vertices of a space–time prism. Between the vertices, given the remaining amount of time ($t_1 - t_0$), and given a maximum possible speed of travel, the set of all locations (that is, space–time coordinates) she/he can reach form a space–time prism. Thus, space-time prisms represent the feasible activity-travel space defined by the spatial and temporal constraints.
8. The STARCHILD approach was extended later by Recker (1995), who introduced a mathematical programming (or operations research) approach to model household activity-travel patterns. Specifically, he casted the household activity-travel pattern modeling problem (HAPP) as a network-based routing problem, while accommodating vehicle assignment, ride-sharing, activity assignment and scheduling behaviors as well as available time window constraints. The resulting mathematical formulation is a mixed integer linear program that provides an optimal path of household members through time and space as they complete a prescribed agenda of activities. Recker (2001) further expanded on this approach by accommodating the inter-personal interactions among the resource (vehicle) allocation decisions made by households. More recently, Gan and Recker (2008) extended the approach to the case of household activity rescheduling, while also incorporating the impact of uncertainties associated with activity rescheduling behaviors such as activity cancellation, insertion, and duration adjustment. In the context of the mathematical programming approach, Recker (2001) indicates that the approach provides a powerful analytical framework to model complex intra-household interactions associated with household activity-based travel modeling. However, as identified in Recker et al. (2008), further work is needed, especially related to the estimation of such models, to operationalize the models for practical transportation planning purposes.

9. Although children are household members, we have listed them a separate category to emphasize the importance of considering children as a major source of inter-personal interactions.

REFERENCES

Arentze, T.A. and H.J.P. Timmermans, 2000, ALBATROSS: A Learning-based Transportation Oriented Simulation System. European Institute of Retailing and Services Studies, Eindhoven University of Technology, The Netherlands.

Arentze, T.A. and H.J.P. Timmermans, 2005, Albatross version 2: A Learning-based Transportation Oriented Simulation System. European Institute of Retailing and Services Studies, Eindhoven University of Technology, The Netherlands.

Arnott, R., A. de Palma and R. Lindsey, 1993, A structural model of peak-period congestion: a traffic bottleneck with elastic demand. *American Economic Review*, **83**(1), 161–179.

Axhausen, K.W. and T. Gärling, 1992, Activity-based approaches to travel analysis: conceptual frameworks, models and research problems. *Transport Reviews*, **12**, 324–341.

Axhausen, K.W., Z. Zimmerman, S. Schönfelder, G. Rindsfuser and T. Haupt, 2002, Observing the rhythms of daily life: a six week travel diary. *Transportation*, **29**(2), 95–124.

Axhausen, K.W., 2005, Social networks and travel: some hypotheses. In K. Donaghy, S. Poppelreuter and G. Rudinger, eds, S*ocial Aspects of Sustainable Transport: Transatlantic Perspectives*. Aldershot, UK: Ashgate, pp. 90–108.

Axhausen, K.W., 2006, Social networks, mobility biographies and travel: the survey challenges. *Arbeitsbericht Verkehrs- und Raumplanung*, **343**, IVT, ETH Zürich, Zürich.

Balmer, M., K.W. Axhausen and K. Nagel, 2005, An agent based demand modeling framework for large scale micro simulations. *Transportation Research Record*, **1985**, 125–134.

Becker, G.S., 1965, A theory of the allocation of time. *The Economical Journal*, **75**(299), 493–517.

Ben-Akiva, M. and J.L. Bowman, 1998, Integration of an activity-based model system and a residential location model. *Urban Studies*, **35**(7), 1131–1153.

Bhat, C.R., 2005, A multiple discrete-continuous extreme value model: formulation and application to discretionary time-use decisions. *Transportation Research Part B*, **39**(8), 679–707.

Bhat, C.R. and J.Y. Guo, 2007, A comprehensive analysis of built environment characteristics on household residential choice and auto ownership levels. *Transportation Research Part B*, **41**(5), 506–526.

Bhat, C.R. and F.S. Koppelman, 1999, Activity-based modeling of travel demand. In *The Handbook of Transportation Science*. R.W. Hall, ed., Norwell, MA: Kluwer Academic Publishers, pp. 35–61.

Bhat, C.R. and R. Misra, 2000, Nonworker activity-travel patterns: organization of activities. Paper presented at the 79th Annual Meeting of the Transportation Research Board, Washington, DC, January.

Bhat, C.R. and S.K. Singh, 2000, A comprehensive daily activity-travel generation model system for workers. *Transportation Research Part A*, **34**(1), 1–22.

Bhat, C.R. and J.L. Steed, 2002, A continuous-time model of departure time choice for urban shopping trips. *Transportation Research Part B*, **36**(3), 207–224.

Bhat, C.R., J.Y. Guo, S. Srinivasan and A. Sivakumar, 2004, A comprehensive econometric microsimulator for daily activity-travel patterns. *Transportation Research Record*, **1894**, 57–66.

Bhat, C.R., S. Srinivasan and K.W. Axhausen, 2005, An analysis of multiple interepisode durations using a unifying multivariate hazard model. *Transportation Research Part B*, **39**(9), 797–823.

Bowman, J.L., 2004, A comparison of population synthesizers used in microsimulation models of activity and travel demand. Working paper.

Bowman, J.L., and M.E. Ben-Akiva, 2001, Activity-based disaggregate travel demand model system with activity schedules. *Transportation Research A*, **35**(1), 1–28.

Bowman, J.L., and M.A. Bradley, 2005–2006, Activity-based travel forecasting model for SACOG. Technical Memos Numbers 1–11, available at http://jbowman.net.

Bradley, M. and J.L. Bowman, 2006, A summary of design features of activity-based microsimulation models for US. MPOs. White Paper for the Conference on Innovations in Travel Demand Modeling, Austin, TX.

Bradley, M., M. Outwater, N. Jonnalagadda and E. Ruiter, 2001, Estimation of an activity-based micro- simulation model for San Francisco. Paper presented at the 80th Annual Meeting of the Transportation Research Board, Washington DC.

Bradley, M.A., Portland Metro, J.L. Bowman and Cambridge Systematics, 1998, A system of activity-based models for Portland, Oregon. USDOT report number DOT-T-99-02, produced for the Travel Model Improvement Program of the USDOT and EPA, Washington DC.

Buliung, R.N. and P.S. Kanaroglou, 2007, Activity-travel behavior research: conceptual issues, state of the art, and emerging perspectives on behavioral analysis and simulation modeling. *Transport Reviews*, **27**(2), 151–187.

Buliung, R.N. and M.J. Roorda, 2006, Spatial variety in weekly, weekday-to-weekend and day-to-day patterns of activity-travel behavior: initial results from the Toronto Travel-Activity Panel Survey. CD Proceedings of the 85th Annual Meeting of the Transportation Research Board, Washington DC, January.

Carpenter, S. and P.M. Jones, 1983, *Recent Advances in Travel Demand Analysis*. Aldershot, UK: Gower.

Carrasco, J.A. and E. Miller, 2006, Exploring the propensity to perform social activities: a social network approach. *Transportation*, **33**(5), 463–480.

Chapin, F.S., Jr., 1974, *Human Activity Patterns in the City: Things People Do in Time and Space*. London: John Wiley and Sons.

Clarke, M.I., 1986, Activity modeling: a research tool or a practical planning technique? In *Behavioral Research for Transport Policy*, Utrecht, The Netherlands: VNU Science Press, pp. 3–15.

Copperman, R. and C.R. Bhat, 2007, An analysis of the determinants of children's weekend physical activity participation. *Transportation*, **34**(1), 67–87.

Davidson, W., R. Donnelly, P. Vovsha, J. Freedman, S. Ruegg, J. Hicks, J. Castiglione and R. Picado, 2007, Synthesis of first practices and operational research approaches in activity-based travel demand modeling. *Transportation Research Part A*, **41**(5), 464–488.

de Graff, T. and P. Rietveld, 2007, Substitution between working at home and out-of-home: the role of ICT and commuting costs. *Transportation Research Part A*, **41**(2), 142–160.

Doherty, S.T., E.J. Miller, K.W. Axhausen and T. Gärling, 2002, A conceptual model of the weekly household activity–travel scheduling process. In E. Stern, I. Salomon and P. Bovy, eds, *Travel Behaviour: Patterns, Implications and Modelling*, pp. 148–155.

Doherty, S.T., E. Nemeth, M. Roorda and E.J. Miller, 2004, Design and assessment of the Toronto area computerized household activity scheduling survey. *Transportation Research Record*, **1894**, 140–149.

Dosi, D., L. Marengo and G. Fagiolo, 1996, Learning in evolutionary environments. Technical report, University of Trento.

Dugundji, E.R. and J.L. Walker, 2005, Discrete choice with social and spatial network interdependencies: an empirical example using mixed GEV models with field and panel effects. *Transportation Research Record*, **1921**, 70–78.

Eluru, N., A.R. Pinjari, J.Y. Guo, I.N. Sener, S. Srinivasan, R.B. Copperman and C.R. Bhat, 2008, Population updating system structures and models embedded within the Comprehensive Econometric Microsimulator for Urban Systems (CEMUS). *Transportation Research Record*, **2076**, 171–182.

Ettema, D., A.W.J. Borgers and H.J.P. Timmermans, 1993, Simulation model of activity scheduling behavior. *Transportation Research Record*, **1413**, 1–11.

Ettema, D., T. Schwanen and H. Timmermans, 2004, Task allocation patterns: an assessment of household-level strategies. Paper presented at the EIRASS conference on 'Progress in Activity-Based Analysis', Maastricht, The Netherlands.

Evans, A., 1972, On the theory of the valuation and allocation of time. *Scottish Journal of Political Economy*, **19**, 1–17.

Fotheringham, A.S., C. Brunsdon and M. Charlton, 2000, *Quantitative Geography: Perspectives on Spatial Data Analysis*. London: Sage Publications.

Franzese, R.J. and J.C. Hays, 2008, Empirical models of spatial interdependence. In J. Box-Steffensmeier, H. Brady and D. Collier, eds, *Oxford Handbook of Political Methodology*, Oxford: Oxford University Press, pp. 570–604.

Gan, L.P. and W. Recker, 2008, A mathematical programming formulation of the household activity rescheduling problem. *Transportation Research Part B*, **42**(6), 571–606.

Gärling, T., K. Brannas, J. Garvill, R.G. Golledge, S. Gopal, E. Holm and E. Lindberg, 1989, Household activity scheduling. In *Transport Policy, Management and Technology Towards 2001: Selected Proceedings of the Fifth World Conference on Transport Research* **IV**. Ventura, CA: Western Periodicals, pp. 235–248.

Gärling, T., M.P. Kwan and R.G. Golledge, 1994, Computational-process modeling of household travel activity scheduling. *Transportation Research Part B*, **28**(5), 355–364.

Gilbert, N. and R. Conte, eds, 1995, *Artificial Societies: The Computer Simulation of Social Life*. London: UCL Press.

Gliebe, J.P. and F.S. Koppelman, 2005, Modeling household activity-travel interactions as parallel constrained choices. *Transportation*, **32**(5), 449–471.

Golledge, R.G. and T. Gärling, 2004, The role of spatial cognition in transport. In *Handbook of Transport Geography and Spatial Systems*, D. Hensher, K.J. Button, K.E. Haynes and P.R. Stopher, eds, Amsterdam: Pergamon/Elsevier, pp. 501–512.

Goulias, K.G. and R. Kitamura, 1996, A dynamic model system for regional travel demand forecasting. In T. Golob, R. Kitamura and L. Long, eds, *Panels for Transportation Planning: Methods and Applications*. Boston, MA: Kluwer Academic Publishers, Ch. 13, pp. 321–348.

246   *A handbook of transport economics*

Gribble, S., 2000, LifePaths: a longitudinal microsimulation model using a synthetic approach. In A. Gupta and V. Kapur, eds, *Microsimulation in Government Policy and Forecasting*. Amsterdam: Elsevier, Ch. 19, pp. 383–394.

Grimm, V., 1999, Ten years of individual-based modeling in ecology: what have we learned, and what could we learn in the future? *Ecological Modelling*, **115**(2), 129–148.

Guo, J.Y. and C.R. Bhat, 2004, Modifiable areal units: problem or perception in modeling of residential location choice? *Transportation Research Record*, **1898**, 138–147.

Guo, J.Y. and C.R. Bhat, 2007a, Population synthesis for microsimulating travel behavior. *Transportation Research Record*, **2014**, 92–101.

Guo, J.Y. and C.R. Bhat, 2007b, Operationalizing the concept of neighborhood: application to residential location choice analysis. *Journal of Transport Geography*, **15**(1), 31–45.

Habib, K.M., E.J. Miller and K.W. Axhausen, 2008, Weekly rhythm in joint time expenditure for all at-home and out-of-home activities: application of Kuhn–Tucker demand system model using multiweek travel diary data. *Transportation Research Record*, **2054**, 64–73.

Hackney, J., 2005, Coevolving social and transportation networks. *Arbeitsbericht Verkehrs–und Raumplanung*, **335**, Institut fur Verkehrsplanung and Trasnportsysteme, ETH Zurich, Zurich.

Hägerstrand, T., 1970, What about people in regional science? *Papers and Proceedings of the Regional Science Association*, **24**, 7–24.

Harvey, A.S. and M.E. Taylor, 2000, Activity settings and travel behaviour: a social contact perspective. *Transportation*, **27**(1), 53–73.

Jara-Diaz, S.R., M. Munizaga, P. Greeven and R. Guerra, 2007, The unified expanded goods-activities-travel model: theory and results. Paper presented at the 11th WCTR conference, Berkeley, June 24–28.

Joh, C.H., T.A. Arentze and H.J.P Timmermans, 2006, Measuring and predicting adaptation behavior in multi-dimensional activity-travel patterns. *Transportmetrica*, **2**, 153–173.

Jones, P.M., 1979, New approaches to understanding travel behaviour: the human activity approach. In D.A. Hensher and P.R. Stopher, eds, *Behavioral Travel Modeling*. London: Redwood Burn Ltd., pp. 55–80.

Jones, P.M., F.S. Koppelman and J.P. Orfeuil, 1993, Activity analysis: state of the art and future directions. In *Developments in Dynamic and Activity-Based Approaches to Travel Analysis*. Aldershot, UK: Gower, pp. 34–55.

Kang, H. and D.M. Scott, 2006, An integrated spatio-temporal GIS system for exploring intra-household interactions. Paper presented at the 53rd Annual North American Meetings of the Regional Science Association International, Toronto, ON, November 16–18.

Kitamura, R., 1988, An evaluation of activity-based travel analysis. *Transportation*, **15**(1–2), 9–34.

Kitamura, R., E.I. Pas, C.V. Lula, T.K. Lawton and P.E. Benson, 1996, The sequenced activity mobility simulator (SAMS): an integrated approach to modeling transportation, land use and air quality. *Transportation*, **23**(3), 267–291.

Kitchin, R.M. and M. Blades, 2002, *The Cognition of Geographic Space*. London: I. B. Tauris.

Koppelman, F.S. and T.A. Townsend, 1987, Task allocation among household members: theory and analysis. Paper presented at the 5th International Conference on Travel Behavior, Aix en Provence, France.

Kurani, K.S. and M.E.H. Lee-Gosselin, 1996, Synthesis of past activity analysis applications. Paper presented at the Travel Model Improvement Program (TMIP) Conference on activity-based travel forecasting, New Orleans, June 2–5.

Kwan, M. and J. Lee, 2004, Geovisualization of human activity patterns using 3D GIS: a time-geographic approach. In M.F. Goodchild and D.G. Janelle, eds, *Spatially Integrated Social Science*. New York: Oxford University Press, pp. 48–66.

Lee, M. and M.G. McNally, 2003, On the structure of weekly activity-travel patterns. *Transportation Research Part A*, **37**(10), 823–839.

Lee, M. and M.G. McNally, 2006, An empirical investigation on the dynamic processes of activity scheduling and trip chaining. *Transportation*, **33**(6), 553–565.

Lin, D.-Y., N. Eluru, S.T. Waller and C.R. Bhat, 2008, Integration of activity-based modeling and dynamic traffic assignment. *Transportation Research Record*, **2076**, 52–61.

Los Alamos National Laboratory (LANL), 2007, TRANSIMS, TRansportation ANalysis and SIMulation System. Los Alamos National Laboratory. Alamos, NM. Available at http://transims.tsasa.lanl.gov, accessed November 2007.

MATSIM, 2007, Multi-Agent Transport Simulation Toolkit. Available at http://www.matsim.org, accessed November 2007.

McDonald, N., 2006, An exploratory analysis of children's travel patterns. *Transportation Research Record*, **1977**, 1–7.

McFadden, D., 1973, Conditional logit analysis of qualitative choice behavior. In *Frontiers in Econometrics*, P. Zarembka, ed., New York: Academic Press, 105–142.

Meloni, I., L. Guala and A. Loddo, 2004, Time allocation to discretionary in home, out of home activities and to trips. *Transportation*, **31**(1), 69–96.

Miller, E.J. and M.J. Roorda, 2003, A prototype model of 24-hour household activity scheduling for the Toronto area. *Transportation Research Record*, **1831**, 114–121.

Mitchell, R. and C. Rapkin, 1954, *Urban Traffic: A Function of Land Use*. New York: Columbia University Press.

Mohammadian, A. and S.T. Doherty, 2006, Modeling activity scheduling time horizon: duration of time between planning and execution of pre-planned activities. *Transportation Research A*, **40**(6), 475–490.

Morrison, R., 1998, Adapted by B. Dussault, 2000, Overview of DYNACAN: a full-fledged Canadian actu-arial stochastic model designed for the fiscal and policy analysis of social security schemes. Available at www.actuaries.org/CTTEES_SOCSEC/Documents/dynacan.pdf.

Odell, J., 2002, Objects and agents compared. *Journal of Object Technology*, **1**(1), 41–53.

Páez, A., 2007, Spatial perspectives on urban systems: developments and directions. *Journal of Geographic Systems*, **9**(1), 1–6.

Páez, A. and D. Scott, 2004, Spatial statistics for urban analysis: a review of techniques with examples. *Geo Journal*, **61**(1), 53–67.

Páez, A. and D.M. Scott, 2007, Social influence on travel behavior: a simulation example of the decision to telecommute. *Environment and Planning A*, **39**(3), 647–665.

Pas, E.I., 1985, State of the art and research opportunities in travel demand: another perspective. *Transportation Research Part A*, **19**(5–6), 460–464.

PB Consult, 2005, The MORPC travel demand model validation and final report. Prepared for the Mid-Ohio Region Planning Commission.

PB Consult, J. Bowman and M.A. Bradley, 2006, Regional transportation plan major update project for the Atlanta Regional Commission, General Modeling Task 13 (Activity/Tour-Based Models). Progress Report for the Year 2005.

Pendyala, R.M., 2004, Phased implementation of a multimodal activity-based travel demand modeling system in Florida. Research report, prepared for the Florida Department of Transportation.

Pendyala, R.M., R. Kitamura, A. Kikuchi, T. Yamamoto and S. Fujii, 2005, FAMOS: The Florida Activity Mobility Simulator. *Transportation Research Record*, **1921**, 123–130.

Pendyala, R.M., T. Yamamoto and R. Kitamura, 2002, On the formulation of time-space prisms to model constraints on personal activity–travel engagement. *Transportation*, **29**(1), 73–94.

Pinjari, A.R., N. Eluru, R. Copperman, I.N. Sener, J.Y. Guo, S. Srinivasan and C.R. Bhat, 2006, Activity-based travel-demand analysis for metropolitan areas in Texas: CEMDAP Models, Framework, Software Architecture and Application Results. Research Report 4080-8, Center for Transportation Research, The University of Texas at Austin.

Pinjari, A.R., R.M. Pendyala, C.R. Bhat and P.A. Waddell, 2007, Modeling the choice continuum: an inte-grated model of residential location, auto ownership, bicycle ownership, and commute tour mode choice decisions. Technical paper, Department of Civil, Architectural and Environmental Engineering, The University of Texas at Austin.

Recker, W.W., 1995, The household activity pattern problem: general formulation and solution. *Transportation Research Part B*, **29**(1), 61–77.

Recker, W.W., 2001, A bridge between travel demand modeling and activity-based travel analysis. *Transportation Research Part B*, **35**(5), 481–506.

Recker, W., J. Duan and H. Wang, 2008, Development of an estimation procedure for an activity-based travel demand model. *Computer-Aided Civil and Infrastructure Engineering*, **23**(7), 483–501.

Recker, W.W., M.G. McNally and G.S. Root, 1986a, A model of complex travel behavior: part I. Theoretical development. *Transportation Research Part A*, **20**(4), 307–318.

Recker, W.W., M.G. McNally and G.S. Root, 1986b, A model of complex travel behavior: part II. An opera-tional model. *Transportation Research Part A*, **20**(4), 319–330.

Roorda, M.J. and E.J. Miller, 2005, Strategies for resolving activity scheduling conflicts: an empirical analysis. In *Progress in Activity-Based Analysis*, H.J.P. Timmermans, ed., Oxford: Elsevier, pp. 203–222.

Salvini, P.A. and E.J. Miller, 2005, ILUTE: an operational prototype of a comprehensive microsimulation model of urban systems. *Networks and Spatial Economics*, **5**, 217–234.

Schlich, R. and K.W. Axhausen, 2003, Habitual travel behaviour: evidence from a six-week diary. *Transportation*, **30**(1), 13–36.

Scott, D.M., and P.S. Kanaroglou, 2002, An activity-episode generation model that captures interactions between household heads: development and empirical analysis. *Transportation Research Part B*, **36**(10), 875–896.

Sener, I.N. and C.R. Bhat, 2007, An analysis of the social context of children's weekend discretionary activity participation. *Transportation*, **34**(6), 697–721.

Shaw, S.-L. and X. Xin, 2003, Integrated land use and transportation interaction: a temporal GIS exploratory data analysis approach. *Journal of Transport Geography*, **11**(2), 103–115.

Small, K.A., 1982, The scheduling of consumer activities: work trips. *American Economic Review*, **72**(3), 467–479.

Spissu, E., A.R. Pinjari, C.R. Bhat, R.M. Pendyala and K.W. Axhausen, 2009, An analysis of weekly out-of-home discretionary activity participation and time-use behavior. *Transportation*, **36**(5), 483–510.

Srinivasan, S. and C.R. Bhat, 2005, Modeling household interactions in daily in-home and out-of-home maintenance activity participation. *Transportation*, **32**(5), 523–544.

Srinivasan, S. and C.R. Bhat, 2008, An exploratory analysis of joint-activity participation characteristics using the American time use survey. *Transportation*, **35**(3), 301–328.

Strauch, D., R. Moeckel, M. Wegener, J. Gräfe, H. Mühlhans, G. Rindsfüser and K.-J. Beckmann, 2003, Linking transport and land use planning: the microscopic dynamic simulation model ILUMASS. In *Proceedings of the 7th International Conference on Geocomputation*, Southampton, UK.

Sundararajan, A. and K.G. Goulias, 2003, Demographic microsimulation with DEMOS 2000: design, validation, and forecasting. In *Transportation Systems Planning: Methods and Applications*, K.G. Goulias, ed., Boca Raton, FL: CRC Press, Ch. 14.

Timmermans, H.J.P., T. Arenze and C.-H. Joh, 2002, Analyzing space–time behavior: new approaches to old problems. *Progress in Human Geography*, **26**(2), 175–190.

Vickrey, W., 1969, Congestion theory and transport investment. *American Economic Review*, **59**(2), 251–260.

Vovsha, P., E. Petersen and R. Donnelly, 2002, Micro-simulation in travel demand modeling: lessons learned from the New York Best Practice Model. *Transportation Research Record*, **1805**, 68–77.

Waddell, P., 2001, Towards a behavioral integration of land use and transportation modeling. In *Travel Behavior Research: The Leading Edge*, D. Hensher, ed. New York: Pergamon, pp. 65–95.

Waddell, P., C.R. Bhat, E. Ruiter, S. Bekhor, M. Outwater and E.L. Schroer, 2001, Review of the literature and operational models. Final report to the Puget Sound Regional Council on land use and travel demand forecasting models.

Waddell, P., A. Borning, H. Ševčíková and D. Socha, 2006, Opus (the Open Platform for Urban Simulation) and UrbanSim 4. Proceedings of the 7th International Conference on Digital Government Research, San Diego, CA.

Yarlagadda, A.K. and S. Srinivasan, 2008, Modeling children's school travel mode and parental escort decisions. *Transportation*, **35**(2), 201–218.

Zhang, J., H. Timmermans and A. Borgers, 2004, Model structure kernel for household task allocation incorporating household interaction and inter-activity dependency. Paper presented at the 83rd Annual Meeting of the Transportation Research Board, Washington DC.

11 Economics of transport logistics
Michel Beuthe

INTRODUCTION

The general organization of a firm and its transportation activities must be approached from a business logistics point of view, which analyses 'the movement, storage and related activities between the place of origin where the company obtains its raw materials, and the place where its products are required for consumption by its customers' (Blauwens et al., 2002). Although logistics was initially associated with inventory management and transport, it encompasses nowadays a complete analysis of the production processes in their relationship with demand, transport, distribution of products, and recycling processes of return items and used goods. Actually, the total logistics approach is in principle concerned with the whole chain of productive activities including transport.

It follows that logistics as a rational analysis of complex processes covers a very large ground. It can be applied to practically all human activities and uses a wide range of disciplines: economics, engineering, management of business, operations research, statistics and mathematics. It is really a multidisciplinary field of analysis, even when attention is focused on a particular activity like in the present case of transport logistics. Actually, it is a field where many studies, experiments and innovations are developed within and for industrial firms. Hence, it is rather difficult to present a synthetic view of the subject: the present review is perforce made of many bits and pieces, elements which must then be chosen, calibrated and assembled in applied logistic analyses.

On the basis of the business literature on logistics, this chapter first gives a view of what has become transport and inventory logistics in a world progressively more open to exchanges and interconnected with transport and telecommunication networks. The second section reviews the basic costs of a given supply chain and shows how they may be influenced by the qualitative characteristics of the means of transport that are used. The third section puts together these elements to set up a simple static partial optimization analysis. Then, the fourth section expands on the presentation of a number of contributions from operations research and mathematical economics: first on routing models, mode choice and plant location; second on game theoretic approaches and bargaining models in a logistic context. Given the composite nature of logistic analysis, which, at this stage, can be compared to a handy toolbox for handling a wide variety of business problems, the conclusions will be rather tentative and general.

THE FIELD OF LOGISTICS AND ITS EVOLUTION

The word 'Logistics' may be relatively new but the problems it covers have always existed. In its most extensive definition 'logistics' is about the rational organization of complex human activities, and, as such, it was already practiced by nomads moving from one feeding place to another according to seasons, for the provisioning of large armies and urban populations, as well as in trading and banking activities. For a long while in modern times, the expertise in these matters was held in-house by well-trained professional accountants and transport managers. The first scientific approach to logistics, the well known 'economic order quantity' (EOQ) formula for replenishing an inventory, was proposed by Harris in 1915. The 'news vendor' model was developed and much used during the World War II, whereas Whitin's fundamental 'Theory of inventory management' was only published in 1953.

Thus, at the beginning, the main focus of logistic analysis was on inventory and transport management. Inbound and outbound logistics were dealt with as a consequence of a production plan and treated as separate activities with inventories playing buffers between inputs provisioning, production and distribution. The costs involved were analyzed in a rather piecemeal way: ordering, transporting, stocking and handling, loading/unloading, transferring, packaging, conditioning and delivering. However, progressively more attention was given to the overall planning of production, to products design, distribution and services quality. Hence, it was no longer sufficient to minimize transport costs and rely on buffer stocks. The planning horizon was shortened to better respond to demand fluctuations and each process was progressively seen as a link in a supply chain that had to be globally optimized through improved coordination (Brewer et al., 1991). The firms came to realize the benefits of better organizing the sequences of their activities from demand and market information backwards through the distribution sequence, up the production flows and finally inputs provisioning, in an inverse sequence to the one they were used to.

Over the last few years, in response to growing environmental concerns, another extension was added to that sequence for the handling of returns items to the manufacturer (bottles, pallets, containers and minor repairs), and for the recycling of waste as well as defective and used durable goods. It is the problem of reverse logistics which can be handled with the same methodologies, but induces an additional layer of complexity for its coordination with supply logistics.

The advent of the internet and other developments in information technology, such as mobile phones and barcodes, supported this demand driven logistics by providing direct connection between consumers and the central decision making via the retailers. Likewise, they gave to the central firm a direct link with their suppliers. Thus, it became possible to organize a fast transfer of information from the retailers to the suppliers to better organise the supply chains while meeting the consumers' demands. As a matter of fact, each of us now is participating in that chain of information when shopping in stores or buying online. Another example of what information technology allows for a better management of transports and inventories is the Cooperative European System for Advanced Information Redistribution (CESAR), which is a centralized tracking and tracing system for shipments made with combined transport operators (www.cesar-online.com, and www.uirr.com).

In 1985, Porter advanced the idea that, to promote their competitiveness, firms should analyze their activities in terms of their relative values. To start with, they should distinguish their primary activities, such as inbound logistics, operations, outbound logistics, marketing, sales and services, from support activities like infrastructure, human resource management, technology development and procurement. The firms should then examine whether the performance of these activities is giving them a competitive advantage, and if not, they should reform their activities or consider outsourcing. This type of 'value chain' analysis is another turn taken by logistic analysis, which has been extensively used over the last two decades for preparing acquisitions of firms or mergers, for restructuring or outsourcing operations.

In a similar vein, Christopher (2005) recommends identifying the various functional costs (purchasing, production, sales, marketing, transport and so forth) attributable to each product's demand segment, so-called 'mission' in business lingo, and examine whether they would be avoidable if that mission was cancelled. Again, comparing the sum of these costs to the revenue they provide gives a good indication whether a product line is worth pursuing. Perret and Jaffeux (2002) give an excellent survey of many other management techniques, whereas Kotzab et al. (2005) provide many applications and case studies of supply logistics.

These trends and the use of the above techniques were reinforced by the progressive liberalization and globalization of economic activities. It allowed firms to further extend their market reach and production facilities, playing on cost differences of inputs and labor between countries, relative exchange rates, subsidies and regulations. The firms also came to outsource some or all of their procurement and production operations to only keep in house, in some cases, the design and development as well as the control of marketing at the end of the chain. That new configuration of firms obviously requires tight coordination of all activities, and lead to the emergence of important logistic intermediaries that can manage supply chains internationally, handling many tasks of transport and distribution, including custom documentation, inventory management, packing and preparing goods for final distribution (Koźlak, 2009; Quinet and Vickerman, 2004).

As a result logistic analysis has become an essential component of the firms' management. Its scope now encompasses the firms' entire organization and all its supply chains from the outputs' markets backward to production and procurement, as well as the flows of information needed to coordinate the sequences of all activities. Even the management structure must be adjusted across the usual functions to provide a better coordinated management. From this viewpoint, competition on the markets can then be seen as a competition between supply chains, each of them organized to minimize their cost but also to insure 'responsiveness' to consumers requirements, 'reliability' of processes and activities, 'resilience' to unexpected disturbances and good 'relationships' with suppliers and customers. These are the often quoted four R's that should guide managers. Since the firm is now driven by the consumers' demands and tastes, Christopher (2005) suggests that it would be more appropriate to use 'demand chain management' as a terminology rather than 'supply chain management'.

The relative importance of freight logistics in a national economy is rather difficult to assess since the sector relies on other branches of activities as suppliers, and logistic activities are often kept in-house in many industries. In Belgium, as an example, a recent report (Lagneaux, 2008) indicates that the logistic sector itself accounted for 3.1 per cent of the Belgian GDP and 3.4 per cent of the Belgian domestic employment in 2005. Including the supply activities to the freight logistic sector, this employment percentage amounted to 5.3 per cent in the same year. Moreover, from some survey data, it can be estimated that the overall employment could reach 8 per cent of domestic employment if in-house transport logistics activities also are added. Table 11.1 gives the relative shares

Table 11.1   Relative shares of direct added value of transport and logistics in Belgium

	Share 2005	Change 2000–2005 per year
Rail	3.1	−6.4
Road	32.2	+2.8
Pipeline	0.1	−5.5
Sea and coastal water	9.6	+43.7
Inland water	0.4	−0.6
Air	0.4	−0.7
Transport sectors	45.8	+5.6
Cargo handling	6.4	+8.6
Cargo storage	6.3	+9.2
Supporting transport	11.9	+21.6
Forwarders	6.7	+3.6
Agencies	4.5	+3.7
Postal services	18.4	+2.3
Other logistic sectors	54.2	+7.1

Source: Compiled from Lagneaux (2008).

of the added values produced by the different branches included as logistic activities in that report.

In this instance, logistic activities other than transport have a larger importance in the global sector of freight logistics. The specific contribution of each branch obviously is influenced by the characteristics of the country. Here, we can see the role played by the Belgian harbors and their associated activities. The numerous centers of distribution to Europe located in Belgium must also have a substantial impact on the non-transport branches.

THE BASIC LOGISTIC COSTS IN A TRANSPORT CHAIN

Transport Costs

These are the charges paid to the carrier(s) for the transport from origin to destination; they may be incurred by the shipping firm if it uses its own vehicles and personnel. These costs depend on the mode used, the volume of the flow and the size of the shipments. They include the costs of packaging, loading, unloading and transhipments. The latter may play an important role in the choice of a transport solution, when comparing direct road transport to waterway or railway transports that often involve some trucking at the origin or destination, or when considering multimodal solutions with transfers between modes.

The rates that are paid are influenced by the market organization. Whereas road and inland waterway transport rates are likely to be close to real cost because of the competitive structure of these modes, railways' rates are better controlled by the carriers. Indeed, the latter are liable to exercise some 'yield management' and discriminate among clients according to their location and available transport alternatives. Focusing on the relationship between cost, volume and transport attributes, the transport unit cost function can be written as

$$P = P(Q, Z),\qquad(11.1)$$

where Q is the total of shipments over the period of analysis, say a year, and Z is the vector of characteristics of the specific transport considered (mode, carrier, means or combination thereof). These characteristics are mainly its reliability R, safety during transport S, transport time T, flexibility F and frequency N (Ben-Akiva et al., 2008; Beuthe et al., 2008).

Administrative and Ordering Costs

The cost of order processing and administration is usually assumed to be proportional to the number of orders. It certainly varies with the transport solution and its organization with various intermediaries or forwarders. The ordering cost per unit can be written

$$A = A(F),\qquad(11.2)$$

since it must be a function of the carrier's flexibility of service.

Inventory Costs

These costs are composed of several elements, mainly the cost of the cycle stock, the cost of in-transit inventory, and the cost of the safety stock.

Cycle stock
With the exception of extreme just-in-time delivery systems, most companies order goods in a quantity that satisfies their needs for a certain period. Hence, stocks are bound to follow a cyclical pattern, since they build up at the consignment arrivals and diminish progressively until the next arrival. If the stock of a particular good is consumed at an even pace, the level of its stock will take the shape of a series of right-angled triangles, and its average level will be equal to half the size of one consignment. Hence, the cost of the cycle stock is

$$G_c = \frac{1}{2} w. q,\qquad(11.3)$$

where $q = Q/N$ is the ordered consignment size, and w is the yearly inventory cost per unit. The latter is based on the unit value of the good, the rate of interest on the capital embedded in the stock, and all the other costs associated with the stock operations (insurance, warehousing, depreciation, etc.). It is obvious that the smaller the size of the consignment q, the smaller is the cost for the consignee.

   In a very simple situation where q is fixed for each period separately, its setting is referred to in the literature as the 'newsboy problem', one of the earliest inventory problems dealt with in management science. Its solution q^* is given by the following simple formula: $D(q^*) = c_s / (c_s + c_o)$, where $D(q^*)$ is the cumulative distribution function of demand over the 0 to q^* range, c_s is the 'shortage cost' per unit, or lost profit from being short, and c_o is the 'overage cost' per unit of leftover copies. Good reviews of this problem's many facets are given by Porteus (1985) and Chan et al. (2004). Below, we will again consider this problem in a competitive situation.

This cycle stock as defined should not be confused with a stock that would be built up because of a seasonal production cycle at the source, or as a speculation on future demand. That is done only to secure goods or materials at a later date. This analysis is set in a relatively stable economic environment. The dynamic management of inventories in an unstable economic context would require a more general analysis.

In-transit inventory
Goods are also in inventory during transportation. The cost of that inventory on wheels depends on the transport duration, the consignment value, the rate of interest and insurance cost. For a particular transport solution, the corresponding unit cost can be written as

$$G_t = v(S) . T,   \tag{11.4}$$

$v(S)$ includes the inventory cost, the goods depreciation and the pilferage cost per unit of time (a fraction of year); it is a function of the transport safety. T is the average transport duration in fraction of year, which includes the time taken by all transport operations including delays incurred at transfers.

Safety stock
Even though we assume a rather stable economic environment, there remains some uncertainty linked to the irregular level of demand from day to day and to possible delivery delays. Hence, some additional inventory is needed beyond what is required to meet the average rate of stock consumption. Besides the marketing policy adopted by the consignee, the safety stock level is mainly a function of the transport mode characteristics Z. Like the cost of cycle stock, it also depends on the value of the good, the rate of interest and insurance cost. It can be estimated as

$$G_s = w . k . \sigma,   \tag{11.5}$$

where w is the yearly inventory cost per unit, which depends on the money value of the goods, k is a parameter that depends on the probability of running out of stock a firm is ready to accept (it can be computed on the daily demand distribution), σ is the standard deviation of demand during lead time, and $k. \sigma$ defines the level of safety stock that is needed.

Several assumptions can be made on the distribution of the daily demands and delivery time, which lead to different estimates of the standard deviation (Zinn et al., 1992). The more common ones are the normal and Poisson distributions (Fetter and Dalleck, 1961; Whitin, 1953). Following Baumol and Vinod, (1970), let us assume here a Poisson distribution so that σ can be approximated by

$$\sigma = [(t + T) Q]^{1/2},   \tag{11.6}$$

where $(t + T) Q$ is an estimate of the unsatisfied demand that may accumulate during the period $(t + T)$ of maximum lead time, the time between two shipments (t) added to transport time T, when an order is just missing a shipment. Hence, more generally, σ can be simply written as $\sigma (Q, Z)$. Indeed, the lead time is a function of the transport characteristics; it decreases with increasing reliability, safety, flexibility and frequency of transport service.

The parameter k is a measure of the willingness to accept a stock-out. It is a somewhat subjective parameter that must be decided by each firm; it depends on the type of good and adopted marketing strategy. It can be assessed for instance by reference to the normal distribution taken as an approximation of the Poisson distribution. k is then the critical value at which the area under the standard normal curve at the right of k equals the accepted risk of running out of stock.

OPTIMIZING THE TOTAL LOGISTIC COSTS OF A TRANSPORT CHAIN

We can aggregate all the above elements to compute the total cost of a particular transport chain for a year during which the total flow is Q:

$$C = P(Q, Z).Q + A(F).N + \tfrac{1}{2}w. Q/N + v(S). T. Q + w. k.\sigma (Q, Z)$$

$$= P(Q, Z).Q + V(Q, Z). \tag{11.7}$$

In Equation (11.7), $P.Q$ can be taken as the external part of the total logistic cost which is determined by the transport supply side, the carrier or the shipper's department in charge of the own transport operations. In contrast, the function V corresponds to the internal part of the logistic cost of the shipper and/or consignee.

Supposing that the shipper already has, somehow, chosen a particular transport mode, it can still minimize the logistic cost by choosing the most appropriate service that is offered by that transport mode. For road transport, for example, it can choose between carriers according to their vehicle sizes and the service levels they offer in terms of reliability, flexibility, frequency, safety, speed and prices. Assuming then well-behaved continuous functions, the first-order conditions for a minimum of the total logistic cost given a total flow Q are

$$\partial C/\partial T = \partial P/\partial T.Q + v(S).Q + w. k. \partial \sigma /\partial T = 0, \tag{11.8}$$

$$\partial C/\partial F = \partial P/\partial F.Q + \partial A/\partial F. N + w. k. \partial \sigma /\partial F = 0, \tag{11.9}$$

$$\partial C/\partial R = \partial P/\partial R.Q + w. k. \partial \sigma /\partial R = 0, \tag{11.10}$$

$$\partial C/\partial S = \partial P/\partial S.Q + \partial v/\partial S. T.Q + w. k. \partial \sigma /\partial S = 0, \tag{11.11}$$

$$\partial C/\partial N = \partial P/\partial N.Q + A(F) - 1/2 w. Q/N^2 + w. k. \partial \sigma /\partial N = 0. \tag{11.12}$$

It is assumed that second-order conditions are satisfied.

The marginal internal value of a transport attribute per unit transported, that is the shipper's marginal willingness to pay for it, can be evaluated from these equations. For example, at the optimal solution, the marginal willingness to pay for a shorter transport time is

$$V_T = -\partial P/\partial T = v(S) + w. k/Q. \partial\sigma/\partial T. \tag{11.13}$$

Similarly, the marginal willingness to pay for a better level of the other (positive) attributes can be derived as:

$$V_F = -(\partial A/\partial F. 1/q + w. k/Q. \partial\sigma/\partial F),$$

$$V_R = -(w. k/Q. \partial\sigma/\partial R),$$

$$V_S = -(\partial v/\partial S. T + w. k/Q. \partial\sigma/\partial S).$$

$$V_N = -(A(F)/Q - 1/2 w/N^2 + w. k/Q. \partial\sigma/\partial N). \tag{11.4}$$

These equations provide a theoretical interpretation of the firms' willingness to pay per transported unit for an attribute within a small variation around a given transport solution. It clearly appears that the safety stock plays an important role in the supply chain organization. Beside this factor, the marginal value of flexibility depends on its impact on ordering cost, the marginal value of safety is determined by its impact on in-transit inventory, whereas the willingness to pay for frequency depends on its impact on both the in-transit and cycle stocks.

From Equation (11.12), the optimal 'economic order quantity' $q*$ also can be easily deduced since $N = Q/q$ and $\partial N/\partial q = -Q/q^2$. Thus, Equation (11.12) can be transformed into

$$\partial C/\partial q = -\partial P/\partial N. Q^2/q^2 - A(F).Q/q^2 + 1/2 w - w. k. \partial\sigma/\partial N.Q/q^2 = 0,$$

$$\text{and } q* = \left[\frac{2[\partial P/\partial N.Q^2 + A(F).Q + w.k.\partial\sigma/\partial N.q]}{w} \right]^{1/2}. \tag{11.15}$$

Although more complex, it is similar to the basic formula with constant parameters that is given in textbooks on inventory theory when neither qualitative attributes nor any safety stock are included:

$$q* = \left[\frac{2A.Q}{w} \right]^{1/2}. \tag{11.16}$$

The conditions (11.8) to (11.12) suppose that the variables are continuous. For a given choice of a transport mode that may be approximately the case, since several levels of service are indeed proposed by carriers. However, there are strong discontinuities from one mode to another so that carriers may not be able to offer the most desirable levels

Table 11.2   An example of logistic costs

	Road haulage	Inland navigation
P: transport costs in € / tonne	10.91	8.43
w : yearly inventory cost in € / tonne	93	93
T : transport time in days	0.19	4.48
v : in-transit value in € / tonne/day	0.26	0.26
q : shipment in tonnes	25	1200
$k. \sigma$: safety stock in tonnes	250	1214
Transport cost/ tonne	10.91	8.43
In-transit inventory cost/ tonne	0.05	1.14
Cycle stock cost / tonne	0.02	1.01
Safety stock cost / tonne	0.18	0.89
Additional fixed cost / tonne[a]	0.09	0.45
Total logistics cost / tonne	11.25	11.92

Notes: [a] Costs that do not vary with the stock level

Source: Vernimmen and Witlox (2001).

of services. For example, the transport time of each mode can only vary within a limited range for technical and structural reasons, and available vehicles' carrying capacity may not be appropriate to transport some given shipment size. It follows that the choice of a transport solution is constrained by the set of available alternatives. In most cases, the analysis of the best logistic solution, including the choice of a mode, has to focus on the valuation of the total logistic cost function and the comparison of values it takes for the set of available solutions. That implies that all the components of the total logistic cost for each transport solution should be estimated by the firms, in particular v, w, k, L and the standard deviation.

Interesting discussions of all these parameters with examples can be found in Ballou (1999) and Blauwens et al. (2002). Table 11.2 drawn from a firm's case-study gives a global comparison between road haulage and inland navigation.

Rather than trying to estimate each of the parameters in Equation (11.7), an alternative approach to estimate the total logistic cost from a transport point of view is to use some econometric methods on revealed or stated choice data to estimate the shippers' willingness to pay for the different transport attributes. These values can then be used to calculate generalized cost functions of logistic chains in mode choice modeling. This approach may provide useful results for analysing transport policies at the aggregate level, but it may also be used for in-depth review of an individual firm's transport organization. Recent examples, and references, of that approach can be found in Ben-Akiva et al. (2008), Beuthe and Bouffioux (2008) for estimates from survey data, and in Beuthe et al. (2008) for estimates from individual data. Empirical results in these papers and others in the literature indicate that the firms' and industries' characteristics, like their location in the spatial network, the type of goods and their value, substantially affect the relative importance and equivalent values attached to transport characteristics.

As shown in Table 11.3, the cost of transport is by far the most important factor,

Table 11.3   Average weights (%)

Variable		Frequency	Time	Reliability	Flexibility	Safety	Cost
Goods value	Low	3.12	11.42	6.56	5.95	2.66	70.30
	Middle	2.97	15.36	8.06	4.48	2.91	66.22
	High	5.26	11.49	6.23	6.30	4.68	66.05
Mode:	Road	3.77	6.91	9.53	5.89	3.85	70.05
	Rail	3.48	22.45	11.20	4.58	3.42	54.87
	Inland waterway	2.96	14.66	5.58	7.19	2.79	66.81
	Others	4.50	14.25	5.11	5.93	3.83	66.38
Goods	Foodstuffs	3.76	4.00	4.61	3.06	3.06	81.51
	Minerals	4.35	22.87	12.21	8.58	3.25	48.73
	Metal products	2.26	3.50	4.43	2.32	1.90	85.58
	Chemical-Pharma.	3.72	3.80	8.00	3.82	2.64	77.92
	Miscellaneous	4.32	11.06	10.43	6.65	4.16	63.38
Firms that could consider a change of mode		2.98	11.45	6.49	5.80	3.11	70.16
Global		3.16	15.92	8.47	5.63	3.15	63.67

Source: Beuthe and Bouffioux (2008), from a survey of 113 Belgian firms.

followed by transport time and reliability, but the latter may be judged more important than time by some firms. Speed is a factor that may solve some procurement problems, but speed has a cost which must be balanced with its relative value to the firm. Taking all qualitative attributes together, we see that they substantially weigh on the choice of a means of transport. Table 11.4 shows a large spread of time value estimates that results from the factors mentioned above but also from data and methodological differences, such as the number of qualitative attributes that are considered in the econometric estimation. This means that before using any time value estimate in applied research one should carefully assess its relevance to the case. Reviews of earlier studies can be found in De Jong (2000) and Zamparini and Reggiani (2007).

CONTRIBUTIONS OF MANAGEMENT SCIENCE AND MATHEMATICAL ECONOMICS

In the above analyses, prices and values were taken as given and used to solve the logistic problem of a single transport flow between an origin and destination. But in many cases, several interdependent flows must be simultaneously handled. This is the case, for example, when the required deliveries are parts of a distribution round to geographically dispersed clients. It is the 'vehicle routing problem' the solution of which corresponds to the minimization of the total cost of the distribution tour. Operations research has developed a number of useful analyses to deal with such more complicated situations.

Furthermore, decision making was assumed to be made in a non-rivalry framework,

Table 11.4   *Comparison of time values for freight*

	Value of one hour per tonne for a mean (a) or median (m) distance				
	Road	Rail	Road/Rail[a]	Inl.W	Road/Inl.W
Beuthe and Bouffioux (€2003) (m)	1.82	0.18	–	0.005	–
Beuthe and Bouffioux (€2003) (a)	2.88	0.17	–	0.009	–
De Jong et al. (€2002) (m)	4.74	0.96	–	0.046	–
Fowkes and Whiteing (€ 2003)	–	–	0.08–1.85		
Kurri et al. (€2002)	1.53	0.09	–	–	–
Danielis (€2001)	–	–	3.05–3.55	–	–
Stratec (€1999)	–	–	0.34–2.56	–	0.11–0.26
Stratec (€ 2005)	–	–	–	–	0.02–0.206[c]
Maggi and Rudel (€2004) (m)	–	–	0.46–1.98[b]	–	–
Blauwens and Van de Voorde (€2002)	–	–	–	0.09	–
HEATCO (€2002) Belgium	3.29	1.35	–	–	–
France	3.32	1.36	–	–	–
EU-25	2.98	1.22	–	–	–
French Ministry (€2000)	0.45	0.01–0.15	–	0.01–1.15	–

Notes:
[a] 'Road/Rail' and 'Road/Inland Waterway' refer to choice analyses involving two modes.
[b] 0.46 € for an 870 km distance, 1.98 € for 142 km.
[c] Actually for choices between inland waterway and all other modes: from 0.02 for bulk to 0.38 for manufactured goods. The value of time tends to be higher for transport in containers.

Source: Beuthe and Bouffioux (2008), Blauwens and Van de Voorde (1988), Danielis (2002), De Jong *et al.* (2005), Fowkes and Whiteing (2006), HEATCO (2004), Kurri et al. (2000), Maggi and Rudel (2008), Ministère des Transports (2006), Stratec (2007).

as if a single agent was concerned by the logistic solution, or under the assumption that the shipper and the consignee shared a common objective. Actually, several agents may be involved that have somewhat conflicting objectives. This is the type of problem studied by game and bargaining theory.

Routing and Modal Choices

Routing problems involve binary variables defining the successive legs of the route, and may lead to complex non-linear integer programs, especially when the number of variables is not small and additional constraints are introduced. Problems of that kind can be solved by ad-hoc heuristic methods that identify a feasible solution through an iterative procedure, a solution that may still correspond only to a local optimum. Meta-heuristics are then needed that provide a structured search from local solutions towards the global one. Examples of such methods are the 'tabu' search that imposes likely restrictions on the search process, population search that generates new solutions by combining previous solutions, and learning mechanisms with feedbacks. An accessible review of these operations research methods is given by Hillier and Lieberman (2005). Additional references can be found in Langevin and Riopel (2005).

One of the first problem studied in transport was the well known case of the 'travelling salesman' who must visit a number of clients on a tour starting from home and passing through each city once and only once to come back home in the end. In that case, the successive legs form a continuous 'chain' without any detour ('sub-tour') from any point on the chain. This condition complicates the analysis that otherwise would boil down to a simpler assignment problem. The first efficient iterative procedure for solving that problem, a branch-and-bound technique, was proposed by Little et al. (1963). This model is a good example of a whole set of distribution problems: delivery of parcels and wholesale distribution to retailers, postal rounds, delivery of cash to ATM machines, pickup of milk, and so forth, which can involve a very high number of variables and intricate constraints.

The basic routing problem assumes the delivery of a given amount q, and its solution corresponds to a fixed route. When demand is stochastic, it may be cheaper sometimes for the carrier to skip some points of delivery and consider semi-fixed routes (Bertsimas, 1992; Waters, 1989). Haughton (1998) analyzed the saving that would result from a strategy of ascertaining before dispatch whether delivery is needed at some points. He also analyzed strategies of demand stabilization that would imply for the client additional logistic costs, particularly a higher safety stock. Such strategies have an obvious impact on the quality of service, as well as on the price and the q quantity that may have to be negotiated. An interesting variation on this theme is the 'inventory routing' problem where levels of inventory and routing are simultaneously analyzed. Raa (2006) proposes such a model where account is taken of the vehicle's fixed cost and of the possibility that a vehicle from a fleet may make multiple tours.

An important constraint that may arise is when the clients request a visit or delivery at a pre-specified time window, a case first considered by Solomon (1987), and developed by Potvin and Rousseau (1993) and Desrosiers et al. (1995). Recently, Dullaert and Bräysy (2003) analyzed the trade-off between freight rates and distribution costs from the point of view of the dispatcher. The freight rates are then devised according to the shipment size and the width of the time window, a lower rate being proposed if the customer accepts a wider time window. Daganzo (1999) gives a good presentation of various routing problems. Cordeau et al. (2005) give a good review of recent heuristics for solving routing problems.

Another avenue of research, which is more related to public planning policies, aims at modeling the process of assigning transport flows of commodities to modes and routes. The main type of model in this field is the well known four-step transport model, whose steps are, successively, the generation of the global demand to be transported over a network, the distribution of that demand between origins and destinations in the network, the choice of modes and means for realizing that task, and finally the assignment on routes (Ortuzar and Willumsen, 2001). Over the last 20 years this model was applied and developed in a number of national transport models and European research programmes (see for instance De Jong et al., 2005).

The first two steps are handled through regional economic analysis. They include the setting of a digitized geographical transport network and the use of spatial gravity models. The third step involves transport cost data gathering and estimation, as well as econometric discrete modal choice analysis. The route choice is mainly treated using shortest path algorithms like the Moore–Dijsktra (Dijkstra, 1959; Moore, 1957) and the Frank–Wolfe (1956) for computing iteratively equilibrium solutions in the most sophisticated models. One difficulty with such models lies in the comprehensiveness of the utility functions. Indeed, as discussed above, many factors influence the choice of a mode. A full description of the costs and logistic factors involved in the different options is needed, including the services' quality levels, the shipment sizes as well as equipments and infrastructure that may be needed to adopt a particular mode (Nash and Whiteing, 1988; Winston, 1985). Part of that problem may be met by analyses specific to different types of commodities, but the analyst is often limited by available data.

Following the development of the STAN model (Crainic et al., 1990), which includes some virtual modes corresponding to combinations of mode or means (Harker, 1987), Jourquin (1995) proposed a new formulation of transport networks based on the concept of virtual links. It is implemented in an assignment model and software (NODUS package) that combine the last two steps (modal choice and routing) by using a complete virtual network automatically created on the basis of the characteristics of the geographical nodes and links. Through the creation of virtual links, all possible operations are represented and their costs can be taken into account (loading, unloading, transfers, customs and technical delays at boundary crossing and so forth); similarly, all types of vehicles using the same geographical infrastructure can be distinguished and all feasible combinations of modes and means can be analyzed (Jourquin and Beuthe, 1996). Hence, many details of logistic operations are integrated in the spatial network of transport opportunities and the entire choice set of modes/means/routes is fully taken into account. The generalized transport cost is then minimized over the virtual network. This modeling allows the convenient analysis of multimodal transport solutions and transport policies or investments (Beuthe et al., 2002; Jourquin and Beuthe, 2006). No estimation of a modal choice 'utility' function is required, but one still needs estimates of the quality factors' monetary values that should be included in an additive or linear generalized cost function. In many cases the transport time, and its value, is used as a proxy, but this is only an ad-hoc solution when lacking more information. To some extent the calibration of the model on observed traffic data may compensate the lack of information. The additive cost function de facto assumes that the implicit utility function also is additive, which is the standard assumption in four-step models. Such a set-up leads in principle to 'all-or-nothing' assignments on the network, but this problem may be mitigated by spreading the flows between alternatives (routes and/or modes) that are close in terms of their costs (Jourquin, 2006). A spreading of the flows also can be achieved through iterative equilibrium analyses with costs that increase with traffic, as in cases where congestion is involved.

These transport models can be useful for analyzing optimal locations of hubs and their market sizes. It is an active research area in the context of transport policies that encourage inter-modality for relieving the road network congestion and as a tool for regional economic development. The standard multiple-hub location problem assumes that hubs on a transport network are directly connected to each other, whereas non-hub nodes are connected to a single hub but not connected between each other by any means. The objective is to minimize the total transport cost. O'Kelly (1987) formulated that problem as a quadratic integer program, under the name of p-hub median problem. Campbell (1994) formulated it as a mixed integer linear program. Limbourg and Jourquin (2009a) applied that methodology to obtain a set of *p* optimal location for large rail/road container terminals (hubs) over the whole European freight transport network. In a second stage, they successively introduce these hubs' networks into the virtual multimodal freight network generated with the NODUS software. Then, minimizing the total transport costs by all transport modes, they identify the best intermodal road/ rail intermodal system, which is made of only seven hubs, and its market share within a competitive multimodal environment. An iterative procedure takes into account how the handled volume affects terminal costs. The relationship between cost and volume of transhipment is provided by Ballis and Golias (2002a) who developed an expert system of analysis that incorporates various platforms' technical characteristics (tracks, handling equipment, sidings, storage and so forth) and knowledge of experts in the field. Limbourg and Jourquin (2009b) also show that the hubs' market areas are comparable to those derived through simple Euclidean distance analysis in traditional market area theory, like in Beuthe (1972) and Niérat (1997).

Ballis and Golias (2002b) also treat the problem of rail/road hubs location in Europe by minimizing the total transport cost with the expert system mentioned above, but they do not take into account the competitive transport alternatives of other modes. Among the seven selected hubs, only two are among those chosen by the above procedure. Similarly, Jeong et al. (2007), using an integer linear programming model for assigning rail traffic that takes into account service frequencies, identify a rail/road network where the eight recommended hubs correspond to those with the largest volume of freight and where a high consolidation rate can be achieved. Only three hubs are among those selected by Limbourg and Jourquin (2009b). Despite these discrepancies, which can be explained by the different spatial scopes of data and the modeling, we note that all the selected nodes are located in the industrial center of Europe and particularly in Germany and France, where the transport flows are important. Note also the rather small number of hubs that are selected.

However, minimizing total cost of transport is not the only objective that may be considered. Campbell (1994) proposes another formulation of the problem with a minimax criterion, the so called p-hub centre problem that minimizes the maximum cost between origin and destination pair. Ernst et al. (2009) formulate it as an integer programming that may be solved through a branch-and-bound approach. Limbourg and Jourquin (2009b) have also tested that formulation. The outcome is very different: again a small number of eight hubs, but with some hubs spread out in Northern England, Southern Sweden and Southern Italy, a solution obviously entailing a higher cost. This could be expected since the p-hub centre problem is based on an equity criterion, whereas the p-hub median problem is based on the efficiency criterion of cost minimization.

Among the many contributions in this area, let us also cite some recent analyses on barge terminal networks by Bontekoning et al. (2004), Konings (2009) and Macharis (2004). Reverse logistics is another relatively new topic. Bostel et al. (2005) offer an interesting review of this field, including specific inventory models and flow optimization. Crainic et al. (1993) treat the problem of allocation of empty containers, whereas Fleischmann (2001) and Lu et al. (2004) provide analyses of reusable products transport.

Finally, we should also mention the development of decision-support models for the design of supply chains with production specialization and outsourcing in a world globalization context. These models necessarily have a wider scope since they involve many different aspects that concern the firms: long term strategies in terms of competitive advantages and core competency, capacity planning of major resources for selecting partners and facilities in the supply chain, tactical production planning for assigning production to plants, lines and subcontractors, scheduling the sequence of procurements and, lastly, concrete execution of the defined tasks and feedback (Voss and Woodruff, 2003). They integrate the transport problem within a larger analysis that includes several layers of successive production facilities and distribution systems down to places of consumption. They become even more intricate in the case of international global supply chain designs, which may include differences in taxes and subsidies according to the countries, trade concessions, differences in labor costs, currency exchange rates and their variability, access to overseas markets and factors related to different cultures, worker skills and quality issues. (Meixell and Gargeya, 2005; Prasad and Babbar, 2000). Obviously, such supply chain analyses may identify optimal global solutions that submit the transport organisation to a sub-optimal solution compared to what could be achieved in a separate optimization. These decision-support systems actually provide to large corporations a better understanding of strategic decision problems they face, like in which world region they ought to locate an assembly plant or a distribution centre, where to outsource a customers tele-service, parts production or a financial branch and so forth.

Again, such decision-support models correspond to complex mixed integer programs that motivated the development of specific software solvers and languages, such as APML, GAMS, MPL and so forth. Heuristics and meta-heuristics also are needed, because the programs may involve intricate non-linear relations.

Game and Bargaining Theories

Economic theory has always been interested in the relationships between several agents on a market and market configurations, from monopoly to duopoly situations, imperfect competition and dynamic models, where agents behave under various hypotheses as in the well known Cournot, Bertrand and Stackelberg models. These are often taken as reference in transport modeling (Quinet and Vickerman, 2004). Interesting reviews of recent developments in the framework of supply chain logistics are given by Cachon and Netessine (2004) and Chan et al. (2004).

Game theory provides a formal framework to analyze many situations with conflict of interests, which can arise in the shaping of a supply chain. It already has a long history starting in the 1940s, but not much of it has yet been applied to logistics and supply chain management. Its first applications dealt with non-cooperative games, in particular, the competition between news vendors and the setting of their order quantities (Cachon and Harker, 2002; Parlar, 1988) or the retailer–wholesaler game, when both hold inventories and sell directly to customers (Netessine and Rudi, 2001b). All these authors lengthily discuss the existence and possible uniqueness of the Nash equilibrium, a solution which constitutes the best response of any particular player to the choice of specific strategies by other players. However, they are quite aware that such a solution may be Pareto inferior. Thus, Cachon (2004) tackles the problem of a supply chain using the concept of Pareto optimum. Dynamic games are also considered, and as there are often dominating players in a supply chain, like a wholesaler versus its clients, some applications of the Stackelberg equilibrium with a leader and a follower can be found (Netessine and Rudi, 2001a).

The framework of cooperative games may seem more useful for analyzing supply chain management since it often leads to negotiations. In contrast with the topic of non-cooperative games, which is focused on the choice of actions and strategies, the topic of cooperative games is rather about the outcome of the game. Its main concern is the possibility of coalitions and the total value they would contribute to their members. How the coalition could be influenced by actions of non-members is not considered, a drawback of that kind of approach in a world of competing coalitions. The central concept here is the 'core' of the game, which is made of a coalition such that there is no other coalition that would make its members as well off and one member at least strictly better off. A core may not exist and it may not be unique (like in the case of the Nash equilibrium). Hartman et al. (2000), followed by Muller et al. (2002), applied this concept to the problem of a central inventory set by several news vendors who split the resulting benefits of the risk pooling. It turns out that the core corresponds to a singleton under some conditions.

Shapley (1953) proposes an axiomatic concept of the value attached to a coalition which can identify a unique outcome to cooperative games. The problem however is that the coalition with the maximum Shapley value may not be in the core of the game, so that there may be another coalition able to derail the Shapley coalition. Groothedde (2005) provides a simulation model for analysing the best design of a hub network in a cooperative framework.

'Biform games' also have been proposed that are made of two successive stages, the first one being a non-cooperative game, the second being a cooperative game. An example is the retailers' non-cooperative decision of stocking goods followed by cooperation on how to transfer goods from one to another in view of the actual demand for goods, and how to share the results of that cooperation (Anupindi et al., 2002).

Other types of games endeavor to take into account the disparity of information among players. In 'signalling games' the party who benefits from better information, say a manufacturer that has an accurate market forecast, moves first by proposing a contract to a component supplier. The latter may wonder whether the forecast is accurate and, in any case, he may wonder whether the manufacturer manipulates the information and tries to induce him to invest at his own cost in a larger capacity than warranted, just in case the demand would be in the upper range (Cachon and Larivière, 2001). The question is how much information should be signalled and of what kind, like a contract which provides for a lump sum payment to begin with, or a commitment to a minimum size order. In a 'screening game', it is the supplier with less information that tries to obtain information through the proposal of a set of contracts that would lead the manufacturer to reveal the appropriate capacity level in the situation. Kreps (1990) proposes a 'revelation principle' that leads to a truth-telling set of contracts.

Bargaining theory is a natural outgrowth of game theory where agents' behaviors are analyzed in their negotiation relationship. Most of the work in this field until now has focused on bargaining between two agents, starting with the axiomatic cooperative bargaining solution of Nash (1950, 1953). Ståhl (1972) and Rubinstein (1982) developed a non-cooperative sequential bargaining process where agents make offers and counteroffers until an agreement is reached. To model a situation of incomplete information, Myerson and Satterthwaite (1983) assume that while the buyer in a supply chain has a willingness to pay value that the supplier does not know, and the supplier has an opportunity cost value unknown to the buyer, both parties may have knowledge of the distribution of each others values, which depend on their respective opportunities. Actually, these distributions reflect the bargaining power of each party.

Regardless of the state of information, the bargaining may proceed directly without an intermediary or with an intermediary who may facilitate the negotiation between conflicting interests. In this particular framework, the intermediary collects the information on the buyer's marginal willingness to pay and the supplier's opportunity cost or, at least, their distributions and, on that knowledge, attempts to propose acceptable terms of trade. If this intervention permits the identification of a solution that could improve the outcome for each party, including him/her/self, then a trade can be concluded that may involve a mechanism of profit distribution between parties. Otherwise, his/her attempt fails and the bargaining parties must fall back on whatever alternatives they may have that actually set their acceptable minima. It is clear that such analyses can be of use in the setting of an efficient supply chain for which reliable and confidential information must be gathered and conflicting interests between buyers and suppliers must be reconciled. It is also a useful tool for analyzing the organization of a supply chain, which may be very extensive or very short and may vary over time with movements towards more or less intermediation. The role of intermediary may be taken by different agents according to the circumstances. It may be played by forwarders in a transport chain, by a wholesaler between producers and retailers, or by contract manufacturers between components suppliers and large brand-carrying original equipment manufacturer (OEM). The intermediation bargaining mechanism must be carefully set up so that its features induce individual participants to participate and reveal their true valuations and lead to a Pareto efficient solution (Myerson, 1979). Nagarajan and Bassok (2002) and Ertogral and Wu (2001) have examined how the agreements between the intermediary and the buyers or suppliers in a supply chain can be negotiated to obtain an acceptable split of the intermediation additional benefit.

With the above assumption on incomplete information, multilateral trade may be analysed as a vertically integrated structure such that one supplier is confronted to a set of buyers or with one buyer facing several suppliers. It can also be approached without a pre-established structure, the buyers and suppliers coming to a central exchange (Wu, 2004). In the case of one supplier, a possible solution could be the one of a discriminating monopolist that produces an amount such that its marginal revenue is equal to its marginal cost and allocates its production to clients with the highest marginal willingness to pay (Bulow and Roberts, 1989). The interested reader will find in Wu (2004) a very good review of the existing applications of bargaining theories to supply chain analysis.

This economic theory part of the logistic literature has contributed more formal analyses than concrete tools to logistics decision makers. However, as in classical market analysis, it provides a better understanding of concrete business arrangements for partnerships and contracting between agents in supply chains. As such, one may think that this type of analysis is, until now, more useful in providing a framework for assessing and regulating business practices than in giving practical advise to managers. This is another facet of the research in this field which may gain in importance in view of the globalization of economic activities. Indeed, the firms now can choose more freely the countries where they want to operate, but different countries have different laws and regulations to which they have to adapt. Nevertheless, large firms that have opportunities for setting or switching supply chains from one region to another may attempt to negotiate more favourable terms from local authorities.

CONCLUSIONS

This chapter has shown how wide is the scope of logistics in scientific literature and the practice of business firms. It is essentially a multidisciplinary subject which aims at solving practical organization problems. It can be extremely useful to business firms and public entities for efficiently organizing daily operations as well as for devising longer term strategies and policies. As such, it is not a field much open to speculation or rival theories. It is more like a toolbox where the practitioner may find ideas and techniques to solve some specific and concrete problems for the management of operations. The operations research part of the logistic literature illustrates that concern by proposing a large variety of techniques and models which address different business situations as well as problems of management organization and strategic positioning. In areas connected to transportation it meets questions such as how to organize inventories, deliveries and supply chains, where to locate production, distribution centers and terminals, whether to outsource production and services or keep them within the firm and so forth.

The organizational problems arising in business and public life are many and often specific. Some problems have been well worked out, but others still remain insufficiently investigated. Large-scale problems with many agents and/or many links in the supply chain are difficult and need more research. Problems of interaction between several production and supply chains also deserve more attention. Additional problems still emerge with new technologies as well as with changing economic and social circumstances. Over the last 20 years, internet and telecommunication facilities have opened up new vistas for restructuring management and setting up new schemes that link online a firm's supply chain to its market demand. Transport and logistic firms as well as analysts strongly responded to this evolving environment by proposing sophisticated analyses, powerful software and practical solutions. It has now become an important industry that will likely lead the way in the field, with the support of the scientific community. Given the multiple facets of logistic analysis, the reader is invited to gather more detailed information on his own specific concerns in some of the specialized review papers and books recommended as references.

REFERENCES

Anupindi, K., Y. Bassok and E. Zemel, 2002, A general framework for the study of decentralized distribution systems. *Manufacturing and Service Operations Management*, **3**, 349–368.

Ballis, A. and J. Golias, 2002a, Comparative evaluation of existing and innovative rail-road freight transport terminals. *Transportation Research Part A*, **36**, 593–611.

Ballis, A. and J. Golias, 2002b, Innovative transhipment in the combined transport sector in Europe: inventory and expert system approach. 81st Annual Meeting of Transportation Research Board, Washington DC, January 13–17.

Ballou, R.H., 1999, *Business Logistics Management: Planning, Organizing and Controlling the Supply Chain*. New York: Prentice-Hall.

Baumol, W.J. and H.D. Vinod, 1970, An inventory theoretic model of freight transport demand. *Mangement S*, **16** (7), 413–421.

Ben-Akiva, M., D. Bolduc and J.Q. Park, 2008, Discrete choice analysis of shippers' preferences. In M. Ben-Akiva, H. Meersman and E. Van de Voorde, eds, *Recent Developments in Transport Modeling*. Bingley, UK: Emerald Group Publishing Ltd., pp. 135–155.

Bertsimas, D.J., 1992, A vehicle routing problem with stochastic demand. *Operations Research*, **40**, 574–585.

Beuthe, M. and Ch. Bouffioux, 2008, Analyzing qualitative attributes of freight transport from stated orders of preference experiment. *Journal of Transport Economics and Policy*, **42**, Part 1, 105–128.

Beuthe M., Ch. Bouffioux, C. Krier and M. Mouchart, 2008, A comparison of conjoint, multi-criteria, conditional logit and neural network analyses for rank-ordered preference data. In M. Ben-Akiva, H. Meersman and E. Van de Voorde, eds, *Recent Developments in Transport Modelling*. Bingley, UK: Emerald Group Publishing Ltd., Ch. 9, 157–178.

Beuthe, M., F. Degrandsart, J.F. Geerts and B. Jourquin, 2002, External costs of the Belgian interurban freight traffic: a network analysis of their internalisation. *Transportation Research D*, **7**, 285–301.

Beuthe, M., 1972, A predictive model of regional demands for freight transportation. *Journal of Regional Science*, **12** (1), 85–93.

Blauwens, G. and E. Van de Voorde, 1988, The valuation of time savings in commodity transport. *International Journal of Transport Economics*, **15**, 77–87.

Blauwens, G., P. De Baere and E. Van de Voorde, 2002, *Transport Economics*. Antwerp: De Boeck.

Bontekoning, Y., C. Macharis and J. Tripp, 2004, Is a new applied transportation research field emerging? A review of intermodal rail-truck freight transport literature. *Transportation Research Part A*, **38**, 1–34.

Bostel, N., P. Dejax and Z. Lu, 2005, The design, planning and optimisation of reverse logistics networks. In A. Langevin and D. Riopel, eds, *Logistics Systems*. New York: Springer, Ch. 6, 171–212.

Brewer, A.M., K.J. Button and D.A. Hensher, eds, 2001, *Logistics and Supply-chain Management, Handbooks in Transport Economics*, Vol. 2. New York: Pergamon.

Bulow, J. and J. Roberts, 1989, The simple economics of optimal auctions. *Journal of Political Economy*, **97** (5), 1060–1090.

Cachon, G. and M. Larivière, 2001, Contracting to assure supply: how to share demand forecasts in a supply chain. *Management Science*, **47**, 629–646.

Cachon, G. and P.T. Harker, 2002, Competition and outsourcing with scale economies. *Management Science*, **48**, 1314–1333.

Cachon, G., 2004, The allocation of inventory risk in a supply chain: push, pull and advanced discount contracts. *Management Science*, **50** (2), 222–238.

Cachon, G. and S. Netessine, 2004, Game theory in supply chain analysis. In D. Simchi-Levi, S.D. Wu and Z.-J. Shen, eds, *Handbook of Quantitative Supply Chain Analysis*. Dordrecht, The Nedarlands: Kluwer Academic Publishers, Ch.2, pp. 13–59.

Campbell, J.F., 1994, Integer programming formulations of discrete hub location problems. *European Journal of Operational Research*, **72** (2), 387–405.

Chan, L.M.A., Z.J.M. Shen, D. Simchi-Levi and J.L. Swan, 2004, Coordination of pricing and inventory decisions. In D. Simchi-Levi, S. D. Wu and Z. -J. Shen, eds, *Handbook of Quantitative Supply Chain Analysis*. Dordrecht, The Nedarlands: Kluwer Academic Publishers, Ch. 9, pp. 335–392.

Christopher, M., 2005, *Logistics and Supply Chain Management*. London: FT Prentice Hall.

Cordeau, J.-F., M. Gendreau, A. Hertz, G. Laporte and J.-S. Sormany, 2005, New heuristics for the vehicle routing problem. In A. Langevin and D. Riopel, eds, *Logistics Systems: Design and Optimization*. New York: Springer, Ch. 9, pp. 279–297.

Crainic, T.G., M. Florian, J. Guélat and H. Spiess, 1990, Strategic planning of freight transportation: Stan, an interactive graphic system. *Transportation Research Record*, **1283**, 97–124.

Crainic, T.G., M. Gendreau and P. Dejax, 1993, Dynamic and stochastic models for the allocation of empty containers. *Operations Research*, **41**, 102–126.

Daganzo, C. F., 1999, *Logistics Systems Analysis*. Berlin: Springer.

Danielis, R., 2002, *Domand a di Transporto Merci e Preferenze Dichiarate/Freight Transport Demand and Stated Preference Experiments*. Milan: Franco Angeli.

De Jong, G., 2000, Value of freight travel-time saving. In D.A. Hensher and K.J. Button, eds, *Handbook of Transport Modelling*. Amsterdam: Pergamon pp. 553–564.

De Jong, G., M. Pieters, A. Daly, I. Graafland, E. Kroes and C. Koopmans, 2005, Using the Logsum as an evaluation measure. Working paper, Rand Europe, Leiden.

Desrosiers J., J. Dumas, M. Solomon and F. Soumis, 1995, Time constraint routing and scheduling. In M. Ball, T. Magnanti, C. Monma and G. Nemhauser, eds, *Handbooks in Operations Research and Management Science 8: Network Routing*. Amsterdam: Elsevier pp. 35–140.

Dijkstra, E.W., 1959, A note on two problems in connection with graphs. *Numerische Mathematik*, **1**, 269–271.

Dullaert W. and O. Bräysy, 2003, Heuristics for the contribution maximising vehicle routing problem with time windows. In W. Dullaert, B. Jourquin and J.B. Polak, eds, *Across the Border: Building Upon a Quarter Century of Transport Research in Benelux*. Antwerp, Belgium: De Boeck, pp. 111–130.

Ernst, A.T., H. Hamacher, H. Jiang, M. Krishnamoorthy and G. Woeginger, 2009, Uncapacitated single and multiple allocation p-hub center problems. *Computers/Operations Research*, **36**, 2230–2241.

Ertogal, K. and S.D. Wu, 2001, A bargaining game for supply chain contracting. Technical report, University of California, Berkeley, CA.

Fetter, R. and W.C. Dalleck, 1961, *Decision Models for Inventory Management*. Homewood, IL: Irwin.

Fleischmann, M., 2001, Quantitative models for reverse logistics. *Lecture Notes in Economics and Mathematical Systems*, **501**. Berlin: Springer.

Fowkes, T. and T. Whiteing, 2006, The value of freight travel time savings and reliability improvements: recent evidence from Great Britain. *Proceedings of the European Transport Conference*, 2006.

Frank, M. and P. Wolfe, 1956, An algorithm for quadratic programming. *Naval Research Logistics Quarterly*, **3**, 95–110.

Groothedde, B., 2005, Collaborative logistics and transportation networks. Ph.D. Thesis, Trail Research School, Technische Universiteit Delft.

Harker, P. T., 1987, *Predicting Intercity Freight Flows*, VNU Science Press.

Harris, F.W., 1915, How much stock to keep on hand. *Factory, The management magazine*, **10**, 240–284.

Hartman, B.C., M. Dror and M. Shaked , 2000, Cores of inventory centralization games. *Games and Economic Behavior*, **31**, 26–49.

Haughton, M.A., 1998, The performance of route modification and demand stabilization strategies in stochastic vehicle routing. *Transportation Research B*, **32** (8), 551–566.

HEATCO, 2004, Proposal for harmonised guidelines (Deliverable 5), IER.

Hillier, F.S. and G.J. Lieberman, 2005, *Introduction to Operations Research*, 8th edn, New York: McGraw-Hill.

Jeong, S.-J., C.-G. Lee and J.H. Bookbinder, 2007, The European freight railway system as a hub-and-spoke network. *Transportation Research Part A*, **41**, 523–536.

Jourquin, B. and M. Beuthe, 1996, Transportation policy analysis with a geographic information system: the virtual network of freight transportation in Europe. *Transportation Research C: Emerging Technologies*, **4** (6), 359–371.

Jourquin, B. and M. Beuthe, 2006, A decade of freight transport modelling with virtual networks: Acquired experiences and new challenges. In A. Reggiani and P. Nijkamp, eds, *Spatial Dynamics, Networks and Modelling*. Cheltenham, UK: Edward Elgar, pp. 181–200.

Jourquin, B., 2006, A multi-flow multi-modal assignment procedure on large freight transportation networks. *Studies in Regional Science*, **35**, 929–946.

Jourquin, B., 1995, Un outil d'analyse économique des transports de marchandises sur des réseaux multimodaux et multi-produits. Le réseau virtuel : concept méthodes et applications. Ph.D. Thesis, Fucam.

Konings, R., 2009, Intermodal Barge transport, network design, nodes and competitiveness. Ph.D. Thesis, TRAIL Research school, Technische Universiteit Delft.

Kotzab H., S. Seuring, M. Müller and G. Reiner, 2005, *Research Methodologies in Supply Chain Management*. Heidelberg: Physica-Verlag.

Koźlak A., 2009, Modern solutions in logistics. In J. Burnewicz, ed., *Innovative Perspective of Transport and Logistics*. Poland: University of Gdansk.

Kreps, D.M., 1990, *A Course in Microeconomic Theory*, New York: Princeton University Press.

Kurri, J., A. Sirkiä and J. Mikola, 2000, Value of time in freight transport in Finland. *Transportation Research Record*, **1725**, 26–30.

Lagneaux, F., 2008, Economic importance of Belgian transport logistics. Report of the National Bank of Belgium.

Langevin, A. and D. Riopel, 2005, *Logistics Systems, Design and Optimization*. Berlin: Springer.

Limbourg, S. and B. Jourquin, 2009a, Optimal rail-road container terminal locations on the European network. *Transportation Research Part E*, **45** (4), 551–563.

Limbourg, S. and B. Jourquin, 2009b, Market area of intermodal rail-road container terminals embedded in a hub-and-spoke network. *Papers in Regional Science*, DOI: 10.1111/j.1435-5957.2009.00255.x.

Little, J.D.C., K.G. Murty, D.W. Sweeney and C. Karel, 1963, An algorithm for the travelling salesman problem. *Operations Research*, **11**, 972–989.

Lu, Z., N. Bostel and P. Dejax, 2004, The simple plant location problem with reverse flows. In A. Dolgui, J. Soldeck and O. Zaikin, eds, *Supply Chain Optimisation*. Kluwer Academic Publishers, pp. 151–166.

Macharis, C., 2004, A methodology to evaluate potential locations for intermodal barge terminals: a policy decision support tool. In M. Beuthe, V. Himanem, A. Reggiani and L. Zamparini, eds, *Transport Developments and Innovations in an Evolving World*. Berlin: Springer, Ch. 11.

Maggi, R. and R. Rudel, 2008, The value of quality attributes in freight transport: evidence from an SP-experience in Switzerland. In M. Ben-Akiva, H. Meersman and E. Van de Voorde, *Recent Developments in Transport Modelling*. Bingley, UK: Emerald Group Publishing Ltd., Ch. 9, pp. 179–190.

Meixell, M.J. and V.B. Gargeya, 2005, Global supply chain design: a literature review and critique. *Transportation Research Part E*, **41** (6), 531–550.

Ministère des Transports, de l'Equipement, du Tourisme et de la Mer, 2006, Recommandations méthodologiques pour l'évaluation socio-économique des projets ferroviaires. Instruction ministérielle (projet), Direction Générale de la Mer et des Transports, mars.

Moore, E.F., 1957, The shortest path through a maze. *Proceedings of the International Symposium on Theory of Switching*, Part II, 285–292.

Muller, A., M. Scarsini and M. Shaked, 2002, The newsvendor game has a non-empty core. *Games and Economic Behavior*, **38**, 118–126.

Myerson, R.B., 1979, Incentive compatibility and the bargaining problem. *Econometrica*, **47** (1), 61–73.

Myerson, R.B. and Satterthwaite, 1983, Efficient mechanisms for bilateral trading. *Journal of Economic Theory*, **29** (2), 265–281.

Nagarajan, M. and Y. Bassok, 2002, A bargaining framework in supply chains: the assembly problem. Technical report, Marshall School of Business, University of Southern California, Los Angeles, CA.

Nash, C.A. and A.E. Whiteing, 1988, Mode choice: a total distribution cost approach. In L. Bianco and A. La Bella, eds, *Freight transport, Planning and Logistics, Lecture Notes in Economics and Mathematical Systems*, **317**, Berlin: Springer-Verlag, pp. 121–149.

Nash, J.F., 1950, The bargaining problem. *Econometrica*, **18**, 155–162.

Nash, J.F., 1953, Two-person cooperative games. *Econometrica*, **21**, 128–140.

Netessine, S. and N. Rudi, 2001a, Supply chain structures on the Internet and the role of marketing-operations interaction. In D. Simchi-Levi, S.D. Wu and Z.-J. Shen, eds, *Handbook of Quantitative Supply Chain Analysis*. Dordrecht, The Netherlands: Kluwer Academic Publishers, Ch. 14, pp. 607–642.

Netessine, S. and N. Rudi, 2001b, Supply chain choice on the Internet. Working paper, University of Pennsylvania. Available online: http://netessine.com.

Niérat, P., 1997, Market area of rail-truck terminals: pertinence of the spatial theory. *Transportation Research Part A*, **31** (2), 109–127.

O'Kelly, M., 1987, A quadratic integer program for the location of interaction hub facilities. *European Journal of Operational Research*, **32**, 393–404.

Ortuzar, J. and L. Willumsen, 2001, *Modelling Transport*. New York: Wiley.

Parlar, M., 1988, Game theoretic analysis of the substitutable product inventory problem with random demands. *Naval Research Logistics*, **35**, 397–409.

Perret, F.-L. and C. Jaffeux, 2002, *The Essentials of Logistics and Management*. Lausanne, Switzerland: Presses Polytechniques et Universitaires Romandes.

Porter, M.E., 1985, *Competitive Advantage*. New York: The Free Press.

Porteus, E.L., 1985, Investing in reduced setups in the eoq model. *Management Science*, **31**, 998–1010.

Potvin, J.Y. and J.M. Rousseau, 1993, A parallel route building algorithm for the vehicle routing and scheduling problem with time windows. *European Journal of Operational Research*, **66**, 331–340.

Prasad, S. and S. Babbar, 2000, International purchasing, inventory and logistics: an assessment and agenda. *International Journal of Operations & Production Management*, **18** (198), 6–37.

Quinet, E. and R. Vickerman, 2004, *Principles of Transport Economics*. Cheltenham, UK: Edward Elgar.

Raa, B., 2006, Models and algorithms for the cyclic inventory routing problem. Ph.D. Thesis, University of Gent.

Rubinstein, A., 1982, Perfect equilibrium in a bargaining model. *Econometrica*, **50**, 97–109.

Shapley, L., 1953, A value for n-person game. In H.W. Kuhn and A.W. Tucker, eds, *Contributions to the Theory of Games*, Volume II. Princeton, NJ: Princeton University Press, pp. 307–317.

Solomon, M., 1987, Algorithms for vehicle routing and scheduling problem with time window constraints. *Operations Research*, **35** (2), 254–265.

Ståhl, I., 1972, *Bargaining Theory*. Stockholm: Stockholm Research Institute, Stockholm School of Economics.

Stratec, 2007, Analyse détaillée des perspectives de trafics fluviaux. Etudes d'avant-projet du Canal Seine-Nord Europe, Voies Navigables de France.

Vernimmen, B. and F. Witlox, 2001, Using an inventory theoretic approach for modal choice: a case study. Working paper 1169/030, Faculty of Applied Economics UFSIA-RUCA, University of Antwerp.

Voss, S. and D.L. Woodruff, 2003, *Introduction to Computational Optimization Models for Production Planning in a Supply Chain*. Berlin: Springer.

Waters, C.D.J., 1989, Vehicle-scheduling problems with uncertainty and omitted customers. *European Journal of the Operational Research Society*, **40**, 1099–1108.

Whitin, T.M., 1953, *The Theory of Inventory Management*. Princeton, NJ: Princeton University Press.

Winston, C., 1985, Conceptual developments in the economics of transportation: an interpretative survey. *Journal of Economic Literature*, **23**, 57–94.

Wu, S.D., 2004, Supply chain intermediation: a bargaining theoretic framework. In D. Simchi-Levi, S.D. Wu and Z.-J. Shen, eds, *Handbook of Quantitative Supply Chain Analysis*, Boston: Kluwer, Ch. 3, pp. 67–115.

Zamparini, L. and A. Reggiani, 2007, Freight transport and the value of travel time savings: a meta-analysis of empirical studies. *Transport Reviews*, **27** (5), 621–636.

Zinn, W., H. Marmorstein and J. Charnes, 1992, The effect of auto-correlated demand on customer service. *Journal of Business Logistics*, **13** (1), 173–192.

PART III

THE COST OF TRANSPORT

12 Cost functions for transport firms

Leonardo J. Basso, Sergio R. Jara-Díaz and
William G. Waters II

INTRODUCTION

There are various components of the total costs of transport: (1) the costs of infrastructure; (2) costs incurred by transport operators; (3) costs borne directly by users (e.g., time and inconvenience costs); and (4) costs borne by society generally (such as pollution and environmental impacts). The primary focus of this chapter is on the second category – the costs incurred by transport operating companies – and on the fundamental economic concept of a transport cost function and how to estimate it, that is, the challenge of empirical measurement of the costs of outputs that are complex and diverse. Characteristics of the other cost components are reviewed in Quinet and Vickerman (2004, Chapters 4 and 5) and the chapter by Berechman et al.

While the focus here is on the costs incurred by operators (item 2 above), there may be interrelationships with other cost components. For example, in the case of railways, some or all infrastructure is supplied by transport operators, and there are interrelationships between infrastructure and operating decisions, for example, the quality of infrastructure can reduce operating costs, and/or operating practices such as speed and size of load can affect infrastructure costs. There can also be a connection between transport operator costs and collective user costs such as waiting times (item 3 above). Nonetheless, operators do attempt to optimize production and costs of whatever they are responsible for and, therefore, it is valid to focus on the theory and empirical estimation of transport operator costs.

The emphasis of this chapter is on the common challenges and methods of analysis across modes rather than dwelling on mode-specific issues. Although we include examples of cost functions for various modes and locations, comprehensive coverage of modes, and freight and passenger operations are not objectives per se. Instead, this chapter focuses on the most recent advances in theoretical and empirical analysis of transport firms and their policy implications whatever the mode and services provided.

The plan of the chapter is as follows. First we review the origins and purpose of transport cost analysis. In the following section, the complexity of transport production and costs is reviewed and some key multioutput concepts are introduced. We discuss in detail what transport output is, and how economies of scale and scope show up in a transport network. We then shift focus from theory to practice and summarize the main issues and findings in empirical cost functions with an emphasis on the concepts of economies of scale and density as usually used in the transport cost functions literature. Because, in many cases, the conclusions on industry structure from empirical studies were not completely satisfactory, in that observed and predicted behavior did not really match, a number of authors in the last 15 years have proposed various methodological improvements. We take on these re-assessments in the penultimate section of the chapter. The final section contains our concluding remarks.

TRANSPORT COST ANALYSIS: ORIGINS AND PURPOSE

The reasons for developing cost functions are varied and have changed over time. The origins of empirical analysis of transport costs were for railways, and began early in the twentieth century (Waters, 2007). Railways provided a multitude of services, to/from many origins and destinations and incurred a variety of costs, at different times and for various durations of time. There was almost no ability to link the various costs incurred with specific services provided. As a result, prices charged were unrelated to costs. This posed problems to firms that wanted to know where they made and lost money, and it was a mystery to economists who could not relate prices to marginal costs and assess the workings of markets. Railway rate theory became one of the dominant areas of study in economics during the 1890s and into the twentieth century. In the same era, fears of rail monopoly power became the stimulus for public control of railways: regulation in North America or public ownership as in many European countries. US regulation required that rail companies file statistics about operations as well as costs incurred. These data would provide the raw material for the first empirical analyses linking costs to production (Clark, 1923; Lorenz, 1916).

There were several purposes for the cost analyses, including both broad characteristics, such as the extent of scale economies, as well as micro interests in determining the costs of individual services. The fundamental premise of regulation (or public ownership) of railways (and public utilities) was the belief that there were substantial economies of scale. Monopoly was the likely market structure with the attendant ability to charge high and discriminatory prices. Further, if competition were to emerge, it would be unstable, pricing at or near marginal costs would lead to financial ruin or survival of the strongest firm. Public control was deemed necessary for transport and utilities, and this belief would persist through the first half of the twentieth century and be extended to other modes of transport as they emerged.

Perhaps the earliest empirical analysis is that of Lorenz (1916). He used data for American railroads and plotted total costs per mile of track versus total ton-miles per mile of track. A downward slope with increased size was taken as evidence of economies of scale. In retrospect, dividing the data by miles of track made the formulation an indicator of economies of greater density of operation, but not necessarily economies of scale; more on this momentarily. The first econometric analyses of cost functions emerged in the 1950s and they found scale economies to be modest or non-existent. This undermined the traditional rationale for regulation (for example, Meyer et al., 1959). Further, not only did analysis of the costs of rail and other modes show scale economies were not important, they showed that regulation was driving up costs. These studies provided significant intellectual support for the deregulation movement that arose in the 1970s and spread through much of the developed world.[1]

On the other hand, significant advances were made on the theoretical side. By the early 1980s, a large new body of knowledge was available: multioutput theory (Baumol et al., 1982). This theory helped to understand more clearly what natural monopolies are, and how and when it would be efficient for a firm to increase its size. Of particular importance was the fact that, for the first time, there was a clear distinction between two ways of increasing *size*: producing more of the current products (economies of scale), or producing a larger set of products (economies of scope). Moreover, multioutput theory generalized and formalized concepts such as marginal cost and incremental costs. These were central to establishing a relation between costs and optimal or second-best pricing of various outputs that are jointly produced (Baumol et al., 1962, discussed the relation between prices and incremental costs; Baumol and Bradford, 1970, the relation between marginal costs and prices when there were shared revenue burdens such as covering over-head costs or required budgetary surpluses).

Nowadays, the estimation of transport cost functions, using fairly sophisticated econometric techniques and with a heavy mode-specific emphasis, is a quite common task. There is still a desire by transport operators and/or regulators to have estimates of the costs of services to compare with prices charged. There are public policy interests in broad characteristics of transport industries such as determining the extent of economies of scale, scope and density. These have implications for the working of competitive forces, and the implications of mergers and possible regulatory actions. Both firms and the public are interested in performance comparisons across companies, over time and across regulatory regimes. A recent interest is in possible interdependencies between the costs of operations and infrastructure. This has arisen in contemplating proposals to separate rail operations from infrastructure provision, but similar issues arise in other modes with implications for the type and extent of public intervention in the industry (for an early discussion of this subject, see Bailey and Friedlaender, 1982).

The flip side of a fuller theory, advanced econometric techniques and a focus on specific modes, is that the interpretation of the estimated cost functions has become more complex. This is so because different authors often employed different definitions of output (both across and within industries), and/or different data sets, which lead to differences in results. The underlying problem is that any definition of output employed is, necessarily, an aggregation of true outputs, and there often is confusion or lack of clarity about what exactly is being measured.

Finally, we close this introductory section by noting that there is another, pragmatic, approach to unit cost estimation, which we will not discuss. This is a method used by transport operators to develop cost estimates for specific services. This approach originated in railways but has been adopted in other modes and industries. There are a number of routine and repetitive activities in the ongoing operations of a transport firm: rail cars must be loaded and unloaded, wagons switched, trains run, engines and wagons maintained, track maintained, billing, marketing and so forth. Various expense categories can be linked to the various activities more easily than expenditures can be linked to final service outputs supplied/demanded. Expense categories are linked to measures of various activities, sometimes by direct accounting allocation but often using regression analysis on data across firms, regions within a firm and/or time periods. Cost coefficients are produced for the various intermediate activities. Then, an estimate of the cost of providing a specific service (output) can be constructed by itemizing the various work activities required to supply that service and multiplying the unit cost for each. This is known as 'activity-based costing.' There are econometric problems with this approach. It must assume that each activity and its costs are separable from all the others, which is unlikely; and usually only simple linear regressions are used. But apparently practitioners are satisfied that the disaggregation into activity components is sufficient for their purposes, and improved estimation procedures have not received much study.[2]

TRANSPORT COST FUNCTIONS: THEORY

A cost function $C(w, Y)$ represents the minimum expense necessary to produce an output Y at given input prices w. When there is only one output – as the 'widgets' per unit of time discussed in elementary economics texts – and hence Y is a scalar, it is easy to derive analytically and graphically the well-known results of marginal cost pricing in the first best case, and average cost pricing in the second-best (that is, cost recovery under scale economies). Transport output, however, is more complex than the output of most other industries as it involves a large number of different services supplied simultaneously in both spatial and temporal dimensions. And since historically there has been an interest in having cost-determined prices, understanding costs of production of transport services has become a persistent and central theme of debate and discussion in transport economics.

The original problem was to relate the price of the different services to the costs of production when some expenses are shared by many outputs. These shared expenses give rise to concepts such as joint, common, indivisible and overhead costs (see, for example, Baumol et al., 1962; Clark, 1923; Kahn, 1970), and there were decades of debate about how to allocate them to the many different outputs in order to then choose prices. Multioutput theory (Baumol et al., 1982) helped to solve the problem by formalizing the concepts of marginal and incremental cost when a firm produces more than one output and some of the expenses may be shared.[3] If a multioutput cost function $C(w, Y)$ is well specified – then the marginal cost of an output y_i is the partial derivative of C with respect to y_i and it represents the cost of (marginally) increasing production of that output keeping everything else constant. In general, then, the marginal cost of one output will depend on production levels of all other outputs. The incremental cost of an output or any subset of outputs of interest is simply the difference between the cost function evaluated at the full output Y and the function when all products in the corresponding subset are zero. Note that the incremental cost will also depend – in general – on the production level of all outputs.

Pricing of interrelated outputs – be that for the first-best case, or any second-best case – will usually require simultaneous solution of the interrelated markets, that is, combining the multiple output cost function with the multiple demands. Thus, rather than ex-ante allocation of joint and/or overhead costs to outputs, these costs will be implicitly allocated to different consumer groups once a pricing rule is chosen. Since this chapter focuses on the properties and interpretation of the cost function (such as economies of scale and scope) and not the cost–demand interrelationships, pricing is not discussed further. Accordingly, we begin our discussion with a formulation of this modern, that is multioutput, theoretical approach to transport output and production.

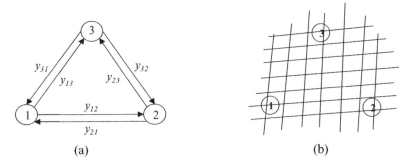

Figure 12.1   Origin–destination demand structure (a) and physical network (b)

Transport Output and Cost Functions

The output of a transport firm is a vector of flows of the form $Y = \{y_{ijkt}\}$ between many origin-destination pairs ij, disaggregated by the type of cargo k and period t (Braeutigam, 1999; Jara-Díaz, 1982a, b; Winston, 1985). In order to produce a flow vector Y, the firm has to take a number of decisions: number and capacity of vehicles (fleet size), design of the ways (location, capacity), design of terminals (location, loading and unloading capacities), frequencies, and so on. Some decisions involve choices about the characteristics of inputs, while others are related to their use, that is, to the way in which inputs are combined in order to produce the flow vector; we shall call the latter type of decisions 'operation rules'. Since transport takes place on a network, the firm also has to choose a *service structure* – the generic way in which vehicles visit the nodes in order to produce the flows – and a link sequence. Together, these two decisions define a *route structure*, which is to be chosen given the *origin–destination (OD) structure of demand* (defined by vector Y), and the *physical network* (Jara-Díaz and Basso, 2003). It is important to note that, in the end, the route structure decision is a consequence of the spatial dimension of transport output.

To illustrate these concepts, consider a three nodes OD system as in Figure 12.1a, together with a physical network as in Figure 12.1b, and let us keep only the spatial dimension of output, that is, transport product is a vector of components $\{y_{ij}\}$. For this given vector, the best combination of inputs and operation rules will depend on many factors. Three possible service structures are shown in Figure 12.2. Structure (a) corresponds to a general cyclical system (Gálvez, 1978), structure (b) to three simple cyclical systems (point-to-point service), and structure (c) to hub-and-spoke, where a distribution node – the hub – has been created (a structure which is pervasive in the airlines industry). Regarding the allocation of vehicles to fleets – one of the components of a service structure – in case (a) there can only be one fleet (and therefore only one frequency), while in cases (b) and (c) there may be up to three different fleets. If the service structure chosen is as in Figure 12.2a, a possible route structure is the one shown in Figure 12.3.

In general, the transformation of inputs X into outputs Y may be conceptually represented through a transformation function $F(X, Y) \geq 0$, which shows all combinations of outputs Y that are feasible to be produced with inputs X. Equality represents an efficient use of inputs and $F(X, Y) = 0$ is the production-possibility frontier. If the vector of

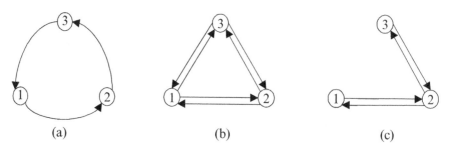

Figure 12.2   Service structures: (a) cyclical system, (b) point-to-point, (c) hub-and-spoke

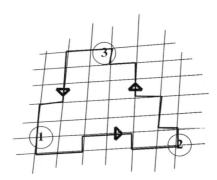

Figure 12.3   A route structure for the cyclical structure

input prices is w and a firm minimizes its expenses subject to $F(X, Y^0) = 0$, it obtains the cost function $C(w, Y^0)$ which represents the minimum expenditure necessary to produce a given output vector Y^0 at input prices w.

As explained earlier, in the case of transport Y is a vector of flows and the decisions of a transport firm are three: quantity and characteristics of the inputs, operating rules and route structure. Given the discrete nature of this latter decision, the underlying cost minimizing process may be seen as a sequence with three stages (Jara-Díaz and Basso, 2003). First, for a given route structure the firm optimizes inputs and operating rules. This leads to establishing the production-possibility frontier (technical optimality). For example, for the simplest multi-output case possible (a back-haul system with two nodes), the frontier

$$y_{ji} = \frac{\mu B}{2} - \left[\left(\frac{d_{12} + d_{21}}{v} \right) \frac{\mu}{2K} + 1 \right] y_{ij},$$

with $y_{ij} > y_{ji}$, $i, j = 1, 2$, $i \neq j$,

represents all vectors (y_{12}, y_{21}) that can be produced efficiently using loading/unloading sites of capacity μ, with B vehicles of capacity K circulating at a speed v on a simple network where d_{ij} is the distance between i and j (Jara-Díaz, 2000).[4]

Below this frontier all combinations (y_{12}, y_{21}) that are technically feasible can be found. Similar frontiers can be found for each route structure possible when there are more than two nodes. Given these frontiers, in the second stage input prices are considered and expenses are minimized. This leads to *conditional cost functions* that give the minimum cost necessary to produce output Y for given route structures. For example, consider a three nodes system (that is, six OD flows) and a hub-and-spoke route structure with the hub in node 2 and one fleet.[5] Jara-Díaz and Basso (2003) found that if link 1–2 carries the largest load (given by $y_{12}+y_{13}$), the conditional cost function would be:

$$C_{HS}(Y) = C_0 + (y_{12} + y_{13}) \cdot (d_{12} + d_{23} + d_{32} + d_{21}) \cdot \Lambda$$

$$+ (y_{12} + y_{13} + y_{32} + y_{21} + y_{31} + y_{23}) \cdot \Omega, \qquad (12.1)$$

with $\Lambda = \left[\dfrac{P_K + w\varepsilon}{vK} + \dfrac{P_g g}{K} \right]$ and $\Omega = \left[\dfrac{2}{\mu}(P_K + w\varepsilon) + \dfrac{2P_S}{\mu} \right]$,

where d_{ij} is the distance between i and j, g is vehicle fuel consumption per kilometer, ε is the number of people required to operate a vehicle, P_S is the expense per hour to operate a loading/unloading site, w is the wage rate, P_g is fuel price, and P_K and P_μ are price per hour of a vehicle of capacity K and a loading/unloading site of capacity μ, respectively (either rental prices or depreciation).

Equation (12.1) shows that it is indeed possible to obtain a transport cost function starting from the technology, and that this function will indeed depend on the prices of the many inputs a transport firm uses and on the vector of OD flows. Furthermore, it is interesting to see in Equation (12.1) the way in which Y enters the cost function. On one hand, there is a pure flow term capturing the expenses that occur while vehicles are not in motion, that is, those due to terminal operations (as evident through Ω); on the other hand, there is a flow-distance term, capturing route expenses (evidently reflected by Λ). From Equation (12.1) it is straightforward to obtain measures of marginal costs; something interesting to note is that only for those flows that determine frequency will marginal costs be related to in-route expenses.

The third and last stage of the cost minimizing process consists of comparing the conditional cost functions, corresponding to alternative route structures, in order to select the route structure that implies the smallest cost to produce Y. By choosing the cost minimizing route structure for any possible value of Y one obtains the global cost function.

Economies of Scale and Scope

Now, as discussed before, the reasons for studying transport cost functions are manyfold but, undoubtedly, one of the main reasons is that from cost functions one can obtain important information regarding economies of scale and scope of firms. These are intimately related to industry structure and the existence of natural monopoly (Baumol et al., 1982) and hence to the possible success or failure of competition in the industry. The multioutput degree of economies of scale, S, measures the rate of change in cost when there is a small and equiproportional expansion of Y (Panzar and Willig, 1977). Formally $C(w, \lambda Y) = \lambda^{1/S} C(w, Y)$ with $\lambda > 1$. A value of S larger, equal or smaller than 1 implies that costs increase in a smaller, the same, or a larger proportion than the output respectively: it is then said that there are increasing, constant or decreasing returns to scale, respectively. Omitting input prices for notational simplicity, S can be calculated from C as,

$$S = \frac{C(Y)}{\sum_i y_i \frac{\partial C}{\partial y_i}} = \frac{1}{\sum_i \eta_i},$$

(12.2)

where η_i is the elasticity of C with respect to the i-th output. Applying this definition to the case of transport, the degree of economies of scale will depend on the operational re-organization that the firm may achieve, after proportional increases of the flow vector. For example, if the flows are small and similar, the OD structure of Figure 12.1a may be well served with small vehicles and a service structure as in Figure 12.2a or 12.2b. If flows were larger, service structures such as Figure 12.2c may become more attractive. Hence, not only are the number and size of inputs relevant, but also the spatial re-design of service. What is important to note here is that the firm chooses its route structure, which is indeed not assumed as fixed in Equation (12.2).

Economies of scale analyze what happens with cost if the output being produced is increased equiproportionally. If one wants to study the advantage or disadvantage of producing different products, then one should use a different concept: economies of scope (Panzar and Willig, 1981). Economies of scope exist if

$$SC_A = SC_B = \frac{C(Y^A) + C(Y^B) - C(Y^D)}{C(Y^D)}$$

(12.3)

is positive, where D is the set of all outputs, $A \cup B = D$ and $A \cap B = \emptyset$ (that is, A and B are an orthogonal partition of D). Y^A is vector Y^D but with $y_i = 0, \forall i \notin A \subset D$; Y^B is defined analogously. Therefore, a negative value for SC_A indicates that it is cheaper to have a second firm producing Y^B, rather than to expand the production line of a firm already producing Y^A. If SC_A is positive, then it is cheaper that a single firm produces everything (Y^D). It is easy to verify that SC should lie in the $[-1; 1]$ interval.

Recalling that in transport the output vector is $Y = \{y_{ijkt}\}$, it is possible to distinguish three types of economies of scope: economies of scope per period of service, economies of scope for type of cargo (these are the ones usually recognized in the literature) and economies of spatial scope, where the expansion of the line of production implies serving new OD pairs. Therefore, in transport, economies of *spatial* scope are analyzed in a context in which *the size of the network* – understood as the OD structure – changes. This does not happen with S. Hence, SC enables one to examine whether it is cheaper for a firm A, that serves PS^A nodes and potentially $PS^A \cdot (PS^A - 1)$ OD flows, to expand its network to PS^D nodes – serving $PS^D \cdot (PS^D - 1) - PS^A \cdot (PS^A - 1)$ new flows – or if it is cheaper for another firm to do it. If firm D produces on the OD structure of Figure 12.1a, a possible partition is the one shown in Figure 12.4 (Jara-Díaz et al., 2001). Note that analyzing this type of economies of (spatial) scope is equivalent to analyzing an increase in one node of firm A's network.

In synthesis, and emphasizing the spatial dimension of output in the transport case, with S one analyzes the behavior of costs after an equiproportional expansion of the OD

(A)
$Y^A = \{y_{12}; y_{21}; 0; 0; 0; 0\}$

(B)
$Y^B = \{0; 0; y_{13}; y_{31}; y_{23}; y_{32}\}$

(D)
$Y^D = \{y_{12}; y_{21}; y_{13}; y_{31}; y_{23}; y_{32}\}$

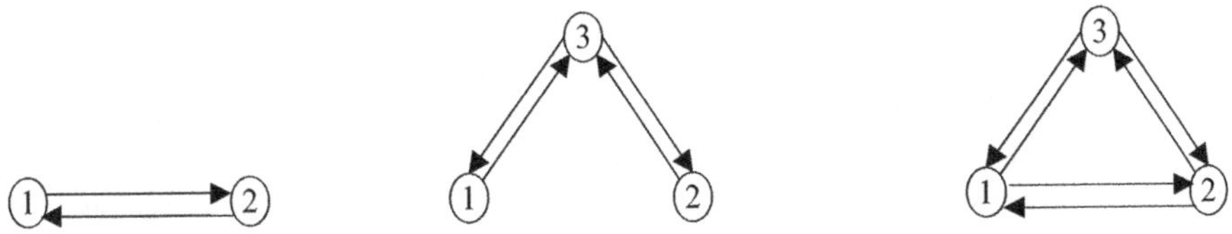

Figure 12.4   A possible orthogonal partition to analyze economies of spatial scope

flows keeping the number of OD pairs constant, while with *SC* one analyzes the behavior of cost when new OD pairs are added.

Technical Efficiency and Cost Functions

Before moving from theory to practice, it is important to comment on the assumption behind a cost function that technical efficiency is achieved: that is, that the firm will minimize the expenses incurred in producing a given output vector Y. There are several reasons why firms may not minimize costs; these have impacts on estimation procedures. One of these reasons is competition and elastic demand: Oum et al. (1995) showed that if airlines face competition or threat of entry, they may offer hub-and-spoke route structures even though it may be cheaper to use point-to-point route structures. Using the nomenclature from this chapter even though the point-to-point conditional cost function is below the hub-and-spoke conditional cost function, airlines choose a hub-and-spoke route structure, *failing* at the third stage of the process. This happens because, with competition and elastic demand, the route structure choice of a firm influences not only its own costs and demand but also the other firms' profit function. The process may be as follows: imagine that the average cost per passenger in a direct connection decreases as traffic increases (for example, because of economies of aircraft size); then by choosing a hub-and-spoke route structure an airline would be able to increase the traffic in the (fewer) direct connections it now serves decreasing its expenses and thus being able to offer lower prices. This will increase its own demand at the expense of the other airline; thus, an airline behaving strategically may choose a hubbing strategy as a means to be aggressive against a competitor or a potential entrant, even though hubbing does not minimize cost.[6]

A second reason why firms may not achieve technical efficiency has to do with regulated services in an asymmetric information environment. In a nutshell, the problem is that of a principal – agent framework in which a regulator asks a transport firm to produce output Y in exchange for some reimbursement, but the network operator has private information about its technology and its cost reducing effort cannot be observed by the authority. In this setting, the regulatory schemes, that is, the type of contract between the regulator and the operator affects the input allocation and cost reducing effort of the latter. In layman's terms, the operators can be lazy or careless and costs increased without being detected by regulators. This problem is obviously not specific to transport – it is a more general problem with regulation – but it has begun to be addressed in transport contexts (see, for example, Gagnépain and Ivaldi, 2002a, b; Piacenza, 2006).

TRANSPORT COST FUNCTIONS: EMPIRICAL ESTIMATION

Early empirical transport cost analyses were cited above, and there are several thorough reviews of this literature, notably Jara-Díaz (1982a) and Oum and Waters (1996); see also Braeutigam (1999), Jara-Díaz (2007) and Pels and Rietveld (2008). This present review is limited to the most recent advances and issues in transport cost estimation. We do not review what is probably the most significant empirical advance, now well established and routine: the formulation of flexible functional forms, which are much more subtle and powerful representations of cost output relationships, in contrast to the early use of simple linear regressions.[7] But a few other empirical issues warrant attention. We first review the need for aggregation of the multiple and diverse outputs in transport. Next are problems associated with fixed or quasi-fixed inputs (notably capital) and their implications for estimating cost functions. Third are issues arising in efficiency comparisons along with the use of frontier estimation techniques. Then, having reviewed how transport cost functions are specified and estimated, we move on to their use and interpretation of scale indices.

Output Aggregation

Both the number of commodities or passengers served as well as the number of OD pairs served are usually huge and therefore output aggregation is necessary in most cases for the econometric estimation of cost functions. Both the strict definition of transport output discussed in the previous section and the need for aggregation have been frequently recognized in the literature.[8]

Many aggregate measures of output have been used in applied work. Some of these indicators have been passenger-kilometers, revenue passengers, seat-kilometers, vehicle-kilometers, ton-kilometers, total tons and number of shipments. But, given that transport occurs in different networks, and under different conditions for different firms, researchers have, additionally, used what has been called 'attributes' in an effort to better capture the conditions under which transport takes place. Some of the attributes that have been used are: average shipment size, average load factor, average length of haul, length of trip, capacity utilization, percentage of less-than-truckload services and so on. Finally, starting in the mid-eighties, network size and network shape variables have been considered; examples are number of route miles, number of points served and some other indicators of network complexity (Filippini and Maggi, 1992). Many reviews and text books provide summaries, by mode, of the products, attributes and network size variables used in the empirical literature; we refer the readers to these articles for specific details (Braeutigam, 1999; Jara-Díaz, 2000, 2007; Jara-Díaz and Cortés, 1996; Oum and Waters, 1996; Pels and Rietveld; 2008).

It is quite natural that, in this context of aggregation and where many different possible output measures are available, the question of which output measures to use would arise. In fact, a discussion that has captured some attention from transport economists (see, for example, Berechman, 1993 or Small and Verhoef, 2007) is whether the analyst should use *final* or *demand-oriented* measures of output, such as passenger- or ton-kilometers, or she should use *intermediate* or *supply-oriented* measures of output, such as seat-kilometers or vehicle-kilometers. According to some authors, whether one should use final or intermediate measures of output will depend upon the purpose of the analysis. A study of the technical efficiency of firms' production would use intermediate outputs, whereas a study of the effectiveness of the firms' service offerings and marketing policies would use final outputs (Small and Verhoef, 2007). The authors that have defended the use of intermediate output measures have argued that, unlike demand-oriented outputs, supply-oriented indicators are, to a larger extent, under the control of operators; the latter are, in reality, the decision variables of transport companies. Yet, as De Borger et al. (2002) argue in the case of transit services, 'since passengers or passenger-km at least partially capture the economic motive for providing the services, demand-oriented output measures must indeed be relevant. After all, if one ignores demand altogether, then the most cost efficient and productive bus operators may be the ones not servicing any passengers.' In the end, the crux of the matter is that implicit in the definition of a cost function for producing *final* outputs is a decision rule for choosing *intermediate* outputs (Small and Verhoef, 2007). This is most clear in Jara-Diaz and Basso (2003), where conditional cost functions were obtained from the technology, starting with the disaggregated output description $Y = \{y_{ij}\}$. One of such cost functions was presented in Equation (12.1). There, it is fairly clear that, at the end, one can write that cost function as depending on two aggregate output measures: the number of seat-km or available ton-km (term that multiplies L), and the number of total passengers or tons (term that multiplies W). The first one is a supply-oriented measure, the second one a demand-oriented measure. The lessons from this are two-fold: first, that indeed in the end firms' expenses are related to supply-oriented measures of output, but this comes from the fact that a certain demand had to be served. Second, that if one is to use aggregate measures in empirical work, it is extremely important to consider not only flow times distance measures, as it is most common, but also pure flow measures since these are the ones capturing terminal expenses.

Although it is not an output, another variable included in any cost regression that involves data over time is a time trend, which is used to estimate any shifts in the cost function over time. It is expected to be negative as any productivity gains imply a downward shift in the cost function.[9]

Disequilibria in Input Use

An ongoing set of issues concerns the treatment and interpretation of inputs that might not be sufficiently variable in a firm's cost function, primarily capital inputs. Theory assumes that firms will combine inputs efficiently for producing any specified output. But some inputs, notably capital, might not be varied except at periodic intervals. The typical data point for cost function analysis is the annual costs and output of a firm. Although many inputs can be adjusted within a year, in practice, planned outputs might be changing during a year, and some input use will be in disequilibrium. Ignoring this disequilibrium can be a source of error and bias in cost function estimation. This problem arises particularly in the case of railways because, unlike other modes, railways generally are responsible for infrastructure investments which are long lived 'lumpy' capital investments.

One approach to lumpy non-variable capital was to postulate a short run cost function (for example, Caves et al., 1981). This approach omits the price of capital from the cost function formulation (since it is assumed that capital cannot be varied in response to its price) and includes a measure of capital stock in the regression. A long-run function can be constructed as an envelope of the sum of the variable cost function plus the costs of fixed capital. (Other examples of this approach are Caves et al., 1984; Friedlaender et al., 1993; and Gillen et al., 1985, 1990). An alternate approach is to impute some measure of capital utilization into the cost function, that is, to use capital utilization rates as a proxy for the consumption of capital (for example, Friedlaender et al., 1993). However, this approach imposed implicit restrictions on the assumed functional form of production technology. Oum and Zhang (1991) showed that some implausible results follow from this approach and introduced a modification which corrected it.

A recent issue is the growing interest in separating rail operations from track infrastructure. By separating costs components related to way and track from those of operations, Bitzan (2000, 2003) estimated a quasi-fixed cost function and found that there were cost complementarities between the two cost categories. Similar results were found by Ivaldi and McCullough (2004, 2007).

Data Anomalies

Scarcity of data means that many empirical cost functions must make use of combined data across firms and over time. But there are risks of hidden anomalies associated with specific firms (for example, unknown sources of efficiency or inefficiency) and/or years (for example, boom years that result in temporarily high output with unusual impacts on costs). It has become customary to employ dummy variables of zero or one, the latter value for data points for a specific firm or year. This has the effect of measuring the average deviation from the regression surface of that family of observations (the specific firm or year) that is not modeled by the other variables in the regression. For example, if a particular year is a boom year accompanied by unusually high outputs without the usual increases in costs, the year dummy would capture this anomaly and the data for that year would be implicitly adjusted to more accurately reflect the primary cost-output relationships that are being estimated.

It should be noted that the inclusion of firm dummies can require some care in whether or not to use them. There could be correlation between key variables which are being estimated – such as economies of scale – and data for specific firms. Suppose a particular firm is much larger than others and also more efficient, perhaps due to economies of scale. The dummy variable for that firm might be capturing part of what should have been measured as scale economies. Caves et al. (1987) point out this potential problem of dummy variables (see also Oum and Yu, 1995).

Another potential data problem is prices of inputs and/or outputs. Any least squares procedure assumes that output and input prices are exogenous. In the literature, authors have usually claimed that output is exogenous because firms are regulated, yet this reason is becoming less and less valid following substantial deregulation in many transport markets. In this case, instrumental variables may be used to account for endogeneity of the regressors or, alternatively, the cost function may be estimated together with the equilibrium of the market. These, however, are not yet standard procedures in the literature.

Frontier Estimation Techniques

The statistical technique of regression analysis estimates a function that accepts both positive and negative deviations from data points. One could say that the function represents some sort of *average* of the data points. But, particularly for evaluating the relative performance of firms, arguably the comparisons should be based on some measure of best performance rather than comparisons with average firms; after all, a cost function is theoretically a frontier since it represents the minimum expense necessary to produce a level of output given input prices. This has given rise to various frontier estimation techniques to form the basis of comparison among the data points. A programming approach is to identify the surface defined by the data points of lowest costs for various values of the arguments in the cost function. Data Envelopment Analysis (DEA) is an example of this approach. However, defining a frontier with specific data points means the efficiency frontier and performance measures are sensitive to data outliers and/or errors in boundary data points. More typically, frontier estimation uses econometric techniques where the assumed distribution of errors are asymmetric and, usually, separable in a term that is symmetric, and another representing inefficiency, that is, a departure from the (stochastic) frontier. Various assumptions can and have been made about error terms and their distribution. Yet, since frontier estimation is not a technique unique to transport, but rather it is a tool of analysis applicable to all fields of inquiry, we believe it is inappropriate to review transport applications in this chapter except to point out the attraction and importance of frontier estimation.[10]

We do want to close this subsection, though, with a comment regarding a recent development. As explained above, it has been usually argued that when transport services are regulated, the regressors will be exogenous since firms take output as given (defined by the regulator). Yet, according to Gagnépain and Ivaldi (2002a) even this may not be enough. They argue that informational asymmetries between the regulator and the monopoly affect the production process: managers may put more or less effort on cost reducing activities depending on the regulation mechanism, making the inefficiency term endogenous. Thus, they argue, asymmetric information models should provide a relevant framework for the estimation of cost frontiers. In fact, they propose a model – applied to urban bus services in France – that is able to elicit a structural relationship between observable variables and the inefficiency term, solving the endogeneity problem.

Returns to Scale and Density

Having reviewed briefly how transport cost functions are specified and estimated, we can now move on to their use and interpretation. In what follows we will call vector Y the *true transport product*, as a way to distinguish it from the vector of aggregates, which we will denote by $\tilde{Y} = \{\tilde{y}_1, .., \tilde{y}_h, .., \tilde{y}_V\}$. In the latter we will include both output and attribute measures and use N to denote variables related to network size. So, let us consider now an estimated cost function $\tilde{C}(\tilde{Y}; N)$, where input prices are suppressed for simplicity. After Caves et al. (1984), it became customary to analyze transport industry structure using two indices: economies of density, *RTD*, and economies of scale with variable network size, *RTS*.[11] As summarized by Oum and Waters (1996), *RTD* refers to the impact on average cost of expanding all traffic, holding network size constant (that is, an increase in the density of traffic), whereas *RTS* refers to the impact on average cost of equi-proportionate increases in traffic and network size. Analytically:

$$RTD = \frac{1}{\sum_{h \in H} \tilde{\eta}_h} \tag{12.4}$$

$$RTS = \frac{1}{\sum_{h \in H} \tilde{\eta}_h + \eta_N}, \tag{12.5}$$

where $\tilde{\eta}_h$ is the elasticity of $\tilde{C}(\tilde{Y}; N)$ with respect to aggregate product $\tilde{y}_h$ and η_N is the elasticity with respect to N. Obviously, these two indices are scale-like measures (see Equation 12.2) and the elasticities involved can be easily obtained from estimated cost functions. For example, if the function is a translog around the mean, first order coefficients are output elasticities at the mean. Both *RTD* and *RTS* have become *the* textbook concepts to analyze transport industry structure (Berechman, 1993; Braeutigam, 1999; Pels and Rietveld, 2008; Small and Verhoef, 2007).

As explicitly shown in Equations (12.4) and (12.5), the sum of the product elasticities is made over a subset *H* of aggregates, something that we did not define. This was on purpose, because the definition of this subset has varied between studies. Most articles do not include the so-called attributes in *H*, as in Friedlaender et al. (1993, railroads), Kumbhakar (1990, airlines) and Bhattacharyya et al. (1995, buses). Other authors argue that the inclusion of certain elasticities will depend on how the product is expanded, as Caves et al. (1985, railroads), who consider the average length of haul elasticity in some of their *RTS* calculations, Windle (1988, buses), who includes the load factor elasticity in a calculation of *RTD*, and Caves and Christensen (1988, buses and airlines), who include the load factor elasticity for some *RTS* calculations.

It may be obvious to the reader that, as *RTD* does not include η_N, it must be the case that $RT > RTS$ because the network size elasticity is positive since, *everything else constant*, serving a larger network implies larger expenses (Pels and Rietveld, 2008). The conclusions that one may derive from calculated values for these indices regarding cost efficiency are quite simple (see Braeutigam, 1999, for a pedagogical example): increasing returns to scale ($RTS > 1$) would suggest that, if possible, both network size and outputs should be increased because serving larger networks would diminish ray average cost; along that ray, the industry would be seen as a natural monopoly. Constant returns to scale ($RTS = 1$) together with increasing returns to density ($RTD > 1$) would indicate that 'costs per passenger mile are reduced not by operating a bigger network, but by increasing the density of traffic over the network' (Braeutigam, 1999). It would follow that firms of all network sizes can compete, as long as they reach large enough density levels. Note, though, that evidently cost efficiency would not be the only effect of an increase in density or scale through, say, a merger; there may be other effects in, for example, market power, which have to be taken into account to correctly assess the performance of the industry. These other effects, though, are not within the scope of this chapter.

There have been numerous empirical calculations of *RTD* and *RTS* in the literature, for different industries. A quite striking result is that, in general, for all industries, there seems to be increasing returns to density ($RTD > 1$) but constant returns to scale ($RTS = 1$). For example, Braeutigam (1999) reports this for railroads, something that is corroborated by the study of Graham et al. (2003). For the airline industry (where the number of points served, *PS*, is the usual network variable), the presence of increasing returns to density and constant returns to scale have been reported by Baltagi et al. (1995), Caves et al. (1984), Gillen et al. (1985, 1990), Keeler and Formby (1994), Kirby (1986), Kumbhakar (1992), and Oum and Zhang (1991) among others. In the case of urban bus operations, De Borger and Kertens (2008) explain that most studies find that bus technology is characterized by economies of traffic density, so that more intensive use of a given network reduces the cost per vehicle-kilometer; regarding *RTS*, the overall picture is one of a U-shaped relation between average cost per vehicle-kilometer and output expressed in vehicle-kilometers, but with very broad ranges of constant returns to scale.[12]

Despite this quite consistent picture, a number of recent studies have found different values for *RTD* and *RTS*. This happened because these papers actually proposed new ways to calculate these indices: these re-assessments are discussed in detail in the next section. Finally, we close this section by discussing other results that can and have been obtained from the estimation of transport firms cost functions. First, regarding economies of scope – a concept that was discussed in the second section – it happens that their calculation has not been really popular in transport studies. Probably, the main reason is the intensive use of the translog form, which precludes the necessary evaluation at 0 for some outputs. Those who have calculated economies of scope have usually focused on partitions that separate different types of cargo. For example, Harmatuck (1991) found that in trucking, economies of scope with respect to truckload and less-than-truckload services were not prevalent; Kim (1987) found diseconomies of scope in railroads with respect to passenger and cargo services. Second, many authors have attempted to study not only economies of density and scale, but also the inefficiency of different transport firms, using frontier estimations. For example, Farsi et al. (2005) found inefficiency estimates of about 6–8 percent on average and 31–38 percent on maximum for Swiss railway companies. Lastly, a few authors have used principal – agent frameworks to look at the best regulatory contracts in terms of cost efficiency (Gagnepain and Ivaldi, 2002b; Piacenza, 2006).

REASSESSMENT OF INDUSTRY STRUCTURE INDICES

As explained in the previous section, most empirical studies of the airline industry have reported the presence of increasing returns to density and constant returns to scale, which would indicate that it would be advantageous for firms to increase traffic densities on their networks, but it would be of little or no cost advantage to expand their networks. Observed industry behavior, however, is different: after deregulation – in the United States first and then in the rest of the world – the air industry has concentrated and the networks served have expanded through mergers, alliances and acquisitions. As increasing network size seems to contradict the finding of constant returns to scale as previously defined, some explanations have been offered in the literature. For example, some see demand-side advantages of size, that is, customers value network coverage and are willing to pay a premium to use carriers with greater market coverage and frequency of service. Furthermore, large firms and incumbents operating hub-and-spoke systems would have strategic advantages if in addition they use some marketing devices, such as frequent flyer programs and reservation systems (see Borenstein, 1992). This could explain a tendency toward consolidation despite lack of any significant cost advantages of size.

Returning to pure cost considerations, some authors have argued that network growth can be understood as an attempt to exploit economies of traffic *density* by attracting traffic (for example, Brueckner and Spiller, 1994; Oum and Tretheway, 1990); this, however, weakens the role of *RTS* as a tool to analyze the advantages of network growth. Some other authors, on the other hand, have proposed rethinking and re-examinations of the methods to calculate scale economies for all transport industries. Gagné (1990), Xu et al. (1994) and Ying (1992) observed that aggregates are usually interrelated, for example, ton-kilometers are equal to total flow times average distance, something that had not been taken into account when calculating estimates of *S*. Along this line these authors considered the interrelations among aggregates ('products' and 'attributes') to calculate a total rather than a partial cost elasticity for the basic product (ton-kilometers). Later on, Oum and Zhang (1997) linked these aggregates to variables representing the network.

The approach to re-examine the calculation of scale economies, based upon the interrelation among the arguments of the estimated cost functions, suffers from two difficulties: first, no single set of output descriptions has been used; second, it has never really been clear which elasticities should be considered in the calculations. All of this gets reflected in the lack of accepted standard definitions for economies of density and economies of scale. As some have pointed out, what is scale in one study may be density in another. Jara-Díaz and Cortés (1996) proposed a new look at the subject. Their approach was based upon the interpretation of the different forms in which output has been described as implicit representations of vector Y, the displacements of goods and persons that transport firms produce. Let us briefly review this.

Behind each component included in the vector of aggregates $\tilde{Y} = \{\tilde{y}_1, \ldots \tilde{y}_h, \ldots \tilde{y}_V\}$, lies the real output Y of a transport firm, that is, the vector of flows. For example, ton-kilometers are obtained as $\Sigma_l y_l d_l$, where d_l is the distance traveled by the flow y_l, tons per unit of time, in the l-th OD pair. Jara-Díaz and Cortés (1996) noted that the inability to use Y in the empirical work does not mean that its definition should be abandoned when using an estimated cost function to make economic inferences. If the estimated function represents the real multioutput cost function well, then the characteristics of the latter should be obtainable from the estimated parameters of the former. Let us take the case of economies of scale. Since economies of scale analyze the behavior of costs when the output vector increases equiproportionally, a correct calculation of economies of scale in transport would be related to an increase in the same proportion of all the flows in Y. This may be analyzed from an estimated cost function $\tilde{C}(\tilde{Y}; N)$ if one examines the behavior of aggregates $\tilde{y}_h$ when Y varies. If the aggregates can be described as functions of Y, that is, $\tilde{y}_h \equiv \tilde{y}_h(Y)$, then $\hat{C}(Y) = \tilde{C}(\tilde{Y}(Y), N)$ can be considered as an approximation of the cost function in terms of Y. By calculating from $\hat{C}(Y) = \tilde{C}(\tilde{Y}(Y), N)$ the elasticities of cost with respect to the components of Y, Jara-Díaz and Cortés developed a method to obtain the degree of economies of scale. The cost elasticity with respect to y_l – where l is and OD pair – is

$$\hat{\eta}_l = \frac{\partial \hat{C}}{\partial y_l} \frac{y_l}{C} = \frac{y_l}{C} \sum_{h=1}^{V} \frac{\partial \tilde{C}}{\partial \tilde{y}_h} \frac{\partial \tilde{y}_h}{\partial y_l} = \sum_{h=1}^{V} \frac{\partial \tilde{y}_h}{\partial y_l} \frac{y_l}{\tilde{y}_h} \frac{\partial \tilde{C}}{\partial \tilde{y}_h} \frac{\tilde{y}_h}{C} = \sum_{h=1}^{V} \varepsilon_{hl} \tilde{\eta}_h \qquad (12.6)$$

with ε_{hl} the elasticity of aggregate output $\tilde{y}_h$ with respect to y_l and $\tilde{\eta}_h$ the elasticity of $\tilde{C}$ with respect to $\tilde{y}_h$. Therefore, the correct calculation for an estimator of S, $\hat{S}$, is

$$\hat{S} = \left[\sum_l \hat{\eta}_l \right]^{-1} = \left[\sum_h \alpha_h \tilde{\eta}_h \right]^{-1} \text{ with } \alpha_h = \sum_l \varepsilon_{hl}. \qquad (12.7)$$

Note that the coefficient α_h is the (local) degree of homogeneity of the h-th aggregate with respect to the disaggregated flows, and that its calculation avoids the discussion regarding which aggregate should be considered in the calculation of S. Importantly, as the number of OD pairs does not change when flows increase, Jara-Díaz and Cortés argued that the elasticity of the network size should never be included in a scale calculation. As discussed earlier, this is also imposed in the calculation of *RTD*, which made Oum and Zhang (1997) argue correctly that the method was an improved version of *RTD*. Moreover, the fact that *RTD* and scale under a strict multioutput definition are related had been brought up before: Panzar (1989) stated that 'returns to density are precisely equal to (what has been previously defined to be) the degree of multiproduct economies of scale!' (pp. 43–44), something also mentioned by Hurdle et al. (1989) and Filippini and Maggi (1992). This shows that, in a rigorous sense, an improved version of what today is understood as economies of density is, in fact, scale under a strict definition.

This, however, is not all because *RTD* assumes not only that network size does not vary, but also that the route structure remains unchanged, as pointed out by Basso and Jara-Díaz (2006a). This condition is required because the idea of estimating the degree of economies of density is to analyze whether 'the average costs of a direct connection decreases with proportionate increases in both flows on that connection' (Hendricks et al., 1995), which means that only the existing links must handle the new traffic. If the route structure changes, some new links may be added while others may disappear. Therefore, Basso and Jara-Díaz (2006a) proposed to distinguish *RTD* from S – the actual multioutput degree of economies of scale – using Equation (12.7) for both, assuming that the route structure is fixed in the case of *RTD* but is variable in the case of S. Obviously, this distinction induces differences in the calculation of the α_j. For example, the coefficient of the average distance in *RTD*, say α_{DM}, will always be zero as flows grow by the same proportion holding the route structure fixed; however, the coefficient of the average distance in the case of S, γ_{DM}, could be different from zero if the minimum cost occurs for a different route structure after flows grow. We consider the distinction between *RTD* and S – and therefore between α_j and γ_j – to be useful and relevant. Economies of density will be useful to know if, for example, there are economies of vehicle size, that is, if larger flows in non-stop routes imply decreasing *average costs* in that route because of larger vehicles. Hub-and-spoke networks would be strongly influenced by the existence of economies of density. On the other hand, multioutput economies of scale S are important because, when traffic increases significantly, it may not be efficient to further increase the size of the vehicles (see, for example, Wei and Hansen, 2003), while a frequency increase may be expensive because of congestion. With a reconfiguration of the route structure, however, it may happen that the increases in flows may be handled without increasing costs very much; for example, through point-to-point service in certain OD pairs (phenomenon that has been observed; see Swan, 2002). Moreover, the distinction may help to find out whether a transport firm is being cost efficient or not because, as elegantly showed by Kraus (2008), if a firm is minimizing cost, the degree of local economies of scale should be the same independently of whether the firm adjusts density alone, or changes its route structure as well. In other words, if the firm is being cost efficient, RTD and S will be equal.

Now, neither RTD nor S helps in analyzing what happens if the network size changes. As explained above, it is RTS that is aimed at examining the behavior of costs when both traffic and network size increase. The increase is applied to the vector of aggregates $\tilde{Y} = \{\tilde{y}_h\}$ (or to a sub-vector) and to the network size variable N and it is done by keeping proportions constant. It is because of this that RTS is said to analyze what happens when the size of the network is increased but the density of traffic movements is unchanged. However, RTS fails to provide insightful conclusions regarding the cost structure of transport firms. To explain this briefly, note that increasing N implies the variation of the number of OD pairs, that is, a variation of the dimension of Y, which is something that should be examined with a (spatial) scope analysis as discussed previously.[13] As shown, it is perfectly possible to find $SC>0$ and $S=1$, that is, increasing returns to spatial scope, but constant returns to scale. This, however, can never be found with RTS because $RTS < RTD$ analytically. A closer look at RTS reveals where the problem lies: as shown by Basso and Jara-Díaz (2006b) the procedure of increasing network size keeping *density* constant imposes analytical conditions on the new OD flows – the ones that are incorporated after the network increase – which seem to be indefensible. For example, depending on the specification of the cost function, RTS may impose that the new flows are, on average, less than half the average of existing flows. Basso and Jara-Díaz conclude that RTS should be abandoned and what should be calculated instead is economies of spatial scope.

The empirical problem is that a direct calculation of SC using Equation (12.3) – an example is Jara-Díaz (1988) – is seldom feasible. However, the approach proposed by Jara-Díaz and Cortés (1996) delivers a way to deal with the problem: since most aggregates $\tilde{y}_h$ are implicit functions of Y, even though the (disaggregate) output vectors Y^A, Y^B and Y^D might be unknown, SC might be calculated correctly if the corresponding aggregate vectors $\tilde{Y}(Y^A)$, $\tilde{Y}(Y^B)$ and $\tilde{Y}(Y^D)$ were known, and a cost function $\tilde{C}(\tilde{Y}; N)$ was available (Jara-Díaz et al., 2001). In other words, considering PS as the network size variable, scope could be calculated as

$$SC_A = SC_B = \frac{\tilde{C}(\tilde{Y}(Y^A), PS^A) + \tilde{C}(\tilde{Y}(Y^B), PS^B) - \tilde{C}(\tilde{Y}(Y^D), PS^D)}{\tilde{C}(\tilde{Y}(Y^D), PS^D)}. \quad (12.8)$$

The problem is then reduced to the calculation of the aggregates under different orthogonal partitions of Y when possible. One advantage of Equation (12.8) is that it allows the calculation of scope even if a translog specification is being used. This is because aggregates (such as total passengers or ton-kilometers) do not go to zero when only some OD flows are zero. Thus, the arguments of $\tilde{C}(\tilde{Y}; PS)$ in Equation (12.8) are likely never evaluated at zero, as is the case with some components of Y^A or Y^B in $C(\cdot)$ in Equation (12.3).

Table 12.1   Summary of the proposed approach

Literature	Proposed calculations
$RTD = \dfrac{1}{\displaystyle\sum_{h \in H} \tilde{\eta}_h} \quad \rightarrow$	$RTD^C = \left[\displaystyle\sum_h \alpha_h \tilde{\eta}_h \right]^{-1}$ constant route structure
	$S = \left[\displaystyle\sum_h \gamma_h \tilde{\eta}_h \right]^{-1}$ variable route structure
$RTS = \dfrac{1}{\displaystyle\sum_{h \in H} \tilde{\eta}_h + \eta_N} \quad \rightarrow$	$SC_A = \dfrac{\tilde{C}(\tilde{Y}(Y^A), PS^A) + \tilde{C}(\tilde{Y}(Y^B), PS^B) - \tilde{C}(\tilde{Y}(Y^D), PS^D)}{\tilde{C}(\tilde{Y}(Y^D), PS^D)}$

It is important to explain that the calculation of Equation (12.8) can be seen from different perspectives. For example, if one knows $\tilde{Y}(Y^A)$ and PS^A – an initial condition – and the functions $\tilde{y}_h \equiv \tilde{y}_h(Y)$, one has to propose the components of Y^D and Y^B (which must be orthogonal to Y^A), plus PS^D and PS^B, in order to generate $\tilde{Y}(Y^B)$, $\tilde{C}(\tilde{Y}(Y^B), PS^B)$, $\tilde{Y}(Y^D)$ and $\tilde{C}(\tilde{Y}(Y^D), PS^D)$. Analytically, the challenge is somewhat different from the calculations behind the coefficients α_h for either RTD or S, because many orthogonal partitions can be analyzed. Basso and Jara-Díaz (2005) proposed a way to calculate all what is needed in Equation (12.8), using the same kind of information that is normally used to calculate RTS. Their procedure relies on replacing the constant density assumption used in RTS by a constant average OD flow assumption, used in the context of spatial scope.

For synthesis, and emphasis of the spatial dimension of output in the transport case, with S one analyzes the behavior of costs after an equiproportional expansion of the OD flows keeping the number of OD pairs constant, while with SC one analyzes the behavior of cost when new OD flows are added. To do this properly from cost functions with aggregate output, the relation between each aggregate and the true output vector has to be revealed in order to calculate scale and scope consistently for policy analysis. We argue that this implies replacing the calculation of RTD and RTS with three measures: corrected RTD, the multioutput degree of scale economies S and spatial SC, as summarized in Table 12.1.

Applying this approach, a series of reassessments have been reported in the literature. For the case of RTD^C, Jara-Díaz and Cortés (1996) provide a number of examples; the methodology was also applied by Mizutani (2004) and Savage (1997) to the case of railways. Regarding S, Basso and Jara-Díaz (2006a) presented an example for US airlines where, while RTD^C was 1.161, S attained a value of 1.378. Finally, regarding economies of spatial scope, using the results from previously published cost models, Basso and Jara-Díaz (2005) found that smaller Canadian airlines (in terms of points served) exhibited economies of spatial scope, implying that enlarging their network was better than having a new company serving the new nodes. This degree of economies of (spatial) scope remained positive as new nodes were added but diminished in value as the network size got larger. Since RTS was found to be one, the authors argued that economies of spatial scope gave a better cost explanation for the observed merging between airlines with non-overlapping networks that took place in Canada. Other applications of these methods are being worked out.

CONCLUDING REMARKS

The estimation of transport cost functions has been one of the most relevant tasks in the field of transport economics in the last 40 years, both empirically and theoretically. Its empirical importance arises because transport is one of the few sectors of the economy in which the policy discussion on the possible presence of natural monopolies and the potential need for regulation has been mostly motivated around the presence or absence of economies of scale, originally associated with diminishing average costs. The theoretical relevance is due to the difficulties in dealing with an activity whose spatial dimension can not be overlooked, which provoked the introduction of new scale concepts. The emergence of the multioutput theory at the beginning of the eighties prompted a review of the way scale economies are conceived and calculated from cost functions where output is described as a vector of aggregates, as became customary in the transport literature during that decade. Viewed in perspective, the main issue was how to deal with an economic activity whose product takes place on a network. The sophisticated econometric tools developed to understand better the supply side in microeconomics, had not been satisfactorily accompanied by an agreed framework to analyze the production process of a transport firm.

In this chapter we have presented an account of the formulation and usage of cost functions for transport firms, hopefully arriving at the state of the art. It is clear that the estimation of transport cost functions will continue to benefit in the future from advances in the field of econometrics, as has happened in the past with, for example, flexible forms or frontier estimation. In this sense, structural estimation is probably something that we will start seeing applied more and more to transport industries. Also, general theoretical advances should have an impact in the analysis of transport cost functions. The link between principal – agent models and frontier estimation of cost functions is a promising avenue for research.

We put, however, a particular emphasis on the concepts of economies of scale and scope. The literature in the last ten years shows a number of very interesting results that have emerged from the discussion around the appropriate ways to capture the advantages or disadvantages of increasing production or enlarging or reshaping the network served. There have been important advances in order to unveil the links between concepts that have been applied in practice for many years in this area – as returns to density (RTD) and returns to scale with variable network size (RTS) – and the characteristics of the actual production process. This has been done by looking at the connections between aggregates and flows and between flows and the operating tools that any transport firm applies on a periodic basis as fleet programming, re-routing and so on. As a result, we have now a better understanding of density, scale and scope in transport production. Future application of these new and/or improved methodologies will then help analysts not only to contrast new against old results, but also to determine the structure of the industry and thus answer the old but always relevant question of whether competition would emerge in the absence of regulation.

ACKNOWLEDGMENTS

This research has been partially funded by Fondecyt, Chile, project 1080140 and the Millennium Institute 'Complex Engineering Systems'. The authors would like to thank Robin Lindsey for helpful comments.

NOTES

1. The estimation of cost functions have been widely used in assessing the impact of regulation on transport operator costs and efficiency. Reviewing this literature (and similar themes such as the impact of government ownership) is beyond the scope of this chapter. This chapter focuses on the fundamentals of formulating and interpreting transport cost functions.
2. A brief but fuller explanation of the practitioner approach to costing and comparison with the economists' approach is in Waters and Tretheway (1989). A fuller discussion of rail cost analysis is provided in Waters (1985) and Talley (1988).
3. The importance of incremental costs for pricing was realized years before multioutput theory was formalized; see, for example, Baumol et al. (1962). In fact, the editor of the journal where this paper was published foreshadowed the importance of developing new theory: he commented on the authors' conclusions that 'the statement, concerned with concepts of costs, should help to provide an essential groundwork of improved techniques for the measurement of relevant costs in specific situations'.
4. The production-possibility frontier comes from: (1) Frequency is defined by y_{ij} – the largest flow by assumption – for a given vehicle capacity K. (2) Given this frequency, one can obtain the load factor in direction ji, which will obviously be smaller than K. (3) The cycle time of one vehicle is then the sum of in-vehicle time plus loading-unloading times, which depend on both load sizes. (4) Finally, the necessary vehicle fleet B is obtained as the frequency multiplied by the cycle time.
5. Obviously, other *hub-and-spoke* structures could be considered as well, like a two fleet operation, one in 1–2 and the other in 2–3. These can be constructed straightforwardly using results from a two nodes system.
6. However, in equilibrium, and in typical prisoner's dilemma fashion, the airlines may end up worse off in terms of profits when choosing the hub-and-spoke route structures.
7. Flexible functional forms came into use by 1980, notably the translog function (first applications were Brown et al., 1979; Caves et al., 1981 and Spady and Friedlaender, 1978). Use of the translog is standard practice in empirical analysis and is not reviewed here (brief expositions can be found in Jara-Diaz, 2000, pp. 40–41 and Oum and Waters, 1996, pp. 428–429).
8. Ying (1992, p. 231) states: 'This multiproduct nature is especially evident for transportation firms, which transport various commodities or passengers from a specific origin to a specific destination over a spatial network [. . .] Empirical studies in transportation have necessarily aggregated output data [. . .]. In these situations, some researchers have tried to capture the heterogeneous nature of this single output through a vector of output quality or attribute variables.' Braeutigam (1999, p. 68) states that 'treating the movement of each commodity from each origin to each destination as a separate product would be desirable. There would be so many outputs however, that estimating a cost function would be impossible'. See also Gillen et al. (1990), Small and Verhoef (2007) and Winston (1985). A debate over output units and their definition in the supply of and demand for transport has persisted for over a century: Locklin (1933) includes discussion of output and its interpretation and implications in the early literature, see also Wilson (1959, 1962). The first modern detailed discussion regarding output definition and aggregation can be traced back to Jara-Díaz (1981).
9. The estimation of productivity gains using transport cost functions is standard practice, yet more sophisticated models and ways to estimate productivity changes exist. For example, one can separate specific technological improvements from general trends, as done by Bitzan and Keeler (2003), who separate the gains from elimination of cabooses (vans) by North American railroads from general productivity gains. Productivity measurement via cost functions is too extensive to be reviewed here and is covered by other surveys of transport cost functions.
10. A brief discussion of frontier estimation in transport is in Oum and Waters (1996, pp. 446–448). An in-depth review of frontier estimation is Kumbhakar and Lovell (2000).
11. Antoniou (1991) traces this distinction back to Koontz (1951), however.
12. In trucking studies the distinction between *RTD* and *RTS* has been less common, as most of the cost functions estimated did not include a network size variable. It follows that the calculation of economies of

scale did not impose a fixed network size and, therefore, represent an *RTS* measure. Indeed, most studies found values close to 1.
13.   Other authors have suggested, either literally or implicitly, that *RTS* and scope are related (Borenstein, 1992; Daughety, 1985; Hurdle et al., 1989).

REFERENCES

Antoniou, A., 1991, Economies of scale in the airline industry: the evidence revisited. *The Logistics and Transportation Review*, **27** (2), 159–184.

Bailey, E.E. and A.F. Friedlaender, 1982, Market structure and multiproduct industries. *The Journal of Economic Literature*, **20**, 1024–1048.

Baltagi, B.H., J.M. Griffin and D.P. Rich, 1995, Airline deregulation: the cost pieces of the puzzle. *International Economic Review*, **36** (1), 245–258.

Basso, L.J. and S.R. Jara-Díaz, 2005, Calculation of economies of spatial scope from transport cost functions with aggregate output (with an application to the airline industry). *Journal of Transport Economics and Policy*, **39** (1), 25–52.

Basso, L.J. and S.R. Jara-Díaz, 2006a, Distinguishing multiproduct economies of scale from economies of density on a fixed-size transport network. *Networks and Spatial Economics*, **6** (2), 149–162.

Basso, L.J. and S.R. Jara-Díaz, 2006b, Is returns to scale with variable network size adequate for transport industry structure analysis? *Transportation Science*, **40**, 259–268.

Baumol, W.J., J.C. Bonbright, Y. Brozen, J. Dean, K.E. Ford, C.B. Hoover, F.P. Dudley, M.J. Roberts and E.W. Williams, 1962, The role of costs in the minimum pricing of railroad services. *Journal of Business*, **35**, 357–366.

Baumol, W.J. and D.F. Bradford, 1970, Optimal departures from marginal cost pricing. *American Economic Review*, **60** (3), 265–283.

Baumol, W.J., J.C. Panzar and R.D. Willig, 1982, *Contestable Markets and the Theory of Industry Structure*. New York: Harcourt, Brace and Jovanovich.

Berechman, J., 1993, *Public Transit Economics and Deregulation Policy*. Amsterdam: North-Holland.

Bhattacharyya, A., S. Kumbhakar and A. Bhattacharyya, 1995, Ownership structure and cost efficiency: a study of publicly owned passenger-bus transportation companies in India. *Journal of Productivity Analysis*, **8** (1), 35–52.

Bitzan, J., 2000, Railroad cost conditions: implications for policy. Report for the Federal Railroad Administration, Washington, DC.

Bitzan, J., 2003, Railroad costs and competition: the implications of introducing competition to railroad networks. *Journal of Transport Economics and Policy*, **37** (2), 201–275.

Bitzan, J. and T.E. Keeler, 2003, Productivity growth and some of its determinants in the deregulation of the US railroad industry. *Southern Economic Journal*, **70**, 232–253.

Borenstein, S., 1992, The evolution of US airline competition. *Journal of Economic Perspectives*, **6** (2), 45–73.

Braeutigam, R.R., 1999, Learning about transport costs. In J. Gomez-Ibañez, W.B. Tye and C. Winston, eds, *Essays in Transportation Economics and Policy*. Washington DC: Brooking Institution Press, pp. 57–97.

Brown, R.S., D.W. Caves and L.R. Christensen, 1979, Modelling the structure of cost and production for multiproduct firms. *Southern Economic Journal*, **46**, 256–273.

Brueckner, J.K. and P.T. Spiller, 1994, Economies of traffic density in the deregulated airline industry. *The Journal of Law and Economics*, **37** (2), 379–413.

Caves, D.W. and L.R. Christensen, 1988, The importance of economies of scale, capacity utilisation and density in explaining interindustry productivity growth. *Logistics and Transportation Review*, **24** (1), 3–32.

Caves, D.W., L.R. Christensen and J.A. Swanson, 1981, Productivity in US Railroads, 1951–1974. *Bell Journal of Economics*, **11**, 161–181.

Caves, D.W., L.R. Christensen and M.W. Tretheway, 1984, Economies of density versus economies of scale: why trunk and local airline costs differ. *Rand Journal of Economics*, **15**, 471–489.

Caves, D.W., L.R. Christensen, M.W. Tretheway and R.J. Windle, 1985, Network effects and the measurement of returns to scale and density for US Railroads. In A. F. Daughety, ed., *Analytical Studies in Transport Economics*. Cambridge: Cambridge University Press, pp. 97–120.

Caves, D.W., L.R. Christensen, M.W. Tretheway and R.J. Windle, 1987, An assessment of the efficiency effects of US airline deregulation via an international comparison. In E. E. Bailey, ed., *Public Regulation: New Perspectives on Institutions and Policies*. Cambridge, MA: MIT Press, pp. 285–320.

Clark, J.M., 1923, *Studies in the Economies of Overhead Costs*. Chicago, IL: University of Chicago Press.

Daughety, A.F., 1985, Transportation research on pricing and regulation: overview and suggestions for future research. *Transportation Research Part A*, **19** (5), 471–487.

De Borger, B. and K. Kerstens, 2008, The performance of bus-transit operators. In D. A. Hensher and K. J. Button, eds, *Handbook of Transport Modelling*, 2nd edn. Amsterdam: Elsevier, pp. 693–714.

De Borger, B., K. Kerstens and A. Costa, 2002, Public transit performance: what does one learn from frontier studies?, *Transport Reviews*, **22** (1), 1–38.

Farsi, M., M. Filippini and W. Greene, 2005, Efficiency measurement in network industries: application to the Swiss railway companies. *Journal of Regulatory Economics*, **28** (1), 69–90.

Filippini, M. and R. Maggi, 1992, The cost structure of the Swiss private railways, *International Journal of Transport Economics*, **19**, 307–327.

Friedlaender, A.F., E.R. Berndt, J.S. Wang Chiang, M. Showalter and C.A. Vellturo, 1993, Rail costs and capital adjustments in a quasi-regulated environment. *Journal of Transport Economics and Policy*, **27** (2), 131–152.

Gagné, R., 1990, On the relevant elasticity estimates for cost structure analysis of the trucking industry. *The Review of Economics and Statistics*, **72**, 160–164.

Gagnépain, P. and M. Ivaldi, 2002a, Stochastic frontiers and asymmetric information models. *Journal of Productivity Analysis*, **18**, 145–159.

Gagnépain, P. and M. Ivaldi, 2002b, Incentive regulatory policies: the case of public transit systems in France. *Rand Journal of Economics*, **33** (4), 605–629.

Gálvez, T., 1978, Análisis de Operaciones en Sistemas de Transporte (Transport systems operations analysis). Working Paper ST/INV/04/78, Civil Engineering Department, Universidad de Chile, Santiago de Chile.

Gillen, D., T.H. Oum and M. Tretheway, 1985, *Airline Cost and Performance: Implications for Public and Industry Policies*. Vancouver, Canada: Centre for Transportation Studies, University of British Columbia.

Gillen, D., T.H. Oum and M.W. Tretheway, 1990, Airlines cost structure and policy implications. *Journal of Transport Economics and Policy*, **24**, 9–34.

Graham, D. J., A. Couto, W.E. Adeney and S. Glaister, 2003, Economies of scale and density in urban rail transport: effects on productivity. *Transportation Research Part E*, **39**, 443–458.

Harmatuck, D., 1991, Economies of scale and scope in the motor carrier industry. *Journal of Transport Economics and Policy*, **21**, 131–153.

Hendricks, K., M. Piccione and G. Tan, 1995, The economics of hubs: the case of monopoly. *Review of Economics Studies*, **62**, 83–99.

Hurdle, G., R. Johnson, A. Toskow, G. Warden and M. Williams, 1989, Concentration, potential entry and performance in the airline industry. *Journal of Industrial Economics*, **38** (2), 119–139.

Ivaldi, M. and G.J. McCullough, 2004, Subadditivity tests for network separation with an application to US Railroads. CEPR Discussion Paper 4392, London.

Ivaldi, M. and G.J. McCullough, 2007, Railroad pricing and revenue-to-cost margins in the post-staggers era. *Research in Transportation Economics*, **20**, 153–178.

Jara-Díaz, S.R., 1981, Transportation cost functions: a multiproduct approach. Ph.D. Thesis, M.I.T.

Jara-Díaz, S.R., 1982a, The estimation of transport cost functions: a methodological review. *Transport Reviews*, **2**, 257–278.

Jara-Díaz, S.R., 1982b, Transportation product, transportation function and cost function. *Transportation Science*, **16**, 522–539.

Jara-Díaz, S.R., 1988, Multioutput analysis of trucking operations using spatially disaggregated flows. *Transportation Research Part B*, **22**, 159–171.

Jara-Díaz, S.R., 2000, Transport production and the analysis of industry structure. In J. Polak and A. Heertje, eds, *Analytical Transport Economics. An International Perspective* Cheltenham, UK: Edward Elgar Publishing, pp. 27–50.

Jara-Díaz S.R., 2007, *Transport Economic Theory*. Amsterdam: Elsevier.

Jara-Díaz, S.R. and L.J. Basso, 2003, Transport cost functions, network expansions and economies of scope. *Transportation Research Part E*, **39** (4), 271–288.

Jara-Díaz, S.R. and C. Cortés, 1996, On the calculation of scale economies from transport cost functions. *Journal of Transport Economics and Policy*, **30**, 157–170.

Jara-Díaz, S.R., C. Cortés and F. Ponce, 2001, Number of points served and economies of spatial scope in transport cost functions. *Journal of Transport Economics and Policy*, **35** (2), 327–341.

Kahn, A.E., 1970, *The Economics of Regulation: Principles and Institutions*, Vol. I. New York: John Wiley & Sons.

Keeler, J.P. and J.P. Formby, 1994, Cost economies and consolidation in the US airline industry. *International Journal of Transport Economics*, **21** (1), 21–45.

Kim, M., 1987, Economies of scale and scope in multiproduct firms: evidence from US railroads. *Applied Economics*, **19**, 155–172.

Kirby, M.G., 1986, Airline economies of 'scale' and the Australian domestic air transport policy. *Journal of Transport Economics and Policy*, **20** (3), 339–352.

Koontz, H.D., 1951, Economic and managerial factors underlying subsidy needs of domestic trunk line air carriers. *Journal of Air Law and Commerce*, **18** (1), 127–156.

Kraus, M., 2008, Economies of scale in networks. *Journal of Urban Economics*, **64**, 171–177.

Kumbhakar, S.C, 1990, A reexamination of returns to scale, density and technical progress in US airlines. *Southern Economic Journal*, **57**, 428–442.

Kumbhakar, S.C, 1992, Allocative distortions, technical progress and input demand in US airlines: 1970–1984. *International Economic Review*, **33** (3), 723–737.

Kumbhakar, S.C. and C.A.K. Lovell, 2000, *Stochastic Frontier Analysis*. Cambridge: Cambridge University Press.

Locklin, D.P., 1933, The literature on railway rate theory. *Quarterly Journal of Economics*, **47**, 167–230.

Lorenz, M.O., 1916, Cost and value of service in railroad ratemaking. *Quarterly Journal of Economics*, **21**, 205–218.

Meyer, J.R., M.J. Peck, J. Stenason and C. Zwick, 1959, *The Economics of Competition in the Transportation Industries*. Cambridge, MA: Harvard University Press.

Mizutani, F., 2004, Privately owned railways' cost function, organization size and ownership. *Journal of Regulatory Economics*, **25** (3), 297–322.

Oum, T.H. and M.W. Tretheway, 1990, Airline hub and spoke system. *Transportation Research Forum Proceedings*, **30**, 380–393.

Oum, T.H. and W.G. Waters, II, 1996, A survey of recent developments in transportation cost function research. *Logistics and Transportation Review,* **32** (4), 423–463.

Oum, T.H. and C. Yu, 1995, A comparative study of productivity and cost competitiveness of the world's major airlines. *Journal of Air Transport Management*, **2**, 181–195.

Oum, T.H., A. Zhang and Y. Zhang, 1995, Airline network rivalry. *Canadian Journal of Economics*, **28**, 836–857.

Oum, T.H. and Y. Zhang, 1991, Utilisation of quasi-fixed inputs and estimation of cost functions. *Journal of Transport Economics and Policy*, **25**, 121–134.

Oum, T.H. and Y. Zhang, 1997, A note on scale economies in transport. *Journal of Transport Economics and Policy,* **31**, 309–315.

Panzar, J. and R. Willig, 1977, Economies of scale in multioutput production. *Quarterly Journal of Economics*, **91**, 481–493.

Panzar, J. and R. Willig, 1981, Economies of scope. *American Economic Review*, **71**, 268–272.

Panzar, J., 1989, Technological determinants of firm and industry structure. In R. Schmalensee and R. Willig, eds, *Handbook of Industrial Organization*. Amsterdam: North-Holland, pp. 3–59.

Pels, E. and P. Rietveld, 2008, Cost functions in transport. In D.A. Hensher and K.J. Button, eds, *Handbook of Transport Modelling*, 2nd edn. Amsterdam: Elsevier, pp. 381–394.

Piacenza, M., 2006, Regulatory contracts and cost efficiency: stochastic frontier evidence from the Italian local public transport. *Journal of Productivity Analysis*, **25**, 257–277.

Quinet, E. and R.W. Vickerman, 2004, *Principles of Transport Economics*. Cheltenham, UK: Edward Elgar.

Savage, I., 1997, Scale economies in United States rail transit systems. *Transportation Research Part A*, **31** (6), 459–473.

Small, K.A. and E.T. Verhoef, 2007, *The Economics of Urban Transportation*. London: Routledge.

Spady, R. and A. Friedlaender, 1978, Hedonic cost functions for the regulated trucking industry. *Bell Journal of Economics,* **9**, 159–179.

Swan, W.M., 2002, Airline route developments: a review of history. *Journal of Air Transport Management*, **8**, 349–353.

Talley, W., 1988, *Transport Carrier Costing*. New York: Gordon and Breach Science Pub.

Waters, W.G., II, 1985, Rail cost analysis. In K.G. Button and D. Pitfield, eds, *International Railway Economics*. Aldershot, UK: Gower Publishing, pp. 101–135.

Waters, W.G., II, 2007, Evolution of railroad economics. In S. Dennis and W. Talley, eds, *Railroad Economics*, Amsterdam: Elsevier Science, pp. 11–67.

Waters, W.G., II and M.W. Tretheway, 1989, The aggregate econometric approach versus the disaggregate activity approach to estimating cost functions. Paper presented at the World Conference on Transportation Research, Yokohama, Japan.

Wei, W. and M. Hansen, 2003, Cost economics of aircraft size. *Journal of Transport Economics and Policy*, **37**, 279–296.

Wilson, G.W., 1959, The output unit in transportation. *Land Economics*, August, pp. 266–76.

Wilson, G.W., 1962, *Essays on Some Unsettled Questions in the Economics of Transportation*. Bloomington, IN: Foundation for Business and Economic Studies, University of Indiana.

Windle, R.J., 1988, Transit policy and the cost structure of urban bus transportation. In J.S. Dodgson and N.

Topham, eds, *Bus Deregulation and Privatization: An International Perspective.* Aldershot, UK: Avebury, pp. 119–40.

Winston, C., 1985, Conceptual developments in the economics of transportation: an interpretive survey. *Journal of Economic Literature,* **23**, 57–94.

Xu, K., R. Windle, C. Grimm and T. Corsi, 1994, Re-evaluating returns to scale in transport. *Journal of Transport Economics and Policy,* **28**, 275–286.

Ying, J., 1992, On calculating cost elasticities. *The Logistics and Transportation Review,* **28** (3), 231–235.

13 Efficiency measurement theory and its application to airport benchmarking

Tae Hoon Oum, Katsuhiro Yamaguchi and Yuichiro Yoshida

INTRODUCTION

Efficiency measurement and benchmarking is an important topic whether one is interested in comparing efficiency of a firm or a sub-unit of a firm (a decision making unit, or a DMU in short) relative to its peers/competitors, learning to improve one's efficiency performance relative to a benchmark unit, or investigating effects of a public policy or a regulation. Efficiency measurement is critical for industries where firms do not face strong competition in the market. Examples include transport infrastructure providers such as airports, seaports, highways, urban transit systems and so forth, public utilities such as electricity, water, public schools, hospitals, and other subsidized programs, and regulated industries where markets can not discipline firms effectively.

Most national and state statistical agencies in OECD countries measure and regularly publish the total factor productivities of the national economy, provinces and various industrial sectors. For example, Statistics Canada computes total-factor productivity (TFP) for the Canadian economy, each province and over 100 different industrial sectors of Canada. The US Bureau of Labor Statistics computes and publishes similar TFPs for the US economy, states' economies, and a large number of its industrial sectors, and the labor share and capital share of the TFP growths. These measures are then used by various industrial sectors to make wage offers to their unions, and for subsequent negotiations with trade unions. For example, Tampa International Airport decided to benchmark various parts of its operations with peer airports in order to see what they can improve vis-à-vis competing airports. This practice became very popular among airport managers. The Airports Council International North America (ACI-NA) has decided to adopt the productivity benchmarking as an annual practice so that its member airports can use their productivity results to identify where they need improvements.

The literature on efficiency measurement and benchmarking has been advanced significantly during the last three decades. The most widely used methodologies for measuring and analyzing efficiency are Data Envelopment Analysis (DEA), econometric production (or cost) function methods, and the productivity index number approach. These and other methodologies, at times, may yield significantly different results on the relative efficiency of firms. Furthermore, especially in transport and logistics industries, the definition of outputs and/or inputs is not always clear, since the production processes often involve many intermediate inputs and outputs. For example, the efficiency rankings of airports vary wildly depending on whether or not non-aeronautical services (commercial services including duty free sales) are included as an output. These and other issues require in-depth investigation in order to enhance credibility of efficiency ranking and to make efficiency benchmarking useful to managers and policy makers.

This chapter starts out in the following section by reviewing the conventional theory of efficiency measurement and its recent developments. One of the most relevant extensions in the theory was made recently in how to treat undesirable outputs (that is, negative externalities) in efficiency measurement. We will present how three different methodologies stated above (namely DEA, econometric method and index number approach) incorporate the undesirable outputs such as greenhouse gas and congestion delay externalities. Then we focus our discussion on the case of airports, by providing a chronological review of the literature. Studies on efficiency measurement on air transport emerged following the deregulation in aviation industries, which advanced through the 1980s in the United States and was then followed by the EU and other parts of the world. The literature on airport efficiency measurement accumulated as the effects of deregulation in aviation industry became manifest. Now, public concern on the global environment is growing, and this gives rise to a new stream of efficiency measurement research in which undesirable outputs are incorporated by treating them as negative outputs. The section on empirical analysis of airport productivity will present these evolutions of the literature on airport efficiency measurement.

THEORY OF EFFICIENCY MEASUREMENT AND RECENT DEVELOPMENTS

Basic Concepts of Efficiency Measurements

Methodologies of measuring the performance of economic entities can be divided into several categories. In what follows, we call these economic entities whose performances are measured DMUs. One natural way of measuring the performance of a DMU is to compare its inputs used and outputs produced. This idea is often referred to as the productivity ratio. When DMUs produce multiple outputs sharing the same set of inputs, measuring their performance is not as straightforward as simply taking the ratio of an output and an input. An alternative is to use a distance function that measures the relative deviation of any given pair of input and output vectors from the production possibility frontier. Another way of defining the performance of a DMU uses cost/revenue/profit functions, where the performance is measured relative to these functions. This section provides these basic concepts of efficiency measurement.

Distance Function Approach

Production possibility set
Let $\mathbf{x}$ be an m-vector of inputs and $\mathbf{y}$ be an n-vector of outputs. Production possibility set S is a set of combinations of input and output such that

$$S = \{(\mathbf{x}, \mathbf{y}) \mid \mathbf{x} \text{ can produce } \mathbf{y}\}. \tag{13.1}$$

Output set $P(\mathbf{x})$ is a set of outputs that can be produced by a given input vector $\mathbf{x}$:

$$P(\mathbf{x}) = \{\mathbf{y}|\ \mathbf{x} \text{ can produce } \mathbf{y}\} \quad (13.2)$$

$$= \{\mathbf{y}|\ (\mathbf{x}, \mathbf{y}) \in S\}. \quad (13.3)$$

Input set $L(\mathbf{y})$ is then a set of inputs that can produce a given output vector y:

$$L(\mathbf{y}) = \{\mathbf{x}|\ \mathbf{x} \text{ can produce } \mathbf{y}\} \quad (13.4)$$

$$= \{\mathbf{x}|\ (\mathbf{x}, \mathbf{y}) \in S\}. \quad (13.5)$$

Properties associated with the production technology include the following (see Chambers (1988) for details.):[1]

- Non-negativity implying that elements of x and y are all positive real numbers, that is, $\mathbf{x} \in R^m_+$ and $\mathbf{y} \in R^n_+$ where m, n are the numbers of inputs and outputs respectively.
- Weak essentiality implying that for any non-zero output vector, its input set does not include the zero vector, that is, $L(\mathbf{y}) \notin 0$ for any $\mathbf{y} \neq 0$.
- Disposability (or monotonicity) in inputs: increase in an input will not decrease output, that is, if $\mathbf{x}_0 \leq \mathbf{x}_1$ and for at least one input, inequality holds with strict inequality, then $P(\mathbf{x}_0) \subset P(\mathbf{x}_1)$.[2]
- Disposability of outputs: any portion of outputs can be disposed without any cost, that is, if $\mathbf{y}_1 \in P(\mathbf{x})$ and $\mathbf{y}_0 \leq \mathbf{y}_1$ then $\mathbf{y}_0 \in P(\mathbf{x})$.
- Concavity in inputs: if $\mathbf{x}_0$; $\mathbf{x}_1 \in L(\mathbf{y})$ then $\lambda\mathbf{x}_0 + (1 - \lambda)\mathbf{x}_1 \in L(\mathbf{y})$, $\forall\lambda \in [0, 1]$ (and similarly for outputs).

Distance functions

Output-oriented distance functions   An output-oriented distance function has a value between 0 and 1, and is the inverse of the maximum ratio by which output vector y can be extended and still remains inside of the output set P (x) for a given input vector x:

$$d_O(\mathbf{x}, \mathbf{y}) = \min\ \{\theta|\ (\mathbf{y}/\theta) \in P(\mathbf{x})\}. \quad (13.6)$$

Technical Efficiency for the output-oriented distance function TE_O is defined as

$$TE_O = d_O(\mathbf{x}, \mathbf{y}). \quad (13.7)$$

Input-oriented distance functions   An input-oriented distance function is, in turn, the maximum ratio by which input vector x can be contracted and still be inside the input set L (y) for a given output vector y:

$$d_I(\mathbf{x}, \mathbf{y}) = \max\ \{\rho|\ (\mathbf{x}/\rho) \in L(\mathbf{y})\}. \quad (13.8)$$

Technical efficiency for the input-oriented distance function $T\ E_I$ is then defined as the inverse of the input-oriented distance function $d_I(\mathbf{x}, \mathbf{y})$ that

$$TE_I = 1/d_I(\mathbf{x}, \mathbf{y}),\tag{13.9}$$

which takes a value between 0 and 1. Input-oriented efficiency measurement captures how efficiently inputs are used for the given output level. See Chapter 3 of Coelli et al. (2005) and Coelli and Perelman (2000) for properties of these concepts and further discussions.

Luenberger productivity index Input-oriented and output-oriented distance functions yield different productivity indices when production is not constant-return-to-scale. The productivity index proposed by Luenberger (1992) yields a value between the input- and output-oriented functions, by computing the distance from (**x**, **y**) to the production frontier in the direction of $(-\mathbf{x}, \mathbf{y})$, relative to the length of the vector (**x**, **y**) itself. The productivity index computed in this way is called the Luenberger productivity index, which we denote by $d_L(\mathbf{x}, \mathbf{y})$ and is defined as follows for a DMU whose input – output combination is (**x**, **y**):

$$d_L(\mathbf{x}, \mathbf{y}) = \max\{\beta|\,((1 - \beta)\,\mathbf{x}, (1 + \beta)\,\mathbf{y}) \in S\}.\tag{13.10}$$

See also Chambers et al. (1996a, b) and Mussard and Peypoch (2006) for the details on Luenberger productivity index.

Scale economies Production transformation function $T(\mathbf{x}, \mathbf{y})$ is defined as an implicit function such that

$$T(\mathbf{x}, \mathbf{y}) = 0\tag{13.11}$$

where $d_O(\mathbf{x}, \mathbf{y}) = d_I(\mathbf{x}, \mathbf{y}) = 1$. That is, production transformation function $T(\mathbf{x}, \mathbf{y})$ is the boundary of the production possibility set S. Then we can define the overall (local) elasticity of scale $E_{y:x}$ as the percentage increase in all outputs in response to a percentage increase in all inputs, when all outputs are increased at the same rate where (x, y) is such that $T(\mathbf{x}, \mathbf{y}) = 0$. Thus it is computed as

$$E_{y:x} = \left[\sum_{i=1}^{n}\left(\sum_{j=1}^{m}E_{y_ix_j}\right)^{-1}\right]^{-1}\tag{13.12}$$

$$s.t.\ T(\mathbf{x}, \mathbf{y}) = 0,\tag{13.13}$$

where x_j (y_i) is the jth (ith) element of input (output) vector, and $E_{y:x}$ is an elasticity of y with respect to x.

Cost, Revenue and Profit Function Approach

Let us continue to consider multi-output, multi-input DMUs. When price data are available, relationship between inputs and outputs can be expressed compactly in one equation as either cost, revenue or profit functions.

Cost function approach
Cost function is represented as

$$c\,(\mathbf{w}, \mathbf{y}) = \min_{\mathbf{x}} \mathbf{w}'\mathbf{x} \tag{13.14}$$

$$s.t.\ (\mathbf{x}, \mathbf{y}) \in S \tag{13.15}$$

where $\mathbf{w}$ is an input-price vector. After specifying appropriate functional form and error distribution, cost function is estimated. Then such minimum (estimated theoretical) cost is compared to the actual cost to obtain cost efficiency. For cost-function approach to be applicable, it must be reasonable to assume that DMUs are cost minimizers.

Applying Shephard's lemma to the cost function gives input demand function:

$$x_i(\mathbf{w}, \mathbf{y}) = \frac{\partial c(\mathbf{w}, \mathbf{y})}{\partial w_i}. \tag{13.16}$$

When the cost function (13.14) is specified as a flexible function using an anonymous approximation function such as translog function, the cost function (13.14) has to be estimated simultaneously with input demand functions (as cost shares) through an appropriate econometric method such as seemingly unrelated regressions (SUR).

Economies of scale can be alternatively computed from cost elasticities:

$$E_c = \left[\sum_{i=1}^{n} \frac{\partial \ln c(\mathbf{w}, \mathbf{y})}{\partial \ln y_i} \right]^{-1}. \tag{13.17}$$

This measure of scale economies E_c does not in general coincide with $E_{y:x}$ as E_c permits unequal rates of increase in inputs so as to minimize the increase in cost, for example if the production technology is not homothetic.

Revenue function approach   Revenue function is represented as

$$r\,(\mathbf{p}, \mathbf{x}) = \max_{\mathbf{y}} \mathbf{p}'\mathbf{y} \tag{13.18}$$

$$s.t.\ (\mathbf{x}, \mathbf{y}) \in S \tag{13.19}$$

where $\mathbf{p}$ is an output-price vector. That is, for a given input vector $\mathbf{x}$, output mix needs to be optimized so as to maximize the revenue. Revenue-function approach is much less utilized than cost-function approach in productivity measurement, and is more popular in the field of macro-economics and international trade.

Applying Shephard's lemma to the revenue function gives revenue-maximizing output allocation given output prices and inputs:

$$y_i(\mathbf{p}, \mathbf{x}) = \frac{\partial r\,(\mathbf{p}, \mathbf{x})}{\partial p_i}. \tag{13.20}$$

Profit function approach   Profit function is represented as

$$\pi (\mathbf{p}, \mathbf{w}) = \max_{\mathbf{x}, \mathbf{y}} \mathbf{p}'\mathbf{y} - \mathbf{w}'\mathbf{x} \qquad (13.21)$$

$$s.t. \ (\mathbf{x}, \mathbf{y}) \in S. \qquad (13.22)$$

The profit function approach is the most comprehensive approach in the sense that it captures all the potential sources of inefficiency of DMUs. However, its data requirement is the highest: both input and output price data are required. Also, it must be reasonable to assume that DMUs are profit maximizers.

Applying Hotelling's lemma to the obtained profit function yields (provided that the profit function is twice continuously differentiable) the supply function:

$$q_i(\mathbf{p}, \mathbf{w}) = \frac{\partial \pi (\mathbf{p}, \mathbf{w})}{\partial p_i}. \qquad (13.23)$$

Other Issues

Identifying the sources of inefficiency
Efficiency can be decomposed into several parts, including (pure) technical efficiency, allocative efficiency, and scale economies. It is possible that a DMU is technically efficient but inefficient in allocative sense or in production scale. Appropriate method and assumptions will separate these sources of inefficiency (see Chapter 3 of Coelli et al., 2005, for details.).

For example, allocative efficiency is defined as follows. Let $\mathbf{x}^*$ be the solution to the cost-minimization problem given in Equation (13.14) and c^* be the resulting minimum cost. Then allocative efficiency of inputs AE_I is

$$AE_I \equiv \frac{\mathbf{w}'\mathbf{x}^*}{(\mathbf{w}'\mathbf{x}) / d_I}. \qquad (13.24)$$

Recall that technical efficiency is

$$TE_I = 1/d_I (\mathbf{x}, \mathbf{y}) \qquad (13.25)$$

and combining together we have the cost efficiency CE:

$$CE = \frac{\mathbf{w}'\mathbf{x}^*}{\mathbf{w}'\mathbf{x}} \qquad (13.26)$$

$$= AE_I \cdot TE_I. \qquad (13.27)$$

Similar argument applies to outputs as well. For outputs, allocation efficiency implies optimal output mix in maximizing revenue r in Equation (13.18), given inputs $\mathbf{x}$ and output prices $\mathbf{p}$.

Technological change and productivity growth: Malmquist index
Performance of a DMU changes not only because of efficiency change of such DMU itself but also due to the technological change. Malmquist index captures both of them and hence decomposing it separates and identifies these two effects. Caves et al. (1982b), Fare and Grosskopf (1992), and Chapter 9 of Fare et al. (1994) explain the concept in

detail; here we review briefly some of their results. Malmquist input-oriented productivity index is defined as follows.

$$M_I^{t+1} \equiv \left[\left(\frac{d_I^t\,(\mathbf{x}^{t+1},\,\mathbf{y}^{t+1})}{d_I^t\,(\mathbf{x}^t,\,\mathbf{y}^t)} \right) \left(\frac{d_I^t\,(\mathbf{x}^{t+1},\,\mathbf{y}^{t+1})}{d_I^t\,(\mathbf{x}^t,\,\mathbf{y}^t)} \right) \right]^{\frac{1}{2}} \tag{13.28}$$

$$= \left[\left(\frac{TE_I|_{\mathbf{x}^t,\mathbf{y}^t,S^t}}{TE_I|_{\mathbf{x}^{t+1},\mathbf{y}^{t+1},S^t}} \right) \left(\frac{TE_I|_{\mathbf{x}^t,\mathbf{y}^t,S^{t+1}}}{TE_I|_{\mathbf{x}^{t+1},\mathbf{y}^{t+1},S^{t+1}}} \right) \right]^{\frac{1}{2}} \tag{13.29}$$

where superscript indicates time of observation and M_I^{t+1} is the Malmquist input-oriented productivity index. Note that M_I^{t+1} above can be alternatively written as

$$M_I^{t+1} = \left\{ \frac{TE_I|_{\mathbf{x}^t,\mathbf{y}^t,S^t}}{TE_I|_{\mathbf{x}^{t+1},\mathbf{y}^{t+1},S^{t+1}}} \right\} \left[\left(\frac{TE_I|_{\mathbf{x}^t,\mathbf{y}^t,S^{t+1}}}{TE_I|_{\mathbf{x}^t,\mathbf{y}^t,S^t}} \right) \left(\frac{TE_I|_{\mathbf{x}^{t+1},\mathbf{y}^{t+1},S^{t+1}}}{TE_I|_{\mathbf{x}^{t+1},\mathbf{y}^{t+1},S^t}} \right) \right]^{\frac{1}{2}}. \tag{13.30}$$

The square root of the terms in square brackets gives the technology change as the geometric mean of the shifts in production possibility set measured at observed inputs and outputs in periods t and $t + 1$. The terms in the curly brackets give the ratio of efficiencies in two periods.

Conventional Methods of Efficiency Measurement

Index numbers and Total Factor Productivity (TFP)
An index is *exact* if it is derived from aggregator functions (for example, production functions and utility functions.) An exact index is *superlative* if the aggregator function is a flexible, second-order approximation function of some anonymous function. One example of a *superlative* index is the Fisher Ideal index, and another is the Tornqvist index (see Fisher, 1922, for Fisher Ideal index, and Tornqvist, 1936, and Theil, 1965, for Tornqvist index). A desirable index number should possess properties such as reversality and circularity (or transitivity). Fisher Ideal index does not satisfy circularity. Caves et al. (1982a) developed a multilateral superlative index based upon Tornqvist Index, which satisfies the circularity. We summarize their results in the following.

As mentioned above, Tornqvist index is superlative and its aggregator function is a homogeneous translog function. For example, Tornqvist output index is derived from a translog production function.[3] Tornqvist multilateral output index δ has the form such that

$$\ln \delta = \frac{1}{2} \sum_{i=1}^{n} (R_i + \overline{R_i})\,[\ln y_i - \overline{\ln y_i}], \tag{13.31}$$

and Tornqvist multilateral input index ρ is such that

$$\ln \rho = \frac{1}{2} \sum_{i=1}^{m} (W_i + \overline{W_i})\,[\ln x_i - \overline{\ln x_i}], \tag{13.32}$$

where $R_i\,(W_i)$ is the revenue (cost) share of the ith output (input), $y_i\,(x_i)$ is the ith element of the output (input) vector $\mathbf{y}\,(\mathbf{x})$, and the bar $(-)$ indicates arithmetic mean. In its derivation, *Tornqvist output (input) index assumes constant-return production technology and revenue maximization (cost minimization) of DMUs.*

Caves et al. (1982a) show that the Tornqvist productivity index, say λ, equals to the ratio between Tornqvist output and input indices:

$$\ln \lambda = \ln\left(\frac{\delta}{\rho}\right) \tag{13.33}$$

$$= \frac{1}{2}\sum_{i=1}^{n} (R_i + \overline{R_i})\,[\ln y_i - \overline{\ln y_i}] - \frac{1}{2}\sum_{i=1}^{m} (W_i + \overline{W_i})\,[\ln x_i - \overline{\ln x_i}]. \tag{13.34}$$

The productivity index λ obtained as above is often called the total factor productivity (TFP). Oum and Yu (1998) applied this index number method to TFP measurement of airlines.

Applications of the index approach in other fields are widely ranged as well. Fuglie (2004) computed Tornqvist index of total factor productivity for crop and livestock production in Indonesia between 1961 and 2000, and examined the trend of agricultural productivity and its impact on agricultural growth. Grifell-Tatje and Lovell (1996) examined the changes in TFP of Spanish savings banks during post-deregulation period with Malmquist productivity index number approach, and investigated the effects of branching and consolidations on the decline of productivity over the period.

Data envelopment analysis
Data envelopment analysis (DEA) is applied to assess relative productivity or efficiency of DMUs that produce multiple outputs using common multiple inputs. Twenty years after the pioneering work by Farrel (1957), an innovative work by Charnes et al. (1978) triggered a rapid accumulation of the research on, and using, data envelopment analysis (DEA). Banker et al. (1984) extended the literature, and Gillen and Lall (1997) applied DEA to airport productivity.

There are many applications of DEA other than airport productivity. Abbott and Doucouliagos (2003) employed DEA to estimate the efficiencies of Australian public universities in 1995 to evaluate their performance. Gregoriou et al. (2005) used DEA to evaluate the performance of hedge funds, and compared the results of DEA models with conventional financial performance indicators, suggesting that the DEA is useful as a complementary tool for the selection of efficient hedge funds. Cullinane and Wang (2006) measured the efficiency of 69 container terminals in Europe with annual throughput of over 10 000 TEUs in 2002 by using DEA, and used the estimated scores to analyze their relationship with production scale and geographical location.

The DEA model   DEA is a non-parametric method of identifying production possibility set and computing efficiency using the distance function approach. The benefit of DEA is that it only requires physical data, and not financial/nominal data; free of a-priori assumptions on functional forms; and applicable to multi-output productions. The weakness is that it is extremely sensitive to outliers; generates multiple best performers; and is inefficient as it utilizes only a subset of observations in identifying production possibility set. See Chapter 6 of Coelli et al. (2005) for a concise explanation and applications of DEA. DEA can be combined with Malmquist approach to separate and measure the technological advance and efficiency improvement over time (see Coelli and Rao, 2005).

In the original DEA model developed in Charnes et al. (1978), the efficiency of a DMU is measured by solving the following maximization problem:

$$\max_{u_i, v_j} \frac{\sum_{i=1}^{n} u_i y_{i0}}{\sum_{j=1}^{m} v_j x_{j0}}$$

$$s.t. \quad \frac{\sum_{i=1}^{n} u_i y_{il}}{\sum_{j=1}^{m} v_j x_{jl}} \leq 1 \quad \forall l = 1, \cdots, L$$

$$u_i, v_j \geq 0 \quad \forall i = 1, \cdots, n, \quad \forall j = 1, \cdots, m \qquad (13.35)$$

where L is the number of DMUs, y_{il} and x_{jl} are the ith output and jth input of the lth DMU respectively. The efficiency of a DMU is measured as the maximum ratio of a linear combination of outputs to a linear combination of inputs, controlling nonnegative parameters u and v, subject to the constraint that such ratio must be less than or equal to unity for every DMU.

The following linear programming problem is a reduced form derived from the above maximization problem:

$$\min_{\lambda_1, \cdots, \lambda_L} h_0$$

$$s.t. \sum_{l=1}^{L} \lambda_l y_{il} = y_{i0} \quad \forall i = 1, \cdots, n$$

$$\sum_{l=1}^{L} \lambda_l x_{jl} = h_0 x_{j0} \quad \forall j = 1, \cdots, m$$

$$\lambda_1, \cdots, \lambda_L, h_0 \geq 0. \qquad (13.36)$$

At the solution of this linear-programming problem, h_0 indicates 'input-oriented' efficiency of each DMU. We focus on this input-oriented DEA efficiency in the following analysis.[4]

Note that the model in (13.36) assumes constant returns to scale (CRS) for production technology. This CRS DEA model can be readily extended to the variable-returns-to-scale (VRS) DEA model. We obtain the VRS specification by adding the following concavity condition as a constraint to the above linear programming problem in (13.36):

$$\sum_{l=1}^{L} \lambda_l = 1. \qquad (13.37)$$

Note that the following inequality is always satisfied:

$$h_0 | V RS \geq h_0 | CRS. \qquad (13.38)$$

As Banker, Charnes, and Cooper (1984) argues, VRS DEA efficiency measured as h_0 above indicates only technical efficiency, and does not include scale efficiency. The difference between CRS and VRS DEA efficiencies then gives such scale efficiency.

Stochastic frontier analysis

Stochastic frontier analysis (SFA) was initiated by Aigner et al. (1977). The idea is to assume that the disturbance term has two components, white noise and inefficiency, when estimating a parametric production frontier. While the white noise is a two-tailed symmetric distribution, inefficiency has only one tail. Maximum likelihood method is conventionally utilized in estimating the production frontier as well as parameters for the noise and inefficiency distributions. This idea can be adopted in estimating not only production functions but also cost/profit functions, which enables efficiency measurement under multiple-output situation.[5]

In the literature, there is a wide range of SFA applications other than airport efficiency measurement. Wang (2007) applied the SFA method using the data of 30 countries to evaluate the efficiency of aggregate R&D activities, and analyzed the relationship between R&D efficiency score and the economic-environment variables of the country. Bonin et al. (2005) used SFA to estimate the profit and cost efficiency of 225 banks in 11 transition countries from 1996 to 2000. They investigated the effect of ownership on the banks' efficiency through the second-stage regression in which measured efficiency scores are regressed against banks' characteristics. Tongzon and Heng (2005) employed SFA to estimate the efficiency of 25 container ports, investigating whether privatization is necessary for them to gain competitive advantage. They also conducted second stage regression to examine the determinants of port competitiveness.

In the following we introduce the empirical model utilized in Oum et al. (2008) in which they estimated cost efficiencies of worldwide airports using SFA. They estimated a variable cost function in the form of

$$\ln C_{it} = \ln C^*(Q_{it}, W_{it}, K_{it}, t) + \Delta_i + \varepsilon_{it}^c \tag{13.39}$$

where ε_{it}^c is the white noise for the airport i in time t; Q_{it}, W_{it} and K_{it} are the vectors of outputs, variable input prices, and fixed capital inputs respectively. Here, Δ_i is the deviation of actual cost for airport i from the cost frontier C^*. Since Δ_i is the inefficiency in the cost, it takes only positive values. Their assumption is that Δ_i is a random draw conditional on the airports' attributes, that is, ownership form. The probability density function of Δ_i is

$$\Delta_i = \exp(Z_i \Gamma_i) \tag{13.40}$$

where

$$\Gamma_i \sim N(\overline{\Gamma}, \Omega), \tag{13.41}$$

and Z_i is the ownership-form dummy vector representing characteristics of airport i. The variance – covariance matrix Ω is assumed to be diagonal. After specifying the minimum cost function $\ln C^*$ as a translog function, they estimate it together with the cost-share function for variable inputs. This improves the efficiency of estimation, as stated above.

Recent Developments in Theory

Production with undesirable outputs

Production of desirable outputs (for example, transport services) is often accompanied by production of undesirable outputs (pollution, congestion delays, noise and risk of accidents) as by-products. Chung et al. (1997) introduced the directional distance function approach to calculate production relationships involving goods and bads. Atkinson and Dorfman (2005) treated the bad as a technology shifter of an input distance function while Pathomsiri et al. (2008) defined a directional output distance function in the framework of DEA to incorporate the delays associated with airport operations. The distance function approach has been applied to the industries other than aviation. Park and Weber (2006) applied it to estimate the efficiency of Korean banks, where loan losses are treated as undesirable output of bank's operation. McMullen and Noh (2007) evaluated the environmental efficiency of US bus transit agencies in 2000. They employed DEA with directional distance function to account for vehicular emissions as undesirable output.

Distance function approach   Let us denote **y**, **b**, and **x** as vectors of desirable outputs (goods), undesirable outputs (bads), and inputs respectively. One way of treating the undesirable outputs is to treat them symmetrically to the ordinary outputs. Then the input distance function with undesirable outputs, d_I^u say, is defined as

$$d_I^u(\mathbf{x}, [\mathbf{y}, \mathbf{b}]) = \max\{\rho|\ (\mathbf{x}/\rho) \in L\ ([\mathbf{y}, \mathbf{b}])\} \tag{13.42}$$

where L ([**y**, **b**]) is the set of input vectors that can produce the output combination of [**y**, **b**].

Unfortunately, when treating desirable and undesirable outputs symmetrically the output-oriented distance function is in general not well defined, even under a standard set of assumptions on the production possibility set. This is due to the fact that the amount of goods and bads can increase together even when the amount of inputs is held constant, unlike ordinary goods that are in trade-offs.

Atkinson and Dorfman (2005) uses input distance function in measuring efficiency of electric utilities industry with air pollution as bads, that are treated as a technology shifter. Let t be the parameter for the state of production technology, which depends on the quantity of bads **b**. That is, production possibility set S (and therefore the input set L) expands as the quantity of bads increases. They specified the input distance function as follows:

$$d_I^u(\mathbf{x}, \mathbf{y}, t|\mathbf{b}) = \max\{\rho|\ (\mathbf{x}/\rho) \in L\ (\mathbf{y}, t|\ \mathbf{b})\}. \tag{13.43}$$

Output distance function can be computed in this specification, and that corresponds to measuring the distance to the production frontier from the output combination (**y**, **b**) in the direction that **y** is increasing while holding **b** as given.[6] Atkinson and Dorfman specifies the distance function as translog, then applies SFA method for econometric estimation.

DEA-based approach   The methodology employed by Pathomsiri et al. (2008) is essentially DEA oriented, and they define the output set P (x) as follows:

$$P(\mathbf{x}) = \{\mathbf{y}, \mathbf{b}|$$

$$\sum_{l \in L} \lambda_l y_{il} \geq y_i, \quad i = 1, \cdots, N,$$

$$\sum_{l \in L} \lambda_l b_{jl} = b_j, \quad j = 1, \cdots, J,$$

$$\sum_{l \in L} \lambda_l x_{kl} \leq x_k, \quad k = 1, \cdots, M,$$

$$\lambda_l \geq 0, \quad l = 1, \cdots, L\} \tag{13.44}$$

where **b** is a *J*-vector of undesirable outputs; on the right-hand side of constraints y_i, b_j and x_k are respectively *i*th, *j*th and *k*th element of **y**, **b** and **x** vectors whereas on the left-hand side, b_{jl} is the *j*th undesirable output of airport *l*, and so on. The production possibility set defined as above is compact and convex, implying that shrinking all three vectors **y**, **b** and **x** in the production possibility set at the same rate will result in a set of vectors that is still in the production possibility set. Also, above expression implies weak disposability of goods **y**, that is, for any given combination of undesirable outputs **b** and inputs **x** one can reduce the amount of desirable outputs **y** and still be in the production possibility set.

In their analysis, inefficiency is computed by using the directional output distance function, not the above-mentioned ordinary output-oriented distance function. Unlike the ordinary DEA, inefficiency cannot be computed by contracting the output vector (**y**, **b**), since as stated above, it will simply reduce to a zero vector. Instead, their method finds the minimum distance to the boundary from the output combination (**y**, **b**) in the direction that **y** is increasing and **b** is decreasing just as Luenberger productivity index, with undesirable-output vector **b** in the place of input vector **x**; that is, in the direction of (**y**, –**b**) (see Pathomsiri et al., 2008, for more details.)

Index-number approach   Pittman (1983) extended the original index-number approach developed by Caves et al. (1982a) to include the undesirable outputs. As in Caves et al., Pittman specifies the production transformation function as translog:

$$F(\ln \mathbf{Y}^k, \ln \mathbf{x}^k, k) = 1 \tag{13.45}$$

$$\mathbf{Y}^k = [\mathbf{y}^k, \mathbf{b}^k] \tag{13.46}$$

where $\mathbf{y}^k$, $\mathbf{b}^k$ and $\mathbf{x}^k$ are respectively desirable and undesirable outputs and inputs, for firm *k*. Production transformation function *F* is firm specific, as it has technology parameter *k* as the last argument. Since it is possible for a firm to increase desirable outputs by increasing the output of undesirable outputs and thus the production of desirable and undesirable outputs are not in trade-offs as stated above, in comparing productive efficiency of two firms, the factor of proportionality δ_k is redefined as the contraction factor for desirable outputs while undesirable outputs are expanded by the same factor, that is,

$$F\left(\ln \frac{\mathbf{y}^k}{\delta_k}, \ln \delta_k \mathbf{b}^k, \ln \mathbf{x}^l, l \right) = 1 \tag{13.47}$$

where $\mathbf{x}^l$ is the output vector for firm l. The bilateral output index that compares the social efficiency of firms k and l is then obtained as

$$\ln \delta_{kl} = -\sum_i \left[\frac{1}{2} F_i(\ln \mathbf{Y}^k, \ln \mathbf{x}^k, k) + \frac{1}{2} F_i(\ln \mathbf{Y}^l, \ln \mathbf{x}^l, l) \right] \ln\left(\frac{Y_i^k}{Y_i^l} \right) \tag{13.48}$$

where Y_i^k is the ith element of a vector $\mathbf{Y}^k = [\mathbf{y}^k, \mathbf{b}^k]$. This expression of output index is identical to the original bilateral output index without the undesirable outputs developed in Caves et al. (1982a). Hence the multilateral output index follows the same way as in the Caves et al., even with the existence of undesirable outputs. It is also shown by Pittman that the multilateral input index has the same form as that of Caves et al., where all outputs are desirable.

One practical difficulty, however, arises due to the fact that the prices for undesirable outputs may well be unobservable. As explained earlier in the section on Tornqvist index, index number approach requires revenue (or cost) share data. To construct such data, Pittman uses the shadow prices of undesirable outputs, obtained through the constrained profit maximization problem, where total admissible amounts of emission of bads are constraints.

Other econometric/methodological developments

Dynamic efficiency and network efficiency   When production uses durable inputs, a DMU's decision process becomes that of dynamic optimization.[7] There, what is an optimal choice in static (or one-time) sense does not have to be optimal in the long-run dynamic sense. Therefore, the measurement of performance requires an appropriate method. One such method is dynamic DEA. In dynamic DEA, there are two kinds of inputs, namely variable inputs and quasi-fixed inputs. The quasi-fixed inputs are durable, and therefore, the choice is to adjust their stocks at every time point, thus entailing dynamic optimization. Dynamic DEA solves for the dynamic cost frontier through linear programming. See Nemoto and Goto (1999, 2003) for details. Yoshida and Yamaguchi (2007) recently developed a parametric counterpart to the dynamic DEA. In these methodologies, overall cost efficiency is decomposed into dynamic and static efficiency. Further, this static efficiency is decomposed into allocation efficiency and technical efficiency, as described above. This framework for dynamic efficiency has been recently adopted in measuring network efficiency, where firms are vertically integrated in the production process and intermediate outputs become the inputs of the downstream firms.

Parametric estimation of production transformation function   DEA is a versatile methodology in the sense that it only requires physical data, can handle multi-outputs, and imposes no a-priori assumptions such as cost minimization or CRS production. However, it generates multiple best performers, cannot allow IRS production and utilizes only a subset of observations in identifying the frontier. Yoshida (2004) and Yoshida and Fujimoto (2004) propose and use parametric approach of estimating productive efficiency called endogenous-weight TFP. Endogenous-weight TFP is a parametric method which estimates production transformation function with multiple outputs directly by using physical data only. Thus it overcomes all of the shortcomings of DEA mentioned above. However, choice of a functional form is critical for a successful measurement of efficiencies.

Corrected ordinary least squares The idea of corrected ordinary least squares (COLS) is to first estimate the production function with OLS, and then to shift it 'upward' as much as the maximum positive error to construct the production frontier. Coelli and Perelman (2000) apply COLS to productivity measurement of European railways using the distance function approach. Greene (1998) provides comprehensive discussion of production frontier estimation using COLS.

EMPIRICAL ANALYSIS OF AIRPORT PRODUCTIVITY: A CHRONOLOGICAL OVERVIEW

This section considers an empirical analysis of airport productivity that uses efficiency measurement techniques discussed in the previous section. It attempts to give a chronological overview of airport productivity analysis. The section concludes by addressing future research opportunities.

Initial Stage of Airport Productivity Analysis

The first series of productivity analyses of airports came out in the late 1990s. Since the advent of deregulation in the airline industry that started in the United States and then in Europe and other areas of the world, there has been growing emphasis on improvement of airport performance. Airlines were now in a position to strategically select airports and develop their network. However, it was not until after airport privatization that took place in the UK and Australia in the late 1980s that productivity analysis was applied to airports.

Gillen and Lall (1997) and Hooper and Hensher (1997) were the first two papers to shed light on this topic. Gillen and Lall (1997) applied Data Envelopment Analysis (DEA) on 21 US airports and used the efficiency measurement of terminal service and aircraft movements derived from DEA in a Tobit regression to identify how much variation in productivity index is attributable to managerial factors. They identified higher terminal efficiency when gates were commonly used by a number of air carriers compared to when gates were used exclusively by specific air carriers. Preferential use of gates enabled airlines to exercise monopoly power and deter new entry. Airports with compensatory financing under which the airport takes full responsibility of the airport finance, had higher level of efficiency for terminal service, while airports with residual financing under which any financial shortfall is imposed on the airlines, had higher efficiency for the air side. Exploratory work by Hooper and Hensher (1997), on the other hand, used the Tornqvist index to measure productivity of six Australian airports. Gross TFP index was regressed against output to compute output-adjusted TFP which significantly altered the overall productivity ranking. This paper served as a lead to subsequent papers that focused on scale economies of airports.

Another important step in airport productivity analysis was to assess the impact of public policy. Parker (1999) was the first to assess efficiency impact of airport privatization. DEA was applied to panel data of 22 UK airports including those managed by British Airports Authority (BAA). He found no evidence of technical productivity improvement from BAA privatization. This paper attracted researchers and policy makers to take a deeper look at the optimal governance structure and regulation of airports.[8]

The Second Stage: Theoretical and Methodological Evolution

A number of studies that followed not only assessed airports in different parts of the world but also adopted new methodological approaches.

Salazar de la Cruz (1999) analyzed 16 major airports in Spain with DEA. Mid-sized airports exhibited constant returns to scale whereas large airports showed signs of decreasing returns to scale. Another DEA analysis of 33 Spanish airports by Murillo-Melchor (1999) broke down productivity change into technical efficiency and scale efficiency. Larger airports were constant or decreasing returns to scale, while small regional airports omitted in Salazar de la Cruz (1999) turned out to be increasing returns to scale. The Malmquist indices derived attempted to reveal the dynamic productivity change.

Sarkis (2000) calculated various efficiency scores using a variety of DEA-based models and provided a robust observation that average efficiency of major US airports experienced general increase during the period. He also performed a non-parametric analysis (Mann–Whitney U-test) of DEA based indices to identify characteristics that affected airport efficiency. Hub airports were more efficient than others, while there was no statistically significant difference between airports in cities with multiple airports and those in single airport cities. Gillen and Lall (2001) updated their previous work on US airports and constructed Malmquist index of productivity change and decomposed it into scale efficiency, technical efficiency and technological change. Significant variation was identified in the 22 airports that they analyzed. They also found that higher productivity for terminal service does not always imply high productivity for airside activities. Another interesting observation was to identify 'innovator airports' that pushed the frontier to a more efficient level.

Pels et al. (2003) analyzed 34 European airports using DEA and stochastic frontier analysis. By calculating most productive airport sizes they contended that given the current input-mix most airports were operating under increasing returns to scale. DEA analysis of 37 Spanish airports by Martin and Roman (2001) concluded that 20 were operating under increasing returns to scale.

Adler and Berechman (2001) introduced an innovative way of reflecting airlines' perception of airport quality into productivity analysis. They collected detailed questionnaires from airlines and after confirming with canonical correlation analysis that these subjective data could be explained by objective data, they applied DEA-based super-efficient techniques on the subjective and objective attributes of 26 airports, of which 16 were European airports. In order to avoid lack of differentiation between DMUs, the number of outputs was reduced by principal component analysis. They found some west European airports such as Geneva and Milan consistently lead the efficiency scores.

Abbott and Wu (2002) conducted DEA analysis of 12 Australian airports and contended that although technological change was recorded during 1990s technical and scale efficiency had not improved. Regression analysis of DEA efficiency against characteristics of airports and operating environments revealed that productivity improvement had been higher for more profitable, heavily asset-accumulating airports. They added 12 airports outside Australia to conduct benchmarking and found that Australia's largest airports such as Sydney and Melbourne appear to be on, or close to, the efficient frontier. Correlation between X-values, the expected efficiency savings ratio, under the price-cap regulation and the efficiency scores derived from DEA was not statistically significant.

Fernandes and Pacheco (2002) analyzed 35 Brazilian airports with DEA and compared the efficient capacity with existing demand forecast to assess the timing of future capacity expansion. They argued that although majority of efficient airports would suffer capacity shortage even in the short-run, some inefficient airports have slacks available to utilize before they reach the capacity limit for the next 15 years.

Bazargan and Vasigh (2003) studied a total of 45 US airports, 15 each from large, medium and small hub airports, to identify efficiency difference between the three airport categories. They introduce virtual super-efficient airports in the DEA analysis to cope with a majority of airports being on, or close to, the frontier. The resulting efficiency scores from the adjusted DEA were statistically verified by non-parametric tests and showed that the small hubs consistently outperformed the large hubs.

Reaching Out Into the World: Global Airport Benchmarking

In 2001, the Air Transport Research Society (ATRS) embarked on the first comprehensive world-wide airport benchmarking. Oum et al. (2003) and Oum and Yu (2004) highlight major findings from the ATRS initiative. Oum et al. (2003) computed productivity of 50 major airports in Asia Pacific, Europe and North America using the endogenous-weight TFP method (EW-TFP). Asia-Pacific airports appeared to be more efficient than those in North America, which in turn were relatively more efficient than European airports. The productivity index was then regressed against factors beyond, and under, managerial control. From the regression analysis, larger airports appear to have higher gross TFP due to economies of scale and not necessarily because they are technically efficient. Airport ownership structure does not seem to have any statistically significant effect on TFP, while diversification into non-aeronautical activities leads to higher productivity. Oum and Yu (2004) focused on operating efficiency of airports. They computed gross Variable Factor Productivity (VFP) that considers labor and soft costs (other non-capital costs and outsourcing cost) as inputs and then residual VFP was estimated by removing factors beyond managerial control. In addition to similar analytical results from Oum et al. (2003), high performers in terms of residual VFP were identified.

A number of productivity analyses were also conducted in different corners of the world. Yoshida and Fujimoto (2004) applied DEA and EW-TFP to 67 airports in Japan and conducted Tobit regression to assess efficiency of local and new airports.

They found inefficiency in small regional airports on the mainland and similar inefficiency in airports opened since the 1990s. Barros and Sampaio (2004) conducted DEA analysis for ten major airports in Portugal and disaggregated productivity into technical and allocative efficiency. The productivity index from DEA was regressed against various spatial factors and suggested that the location of an airport plays an important role in determining its efficiency. Fung et al. (2008) applied DEA to 25 airports in mainland China and found the average rate of productivity growth to be 3 per cent, although significant discrepancy existed between airports in different geographical locations. Airports in the southwest region of China, for instance, were the most efficient on average. Using a Gaussian kernel smoothing technique the source of growth was attributed mostly to technological improvement rather than technical efficiency gains.

New Avenues of Airport Productivity Analysis

Pacheco and Fernandes (2003) conducted a bi-dimensional analysis of 35 Brazilian airports through DEA analysis of variables that are related to ability to raise financial returns and capacity utilization. They plotted the outcome into an efficiency matrix to identify which airports needed capacity expansion and also needed to increase management efficiency. Pels et al. (2003) conducted stochastic frontier analysis and DEA for 33 European airports. In SFA, an efficient frontier of air transport movements (ATM) is first estimated and predicted value of ATM is then used to estimate air passenger movements (APM). Similarly, in DEA, the number of runways is used as fixed factor. This allowed Pels et al. to distinguish between efficiency in terms of aircraft movement and passenger throughput. They contend that an average airport is operating under constant returns to scale for ATM and increasing returns to scale for APM. This is consistent with Gillen and Lall (1997). Overall, they identified room for efficiency improvement in many European airports and found no specific correlation between region and airport efficiency.

Sarkis and Talluri (2004) applied DEA to 44 major US airports and conducted cross-efficiency analysis to rank their performance. It appears that Fort Lauderdale and Oakland were good performers, while Jacksonville, Kansas City, Milwaukee and New Orleans were least efficient. They utilized these results to perform hierarchical clustering analysis so as to identify different categories of benchmarking. Thirteen clusters were identified. Similar to the result in Sarkis (2000), airports in warm and stable weather regions, as well as large hub airports turned out to be performing well.

A number of recent studies have started to take undesirable outputs into consideration. Yu (2004) introduced social cost of aircraft noise as an undesirable output as well as population as environmental factors into a DEA analysis of airports. He calculated DEA productivity scores for 14 airports in Taiwan and argued that conventional methodology that uses normal outputs underestimates the relative efficiency performance of these airports. Yu et al. (2008) assessed productivity growth of four Taiwanese airports using a modified Malmquist index that accommodated undesirable output, the aircraft noise. Omission of undesirable outputs overestimated TFP growth by almost threefold. Considering that TFP growth on average was found to be driven mainly by efficiency gains, the authors stress the importance of upgrading air traffic facilities to enhance efficiency through reduction in aircraft noise. Pathomsiri et al. (2008) incorporated delays as an undesirable output into a DEA analysis of 56 US airports. The Luenberger productivity index was used to assess inter-temporal productivity change. When delay was excluded from outputs many large and congested airports were the ones on the efficient frontier. However, when delay was accounted for, many small and less congested airports joined the group of efficient airports.

CONCLUDING REMARKS

Efficiency measurement and benchmarking is an important topic whether one is interested in comparing efficiency of a firm or a sub-unit of a firm relative to its peers/competitors, learning to improve one's efficiency performance relative to a benchmark unit, or investigating effects of a public policy or a regulation. Efficiency measurement is critical for industries where firms do not face strong competition in the market. Examples include transport infrastructure providers such as airports, seaports, highways, urban transit systems and so forth, public utilities such as electricity, water, public schools, hospitals, and other subsidized programs, and regulated industries where markets can not discipline firms effectively. One complication here is that these firms provide multiple outputs sharing a common set of inputs in producing these multiple outputs. This calls for a delicate and sophisticated treatment in measuring their efficiencies.

This chapter began by presenting various methodologies to measure efficiencies under these difficulties. They include DEA, Stochastic Frontier method and Productivity Index approaches. Also, it presented recent developments in efficiency measurement theory, especially in the case with undesirable outputs. It then reviewed the literature on airport efficiency measurement results and recent advances in the airport efficiency measurement with the existence of undesirable outputs such as pollution and congestion. It is clear that deregulation of the aviation industry motivated airport efficiency measurement. Growing concern over environmental degradation has started a new stream of research on airport efficiency measurement incorporating undesirable outputs.

NOTES

1. Note, however, that in productivity/efficiency measurement, not all of these properties are assumed a priori.
2. This is often termed strong disposability (see Section 2.3 of Fare, Grosskopf, and Lovell, 1994). Weak disposability requires instead that $\forall \lambda > 1$ and $\mathbf{x} \neq \mathbf{0}$, $P(\mathbf{x}) \subset P(\lambda\mathbf{x})$. Thus weak disposability allows isoquants to be 'bending backward' or 'upward sloping'.
3. For details of derivation see Caves et al. (1982a). For translog function and its properties see, for example, Berndt and Christensen (1973).
4. While output-oriented DEA efficiency can be similarly defined, Tone (2001) proposes non-radial measures of efficiency in the framework of DEA, called slacks-based measures (SBM). Unlike the conventional method, SBM contracts the input vector non-radially. This measure provides efficiency as a unique intermediate value between input- and output-oriented efficiencies.
5. See Greene (1998) and Kumbhakar and Lovell (2000) for more comprehensive discussions of SFA.
6. That is, output distance function with undesirable output d_o^u is given as

$$d_o^u(\mathbf{x}, \mathbf{y}, t|\mathbf{b}) = \min\{\theta| \, (\mathbf{y}/\theta) \in P\,(\mathbf{x}, t|\mathbf{b})\}$$

where P (**x**, t|**b**) is the output set for a given input vector **x**, which also depends on the level of undesirable output **b** via the technology shifter t.
7. Contrast with the Malmquist concept, which is merely comparative statics.
8. Editor note: see the chapter on airport governance and regulation by David Gillen.

REFERENCES

Abbott, M. and C. Doucouliagos, 2003, The efficiency of Australian universities: a data envelopment analysis. *Economics of Education Review*, **22**, 89–97.
Abbott, M. and S. Wu, 2002, Total factor productivity and efficiency of Australian airports. *The Australian Economic Review*, **35**, 244–260.
Adler, N. and J. Berechman, 2001, Measuring airport quality from the airlines' viewpoint: an application of data envelopment analysis. *Transport Policy*, **8**, 171–181.
Aigner, D., C.A.K. Lovell and P. Schmidt, 1977, Formulation and estimation of stochastic frontier production function models. *Journal of Econometrics*, **6**, 21–37.
Atkinson, A.E. and J.H. Dorfman, 2005, Bayesian measurement of productivity and efficiency in the presence of undesirable outputs: crediting electric utilities for reducing air pollution. *Journal of Econometrics*, **126**, 445–468.
Banker, R.D., A. Charnes and W.W. Cooper, 1984, Some models for estimating technical and scale inefficiency in data envelopment analysis. *Management Science*, **30**, 1078–1092.
Barros, C.P. and A. Sampaio, 2004, Technical and allocative efficiency in airports. *International Journal of Transport Economics*, **31**, 355–377.
Bazargan, M. and B. Vasigh, 2003, Size versus efficiency: a case study of US commercial airports. *Journal of Air Transport Management*, **9**, 187–193.
Berndt, E.R. and L.R. Christensen, 1973, The translog function and the substitution of equipment, structures, and labor in US manufacturing, 1929–1968. *Journal of Econometrics*, **1**, 81–114.
Bonin, J.P., I. Hasan and P. Wachtel, 2005, Bank performance, efficiency and ownership in transition countries. *Journal of Banking and Finance*, **29**, 31–53.
Caves, D.W., L.R. Christensen and W.E. Diewert, 1982a, Multilateral comparisons of output, input, and productivity using superlative index numbers. *The Economic Journal*, **92**, 73–86.
Caves, D.W., L.R. Christensen and W.E. Diewert, 1982b, The economic theory of index numbers and the measurement of input, output, and productivity. *Econometrica*, **50**, 1393–1414.
Chambers, R.G., 1988, *Applied Production Analysis: A Dual Approach*. New York: Cambridge University Press.
Chambers, R.G., Y. Chung and R. Fare, 1996a, Benefit and distance functions. *Journal of Economic Theory*, **70**, 407–419.
Chambers, R.G., R. Fare and S. Grosskopf, 1996b, Productivity growth in APEC countries. *Pacific Economic Review*, **1**, 181–90.
Charnes, A., W.W. Cooper and E. Rhodes, 1978, Measuring the efficiency of decision making units. *European Journal of Operational Research*, **2**, 429–444.
Chung, Y.H., R. Fare and S. Grosskopf, 1997, Productivity and undesirable outputs: a directional distance function approach. *Journal of Environmental Management*, **51**, 229–240.
Coelli, T.J. and S. Perelman, 2000, Technical efficiency of European railways: a distance function approach. *Applied Economics*, **32**, 1967–1976.
Coelli, T.J. and D.S.P. Rao, 2005, Total factor productivity growth in agriculture: a Malmquist index analysis of 93 countries, 1980–2000. *Agricultural Economics, International Association of Agricultural Economics*, **32s1**, 115–34.
Coelli, T.J., D.S.P. Rao, C.J. O'Donnell and G.E. Battese, 2005, *An Introduction to Efficiency and Productivity Analysis*, 2nd edn, Berlin: Springer.
Cullinane, K.P.B. and T. Wang, 2006, The efficiency of European container ports: a cross-sectional data envelopment analysis. *International Journal of Logistics: Research and Applications*, **9** (1), 19–31.
Fare, R. and S. Grosskopf, 1992, Malmquist productivity indexes and Fisher ideal indexes. *The Economic Journal*, **102** (410), 158–160.
Fare, R., S. Grosskopf and C.A.K. Lovell, 1994, *Production Frontiers*. Cambridge: Cambridge University Press.
Farrel, M.J., 1957, The measurement of productive efficiency. *Journal of the Royal Statistical Society, Series A General*, **120** (3), 253–290.
Fernandes, E. and R.R. Pacheco, 2002, Efficient use of airport capacity. *Transportation Research Part A*, **36**, 225–238.

Fisher, I., 1922, *The Making of Index Numbers*. Boston: Houghton-Mifflin.

Fuglie, K.O., 2004, Productivity growth in Indonesian agriculture, 1961–2000. *Bulletin of Indonesian Economic Studies*, **40** (2), 209–225.

Fung, M.K.Y., K.K.H. Wan and Y.V. Hui, 2008, Productivity changes in Chinese airports 1995–2004. *Transportation Research Part E*, **44** (3), 521–542.

Gillen, D. and A. Lall, 1997, Developing measures of airport productivity and performance: an application of data envelopment analysis. *Transportation Research Part E*, **33**, 261–273.

Gillen, D. and A. Lall, 2001, Non-parametric measures of efficiency of US airports. *International Journal of Transport Economics*, **28**, 283–306.

Greene, W.H., 1998, Frontier Production Functions. In H. Peasaran and P. Schmidt, eds, *Handbook of Applied Econometrics*, Vol. II. Oxford: Blackwell Publishers, pp. 81–166.

Gregoriou, G.N., K. Sedzro and J. Zhu, 2005, Hedge fund performance appraisal using data envelopment analysis. *European Journal of Operational Research*, **164**, 555–571.

Grifell-Tatje, E. and C.A.K. Lovell, 1996, Deregulation and productivity decline: the case of Spanish savings banks. *European Economic Review*, **40**, 1281–1303.

Hooper, P.G. and D.A. Hensher, 1997, Measuring total factor productivity of airports: an index number approach. *Transportation Research Part E*, **33**, 249–259.

Kumbhakar, S.C. and C.A.K. Lovell, 2000, *Stochastic Frontier Analysis*. Cambridge: Cambridge University Press.

Luenberger, D.G., 1992, Benefit functions and duality. *Journal of Mathematical Economics*, **21** (5), 461–481.

Martin, J.C. and C. Roman, 2001, An application of DEA to measure the efficiency of Spanish airports prior to privatization. *Journal of Air Transport Management*, **7**, 149–157.

McMullen, B.S. and D. Noh, 2007, Accounting for emissions in the measurement of transit agency efficiency: a directional distance function approach. *Transportation Research Part D*, **12**, 1–9.

Murillo-Melchor, C., 1999, An analysis of technical efficiency and productivity changes in Spanish airports using the Malmquist index. *International Journal of Transport Economics*, **26**, 271–292.

Mussard, S. and N. Peypoch, 2006, On multi-decomposition of the aggregate Luenberger productivity index. *Applied Economics Letters*, **13** (2), 113–116.

Nemoto, J. and M. Goto, 1999, Dynamic data envelopment analysis: modeling intertemporal behavior of a firm in the presence of productive inefficiencies. *Economic Letters*, **64**, 51–56.

Nemoto, J. and M. Goto, 2003, Measurement of dynamic efficiency in production: an application of data envelopment analysis to Japanese electric utilities. *Journal of Productivity Analysis*, **19**, 191–210.

Oum, T.H., J. Yan and C. Yu, 2008, Ownership forms matter for airport efficiency: a stochastic frontier investigation of worldwide airports. *Journal of Urban Economics*, **64** (2), 422–435.

Oum, T.H. and C. Yu, 1998, *Winning Airlines: Productivity and Cost Competitiveness of the World's Major Airlines*. Boston: Kluwer Academic Press.

Oum, T.H. and C. Yu, 2004, Measuring airports' operating efficiency: a summary of the 2003 ATRS global airport benchmarking report. *Transportation Research Part E*, **40**, 515–532.

Oum, T.H., C. Yu and X. Fu, 2003, A comparative analysis of productivity performance of the world's major airports: summary report of the ATRS global airport benchmarking research report 2002. *Journal of Air Transport Management*, **9**, 285–297.

Pacheco, R.R. and E. Fernandes, 2003, Managing efficiency of Brazilian airports. *Transportation Research Part A*, **37**, 667–680.

Park, K.H. and W.L. Weber, 2006, A note on efficiency and productivity growth in the Korean Banking Industry, 1992–2002. *Journal of Banking and Finance*, **30**, 2371–2386.

Parker, D., 1999, The performance of BAA before and after privatization. *Journal of Transport Economics and Policy*, **33**, 133–145.

Pathomsiri, S., A. Haghani, M. Dresner and R.J. Windle, 2008, Impact of undesirable outputs on the productivity of US airports. *Transportation Research Part E*, **44**, 235–259.

Pels, E., P. Nijkamp and P. Rietveld, 2003, Inefficiencies and scale economies of European airport operations. *Transportation Research Part E*, **39**, 341–361.

Pittman, R.W., 1983, Multilateral productivity comparisons with undesirable outputs. *The Economic Journal*, **93**, 883–891.

Salazar de la Cruz, F., 1999, A DEA approach to the airport productivity function. *International Journal of Transport Economics*, **26**, 255–270.

Sarkis, J., 2000, An analysis of the operational efficiency of major airports in the United States. *Journal of Operations Management*, **18**, 335–351.

Sarkis, J. and S. Talluri, 2004, Performance based clustering for benchmarking of US airports. *Transportation Research Part A*, **38**, 329–346.

Theil, H., 1965, The information approach to demand analysis. *Econometrica*, **33** (1), 67–87.

Tone, K., 2001, A slacks-based measure of efficiency in data envelopment analysis. *European Journal of Operational Research*, **130**, 498–509.

Tongzon, J. and W. Heng, 2005, Port privatization, efficiency and competitiveness: Some empirical evidence from container ports (terminals). *Transportation Research Part A,* **39**, 405–424.

Tornqvist, L., 1936, The Bank of Finland's consumption price index. *Bank of Finland Monthly Bulletin*, **10**, 1–8.

Wang, E.C., 2007, R&D efficiency and economic performance: a cross-country analysis using the stochastic frontier approach. *Journal of Policy Modeling*, **29**, 345–360.

Yoshida, Y., 2004, Endogenous-weight TFP measurement: methodology and its application to Japanese-airport benchmarking. *Transportation Research Part E*, **40**, 151–182.

Yoshida, Y. and H. Fujimoto, 2004, Japanese-airport benchmarking with the DEA and endogenous-weight TFP methods: testing the criticism of over investment in Japanese regional airports. *Transportation Research Part E*, **40**, 533–546.

Yoshida, Y. and K. Yamaguchi, 2007, Dynamic and static productivity measurements of Japanese airlines: can they really compete through the liberalization in Asian aviation industry? GRIPS Research Report Series, National Graduate Institute for Policy Studies.

Yu, M.M., 2004, Measuring physical efficiency of domestic airports in Taiwan with undesirable outputs and environmental factors. *Journal of Air Transport Management*, **10**, 295–303.

Yu, M.M., S.H. Hsu, C.C. Chang and D.H. Lee, 2008, Productivity growth of Taiwan's major domestic airports in the presence of aircraft noise. *Transportation Research Part E*, **44** (3), 543–554.

14 Theory of external costs
Stef Proost

INTRODUCTION

This chapter explores the concept and use of external costs in transport economics. External costs of transport are real costs that are not included in the market price of transport and are therefore not borne by the user. This covers a wide range of problems: airport noise, air pollution by cars and trucks, car accidents, road congestion and so forth. External costs are considered an important market failure. This means that government intervention (taxes, regulations and so forth) could improve the unregulated market outcome. Neither the exact magnitude of the external costs, nor the best policy intervention are easy to determine. For this reason, external costs have been at the origin of fierce policy debates, ranging from the introduction or not of congestion pricing to the promotion of electric vehicles and speed limits on highways.

In this chapter we return to the basics. What is an external cost, why does it exist in a market economy, is there any difference between external costs generated by producers (trucks) and consumers (cars), how do external costs interact with the other market failures (income distribution, revenue raising taxes) and what does this imply in terms of policy instruments? According to Laffont (2008), the discussion of external costs took off really with Pigou (1920). Coase (1960) has shown how external costs are dealt with in the small number case by negotiation and contracts. Samuelson (1954) has shown how external costs and public bads affect the properties of the competitive economy. Baumol and Oates (1975) were the first to discuss environmental externalities; a more modern treatment can be found in Kolstad (2010). Atkinson and Stiglitz (1980) and Starrett (1988) discuss the role of externalities and policy interventions in a wider context. Policies on transport externalities are discussed in more detail in Small and Verhoef (2007).

The chapter contains eight sections. In the next section, a theoretical general equilibrium model is used to define the concept of external cost and how the marginal external cost is related to the efficiency properties of the standard competitive equilibrium. The general equilibrium model is rather cumbersome to work with and therefore we illustrate the use of the external cost concept for policy analysis with the help of two simple illustrations in the two following sections: the optimal pollution model and the partial equilibrium model. In the transport sector there are several external costs and we discuss the principal external costs briefly. The properties of different policy instruments are analyzed in another section with the help of an analytical model for the case of conventional air pollution by cars. Then a section discusses briefly issues of time and uncertainty. The final section discusses the use of external cost concepts and policy instruments in a second best context where more than one market failure is present.

DEFINITION OF EXTERNAL COSTS IN THE NEO-CLASSICAL MODEL

The concept of external cost only makes sense in a well-defined economic model. This is the neo-classical model for public goods (and bads) defined by Samuelson (1954) that incorporates earlier contributions from Pigou. We define this elementary model using utility functions and production functions, private goods and public goods or bads, perfect competition for the private goods and finally lump-sum redistributive transfers as government instruments. Under these assumptions the external cost concept can be readily applied to define congestion, air pollution, noise and other externality problems related to transport.

We start by presenting this very general framework and the concept of external cost. We rely partly on Sandmo's (2000) presentation of the Samuelson model.

We consider an economy with $J + 2$ private goods. Individual i's consumption of good j is written x_j^i and total consumption is written as x_j for goods $j = 0,\ldots, J$. Good K is only used as intermediate input in the production process. All individuals consume the same quantity z of a public good. Individuals also consume the same quantity of a public bad e where:

$$e = e(x_J, x_K, a) \tag{14.1}$$

The public bad is called an *externality* in the rest of this chapter. Equation (14.1) shows that the externality is generated by the total consumption of private good x_J and the use of the intermediate input x_K and can be mitigated by the abatement effort a. We focus on two interpretations of function (14.1). One is that e is the level of *air pollution* generated by the use of cars and trucks and a as the level of public abatement efforts (reduced emissions by the public sector). Assumptions used to simplify the representation of the air pollution externality are that only total emissions matter and that everybody experiences the same total pollution effect e. This can easily be generalized. In fact, (14.1) is the reduced form of a complex physical – chemical transformation process (called pathway approach in Friedrich and Quinet chapter of this handbook) that translates emissions (x_J, x_K) into pollution effects.

The second interpretation of Equation (14.1) that we use is road *congestion*. The externality e can then be seen as the extra time necessary to make a given trip by car or truck. This is extra time on top of the minimum time necessary when there is no traffic on the road. In transport economics, one often uses an average time cost function where the aggregate flow determines the time and time cost per trip and where the time in excess of the time at maximum speed is called congestion time loss (see the chapter by Santos and Verhoef). The public abatement a can now be seen as the road capacity. Larger road capacity reduces the time losses for significant traffic flows.

Consumer preferences are now defined for all individuals $i = 1,\ldots, I$ as:

$$u^i = u^i(x^i, z, e) \tag{14.2}$$

Utility is typically increasing in x and z, but decreasing in e. The impact of e on utility will require the translation of the physical externality (particles, reduced speed) into effects valued by the individual and therefore a more precise specification of the utility function. In the case of pollution this can take the form of reduced health conditions and lower labor capacity, discomfort and so forth. In the case of congestion, this translates into a reduction of time for leisure and labor.

Production possibilities in our economy are represented by an aggregate production constraint where we assume constant returns to scale:

$$F(x_0, \ldots, x_J, x_K, z, a, e) = 0 \tag{14.3}$$

The dependence of $F(\,)$ on the inputs and outputs (x) describes the traditional production possibilities in an economy. This economy can also devote part of the production possibilities to produce public goods z and abatement a. The level of the externality e typically affects production possibilities negatively. The higher the level of road congestion, the more time truck drivers need to make any deliveries. Cars and trucks contribute to the level of congestion. We assume that there are many firms and many individuals that take the level of externality as given. A very simple example of an aggregate production constraint is:

$$a + z + x_0 + x_J + x_{J-1} + \frac{x_K}{1 + e} \leq 0 \tag{14.4}$$

where the four first terms are outputs from the production process (a, z, x_0, x_J) and the two last terms are inputs : labor (x_{J-1}) and truck use (x_K). If e stands for congestion, the level of congestion decreases the productivity of trucks.

Economists are interested in using as benchmark the 'First Best' solution where an omniscient planner controls without cost all consumption and production activities and maximizes a social welfare function W of the Bergson – Samuelson type (see first part of Equation (14.4)).

$$\Gamma = W(u^1, \ldots, u^I) - \gamma F(x_0, \ldots, x_J, x_K, z, a) \tag{14.5}$$

The social welfare function represents the preferences of society and can be given a normative and a positive interpretation. A minimum requirement often imposed is that it respects the Pareto principle: when the utility of one individual is increased, and the utility of the others stays constant, social welfare increases. This welfare function can also embed preferences on the distribution of income. The more quasi-concave is W and the higher the concavity chosen for the utility functions, the higher is the aversion to inequality. When W consists of a simple sum of utility functions that are all linear in income, the welfare function contains no inequality aversion and only the sum of the income equivalents matters as objective for the planner. The latter assumption is often implicit in many discussions but needs to be spelled out clearly to have a sound debate on efficiency and equity of policies. When the function W is given a positive interpretation, this function represents the weights of different groups of voters and lobbies in the political decision process (see Dixit et at., 1997).

The first best solution will satisfy the following first order conditions for a maximum when problem (14.5) does have an interior solution (we will later use good 0 as numéraire):

$$\frac{u_j^i}{u_0^i} = \frac{F_j}{F_0} \quad i = 1, \ldots, I; j = 1, \ldots, J-1 \tag{14.6}$$

$$\sum_i \frac{u_z^i}{u_0^i} = \frac{F_z}{F_0} \tag{14.7}$$

$$\frac{u_J^i}{u_0^i} - \frac{F_J}{F_0} = -\sum_i \frac{u_e^i}{u_0^i} e_J + \frac{F_e}{F_0} e_J \quad i = 1, \ldots, I \tag{14.8}$$

$$\frac{F_K}{F_0} = \sum_i \frac{u_e^i}{u_0^i} e_K - \frac{F_e}{F_0} e_K \tag{14.9}$$

$$\frac{F_a}{F_0} = \sum_i \frac{u_e^i}{u_0^i} e_a - \frac{F_e}{F_0} e_a \tag{14.10}$$

$$\frac{\delta W}{\delta u^i} \frac{\delta u^i}{\delta x_0} = \frac{\delta W}{\delta u^h} \frac{\delta u^h}{\delta x_0} \quad i, h = 1, \ldots, I \tag{14.11}$$

To understand these conditions, it is useful to see good 0 as the numéraire good; F_0 then denotes the opportunity cost of producing good 0 (choose it equal to 1). Conditions (14.6) are well known: the marginal rate of substitution between any pair of goods and for any consumer should equal the marginal rate of transformation in production. Equivalently, the willingness to pay for good j (in terms of the numéraire good 0) should equal the opportunity cost of good j (in terms of the numéraire good 0). Condition (14.7) is the Samuelson condition for the optimal supply of public goods: as the public good serves everybody, optimal supply requires that the sum of the marginal willingnesses to pay for the public good equals the opportunity cost to produce this good. Condition (14.11) is the condition that resources are optimally distributed over the population. Conditions (14.6), (14.7) and (14.11) hold for any economy without externalities.

Condition (14.8) specifies the optimal level of consumption of the externality generating good x_J. For every individual i the individual marginal benefit of good J minus the opportunity cost in production should equal the marginal utility loss for all individuals caused by the externality plus the marginal production loss generated by the increase in the externality. Compared with the other private goods, the real contribution of a unit of consumption of good J is lower as there is a negative side effect on the utility of the others and the production possibilities in the economy. Compared to a pure public good, good J is a good that generates private benefits for the individual who consumes it but is at the same time a public bad for all the others.

Condition (14.9) specifies the optimal use of the externality generating intermediate input x_K by the producers: it should be used up to the point where its marginal product (LHS) equals the RHS: the value of the negative impacts on consumers and other producers.[1] Condition (14.10) determines the optimal supply of public abatement for pollution (or optimal supply of road capacity to relieve congestion). The LHS is the opportunity cost of public abatement in terms of the numéraire good; the RHS is the benefit of public abatement: a reduction of the externality e valued at the marginal willingness to pay of all individuals and all firms to avoid the externality.

The next step is to examine whether the first best can be reached via a corrected market economy. We know that using perfect competition assumptions for all private goods markets and a set of individualized lump-sum taxes and transfers (T_i) to redistribute resources and to finance the pure public good as well as the public abatement good a, one can obtain the first-best solution. Set the price of numéraire good 0 to 1 and denote the price of good j by P_j. When all producers and consumers face identical prices, conditions (14.6) are satisfied, the level of public good is determined by the government according to (14.7) and individualized lump-sum transfers assure that the conditions for an optimal income distribution (14.11) are satisfied. We obtain the following conditions:

$$\frac{u_j^i}{u_0^i} = p_j = \frac{F_j}{F_0} \quad i = 1, \ldots, I; j = 1, \ldots, J-1 \tag{14.12}$$

$$\sum_i \frac{u_z^i}{u_0^i} = p_z = \frac{F_z}{F_0} \tag{14.13}$$

$$\frac{u_J^i}{u_0^i} - p_J = -\sum_i \frac{u_e^i}{u_0^i} e_J + \frac{F_e}{F_0} e_K \quad i = 1, \ldots, I \tag{14.14}$$

$$\frac{F_K}{F_0} + p_K = \sum_i \frac{u_e^i}{u_0^i} e_K - \frac{F_e}{F_0} e_K \tag{14.15}$$

$$\frac{F_a}{F_0} = p_a = \sum_i \frac{u_e^i}{u_0^i} e_a + \frac{F_e}{F_0} e_a \tag{14.16}$$

Conditions (14.14) and (14.15) can now be used to define the *marginal external costs*: the marginal external cost is the value of the utility loss for all individuals and value of the productivity loss for all firms associated to the consumption or use of one unit of the externality generating goods J and K:

$$MEC_J = -\sum_i \frac{u_e^i}{u_0^i} e_J + \frac{F_e}{F_0} e_J$$

$$MEC_K = -\sum_i \frac{u_e^i}{u_0^i} e_K + \frac{F_e}{F_0} e_K \tag{14.17}$$

We see that the marginal external cost (MEC) is here an unweighted sum of marginal damages in income terms (numéraire good) to consumers and producers caused by the externality. We note the following properties of the MEC:

1. It is defined as the extra damage caused to other agents in the economy (consumers and producers). The damage the agent causes to himself is already incorporated in his consumption or production decision. Sometimes agents are responsible for an important share of the externality and also experience themselves the damage. This part of the damage is not included in the MEC. Take congestion at the premises of one single firm (for example, the terminal operated by one airline): this part of the time losses is taken into account by the firm itself when it minimizes overall

production costs. The delay imposed on other firms and consumers on the public road or air space is not taken into account.

2. The MEC is a function whose value is determined by the levels of the externality-generating goods, by the level of (public) abatement a and by levels of many other production and consumption activities. In the case of congestion, it is often the ratio of the weighted sum of volumes of cars and trucks to road capacity that determines the level of the external congestion costs. As trucks cause typically more congestion than a car, their MEC is two or more times larger than for cars.

3. Information on the MEC function is in general insufficient to determine the optimal level of the externality: one needs to equate the marginal external damage (RHS of (14.14) and (14.15)) to the marginal cost of reducing the consumption of the externality-generating good (LHS of (14.14) and (14.15).

4. The MEC is a simple sum of damages without any distributional weights. Weights are unnecessary as the omniscient planner can equalize the social marginal utility of income by redistributing private goods between individuals without any efficiency cost.

5. We derived the MEC definition from the first order conditions for an interior optimum. The optimum can very well entail corner solutions and then the MEC is of much less use. There are many examples of this: it could make sense to ban the use of very poisonous goods or ban the use of motorways by pedestrians and so forth.

6. The value of the MEC needs to be estimated; it can not be observed directly from market transactions because the victims have no incentive to report correctly the damage. The same problem exists for public goods.

7. One could also consider external benefits rather than external costs. Agglomeration externalities are an example of positive externalities generated by the concentration of production activities: within a given range, the average product increases with the number of commuters to a city. In this case there is a negative externality (increased transport time for commuters) but also a positive externality (higher average product).

The *total and average externality costs* are in general not used by economists but can be defined. The total external cost requires a comparison of the social welfare function for different levels of the externality. This could be done by optimizing (14.5) for different levels of the externality and by simultaneously adjusting all the other conditions for an optimal solution in our economy. The difference in social welfare expressed in units of the numéraire good is then the total externality cost. The average external cost is then defined by dividing through the total external cost by the total quantity of good J.

One could reach the first-best optimum described above by assuming a perfectly competitive market economy, lump-sum taxes and transfers and by imposing so called *Pigouvian taxes* t_J, t_K equal to their MEC. The market price of goods J and K would then include an excise tax equal to the MEC. It is the interpretation of the MEC as a market imperfection to be corrected by appropriate taxes that makes the MEC a central concept in transport and environmental economics.

It is important to note all the conditions that need to be satisfied for the Pigouvian taxes to be the right instrument to achieve the first best: interior optimum, no other distortions in the economy (no other taxes), perfect redistribution instruments (lump-sum taxes and subsidies) and, finally, no transaction or enforcement costs.

The full general equilibrium model necessary to discuss external costs and their role in the choice of instruments is rather cumbersome. It is common to use simplified models to analyze policy implications of external costs in a sectoral context like transport. In this chapter we use two simplified models to analyze policies: the optimal pollution model and the partial-equilibrium transport model.

ILLUSTRATION WITH THE OPTIMAL POLLUTION MODEL

Two simplifying assumptions allow defining and using the *optimal pollution* or *optimal externality model* to discuss the marginal, average and total external cost and to discuss the use of different policy instruments. The assumptions are: income distribution does not matter (or redistribution is taken care of by other instruments in an efficient way) and the utility and production functions are separable in private goods and in the external-ity. The latter assumption means that the choice among private goods is not affected by the level of the externality. Finally, we still assume perfect competition and the absence of distortionary taxes in the rest of the economy. The model is particularly useful to discuss pollution externalities because for such externalities there is in general no feed-back between the level of the damage (local air pollution) and the consumption of the pollution-generating good *J* (say fuel use). This is not the case for an externality like road congestion where the level of congestion influences strongly the consumption of road transport services. In that case a partial equilibrium model is easier. We will illustrate that second model in the next section.

Figure 14.1 is an example of an optimal pollution model with four individuals: two victims (*1,2*) and two polluters (*A, B*). The horizontal axis measures the physical level of the externality, the vertical axis the marginal damages of the externality (MD, MEC) and

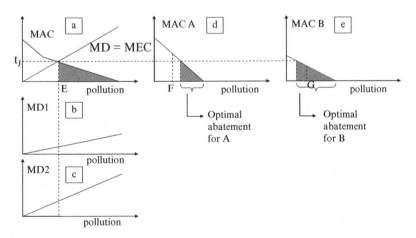

Figure 14.1   The optimal pollution model

the marginal abatement costs (MAC) to reduce pollution. The externality is a simple sum of use of commodity J by A and B:

$$e = x_J^A + x_J^B \tag{14.18}$$

The utility functions of the victims are given by (14.19), the marginal damage is then a linear function of the pollution level.

$$U^i = x_0^i - 0.5\,\alpha^i e^2 \quad i = 1, 2 \tag{14.19}$$

The total marginal damage is the sum of the individual marginal damages – in Figure 14.1 this is the horizontal sum of the individual marginal damages in b and c. The total marginal damage is here equal to the MEC. It is increasing in the pollution level.

In general one can reduce pollution by reducing the use of the externality generating commodities J or K and by increasing public abatement a. In this graphical example the only way to reduce pollution is to reduce the consumption of good J. The two polluters have the following utility function:

$$U^i = x_0^i + \left(\gamma^i - \frac{\beta^i}{2}x_J^i\right)x_J^i \text{ with } i = A, B, \tag{14.20}$$

and face a price p_J equal to the marginal cost of producing good J. Reducing the consumption of good J has a marginal cost that is increasing in the reduction of consumption: $\gamma^i - \beta^i x_J^i - p_J$. This is the willingness to pay for good J minus the marginal production cost of good J. This corresponds to the loss of consumer's surplus from decreasing consumption starting from the uncorrected market equilibrium. In Figure 14.1, the marginal abatement costs are the upward-sloping linear marginal abatement costs MAC in Figure 14.1d and e. Reducing total pollution at lowest cost, requires that the marginal abatement costs of both polluters are equalized (LHS of condition (14.13) is per individual but all individuals face the same RHS). Repeating this exercise for different target pollution levels generates the aggregate marginal abatement cost curve MAC in Figure 14.1a. In our example, where pollution can only be reduced by lowering consumption of good J, the aggregate MAC function corresponds to the aggregate demand function for good J, and the abatement cost corresponds to the loss of consumer surplus.

Figure 14.1a represents the optimal pollution or optimal externality level: the level where the marginal cost of extra reductions in the externality (using the cheapest combinations of measures to reduce pollution) equals the marginal damage to all the victims. This can also be interpreted as the optimal supply of a public bad.

One way to implement the optimal solution is to use a Pigouvian tax t_J. The Pigouvian tax is the horizontal line where aggregate MD (or MEC) equals the MAC. As the tax is identical for all polluters, one guarantees a cost-effective reduction of the pollution. The MEC is here a function. Knowing the marginal damages is insufficient to compute the Pigouvian tax: one needs also information on the aggregate marginal cost of abatement.

It is easy to illustrate corner solutions with the help of Figure 14.1a. If the marginal damage is very high, the MD curve lies above the MAC curve and the best solution is to ban the consumption of good J.

THE PARTIAL EQUILIBRIUM MODEL

When only one good is generating the externality *a partial equilibrium model* is a better shortcut. The partial equilibrium model allows an explicit representation of the demand for the externality-generating good J and the possible feedback effect of the externality on the demand for good J. Most appropriate is a representation where the demand for good J is a function of the generalized cost of good J. In the case of perfect competition, the generalized cost equals the sum of the marginal cost plus the time cost of the trip. This representation of the demand function allows to incorporate easily the feedback effect of the level of the congestion externality on the use of the externality-generating good (cars). Figure 14.2 uses this technique to illustrate congestion externalities.

In Figure 14.2 we use a linear time cost function that, for a given infrastructure capacity, increases in overall use. This generates level of use X°_J when no externality tax is used. At this volume of car use, the willingness to pay for the last unit of car use equals the sum of the marginal production cost and the average time cost for a trip. The externality is the extra time loss imposed by one car user on all other users. The average time cost is increasing and this means that an extra user imposes this increase in average time costs on all other users. The total increase of time costs for all drivers when there is one extra driver equals the marginal time cost. The marginal external cost is the difference between the marginal time cost and the average time cost because the average time cost is already paid by the user. In terms of our general equilibrium model condition (14.13) requires that, for each individual, the willingness to pay for travel by car (demand function) equals his marginal production cost + average time cost + marginal external cost (the increase in average time cost imposed on all other drivers). This generates a first best equilibrium X^*_J. The same simplified model can be used to discuss other types of externalities: air pollution, climate change, noise, accidents and so forth. In these cases,

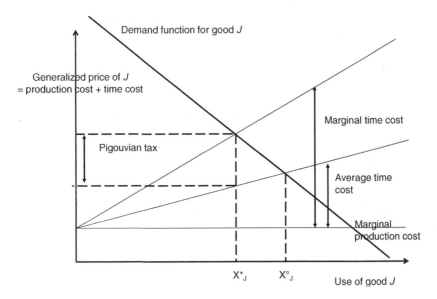

Figure 14.2   Partial equilibrium representation of the congestion externality

the marginal external cost can be increasing, constant or decreasing in the volume of traffic.

The presentation of the external cost of congestion in a partial equilibrium model relies on many simplifying assumptions: no income distribution issues, perfect competition, homogeneous drivers and neglect of choice decisions other then whether to travel such as choice of route. We also require the absence of distortionary taxes in the rest of the economy.

A similar representation can be used to discuss accident externalities. The average accident risk cost function replaces the average time cost function. The average risk cost function can be increasing or decreasing in the volume of traffic. The individual driver is, in principle, aware of this cost and adapts the volume of travel accordingly. If the average risk cost is decreasing in the volume of traffic, we have an external benefit and one needs to give a 'Pigouvian' subsidy to achieve the first best.

REVIEW OF EXTERNALITIES IN THE TRANSPORT SECTOR

Table 14.1 (inspired by Calthrop and Proost, 1998) describes the most common externalities in the transport sector. This list is by no means exhaustive and is intended to cover all modes of transport. A more detailed review of transport externalities and their estimates is given in the chapters of this Handbook by Delucchi and McCubbin and by Friedrich and Quinet. Parry et al. (2007) discuss the definition and estimates for the US transport sector. We survey five externalities: congestion, traffic safety, air pollution, noise and climate change. For each externality, we describe its source (what consumption or production activity creates the externality), the presence or not of public abatement (government investment that can influence level of externality), whether there is a feedback from the externality on the source of the externality (does the level of the externality itself discourage or encourage the source of the external effect), the nature of the MEC and finally the type of policy instruments commonly used to correct the source of the externality. In transport, one often encounters a combination of externalities: a car generates congestion, accidents, conventional air pollution, noise and climate change and this is an extra challenge to design a good policy as one needs joint optimization of all the policies. In the definition of external costs, we concentrate on the costs that are a direct consequence of the transport decision itself and we exclude the downstream externalities (example: air pollution in car manufacturing). In general it is better to deal with these externalities at the level of the downstream sector because more information is available of all the options and their relative merits.

REVIEW OF POLICIES TO ADDRESS EXTERNALITIES IN TRANSPORT

We discuss five types of policy instruments to correct the source of the externality. Their properties in a context close to a first best world are discussed in Table 14.2. We define this as a first best world because we neglect income distribution issues, other taxes and other market distortions in the economy. Second best issues will be discussed in a later section.

Table 14.1   Most commonly considered external costs in transport

	Source	Public abatement	Feedback	Nature of the MEC	Policy instruments used
Congestion	Too many users of the same facilities increase in-vehicle travel cost and schedule delay costs	Capacity (road, airports, rail platforms etc)	Negative: more congestion decreases travel demand	Mainly time and schedule delay costs	Congestion pricing, gasoline taxes, regulation (truck delivery times), ...
Traffic accidents	More intensive or more mixed use influences the average probability and severity of accidents	Adaptation of road equipment, emergency services etc.	Negative: larger risk of accidents, decreases travel demand	Mainly health, loss of life, material damage	Traffic regulations (max speed and so forth) Pricing (experience rating of insurance premiums)
Air pollution	Exhaust of combustion engines (car, trucks, bus, airplane, power stations)			Mainly health, loss of life	Standards on car emissions and quality of fuels (sulfur content of gasoline and diesel)
Noise	Vehicles, trains, airplanes	Noise walls, more silent road surfaces, tire design		Discomfort, health	Standards on cars, banning use of certain equipment at night Tradable permits for night flights
Climate change	Fossil fuel use by vehicles, diesel-fuel-powered trains, airplanes			Long-term disruption of climate (sea level, cooling costs, water supply ...)	Standards on fuel consumption (minimum efficiency) CO_2 taxes Tradable permits

For each instrument we discuss three properties. First we discuss how the instrument affects the externality levels by tracking the possible responses of the polluters. Take the case of air pollution by a car. A car user has two options at his disposition: reduce the level of car use ('reduced activity') and use a cleaner car ('greener activity'). For externalities such as air pollution, noise and traffic safety, the way the vehicle is used and the type of vehicle are sometimes more effective in reducing the externality than the volume of activity. This is not the case for congestion where the volume of transport at a given time is the main driver of the externality. Next we discuss the *cost-efficiency property*: does the instrument guarantee that a given pollution reduction is realized at lowest cost (condition (14.8) has the same RHS for all polluters, or graphically in Figure 14.1 the efforts are distributed efficiently over the two polluters).

Table 14.2   Properties of different instruments

	Effects	Cost-efficiency	Transaction and enforcement costs
Emission taxes	Greener and reduced activity	Yes	Measuring emissions can be difficult: car exhausts (NO_x, VOC difficult, CO_2 is easy), congestion requires time of day and link-specific tolling
Emission reduction subsidies	Greener activity	Yes – partly	One needs to measure emissions both before and after introduction of subsidies
Tradable Emission permits	Greener and reduced activity	Yes	Measure emissions, initial emissions if one uses grandfathering and one needs to keep track of permits
Standards	Greener activity	Only if perfect information on costs of compliance with standards	Can be lower: car equipment can be checked more easily than emissions
Other: Negotiation, Liability		When number of parties is small	Can be high when many parties are involved

The third but not least important criterion to judge policies are *transaction and enforcement costs*. We discuss the general properties of the five instruments one by one. The discussion is kept very general as the application of an instrument to correct a particular externality for a given mode requires a detailed study.

We illustrate the effect of different instruments using a simple analytical example that focuses on air pollution (relying on Calthrop and Proost, 2002). Assume that a unit of car use costs c° before taxes is imposed or abatement equipment is installed. The car industry is perfectly competitive and there is no congestion. Every unit of car use generates a constant pollution damage d. To have a meaningful solution the damage must be smaller than the maximum willingness to pay for the good. The maximum is normalized to 1, so the constraint is $d < 1$. Car manufacturers can reduce the damage by a proportion z at an extra cost per unit of car use of $0.5 cz^2$. The willingness to pay for car use equals $1 - x$ where x represents car use.

Before discussing different instruments, it is necessary to identify the first best solution. Should car use be reduced and how green should cars be? The solution is given by the following maximization problem:

$$\max_{z,\, y} \int_0^y (1 - x - d(1 - z) - 0.5cz^2) dx.$$

The solution is:

$$y:\ x^* = 1 - c^\circ - d(1 - z) - 0.5cz^2 = 1 - c^\circ - d + 0.5\frac{d^2}{c}$$

$$z:\ z^* = \frac{d}{c} \tag{14.21}$$

We see that the optimal car use x^* depends on the remaining damage $d(1-z)$ of a vehicle km and on the extra production costs of a greener car. (The final expression for x^* is obtained by substituting the optimal value of z^*.) The optimal proportion of abatement z^* is increasing in the environmental damage and decreasing in the cost parameter c. Because the price of car use has increased, the optimal abatement is a combination of reduction of car use and cleaner cars.

The *externality tax* is defined as a tax on the source of the externality proportional to the externality damage caused. It can be a tax on air pollution emissions (NO_x, SO_2, ...), a congestion tax on road use during the peak hours etc. An externality tax gives an incentive to 'cleaner' consumption (using less polluting vehicles and so forth) as the polluter will change his vehicle and his driving style up to the point where the marginal cost of using a cleaner vehicle plus the externality tax on the remaining emissions is minimized. The cleaner car will be more expensive (production cost of a cleaner car + the tax on the remaining emissions) and so the emission tax will also have a volume effect. As long as the externality tax is applied to all sources of the externality, it will achieve a cost-efficient reduction of the externality. A strong point of an emission tax is that no information is needed on the individual abatement costs (LHS of Equation (14.7)) because it is in the interest of the individual to equate his MAC to the tax level. However, an externality tax will only guarantee an optimal level of the externality if the externality tax equals the aggregate marginal damage. This requires the solution of the equation MAC = MEC (cf. Figure 14.1 and conditions (14.8) and (14.9)) and this is very demanding in terms of information. The transaction and enforcement cost of a tax on emissions will be small when one can easily measure the emissions. In the case of air pollution, this is easy if the emissions are directly proportional to the type and quantity of fuel. This is the case for carbon emissions and sulfur content but much less for NO_x content or other pollutants. In our analytical example the optimal tax on emissions is constant and equal to d. Car manufacturers will now have to pay $c^\circ + t(1-z) + 0.5cz^2$ for every unit of car use they deliver. They have an interest to minimize this cost and they can do that by choosing $z = d/c = z^*$. With this choice of the tax rate, the producers will offer cars at a price $c^\circ + d - 0.5d^2/c$ and this generates the optimal car use x^*. We summarize the effects of this instrument in the first column of Table 14.3.

A *tradable permits system* where the total pollution that is allowed is exactly equal to the result obtained with an emission tax, has in principle the same economic effects as an emissions tax. In a tradable pollution permit system the government fixes the total level of externality it wants to accept. This quantity is translated into a total quantity of emission rights that are allocated directly to the polluters or sold in an auction. The polluters trade emission rights among themselves up to the point where their marginal abatement cost equals the price of a permit on the market. This policy instrument gives rise to greener cars and also increases the users' price of the externality-generating good so that the volume of car use is also reduced. Because there is only one market price, the marginal abatement costs of all polluters will be equalized and this guarantees a cost-efficient solution. If the total quantity of emission rights is selected so as to satisfy MAC = MEC, tradable emission rights produce the optimal quantity of emissions. But this requires the knowledge of the aggregate MEC and the MAC curve and this is rarely available.

The tradable emission rights instrument may entail high transaction and enforcement costs. One needs to measure the initial emissions (if one distributes the emission rights as

Table 14.3   *Illustration of properties of different instruments to correct external pollution costs of cars*

	Emission tax	Emission reduction subsidy	Product tax	Emission standard
Instrument	$t = d/c$	$s = d/c$	$tt = d$	$z^{min} = d/c$
"Green car" (pollution/veh km)	d/c	d/c	0	d/c
Consumer price	$c° + d - 0.5d^2$	$c° - 0.5d^2$	$c° + d$	$c° + 0.5d^2$
Car use		Larger than with emission tax	Smaller than with emission tax	Larger than with emission tax
Remaining pollution		Larger than with emission tax	?	Larger than with emission tax
Government revenues	positive	negative	positive	none
Transaction costs	large	large	small	smallest
Efficiency in numerical example	100%	89%	11%	99%

a function of emissions in the past, the so called 'grandfathering') and one needs to set up a market for emissions rights. In the case of air pollution one could allocate the rights to the producers of cars (if mileage per vehicle is fixed) or to all the car users. The latter alternative will certainly generate significant transaction costs.

An *externality reduction subsidy* is a subsidy that is proportional to the reduction of the externality. An externality reduction subsidy ($s = d/c$) has the same effect on the greening of vehicles as an emission tax but the volume effect will be different. Car manufacturers that receive a subsidy s for every unit of emission reduction will only accept the subsidy if it allows them to offer cheaper cars on the market and this results ultimately in a cheaper car for consumers. A cheaper car means more, instead of less, car use. A subsidy for emission reduction does not guarantee that one achieves the optimal level of pollution. Returning to our analytical example, using a subsidy $s = d$ we find that car manufacturers try to minimize the following cost of car use: $c° - sz + 0.5cz^2$. This gives us a cleaner car: $z = d/c = z^*$, but the car use is now offered to consumers at a price $c° - 0.5d^2/c$ and this gives a level of car use that is larger than initially and higher than is optimal. The reason is that the remaining damage is not taxed and the polluting good is even subsidized.

The transaction and enforcement costs will only be low if one can measure easily the initial emission level as well as the emission reduction. Emission reduction subsidies present an additional disadvantage: every polluter has an incentive to overstate his initial emission so as to receive more subsidies. In reality one finds almost no pure emission reduction subsidy systems but many subsidy systems that pay part of the costs of emission reductions. These more realistic subsidy systems are less efficient in stimulating the right mix of emission reduction, but they have lower transaction costs. As subsidy schemes make politicians more popular, we find more of them. The emission reduction subsidy is compared with the other instruments in Table 14.3.

The third instrument that is analyzed is a *product tax*. This is a tax per vehicle kilometer for a reference level of pollution. Making the product greener has no influence whatsoever on the product tax paid. The main effect of this instrument is to reduce the volume. This is efficient if the externality is mainly volume related but this is only the case with congestion. Product type taxes are widely used: taxes on automotive fuels are proportional to greenhouse gas emissions but are not a good instrument to reduce conventional air pollution or time-and-place-dependent congestion. The main advantage of a product tax is its low transaction and enforcement cost.

Standards are one of the most widely used policy instruments. There are many standards systems in use: the government fixes the type of emission regulation equipment, the maximum emission per unit of input or output and so forth. A property of a standard is that the government fixes the emission reduction effort of each polluter, whereas for the previous instruments it was fixed by the polluter himself. A government that has good information about the abatement costs of homogenous categories of polluters can achieve a relatively efficient solution using a standard. Imposing a standard makes car use more costly and has therefore also a small volume effect. The volume effect is, however, too small compared to an emission tax because the remaining pollution is not taxed. Standards that require only monitoring at the moment of installation have relatively low monitoring and enforcement costs. A famous standard for cars is the corporate fuel efficiency standard in the United States that has given rise to many debates (see Fischer et al., 2007).

Table 14.3 compares the efficiency of the four instruments discussed. In the last line, we use the analytical model to show the relative welfare effect of the different instruments to address conventional air pollutants in the EU. We assume a uniform and constant mileage per car, and assume that the catalytic converter standard (EURO IV) imposed in the EU reduces damage of conventional air pollutants by 90 percent This corresponds to using parameters $d = 0.10$ and $c = 0.11$. Ignoring monitoring and enforcement costs, the last line in Table 14.3 shows that, compared to the (welfare) efficiency of an emission tax, a standard and an emission reduction subsidy perform relatively well. A product tax performs very poorly. The main reason is that a catalytic converter is a very cost-efficient way to reduce conventional air pollution: they cost about 1000 € and reduce pollution per mile by some 90 percent. Reduction in car use is much less efficient to reduce conventional air pollution and so a product tax is a poor choice of instrument.

In the analytical example, each policy instrument is used in isolation. Combinations of instruments to address one externality can outperform the use of a single instrument. Fullerton and West (2000) test the effects of a combination of a standard and a mileage tax. In our simple model this can produce the same optimal outcome as the emission tax at a much lower monitoring and enforcement cost. Fullerton and West find that the efficiency equivalence breaks down with heterogeneous individuals and that, excluding monitoring and enforcement costs, a combination of gasoline, age and engine size achieves some 71 percent of the efficiency of emission taxes.

Another policy that is used regularly is a scrapping subsidy for old cars. This type of instrument raises moral hazard problems because only old cars that are hardly used get scrapped and the effects are mostly temporary. A simple scrapping subsidy will also increase the car stock and overall car use.

TIME AND UNCERTAINTY ISSUES

In the neo-classical model one can introduce the time dimension by a redefinition of the commodity concept. The same commodity available next year is a different commodity. Adding a full set of capital markets to trade off income over time one can define the external cost associated to a stock externality. A stock externality is an externality where the damage is a function of the stock of emissions. Limiting ourselves to externalities at the level of consumption, it can be defined as:

$$e_\tau = e(x_{J0}, \ldots, x_{J\tau}; a_0, \ldots a_\tau) \qquad (14.22)$$

The Pigouvian tax for the consumption of commodity J in period 0 is equal to the discounted sum of the marginal external damage cost of using good J in all periods where the initial emissions contributes to the externality:

$$t_{J0} = -\sum_{\tau=0}^{\infty}(1 + r)^{-\tau}\sum_{i=1}^{I}\frac{u_{e\tau}^i}{u_{0\tau}^i}\frac{\delta e_\tau}{\delta x_{J0}} \qquad (14.23)$$

So the Pigouvian tax equals the discounted sum of marginal damage in every future period. For every future period, we have the unweighted sum of individual damages. With perfect capital markets, all intertemporal rates of substitution are equal to the same discount rate and this gives us Equation (14.23).

The application of (14.23) to environmental problems such as climate change with damages that extend far into the future raises two concerns. The first is the absence of very long-term capital markets. The second is intertemporal equity. Transactions on capital markets are possible at a horizon of 30 to 40 years maximum. Beyond this term, individuals cannot trade off resources over time because of their individual lifetime. Also the government can not easily redistribute resources over a very long term and this means that perfect redistribution instruments for the very long term are not available. Using a discounted sum of future damages is then not appropriate. This has given rise to a lively discussion among environmental economists (see Stern, 2008). The discount rates (on consumption) used range between 1 and 5 percent. Using an infinite horizon, the discounted sum (and Pigouvian tax) of a yearly extra damage of 1 € associated to one ton of pollution now would range between 100€ (1/0.01) and 20€ (1/0.05) so it is difficult to understate the importance of this discount parameter.

A second important issue is the uncertainty in damages and in costs. For uncertain damages, the marginal external cost becomes now the expected value of the marginal damage. It is the expected value that forms the basis for Pigouvian taxes. The uncertainty in abatement costs has important implications for the choice of policy instruments. Weitzman (1974) showed that when the slope of the marginal damage function is steeper than the slope of the marginal abatement cost function, it is preferable to use a quantity instrument (tradable permits) rather than a price instrument (Pigouvian tax). The intuition is that very steep marginal damage functions correspond to more catastrophic events and these can be more easily avoided using restrictions on the overall quantity of pollution. Figure 14.3 illustrates the argument. In Figure 14.3 there is only uncertainty on the slope of the aggregate marginal abatement cost function: it can be high (difficult

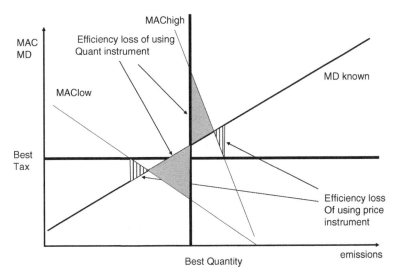

Figure 14.3   Choice between a tax instrument and tradable permits when the MAC is uncertain

to reduce emissions) or low and both have a 50 percent probability. If a quantity instrument is used it is best to use a tradable permit system, this guarantees that one distributes efforts cost-efficiently over all individual polluters and that one can indeed use the aggregate marginal abatement cost function. The best overall limit on emissions is the vertical line that minimizes the two shaded areas next to the vertical line. The shaded area to the left of the quantity limit is the loss of efficiency if the MAC happens to be low. When the MAC happens to be low, the allowed emission quantity is too high as a further emission reduction would avoid damages given by the MD curve at a cost lower than the MD. Consider now the efficiency loss if one used the best price instrument. The best Pigouvian tax is here the horizontal line and the efficiency losses associated to the use of a price instrument are given by the hatched areas. The hatched area at the left side is the loss of efficiency when the MAC happens to be low: in that case, the tax on pollution is too high compared to the MD and one pushes the abatement efforts too far. In Figure 14.3, the slopes of the MAC and MD curves are chosen such that a price instrument is more efficient, other relative slopes can give the reverse result.

The marginal damage can also be uncertain (as for climate change) but there exists no parallel theorem on instrument choice for this case.

SECOND BEST WORLD

In the previous sections we started from a first best economy in which the government used lump-sum taxes and subsidies as perfect redistribution instruments and where there was only one externality to deal with. The externality was the only market distortion, all other markets were functioning perfectly: there is perfect competition and there are no product or income taxes (other than externality taxes).

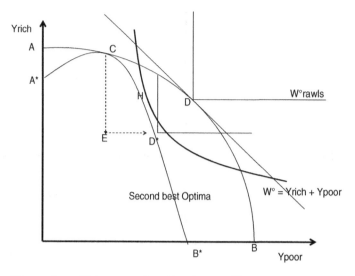

Figure 14.4   The equity–efficiency trade-off and second best optima

This first best world does not exist: the government does not have perfect information about the skills of the individuals and it is therefore forced to use income taxes and product taxes. Such taxes allow correcting the income distribution but do this at an efficiency cost. There is an equity – efficiency trade-off. We illustrate in Figure 14.4 for the case of two individuals: a rich individual with a high productivity whose equivalent income is measured on the *y*-axis, and a poor individual whose equivalent income is measured on the *x*-axis (inspired by Atkinson and Stiglitz, 1980). The benevolent planner (as represented by his SWF, cf. (14.4)) can attach a large value to income distribution and then he ranks alternatives according to level curves of the Rawls type or he can attach much less attention to income distribution and then he maximizes a simple sum of equivalent incomes. All first best equilibria are on the frontier AB. With perfect income distribution one can reach many points; nothing prevents the planner from choosing point D. Point C could be seen as the outcome under laissez-faire.

Consider now a second best world where redistribution of income requires the use of income taxes. If one does not care about income distribution, one ends up at point C and the rich stay rich and the poor very poor. In most societies one wants to redistribute income. The second best frontier is now A*CB* and represents the trade-off between efficiency and equity: the more one wants to redistribute to the poor, the higher the income tax rates one needs and the higher the efficiency loss. (If one reverses the tax system and makes it regressive so that one takes more away from the poor using labor taxes (curve A*C), the lower the incentives of the poor to work and the less one can offer to the rich.) In order to reach point D* starting from point C, one needs to give up two units of equivalent income from the rich in order to add one unit of income to the poor. In fact one loses one unit of income under the form of efficiency losses. The planner with less extreme income redistribution preferences may end up at a point like H.

An important question is whether in this second best world, the policy rules we derived for a first best world can still be used. This is a difficult question. We distinguish between three perspectives: the optimal income tax perspective, the tax reform perspective and the pure efficiency perspective. For each of these perspectives we derive the consequences of the Second Best setting for the choice of instruments to correct external costs.

The Optimal Income Tax Perspective

There is one general property of interest mentioning at the outset. Diamond and Mirrlees (1971 a, b) showed that, when there are indirect taxes on consumers as well as income taxes, it is in general desirable not to introduce any distortions in the production sector. The reasoning is that with a full set of indirect and income taxes one can always achieve the same result as achieved with taxes inside the production sector. This has large implications: as long as externalities are inside the production sector, Pigouvian taxes are optimal as these restore the efficiency conditions in the production sector: they assure that, for a given input vector, the maximum output is produced.

If we assume furthermore that the government can use a non-linear income tax and that the utility function is separable between the externality and labor, $(U = U\{(x_0, \ldots, x_J, e), l\})$, the best tax is still the Pigouvian tax equal to the MEC. The intuition is that deviating from the Pigouvian tax would only decrease the total resources available for redistribution in the economy (Gauthier and Laroque, 2009). The same reasoning holds for the optimal supply of public goods and public abatement. This implies that for transport externalities other than congestion, one could largely continue to use the principles we derived for the first best. The main intuition is the presence of the non-linear income tax that fulfills the income distribution task. In general congestion is also related to labor supply, and in this case the separability between efficiency and equity no longer holds.

The Tax Reform Perspective

The starting point here is not an equilibrium with optimized income redistribution via non-linear income taxes, but a set of indirect and labor taxes, as well as a set of distributional weights of the policy maker and an externality. An environmental tax reform is then an increase or decrease of the environmental tax and a corresponding decrease or increase of another tax that keeps the government budget in equilibrium. Consider a tax increase on the polluting good J, compensated by a tax decrease on good h. Then the welfare effect of this tax reform equals dW:

$$dW = -MSCF_J dt_J - MSCF_h dt_h$$

where

$$MSCF_J = \frac{\displaystyle\sum_{i=1}^{I} \lambda^i x_J^i - \sum_{i=1}^{I} \lambda^i \frac{\dfrac{\delta U^i}{\delta e} \dfrac{\delta e}{\delta x_J} \dfrac{\delta x_J}{\delta t_J}}{\delta U^i}}{\displaystyle\sum_{j=0}^{J} t_j \frac{\delta x_j}{\delta t_J}}$$

$$MSCF_h = \frac{\displaystyle\sum_{i=1}^{I}\lambda^i x_h^i}{\displaystyle\sum_{j=0}^{J}t_j\frac{\delta x_j}{\delta t_h}}$$ (14.24)

The welfare effect is the marginal social cost of funds (MSCF) of raising one euro by raising the tax on good J minus the marginal social cost of funds of raising one euro less government revenue from good h. If the cost of raising taxes on good J is lower than on good h, it makes sense to increase the tax on good J and to reduce the tax on good h. The cost for individual i of a marginal tax increase on good J is the actual consumption of good J minus the environmental gain that he experiences.

The MEC now intervenes with income distribution weights in the marginal social cost of raising one more unit of revenue on good J. if raising the tax has important environmental benefits, the cost of raising one euro of revenue is low, and when this allows to decrease an existing tax on good h that has a high efficiency cost, this can generate a net welfare benefit. The important insight from this formulation is that the ultimate incidence of an environmental tax depends strongly on how the revenue of the tax is used and is only partly influenced by the relative consumption by income group of the taxed commodity. For an application to passenger transport taxes see Mayeres and Proost (2001). Parry and Small (2005) apply the tax reform framework to gasoline taxes for the United States and the UK. Bento et al. (2009) look at the distributional impact of gasoline taxes, including their effects on markets of new cars and second-hand cars.

The Pure Efficiency Perspective

The starting point here is again a set of indirect and income taxes. One disregards the income distribution issues and identifies the best policy instrument to use in the presence of existing taxes. This question has received most attention and was at the core of the 'double dividend' controversy. In most economies labor taxes are the most important tax in terms of revenues. When one disregards the income distribution concern, labor taxes are a pure distortion and this has two large implications for the choice of instruments. First, a Pigouvian tax on the externality generating good J will decrease the externality and this is a benefit. The revenue raised can be used to decrease the existing labor tax and this is also a benefit. Is this a 'real double dividend'? No, because at the same time the real cost of the consumption bundle of the individual is increased and this decreases the purchasing power of the wage and acts in fact as a higher labor tax. Summing all the effects implies in general that the presence of labor taxes leads to an optimal Pigouvian tax that is somewhat lower than in the first best. The higher is the existing labor tax, the lower will be the optimal second best Pigouvian tax.

There is a second implication for the choice of instruments. The best instrument is an externality tax if the revenues are used to reduce existing labor taxes. The worst instrument are grandfathered tradable permits because they increase the implicit labor tax (by making good J more expensive) but do not generate tax revenues that can be used to decrease existing labor taxes. Goulder et al. (1999) illustrate the effects of different instruments in a first and second best setting for the case of NO_X emissions in industry.

Another illustration is given in Parry and Bento (2002) who examine the appropriate congestion taxes on commuting traffic in the presence of labor taxes. If congestion externalities are only due to commuting traffic that chooses between correctly priced public transport and congested roads, and if revenue is used to reduce labor taxes, then the optimal congestion tax equals the marginal external congestion cost. The intuition is the following. All labor has to commute, and since public transport is priced correctly, there is no distortion in redirecting commuters from road to public transport. As long as tax revenue is used to reduce labor taxes, there is no extra distortion on labor supply. There is even a time gain on the road due to lower congestion. Parry and Bento find that a congestion tax whose revenues are recycled via a lower labor tax generates a double dividend as the congestion tax improves the efficiency of the journey to work. De Borger and Wuyts (2009) consider congestion and other transport related features of the labor market like free parking, company cars and so forth. They find that the tax on commuters has to be larger than the marginal external congestion cost so as to correct underpricing of parking. In addition, recycling via public transport subsidies may be superior to labor tax recycling because this decreases the free parking distortion.

Calthrop et al. (2010) use the tax reform approach to set up rules for a cost–benefit analysis of infrastructure investments when there are several markets with distortions. Whatever the source of funds, for a given investment the expressions for the welfare assessment include three terms. The first is the direct benefit of the investment holding fixed all traffic flows and all taxes; this term is independent of the source of funding. Next, is the direct cost of financing the investment, measured at the marginal cost of funds of the tax instrument used. Third, are the induced distortions of the investment on all the markets measured at existing tax rates. The distortion equals the difference between the tax, corrected for the marginal cost of funds, and the marginal external costs. The marginal social cost of funds (cf. Equation (14.23)) is the cost of collecting one euro of revenue via a particular tax when the revenue of the tax is not spent in the economy. For income taxes, this marginal cost of public funds can range between one and more than two according to Kleven and Kreiner (2006).

NOTE

1. When firms also inflict external costs upon each other it is important to keep in mind that the production sector is an aggregate of a large number of firms and that the number of firms is fixed. Otherwise a merger of firms would reduce the level of the externality. See Mayeres and Proost (1997) who have firms and consumers generating transport externalities in a model analogous to the one used here.

REFERENCES

Atkinson A. B. and J. Stiglitz, 1980, *Lectures on Public Economics*, McGraw-Hill.
Baumol W. and W. Oates, 1995, *The Theory of Environmental Policy*. Englewood Cliffs, NJ: Prentice Hall.
Bento, A., Goulder, L., Jacobsen, M. and R. von Haefen, 2009, Distributional and efficiency impacts of increased US gasoline taxes. *American Economic Review*, **99** (3), 1–37.
Calthrop E. and S. Proost, 1998, Road transport externalities: interaction between theory and empirical research. *Environmental and Resource Economics*, **11** (3/4), 335–348.

Calthrop, E. and S. Proost, 2002, Environmental pricing in transport. In *Handbook of Transport: Vol. 4. Transport and the Environment*. Pergamon Press, p. 1–18.

Calthrop, E., B. De Borger S. Proost, 2010, Cost-benefit analysis of transport investments in distorted economies. *Transportation Research Part B*, **44**, 850–869.

Coase, R.H., 1960, The problem of social cost. *Journal of Law and Economics*, **3**, 1–44.

De Borger, B. and B. Wuyts 2009, Commuting, transport tax reform and the labour market: employer-paid parking and the relative efficiency of revenue recycling instruments. *Urban Studies*, **46** (1), 213–233.

Diamond, P. and J. Mirrlees 1971a, Optimal taxation and public production I: production efficiency. *American Economic Review*, **61** (1), 8–17.

Diamond, P. and J. Mirrlees, 1971b, Optimal taxation and public production II: tax rules. *American Economic Review*, **61** (3), 261–278.

Dixit, A., G.M. Grossman and E. Helpman, 1997, Common agency and coordination: general theory and application to government policy making. *Journal of Political Economy*, **104** (4), 752–769.

Fischer, C., W. Harrington and I.W.H. Parry, 2007, Should corporate average fuel economy (CAFE) standards be tightened? *Energy Journal*, **28**, 1–29.

Fullerton, D. and S. West, 2002, Can taxes on cars and on gasoline Mimic an unavailable tax on emissions? *Journal of Environmental Economics and Management*, **43**, 135–157.

Gauthier, S. and G. Laroque, 2009, Separability and public finance. *Journal of Public Economics,* **93**, 1168–1174.

Goulder L.H., I.W.H. Parry, R.C. Williams III and D. Burtraw 1999, The cost-effectiveness of alternative instruments for environmental protection in a second-best setting. *Journal of Public Economics*, **72**, 329–360.

Kleven H.J. and C.T. Kreiner, 2006, The marginal cost of public funds in OECD countries: hours of work versus labor force participation. *Journal of Public Economics*, **90**, 1955–1973.

Kolstad, C., 2010, *Environmental economics*, 2nd edn. Oxford: Oxford University Press.

Laffont, J.J., 2008, Externalities. *The New Palgrave Dictionary of Economics,* 2nd edn. N. Durlauf and L.E. Blume. London: Palgrave Macmillan.

Mayeres, I. and S. Proost, 1997, Optimal tax and public investment rules for congestion type of externalities. *Scandinavian Journal of Economics*, **99** (2), 261–279.

Mayeres, I. and S. Proost, 2001, Marginal tax reform, externalities and income distribution. *Journal of Public Economics,* **79** (2), 343–363.

Parry, I.W.H. and A. Bento, 2002, Revenue recycling and the welfare effects of road pricing. *Scandinavian Journal of Economics*, **103** (4), 645–671.

Parry, I.W.H. and K. Small, 2005, Does Britain or the United States have the right gasoline tax? *American Economic Review*, **95**, 1276–1289.

Parry, I.W.H., M. Walls and W. Harrington, 2007, Automobile externalities and policies. *Journal of Economic Literature*, **XLV**, 374–400.

Pigou, A.C., 1920, *The Economics of Welfare*, London: Macmillan.

Samuelson, P.A., 1954, The pure theory of public expenditure. *Review of Economics and Statistics*, **36** (4), 387–389.

Sandmo, A., 2000, *The Public Economics of the Environment*. Oxford: Oxford University Press.

Small, K.A. and E. Verhoef, 2007, *Urban Transport Economics*. London: Routledge.

Starrett, D.A., 1988, *Foundations of Public Economics*. Cambridge: Cambridge University Press.

Stern, N., 2008, The economics of climate change. *American Economic Review, Papers and Proceedings*, **98** (2), 1–37.

Weitzman, M.L., 1974, Prices versus taxes. *Review of Economic Studies*, **41** (4), 477–491.

15 External costs of transport in the United States
Mark Delucchi and Don McCubbin

INTRODUCTION

In this chapter we report estimates of the external costs of transport in the United States.[1] Generally, we cover road, rail, air and water transport; passenger transport and freight transport; and congestion, accident, air pollution, climate change, noise, water pollution and energy-security costs. However, we were not able to find estimates for all cost categories; in particular, there are fewer estimates for freight transport than for passenger transport, fewer estimates for water transport than for other modes, and fewer estimates of water pollution costs than of other costs. Table 15.1 summarizes the quality of estimates in each category.

In our review, negative externalities are the *unaccounted for* or *unpriced* costs of an action. This means that they are the result of individual decisions or actions, such as whether to drive or take a train, or freight something by ship or plane, and are related to the explicit prices and unaccounted-for costs of those choices.

Estimates of the external costs of transport may be used for several purposes: as a guide to more economically efficient pricing (given that the optimal price is equal to the private market price plus the estimated marginal external costs); as a guide to allocating research and development funds to mitigate the largest external costs; as part of a cost-benefit analysis of optimal investment in transportation modes and infrastructure; and as part of historical or comparative analyses.

As indicated in Table 15.1, the available estimates do not fully characterize all costs for all modes. Moreover, the wide variations in estimation methods, data, and assumptions among even the 'good' estimates confound the comparison of estimates across modes.

Table 15.1 Quality of estimates of external costs by transport mode and cost category

	Road		Rail		Air		Water	
	Pass.	Freight	Pass.	Freight	Pass.	Freight	Pass.	Freight
Congestion delay	good	good	poor	poor	poor	n.e.	n.e.	n.e.
Accident	good	good	n.e.	poor	poor	n.e.	n.e.	n.e.
Air pollution, health	good	good	fair	fair	fair	fair	fair	fair
Air pollution, other	good	good	n.e.	n.e.	n.e.	n.e.	n.e.	n.e.
Climate change	good	good	good	good	fair	fair	fair	good
Noise	good	good	poor	poor	fair	n.e.	n.e.	n.e.
Water pollution	poor	poor	n.e.	n.e.	n.e.	n.e.	n.e.	n.e.
Energy security	fair	fair	fair	fair	fair	n.e.	n.e.	fair

Notes: Pass. = passenger; n.e. = not estimated.

As a result, we are able to make only general comparisons among modes and general statements about total costs of transport.

In the following sections we review recent estimates of external costs by mode in the United States. In each section we first review methods and issues in the estimation of the cost, and then present estimates of the costs. For each cost category (for example, congestion delay, accidents), we summarize estimates of the cost by mode and study. Presenting the estimates in this way indicates where more research and analysis is needed.

CONGESTION DELAY COSTS

Brief Review of Methods and Issues

The congestion caused by additional travel generates a number of external costs, including opportunities foregone due to travel delay, the discomfort of crowding, and the impact of travel-time uncertainty on the reliability of arrival and delivery times. Table 15.2 provides a comprehensive classification of the external costs of congestion, by mode, with a qualitative indication of the likely magnitude of the externality.

Most analyses have focused on the opportunity cost of activities foregone due to travel delay due to road congestion; there has been less work on the external costs of congestion for other modes, or on the other kinds of external costs of road congestion, such as the impact on the reliability of arrival and delivery times. In this review we consider only those impacts of congestion that are properly considered externalities, as we define the term above. Thus, we do not count for example congestion at freight train yards or at airport terminals used by a single carrier, because in both instances the full cost of the congestion is recognized by the entities making the travel decisions.

At the simplest level, congestion delay costs on the road are equal to hours of delay multiplied by the value of opportunities foregone during an hour of delay. Hours of delay are estimated on the basis of the difference between the average speed in a baseline travel situation and the average speed in a scenario with increased travel; this difference, in turn, is based on empirical relationships between average speed and travel volume, which in the case of road traffic can be fairly complex. The value of an hour of delay depends on the type and value of the activity being displaced and the conditions of the delay. If it is possible to work or relax during the delay, the opportunity time 'cost' may be small.[2] Accordingly, analysts often distinguish displacement of unpaid activities from displacement of paid work, and estimate the value of travel time as a function of the income of the persons affected and the 'amenity' conditions of the travel per se.[3]

We do not consider here what are sometimes referred to as 'scarcity' costs, which are related to infrastructure capacity. Maibach et al. (2007) write that 'scarcity costs denote the opportunity costs to service providers for the non-availability of desired departure or arrival times' (p. 23). Although it is true that there is a cost to expanding (or failing to expand) capacity, it is not clear that this ought to be viewed as an *external* cost of individual travel choices, because the individual fares charged by service providers ideally are supposed to include capacity fees. Thus, in our review, congestion externalities for, say, rail travel are related to the actual delays and disamenities caused by crowding per se, or to the delay in road traffic caused by road crossings (Table 15.2), but do not include

Table 15.2 Qualitative classification of congestion externalities by mode

Marginal travel by → External effect on ↓	Road	Rail	Air	Water	*Remarks*
Travel time underway (opportunity cost of time)	++	0	0	0?	Additional drivers and vehicles slow down other vehicles on the road, but additional passengers, trains or planes do not slow down other trains or planes while underway, because for safety reasons rail and air lanes en route are not permitted to become congested. It might be possible for some short-haul shipping lanes to become crowded.
Crowding, comfort of passenger travel	+	+	+	0?	Highway congestion can make drivers anxious. Crowding on trains can make people stand, which can be uncomfortable. While passengers on planes have reserved seats, crowded flights are less comfortable because there is less room to 'stretch out,' less overhead luggage space and so forth.
Reliability of arrival time (passenger, freight)	++	0	+	0	The greater the variation in delay times the greater the uncertainty about arrival times (Small et al., 1999). Congestion can occur at airports due to too many incoming and outgoing flights (Poole and Dachis, 2007).
Boarding or disembarking time	n.a.	+	+	0	Large crowds can cause minor delays in boarding trains and planes, increase dwell time at stations and slow disembarkation.
Time spent at garage/ station/terminal/ port (opportunity costs, comfort costs, reliability costs)	+?	0	++	+?	Road congestion can result in extra search time for parking spaces. Passenger rail lines have one train per station per track on fixed schedules, and although freight trains can experience crowding at rail yards, the costs are faced by the operator. At airports with different carriers and limited terminal capacity, additional flights can cause significant airport delays for all other flights (Brueckner, 2002).
Cars and trucks waiting at rail or raised-bridge crossings.	n.a.	+	0	+	Additional train cars increase the time that cars and trucks must wait at rail crossings. Additional ships can increase the time that cars and trucks wait at raised-bridge crossings.
Energy use	+	0	+	0	Idling due to congestion on highways or at airport terminals increases energy use per ton-mile or passenger mile.
Accidents	+	0	0	0	Changes in average vehicle speed can affect the frequency and severity of accidents.
Vehicle wear and tear	+	0	0?	0	Driving in congested conditions increases vehicle wear and tear

Notes: ++ = large effect; + = small effect; 0 = no effect; n.a. = not applicable.

scarcity/capacity effects. Put another way, for privately operated non-road modes, there is in theory nothing to prevent the carrier from figuring out the optimal capacity assuming full-cost prices and then charging the passengers those full-cost prices; in this situation, there is no externality (see, for example, Gorman, 2008, p. 7). We hasten to add, however, that a complete social cost–benefit analysis of transport modes, as opposed to a study of the external costs of transport, certainly would include all actual infrastructure and capacity costs as well as congestion delay costs.

Because there has been considerable research on all of the factors in the estimation of road delay, and because the theory is relatively well developed and most of the parameters (that is, traffic volumes, average speed and personal income) are relatively easy to estimate (compared, for example, with the estimation of parameters in the calculation of climate-change externalities), estimates of national average-annual delay costs for roads tend to be relatively robust. For more information on estimates of the cost of travel time, see Calfee and Winston (1998), Morrison and Winston (1989), Small et al. (1999) and Zhang et al. (2004). For more information on estimates of hours of delay on highways in the United States, see reports by the Texas Transportation Institute (Schrank and Lomax, 2007).

Estimates of US Costs by Mode and Intermodal Comparisons

Table 15.3 summarizes recent estimates of congestion delay costs by mode. Most authors focus on time-delay costs of road congestion, and estimate these to be in the range of 1 to 7 cents per mile (2006 USD) on average. Of course, congestion costs on particular roadways can be much higher than this; for example, Ozbay et al. (2007) estimate that congestion costs on some routes in New Jersey can exceed 30 cents per mile.

We did not find a study that estimated congestion costs by water mode (as indicated in Table 15.2, these primarily would be related to congestion at port terminals). Maibach et al. (2007) suggest that presently congestion costs at seaports are small, but could become significant in the future, especially in North America where 'capacity . . . is approaching its limits and . . . congestion at cargo handling and storage facilities is a priority issue' (p. 35).

ACCIDENT COSTS

Brief Review of Methods and Issues

The estimated costs of accidents include medical costs, property damage, lost productivity, insurance administration, emergency services and the nonmonetary costs of lost quality of life and pain and suffering as a result of death and serious injury. In the case of travel by road, the estimated cost of accidents is greater than every other social cost except travel time (Delucchi, 2004b). The threat of motor vehicle accidents also gives rise to 'fear and avoidance costs' – for example, the opportunity costs of making people afraid to walk (Evans, 1994; Newbery, 1998) – and to 'extra attentiveness costs' (that is, extra effort to avoid accidents) (Edlin 2002; Hensher, 2006; Newbery, 1998; Steimetz, 2003), but these are not included in the external-cost estimates reviewed here.

Table 15.3   Estimates of congestion delay costs by mode (year-2006 cents)

	Road	Rail	Air	Water
Gorman et al. (2008)	0.22 to 0.54/tm[a] (freight)	0.03/gtm[b] (freight)	–	–
Lemp and Kockelman (2008)[c]	4.75/pmt	–	–	–
Parry et al. (2007)[d]	3.80 /pmt	–	–	–
Delucchi (2004a)[e]	1.93 to 7.46/pmt	–	–	–
Levinson et al. (1998)	0.88/pmt[f]	–	0.35/pmt[g]	–

Notes: pmt = passenger-mile of travel; gtm = gross ton-mile; vmt = vehicle-mile of travel; tm = ton-mile.
[a]   Using forecasted year 2000 congestion costs due to trucks of $5.0 billion (year-1994 USD) and 198 789 million vehicle miles for trucks reported by FHWA (1997, Tables 1 and 17), Gorman (2008, p. 7) assumes a 14.8-ton average payload and estimates $0.0022 per tm (year-2006 USD). However, Gorman's payload estimate implies an unrealistically high 2 942 billion ton-miles for trucks in 2000. Using an estimate of 1 203 billion ton-miles for all trucks (Dennis, 2004, Figure 4), we estimate $0.0054 per tm (year-2006 USD). We recognize that our estimate for ton-miles excludes certain categories, such as shipments by households, retail, service, and government establishments (including US Mail); and certain non-commercial freight shipments, such as municipal solid waste (as discussed by Dennis, 2004, p. 9).
[b]   This is an estimate of the delay to road traffic caused by freight trains crossing the road network. Gorman et al. (2008, pp. 7–8) evaluate the frequency, duration and intensity of rail interaction with road transportation, and estimate a $465 million total congestion delay cost to road traffic, based on $20/delay-hour and 1.4 billion gross ton-miles of rail traffic.
[c]   To estimate the delay caused per mile of additional travel by specific vehicle types, Lemp and Kockelman (2008) use a formula that predicts delay as a function of traffic volume, estimates of differences in delay caused by different vehicle types, and an assumption that travel time costs $8/vehicle-hour. Estimates appear to be in year-2006 USD. We converted to PMT, assuming 1.6 passengers per vehicle (US Department of Transport, 2008, Table 4-22).
[d]   Parry et al. (2007) report FHWA's (2000) estimate of the 'weighted-average' marginal external delay cost at '5 cents per passenger mile' (p. 380). According to Parry et al. (2007), FHWA estimated marginal external costs for representative urban and rural roads at different times of day, and then weighted each estimate by its share of total VMT. However, in reviewing FHWA (2000, Table V-23) we found that the estimate is in terms of cents per vehicle-mile – not per passenger-mile – so we assumed cents per VMT here. Original estimate is in year-1994 USD. We converted to PMT, assuming 1.6 passengers per vehicle (US DOT, 2008, Table 4-22).
[e]   Delucchi (2004a) estimates low and high external delay costs on the basis of low and high assumptions regarding the value of travel time by trip purpose, delay by trip purpose, and other factors. Estimates in year-1991 USD.
[f]   The estimate from Levinson et al. (1998, Table 12) appears to be in year-1995 USD. We converted to pmt, assuming 1.6 passengers per vehicle.
[g]   According to Levinson et al. (1998, p. 235), this is consistent with data representing the San Francisco to Los Angeles trip by air plane. The estimated congestion arises due to airport use exceeding its capacity. Estimate appears to be in year-1995 USD.

Although estimating the total costs of accidents can be relatively straightforward – the biggest challenge is the estimation of the value of non-monetary impacts such as pain and suffering and lost quality of life, but there is a large literature on this (See Riera et al., 2006, for a estimation of the value of statistical life in the context of motor-vehicle accidents) – estimating the *external* costs of accidents is difficult. The external costs of accidents are those that: (1) are inflicted on party *B* as a result of a trip made by party *A* (that is, would not have occurred had party *A* not made the trip) and (2) are not accounted for, in any way, by party *A* in its trip-making decision.[4] Neither of these conditions is easy to estimate. Consider the first condition. It might seem that any time that car *A* is involved in an accident with car *B*, there is a potential externality, ignoring for now condition 2: if *A* had not been there, it appears at first glance that *B* would not have incurred costs. But although it is true that had *A* not made the trip, that *exact* accident involving *A* and *B* would not have occurred, it is possible that *B* or some other party would have gotten in an accident anyway. The relevant question is whether the trip by *A* affects the accident *risk* that all others face; if the accident risk is independent of *A's* travel, then *A's* trip does not generate external costs (Elvik, 1994; Jansson, 1994).[5] And the relationship between marginal trips and the overall accident rate for everyone else is not straightforward, in part because, as mentioned above, people may compensate for increased exposure by driving more carefully.[6]

As regards the second condition, the issue is the extent to which insurance liability payments, altruism, and the prospect of court-awarded damages together adequately reflect to party *A* the increased risk that *A's* actions impose on party *B*. One complication here is that it is not clear how much insurance liability payments, which may be made annually, influence daily trip-making decisions. If insurance rates do not affect driving decisions, then any change in overall risk resulting from additional driving is effectively unpriced and hence an externality.

The upshot is that estimates of the external portion of accident costs can be quite uncertain and can vary significantly from mode to mode. For example, accidents involving passenger transport by rail, air or water can have large total *social* (private + external) costs, as noted by Levinson et al. (1998), but typically the external-cost portion of the total is relatively small, because marginal travel by these modes does not appreciably increase the average risk for everyone – and as discussed above if the average risk does not change, there is no externality. The risk to persons and property not traveling on the mode is an externality if it is not reflected in insurance or insurance-like prices paid by the operator of the mode, but this presumably is a small fraction of the total accident cost. Thus, for all modes, improving estimates of external accident costs will require better models of accident rates as a function of travel, and better information on the magnitude and effect of liability insurance payments and related quasi-prices.

Finally, we note that accident costs and delay costs are inter-related. Accidents usually cause delay, and changes in vehicle speed and density due to congestion can affect the frequency and severity of accidents. Hensher (2006) discusses the interrelationships in the context of speed limits in urban areas.

Estimates of US Costs by Mode and Intermodal Comparisons

Table 15.4 summarizes recent estimates of external accident costs by mode. Again, we found relatively few estimates for rail and air, and no estimates for water. The estimates of the external costs of road accidents vary by about an order of magnitude or more, due mainly to differences in key valuation parameters, such as the value of life lost or of pain and suffering, and in the definition and estimation of externalities. Differences due to different base years are minor, because the accident rate per vehicle mile of travel has declined only modestly over the past 20 years; for example, from 1996 to 2005 the fatality rate per vehicle mile traveled declined by 14 percent (Starnes, 2008), which is trivial compared with the roughly 1000 percent variation in the estimates.

Again, we did not find estimates of the external accident cost of passenger or freight transport by water for the United States. Zhang et al. (2004) estimate accident costs for

Table 15.4   Estimates of external accident costs by mode (year-2006 cents)

	Road	Rail	Air	Water
Lemp and Kockelman (2008)[a]	4.1 to 14.4/pmt (6.6/pmt weighted avg)			
Parry et al. (2007)[b]	1.9/pmt			
Delucchi (2004b)[c]	1.4 to 4.9/pmt $0.1/tm to $2.0/tm (freight)			
Forkenbrock (1999, 2001)	0.76/tm (freight)	0.22/tm[d] (freight)		
Miller (1997)[e]	1.9 to 4.0/pmt			

Notes: pmt = passenger-mile of travel; tm = ton-mile.
[a]   To estimate external crash costs for different vehicle types, Lemp and Kockelman (2008) use data on national average crash rates, a model of crash severity by vehicle type (given a crash), and estimates of economic and non-economic costs by severity of injury (from the widely used work of Blincoe et al., 2002). They assume that 50 percent of the costs are externalities. The variation pertains to different vehicle types. Estimates appear to be in year-2006 USD. We converted to pmt, assuming 1.6 passengers per vehicle.
[b]   The $ year of the estimate from Parry et al. (2007) is unclear; we assume year-2005 USD is reasonable. We converted to pmt, assuming 1.6 passengers per vehicle.
[c]   Delucchi (2004b, Tables 1-8 and 1-9a) estimates low and high external accident costs for the entire US vehicle fleet in 1991 on the basis of low and high assumptions regarding the fraction of costs internalized by insurance liability premiums and other factors. We assume here that 10 percent of the total estimated by Delucchi (2004b) is attributable to heavy-duty freight trucks, and that 89.3 percent is attributable to light-duty passenger vehicles (based on Miller et al., 1998); the remaining 0.7 percent is attributable to buses, which we do not consider here. We then divide heavy-duty freight-vehicle costs by ton-miles of truck shipment in 1991 (low-cost estimate from Table 1-A5 of Delucchi, 2004b, high-cost estimate from www.bts.gov/publications/national_transportation_statistics /html/table_01_46b.html), and divide light-duty passenger-vehicle costs by passenger miles of travel (equal to vehicle miles from Table 1-A5 of Delucchi, 2004b, multiplied by 1.6 passengers per vehicle). Original estimates in year-1991 USD.
[d]   Forkenbrock (2001) explains his method: 'In summary, Class I freight railroads were involved in accidents that cost society a total of $3 323 980 000 in 1994, and they paid a total of $1 263 000 000 in various kinds of compensation for accidents. The net uncompensated accident cost of freight rail operations in 1994 was therefore $2 060 980 000. Dividing this figure by the 1 200 701 000 000 Class I rail ton-miles in 1994 . . . results in an uncompensated cost of 0.17 cent per ton-mile.' (p. 330). Estimates in year-1994 USD.
[e]   Miller (1997) estimates that the external costs of road accidents in the United States in 1993 were $56 billion or $116 billion (in year-1995 USD), depending on how insurance payments are treated. We divided these estimates by 2 296 billion vehicle miles in 1993 (www.fhwa.dot.gov/ohim/summary95/vm201.pdf) and then converted to pmt, assuming 1.6 passengers per vehicle.

marine ferries in Canada, but they express the results per trip rather than per passenger-mile, and they classify all of the costs as 'internal' rather than 'external' (see their Table 4.22).[7] Maibach et al. (2007) write that 'for inland waterways and maritime transport information on accident costs is almost entirely lacking' (pp. 36–37).

AIR POLLUTION COSTS: HEALTH IMPACTS

Brief Review of Methods and Issues

All transportation modes emit significant quantities of air pollutants. Air pollution harms human health, damages materials, reduces visibility, and stresses crops and forests. In this chapter, we consider two categories: (1) impacts on human health and (2) other impacts, on materials, visibility, crops, and forests. We make this distinction for two reasons. First, there has been much more research on the health impacts of air pollution than on the other impacts. Second, the value of the health impacts of air pollution markedly exceeds the value of the other impacts combined.

An extensive epidemiological literature indicates that air pollution causes a variety of effects including premature mortality, chronic illness and hospital admissions for respiratory and cardiovascular illnesses (Bascom et al., 1996; Cohen et al., 2005; Samet and Krewski, 2007). To quantify the health impacts of air pollutants due to emissions from transportation sources, the most detailed analyses proceed in four steps, which constitute the 'damage function' approach (McCubbin and Delucchi, 1999; Muller and Mendelsohn, 2007):

1.   Estimate the relationship between changes in transportation activity (for example, vehicle miles of travel) and changes in emissions of air pollutants.
2.   Estimate the relationship between changes in emissions and changes in air quality; this can be done with sophisticated three-dimensional atmospheric chemistry models, or, more crudely, with simple functions relating air quality to emissions.
3a. Estimate the relationship between changes in air pollution and changes in human exposure to air pollution (see Brauer et al., 2008).
3b. Estimate the relationship between changes in exposure and changes in health impacts such as mortality, chronic illness and asthma attacks. This step often is combined with step 3a, so that one estimates the relationship between changes in air pollution and changes in health impacts.
4.   Estimate the relationship between changes in health impacts and changes in economic welfare. This step typically is called 'valuation', because the objective is to estimate the dollar value of the physical health impacts.

All of these steps are uncertain, but the last two are especially uncertain. For example, air quality models and emissions models probably have prediction errors of less than 50 percent,[8] but uncertainty in the relationships between air quality and human health, and in valuation, can be several-fold, or even an order of magnitude. The biggest potential health impact of air pollution – mortality related to particulate matter – is potentially very uncertain, for example, due to questions regarding the toxicity of different types of particulate matter (Reiss et al., 2007), and the value of an average statistical life based on, say, wage-risk studies can be an order of magnitude higher than the value of statistical life based on life-years lost if relatively few years are lost (Leksell and Rabl, 2001; Viscusi and Aldy, 2003).

Because there is no mechanism by which air pollution costs are transmitted to those whose activities cause the pollution (aside from the very small effect of one's own pollution on oneself), essentially all air pollution is reasonably regarded as an externality.

Estimates of US Costs by Mode and Intermodal Comparisons

Table 15.5 summarizes several estimates of the health costs of air pollution, by mode. In this case, there are estimates for all modes, although there are many more estimates for

Table 15.5   Estimates of air-pollution health costs by mode (year-2006 cents)

	Road	Rail	Air	Water
Author estimates using COBRA[a]	LDGV: 0.91/pmt HDDV: 1.55/tm	0.35 /tm	0.39/pmt 1.88/tm	1.74/tm
National Research Council (2010)[b]	LDGV 2005: 0.3/pmt LDGV 2030: 0.2/pmt HDDV 2005: 1.2/tm HDDV 2030: 0.2/tm			
Lemp and Kockelman (2008)[c]	0.11 to 1.53/pmt			
Parry et al. (2007)[d]	1.29/pmt			
Zhang et al. (2004)[e]	car: 0.09/pmt (intercity) car: 0.87/pmt (urban) bus: 0.10/pmt (intercity) transit: 0.34/pmt (urban) truck: 0.52/tm (freight)	0.49/pmt (intercity) 0.18/tm (freight)	0.01/pmt 0.003/tm (freight)	1.13/pmt 0.08/tm (freight)
Forkenbrock (1999, 2001)[f]	0.10/tm (freight truck)	0.01 to 0.03/tm (freight)		
McCubbin and Delucchi (1999)[g]	LDGV: 0.50 to 6.66/pmt HDDV: 1.04 to 19.35/tm			
Levinson et al. (1998)[h]	0.71/pmt		0.18/pmt	
Small and Kazimi (1995)[i]	1977 car: 5.61/pmt Tier II car: 0.24/pmt ULEV: 0.21/pmt 2000HDDT: 8.08/tm			

Notes: pmt = passenger-mile of travel; gtm = gross ton-mile; vmt = vehicle-mile of travel; tm = ton-mile; ULEV = ultra-low-emission vehicle; 2000HDDT = heavy-duty diesel truck, fleet average in the year 2000; Tier II car = automobile meeting US government Tier II emission standards; LDGV = light-duty gasoline vehicle; HDDV = heavy-duty diesel vehicle.

[a]   COBRA refers to the Co-Benefits Risk Assessment (COBRA) Screening Model (Abt Associates, 2006). We ran the model in late 2008. COBRA estimates the value of health damages due to changes in fine particulate matter (PM) air quality due to changes in emissions in PM precursors, including SO_2, NO_2, and NH_3. 'Built into COBRA are emissions inventories, a simplified air quality model, health impact equations, and economic valuations ready for use, based on assumptions that EPA currently uses as reasonable best estimates' (Abt Associates, 2006, p. 4). Estimates are in 2006 USD. To produce estimates in dollars per unit of activity, we divided by estimates of total activity data for 2010: VMT by vehicle class from the EPA (2005, Table 3, p. G-8), and air, rail, and water ton-miles of shipment from the Bureau of Transportation Statistics (BTS) (Dennis, 2007, Figure 4). (The BTS shows data through 2005; we have projected data for 2010 assuming the rate of change from 2000 to 2005.) We assume that all rail effects are due to freight; and we assume that 90 percent of air travel effects are due to passenger travel and 10 percent due to freight, based on ton-weighted departures (FHWA, 2005, Table 2-4). We calibrated the rail and water estimates to be consistent with the emission inventory reported by EPA (2008) for the Locomotive and Marine Diesel rule, and we assumed that 5 percent of emissions were due to foreign ships not included in the BTS domestic ton-mile estimates.

[b]   The National Research Council (NRC) (2010) uses the GREET lifecycle emissions model (Wang, 1999) and the damage-cost model of Muller and Mendelsohn (2007) to estimate health and other non-climate costs of air pollution from the lifecycle of light-duty-gasoline vehicles and a range of heavy-duty diesel vehicles in the United States in 2005 and 2030. The NRC estimates are in year-2007 US cents per VMT; we converted to pmt assuming 1.6 passengers per vehicle, and to ton-miles assuming 5.8 tons per truck

Table 15.5   (continued)

(see footnote g). For HDDVs, we use NRC estimates for class 8A HDDVs. For consistency in comparing the NRC estimates with the estimates from the other studies in this table, we show here the NRC's estimates of air-pollution damages from the fuel-use stage only (tailpipe and evaporative emissions) (based on NRC Figures 3.7 and 3.9). The NRC estimates that air-pollution damages from *all* parts of the vehicle lifecycle (energy-feedstock production, fuel manufacture, fuel use in vehicles, and vehicle manufacture) are 0.8 cents/pmt for LDGVs in 2005 and 2030, and 1.2 cents/tm in 2005 and 0.4 cents/tm in 2030 for class 8A HDDVs.

[c] Lemp and Kockelman (2008) multiply vehicle emission rates, which they get from US EPA emission indices, by unit health damage costs from Ozbay and Berechman (2001), for specific models of light-duty vehicles. The variation is due to different emission levels for different vehicles. Estimates appear to be in year-2006 USD. We converted to pmt, assuming 1.6 passengers per vehicle.

[d] Parry et al. (2007, Table 2) appear to report their estimate in year-2005 USD. We converted to pmt, assuming 1.6 passengers per vehicle.

[e] Zhang et al. (2004) calculated the increases in mortality and morbidity cases due to the change in the concentration of each pollutant, and then estimated the monetary valuation of different impacts due to air pollution. Data from Table 6.22 of Zhang et al. (2004). Estimates are in year-2002 Canadian $. We converted to US $ using a typical year 2002 US/Canadian exchange rate (C$1.55 = USD1.00), and then updated to year-2006 USD.

[f] Forkenbrock's (2001, Table 9; 1999, p. 515) estimates are based on the work of Haling and Cohen (1995), who use results of National Economic Research Associates (NERA, 1993) to assign costs of air pollution in 2233 rural US counties in various states. NERA's estimates include impacts on health, materials, agriculture and aesthetic quality. NERA's estimates of health costs include mortality and nonfatal effects ranging from minor irritations to more serious ailments that require medical treatment. Estimates are in 1994 $.

[g] McCubbin and Delucchi (1999, Table 4) use a detailed damage-function approach to estimate the health effects of air pollution from the on-road vehicle fleet in every county in the United States in 1990. Only emissions from motor vehicles themselves are included here; emissions from petroleum refineries and emissions of road dust are reported in McCubbin and Delucchi (1999) but not included here. The low-high range reflects uncertainty in emissions, air quality, health impacts, and valuation. Estimates are in 1991 USD/vmt. We converted to pmt, assuming 1.6 passengers per vehicle; and for trucks we converted to ton-miles assuming 5.8 tons per truck, based on year 2000 VMT (FHWA, 2000, Table VM-1) and ton-miles (Dennis, 2007, Figure 4).

[h] Levinson et al. (1998, Table 12) synthesized earlier studies to develop cost estimates of air pollution caused by air travel, considering the health, material, and vegetation damages from particulates, sulfur oxides, hydrocarbons, carbon monoxide and nitrogen oxides, plus the greenhouse damages due to carbon. Estimates are in 1995 USD. We converted to pmt, assuming 1.6 passengers per vehicle.

[i] Small and Kazimi (1995) estimate air pollution costs by pollutant and vehicle type in Los Angeles. Their baseline results, which are presented here, use a $4.87 million value of life, the geometric average of the high and low particulate mortality coefficients, the geometric average of two ozone morbidity figures with the costs equally attributed to NO_x and VOC, and the only particulate morbidity figure. Estimates are in 1992 USD. We converted to pmt, assuming 1.6 passengers per vehicle and 5.8 tons per truck (as noted in note *g*).

---

road than for the other modes. The estimates of damage costs span a very wide range, mainly because of different assumptions regarding key parameters such as the mortality impacts of pollutants, the value of mortality, and the base year of analysis. The base year is important in the case of air pollution because air-pollutant emissions have declined dramatically over the past 20 years due to improvements in engine design and fuel quality, and are projected to decline further over the next 20 years dues to regulatory changes both in the United States and internationally.

Combining data on national emissions from highway vehicles in the United States with total travel by highway vehicles in the United States, we calculate that fleet-average per-mile emission rates declined by around 70 percent from 1990 to 2006 (by comparison, on a per-mile basis oil use, GHG emissions, noise emissions, and accidents have changed much less).[9] Moreover, there can be a significant difference between fleet-average emissions in year *Y* and emissions from a new model-year *Y* vehicle. Thus, if the method of McCubbin and Delucchi (1999) was applied to new recent-model-year cars (as opposed to the 1991 fleet average), the estimates reported for them in Table 15.7 would be reduced by an order of magnitude. For these reasons, we suggest that researchers estimate air pollution damages from road transport by multiplying an estimate of the damages per kg emitted by the emission rate in kg/mi, rather than by using other analysts' estimates of the cost per mile.

Similarly, care should be taken with rail and water estimates because of recent regulatory changes in the United States (EPA, 2008) and likely implementation of more stringent international fuel standards for ocean-going ships (McCarthy, 2008). Ships have historically used fuel with extremely high sulfur levels and have generated significant global health impacts that have been estimated only recently (Corbett et al., 2007).

AIR POLLUTION COSTS: OTHER IMPACTS (VISIBILITY, AGRICULTURE, MATERIALS, FORESTRY)

Brief Review of Methods and Issues, and Estimates of Costs

There have been very few recent estimates of visibility, agriculture, materials, and forestry costs of transportation air pollution in the United States. As mentioned above, Forkenbrock's (1999; 2001) estimates are based on studies that include impacts on materials, agriculture and 'aesthetic quality', but his estimates are not disaggregated by type of impact. The air-pollution damage estimates of Levinson et al. (1998) also are based on studies that include damage to materials and vegetation, but like Forkenbrock, Levinson et al. (1998) do not disaggregate their results by type of impact.

We have found one set of estimates of the costs of the other (non-health) impacts of transportation air pollution in the United States, and another set pertaining to all air pollution in the United States. Delucchi et al. (2002) estimate the visibility cost of motor-vehicle air pollution, and Murphy et al. (1999) estimate the agricultural cost of motor-vehicle air pollution. These estimates, along with much less detailed estimates of the materials and forestry cost of motor-vehicle air pollution, are summarized in Delucchi (2000). On the basis of the information presented in Delucchi (2000), we can estimate the cost of the non-health impacts as a percentage of the cost of health impacts for road. This is shown in Table 15.6.

Muller and Mendelsohn (2007) estimate air pollution damages to health, visibility, materials, and agricultural, from all sources of emissions in the United States in the year 2002. Table 15.6 includes their estimates. They estimate smaller damages from non-health impacts relative to health impacts than does Delucchi (2000), though both studies find that health impacts dominate. We suspect that in a table like this constructed for rail, air and water modes, the costs of non-health impacts, in total, generally will be much less than the estimated health damages.

Table 15.6   The costs of the non-health impacts of motor-vehicle air pollution as a percentage of the cost of the health impacts

Non-health impact	Delucchi (2000), motor-vehicle air pollution low-damage case to high-damage case[a]	Muller and Mendelsohn (2007), all air pollution in United States
Visibility	19% to 10%	4%
Agriculture	17% to 2%	2%
Materials	5% to 3%	~0%
Forestry	1% to 1%	~0%
All	43% to 15%	6%

Notes: [a] In Delucchi (2000), percentages are the ratio of visibility + agricultural + materials + forestry damages to health damages excluding damages from 'upstream' emissions (for example, at petroleum refineries) and from road-dust emissions. The range is the low-damage case to the high-damage case. Estimates are based on 1990–91 US emission levels.

CLIMATE CHANGE COSTS

Brief Review of Methods and Issues

All transportation modes emit pollutants that can affect global climate. These climate-forcing pollutants, sometimes called 'greenhouse gases' (even though some of the pollutants are aerosols rather than gases), include carbon dioxide (CO_2), methane (CH_4), nitrous oxide (N_2O), carbon monoxide (CO), nitrogen oxides (NO_2), ammonia (NH_3), sulfur oxides (SO_2), volatile organic compounds (VOCs), chlorofluorocarbons (CFCs) and various forms of particulate matter (PM). The Intergovernmental Panel on Climate Change (IPCC) provides an exhaustive review of research on the effects of GHGs on global climate (IPCC, 2007).

The climate change costs of transport can be estimated as the product of the two factors: CO_2-equivalent emissions of GHGs (in kg/ton-mile, kg/passenger-mile or kg/vehicle-mile), and the damage cost of a unit of GHG emissions (in \$/kg-CO_2). Ideally, CO_2-equivalent emissions are estimated for the entire lifecycle of a transportation mode, where 'lifecycle' refers to all of the activities directly or indirectly involved in transportation, including for example the production and transport of the fuel used by the transport mode and the production and transport of finished materials used by the transport mode. 'CO_2-equivalency' means that one gram of emission of non-CO_2 GHG P is expressed as the number of grams of CO_2 that have an effect equivalent to that of one gram of P, where 'equivalency' ideally is in terms of the damages from climate change (Bradford, 2001; Manne and Richels, 2001). The Lifecycle Emissions Model (LEM) (Delucchi et al., 2003) and the widely used Greenhouse-gases, Regulated Emissions, and Energy-use in Transportation (GREET) model (Wang, 1999) estimate lifecycle, CO_2-equivalent emissions from transport modes except air.

The cost of a unit of GHG emissions has been estimated in numerous studies. Anthoff et al. (2009), Delucchi (2004c), Pearce (2003), Tol (2003) and Wahba and Hope (2006), review or develop original estimates of the marginal damage cost of CO_2 emissions.

Anthoff et al. (2009) show that damage estimates can span several orders of magnitude, depending on the pure rate of time preference (a component of the social discount rate), the relationship between changes in consumption (or income) and changes in welfare (also known as equity weighting), and the per-capita income level to which the results are normalized. This wide range makes it difficult even to establish reasonable upper and lower bounds.

Estimates of US Costs by Mode and Intermodal Comparisons

Table 15.7 shows estimates of the climate change cost. Not included in Table 15.7 are studies that estimate GHG emissions and radiative forcing changes due to transport modes but do not value the changes in dollars (Capaldo et al., 1999; Eyring et al., 2005; Fuglestvedt et al., 2008; Sausen et al., 2005). Eyring et al. (2005) summarize the emissions from international shipping over the past several decades. Capaldo et al. (1999) use a global chemical transport model to estimate that the emissions from international shipping can be a dominant contributor to atmospheric sulfur dioxide concentrations, and that particulate matter emissions from ships result in a global radiative forcing of $-0.11\,Wm^{-2}$, due to cloud effects. Sausen et al. (2005) estimate that in the year 2000, aviation had a radiative forcing of $77.8\,mWm^{-2}$, including the effect of cirrus clouds induced by aviation. Fuglestvedt et al. (2008) calculate the global mean net radiative forcing due to each transport sector in the year 2000 relative to preindustrial times: $175\,mWm^{-2}$ for the road sector, about $5\,mWm^{-2}$ for the rail sector, $70\,mWm^{-2}$ for aviation, and $-70\,mWm^{-2}$ for shipping. Shipping has a negative radiative forcing because of relatively high emissions of sulfur dioxide, due to the high sulfur content of marine fuel oil.[10]

The estimates developed for this chapter, shown as 'Author estimates' in Table 15.7, span the range of the other estimates presented in Table 15.7. The nearly 100-fold difference between our low and high results is due entirely to the uncertainty in the $/kg damage cost of GHG emission, as discussed above. Note that our estimates include the full lifecycle, and a wide range of GHGs, whereas the other estimates in Table 15.7 include only end-use emissions of CO_2.

NOISE COSTS

Brief Review of Methods and Issues

In many urban areas, noise is a serious problem. Roadways with large volumes of high-speed traffic, high-speed rail lines and airports can be very noisy. This noise can disturb sleep, disrupt activities, hinder work, impede learning and cause stress. As a result, homes near major roadways and airports have less value than similar homes further away.

The external cost of noise from transport includes the value of the damages from excess noise experienced plus the cost of any defensive actions or avoidance behavior, although this second factor (defensive/avoidance behavior) rarely is estimated. To estimate damages from excess noise from a particular transport mode, one needs a model of noise generation from the source, a method for estimating exposure to the noise, and a method for valuing the damages of exposure above a threshold. Noise generation and

Table 15.7   Estimates of climate-change damage costs by mode (year-2006 cents)

	Road	Rail	Air	Water
Author estimates[a]	car: 0.06 to 4.78/ pmt (26 mpg) scooter: 0.02 to 1.23/pmt mini-bus: 0.02 to 1.47/pmt city bus: 0.04 to 3.46/pmt truck: 0.03 to 2.74/ tm (freight)	0.02 to 1.68/pmt (intracity rail transit) 0.006 to 0.47/tm (freight)		0.002 to 0.23/tm (freight)
Lemp and Kockelman (2008)[b]	0.84 to 3.81/pmt			
Parry et al. (2007)[c]	0.19/pmt			
Zhang et al. (2004)[d]	car: 0.06/pmt (intercity) car: 0.12/pmt (urban) bus: 0.01/pmt (intercity) transit: 0.04/pmt (urban) truck: 0.06/tm (freight)	0.07/pmt (intercity) 0.01/tm (freight)	0.08/pmt 0.45/tm (freight)	0.16/pmt (passenger ferry) 0.01/tm (freight – presumably a large cargo ship)
Forkenbrock (1999, 2001)[e]	0.19/tm (freight)	0.03/tm (freight)		

Notes: pmt = passenger-mile of travel; tm = ton-mile.
[a]   We multiply estimates of lifecycle CO_2-equivalent emissions, in grams/passenger-mile or grams/ton-mile, by an assumed GHG global damage cost of $1.0/10^6$-g-CO_2-equivalent (low-cost case) to $80/10^6$-g-CO_2-equivalent (high-cost case) ($0.91/ton to $73/ton). The estimates of lifecycle emissions are from an updated version of the model documented in Delucchi et al. (2003), and include the CO_2 equivalent of CH_4, N_2O, CO, NO_2, SO_2, VOCs, PM and CFCs. The damage cost estimates are based on our review of Anthoff et al. (2009), Delucchi (2004c), Pearce (2003), Tol (2003) and Wahba and Hope (2006). Estimates in year-2006 USD.
[b]   Lemp and Kockelman (2008) multiply end-use (not lifecycle) emissions of CO_2 (not including other GHGs), estimated on the basis of the carbon-content of the fuel and the fuel economy, by an assumed damage value of $50/ton-$CO_2$, for specific models of light-duty vehicles. Estimates appear to be in year-2006 USD. We converted to pmt, assuming 1.6 passengers per vehicle.
[c]   Parry et al. (2007, Table 2) multiply end-use (not lifecycle) emissions of CO_2 (not including other GHGs) by an assumed damage value of $14/ton-$CO_2$, (They consider a range of $5.50/ton to $82/ton.) They appear to report their estimate in year-2005 USD. We converted to pmt, assuming 1.6 passengers per vehicle.
[d]   Zhang et al. (2004) multiply end-use (not lifecycle) emissions of CO_2 (not including other GHGs) by an assumed damage value of $5.50/ton-$CO_2$ (year 2002 Canadian $), which they derived starting with a value of $3.50/ton-$CO_2$ in 1990 US $. Original estimates are in year-2002 Canadian $. We converted to USD using a typical year 2002 US/Canadian exchange rate (C$1.55 = US$1.00), and then updated to year-2006 USD.
[e]   Forkenbrock (1999, p. 516, 2001, Table 7) multiplies end-use (not lifecycle) emissions of CO_2 (not including other GHGs) by an assumed damage cost of $10 per ton of CO_2. Estimates are in 1994 USD.

exposure models have been developed for all modes; see Miedema and Oudshoorn (2001) for a review of models of annoyance due to exposure to noise from road, air, and rail transport, and Delucchi and Hsu (1998) for an application of noise-generation models to road noise and the resultant damages. Noise damage values generally are estimated on the basis of 'hedonic' price analyses, which are discussed next.

As mentioned above, noise is a prominent enough problem that it measurably affects the value of homes. Econometric or 'hedonic' price analyses measure this effect by estimating the sales price of a house as a function of a number of important characteristics, including the ambient noise level or distance from a major noise source (Nelson, 2008). If such an analysis does not omit important determinants of sales price, it can tell us how much an additional decibel of noise (above a certain threshold) reduces the value of a home. This reduction in value per decibel, multiplied by the average value of homes, the number of homes exposed to noise above a threshold, and the amount of noise above a threshold, will tell us the external 'damage cost' of transport noise in and around the home. (See Nelson, 2008, for a comprehensive discussion of issues in hedonic property value studies of noise from aircraft and road traffic.)

In the estimation of noise damages from transport a number of factors are uncertain. Delucchi and Hsu (1998) show that in the case of road-noise damages, the primary uncertainty regards the cost of noise per decibel above a threshold, the interest rate, the amount of noise attenuation due to ground cover and intervening structures, the threshold level below which damages are assumed to be zero, the density of housing alongside roads, average traffic speeds and the cost of noise away from the home. The case of noise from air travel may be less complicated, because exposure is not attenuated by structures in complex ways.

Estimates of US Costs by Mode and Intermodal Comparisons

Table 15.8 presents several estimates of noise damage costs. Most studies focus on noise from highway vehicles or airplanes, because noise from trains and ships generally is thought to be relatively minor. For example, Andersson and Ögren (2007) state that several studies have shown that individuals perceive noise from road traffic as more annoying than from rail traffic, and Bickel et al. (2006, p. 397) assume that ship noise is negligible.

Note that the studies of Table 15.8 estimate damages from each transport mode under the assumption that the mode is the only source of noise. Because noise from different sources does not simply add up, the net effect of 'marginal' noise from a particular transport mode can depend on the magnitude and characteristics of other sources of noise (Moore, 1978).

WATER POLLUTION

Brief Review of Methods and Issues

Fuels and chemicals from transportation modes can spill and leak into oceans, rivers, lakes and groundwater. This water pollution can harm human health, injure and kill

Table 15.8   Estimates of noise damage costs by mode (year-2006 cents)

	Road	Rail	Air	Water
Forkenbrock (1999, 2001)	0.05/tm (freight)	0.05/tm (freight)[a]		
Delucchi and Hsu (1998)[b]	LDVs: 0.00 to 3.45/pmt HDTs: 0.00 to 5.48/tm			
Levinson et al. (1997, 1998)	0.87/pmt[c]	0.52/pmt to 0.89/pmt[d]	0.88/pmt[e]	

Notes: pmt = passenger-mile of travel; tm = ton-mile; LDV = light-duty vehicle; HDT = heavy-duty truck.
[a]   Forkenbrock (2001) looked at the external costs of freight rail in rural areas in the United States. He argued that in sparsely settled rural areas, exposure to rail noise is similar to exposure to noise from trucks operating on highways, and that both are small. Accordingly, he assumed for rail noise the same cost per ton-mile he estimated for trucks in Forkenbrock (1999, p. 518). Original estimates are in year-1994 USD.
[b]   See discussion of Delucchi and Hsu (1998) in the text. Range is damages from travel on local roads, in the low-cost case, to damages from travel on interstate freeways, in the high-cost case (note that Delucchi and Hsu, 1998, consider the high-cost case to be unlikely). Estimates are in year-1991 USD. We converted to pmt, assuming 1.6 passengers per vehicle; and for trucks we converted to ton-miles assuming 5.8 tons per truck, based on year 2000 vehicle miles traveled (FHWA, 2000, Table VM-1) and ton-miles (Dennis, 2007, Figure 4).
[c]   Levinson et al. (1998, Table 12) use a noise-generation model to estimate the cost of motor-vehicle noise. They assume that there is zero background noise (Levinson et al., 1997, p. 209). Estimates are in year-1995 USD. We converted to pmt, assuming 1.6 passengers per vehicle.
[d]   Levinson et al. (1997, p. 210) analyzed the noise costs caused by high-speed rail for two train speeds: 125 mph and 200 mph. The $ year is unclear; we assume year-1994 USD.
[e]   Levinson et al. (1998, Table 3) review estimates of noise damage costs from air planes in Europe, and then assume that the average value applies to the United States (Zhang et al., 2004, make the same assumption). Estimates are in year-1995 USD.

wildlife, corrode materials and despoil scenic recreation areas (see Freeman, 2000, for a discussion of the costs and benefits of water pollution policy). Transportation modes also can cause water pollution indirectly: emissions of nitrogen oxide from fuel combustion can eventually deposit as nitrate and cause nitrogen pollution in aquatic systems (see Galloway et al., 2004, for a comprehensive discussion of the nitrogen cycle).

In general there has been much less research on the dollar cost of the impacts of water pollution than on the dollar cost of the impacts of air pollution. A few studies have quantified the economic cost of oil spills (for example, Carson et al., 2004; Grigalunas et al., 1986), but there is essentially no systematic research on the costs of the other impacts of water pollution. Gaffield et al. (2003) estimate that gastrointestinal illnesses due to water pollution (apparently from storm runoff) cost $2 to $14 billion per year (2002 USD), but it is difficult to apportion to this to transportation. In any event, quantifying the cost of water pollution is a relatively low priority, because it appears to be small compared to the other external costs of transport (see Table 15.9).

Estimates of US Costs by Mode and Intermodal Comparisons

We found in the peer-reviewed literature one relatively recent estimate of water pollution damage costs from road transport. This estimate is presented in Table 15.9.

Table 15.9   Estimates of water-pollution costs by mode (year-2006 cents)

	Road	Rail	Air	Water
Delucchi (2000, 2004b)[a]	0.014 to 0.051/pmt $0.003/tm to $0.051/tm (freight)			

Notes: pmt = passenger-mile of travel; tm = ton-mile.
[a] Equal to Delucchi's (2000) estimate of damages from oil spills, leaking storage tanks, and urban runoff
   due to oil use by all highway vehicles in the United States in 1990–91 ($0.4 to $1.5 billion), allocated
   between light-duty vehicles and heavy-duty vehicles according to fuel use in 1991 (78.1 percent LDVs, 21.2
   percent HDVs, 0.7 percent buses; Table 1-A5 of Delucchi, 2004b, for LDVs and HDVs and www.fhwa.
   dot.gov/policy/ohpi/qftravel.cfm for buses), then divided by pmt for LDVs and ton-miles for HDVs per
   Table 15.4 note *c*. Original estimates are in 1991 USD.

Note that the estimates in Table 15.9 do not include the costs of the water-quality impacts of highway de-icing, which can disintegrate pavement, corrode vehicles and bridges, pollute groundwater, and harm vegetation (Granato et al., 1996; Vitaliano, 1992; EPA, 1996). Murray and Ernst (1976) estimated that in the United States in the 1970s, the environmental impacts of highway de-icing, including pollution of water supply and damage to human health, damage to vegetation, and corrosion of vehicles and infrastructure cost $2.9 billion/year (1973–74 USD). Vitaliano (1992) also estimates the social costs of highway de-icing, and although he does not report national totals, his estimates of damages per ton of salt appear to be similar to Murray and Ernst's (1976). We do not include de-icing water-quality costs here because they either are not externalities at all (in the case of vehicle corrosion costs), or in any case are not external costs of marginal travel. However, these costs should be included in full social cost–benefit analyses of transportation investments.

Our estimate also excludes indirect water pollution impacts, such as NO_x/nitrate pollution of aquatic ecosystems, as mentioned above. These are marginal external costs of transport fuel use, but as far as we know they have not been quantified.

ENERGY SECURITY/OIL-IMPORTING COSTS

Brief Review of Methods and Issues

The United States consumes about a fourth of the world's petroleum, and imports nearly 60 percent of its own consumption (Davis et al., 2008). Over two-thirds of US oil consumption goes to the transportation sector, which with the exception of some electric rail systems is fueled entirely by petroleum.

The heavy use of imported oil by the transportation sector gives rise to several kinds of economic costs that are not reflected in the price of oil: the cost of the Strategic Petroleum Reserve (SPR), defense expenditures to protect US oil interests, macroeconomic disruption/adjustment costs due to price volatility, and pure wealth transfers from US consumers to foreign producers. These external costs ultimately derive from the concentration of large amounts of oil in relatively unstable regions of the world, in particular the Persian Gulf.

Strategic Petroleum Reserve (SPR)
The SPR is meant to buffer the effects of sudden supply shortfalls or sudden price spikes (www.fe.doe.gov/programs/reserves/index.html). The cost of the SPR includes the annualized construction costs, ongoing maintenance and repair costs, and costs related to changes in the value of oil over the period it is stored. Delucchi (2007) estimates the total cost of the SPR is very small, and so consequently we do not include it in our quantitative estimates here.[11]

Defense expenditures
A substantial fraction of the US defense goes towards protecting US interests in Middle East – interests that center mainly on oil (Delucchi and Murphy, 2008a). Delucchi and Murphy (2008a) attempt to quantify the relationship between the size of the defense budget and various aspects of US oil interests in the Middle East. Because there is little real information on which to base this quantification, the estimates of Delucchi and Murphy (2008a) span a wide range (see Table 15.10).

Macroeconomic adjustment costs
The inability of the macro economy to adjust efficiently to rapid changes in the price of oil can cause a real decrease in economy-wide output, manifest as a reduction in gross domestic product (GDP). This 'macroeconomic adjustment cost' (MEAC) is a function of the total level of petroleum consumption, the magnitude of the price change, the substitutability of oil in the economy and other factors. To the extent that the MEAC is a real resource cost, a function of oil consumption, and not reflected in the price of oil, it is a marginal external cost of oil use. Jones et al. (2004) review research from 1996 to 2004 on the relationship between oil price shocks and the macroeconomy, and conclude that a one percent change in oil price causes a -0.055 percent change in GDP. Leiby (2007) provides the best recent estimate of the external macro-economic adjustment cost. The most important factors in the estimate of this external cost are the size of the US economy, the level of imports, the world oil price, the likelihood of a disruption, and the responsiveness of regional oil supply and demand.

Wealth transfer cost
Because the world price of oil generally is well above the long-run marginal production costs of most of the major oil exporters, consumers of imported oil generally transfer a large amount of wealth to oil exporters. Greene and Ahmad (2005) estimate that from 1970 to 2004 this oil/wealth transfer cost exceeded one trillion dollars. However, because this cost is a transfer among nations we do not count it as an external cost here.

Estimates of US Costs by Mode and Intermodal Comparisons

Few analyses estimate the external costs of oil importing. For this chapter, we have made original estimates by multiplying the energy-use intensity of different modes by the oil-importing damage cost. Table 15.10 shows the estimates; details are given in the notes to the table.

Because a single national damage cost per energy unit applies to all modes, differences in damages among modes depend entirely on differences in energy consumption per mile

Table 15.10 Estimates of energy-security/oil-importing costs by mode (year-2006 cents)

	Road	Rail	Air	Water
Author estimates[a]	car: 0.20 to 0.75/pmt light truck: 0.22 to 0.84/pmt transit bus: 0.23 to 0.89/pmt freight truck: 0.22 to 0.84/tm	passenger: 0.15 to 0.58/pmt freight: 0.02 to 0.07/tm	passenger: 0.18 to 0.69/pmt	freight: 0.03 to 0.11/tm
Parry et al. (2007)[b]	0.39/pmt			

Notes: pmt = passenger-mile of travel; tm = ton-mile; MEAC = macroeconomic adjustment/disruption cost; EIA = Energy Information Administration.

[a]**Oil importing damage cost**. Leiby (2007) estimates the MEAC in the United States to be $2.10 to $7.40 per barrel (bbl) of imported oil (2005 USD) and reports that imported oil is 58.6 percent of total oil demand, which results in $1.20 to $4.30/bbl of all oil demanded in the United States. We update to 2006 USD using the GDP implicit price deflator (Table 1.1.9 of the National Income Product Accounts from the Bureau of Economic Analysis, www.bea.gov/national/nipaweb/index.asp), and then multiply the high value by a factor of 1.2 to account for the MEAC due to use of domestic oil, which as Leiby (2007) suggests is less than the cost of imported oil but not zero. The result is $1.27/bbl-oil to $5.36/bbl-oil.

Delucchi and Murphy (2008a) estimate that the military cost of consuming Persian-Gulf oil in the United States in 2004 was $13.4 billion to $47.0 billion, or $1.80/bbl to $6.20/bbl of all oil supplied in the United States in 2004 (given 7.6 billion bbl of crude and products supplied in 2004, EIA, 2008). Updating to 2006 USD using the GDP implicit price results in a range $1.88/bbl-oil to $6.59/bbl-oil.

Leiby (2007) also estimates 'monopsony' or demand-related wealth-transfer costs, but because these are transfers from US consumers to foreign producers we ignore them here. We ignore the annualized cost of the SPR because it is trivial (Delucchi, 2007).

The MEAC and the military cost total $3.15/bbl to $11.95/bbl. Multiplying the total by 1-bbl-crude-oil/1.063-bbl-products and 1-bbl-product/5.353×10^6-BTU-product (higher heating value) in 2006 (both conversions from the EIA [2008]) gives a range $0.55/10^6-BTU-product to $2.10/10^6-BTU-product in the United States in 2006 $.

Energy intensities by mode. We assume the following end-use (not lifecycle) intensities (based on higher heating values, using the same energy conversion factors that the EIA uses):

Mode	Energy intensity		Source and notes
cars	3571	BTU/pmt	Davis et al. (2008) Table 2.13, year 2005
personal trucks	~4008	BTU/pmt	Our estimate for year 2005 based on Davis et al. (2008)
transit bus	4235	BTU/pmt	Davis et al. (2008) Table 2.13, year 2005
air travel	3264	BTU/pmt	Davis et al. (2008) Table 2.14, year 2005
passenger rail	2759	BTU/pmt	Approximate weighted average of intercity rail, rail transit, and commuter rail, in Davis et al. (2008) Table 2.14, year 2005 (uses weights based on year 2006 energy use)
water (freight)	514	BTU/tm	Davis et al. (2008) Table 2.14, year 2005
rail (freight)	337	BTU/tm	Davis et al. (2008) Table 2.14, year 2005
road (freight)	4009	BTU/tm	Energy use of medium/heavy trucks divided by ton-miles of freight hauled by trucks, Davis et al. (2008) Tables 2.7 and 5.12, year 2002

[b]Parry et al (2007, Table 2) appear to report their estimate in year-2005 USD. We converted to pmt, assuming 1.6 passengers per vehicle.

(on the assumption that all modes use petroleum). As shown in the notes to Table 15.10, all passenger transport modes have roughly similar energy intensities per passenger mile, at current average occupancies, but freight shipment by road is an order of magnitude more energy intensive than shipment by water or rail.

OTHER COSTS (NOT ESTIMATED HERE)

The construction and use of transportation modes can create 'external' or non-market costs beyond those estimated here. For example, all modes create unsightly infrastructure and waste, which presumably have an aesthetic cost. Surveys have found, not unexpectedly, that the general public feels that the world would be prettier without roads (Huddart, 1978) and the unsightliness of scrapped autos and junkyards has been formally condemned by the courts (Woodbury, 1987).

Poorly designed and thoughtlessly placed transportation infrastructure can divide communities, impede circulation and create barriers to social interaction.[12] Indeed, the 'freeway revolts' that began in the late 1960s and shut down freeway projects in several cities in the United States – the dead-end Embarcadero Freeway in San Francisco, torn down after the 1989 Loma Prieta earthquake, is perhaps the most famous example – were spawned in part by these sorts of negative social impacts. Soguel (1995) cites a study by Appleyard that shows that 'residents of San Francisco with light volumes of traffic have three times as many local friends and twice as many acquaintances as those on heavily traveled streets' (p. 302).[13]

Transportation infrastructure also can fragment sensitive environmental habitat and thereby disturb and possibly even eliminate plants and other (non-human) animals. Van Bohemen (1995, p. 133) distinguishes four kinds of fragmentation: destruction, disturbance, barrier action, and collisions with vehicles. Valuing these impacts is a complex undertaking (see Nijkamp et al., 2008, for a review issues in estimating the economic value of biodiversity). Willis et al. (1998) review studies of the 'wildlife value' and 'landscape value' of land used for roads in Britain. They report a very wide range of values, from less than £10/ha/yr to more than £10 000/ha/yr, depending, naturally, on the type of land (forest, meadow, farm and so forth), and the type of values solicited (use value, option value, existence value and so forth).

Finally, taxes and fees paid by users of transportation modes and transportation fuels may be considered to be insufficient or excessive with respect to some standards of equity or social-cost accounting. Delucchi (2007) and Delucchi and Murphy (2008b) review these issues and offer estimates of various financial 'subsidies' to motor vehicle use in the United States.[14] We do not include financial subsidies here because generally they are matters of equity rather than economic efficiency and hence do not constitute externalities as we define them.

SUMMARY AND CONCLUSION

Table 15.11 presents the low and high estimates of the external cost of each of the impacts reviewed here. We can draw three general conclusions from this review. First, per passenger-mile or per ton-mile, the road mode generally has higher external costs than do the other modes. This is due to the relatively high energy intensity of road travel, the relatively close proximity of road vehicles to people, and to individuals operating the vehicles. Second, accident and congestion costs generally are the largest, followed by air pollution and climate change costs. Third, there is a great deal of uncertainty in many of the estimates, often having to do with the step of valuing physical impacts. Ongoing research will reduce this uncertainty.

Table 15.11 *Summary of estimates of external costs by transport mode and cost category (year-2006 cents)*

	Passenger (per passenger-mile)				Freight (per ton-mile)			
	Road	Rail	Air	Water	Road	Rail	Air	Water
Congestion delay	0.88–7.5	n.e.	0.35	n.e.	0.54	0.03	n.e.	n.e.
Accident	1.4–14.4	n.e.	n.e.	n.e.	0.11–2.0	0.22	n.e.	n.e.
Air pollution, health	0.09–6.7	0.49	0.01–0.39	1.1	0.10–18.7	0.01–0.35	0.0–1.9	0.08–1.7
Air pollution, other	n.e.	n.e.	n.e.	n.e.	n.e.	n.e.	n.e.	n.e.
Climate change	0.06–4.8	0.02–1.7	0.08	0.16	0.02–5.9	0.01–0.47	0.45	0.00–0.23
Noise	0.0–3.5	0.52–0.89	0.88	n.e.	0.0–5.3	0.05	n.e.	n.e.
Water pollution	0.01–0.05	n.e.	n.e.	n.e.	0.003–0.05	n.e.	n.e.	n.e.
Energy security	0.20–0.84	0.15–0.58	0.18–0.69	n.e.	0.22–0.84	0.02–0.07	n.e.	0.03–0.11

Notes: n.e. = not estimated.

We have presented here estimates of the external costs of transport per passenger-mile and per ton-mile for recent years in the United States. It also is interesting to ask what the *total* external costs of transport, as opposed to the costs per mile, might be in the future. Total external costs are the product of the total activity (for example, passenger-miles of travel) and the average external cost per unit of activity (for example, cost per passenger-mile of travel). We therefore conclude this chapter with discussions of trends in activity levels and costs per unit of activity, for the major external costs of road transportation.

Congestion

By any measure, road congestion has increased rapidly and dramatically over the past two decades (Schrank and Lomax, 2007). The dramatic rise in congestion is due to increases in vehicle-miles of travel and reductions in vehicle speeds. In the case of congestion – unlike in the cases of accidents and air pollution – there has been no reduction in impacts per mile to offset the increases in total miles driven.

Constraints on adding road capacity and the difficulty of discouraging or re-directing motor-vehicle use make large, widespread decreases in travel unlikely, although recent transportation planning efforts focused on better matching of origins and destinations may dampen VMT growth in some areas of the United States. More promising are efforts to reduce congestion impacts per mile by re-allocating travel over time and space. (Congestion impacts per mile also can be reduced by making vehicles smaller, but the prospects for this seem unlikely.) Travel can be re-allocated by traffic control or by pricing; in the United States, policy makers appear to favor pricing. The federal government and several states are developing congestion-pricing programs (Congressional Budget Office, 2009; Federal Highway Administration, 2008), including some designed to ease truck congestion at ports (Mani and Fischer, 2009).

Accidents

The fatality and injury rate per mile of vehicle travel have declined steadily for many years, due to reduced involvement of alcohol, increased use of seatbelts, improved vehicle safety, and other factors (Blincoe et al., 2002; Starnes, 2008). However, these reductions have been offset by growth in vehicle miles of travel, with the result that total road fatalities have remained roughly constant. Absent substantial changes in travel or traffic safety patterns, these trends are likely to continue in the near term.

Air Pollution

Dramatic reductions in emissions per mile from motor vehicles, due to improved emission-control technology spurred by tougher emission standards, have outpaced the growth in total vehicle travel, with the result that total emissions of all air pollutants from the highway transportation sector in the United States have declined dramatically since 1990 (www.epa.gov/ttn/ chief/trends/index.html). However, damage-cost trends may not have followed these emissions trends exactly, because the exposed population and the value of impacts have increased.

In the future, continued reductions in emissions per mile, particularly from diesel vehicles – which emit the most damaging pollutants (PM, SO_X, and NO_X) – may result in sharp decreases in total transportation-related air pollution damages, in spite of increasing travel and greater exposed population. Note that as vehicular air pollution is reduced, air-pollution-damage costs will become less important compared with accident, congestion, climate-change and energy-security costs.

Climate Change and Energy Security

Motor-vehicle energy use, petroleum use, and greenhouse-gas emissions have been increasing since 1970 because VMT has increased steadily while fuel use per mile has declined only modestly. Since the mid-1990s, petroleum use has increased with VMT, which implies that fuel-use per mile has remained constant (Davis et al., 2008). Oil-importing 'energy-security' costs have increased since the 1990s because of increasing petroleum use, increasing oil imports, higher oil prices, and more regional conflicts over oil (Leiby, 2007). Similarly, climate-change costs have increased with petroleum use, population and income.

In the near term, these trends in climate-change and energy-security costs are likely to continue. The middle term is uncertain, because of uncertain prospects for fuel-economy improvements and fuel substitution, and uncertainty about oil prices. In the long run (at least 30 years hence), we expect to see the energy-security and climate-change costs of transportation mitigated greatly by the widespread use of non-petroleum fuels.

We conclude that safety and congestion costs will remain large until there are very broad changes in transportation activity. The mitigation of energy-security costs and climate-change costs depends on the pace of introduction of non-petroleum fuels, which is difficult to predict. Air pollution costs are likely to be of diminishing importance.

NOTES

1. Estimates of the external costs of transport in Europe can be found in Bickel et al. (2006), Janic (2007), Link (2005), Nash et al. (2001), Quinet (2004) and the chapter by Friedrich and Quinet.
2. See Lyons et al. (2007) for a discussion of this for rail passengers in Britain.
3. See Small et al. (1999) for a general discussion of valuing travel time and predictability.
4. This conceptualization goes back at least to Vickrey (1968).
5. This is analogous to the case of congestion: a congestion externality arises if an additional trip increases the average travel time for everyone else.
6. To see the subtleties, consider the case of cars hitting pedestrians. It might seem that every additional car creates additional risk for pedestrians, and hence gives rise to potential external costs, but to the extent that pedestrians adjust to the increased exposure by being more careful, then part of the potential external cost is manifest as the cost of extra care rather than as the cost of more accidents.
7. Zhang et al. (2004) also estimate accident costs for air transport in Canada, but express the results per flight hour rather than per passenger-mile or ton-mile, and classify all of the costs as 'internal'.
8. Tesche (1988) found that ozone air quality models had prediction errors of 35 percent to 40 percent. More recent ozone air quality models are more accurate than this (Davidson et al., 2008; Gilliland et al., 2008; Hogrefe et al., 2008), but aerosol air-quality models are not yet as well developed, and the errors appear to be slightly larger than the errors in ozone air-quality models (Davidson et al., 2008; Fisher, 2008; Gilliland et al., 2008). The status of aerosol air-quality modeling is particularly relevant because aerosol levels are associated with premature mortality (for example, Samet and Krewski, 2007).
9. We used emissions data from: www.epa.gov/ttn/chief/trends/ and highway travel numbers from: www. fhwa.dot.gov/policy/ohpi/qftravel.cfm.
10. Our 'author estimates' in Table 15.7 also account for the high emissions of sulfur from shipping and the negative radiative forcing effect of sulfate.
11. Delucchi (2007) probably underestimates the future price of oil in his low-cost case, but the higher the future price, the higher the present value of future oil sales, and hence the lower the cost of holding oil for future use.
12. Along these lines, some researchers suggest that roads and cars cause urban 'sprawl' and that sprawl has external costs (not paid by transportation users), such as higher infrastructure costs and reduced social interaction. However, Brueckner and Largey (2008) find that the effect of low density on social interaction actually is positive, or beneficial, rather than negative: as density decreases, social interaction *increases.*
13. Soguel (1995) surveyed residents in the Swiss town of Neuchâtel (population 32 000) and found that they were willing to pay $1.9 to $2.6 million per year, or $58 to $82/person/year, to divert traffic on five urban streets to underground bypasses (for a total of 750 m), in order to provide unimpeded access to the city center.
14. A related issue is whether unpriced (free) parking is an external cost. The answer to this depends in part on considerations of the size of transaction costs and the 'efficiency' of bundling, and partly on how one views environmental and congestion externalities that are indirectly related to parking supply. See Button (2006), Feitelson and Rotem (2004) and Shoup (2005) for a discussion of some of the issues; see Shoup (2005) for a discussion of the costs and impacts of 'free' parking. This issue receives considerable attention because the total annualized cost of unpriced parking is at a minimum several tens of billions dollars per year (Delucchi, 2004b).

REFERENCES

Abt Associates Inc., 2006, *User's Manual for the Co-Benefits Risk Assessment (COBRA) Screening Model.* Washington DC: Clean Energy-Environment State Partnership Program, US Environmental Protection Agency.

Andersson, H. and M. Ögren, 2007, Noise charges in railway infrastructure: a pricing schedule based on the marginal cost principle. *Transport Policy,* **14,** 204–213.

Anthoff, D., C. Hepburn and R.S.J. Tol, 2009, Equity weighting and the marginal damage costs of climate change. *Ecological Economics,* **68,** 836–849.

Bascom, R., P.A. Bromberg, D.A. Costa, R. Devlin, D.W. Dockery, M.W. Frampton, W. Lambert, J.M. Samet, F.E. Speizer and M. Utell., 1996, Health effects of outdoor air pollution. *American Journal of Respiratory and Critical Care Medicine,* **153** (1), 3–50.

Bickel, P., R. Friedrich, H. Link, L. Stewart and C. Nash, 2006, Introducing environmental externalities into transport pricing: measurements and implications, *Transport Reviews*. **26** (4), 389–415.

Blincoe, L.J., A. Seay, E. Zaloshnja, T. Miller, E. Romano, S. Luchter and R. Spicer, 2002, *The Economic Impact of Motor Vehicle Crashes, 2000*. DOT-HS-809-446. Washington DC: National Highway Traffic Safety Administration, US Department of Transportation. Available at: www.nhtsa.dot.gov/staticfiles/ DOT/NHTSA/Communication & Consumer Information/Articles/Associated Files/EconomicImpact2000. pdf.

Bradford, D.F., 2001, Time, money, and tradeoffs. *Nature*, **410**, 649–650.

Brauer, M., et al., 2008, Models of exposure for use in epidemiological studies of air pollution health impacts. In C. Borrego and A.I. Miranda, eds, *Air Pollution Modeling and Its Application XIX*, NATO Science for Peace and Security Series. Dordrecht, The Netherlands: Springer Science + Business Media B.V., Chapter 7.1, pp. 589–604.

Brueckner, J.K., 2002, Internalization of airport congestion. *Journal of Air Transport Management*, **8**, 141–147.

Brueckner, J.K. and A.G. Largey, 2008, Social interaction and urban sprawl. *Journal of Urban Economics*, **64**, 18–34.

Bureau of Transportation Statistics, 2007, Transportation Statistics Annual Report 2007. US Department of Transportation, Washington DC. Available at: www.bts.gov/publications/transportation_statistics_ annual_report/2007/.

Button, K., 2006, The political economy of parking charges in 'first' and 'second-best' worlds. *Transport Policy*, **13**, 470–478.

Calfee, J. and C. Winston, 1998, The value of automobile travel time: implications for congestion policy. *Journal of Public Economics*, **69**, 83–102.

Capaldo, K., J.J. Corbett, P. Kasibhatla, P. Fischbeck and S.N. Pandis, 1999, Effects of ship emissions on sulphur cycling and radiative climate forcing over the ocean. *Nature*, **400**, 743–746.

Carson, R.T., R.C. Mitchell, M. Hanemann, R.J. Kopp, S. Presser and P.A. Ruud, 2004, Contingent valuation and lost passive use: damages from the Exxon Valdez Oil spill. *Environmental and Resource Economics*, **25** (3), 257–286.

Cohen, A.J., H. Ross Anderson, B. Ostro, K.D. Pandey, M. Krzyzanowski, N. Kunzli, K. Gutschmidt, A. Pope, I. Romieu, J.M. Samet and K. Smith., 2005, The global burden of disease due to outdoor air pollution. *Journal of Toxicology and Environmental Health A*, **68** (13–14), 1301–1307.

Congressional Budget Office, 2009, *Using Pricing to Reduce Traffic Congestion*. Pub. No. 3133, The Congress of the United States, Washington, DC. Available at: www.cbo.gov/ftpdocs/97xx/doc9750/03-11-CongestionPricing.pdf.

Corbett, J.J., J.J. Winebrake, E.H. Green, P. Kasibhatla, V. Eyring and A. Lauer, 2007, Mortality from ship emissions: a global assessment. *Environmental Science and Technology*, **41**, 8512–8518.

Davidson, P., K. Schere, R. Draxler, S. Kondragunta, R.A. Wayland, J.F. Meagher and R. Mathur, 2008, Toward a US national air quality forecast capability: current and planned capabilities. In C. Borrego and A.I. Miranda, eds, *Air Pollution Modeling and Its Application XIX*, NATO Science for Peace and Security Series. Dordrecht, The Netherlands: Springer Science + Business Media B.V., Chapter 2.15, pp. 226–234.

Davis, S.C., S.W. Diegel and R.G. Bundy, 2008, *Transportation Energy Data Book*, ORNL-6981. Oak Ridge, TN: Oak Ridge National Laboratory. Available at: http://cta.ornl.gov/data/index.shtml.

Delucchi, M.A., 2000, Environmental externalities of motor-vehicle use in the US. *Journal of Transport Economics and Policy*, **34**, 135–168.

Delucchi, M.A., 2004a, Personal nonmonetary costs of motor-vehicle use. UCD-ITS-RR-96-3(4) rev. 1. Institute of Transportation Studies, University of California, Davis. Available at: www.its.ucdavis.edu/ people/faculty/delucchi.

Delucchi, M.A., 2004b, The annualized social cost of motor-vehicle use in the U.S., 1990-1991: Summary of Theory, Data, Methods, and Results. UCD-ITS-RR-96-3(1) rev. 1. Institute of Transportation Studies, University of California, Davis. Available at: www.its.ucdavis.edu/people/faculty/delucchi.

Delucchi, M.A., 2004c, Summary of the Nonmonetary Externalities of Motor-Vehicle Use. UCD-ITS-RR-96-03(9) rev. 1. Institute of Transportation Studies, University of California, Davis. Available at: www.its. ucdavis.edu/people/faculty/delucchi.

Delucchi, M.A., 2007, Do motor-vehicle users in the US pay their way? *Transportation Research Part A*, **41**, 982–1003.

Delucchi, M.A. and S.-L. Hsu, 1998, The external damage cost of noise from motor vehicles. *Journal of Transportation and Statistics*, **1** (3), 1–24.

Delucchi, M.A. and J. Murphy, 2008a, US Military expenditures to protect the use of Persian-Gulf oil for motor vehicles. *Energy Policy*, **36**, 2253–2264.

Delucchi, M.A. and J. Murphy, 2008b, How large are tax subsidies to motor-vehicle users in the US?, *Transport Policy*, **15**, 196–208.

Delucchi, M.A., J.J. Murphy and D.R. McCubbin, 2002, The health and visibility cost of air pollution: a comparison of estimation methods. *Journal of Environmental Management*, **64**, 139–152.

Delucchi, M.A., et al., 2003, A lifecycle emissions model (LEM): lifecycle emissions from transportation fuels, motor vehicles, transportation modes, electricity use, heating and cooking fuels, and materials. UCD-ITS-RR-03-17. Davis, California: Institute of Transportation Studies, University of California, Davis. Available at: www.its.ucdavis.edu/people/faculty/delucchi.

Dennis, S.M., 2004, Improvement in BTS estimation of ton-miles. Working paper 2004-002-OAS, Bureau of Transportation Statistics, US Department of Transportation. Available at: www.bts.gov/programs/bts_working_papers/2004/paper_02/pdf/entire.pdf.

Dennis, S.M., 2007, A decade of growth in domestic freight. Special Report SR-002, Bureau of Transportation Statistics, US Department of Transportation. Available at: www.bts.gov/publications/bts_special_report/2007_07_27/.

Edlin, A.S., 2002, Per-mile premiums for auto insurance. Working paper no. E02-318, Department of Economics, University of California, Berkeley. Available at: http://repositories.cdlib.org/iber/econ/.

Elvik, R., 1994, The external costs of traffic injury: definition, estimation, and possibilities for internalization. *Accident Analysis and Prevention*, **26**, 719–732.

Energy Information Administration (EIA), 2008, Annual Energy Review 2007, DOE/EIA-0384(2007), Department of Energy, Washington, DC. Available at: www.eia.doe.gov/emeu/aer/contents.html.

Environmental Protection Agency (EPA), 1996, Indicators of the Environmental Impacts of Transportation. Final report, Washington DC: Office of Policy, Planning, and Evaluation, June.

Environmental Protection Agency (EPA), 2005, Clean Air Interstate Rule: Emissions Inventory Technical Support Document. March 4. Available at: http://epa.gov/CAIR/pdfs/finaltech01.pdf.

Environmental Protection Agency (EPA), 2008, Regulatory impact analysis: control of emissions of air pollution from locomotive engines and marine compression ignition engines less than 30 liters per cylinder. EPA report # EPA420-R-08-001. Washington DC, March.

Evans, A., 1994, Editorial: transport safety. *Journal of Transport Economics and Policy,* **27** (1), 3–6.

Eyring, V., H.W. Köhler, J. can Aardenne and A. Lauer, 2005, Emissions from international shipping. *Journal of Geophysical Research,* **110**, D17305, doi:10.1029/2004JD005619.

Federal Highway Administration (FHWA), 1997, Highway Cost Allocation Study (HCAS). US Department of Transportation, Government Printing Office, Washington DC.

Federal Highway Administration (FHWA), 2000, Highway Statistics 2000. US Department of Transportation, Washington DC. Available at: http://www.fhwa.dot.gov/ohim/hs00/index.htm.

Federal Highway Administration (FHWA), 2005, Assessing the effects of freight movement on air quality at the national and regional level. Final Report, Washington DC. Available at: http://www.fhwa.dot.gov/environment/freightaq/.

Federal Highway Administration (FHWA), 2008, Congestion Pricing, A Primer: Overview. FHWA-HOP-08-039, Office of Transportation Management, Federal Highway Administration, US Department of Transportation, Washington DC. Available at: http://ops.fhwa.dot.gov/publications/fhwahop08039/fhwahop08039.pdf.

Feitelson, E. and O. Rotem, 2004, The case for taxing surface parking. *Transport Research Part D,* **9**, 319–333.

Fisher, B., 2008, Uncertainty in air quality decision making. In C. Borrego and A.I. Miranda, eds, *Air Pollution Modeling and Its Application XIX*, NATO Science for Peace and Security Series. Dordrecht, The Netherlands: Springer Science + Business Media B.V., Chapter 4.4, pp. 376–384.

Forkenbrock, D.J., 1999, External costs of intercity truck freight transportation. *Transportation Research Part A,* **33**, 505–526.

Forkenbrock, D.J., 2001, Comparison of external costs of rail and truck freight transportation. *Transportation Research Part A,* **35**, 321–337.

Freeman, A.M., 2000, Water pollution policy. In *Public Policies for Environmental Protection*, 2nd edn, P.R. Portney and R.N. Stavins eds. Washington DC: Resources for the Future, pp. 169–214.

Fuglestvedt, J., T. Berntsen, G. Myhre, K. Rypdal and R.B. Skeie, 2008, Climate forcing from the transport sectors. *PNAS*, **105** (2), 454–458.

Gaffield, S.J., R.L. Goo, L.A. Richards and R.J. Jackson, 2003, Public health effects of inadequately managed stormwater runoff. *American Journal of Public Health*, **93**, 1527–1533.

Galloway, J.N., et al., 2004, Nitrogen cycles: past, present, and future, *Biogeochemistry,* **70**, 153–226.

Gilliland, A.B., J.M. Godowitch, C. Hogrefe and S.T. Rao, 2008, Evaluating regional-scale air quality models. In C. Borrego and A.I. Miranda, eds, *Air Pollution Modeling and Its Application XIX*, NATO Science for Peace and Security Series. Dordrecht, The Netherlands: Springer Science + Business Media B.V., Chapter 4.8, pp. 412–419.

Gorman, M.F., 2008, Evaluating the public investment mix in US freight transportation infrastructure. *Transportation Research Part A,* **42**, 1–14.

Granato, G.E., P.E. Church, and V.J. Stone, 1996, Mobilization of major and trace constituents of highway runoff in groundwater potentially caused by deicing chemical migration. *Transportation Research Record*, **1483**, 92–104.

Greene, D.L. and S. Ahmad, 2005, Costs of U. S. Oil Dependence: 2005 Update. ORNL/TM-2005/45, Oak Ridge National Laboratory, Oak Ridge, Tennessee. Available at: http://cta.ornl.gov/cta/Publications/Reports/ORNL_TM2005_45.pdf.

Grigalunas, T.A., R.C. Anderson, G.M. Brown Jr., R. Congar, N.F. Meade and P.E. Sorensen, 1986, Estimating the cost of oil spills: lessons from the Amoco Cadiz incident. *Marine Resource Economics*, **2** (3), 239–262.

Haling, D. and H. Cohen, 1995, Air quality cost analysis spreadsheet. Provided to Forkenbrock et al., 2001, Cambridge Systematics, Inc., Washington DC.

Hensher, D.A., 2006, Integrating accident and travel delay externalities in an urban speed reduction context. *Transport Reviews*, **26** (4), 521–534.

Hogrefe, C., J.-Y. Ku, G. Sistla, A. Gilliland, J.S. Irwin, P.S. Porter, E. Gégo, P. Kasibhatla, and S.T. Rao, 2008, Has the performance of regional-scale photochemical modelling systems changed over the past decade? In C. Borrego and A.I. Miranda, eds, *Air Pollution Modeling and Its Application XIX*, NATO Science for Peace and Security Series. Dordrecht, The Netherlands: Springer Science + Business Media B.V., Chapter 4.6, pp. 394–403.

Huddart, L., 1978, An evaluation of the visual impact of rural roads and traffic. Supplementary Report 355, Crowthorne, England: Transport and Road Research Laboratory.

Intergovernmental Panel on Climate Change (IPCC), 2007, Climate Change 2007: The Scientific Basis. Contribution of Working Group I to the Fourth Assessment Report of the IPCC, S. Solomon, D. Qin, M. Manning, Z. Chen, M. Marquis, K.B. Averyt, M. Tignor and H.L. Miller, eds. Cambridge: Cambridge University Press. Available at: www.ipcc.ch/ipccreports/ar4-wg1.htm.

Janic, M., 2007, Modelling the full costs of an intermodal and road freight transport network. *Transportation Research Part D*, **12**, 33–44.

Jansson, J.O., 1994, Accident externality charges. *Journal of Transport Economics and Policy*, **27** (1), 31–43.

Jones, D.W., P.N. Leiby and I.K. Paik, 2004, Oil price shocks and the macroeconomy: what has been learned since 1996. *The Energy Journal*, **25** (2), 1–32.

Leiby, P.N., 2007, Estimating the energy security benefits of reduced US oil imports. ORNL/TM-2007/028, Oak Ridge National Laboratory, Oak Ridge, Tennessee, February 28 (revised March 14, 2008). Available at: www.epa.gov/otaq/renewablefuels/ornl-tm-2007-028.pdf.

Leksell, I. and A. Rabl, 2001, Air pollution and mortality: quantification and valuation of years of life lost. *Risk Analysis*, **21** (5), 843–857.

Lemp, J.D. and K.M. Kockelman, 2008, Quantifying the external costs of vehicle use: evidence from America's top-selling light-duty models. *Transportation Research Part D*, **13**, 491–504.

Levinson, D., D. Gillen and A. Kanafani, 1998, The social costs of intercity transportation: a review and comparison of air and highway. *Transport Reviews*, **18** (3), 215–240.

Levinson, D., J.M. Mathieu, D. Gillen and A. Kanafani, 1997, The full cost of high-speed rail: an engineering approach. *Annals of Regional Science*, **31**, 189–215.

Link, H., 2005, Transport accounts: methodological concepts and empirical results. *Journal of Transport Geography*, **13**, 41–57.

Lyons, G., J. Jain and D. Holley, 2007, The use of travel time by rail passengers in Great Britain. *Transport Research Part A*, **41**, 107–120.

Maibach, M. , C. Schreyer, D. Sutter, H.P. van Essen, B.H. Boon, R. Smokers, A. Schroten, C. Doll, B. Pawlowska and M. Bak, 2007, *Handbook on Estimation of External Cost in the Transport Sector*. The Netherlands: CE Delft. Available at: www.rapportsysteem.nl/artikel/index.php?id=702&action=read.

Mani, A., and M. Fisher, 2009, Port peak pricing program evaluation. FHWA-HOP-09-014, Federal Highway Administration, US Department of Transportation, Washington DC. Available at: www.ops.fhwa.dot.gov/publications/fhwahop09014/index.htm.

Manne, A.S. and R.G. Richels, 2001, An alternative approach to establishing trade-offs among greenhouse gases. *Nature*, **410**, 675–677.

McCarthy, J.E., 2008, Air Pollution from Ships: MARPOL Annex VI and Other Control Options. Congressional Research Service, Washington DC. Available at: http://ncseonline.org/nle/crsreports/08July/RL34548.pdf.

McCubbin, D.R. and M.A. Delucchi, 1999, The health costs of motor-vehicle related air pollution. *Journal of Transport Economics and Policy*, **33**, 253–286.

Miedema, H.M.E. and C.G.M. Oudshoorn, 2001, Annoyance from transportation noise: relationships with exposure metrics DNL and DENL and their confidence intervals. *Environmental Health Perspectives*, **109** (4), 409–416.

Miller, T.R., 1997, Societal costs of transportation crashes. In D.L. Greene, D.W. Jones and M.A. Delucchi, eds, *Measuring the Full Social Costs and Benefits of Transportation*. Heidelberg, Germany: Springer-Verlag, pp. 281–314.

Miller, T.R., D. Levy, R. Spicer and D. Lestina, 1998, Allocating the cost of motor vehicle crashes between vehicle types. *Transportation Research Record,* **1635**, 81–97.

Moore, J.E., 1978, *Design for Good Acoustics and Noise Control*. New York: Macmillan Press Ltd.

Morrison, S.A., and C. Winston, 2008, The effect of FAA expenditures on air travel delays. *Journal of Urban Economics,* **63**, 669–678.

Muller, N.Z. and R. Mendelsohn, 2007, Measuring the damages of air pollution in the United States. *Journal of Environmental Economics and Management,* **54**, 1–14.

Murphy, J.J., M.A. Delucchi, D.R. McCubbin and H.J. Kim, 1999, The cost of crop damage caused by ozone air pollution from motor vehicles. *Journal of Environmental Management,* **55**, 273–289.

Murray, D.M., and U.F.W. Ernst, 1976, An economic analysis of the environmental impact of highway deicing. EPA-600/2-76-105, Cincinnati, Ohio, US Environmental Protection Agency.

Nash, C., T. Sansom and B. Still, 2001, Modifying transport prices to internalise externalities: evidence from European case studies. *Regional Science and Urban Economics,* **31**, 413–431.

National Research Council, Committee on Health, Environmental, and Other External Costs and Benefits of Energy Production and Consumption, 2010, *Hidden Costs of Energy: Unpriced Consequences of Energy Production and Use*. Washington DC: National Academies Press. Available at: http://www.nap.edu/catalog/12794.html.

Nelson, J.P., 2008, Hedonic property value studies of transportation noise: aircraft and road traffic. In A. Baranzini, J. Ramirez, C. Schaerer and P. Thalmann, eds, *Hedonic Methods in Housing Markets*. Berlin: Springer, pp. 57–82.

Newbery, D.M., 1998, Fair payment from road users. A review of the evidence on social and environmental costs, Hampshire, England. AA Group Public Policy.

Nijkamp, P., G. Vindigni, and P.A.L.D. Nunes, 2008, Economic valuation of biodiversity: a comparative study. *Ecological Economics,* **67**, 217–231.

Ozbay, K., and J. Berechman, 2001, Estimation and evaluation of full marginal costs of highway transportation in New Jersey. *Journal of Transportation and Statistics* **4**, 81–104.

Ozbay, K., B. Bartin, O. Yanmaz-Tuzel and J. Berechman, 2007, Alternative methods for estimating full marginal costs of highway transportation. *Transportation Research Part A,* **41**, 768–786.

Parry, I.W.H., M. Walls and W. Harrington, 2007, Automobile externalities and policies, *Journal of Economic Literature,* **45**, 373–399.

Pearce, D., 2003, The social cost of carbon and its policy implications. *Oxford Review of Economic Policy,* **19**, 362–384.

Poole, R.W. and B. Dachis, 2007, Congestion pricing for the New York airports: reducing delays while promoting growth and competition. Reason Foundation, Policy Study 366.

Quinet, E., 2004, A meta-analysis of Western European external cost estimates. *Transportation Research Part D,* **9**, 456–476.

Reiss, R., E.L. Anderson, C.E. Cross, G. Hidy, D. Hoel, R. McClellan and S. Moolgavkar, 2007, Evidence of health impacts of sulfate-and nitrate-containing particles in ambient air. *Inhalation Toxicology,* **19** (5), 419–49.

Riera, P., A. Mhawej, R. Mavsar and R. Brey, 2006, Fixed-effects hedonic price model for statistical value of life estimations. *Transport Reviews,* **26** (4), 487–500.

Samet, J. and D. Krewski, 2007, Health effects associated with exposure to ambient air pollution. *Journal of Toxicology and Environmental Health A,* **70** (3-4), 227–242.

Sausen, R., I. Isaksen, V. Grewe, D. Hauglustaine, D.S. Lee, G. Myhre, M.O. Köhler, G. Pitari, U. Schumann, F. Stordal and C. Zerefos, 2005, Aviation radiative forcing in 2000: an update on the IPCC (1999). *Meteorologische Zeitschrift,* **14** (4), 555–561.

Sawyer, D. and S. Stiebert, 2007, *Evaluation of Total Cost of Air Pollution Due to Transportation in Canada*. Ottawa, Ontario, Marbek Resource Consultants Ltd. Available at: http://dsp-psd.pwgsc.gc.ca/collection_2008/tc/T22-148-2007E.pdf.

Schrank, D. and T. Lomax, 2007, *The 2007 Urban Mobility Report*. Texas Transportation Institute, The Texas A&M University System, September. Available at: http://mobility.tamu.edu.

Shoup, D., 2005, *The High Cost of Free Parking*. Chicago, IL: APA Planners Press.

Small, K.A., R. Noland, X. Chu and D. Lewis, 1999, *Valuation of Travel-Time Savings and Predictability in Congested Conditions for Highway User-Cost Estimation*. National Highway Cooperative Research Program Report 431, Washington, DC, National Academy Press. Available at: http://pubsindex.trb.org/document/view/default.asp?lbid=492077.

Small, K.A. and C. Kazimi, 1995, On the costs of air pollution from motor vehicles. *Journal of Transport Economics and Policy,* **29** (1), 7–32.

Soguel, N.C., 1995, Costing the traffic barrier effect: a contingent valuation survey. *Environmental and Resource Economics,* **6**, 301–308.

Starnes, M., 2008, *Trends in Non-Fatal Traffic Injuries: 1996-2005*, DOT-HS-810-944, National Highway Traffic Safety Administration, US Department of Transportation, Washington DC. Available at: http://www-nrd.nhtsa.dot.gov/Pubs/810944.pdf.

Steimetz, Seiji S.C., 2003, Defensive driving and the external costs of accidents and travel delays. Job-Market Paper, Department of Economics, University of California, Irvine.

Tesche, T.W., 1988, Accuracy of ozone air quality models. *Journal of Environmental Engineering*, **114** (4), 739–752.

Tol, R.S.J., 2003, Is the uncertainty about climate change too large for expected cost–benefit analysis? *Climatic Change*, **56**, 265–289.

US Department of Transportation, 2008, *National Transportation Statistics*. Research and Innovative Technology Administration, Bureau of Transportation Statistics. Available at: http://www.bts.gov/publications/national_transportation_statistics/.

Van Bohemen, H.D., 1995, Mitigation and compensation of habitat fragmentation caused by roads: strategy, objectives, and practical measures. *Transportation Research Record*, **1475**, 133–137.

Vickrey, W., 1968, Automobile accidents, tort law, externalities, and insurance: an economist's critique. *Law and Contemporary Problems*, **33**, 464–487.

Viscusi, W.K. and J.E. Aldy, 2003, The value of a statistical life: a critical review of market estimates throughout the world. *The Journal of Risk and Uncertainty*, **27** (1), 5–76.

Vitaliano, D.F., 1992, An economic assessment of the social costs of highway salting and the efficiency of substituting a new deicing material. *Journal of Policy Analysis and Management*, **11** (3), 397–418.

Wahba, M. and C. Hope, 2006, The marginal impact of carbon dioxide under two scenarios of future emissions. *Energy Policy*, **34**, 3305–3316.

Wang, M.Q., 1999, Greet 1.5: Transportation Fuel-Cycle Model. ANL/ESD-39, Argonne, Illinois, Center for Transportation Research, Argonne National Laboratory, August. See the GREET website at: www.transportation.anl.gov/modeling_simulation/GREET/index.html.

Willis, K.G., G.D. Garrod, and D.R. Harvey, 1998, A review of cost–benefit analysis as applied to the evaluation of new road proposals in the UK. *Transportation Research Part D*, **3**, 141–156.

Woodbury, S., 1987, Aesthetic nuisance: the time has come to recognize it. *Natural Resources Journal*, **27**, 877–886.

Zhang, A., A.E. Boardman, D. Gillen and W.G. Waters II, 2004, *Towards Estimating the Social and Environmental Transportation in Canada*. Centre for Transportation Studies, Sauder School of Business, The University of British Columbia, Vancouver, Canada. Available at: www.tc.gc.ca/pol/en/Report/FullCostInvestigation/Transmodal/t003/t003.pdf.

16 External costs of transport in Europe
Rainer Friedrich and Emile Quinet

INTRODUCTION

Many European countries show a strong tradition of state intervention into various economic sectors, especially agriculture, energy and transport. This tradition has entailed a special attention to externalities, a major cause of public intervention. This is one of the reasons why the Commission of the European Union has devoted a lot of care to study transport externalities. Two specific motivations have reinforced this tendency.

The first one is the idea that, in order to support an efficient transport market, it is necessary that the users pay their fair cost, which is composed of private costs, infrastructure costs and also external costs, and therefore it is important to be able to measure these external costs as a basis for determining transport taxes and charges. The second one is the growth of environmental concerns in Europe, exemplified by the rise of green political parties which became a prominent actor in the political life of many countries of this continent.

Due to these reasons, it is commonly acknowledged in Europe that a fair transport pricing would have a strong impact on transport modal splits and on mobility, and it would enhance rail transport which is acknowledged to be more environmentally friendly but has been losing market share for freight transport. It would also contribute to reverse the long term growth of road transport, which is accompanied by a rise of congestion and emissions of greenhouse gases.

Consequently, a large number of studies on external transport costs in Europe have been conducted over the years. An overwhelming proportion of them have been funded by public authorities, either at the country level or at the European Union level in the framework of the European Research Programs. These studies have been commissioned to help public decision makers for various purposes. The first one is to support pricing decisions on infrastructure charges incorporating externalities. The second one is to aid decisions on infrastructure investment as in many countries and at the European Union level the project assessment methodology relies heavily on cost–benefit analysis, which implies monetisation of externalities. A third purpose is to contribute to developing national accounts of externalities in order to complement the usual national accounts and to provide information for strategic decisions. Some of the many studies carried out are listed in Table 16.1. This list is not exhaustive, but tries to list some of the more important studies at country or EU level.

The next section presents the general features of European studies. The methodologies and issues for the estimates are analyzed more in depth in the following section. Then a final section is devoted to the results and to their comparisons with estimates found in North America as presented in the previous chapter.

Table 16.1   List of major studies on external costs of transport in Europe

Title of the study and year of publication	Main objective	Scope of costs estimates
ECMT 1998	Summarize recent estimates of external costs.	Provide estimates of external costs based on the expertise of the representatives of Member-States.
TRENEN (Proost and Van Dender, 1999)	Set up a general equilibrium model for determination of optimal infrastructure charges	Calculation of actual external costs and optimal charges for some cities and for some countries
CAPRI (Nash, 1999)	Exchange of information and results on external costs.	Recommendations for the estimation of external costs
QUITS 1998	Set up tools to evaluate costs and quality of service for some international corridors	Estimates of marginal costs based on ExternE methodology, for some European corridors.
COWI Civil Aviation in Scandinavia (2000)	Comparison of air and road costs	Estimates of average costs of air pollution, global warming, noise for air and road transport for some Scandinavian corridors.
Infras-IWW 2000 and 2004	Calculation of external costs of transport in Europe	Average, marginal and total external costs, both at country level and for some corridors.
Surface transport costs . . . (Samson *et al.*, 1998)	Costs and transport charges in Great Britain	Distinguish between marginal and average costs for rail and road in several specific situations
RECORDIT (ISIS, 2001)	Calculation of infrastructure charges for freight transport on several international corridors.	Calculation of marginal external costs
Boiteux (2000)	Transport costs	Taking account of externalities
Friedrich and Bickel (2001)	Environmental external costs of transport	Marginal and total environmental external costs of transport
External costs of aviation (Dings et al., 1999)	Calculation of external costs of aviation for several types of airplanes.	Calculation of average external costs
Amici della terra 2002	Calculation of external costs of transport for Italy	Calculation of marginal external costs
FIFI (Roy, 2000)	Compares current and optimal charges for several situations (urban areas, rural areas) for six countries	Calculation of both optimal and present marginal external costs in several situations
UNITE (2004)	Aims at defining a concept of transport accounts in accordance with marginal costs calculation.	Provides methodologies to reckon marginal costs and applies it to some specific situations

Table 16.1 (continued)

Title of the study and year of publication	Main objective	Scope of costs estimates
HEATCO (2006)	Recommendation of a harmonized methodology for transport project appraisal within the EU	Proposes methodology and provides recommended unit values of external costs in European countries
GRACE (2006)	Develop means to calculate marginal costs in Europe and provide tools for transferring results	Marginal external costs for transport case studies and software allowing calculation
TREMOVE (2009)	Transport emission simulation model	Estimates transport demand and emissions from transport for transport policy scenarios
IMPACT (Maibach et al., 2008)	Survey of external costs estimates in European countries providing best practices for these estimates	A very comprehensive survey of estimates and methodologies
NEEDS (2009)	Methodology and tool for assessment of energy scenarios and related external costs	Provides external costs of energy supply
CAFÉ (2005)	Cost benefit analysis of integrated environmental strategic policies for air pollution	Provides estimates of external costs for different air pollution control strategies.
NEWEXT (2004)	Updating of the ExternE studies	Updates external costs of transport of ExternE

THE GENERAL FEATURES OF EUROPEAN EXTERNAL COST STUDIES

One of the characteristics of European external cost studies is that the indicator used to express external costs varies according to the purpose of the study. All studies differentiate between marginal external costs caused by marginal changes in the transport system, for example, one more kilometer driven with a specific vehicle at a specific time, and non-marginal cost differences caused by larger changes in the transport system. Marginal costs are useful for pricing considerations as the European Union and many countries rely on the doctrine of marginal social cost pricing. For project appraisal,[1] however, the difference in external costs between a scenario without and a scenario with the project is calculated. For national accounting the overall external costs caused by a sector, for example, transport or road transport, are estimated. Another concern is to determine what parts of the estimated risks are internalized and thus not external; this point is especially important for accident risks.

Another specific characteristic of European studies concerns the evaluation process for

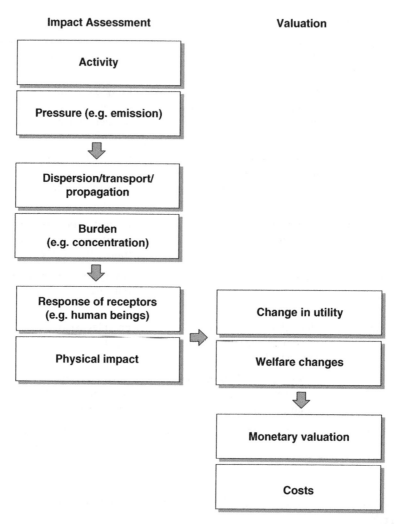

Figure 16.1   The Impact Pathway Approach for the estimation of environmental costs

environmental externalities, which is best described by the Impact Pathway Approach (IPA) developed by Bickel and Friedrich (2005). The IPA is illustrated in Figure 16.1 for the case of air pollution (roughly the same procedure is used for noise).

The IPA follows the complete chain of causal relationships, starting with the emission of a burden through its diffusion and conversion in the environmental media to its impact on the various receptors and finally the monetary valuation of its impacts. More precisely, a transport activity causes changes in environmental pressures (for example, air pollutant emissions), which are dispersed, leading to changes in environmental burdens and associated impacts on various receptors, such as human beings, crops, building materials or ecosystems (for example, emissions of air pollutants leading to respiratory diseases). This change in impacts leads either directly or indirectly (for example, through health effects caused by air pollutants) to a change in the utility of the affected persons. Welfare changes resulting from these impacts are assigned monetary values in the last steps of the process.

One of the strengths and main principles of the IPA is the valuation of damages (for example, additional respiratory hospital admissions) rather than pressures or effects (for example, emissions of fine particles), which implies, that pressures are transformed into impacts, before they are assessed. The assessment is then made by allocating monetary values to each of the impact categories. This monetary weighting factor is achieved by using the willingness to pay approach, that is by asking the affected population about their willingness to pay to avoid a certain risk or damage. In practice, such contingent valuation surveys are not made for each study and each impact, but results of already existing surveys are used and transformed to the situation in the new analysis by using a method called benefit transfer.

Principally, impacts and costs from two scenarios have to be calculated: a reference scenario reflecting the base case concerning the amount of pollutants or noise emitted without the project or activity or policy to be assessed included, and a modified scenario, which is based on the reference scenario, but with changes in activities and emissions due to the project or policy or activity change considered. The difference in physical impacts and resulting damage costs of both scenarios represents the effect of the project/policy/ activity.

A very important outcome of using this approach is that it reveals that the results depend considerably on site and time of the activity to be assessed. Cars driving with a certain speed, but at different times and on different road segments, might emit the same amount of pollutants and noise, but the damage caused varies with population density, meteorological conditions and concentrations of other pollutants in air or soil, which react with the emitted pollutants to form secondary pollutants.

This bottom-up methodology for calculating environmental external costs is widely accepted, and all recent studies use it, sometimes in a simplified version. Thus a harmonization with regard to method and unit results (that is, external costs per t of pollutant emitted or per kilometer driven with a vehicle with EURO 4 emission standard in an urban street) has taken place in Europe.

The following table, updated from a meta-analysis by Quinet (2004), shows a sample of results for some of the major studies listed in Table 16.1 which estimated costs for a comprehensive set of external effects which can be expressed in terms of Euros per passenger-km or per ton-km.

Quinet (2004) lists several reasons for the large variation in estimates: the specificities of the situations, the type of cost under consideration, the external effects under consideration, the physical relations between emission and damages, and the unit values used for monetization. He concludes that, apart from the fact that studies differ in the list of external costs taken into consideration, the main sources of variation in estimates are the type (marginal or average) of cost; the location (metropolitan area, other urban area, inter-urban area); and scientific differences of opinion on some physical impacts such as air pollution, and to a lesser extent the value of CO_2 emissions. Encouragingly, the results of the various studies are therefore not as chaotic as it may appear, but rather display a large degree of coherency.

But this does not tell us whether the estimates actually reflect the costs of externalities. It may be that there is an imitation syndrome at work and that, after a first estimate has

Table 16.2   Data on external costs per passenger-km or ton-km drawn from some comprehensive studies

Mode and vehicle type	Car	Coach	Rail passenger	Air passenger	Truck	Rail Freight
Number of observations	55	32	47	31	40	32
Mean	0.093	0.043	0.004	0.041	0.054	0.009
Standard deviation	0.099	0.088	0.013	0.046	0.038	0.011

Notes: Units are €/passenger-km or €/ton-km

been published, later ones do not dare diverge too much. But the reverse can happen too; it is a rewarding task for a scholar to gain renown for discovering a result that is at odds with the current wisdom, and which can lead to financial support from relevant pressure groups. Overall it seems fair to say that such a meta-analysis suggests that the estimates are accurate, but it does not provide a proof.

METHODOLOGY AND ISSUES FOR EACH EXTERNAL COST

In the following, we analyze the different cost categories in more detail. The following categories are considered:

- Congestion and scarcity
- Accidents
- Air pollution
- Climate change
- Noise
- Water and soil pollution
- Energy security
- Landscape effects
- Urban (barrier) effects
- Life-cycle impacts
- Positive externalities

We will briefly review each external cost category, analyzing the methods of monetization, the transfer processes and assessing the accuracy of the estimates.

Congestion and Scarcity

Congestion poses an issue of definition. What constitutes a 'congestion cost'? Is it the cost above the normal travel time, and if so what is 'normal'? Or the total travel time, or the marginal cost?[2] We will not debate this question, but instead adopt the most frequent definition according to which congestion cost is the marginal cost that a user imposes on other users; this definition is especially relevant for pricing purposes, while changes in total travel time would be relevant for project assessment. With this definition, congestion cost is clearly an external cost that would not exist if travel time were independent of traffic volume.

Congestion has various aspects in each mode. It has been widely considered for road transport. Its calculation requires several ingredients: mainly a speed-flow relation and values of travel time. Speed flow relations are rather uncertain; many specifications are proposed that differ somewhat across countries,[3] and none dominates the others. These relations are used as inputs to traffic models; but in general these traffic models do not take into account queuing for which a dynamic traffic model is desirable but rarely used.

Recommendations regarding values of time for both passenger transport (per passenger hour) and freight transport (per freight ton hour) can be found in the HEATCO (2006) final report. For passenger transport the report recommends that considerably higher values of time be used for time spent waiting, standing or walking than for time spent in the vehicle.

Congestion not only affects average travel time but also reliability of travel time, about which relatively little is yet known although it is now the subject of intense research. Several studies give evidence on the value of reliability and on the cost of early or late arrival vis-à-vis the ideal schedule. But we do not have enough information on preferred arrival times or on the distribution of travel times to include this effect in the calculations of comprehensive external costs. This is unfortunate as it has been established, that the cost of unreliability can be comparable to the cost of predictable congestion delay.[4] Compared to the changes in travel time and reliability, other externalities caused by congestion like more pollution, greenhouse gas emissions and noise are less important.

Good estimates of congestion are also needed for air and rail transport as infrastructure management and service operations are vertically separated and service operators compete for customers. In such a market regime congestion costs are not fully internalized. For those modes where the timetables are planned ex ante, congestion does not imply increased travel time, instead three other indicators are relevant. First, changes in the timetables, that is, a shift in the planned departure time; second, in situations of high congestion, the unreliability of the planned timetable increases; and third, the scarcity of infrastructure may prevent some profitable services from being provided. We know little about these various aspects; the estimates of congestion in public transport usually only take the unreliability of public urban transport, train services and air flights into account.[5]

Table 16.3 reports estimates of van den Bossche et al. (2002) which show that the costs of congestion vary strongly by time of day and location

Accidents

The estimation of the external costs of accidents is in no way straightforward. The cost categories that should be included depend on the decision that is intended to be supported by the estimation. If the task is to carry out an appraisal of a transport infrastructure option, one would construct a scenario without the option and another one with the option, would estimate the number and severity of accidents for both scenarios and would then allocate the difference between the scenarios to the option and use it for a cost–benefit analysis. So all additional or avoided accidents with all cost categories would count.

If, alternatively, the task is to assess the marginal external costs of a transport user

Table 16.3   Estimates of external costs of congestion by van den Bossche et al. 2002, in Euro1998 per vehicle-km

COST DRIVERS		COST ESTIMATION BY ROAD TYPE		
Vehicle Type	Traffic situation	Motorway	Rural road	Urban road
Passenger car	Uncongested	0.012	0.039	0.028
				0.004
	Dense	2.102	1.333	2.879
	Congested	2.161	2.074	3.292
				1.315
Motorcycle	Uncongested	0.005	0.020	0.014
	Dense	1.052	0.667	1.440
	Congested	1.080	1.037	1.646
Bus	Uncongested	0.022	0.080	0.055
				0.007
	Dense	4.205	2.666	5.759
	Congested	4.321	4.149	6.584
				2.461
LGV	Uncongested	0.017	0.060	0.041
	Dense	3.154	1.999	4.319
	Congested	3.241	3.111	4.938
HGV	Uncongested	0.029	0.009	0.069
		0.010–0.260		0.007
	Dense	5.257	3.332	7.198
	Congested	5.401	5.186	8.230
				2.461

(perhaps for the purpose of computing an accident externality charge), only the additional accident risk the user imposes on others is relevant. The user's own risk does not count as long as he is aware of it because the risk is then internalized. In addition, the premiums paid for third-party liability insurance might be seen as an internalization of a (small) part of the risk to others, so might be subtracted from the resulting external costs.

Concerning public transport, the marginal external accident costs of users are close to zero as long as some seats remain free. Thus usually 'marginal' costs are calculated by assuming the operation of one additional vehicle (plane, bus, train. . .) and then distributing the external costs per km evenly among the users of the vehicle.

Change in accident risks
The ideal procedure to determine the change in risk due to a project or activity would be to use a risk function that depends on infrastructure characteristics, traffic composition and volumes. However, such a function could become quite complex. For instance, on a sparsely used road an additional user might cause a considerable risk, while on the same road with denser traffic the risk might be relatively low since overtaking would be difficult and traffic flow would be fairly smooth. In principle, the relationship between accident risk, speed and traffic density is influenced by the trade-off that drivers make between travel time and safety. The congestion and accident externalities are interdependent since

Table 16.4   *Recommendation for European average correction factors for unreported road accidents (HEATCO, 2006)*

	Fatality	Serious injury	Slight injury	Average injury	Damage only
Average	1.02	1.50	3.00	2.25	6.00
Car	1.02	1.25	2.00	1.63	3.50
Motorbike/moped	1.02	1.55	3.20	2.38	6.50
Bicycle	1.02	2.75	8.00	5.38	18.50
Pedestrian	1.02	1.35	2.40	1.88	4.50

congestion imposes a cost in risk and driving effort. According to estimates by Hensher (2006) and Steimetz (2008), the accident risk plus effort externality per vehicle-kilometer of travel for cars is similar in magnitude to the travel-delay externality.

A detailed analysis taking these relations into account would be necessary for assessing a policy for the reduction of risk, for example, the replacement of railway grade crossings. In general, however, a pragmatic approach is taken in which uniform risk values per km for different vehicles, modes, types of roads, and urban/non-urban settings, are derived by dividing statistical accident data by traffic volumes. In addition to national statistics, the CARE database contains information about road accidents in the EU. For air, most occur during landing and take-off; people at risk include those living below the landing and take-off routes.

The information about accident impacts that is available, and thus can be used for the estimation of external costs, usually contains four categories of impacts:

- Fatalities: death arising from the accident.
- Serious injuries: casualties which require hospital treatment and have lasting injuries, but the victim does not die within the fatality recording period.
- Slight injuries: casualties whose injuries do not require hospital treatment or, if they do, the effect of the injury quickly subsides.
- Damage-only accidents: accidents without casualties.

Especially for road transport, the use of this statistical information leads to an underestimation of accident risks as not all non-fatal accidents are reported and thus included in the statistics. Fatalities are reported, however, only those that occur within 30 days of an accident. Thus, for road accidents in the EU it is recommended to use correction factors given in Table 16.4 (based on HEATCO (2006)). For other modes no correction is necessary.

Valuation of accident risks
Costs that have to be taken into account comprise direct economic costs, indirect economic costs and a value of safety per se.

Direct and indirect economic costs include:

- Medical and rehabilitation cost: The major direct cost of accidents is medical and rehabilitation costs. The cost includes both the cost incurred in the year of the accident and, for some injury types, future cost over the remaining lifetime. The future cost is expressed as the present value over the expected lifetime of the patient, taking into account advancements in hospital efficiency.

- Legal court and emergency service cost: The administrative cost of an accident consists of the cost for police, the court, private crash investigations, the emergency services and administrative costs of insurances.
- Material damages: Compared to the values for casualties, material damages are less important.
- Production losses: The indirect economic cost of accidents consists of the value to society of goods and services that could have been produced by the person if the accident had not occurred. The (marginal) value of a person's production could be assumed to be equal to the gross labour cost, wage and additional labour cost paid by the employer. The value of the lost production will grow over time in a growing economy. Three types of production losses can be found:

(i)   due to premature death,
(ii)   due to reduced working capacity and
(iii) due to days of illness.

In the case of a fatality, the gross lost production has to be corrected by subtracting the value of the goods and services that the deceased person would have consumed without the accident.

The value of safety per se is usually determined by measuring the willingness to pay (WTP) to avoid the accident risk. It is by far the largest part of the accident costs. Numerous studies have measured this WTP using revealed preference or stated preference methods.

Nearly all EU countries have an appraisal framework for decisions about transport infrastructure. The VSLs (values of a statistical life) that are recommended for use vary to some extent. They are – as expected – lowest in the East European countries with lower per capita income ranging from about 150 000 € to 400 000 €. The highest values can be observed in Northern and Western Europe ranging from 1.1 million € to ca. 2.2 million €, while Southern European values are considerably lower.

In the HEATCO (2006) project, which was carried out for the European Commission, DG TREN, an attempt has been made to propose guidelines harmonized throughout Europe. For transnational projects HEATCO recommends a value of the safety per se of 1.25 million $€_{2002}$ (factor prices) for a fatality, 162 500 $€_{2002}$ for a severe injury and 12 500 $€_{2002}$ for a slight injury. For national projects these values should be adjusted according to income weighted with the purchasing power parity. Direct and indirect economic costs may roughly be estimated as 10 per cent of the value of safety per se; an estimation for the economic costs of injuries can be found in European Commission (2002). The outcome for some European countries is shown in Table 16.5.

As it can be assumed that WTP for risk avoidance is increasing with increasing income, these values are often considered to increase in the future based on a default intertemporal elasticity to GDP per capita growth of 0.7 to 1.0. Some studies imply a larger WTP to avoid risks for users of public transport than for car drivers due to two selection

Table 16.5   Recommended values for casualties avoided for selected European countries (Euro2002 PPP, factor prices) for the year 2005

Country	Fatality	Severe injury	Slight injury
Belgium	1 603 000	243 200	15 700
Czech Republic	932 000	125 200	9 100
France	1 548 000	216 300	16 200
Germany	1 493 000	206 500	16 700
Greece	1 069 000	139 700	10 700
Italy	1 493 000	191 900	14 700
Latvia	534 000	72 300	5 200
Netherlands	1 672 000	221 500	17 900
Norway	2 055 000	288 300	20 700
Poland	630 000	84 500	6 100
Spain	1 302 000	161 800	12 200
Sweden	1 576 000	231 300	16 600
United Kingdom	1 617 000	208 900	16 600

Source: HEATCO 2006

biases: first, car drivers having a lower income adjusted WTP should be more risky drivers and have more accidents than the average; so the average casualty on road corresponds to a lower Value of Life than the average population; second, people using public transport are, all other causes being held equal, on average more risk adverse than the car drivers.

On the whole, the uncertainty about accident costs derives mainly from uncertainty in the estimation of changes in risk. Compared to this, uncertainty about the appropriate value of a statistical life seems to be less important.

Air Pollution

Impacts of air pollution
Air pollution causes health risks, biodiversity losses, reductions in crop yield and damage to materials. To assess the impacts of air pollutants, it is important to measure the effects of emissions on the utility of individuals so that they can be valued. For instance, it is not useful to ask for the WTP to avoid an amount of emissions, say 5 tonnes of NO_x, as no one – at least without further information or knowledge – can judge the severity of this or the damage or loss of utility caused by this emission. On the other hand, if somebody is asked for an assessment of a concrete health risk imposed on him, for example, a cough day, he can compare this impact with other impacts and changes of utility that he experiences. Thus, it is important to transform pressures or emissions into damages and risks.

An important aspect here is that impacts depend on the time and site of the emissions. For instance, if emissions of air pollutants occur in a densely populated area, the health of more people is at risk than for a site where equal amounts of pollutants are emitted but in a less densely populated area. Thus, the impacts depend on meteorological conditions, population density and height of release. They also depend on the chemical composition of the atmosphere. The emissions of sulphur dioxide are more harmful in areas where ammonia concentrations in the atmosphere are higher, because then more ammonium sulphate is formed, which – as part of PM2.5 – may cause more health damage than SO_2. Furthermore, environmental costs vary considerably with the characteristics of the vehicles, trains, vessels or aircraft. A detailed bottom-up approach is required to be able to consider technology and site specific parameters, and variations of costs with time. All newer European studies on external costs of transport are meanwhile based on bottom-up calculations using the IPA approach already presented above (see Figure 16.1).

One of the strengths and main principles of the IPA is the valuation of damages (for example, additional respiratory hospital admissions) and not pressures or effects (for example, emissions of fine particles). The monetary valuation of concrete casualties (for example, hospital admissions) is more reliable and transparent than deriving a general WTP for reducing air pollution.

Many of the impact pathways include non-linearities, due to air chemistry, for example. Therefore, impacts and costs from two scenarios are calculated: a reference scenario reflecting the base case concerning the amount of pollutants or noise emitted, and a modified scenario, which is based on the reference scenario, but with changes in emissions due to the activity considered. The difference in physical impacts and resulting damage costs of both scenarios represents the effect of the activity considered.

It is obvious that not all impacts can be modeled for all pollutants in detail. For this reason the most important pollutants and damage categories (so-called 'priority impact pathways') are selected for a detailed analysis. For transport, the relevant pollutants should cover at least primary $PM_{2.5}$ (especially from engine exhaust), primary PM_{10} (for example, from brake and tyre wear, road abrasion and resuspension processes), NO_x (as precursor of nitrate aerosols and ozone), SO_2 (direct effects and as precursor of sulphate aerosols) and non-methane volatile organic compounds (NMVOC, as precursor of ozone). Depending on the question to be answered, life cycle emissions have to be included. The most important impacts caused by these pollutants are shown in Table 16.6.

The estimation of damage to semi-natural ecosystems is much less established than the exposure response relationships for health impacts and for material and crop damage. The current state-of-the-art method is to first calculate the deposition of acidifying substances (especially sulphuric acid and nitric acid) and nutrients (here substances containing nitrogen). Then, with a methodology described in Ott et al. (2006), a 'pdf' value is estimated that describes the fraction of species in a certain ecosystem that would potentially disappear, that is, become extinct in this ecosystem due to this deposition. In some earlier studies, an approach described in INFRAS/IWW 2004 is used, which is based on estimating repair costs; this approach however is now being replaced by the Ott et al. (2006) procedure.

Monetary valuation of impacts from air pollution
Given the physical impacts, appropriate monetary values are needed to derive damage costs. For material damage and crop losses, market prices can be used. This is not the case for major aspects of health impacts, for which three components of welfare change can be distinguished (see, for example, Bickel and Friedrich, 2005):

1. Resource costs, that is, medical costs paid by the health service.
2. Opportunity costs, that is, mainly the costs in terms of productivity losses.
3. Disutility, that is, other social and economic costs of the individual or others.

Table 16.6   Important health and environmental effects to be taken into account for estimating external costs of air pollution as minimum requirement

Impact category	Pollutant	Effects included
Public health – mortality	$PM_{2.5}$, PM_{10}[a]	Reduction in life expectancy due to acute and chronic effects
	O_3	Reduction in life expectancy due to acute effects
Public health – morbidity	$PM_{2.5}$, PM_{10}[a], O_3	Respiratory hospital admissions (Minor) Restricted activity days Days of bronchodilator usage Days of lower respiratory symptoms
	$PM_{2.5}$, PM_{10}[a] only	New cases of chronic bronchitis Cardiac hospital admissions
	O_3 only	Cough days
Material damage	SO_2, acid deposition	Ageing of galvanized steel, limestone, natural stone, mortar, sandstone, paint, rendering, zinc
Crops	SO_2	Yield change for wheat, barley, rye, oats, potato, sugar beet
	O_3	Yield loss for wheat, potato, rice, rye, oats, tobacco, barley
	Acid deposition	Increased need for liming
	N	Fertilizer effects
Ecosystems	NOx, SO_2	Biodiversity loss due to eutrophication and acidification

Notes: [a] Including secondary particles (sulphate and nitrate aerosols).

Source: Bickel and Friedrich (2005)

Components (1) and (2) can be estimated using market prices and are known as 'Cost of illness' (COI). To this must be added a measure of the individual's loss of welfare (3) due to any restrictions on, or reduced enjoyment from, desired leisure activities; discomfort or inconvenience (pain, suffering); anxiety about the future; and concern and inconvenience to family members and others. Stated preference methods are the state-of-the-art method for valuing component (3).

Mortality risks are generally valued by using the life years lost as indicator. The dominant health impacts of air pollution are chronic effects that occur after a latency period of sometimes several decades. And the damage to be evaluated is the risk of experiencing a premature death, however, it is not the risk of an 'additional' death, as everybody only dies once. Thus the value of a life year lost multiplied by the number of lost life years (and not the value of a statistical life) is considered to be the appropriate measure. A survey designed to directly assess latent mortality effects due to air pollution resulted in an average value of 40 000 € as EU average value for a latent life year lost (NEEDS, 2009) and this value is retained in most recent studies.

As discussed above, results depend on motorization of the vehicle, on the site, time

Table 16.7   Cost factors for road transport emissions[a] per tonne of pollutant emitted in Euro2002 PPP (factor prices)

Pollutant emitted	NO_x	NMVOC	SO_2	$PM_{2.5}$	
Effective pollutant	O_3, nitrates,	O_3	sulphates, acid deposition	Primary $PM_{2.5}$	
Local environment				urban	outside built-up areas
Austria	4300	600	3900	430 000	72 000
Belgium	2700	1100	5400	440 000	95 000
Czech Republic	3200	1100	4100	270 000	67 000
Denmark	1800	800	1900	400 000	47 000
Estonia	1400	500	1200	160 000	27 000
Finland	900	200	600	360 000	30 000
France	4600	800	4300	410 000	82 000
Germany	3100	1100	4500	400 000	78 000
Greece	2200	600	1400	270 000	38 000
Hungary	5000	800	4100	230 000	59 000
Ireland	2000	400	1600	440 000	46 000
Italy	3200	1600	3500	390 000	71 000
Latvia	1800	500	1400	140 000	26 000
Lithuania	2600	500	1800	160 000	32 000
Luxemburg	4800	1400	4900	730 000	104 000
Netherlands	2600	1000	5000	440 000	86 000
Poland	3000	800	3500	190 000	57 000
Portugal	2800	1000	1900	270 000	40 000
Slovakia	4600	1100	3800	200 000	54 000
Slovenia	4400	700	4000	280 000	58 000
Spain	2700	500	2100	320 000	44 000
Sweden	1300	300	1000	370 000	36 000
Switzerland	4500	600	3900	460 000	76 000
United Kingdom	1600	700	2900	410 000	64 000

Notes: Cost categories included are: human health, crop losses, material damages.
[a] Values are applicable to all emissions at ground level (for example, diesel locomotives).

and height of the emissions. Ideally, for each scenario a detailed calculation using atmospheric transport models would be made. However, this requires a lot of effort. An alternative and approximate method is to calculate external costs per unit of pollutant released for typical source features and then multiply these values by the emissions of the vehicle type to be assessed. Source classes have to distinguish at least between the country of the release, release in an large or a small agglomeration or outside urban areas, release from low sources (for example, exhaust pipes near the surface) or medium or high stacks (for example, from power plants for electricity production).

As an example, Table 16.7 shows cost factors in euros per tonne of pollutant emitted by road and other ground level transport (for example, diesel trains), drawn from HEATCO (2006). The estimates are based on EcoSense calculations for ground level emissions, using 1998 background emissions and meteorology. The values include estimates for local effects of $PM_{2.5}$. A distinction was made between urban sites with high population density around the site, and non-urban areas. For the other pollutants, no local urban effects are shown as the emitted substances are chemically transformed in the atmosphere into other toxic substances, and this transformation takes some time during which the pollutants are transported away from the site of the emission.

The numbers provided are estimated average values based on the spatial distribution of emissions within a country. The impacts and costs may vary within one country, particularly in large ones. The variation in costs due to NO_x, NMVOC and SO_2 between countries is mainly caused by air chemistry (including ozone formation) and the population affected. For primary particles, no air chemistry is involved; therefore differences reflect the population affected, which is determined mainly by distance to the emission source and the prevailing wind direction.

Climate Change

The estimation of the damage and risks caused by the release of one unit of a greenhouse gas is not an easy task, as the future climate change resulting from the release can only be predicted with large uncertainties and as the impacts from this climate change are only known partly and with a large uncertainty. Several integrated models aim at assessing climate change impacts; two of the most currently advanced and used in Europe are FUND (Tol and Anthoff, 2010) and RICE (Nordhaus, 2010). Table 8 shows a result of FUND. The figures show average external costs in [$Euro_{2000}$ per ton of CO_2] discounted to the year of emission for an emission scenario that is close to the IPCC A1 balanced scenario, so no climate policy is implemented. A pure discount rate of 1 per cent is used. The first row shows the result without equity weighting, the willingness to pay to avoid a risk is proportional to the income. This is sometimes seen as unjust, and instead it is argued that for ethical reasons we should assess risks with the same value no matter where they occur – this is named 'equity weighting'. That is why two different weightings are presented, the first uses worldwide weights, adjusting monetary values by a world average income; the second uses regional average income weights (see Box 16.1).

Another consideration is that the precautionary principle might not be properly reflected in these figures. When estimating impacts from climate change, large uncertainties and gaps exist. This, however, does not mean that the full impacts are automatically higher than the estimated ones, as new effects might also be benefits and new adaptation measures might be developed that reduce impacts. There is, however, a discussion about risks that in the long run could create quite high damages, although the probability is seen either as low or is unknown. So one could argue that according to the precautionary principle for cases where unknown, but important impacts might occur, a risk-averse assessment might be applied.

A way to take the precautionary principle into account is to apply the standard price approach, that is, to use agreed political or societal decisions about environmental standards by using the marginal avoidance costs leading to the fulfillment of these standards. Here we assume that the decision maker has – under consideration also of the precautionary principle, that is, of knowledge gaps about possibly occurring impacts – fixed an environmental aim and that reaching this aim is Pareto optimal. Thus it is assumed

---

BOX 16.1   ALTERNATIVE POSSIBILITIES TO WEIGHT MONETARY VALUES

We consider here two alternative weights, implying various equity considerations. The first is to use world average weights, that is, adjust regional monetary values by a world average income (central row: 'AvEW'). Clearly this would mean that in Europe we would use less effort to reduce risks stemming from greenhouse gas emissions than we would for reducing similar risks caused by other environmental stressors, for example, air pollution. For Europe itself, this distortion, that is, welfare loss, stemming from different assessments for the same risk in Europe, might not be so large, as most impacts from global warming occur outside Europe in developing countries.

But an ethical argument might be that – at least for risks caused by Europeans – the European values should be used. This would lead to regional equity weighting, which means that regional decision makers would base their decisions on their own monetary values for impacts occurring anywhere in the world (REW). First note that this would mean that marginal avoidance costs for reducing greenhouse gas would be different in different regions, for example, lower in India than in Europe, which would result in a less efficient policy (if the same marginal avoidance costs would be applied all over the world, and in addition a burden sharing mechanism would be installed, the same reduction could be achieved with fewer costs). Furthermore, as most of the greenhouse gas emissions occur in rich countries, much more abatement would take place than with the non-equity weighted results. Again, this clearly entails welfare losses compared to a Pareto-optimal state, as for developing countries much more would be spent for reducing risks from global warming than for the reduction of similar risks and impacts from other causes. Thus, all kinds of equity weighting lead to welfare losses. It would obviously be better to use non-equity weighting for decisions on greenhouse gases, and make some additional burden sharing or transfers to poorer countries to deal with equity issues and the polluter-pays principle.

---

that the marginal avoidance costs for reaching this aim are a (second best) proxy for the estimation of the marginal damage costs, as in the optimal state the marginal avoidance costs of course must be equal to the marginal damage costs.

But this point of view entails some problems. For the countries that have signed the Kyoto Agreement, which includes the countries of the European Union, it is clear that for the present, obviously the objectives of the Kyoto protocol which have been agreed should be chosen. For the future, however, no world wide agreement has yet been made. For 2020, in negotiations the EU has offered and agreed upon a reduction of 20 per cent compared to 1990 emissions, with the option of increasing this to 30 per cent if a post-Kyoto agreement comes into force. (Within such an agreement carbon trading would certainly be allowed, so that the aim of 30 per cent reduction, while using the Clean Development Mechanism (CDM), might result in lower marginal avoidance costs than a 20 per cent aim

Table 16.8   *Damage costs of the emission of 1 ton of CO_2 eq in Euro2000 for a reference scenario without greenhouse gas mitigation measures calculated with FUND*

Year of emission	NoEW	AvEW	REW
2005	7	20	97
2015	11	25	122
2025	14	29	148
2035	15	27	137
2045	17	28	143
2055	27	40	196
2065	25	35	164
2075	32	39	175
2085	40	48	203
2095	45	50	201

Notes: NoEW = no equity weighting, AvEW = equity weighting with world average income, REW = regional equity weighting, here for European emissions with EU income.

with trading within the EU, but not outside.) For Kyoto, current (2010) CO_2 certificate prices are around 12–15 €/t CO_2; on the other hand, the full implementation of the reduction goals might lead to higher marginal prices in economic sectors not involved in the trading. Furthermore, the (unexpected) economic crisis also helped to reducing certificate prices; thus an average carbon price of 23 €/t CO_2 could be used for 2010.

Marginal abatement costs for the −20 per cent target of the EU differ widely, and are extremely sensitive to which instruments (for example CDM, Joint Implementation) are allowed to be used. Thus, we assume that the definition of the future policy will be made in such a way that marginal abatement costs (MACs) will increase with the annual discount rate of 3 per cent, a value which is often recommended for the next decades, thus leading to costs of 77 €/t CO_2 in 2050. This result is in line with recommendations of the HEATCO (2006) and the Watkiss (2005) study. The reasoning is also similar to the one in Quinet et al. (2008).

With these marginal abatement costs the 2° target, that is, the target that the average earth surface temperature would not increase by more than 2° compared to preindustrial times, will most likely be violated. According to Kuik's meta model (Kuik et al., 2007), we would end up at about 450 ppm CO_2 (not CO_2-eq.) or roughly 2.8° warming.

Whereas the aim of 20 per cent reduction has been firmly decided within the EU, the target of not exceeding 2° of temperature increase is not a fixed commitment but a nonbinding declaration of intent. That means that it could become valid under the condition that the fulfillment of the aim is economically and socially feasible, which has not yet been fully discussed. However, to get an upper estimate of external costs of carbon, marginal avoidance cost for reaching the 2°C limit could be used. Values from a meta model developed by Kuik et al. (2007) within the CASES project which analyses a number of different models could be used. The meta model gives results of ca 100 €/t CO_2 for 2025 and c. 200 €/t for 2050 for reaching the 2° goal. The value for 2025 is considerably higher than in a JRC report (Russ et al., 2007), which estimates only 37 €/t for 2020 and 64 €/t for 2030 for reaching the 2° aim; however, no values beyond 2030 are given. Based on

Table 16.9   *Values in Euro2005 per tonne of CO_2 equivalent for the assessment of greenhouse gas emissions*

[Euro 2005 per tonne CO_2 eq]	2010	2015	2025	2035	2045	2050
(1) MDC_NoEW	9	11	14	15	17	22
(2) MAC_Kyoto+	23.5	27	32	37	66	77
(3) MAC_2°_aim	23.5	31	52	89	152	198

Notes: MDC = marginal damage costs, MAC = marginal avoidance costs, NoEW = no equity weighting

these considerations, using the value of c. 200 €/t CO_2 from Kuik et al. (2007) for 2050, but interpolating exponentially between 2010 and 2050, brings the values for 2020 closer to the JRC and NEEDS estimates. This might be seen as a best guess, although one has to acknowledge that the figures after 2030 are still less reliable, and might change once better results become available.

As a whole, there is some coherency between the estimates of the various studies, which are compatible, both with the present agreements, with the range of possible future agreements and the scientific knowledge on damages. But as shown by Table 16.9, the range of estimates is still wide.

Noise

For noise, the dependence of impacts on the location is of paramount importance. Noise has purely local impacts, whereas air pollutants can be transported hundreds of kilometers and greenhouse gases have worldwide impacts. The perception of sound follows a logarithmic scale, which results in considerable non-linearities of the impacts and associated costs due to a change in noise levels (in the following we refer to the equivalent noise level L_{Aeq}). The background noise level plays an important role. Assume we have a source that creates in a totally quiet environment a noise level of 40 dB(A). In a rather quiet environment with a background noise also of 40 dB(A) the doubling of the noise energy would lead to level of 43 dB(A); the same source in a noisier environment with a background noise level of 60 dB(A) would lead to a noise level of 60.04 dB(A) and no difference can be heard. Besides this peculiarity of energetic addition of noise levels, the annoyance caused by a certain noise level can be very different. Depending on the features of noise, very loud noise levels (for example, during a rock concert) can be perceived very differently by the concert visitors and the persons living near the concert site. This, together with the very local character of noise makes impact assessment a challenging task, and the models used to quantify noise exposure must be able to map the environment (receptors, buildings), the mode and vehicle technology (PC, HGV passenger cars, heavy goods vehicles and so forth) and the driving patterns adequately.

Noise impacts

The general procedure for taking into account the site- and technology-specific characteristics of noise disturbance is the same as for air pollution. Two scenarios are cal-

Table 16.10 Categorization of effects and related impact categories

Category	Measure given	Impacts
Stress related health effects	RR	Hypertension and ischemic heart disease
Psychosocial effects	AR	Annoyance
Sleep disturbance	AR	Awakenings and subjective sleep quality

Notes: RR = relative risk; AR = absolute risk

Source: De Kluizenaar et al., 2001

culated: a reference scenario reflecting the present situation with traffic volume, speed distribution, vehicle technologies and so forth, and the case scenario which is based on the reference scenario, but includes the changes due to the project alternative considered. The difference in damage costs between both scenarios represents the noise costs due to the project assessed. It is important to quantify total exposure levels and not only exposure increments, because for certain impacts thresholds have to be considered. For instance, some exposure-response functions for health impacts are applicable only above a threshold of 70 dB(A) (see De Kluizenaar et al., 2001).

If the task is to identify marginal costs of an additional vehicle, the calculations may lead to rather small costs if the considered road already has a high traffic density and thus noise level.

Depending on the exposure-response relationships available different noise indicators are required for the quantification of impacts. Examples of indicators that are commonly used are equivalent noise levels for different times of day, for example, $L_{Aeq}(7.00-19.00)$, $L_{Aeq}(19.00-23.00)$, $L_{Aeq}(23.00-7.00)$ and the compound day–evening–night noise indicator L_{DEN} (see European Commission, 2002, for details on noise indicators). Usually noise levels are calculated as incident sound at the façade of the buildings. Empirical noise propagation models have been established in several member states (see, for example, Nordic Council of Ministers, 1996 or Arbeitsausschuss Immissionsschutz an Straßen, 1990), which can be used to model traffic noise exposure.

Two major impacts are usually considered when assessing noise impacts:

- Annoyance, reflecting the disturbance which individuals experience when exposed to (traffic) noise.
- Health impacts, related to the long-term exposure to noise, mainly stress-related health effects like hypertension and myocardial infarction.

It can be assumed that these two effects must be added, that is, the potential long-term health risk is not taken into account in people's perceived noise annoyance, though there is no real evidence of this fact.

A large amount of scientific literature on health and psychosocial effects considering a variety of potential effects of transport noise is available. For instance, De Kluizenaar et al. (2001) reviewed the state of the art, reporting risks due to noise exposure in the living environment. They identified quantitative functions for risks for the effect categories presented in Table 16.10.

Table 16.11   Monetary values for different noise levels (LDEN = day–evening–night-level) in Germany (for other countries and levels see HEATCO, 2006) in € per person affected and per year

Based on	Stated preference Noise Level			Stated preference Annoyance Level			Hedonic pricing		
LDEN dB(A)	road	rail	air	road	rail	air	road	rail	air
43	0	0	0	5	2	8	0	0	0
51	9	0	14	11	6	18	20	0	31
60	88	44	136	21	12	29	200	100	310
75	291	248	412	113	98	119	573	473	848

Existing work has shown that quantifiable health effects are of minor importance compared to the willingness to pay for reducing disamenity and annoyance.

Monetary valuation of noise

Given its high importance for the results and the challenges in its measurement, the value of annoyance caused by noise requires particular consideration. The main cost component of annoyance is disutility experienced. Stated preference (SP) and revealed preference (RP) methods have been employed to estimate the economic value of changes in noise levels. The noise valuation literature is dominated by hedonic price (HP) studies (most of them old) on road traffic and aircraft noise of varying quality. HP studies analyze the housing market to explore the extent to which differences in property prices reflect individuals' WTP for lower noise levels. Resulting values seem to be problematic to transfer, however, both theoretically and in practice (Day, 2001). HP studies tend to give higher values than SP studies. A choice of values has been carried out in the EU project UNITE (2004).

A newer approach is to transfer the noise level (in dB(A)) into an annoyance indicator that expresses the annoyance due to noise in three or five categories from not annoyed to highly or extremely annoyed, before assessing it by using stated preferences. In HEATCO (2006) a stated preference survey in five European countries was carried out. Based on surveys in Germany, Hungary, Norway, Spain, Sweden and the UK, values for application in Europe were derived for the annoyance levels highly annoyed, annoyed and little annoyed.

Table 16.11 shows external costs of noise per person exposed to different noise levels. The columns on the left show values for the willingness to pay for avoiding health impacts and annoyance based on 'stated preference' studies, the central columns present the willingness to pay to avoid health impacts and annoyance levels based on the HEATCO (2006) survey, the values in the right columns are based on hedonic pricing studies.

Water and Soil Pollution

These effects are considered only by a few studies, the main ones being Infras-IWW and ExternE, the results of which have been reused by IMPACT and by UNITE.

The methodology is to assess the repairs necessary for areas polluted by salt, heavy metals and various chemical products. The health impacts are also assessed. The IPA is

Table 16.12   Soil and water pollution unit costs for road and rail transport in Switzerland

	Transport mode	Costs in €-cent per vehicle kilometre
Road	Passenger cars	0.06
	Busses (public transport)	1.07
	Coaches	1.05
	Motorcycles	0.04
	Vans	0.17
	Heavy duty vehicles	1.05
Rail	Rail total	0.43
	Rail passenger	0.29
	Rail freight	1.02

used, starting from the emissions of soil and water pollutants by vehicles and coming to the impact on health using epidemiological studies.

The following results (Table 16.12) are drawn from a Swiss study (OSD 2006).

Energy Security

The main studies on the cost of energy security are based on the United States and their results cannot be transferred to Europe. These studies take into account (cf. the Delucchi and McCubbin chapter in this *Handbook*) the cost of the strategic petroleum reserve, the defense expenditures and costs due to the imperfectly competitive petrol market and to macroeconomic adjustments. It is clear that these types of costs cannot be transferred to Europe. The mandatory storage of oil (for example, in Germany) is paid by the oil suppliers and thus internalized. No serious attempt has been made in Europe to quantify external costs (for example, per unit of oil consumed). In the EC project ExternE-Pol an estimate is made, based on a meta-analysis of other studies, that a $5 increase of a price per barrel of oil would result in a 0.4 per cent decline in annual GDP for the first year. However, this would only be an externality if this price increase occurred unexpectedly, as otherwise market participants would take this increase into account.

Landscape Effects

The estimation of impacts to ecosystems due to air pollution, especially eutrophication and acidification, is already described in section 'air pollution' above. The damage due to land use change (for example, from forests to built land) can also be estimated by estimating the pdfs (potentially disappeared fraction of species) for the different land use types; obviously built-up areas would have a pdf of 100 per cent. A method widely used to estimate the corresponding costs is the repair cost approach: what is the cost to eliminate the damages or to re-create similar ecosystems. However, a few results from contingent valuation studies are also available.

These methods were first implemented by the Infras-IWW study and later by UNITE and NEEDS. The results of Infras-IWW are shown in Table 16.13.

Table 16.13   Marginal costs for nature and landscape

Marginal costs for nature and landscape	Short run marginal cost	Long run marginal cost	
		€ per 1000 vkm	€ per 1000 pkm/tkm
Passenger car urban	0	0.0	0.0
Passenger car interurban	0	4.0	2.1
Urban bus	0	0.0	0.0
Coaches	0	25.7	1.3
Two-wheelers	0	2.1	1.9
LDV	0	3.6.2	10.9
HDV	0	11.5	0.8
Train passenger	0	232	1.2
High speed train	0	232	0.7
Train freight	0	75	0.1
Aviation passenger	0	79	1.1
Aviation freight	0	83	6.5
Waterborne freight	0	922	0.8

Table 16.14   Marginal separation costs for urban transport

Marginal separation costs for urban transport means urban main roads	€/1000 vkm	€/1000 pkm resp. tkm
Pass. car	16.0	9.6
Bus	39.9	2.2
Motorcycle	8.0	7.1
LDV	24.0	32.3
HDV	47.9	7.1
Inter-city train passenger	0	0

Urban (Barrier) Effects

Infrastructures cause barrier effects in agglomerations, people cannot move freely in a city, for example, from one side of a street to the other. Barrier effects depend on the traffic flow on a road. The calculation of the damage costs is based on the time lost by pedestrians for crossing the infrastructure. This type of cost has been calculated by Infras-IWW and the results have been re-used in other studies such as UNITE.

Life-cycle Impacts

When estimating marginal external costs, the analysis should not be restricted to the operation phase of a vehicle, but should include the whole life cycle of the vehicle (that is, well to wheel). For instance, for an electric vehicle the direct external costs during use might be close to zero, but the electricity production and the production of car and battery might cause quite considerable external costs.

The most important impact categories of the life cycle are global warming and air pollution. The most important life cycle processes are the supply of fuel, for example, the extraction and transport of primary energy carriers (crude oil, coal) and the generation of electricity in a power plant or the production of gasoline in a refinery, and the production of the vehicle. The emissions for such processes can generally be found in LCA databases like ECOINVENT (2010). The methodology to calculate external costs would then be the same as described above. For greenhouse gases, the same monetary values per ton of CO_2 eq. as for the operation phase would apply. For air pollution, however, the use of the bottom-up methodology described above would lead to different monetary values per ton of pollutant emitted, as the site and height of release are different. (Typical values per tonne of pollutant can be found, for example, at www. externe.info.)

Positive Externalities: The Mohring Effect

Some attention has been given in Europe to positive externalities. Attention is restricted here to two types of positive externalities: the agglomeration effect and the Mohring effect.

The agglomeration effect concerns the links between agglomeration, productivity and transport. If improvements in transport systems give rise to changes in the mass of economic activity accessible to firms, for instance, by reducing travel times or the costs of travel, then they can induce positive benefits via agglomeration economies. The point and its consequences on transport investments are developed in the chapter by Mackie et al. But its implications for total external costs have never been considered by any study.

This is not the case for the Mohring effect, a form of user economy of scale in public transport services. As traffic on a particular route increases, so public transport operators tend to improve the frequency of service, and to provide benefits to passengers, which are clearly external benefits, or external negative costs. Only a few studies have considered this externality – among them the UNITE study.

This external effect depends on the reaction of the supplier to the increase of traffic. If the result is simply increased load factors, then there is no Mohring effect. If an increase in passengers on public transport is met with a proportionate increase in services, there are clearly benefits to existing users from increases in traffic. Benefits also accrue if the supplier maximizes welfare and, in the simple Mohring model, service frequency varies according to the square root of the traffic.

The hypothesis assumed in the UNITE study is that the occupancy rate or load factor is kept constant when traffic changes. Estimates of the Mohring effect are given for rail intercity traffic and for air traffic, using both simulation and regression methods. The results are, depending on headway time, −0.0005 to −0.0035 € per passenger km assuming load of 150 pax for rail traffic and −€0.239 to −1.347€ per plane km, based on line density of 150 000–250 000 pax per year, flight length of 525–1815 km and occupancy of 130.

COMPARISON WITH NORTH AMERICAN VALUES

As explained above, external transport costs vary according to site, time and technology and thus have to be calculated for each case individually. Thus 'typical' values do not exist. Furthermore, the methodology to estimate external costs and also the input data like monetary values per unit of impact have progressively improved in successive research projects, which means that results will change with these improvements. Nevertheless, in order to give a picture of the overall unit costs per vehicle km resulting from the application of the methodology described above, some exemplary European unit values are shown in the following. These values are derived from the *Handbook on estimation of external costs in the transport sector* (Maibach et al. 2008), where the results of all recently finished European research projects on externality estimation have been exploited and used to describe a European methodology and data set, including NEEDS, CASES, GRACE, UNITE, RECORDIT, ExternE, HEATCO, ASSET and REFIT. Figures are exemplary for a selection of vehicle categories, emission standards and traffic situations.

It is interesting to compare these estimates to those established for the United States by Delucchi and McCubbin (this volume). Table 16.15 shows the ranges of figures for each type of costs, expressed in their original units: $ per mile for the United States and € per km for Europe. Roughly speaking, taking into account those units, a value x in the United States is equivalent to x/2 in Europe. Let us say a word of caution about the figures. The European figures and their ranges reflect results of a sensitivity analysis, where vehicle categories, emission standards and traffic situations are varied; the uncertainty plays a minor role in the bandwidths. Conversely, the bandwidths in the US studies cover both the variety of situations and scientific uncertainty. But the bandwidths do not have a precise definition; they do not correspond to a precise quantile of the distribution. Nevertheless it appears that there is more scientific consensus in Europe than in the United States.

With this caveat, some conclusions can be drawn from this table. Looking first at the total figures (the last row), we see that the estimates in both continents are roughly similar: the ranges largely overlap and the outer limits of the ranges can clearly be explained by the diversity of situations.

Let us now look at the individual external costs. First, some costs are evaluated in Europe and not in the United States (lifecycle, water pollution, nature and landscape) and others in the United States and not in Europe (energy security). But the estimates of both groups are roughly equivalent. The reasons for variations in the total costs differ: they come from congestion in Europe and from noise and air pollution in the United States. This difference may reflect the diversity of situations of congestion in Europe where road widths, car performances, traffic densities are widely dispersed; it can also reflect the fact that in the United States the consensus on the scientific effects is not as wide as in Europe.

Turning now to the commonly estimated external costs, in both continents the hierarchy of external costs is the same: the largest cost is congestion followed by accidents, air pollution and noise, the climate change being the smallest. The relative unimportance of climate change may seem strange, owing to the political momentum on this cost; this paradox can be explained by the fact that the cost of climate change is not all that large presently, but will increase sharply in the future years. Finally, it is clear that in both continents the ranking of modes and types of traffic (freight and passengers) is the same. And on the whole it turns out that the estimates are rather similar in both continents.

Table 16.15   *Summary of estimates of external costs by transport mode and cost category*

	Passenger ($per passenger-mile for United States and € per passenger-km for EU)				Freight ($per ton-mile for United States and € per ton-km for EU)			
	Road	*Rail*	*Air*[a]	*Water*	*Road*	*Rail*	*Air*	*Water*[b]
Congestion delay and scarcity	*0.88–7.5*	n.e.	*0.35*	n.e.	*0.54*	*0.03*	n.e.	n.e.
	0.00–30.0	0.05	n a	n a	0.75	0.05	n a.	n a.
Accident	*1.4–14.4*	n.e.	n.e.	n.e.	*0.11–2.0*	*0.22*	n.e.	n.e.
	0.97–2.50	0.05	0.7	n a	0.23–0.92	0.02	n a	n a
Air pollution (only health effects for United States)	*0.09–6.7*	*0.49*	*0.01–0.39*	*1.1*	*0.10–18.7*	*0.01–0.25*	*0.0–1.9*	*0.08–3.2*
	0.05–0.97	0.00–1.50	0.7	n a	0.73–0.93	0.00–1.05		0.06–0.8
Climate change	*0.06–4.8*	*0.02–1.7*	*0.08*	*0.16*	*0.02–5.9*	*0.01–0.47*	*0.45*	*0.00–0.23*
	0.23–0.40	0.00–1.51	3.5	n a	0.19–0.23	0.00–0.08		0.00–0.07
Noise	*0.0–3.5*	*0.52–0.89*	*0.88*	n.e.	*0.0–5.3*	*0.05*	n.e.	n.e.
	0.07–0.83	0.14–0.82	1.5	n a	0.09–1.12	0.11–0.49	n a	n a
Water pollution	*0.01–0.05*	n.e.	n.e.	n.e.	*0.003–0.05*	n.e.	n.e.	n.e.
	0.04	0.002	n a	n a	0.09	0.02	n a	n a
Life cycle	n a	n a	n a	n.e.	n a	n a	n.e.	n a
	0.28–0.60	0.07–0.26	4.0	n a	0.23–0.27	0.10–0.13	n a	0.00–0.07
Nature and landscape	n a	n a	n a	n a	n a	n a	n a	n a
	0.00–0.25	0.00–0.16	n a	n a	0.00–0.10	0.00–0.02	n a	n a
Energy security	*0.20–0.84*	*0.15–0.58*	*0.18–0.69*	n.e.	*0.22–0.84*	*0.02–0.07*	n.e.	*0.03–0.11*
	n a	n a	n a	n a	n a	n a	n a	n a
Total	*2.64–24.83*	*1.18–3.17*			*0.99–15.83*	*0.32–1.07*		
	1.64–35.59	0.31–4.35			2.31–4.41	0.30–1.86		

Notes:
[a] Drawn from *Handbook* estimates per flight, with the hypothesis of an occupancy rate of 150 passengers per flight
[b] Drawn from *Handbook* estimates per vessel, with the hypothesis of 1500 tons per vessel

NOTES

1. The word 'project' is taken in a broad sense, including for instance changes in transport prices, changes in regulation (for example, emissions control standards)
2. Some authors consider congestion to be the deadweight loss due to imperfect pricing. But this definition does not match the usual meaning of the word 'cost'.
3. These differences are to some extent justified by differences in infrastructure standards.
4. See, for instance, Bates et al. (2001), de Palma and Marchal (2001) and Small et al. (2005).
5. See, for instance, Marquès and Simões (2010) for airports and UNITE D7 (Doll, 2002) for rail and air congestion and scarcity.

REFERENCES

Amici della terra, Ferrovie dello Stato, 2002, The environmental and social costs of mobility in Italy, fourth report. Amici della terra, Rome.

Arbeitsausschuss Immissionsschutz an Straßen, 1990, Richtlinie für den Lärmschutz an Straßen – Ausgabe 1990 – RLS-90. Forschungsgesellschaft für Straßen- und Verkehrswesen, Bonn.

ASSET, 2006, EU 6th RTD framework programme: assessing sensitiveness to transport. Available at: http://www.asset-eu.org/.

Bates J., J. Polak, P. Jones and A. Cook, 2001, The valuation of reliability for personal travel. *Transportation Research Part E*, **37**, 191–229.

Bickel, P. and R. Friedrich, eds, 2005, Externalities of energy methodology 2005 update. Luxembourg: European Commission, 2005. Available at: http://www.externe.info/.

Boiteux, M., 2000, Transports: choix des investissements et prise en compte des nuisances. La Documentation Française, Paris.

van den Bossche, M. A., C. Certan, S. Veldman, C. Nash, D. Johnson, A. Ricci and R. Enei, 2002, UNITE D15 guidance on adapting marginal cost estimates. UNITE (UNIfication of accounts and marginal costs for Transport Efficiency) Deliverable, Funded by 5th Framework RTD Programme, Netherlands Economic Institute (NEI), Rotterdam.

CAFÉ, 2005, Methodology for the cost–benefit analysis for CAFÉ. AEAT technology. Available at http://www.cafe-cba.org/reports/.

COWI in co-operation with TØI and INREGIA, 2000, Civil aviation in Scandinavia: an environmental and economic comparison of different transport modes. COWI, Copenhagen, TØI, Oslo, and INREGIA, Stokholm.

Day, B., 2001, The theory of hedonic markets: obtaining welfare measures for changes in environmental quality using hedonic market data. Economics for the Environment Consultancy (Eftec), London.

De Kluizenaar, Y., W. Passchier-Vermeer and H.M.E. Miedema, 2001, Adverse effects of noise exposure on health: a state of the art summary. TNO report 2001.171, Leiden.

De Palma, A., and F. Marchal, 2002, Real cases applications of the fully dynamic METROPOLIS tool-box: and advocacy for large scale mesoscopic transportation systems. *Network and Spatial Economics*, **2**, 347–369

Dings, J.M.W., R.C.N. Wit, B.A. Leurs, S.M. de Bruyn and M.D. Davidson 1999, External costs of aviation, solutions for environment, economy and technology. Delft 180, 2611 HH Delft, The Netherlands.

Doll, C., 2002, Transport user cost and benefit case studies. UNITE (UNIfication of accounts and marginal costs for Transport Efficiency) Deliverable 7, Funded by 5th Framework RTD Programme, ITS, University of Leeds, Karlsruhe.

ECOINVENT, 2010, Life cycle inventory (LCI) database. Available at: www.ecoinvent.org.

European Commission, 2002, Position paper on dose response relationships between transportation noise and annoyance, EU's Future Noise Policy, WG2 – Dose/Effect. Office for Official Publications of the European Communities, Luxembourg.

European Ministers of Transport (ECMT), 1998, Efficient transport for Europe. European Conference of Ministers of Transport, Paris.

Friedrich, R. and P. Bickel, eds, 2001, *Environmental External Costs of Transport*. Berlin: Springer.

GRACE, 2006, EU RTD 6th RTD framework programme: generalisation of research on accounts and cost estimation. Available at: http://www.grace-eu.org.

HEATCO, 2006, EU RTD 6th RTD framework programme: developing harmonised European approaches for transport costing and project assessment. Available at: http://heatco.ier.uni-stuttgart.de/.

Hensher, D.A., 2006, Integrating accident and travel delay externalities in an urban speed reduction context. *Journal of Urban Economics*, **26** (4), 521–534.

INFRAS/IWW, 2000, External costs of transport: accident, environmental and congestion costs of transport in Western Europe. Report for the IRU-UIC, Paris.

INFRAS/IWW, 2004, External costs of transport: update study. International Union of Railways (UIC), Paris.

ISIS (RECORDIT), 2001, Real cost reduction of door-to-door intermodal transport, 2001. Project funded by the European Commission Commission under the Transport RTD Programme of the 4th Framework Programme, ISIS, Roma. Available at: www.recordit.org.

Kuik, O., L. Brander, N. Nikitina, S. Navrud, K. Magnussen and H. Fall, 2007, Energy-related external costs due to land use changes, acidification and eutrophication, visual intrusion and climate change. CASES: Cost assessment of Sustainable Energy systems, Deliverable D 3.2. Available at: http://www.feem-project.net/cases/documents/deliverables.

Maibach, M. and C. Schneider, 2002, External costs of corridors: a comparison between air, road and rail. Final Report for the Air Transport Action Group, Zurich.

Marques, R.C. and P. Simões, 2010, Measuring the influence of congestion on efficiency in worldwide airports. *Journal of Air Transport Management*, doi:10.1016/j.jairtraman.2010.03.002.

Nash, C., 1999, CAPRI, *Concerted Action on Transport Pricing Research Integration*. Project funded by the European Commission under the Transport RTD programme of the the 4th programme framework, Institute for Transport Studies, University of Leeds, Leeds.

NEEDS, 2009, *New Energy Externalities Development for Sustainability*. EU 6th RTD framework programme. Available at: www.needs-project.org.

NEWEXT, 2004, *New Elements for the Assessment of External Costs from Energy Technologies*. Project of the EU 5th framework programme. IER, University of Stuttgart. Available at: www.ier.uni-stuttgart.de/forschung/projektwebsites/newext/.

Nordhaus, 2010, Available at: http://nordhaus.econ.yale.edu/RICEmodels.htm.

Nordic Council of Ministers, 1996, Nordic prediction method. Road Traffic Noise, TemaNord 1996:525, Rail Traffic Noise, TemaNord 1996:524.

OSD, 2006, Externe Kosten des Strassen- und Schienenverkehrs 2000 : Klima und bisher nicht erfasste Umweltbereiche, städtische Räume sowie vor- und nachgelagerte Prozesse Bern: Bundesamtes für Raumentwicklung (ARE).

Ott, W., M. Baur, Y. Kaufmann, R. Frischknecht, R. Steiner, 2006, Assessment of biodiversity losses. Available at: http://www.needs-project.org/RS1b/RS1b_D4.2.pdf.

Proost, S. and K. Van Dender, 1999, TRENEN II STRAN. Centre for Economic Studies, Katholieke Universiteit, Leuven.

Quinet, E. 2004, A meta-analysis of Western European External Costs Estimates. *Transportation Research Part D*, **9**, 465–476.

Quinet, A., L. Baumstark and J. Celestin-Urbain, 2008, La valeur tutélaire du carbone. Centre d'Analyse Stratégique, Paris.

QUITS, 1998, QUITS (Quality Indicators for Transport Systems). Project funded by the European Commission under the Transport RTD Programme of the 4th Framework Programme, ISIS, Rome.

REFIT, 2004, Refinement and Test of Sustainability Indicators and Tools with Regard to European Transport. EU 6th RTD framework programme. Available at: http://refit.bouw.tno.nl/index.htm.

Roy, R., 2000, Revenues from efficient pricing; evidence from the member states. Final study report edited by Dr. Roy, London, UIC/CER/European Commission DG-TREN Study.

Russ, P., P.T. Wiesenthal, D. van Regemorter and J.C. Ciscar, 2007, Global climate policy scenarios for 2030 and beyond. JRC Reference Reports, Luxembourg, European Communities 2007.

Samson, T., C. Nash, P.J. Mackie, J. Shires and P. Watkiss, 1998, Surface transport costs and charges Great Britain 1998. Institute for Transport Studies, University of Leeds, Leeds.

Small K., C. Winston and J. Yan, 2005, Uncovering the distribution of motorists' preferences for travel time and reliability. *Econometrica*, **73** (4), 1367–1382.

Steimetz, S., 2008, Defensive driving and the external costs of accidents and travel delays. *Transportation Research Part B*, **42** (9), 703–724.

Tol, R.S.J. and D. Anthoff, 2010, Climate policy under fat-tailed risk: an application of FUND. Papers WP348, Economic and Social Research Institute (ESRI)

TREMOVE, 2009, A policy assessment model to study the effects of different transport and environment policies on the transport sector for all European countries. Available at: http://www.tremove.org/index.htm.

UNITE, 2004, UNification of accounts and marginal costs for Transport Efficiency (UNITE), EU 6th RTD framework programme. Available at: http://www.its.leeds.ac.uk/projects/unite/.

Watkiss, P., 2005, The social cost of carbon (SCC) review: methodological approaches for using SCC estimates in policy assessment. Final Report. London: UK Defra, 2005.

17 The value of a statistical life
Henrik Andersson and Nicolas Treich

INTRODUCTION

Modern societies rely on a well-functioning transportation infrastructure. Policies taken to maintain and/or improve an infrastructure come at a cost; and the scarcity of resources forces policy makers to prioritize between policies. The use of a common metric for benefits and costs may facilitate the evaluation of different policies, which in turn, enables policy makers to allocate resources more efficiently. Monetary values often act as this common metric. Another good reason for monetizing non-marketed goods is that this common ground for comparisons makes the prioritization process more transparent to those not directly involved in the process (for example, the public).

Many of the benefits and costs induced by policies within the transport sector have monetary values. Material expenditures, for example, for road improvements in order to increase safety and reduce travel time, are easily obtainable since the materials are traded on markets and have market prices. However, many of the costs are not 'construction costs' and do not have monetary market prices. For instance, road improvements might increase road traffic, resulting in increased noise and emission levels; in addition, when a new road is constructed recreation areas may be lost, wildlife may be adversely affected and so forth. Similarly, whereas expected benefits from avoided material damage caused by crashes can be calculated using available market prices, the benefits from a reduced risk exposure and/or a reduced travel time have no market prices.

In this chapter, we are interested in the monetary value of increased safety, and more specifically, in the value of reducing the risk of mortality. Economists often refer to the monetary value of reducing mortality risks as the 'value of life'. For those initiated in the vocabulary, this expression has a clear and precise meaning and is quite uncontroversial. For others it may be controversial since it seems to imply that human life can be valued while it should be 'priceless'.[1] The expression 'value of life' is an unfortunate reduced form of the *the value of a statistical life* (VSL),[2] which defines the monetary value of a (small and similar among the population) mortality risk reduction that would prevent one *statistical* death and, therefore, should not be interpreted as how much individuals are willing to pay to save an *identified* life.[3]

A procedure often used to estimate benefits from reduced mortality is the human capital approach, in which the value of a person's life is determined by this person's market productivity. For several reasons, this approach is no longer popular. The dominant approach nowadays is based on individuals' willingness to pay (WTP). This approach assumes that individuals' preferences are the basis for economic welfare. The WTP-approach to value mortality risk reductions was introduced by Drèze (1962). Drèze's paper was written in French and the concept became widely known only after Schelling's (1968) seminal paper. The theoretical foundation of the concept was further developed within the expected utility framework by Mishan (1971) and Jones-Lee (1974). A key contributor to the empirical literature on VSL is Viscusi, in particular for his analysis of compensating wage differentials (Viscusi, 1993; Viscusi and Aldy, 2003).[4]

To understand the VSL concept, it may be useful to take an example. Suppose that in a city composed of 100 000 identical individuals, there is an investment project that will make the city's roads safer. It is known that on average five individuals die every year on these roads, and the project is expected to reduce from five to two the number of expected fatalities per year. Suppose now that each member of the city is willing to pay $150 annually to benefit from this reduction in mortality risk induced by the project. Then the corresponding VSL would be $150 × 100 000/3 = $5 million. Indeed, $15 million could be collected in this city to save three statistical lives, and so the value of a statistical life could be established at $5 million. This example also illustrates why estimates about individuals' VSL can be useful. Suppose indeed that one ignores the WTP of city members from this specific project; but one has some information about money/risk tradeoffs observed from the city members' choices (or from survey studies) concerning other mortality risks. Then it can be useful to compute an average implicit VSL in this city based on these choice data, and use this VSL to estimate the benefits of this specific risk-reduction road safety project that one wants to evaluate.

If individuals treat longevity, or small changes in mortality risk, like any other consumption good, there should be no or little controversy to use the concept of WTP to value a reduction in the probability of death (Freeman, 2003).[5] A source of controversy may arise, however, as there is evidence that individuals misperceive mortality risks and thus may give inconsistent WTP (Hammitt and Graham, 1999). Also, while standard preferences assume self-interested behavior, individuals may care about the risks to life of others (for example, relatives or identified victims). Thus, altruistic concerns may matter in the WTP for reduction in mortality risks. Another and more classical issue is linked to the distributional effects of the WTP approach, that may for instance give disproportionate weight to wealthier individuals in the society. The heterogeneity of population risk-exposure is a sensitive topic. A challenge faced by policy makers consists in determining whether and how the VSL should be adjusted to account for the differences in the types of risks and in individuals' characteristics.

The chapter's first objective is to survey some classical theoretical and empirical findings on the VSL literature; but it also attempts to clarify some of these issues often raised by the application of the WTP approach to study of mortality risks. The chapter is divided into two main sections, one theoretical and one empirical. In the following section, we outline the standard VSL model, describe how VSL is influenced by different factors and discuss some welfare implications. In the empirical part, we briefly discuss estimation approaches, as well as empirical findings and the use of the VSL in transport. The chapter ends with some conclusions.

THEORETICAL INSIGHTS

In this section, we first introduce the VSL concept using a standard economic model and present some common extensions of the basic framework initially introduced. We then

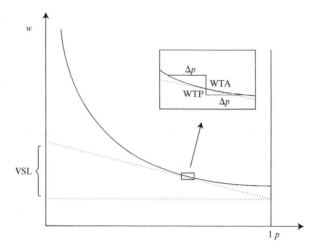

Notes: Indifference curve over survival probability (p) and wealth (w). The slope of the curve represents the marginal rate of substitution between p and w. The WTP (WTA) represents the maximal amount that an individual is willing to pay (accept) for a mortality risk reduction (Δp) (increase).

Source: James Hammitt, Lecture notes, School of Public Health, Harvard University.

Figure 17.1   The value of a statistical life

justify the policy use of the average VSL across individuals using a public goods model, and discuss some distributional implications of the economic approach. We finally present some comparative statics results.

The VSL Model

The standard model

We consider a standard single-period VSL model. The individual maximizes his (state-dependent) expected indirect utility which is given by

$$V \equiv pu(w) + (1 - p)v(w) \qquad (17.1)$$

where p is the probability of surviving the period, $u(w)$ is the utility of wealth w if he survives the period, and $v(w)$ is the utility of wealth w if he dies (typically, the utility of a bequest). This model was introduced by Drèze (1962) and Jones-Lee (1974) and has been commonly used in the VSL literature.[6]

We adopt the standard assumptions that u and v are twice differentiable with

$$u > v, u' > v' \geq 0, u'' \leq 0 \text{ and } v'' \leq 0. \qquad (17.2)$$

That is, state-dependent utilities are increasing and weakly concave. At any wealth level, both utility and marginal utility are larger if alive than dead. Under these standard assumptions, indifference curves over (w, p) are decreasing and strictly convex, as illustrated in Figure 17.1.

The willingness to pay (WTP) for a mortality risk reduction $\Delta p \equiv \varepsilon$ is denoted $C(\varepsilon)$ and is given by the following equation

$$(p + \varepsilon)u(w - C(\varepsilon)) + (1 - p - \varepsilon)v(w - C(\varepsilon)) = V \qquad (17.3)$$

where V is defined in Equation (17.1). Similarly, the willingness to accept (WTA) for a mortality risk increase $\Delta p \equiv \varepsilon$ is denoted $P(\varepsilon)$ and is given by the following equation

$$(p - \varepsilon)u(w + P(\varepsilon)) + (1 - p + \varepsilon)v(w + P(\varepsilon)) = V. \qquad (17.4)$$

The WTP and WTA are represented in Figure 17.1. From Equations (17.3) and (17.4) it is obvious that WTP and WTA should be sensitive to the size of ε. For small ε it is important to stress, however, that we also expect that WTP and WTA should be nearly equal in magnitude and near-proportional to ε (Hammitt, 2000a).[7]

The VSL does not measure what an individual is willing to pay to avoid death with certainty, nor what he is willing to accept to face death with certainty. It measures the WTP or the WTA for an *infinitesimal* change in risk. It can be obtained by taking the limit of the WTP or the WTA when the change in risk is infinitely small, that is when $\varepsilon \cong 0$.[8] In other words, the VSL is the marginal rate of substitution (MRS) between wealth and survival probability, that is, (the negative of) the slope of the indifference curve at (w, p). It is defined as follows

$$\text{VSL} \equiv \frac{-dw}{dp} = \frac{u(w) - v(w)}{pu'(w) + (1 - p)v'(w)}. \qquad (17.5)$$

The VSL thus depends separately on the characteristics of the baseline risk through p and on those of the individual through u, v and w. Notice that the properties exhibited in (2) imply that the VSL is always strictly positive.

The dead-anyway effect and the wealth effect

The expression obtained for the VSL in Equation (17.5) is useful for identifying two standard effects. First, the dead-anyway effect (Pratt and Zeckhauser, 1996) describes how VSL increases with baseline risk $(1 - p)$, that is, how VSL decreases with survival probability p. Intuitively, an individual facing a large probability of death has little incentive to limit his spending on risk reduction since he is unlikely to survive. In Equation (17.5) the value of the numerator is independent of p and a decrease in p reduces the value of the denominator (since $u' > v'$).[9]

Second, the wealth effect describes how VSL increases with wealth w. The intuition for the wealth effect is two-fold. First, wealthier people have more to lose if they die, that is, the numerator in Equation (17.5) increases with w (since $u' > v'$). Second, the utility cost of spending is smaller due to weakly diminishing marginal utility (risk aversion) with respect to wealth, that is, the denominator in Equation (17.5) does not increase (because $u'' \leq 0$ and $v'' \leq 0$). As a consequence, due to these two effects, the VSL increases as one moves upward and leftward along an indifference curve such as the one depicted in Figure 17.1.

To illustrate the two effects, it can be useful to consider specific functional forms.

Assume that the (marginal) utility of bequest is zero, $v(w) = 0$, and that the utility function is isoelastic, $u(w) = w^{1-\gamma}/(1 - \gamma)$ with $\gamma \in [0, 1]$. Then we get

$$\text{VSL} = \frac{w}{p(1 - \gamma)} \tag{17.6}$$

which increases in wealth w, and decreases in the survival probability p.

Risk aversion and background risks

It is often suggested that the VSL obtained from compensating wage differential studies underestimates the average VSL in the population because those who choose to work in hazardous industries are less risk averse. This suggestion, however, requires a more precise specification about what we mean by 'less risk averse'. For state-independent utility functions, it is usual to define risk aversion by the coefficient of curvature of the utility function introduced by Pratt (1964) and Arrow (1971, ch. 3). Yet, the above framework considers the case of state-dependent utility functions, that is, a case in which the utility assigned to any given level of wealth w varies with the state of nature (being alive or dead). And how to characterize risk aversion is not clear in the case of state-dependent utility functions (Karni, 1983).[10]

Eeckhoudt and Hammitt (2004) consider the standard model (17.1) and examine the effect of an increase in risk aversion in the sense of Arrow-Pratt of the utility contingent on being alive, that is of u. They show that more risk aversion increases the VSL when the marginal utility of bequest is zero and in a few other situations.[11] But in general, Eeckhoudt and Hammitt (2004) show that the effect of risk aversion on the VSL, or on the WTP/WTA for a risk change, is ambiguous. Moreover, Eeckhoudt and Hammitt (2001) and Kaplow (2005) show in model (17.1) that a high coefficient of relative risk aversion, $-wu''(w)/u'(w)$, usually implies high values for the income elasticity of the VSL.

Eeckhoudt and Hammitt (2001) examine the effect of background financial and mortality risks on the VSL. Under reasonable assumptions about risk preferences with respect to wealth in the event of survival and death, they show that background mortality and financial risks decrease VSL. Andersson (2008) extends their analysis on background mortality risk and shows, that when individuals perceive the risks to be mutually exclusive, the background risk increases VSL.

Multiperiod models

We have presented so far a single-period model. In more realistic multiperiod models, individuals have preferences over probability distributions of the length of life and over consumption levels at each period of life. We illustrate this using the simplest two-period model:

$$J \equiv \max_{c} u(c) + \beta p u(r(w - c)) \tag{17.7}$$

where β is a discount factor, r the interest factor, c consumption in period 1 and p the survival probability from period 1 to period 2. Observe that there is no bequest motive, and that an individual surviving period 1 will die for sure in period 2. The VSL, as defined as the MRS between wealth w and survival probability p, then equals

$$\text{VSL} = \frac{-dw}{dp} = \frac{\partial J/\partial p}{\partial J/\partial w} = \frac{u(r(w - c^*))}{pru'(r(w - c^*))} \quad (17.8)$$

in which c^* is optimal consumption. Observe that the obtained formulae for the VSL is not much different from the one of the single-period model (17.5) (assuming no bequest).

Several authors have used multiperiod life-cycle consumption models to derive an expression for the VSL (Bergstrom, 1982; Conley, 1976; Garber and Phelps, 1997; Shepard and Zeckhauser, 1984).[12] A recurrent problem overlooked in the formulation (17.7) is that future earnings may stop when the consumer dies, and so the wealth constraint should be carefully specified. Following Yaari (1965), two cases are often considered. In one case, the individual can purchase actuarially fair annuities. In the other case, the individual can borrow and lend at the riskless rate $r - 1$, but can never be a net borrower. The results of each case differ, as illustrated by Shepard and Zeckhauser (1984) for instance.

One advantage of multiperiod models is that the effect of age can be studied. Although there is a widespread belief that VSL should decline with age (for example, European Commission, 2000), there is no theoretical support for this belief. In particular, Johansson (2002) suggests that VSL should track the life-cycle pattern of consumption. Therefore, the relationship between age and VSL need not be monotonic. Some theoretical as well as some numerical results have suggested that there should be an inverted-U relationship between VSL and age (Aldy and Viscusi, 2007).

Human capital and annuities

Before the concept of WTP became widely accepted among economists as the appropriate evaluation method, the human capital (HC) approach was the dominant procedure to appraise the social value of a lost life. According to the HC approach the 'value of life' is the value of the individual's market productivity, a value assumed to be reflected by the individual's earnings (Mishan, 1982). The HC is calculated as the individual's present value of future expected earnings and the approach has two major drawbacks: (1) it assigns a zero value to non-market production implying that, for example, unemployed and retired persons have a value equal to zero and (2) it does not reflect individual preferences for safety. Attempts to also incorporate non-market earnings have been made by imputing, for example, earnings to services carried out in the household (Max et al., 2004), or as in Keeler (2001) where leisure was given a monetary value. However, the main objection against HC is that it does not reflect individual preferences for safety, a problem which cannot be solved by assigning monetary values to non-market production or leisure.

To compare the VSL and the HC approach consider the following example. Assume a population of n identical people, in which $n(1 - p)$ are expected to die. Consider a project that may save $n\varepsilon$ statistical lives. Using the WTP approach, one collects ex ante $n \times C(\varepsilon)$ – see Equation (17.3) – which represents the monetary-equivalent benefits of the life savings project. In contrast, using the HC approach, one collects $n\varepsilon w$. That is, the monetary-equivalent benefits of the project is obtained by multiplying number of people who may be saved by their HC w (for example, we interpret w as the discounted lifetime labor income). Notice then that comparing $n \times C(\varepsilon)$ to $n\varepsilon w$ amounts to compare $C(\varepsilon)/\varepsilon$ to w, which for small ε, amounts to compare VSL to w. However, notice that the VSL is usually larger than w, as illustrated by Equation (17.6). The general idea that we want to put forward is that the HC approach may underestimate the value of preventing death.

Bergstrom (1982), Conley (1976), Cook (1978) and Rosen (1988) examine the relationship between the HC and VSL approach in a model with fair annuities. An annuity contract leads to specify ex ante how survivors will share ex post the wealth of those who will die. Overall, these papers suggest that HC may serve as a lower bound for the VSL under some (fairly plausible) restrictions on the utility functions. These restrictions usually include the concavity of u and a low bequest motive expressed through v.

VSL and Welfare Economics

Public provision of safety

We now introduce a model of public provision of safety (for example, public investments in road safety) in a society with heterogenous individuals. We consider a particular case of the textbook model of provision of a public good (Samuelson, 1954) in order to underline the links between this textbook model and the VSL concept, as introduced above.

The economy is composed of n individuals. The level of safety expenditure z is a public good. Safety expenditure increases each individual i's survival probability $p_i(z)$, that is $p_i'(z) > 0$. Individual i's expected utility is given by

$$V_i \equiv p_i(z)u_i(w_i) + [1 - p_i(z)]v_i(w_i) \qquad (17.9)$$

The objective of the benevolent social planner is to choose the level of public safety expenditure z together with the level of individual tax t_i in order to maximize

$$\sum_{i=1}^{n} \lambda_i \{ p_i(z) u_i(w_i - t_i) + [1 - p_i(z)]v_i(w_i - t_i) \} \qquad (17.10)$$

under the budget constraint

$$\sum_{i=1}^{n} t_i = z \qquad (17.11)$$

Notice that λ_i is the Pareto weight associated with each individual i in the social planner's objective.

The first order conditions of this optimization program are given by

$$\sum_{i=1}^{n} \lambda_i p_i'(z) [u_i(w_i - t_i) - v_i(w_i - t_i)] = \mu \qquad (17.12)$$

$$\lambda_i \{ p_i(z)u_i'(w_i - t_i) + [1 - p_i(z)]v_i'(w_i - t_i) \} = \mu, \text{ for all } i \qquad (17.13)$$

where μ is the Lagrange multiplier associated to the constraint (17.11). Equation (17.12) is the social marginal benefit condition while Equation (17.13) is the individual equalized marginal costs condition. Eliminating λ_is and μ in the $n + 1$ first order conditions above, we obtain

$$\sum_{i=1}^{n} p_i'(z)\,\mathrm{VSL}_i = 1 \qquad (17.14)$$

where VSL_i is the value of a statistical life corresponding to each individual i:

$$\mathrm{VSL}_i \equiv \frac{u_i(w_i - t_i) - v_i(w_i - t_i)}{p_i(z)u_i'(w_i - t_i) + (1 - p_i(z))v_i'(w_i - t_i)}. \qquad (17.15)$$

The equality (17.14) is therefore the efficiency condition that characterizes the optimal public provision of safety in this economy. It corresponds to the Samuelson's condition that the sum of MRSs equals the marginal rate of transformation (which is equal to one here). Observe that if individual increases in survival probability $p'_i(z)$ are uncorrelated with VSL_i then the efficiency condition becomes

$$1 \Big/ \left(\sum_{i=1}^{n} p_i'(z) \right) = \frac{1}{n} \sum_{i=1}^{n} \mathrm{VSL}_i \qquad (17.16)$$

that is, the marginal cost to save a life in the society should be equal to the overall population arithmetic mean of VSL. Therefore, this efficiency condition justifies the use of the average VSL as the economic criterion to determine the value of a social life when public projects affecting mortality risks in the society are implemented.

Distributional effects
The efficiency condition (17.16) relies on two critical assumptions: (1) there are no restrictions on the tax levied on individuals, (2) the individual risk reductions are uncorrelated with individuals' VSLs.

Assumption (1) relies on the possibility for the social planner to implement individualized lump-sum transfers t_i that are given by Equation (17.12) and (17.13). However, governments usually do not have the information, nor possess the power to implement such optimal lump-sum transfers. Assumption (1) is thus difficult to justify empirically. It is no surprise that it has been extensively discussed in the public economics literature (see, for example, Drèze and Stern, 1987). If this assumption is relaxed, the efficiency rule is different, and therefore the efficient level of public safety should be different as well (see, for example, Ballard and Fullerton, 1992).[13] Moreover, notice that assumption i) implies that the tax levied is such that all individuals end up with the same marginal utility of income, see (17.13). Hence the notion of equality that is put forward in economic analysis is that of marginal utility, and not a notion based on equal levels of risks to life for instance (Sen, 1973) or equal levels of differences in risks to life (Somanathan, 2006).[14]

It is unlikely that individual risk reductions are uncorrelated with individual VSL, as assumption (2) requires. Suppose indeed that a program principally affects a higher (lower) income group. Since VSL is expected to increase with wealth, individual risk reductions are positively (negatively) correlated with individual VSL. The same observation holds if the program principally affects high risk (low risk) people, due to the dead anyway effect.

These observations suggest that the use of the average VSL may lead to a bias in risk policies that may disproportionately favor the rich, or the most exposed individuals for instance. One solution to 'debias' risk policies is to weight individual VSL (for a general argument, see, for example, Blackorby and Donaldson, 1990). The well-known problem is that there is no evident choice for the weights, as it has been discussed at length in the literature, and most economists prefer not to use weights at all (Harberger, 1971).[15] Baker et al. (2008) recently re-examine these arguments using the same framework that we introduced above. Specifically, they 'adjust' the underlying social welfare function, in particular by adapting the Pareto-weights λ_is, so that the welfare function justifies the use of a 'common' VSL.

Statistical versus identified lives

Economists make clear that the VSL approach applies only when changes in risk are small and similar among the affected population (for example, Viscusi, 1992, ch. 2).[16] Therefore, the focus on statistical lives leaves open the question of how to evaluate a project that may instead save, or threaten, the lives of identified people. It also meets a well-known conceptual issue, 'Broome's paradox'. Assume that a project may kill one person from a population of similar individuals. If the identity of the victim is unknown, the project may be adopted. Yet, if the victim's identity is known, the potential victim might require infinite compensation for the loss of his life and the project would be rejected.[17]

Hammitt and Treich (2007) examine formally the Broome's paradox in the framework introduced above. They explain that the paradox is related to the distributional effect discussed above, and arises because adding monetary compensations is only a good proxy for welfare if marginal utilities are equal across individuals. Along the same lines, Hammitt and Treich study the effect of information about the heterogeneity of risk in the population – that is, the effect of individual identifiability – on the average WTP or WTA for a mortality risk change. They show that the average WTA is usually larger with more information about how the project affects individuals' risks. Hence individual-specific information may lead to rejecting a risk-increasing project that would have been accepted without information, as in Broome's paradox. In contrast, they show that average WTP is usually smaller with more information about heterogeneity of the risk change. Hammitt and Treich (2007) thus conclude that there is no necessary relationship between the extent to which risk changes are statistical or identifiable and the level of safety endorsed by an economic analysis.

Altruism

The relationship between altruism and life-savings has been discussed in the early stage of the economic literature on VSL (Jones-Lee, 1976; Mishan, 1971; Needleman, 1976; Schelling, 1968) and has been more recently addressed in the psychology literature (see, for example, Jenni and Loewenstein, 1997).

The benchmark economic result dates back to a point initially raised by Bergstrom (1982). Consider an altruistic economy in which individual i's utility $U_i \equiv U_i(V_1, \ldots, V_n)$ increases in each of its arguments and strictly increases in V_i, as defined in Equation (17.9). This is the case of pure altruism. Bergstrom's point is that since preferences in this altruistic economy increase in everyone's utilities, every Pareto optimum in the altruistic economy must also be a Pareto optimum in the selfish economy described above. As a consequence, the necessary conditions (17.12) and (17.13) for an optimum in the altruistic economy are identical to those in the selfish economy.

The important implication of this point is that the presence of altruism should not lead to any adjustment upward or downward of the VSL but should be kept the same as if individuals were selfish. The intuitive argument is simple. A pure altruist benefits when another person's risk is reduced but is harmed when one imposes a financial cost on this person. The sign of one person's altruistic valuation for another is thus the same as the sign of the net private benefits to the other and so pure altruism cannot alter the sign of the social net benefits. This argument was recently generalized by Bergstrom (2006). Jones-Lee (1991) extended Bergstrom's analysis and showed that people's WTP for others' safety should only be taken account of when the altruism is 'exclusively focused upon other people's safety' (p. 217). Individuals with this form of altruism are defined as safety paternalists, and disregard all factors besides safety that contribute to the utility of other people.[18]

We must finally notice that the above arguments do not exhaust the rich set of research questions that pose relations to others for VSL. These questions include those related to the modelling of intra-household interactions (for example, patriarchal versus bargaining models), to whether and how the relative position (with respect to utility, income, safety and so forth) of an individual compared to others matters for welfare and to the various pecuniary effects posed by mortality risks in our societies (life insurance, externalities due to increased longevity).

EMPIRICAL ASPECTS

In the following sections, we first briefly describe preference elicitation of non-marketed goods, followed by a presentation of results from the empirical literature. This presentation contains: (1) empirical estimates of VSL in transport, (2) findings from the VSL literature in general and (3) a discussion of individuals' risk perception and how it relates to VSL. We finally discuss how VSL is used in policymaking.

Preference Elicitation

Since the concept of WTP was developed 40 years ago, the VSL has been estimated in a number of studies, and in a variety of areas. As mortality risk reductions per se are non-marketed goods, we have to rely on non-market valuation methods in order to estimate VSL.[19] These methods can be classified into two types, revealed- and stated-preferences methods. Both approaches have their strengths and weaknesses. Revealed preference (RP) methods use the information from choices made by individuals in existing markets, whereas stated preference (SP) methods employ hypothetical market scenarios.[20]

Revealed preferences
In RP studies, information is obtained from situations where individuals make actual trade-off decisions, either implicitly or explicitly, between wealth (foregone consumption) and physical risk. Economists usually prefer RP to SP methods when non-marketed amenities are to be evaluated. With actual (and often repeated) choices, individuals have incentives to identify and understand the choice alternatives. Hence, preferences elicited in RP studies are not only based on actual behavior and thus are expected to be more

consistent, but are also assumed, compared to hypothetical choices made by respondents in SP studies, to be made on a more informed basis.

Many RP studies to estimate VSL have used compensating wage differentials but individual consumption decisions have been employed as well (for a review, see Viscusi and Aldy, 2003). In transport, consumers' decisions on, for example, the purchase of car models (Atkinson and Halvorsen, 1990), safety products such as bicycle helmets (Jenkins et al., 2001), and car drivers' decision whether to use a seat-belt or not (Blomquist, 1979; Hakes and Viscusi, 2007) have been used to estimate VSL.

A common problem of using consumption data on safety equipment, for example, airbags or bicycle helmets, is that it provides a lower bound of consumers' WTP for safety, that is, a lower bound for those who decide to buy the safety equipment. Since the consumers are faced with a binary decision, the decision to buy or not the safety device can only reveal whether the benefit from the product is at least as large as the cost of the product (Viscusi, 1993). The use of the car market with a wide variety of different models therefore provides an advantage compared with the use of most safety products, since it reveals the consumers' total WTP for safety (see below). The technique that has been used to estimate VSL in the car market is the hedonic regression technique (Andersson, 2005a; Atkinson and Halvorsen, 1990; Dreyfus and Viscusi, 1995).

The hedonic regression technique was formalized in a seminal paper by Rosen (1974). According to this technique, the price (P) of a composite good, defined as a vector of its attributes $\mathbf{A} = [a_1, \ldots, a_n]$, is a function of its utility-bearing characteristics, that is, $P(\mathbf{A})$. The relationship between the price of the composite good and its characteristics is illustrated in Figure 17.2a in the $P - a_1$ plane. Let θ^i and ϕ^i in Figure 17.2a denote individual i's bid function (indifference curve) and firm i's offer function (isoprofit curve), and let a_1 denote survival probability. The market equilibria, observable by the analyst, are characterized by tangency between the bid and offer functions, where marginal valuation equals marginal cost. Since the bid function is equivalent to the indifference curve, the marginal WTP for a utility maximizing individual is proportional to the MRS between survival probability and other consumption. Since the hedonic price function (HPF) is derived from these equilibria, we can use it to estimate the population mean MRS (P, a_1), *i.e.* VSL. Deriving the HPF and estimating marginal WTP is sometimes referred to as the *first step* of the hedonic regression technique.

The HPF does not, as illustrated in Figure 17.2a, contain any information concerning the shape of the underlying bid and offer functions, however. Thus, in order to estimate non-marginal WTP using the hedonic regression technique, we need to derive the individuals' marginal bid functions, $\theta^i_{a_1}$, which are drawn in Figure 17.2b for two individuals, together with the marginal price locus, P_{a_1}, and two marginal offer functions, $\phi^i_{a_1}$.[21] Rosen (1974) proposed that a *second step* should be carried out in order to identify these marginal bid and offer functions, where the results from step one, together with information on consumer and firm attributes, should be used.[22]

The fact that RP methods rely on the existence of markets where individuals are assumed to make informed decisions about alternatives that differ in risk levels is also its potential weakness. Moreover, RP methods also require that the analyst is able to identify the alternatives identified by the consumers. For instance, if consumers base their decision on subjective risks, this is the information that should be used in principle by the analyst. Further, since real market situations are required: (1) estimates are based

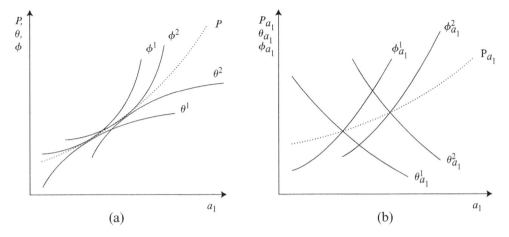

Source: Andersson, 2005b

Figure 17.2   *(a) The hedonic price function (P) and the bid (θ^i) and offer functions (φ^i) for two utility- and profit-maximizing consumers and firms, respectively. Tangency between a bid and an offer function denotes a market equilibrium. (b) The marginal price locus (P_{a_1}) and two marginal bid ($\theta^i_{a_1}$) and offer functions ($\varphi^i_{a_1}$), respectively. Marginal WTP equals marginal cost at intersections between the marginal bid and offer functions.*

on the market population (for example, car owners) and not the general population and (2) it limits the applicability to specific situations that analysts and policymakers are interested in.

Stated preferences

SP methods have an important role to play when knowledge among analysts about the decision alternatives, the beliefs and consequences individuals face is limited, or when market data does not exist for the amenity of interest. SP methods are also more flexible than RP which allows the analyst to tailor the surveys to elicit the desired information, and they have, therefore, been employed in a wide variety of areas to estimate VSL (see, for example, Hammitt and Graham, 1999). There exists a wide range of techniques to elicit preferences using hypothetical market scenarios. Some recent studies in traffic safety have used a stated-choice approach to estimate VSL (for example, Rizzi and Ortúzar, 2006a, b), but the method that dominates in the evaluation literature on VSL in traffic is the contingent valuation method (CVM) (Bateman et al., 2002; Mitchell and Carson, 1989).

The CVM is a SP method where individuals are asked directly how much they are willing to pay (or are willing to accept) for a change in the quantity of a good, or alternatively, how much they would require in compensation for a change that was not carried out. There are several CVM-formats for eliciting respondents' preferences. These can be divided into two subgroups, 'open-ended' and the referendum format (see, for example, Bateman et al., 2002). In open-ended questions the respondents are asked to state their

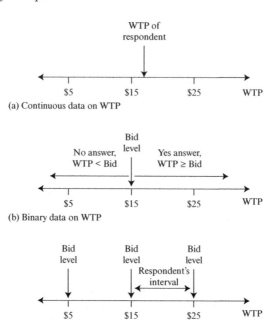

Figure 17.3   Data on WTP from CVM surveys

maximum WTP for the good, without being provided any choice alternatives. This provides the analyst with a continuous data on WTP, as illustrated in Figure 17.3a. In the referendum format the respondents are asked to answer *yes* or *no* to questions on whether or not they are willing to pay a certain amount for a specific good. Figure 17.3b shows the data from a dichotomous single-bounded WTP question, where the analyst only knows whether the true WTP is above or below the asked bid level. The analyst also has the option to collect interval data, Figure 17.3c. This can be done using either follow-up questions to a dichotomous choice question, or to provide the respondents with series of bid levels.

The major drawback of the SP methods is that they are based on hypothetical choices. In a hypothetical setting respondents may have little incentives to truthfully state their preferences. Results from experiments suggest that respondents overstate their WTP (or WTA), that is, SP studies are plagued by what is often referred to as 'hypothetical bias'. It has been suggested that the hypothetical bias can be related to unfamiliarity with the good and preference uncertainty among the respondents (Blumenschein et al., 2008; List and Gallet, 2001). To mitigate this bias, it is common practice to include questions about preference certainty, either as a quantitative or a qualitative measure, and to restrict the sample to those who are certain about their answer (Blumenschein et al., 1998, 2001, 2008; Champ et al., 1997; Champ and Bishop, 2001; Hultkrantz et al., 2006).[23]

In order to receive answers in CVM-studies that reflect the respondents' 'true' preferences, the hypothetical market scenario should be meaningful and understandable for the respondents (Carson et al., 2001). Empirical evidence suggest that people are imprecise when stating their preferences in studies on safety (Dubourg et al., 1997) and Carson et al. (2001) conclude that preference elicitation of small changes of probability using CVM is particulary problematic. This may be due to peoples difficulties in understanding small (changes in) probabilities, for which there is a wealth of evidence. Whether the problem of insensitivity to scale found in CVM studies (Hammitt and Graham, 1999) could be linked to the lack of understanding has been examined. Alberini et al. (2004) and Corso et al. (2001) find that by using proper visual aids and by training the respondents in trading wealth for safety, scale sensitivity in line with the theoretical predictions could be reached.[24] Moreover, Andersson and Svensson (2008) examine the correlation between cognitive ability among respondents and scale sensitivity. They find that respondents with a higher cognitive ability were more likely to state a WTP more in line with the theoretical predictions.

Results from the Literature

Empirical estimates of VSL

Most studies that have elicited individuals' preferences for transport safety, have done so for road fatality risk. This attention towards road risk is not surprising considering it is by far the transport mode that causes most fatalities (see, for example, Evans, 2003). Table 17.1 shows an overview of estimates of VSL, all related to road traffic.[25] As shown in the table, the magnitude of the estimates are vastly different, ranging from 150 000 (Bhattacharya et al., 2007) to ca. 36 million (McDaniels, 1992), in USD 2005 price level.

VSL is intended to reflect an affected population's preferences for a reduction in its mortality risk. Values might therefore differ, since there are 'no a priori grounds for supposing these preferences, perceptions, and attitudes need necessarily be the same' (Jones-Lee and Loomes, 1995, p. 184) across populations. For instance, Carlsson et al. (2004) examine respondents' WTP for two transport modes (without estimating VSL, therefore not included in Table 17.1), travelling by air or taxi. For the same baseline and reduction in risk, they find that WTP is significantly higher when travelling by air compared with by taxi. One explanation for their result is that respondents perceived travelling by air to be riskier, even though the risks were the same size in the survey. This could be related to how travellers perceive the controllability, voluntariness and responsibility of a risk of a specific mode. If travellers perceive risks in surface transport to be less dreadful than other transport modes (air, underground, and so forth), we expect WTP to be greater for the latter which was the finding in Carlsson et al.(2004).[26]

In Table 17.1 all studies have been conducted on road safety, but since the studies have been conducted under different contexts (for example, in different locations or point of time) and for different populations, we can still expect the values to differ. For instance, the range of values in Blomquist et al. (1996) depends on transport modes (lowest value is for motorcyclists) and who benefits from the safety measure (highest value is parents' WTP for child safety). However, values are usually more sensitive to the context, the affected population, the survey design, etc., than predicted by theory. For instance, the large interval in: (1) Andersson (2007) is due to insensitive to scale (2) Hultkrantz et al. (2006) whether the good is a public (lower value) or private safety measure and (3) McDaniels (1992) if WTP (lower value) or WTA is estimated. The findings in these three studies are representative of the WTP literature on fatality risk, as well as other non-marketed amenities (de Blaeij et al., 2003; Hammitt and Graham, 1999; Horowitz and

Table 17.1 *Empirical estimates of the value of a statistical life in road traffic, in USD 2005 (×1000)[a]*

Authors	Country	Year of data, study type	No. of esti- mates[b]	Range of VSL estimates		
				Single	Lowest	Highest
Andersson (2005a)	Sweden	1998, RP	1	1425		
Andersson (2007)	Sweden	1998, SP	8		3017	15297
Atkinson and Halvorsen (1990)	United States	1986, RP	1	5521		
Beattie et al. (1998)	UK	1996, SP	4		1510	17060
Bhattacharya et al. (2007)	India	2005, SP	1	150		
Blomquist (1979)	United States	1972, RP	1	1832		
Blomquist et al. (1996)	United States	1991, RP	4		1434	7170
Carthy et al. (1999)	UK	1997, SP	4		4528	5893
Corso et al. (2001)	United States	1999, SP	2		3517	4690
Desaigues and Rabl (1995)	France	1994, SP	6		1031	23984
Dreyfus and Viscusi (1995)	United States	1987, RP	1	4935		
Ghosh et al. (1975)	UK	1973, RP	1	1901		
Hakes and Viscusi (2007)	United States	1998, SP	5		2396	6404
	United States	1998, RP	6		2288	10016
Hojman et al. (2005)	Chile	2005,[c] SP	1	541		
Hultkrantz et al. (2006)	Sweden	2004, SP	2		2192	5781
Iragüen and Ortúzar (2004)	Chile	2002, SP	1	261		
Jara-Diaz et al. (2000)	Chile	1999, SP	1	4555		
Jenkins et al. (2001)	United States	1997, RP	9		1350	4867
Johannesson et al. (1996)	Sweden	1995, SP	4		5798	6981
Jones-Lee et al. (1985)	UK	1982, SP	1	4981		
Kidholm (1995)	Denmark	1993, SP	3		898	1338
Lanoie et al. (1995)	Canada	1986, SP	2		1989	3558
Maier et al. (1989)	Australia	1989,[c] SP	6		1853	5114
McDaniels (1992)	United States	1986, SP	3		10131	36418
Melinek (1974)	UK	1974,[c] RP	1	881		
Persson et al. (2001)	Sweden	1998, SP	1	2551		
Rizzi and Ortúzar (2003)	Chile	2000, SP	1	486		
Schwab Christe (1995)	Switzerland	1993, SP	1	1094		
Vassanadumrongdee and Matsuoka (2005)	Thailand	2003, SP	2		3208	5458
Viscusi et al. (1990)	United States	1991,[c] SP	1	11091		
Winston and Mannering (1984)	Unites States	1980, RP	1	2315		

Notes: VSL estimates in USD 2005. Values transformed using purchasing power parities (PPP) and consumer price indices (CPI) from http://stats.oecd.org, 09/02/07. (For Chile and Thailand PPP and CPI from http://www.imf.org/external/data.htm were used.)
[a] Many of the VSL estimates are from de Blaeij *et al.* (2003).
[b] Several studies contain more estimates than stated here. When available, 'preferred' values have been used.
[c] Refers to year of study rather than data, since the latter not available.

McConnell, 2002; Miller, 2000; Plott and Zeiler, 2005). Moreover, in their meta-analyses on VSL in road safety, Miller (2000) and de Blaeij et al. (2003) found that estimates from SP studies were significantly higher than estimates from RP studies.

Miscellaneous empirical findings
How VSL is influenced by different factors is important not only to examine how values may differ between socio-economic or demographic groups. The analysis also plays an important role for validity testing. The list below contains a brief review of the empirical literature on how different attributes have been found to affect the VSL.

Wealth level We know that VSL is predicted to increase with the wealth level. Even if RP and 'CVM studies do not always find a statistically significant relationship with income. . .' (Hammitt, 2000a, p. 15), the evidence that VSL increases with wealth is quite strong (de Blaeij et al., 2003; Liu et al., 1997; Miller, 2000; Mrozek and Taylor, 2002; Viscusi and Aldy, 2003). Moreover, the evidence from the RP and SP literature suggests that the income elasticity is between zero and one (Hammitt et al., 2006; Viscusi, 1993).

Baseline risk We also know that VSL should increase with the level of the baseline risk. Here the empirical evidence is mixed, with, for example, the relationship found to be: (1) positive in de Blaeij et al. (2003) and Persson et al. (2001), (2) negative in Andersson (2007) and Viscusi and Aldy (2003) and (3) non-monotonic and concave in Mrozek and Taylor (2002). Explanations why baseline risk does not always affect VSL according to theory could be sorting in the market and a difference between the perceived (that is, the risk the consumer/respondent bases his decision on) and the objective (that is, observed by the analyst) risk.

Background risk As described above, the effect of a physical background risk depends on how individuals regard it to be related to the specific risk, that is, the risk for which VSL is estimated. The empirical evidence is limited; results from a Swedish SP study suggest that the risks are perceived to be independent, that is, VSL decreases with the background risk (Andersson, 2007), whereas a Swedish RP study using the car market does not find any statistically significant correlation between the VSL and the background risk (Andersson, 2008).

Age The theoretical prediction of the effect of age on VSL is indeterminate, since the relationship is determined by the optimal consumption path which depends on assumptions on discount factors, saving opportunities and so forth. Regarding empirical evidence, the findings in most studies support that VSL follows an inverted U-shape, is declining, or is independent of age (Alberini et al., 2004, 2006b; Andersson, 2007; Hammitt and Liu, 2004; Johannesson et al., 1999; Jones-Lee et al., 1985; Krupnick, 2007; Viscusi and Aldy, 2007).[27]

Health status It is intuitive to expect that people in good health should be willing to pay more to reduce the risk of fatality, since they in a sense have more to lose. However, health may also affect the marginal utility of wealth, which may potentially have some offsetting effects (Hammitt, 2002; Strand, 2006). Moreover, health is expected to affect negatively the VSL through its positive effect on survival probabilities (the dead-anyway effect) and to affect positively the VSL through its positive effect on the future flow of incomes and from reduced health care expenditures (the wealth effect). The effect of health status on VSL is ambiguous, and the empirical evidence suggests that VSL does not vary with health status (Alberini et al., 2004, 2006b; Andersson, 2007; Smith et al., 2004).

Altruism   Regarding individuals' WTP for others' safety (health), the overall evidence seems inconclusive. Several studies have found evidence which implies that individuals are safety-paternalistic (Andersson and Lindberg, 2009; Holmes, 1990; Jacobsson et al., 2007; Vázquez Rodríguez and León, 2004). Others have found that WTP is higher among parents for their children than for themselves (Chanel et al., 2005; Dickie and Messman, 2004; Liu et al., 2000), and that WTP is higher for a safety measure for the entire household than for a measure which can only be used individually (Bateman and Brouwer, 2006; Chanel et al., 2005). However, it also seems that individuals are not willing to pay as much for others' safety as they are for their own safety, which is manifested by the empirical evidence which shows that individuals are not prepared to pay as much for a public safety measure as for a private measure (de Blaeij et al., 2003; Hultkrantz et al., 2006; Johannesson et al., 1996).

Scale sensitivity   A necessary (but not sufficient) condition for WTP answers in SP studies to be valid estimates of individuals' preferences for small mortality risk reductions is that WTP is near-proportional (increasing and slightly concave) to the size of the risk reduction (Hammitt, 2000a).[28] Corso et al. (2001) distinguish between weak and strong scale sensitivity, where weak and strong refer to an increasing and near-proportional WTP to the magnitude of the risk reduction, respectively. A consequence of a rejection of near-proportionality is that the VSL is sensitive to the change in the mortality risk (Andersson, 2007). Whereas there is often support for weak sensitivity in the empirical literature, strong sensitivity is often rejected, even though there have been some recent promising results regarding the latter (Alberini et al., 2004; Andersson and Svensson, 2008; Hammitt and Graham, 1999; Corso et al., 2001).

Mortality risk perceptions
The VSL depends on how individuals perceive mortality risks, in particular it depends on their perception of baseline risks and of probability changes. If, for instance, they perceive risks to be higher than they actually are, monetary estimates of the value of risk reductions are expected to be higher than if the public was better informed (Bleichrodt and Eeckhoudt, 2006; Gayer et al., 2000).

There is extensive, and 'strong and quite diverse' (Viscusi, 1992, p. 108) evidence that individuals are rational in their decision making involving risks in the market (Blomquist, 2004; Viscusi and Aldy, 2003), but there are also results which imply that the estimated 'risk-dollar' trade-offs may not always be accurate (Viscusi and Magat, 1987). When hypothetical markets are used to elicit individuals' WTP, there is evidence of ordinal but not cardinal risk comprehension (Hammitt and Graham, 1999). Hence, individuals seem to respond in a correct way to risks, both in hypothetical and market scenarios, but 'their ability to perceive risk in a cardinally correct way is questioned' (Blomquist, 2004, p. 99).

Lichtenstein et al. (1978) showed that individuals overassess small fatality risks and underassess large fatality risks, a pattern confirmed by the results in several other studies and today regarded as an established fact (Armantier, 2006; Benjamin and Dougan, 1997; Hakes and Viscusi, 2004; Morgan et al., 1983; Viscusi et al., 1997). Studies on risk perception have, however, used automobile risk as the 'standard anchor' (Hakes and Viscusi, 2007, p. 668). We, therefore, need to turn to the literature that has specifically examined respondents' perception of road-traffic risks to be able to draw any conclusions whether road users underassess or overassess their risk exposure from road-traffic. For instance, Hammerton et al. (1982) find evidence that 'on average subjective assessments are of a broadly similar order of magnitude to the objective ratio' (p. 192), and Persson and Cedervall (1991) that the median of the respondents' perceived risk is equal to the calculated objective risk. Andersson and Lundborg (2007) who examined respondents' perception of their own risk, find that the respondents underassess their risk, which is a result of men underassessing their fatality risk. In their study: (1) the risk perception among females is not statistically significantly different from the objective risk and (2) a similar pattern to Lichtenstein et al. (1978) is observed with only those with the lowest objective risk level (women aged 25–54) overassessing their risk.[29]

RP studies only observe individuals' choices and do not observe individuals' risk perceptions. Analysts thus need to make some assumptions about individuals' risk perceptions. They usually assume that individuals hold unbiased beliefs about mortality risks. When examining which car attributes are important for car consumers, Johansson-Stenman and Martinsson (2006) find that nearly all car consumers considered safety to be very (ca. 85 per cent) or fairly (ca. 15 per cent) important. When car dealers were asked how important car attributes were for the consumers, they stated that safety was very (ca. 54 per cent) or fairly (ca. 37 per cent) important for more than 90 per cent. If this translates into consumers seeking information, they will become well-informed and any potential bias from RP studies could be small.

Policy Use of VSL in Transport

Benefit–cost analysis (BCA) of road safety projects goes back at least 30 years (Elvik and Vaa, 2004). Early monetary values of preventing a fatality were commonly based on the HC approach (Abraham and Thedie, 1960; Persson, 2004; US DoT, 2004) and many countries still use values based on this approach (Bristow and Nellthorp, 2000; Trawén et al., 2002). Other countries adopted the concept of WTP in the early 1990s; Sweden 1990 (Persson, 2004), New Zealand 1991 (Guria et al., 2005), followed by the UK and the US in 1993 when the Department of Transport in each country decided to replace their previous policy value by preference based values (US DoT, 2004; UK DoT, 2007).

Table 2 shows policy VSL used in New Zealand, Norway, Sweden, UK and US.[30] For ease of comparison between countries and to the estimated values in Table 17.1, values have been converted to USD 2005 price level. The table reveals that the values are based on relatively old studies, that is, from the early 1990s.[31] Values have been revised since they were implemented, and new research have on those occasions been considered (Robinson, 2007; SIKA, 2005). However, policy makers have been reluctant to revise the values on grounds other than price and real income changes, which is probably a result of the uncertainty still surrounding VSL estimates.

Table 17.2   Policy VSL in use, in USD 2005 (×1000)[a]

Country	Source	Official value based on ...	VSL
New Zealand	Trawén et al. (2002)	SP study (Miller and Guria, 1991).	1790
Norway	Trawén et al. (2002)	meta-analysis (Elvik, 1993).	2051
Sweden	SIKA (2005)	SP study (Persson and Cedervall, 1991).	1996
United Kingdom	UK DoT (2007)	multi-stage approach (Carthy et al., 2000).	2308
United States	US DoT (2002)	meta-analysis (Miller, 1990).	3309

Notes: VSL estimates in USD 2005. Values transformed using purchasing power parities (PPP) and consumer price indices (CPI) from http://stats.oecd.org, 9 February 2007.
[a] In this table we only show examples of VSL used in policy. For other policy values in use of preventing a fatality see Boiteux and Baumstark (2001), Bristow and Nellthorp (2000), and Trawén et al. (2002).

It is important to recognize that individual WTP may not fully reflect the social value of traffic safety. The individual WTP may not reflect a reduction in costs to society such as medical, police surveillance, damage, and lost productivity. Jones-Lee et al. (1985) found evidence that the respondents did not take account of such other effects of the safety improvements. Therefore, in, for example, Sweden, the UK and the US, the VSL is augmented by a value that reflects these other effects (Robinson, 2007; SIKA, 2005; UK DoT, 2007). For instance, the Swedish value in Table 17.2 consists of two components: (1) marginal WTP to reduce fatality risk and (2) what is referred to as 'material costs' and consists of net loss production, other costs and medical costs (Trawén et al., 2002). Material costs are only a fraction of the total value, 7 per cent, though.

The VSL has been mostly developed and used by policy makers in the US. The major impetus for this may be related to the US executive order which imposed the use of BCA almost 30 years ago. We, therefore use the United States to relate the policy values in Table 17.2 to other areas where policy values are also used. The Office and Management Budget (OMB) has primary responsibility for writing guidelines to assist regulatory assessment and for coordinating and reviewing analyses across US federal agencies (Robinson, 2007). The OMB Circular A-4 OMB03 reports that the range of VSL estimates is usually between USD 1 and 10 million, and agencies generally use values in this range. The Environmental Protection Agency (EPA) (which is responsible for more costly federal policies and has played a significant role in the increasing use of VSL) depending on context, use values within the range USD 1 to 10 million, with a mean estimate of USD 5.5 million, whereas the Food and Drug Administration (FDA) uses a slightly lower value, USD 5 million (EPA 1999 prices, FDA no price year reported, Robinson, 2007). These values are, thus, higher than the value used by the Department of Transportation as reported in Table 17.2.[32]

Based on theoretical and empirical evidence there may sometimes be a motivation to use different VSLs for different populations. However, this suggestion is controversial since it raises issues about the equitable treatment of different segments of the population. Therefore, the adjustment of VSL made by regulatory agencies is very modest, and does not reflect the large WTP differences observed in individuals' choices. In the UK for instance, the value in Table 17.2 is used for all causes of death except cancer, where a value twice this size is applied (Baker et al., 2008). Regarding wealth levels, adjustments are made longitudinally (over time) but not cross-sectionally (across populations) since the latter is considered controversial from an ethical perspective (European Commission, 2000; Robinson, 2007). Moreover, it is noticeable that public recommendations may openly prohibit the used of differentiated VSL. OMB for instance issued a memorandum advising agencies against adjusting VSL for age (Robinson, 2007). Similarly, the European Commission states that 'it is not recommended that [VSL] values be changed according to the income of the population affected' (European Commission, 2000).

CONCLUSIONS

In this chapter, we have described from a theoretical and empirical perspective how to estimate monetary values of reducing the mortality risk in transport. We presented the standard theoretical expected utility model in a static framework, which we then extended to a multiperiod model and how different attributes affect VSL, and issues related to public provision of safety. In the empirical part, we described how preferences can be elicited, showed empirical results, and discussed how the values are used in policy making. Since the VSL concept is based on preference elicitation, it adopts the standard economic concept that individuals are the best judges of their own interests (that is, individual sovereignty). Preference elicitation requires not only good econometric practice but also a solid theoretical foundation.

The elicitation of preferences for safety has come a long way since it was introduced about four decades ago. However, old findings can be improved and new questions are raised continuously. For instance, in the example we give, the decision problem is that of a social planner who must select optimal public safety expenditures. In this framework, individuals make no decisions. However, in reality, individuals make decisions that may directly interact with the public decision. It has been argued for instance that road safety measures or automobile safety standards (for example, seat belts) may fail to save lives because safer roads or safer cars induce more dangerous driving (Peltzman, 1975). Thus the behavioral response of individuals to public action should not be ignored.[33]

Model (17.1) is based on the expected utility model. Although this model is still the dominant model in the theory of choice under risk, many alternative models have been proposed. These alternative models may better account for empirical or experimental evidence that is often inconsistent with the theoretical predictions based on expected utility. However, few studies have studied VSL using these alternative models. An exception is Bleichrodt and Eeckhoudt (2006) who assume that individuals do not evaluate probabilities linearly (Quiggin, 1982) and show that this may affect the WTP for reduction in mortality risks.[34]

Finally, it is important to remember that model (17.1) relies on a state-dependent utility framework. The comparative statics results that we have presented depend on the assumptions in (17.2), in particular, on those on the utility of death, that is, on the bequest utility. But we observe that we have little sense of what should be the sensible properties on the bequest utility, and how it should vary across the population and time. Presumably, it may vary with family structure. Moreover, there is a well known identification problem here because the subjective probabilities and the relative units of scales and origins of the state-dependent utility cannot usually be separately identified (Drèze and Rustichini, 2004; Karni, 1985), unlike within the state-independent framework.

These questions were raised relatively recently in the VSL literature, and may be the object of future research efforts. There are obviously many factors that may influence VSL, and we have considered just a few of them.

ACKNOWLEDGEMENT

We would like to thank James Hammitt and the editors, André de Palma, Robin Lindsey, Emile Quinet and Roger Vickerman, for useful comments on earlier drafts of this chapter. Financial support from the *Swedish National Road and Transport Research Institute* (VTI) and the *Chair Finance Durable et Investissement Responsable* is gratefully acknowledged. The usual disclaimers apply.

NOTES

1. For a critical discussion, see Ackerman and Heinzerling (2004).
2. Alternative terms for VSL used in the literature include micromorts (Howard, 1984), value per statistical life (Hammitt, 2000b), value per life saved (Jones-Lee, 1976) and value of prevented fatality (Jones-Lee, 2004).
3. This difference between identified and statistical lives has been illustrated by how easy it is to collect money for the treatment of a young girl, who needs expensive care to prolong her life by a short time period, once the public is aware of her condition, compared with how hard it can be to get acceptance for, for example, a tax-rise to finance health-care expenditures that would reduce the mortality risk for many, but unidentified, individuals (Josefsson et al., 1994; Pratt and Zeckhauser, 1996; Schelling, 1968). Whereas the girl constitutes an identified life, the small risk reductions enjoyed by unidentified individuals can be converted into statistical lives.
4. In compensating wage differential studies, researchers estimate additional wages paid to worker in riskier jobs, using econometric methods to control for other factors (such as education or the activity sector). The idea of compensating wage differentials dates back to Adam Smith, who noted in *The Wealth of Nations*, 'The wages of labor vary with the ease or hardship, the cleanliness or dirtiness, the honorableness or dishonorableness of the employment.' (Smith, 1776 [1976], p. 112).
5. In Ezra Mishan's words, 'there is no call for evaluating loss of life on a criterion different from that which is basic to the economist's calculation of all the other effects comprehended in cost–benefit analysis' (Mishan, 1982, p. 324).
6. See for example the following significant contributions: Bergstrom (1982), Weinstein et al. (1980), Viscusi (1993) and Viscusi and Aldy (2003).
7. For large changes in risk or when the risk change has no close substitutes (Hanemann, 1991) differences between WTP and WTA can arise.
8. The VSL can be obtained using first-order approximations of the WTP and WTA, that is by computing $C'(0)$ and $P'(0)$. We notice here that two other expressions – using equivalent variations instead of compensating variations – could also be used: i) the WTA for not implementing a risk-decreasing project and ii) the WTP for not implementing a risk-increasing project.
9. Breyer and Felder (2005) show that the dead-anyway effect does not hold anymore when annuity markets are introduced.
10. Karni (1983) introduces such a general characterization, based on the equality of the marginal utility of wealth across states.
11. Also, observe in Equation (17.6) that VSL increases in the constant relative risk aversion parameter γ.
12. The multiperiod model has also been used to examine how VSL is related to latent health risks, that is, when there is a time lag between a change in exposure and a change in health risk (for example, air pollution) (Alberini et al., 2006a; Hammitt and Liu, 2004; Johannesson and Johansson, 1996). Since the risk reduction usually is immediate in transport, this topic is not discussed in this chapter.
13. Armantier and Treich (2004) examine the social value of a project affecting mortality risks and that is

financed by distortionary taxation, *but* assume that this project is evaluated by the average VSL rule (as if there were optimal lump-sum transfers). They exhibit some conditions such that the project will be overestimated or underestimated, and thus leads to a too high or too low level of safety provision.

14. See Viscusi (2000) for an extensive discussion.
15. As Arnold Harberger (1971) put it in one of his three postulates for applied welfare economics: '[C]osts and benefits accruing to each member of the relevant group (e.g. a nation) should normally be added without regard to the individual(s) to whom they accrue' (p. 785).
16. This observation is reminiscent to the first sentence of the Thomas Schelling's seminal paper: 'It is not the worth of human life that I shall discuss, but of "life-saving", of preventing death. And it is not a particular death, but a statistical death.' (Schelling, 1968).
17. This is a paradox in the sense that the only difference between the two situations is knowing the identity of the victim. This, it may be argued (Broome, 1978), should not ultimately affect the social decision rule. Broome's (1978) provocative paper raises a number of other conceptual issues for the application of the VSL framework. Most of these issues are discussed in a set of critical papers (Buchanan and Faith, 1979; Jones-Lee, 1979; Williams, 1979).
18. Also, Jones-Lee (1992) proves that the benchmark result of Bergstrom also holds in an economy with 'pure paternalism'. An individual *i* is a pure paternalist if his 'marginal rate of substitution of *j*'s wealth for *j*'s survival probability is the same as *i*'s marginal rate of substitution of own wealth for own survival probability' (Jones-Lee, 1992, p. 86).
19. This chapter only gives an introduction and brief overview of non-market valuation. We do not discuss the econometric aspects of preference elicitation. Instead we refer to the references provided in this section, in which many econometric aspects are discussed, together with other literature on non-market valuation (for example, Bateman et al., 2002; Haab and McConnell, 2003) as well as textbooks on econometrics (for example, Wooldridge, 2002, 2003).
20. An alternative to derive society's WTP for a mortality risk reduction is 'implicit valuation' (Schelling, 1987), where social policy is assumed to express the value for the society to save 'lives'. The critique against using 'implicit valuation' to estimate VSL is that 'public tradeoffs do not directly inform about individual WTP' (Blomquist, 2004, p. 95). An interesting example of 'implicit valuation' is Ashenfelter and Greenstone (2004a, b). Ashenfelter and Greenstone use speed legislation to derive VSL. They estimated a value approximately equal to USD 1.5 million (in 1997 prices).
21. Subscripts in Figure 17.2b denote derivatives of functions with respect to the argument in the subscript.
22. Whether the demand function can be identified using single market data in Rosen's two-step procedure has been under considerable debate (Brown and Rosen, 1982; Ekeland et al., 2002). One of two approaches can be followed to recover the preference parameters: i) impose a structure of non-linearity of the system (Ekeland et al., 2002, 2004), or ii) use multi market data where the HPFs differ between the markets (Brown and Rosen, 1982; Palmquist, 1991). Both approaches have been criticized, the former since often restrictions on the model are imposed that are unjustified from an economic perspective (Ohsfeldt and Smith, 1985; Epple, 1987), and the latter since the identification strategy often is "logically inconsistent" (Ekeland et al., 2002, p. 307).
23. The hypothetical nature of preference elicitation also gives rise to other types of bias (see *e.g.*, Bateman et al., 2002, pp. 302-303).
24. The visual aid that worked the best in Corso et al. (2001) was an array of dots. The same aid has been used in other studies with less success (Andersson, 2007; Jones-Lee et al., 1985; Persson et al., 2001).
25. The inclusion of VSL only for road traffic was a result of our literature review and was not intentional. We make no claim that the list of VSL studies in transport is complete, though.
26. Jones-Lee and Loomes (1995), using an implicit valuation approach, found that a WTP based VSL for Underground (Subway) risk should be approximately 50 per cent higher compared with its road counterpart.
27. VSL is sometimes converted to the value per statistical life-year (VSLY) (Alberini and Krupnick, 2002). This conversion relies on the assumption that VSL declines with age (Hammitt, 2007).
28. Note that in the first step of the hedonic technique, marginal WTP is estimated and therefore scale sensitivity is not an issue.
29. The pattern of overassessment of small risks and underassessment of large risks may follow the prediction that individuals update their risk perceptions in a Bayesian fashion (Dickie and Gerking, 1996; Gayer et al., 2000; Hakes and Viscusi, 1997; Smith and Johnson, 1988; Viscusi, 1989). This updating process is of interest to SP studies on mortality risk, since respondents might combine their prior beliefs with the values in the survey and state their WTP for this updated risk reduction (instead of the one presented in the survey) (Corso et al., 2001; Hammitt and Graham, 1999).
30. We again make no claim that the list of values is complete.
31. After the Exxon Valdez oil spill the NOAA (National Oceanic and Atmospheric Administration) panel was formed to examine issues in damage compensation (NOAA, 1993). The NOAA Panel's

recommendations of preference elicitation using SP techniques have had a major impact on later studies and contributed to more precise SP estimates, which is why studies conducted prior to NOAA can be considered relatively old.

32. As a comparison, recommended policy value for EU is € 1.0 million with a range of € 0.65 to 2.5 million (2000 prices) (European Commission, 2000).
33. See Gossner and Picard (2005) and Viscusi (1994) for some early studies on the interaction of private and public protection measures.
34. See also Treich (2007) who shows that VSL is always higher under ambiguity aversion (Klibanoff et al., 2005). Other models that could potentially be applied to VSL may include the prospect theory model (Kahneman and Tversky, 1979), regret/disappointment models (Bell, 1985; Loomes and Sugden, 1982) and the more recent reference-dependent models (see, for example, Köszegi and Rabin, 2007).

REFERENCES

Abraham, C. and J. Thedie, 1960, Le prix d'une vie humaine dans les décisions économiques. *Revue Française de Reserche Opérationnelle*, **4**, 157–167.

Ackerman, F. and L. Heinzerling, 2004, *Priceless: On Knowing the Price of Everything and the Value of Nothing*. New York: The New Press.

Alberini, A., M. Cropper, A. Krupnick and N.B. Simon, 2004, Does the value of a statistical life vary with the age and health status? Evidence from the USA and Canada. *Journal of Environmental Economics and Management*, **48** (1), 769–792.

Alberini, A., M. Cropper, A. Krupnick and N.B. Simon, 2006a, Willingness to pay for mortality risk reductions: does latency matter? *Journal of Risk and Uncertainty*, **32** (3), 231–245.

Alberini, A., A. Hunt and A. Markandya, 2006b, Willingness to pay to reduce mortality risks: evidence from a three-country contingent valuation study. *Environmental and Resource Economics*, **33** (2), 251–264.

Alberini, A. and A. Krupnick, 2002, *The International Yearbook of Environmental and Resource Economics 2002/2003*. In T. Tietenberg and H. Folmer, eds, Cheltenham, UK: Edward Elgar, pp. 233–277.

Aldy, J.E. and W.K. Viscusi, 2007, Age differences in the value of statistical life: revealed preference evidence. *Review of Environmental Economics and Policy*, **1** (2), 241–260.

Andersson, H., 2005a, The value of safety as revealed in the Swedish car market: an application of the hedonic pricing approach. *Journal of Risk and Uncertainty*, **30** (3), 211–239.

Andersson, H., 2005b, Willingness to pay for a reduction in road mortality risk: evidence from Sweden. Ph.D. Thesis, Lund Economic Studies 126, Dept. of Economics, Lund University, Lund, Sweden.

Andersson, H., 2007, Willingness to pay for road safety and estimates of the risk of death: evidence from a Swedish contingent valuation study. *Accident Analysis and Prevention*, **39** (4), 853–865.

Andersson, H., 2008, Willingness to pay for car safety: evidence from Sweden. *Environmental and Resource Economics*, **41** (4), 579–594.

Andersson, H. and G. Lindberg, 2009, Benevolence and the value of road safety. *Accident Analysis and Prevention*, **41** (2), 286–293.

Andersson, H. and P. Lundborg, 2007, Perception of own death risk: an analysis of road-traffic and overall mortality risks. *Journal of Risk and Uncertainty*, **34** (1), 67–84.

Andersson, H. and M. Svensson, 2008, Cognitive ability and scale bias in the contingent valuation method. *Environmental and Resource Economics*, **39** (4), 481–495.

Armantier, O., 2006, Estimates of own lethal risks and anchoring effects. *Journal of Risk and Uncertainty*, **32** (1), 37–56.

Armantier, O. and N. Treich, 2004, Social willingness to pay, mortality risks and contingent valuation. *Journal of Risk and Uncertainty*, **29** (1), 7–19.

Arrow, K.J., 1971, *Essays in the Theory of Risk-Bearing*. Wisbech, UK: Markham Publishing Company.

Ashenfelter, O. and M. Greenstone, 2004a, Estimating the value of a statistical life: the importance of omitted variables and publication bias. *American Economic Review*, **94** (2), 454–460.

Ashenfelter, O. and M. Greenstone, 2004b, Using mandated speed limits to measure the value of a statistical life. *Journal of Political Economy*, **112** (1), 226–267.

Atkinson, S.E. and R. Halvorsen, 1990, The valuation of risks to life: evidence from the market for automobiles. *Review of Economics and Statistics*, **72** (1), 133–136.

Baker, R., S. Chilton, M. Jones-Lee and H. Metcalf, 2008, Valuing lives equally: defensible premise or unwarranted compromises? *Journal of Risk and Uncertainty*, **36** (2), 125–138.

Ballard, C.L. and D. Fullerton, 1992, Distortionary taxes and the provision of public goods. *Journal of Economic Perspectives*, **6** (3), 117–131.

Bateman, I.J. and R. Brouwer, 2006, Consistency and construction in stated WTP for health risk reductions: a novel scope-sensitivity test. *Resource and Energy Economics*, **28** (3), 199–214.

Bateman, I.J., R.T. Carson, B. Day, M. Hanemann, N. Hanley, T. Hett, M. Jones-Lee, G. Loomes, S. Mourato, Özdemiroglu, D.W. Pearce, R. Sugden and J. Swanson, 2002, *Economic Valuation with Stated Preference Techniques: A Manual.* Cheltenham, UK: Edward Elgar.

Beattie, J., J. Covey, P. Dolan, L. Hopkins, M.W. Jones-Lee, G. Loomes, N. Pidgeon, A. Robinson and A. Spencer, 1998, On the contingent valuation of safety and the safety of contingent valuation. Part 1: Caveat Investigator. *Journal of Risk and Uncertainty*, **17** (1), 5–25.

Bell, D.E., 1985, Disappointment in decision making under uncertainty. *Operations Research*, **33** (1), 1–28.

Benjamin, D. and W.R. Dougan, 1997, Individuals' estimates of the risks of death. Part I: a reassessment of the previous evidence. *Journal of Risk and Uncertainty*, **15** (2), 115–133.

Bergstrom, T.C., 1982, When is a man's life worth more than his human capital? M.W. Jones-Lee, ed., Chapt. *The Value of Life and Safety* Amsterdam, The Netherlands: North-Holland, pp. 3–26.

Bergstrom, T.C., 2006, Benefit–cost in a benevolent society. *American Economic Review*, **96** (1), 339–351.

Bhattacharya, S., A. Alberini and M.L. Cropper, 2007, The value of mortality risk reductions in Delhi, India. *Journal of Risk and Uncertainty*, **34** (1), 21–47.

Blackorby, C. and D. Donaldson, 1990, A review article: the case against the use of the sum of compensating variations in cost–benefit analysis. *Canadian Journal of Economics*, **23** (3), 471–494.

Bleichrodt, H. and L. Eeckhoudt, 2006, Willingness to pay for reductions in health risks when probabilities are distorted. *Health Economics Letters*, **15** (2), 211–214.

Blomquist, G.C., 1979, Value of life saving: implications of consumption activity. *Journal of Political Economy*, **87** (3), 540–558.

Blomquist, G.C., 2004, Self-protection and averting behavior, values of statistical lives, and benefit cost analysis of environmental policy. *Review of Economics of the Household*, **2** (1), 89–110.

Blomquist, G.C., T.R. Miller and D.T. Levy, 1996, Values of risk reduction implied by motorist use of protection equipment. *Journal of Transport Economics and Policy*, **30** (1), 55–66.

Blumenschein, K., G.C. Blomquist, M. Johannesson, N. Horn and P. Freeman, 2008, Eliciting willingness to pay without bias: evidence from a field experiment. *Economic Journal*, **118** (525), 114–137.

Blumenschein, K., M. Johannesson, G.C. Blomquist, B. Liljas and R.M. O'Conor, 1998, Experimental results on expressed certainty and hypothetical bias in contingent valuation. *Southern Economic Journal*, **65** (1), 169–177.

Blumenschein, K., M. Johannesson, K.K. Yokoyama and P.R. Freeman, 2001, Hypothetical versus real willingness to pay in the health care sector: results from a field experiment. *Journal of Health Economics*, **20** (3), 441–457.

Boiteux, M. and L. Baumstark, 2001, Transports: choix de investissements et coût des nuisances. Mimeo, Commissariat General du Plan.

Breyer, F. and S. Felder, 2005, Mortality risk and the value of a statistical life: the dead-anyway effect revis(it) ed. *The Geneva Papers on Risk and Insurance Theory*, **30** (1), 41–55.

Bristow, A.L. and J. Nellthorp, 2000, Transport project appraisal in the European Union. *Transport Policy*, **7**, 51–60.

Broome, J., 1978, Trying to value a life. *Journal of Public Economics*, **9**, 91–100.

Brown, J.N. and H.S. Rosen, 1982, On the estimation of structural hedonic price models. *Econometrica*, **50** (3), 765–768.

Buchanan, J.M. and R.L. Faith, 1979, Trying again to value a life. *Journal of Public Economics*, **12** (2), 245–248.

Carlsson, F., O. Johansson-Stenman, and P. Martinsson, 2004, Is transport safety more valuable in the air. *Journal of Risk and Uncertainty*, **28** (2), 147–163.

Carson, R.T., N.E. Flores and N. F. Meade, 2001, Contingent valuation: controversies and evidence. *Environmental and Resource Economics*, **19** (2), 173–210.

Carthy, T., S. Chilton, J. Covey, M.W. Hopkins, Lorraine Jones-Lee, G. Loomes, N. Pidgeon and A. Spencer, 1999, On the contingent valuation of safety and the safety of contingent valuation. Part 2: The CV/SG Chained Approach. *Journal of Risk and Uncertainty*, **17** (3), 187–213.

Carthy, T., S. Chilton, J. Covey, M.W. Hopkins, Lorraine Jones-Lee, G. Loomes, N. Pidgeon and A. Spencer, 2000, Valuation of benefits of health and safety control. Final report, Health and Safety Executive Publications Unit, London, UK.

Champ, P.A., and R.C. Bishop, 2001, Donation payment mechanism and contingent valuation: an empirical study of hypothetical bias. *Environmental and Resource Economics*, **19** (4), 383–402.

Champ, P.A., T.C. Brown and D.W. McCollum, 1997, Using donation mechanisms to value nonuse benefits from public goods. *Journal of Environmental Economics and Management*, **33** (2), 51–162.

Chanel, O., S. Luchini and J. Shogren, 2005, Does charity begin at home for pollution reductions? Document de Travail 57, GREQAM.

Conley, B., 1976, The value of human life in the demand for safety. *American Economic Review*, **66** (1), 45–55.

Cook, P.J., 1978, The value of human life in the demand for safety: comment. *American Economic Review*, **68** (4), 710–711.

Corso, P.S., J.K. Hammitt and J.D. Graham, 2001, Valuing mortality-risk reduction: using visual aids to improve the validity of contingent valuation. *Journal of Risk and Uncertainty*, **23** (2), 165–184.

de Blaeij, A., R.J.G.M. Florax, P. Rietveld and E. Verhoef, 2003, The value of statistical life in road safety: a meta-analysis. *Accident Analysis and Prevention*, **35** (6), 973–986.

Desaigues, B. and A. Rabl, 1995, Reference values for human life: an econometric analysis of a contingent valuation in france. In N.G. Schwab Christe and N.C. Soguel, eds. *Contingent Valuation, Transport Safety and the Value of Life*. Norwell, MA: Kluwer Academic Publishers, pp. 87–112.

Dickie, M. and S. Gerking, 1996, Formation of risk beliefs, joint production and willingness to pay to avoid skin cancer. *Review of Economics and Statistics*, **78** (3), 451–463.

Dickie, M. and V.L. Messman, 2004, Parental altruism and the value of avoiding acute illness: are kids worth more than parents? *Journal of Environmental Economics and Management*, **48** (3), 1146–1174.

Dreyfus, M.K. and W.K. Viscusi, 1995, Rates of time preference and consumer valuations of automobile safety and fuel efficiency. *Journal of Law and Economics*, **38** (1), 79–105.

Drèze, J.H., 1962, L'Utilité Sociale d'une Vie Humaine. *Revue Française de Reserche Opérationnelle*, **6**, 93–118.

Drèze, J.H. and N.H. Stern, 1987, The theory of cost–benefit analysis. In A.J. Auerbach and M. Feldstein, eds, *Handbook of Public Economics,* Amsterdam: North-Holland, pp. 909–989.

Drèze, J.H. and A. Rustichini, 2004, State-dependent utility and decision theory. In S. Barbera, P.J. Hammond and C. Seidl, eds, *The Handbook of Utility Theory,* Dordrecht, The Netherlands: Kluwer Academic Publisher, pp. 839–892.

Dubourg, W.R., M.W. Jones-Lee and G. Loomes, 1997, Imprecise preferences and survey design in contingent valuation. *Economica*, **64**, 681–702.

Eeckhoudt, L.R. and J.K. Hammitt, 2001, Background risks and the value of a statistical life. *Journal of Risk and Uncertainty*, **23** (3), 261–279.

Eeckhoudt, L.R. and J.K. Hammitt, 2004, Does risk aversion increase the value of mortality risk? *Journal of Environmental Economics and Management*, **47** (1), 13–29.

Ekeland, I., J.J. Heckman and L. Nesheim, 2002, Identifying hedonic models. *American Economic Review*, **92** (2), 304–309.

Ekeland, I., J.J. Heckman and L. Nesheim, 2004, Identification and estimation of hedonic models. *Journal of Political Economy*, **112** (1), 60–109.

Elvik, R. and T. Vaa, 2004, *The Handbook of Road Safety Measures*. Oxford: Elsevier.

Elvik, R., 1993, Økonomiskt versetting av velferdskap ved traikkulykker. TØI Rapport 203/1993, The Institute of Transport Economics, Oslo, Norway.

Epple, D., 1987, Hedonic prices and implicit markets: estimating demand and supply functions for differentiated products. *Journal of Political Economy*, **95** (1), 59–80.

European Commission, 2000, Recommended interim values for the value of preventing a fatality in DG environment cost benefit analysis. Mimeo Available at: http://europa.eu.int/comm/environment/enveco/others/recommended _interim_values.pdf.

Evans, A.E., 2003, Accident fatalities in transport. *Journal of the Royal Statistical Society*, **166** (2), 253–260.

Freeman, A.M., 2003, *The Measurement of Environmental and Resource Values*, 2nd edn. Washington DC: Resources for the Future.

Garber, A.M. and C.E. Phelps, 1997, Economic foundations of cost-effectiveness analysis. *Journal of Health Economics*, **16** (1), 1–31.

Gayer, T., J.T. Hamilton and W.K. Viscusi, 2000, Private values of risk tradeoffs at superfund sites: housing market evidence on learning about risk. *Review of Economics and Statistics*, **82** (3), 439–451.

Ghosh, D., D. Lee and W. Seal, 1975, Optimal motorway speed and some valuations of time and life. *The Manchester School*, **43**, 134–143.

Gossner, O. and P. Picard, 2005, On the consequences of behavioral adaptations in the cost-benefit analysis of road safety measures. *Journal of Risk and Insurance*, **72** (4), 577–599.

Guria, J., J. Leung, M. Jones-Lee and G. Loomes, 2005, The willingness to accept value of statistical life relative to the willingness to pay value: evidence and policy implications. *Environmental and Resource Economics*, **32** (1), 133–127.

Haab, T.C. and K.E. McConnell, 2003, *Valuing Environmental and Natural Resources: The Econometrics of Non-Market Valuation*. Cheltenham, UK: Edward Elgar.

Hakes, J.K. and W.K. Viscusi, 1997, Mortality risk perceptions: a bayesian reassessment. *Journal of Risk and Uncertainty*, **15** (2), 135–150.

Hakes, J.K. and W.K. Viscusi, 2004, Dead reckoning: demographic determinants of the accuracy of mortality risk perception. *Risk Analysis*, **24** (3), 651–664.

Hakes, J.K. and W.K. Viscusi, 2007, Automobile seatbelt usage and the value of statistical life. *Southern Economic Journal*, **73** (3), 659–676.

Hammerton, M., M.W. Jones-Lee and V. Abbott, 1982, The consistency and coherence of attitudes to physical risk. *Journal of Transport Economics and Policy*, **16** (1), 181–199.

Hammitt, J.K., 2000a, Evaluating contingent valuation of environmental health risks: the proportionality test. *AERE (Association of Environmental and Resource Economics) Newsletter*, **20** (1), 14–19.

Hammitt, J.K., 2000b, Valuing mortality risk: theory and practice. *Environmental Science and Technology*, **34** (8), 1396–1400.

Hammitt, J.K., 2002, QALYs versus WTP. *Risk Analysis*, **22** (5), 985–1001.

Hammitt, J.K., 2007, Valuing changes in mortality risk: lives saved versus life years saved. *Review of Environmental Economics and Policy*, **1** (2), 228–240.

Hammitt, J.K. and J.D. Graham, 1999, Willingness to pay for health protection: inadequate sensitivity to probability? *Journal of Risk and Uncertainty*, **18** (1), 33–62.

Hammitt, J.K. and J.-T. Liu, 2004, Effect of disease type and latency on the value of mortality risk. *Journal of Risk and Uncertainty*, **28** (1), 73–95.

Hammitt, J.K. and N. Treich, 2007, Statistical vs. identified lives in benefit-cost analysis. *Journal of Risk and Uncertainty*, **35** (1), 45–66.

Hammitt, J.K., J.-T. Liu and J.-L. Liu, 2006, Is survival a luxury good? The increasing value of a statistical life. Mimeo, Harvard Center for Risk Analysis, Boston, USA.

Hanemann, W.M., 1991, Willingness to pay and willingness to accept: how much can they differ? *American Economic Review*, **81** (3), 635–647.

Harberger, A.C., 1971, Three basic postulates for applied welfare economics: an interpretative essay. *Journal of Economic Literature*, **9** (3), 785–797.

Hojman, P., J. d. D. Ortúzar, and L.I. Rizzi, 2005, On the joint valuation of averting fatal and severe injuries in highway accidents. *Journal of Safety Research*, **36**, 377–386.

Holmes, T.P., 1990, Self-interest, altruism, and health-risk reduction: an economic analysis of voting behavior. *Land Economics*, **66** (2), 140–149.

Horowitz, J.K. and K.E. McConnell, 2002, A review of WTA/WTP studies. *Journal of Environmental Economics and Management*, **44**, 426–447.

Howard, R.A., 1984, On fates comparable to death. *Management Science*, **30** (4), 407–422.

Hultkrantz, L., G. Lindberg and C. Andersson, 2006, The value of improved road safety. *Journal of Risk and Uncertainty*, **32** (2), 151–170.

Iragüen, P. and J. d. D. Ortúzar, 2004, Willingness-to-pay for reducing fatal accident riks in urban areas: an internet-based web page stated preference survey. *Accident Analysis and Prevention*, **36**, 513–524.

Jacobsson, F., M. Johannesson and L. Borgquist, 2007, Is altruism paternalistic? *Economic Journal*, **117**, 761–781.

Jara-Diaz, S., T. Galvez and C. Vergara, 2000, Social valuation of road accident reductions. *Journal of Transport Economics and Policy*, **34**, 215–232.

Jenkins, R.R., N. Owens and L. B. Wiggins, 2001, Valuing reduced risks to children: the case of bicycle safety helmets. *Contemporary Economic Policy*, **19** (4), 397–408.

Jenni, K.E. and G. Loewenstein, 1997, Explaining the identifiable victim effect. *Journal of Risk and Uncertainty*, **14** (3), 235–257.

Johannesson, M. and P.-O. Johansson, 1996, To be, or not to be, that is the question: an empirical study of the WTP for an increased life expectancy at an advanced age. *Journal of Risk and Uncertainty*, **13** (2), 163–174.

Johannesson, M., G.C. Blomquist, K. Blumenschein, P.-O. Johansson, B. Liljas and R.M. O'Conor, 1999, Calibrating hypothetical willingness to pay responses. *Journal of Risk and Uncertainty*, **18** (1), 21–32.

Johannesson, M., P.-O. Johansson and R.M. O'Connor, 1996, The value of private safety versus the value of public safety. *Journal of Risk and Uncertainty*, **13** (3), 263–275.

Johansson-Stenman, O. and P. Martinsson, 2006, Honestly, why are you driving a BMW? *Journal of Economic Behavior & Organization*, **60** (2), 129–146.

Johansson, P.-O., 2002, On the definition and age-dependency of the value of a statistical life. *Journal of Risk and Uncertainty*, **25** (3), 251–263.

Jones-Lee, M.W., 1974, The value of changes in the probability of death or injury. *Journal of Political Economy*, **82** (4), 835–849.

Jones-Lee, M.W., 1976, *The Value of Life: An Economic Analysis*. Chicago, IL: University of Chicago Press.

Jones-Lee, M.W., 1979, Trying to value a life: why Broome does not sweep clean. *Journal of Public Economics*, **12** (2), 249–256.

Jones-Lee, M.W., 1991, Altruism and the value of other people's safety. *Journal of Risk and Uncertainty*, **4**, 213–219.

Jones-Lee, M.W., 1992, Paternalistic altruism and the value of statistical life. *Economic Journal*, **102** (410), 80–90.

Jones-Lee, M.W., 2004, Valuing international safety externalities: does the golden rule apply? *Journal of Risk and Uncertainty*, **29** (3), 277–287.

Jones-Lee, M.W. and G. Loomes, 1995, Scale and context effects in the valuation of transport safety. *Journal of Risk and Uncertainty*, **11** (3), 183–203.

Jones-Lee, M.W., M. Hammerton and P. Philips, 1985, The value of safety: results of a national sample survey. *The Economic Journal*, **95** (377), 49–72.

Josefsson, J., G. Hermerén and N.-E. Sahlin, 1994, Ethical Aspects of Valuing Lives. In B. Brehmer and N.-E. Sahlin,eds., *Future Risks and Risk Management*. Dordrecht, The Netherlands: Kluwer Academic Publishers, pp. 93–123.

Kahneman, D. and A. Tversky, 1979, Prospect theory: an analysis of decision under risk. *Econometrica*, **47** (2), 263–291.

Kaplow, L., 2005, The value of a statistical life and the coefficient of relative risk aversion. *Journal of Risk and Uncertainty*, **31** (1), 23–34.

Karni, E., 1983, Risk aversion for state-dependent utility functions: Measurement and applications. *International Economic Review*, **24** (3), 637–647.

Karni, E., 1985, *Decision-Making under Uncertainty: The Case of State-Dependent Preferences*. Cambridge, MA: Harvard University Press.

Keeler, E.B., 2001, The value of remaining lifetime is close to estimated values of life. *Journal of Health Economics*, **20** (1), 141–143.

Kidholm, K., 1995, Assessing the value of traffic safety using contingent valuation technique: the Danish Survey. In N.G. Schwab Christe and N.C. Soguel, eds, *Contingent Valuation, Transport Safety and the Value of Life*. Norwell, MA: Kluwer Academic Publishers, pp. 45–62.

Klibanoff, P., M. Marinacci and S. Mukerji, 2005, A smooth model of decision making under ambiguity. *Econometrica*, **73** (6), 1849–1892.

Köszegi, B. and M. Rabin, 2007, Reference-dependent risk attitudes. *American Economic Review*, **97** (4), 1047–1073.

Krupnick, A., 2007, Mortality risk valuation and age: stated preference evidence. *Review of Environmental Economics and Policy*, **1** (2), 261–282.

Lanoie, P., C. Pedro and R. Latour, 1995, The value of a statistical life: a comparison of two approaches. *Journal of Risk and Uncertainty*, **10**, 235–257.

Lichtenstein, S., P. Slovic, B. Fischhoff, M. Layman and B. Combs, 1978, Judged frequency of lethal events. *Journal of Experimental Psychology: Human Learning and Memory*, **4** (6), 551–578.

List, J.A. and C.A. Gallet, 2001, What experimental protocol influence disparities between actual and hypothetical stated values. *Environmental and Resource Economics*, **20**, 241–254.

Liu, J.-T., J.K. Hammitt, and J.-L. Liu, 1997, Estimated hedonic wage function and value of life in a developing country. *Economics Letters*, **57** (3), 353–358.

Liu, J.-T., J.K. Hammitt, J.-D. Wang and J.-L. Liu, 2000, Mother's willingness to pay for her own and her child's health: a contingent valuation study in Taiwan. *Health Economics*, **9** (4), 319–326.

Loomes, G. and R. Sugden, 1982, Regret theory: an alternative theory of rational choice under uncertainty. *Economic Journal*, **92** (368), 805–824.

Maier, G., S. Gerking and P. Weiss, 1989, The economics of traffic accidents on Australian roads: risk lovers or policy deficit? *Empirica-Australian Economic Papers*, **16**, 177–192.

Max, W., H.-Y. Sung, D.P. Rice and M. Michel, 2004, Valuing human life: estimating the present value of lifetime earnings. Mimeo, University of California, San Francisco.

McDaniels, T.L., 1992, Reference points, loss aversion, and contingent values for auto safety. *Journal of Risk and Uncertainty*, **5** (2), 187–200.

Melinek, S.J., 1974, A method of evaluating human life for economic purposes. *Accident Analysis and Prevention*, **6**, 103–114.

Miller, T.R., 1990, The plausible range for the value of life: red herrings among the mackerel. *Journal of Forensic Economics*, **3**, 17–40.

Miller, T.R., 2000, Variations between countries in values of statistical life. *Journal of Transport Economics and Policy*, **34** (2), 169–188.

Miller, T.R. and J. Guria, 1991, The value of statistical life in New Zealand. Land Transport Division, Ministry of Transport, Wellington, New Zealand.

Mishan, E.J., 1971, Evaluation of life and limb: a theoretical approach. *Journal of Political Economy*, **79** (4), 687–705.

Mishan, E.J., 1982, *Cost–Benefit Analysis*, 3rd edn. London: George Allen & Unwin.

Mitchell, R.C. and R.T. Carson, 1989, *Using Surveys to Value Public Goods. Resources for the Future*, Oxford: RFF Press.

Morgan, M.G., et al., 1983, On judging the frequency of lethal events: a replication. *Risk Analysis* 3(1), 11–16.

Mrozek, J.R. and L.O. Taylor, 2002, What determines the value of life? A meta-analysis. *Journal of Policy Analysis and Management*, **21** (2), 253–270.

Needleman, L., 1976, Valuing other people's lives. *Manchester School of Economic and Social Studies*, **44** (4), 309–342.

NOAA, 1993, Report of the NOAA Panel on Contingent Valuation. Federal Register 58.

Ohsfeldt, R.L. and B.A. Smith, 1985, Estimating the demand for heterogenous goods. *Review of Economics and Statisitcs*, **67** (1), 165–171.

Palmquist, R.B., 1991, Hedonic methods. In J.B. Braden and C.D. Kolstad, eds, *Measuring the Demand for Environmental Quality*. Amsterdam, The Netherlands: Elsevier Science Publishers (North-Holland), pp. 77–120.

Peltzman, S., 1975, The effects of automobile safety regulation. *Journal of Political Economy*, **83** (4), 677–725.

Persson, U., 2004, Valuing reductions in the risk of traffic accidents based on empirical studies in Sweden. Ph.D. Thesis, Bulletin 222, Dept. of Technology and Society, Lund University, Lund, Sweden.

Persson, U. and M. Cedervall, 1991, The value of risk reduction: results of a Swedish sample survey. IHE Working Paper 1991:6, The Swedish Institute for Health Economics.

Persson, U., A. Norinder, K. Hjalte and K. Gralén, 2001, The value of a statistical life in transport: findings from a new contingent valuation study in Sweden. *Journal of Risk and Uncertainty*, **23** (2), 121–134.

Plott, C.R. and K. Zeiler, 2005, The willingness to pay-willingness to accept gap, the 'endowment effect', subject misconceptions, and experimental procedures for eliciting valuations. *American Economic Review*, **95** (3), 530–545.

Pratt, J.W., 1964, Risk aversion in the small and in the large. *Econometrica*, **32**, 122–136.

Pratt, J.W. and R.J. Zeckhauser, 1996, Willingness to pay and the distribution of risk and wealth. *Journal of Political Economy*, **104** (4), 747–763.

Quiggin, J., 1982, A theory of anticipated utility. *Journal of Economic Behavior and Organization*, **3** (4), 323–343.

Rizzi, L.I. and J.d.D. Ortúzar, 2003, Stated preference in the valuation of interurban road safety. *Accident Analysis and Prevention*, **35**, 9–22.

Rizzi, L.I. and J.d.D. Ortúzar, 2006a, Estimating the willingness-to-pay for road safety Imporvements. *Transport Reviews*, **26** (4), 471–485.

Rizzi, L.I. and J.d.D. Ortúzar, 2006b, Road safety valuation under a stated choice framework. *Journal of Transport Economics and Policy*, **40** (1), 69–94.

Robinson, L.A., 2007, How US government agencies value mortality risk reductions. *Review of Environmental Economics and Policy*, **1** (2), 283–299.

Rosen, S., 1974, Hedonic prices and implicit markets: product differentiation in pure competition. *Journal of Political Economy*, **82** (1), 34–55.

Rosen, S., 1988, The value of changes in life expectancy. *Journal of Risk and Uncertainty*, **1** (3), 285–304.

Samuelson, P.A., 1954, The theory of pure provision of public expenditures. *Review of Economics and Statistics*, **36**, 387–389.

Schelling, T.C., 1968, The life you save may be your own. In S.B. Chase, ed., *Problems in Public Expenditure Analysis*. Washington DC: The Brookings Institution, pp. 127–162.

Schelling, T.C., 1987, *The New Palgrave: A Dictionary of Economics*. London: Macmillan Press Limited.

Schwab Christe, N.G., 1995, The valuation of human costs by the contingent valuation method: the Swiss experience. In N.G. Schwab Christe and N.G. Soguel, eds, *Contingent Valuation, Transport Safety and the Value of Life*. Norwell, MA: Kluwer Academic Publishers, pp. 19–44.

Sen, A.K., 1973, *On Economic Inequality*. Oxford: Oxford University Press.

Shepard, D.S. and R.J. Zeckhauser, 1984, Survival versus consumption. *Management Science*, **30** (4), 423–439.

SIKA, 2005, Kalkylvärden och kalkylmetoder – En sammanfattning av Verksgruppens rekommendationer 2005. Pm 2005:16, SIKA (Swedish Institute for Transport and Communications Analysis), Stockholm, Sweden.

Smith, A., 1776 [1976], *An Inquiry into the Nature and Causes of The Wealth of Nations*. Chicago IL: The University of Chicago Press.

Smith, V.K. and F.R. Johnson, 1988, How do risk perceptions respond to information? The case of Radon. *Review of Economics and Statistics*, **70** (1), 1–8.

Smith, V.K., M.F. Evans, H. Kim and D.H. Taylor, 2004, Do the near-elderly value mortality risks differently? *Review of Economics and Statistics*, **86** (1), 423–429.

Somanathan, E., 2006, Valuing lives equally: distributional weights for welfare analysis. *Economic Letters*, **90**, 122–125.

Strand, J., 2006, Valuation of environmental improvements in continuous time with mortality and morbidity effects. *Resource and Energy Economics*, **28** (3), 229–241.

Trawén, A., P. Maraste and U. Persson, 2002, International comparison of costs of a fatal casualty of road accidents in 1990 and 1999. *Accident Analysis and Prevention*, **34**, 323–332.

Treich, N., 2007, The value of statistical life under ambiguity aversion. Mimeo, LERNA, Toulouse School of Economics.

UK DoT, 2007, 2005 Valuation of the benefits of prevention of road accidents and casualities. Highway Economics Note No. 1, UK Department of Transportation (DOT).

US DoT, 2002, Revised departmenatal guidance: treatment of value of life and injuries in preparing economic evaluations. Memorandum, US Department of Transportation (DOT).

US DoT, 2004, Revision of departmenatal guidance on treatment of value of life and injuries. US Department of Transportation (DOT): Office of Economic and Strategic Analysis. Available at: http://ostpxweb.ost.dot.gov/policy/EconStrat/treatmentoflife.htm, 10/4/07.

US OMB, 2004, Circular A-4, Regulatory analysis. Office and Management Budget (OMB), Information qualilty guidelines.

Vassanadumrongdee, S. and S. Matsuoka, 2005, Risk perceptions and value of statistical life for air pollution and traffic accidents: evidence from Bangkok, Thailand. *Journal of Risk and Uncertainty*, **30** (3), 261–287.

Vázquez Rodríguez, M.X. and C.J. León, 2004, Altruism and the economic values of environmental and social policies. *Environmental and Resource Economics*, **28** (2), 233–249.

Viscusi, W.K., 1989, Prospective reference theory: toward an explanation of the paradoxes. *Journal of Risk and Uncertainty*, **2** (3), 235–263.

Viscusi, W.K., 1992, *Fatal Tradeoffs: Public and Private Responsibilities for Risk*. New York: Oxford University Press.

Viscusi, W.K., 1993, The value of risks to life and health. *Journal of Economic Literature*, **31** (4), 1912–1946.

Viscusi, W.K., 1994, Mortality effects of regulatory costs and policy evaluation criteria. *Rand Journal of Economics*, **25**, 94–109.

Viscusi, W.K., 2000, Risk equity. *Journal of Legal Studies*, **29** (2), 843–871.

Viscusi, W.K. and J.E. Aldy, 2003, The value of a statistical life: a critical review of market estimates throughout the world. *Journal of Risk and Uncertainty*, **27** (1), 5–76.

Viscusi, W.K. and J.E. Aldy, 2007, Labor market estimates of the senior discount for the value of a statistical life. *Journal of Environmental Economics and Management*, **53** (3), 377–392.

Viscusi, W.K. and W.A. Magat, 1987, *Learning About Risk: Consumer and Worker Response to Hazard Warnings*. Cambridge, MA: Harvard University Press.

Viscusi, W.K., J.K. Hakes and A. Carlin, 1997, Measures of mortality risks. *Journal of Risk and Uncertainty*, **14** (3), 213–233.

Viscusi, W.K., W.A. Magat and J. Huber, 1990, Pricing environmental risks: survey assessment of risk-risk and risk-dollar trade-offs for chronic bronchitis. *Journal of Environmental Economics and Management*, **21**, 32–51.

Weinstein, M.C., D.S. Shepard and J.S. Pliskin, 1980, The economic value of changing mortality probabilities: a decision-theoretic approach. *Quarterly Journal of Economics*, **94** (2), 373–396.

Williams, A., 1979, A note on trying to value a life. *Journal of Public Economics*, **12** (2), 257–258.

Winston, C. and F. Mannering, 1984, Consumer demand for automobile safety: new evidence on the demand for safety and the behavioral response to safety regulation. *American Economic Review*, **72** (2), 316–319.

Wooldridge, J.M., 2002, *Econometric Analysis of Cross Section and Panel Data*. Cambridge, MA: Massachusetts Institute of Technology.

Wooldridge, J.M., 2003, *Introductory Econometrics: A Modern Approach*, 2nd edn. Mason, OH: Thomson, South-Western.

Yaari, M.E., 1965, Uncertain lifetime, life insurance, and the theory of the consumer. *Review of Economics Studies*, **32** (2), 137–150.

18 Transport and energy
Kenneth Button

INTRODUCTION

To move anything requires an expenditure of energy. Transport, therefore, is by definition a user of energy. The amount and types of energy that are used, however, have varied considerably over time as technology has changed. For a long time, much it used to be in the form of the food given to animals, beasts-of-burden or simply human consumption of calories in various forms. Renewable sources of energy, wind and water-power in particular, have been widely exploited and still are although often in somewhat different ways. Wind power, for example, is more often used indirectly as a means of generating electricity than for propelling ships or Chinese wheelbarrows. With the exception of some less developed countries where the beast of burden often still plays a major role, much of modern transport since the advent of the steam engine has relied on non-renewable sources of energy such as coal, oil and natural gas.

The levels of current and projected future use of oil by the transport industries are particularly impressive. While there are national differences between countries, Table 18.1, for example, provides some information on both the absolute and relative final demand for energy in the European Union, including forecasts of likely use in the future. The transport sector accounted for some 80 per cent of the energy demand growth between 1990 and 2000, and became the largest demand sector. The predominant role of the transport sector in final energy demand growth is projected to continue under EU baseline assumptions until 2010 but beyond that policy initiatives and technological progress lead to a deceleration and an eventual decline of transport energy needs.

Table 18.1   *Final energy demand by sector in EU-25 in million tons of oil equivalent (Mtoe)*

	Mtoe				
	1990	2000	2010	2020	2030
Industry	341.1	330.1	356.4	382.4	391.6
energy intensive	216.8	211.6	220.8	228.4	224.9
other	124.3	118.4	135.7	154.0	166.6
Domestic	407.6	432.3	500.5	550.6	576.6
residential	261.0	273.3	312.0	338.7	351.3
tertiary	146.6	159.0	188.5	211.9	225.3
Transport	273.2	333.0	381.1	405.5	402.3
Total	1021.9	1095.4	1238.0	1338.5	1370.5

Source: European Commission (2006); forecasts for 2010, 2020 and 2030.

Transport, however, is still expected to account for 30 per cent of final energy demand in 2030, remaining the largest single consumer.

One factor contributing to the rise in energy demand for transport is the technology changes that have taken place, and in particular the increasing use of road transport. In 2003, the number of registered cars and heavy vehicles (trucks and buses) was, respectively, around 589 million and 224 million worldwide, and had increased at rates of 2.7 per cent and 3.0 per cent annually between 1993 and 2003. The US Department of Energy has estimated that unchecked, the global vehicle fleet will increase to 3500 million by 2050 with vehicle numbers in developed countries doubling and those in developing nations increasing 15-fold. The International Energy Agency (2005) reports that nearly 58 per cent of global petroleum consumption was by transport in 2003, and forecasts are for this proportion growing at least to 2020. In the United States, some 21 million barrels of oil are consumed daily, with 5.8 million being burned by transport, and forecast by the US Department of Energy, Energy Information Administration (2006) to rise to 26 million barrels by 2030, with gasoline accounting for about 45 per cent of this.

It is not just the number of vehicles that matter, but also technology. For example, the average new passenger car in Europe consumes about 6.5 liters of fuel per 100 kilometers, whereas the average passenger car in the United States uses over 40 per cent more over the same distance. Part of this can be explained in terms of distances traveled: more frequent and longer trips in the United States may be seen to justify more 'comfortable' vehicles but, in addition, there are important taxation differences. Retail gasoline prices in Europe include taxes in the range of 60 per cent to 75 per cent, compared with only 20 per cent to 25 per cent in the United States. There may also be cultural differences in the ways various societies see large, less fuel-efficient vehicles, but these are more difficult to quantify.

In the past, interest in energy use was largely parochial in nature, concerned with the short- to medium-term needs for commerce and military activities. An army marched on its stomach, and on the stomachs of the mules, horses and oxen in its baggage train. The prime objective of logistics in this context was to supply the energy, largely fodder, which had to go into those stomachs. Empires have always been dependent on reliable transport and as they expanded one of their primary logistics concerns was to have adequate energy to ensure such communications were secured; the British Empire's 'coaling stations' for its military and commercial marine activities in Victorian times are a classic example. But recently, with the expansion of globalization, the extensive use of motorized transport and the widespread depletion of liquid based carbon fuel reserves, combined with the environmental damage associated with their use, the interest in energy has ceased to be purely a local affair. Not only is the energy used in transport substantial, its combustion is also a major contributor to greenhouse gas emissions and security in its supply is central consideration in the geopolitical power game.

THE USE OF ENERGY BY THE TRANSPORT INDUSTRIES

Transportation is not homogeneous and can be broken down in a number of ways to reflect its use of energy. The focus here is largely on the use of non-renewable energy resources, and especially oil, but the data is not always transparent in that sense.[1] For

Table 18.2   Fuel consumption by main transport modes (United States)

	1980	1990	2000	2003	2004
Highway					
Gasoline, diesel and other fuels (million gallons)	114960	130755	162555	170069	173750
Truck;	19960	24490	35229	32696	33968
Single-unit 2-axle 6-tire or more truck	6923	8357	9563	8880	9263
Combination truck	13037	16133	25666	23815	24705
Truck (percent of total)	17.4	18.7	21.7	19.2	19.6
Rail, Class I (freight service)					
Distillate/diesel fuel (million gallons)	3904	3115	3700	3826	4059
Water					
Residual fuel oil (million gallons)	8952	6326	6410	3874	4690
Distillate/diesel fuel oil (million gallons)	1478	2065	2261	2217	2140
Gasoline (million gallons)	1052	1300	1124	1107	1005
Pipeline					
Natural gas (million cubic feet)	634622	659816	642210	591492	571853

Source: Association of American Railroads (2005); US Department of Energy (2004); US Department of Energy, Energy Information Administration (2005); US Department of Transportation, Federal Highway Administration (2005).

example, electricity may be the direct energy source for many rail systems and local trams, but electricity can be generated in a variety of ways; from oil, natural gas, coal, nuclear sources, hydro power, wind-power and so on. Given considerable variations in the efficiency of generating plants, what one would really like is an indicator of the amount of fossil fuel used to provide the energy to produce a given unit of transportation. Additionally, most of the data available on energy consumed in transport relates to the final movement. It offers few insights into the full costs of transport provisions that embrace also the energy needed to supply and maintain transport infrastructure and the manufacture and maintenance of vehicles. We also have limited knowledge on the way transport affects use of resources in the broader economy – for example, on the effect that transport intensive industries such as tourism have on energy consumption in final production such as hotels, restaurants and the manufacturing of souvenirs, as well as in the movement of the tourists themselves.[2]

Table 18.2 looks at energy consumption by various transport modes in the United States. The dominant role of gasoline as an energy source is clear and reflects the widespread use of automobiles for personal travel. Other countries have somewhat different relative patterns that depend, in part, on the nature and size of their national economies and geography – for example, whether they produce and move large amounts of raw materials – but also on the transport policies that have been favored – for example, whether public transport has been strongly supported and the levels of fuel taxation that have been deployed.

Table 18.3   Transport modes energy use: absolute and relative, China, 1990–2000 in thousand tons of oil equivalent (ktoe).

Mode	Energy Consumption in ktoe		Ratio	Consumption Share		Change
	1990	2000	2000/1990	1990	2000	
Railways	14851	13017	0.88	27.8%	13.5%	−14.2%
Highways	25495	65516	2.57	47.6%	68.1%	+20.5%
Waterways	11407	11 988	1.05	21.3%	12.5%	−8.8%
Civil Aviation	1222	5 090	4.16	2.3%	5.3%	+3.0%
Pipelines	550	605	1.10	1.0%	0.6%	−0.4%
Total	53 524	96 214	1.80	100.0%	100.0%	0.0%

Source: China Energy Research Society (2002).

Until 1990, much of the policy interest in energy consumption by transport and resultant public debates focused on its use in developed Western economies. The subsequent rapid economic expansions of large developing countries, especially India and China, have led to a shift in focus. With rapid economic growth and aggressive expansion of transportation infrastructure, for example, China saw a four-fold increase in freight traffic and a six-fold increase in passenger traffic between 1980 and 2000. Cars for short trips and planes for long trips increasingly dominate passenger traffic in the country, as growing incomes have allowed more people to utilize these fast and comfortable means of travel. From 1980 through 2002, passenger traffic grew over six-fold, from 228 billion to 1413 billion person-km. Passenger highway traffic grew ten-fold, its share of total passenger traffic increasing from 32 per cent to 55 per cent. Passenger aviation traffic grew more than 30-fold, its share of passenger traffic growing five-fold to 9 per cent. Railway passenger traffic, while nearly quadrupling in volume, saw its share of passenger traffic decline from 61 per cent to 35 per cent. However, average annual growth in highway traffic share has slowed from 3.7 per cent in the late 1980s to 1.9 per cent in the early 1990s to 1.2 per cent in the late 1990s to 0.9 per cent between 2000 and 2002.

As the result of the rapid traffic growth and the changing modal split, the transport share of national energy use grew from under 5 per cent in 1996 to nearly 9 per cent in 1999. The share of energy used by road transport in China officially grew from roughly 48 per cent in 1990 to 68 per cent in 2000, and most of this is in the form of oil consumption (Table 18.3). The share of civil aviation also grew rapidly albeit from a very much lower base.[3]

Most of the analysis of transport energy use focuses on its importance in moving vehicles of one form or another, but both the mobile plant used in transporting goods and people and the infrastructure it relies on require significant amounts in their construction and maintenance. While difficult to quantify, for example, the production of over 50 million cars, nearly 14 million light commercial vehicles and three million heavy commercial vehicles in 2006 obviously consumed an immense amount of energy.

TRANSPORT AND DISTORTIONS IN THE ENERGY MARKET

There is an intellectual curiosity about the links between transport and energy use, but there are also important public policy issues to be considered. Energy is used in virtually all forms of activity and there is a need to ensure that it is used to maximum effect and in ways that ensure any external effects are not excessive. In economic terms, the market for energy is, however, far from perfect for a variety of reasons. These stem partly from the intrinsic nature of the 'commodity' (largely associated with market failures linked to economies of scale in supply and externalities), but can also be due to the institutional environment in which energy is provided (especially government intervention failures that often are seen in terms of allocating property rights and regulatory capture). These imperfections, in turn, affect the ways in which transport users view energy and the ways in which they use it, and the forms and quantities in which it is supplied.

Renewability of Resources

Much of the energy used in transport comes from finite sources – oil reserves, coal and natural gas. In economic terms, this is not a major issue if prices are appropriate and reflect the genuine, long-term opportunity cost of the use of these resources. In many cases the drawing down of the reserves of these resources may still be consistent with a genuinely sustainable scenario in the Brundtland Report sense, if at the same time alternative energy sources are being created – for example, the creation of hydroelectric or wind capacity. In terms of the notion of sustainable development, future generations will still have the same resource base as the current one, albeit it in a different form.

The challenge with this situation is to ensure that there are mechanisms and signals to ensure that the energy base is not depleted by excessive use for transport. In the past there have been significant shifts in the energy used in transport, with coal, and then oil, taking over from oars and sail for shipping, for example. Market forces have largely been driving these shifts; slaves became expensive as rowers, and sailing ships being too unreliable for expanding trade networks and hence steam ships took over. One thing that has been learned, however, is that predicting the depletion rate of a resource, and thus trying to plan for alternatives, is difficult. Stanley Jevons's famous concern in 1865 that coal supplies would soon be exhausted and, in consequence, the rail and steam ship industry would, amongst others, become nonviable is a good example of how static analysis linking non-renewable resource depletion and transport can be misleading. But equally, the move from wood to coal, and then to oil boilers on ships showed how the market can respond to potential shortages through stimulating the development of alternative technologies and leading to efforts to extract economically more of the scarce resource.

The economic problem here is that, for markets to function, they must have appropriate price signals. The semi-cartelization of many energy markets, with institutions such as OPEC (Organization of the Petroleum Exporting Countries), and also of many markets that supply the hardware (mobile plant) of transport, such as the automobile and airframe manufacturers, coupled with political involvement means that these signals are far from perfect. Consequently, the exploitation of non-renewable resources is seldom optimal. And this is irrespective of any externality considerations. The issue

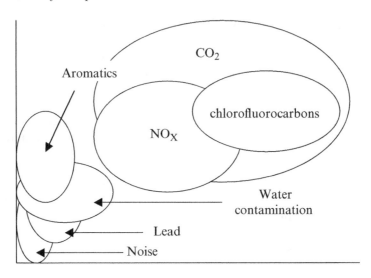

Figure 18.1   The range and duration of transport produced environmental effects

here, however, is more of a generic one rather than being transport specific because these market and institutional failures extend across all uses of energy.

Energy Use and the Environment

The physical external environmental effects associated with the energy consumed by transport come in various forms and impact on different groups. Transport is now generally recognized as a major contributor to greenhouse gas emissions, most notably CO_2, as well as imposing other, more localized environmental costs on society (Figure 18.1). The results of these side effects can be damage to human health, as with potential brain damage to children from lead additives used to improve the efficiency of internal combustion engines or the cancer inducing effects of aromatics.[4] Traffic noise of various types affects sleep and can cause hearing problems at extreme levels. The environmental effects may also take the form of damage to flora and fauna, as with sulphur and NO_x emissions that can produce acid rain. Geography can influence the effects of atmospheric pollution. A number of major cities in the world, for example, including Mexico City, Athens and Los Angeles suffer from periodic build-ups of local pollution because of their microclimates while acid rain is blown from industrial areas of Europe over areas of forest in Scandinavia. The movement of transportation fuels can also pose environmental hazards as seen in storage tank fires and leaks, and in maritime oil spills. While not considered in detail here, some countries, such as France, use significant amounts of nuclear energy both for electric-powered transport and also in the transport hardware-producing industries, such as car manufacturing, that may result in longer term environmental concerns about storage of expended fuels, potential radiation leaks and movement of fuels.

While many of the links between the various implications of the pollutants emitted by transport and the energy used result in local or regional environmental and health problems, some are much more wide ranging as, for example, in the link between carbon fuels

Table 18.4 *Contributions of individual transport modes to overall transport CO$_2$ emissions and to total CO$_2$ emissions in the UK (2006)*

	Million tons	% of UK domestic transport CO$_2$ emissions	% of UK total CO$_2$ emissions
Road transport	120.5	69.5	20.2
Railways	2.2	1.3	0.2
Domestic aviation	2.3	1.3	0.2
Domestic shipping	5.5	3.2	0.9
All domestic transport	*130.5*	*75.3*	*21.5*
International aviation	35.6	20.5	6.0
International shipping	6.8	3.9	1.1
Other transport	0.5	0.3	0.1
All transport emissions	*173.4*	*100*	*28.7*
UK CO$_2$ emissions	597.2		

Source: European Environmental Agency.

use and CO$_2$, the main global warming gas, emissions. CO$_2$ and other greenhouse gas emissions are a global concern and their exact implications for particular geographical regions over time are still uncertain. What is generally agreed is that if global warming is a long-term phenomenon it will adversely affect the economies of lower lying areas and reduce the agricultural output of some other areas.

The nature and scale of emissions vary according to mode of transport, the ways in which transport is used and across countries. The United States transport system, as an example, is estimated to contribute about 37 per cent of global CO$_2$ emissions stemming from transport use, mainly because of the country's high level of automobile ownership and the low fuel efficiency of its car fleet. The situation is somewhat different in most European countries that tend to be relatively less transport intensive in general and where vehicle fleets are more fuel efficient, In more detail, Table 18.4 offers some data on the amounts of CO$_2$ emissions associated with UK transport[5] in aggregate it contributes slightly less than 30 per cent of national emissions for that country.[6]

Road transport is the largest direct contributor to global transport greenhouse gas emissions, accounting for 76 per cent of the sector's contribution, with rail transport contributing another 2 per cent water transport 10 per cent and international air transport 7 per cent (World Business Council for Sustainable Development, 2004). These figures do not include the emissions associated with the electricity generated from oil and coal for railway use and with the energy used up in the production and maintenance of transport vehicles and infrastructure.

While there is a correlation between the energy expended by transport and the environmental damage that may result, the link is far from perfect. Table 18.5 provides some information on energy use and a somewhat wider range of pollutants.[7] Again this is in aggregate and the details can differ considerably by particular circumstance. There is clearly a strongly link between energy use and CO$_2$ emissions, but the correlations involving other environmental effects are far more varied.

Table 18.5   Energy use and emissions per passenger kilometer for long-distance trips

		Energy (MJ/p-km)	CO_2	Emissions (g/p-km)		
				NO_X	Volatile organic compounds	SO_2
Aircraft	500 km	2.2	160	0.47	0.06	0.05
	1500 km	1.6	115	0.40	0.03	0.05
Car	Gasoline, 2 occupants	1.5	110	0.08	0.03	0.02
	Diesel, 2 occupants	1.3	100	0.39	0.05	0.03
	Diesel, 1 occupant	3.2	235	0.76	0.09	0.07
Train	High speed	0.7	40	0.24	0.01	0.06
	Conventional	0.8	50	0.28	0.01	0.07
Coach		0.3	20	0.29	0.02	0.01

Source: Roos et al. (1997).

The market distortions come not from the environmental damage per se but rather from situations where the perpetrators are not paying for the implications of their actions. The users of energy in their transportation activities are seldom cognizant of the environmental costs that they are imposing, and even less often made to pay for these costs in any way. The various energy sources exploited in transport have differing impacts on the environment and, as was seen in Table 18.4, even where a single source is deployed its impact can vary with how the mode is used, in this case by distance.

Institutional Issues

The prices of energy alternatives confronting transport users are heavily distorted, not just because of market failures but also by institutional intervention failures. The energy market is manipulated not simply in an attempt to correct for externalities and other failures, but also to meet a range of other objectives such as securing supplies for national defense or ensuring universal minimum supplies. Energy is also a large part of many people's expenditure, and manipulation of its price is widespread to meet political objectives. Even when interventions are aimed at remedying market distortions, they can fail to meet their objectives or do so with unforeseen adverse consequences (Organisation for Economic Cooperation and Development, 1992).

Conflicting policy objectives can often lead, for example, to the exacerbation of market failures or changes in their nature. The widespread removal of lead from gasoline in most industrial economies during the 1980s was aimed at reducing brain damage to children, for example, but it also not only resulted in the introduction of cancer-inducing aromatics into fuel to retain its performance but also reduced fuel efficiency with consequential impacts on greenhouse gas emissions. Equally, high taxes on diesel fuel can have the effect of reducing sulphur and particulate emissions but, given lower pump prices for gasoline, discourage the use of more fuel-efficient diesel vehicles.

Many of these types of problems arise from simple lack of information – for example, the replacement of lead with aromatics was at a time when the adverse health effects of the latter were not fully appreciated. It should also be remembered that concerns with global warming are relatively recent, and, therefore social attitudes to CO_2 emissions have not traditionally focused on them. This type of information paucity is common in many markets and influences the formulation of regulations in most sectors. It could be argued that many of these issues are independent of market or regulatory considerations; we simply do not know the information and it takes time to gain it. But counter to this, governments set much of the framework in which research is done, establishes priorities, and often provides considerable funding to support it. It is thus, perhaps, more of an issue of whether this information gathering is done and disseminated effectively rather than it being captured by vested interests or the subject of poor management.

There are also larger institutional challenges confronting policy makers. Political boundaries, both between countries and within many countries, are often arbitrary in nature and frequently the result of some historical 'accident'. They seldom provide sensible geographical entities for making optimal decisions in any area, and transport and energy concerns are no exceptions. Transport is a mobile user of energy, making local policy making problematic, and is increasingly crossing legal jurisdictions, making policies with more global significance difficult to formulate and enforce. The generation of NO_X is largely in urban areas but its adverse impacts are mainly felt downwind in agricultural regions, often in another country, that have no say in what cities do. Equally, the main transport sources of CO_2 emissions are wealthier nations, but it is the poorer agricultural and coastal nations that are forecast to be most severely affected by global warming.

International Energy Markets

Market forces largely determine the price of oil, which is the main transport energy source, although there are imperfections due to the oligopolistic nature of the oil extracting and refining companies, and efforts to control the market by international cartels, notably OPEC. While the market may be seen as 'effectively competitive' in the short term, there are periodic exogenous shocks that affect the market. These are generally associated with political instability in oil producing countries; 'political risk'. It is in this context that bodies such as the International Energy Agency (IEA) have been created to provide both information about trends and potential disruptions and to facilitate an easiest transition at times of shocks to the market.

The international nature of the energy market inevitably influences national policies regarding transport. Oil is increasingly supplied from countries with unstable political regimes and in many places, proven reserves have, for political reasons, previously been overstated. These two reasons have encouraged the industrialized economies to economize on fuel consumption in general, and to seek alternative sources of energy, both in terms of new deposits of conventional fuels and the development of new fuels. This international uncertainty, coupled with rising demands, largely explain the eight-fold rise in crude oil prices in the decade to 2007.

Second-best Issues

While markets for the fuel used in transport seldom produce a Pareto optimal outcome, the extent to which this results in serious resource misallocations also depends upon the price of other resources used in transport as well as on other activities that are either complements or substitutes for transport. For overall relative efficiency, if there are deviations from optimal pricing elsewhere this may require second-best adjustments in transport energy markets to compensate.

The second-best issue, when prices other than those for fuel are not set to marginal price, may involve the relative share of different forms of transport (for example, the differential taxation of aviation fuel compared with automobile fuel) or alternative fuels for the same mode of transport (for example, the taxation of fuel used in the business use of a vehicle and its use for leisure purposes). The difficulty here is that while market manipulations using, say, subsidies or taxes may bring balance to the various transport markets, they may well distort markets overall. Transport subsidies, say, to public transit to attract travelers from private cars for fuel economy reasons will, if energy prices elsewhere in the economy reflect marginal costs, lead to an excess of energy consumption in the transport sector overall. In simple terms, a subsidy to one mode reduces the overall costs of transport in aggregate.

Because of the nature of institutional structures, however, it is seldom possible to bring a holistic focus when policy making. The result is thus generally a second-best situation with individual government departments setting targets based upon political criteria and incomplete information, and there being further fragmentation of the process as one moves down through the state (in federal systems) and local levels.[8]

Strategic Issues

Transport is a major lubricant of modern economies and relies heavily on oil for its energy source. There is a mismatch, however, between those nations that produce oil, or have significant reserves for future exploitation, and those that are the major consumers. For example, the United States imports about 60 per cent of its oil and Japan nearly 100 per cent. Additionally, many of the sources of oil are in some of the least politically stable parts of the world, not to say the least physically hospitable, leading to uncertainties in long-term supply and volatile price fluctuations in the short-term global market.

From an economic perspective, the question is the extent to which this uncertainty (in Knight's (1921) sense of there being no calculable probability) represents a market failure or whether it is a matter of risk that markets handle through a variety of 'insurance' mechanisms. The availability of such things as strategic reserves and the coordinating functions of bodies such as the International Energy Agency, offer, at a cost, some degree of protection against short-term volatility in the transport energy market. A similar function is served by the availability of non-oil based sources of energy – for example, nuclear and hydro-generated energy – as well as 'gasoline' produced from vegetable products such as sugar cane and maize. Some defense expenditures may also come into this category – Dellucchi and Murphy (2004), for example, estimated that the United States spends about $0.005 to $0.60 per US gallon of gasoline in this way, a rather large amount compared to estimates of the uninternalized cost of gasoline (that is, that not covered by some insurance mechanism) that have been put at zero to $0.20 per US barrel of gasoline in 2005 prices by other authors (Leiby et al., 1997).

POLICY OPTIONS FOR ALTERING ENERGY USE

In theory, a wide-range of policy tools can be deployed to affect the energy use of transport. Each has its particular characteristics and usefulness depending on the context in which they are deployed. The aim here is not to attempt to be comprehensive and try to discuss all possible measures, nor to go into great depth regarding those that are covered, but rather to be selective and focuses on some of the more important efforts that have been made to influence fuel consumption in transport. In particular, longer-term policies involving land-use and such policies as 'compact-city' design are explicitly omitted. These are large and multi-dimensional topics in their own rights and take us beyond the boundaries of a chapter such as this.

Although theoretically there are numerous ways to influence energy use, a wide range of practical and political factors determine the policies that have been initiated to influence the energy consumption in transportation.[9] In some cases the costs of introducing, monitoring, and policing some policies simply make them impractical, or at least in the purest forms.[10] In other cases there may also be trade-offs between improving energy efficiency and meeting other objectives, such as removing pollutants from the atmosphere or ensuring an acceptable level of traffic safety. An example of the former has been the removal of lead from gasoline in many countries that reduces the fuel efficiency of internal combustion engines.[11]

Politically, issues of technological efficiency, including energy efficiency, are often seen as less important than other objectives such as equity. This, for example, is often an argument that is used against fuel or carbon taxes that are seen as being regressive in their impacts. Politics is also, even in democracies, prone to capture by particular groups, or more often coalitions of interests, that may be hostile to certain types of instruments that will impact adversely on them. The most obvious of these lobbying groups involve energy producing industries but also can involve those with an interest in providing transport equipment or hardware.

The policy tools that are in place, or have been used, to influence the type of fuel used in transport, as well as the aggregate consumption, are, nevertheless, quite extensive.

The Role of the Market

One policy option that is often forgotten is to leave things to the market. After all while there are market failures, there are also government intervention failures that may either worsen an existing market failure or cause serious and unexpected distortions elsewhere in the system (Organisation for Economic Co-operation and Development, 1992).

In practice, the market has been a significant influence on the types and amount of energy used by transport. Historically, for example, changes in prices have demonstrable medium and long term impacts on overall energy consumption in transport, most of which have only been appreciated in retrospect. Not all these, however, have been directly related to the price of fuel. A simple transmission mechanism illustrates the difficulty that policy makers encounter in trying to foresee energy changes and plan for the development of new technologies. At the beginning of the twentieth century, automobiles were expensive and coal-powered (either directly or after transformation into electricity) railways systems dominated surface transport. The energy effect came about following

Table 18.6   Fuel efficiency of US cars following the 1973 and 1979 'oil crises'

Miles per US gallon	Real price of gasoline			(1967 = 100)
	City	Highway	Harmonic mean	
1968	12.59	18.42	14.69	97.3
1969	12.60	18.62	14.74	95.4
1970	12.59	19.0'	'4.85	98.0
1971	12.27	18.18	14.37	87.6
1972	12.15	18.90	14.48	85.9
1973	12.01	18.07	14.15	88.7
1974	12.03	18.23	14.21	108.3
1975	13.68	19.45	15.79	106.0
1976	15.23	21.27	17.46	105.3
1977	15.99	22.26	18.31	103.7
1978	17.24	24.48	19.89	100.5
1979	17.70	24.60	20.25	122.2
1980	20.35	29.02	23.51	149.6
1981	21.75	31.12	25.16	150.8
1982	22.32	32.76	26.06	134.7
1983	22.21	32.90	26.01	126.1
1984	22.67	33.69	26.59	119.2

Source: Crandall et al. (1986).

the introduction of mass production initially by Fiat in Italy, and then on a larger scale by Henry Ford in the United States, to take advantage of the high car prices of the time. This brought down the costs of car production and subsequently the price of cars (from $910 in current dollars for a touring Model-T in 1910 to $367 in 1925). In turn, this led to more use of cars and trucks (sales of the touring models were 16 890 units in 1910 rising to 691 212 in 1925) with a resultant switch in transportation away from coal, then the primary energy source, to oil. In the East German economy of the 1960s, market forces were largely ignored when policy moves towards greater car ownership at administered prices were initiated. The resultant centrally planning outcomes were the Wartburg and Trabant cars, and, by the time the Berlin Wall came down, there was a waiting time of nearly ten years to receive your not very comfortable, reliable or efficient vehicle. The complexity of planning the design and production of cars proved too complex for even the highly skilled planners of East Germany.

   Fuel prices themselves have also powerful influences on consumption. Where there have been shortages of some forms of energy, either because of physical factors or institutional, markets can bring about changes. In the past there have been shortages of oil for political reasons. While there are short-term adjustment issues, the long-term effect of fuel shortages and price increases is that fuel is used more efficiently. As an example, Table 18.6 shows the impact on the fuel efficiency of the US car fleet after the oil crises of 1973 and 1979. It is clear that the average energy efficiency of vehicles rose following both crises, albeit with a lag as the adjustment took place.[12] A more recent survey bringing together work on long term gasoline fuel price elasticities indicates that about 20 per cent to 60 per cent of the effect of price on fuel consumption appears to be due to changes in the vehicle miles driven, with 40 per cent to 80 per cent being due to changes in fleet composition (Parry et al., 2007).[13] A more general rule of thumb, suggested by Goodwin et al. (2004) after reviewing numerous empirical studies, is that fuel consumption elasticities are greater than traffic elasticities, generally by factors of 1.5 to 2.00.

Taxes

Energy, because of the relative inelasticity of aggregate demand for its use, has traditionally been the subject of taxation. In many cases this has been for purely sumptuary purposes, but in other cases, as with the federally earmarked gasoline tax in the United States, it has been used as proxy charge for some related consumption item; in the United States case to pay for the use of the road. In other cases, there have been environmental motivations, for example, the differential taxes applied to gasoline and diesel fuels in many countries.

Examples of taxes on the energy used by transport abound. The US Energy Tax Act of 1979, for instance, is a law passed as part of the National Energy Act. One element of the act created the 'gas-guzzler tax' applying to sales of vehicles with official estimated gas mileage below certain levels. In 1980, the tax was $200 for a fuel efficiency of 14 to 15 miles per gallon, and was increased to $1800 in 1985. In 1980, the tax was $550 for fuel efficiencies of 13 mpg and below, and was changed in 1986 to $3850 for ratings below 12.5 mpg. The gas-guzzler tax only applied to cars under 6000 pounds, which made sports utility vehicles and other large passenger cars exempt.

In terms of using taxation as an instrument for encouraging energy conservation, or changes in the energy source used for environmental reasons, carbon taxes have been adopted in a number of countries. These are not transport specific but are more holistic in their intent of making optimal use of resources more generally, although their impacts on transport are often large. In 1991, Sweden, for example, placed a tax of $100 per ton on the use of oil, coal, natural gas, liquefied petroleum gas, petrol and aviation fuel used in domestic travel. Industrial users paid half the rate (between 1993 and 1997, 25 per cent of the rate), and certain high-energy industries such as commercial horticulture, mining, manufacturing and the pulp and paper industry were fully exempted from these new taxes. In 1997, the rate was raised to $150 per ton of CO_2 released. Finland, the Netherlands and Norway also introduced carbon taxes in the 1990s.

In other cases, however, efforts at introducing such policies have failed. In 2005, New Zealand proposed a carbon tax to take effect from April 2007, and applied across most economic sectors but the policy was abandoned in December 2005. Similarly, in 1993, President Bill Clinton proposed a British Thermal Unit (BTU) tax that was never adopted.[14]

Subsidies

To try to stimulate the use of more fuel efficient modes of transport there has traditionally been a fairly widespread use of subsidies. These are politically attractive, largely because they involve a defuse contributor base but a focused receptor base. We exclude here the plethora of subsidies that are designed primarily to meet social objectives, such as ensuring acceptable levels of mobility, meeting the needs of the physically disadvantaged and providing access to remote regions, but are concerned explicitly with subsidies aimed at changing travel patterns with the objective of encouraging more energy efficient travel.[15]

In terms of surface personal travel, the conventional wisdom is that an efficient public transport system, with adequate load factors is more energy efficient than the automobile.[16] There are general issues regarding subsidies, such as whether it is reasonable to use taxes collected from the general public to essentially subsidize public transport and car users, and whether it is possible to have an efficient subsidy regime that is not highly X-inefficient and captured by the transport providing agencies and their employees. But from a pure efficiency perspective, there has to be a significant cross elasticity of demand between modes for public transport subsidies to be effective. Dargay and Hanly (1999), however, found that the long run cross-elasticity of car ownership with respect to transit fares is 0.4, while the elasticity of car use with respect to transit fares is 0.3.[17] In general, a relatively large fare reduction is required to attract motorists to use public transport, and in particular buses, although there seems to be more sensitivity to public transport service improvements (service frequency, reliability, and so forth). Over time, however, as incomes have risen public transport demand has in general become more price inelastic and, indeed, is often seen as an inferior good.

Vehicles Standards

Rather than directly regulate or use the pricing mechanism, there have been efforts to influence energy consumption by legislating on the design of vehicles. The details adopted vary and here we just highlight some of the issues by looking at the US case. The corporate average fuel economy (CAFE) standards, first enacted by the US Congress in 1975, are federal regulations sought to improve fuel economy in the wake of the 1973 Arab oil embargo. The regulations initially applied to the sales-weighted average fuel economy, expressed in miles per gallon, of a manufacturer's fleet of current model year passenger cars or light trucks with a gross vehicle weight rating of 8500 lbs or more, manufactured for sale in the United States. Light trucks not exceeding 8500 lbs gross vehicle weight rating do not have to comply with CAFE standards; some half a million vehicles in 1999. From early 2004, the average new car has had to exceed 27.5 mpg and light trucks exceed 20.7 mpg. Trucks under 8500 lbs must average 22.5 mpg in 2008, 23.1 mpg in 2009 and 23.5 mpg in 2010. After this, new rules set varying targets based on truck size 'footprint'.

The US National Highway Traffic Safety Administration (NHTSA) regulates CAFE standards and the Environmental Protection Agency (EPA) measures vehicle fuel efficiency. Congress specifies that CAFE standards must be set at the 'maximum feasible level' given consideration for technological feasibility; economic practicality; effect of other standards on fuel economy; and need of the nation to conserve energy. If the average fuel economy of a manufacturer's annual fleet of car and/or truck production falls below the defined standard, the manufacturer pays a financial penalty. Fuel efficiency is highly negatively correlated to vehicle weight, but weight has been considered by many safety experts to be positively correlated with safety, intertwining the issues of fuel economy, road-traffic safety, air pollution and global warming. Hence, historically, the EPA has encouraged consumers to buy more fuel-efficient vehicles while NHTSA has expressed concerns that this leads to smaller, less safe vehicles. More recent studies tend to discount the importance of vehicle weight to traffic safety, concentrating instead on the quality of engineering design of vehicles.[18] However, there is concern that safety is compromised with a mix of vehicles that vary greatly in weight (White, 2004).

Speed Limits

Engines of all types perform differently at different speeds and each has an optimal fuel performance speed. Given the operational cycle of any transport activity, as a generalization more energy is expended at the beginning of a movement, and in some cases at the end, than during cruise. It is possible, therefore, to influence the energy efficiency of a transport system by regulating the speeds at which individual units operate over it. Privately supplied transport operations, such as shipping and airlines, have financial incentives to conserve energy and, other things being equal, route ships and planes accordingly and set fuel-efficient schedules. The public authorities, cognizant of the wider impacts of transport, often bypass these energy goals to attain other objectives. The most obvious case are the take-off and landing patterns at airports that seldom are energy efficient but take cognizance of noise nuisance envelopes.

While speed limits are usually imposed for reasons of improving traffic flows and for safety, there are examples of explicit, speed-based energy policies in transport. As an emergency response to the 1973 oil crisis, the US Congress effectively imposed a national 55 mph speed limit in 1974 under the Emergency Highway Energy Conservation Act by requiring the limit as a condition of each state receiving highway funds. The limit was unpopular, especially in western states that have long distances between cities or points of interest. Subsequent analysis was somewhat unclear on the implications of the measure on energy consumption.[19] Congress lifted all federal speed limit controls in the November 28, 1995 National Highway Designation Act, fully delegating speed limit authority to the states.

Fostering Alternative Technologies

Taxation, vehicle design standards and other measures, in addition to market forces, can, and have in many cases, affected the technology of transport and, *ipso facto*, energy use and efficiency. The higher fuel prices after the Israeli wars of the 1970s led to lighter vehicles using alternative materials for bodywork and more fuel efficient engines. In addition, however, there have also been a number of other explicit policies aimed at technology shifts with the aim of reducing the use of oil-based fuels.

There has been a long history, for example, of policies aimed at developing viable electric cars that can effectively be powered from a variety of energy sources, including hydro-generated electricity.[20] These are sometimes called, as in California, 'zero-emissions vehicles', although from the wider geographical perspective, given the primary source of energy, this is very seldom the case, and even if solar panels are used on vehicles, there is still the pollution associated with the production of these panels. National governments have regularly tried to foster the development of economically feasible electric car technologies by investing in R&D programs. At a more local level, the California Zero Emission Vehicle (ZEV) program, initiated in 1990, and followed by some other states as partial zero emissions vehicles (PZEV) programs, was designed to catalyze the commercialization of advanced-technology vehicles that would not have any tailpipe or evaporative emissions. It initially required that 2 per cent of new vehicles produced for sale in 1998 and 10 per cent of new vehicles produced for sale in 2003 would be zero emission vehicles. After automakers argued they could not meet the 1998 deadline, full implementation of the program was delayed until 2003 with interim measures to encourage the use of more PZEVs. In 2002, automakers sued the state over the program and were granted a preliminary injunction barring its implementation pending a final court ruling. In the midst of the ensuing legal debate, the state decided to go ahead and make revisions to the rule to sidestep the legal challenge, with the aim of restoring the ZEV program by 2005. Overall, these types of policy have not been conspicuously successful in bringing about sea-changes in transport technology.[21]

The European Union, through Joint Technology Initiatives in the 7th Research Framework Program running from 2007 to 2013, is providing increasing levels of funding for research into fuel cells and hydrogen with the intention of reducing the time needed to market such technologies by between 2 and 5 years.

While fully electric- or hydrogen-propelled vehicles have proved elusive to develop on a commercial scale, the hybrid-vehicle, such as the Honda Insight and the Toyota Prius, that combines electric propulsion with, generally, a gasoline engine has proved more successful. It offers, at prevailing prices, fuel efficiency, although at a higher capital cost, and, in many cases, is economically justified in the market place. Policy has been instrumental by both financing part of the R&D costs of the underlying technology, but in many cases local policies have provided an added inducement for its up-take. In the United States many local jurisdictions, for example, allow hybrids to use high-occupancy vehicle lanes (HOV) on highways even if not meeting the passenger occupancy requirements.[22]

There are also initiatives to foster the use of telecommunications as an alternative to trips that are primarily for information exchange. This can apply to such things as teleworking (rather than commuting to work in an office) and teleshopping. While the debate over whether advanced telecommunications (ATIC, Advanced Technologies of Information and Telecommunications) have added to travel because of the complementary nature of the 'product' or reduced it because of its substitutability features is still the subject of much debate (Salomon and Mokhtarian, 2007). Policy makers have launched a number of initiatives to increase the use of ATIC as a transport energy policy initiative.[23] Some of this has been in the form of information – for example, the US Office of Personnel Management and the General Services Administration have established a joint web site on telework to provide access to guidance issued by both agencies and facilitation; for example, under US law, federal executive agencies must establish policies under which eligible employees may participate in telecommuting to the maximum extent possible. Again in the United States, in 1996 the Clean Air Act, amongst other things, required companies with over 100 employees to encourage telecommuting. The European Union also reached a framework agreement to encourage more teleworking and to put in place laws that would help facilitate it across the member countries.

CONCLUSIONS

Transport is a major user of energy, and that consumption is growing as affluence spreads and the demands for transport rise with it. The ownership of a car is widely seen as a symbol of success, as much as a mode of transport and the number of vehicles grows as industrialization and urbanization continue. On the freight side, sophisticated international logistics systems now contribute significantly to global economic growth and rely heavily on 'cheap' transport, and in many cases on governments subsidizing that transport. While not exact, there is thus a strong correlation between income, transport demand and the use of energy by the transportation sector. This use of energy does not, however, take place within a fully competitive market with complete contracts with the outcome being significant misallocations of resources. As a result there has been a tendency for the over exploitation of many non-renewable energy sources, together with serious adverse impacts on the environment at the local, regional and global levels.

The problems associated with the increasing use of energy, and in particular oil-based fuels, are fairly well documented. Some problems need clarification such as the exact amount of carbon fuel available for future generations, the detailed links between CO_2 and global warming at the global level, and the effects of lead on the brain development of children. But the general pictures are agreed upon. The challenge is much less in terms of fine tuning the science, although further work is unquestionably needed, than in the need for examining the optimal trade-offs society must make in terms of how transport is to use scarce resources in the future and for developing institutional frameworks that allow the optimal path of use to be realized. Given the diverse uses to which gasoline in particular is put – for example, transportation, heating, refrigerating, lighting and manufacturing – perhaps the greatest challenge is not within the transport sector, but rather developing much broader mechanisms to efficiently allocate its consumption across all of these uses.

NOTES

1. The use of draught animals is still extensive in many developing countries, and in some special circumstances in industrialized nations, but is not covered in this contribution.
2. Reliance on case studies and academic analysis rather than official statistics often helps to fill, although not completely, gaps in the full energy profile of transport modes and trips.
3. In official data, energy used for transport only covers that use for enterprises whose main business is transport and excludes use by other enterprises and individuals. Adding the latter is thought to push energy by up to 6 per centage points; the Institute of Energy Economics Japan (2003), for example estimates transport's share in 2000 as 13.3 per cent.
4. Even if these externalities were brought directly within the decision-making framework, there would still be adverse environmental and health effects associated with transport. The difference is that society would make informed judgments about the benefits of transportation against the full costs that are associated with it.
5. For more details of the UK case, see UK Treasury (2006).
6. Countries such as Sweden, that have significant hydroelectricity-generating capacity, and France, that use a lot of nuclear energy for stationary energy, have a much higher per centage of their aggregate CO_2 emissions associated with their transport activities.
7. Dings and Dijkstra (1997) offers a comparable set of data for European freight transport.
8. For example, the UK's fuel tax escalator that automatically increased fuel taxes by 3 per centage points a year above inflation between 1993 and 1997, and by 6 per cent between 1997 and 1999, only applied to road fuel.
9. Flynn (2002), for example, discusses some of the issues of encouraging natural gas as a major fuel source.

10. In some cases there are larger, national political positions that influence which policies are achievable. For example, the United States has a history of aversion to supranational bodies or regulations and this has in part influenced its position regarding signing the Kyoto Convention on greenhouse gas emissions.
11. Although tradable or marketable permits are not discussed here they are very relevant from a more macro-perspective given the carbon trading policies that have emerged since the Kyoto Conference. At the more micro-level, they were used in the United States to facilitate the efficient removal of lead from gasoline (Hahn, 1989).
12. The United States introduced the CAFÉ standards, that *de jure* from 1975 but de facto from 1978, affected the average miles per gallon permitted for new cars. This may have affected marginally the pattern of fuel efficiency after the second oil crisis but the price rise was so large this provided the dominant effect.
13. Another synthesis of elasticities of gasoline demand by passenger automobiles conducted by Basso and Oum (2007) suggests a short-run elasticity of 0.2 to 0.3 and a long-run elasticity of 0.6 to 0.8.
14. In July 2008, British Columbia introduced a tax on carbon-based fuels that covers gasoline, diesel, natural gas and home heating fuel. The initial rate was $10 a tonne, to be increased by $5 a tonne per year up to $30 per tonne in 2012. The initial tax adds 2.4 cents per liter to the tax on gasoline (http://www.cbc.ca/canada/british-columbia/story/2008/06/30/bc-carbon-tax-effective.html).
15. These are not, however, normally Pigouvian (Pigou, 1920) subsidies that are explicitly paid to individuals to desist in generating external costs, but rather indirect subsidies to encourage the adoption of activities that are associated with lower levels of external or other adverse economic impacts.
16. It may not be more efficient than other forms of personal transport such as the moped or motorcycle. In addition, low load factors on public transport can make it a very unattractive proposition from an energy and environmental perspective. Buses in Washington DC, for example, emit more pollution per mile person trip than do cars.
17. Particular care, however, must be taken in generalizing too much regarding cross-elasticities. As Oum et al. (2007) point out they tend to be highly context specific.
18. For economic assessments of the CAFE standards see, Crandall et al. (1986), Kleit (1990), Fischer et al. (2007) and National Research Council (2002).
19. The Heritage Foundation claimed that the total fuel savings during the national speed limit was no more than 1 per cent (Copulos, 1986). See Forester et al. (1984) for a more general assessment of the policy.
20. Historically, in the early days, electric-driven cars were as numerous as gasoline, steam or diesel cars, the first electric car being developed somewhere between 1832 and 1839, but seem to have gone out of favor because of maintenance issues and the costs of mass production.
21. For example, of the 4000 to 5000 electric cars built for California's ZEV mandate in the late 1990s, only about 1000 remain on the road.
22. Whether a situation with two hybrid cars each with only a driver in it is more fuel efficient and less environmentally damaging than a single conventional car with a driver and passenger is a moot point, as is the implications of a large hybrid vehicle with a passenger vis-à-vis a small gasoline-propelled car.
23. The evidence seems to be moving towards the position that, in the absence of complementary traffic restraint measures, policies to foster teleworking only marginally change energy use in transport. The reason is that while teleworking gets commuters off the road, road-space is filled by non-commuters or commuters who shift from other modes (the effects of 'latent demand' to adopt traffic engineering jargon). This traffic is often non-radial and hits junctions that impede traffic flows. The result is that traffic speeds revert back to their original levels. Any energy saving is because with the impedance effect, you actually have fewer vehicles at this speed (that is, flow is lower).

REFERENCES

Association of American Railroads, 2005, *Railroad Facts*. Washington DC: AAR.
Basso, L. and T.H. Oum, 2007, A survey of models of gasoline demand by passenger automobiles. *Transport Reviews*, **27**, 449–484.
China Energy Research Society, 2002, *Energy Policy Research 2002.1*. Beijing (in Chinese).
Copulos, M.R., 1986, *The High Cost of the 55 MPH Speed Limit*. Washington DC: The Heritage Foundation.
Crandall, R.W., H.K. Gruenspecht, T.E. Keeler and L.B. Lave 1986, *Regulating the Automobile,* Brookings Institution, Washington DC.
Dargay, J. and M. Hanly, 1999, Bus fare elasticities. ESRC Transport Studies, Unit, University College London. Available at: www.ucl.ac.uk/ucetmah.

Delucchi, M.A. and J. Murphy, 2004, US military expenditures to protect the use of Persian Gulf oil for motor vehicles. University of Davis Research Report UCD-ITS-RR-96-03(15).

Dings, D. and W. Dijkstra, 1997, *Specific Energy Consumption and Emissions of Freight Transport.* Delft, The Netherlands: CE Delft.

European Commission, 2006, European energy and transport trends to 2030: update 2005. Office for Official Publications of the European Communities, Luxembourg.

Fischer, C., W. Harrington and I.W.H. Parry, 2007, Should automobile fuel economy standards be tightened? *Energy Journal,* **28**, 1–29.

Flynn, P.C., 2002, Commercializing an alternate vehicle fuel: lessons learned from natural gas for vehicles. *Energy Policy,* **30**, 613–619.

Forester, T.H., R.F. McNown and L.D. Singell, 1984, A cost-benefit analysis of the 55 mph speed limit. *Southern Economic Journal,* **50**, 631–641.

Goodwin, P., J. Dargay and M. Hanly, 2004, Elasticities of road traffic and fuel consumption with respect to price and income: a review. *Transport Reviews,* **24**, 275–292.

Hahn, R.W., 1989, Economic prescriptions for environmental problems: how the patient followed the doctor's orders. *Journal of Economic Perspectives,* **3**, 95–114.

Institute of Energy Economics Japan, 2003, *Handbook of Energy and Economic Statistics in Japan.* Tokyo: IEER.

International Energy Agency, 2005, *Key World Energy Statistics 2005.* Paris: IEA.

Kleit, A.N., 1990, The effect of annual changes in automobile fuel economy standards. *Journal of Regulatory Economics,* **2**, 151–172.

Knight, F. H., 1921, *Risk, Uncertainty and Profit.* New York: Houghton Mifflin.

Leiby, P.N., D.W. Jones, T.R. Curlee and R. Lee, 1997, Oil imports: an assessment of benefits and costs. Oak Ridge National Laboratories Report ORNL-6851.

National Research Council, 2002, *Effectiveness and Impact of Corporate Average Fuel Economy (CAFE) Standards.* Washington DC: National Research Council, National Academy Press.

Organisation for Economic Co-operation and Development, 1992, *Market and Government Failures in Environmental Policy: The Case of Transport.* Paris: OECD.

Oum, T.H., W.G. Waters and X. Fu, 2007, Transport demand elasticities. In D.A. Hensher and K.J. Button, eds, *Handbook of Transport Modelling,* 2nd edn. Oxford: Elsevier, pp. 240–255.

Parry, I.W.H., M. Walls and W. Harrington, 2007, Automobile externalities and policies. *Journal of Economic Literature,* **45**, 373–399.

Pigou, A., 1920, *The Economics of Welfare.* London: Macmillan.

Roos, J., A. Bleijenberg and W. Dijkstra, 1997, *Energy Use and Emissions from Aviation and Other Modes for Long Distance Travel in Europe.* Delft, The Netherlands: CE Delft.

Salomon, I. and P.L. Mokhtarian, 2007, Can telecommunications help solve transportation problem? A decade later: are prospects better? In D.A. Hensher and K.J. Button, eds, *Handbook of Transport Modelling,* 2nd edn. Oxford: Elsevier, pp. 240–255.

UK Treasury, 2006, *The Economics of Climate Change: the Stern Review.* London: UK Treasury.

US Department of Energy, 2004, *Natural Gas Annual 2004.* DOE/EIA-0131(04), Washington DC: US Department of Energy.

US Department of Energy, Energy Information Administration, 2005, *Fuel Oil and Kerosene Sales 2004.* Washington DC: US Department of Energy.

US Department of Energy, Energy Information Administration, 2006, *Annual Energy Outlook 2006: With Projections to 2030.* Washington DC: US Department of Energy.

US Department of Transportation, Federal Highway Administration, 2005, *Highway Statistics 2004.* Washington DC: US Department of Transport.

White, M.J., 2004. The arms race on American roads: the effect of sport utility vehicles and pickup trucks on traffic safety. *Journal of Law and Economics,* **47**, 333–355.

World Business Council for Sustainable Development, 2004, *Mobility 2030: Meeting the Challenges to Sustainability.* Geneva: WBCSD.

19 The full marginal costs of highway travel: methods and empirical estimation for North America

Yossi Berechman, Bekir Bartin, Ozlem Yanmaz-Tuzel and Kaan Ozbay

INTRODUCTION

Sound transportation policy making requires the correct estimation of the Full Marginal Costs (FMC) of highway travel. This information is essential for allocating resources efficiently, for ensuring equity among users and for developing effective pricing mechanisms. FMC is defined as the overall costs incurred by society from servicing an additional unit of transportation output (for example, car traffic). It is composed of direct costs to users and indirect costs to society (non-internalized externalities).[1] Thus, the main objectives of this chapter are, first, to analytically examine the key components of FMC; subsequently, to empirically estimate these variables using pertinent case-study data from North America (the Northern New Jersey highway network) at the origin–destination (O–D) spatial level.

A critical issue in transportation cost analysis is the definition of output. One approach is to distinguish between intermediate and final outputs, depending on the purpose of the analysis (Berechman and Giuliano, 1984). Intermediate outputs such as vehicle-miles, vehicle-hours or distance-traveled, are adequate for the evaluation of the technical efficiency of a transportation system. Final outputs, such as the number of trips or number of passengers, on the other hand, are most appropriate for analyzing the overall effectiveness of the system. It has been argued that models, which use intermediate outputs (for example, distance-traveled) may be inapt for analyzing users' and social costs of transportation (for example, Jara-Diaz et al., 1992). Moreover, the use of such output variables may be inadequate for the computation of the degree of scale economies in capacity expansion, a key factor in capacity investment models (Mohring, 1976; Small and Verhoef, 2007). Finally, an intermediate output type can also lead to erroneous results when performing a cost–benefit analysis (CBA) of transportation improvements.

In this chapter we use the term 'output' to represent the overall level of utilization of a transportation system such as a highway network. This type of definition corresponds to 'final output' explained above. Thus, the question that we intend to examine is: what are the changes, in direct and indirect costs, incurred by society from a marginal increase in highway utilization? In many cases, CBA is carried out at the facility level thus ignoring network effects relative to the magnitude and distribution of users and externality costs, before and after the investment, and over the network's links and O–D pairs. The FMC computations, done in this chapter, demonstrate how such network analysis can be carried out. We further demonstrate how total network costs change following actual capacity improvements.

The structure of the chapter is as follows. The next section provides the general analytical framework for FMC analysis, followed by examination of the question of scale economies in highway capacity expansion. The subsequent section, 'Type of marginal cost functions', defines the various cost categories used in FMC analysis. The section titled 'Case study' presents analysis of actual highway capacity improvements and their impact on FMC values using the New Jersey highway network. Summary and conclusions are in the final section.

ANALYTICAL FRAMEWORK

To analyze the FMC of travel, in this section we first derive optimal traffic volume and capacity that ensure optimal social welfare from highway investments.

Formulation

Consider a one-mile of roadway segment per time unit (for example, hour[2]).[3] Let V be traffic volume, K be the capacity; $P(V)$ is users' inverse demand function; $C(V, K)$ is users' average cost function of travel; and $F(K)$ is the highway capacity investment function. All variables are defined per one-mile of roadway. The objective is to maximize a social welfare function W, $(W = W(V, K))$ with respect to V and K, where W is defined as the difference between the benefits attained from an investment in the form of total users' welfare gains $(\int_0^V P(z) \cdot dz)$, total users' costs, $(V \cdot C(V, K)$, and the investment's cost of capital $(F(K))$. That is:

$$W = \int_0^V P(z) \cdot dz - V \cdot C(V, K) - F(K) \tag{19.1}$$

First order conditions are:

$$\frac{\partial W}{\partial V} = P(V) - C(V, K) - V \cdot \frac{\partial C(V, K)}{\partial V} = 0, \tag{19.2}$$

$$\frac{\partial W}{\partial K} = -V \cdot \frac{\partial C(V, K)}{\partial K} - \frac{\partial F(K)}{\partial K} = 0. \tag{19.3}$$

The expression $C(V, K) + V \cdot \partial C(V, K)/\partial V$ is the social marginal cost curve, where $V \cdot \partial C(V, K)/\partial V$ represents the external cost, borne by users collectively. From Equation (19.2), we obtain that at social equilibrium, the user price $P(V)$ should be equal to the social marginal cost, which is comprised of average user cost and the externality cost:

$$P(V^*) = C(V^*, K) + V^* \cdot \frac{\partial C(V^*, K)}{\partial V} \tag{19.4}$$

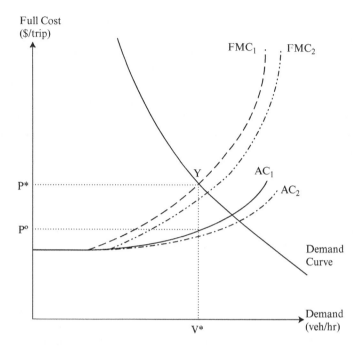

Notes: AC: average cost, FMC: full marginal cost

Figure 19.1   Hypothetical full marginal and average cost curves

where, $P(V^*)$ is the socially optimal price that users need to pay to internalize the externality cost, and the second term on the right-hand side of the equation is equal to the optimal congestion toll.

From Equation (19.3), we obtain the cost–benefit rule for the capital investment. At optimum, the marginal dollar invested in the capacity of the road segment, $\partial F(K)/\partial K$, should generate benefits that are equal to the reduction in total users' costs from that investment, $-V \cdot \partial C(V, K)/\partial K$.

These conditions are shown in Figure 19.1. Point Y represents the social equilibrium when AC_1 is the average cost curve, and V^* is the optimal level of traffic, given optimal roadway capacity. The realization of maximum social welfare, W, requires that these two conditions hold simultaneously. Therefore, cost–benefit rule for capacity expansion applies when calculated for the optimal volume, V.

The full price that users need to cover which equals to the social marginal cost at point Y is composed of congestion externality, private user costs and the investment costs. Total revenue, R, can be expressed as:

$$R = V^{*2} \cdot \frac{\partial C(V^*, K)}{\partial V} \tag{19.5}$$

When $C(V, K)$ depends only on the volume-capacity ratio, V/K, and is homogenous of degree zero, then marginal cost at social equilibrium, $\partial C(V^*, K^*)/\partial V$, can be expressed as $\partial C(V^*, K)/\partial V = -K/V \cdot \partial C(V^*, K)/\partial K$ using the quotient rule and the chain rule, as shown in Small (1992). Then, the total revenue, R, becomes:

$$R = -V^* \cdot K \cdot \frac{\partial C(V^*, K)}{\partial K} = K \cdot \frac{\partial F(K)}{\partial K} \tag{19.6}$$

Equation (19.6) can be simplified by using the economies-of-scale of capacity investment, S_K, defined as the ratio of average to marginal capacity costs. That is,

$$S_K = \frac{F(K^*)}{K^* \cdot \frac{\partial F(K)}{\partial K}} \tag{19.7}$$

Using Equation (19.7), total revenue, R, can be expressed as:

$$R = \frac{F(K^*)}{S_K} \tag{19.8}$$

Interpretation of Equation (19.8) is straightforward. Revenue through optimal congestion fee covers the cost of providing capacity only if there are neutral economies of scale, that is, $s_K = 1$. Revenue is greater than capital cost if $s_K < 1$ (that is, diseconomies of scale), and less than capital cost if $s_K > 1$ (that is, economies of scale). Note that the highway capacity investment function, $F(K)$, includes the cost of construction, maintenance and land-acquisition costs.

The above discussion helps to highlight the fact that a correct evaluation of benefits from a highway investment should be carried out at the point of social equilibrium (point Y in Figure 19.1). At this point the value of the congestion externality is priced to users as a congestion toll, which equals $P^* - P^o$ in Figure 19.1.

Capacity expansion causes the FMC curve to shift to the right from FMC_1 to FMC_2 as shown in Figure 19.1. This shift is due to the decrease in time cost, vehicle operating cost and the congestion externality.[4] New average cost of serving the traffic volume would be reduced as well (from AC_1 curve to AC_2 curve), which is the desired effect of capacity expansion.

A major caveat to this analysis is related to the estimation of marginal costs when the expanded highway segment is part of a large complex network. In a network setting, the social equilibrium conditions presented above need to be modified to account for users' route choices. That is, unlike the single link case, when faced with multiple links a user is inclined to choose the most attractive route to travel. In other words, a user would select the route that maximizes his/her utility, irrespective of other users. As a result, the system reaches equilibrium (called 'user equilibrium') at a point where no user can reduce his/her travel cost by switching routes (Berechman, 2009, Chapter 8). Thus, the estimation of FMC at the network level must be carried out at user equilibrium, employing a proper trip assignment algorithm.

Small and Verhoef (2007, Section 5.1) have pointed out that the self-financing result shown in Equation (19.8), and which refers explicitly to congestion technology, requires three conditions to hold: (1) neutral scale economies in capacity provision, (2) constant returns to scale in congestion technology and (3) perfect divisibility of capacity.

Condition (2) holds for cost functions that depend only on volume-capacity ratios, such as the Bureau of Public Roads (BPR) function.[5] In this function travel time is homogeneous of degree zero, that is, the same proportional increase in volume and capacity will not affect users' congestion costs. It may not hold for other types of cost functions such as queuing type cost functions (for example, Mun, 1994). Turning to condition (3), roadway capacity often varies as a result of its physical attributes, such as lane width, shoulder width and horizontal and vertical alignment. Therefore, although controversial, the divisibility of capacity can be regarded as an acceptable approximation (see Starkie, 1982, for a detailed discussion regarding the divisibility of roadway capacity). Next we examine evidence on scale economies in capacity – condition (1) for the self-financing result.

Empirical Evidence on Scale Economies in Capacity Provision

Following the above discussion (see also Arnott and Kraus, 2003) we now review several empirical studies, which attempted to estimate highway capacity scale economies.

Meyer et al. (1965) reformulated the construction cost function of expressways in Chicago (originally estimated by Joseph, 1960), with a 35-year lifespan, as follows:

$$C_k = w_c \cdot (21{,}451 + 4{,}883 \cdot NRD) + 5{,}931 \cdot N \tag{19.9}$$

where, C_k is the sum of annual construction and maintenance costs per mile of roadway, w_c is an index of the width of various highway facilities as a ratio of the width of an eight-lane highway,[6] NRD is the net residential density in thousand persons per square mile and N is number of lanes. They further related the right-of-way to construction costs for an N-lane roadway as:

$$C_{row} = 0.005 \cdot NRD \cdot C_k \tag{19.10}$$

Based on Equations (19.9) and (19.10), for an area with a net residential density of 15 000 persons per square mile, we can estimate scale economies for two-, four-, six- and eight-lane highways as: 3.22, 2.11, 1.74 and 1.55, respectively.[7]

The high economies of scales values derived from this analysis are largely the result of the values given to w_c in Equation (19.9). These arbitrary values (Table 11 in Meyer et al., 1965) imply high economies of scale for highway construction work, simply because the authors take a fixed median and shoulder width of 38 ft, regardless of the number of lanes. Therefore, as Keeler and Small (1977) and Small and Verhoef (2007) correctly point out, these high economies of scale values arise from engineering design assumptions (regarding fixed median and shoulder width independent of the number of lanes) rather than from empirical evidence.

Mohring (1976) argues that there should be substantial economies of scale simply because of the geometric design of a typical roadway. That is, the addition of one more lane would be less expensive due to less earth-work and right-of-way required, and fixed costs of administration and equipment. However, he also points out that within a network setting, adding new roads to a network would require more intricate construction designs (for example, overpasses, tunnels, sloped-embankments and so forth), and would have higher right-of-way costs, which would therefore increase costs more than the provided capacity. Therefore, he concludes that: 'it seems plausible to argue that diseconomies of scale prevail' (Mohring, 1976, p. 144).

Kraus (1981) has suggested that the estimation of economies of scale for highway capital projects should be conducted by holding fixed the right-of-way and design costs (number of interchanges, overpasses and so forth). He estimated highway capital cost functions for various facility types such as individual freeway and arterial roadway segments, diamond interchange, cloverleaf interchange, overpasses and directional interchanges. These estimated cost functions are based on unit costs of roadway work, paving, right-of-way that vary with facility type, an approach similar to the one used in Meyer et al. (1965). His estimates indicate substantial economies of scale ($s_K = 2$) for individual freeway segments for a typical four-lane freeway in the outskirts of the London urban area. He found economies of scale in all types of interchange designs, but neutral economies of scale for arterial roads. He also estimated significant diseconomies of scale ($s_K = 0.53$) in overpass construction. He concluded that for a combination of various roadway facilities, scale economies vary between 1.12 and 1.27, depending on the urbanization degree.[8]

Keeler and Small (1977) estimated highway construction costs from a database that includes 57 state-maintained arterials, expressways and rural roads in the San Francisco Bay Area. Using these authors' notation, the construction cost formula is estimated as: [9]

$$C = \exp(11.609 \cdot CRS + 12.767 \cdot CUC + 12.993 \cdot FR + 13.255 \cdot$$

$$FSU + 1.1151 \cdot FC) \cdot w^{-0.0305} \tag{19.11}$$

where, C is the construction cost per lane-mile (in 1972 USD); CRS is the percentage of non-freeway road length outside city limits; CUC is the percentage of arterial roads within city limits; FR is the percentage of rural freeways; FSU is the percentage of urban or suburban freeways; FC is the percentage of freeways within city limits; and w is average width of road in lanes. From Equation (19.11) it can be deduced that lane width has an economically insignificant effect on the construction cost, and the cost is proportional to number of lanes, suggesting neutral economies of scale in highway construction. The authors further estimated right-of-way costs as a proportion of construction cost with the same parameters employed in Equation (19.11). Therefore, their formulation of right-of-way also suggests that there exist neutral economies of scale in land acquisition costs.

Kane and Morlok (1970) have investigated highway construction costs from a database compiled from a survey of various state highway departments. The database includes 82 freeway construction projects from 23 cities where the key variables are number of lanes, road length, gross residential density, right-of-way, and construction costs. They argue that the terrain, soil conditions and regional development in the construction area substantially influence construction costs. Thus, they estimate three equations for different type of soil and regional classes. Their construction and right-of-way cost formulations are in the form of: [10]

$$C = a + b \cdot N + c \cdot DEV + d \cdot GRD + e \cdot RLF \tag{19.12}$$

In Equation (19.12) C is cost per mile, N is number of lanes, DEV is development (annual tax revenue in dollar-thousands per square mile), GRD is gross residential density in persons per square mile and RLF is the relief index.[11] Kane and Morlok (1970, p. 332) state that 'construction costs by lane size increase with increasing density, and therefore one might expect that the economies of scale savings might be met or exceeded by the increased costs due to more dense locations.'

The choice of variables in Equation (19.12), especially RLF, makes it difficult to determine whether the cost function indicates economies of scale. Using the estimated parameters Kane and Morlok (1970) concluded that scale economies are greater than 1.0 when capital costs are higher than $1.1 million (in 1970 USD) per lane-mile of a freeway.

In a more recent study, Levinson and Karamalaputi (2003) attempted to predict the location of new highway construction based on the status of the network, traffic demand, estimated cost of construction and budget constraints. They employed a database consisting of newly constructed roadways and expanded existing roadways between 1978 and 1998. Their estimated construction cost function is given as follows:[12]

$$\ln(C) = 5.79 + 0.50 \cdot \ln(L \cdot \Delta N) + 0.39 \cdot I_1 + 1.97 \cdot I_2 + 0.56 \cdot I_3$$

$$+ 0.75 \cdot \ln(Y - 1979) + 0.16 \cdot \ln(P) - 0.03 \cdot X \qquad (19.13)$$

where, C is the construction cost (in nominal thousands of dollars), $L \cdot \Delta N$ is the lane kilometers of construction (length multiplied by the change in number of lanes), I_1 is dummy variable (1 if new construction, 0 if expansion), I_2 and I_3 are dummy variables for interstate and state highways, respectively; Y is the year of completion, P is the project duration in years and X is the distance of the roadway from the nearest downtown in kilometers.

Equation (19.13) indicates strong scale economies in highway construction of 2.0; that is, construction cost increases only by 41 per cent when the road length is doubled. This function yields $294.5 million nominal (2008) dollars of construction cost for a new 5 mile (8 km) 6-lanes interstate highway that is 5 miles away from a downtown area, with construction duration of 4 years

Wilmot and Cheng (2003) have estimated highway construction costs in Louisiana using a database that comprises of highway construction projects undertaken by the Louisiana Department of Transportation and Development between 1984 and 1997. Their cost model includes five sub-models, each aimed at estimating the cost function of a construction item such as excavation and embankment, concrete pavement, asphalt pavement, reinforcing steel concrete and structures.[13] A key finding is that costs are highly influenced by the average annual bid volume, number of plan changes and the changes in practices and standards. Their results indicate varying economies of scale with respect to quantity, equipment, material and labor for different work types. Therefore, it is not clear from their analysis whether scale economies exist in highway construction.

Link (2006) estimated highway maintenance costs using a database of 221 cross-sectional observations of motorway renewal costs and traffic volume in Germany during the period of 1980–1999. She related maintenance cost to several variables including labor, material and capital costs, number of lanes and length, and traffic volume. She reported economies of scale with respect to renewed area (m²) to be 1.52.

Equation (19.8) reveals that the ability to recover capital costs in highway construction depends, among other things, on the presence or absence of scale economics in capacity construction. The literature reviewed in this section does not produce an unequivocal answer on these scale economies. Results depend on the cost function that is estimated, the database and the network and geography of the area where construction takes place. As further shown by the summary of studies in Appendix 19A.1, there are no systematic tests for determining scale economies in highway construction. The use of macroeconomic data on variables such as wages, capital equipment, raw material and cost of capital might improve these estimates; yet local conditions such as the right-of-way, geometric design and network structure might have significant effects on the estimated cost function. These estimates further depend on characteristics of the project such as whether it is a new construction or an improvement project.

Next we focus on the specification of an FMC function and then estimate it using data from the Northern New Jersey network.

TYPE OF MARGINAL COST FUNCTIONS

The majority of highway travel cost studies reported in the literature focus on vehicle operating, congestion, accident, air pollution, noise and infrastructure costs. Some studies have also estimated water pollution and climate change costs. In addition, many of these studies use intermediate outputs in their analysis, that is, they estimate transportation costs based on distance traveled.[14] In contrast, in this chapter, we use a trip-based FMC, estimated on a set of feasible paths of a given highway network, between all O–D pairs faced by trip makers. In addition, we use network utilization, in terms of number of actual trips made, as our output measure.

For this analysis we have grouped highway-travel-related costs into three major categories: (1) user costs, (2) infrastructure costs and (3) environmental costs. Each of these contains several cost items which are reviewed in detail. Subsequently, total and marginal cost functions are developed for each cost category.

User Costs

Vehicle operating costs

Vehicle operating costs include *ownership* variable costs (insurance, depreciation) and *operating* costs (maintenance, repair, fuel, parking and tolls), which increase with mileage driven. Total and marginal vehicle operating cost functions are:[15]

$$C_{opr} = (C_f + C_o + C_t + C_{pt}) \cdot m + (C_d + C_{ins}) \cdot a \qquad (19.14)$$

$$MC_{opr} = \frac{\partial C_{opr}}{\partial m} \qquad (19.15)$$

where:

C_{opr} = cumulative user cost over n years ($)
MC_{opr} = marginal user cost ($/mile)
C_f = cost of fuel ($/mile)

Table 19.1   Unit costs (in 2008 USD)

Operating Expenses	Unit Costs
Gas & oil	0.087 ($/mile)
Maintenance	0.056 ($/mile)
Tires	0.0064 ($/mile)
Insurance Cost	1 370 ($/year)
Parking and Tolls	0.021 ($/mile)

Source: AAA (2005), USDOT (2003).

C_o = cost of oil ($/mile)
C_t = cost of tires ($/mile)
C_{pt} = cost of parking and tolls ($/mile)
C_d = total depreciation cost over n years ($)
C_{ins} = cost of insurance depending on the age of the car ($/year)
m = mileage over n years (miles)
a = age of vehicle (years)

All vehicle-operating costs, except depreciation, are defined by their respective unit cost values per mile, obtained from AAA (2005) and USDOT (2003) reports. Table 19.1 shows the unit costs for the vehicle operating function in the United States.

Following Levinson (1997), depreciation costs are specified as a function of mileage (m) and auto age (a).[16] In this chapter, depreciation cost function is estimated for the Ford Taurus car model. The resulting total and marginal vehicle operating costs are shown below. Since automobile depreciation rate and car value (thus insurance costs) are highest at the first five years, marginal vehicle operating costs decrease as the vehicle age increases, mainly due to the depreciation and insurance costs effects.

$$C_{opr} = 7,508.73 + 0.12 \cdot (m/a) + 2,783.3 \cdot a + 0.143 \cdot m \quad R^2 = 0.77 \quad (19.16)$$

$$MC_{opr} = \frac{\partial C_{opr}}{\partial m} = 0.143 + 0.12/a \quad (19.17)$$

Travel time costs
In general, total travel time costs are composed of two major components: direct or own travel time costs and non-internalized congestion externality costs. The amount of time lost, $T_{r,s}(V, d_{r,s})$, depends on trip characteristics, that is, the distance between O–D pair ($d_{r,s}$), and traffic volume (V), and can be determined through the use of a travel time function such as the BPR. On the other hand, the monetary value of time lost is determined by the use of Value of Time (VOT) parameter. For VOT calculations two vehicle types are considered: passenger cars and trucks. VOT for passenger cars during peak and off-peak hours are taken as 80 per cent and 35 per cent of the average hourly wage, respectively (USDOT, 1997). For trucks VOT is taken as 100 per cent of the average hourly wage during peak and off-peak periods (USDOT, 1997).[17] The US Department of

Labor (2007) has reported that in 2007 the average hourly wage for all occupations was $22.64/hour. The hourly wage in trucking was reported as $19.90/hour.[18,19]

Total and marginal travel time costs for all users on a roadway connecting the O–D pair (r,s) is formulated as follows:

$$C_{cong} = V.T_{r,s}(V, d_{r,s}).\text{VOT} = V.\frac{d_{r,s}}{S_o}\left(1 + 0.15\left(\frac{V}{K}\right)^4\right).\text{VOT} \qquad (19.18)$$

$$MC_{cong} = T_{r,s}(V, d_{r,s}) \cdot \text{VOT} + V \cdot \text{VOT} \cdot \frac{\partial T_{r,s}(V, d_{r,s})}{\partial V} = \frac{d_{r,s}}{S_o} \cdot \left(1 + 0.75\left(\frac{V}{K}\right)^4\right) \cdot \text{VOT} \qquad (19.19)$$

where:

C_{cong} = total congestion cost ($)
MC_{cong} = marginal travel time cost ($/trip)
$d_{r,s}$ = distance between points r and s, (miles)
V = traffic volume (vehicles/hour)
$T_{r,s}$ = direct travel time (hours)
VOT = value of time ($/hour)
K = capacity of the roadway segment between nodes r and s (vehicles/hour)
S_o = free flow speed (mile/hour)

The first term of the marginal cost function (Equation 19.19) represents user's direct time costs, whereas the second term represents the congestion externality costs.

Accident costs
Accident costs refer to the economic value of total damages (human and property) caused by vehicle crashes. The analysis is composed of two stages. In the first stage we estimate the number of accidents by severity. In the second stage we monetize 'damages', which include damage to vehicles, medical expenses, disability compensation and value of life. The number of accidents is correlated with highway type and its geometric design. These include: number of lanes, horizontal and vertical alignment and sight clearance/obstructions. For the purpose of estimating an accident rate function, highways are grouped into three categories according to their functional properties: (1) freeways, expressways and interstate highways; (2) principal arterial roads and (3) arterial-collector-local roads. The generalized total accident cost function can be expressed as:

$$C_{acc} = \sum_{r=1}^{3} C_f P_f^r + C_i P_i^r + C_p P_p^r \qquad (19.20)$$

where:

C_{acc} = total accident cost ($/year)
P_f^r, P_i^r, P_p^r = number of fatal (f), injury (i) and property damage (p) accidents per year for highway type r.
C_f, C_i, C_p = Unit cost of fatal (f), injury (i) and property damage (p) accidents ($)

Table 19.2   Average comprehensive cost per person by accident type

Accident type	Cost
Fatality	$4 100 000
Incapacitating Injury	$208 500
Non-incapacitating injury	$53 200
Possible injury	$25 300
Property damage	$2 300

Source: National Safety Council (2007).

Table 19.3   Average comprehensive cost by accident type

Accident type	Cost
Fatality	$3 673 732
Incapacitating injury	$254 335
Evident injury	$50 867
Possible injury	$26 847
Property damage	$2 826

Notes: All costs are in 2008 dollars, converted from 1994 values using 2.5 percent inflation rate.

Source: Federal Highway Administration (1994).

The National Safety Council (2007) reported the average unit cost per person for each accident type, as shown in Table 19.2. These values are comprehensive costs that include a measure of the value of lost quality of life, which was obtained through empirical studies of what people actually pay to reduce their safety and health risks.

Accident cost estimation is hardly exact; it can only be approximated. The studies in the relevant literature show varying unit costs for accidents. For example, the National Highway Traffic Safety Administration (NHTSA) study (2000) reports the lifetime economic cost of each fatality as $977 000. Over 80 per cent of this amount is attributable to lost workplace and household productivity. The same study reports that the cost of each critically injured survivor is $1.1 million. A study by Federal Highway Administration (1994) reports the comprehensive costs of each accident by severity, as shown in Table 19.3.

A recent poll conducted by American Association of State Highway and Transportation Officials (2007) reports accident costs by severity. The reported figures, shown in Table 19.4, reflect the average accident costs used in 24 states used for prioritizing safety projects.

In our analysis, we use the unit accident costs shown in Table 19.3, which were reported by the FHWA (1994) study. In order to accommodate the cost figures based on the accident types available in the NJDOT accident database, and for brevity, we regroup accident types in FHWA (1994) into three categories of accidents: fatality, injury (incapacitating) and property damage.

Table 19.4   Average cost by accident type

Accident type	Cost
Fatality	$2 435 134
Major injury	$483 667
Incapacitating injury	$245 815
Minor injury	$64 400
Non-incapacitating evident injury	$46 328
Injury	$59 898
Possible or unknown injury	$23 837
Property damage	$6 142

Source: American Association of State Highway and Transportation Officials (2007).

Given these figures and actual accident data in New Jersey (NJDOT, 2005), the total, marginal and accident cost functions are calculated. The accident cost functions, by severity level, were specified as a function of traffic volume (V), length (M) and number of lanes (L) of the route section. Table 19.5 presents these functions.

In Table 19.5, the cost function for fatality type accidents is given for freeways/interstates only. Results of regression analysis of fatality accidents were not statistically significant for principal arterial and arterial/local type roads. The weakness in these results can be explained by the fact that fatality type accidents are relatively small in number on these roads. Therefore, fatality accident functions are excluded for principal arterial and arterial/local roads.

Note that the components of accident costs in Table 19.5 increase less than proportionally with traffic volume (V). One explanation is that the likelihood and severity of accidents decreases with lower traveling speed, caused by increased traffic volume, thus density.

Infrastructure Costs

Infrastructure costs include capital expenditures for building roadway capacity, such as land acquisition, facility construction, costs of material, labor and administration costs. They further include regular maintenance costs to maintain a state of good repair and occasional improvement expenditures due to changes in traffic makeup and volume. Statistical models are estimated for new construction, maintenance and right-of-way costs.

Costs of new construction
The database used to estimate the cost function includes 14 new construction projects that were completed between 1991 and 1994 in New Jersey. Each observation consists of the final contract amount and detailed project blueprints, which were used to obtain detailed construction information, such as the actual project work length and highway width. The database consists of nine interstate highways, four arterial roadways and one country route.

Table 19.5 *Accident total and marginal cost functions by road type*

Cost type	Freeway/interstate	Principal arterial	Arterial/local
Total accident cost	$127.5 \cdot V^{0.77} \cdot M^{0.76} \cdot L^{0.53}$ $+ 114.75 \cdot V^{0.85} \cdot M^{0.75} \cdot L^{0.49}$ $+ 198,900 \cdot V^{0.17} \cdot M^{0.42} \cdot L^{0.45}$	$178.5 \cdot V^{0.58} \cdot M^{0.69} \cdot L^{0.43}$ $+ 18,359 \cdot V^{0.45} M^{0.63} \cdot L^{0.47}$	$229.5 \cdot V^{0.58} \cdot M^{0.77} \cdot L^{0.77}$ $+ 9,180 \cdot V^{0.74} \cdot M^{0.81} \cdot L^{0.75}$
Marginal accident cost	$98.18 \cdot V^{-0.23} \cdot M^{0.76} \cdot L^{0.53}$ $+ 97.53 \cdot V^{-0.15} \cdot M^{0.75} \cdot L^{0.49}$ $+ 33,813 \cdot V^{-0.83} \cdot M^{0.42} \cdot L^{0.45}$	$103.5 \cdot V^{-0.42} \cdot M^{0.69} \cdot L^{0.43}$ $+ 8,261.5 \cdot V^{-0.55} \cdot M^{0.63} \cdot L^{0.47}$	$133.11 \cdot V^{-0.42} \cdot M^{0.77} \cdot L^{0.77}$ $+ 6,793.17 \cdot V^{-0.26} \cdot M^{0.81} \cdot L^{0.75}$

Source: Compiled by the authors.

Table 19.6   New construction costs: regression results

	Coefficient	Standard Error	t	$p > \lvert t \rvert$
Constant	6.979	2.480	2.81	0.017
ln(S)	0.554	0.125	4.43	0.001
ln(NRD)	0.421	0.142	2.96	0.013
$R^2 = 0.58$				
Constant	8.446	2.166	3.90	0.002
ln(TM)	0.448	0.100	4.45	0.001
ln(NRD)	0.381	0.137	2.78	0.018
$R^2 = 0.59$				

In the section titled 'Analytical framework' we highlighted the impact that the degree of urbanization at the project's location has on the total construction costs. Even if other variables are held constant, building a roadway in a dense urban area is more expensive than building it in a sparsely populated area. One key reason is the ease of access to the construction sites. Other reasons are the ease of grading and the extent of demolition (Small, 1992). Here we follow Meyer et al. (1965) who use net residential density as the urbanization indicator. The following log-linear cost function was estimated:[20]

$$\ln (C) = a + b \cdot \ln (S) + c \cdot \ln (NRD) \tag{19.21}$$

In Equation (19.21) C is the construction cost (in 2008 USD);[21] S is the total new roadway surface (in ft^2) including lanes, shoulder width, emergency lanes and so forth; NRD is net residential density in persons per square mile, and a, b and c are parameters. Note that the parameter '1/b' measures scale economies in capacity provision; scale economies exist if $b < 1$, and scale diseconomies exist if $b > 1$.

Given the importance of capital costs in this analysis, it is worthwhile to provide a detailed discussion of the estimation process. First, we have extracted the approximate amount of pavement material (surface, base and sub-base) and earthwork (excavation and embankment) in cubic feet for each project in the database. Using this information a cost model, similar to Equation (19.21), is estimated with total pavement material (TM) used in cubic feet and NRD as the model variables.[22] The estimated results are shown in Table 19.6.

The results shown in Table 19.6 indicate a strong degree of scale economies in new road construction of 1.81 (= 1/0.554). Based on these estimates, the construction costs of a 5-mile, 6-lane highway within a net residential density of 15000 persons per square mile is approximately $225 million.

Analysis of the data shows that the correlation coefficient between total pavement material and roadway surface is 0.85; and between total earthwork and roadway surface is 0.62. This high value indicates that for this particular database, the earthwork and pavement material can be represented by the total surface provided. Therefore Equation (19.21) seems a suitable cost model for new construction.

Finally, it should be re-emphasized that construction costs of new roadways vary significantly with location, complexity and size of the project (for example, the need for interchanges, overpasses and noise walls), duration, material, labor and equipment. Construction costs might also vary due to administrative issues such as government's regulation, plan changes, quality of the management team, and the total volume of annual contract bids. Gathering this information is not a straight-forward task.

Costs of capacity improvement

We have already noted that capacity investment take several forms including new construction and capacity improvement. Since a significant number of highway investment projects are capacity improvements it is worth asking whether the cost function estimated above (Equation (19.21)) is also suitable for this type of investment. Capacity improvements include safety improvements, drainage, signage and pavement restoration costs. Usually, they do not account for the costs of noise, dust or delays.

The database used to estimate a cost model for highway capacity improvements was obtained from the NJDOT's roadway pavement system report (NJDOT, 2006). This database consists of 18 awarded rehabilitation and reconstruction projects in 2006, which are large-scale projects with various activities such as bridge rehabilitation, traffic signals, safety improvements, sidewalks and curbs. Given the significant importance of pavement restoration in capacity improvement projects the following cost model was estimated:

$$\ln (C_p) = -1.606 + 0.3283 \cdot \ln (N \cdot L) + 0.362 \cdot \ln (NRD) \quad R^2 = 0.63 \quad (19.22)$$

In Equation (19.22) C_p is the cost of pavement restoration in millions of dollars; N is number of lanes and L is project length in miles.[23] Equation (19.22) indicates that pavement restoration costs, in major reconstruction and rehabilitation projects, exhibit a high degree economies of scale ($s_K = 3.05$). The databases used to estimate models (19.21) and (19.22) were quite different in terms of project type and time period. Therefore, it is rather difficult to explain the difference between the degrees of scale economies obtained for these models. Variations in unobserved factors, such as administrative and contractor's efficiency or volume of bids at a given year, may have also impacted these results.

Costs of pavement resurfacing

Pavement resurfacing work is conducted when pavement deterioration is not severe enough to require a complete reconstruction. The pavement resurfacing includes milling a depth of the hot mix asphalt pavement and resurfacing with new material (NJDOT, 2006, 2007). The sample dataset used here to estimate a pavement resurfacing cost function includes 45 projects that were awarded in 2006 and 2007 by the NJDOT. Regression analysis yields the following cost model:

$$\ln (C_r) = -0.716 + 0.8197 \cdot \ln (N \cdot L) \quad R^2 = 0.68 \quad (19.23)$$

In Equation (19.23) C_r is the pavement resurfacing cost in million dollars, N is number of lanes and L is project length in miles.[24] Equation (19.23) indicates economies of scale in roadway resurfacing work in the scale of 1.22.

A roadway is resurfaced when the pavement reaches a predetermined terminal state, which occurs several times during the lifetime of a roadway (Newbery, 1988a, 1988b; Small et al., 1989). Equation (19.23) can be used to assess the costs involved. Small et

Table 19.7   Right-of-way cost model: regression results

	Value	Standard Error	t – value	Pr>|t|
a	8.74	1.409	6.035	0.000
b	0.717	0.138	5.194	0.000
c	0.509	0.182	2.794	0.015
R^2	0.76	16 Data Points		

al. (1989) suggest the following ratio to determine the time when a pavement reaches its terminal state.[25]

$$P = G/E \tag{19.24}$$

where, P is the resurfacing cycle in years, G is the number of load repetitions before the pavement reaches its terminal state (ESALs[26]), and E is the total load repetitions created by the vehicular traffic per unit of time (*ESALs*). Using Equations (19.23) and (19.24), it is possible to estimate annual resurfacing costs as follows:

$$C_{Resurf} = \frac{0.489 \cdot (N \cdot L)^{0.8197} \cdot i}{[(i + 1)^P - 1]} \tag{19.25}$$

where C_{Resurf} is the annual resurfacing cost, and i is the interest rate.

Right-of-way cost
Right-of-way costs vary considerably depending on location, amount of land acquired and the time of acquisition. In the following model we assume that land acquisition costs are a function of the amount of land procured and net residential density.

The database includes information on various construction projects. For each, recorded land value was obtained from government's appraisal. Each data point contains land size, the actual amount of money paid to the owner, the place where the land is located and the settlement date of purchase. The final database includes 16 observations. The estimated right-of-way cost model is:[27]

$$\ln (C_{row}) = a + b \cdot \ln (A) + c \cdot \ln (NRD) \tag{19.26}$$

where C_{row} is right-of-way cost, A is area of land in acres, and a, b and c are the coefficients of the model parameters. Estimation results are given in Table 19.7.

In the infrastructure cost estimates presented above, only the resurfacing cost function varies with traffic volume. Thus, while all of the above costs functions are used to compute total costs, only Equation (19.25) is used to estimate the marginal costs in our analysis.

Environmental Costs

This category of costs includes air and noise pollution costs, both of which are non-internalized externalities that vary with traffic level and makeup.

Air pollution costs[28]

Highway transportation contributes to air pollution due to the release of pollutants during motor vehicle operations. Its contribution is either through the direct emission of pollutants from chemical reactions of the emitted pollutants with each other or with the existing materials in the atmosphere or ground. The Environmental Protection Agency (EPA) recommends that air pollution costs should be calculated on the basis of several pollutants, namely VOC, CO, NO_x and PM_{10}.

In this chapter, a fuel consumption function, $F(V)$ where V is traffic level, was adopted to estimate the quantities of these pollutants, which are generated by motor vehicles. Unit cost values of each pollutant were calculated based on EPA reports (EPA, 1995). Thus, the total and marginal air pollution cost functions compatible with the US regulations are:

$$C_{air} = V \cdot (0.01094 + 0.2155 \cdot F) \tag{19.27}$$

$$MC_{air} = 0.010904 + 0.2155 \cdot \left(F + \frac{\partial F}{\partial V} \right) \tag{19.28}$$

where:

C_{air} = total air pollution cost ($)
MC_{air} = marginal air pollution cost ($/trip)

$$F = 0.0723 - 0.00312 \cdot S + 5.403 \times 10^{-5} \cdot S^2 \tag{19.29}$$

V = traffic volume (per mile)
S = average speed (miles/hour)

Noise costs

The literature regards noise levels above 50 dB(A) as a nuisance that imposes costs on people (Delucchi and Hsu, 1998; see also Chapter 15 by Delucchi and McCubbin). Noise costs are usually estimated by calculating the reduction in the value of residential units alongside highways and which tend to abate with distance away. In this chapter, the Noise Depreciation Sensitivity Index (NDSI) is taken as 0.85 per cent and the property value depreciation function is:

$$ND = N_h \cdot (L_{eq} - L_{Max}) \cdot D \cdot W_{avg} \tag{19.30}$$

where:

ND = depreciation value ($)
N_h = number of houses affected (houses/mile^2)
L_{eq} = equivalent noise level (dB(A))
L_{max} = maximum acceptable noise level (50 dB(A)), which is the lower bound of annoyance
D = percentage discount in value per increase in the ambient noise level (NDSI = 0.85%)

W_{avg} = average housing value (\$246 628 in year 2005)

The value of L_{max} is assumed to be 50 dB(A), which corresponds to normal conversational speech level. The formula for the equivalent noise level, L_{eq}, is obtained from the FHWA's Traffic Noise Level Model (Delucchi and Hsu, 1998).[29] The expression for L_{eq} is:

$$L_{eq} = 10 \cdot log(V) + 10 \cdot log(K) - 10 \cdot log(r) + 1.14 \tag{19.31}$$

In Equation (19.31), r is the distance to roadway (feet) and K is the aggregate noise-energy emission from all vehicle classes. For cars and trucks, the expression for noise-energy emission is as follows (Delucchi and Hsu, 1998):

$$K = K_c + K_{tr} \tag{19.32}$$

$$K = \frac{F_c}{S_c} \cdot (S_c^{4.174} \cdot 10^{0.115} + 10^{5.03 \cdot F_{ac} + 6.7 \cdot (1 - F_{ac})}) + \frac{F_{tr}}{S_{tr}} \cdot (S_{tr}^{3.588} \cdot 10^{2.102} + 10^{7.43 \cdot F_{atr} + 7.4 \cdot (1 - F_{atr})}) \tag{19.33}$$

where:

K_c = noise-energy emission from autos
K_{tr} = noise-energy emission from trucks
F_c = percent of autos in the traffic
F_{tr} = percent of trucks in the traffic
F_{ac} = percent of free-flow traffic, which travel at free-flow speed
F_{atr} = percent of trucks, which travel at free-flow speed, in total traffic
S_c = speed of autos in the traffic (mph)
S_{tr} = speed of trucks in the traffic (mph)

The number of units affected by traffic noise, N_h, is calculated by multiplying the average residential density, RD, (housing units/square mile) near a highway by the distance to that highway, r (miles) and the length of relevant highway section, d (miles). That is:

$$N_h = 2 \cdot (RD) \cdot r \cdot d \tag{19.34}$$

In order to calculate the noise level around a specific highway (a link in the network), we take a distance range of 50 ft, which is equivalent to the distance where L_{eq} is equal to L_{max}, that is, r_{max} 50 ft. In other words, for the calculations of the costs of noise, we consider the area where the generated noise can be regarded as effective. Residential density is regarded as a function of the degree of urbanization of the area where a specific link is located. Thus, residential density is set as follows: central business district = 4/acre, urban = 3/acre, suburban = 2/acre and rural = 1/acre. Based on these specifications total and marginal noise cost functions are given as follows:

$$C_{noise} = 2 \int_{r_1 = 50}^{r_2 = r_{max}} (L_{eq} - 50) \cdot D \cdot W_{avg} \cdot \frac{RD}{5280} \cdot dr \tag{19.35}$$

$$MC_{noise} =$$

$$W_{avg} \cdot \frac{RD}{264} \cdot \left[\frac{\partial r_2}{\partial V} \cdot (log(V) + log(K) - log(r_2) - 4.89) + \frac{r_2 - r_1}{ln10} \cdot \left(\frac{1}{V} + \frac{\frac{\partial K}{\partial V}}{K} \right) \right]$$

(19.36)

where:

C_{noise} = total noise cost ($)
MC_{noise} = marginal noise cost ($/trip)

Equation (19.35) calculates the total noise cost within a rectangular area around the roadway affected by a noise level above the allowable 50 dB(A). Next, we report the empirical results from a specific case study, carried out in order to assess the FMC of highway capacity expansion.

CASE STUDY

Traditional transportation models make use of network traffic assignment, mainly static assignment, to assess the impact of capacity improvements on traffic flow. Here we compute FMC using a transportation model (NJRTM), which includes an assignment algorithm and which provides a comprehensive and consistent approach for the measurement of all transportation costs with respect to different O–D pairs and road sections.[30] The objective is to estimate the changes in traffic flows both at the local and network levels, caused by capacity improvements. Based on these changes we compute FMC values, engendered by these improvements.[31]

The modeled area consists of 13 counties in the North Jersey region.[32] The network consists of 1377 traffic zones and 74 external zones (NJTPA, 2008). The input variables include traffic volumes, travel times, link capacities, node and link IDs, highway type, number of lanes, free flow speed and free flow travel time for each link, residential units' distance to highways and residential area type. The cost functions, presented in the previous sections, are used to estimate trip costs between O–D pairs.[33] Using the NJRTM model, it was possible to estimate the transportation costs for the original and modified (that is, following capacity enhanced) network conditions.

For this analysis we have selected three major roadway-widening projects, completed between 2004 and 2009, in Northern NJ. Table 19.8 summarizes key features of the selected projects. Details of these projects, along with the network map showing their locations, are provided in Appendix 19A.2.

After increasing the capacity of these road sections, using the same O–D demand matrices, traffic is reassigned onto the modified network. Subsequently, the output information obtained from the traffic assignment is used for comparison of 'before' and 'after' costs. The difference represents the benefits (that is, the reduction in costs) attributable to each specific project. It should be noted that impacts of each capacity investment are

Table 19.8   The selected widening projects in northern New Jersey

Route	Location	Length	Work Type	Cost
Route 17	Bergen County	0.50 miles	Roadway widening and bridge reconstruction	$84.4 million
Route 18	Middlesex County	1.54 miles	Roadway widening and extension	$82 million
Route 35	Middlesex Country	1.38 miles	Roadway widening and bridge reconstruction	$129.6 million

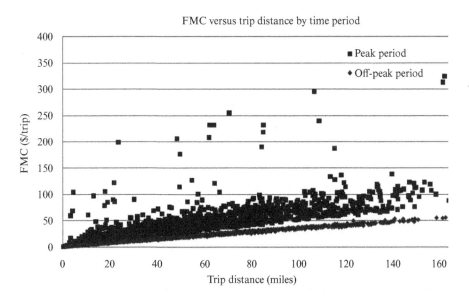

Figure 19.2   FMC values during peak and off-peak hours as a function of trip distance

investigated separately, that is, three different modified networks are created for the three different capacity investments.

For this analysis 1500 random O–D pairs were selected and peak and off-peak period FMC values were estimated for the base network (without capacity improvements).[34] Figure 19.2 depicts the difference in FMC values between peak and off-peak hours as a function of trip distance. As expected, peak-hour FMC values are higher than off peak-hour values, and this difference is more evident as trip distance increases. Moreover, due to high variation in traffic volume during peak-hours, the variability of the FMC values are much higher during the peak-hours compared with off-peak hours.

Tables 19.9 and 19.10 summarize the different cost categories that compose the FMC model. Full Average Cost (FAC) values for the same O–D pairs were also estimated. During the peak period mean FMC value for the randomly selected O–D pairs is found to be $48.2/trip, while the corresponding FAC value is $36.0/trip, indicating scale diseconomies associated with traffic flow. That is, a unit increase in traffic will generate more than proportional increase in total costs (direct and social). In particular, travel time,

Table 19.9   Breakdown of FMC and FAC categories for peak period

Cost Category	Average ($/trip)		Max ($/trip)		Min ($/trip)		Standard Deviation ($/trip)		Cost/mile ($/mile)	
	FMC	FAC	FMC	FAC	FMC	FAC	FMC	FAC	FMC	FAC
Operating	9.8	9.62	33.7	32.56	0.06	0.06	6.3	6.01	0.167	0.165
Travel time	38.3	26.1	306.1	74.6	0.44	0.46	32.1	13.4	0.78	0.51
Accident	0.17	0.038	0.87	0.14	0.01	0.0	0.12	0.027	0.004	6E-4
Air pollution	–0.075	0.02	5.53	0.17	–11.44	0.0	2.27	0.029	0.009	3E-4
Noise	–0.027	0.248	0.159	4.23	–0.33	0.01	0.058	0.332	–3E-4	0.005
Maintenance	0.021	0.009	0.171	0.23	0.0	0.0	0.029	0.017	3E-4	1.2E-4
Total	48.2	36.0	335.3	110.1	0.592	0.54	35.8	19.2	0.96	0.68

Table 19.10   Breakdown of FMC and FAC categories for off-peak period

Cost Category	Average ($/trip)		Max ($/trip)		Min ($/trip)		Standard Deviation ($/trip)		Cost/mile ($/mile)	
	FMC	FAC	FMC	FAC	FMC	FAC	FMC	FAC	FMC	FAC
Operating	9.78	9.42	31.4	30.2	0.23	0.25	6.06	5.8	0.167	0.161
Travel time	9.50	9.45	30.6	29.8	0.70	0.77	5.23	5.1	0.178	0.177
Accident	0.23	0.05	1.41	0.16	0.02	0.0	0.16	0.03	0.5002	8E-4
Air pollution	2.38	0.037	7.55	0.26	–0.57	0.0	1.32	0.05	0.046	6E-4
Noise	0.026	0.606	0.088	10.2	–0.123	0.02	0.02	0.84	4E-4	0.012
Maintenance	0.037	0.024	0.26	0.51	0.0	0.0	0.047	0.041	6E-4	4E-4
Total	21.96	19.6	66.8	61.3	1.12	1.16	12.33	11.4	0.40	0.35

vehicle operating costs and accident costs exhibit diseconomies of scale, reflecting the fact that, given the New Jersey network and traffic demand levels, an additional trip will impose a disproportional increase in private and social costs. The difference between FMC and FAC is larger during peak-periods compared with off-peak periods. As shown in Table 19.10, FMC and FAC estimated during off-peak period are $21.96/trip and $19.6/trip, respectively.

Notice the negative values in Tables 19.9 and 19.10, for the FMC of air pollution and noise. These results are due to reductions in travel speed, which produce lower air and noise pollution values; the zero values indicate very low values and are due to rounding off.

For both FMC and the FAC values, travel time and operating costs dominate all other cost categories. Similarly, travel time costs vary the most among different O–D pairs compared with the other cost categories. The relative order of per mile cost values reported above is similar to the short-run US urban commuters' transportation cost values shown in Small and Verhoef (2007), except for the accident cost category. This difference may be explained by the fact that, during peak hours, traffic volume is much higher compared with off peak hours, resulting in reduced traffic speeds, thus reduced rate of fatal accidents.

After increasing the capacity of the roadway sections, corresponding to the selected projects given in Table 19.8, traffic is reassigned onto the modified network using the same O–D demand matrices. The output information obtained from the traffic assignment is then used for comparison of before and after costs. The differences are the benefits (that is, the reduction in costs) attributable to the project.

Table 19A.2 of Appendix 19A.3 shows the 'before' and 'after' FMC results with respect to morning peak, midday, afternoon peak and night periods for each of the three roadway projects.[35] The estimates are shown in 95 per cent confidence interval. Note that 'before' network for Route 17 project is denoted by 'Base Bergen' and for Route 18 and Route 35 projects it is denoted by 'Base Middlesex'.

From these results it is evident that for the majority of the cases FMC values do not change significantly following the capacity improvements. The reduction in costs, if any, mostly appears in the 'congestion' category. Moreover, there are several cases where FMC values are higher after the capacity improvements. One explanation is the way the set of O–D pairs were selected. That is, O–D pairs were selected randomly, which does not guarantee that the route between each O–D pair will include the improved highway segment. In fact, we found out that out of 500 random pairs selected for the FMC analysis each project, on average only three paths included the improved highway segment. Another explanation is that congestion costs are expected to fall on parallel links as traffic diverts off them to the expanded links. Similarly, costs are expected to rise on links that are in immediately upstream or downstream of the expanded links because they now carry more traffic. Overall, despite the local effects on traffic of these projects, at the network level their impact on reduced travel times and costs is quite marginal. Unfortunately, a smaller coded network does not exist that could be used to assess FMC results at that network scale.

Using the available transportation network, it is also possible to estimate the transportation costs for original and modified (that is, capacity enhanced) network conditions. A link-based approach was used to calculate the total network costs for the original and modified networks. The cost on each link was calculated as the product of its traffic volume and estimated total cost, and aggregated over all links in the network. The estimates of 'before' and 'after' total costs with respect to morning peak, midday, afternoon peak and night periods for each of the three projects shown in Table 19.8 are presented in Table 19A.3 of Appendix 19A.3. The total network costs before capacity improvements are presented as 'Before' total costs. The values given for Route 17, Route 18 and Route 35 represent the total network costs after the capacity improvements due to each of these projects. For example, the reduction in total costs as a result of Route 17 project can be calculated as the difference between the total costs of the 'before' network and the total costs of the Route 17 project. Table 19A.3 shows that the daily reduction in total network costs for Route 17 project is $2.15 million, for Route 18 project is $1.95 million and for Route 35 project is $1.62 million.

It should be noted that the transportation demand model of North Jersey was validated for an average workday. Currently there are no available weekend travel demand models for this network. Therefore, the results in Table 19A.3 represent an estimated change in total costs due to capacity expansion on a given work-day.

SUMMARY AND CONCLUSIONS

This chapter is concerned with the estimation of the Full Marginal Costs (FMC) of highway travel with respect to various direct and indirect (externality) impacts. The main cost categories analyzed here include: user, infrastructure, and environmental costs. For each category, a specific cost function was estimated with O–D based trips as output measures. The estimated parameters were then used to analyze the impacts of three capacity improvements projects on FMC values at the highway network level (that of Northern New Jersey). Key results from the analysis indicate that travel time, vehicle operating and accident costs dominate all other cost categories. During peak hours, the FMC were much higher than the Full Average Costs (FAC). This phenomenon, in turn, implies that an additional trip unit imposes a disproportional total costs.

A key caveat to this analysis is the short-term nature of capacity expansion impact on FMC values. In the long-run, due to latent or induced demand, as well as activity relocation, travel behavior and trip patterns might change. In turn, the short-term FMC results may reverse and, under some conditions (for example, mode switching), may produce higher FMC values than before the capacity changes. However, once such long-run changes are modeled, the FMC methodology developed here can be used to evaluate their effect on highway costs.

A major result from the above case studies is the fact that although FMC can be reduced by capacity modifications along the improved roadway, when network-wide effects are considered (that is, trips that do not include the improved roadway) reductions in FMC are rather minor. As mentioned before, in large and complex transportation networks drivers change their travel patterns to maximize utility, resulting in different traffic volumes along the roadways. Therefore, estimating the travel cost changes of capacity improvement only on the expanded roadway will not produce a complete picture of the overall impacts of those improvements. This is clearly shown by the results obtained for the above three capacity improvement projects.

NOTES

1. The costs incurred by transport operating companies are treated in detail in the chapter by Basso et al.
2. In the case study calculations will be carried out for peak and off-peak hours.
3. Here, we use the formulation with the same notation as presented in Banister and Berechman (2000). A similar analysis is presented in Small (1992) and Small and Verhoef (2007, Section 5.1).
4. Possible other changes include accident and environmental costs, though the direction of these changes is a priori not clear.
5. The BPR function has the form: $T = T_0 \cdot [1 + \alpha \cdot (V/K)^\beta]$, where T_0 is the free-flow travel time, V is traffic volume, K is road capacity and α, β are parameters that describe how the ratio of traffic volume to capacity (V/K) affects travel time. The generally accepted values are $\alpha = 0.15$ and $\beta = 4.0$.
6. Meyer et al. (1965) utilized the construction cost function that Joseph (1960) estimated for eight-lane expressways. Therefore, they assume percentages with respect to the width of a typical eight-lane expressway, w_c, to adjust Equation (19.9) for roadways of varying number of lanes (Table 61, p. 203). They assume that a typical eight-lane expressway would occupy 206 ft; and that typical roadways with two, four and six lanes would occupy, 134 ft, 158 ft and 182 ft, respectively. A simple linear regression of this database gives: $w_c = 0.058 \cdot N + 0.535$, where N is number of lanes.
7. Meyer et al. (1965) do not provide information on goodness-of-fit or any other relevant statistics.
8. Kraus assumes a fixed width of 100 ft for median, shoulder and buffer zone for freeway construction (Kraus (1981, p. 10).

9. No goodness of fit information is reported except for R^2 of 0.51 for the regression.
10. Estimated parameters were presented in Kane and Morlok (1970, p. 335). The cost equation for soil and regional type A1 in their classification has the following estimated parameters: $a = -3.948$, $b = 1.11814$, $c = 0.01092$, $d = 0.00012$, $e = -0.10074$.
11. Relief index, *RLF* represents indirect information regarding the terrain of construction areas from topographic maps. Kane and Morlok (1970, p. 330) recognize that *RLF* is a crude measure of terrain. It is hard to deduce from their definition of *RLF* the range of this variable.
12. Levinson and Karamalaputi (2003) report R^2 of 0.77 with all parameters being statistically significant at 90 per cent confidence interval. Their database included 76 observations.
13. They report that more than 50 per cent of all highway construction costs occur in these construction categories.
14. Notable exceptions are: Jara-Diaz et al. (1992), Ozbay et al. (2001, 2007a, 2007b, 2007c), Safirova et al. (2007).
15. Data on these costs are in dollars per mile. The assignment algorithm is trip-based with subsequent conversion to distance traveled.
16. Depreciation data required were obtained from the official Website of *Kelley Blue Book* (2006).
17. USDOT's (1997) figures apply to all combinations of in-vehicle and other travel times. Walk, access, waiting and transfer time are taken at 100 per cent of the wage rate.
18. Here we use the lower bound of the range of hourly wages suggested by USDOT (1997), which results in VOT for passenger cars of \$18.1 and \$7.9 during peak and off-peak hours, respectively; and \$19.9 for trucks for all time periods.
19. For trucking, VOT only includes the driver's time. However, a comprehensive VOT of trucking should include also the time cost of the cargo and constraints imposed by the supply chain. In that case, VOT can amount to several times the wage rate.
20. It should be noted that the following construction cost function does not apply to arterials, collectors and local roadways.
21. Final cost amount of each project was converted into 2008 dollars using a 2.5 per cent discount rate.
22. Total earthwork variable was not significant in the estimation results and, therefore, dropped from the model.
23. All coefficients are significant at 95 per cent confidence interval.
24. All coefficients are significant at 95 per cent confidence interval.
25. Here, we disregard other factors, such as weather, which might affect the aging of the pavement.
26. $ESAL = (ADT0) \cdot (T) \cdot (Tf) \cdot (D) \cdot (L) \cdot (365)$ Where $(ADT0)$ = initial average daily traffic, T = percentage of trucks, Tf = truck factor, D = directional distribution factor, L = lane distribution factor. See Huang (1993) for truck factors for various roadway functional types.
27. As Keeler and Small (1977) noted, conversion of the costs of 'old' projects to present-day values is quite problematic. Here we used a discount rate of 2.5 per cent to convert the amount paid in the past to current US dollars.
28. Editor note: Air pollution costs in the United States are discussed by Delucchi and McCubbin in their chapter on the external costs of transportation in the United States.
29. This model is based on recent measurements of noise from different motor vehicles: autos, light trucks, medium trucks, heavy trucks and buses. Its parameters relate to intermediate obstructions including road surface type and noise emitted by accelerating vehicles.
30. The model, NJRTM, is currently used by the North Jersey Transportation Planning Authority (NJTPA).
31. Only short-run impacts (that is, reduction in costs) are investigated in this chapter, thus disregarding longer-term effects such as induced demand.
32. To represent travel to and from places outside the region, including New York City, we have used external Travel Zone Areas (or stations), which represent zones that fall outside the model's network.
33. Estimation of FMC values were performed using NJCOST program developed by Ozbay et al. (2008).
34. Average trip-length of these O–D pairs is 58.7 miles with minimum, maximum and standard deviation of 1.4, 188.1 and 36.3 miles, respectively.
35. In order to estimate the change in FMC values, due to each project, we randomly selected 500 O–D pairs in the vicinity of each project. The results reported in Appendix 19A.3 are for these zones.

REFERENCES

AAA, 2005, Your driving costs 2005. American Automobile Association. Available at: www.ouraaa.com.
American Association of State Highway and Transportation Officials, 2007, Poll results: crash costs used for prioritizing safety projects. Available at www.transportation.org/?siteid=62&pageid=1622.

Anderson, D. and G. McCullough, 2000, The full cost of transportation in the twin cities region. Center for Transportation Studies, CTS 00-04.

Apogee Research, 1994, The Costs of Transportation. Boston, MA: Conservation Law Foundation.

Arnott, R. and M. Kraus, 2003, Principles of transport economics. In R.W. Hall, ed., *Handbook of Transportation Science*, 2nd ed. Dordrecht, The Netherlands: Kluwer Academic, pp. 689–726.

Banfi, S., C. Boll, M. Maibach, W. Rothengatter, P. Schenkel, N. Sieber and J. Zuber, 2000, *External Costs of Transport: Accident, Environmental and Congestion Costs in Western Europe*. Zurich: INFRAS.

Banister, D. and J. Berechman, 2000, *Transport Investment and Economic Development*. London: University College London Press.

Berechman, J., 2009, *The Evaluation of Transportation Investment Projects*. New York: Routledge.

Berechman, J., and G. Giuliano, 1984, Analysis of the cost structure of an urban bus transit property. *Transportation Research Part B*, **18**, 273–287.

Black, W., D. Munn, R. Black and J. Xie., 1996, Modal choices: an approach to comparing the costs of transportation alternatives. Technical Report Transportation Research Center, Indiana University, Bloomington.

Cipriani, R., M.J. Porter, N. Conroy, L. Johnson and K. Semple, 1998, The full costs of transportation in the Central Puget Sound region in 1995. TRB Preprint: 980670, Transportation Board 77th Annual meeting, Washington DC.

Decorla-Souza, P. and R. Jensen-Fisher, 1997, Comparing multimodal alternatives in major travel corridors. *Transportation Research Record*, **1429**, 15–23.

Delucchi, M., 1996, Annualized social cost of motor vehicle in use in the United States, based on 1990–1991 data. Technical Report, University of California at Davis, No. 8, 7–13.

Delucchi, M. and S. Hsu, 1998, The external damage cost of noise emitted from motor vehicles. *Journal of Transportation and Statistics*, **1**, 1–24.

Ellwanger, G., 2000, *External Environmental Costs of Transport: Comparison of Recent Studies, Social Costs and Sustainable Mobility*. ZEW, Mannheim, Germany: Physica-Verlag, pp. 15–20.

Environmental Protection Agency (EPA), 1995, *National Emission Trends*. Washington DC: EPA Publications.

Federal Highway Administration, 1994, Motor vehicle accident costs. Available at www.fhwa.dot.gov/leg-sregs/directives/techadvs/t75702.htm.

Federal Highway Administration, 1997, Federal highway cost allocation study final report (and addendum). FHWA, Department of Transportation. Available at: www.fhwa.dot.gov/policy/hcas/final/index.htm.

Fuller, J.W., J.B. Hokanson, J. Haugaard and J. Stoner, 1983, Measurements of highway interference costs and air pollution and noise damage costs, final report 34. Washington DC: US Department of Transportation, Federal Highway Administration.

Gibbons, E. and M. O'Mahony, 2002, External cost internalisation of urban transport: a case study of Dublin. *Journal of Environmental Management*, **64**, 401–410.

Huang, Y.H., 1993, *Pavement Analysis and Design*. Upper Saddle River, NJ: Prentice Hall.

IBI Group, 1995, Full cost transportation pricing study. Transportation and Climate Change Collaborative, Toronto, November 1995.

Jara-Diaz, S.R., P.P. Donoso and J.A. Araneda, 1992, Estimation of marginal transport costs: the flow aggregation function approach. *Journal of Transport Economics and Policy*, 35–48.

Joseph, H., 1960, Construction costs of urban freeways. CATS Research News 4.

Kane, A.R. and E. Morlok, 1970, Road capital cost functions: theory and estimation. *Transportation Research*, **4**, 325-337.

Keeler, T.E., 1975, The full costs of urban transport. Intermodal Comparisons, Technical Report, Institute of Urban and Regional Development, Berkeley.

Keeler, T.E. and K.A. Small, 1977, Optimal peak-load pricing, investment, and service levels on urban expressways. *Journal of Political Economy*, **85**, 1–25.

Kelley Blue Book Website, 2006, Available at www.kbb.com.

KPMG, 1993, The cost of transporting people in the British Columbia lower mainland. Technical Report Transport 2021/Greater Vancouver Regional District. Available at www.gvrd.bc.ca/growth/transport2021/Report11.pdf.

Kraus, M., 1981, Scale economies analysis for urban highway networks. *Journal of Urban Economics*, **9**, 1–22.

Lee, D.B., 1995, Full cost pricing of highways. US Department of Transportation, Research and Special Programs Administration, Volpe National Transportation Systems Center.

Levinson, D., 1997, An econometric analysis of network deployment and application to road pricing. California PATH Working Paper, UCB-ITS-PWP-98-1, Berkeley CA, 1997.

Levinson, D. and D. Gillen, 1998, The full cost of intercity highway transportation. *Transportation Research Part D*, **3**, 207–223.

Levinson, D. and R. Karamalaputi, 2003, Predicting the construction of new highway links. *Journal of Transportation and Statistics*, **6** (2/3), 1–9.

APPENDIX 19A.1　HIGHWAY COST FUNCTION STUDIES

The table below summarizes transportation cost function estimation studies by area of application and cost category. The majority of these studies focus on vehicle operating, congestion, air pollution, noise and infrastructure costs; whereas only a few studies focus on water pollution and climate change costs.

Most studies in the table below focus on the estimation of average cost of highway transportation. Very few studies deal with the estimation of marginal costs, which are essential for congestion pricing (Levinson et al., 1996; Levinson and Gillen, 1998; Mayeres et al., 1996; Ozbay et al., 2001). Ozbay et al. (2001), deal with both marginal and full costs of supplying transportation services. Mayeres et al. (1996), deal with the estimation of marginal external costs only. The 'British Columbia Lower Mainland' study (KPMG, 1993) uses societal costs such as cost of roadway land value, cost of air and water pollution, cost accidents, and cost of loss of open space and user costs. Ozbay et al. (2001) estimate FMC based on one additional trip, presenting variations in FMC with respect to trip distance, facility type, urbanization degree and the time of the day.

Table 19A.1　Studies of transportation costs functions

Cost category	Study and area
Vehicle operating, congestion, air pollution, noise and infra-structure costs	Keeler (1975) – San Fransisco Bay Area, Mackenzie et al. (1992) – US general, Jara–Diaz et al. (1992) – Chile, KPMG (1993) – Vancouver, Miller and Moffet (1993) – US general, Apogee (1994) – Boston, OTA (1994) – US general, IBI (1995) – Canada, Lee (1995) – US general – no congestion cost, Mayeres et al. (1996) – Brussels, Black et al. (1996) – US general, Delucchi (1996) – US general, Levinson (1997), Levinson and Gillen (1998), Levinson et al. (1996) – California, Decorla–Souza and Jensen–Fisher (1997) – US general, Zegras and Litman (1997) – Chile, Cipriani et al. (1998) – Central Puget Sound, Anderson and McCullough (2000) – Twin Cities, Banfi et al. (2000) – Europe, Ellwanger (2000) – Europe – only environmental costs, Small, K. and Kazimi, C. (1995), Small, K. (1977) US general, Ozbay et al. (2001) – New Jersey, Sansom et al. (2001) – UK, Quinet (2004) – Europe, Ozbay et al. (2001, 2007a, 2007b, 2007c) – New Jersey. [Only Congestion: Fuller et al. (1983) – US general, Maddison et al. (1996) – U.K. general, Link (2006) – maintenance costs only, Germany, Gibbons and O'Mahony (2002) – Dublin, Safirova et al. (2007) – Washington], [Studies not considering operating or infrastructure costs: Verhoef (2000), FHWA (1997, 2000) – US general, Proost et al. (2002) – Europe]
Water pollution cost	KPMG (1993) – Vancouver, Apogee (1994) – Boston, OTA (1994) – US general, Lee (1995) – US general, Black et al. (1996) – US general, Delucchi (1996) – US general, Decorla–Souza and Jensen–Fisher (1997) – US general
Climate change cost	Mackenzie et al. (1992) – US general, IBI (1995) – Canada, Mayeres et al. (1996) – Brussels, Anderson and McCullough (2000) – Twin Cities, Banfi et al. (2000) – Europe

APPENDIX 19A.2   DETAILS OF THE SELECTED PROJECT USED FOR THE FMC ANALYSIS

Route 17: The project replaced the existing deficient structure of four-lane Essex Street Bridge with a new, wider structure of six lanes that is compatible with the planned future improvements on Route 17. The demolished bridge was 76 years old. The construction of the new bridge and the improvements at the ramps to Route 17 were completed in the summer of 2008. The total construction cost, inflated to year 2008 dollars using a 2.5 per cent discount rate, is $84.4 million (NJDOT, 2005).

Route 18: It links the New Brunswick area with north-central New Jersey shore communities. In 2001, the NJDOT approved a reconstruction as part of its 5-year capital program. The project was completed in 2004 replacing an existing two-lane roadway with a new four-lane limited access highway. The allocated fund for this project was $75.6 million in 2002. The total construction cost is calculated as $87.4 million for the year 2008 by compounding the costs using a 2.5 per cent interest rate (NJDOT, 2005).

Route 35: The Victory Bridge in New Jersey carries Route 35 over the Raritan River, connecting Perth Amboy and Sayreville. The new bridge replaced a bridge constructed in 1926. The old bridge carried four 9.5-foot travel lanes with no shoulders. The objective of the new bridge was to boost the regional economy and significantly alleviate congestion and improve safety. The new bridge consists of twin structures (northbound and southbound) each carrying two 12-foot lanes, a 10-foot bike lane/outside shoulder and a three foot shoulder. The bridge was designed with a 440-foot main span. The construction was completed in December 2005. (NJDOT, 2005).

The adjusted cost of the project in 2008 dollars was $129.6 million. The allocated fund for this project was $75.6 million in 2002. The total construction cost is calculated as $87.4 million for the year 2008 by inflating the costs using a 2.5 per cent inflation rate

The exact locations of these projects relative to the Northern New Jersey highway network are shown in Figure 19A.1.

Figure 19A.1 Locations of the selected roadway projects

APPENDIX 19A.3

Table 19A.2   The 'before' and 'after' FMC results ($)

	Vehicle operating	Congestion	Accident	Air Pollution	Noise	Maintenance	FMC Total
Morning peak							
Base Middlesex	[2.196,2.503]	[11.188,12.958]	[0.104,0.118]	[0.233,0.437]	[-0.004,0.00]	[0.003,0.006]	[13.72,16.02]
Base Bergen	[1.747,2.019]	[6.860,7.720]	[0.084,0.094]	[0.471,0.596]	[-0.003,-0.001]	[0.0006,0.001]	[11.02,13.19]
Route 17	[1.706,1.937]	[8.643,10.062]	[0.087,0.097]	[0.483,0.607]	[-0.003,-0.0009]	[0.0008,0.0011]	[10.92,12.70]
Route 18	[2.289,2.598]	[10.960,12.767]	[0.103,0.117]	[0.371,0.575]	[-0.003,0.0009]	[0.0048,0.0079]	[13.73,16.07]
Route 35	[2.204,2.509]	[10.719,12.518]	[0.097,0.110]	[0.179,0.450]	[-0.006,-0.0016]	[0.003,0.006]	[13.20,15.59]
Afternoon peak							
Base Middlesex	[2.241,2.559]	[12.768,14.920]	[0.098,0.111]	[0.402,0.568]	[0.000,0.002]	[0.004,0.006]	[15.51,18.17]
Base Bergen	[1.843,2.096]	[10.559,13.057]	[0.079,0.089]	[0.281,0.432]	[-0.005,-0.003]	[0.0008,0.001]	[12.76,15.67]
Route 17	[1.801,2.084]	[10.701,13.552]	[0.080,0.091]	[0.311,0.450]	[-0.006,-0.003]	[0.0007,0.0011]	[12.89,16.18]
Route 18	[2.303,2.622]	[13.562,15.995]	[0.102,0.115]	[0.206,0.449]	[-0.004,-0.0003]	[0.004,0.006]	[16.17,19.19]
Route 35	[2.280,2.589]	[12.912,15.075]	[0.096,0.109]	[0.322,0.532]	[-0.003,0.0008]	[0.003,0.005]	[15.61,18.31]
Midday							
Base Middlesex	[2.104,2.405]	[3.045,3.384]	[0.107,0.121]	[0.715,0.815]	[0.004,0.005]	[0.007,0.010]	[5.98,6.74]
Base Bergen	[1.590,1.825]	[2.420,2.690]	[0.092,0.104]	[0.763,0.888]	[0.003,0.004]	[0.001,0.002]	[4.87,5.51]
Route 17	[1.637,1.860]	[2.496,2.748]	[0.097,0.109]	[0.781,0.899]	[0.003,0.004]	[0.001,0.002]	[5.01,5.62]
Route 18	[2.253,2.552]	[3.177,3.518]	[0.107,0.121]	[0.760,0.863]	[0.005,0.006]	[0.007,0.011]	[6.31,7.07]
Route 35	[2.042,2.345]	[2.976,3.304]	[0.106,0.120]	[0.708,0.814]	[0.004,0.005]	[0.006,0.009]	[5.84,6.60]
Night							
Base Middlesex	[2.157,2.469]	[2.960,3.297]	[0.143,0.162]	[0.752,0.860]	[0.005,0.006]	[0.007,0.011]	[6.02,6.81]
Base Bergen	[1.728,1.968]	[2.448,2.703]	[0.121,0.137]	[0.836,0.976]	[0.003,0.004]	[0.001,0.002]	[5.14,5.79]
Route 17	[1.615,1.827]	[2.400,2.648]	[0.127,0.142]	[0.790,0.916]	[0.003,0.004]	[0.001,0.002]	[4.94,5.54]
Route 18	[2.049,2.348]	[2.884,3.204]	[0.145,0.164]	[0.728,0.836]	[0.005,0.006]	[0.005,0.008]	[5.82,6.56]
Route 35	[2.154,2.432]	[3.026,3.328]	[0.157,0.178]	[0.752,0.865]	[0.005,0.006]	[0.005,0.008]	[6.09,6.82]

Notes:
Brackets represents the 95 percent confidence level of the cost estimates.
Route 17, 18 and 35 show the results *after* the capacity improvements at these highways. The FMC value *before* the capacity improvements on Route 17 is given in Base Bergen. Similarly the FMC value *before* the improvements on Route 18 and 35 are given in Base Middlesex.

Table 19A.3 The 'before' and 'after' total cost results ($)

	Vehicle operating	Congestion	Accident	Air pollution	Noise	Maintenance	Total
Morning peak							
Before	12269130	39133860	3090104	1866980	42316.2	688671.8	57091062
Route 17	12201810	37791990	3054356	1865848	42233.3	731113.8	55687351
Route 18	12181890	37494590	3045857	1864648	42199.3	731733.3	55360918
Route 35	12202720	37776420	3055329	1865782	42235.1	731017.6	55673504
Midday off-peak							
Before	13290220	14092140	4131658	2538840	65369.9	1584298	35702526
Route 17	13290210	14091140	4131628	2538710	65327.9	1584178	35701194
Route 18	13290190	14091990	4131689	2538826	65369.4	1584272	35702336
Route 35	13290120	14091140	4131627	2538840	65364.9	1584298	35701390
Afternoon peak							
Before	13737490	45214080	3422373	2054029	45853.5	740909.6	65214735
Route 17	13705500	44701830	3407008	2052287	45835.8	741083.9	64653545
Route 18	13734350	45176190	3421061	2054931	45900.4	740835.8	65173268
Route 35	13740870	45187420	3420469	2054826	45889.4	740848.1	65190323
Night off-peak							
Before	9350579	9712229	3744627	1805579	46189	2293476	26952679
Route 17	9335390	9562083	3726513	1799889	45673.3	2303998	26773546
Route 18	9335382	9562021	3726508	1799894	45673.7	2303998	26773477
Route 35	9335390	9562163	3726513	1799889	45673.3	2303998	26773626
Total daily change							
Route 17							**2145366**
Route 18							**1951003**
Route 35							**1622160**

Notes:
Route 17, 18 and 35 show the results *after* the capacity improvements at these highways. The original network without the capacity improvements at these highways are the same for each project and labeled *Before* in the table.
The impacts of each capacity investment are investigated separately, *i.e.* three different modified networks are created for the three different capacity investments.

PART IV

OPTIMAL PUBLIC DECISIONS

20 Surplus theory
Yoshitsugu Kanemoto

INTRODUCTION

Cost–benefit analysis (CBA) is the main tool for economic evaluation of transportation projects and policies. It measures the social benefits and costs in monetary units as far as possible to check whether they are desirable from the viewpoint of society as a whole. In practice, CBA is supplemented by other types of analysis because it cannot deal with many important policy issues. For example, the distribution of benefits and costs may have to be forecasted to determine whether poor or special social groups bear disproportionately large burdens. Financial appraisals are also necessary to ensure that a project will be sustainable financially.

The concept of consumer surplus constitutes the core of CBA. It was developed in the middle of the nineteenth century by the French engineer/economist Jules Dupuit (1844). In the twentieth century, the practical application of CBA spread to a variety of public infrastructure projects, such as waterways (in the Federal Navigation Act of 1936, the Corps of Engineers in the United States were required to carry out project improvements of the waterway system when benefits exceeded project costs), flood control (the Flood Control Act of 1939), highway investments and public transits. In 1981, President Reagan issued Executive Order 12291, which required regulatory impact analysis that contains 'A determination of the potential net benefits of the rule, including an evaluation of effects that cannot be quantified in monetary terms'. *(Executive Order 12291, 1981)*. Since then, the use of CBA has become so widespread in the government that Adler and Posner (2000) even note, 'But deregulation seems to be running out of steam, whereas cost–benefit analysis seems thoroughly entrenched in the federal bureaucracy' (Adler and Posner, 2000, p. 5).

CBA in the transportation sector typically measures direct impacts on users, operators, governments and externalities such as environmental costs. According to the World Bank (2005), its main parts are

1. Changes in transport user benefits (consumer surplus);
2. Changes in system operating costs and revenues (producer surplus and government impacts);
3. Changes in costs of externalities (environmental costs, accidents, etc.); and
4. Investment costs (including mitigation measures).

The first part measures the benefits of direct impacts on users. The second and the fourth parts capture impacts on operators and governments, where the fourth part represents capital costs, and operating costs and revenues are included in the second part. The third part measures the external effects on those who are not users or suppliers. This chapter reviews the theoretical foundation of the first of the four parts, consumer surplus.

Transportation investments often entail significant indirect impacts on production and consumption patterns. These induced effects are usually ignored in CBA. We will see later that, if measured in monetary units, the benefits and costs of the induced effects cancel out each other as long as there are no price distortions, that is, no divergence between prices and marginal social costs.

CBA differs from a financial appraisal in that CBA's viewpoint is society as a whole, whereas a financial appraisal looks at the impact on one organization responsible for the transportation project. It corresponds roughly to the second part of CBA (producer surplus and government impacts), but there are some differences because the main purpose of a financial appraisal is to check the financial sustainability of a project. The most important difference is that it uses market prices and market interest rates whereas CBA uses shadow prices.

CBA provides a simple sum of the benefits and costs measured in monetary units. If their distribution is important, we have to disaggregate them into different groups or regions. Because the distribution of benefits is determined through general equilibrium repercussions, we have to simulate a general equilibrium model of the entire economy for this purpose. In practice, the evaluation of distributional impacts is not done very often because a general equilibrium model is costly to build and, because of its complexity, it is difficult to evaluate the reliability of the simulation results.

The organization of the rest of this chapter is as follows. The first part introduces the money-metric utility function as a theoretical basis for consumer surplus and examines compensating variation, equivalent variation and Marshallian consumer surplus. The second part considers the benefit evaluation of a transportation project in a general equilibrium framework. The last part deals with consumer surplus measures in random utility discrete choice models that are used widely in transportation demand modeling.

THEORETICAL FOUNDATIONS OF CONSUMER SURPLUS

The theoretical foundations of consumer surplus lie in the fact that rational consumer preferences can be represented by a utility function measured in monetary units. Consumer surplus can be derived from these money-metric utility functions.

Money-metric Utility Functions

The fact that the benefits that an individual receives can be measured in monetary units has been known for a long time. Mathematical formulation dates back to McKenzie (1957), and Samuelson (1974) attached the catchy expression, money-metric, to the utility function.

If consumers are rational in the sense that they make decisions according to consistent preferences, then their preferences can be represented by utility functions. More specifically, if a household has a preference ordering over possible bundles of goods, $\mathbf{x} \equiv (x_0, \cdots, x_N)$, that satisfy three conditions for consistency, completeness, reflexivity and transitivity, and two mathematical regularity conditions, continuity and monotonicity, then there exists a continuous utility function, $U(\mathbf{x})$, that represents the preferences.

Please refer to standard textbooks in advanced microeconomics, such as Varian (1992), for more complete discussions of this result.

By construction, many different utility functions represent the same preferences. In particular, any strictly increasing function of a given utility function preserves preference rankings and can be used as another utility function. Particularly attractive for policy evaluation is the money-metric utility function that measures utility in monetary units. The money-metric utility function can be constructed easily by computing the amount of money a consumer needs at a given price vector $\mathbf{p} \equiv (p_0, \cdots, p_N)$ to be indifferent to consuming a given bundle of goods, $\mathbf{x}$. Using the expenditure function that minimizes the expenditure necessary to attain a given utility level, u, as follows,

$$E(u, \mathbf{p}) = \text{Min}\{\mathbf{p} \cdot \mathbf{x} \text{ such that } U(\mathbf{x}) \geq u\},$$

we obtain the money metric utility function, $M(\mathbf{x}; \mathbf{p}) = E(U(\mathbf{x}), \mathbf{p})$. For a given price vector, this function gives a utility function in monetary units. Depending on the choice of the price vector, we have different money metric utility functions. The most common examples are those used in compensating variation (CV) and equivalent variation (EV). EV uses the price vector before the change, $\mathbf{p}^0$, to evaluate utility $M(\mathbf{x}; \mathbf{p}^0) = E(U(\mathbf{x}), \mathbf{p}^0)$, and CV the price vector after the change, $\mathbf{p}^1$, $M(\mathbf{x}; \mathbf{p}^1) = E(U(\mathbf{x}), \mathbf{p}^1)$.

CV and EV

Let us summarize briefly the definitions and properties of CV and EV. Consider a public policy or a public project that changes prices from $\mathbf{p}^0$ to $\mathbf{p}^1$ and the income of a house-hold from m^0 to m^1. The consumption bundles chosen before and after the change are denoted by $\mathbf{x}^0$ and $\mathbf{x}^1$. The utility level then changes from $u^0 = U(\mathbf{x}^0)$ to $u^1 = U(\mathbf{x}^1)$, and m^0 and m^1 satisfy $m^0 = M(\mathbf{x}^0, \mathbf{p}^0) = E(U(\mathbf{x}^0), \mathbf{p}^0)$ and $m^1 = M(\mathbf{x}^1, \mathbf{p}^1) = E(U(\mathbf{x}^1), \mathbf{p}^1)$. The compensating variation of this change is defined as $CV = m^1 - E(u^0, \mathbf{p}^1)$. Because $E(u^0, \mathbf{p}^1)$ shows the income level necessary to achieve the same utility level as before at after-the-change prices $\mathbf{p}^1$, CV can be interpreted as the subsidy necessary to restore the initial utility level. In other words, CV is the compensation needed to persuade the consumer to accept the change. In this sense, CV is a measure of willingness to accept (WTA) the proposed policy.

The equivalent variation (EV) is $EV = E(u^1, \mathbf{p}^0) - m^0$, which shows the amount of money that the household is willing to pay for the proposed change at the current prices $\mathbf{p}^0$. EV is therefore a measure of willingness to pay (WTP) for the change. Next, we show that CV and EV can be expressed using Hicksian compensated demand curves. Suppose that only the price of good 1, p_1, changes and income remains the same. Then, we have $m^1 = E(u^1, \mathbf{p}^1) = m^0 = E(u^0, \mathbf{p}^0)$ and CV and EV become $CV = E(u^0, \mathbf{p}^0) - E(u^0, \mathbf{p}^1)$ and $EV = E(u^1, \mathbf{p}^0) - E(u^1, \mathbf{p}^1)$. Because the compensated demand function is the derivative of the expenditure function with respect to the price, that is, $h_1(u, \mathbf{p}) = \partial E(u, \mathbf{p})/\partial p_1$, we can rewrite CV and EV as the integrals of the compensated demand functions as follows:

$$CV = E(u^0, \mathbf{p}^0) - E(u^0, \mathbf{p}^1) = \int_{p_1^1}^{p_1^0} h_1(u^0, \mathbf{p}) dp_1,$$

$$EV = E(u^1, \mathbf{p}^0) - E(u^1, \mathbf{p}^1) = \int_{p_1^1}^{p_1^0} h_1(u^1, \mathbf{p})\,dp_1.$$

CV is the area to the left of the compensated demand curve with utility fixed at the initial level, whereas in EV the utility is fixed at the after-the-change level.

Marshallian Consumer Surplus

Marshallian consumer surplus uses the uncompensated demand function instead of the compensated demand function: $CS = \int_{p_1^1}^{p_1^0} x(m, \mathbf{p})\,dp_1$. In general, Marshallian consumer surplus does not provide a money-metric utility function. To make matters worse, it is well known that Marshallian consumer surplus depends on the path of integration. This is a serious problem because we have many different values of the surplus depending on the path along which we calculate it, and there is no theoretical basis for choosing one of them. Nevertheless, Marshallian surplus is commonly used in practice because it is much easier to handle. Willig (1976) showed that the difference between the Marshallian surplus and CV or EV is small when the expenditure share of the good in question is small. In fact, Hicks himself did not think that the difference between them is important, as noted by Hines (1999, p. 179):

> *Hicks was himself unimpressed by the likely importance of the distinction between welfare measures constructed using compensated and Marshallian demand curves. It is easy to see why, since a compensated demand elasticity differs from the corresponding uncompensated demand elasticity only by the consumer's marginal propensity to spend on the good in question. Unless a commodity represents an extremely large fraction of a consumer's budget, compensated and uncompensated demand elasticities will not differ greatly and any differences between them are likely to be much smaller than the statistical uncertainty associated with demand elasticity estimates.*

If the utility function is quasilinear, as in $U(\mathbf{x}) = x_0 + u(x_1, \cdots, x_N)$, then the Marshallian consumer surplus coincides with CV and EV, and it can be used as a welfare measure. In most parts of the following sections, we use the quasilinear form to simplify exposition.

Allais (1943, 1977) developed another approach to consumer surplus. His idea is to compute the maximum amount of the numeraire good that can be extracted, while fixing the utility levels of all households and keeping the economy in equilibrium. As we will see later, this Allais surplus is an attractive choice when we have to incorporate general equilibrium repercussions into the CBA.

Irrational Behavior

Numerous studies in behavioral economics and economic psychology have shown that people often behave irrationally. It appears that there is no consensus as to how a standard CBA should be modified when people are not rational. Sunstein (2004) argued that the framework of CBA is an effective tool to let people think rationally when confronted by difficult decision problems such as risk policies involving recognition biases and informational cascades. Thaler and Sunstein (2008) proposed the approach of designing the choice architecture to induce people to make more rational decisions.

Aggregation Over Individuals

Any public policy affects many households, often in opposite directions. CBA usually uses the simple aggregation of the consumer surpluses of all households. Problems with this approach are well known. Most important among them is the lack of concern about the distributional impacts of a project. Kaldor (1939) and Hicks (1939) proposed the compensation principle, which permits hypothetical transfers from those who gain from a project to those who lose. According to Kaldor's compensation principle, state A is preferable to state B if those who gain at state A remain better off than at state B, even after compensating (hypothetically) those who lose. Hicks' criterion is reverse: state A is preferable to state B if at state B the losers are unable to compensate the gainers to remain as well off as in state A. The aggregate values of *CV* and *EV* have close relationships to the compensation tests. A positive aggregated *CV* is necessary for the Kaldor test to be passed, and a nonpositive aggregated *EV* is necessary for the Hicks test to be failed.[1]

It has been pointed out that there are serious weaknesses in this rationale. First, the compensation is hypothetical and does not solve the equity issue because compensation does not take place. Second, the compensation principle does not provide a consistent ranking. Scitovsky (1941) pointed out that reversals may occur: it is possible that both at state A and at state B the gainers can compensate losers so that nobody is made worse off. This means that aggregated *CV* and *EV* do not provide a consistent ranking of alternatives. Furthermore, Blackorby and Donaldson (1990) showed that 'in order to eliminate preference reversals and intransitivities, all households must have almost identical quasi-homothetic preferences'. This is close to assuming a representative consumer.

Although these criticisms are valid theoretically, CBA is a useful tool in practice. As argued by Adler and Posner (2000, p. 2), the practical value of CBA does not lie in the theoretical justification based on the compensation principle: 'Most, perhaps all, of the contributors would apparently agree that if government agencies should employ cost–benefit analysis, then they should do so because it is a beneficial tool, not because the sum-of-compensating-variations test or any related test has basic moral weight.'

It is of course true that a simple aggregation of consumer surpluses ignores equity issues. If distributional concerns are important, the only way out is to estimate the distribution of benefits and losses over different households or groups of households.

CONSUMER SURPLUS IN GENERAL EQUILIBRIUM

This section examines the benefit of a transportation investment project in a general equilibrium model of a single consumer economy. The utility function of a representative household is $U(\mathbf{x})$, where $\mathbf{x}$ is a vector of consumption goods. The household is faced with price vector, $\mathbf{p}$, where good 0 is the numeraire, that is, $p_0 = 1$, and transportation is good 1. To simplify notation, we assume a separable production function where good 0 is a ubiquitous input (such as labor) that is used to produce all other goods. The aggregate production function is

$$y_0 = \bar{y}_0 - C_1(y_1, k) - \sum_{i=2}^{N} C_i(y_i), \qquad (20.1)$$

where $\mathbf{y} = (y_0, y_1, \cdots, y_N)$ is a net output vector, k is transportation capacity and $\bar{y}_0$ is a fixed constant representing the total endowment of the numeraire good. We can interpret C_i as the cost of producing good i measured in the numeraire unit. We further assume that the marginal cost of transportation denoted by $c(k)$ is constant and depends on transportation capacity as follows:

$$C_1(y_1, k) = c(k)y_1 + k, \qquad (20.2)$$

where $c'(k) < 0$. Extension to a more general case is not difficult, although notationally messy.

A transportation investment project increases the transportation capacity from $k = 0$ to $k = K$ with investment cost K, which reduces the marginal cost from $c_1^0 = c(0)$ to $c_1^1 = c(K)$. This changes the equilibrium prices and quantities from $(\mathbf{p}^0, \mathbf{x}^0)$ to $(\mathbf{p}^1, \mathbf{x}^1)$. The resulting change in utility is

$$\Delta U = U(\mathbf{x}^1) - U(\mathbf{x}^0). \qquad (20.3)$$

Gross Consumer Surplus and Real National Income

Let us first examine an infinitesimally small change dk in capacity k. The equilibrium prices, consumption, production, and the total cost at k are denoted by $\mathbf{p}^*(k)$, $\mathbf{x}^*(k)$, $\mathbf{y}^*(k)$ and $C^*(k)$, respectively. Dividing the utility increase by the marginal utility of the numeraire, $\partial U/\partial x_0$, yields

$$\frac{dU^*(k)}{dk} \Big/ \frac{\partial U}{\partial x_0} = \sum_{i=0}^{N} \left(\frac{\partial U}{\partial x_i} \Big/ \frac{\partial U}{\partial x_0} \right) \frac{dx_i^*}{dk} = \sum_{i=0}^{N} p_i \frac{dx_i^*}{dk}, \qquad (20.4)$$

where the second equality results from the first-order condition for utility maximization, $p_i = (\partial U/\partial x_i)/(\partial U/\partial x_0)$. This shows that the benefit of a small change equals the change in consumption evaluated at consumer prices. At least for a small change, an increase in real national income provides a measure of the utility change in monetary units.

Next, we examine discrete changes in a special case where the marginal utility of income is constant. As noted earlier, this case is obtained when the utility function is quasilinear. Integrating Equation (20.4) from 0 to K yields the change in *social surplus* as follows:

$$\Delta SS \equiv \frac{1}{\partial U/\partial x_0} \Delta U = \int_0^K \sum_{i=0}^{N} \left[p_i^*(k) \frac{dx_i^*(k)}{dk} \right] dk. \qquad (20.5)$$

If $x_i = x_i^*(k)$ is invertible, we can write k as a function of x_i, that is, $k = k_i^*(x_i)$ for each x_i. This yields the general equilibrium (inverse) demand function,[2] $p_i^*(k_i^*(x_i))$, which traces the path of the price and quantity pair as k moves from 0 to K. Using this, we can rewrite the utility increase as

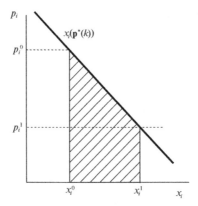

Figure 20.1   Gross consumer surplus in general equilibrium

$$\Delta SS = \sum_{i=0}^{N} \Delta GCS_i \text{ with } \Delta GCS_i = \int_{x_i^0}^{x_i^1} p_i^*(k_i^*(x_i)) dx_i, \qquad (20.6)$$

where ΔGCS_i is the area below the demand curve of good i as in Figure 20.1. The area is called 'social benefit' in the public finance literature and sometimes called 'gross consumer surplus'. We use the latter terminology in this chapter. The formula above shows that the change in utility caused by a public project can be measured by summing the areas below the demand curves (GCSs) of all the consumer goods.

If the general equilibrium demand curves are downward sloping, the GCS in each market is larger than the consumption increase multiplied by the pre-project price and smaller than that multiplied by the post-project price. Hence, the social surplus is between the Paasche and Laspeyres quantity indices as follows:

$$\sum_{i=0}^{N} p_i^1 \Delta x_i \leq \Delta SS \leq \sum_{i=0}^{N} p_i^0 \Delta x_i. \qquad (20.7)$$

Thus, the real national income evaluated at the pre-project prices (Laspeyres index) gives an upper bound for the social surplus and that at the post-project prices (Paasche index) a lower bound. Hicks (1942) obtained a more general version of this result that a Laspeyres index gives an upper bound for the equivalent variation and a Paasche index gives a lower bound for the compensating variation.

Consumer Surplus

To compute the change in real national income, we have to forecast consumption of all goods and services, which is difficult to do in practice. CBA uses a different formula that is derived by eliminating the numeraire from Equation (20.4) using market-clearing conditions and the production function.

Along the equilibrium path, all of the markets clear so that we have

$$\mathbf{x}^*(k) = \mathbf{y}^*(k), 0 \leq k \leq K, \text{ and } dx_i^*/dk = dy_i^*/dk \text{ for any } i. \qquad (20.8)$$

Furthermore, differentiating the production function (20.1) with respect to k and rearranging terms yields

$$\frac{dy_0^*}{dk} = -y_1 c'(k) - 1 - \sum_{i=1}^{N} MSC_i \frac{dy_i^*}{dk}, \tag{20.9}$$

where $MSC_1 = c(k)$ and $MSC_i = \partial C_i(y_i)/\partial y_i$, $i = 2, \cdots, N$ are the marginal social costs of producing good 1 and good i, respectively. Substituting Equations (20.8) and (20.9) into (20.4) yields

$$\frac{dU^*(k)}{dk} \bigg/ \frac{\partial U}{\partial x_0} = -x_1^* c'(k) - 1 + \sum_{i=1}^{N} [p_i - MSC_i] \frac{dx_i^*}{dk}. \tag{20.10}$$

The first term on the right-hand side is the reduction in transportation costs caused by capacity expansion, and the second term (-1) is the increase in the cost of capacity investment. These two terms capture the direct impacts of capacity expansion. The third term is the sum of prices minus marginal social costs of all goods except the numeraire. This term represents the indirect effects through induced changes in production. In a first best world where all prices equal marginal social costs, we have

$$\frac{dU^*(k)}{dk} \bigg/ \frac{\partial U}{\partial x_0} = -x_1^* c'(k) - 1. \tag{20.11}$$

In this case, the benefit can be measured by the cost decrease in the transportation sector alone. The general equilibrium repercussions in other markets cancel out each other in a first best world.

We next consider a discrete change from $k = 0$ to $k = K$. Integrating Equation (20.10) from 0 to K yields the social surplus as follows:

$$\Delta SS = \int_{c_1^1}^{c_1^0} x_1^*(\hat{k}(c)) dc - K + \sum_{i=1}^{N} \left\{ \int_{x_i^0}^{x_i^1} [p_1^*(k_1^*(x_1)) - MSC_i(x_i)] dx_i \right\}, \tag{20.12}$$

where $\hat{k}(c)$ is the inverse of $c(k)$ and we define $MSC_1(x_1) \equiv c(k_1^*(x_1))$. In a first best world where all prices equal the corresponding marginal costs, the last term drops out and we obtain

$$\Delta SS = \int_{c_1^1}^{c_1^0} x_1^*(\hat{k}(c)) dc - K. \tag{20.13}$$

The integral on the right-hand side is the increase in consumer surplus in the transportation sector, which is shown in Figure 20.2 as the area to the left of the demand curve. If this exceeds the cost of capacity expansion, K, the net surplus is positive.

The intuition behind the result that the induced effects cancel each other out in a first best world is as follows. An induced increase in consumption benefits the consumer but increases the cost of production. The value of the former equals the consumer price multiplied by the change in quantity, and the cost of the latter is the marginal cost of production times the change in quantity. In a first best economy where prices equal marginal costs, the two are equal when demand equals supply.

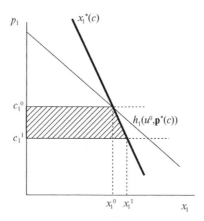

Figure 20.2   Consumer surplus in general equilibrium

We can offer another intuitive explanation. Let us define the direct effect as the change that would occur if prices in other markets remained unchanged and the indirect effect is the induced change caused by changes in prices. Defined in this way, it is straightforward to see that the indirect effects cancel out each other when evaluated in pecuniary terms. A one-cent rise in price reduces the welfare of demanders by the quantity demanded times one cent, and increases the welfare of suppliers by the quantity supplied times one cent. The two are equal when the market is in equilibrium.

Equation (20.12) is difficult to use in practice because marginal costs are not easy to estimate. When we know the size of the price distortion, however, this formula is useful. For example, if the price distortion is caused by taxes, this formula becomes

$$\Delta SS = \int_{c(K)}^{c(0)} x_1^*(\hat{k}(c))\,dc - K + \sum_{i=1}^{N} t_i(x_i^1 - x_i^0),\tag{20.14}$$

where t_i is the tax per unit on good i.

The average cost is easier to estimate than the marginal cost. We can rewrite equation (20.12) using average costs. First, noting that the change in the total cost can be written as the integral of the marginal cost, we obtain

$$\Delta SS = \sum_{i=1}^{N} [\Delta GCS_i - \Delta C_i],\tag{20.15}$$

where $\Delta C_i = C_i^1 - C_i^0$ satisfies[3]

$$\Delta C_1 = \int_{x_1^0}^{x_1^1} MSC_1(x_1)\,dx_1 - \int_{c(K)}^{c(0)} x_1^*(\hat{k}(c))\,dc + K\tag{20.16}$$

and

$$\Delta C_i = \int_{x_i^0}^{x_i^1} MSC_i(x_i)\,dx_i,\ i = 2, \cdots, N.\tag{20.17}$$

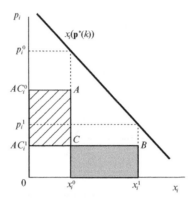

Figure 20.3   Change in production cost: average cost representation

Next, using the average cost, $AC_i = C_i/y_i$, the surplus becomes

$$\Delta SS = \sum_{i=1}^{N} [\Delta GCS_i - (AC_i^1 \times x_i^1 - AC_i^0 \times x_i^0)]. \tag{20.18}$$

Figure 20.3 shows the change in the total cost using the average costs. Rectangles $(AC_i^1, B, x_i^1, 0)$ and $(AC_i^0, A, x_i^0, 0)$, respectively, give the costs with and without the project. Because they share the rectangle $(AC_i^1, C, x_i^0, 0)$, the shaded area represents an increase in costs and the hatched area a decrease in costs, and the difference between them is the net increase in costs. Superimposing Figure 20.1 and Figure 20.3, we obtain the net benefit as in Figure 20.4.

In practice, demand curves are often assumed to be straight lines. In such a case, we have a simple cost–benefit formula, called the rule of a half or the trapezoid rule. The increase in gross consumer surplus is

$$\Delta GCS_i = \frac{1}{2}(p_i^0 + p_i^1)(x_i^1 - x_i^0) \tag{20.19}$$

and social surplus becomes

$$\Delta SS = \sum_{i=1}^{N} \left[\frac{1}{2}(p_i^0 + p_i^1)(x_i^1 - x_i^0) - \Delta C_i \right]. \tag{20.20}$$

In markets other than the transportation sector, social surplus is zero if there is no price distortion, that is, if all prices equal marginal social costs.

Another way of writing the social surplus uses consumer surplus and producer surplus. Suppose that the tax rate for good i is t_i. Then, changes in consumer surplus CS_i, producer surplus PS_i and tax revenue T_i are, respectively,

$$\Delta CS_i = \Delta GCS_i - (p_i^1 x_i^1 - p_i^0 x_i^0),$$

$$\Delta PS_i = [(p_i^1 - t_i)x_i^1 - C_i^1] - [(p_i^0 - t_i)x_i^0 - C_i^0],$$

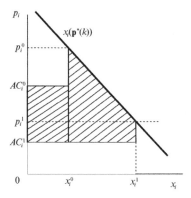

Figure 20.4   Change in net surplus

and

$$\Delta T_i = t_i^1 x_i^1 - t_i^0 x_i^0.$$

Using these definitions, we can rewrite social surplus as

$$\Delta SS = \sum_{i=1}^{N} (\Delta CS_i + \Delta PS_i + \Delta T_i), \qquad (20.21)$$

where in the linear demand curve case, we have the rule of a half for consumer surplus,

$$\Delta CS_i = \frac{1}{2}(p_i^0 - p_i^1)(x_i^0 + x_i^1). \qquad (20.22)$$

If consumption of good i entails external costs, EC_i, then we must add their changes as in

$$\Delta SS = \sum_{i=1}^{N} (\Delta CS_i + \Delta PS_i + \Delta T_i - \Delta EC_i). \qquad (20.23)$$

Compensating Variation in General Equilibrium

So far, we have assumed that the marginal utility of income is constant. If this assumption is not satisfied, the Marshallian consumer surplus does not represent a money-metric utility function. As noted in the preceding section, this measure has another drawback of being path dependent, and it provides neither a sufficient nor a necessary condition for a proposed project to satisfy a compensation test. If we assume that the utility function is quasilinear, however, these problems disappear. In practice, the bias caused by assuming a quasilinear form is not important quantitatively compared with other problems, such as forecasting errors of transportation demand and the value of time. Willig (1976) showed that the difference between the Marshallian consumer surplus and the CV (or EV) is small if the product of the income elasticity of demand and the ratio of the change in consumer surplus to income is small. He gave an example:

'if the consumer's measured income elasticity of demand is 0.8 and if the surplus area under the demand curve between the old and new prices is 5 percent of income, then the compensating variation is within 2 percent of the measured consumer's surplus'. (Willig, 1976, p. 590).

Transportation constitutes a small share of income and the magnitudes of the error would rarely exceed 5 percent. Transportation demand forecasting involves much larger errors and if the error is within 10 percent, one should feel very lucky.

Next, let us examine the CV. Adding and subtracting the same term, $E(u^0, \mathbf{p}^0)$, to the definition of CV, we can rewrite CV as

$$CV = E(u^1, \mathbf{p}^1) - E(u^0, \mathbf{p}^1)$$

$$= [E(u^0, \mathbf{p}^0) - E(u^0, \mathbf{p}^1)] + [E(u^1, \mathbf{p}^1) - E(u^0, \mathbf{p}^0)]. \tag{20.24}$$

Converting to an integral form, the first square bracket on the right-hand side becomes

$$E(u^0, \mathbf{p}^0) - E(u^0, \mathbf{p}^1) = -\int_0^K \frac{dE(u^0, \mathbf{p}^*(k))}{dk} dk$$

$$= -\int_0^K \sum_{i=0}^N h_i(u^0, \mathbf{p}^*(k)) \frac{dp_1^*}{dk} dk, \tag{20.25}$$

where $h_i(u, \mathbf{p})$ is the compensated demand function as in the preceding section and we use the well-known property that the derivative of the expenditure function with respect to a price yields a compensated demand function.

The second square bracket in (20.24) can be rewritten as

$$E(u^1, \mathbf{p}^1) - E(u^0, \mathbf{p}^0) = \mathbf{p}^*(K) \cdot \mathbf{x}^*(K) - \mathbf{p}^*(0) \cdot \mathbf{x}^*(0)$$

$$= \int_0^K \sum_{i=0}^N \frac{d(x_i^*(k)p_i^*(k))}{dk} dk$$

$$= \int_0^K \sum_{i=0}^N \left[x_i^*(k) \frac{dp_i^*(k)}{dk} + p_i^*(k) \frac{dx_i^*(k)}{dk} \right] dk. \tag{20.26}$$

Now, because the aggregate production function (20.1) is satisfied at any k along the equilibrium path, differentiating

$$\bar{y}_0 - y_0^*(k) - [c(k)y_1^*(k) + k] - \sum_{i=2}^N C_i(y_i^*(k)) = 0 \tag{20.27}$$

with respect to k yields

$$\sum_{i=0}^N MC_i(y_i^*(k)) \frac{dy_i^*(k)}{dk} + c'(k)y_1^*(k) + 1 = 0. \tag{20.28}$$

Inserting this equation into the integrand of (20.26), we obtain

$$
\begin{aligned}
&E(u^1, \mathbf{p}^1) - E(u^0, \mathbf{p}^0) \\
&= \int_0^K \left\{ \sum_{i=0}^N \left[x_i^*(k) \frac{dp_i^*(k)}{dk} + p_i^*(k) \left(\frac{dx_i^*(k)}{dk} - \frac{dy_i^*(k)}{dk} \right) \right] - c'(k) y_1^*(k) \right\} dk - K.
\end{aligned}
\tag{20.29}
$$

Because along the equilibrium path we have $x_i^*(k) = y_i^*(k)$ and $dx_i^*/dk = dy_i^*/dk$, we can simplify this equation to

$$
E(u^1, \mathbf{p}^1) - E(u^0, \mathbf{p}^0) = \int_0^K \sum_{i=0}^N x_i^*(k) \frac{dp_i^*(k)}{dk} dk + \int_{c_1^1}^{c_1^0} x_1^*(\hat{k}(c)) dc - K, \tag{20.30}
$$

where we have applied integration by substitution to derive the second integral on the right-hand side. Combining (20.25) and (20.30), we can rewrite CV as

$$
CV = \int_{c_1^1}^{c_1^0} x_1^*(\hat{k}(c)) dc - K + \int_0^K \sum_{i=0}^N [x_i^*(k) - h_i(u^0, \mathbf{p}^*(k))] \frac{dp_i^*(k)}{dk} dk. \tag{20.31}
$$

Thus, in general, CV does not equal the area to the left of the general equilibrium demand curve, or that of the compensated demand curve. The reason is that the compensated demand functions do not necessarily satisfy the market clearing conditions along the equilibrium path.[4]

The Allais Measure in General Equilibrium

As noted earlier, Allais (1943, 1977) developed a consumer surplus measure based on the idea of computing the maximum amount of the numeraire good that can be extracted, while fixing the utility levels of all households. Debreu (1951) proposed a variant of the Allais measure because of its dependence on the choice of numeraire, noting (p. 287): 'its exposition and its results rely entirely on the asymmetrical role played by a particular commodity'.

Instead of using the numeraire, Debreu's coefficient of resource utilization reduces all primal inputs proportionally. Although Debreu's criticism about asymmetry is a valid one, the Allais surplus is attractive for two reasons. First, measured in monetary units, it is easy to use in practice. Second, unlike the CV, it coincides with the area to the left of the equilibrium demand curve, as we will see next.

The Allais surplus measure, AS, is defined as

$$
AS = AS^*(K) - AS^*(0), \tag{20.32}
$$

where $AS^*(k)$ is the surplus of the numeraire good that can be extracted when the transportation capacity is k:

$$
x_0^*(k) + AS^*(k) = y_0^*(k) \tag{20.33}
$$

$$x_i^*(k) = y_i^*(k), \quad i = 1, \cdots, N. \tag{20.34}$$

Differentiating $AS^*(k)$ yields

$$\frac{dAS^*(k)}{dk} = \frac{dy_0^*(k)}{dk} - \frac{dx_0^*(k)}{dk}. \tag{20.35}$$

Because the utility level is fixed along the equilibrium path, we have

$$\frac{dU}{dk} = \sum_i \frac{\partial U}{\partial x_i} \frac{dx_i^*}{dk} = \frac{\partial U}{\partial x_0} \sum_i p_i \frac{dx_i^*}{dk} = 0,$$

which yields

$$\frac{dx_0^*(k)}{dk} = -\sum_{i=1}^{N} p_i \frac{dx_i^*(k)}{dk}. \tag{20.36}$$

Because the production function must also be satisfied in this case, Equation (20.28) continues to hold. Substituting (20.36) and (20.28) into (20.35) yields

$$\frac{dAS^*}{dk} = \sum_{i=1}^{N} p_i \frac{dx_i^*}{dk} - \sum_{i=1}^{N} p_i \frac{dy_i^*}{dk} - [c'(k)y_1^*(k) + 1] = -[c'(k)x_1^*(k) + 1], \tag{20.37}$$

where we use the market clearing condition to obtain the second equality. Critical in this derivation is (20.34), that is, the markets for goods other than the numeraire are cleared along the equilibrium path. Integrating (20.34) from 0 to K yields

$$AS = -\int_0^K [c'(k)x_1^*(k) + 1]dk = \int_{c_1^1}^{c_1^0} x_1^*(\hat{k}(c))dc - K. \tag{20.38}$$

The reason the Allais measure coincides with the area to the left of the demand curve is that, along the equilibrium path, demand and supply are equal for any good other than the numeraire. They are not equal for the numeraire but this does not matter because the price of the numeraire does not change.[5]

Shadow Pricing Rules with Tax Distortions

By construction, the Allais measure does not have to specify how a public project is financed. Another stream of literature deals with this issue explicitly and derives appropriate shadow prices for a small project. This approach started with Diamond and Mirrlees (1971), who obtained the remarkable result that it suffices to use producer prices as shadow prices. Their result depends on the assumption that commodity taxes are chosen optimally. If commodity tax rates are fixed and the government can change only lump-sum transfers, then Harberger's (1971) weighted average shadow pricing rule is obtained, as shown by Bruce and Harris (1982). Diewert (1983) derived these results rigorously in a general framework.

DISCRETE CHOICE AND CONSUMER SURPLUS

Random utility discrete choice models are commonly used in estimating transportation demand. Williams (1977) and Small and Rosen (1981) derived expected consumer surplus measures for those models. Small and Verhoef (2007) offered a concise and clear explanation of the discrete choice models including short discussions on consumer surplus measures, and Walker and Ben-Akiva chapter in this *Handbook* provided an excellent review of recent developments in mixture models. Concentrating on the logit and nested logit models, we review the major results on consumer surplus in discrete choice models. Our focus is on a variety of ways in which the expected consumer surplus can be expressed, that is, those using the logsum formula and the areas to the left of demand curves.

Let us consider a consumer faced with a choice among J alternatives. The utility that a consumer obtains from alternative j is

$$U_j = V(x_j) + \varepsilon_j, \tag{20.39}$$

where ε_j is a random variable that captures the unobserved portion of a consumer's utility. The nonrandom part $V(x_j)$ is called the systematic utility. U_j is often called conditional indirect utility, indicating that the utility is conditional on the choice of alternative j and that it is written as a function of income and prices. A consumer chooses the alternative that maximizes the utility. The probability that the consumer chooses alternative i is given by

$$P_i = \mathrm{Prob}(V_i + \varepsilon_i \geq V_j + \varepsilon_j \; \forall j \neq i). \tag{20.40}$$

Logit

Depending on the specification of the random variable ε_j, we obtain different discrete choice models. The most commonly used is the logit model that assumes the independent and identically distributed (iid) Type I extreme value distribution. The probit model assumes the normal distribution. In this chapter, we concentrate on logit type models because they are more often used in practice. The logit model assumes a double exponential distribution function as follows:

$$F(\varepsilon) = \exp\left\{-\exp\left(-\frac{\varepsilon - \eta}{\mu}\right)\right\}, \tag{20.41}$$

where η is the location parameter usually set equal to zero and μ is the scale parameter. Parameter μ is usually set equal to one. In the logit model, the probability of choosing alternative i is

$$P_i = \frac{\exp(V_i/\mu)}{\sum_{j=1}^{J} \exp(V_j/\mu)}, \quad i = 1, \cdots, J. \tag{20.42}$$

Now, suppose that there are a fixed number, X, of consumers with the same deterministic part of the utility function, V_j, but different draws of the random variable ε_j. The market demand for alternative i is then

$$x_i = \frac{\exp(V_i/\mu)}{\sum\limits_{j=1}^{J} \exp(V_j/\mu)} X, \quad i = 1, \cdots, J. \tag{20.43}$$

This gives the transport demand function in the logit model.

A consumer surplus measure is obtained by dividing the maximized utility level by the marginal utility of income β, which we assume to be constant. As shown by Williams (1977) and Small and Rosen (1981), if ε_j is an iid extreme value, taking the expectation of this consumer surplus, $CS = (1/\beta)\mathrm{Max}_j(U_j)$ yields

$$E(CS) = \frac{1}{\beta}\left\{ \ln\left(\sum_{j=1}^{J} \exp(V_j) \right) + \gamma \right\}, \tag{20.44}$$

where $\gamma \approx 0.577$ is Euler's constant. In project evaluation, we compare cases with and without a project. Denoting the with case by superscript W and the without case by WO, the benefit of the project is

$$\Delta E(CS) = E(CS^W) - E(CS^{WO})$$

$$= \frac{1}{\beta}\left\{ \ln\left(\sum_{j=1}^{J} \exp(V_j^W) \right) - \ln\left(\sum_{j=1}^{J} \exp(V_j^{WO}) \right) \right\}, \tag{20.45}$$

where

$$S = \ln\left(\sum_{j=1}^{J} \exp(V_j) \right) \tag{20.46}$$

is called the logsum variable.

The expected consumer surplus in the market as a whole is obtained by summing the consumer surpluses of all consumers. If all consumers are homogeneous and the number of consumers is fixed at X, we obtain the benefit of the project in a logsum form as follows:

$$\Delta B = \Delta E(CS) X = \frac{X}{\beta}\left\{ \ln\left(\sum_{j=1}^{J} \exp(V_j^W) \right) - \ln\left(\sum_{j=1}^{J} \exp(V_j^{WO}) \right) \right\}. \tag{20.47}$$

Thus, in the logit model, the benefit can be written as an elementary function that is easy to compute in practical applications. This is an attractive feature of the logit model.

Dividing the logsum variable by the marginal utility of income β and adding a minus sign, we obtain what is called the 'inclusive price' or 'composite cost':

$$c = -\frac{1}{\beta} \ln\left(\sum_{j=1}^{J} \exp(V_j) \right). \tag{20.48}$$

The inclusive price represents the minimum expected cost of transportation. The generalized cost P_i is the 'price' of alternative i, whereas the inclusive price is the 'price' of the bundle of alternatives. If the alternatives are routes between an origin–destination (OD) pair, the inclusive price is the price of the OD pair and the generalized cost is the price of a route. Using the inclusive price, we can write the benefit as

$$\Delta B = (c^{WO} - c^W) X. \tag{20.49}$$

When the total transportation demand is fixed, the benefit equals the change in the inclusive price, $c^{WO} - c^W$, multiplied by the total transportation demand X.

In the preceding section, we have seen that when the utility function is quasilinear, the area to the left of the demand curve yields the consumer surplus. We now show that the same result holds in the logit model.[6] Let us take a linear conditional indirect utility function commonly used in transportation demand as follows:

$$U_i = \beta(m - p_i) + a_i + \varepsilon_i, \text{ with } p_i = M_i + \theta T_i, \tag{20.50}$$

where m is income, p_i is a generalized cost, and M_i, T_i and a_i are, respectively, monetary costs, travel time and a dummy variable that represents the other characteristics of an alternative. Coefficients β and θ are the marginal utility of income and the value of time, respectively.

Differentiating the logsum variable with respect to the generalized cost, p_i, of alternative i, we obtain demand for the alternative as follows:

$$x_i = P_i X = -\frac{X}{\beta} \frac{\partial}{\partial p_i} \left\{ \ln \left(\sum_{j=1}^{J} \exp(\beta(m - p_j) + a_j) \right) \right\}. \tag{20.51}$$

Using this result, the change in consumer surplus caused by a change in the generalized cost from p_j^{WO} to p_j^W is

$$\begin{aligned}
\Delta B &= \frac{X}{\beta} \left\{ \ln \left(\sum_{j=1}^{J} \exp(\beta(m - p_j^W) + a_j) \right) - \ln \left(\sum_{j=1}^{J} \exp(\beta(m - p_j^{WO}) + a_j) \right) \right\} \\
&= \sum_{j=1}^{J} \left(\int_{p_j^W}^{p_j^{WO}} x_j \, dp_j \right), \tag{20.52}
\end{aligned}$$

where the integral on the right-hand side is the area to the left of the demand curve for each alternative.[7] We can therefore estimate the benefit using the demand curve for each alternative. Thus, in the logit model, the benefit of the project can be computed by using two formulae: the logsum formula (20.47) or its equivalent using the inclusive price (20.49), and the consumer surplus formula with the areas to the left of the demand curves of alternatives (20.52).

As shown by Anderson et al. (1992), the demand function (20.43) can be derived from the utility maximization problem of a representative consumer as follows:

$$\max_{\{z, x_j\}} U = z + \frac{1}{\beta} \sum_{j=1}^{J} \left[a_j - \ln \left(\frac{x_j}{X} \right) \right] x_j$$

$$\text{s.t.} \quad m = z + \sum_{j=1}^{J} p_j x_j$$

$$\sum_{j=1}^{J} x_j = X, \tag{20.53}$$

where m is income and z is the composite consumer good whose price is set equal to one (1). Substituting the demand function (20.43) into the utility function yields the indirect utility function

$$U = m + \frac{X}{\beta} \ln\left(\sum_{j=1}^{J} \exp(V_j)\right). \tag{20.54}$$

Kidokoro (2006) showed that this utility function yields the same consumer surplus as that in (20.48). We can therefore apply the results in the preceding section to derive the properties of the consumer surplus measure, instead of deriving them directly as we have done here.

Nested Logit

The logit model has a very restrictive substitution pattern across alternatives, referred to as independence from irrelevant alternatives (IIA). The nested logit model and, more generally, generalized extreme value (GEV) models permit more general substitution patterns. Let us examine consumer surplus in the nested logit model.

As an example of a nested logit model, we consider a combination of destination and route choices. A consumer chooses the best route for each destination k ($= 1, \cdots, K$), and based on this choice, the best destination is chosen. We denote by j ($= 1, \cdots, J$) all possible routes for all possible destinations. The set of all possible routes for destination k is denoted by B_k and is called nest k. In the nested logit model, the distribution function of ε_j has the form

$$F(\varepsilon_j) = \exp\left(-\sum_{k=1}^{K}\left(\sum_{j \in B_k} \exp(-\varepsilon_j/\lambda_k)\right)^{\lambda_k}\right). \tag{20.55}$$

Parameter λ_k indicates the degree of independence among error terms in nest k, where a larger λ_k corresponds to a smaller correlation. When $\lambda_k = 1$, they are independent and we obtain the standard logit model.

The choice probability of route i in nest k is

$$P_i = \frac{\exp(V_i/\lambda_k)\left(\sum_{j \in B_k} \exp(V_j/\lambda_k)\right)^{\lambda_k - 1}}{\sum_{l=1}^{K}\sum_{j \in B_l}\left(\sum_{j \in B_k} \exp(V_j/\lambda_l)\right)^{\lambda_l}}. \tag{20.56}$$

This can be expressed as the product of the probability of choosing destination k, P_{B_k}, and that of choosing route i, $P_{i|B_k}$, conditional on the destination choice k as follows:

$$P_i = P_{i|B_k} P_{B_k}, \text{ with } P_{B_k} = \frac{\exp(S_k)}{\sum_{l=1}^{K} \exp(S_l)} \text{ and } P_{i|B_k} = \frac{\exp(V_i/\lambda_k)}{\sum_{j \in B_k} \exp(V_j/\lambda_k)}, \tag{20.57}$$

where

$$S_k = \lambda_k \ln \sum_{j \in B_k} \exp(V_j/\lambda_k) \tag{20.58}$$

is the logsum variable for nest k, which is called the inclusive value. The inclusive value represents the expected value of the maximum utility from routes in nest k. In the same way as in (20.48) in the standard logit model, we obtain the inclusive price (or the composite cost) by dividing this by the marginal utility of income and attaching a minus sign as follows:

$$c_k = -\frac{\lambda_k}{\beta} \ln \sum_{j \in B_k} \exp(V_j/\lambda_k). \tag{20.59}$$

This can be interpreted as the 'price' of nest k.

The expected consumer surplus in the nested model is

$$E(CS) = \frac{1}{\beta} E\left[\max_j (V_j + \varepsilon_j) \right] = \frac{1}{\beta}(S + \gamma), \tag{20.60}$$

where S is the logsum variable of the logsums of all nests as follows:

$$S = \ln \left(\sum_{k=1}^{K} \exp(S_k) \right). \tag{20.61}$$

The change in the expected consumer surplus in the case where the deterministic part of utility moves from V_j^{WO} to V_j^{W} is then

$$\Delta E(CS) = \frac{1}{\beta} \left\{ \ln \left(\sum_{k=1}^{K} \left(\sum_{j \in B_k} \left(\exp(V_j^{W}/\lambda_k) \right)^{\lambda_k} \right) - \ln \left(\sum_{k=1}^{K} \left(\sum_{j \in B_k} (\exp(V_j^{WO}/\lambda_k) \right)^{\lambda_k} \right) \right\}. \tag{20.62}$$

If the total transportation demand is fixed at X, the change in total consumer surplus is

$$\Delta B = \frac{X}{\beta} \left\{ \ln \left(\sum_{k=1}^{K} \left(\sum_{j \in B_k} \left(\exp(V_j^{W}/\lambda_k) \right)^{\lambda_k} \right) - \ln \left(\sum_{k=1}^{K} \left(\sum_{j \in B_k} (\exp(V_j^{WO}/\lambda_k) \right)^{\lambda_k} \right) \right\}. \tag{20.63}$$

Using the logsum variable for each destination, we can rewrite this as

$$\Delta B = \frac{X}{\beta} \left\{ \ln \left(\sum_{k=1}^{K} \exp(S_k^{W}) \right) - \ln \left(\sum_{k=1}^{K} \exp(S_k^{WO}) \right) \right\}, \tag{20.64}$$

which can be written as

$$\Delta B = \frac{X}{\beta} \left\{ \ln \left(\sum_{k=1}^{K} \exp(-\beta c_k^W) \right) - \ln \left(\sum_{k=1}^{K} \exp(-\beta c_k^{WO}) \right) \right\}, \tag{20.65}$$

using the inclusive price, c_k, defined in (20.59).

Furthermore, by differentiating (20.61) with respect to the generalized cost p_j and integrating it from p_j^{WO} to p_j^W, we can rewrite (20.63) as

$$\Delta B = \sum_{k=1}^{K} \sum_{j \in B_k} \left(\int_{p_j^W}^{p_j^{WO}} x_j dp_j \right). \tag{20.66}$$

Hence, one can estimate the benefit by using the demand curves at the route level. In the same way, applying differentiation and integration to (20.65) from c_k^{WO} to c_k^W, we obtain

$$\Delta B = \sum_{k=1}^{K} \left(\int_{c_k^W}^{c_k^{WO}} X_k dc_k \right), \tag{20.67}$$

where

$$X_k = \sum_{j \in B_k} x_j \tag{20.68}$$

is the total demand for destination k. Hence, using the OD level demand function with the inclusive price as its 'price' yields the same result as the consumer surplus calculated by the route level demand functions.[8]

Summing up, the benefit of a project in the nested logit model can be written in a number of ways. The first one is a composite logsum formula using the route level utilities, (20.63). Alternatively, by defining the logsum variable for a nest (an OD pair), we can derive a logsum formula with logsum variables for OD pairs (20.64), or equivalently, a formula with the inclusive prices of OD pairs, (20.65). Furthermore, using demand curves at the route and OD levels, we obtain a consumer surplus formula at the route level (20.66) and at the OD level (20.67).

As in the standard logit model, the nested logit model can be reformulated as the utility maximization of a representative consumer. As shown by Kidokoro (2006), this model yields the same consumer surplus measure as that in the nested logit model.

ACKNOWLEDGMENTS

I would like to thank the editors of this book and Yukihiro Kidokoro for helpful comments.

NOTES

1. More precisely, these results hold for the weak compensation principle. Please refer to Boadway and Bruce (1985) for explanations of strong and weak compensation principles.

2. The terminology of the general equilibrium demand function was used by Boadway and Bruce (1985), Kidokoro (2004, 2006), and Kanemoto (2006). Because demand equals supply along the equilibrium path, the term 'demand function' is misleading. As we shall see below, however, the area to the left of the general equilibrium demand curve is the consumer surplus, and in the context of welfare evaluation it is the counterpart of the demand curve in a partial equilibrium model.
3. Equation (20.16) follows from

$$\Delta C_1 = \int_0^K \frac{dC_1(y_1^*(k), k)}{dk} dk = \int_0^K \left\{ \frac{\partial C_1}{\partial y_1} \frac{dy_1^*(k)}{dk} + \frac{\partial C_1}{\partial k} \right\} dk = \int_{x_1^0}^{x_1^1} MSC_1(x_1) dx_1 - \int_{c(K)}^{c(0)} x_1^*(\hat{k}(c)) dc + K,$$

where the last equality uses the relationship, $\partial C_1 / \partial k = 1 + y_1^*(k) c'(k)$.
4. See Kanemoto and Mera (1985) for this result.
5. See Kanemoto and Mera (1985) for the property of the Allais surplus measure in a general equilibrium setting. They called the Allais measure 'compensating surplus'.
6. See McFadden (1999) and Dagsvik and Karlström (2005) for the analysis of the case where utility is non-linear in income.
7. See Kidokoro (2006) for details.
8. Refer to Maruyama (2006) for a more general analysis of this result.

REFERENCES

Adler, M.D. and E.A. Posner, 2000, *Cost-Benefit Analysis: Legal, Economic, and Philosophical Perspectives.* Chicago, IL: University of Chicago Press.

Allais, M., 1943, *A la Recherche d'une Discipline Économique.* Tome 1, Paris: Imprimerie Nationale.

Allais, M., 1977, Theories of general economic equilibrium and maximum efficiency. In E. Schwödiauer, ed., *Equilibrium and Disequilibrium in Economic Theory.* Dordrecht, Holland: D. Reidel Publishing.

Anderson, S.P., A. De Palma and J.-F. Thisse, 1992, *Discrete Choice Theory of Product Differentiation.* Cambridge, MA: MIT Press.

Blackorby, C. and D. Donaldson, 1990, A review article: the case against the use of the sum of compensating variations in cost–benefit analysis. *Canadian Journal of Economics,* **23** (3), 471–494.

Boadway, R. and N. Bruce, 1985, *Welfare Economics.* Milton Keynes, UK: Lightning Source Inc.

Bruce, N. and R. Harris, 1982, Cost–benefit criteria and the compensation principle in evaluating small projects. *Journal of Political Economy,* **90**, 755–776.

Dagsvik, J.K. and A. Karlström, 2005, Compensating variation and Hicksian choice probabilities in random utility models that are non-linear in income. *Review of Economic Studies,* **72**, 57–76.

Debreu, G., 1951, The coefficient of resource utilization. *Econometrica,* **19**, 273–292.

Diamond, P.A. and J.A. Mirrlees, 1971, Optimal taxation and public production: I-II. *American Economic Review,* **61**, 8–27, 261–278.

Diewert, W.E., 1983, Cost benefit analysis and project evaluation: a comparison of alternative approaches. *Journal of Public Economics,* **22**, 265–302.

Dupuit, J., 1844, *De la Mesure de l'Utilité des Travaux Publics,* Annales de Ponts et Chaussées, Second Series, Volume 8. Translated as: Dupuit, J., 1952, On the measurement of utility of public works. *International Economic Papers,* **2**, 83–110.

Harberger, A.C., 1971, Three basic postulates for applied welfare economics: an interpretive essay. *Journal of Economic Literature,* **9**, 785–797.

Hicks, J.R., 1939, The foundations of welfare economics. *Economic Journal,* **49** (196), 696–712.

Hicks, J.R., 1942, Consumers' surplus and index numbers. *Review of Economic Studies,* **9**, 126–137.

Hines, J.R., 1999, Three sides of Harberger triangles. *Journal of Economic Perspectives,* **13**, 167–188.

Kaldor, N., 1939, Welfare propositions in economics and interpersonal comparisons of utility. *Economic Journal,* **49** (195), 549–552.

Kanemoto, Y., 2006, Urban transport economic theory. In R.J. Arnott and D.P. McMillen, eds, *A Companion to Urban Economics.* Oxford: Blackwell Publishing, pp. 245–260.

Kanemoto, Y. and K. Mera, 1985, General equilibrium analysis of the benefits of large transportation improvements. *Regional Science and Urban Economics,* **15**, 343–363.

Kidokoro, Y., 2004, Cost-benefit analysis for transport networks: theory and applications. *Journal of Transport Economics and Policy,* **38**, 275–307.

Kidokoro, Y., 2006, Benefit estimation of transport projects: a representative consumer approach. *Transportation Research Part B,* **40**, 521–543.

Maruyama, T., 2006, Equivalence of benefit measures for each level of travel demand, *Doboku Gakkai Ronbunshuu D* [*JSCE, Journal of Infrastructure Planning and Management*], **62** (3), 460–473 (in Japanese).

McFadden, D.L., 1999, Computing willingness-to-pay in random utility models. In J. Moore, R. Riezman and J. Melvin, eds, *Trade, Theory and Econometrics: Essays in Honour of John S. Chipman*. London: Routledge.

McKenzie, L.W., 1957, Demand theory without a utility index. *Review of Economic Studies*, **24**, 185–189.

Samuelson, P.A., 1974, Complementarity: an essay on the 40th anniversary of the Hicks–Allen revolution in demand theory. *Journal of Economic Literature*, **64**, 1255–1289.

Scitovsky, T., 1941, A note on welfare propositions in economics. *Review of Economic Studies*, **9**, 77–88.

Small, K. and H. Rosen, 1981, Applied welfare economics of discrete choice models. *Econometrica*, **49**, 105–130.

Small, K.A. and E.T. Verhoef, 2007, *The Economics of Urban Transportation*. New York: Routledge.

Sunstein, C.R., 2004, *Risk and Reason: Safety, Law, and the Environment*. Cambridge: Cambridge University Press.

Thaler, R. and C.R. Sunstein, 2008, *Nudge: Improving Decisions about Health, Wealth, and Happiness*. New Haven, CT: Yale University Press.

Varian, H.R., 1992, *Microeconomic Analysis*, 3rd edn. New York: W.W. Norton & Company, Inc.

Williams, H., 1977, On the formation of travel demand models and economic evaluation measures of user benefits. *Environment and Planning A*, **9**, 285–344.

Willig, R.D., 1976, Consumer's surplus without apology. *American Economic Review*, **66**, 589–597.

World Bank, 2005, A framework for the economic evaluation of transport projects. Transport Note No. TRN-5.

21 The direct and wider impacts of transport projects: a review

Peter Mackie, Daniel Graham and James Laird

INTRODUCTION

Economic appraisal of transport projects, if dated from the studies of Coburn et al. (1960) and Foster and Beesley (1963), is approaching its fiftieth birthday. Many books and reports have been written on this subject and the aim of this chapter is to review specifically the linkage between transport and the economy. With that in mind we review the measurement of the principal direct benefits that when transmitted through into the wider economy give rise to the indirect benefits – the measurement of which we also review. To illustrate the discussion we draw heavily on European, but particularly UK, practice. To define our boundaries further, this chapter does not cover transport and land-use modeling, environmental and safety impacts of transport projects, nor most aspects of capital budgeting. These are all important appraisal topics, but out of scope.

The context we are assuming is that of a layered approach to the assessment of projects. The top layer is some form of strategic goal setting and broad analysis of policy and strategies against those goals. The recent paper by the UK Department for Transport 'Developing a Sustainable Transport System' (DfT, 2008) is an example, although the analytical content to support it is not yet fully developed. The bottom level is that of detailed design and choice between numerous technical alternatives, which is likely to be conducted on cost-effectiveness and value-engineering principles. Economic appraisal of transport projects is a pivotal intermediate layer in the overall assessment process, providing a link between the top level goals and the process of optioneering. Good quality appraisal is an important ingredient of decision making but should not be confused with decision taking itself.

This chapter adopts as its framework for economic appraisal the neoclassical, comparative static framework of cost–benefit analysis (CBA). This approach could be criticized as being too limiting. Theories such as prospect theory offer alternatives to utility maximization, but have not yet been operationalized for practical appraisal, nor has a consensus developed on their general applicability. Loss aversion is for example intrinsically linked to uncertainty and some authors argue that theories on utility maximization can therefore be extended to capture it (for example, McFadden, 2009). Another critique is the failure to consider disequilibrium and paths to equilibrium. Real transport projects cause shocks to the economic system – households change location, firms enter the market in location A and leave in location B, forces are unleashed which take time to play out. This is true, but then there are all sorts of shocks to the economic system of which those from the transport system are just one. We believe the paradigm of comparative static equilibrium, comparing 'with' and 'without' states of the world, all else held constant, remains the essential discipline for infrastructure appraisal, including transport.

Table 21.1   Impacts by stakeholder of a transport project

Stakeholder group	Impacts (changes in)
Transport users	Time
	Reliability
	Fares/costs
	Journey quality
	Perceived accident costs
	Option values
Transport operators/infrastructure providers	Revenues
	Operating costs
	Capital costs
Non-users	External accident costs
	Environmental impacts
	Option values
	Altruistic non-use values
Rest of economy outside transport	Agglomeration
	Competitiveness
	Labor markets
Government	Subsidies
	Taxes
	Charges
	Grants

The structure of this chapter is as follows. In the next section, we set out the framework of appraisal. Then we describe the state of the art in relation to the principal direct transport benefits that feed into the wider economy. Then we examine the measurement of indirect benefits the so-called wider economic benefits. Finally the main problems and prospects are summarized.

THE FRAMEWORK

The Appraisal Framework

In an ideal world, we would like to measure, model and value all the impacts on society of a project or policy measure. Typically, the project impacts might fall on a range of stakeholders as presented in Table 21.1.

Some entries in the table appear twice – for example, increases in revenue will be positive for operators and negative for users. The fundamental theorem is that, suitably discounted,

Present Value of Net Social Benefit =

    (1) Δ consumer surplus (ΔCS)
  + (2) Δ revenues to transport operators
  + (3) Δ environmental and safety externalities

+ (4) Δ option and altruistic non-use values
+ (5) Δ wider economic impact
– (6) Δ costs

and that a simple indicator of benefit–cost ratio, if required, is:

$$[(1) + (2) + (3) + (4) + (5)] / (6)$$

A number of ground rules need to be spelled out at this point. First, although in an ideal world, all items of cost and benefit might be capable of monetary valuation, practice falls short of this – and 'unique' natural and heritage assets pose ethical as well as practical problems for valuation. In practice therefore, the framework is likely to be partly in money, partly in physical impacts and partly in descriptive terms, so that conventional measures of welfare change such as the Kaldor–Hicks test need to be applied in practice with a strong element of judgement.

Second, within the monetized entries, consistency of valuation numeraire or metric is essential. There are two practical options.

- Factor costs: value all inputs net of indirect taxes, so that the metric for the appraisal is £1 of real resources capable of producing (say) £1.209 of goods in the shops at market prices ;
- Market prices: value all input gross of indirect taxes so that the metric for the appraisal is £1 of goods in the shops, say, £1/1.209 of real resources.

It does not matter which metric is used provided it is followed consistently, taking proper account of taxes and subsidies in the second option. In the UK, practice switched from factor costs to market prices following Sugden (1999). The particular issues of importance here concern consistent valuation of non-working time (valued through stated preference studies at market prices) versus fares, operating costs and capital costs (dependent on the tax regime) versus employers' business time (factor costs).

Third, classic capital budgeting questions need to be addressed including the choice of discount rate and decision rules under capital rationing, choice between mutually exclusive alternatives and optimal timing. Then there is the issue of the distributive impacts. Some authors such as Harberger and Sugden view CBA as a proxy for commercial appraisal in conditions where markets are incomplete or fail. On this view, willingness to pay values are relevant for appraisal at sector level with distributive issues being handled through tax and benefit policy. Others, such as Pearce and Nash (1981), view CBA as a form of social calculus which needs to embody explicit consideration of distributive impacts. For mixed reasons of principle and pragmatism, standard values of time and safety are widely used in appraisal practice. These do have the effect of reweighting the time benefits relative to their raw willingness to pay values. For a discussion see Galvez and Jara-Diaz (1998).

Finally, and unlike some planning balance sheets, the purpose of the transport economic efficiency table shown in Table 21.1 is to estimate the net gain from doing something relative to some appropriate reference case such as do minimum. Therefore, we must avoid double counting. So for example, if a transport improvement is reflected in an increase in user benefit (ΔCS) which is then transmitted into a change in housing or land rents, which is then transmitted again into a change in prices and wages in the rest of the economy, we cannot credit the project with the same benefit at three different stages of the economic transmission system. This poses a challenge for measuring the wider economic impacts of transport projects. It is not sufficient to demonstrate that the direct transport impacts such as time, reliability and cost changes are transmitted into the real economy. It is necessary to show that the wider economic impacts credited to the project are *additional* to the direct transport impacts. We shall return to this point below.

Transport Cost–Benefit Analysis

At the core of transport CBA lies the computation for particular schemes or policies of the so-called 'rule of a half' measure of benefits (Neuberger, 1971). A transport improvement is associated with a change in generalised user costs ($TC_0 - TC_1$ in Figure 21.1a) so that the rule of a half measure of user benefit is ½ $(TC_0 - TC_1)(X_0 + X_1)$.

Much of the effort in practical appraisal involves measuring this in time and space (zones, links, peak, off-peak, this year, in ten years time) and then in aggregating the benefit over the life of the project. Although conceptually clear, this is quantitatively challenging because the single demand curve in Figure 21.1 is a representative of a family of interdependent travel demand curves which interact when costs in one part of the demand system change (Mackie and Nellthorp, 2001).

This is the framework of transport cost–benefit analysis (TCBA), but how has its content changed over the years? A useful review of appraisal policy in the UK was conducted recently (Department for Transport, 2009a). Developments include:

- Improved modeling of the cost and volume changes associated with improvements;
- Improved evidence base for value of time, safety and more recently journey quality;
- Extensions of application from infrastructure to fares policy, service levels and traffic management;
- Greatly improved treatment of environmental impacts of all kinds;
- A multi-agency approach capable of showing not just the total benefits and costs but also their allocation among the affected parties;
- Increasingly, an attempt to nest TCBA within a higher order framework of objectives for transport policy so as to achieve greater consistency between top down goals and bottom up appraisal; and
- Much more interest in the linkages between transport and the rest of the economy.

Transport–economy linkages are one of those topics which have gone in and out of fashion. In the 1950s and 1960s, the economic impact of transport infrastructure such as the Severn Bridge (Cleary and Thomas, 1973) and the Transpennine M62 motorway (Dodgson, 1974) were studied, and theory was developed to a satisfactory state of the art (Dodgson, 1973; Mohring, 1976). In essence, transport user benefits, the direct benefits of a transport project, link into other markets by lowering input costs of production leading, under competitive conditions, to a fall in outturn prices (P_0 to P_1 in Figure 21.1b). With elastic demand this leads to an expansion in output and employment, possibly generating second order effects in all markets, until a new equilibrium is reached. This is depicted in Figure 21.1 for the case

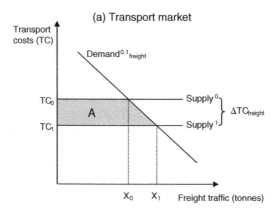

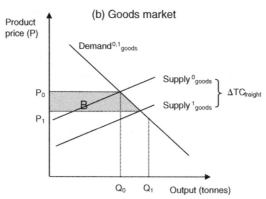

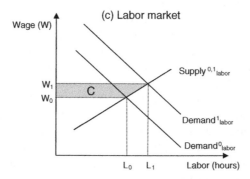

Figure 21.1   *Direct and indirect benefits of a freight related transport quality improvement in competitive conditions*

of a reduction in business and freight costs. Theory indicates that the surpluses generated in the wider economy, that is the indirect benefits represented by Areas *B* and *C* in Figure 21.1b and c double count the direct benefits of the project (Area *A*).

Furthermore, with an elastic supply of products/services, labor or any other input to the production process (for example, land) the transport market is the only market in which a full measure of the benefits of the transport quality improvement can be measured. In 1978, the UK Advisory Committee on Trunk Road Assessment (Leitch, 1978) concluded that practical assessment of the so-called secondary or indirect benefit of transport projects (that is, surpluses *B* and *C* and the changes in employment and output) was too difficult to undertake as part of standard appraisal practice. While very understandable in technical terms, particularly given the tools and computing power available at the time, that conclusion left a critical gap. On the one hand, transport appraisal focused on the direct benefits – time, cost, quality, changes – together with the environmental impacts. On the other hand, transport scheme promoters, especially politicians, were really interested in the impact of building a piece of new infrastructure on the local or regional economy.

There is an apparent disconnect, but is it real? This was the question posed to the SACTRA Committee and addressed in their 1999 report, which has helped to stimulate a further round of interest in transport – economy linkages and their representation in appraisal. A key first step in understanding transport – economy linkages is the measurement of the direct benefits of transport. The next section is devoted to that with a particular emphasis on identifying issues relevant to the link with the wider economy, before the question of additionality of impacts in markets outside of transport is raised in the following section.

DIRECT TRANSPORT BENEFITS FOR BUSINESS AND FREIGHT

This section of the chapter reviews the evidence on the main components of the direct transport benefits that link through to other economic sectors – namely business- and freight-user benefits. The components of the change in user benefit are time related (time savings and reliability) and money related (vehicle operating costs and out of pocket costs/fares/tolls). Time and reliability benefits for all journey purposes typically account for around 80 percent of the monetized benefits in the benefit:cost ratios of transport infrastructure projects, and around half of this 80 percent accrues to employers' business and freight traffic, with the other half being for commuting and other non-work purposes. Time and reliability impacts also raise the most challenging questions about the nature of the feed from the transport impacts through to the final economic impacts, since the wider impacts are driven by accessibility change which in turn is dominated by change in travel time. If the assumptions we make in measuring direct benefits are untenable the impacts on the wider economy (that is the indirect benefits) may well be overstated. This section complements the chapter by David Hensher on the valuation of travel time savings. It is distinct from that chapter in that its focus is on appraisal related issues and linkages with the wider economy.

Values of Travel Time Savings for Business and Freight

Travel time on employers' business

The value of travel time savings (VTTS) on employers' business is important and difficult to study. Although employers' business car traffic is only, say, one-sixth of total traffic, the fact that the unit values for this category of traffic are typically four to five times the non-work time values means that employers' business travel time savings are extremely important in appraisal, often accounting for around half the time saving benefits. The most popular approach adopted in valuing savings in travel time during the course of work is the cost saving approach (Odgaard et al., 2005). This says that in a competitive labor and product market, firms hire labor to the point at which the value of the marginal product is equal to the wage rate; thus the value of the time saving is equal to the marginal gross cost of labor including labor related overheads. To arrive at this conclusion a number of well-documented assumptions are implied regarding the labor market and the allocation of time between work and leisure (for example, Harrison, 1974; Hensher, 1977):

- All released time goes into work, not leisure;
- Travel time is 0 percent productive in terms of work (that is, no work can be undertaken while travelling);
- The marginal value of working to the individual and the marginal value of travelling to the individual have zero value or they are equal and opposite in value;
- The wage rate in the labor market equals the marginal value product which the labor yields (which may not be the case if firms are monopoly employers or if workers through either union power or skill shortages have strong market power).
- There are no indivisibilities in the use of time for production so every minute and every second is equally valuable.

The first three of these assumptions were challenged by Hensher (1977), in the context of white-collar workers accessing an airport. Over the intervening period, developments such as flexitime, the mobile office (phones, wi-fi and so forth) have made the assumptions underpinning the cost-saving approach less plausible. David Hensher, in the chapter in this volume, sets out the mathematical models underpinning the cost saving approach and the alternative Hensher model. He also presents some empirical results.

The two remaining principal criticisms of the cost-saving approach – which are equally applicable to the Hensher approach – are the validity of taking the wage rate to be the marginal productivity of labor (that is, the validity of assuming that the labor and goods market are competitive) and that there are no indivisibilities in the use of time for production. We discuss the latter below in the context of small savings in travel time, and for the moment focus on the critique regarding the marginal product of labor. The principal criticisms of the taking the wage rate to equal the marginal product of labor are that:

- Economies, even developed economies, do not operate in perfect competition. Monopolies will restrict output, therefore the marginal value of the product will be higher than the wage rate. Conversely monopoly power by groups of workers may result in the wage rate exceeding the value of the marginal product.
- If the economy is not in full employment then when a travel time saving occurs there may not be any additional work for the labor to do (within the firm) and if it is released into the market place it is not re-hired elsewhere in the economy at the going wage rate for that class of labor. In such conditions there is a divergence between the value of the saving to the firm and the value of the saving to society.

It is generally considered that in developed economies the wage rate is a reasonable approximation to the value of the marginal product of labor. It is only in the situation that there are particularly regional labor market imperfections or if an appraisal is being undertaken in a developing country that these imperfect labor market issues become relevant. In such situations they may be better dealt with within a general equilibrium framework which can also incorporate the modeling of wider economic impacts (for example, Elhorst and Oosterhaven, 2008; Venables and Gasiorek, 1999).

Empirically, a number of authors have cast doubt on whether VTTS for employers' business varies proportionately with the wage rate (that is, an elasticity to the wage of unity), as would be implied by the cost saving approach (for example, Gunn et al., 1996; Hensher and Goodwin, 2004). In a recent meta-analysis of 77 studies from 30 countries for passenger transport, and 33 studies from 18 countries for freight Shires and de Jong (2006) found a cross-sectional elasticity to income of between 0.4 and 0.5 for work (employers' business) VTTS. This is an observational finding and does not explain why the result occurs. Thus we cannot discount the possibility that the value for employers' business trips is influenced by the traveler as well as the firm (the Hensher model), or that as wage rates increase the travel time for workers becomes more useable, valuable and comfortable (in-vehicle entertainment, mobile phones, lap-tops on trains and so forth). For example, those on higher incomes may have access to facilities that improve the journey experience. Higher paid 'white-collar' business travelers may reflect on a business meeting or a project whilst driving a car – which is a productive use of time – whilst lower paid manual workers may not be able to undertake any productive work whilst travelling.

The cost-saving approach is still the dominant method used to value employers' business travel time savings, but increasingly it is being challenged for plausibility. If modifications to the cost-saving approach are made, then care has to be taken in multi-modal appraisals where some modes (such as inter-city rail) can be used for working while others such as car are less work-friendly. Obtaining willingness to pay (WTP) values, which adequately represent the sum of employer and employee value, has proven, and is likely to remain, challenging. On the other hand if by using the cost-saving approach we are consistently overestimating business-related time savings, this will have consequences for our estimates of impacts in the economy outside the transport sector.

Value of time savings for freight
The value of time savings for freight is bound up with a number of related issues. These include the type of vehicle/mode that carries the freight, what the time-variant costs of operating that vehicle are, whether the freight will depreciate with journey time and reliability. With respect to the latter an extreme case is outlined by de Jong et al. (2004, p. 7), where shippers considered that reliability in delivery time was more important than actual travel time. Some qualitative studies have drawn similar, striking conclusions. More generally, the value of mean travel time appears to be sensitive to the level of variability, or the likelihood of delay. Thus it would be artificial to consider the value of freight time savings without taking into account the contribution of reliability.

Two approaches exist for measuring the value of time savings for freight.

1. Cost saving approach: measure the change in freight operators' costs directly;
2. To measure willingness-to-pay (WTP) for freight time savings by shippers and operators.

Most countries use some variant of the cost-saving approach in determining values to be used in appraisal. The one significant exception is the Netherlands who use the WTP approach. In the cost-saving approach, the aim is to estimate the marginal social cost of one unit of travel time ($\Delta GC/\Delta t$ where GC is generalized cost and t is time) from the bottom up. The key items are time dependent vehicle operating costs include driver and crew wages; the associated overheads (for example, social security payments, subsistence costs, training and licensing); and those vehicle costs that vary with respect to time, including fuel and non-fuel elements (for example, fuel, tyres, maintenance, depreciation, vehicle taxes and insurance). Sometimes the depreciated value of the cost of goods whilst in transit is included. This is based on an estimate of their capital value and the loss of that value in interest whilst in transit – and therefore effectively stored.

In the WTP approach, survey data on freight users' actual and hypothetical (stated preference) choices between alternatives is used to model the marginal WTP for a saving in travel time. The methods bear some similarities to those used for business passenger time, however in this case there are potentially two different 'users' who stand to benefit from a time saving:

● The 'shipper' who initially owns the goods and wishes to see them delivered to their destination, and who might stand to benefit from a cheaper or quicker delivery;
● The 'freight operator' who provides the delivery service and might stand to benefit from a reduction in his costs (unless the saving is completely passed on to the shipper).

Reconciling the two approaches – the bottom-up cost-saving approach, and the top-down WTP approach – has in the past been problematic, with the WTP approach generating significantly higher values. Fowkes (2001, pp. 1–9) provided a careful reconciliation of the Dutch and UK values derived using WTP and cost savings, respectively. He concluded that the cost-saving approach may underestimate WTP for freight time savings if the assumption that freight vehicle occupancy equals 1.0 used in the UK is unrealistically low. He also found that the results from one SP experiment in an early Dutch study (AHCG, 1994) could be reconciled quite closely with the UK values, whilst results from the other SP experiment within the Dutch study gave a higher value of freight time savings (40 percent higher for 'own account') – but this may have been a consequence of sampling issues. A finding throughout the literature is that freight VTTS are very heterogeneous, for example, with load volume and weight, load value, commodity group, distance, international/domestic only, time sensitivity, even time of day or day of week.

Reliability

Reliability in passenger traffic
Unreliability is considered to impose a significant cost on business travellers (see, for example, SACTRA, 1999; McQuaid et al., 2004). The literature distinguishes between

reliability problems arising through travel time variability and those arising through large unexpected delays. The distinction between them is that travel time variability is considered to probabilistic, whilst it is not possible to attach a probability to the likelihood of an 'unexpected delay'. From a theoretical perspective, there is a degree of consensus that the economic cost of a lack of reliability can be captured through an extension to Small's (1982) model of scheduling (Noland and Small, 1995). This framework is particularly useful as it identifies the link between utility and variability in travel times within the model of time allocation that underpins the value of travel time savings. The Noland and Small framework also lends some theoretical support to the concept of a reliability ratio[1] – in which the variance of the travel times directly enters the utility function of the traveler.

The literature contains quite a range of values for the reliability ratio, from 0.35 to 2.4 (see literature reviews of de Jong et al., (2004b) Eliasson, 2004; Noland and Polak, 2002). Large variations in 'unexpected' delay are also found. For example Bates et al. (2000) found that the value of a reduction in one minutes delay ranged from between 1 and 5 times the value of in-vehicle-time depending on journey length and purpose. Wardman (2001) in his meta-analysis of 143 British studies found values of 'late time' to be over 7 times the value of in-vehicle-time. Large unexpected delays are also valued quite highly. Eliasson (2004) in a large Swedish study found values around 3.5 times the value of in-vehicle-time (per minute of delay) for car drivers, whilst a UK study found values between 7 and 10 times in-vehicle-time for rail travelers who experience very large delays (Steer Davies Gleave, 1995 cited in ATOC, 2002).

A key challenge that often limits the ability to include reliability in an appraisal is the ability to model the supply side effects. That is how reliability will vary in response to a project intervention. As evidenced by the UK work in this field (Ove Arup and Partners et al., 2004) this is a far from trivial task and has meant that UK advice is restricted to inter-urban dual carriageways (DfT, 2009b). The difficulties in modeling the supply-side aspect of reliability often prevent the inclusion of reliability effects in a transport appraisal and therefore raise a practical barrier to developing a full understanding as to how transport interventions impact on the wider economy.

Reliability in freight traffic

For goods traffic reliability is treated explicitly in some VTTS studies, for example, Bruzelius (2001), de Jong et al. (2004a), Vandaele et al. (2004). These studies make clear how reliability changes can be valued on any mode, although it may take some time to conduct similar studies in other member states. For example, the results of de Jong et al. (2004a), for the Netherlands indicate that a 10 percent change in reliability (by road), measured as the percentage of deliveries not on time, can be valued between 1 euro and 2.85 euros depending on the load carried.

A common approach is also to use a multiplier on the value of expected travel time savings, to represent reductions in 'delay' time. Typically factors of 2.0–2.5 are used. Bruzelius (2001) put forward a specific factor, 2.0, but also suggested that further research is required in order to validate it for use. Fowkes (2001, p. 7) cites evidence gathered on behalf of the Highways Agency in the UK, that the ratio of the value of delay time to expected goods travel time is in the region of 2 for chemicals, paints, food, drink and groceries, and 3 for other commodities. Again, it seems that the commercial goods VTTS is sensitive to the nature and value of the goods being transported.

There is limited data on the value of reliability for freight traffic, but there is no doubt, given the qualitative and increasing quantitative evidence, that the benefits from increased reliability of commercial goods traffic will make a substantial contribution to the total time-related benefits to commercial goods traffic.

Value of Small Time Savings

Given that the majority of individual transport projects give rise to a lot of relatively small time savings (for example, less than 5 minutes) then the results of a CBA and forecasts of impacts on the wider economy can be extremely sensitive to the treatment of the value of such time savings. Welch and Williams (1997) showed in an urban case study of that between 25 percent and 50 percent of time saving benefits from fairly major infrastructure projects (for example, a city bypass and peripheral distributor road) could be attributed to such small savings. Furthermore, every year congestion levels increase and these annual increments in delay are small. What, therefore, is the value of both year on year small increases in delay and small savings in time that result from an infrastructure improvement?

With one exception (Germany), all the EU countries and Switzerland use a constant VTTS value irrespective of the size of the time saving in their appraisals (Odgaard et al., 2005). The principal objections to the 'constant unit value' of VTTS fall into three broad groups:

- Threshold arguments: small amounts of time are less useful than large amounts;
- Perception arguments: small time savings (or losses) might not be noticed by travelers and any that are not noticed cannot be valued by those affected and so should not be valued by society; and
- Measurement error arguments: small time savings are said to often account for a large proportion of scheme benefits, and that the measurement error is proportionately higher for a mean saving of 10 seconds than for a saving of 10 minutes.

The counter-arguments to these points are well rehearsed (see for example Mackie et al., 2001). Fowkes (1999) has demonstrated that if there is a threshold below which a time saving has no (or reduced value) because of inability to reschedule, then there must be a uniform distribution of such amounts of time from zero up to the threshold starting position. It is further demonstrated that a given small time saving in that range will move exactly the right proportion of people over the threshold that the outcome is the same as valuing all time savings at the same unit value. The perception argument is countered in that it is argued that the world is full of misperception and that this is not just confined to small time savings, it is also applicable to large time savings, changes in accident risk, differences in shop prices and so on. Just because the benefit or cost is not perceived at the point of use does not necessarily imply that it is not real and over time may well become perceived as behavior adjusts to it. Additionally, within transport infrastructure investment policy one is typically concerned with small incremental changes to the transport network which, when put together, meet an overall objective of for example a complete route upgrade. The argument that the time savings associated with each project are not perceived and, therefore, have no or minimal value, but that if the route upgrade was completed as a single project the time savings would be perceived seems inconsistent. Similarly, where there are multiple design options for a scheme (horizontal and vertical alignment, junction layouts) consistency requires simple unweighted aggregation of time units, which is only achieved by use of a constant unit value.

There are two potential sources of measurement error regarding time savings. Firstly, there is the error associated with what the VTTS value is and secondly there is an error associated with the absolute amount of time that will be saved (in minutes). Regarding the first source of error Fowkes demonstrates that the measurement error in the actual VTTS will only have a modest impact on the scheme appraisal. The second source of error is potentially more significant and relates to the accuracy of the transport model used to forecast the travel time saving. An old model with a weak representation of transport supply and travel demand patterns will give more unreliable estimates of travel time savings than would a 'state of the art' model. There therefore appears to be some strength in the argument that the size of the travel time savings (in minutes) predicted by a transport model should be analyzed and a judgement made as to whether the transport model is sufficiently robust to give reliable estimates of such changes.

Empirically, differences have been found in values for small time savings (less than 5 minutes) compared to values for larger time savings, such as in the UK value of time study dataset. However, Bates and Whelan (2001) were inclined not to take these results at face value as they were inconsistent with the expected shape of the indifference curve. In fact, they query whether stated preference experiments are the correct vehicle to investigate responses to small time savings.

So, the issue of the treatment of small time savings remains a live one. The issue is both whether the world is one of indivisibilities, buffers and slack, and whether, in a context where travel times are changing over time anyway due to changes in congestion levels, the best unbiased estimator of the benefits is or is not given by linear additivity. Current practice is to assume a constant unit value of time, but if convincing evidence were to surface to overturn this practice, there would also be consequences for the transmission between the transport impacts and final economic benefits. So, to summarize, the approach taken in the computation of the direct transport benefits, at least conceptually, is a rather open competitive market approach. Changes in travel conditions flow through into lower transport costs unhindered by legal or institutional blockages of any kind. Lower transport costs feed through into improved accessibility, which, in turn, is converted into higher output and lower prices. Provided the demand and supply response properties of the system are correctly represented, the measured transport benefits are a correct proxy for the final economic system benefits. This is the all-round perfect competition benchmark case. However, it is more generally the case that the direct transport benefits will be the dominant component of total economic system benefits. Only in developing country examples, such as feeder roads opening up production of agriculture or minerals for the market is this not the case. For this reason, the traditional prescription for CBA of transport projects has been 'look after the direct benefits and the indirect benefits will look after themselves'. Even in the imperfect market context, the evaluation of the direct benefits is of crucial importance since failure to measure the direct benefits correctly will have consequences also for the estimation of the wider impacts.

WIDER IMPACTS

The interaction between transport and the wider economy, and its treatment in appraisal, is one of the most controversial and lively topics. Historically, there are different traditions – for example, the German approach has been to view transport infrastructure as a tool of regional economic policy and therefore to pay little attention to transport cost-benefit analysis (TCBA) in favor of a broader regional impact approach. By contrast, the UK has relied on TCBA, assessing the user benefits, costs, revenues and environmental impacts, and assuming that the transport benefits were a good proxy for the total economic system benefits (ACTRA, 1978). In the last decade, following the impetus of the SACTRA report of 1999, there has been a resurgence of interest in the wider economy impacts.

What are the motives for this reassessment? In part they are technically driven – enhanced computing power makes tools such as Spatial Computable General Equilibrium (SCGE) more practically usable than before, giving a framework within which transport-economy linkages can be represented. But mainly they are politically driven by the desire to demonstrate to decision-makers the impact of transport infrastructure on the final economy. Time savings are the base metal of the system, but impact on GDP is the gold. In considering these questions, it is essential to distinguish two propositions:

- Transport infrastructure impacts on the final economy via mechanisms of cost, accessibility and quality, changing the opportunity set for producers and consumers. To take one example, it would be difficult to imagine that the supermarket retailing market would be quite the same without the motorway and trunk road network.
- Transport infrastructure yields benefits over and above the direct transport benefits. This is the so-called additionality question. It is difficult to dissent from the first proposition, but it is sometimes presented as if it were the second. Focusing on the second question, it is useful to consider 'additionality' at two levels – first at the conceptual level, and then at the practical level. Conceptually, as discussed in the previous section, in conditions of perfect competition and constant returns to scale and no externalities outside the transport sector, there is no additionality. Additionality only occurs if a market failure exists and the transport project impacts on that market. The UK Department of Transport's advice note (DfT, 2007), three sources of additional wider impacts (WIs) are identified. These are:
    - Agglomeration economics – external economies of access to economic mass not captured by individual firms or transport users
    - Imperfect competition benefits due to output effects in markets where price does not equal marginal cost
    - Labor supply effects and shifting to more productive jobs.

Presently, the bulk of research effort has focused on the possible effect of transport via agglomeration. This is partly because there is a long tradition of theoretical and empirical research on agglomeration, but also because this effect is thought to be by far the largest of the WIs set out above. Below, we review some of the theoretical and empirical work that has been done on agglomeration and comment on the prospects for including this effect with appraisal methodology.

Agglomeration Economies

Agglomeration economies are said to exist when the spatial concentration of economic activity gives rise to increasing returns. Theory tells us that these scale economies arise from the advantages that spatial proximity offers in terms of labor market pooling, knowledge spillovers, specialization and the sharing of inputs and outputs (for the theory of agglomeration see Duranton and Puga, 2004; Fujita and Thisse, 2002; Fujita et al., 1999; and the chapter by Lafourcade and Thisse in this volume). It is thought that the positive effects of agglomeration can be observed in increased productivity and lower average costs for firms.

One way in which the spatial scale of an economy can be effectively increased is through a reduction in the generalized cost of travel. So if the theory of agglomeration economies holds good, we might expect investments in transport infrastructure to induce external benefits via agglomeration economies. Essentially, the argument is as follows: if there are increasing returns to economic mass, and if transport in part determines the level of access to economic mass experienced by firms, then investments in transport which serve to increase proximity may induce some shift in the productivity of firms via economies of agglomeration.

A crucial issue here is that agglomeration economies are externalities, that is, they arise as a side effect of the activities of firms which have consequences for the wider economy. This is very important from the point of view of transport appraisal because traditional methods of appraisal based on valuation of travel times do not recognize these types of externalities. For this reason agglomeration effects of transport investment can be classed as 'wider economic impacts' because they represent market imperfections that are not accounted for in a standard cost-benefit appraisal.

Venables (2007) formalizes this argument in a theoretical model of an urban economy that links productivity to transport investment via effects on city size. His objective is to distinguish real income changes that result from transport investment due to a productivity-city size (agglomeration) effect, from those economic benefits that are captured in standard transport appraisals and which arise from resources saved in commuting and from an increase in urban output.

A diagrammatic representation of the model given in Venables' paper is reproduced as Figure 21.2. Figure 21.2a shows an urban equilibrium in which the size of the city is determine at point X, where the wage gap between city workers and non-city workers is taken up in the travel costs of the city worker who is most distant from the CBD.

Figure 21.2b shows that when a transport improvement is made, commuting costs are shifted downwards and consequently the city expands to point X^*. The total change in the resources used in commuting is $\eta - \alpha$, which combined with the change in output $(\beta + \eta)$, yields a net benefit from the transport improvement of $\alpha + \beta$

In Figure 21.2c, Venables shows the implications of the existence of a city size productivity gradient. If larger cities have higher productivity due to agglomeration externalities then the wage gap can be expressed, not as a constant gap, but as a concave curve that increases with city size. Equilibrium is found at the intersection of the commuting cost and wage gap curves. The fact that productivity is non-constant with respect to city size

(a) Urban equilibrium

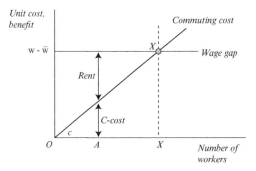

(b) Net gains from transport improvement

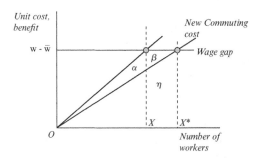

(c) Net gains from transport improvement with endogenous productivity

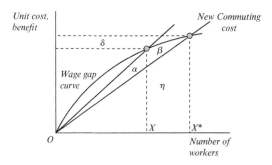

Figure 21.2   Agglomeration economies and transport user benefits

means that the real income gain from a transport improvement is $\alpha + \beta + \delta$, where δ measures the increase in productivity associated with city size.

In this way, Venables demonstrates that there may be external benefits from transport investment related to agglomeration and that these could be quantified quite simply if we know : (1) the change in urban agglomeration that will result from making some transport intervention; and (2) the amount by which productivity will rise in response to an increase in agglomeration.

There are well-established transport modeling tools that can be used to predict the changes in access to economic mass that might result from some investment. The latter quantity, the elasticity of productivity with respect to agglomeration, is slightly more elusive and requires estimation using spatial economic data. The standard approach is to estimate a production function or factor price equation with some measure of variance in the levels of agglomeration experienced at different locations included as an independent variable.

Agglomeration can be modeled using an 'effective density', or market potential, measure such as

$$A_i = \Sigma_j E_j/d_j^\alpha, \, i = j,$$

where E_j is employment in location j, d_{ij} is the distance between locations i and j, and the parameter α measures decay of agglomeration economies over distance (see Graham, 2007a). Although referred to as effective *density*, this representation of agglomeration actually measures access to economic mass, not the physical density of economic activity. Note that we could use travels times or the generalized cost of travel rather than distance as the denominator (see Graham, 2007b).

The agglomeration measure can then be regressed against some measure of productivity to obtain an estimate of the elasticity of productivity with respect to agglomeration. This is sometimes done using wage equations, but more commonly within some production function model, preferably specified at the firm level. For instance, let $y_i = f(X_i, Z_i, A_i)$ be the production function for the ith firm in which y is the output of the firm, X_i is a vector of factor inputs, Z_i is a vector of covariates which affect productivity, and A_i is a measure of the level of agglomeration experienced by the firm.

The hypothesis being tested is whether the agglomeration variable has any statistically significant effect on productivity; that is, whether A_i affects the relationship between y_i and X_i given Z_i. Generally agglomeration is found to be positively associated with agglomeration, though there is substantial variance in the magnitude of the reported estimates. For manufacturing industries agglomeration economies are typically found to be somewhere between 2 percent and 10 percent, but they can be as high as 20 percent for some service industries (for reviews see Eberts and McMillen, 1999, Melo et al., 2009 and Rosenthal and Strange, 2004).

Melo et al. (2009) show that variance in the estimates of agglomeration economies can largely be explained by a few simple characteristics of the study, each of which have relevance for the application of agglomeration within transport appraisal.

Industrial composition of the sample – the industrial category under consideration matters. Estimates for service industries tend to be substantially higher than for manufacturing industries, and intuitively this makes sense since the most urbanized locations of the economy (that is, the central business districts) tend to be composed predominantly of service industries. For the purposes of transport appraisal, we want to estimate the impacts that investments will have across the economy, and so we need some kind of sectoral breakdown in agglomeration effects because local economies differ in industry mix.

Correction for reverse causality – it seems likely that agglomeration could be determined jointly with productivity. Indeed, there is empirical evidence for the existence of bi-directionality (Graham et al., 2009a). The extent to which estimation of the production function allows for reverse causality between productivity and agglomeration can affect the magnitude of estimates obtained. If endogeneity exists, and remains untreated, estimates of agglomeration economies may be biased and inconsistent. This is clearly of first-order importance for the evaluation of transport investments. If agglomeration economies are endogenous, if the direction of causality runs substantially the opposite way proposed by theory, then we may not realize the benefits we expect by increasing densities through investment.

Confounding/omitted variables – the representation of *exogenous* factors that affect productivity (that is, the elements of vector Z_i in the production function above) can have a very important impact on estimates of agglomeration. When we measure variance in 'agglomeration', we need to be clear about what this actually represents. Does it capture the effect of changing access to economic alone, or does it also capture other 'confounding' effects which underlie the agglomeration–productivity relationship? The literature has identified variance in labor quality or unobserved functional heterogeneity, as perhaps the most relevant confounder. The argument here is that the functions undertaken within an industry may be distributed unevenly across the urban system, such that larger cities will tend to capture a higher share of inherently high productivity activities (for example, Duranton and Puga, 2004, Rice et al., 2006). Again, for transport appraisal, this is an important consideration because while transport investments may change access to economic mass, they may make little difference to labor quality or the functional mix of industries.

Context specific – estimates of agglomeration economies tend to be specific to the empirical context within which they are estimated. For instance, there is strong evidence that the strength of agglomeration economies can vary substantially across nations, even for the same industrial groups. The implication is that agglomeration estimates from any one empirical setting may have little relevance elsewhere.

The key point to emphasize is that there are a number of uncertainties involved in the estimation of agglomeration economies, in particular, whether any confounding covariates have been fully and correctly specified and whether the approach to endogeneity is legitimate. For this reason, it is important to view this body of research as ongoing and rapidly developing, seeking to find ever more robust ways of estimating these effects.

For the purposes of transport appraisal, the latest set of agglomeration elasticities used in the UK are those provided by Graham et al. (2009b). These elasticities are derived from a production function model estimated using extensive firm level panel data for the UK taken from the Office for National Statistics Annual Respondents Database (ARD). The model uses a control function approach to address endogeneity and includes measures of labor force skills within the exogenous covariate vector to control for the problem of unobserved labor quality. A novel characteristic of this particular study is that it estimates the value of the distance decay parameter α simultaneously with the agglomeration elasticities. A summary of results from this study for four broad sectors of the economy are given in Table 21.2 below.

These estimates show an agglomeration elasticity of 4 percent for the economy as a whole. While this might seem small, an important point to remember is that even small shifts in productivity can give rise to very large financial benefits. For business services, the effect of agglomeration on productivity is 8 percent while for manufacturing and

Table 21.2   Agglomeration elasticity estimates from Graham et al. (2009b)

		agglom	
	SIC	elas	alpha
Manufacturing	15–40	0.021	1.097
Construction	45	0.034	1.562
Consumer services	50–64	0.024	1.818
Business services	65–75	0.083	1.746
Economy (weight average)	all	0.043	1.655

consumer services it is closer to 2 percent. It is worth noting that these elasticities correct for labor quality through the inclusion of a skills variable, without this correction the elasticity estimates are approximately twice as large. This, of course, implies that much of the productivity differential we casually observe across levels of the urban system can be explained by differences in economic functions, rather than by fundamental productivity differences within like activities. In terms of distance decay, the results show that decay occurs much more rapidly in the service than manufacturing industries, with the estimate for construction falling between these values.

These results and, more generally, those from the existing literature, indicate that there are positive agglomeration effects and these are found to be particularly strong for services. Whether such evidence actually indicates a causal link between transport investment and productivity is, however, questionable. It certainly shows an association between access to economic mass and higher productivity, but does it tell us for sure that by increasing accessibility through transport investments we will necessarily raise productivity? Can we really use agglomeration elasticities to make calculations of the wider economic impacts of transport investments as suggested in Venables' model?

The key issue to consider here relates to the use of a statistical association to infer causality. It does in fact require a leap of faith to suppose that by making accessibility improvements through transport we will thereby induce some direct effects on the microfoundations of agglomeration. This link is assumed in the new guidance, but it has not been verified. The problem is that there is currently very little empirical understanding of why the association between productivity and agglomeration exists. We have reasons proposed by theory – that is, thick labor markets, specialization, knowledge spillovers and so on – but no empirical evidence that has actually linked particular mechanisms to productivity via access to economic mass. In a sense, the elasticities point us towards a black box relationship, which is currently supported by various theories, but in the absence of empirics. This lack of substantial evidence on the mechanisms of agglomeration certainly leaves room for doubt over the role of transport investment in generating wider economic impacts. We face a classic problem of observational equivalence: we observe a positive association between agglomeration and productivity, but there are numerous potential explanations as to why that association exists, and the explanations will tend to be correlated. This leaves a number of unanswered questions. Do positive agglomeration effects result predominantly from the microfoundations proposed by theory? And if so, what are the relative contributions of the various mechanisms? Or are there other unaccounted factors that should be included in the exogenous covariate vector which can explain the observed association? More fundamentally, are we really identifying genuine externalities, or are we also mapping out the supply curve for land or other spatial distortions in the prices of goods?

These are valid questions that can only be addressed by improving our *empirical* understanding of the mechanisms underpinning agglomeration economies. Then we way be able to assess much more accurately how improvements in transport accessibility will increase the performance of these mechanisms. The crucial point is that for accurate appraisal the observed association between agglomeration and productivity has to actually describe a *causal* process and one that can be *initiated* by transport interventions. The empirical evidence as it exists at the moment does not guarantee these two conditions.

Finally in this section, there are three other conceptual issues surrounding the appraisal of agglomeration benefits that are currently being debated and that are worth mentioning.

Applicability of elasticities over different magnitudes of change in agglomeration
Agglomeration elasticities are typically estimated using observations from across the entire urban system. In others words, they are point estimates which tell us *on average* how productivity changes with agglomeration. For these point elasticity estimates to be relevant for the assessment of agglomeration benefits within transport appraisal, however, they have to satisfy two conditions: (1) they must be independent of the magnitude of change in agglomeration and (2) they must be constant over levels of agglomeration. In other words, we require that the agglomeration elasticities be reasonably stable over different levels of magnitude of change in agglomeration. This is important, because changes to the transport system will typically result in only minor shifts in access to economic mass. So we need to know whether small changes in agglomeration have the same proportional effect on productivity as large changes do.

Distance versus generalized cost based agglomeration elasticities
As mentioned above, in the empirical representation of agglomeration we can use distance or some measure of generalized cost (GC) as the denominator in the accessibility equation. The DfT have decided against the use of GC based elasticities on the grounds that it would incorporate an element of double counting with conventional travel time savings. However, a distance based approach can give rise to difficulties when trying to assess the benefits of schemes such as high speed rail projects, which cover large distances but over relatively small travel times. This issue, which is far from resolved, needs careful attention. On the one hand, for econometric estimation the use of GC based measures presents serious challenges in terms of reverse causation because congestion is the flip side of productivity. But, on the other, the effect of agglomeration on economic interactions clearly depends on the GC of travel not Euclidean distance.

The legitimacy of the pass-through assumption
For transport-user benefits to have an impact on the wider economy, the consumer surplus enjoyed by transport users must be passed to agents in other markets particularly the product market and the labor market. If frictions exist in the transfer of any of these benefits then this can limit the impact of transport investment on the wider

economy. One of the key mechanisms in which transport-user benefits are passed through to the wider economy is that time savings to those travelling for business and to freight are assumed to increase the output of the business traveler and the goods vehicle. Frictions that may limit the amount of benefit that is passed through to the wider economy have been discussed above. The Hensher model suggests that not all of business traveler time savings will be used to increase output, some will be directed to leisure, whilst the arguments regarding the usability of small time savings are particularly pertinent to the context of impacts in the wider economy. The time saving may not be sufficiently large to enable a goods vehicle to make an extra delivery a day. Beyond that there is the broad question of whether transport cost savings are fully passed through into final prices and output or are partly captured and capitalized, for example, in increased land rents or sticky wages. This in turn depends on factor supply conditions.

Imperfect Competition Effects

In Figure 21.1, there is an explicit assumption of competitive markets. This means that even though there is an increased output of goods and services there is no additionality. This is because the non-transport price of those goods is equal to their marginal cost of production. Suppose, however, that industries outside the transport sector are generally in some form of imperfect competition so that price is greater than marginal cost. This is depicted in Figure 21.3b. As in Figure 21.1b, a transport improvement reduces delivered price from P_0 to P_1, increasing output from Q_0 to Q_1. Area D represents the resulting change in producers' surplus, which is not counted in transport CBA.

As with agglomeration, the issues associated with measuring area D are practical rather than theoretical:

- Estimating relevant market output elasticities and price: marginal cost mark ups. Different authors for the SACTRA report (1999) produced results ranging from 4 percent to 20 percent of the transport benefits.
- Ensuring that net rather than gross estimates are used. For example, if a road scheme improves the market position of firms inside the study area at the expense of firms elsewhere outside the study area, there is a difference between the gross effect on the study area and the net effect on the wider economy.
- The comparative static approach does not allow for dynamic interactions between transport infrastructure and market structures. It is not implausible that the number of major brewers or supermarket retailers, and hence the mark-ups, would be different with a different transport infrastructure.

Tax Wedge Effects

The third effect is also related to the net changes in the rest of the economy induced by a transport improvement normally presented as a labor market effect. Suppose the improvement results either in an increase in employment to supply the additional output as in Figure 21.1c and Figure 21.3c, or a reshuffling in the labor market with a more efficient match of people to jobs. People will be choosing based on their net of tax usage,

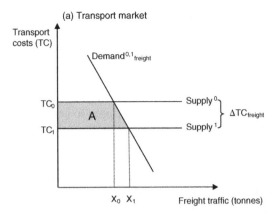

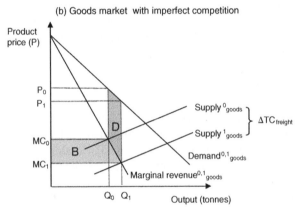

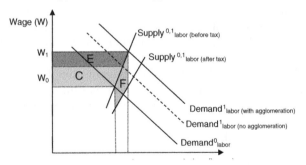

Figure 21.3   Direct and indirect benefits of a freight related transport quality improvement with market failures in the product and labor markets

but the value of their output will be their gross of tax wage. There is a tax benefit equal to the difference between the two which is not counted in transport CBA.

As with the imperfect competition effect, the size of this impact depends on relevant elasticities and the extent to which changes in transport costs are reflected in prices and wages. There is also similar scope for over-counting if the study area is too small to take proper account of the position in the losing as well as gaining locations.

There is also a conceptual issue about the treatment of the labor taxes in the transport sector. Approximately half of the direct transport benefits are typically derived from time savings on employers' business trips including professional drivers of goods vehicles and coaches. It is to be expected that increased transport productivity through higher speeds will in the end result in a smaller labor force required to carry out the base transport activity, partially (dependent on elasticities) offset by the induced traffic effect. It is not clear that the tax wedge approach being taken creates parity of treatment between transport sector labor and labor in the rest of the economy.

Beyond these points, the tax wedge argument raises questions about the definition of the numeraire in transport CBA. Our view is that the numeraire should be one pound's worth of resources in the hands of the Government. CBA is about measuring the value for money from using that pound in different ways. If that is so, then most fiscal or monetary policy has employment effects. It may be that transport expenditure has *exceptional* tax wedge effects, but conceptually we should then be counting the *net* tax wedge effect of a pound's worth of public expenditure on transport, not the gross.

Measurement of Wider Impacts

Two methods exist to incorporate the effect of market failures in the wider economy into a TCBA: the partial equilibrium approach, as exemplified by DfT (2005), and a more sophisticated general equilibrium approach using SCGE models. To date the partial equilibrium approach has been applied to more projects than the alternative SCGE approach, primarily for reasons of practicality.

Conceptually the use of SCGE models is preferable as with the partial equilibrium approach changes induced in other sectors of the economy (the general equilibrium effects) are assumed to have no net social value. However, SCGE model applications to transport are only in their infancy and experience of their use in a decision-making context as opposed to laboratory experiments is extremely limited (Gunn, 2004, and see the chapter by Bröcker and Mercenier in this volume). Furthermore simplifications in the representation of labor markets, labor migration, household behavior, the product market, the land market and the level of industrial disaggregation have to be made. This and the need to interact it with a transport model mean that the application of a SCGE model to the appraisal of a transport improvement is a far from trivial task (Laird et al., 2005).

The essence of the partial equilibrium approach is that the direct benefits of the transport intervention are measured in the transport market. This is Area A in Figure 21.3a. This double counts some of the impacts in the product market (Area B) and the labor market (Area C) – even if market failures exist in these markets. If market failures exist, then additional to transport user benefits is the producer surplus from increased output of goods and services in the product market (Area D), the increase in productivity due to increases in agglomeration (Area E) and the additional tax revenue that falls to government as a result of an increase in labor supply (Area F). The UK's Department for Transport provides detailed guidance on the estimation of each of these surpluses for the UK context (DfT, 2005). By far and away the most complex surplus to estimate is that associated with agglomeration (Area *E*). Here it is necessary to estimate changes in access to economic mass and then using elasticities of productivity to proximity to economic mass to estimate the expected change in the wage for all workers affected. The elasticities reviewed in this chapter form the basis of this assessment. In contrast, the most simplistic effect to estimate is the producer surplus effect in the presence of imperfect competition (Area *D*). This is estimated as a proportion of inputs already calculated – namely business and freight travel time savings.

The measurement of all three additional effects depends on the behavioral response to the transport improvement. Agglomeration economies are the benefits to existing economic activities from the increased access to economic mass facilitated by improved transport. Any attempt at measuring these must therefore take into account existing land uses, and ideally should also take into account how land uses will alter in both response to the transport intervention but also to an increase in the size and productivity of an agglomeration. Practical questions also arise in the specification of accessibility across modes, time periods and trip purposes. The imperfect competition and labor supply effects are associated with the response properties of the system in terms of increased outputs/inputs. Accounting for these benefits, therefore, places emphasis on ability to represent the elasticity properties of the system – traditionally regarded as difficult, and inconsistent with for example doubly constrained gravity models. We are in technically challenging territory. Therefore, whilst many questions regarding whether wider impacts are relevant, measurable and independent from direct benefits have been answered, the practical work of incorporating WIs into TCBA remains at an early stage.

CONCLUDING REMARKS

In many respects, the framework of CBA in transport has changed little since it was developed and can be regarded as mature. The place of TCBA in the overall decision process and its positioning relative to political and social goals on the one side and engineering design on the other is more open to question and revision. Different countries and cultures view this differently.

A great deal of work has gone into updating and maintenance of the content of TCBA and, the UK Department's WebTAG compendium illustrates the sheer volume of supporting evidence (DfT, updated April 2009). In a number of respects, though, appraisal is in the process of change, intensified by the economic, environmental and public finance crises through which we are living. In that context, appraisal is increasingly focused on better use of existing capacity and alternative choices in the management of that capacity.

Two of the key challenges are addressed in this chapter. One of these is the treatment of reliability, the other is improving representation of the wider impacts of transport interventions. Modeling and appraisal of system reliability and robustness is becoming much more important. The biggest challenges are in modeling – how to represent the effect of alternative supply-side strategies such as speed controlled motorways or urban bus priorities on the relevant travel time distributions. Then, having done that, there is the appraisal challenge of achieving more robust valuation of the benefits of increasing the chance of travelling from A to B in 'standard time'. This is particularly important for freight and employers' business trips, indeed all purposes where there are scheduling constraints at the destination. The difficulties of moving forward from deterministic models of the supply side to the next generation have limited the use of values of reliability benefits in economic appraisal. Particularly against the background of tight finance, they require a much higher weight in practical appraisal.

During the last decade, increasing attention has been devoted to the relationship between transport and the real economy. This is very challenging, but progress is being made. The research effort has focused on better understanding agglomeration economies, as this is expected to be the largest source of wider impacts. For the case of the UK, we now have empirical relationships linking access to economic mass with changes in productivity. Unanswered empirical questions still remain, not least substantiating the direction of causality that theory suggests exists and identifying the underlying sources of agglomeration effects. The interest in the wider economy also brings back into focus the debates on the value of travel time, specifically the cost saving approach as a means of valuing business and freight travel time savings and the treatment of small time savings. In the context of wider impacts, whether time savings are fully passed through or partially capitalized in higher rents or real wages is important. We should also not understate the significant practical problems in giving effect to transport-economy linkages in a coherent and consistent manner. For example, the size of the study area for modeling and appraisal of an intervention needs to be large enough to enable representation of the net agglomeration effects. That is to say, it is necessary to compute the balance of the effects on the places activity is displaced from and on the places it moves to. There is a natural inclination on the part of local and regional government to focus on the gross impacts at a local level rather than the net impacts over a region or several regions. Also the methods used must be capable of distinguishing between the effects of different types of interventions – orbital versus radial; investment versus pricing; roads versus public transport. This raises the practical question of the specification of accessibility across modes, time periods and trip purposes in the analysis of wider impacts. It would be wrong as well as futile to uplift all the benefit/cost ratios in the sector by a fixed percentage : on the contrary, we need this apparatus in order to tell us about differential effects of policy options in a context of acute scarcity of public funds.

NOTE

1.   The reliability ratio is defined as the ratio between the value of a 1 minute change in the standard deviation of travel time and a minute's travel time saving.

REFERENCES

Accent Marketing and Research and Hague Consulting Group (AHCG), 1994, Willingness of users to pay tolls. Report to the Department of Transport, The Hague Consulting Group, The Hague, Netherlands.

ACTRA, 1978, Report of the [UK] Advisory Committee on Trunk Road Assessment (the Leitch Committee Report). London, HMSO.

Association of Train Operating Companies (ATOC), 2002, Passenger Demand Forecasting Handbook (PDFH), 4th edn. London: ATOC.

Bates, J. and G.A. Whelan, 2001, Size and sign of time savings. Working Paper 561, Institute for Transport Studies, University of Leeds, Leeds, UK.

Bates, J., P. Jones, J. Polak, and A. Cook, 2000, The investigation of punctuality and reliability. A report to the PDFC.

Bruzelius, N., 2001, The valuation of logistics improvements in CBA of transport investments: a survey. Report to the SAMGODS group, Swedish Institute for Transport and Communications Analysis (SIKA).

Cleary, E.J. and R.E. Thomas, 1973, *The Economic Consequences of the Severn Bridge*. Bath, UK: Bath University Press.

Coburn, T.M., M.E. Beesley, and D.J. Reynolds, 1960, The London–Birmingham Motorway. Road Research Technical Paper 46, London, HMSO.

Department for Transport, 2005 (modified 2006), *Transport, Wider Economic Benefits and Impacts on GDP*. London: Department for Transport.

Department for Transport, 2007, The additionality of wider economic benefits in transport appraisal. Available at: www.dft.gov.uk/pgr/economics/rdg/webia/webtheory/additionalityweb.

Department for Transport, 2008, *Developing a Sustainable Transport System*. London: DfT Publications.

Department for Transport, 2009a, *NATA Refresh : Appraisal for a Sustainable System*. London: DfT Publications.

Department for Transport, 2009b, The reliability sub-objective. Transport Appraisal Guidance (TAG) Unit 3.5.7, London: Department for Transport.

Department for Transport, updated April 2009, Transport Analysis Guidance: WebTAG. Available at: www.dft.gov.uk/webtag/.

Dodgson, J.S., 1973, External effects and secondary benefits in road investment appraisal. *Journal of Transport Economics and Policy*, **7** (2), 169–185.

Dodgson, J.S., 1974, Motorway investment, industrial transport costs and sub-regional growth: a case study of the M62. *Regional Studies*, **8** (1), 75–91.

Duranton, G. and D. Puga, 2004, Microfoundations of urban agglomeration economies. In J. V. Henderson and J. F. Thisse, eds, *Handbook on Urban and Regional Economics. Volume 4: Cities and Geography*. Oxford: Elsevier.

Eberts, R.W. and D.P. McMillen, 1999, Agglomeration economies and urban public infrastructure. In H.P. Cheshire and E.S. Mills, eds, *Handbook of Regional and Urban Economics*, Vol. III. New York: North Holland.

Elhorst, J.P. and J. Oosterhaven, 2008, Integral cost-benefit analysis of Maglev projects under market imperfections. *Journal of Transport and Land Use*, **1** (1), 65–87.

Eliasson, J., 2004, Car drivers' valuations of travel time variability, unexpected delays and queue driving. Proceedings of the European Transport Conference, Strasbourg October 2004. London: AET Transport.

Foster, C.D. and M.E. Beesley, 1963, Estimating the benefits of constructing an underground line in London. *Journal of the Royal Statistical Society, Series A*, **126** (1) 46–58.

Fowkes, A.S., 1999, Issues in evaluation. A justification for awarding all time savings, both small and large, equal unit value in scheme evaluation. In AHCG (1999) op. cit., pp. 341–359.

Fowkes, A.S., 2001, Principles of valuing business travel time saving. ITS Working Paper 562, Institute for Transport Studies, University of Leeds, UK.

Fujita, M. and J. Thisse, 2002, *The Economics of Agglomeration: Cities, Industrial Location and Regional Growth*. Cambridge: Cambridge University Press.

Fujita, M., P. Krugman and A. Venables, 1999, *The Spatial Economy: Cities, Regions and International Trade*. Cambridge, MA: MIT Press.

Galvez, T. and S. Jara-Diaz 1998, On the social valuation of travel time savings. *International Journal of Transport Economics*, **25**, 205–219.

Graham, D.J., 2007a, Agglomeration, productivity and transport investment. *Journal of Transport Economics and Policy*, **41**, 317–343.

Graham, D.J., 2007b, Variable returns to agglomeration and the effect of road traffic congestion. *Journal of Urban Economics*, **62**, 103–120.

Graham, D.J., S. Gibbons and R. Martin, 2009b, Transport investments and the distance decay of agglomeration benefits. Working Paper, Imperial College of London.

Graham, D.J., P. Melo, P. Jiwattanakulpaisarn and R. Noland, 2010, Testing for bi-directional causality between productivity and agglomeration economies, *Journal of Regional Science*, **50**, 935-951.

Gunn, H. 2004. *SCGE MODELS: Relevance and Accessibility for Use in the UK, with Emphasis on Implications for Evaluation of Transport Investments*. Cambridge: RAND Europe.

Gunn, H.F., M.A. Bradley, and C.L. Rohr, 1996, The 1994 national value of time study of road traffic in England. In PTRC, 1996, The Easthampsted Conference on the Value of Travel Time Savings.

Harrison, A.J., 1974, *The Economics of Transport Appraisal*. London: Croom Helm.

Hensher, D.A., 1977, *Value of Business Travel Time*. Oxford: Pergamon Press.

Hensher, D.A. and P. Goodwin, 2004, Implementation values of travel time savings: the extended set of considerations in a toll road context. *Transport Policy*, **11** (2), 171–181.

Jong, G.C. de, S. Bakker, M. Pieters, and P. Wortelboer-van-Donselaar, 2004a, New values of time and reliability in freight transport in the Netherlands. Proceedings of the European Transport Conference, 2004.

Jong, G.C. de, E.P. Kroes, R. Plasmeijer, P. Sanders and P. Warffemius, 2004b, The value of reliability. Proceedings of the European Transport Conference, 2004.

Laird, J.J., J. Nellthorp and P.J. Mackie, 2005, Network effects and total economic impact in transport appraisal, *Transport Policy*, **12**, 537-544.

Leitch, G., 1978, Report of the advisory committee on trunk road assessment (ACTRA). London, HMSO.

Mackie, P.J., S. Jara-Diaz, and A.S. Fowkes, 2001, The value of travel time savings in evaluation. *Transportation Research Part E*, **37**, 91–106.

Mackie, P.J. and J. Nellthorp, 2001, Cost benefit analysis in transport. In K.J. Button and D.A. Hensher, *Handbook of Transport Systems and Traffic Control*. Oxford: Pergamon, pp. 143–174.

McFadden, D., 2009, Sociality, rationality, and the ecology of choice. In: S. Hess, and A. Daly, eds, 2009, *Choice Modelling: The State-of-the-art and the State-of-practice*, Proceedings from the Inaugural International Choice Modelling Conference. Bingley, UK: Emerald, pp. 3–18.

McQuaid, R.W., M. Greig, A. Smyth and J. Cooper, 2004, The Importance of transport in business' location decisions. Report to the DfT. DfT, London.

Melo, P., D.J. Graham and R.B. Noland 2009, A meta-analysis of urban agglomeration economies. *Regional Science and Urban Economics*, **39**, 332–342.

Mohring H., 1976, *Transportation Economics*. Cambridge: Ballinger Press.

Neuberger, H., 1971, User benefit in the evaluation of transport and land use plans. *Journal of Transport Economics and Policy*, **5** (1), 52–75.

Noland, R.B. and J.W. Polak, 2002, Travel time variability: a review of theoretical and empirical issues. *Transport Reviews*, **22** (1), 39–54.

Noland, R.B. and K.A. Small, 1995, Travel time uncertainty, departure time choice, and the cost of the morning commutes. *Transportation Research Record*, **1493**, 150–158.

Odgaard, T., C.E. Kelly and J.J. Laird, 2005, Current practice in project appraisal in Europe European Policy and Research. European Transport Conference, 3–5 October 2005. Strasbourg: AET Transport, UK.

Ove Arup and Partners Ltd., J. Bates, I. Black and J. Fearnon, 2004 Frameworks for modelling the variability of highway journey times. Report to the Department for Transport, UK.

Pearce, D.W. and C.A. Nash, 1981, *The Social Appraisal of Project: A Text in Cost-Benefit Analysis*, London: MacMillan.

Rice, P., A. J. Venables and E. Patacchinni, 2006, Spatial determinants of productivity: analysis for the regions of Great Britain. *Regional Science and Urban Economics*, **36**, 727–752.

Rosenthal, S. S. and W. C. Strange, 2004, Evidence on the nature and sources of agglomeration economies. In J. V. Henderson and J. F. Thisse, eds, *Handbook on Urban and Regional Economics Volume 4 Cities and Geography*. Oxford: Elsevier.

Shires, J.D. and G.C. de Jong, 2006, An international meta-analysis of values of time. In Bickel et al., 2006 Annex 1, *Proposal for Harmonised Guidelines, Developing Harmonised European Approaches for Transport Costing and Project Assessment (HEATCO), Report to the European Commission*. Stuttgart: IER, University of Stuttgart.

Small, K.A., 1982, The scheduling of consumer activities: work trips. *American Economic Review*, **72** (2), 467–479.

Standing Advisory Committee on Trunk Road Assessment (SACTRA), 1999, *Transport and the Economy*. London: The Stationery Office.

Sugden, R., 1999, Developing a consistent cost-benefit framework for multi-modal transport appraisal. Report to Department for Transport, University of East Anglia.

Vandaele, E., F. Witlox and G. Verleye, 2004, The use of correlation analysis to explain the monetary value of quality attributes of transportation. *Proceedings of the European Transport Conference, 2004*.

Venables, A. J., 2007, Evaluating urban transport improvements: cost–benefit analysis in the presence of agglomeration and income taxation. *Journal of Transport Economics and Policy*, **41** (2), 173–188.

Venables, A. J. and M. Gasiorek, 1999, The welfare implications of transport improvements in the presence of market failure. In SACTRA, ed., *The Welfare Implications of Transport Improvements in the Presence of Market Failure and the Incidence of Imperfect Competition in UK Sectors and Regions*. London: Department for the Environment, Transport and the Regions, pp. 3–58.

Wardman, M., 2001, A review of British evidence on time and service quality valuations. *Transportation Research Part E*, **37**, 107–128.

Welch, M. and H. Williams, 1997, The sensitivity of transport investment benefits to the evaluation of small travel-time saving. *Journal of Transport Economics and Policy*, **31**, 231–254.

22 Price discrimination
Simon P. Anderson and Régis Renault

INTRODUCTION

Whenever we take a trip by train or by plane, we are often well aware that the price we paid was quite different from that paid by our fellow passengers with whom we are sharing the carriage or cabin. We can bemoan this situation, if we booked late and do not qualify for an age discount and our ticket was one of the more expensive ones or perhaps be pleased at having gotten a good price. The different prices are illustrations of what economists call discriminatory pricing. This seems to be a textbook case where a service which is identical (same journey, same date, same time, same comfort class) is sold at different prices.[1]

Looking closer, it is a little oversimplified to claim that all travelers have actually received the same level of service. Less expensive tickets are often associated with numerous restrictions which clearly indicate a lower level of service. It is often necessary to buy the ticket a long time in advance, with restrictive conditions on cancellation and reimbursement. The traveler can then enjoy the same service as she would have had if she had paid full price – unless, of course, her plans change at the last minute. However, to get the cheap fare she has to accept some risk, had she been obliged to change or cancel her ticket, or indeed she might have had to put up with some inconvenience due to having not changed her ticket in order to not lose money. There are also reduced fares for those satisfying certain 'demographic' considerations. Senior citizens and children often pay lower fares.

On 5 May, for 18 May 2007, the prices for one-way second class travel between Charleroi Sud (Belgium) and Paris Nord (France), proposed on the internet site www.thalys.com were as follows: Librys 59 €; Mezzo 44.5 €; Mezzo+ 32.5 €; and Smilys 20.5 €. The rates for Mezzo+, Mezzo and Smilys can be reserved only if sufficient seats are still available, and only if one buys a round trip ticket. It is less expensive to buy a round-trip Smilys ticket than to buy a one-way Librys ticket. However, Smilys can only be bought when reserving two weeks before the departure date and it is the only fare which is non-exchangeable and completely non-reimbursable. Mezzo and Mezzo+ are reimbursable up to 50 percent of the price of the ticket, up to the departure date. The only difference between the two tickets is that the quota for Mezzo+ is sold out quicker than for Mezzo. It is also possible to get a Lys fare for 26 € if one has a membership in the program. This is an example of a two-part tariff.

For these examples, the menu of prices that are proposed must take into account the fact that travelers can personally arbitrage (or choose between) the different options. There are also fare categories which are not subject to such arbitrage, such as: Kid (15 €), for children under 12 years old; Kid & Co. (29.5 €), for adults accompanying a child under 12; Youth (29.5 €) for travelers under 26; and Senior (41.5 €) for travelers over 59. All of these classes, except for Smilys, are also available in first class – Librys, for example, costs 100 €.

Price discrimination arises when a firm sells different units of the same good at different prices. This applies perfectly to cases in which certain groups of customers benefit from special tariffs (for example, students or senior citizens), or nonlinear pricing where the price per unit depends on the number of units brought (such as the price of a French Metro ticket when bought singly or in a pack of ten).[2]

Nevertheless, several practices that involve selling different services can be viewed as discriminatory. In such cases, price differences might also be explained by cost differences without necessarily invoking a discriminatory motive (see, for example, Lott and Roberts, 1991). To address this concern, some writers have proposed definitions based on the comparison of price differences relative to cost differences. Stigler (1987) proposed comparing the ratio of the prices of two services with the ratio of their marginal production costs. By this criterion, a situation is discriminatory if the two ratios are unequal. Phlips (1983) on the other hand proposes comparing absolute differences. Then prices are discriminatory if the difference in marginal costs is not equal to the difference in prices.

It is difficult to find a decisive argument for one definition over the other.[3] Both definitions indicate that prices can be discriminatory even if price differences are small, just as it can be discriminatory if price differences are large. Suppose an airline brings passengers to a Parisian airport from which its international flights leave, and has everyone pay the same price for a flight to New York. This pricing discriminates against travelers living near Paris (see Tirole, 1988, 1993, for a similar example).[4] The definitions do not say whether such discrimination harms economic efficiency: the airline's pricing scheme allows it to more effectively exploit its market power by bringing its trans-Atlantic travelers to Paris.

A firm with some market power and proposing different services can set its prices to get the greatest profit, and its prices will not bear any simple relation (absolute or relative) to marginal costs. Exercising market power is channelled through the ability to price above marginal cost. Offering diverse services can be seen as a way of discriminating insofar as it allows the firm to adjust the service proposed and its pricing to a demand that differs from customer to customer.[5]

Just as it is difficult to define discriminatory pricing, it is not easy to classify different discriminatory practices. The classic reference is Pigou (1938), who distinguishes between three possible degrees of discrimination, depending on the ability of the firm to distinguish between buyers who are prepared to pay a higher price and those inclined to pay less. Pigou defines first-degree discrimination as when consumers show pay their maximal willingness to pay for each unit. This is also called *perfect price discrimination*.

Pigou recognized that this first form of price discrimination might not have great practical relevance. He notes that the firm is better able to segment the market between different groups of buyers who have different demands. Ideally, the firm would like to segment the market into groups with similar willingness to pay; such segments could be ranked from highest to lowest willingness to pay.

Such idealized segmentation constitutes second-degree price discrimination. As Pigou notes, however, in practice a firm can only imperfectly compartmentalize consumers according to their willingness to pay. The firm must use characteristics which it can directly monitor, such as the type of good that is being transported (for example, livestock or pig iron[6]) for a railroad that transports freight, or the location of the buyer. This latter practice is third-degree price discrimination.

Pigou's classification underlines the fact that discriminatory pricing is meant for the firm to exercise its market power as well as possible. Rather than proposing a reference case corresponding to no discrimination, as did Stigler and Phlips, Pigou defined the benchmark where the ultimate objective of discrimination is attained, that is, where each unit is sold at the highest possible price.

From this viewpoint, first-degree price discrimination is the theoretical benchmark. We will see, nonetheless, that third-degree discrimination is very relevant to the understanding of the discriminatory practices which are based on directly observable characteristics such as age, departure location and time and date of the journey.

On the other hand, second-degree discrimination only seems to be a particular case of third-degree discrimination which, as we will see, corresponds to a situation which is particularly favorable for the firm, where the verifiable information that allows the firm to discriminate is perfectly correlated with willingness to pay (for example, if older people are willing to pay more).

Nevertheless, numerous types of discriminatory pricing such as nonlinear pricing or offering different comfort classes within a train or plane do not rely on a verifiable criterion and allow the user to choose her preferred option. Such practices therefore cannot be viewed as third-degree price discrimination, and economists have gotten into the habit of calling such practices second-degree price discrimination (see Mougeot and Naegelen, 1994; Phlips, 1983; Tirole, 1988; 1993, chapter 3; Varian, 1989). This term is therefore currently used to cover practices that are quite different from those originally envisaged by Pigou.

The discussion above suggests that discriminatory pricing is tightly tied to the exercise of market power.[7] Under perfect competition, firms are constrained to sell their output at the price that is imposed by the market. It is then obviously impossible to sell different units of a good at different prices, or to try to affect prices by proposing a range of different services (at least as long as such services are sold in a competitive market). Even if the firm has some market power, its ability to discriminate between different buyers can be undone or mitigated by the buyers' ability to arbitrage between the different options proposed.[8]

This arbitrage can take two forms, depending on whether one or several buyers are involved. If it is possible to transfer the good, buyers can exchange the good or service between themselves and the firm cannot charge different prices, because those buyers who benefit from the lowest price will be able to buy in order to resell to those who would otherwise have to pay more. For example, if someone has a membership card which allows her to obtain her tickets at a cheaper price, she could buy a large number of them and resell them to those without a membership card.

Similarly, if a low fare is offered under the condition that the ticket should be bought sufficiently far in advance, then entrepreneurial individuals could buy a large quantity of these cheap tickets in order to sell them just before the date when the tickets are valid. Even though this type of arbitrage can be limited by transactions costs, it nonetheless represents a significant constraint on firms' pricing strategies, so much so that firms often put in place several techniques to stop it. They often require one to present the membership card during the trip or, for airlines, present a piece of identification which has on it the name matching that of the ticket holder. This type of rule also allows the firm to circumvent the second type of arbitrage, in which one customer with several options does not choose the one which was designed for her. For example, if a firm wants to discriminate on the basis of age, by presenting a driver's license the customer verifies that she is paying the price that she should. When buyers can practice such arbitrage between the different pricing options that are offered, Pigou (1938) says that demand is transferrable.

In practice, firms can often discriminate without explicitly forbidding arbitrage. The firm then has to explicitly worry about potential arbitrage when it is setting up a discriminatory tariff structure. While the firm cannot force its customers to not arbitrage, it has to set up the right incentives in its pricing plan.

The analysis of arbitrage behavior across consumers is relatively complicated, and most of the literature on discriminatory pricing simply supposes that transactions costs are high enough to render it impossible. We, too, will implicitly invoke this assumption throughout the chapter.[9] On the other hand, so-called personal arbitrage – by which a user can choose an option which is not intended for her purchase – has been the subject of numerous studies, especially over the last three decades.

The next section 2 presents a certain number of base concepts and general principles which are needed to understand the rest of the paper.[10] Following this, we will show how a firm can exploit information about customer demand in order to discriminate, by supposing that buyers do not indulge in personal arbitrage. We will distinguish between perfect discrimination, discrimination between several categories of buyers who are purchasing the same good, and market segmentation where the firm offers different services for which it can perfectly determine the buyers who are prone to buying each service. The Section after this looks at strategies which allow the firm to motivate buyers to not engage in personal arbitrage when the firm cannot stop it by using verifiable information. We first consider using nonlinear tariffs and then the possibility of discriminating by offering different qualities. In the final section, we conclude and also discuss the link between discriminatory pricing and competition. This discussion allows us to evaluate the robustness of the results obtained for monopolies.

PRELIMINARY RESULTS AND BASIC CONCEPTS

Uniform Monopoly Pricing

We start with the simplest pricing structure, uniform pricing, where all units of the same good are sold at the same price, such as a given journey where there is only one comfort class and all travelers pay the same price.

Let $D(p)$ be the quantity demanded at the price p. The simplest interpretation is to suppose that D describes the distribution of willingness to pay over different travelers. Each traveler only wants a single trip, and $D(p)$ then indicates the number of travelers willing to pay at least p.

It is also useful to define the inverse demand for each quantity q. This is the maximum price at which this number of trips can be sold, $P(q)$. When each traveler only wants

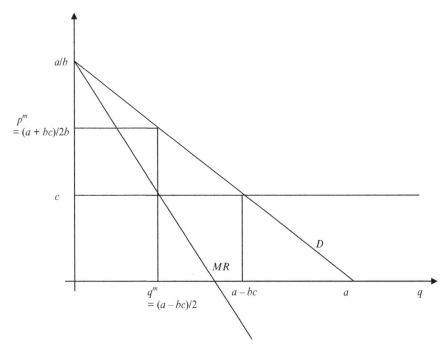

Figure 22.1 Uniform monopoly pricing

a single trip, $P(q)$ is the willingness to pay of the marginal consumer: the individual who would not travel if the price were slightly higher. In order to simplify the analysis, suppose that the marginal cost of production is constant at rate c per unit, which is also therefore the average variable production cost (and is the cost generated by each traveler). Under perfect competition, the price would be given by this marginal cost, and the number of travelers would be $D(c)$. We assume that services are provided by a private monopolistic firm, whose objective is to maximize its profit. We start with the case where demand is linear,

$$q = D(p) = a - bp, \quad a > 0, \quad b > 0, \quad \text{and } \frac{a}{b} > c. \quad (22.1)$$

The latter condition ensures that it is optimal to produce a strictly positive quantity. This situation is illustrated in Figure 22.1. The firm is constrained under uniform pricing to choose a single point on the demand curve. If it wants to carry q travelers, the highest uniform price that it could charge is:

$$p = P(q) = \frac{a - q}{b}. \quad (22.2)$$

The producer surplus, *PS*, which is profit gross of fixed costs, is represented by the rectangle above marginal cost (that is the mark-up per traveler), $p - c$, multiplied by the number of travelers q.[11] The optimal quantity must therefore maximize:

$$\left[\frac{a-q}{b} - c\right]q,$$ (22.3)

and the first order conditions for an optimal quantity can be written as:

$$\frac{a-2q}{b} = c.$$ (22.4)

The left-hand side of this expression is marginal revenue, MR. This is a straight line with the same price intercept as inverse demand D, but its slope is twice as steep. It is easy to see from Figure 22.1 that the condition for equality between marginal cost and marginal revenue is satisfied for a quantity:

$$q^m = \frac{D(c)}{2} = \frac{a-bc}{2},$$ (22.5)

which is therefore half the quantity produced under perfect competition. The uniform price chosen is therefore:

$$p^m = P(q^m) = \frac{a+bc}{2b},$$ (22.6)

and this generates a producer surplus, PS, equal to:

$$(p^m - c)\, q^m = \frac{(a-bc)^2}{4b},$$ (22.7)

which corresponds to the rectangle PS in Figure 22.2.

In the general case, the equality of marginal revenue and marginal cost allows us to determine the optimal quantity.[12] When we describe discriminatory pricing, we will often use first order conditions for *prices* (rather than quantities). Under uniform pricing, the firm chooses a uniform price p^m in order to maximize $D(p^m)\,(p^m - c)$. The first order necessary condition for a maximum can be written in the form:

$$\frac{p^m - c}{p^m} = \frac{1}{|\eta(p^m)|}, \text{ where } \eta(p^m) = p^m \frac{D'(p^m)}{D(p^m)} < 0,$$ (22.8)

where $\eta(p^m) < 0$ is the elasticity of demand. The left-hand side is the mark-up rate, also known as the Lerner Index. it is therefore higher when demand is inelastic (meaning an elasticity closer to zero). Note that the elasticity of demand at the uniform price chosen by the monopolist is always less than -1.

Welfare Analysis and Public Policy

We have just seen that a private firm which maximizes its profit will choose a price that is higher than the perfectly competitive price, and can thus increase its profit. Obviously, this is done at the expense of the consumers (travelers), who face higher prices. We now show how this loss of consumer well-being can be measured in monetary terms in a way that can be compared with the extra profit extracted by the firm.

An individual's consumer surplus is the difference between the maximum price that

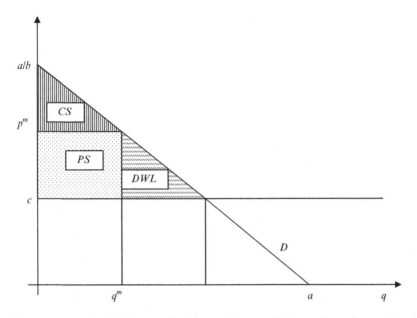

Notes: *CS*: consumer surplus (darker grey triangular area between the inverse demand curve, *D*, and price *p^m*); *PS*: producer surplus (black rectangular area above marginal cost); *DWL*: deadweight loss (lighter grey triangular area).

Figure 22.2   Surpluses and deadweight loss

the consumer is willing to pay for a trip and the price that she actually pays. The inverse demand curve is constructed by ranking willingness to pay in decreasing order, so that the q trips are sold to the q travelers willing to pay most. Aggregate consumer surplus, *CS*, generated by the sale of quantity $D(p)$ at price p, therefore corresponds to the area between inverse demand and the quantity from 0 to $D(p)$.[13] For the solution described in Figure 22.1, this is represented by the triangle *CS* in Figure 22.2. The loss in consumer surplus resulting from a change from pricing *at* marginal cost to pricing at the monopoly level is given by the monopoly producer surplus plus the area *DWL* in Figure 22.2. This loss of consumer surplus can be interpreted as the sum of what travelers would have been willing to pay, collectively, in order to be able to access tickets priced at marginal cost as opposed to the monopoly price. Insofar as this total is larger than the monopoly producer surplus, there is a beneficial exchange possibility for all market participants which has not been realized (the firm would be ready to cut its price down to marginal cost if, in exchange, it could receive compensation that is at least as large as its producer surplus).

Monopoly pricing therefore introduces an inefficiency which can be measured by that part of the loss of consumer surplus which is not offset by an increase in producer surplus. This *deadweight loss* is the area *DWL* in Figure 22.2. To understand this inefficiency more concisely, it is convenient to introduce the concept of *social surplus*. This is the sum of producer surplus and consumer surplus. Pricing at marginal cost enables the maximal social surplus to be attained. Deadweight loss is the reduction of social surplus caused by a higher price.[14]

One reasonable objective for public policy could be to minimize deadweight loss. This objective could be obtained by a public firm, or one subject to regulation, pricing at marginal cost. Such a solution is not generally very satisfactory. When there are increasing returns to scale, such pricing will not cover production costs. For example, when marginal cost is constant, marginal cost pricing will generate zero producer surplus, so the firm will not cover its fixed costs.

It follows that the firm must be partly financed by taxpayers. It may then be desirable to suffer some deadweight loss in order to avoid an overly large deficit. Pricing at marginal cost might then be replaced by pricing at average cost, so that the firm just covers its costs. Nevertheless, it seems rather arbitrary to impose the condition that the firm should not make losses. An alternative argument against pricing at marginal cost is that taxation induces inefficiency in the allocation of resources (see Meade, 1944). Optimal pricing must therefore strike a balance between maximizing social surplus in the markets served by the firm and the efficiency cost of raising tax revenue in the rest of the economy. The latter cost can be measured by the deadweight losses caused by the taxes in the markets where they are levied.[15] Under such circumstances, the firm will only be fully financed by its users if the cost of raising public funds is too large. This reasoning also implies that if the cost of raising public funds is too large, and if the government can appropriate the firm's profits (which is effectively the case if the firm is public), it may be desirable to earn a return exceeding production costs. This extra revenue will enable the government to reduce fiscal pressure on the rest of the economy.

We can now address the pricing problem of a public or regulated firm. Following Laffont and Tirole (1993), we introduce a parameter λ which is the marginal deadweight loss of raising public funds: an extra euro raised means a cost of $1 + \lambda$ euros.[16] The firm's objective function can then be written as:

$$CS + (1 + \lambda)\, PS. \tag{22.9}$$

When λ becomes large, the firm pays no heed to consumer surplus. This case correspond to a private firm maximizing its profits. Otherwise, the firm chooses p to maximize:

$$CS(p) + (1 + \lambda)D(p)\,(p - c). \tag{22.10}$$

Using the relationship $CS'(p) = -D(p)$[17] gives the first order necessary condition of:

$$\frac{p - c}{p} = \frac{\lambda}{1 + \lambda} \frac{1}{|\eta\,(p)|}. \tag{22.11}$$

The price thus obtained is a special case of what are called Ramsey–Boîteux prices, which ensure maximization of social surplus under the constraint that the firm returns a particular level of profits, for example to cover its fixed costs. Under this interpretation, λ therefore indicates the severity of the budget constraint and is the marginal social surplus gain that could be obtained by reducing the profit level to be earned by one euro (see Boîteux, 1956, and Ramsey, 1927).

In the interpretations above, λ is necessarily positive, so that more weight is placed on producer surplus than on consumer surplus. A higher λ leads to a higher mark-up over marginal cost (with monopoly pricing resulting as λ goes to infinity).[18] This outcome is rather unsatisfying insofar as we might wish for public policy to respond not only to economic efficiency but also to redistribution. The current analysis does not need to take a stand on these issues.

Thus, if a higher price (of a train ticket) allows the government to efficiently collect revenues, these could be used to give lump sum transfers to consumers. Nevertheless, a system of monetary transfers creates difficulties in itself because of the perverse incentives it may induce, as well as perhaps for reasons of political viability. If indeed transfers are not to be made directly from government revenues because it is intrinsically costly to do so, then the pricing scheme may be used directly for transfers, and it may therefore be reasonable to put a larger weight on consumer surplus than on producer surplus. This translates in our formal analysis to $-1 < \lambda < 0$.[19] This allows us to understand why we might want to heavily subsidize certain services such as public transportation, even pricing below marginal cost. Finally, there may be other reasons for pricing below marginal cost, especially for transportation services. Up until now, we have not taken into account the possibility of positive or negative externalities such as pollution or congestion. This omission can easily be rectified by replacing, in our analysis, marginal private cost with marginal social cost, which would be greater or smaller depending on whether the externality were negative or positive.

DISCRIMINATION AND VERIFIABLE CONSUMER CHARACTERISTICS

Perfect Discrimination

We first consider the case which is most advantageous to the seller. This arises when the seller has perfect information about the demand from each possible buyer. Perfect discrimination arises when the firm can use this information fully (first-degree discrimination, in Pigou's terminology). In order to use the information, the seller must be able to control the price and the characteristics of each unit sold to each buyer. For example, if an airline perfectly knew the needs and desires of all of its customers it could choose the price at which each client would take the price, and dictate the date, time and comfort class.

This principle can be illustrated very simply by supposing that the good sold is perfectly homogeneous, and that each buyer only wants a single unit. In this case, the tastes of the buyer are completely described by her willingness to pay. A profit-maximizing monopolist will then have each buyer pay her maximum willingness to pay, leaving the consumer no surplus. The firm will therefore want to sell to all those whose valuations exceed marginal cost. This situation is shown in Figure 22.1 for constant marginal cost and linear demand. We see here that this pricing policy leads to maximal social surplus, all of which is captured by the firm.

The above approach can easily be extended to deal with elastic individual demand (so the quantity demanded decreases as the price rises). For illustration, suppose that the demand curve in Figure 22.1 represented a single consumer. The inverse demand would then indicate the highest price that she would pay to consume one extra unit. If the quantity q were sold at the uniform price $P(q)$, the net consumer surplus would be $CS(P(q))$;

we can then define the gross consumer surplus (for an individual[20]) as $V(q) = CS(P(q)) + P(q)q$. Optimal discriminatory pricing would then mean paying the willingness to pay for each unit, and selling units as long as this willingness to pay exceeds marginal cost. This then induces the quantity $q^* = D(c)$ sold at a tariff equal to the corresponding gross consumer surplus, $V(q^*)$ which is the surplus that the consumer would enjoy if she could consume the quantity q^* for free.

Another method for getting to the same result would be to use a two-part tariff (see also Oi, 1971). Such a tariff would specify an entry, or membership, fee A that the consumer must pay in order to consume the good at all. If she joins, then she can buy as much as she wants at a price p. Setting $p = c$ ensures that the consumer will therefore choose q^*, and she will therefore enjoy a surplus of $V(q^*) - cq^*$. She will join as long as the entry fee is not larger than this, and so the seller will set a fee as large as possible subject to this individual constraint; namely it will set an entry fee of $A = V(q^*) - cq^*$. The total price paid by the consumer is then $A + cq^* = V(q^*)$, which means that her full surplus is extracted by the firm. The outcome is thus just the same as for the preceding pricing system. Even though a two-part tariff seems simpler, it still needs just as much information: while it may be easy to fix price at marginal cost, calculating the entry fee means knowing the consumer's surplus, and hence her full demand curve.[21]

The pricing solution for a public firm under the similar assumption of perfect knowledge and ability to discriminate is straightforward: it should choose exactly the same tariff structure. This is because all surplus is extracted from the consumer and earned by the firm for the public purse.

One Good and Several Groups of Buyers

We next consider a situation in which a firm can observe a characteristic or characteristics of buyers – such as age, job, or residential address – and observing these characteristics allows the firm to infer something about demand. The firm can exploit some correlation between the observed variable and the individual demand in order to discriminate (perhaps such discrimination is not legal or socially acceptable, for example if it is based on gender or race).

The firm can then choose a price that depends on the observed characteristic, and the individual who does not have this characteristic can be excluded from prices not meant for her. However, discrimination is imperfect insofar as consumers are bundled together onto the same characteristics (for example, the same age group), and individuals still may differ by willingness to pay within the group (within a group, selling different quantities with nonlinear pricing or introducing differentiation can be used to get potential buyers to reveal their tastes). The firm is therefore obliged to set a uniform price for each category (or group). Suppose, for example, there are two classes of buyers: youths under 26 and the rest of the population. Asking for identification (in the absence of fake IDs), the firm can know which category the buyer is in. It can therefore exclude arbitrage by which people in one group buy the good or service in order to sell it to people in the other group (for example, airline tickets with the traveler's name on them). In the absence of such arbitrage, demand from each group depends only on the price charged to members of the group.

Consider the case of a public firm: the specialization to a private firm will simply be given by letting λ become arbitrarily large. Let p_i be the price applied to group i, and let D_i (p_i) be the resulting demand curve, and CS_i (p_i) be the corresponding consumer surplus. We assume that marginal cost is constant at rate c, so that the firm can choose prices for groups independently of each other.[22] The firm therefore chooses p_i to maximize:

$$CS_i(p_i) + (1 + \lambda)D_i(p_i) \ (p_i - c). \tag{22.12}$$

This leads to a first order condition which simply generalizes that, for a single market:

$$\frac{p_i - c}{p_i} = \frac{\lambda}{1 + \lambda} \frac{1}{\eta_i(p_i)}. \tag{22.13}$$

This type of discrimination benefits the firm because it faces groups of consumers whose elasticities differ. The less elastic demand is (the closer η is to zero), the higher the price charged to the group. Thus, youths enjoy lower train fares and airfares because they are more likely to reduce their demand if prices were higher. Clearly the firm benefits from discrimination because it can always opt to charge the same price across groups. However, only consumers for whom demand is quite elastic benefit, to the detriment of the other consumers.[23]

For a profit-maximizing firm, we can determine whether discrimination is socially beneficial. Suppose for simplicity that $\lambda = 0$, so that social surplus is simply the sum of consumer surplus and producer surplus. Note first that, for a fixed total output, discrimination induces inefficiency in the allocation of this quantity between two groups. The price paid by the consumers in a group reflects what they are willing to pay in order to buy one extra unit. Social surplus can be increased by shifting consumption from those willing to pay less at the margin to those willing to pay more. Furthermore, since the output of a monopolist under uniform pricing is too low, discrimination can only improve welfare if it increases production. This necessary 'output condition' was first proposed by Schmalensee (1981).

In general, the impact of discriminatory pricing on the total quantity produced is ambiguous. For example, suppose that the demand in each group i is linear and given by:

$$D_i(p) = a_i - b_i p. \tag{22.14}$$

Applying the earlier analysis of linear demand, if both groups are served under uniform pricing the total output is:

$$\frac{a_1 + a_2 - (b_1 + b_2) \ c}{2}, \tag{22.15}$$

while the quantities allocated to each group of buyers under discrimination are, respectively:

$$\frac{(a_1 - b_1 c)}{2} \quad \text{and} \quad \frac{(a_2 - b_2 c)}{2}. \tag{22.16}$$

The total output is therefore identical,[24] and discrimination is necessarily harmful to social welfare. This conclusion is invalid if only one group is served by the non-discriminating monopolist. Then, if marginal cost is constant, discriminatory pricing is clearly preferable because it allows more markets to be served. In this case, the group which is served under both pricing schemes is not worse off because it pays the same price under both, while the other group would not have been served at all under uniform pricing.

The above reasoning also gives us an unambiguous result when capacity is fixed. Discriminatory pricing cannot increase output, and is therefore clearly detrimental. If an airplane is full, it is therefore better that all passengers pay the same price. Nevertheless, this reasoning is only valid in the short run, because in the longer run the possibility of discrimination can motivate the airline to increase the number of flights. In this context, too, discrimination can engender a greater diversity amongst the traveling population.

As we argued in the Introduction, second-degree discrimination as originally envisaged by Pigou (1938) can be seen as a special case of the above analysis of discrimination between different groups of buyers. If the observable characteristic used by the firm to discriminate can allow it to perfectly separate buyers into groups that can be ordered according to willingness to pay, then it can practice second-degree price discrimination à la Pigou.

To illustrate, consider the following example given in Anderson and Renault (2003b). Suppose that a traveler wishes to take a train trip and her willingness to pay is perfectly positively correlated with age. Even though this would seem to allow the firm to practice perfect discrimination (because the client's age perfectly reveals her demand), it might in practice be costly to specify too many different prices. For example, it may be only possible to offer two prices. The railroad company must then set a threshold age above which people cannot get the low price.

Suppose, for example, that the inverse demand is given by $P(q) = 1 - q$. With zero marginal cost, the monopoly price and output are both one-half. It is then easy to see that the firm's optimal strategy is to charge full fare of 2/3 for the oldest third of the population, and to set a reduced fare of 1/3 for the younger ones. In this context, we can also determine the second best policy of choosing the critical age with the objective of maximizing social surplus, subject to the firm choosing its prices given this critical age. The second best solution is that the firm only offers the reduced fare to the younger half of the population. The firm would then choose a full fare of 1/2 for the older half of the population and a half-priced fare of 1/4 for the younger travelers. In this sense, the critical age chosen by the profit maximizing firm is too high.

Backhauling

We have assumed so far that the product is produced at constant marginal cost. In the case of transportation, services are provided and these depend upon the capacity offered. While it is out of our scope to cover the full range of issues associated with proper cost attribution, scheduling of service and route network choice of passenger services, we nevertheless broach this issue with a simple example of capacity that is provided on an outbound trip: the train has to get back to the origin to make the next trip to the destination.

The analysis can be framed in terms of a monopoly passenger railway service (see Rietveld and Roson, 2002, for a recent application in this vein). Many commuters might wish to make the trip to the Central Business District in the morning rush-hour commute, but few people want to go in the reverse direction soon afterwards.[25]

The analogue in the context of freight transportation is when a product is shipped to a destination and there is a relatively weak demand for shipping goods in the opposite direction. However, the trucks, ships, or freight trips must still make the return trip to pick up another load. This is termed the 'backhaul problem'.[26] We therefore frame the application to passenger transportation in the classic fronthaul and backhaul context (for example, Mohring, 1976). This is well known in economic theory as a joint production problem, much as the textbook mutton and wool joint production in raising a sheep. Analogously, once an outbound trip to the final market is created (fronthaul), then a return trip is also created (backhaul).

The economic theory of pricing for competitive markets with backhaul is well understood. Suppose, as above, that the round trip costs c, and that the demand for such trips is given by a well-behaved downward-sloping demand, $D(p)$. Suppose too that the demand for trips back from the final market is $D_b(p)$. Denote the inverses of these demand curves as $P(Q)$ and $P_b(Q)$ respectively. For simplicity we assume that the incremental cost when carrying passengers for the trip back is zero. The relevant demand price for round trips is, therefore, the sum of the demand prices for the outbound and inbound trips, censored to be non-negative (because the transporter can always come back empty). That is, if Q is quantity, the demand price for the round trip is $P(Q) + P_b(Q)$ (where it is understood the demand prices are non-negative) and this sum is equal to p in equilibrium. Denote the solution as $\hat{Q}$: transport prices for each leg are then $P(\hat{Q})$ and $P_b(\hat{Q})$. Clearly, if the backhaul demand is weak then $P_b(\hat{Q})$ can very well be zero. Some passengers can be carried, but backhaul demand is not contributing anything to reducing the price on the front haul, and effectively $\hat{Q}_b < \hat{Q}$ where $\hat{Q}_b$ is the number of travelers transported on the backhaul.

It is now simple enough to see how to introduce incremental costs for backhaul: they can be netted off the demand price for the backhaul. The same principle applies in what follows: it suffices to net the incremental costs off the demand price.

For a monopolist, say the commuter train where it has a large cost advantage and is unconstrained, the appropriate principle for determining the quantity to carry (and the corresponding prices) is that the sum of the marginal revenues equal the marginal cost. Here again, the monopolist is not obligated to carry as much back as it carries out, and so we truncate the marginal revenues at zero. Then the solution for the fronthaul quantity, Q^*, is given as the solution to $\max \{MR(Q), 0\} + \max \{MR_b(Q), 0\} = c$, where $MR(.)$ denotes the marginal revenue to the outbound demand curve (and $MR_b(Q)$ for the backhaul demand). In this case, with a weak backhaul demand the price charged will not be zero but rather the revenue maximizing point on the (net) backhaul demand curve. This 'zero-cost monopoly price' (which is equivalently the revenue maximizing price) will prevail when some backhauls carry no passengers. Equivalently, any solution with $Q_b^* < Q^*$ involves $Q_b^* = MR_b^{-1}(0)$. For any solution to the monopoly problem, the prices on the two legs are given from the inverse demand curves as $P(Q^*)$ and $P_b(Q_b^*)$.

In the preceding analysis, the discriminating firm behaves just like a firm that offers different products with perfectly independent demands. In practice, discrimination founded on observable characteristics is often associated with multi-product production. The next section addresses the application of discriminatory pricing in such a context.

Yield Management

To set the stage, assume that a transportation vehicle (such as a train) has a single seat to fill.[27] The operator knows that one traveler will purchase the ticket, and that the traveler's reservation price for the trip is uniformly distributed on [0, 1] (think linear demand curve, as in Figure 22.1). There is no cost associated with selling the ticket or filling the seat. The operator is to set a price to maximize its expected profit. Given that the associated demand curve is linear, the price the operator should set solves the classic monopoly problem, so $p = q = \frac{1}{2}$ and the associated profit is $\pi = \frac{1}{4}$.

Now consider the case where two travelers will arrive, one after the other, and their reservation prices are independently distributed on [0, 1]. The operator sets a single price for both. What price should it set? To find the answer, we first determine its profit. It is more transparent to write out the more general problem with $F(p)$ the probability an individual traveler's reservation price is below p (so $F(.)$ is the cumulative distribution). Then the profit is $\pi = p[1 - F(p) + F(p)(1 - F(p))]$, where the term in brackets is the probability that the first traveler buys, plus the probability that she does not $(F(p))$ times the probability that the second one does $(1 - F(p))$. In the case of linear demand, $F(p) = p$ for p [0, 1] and the first-order condition implies that:

$$p = \frac{1}{\sqrt{3}} > \frac{1}{2} \tag{22.17}$$

The second order condition is readily seen to be satisfied; and profit is approximately 0.385. This is more profit because the operator can take a shot at a higher price given that the second customer provides some insurance in case the first one refuses. This logic is fine-tuned in the next example. Note that the price charged (in the current case of a single price for all) is increasing in the number of consumers, and the profit is too. As the number of travelers gets large, retaining a single seat, the price goes to the highest possible in the population (1) and the profit goes to 1 too since the probability of acceptance also tends to 1.

Profit is even higher if the operator can choose a separate price for each arriving guest. Suppose there are again two travelers and they arrive sequentially. We want to find what price will the operator will set for the first one to arrive, and what it will charge the second one if the first traveler declines the seat. To find these prices, we work backwards. If the first traveler does not buy, we can simply use the answer from the monopoly case with one seat. This gives the expected profit of 1/4 if the room is not filled on the first shot. We can now determine the profit for the choice of a price p_1 to the first traveler. Noting that the probability that the first traveler does not buy is $F(p1)$, this is $\pi = p_1(1 - F(p_1)) + F(p_1)\frac{1}{4}$. The uniform distribution entails an optimal price of 5/8. Plugging back into profit, this means a profit of $\pi = \frac{53}{88} + \frac{51}{84} = \frac{25}{64} = 0.39$. This discriminatory strategy is larger than when a single price must be set for both travelers, since the discriminatory problem subsumes the non-discriminatory one.

We next consider the case of three travelers and two places. Recall first that with simple linear demand, the monopoly price is 1/2 and profit is 1/4. These are indeed the price and expected profit that are earned on the last traveler if one place has already been sold. Likewise, if the very first sale is a failure, there are two places left and two travelers, so then the price is again 1/2 in each period and the expected profit coming out of the failed first sale is 1/2. If the first sale was a success, there is one place left and there are two remaining consumers. The continuation profit is then that derived just above, that is, $\pi = \frac{25}{64}$.

We are now in a position to analyze the first period's price. This is given by the solution to

$$\max_{p} \pi = (1 - F(p))\left[p + \frac{25}{64}\right] + F(p)\frac{1}{2}. \tag{22.18}$$

With a uniform distribution, the profit expression is $\pi = (1 - p)[p + \frac{25}{64}] + p\frac{1}{2}$, which generated a first order condition $(1 - 2p) + \frac{7}{64} = 0$, and hence the solution $p = \frac{71}{128}$. The corresponding sequence of prices is then 71/128, followed by 5/8 (an increase) if the sale was a success or 1/2 (a decrease) if it was a failure. The last price is 1/2, if at least one previous sale foundered.

The type of exercise above can be applied to various other different pricing practices observed in transportation. For example, the SNCF sells a first batch of tickets at a lower price than a second tranche, which in turn is lower than the third tranche. The simplest set-up to analyze this practice is to assume that there are three travelers, and two seats. In contrast to what was just described, the pricing is now per seat, instead of the operator being able to condition per traveler. This implies that this is a special (constrained) case of the earlier analysis, and so leads to lower profits.[28]

The analysis can also be expanded to deal with uncertainty in the number of buyers, possibility of 'strategic' buyers (or coming back after observing a first price), correlation in traveler values, and so forth. We pick up on this last topic because it is germane to transportation when firms may use the strength of early demand response to gauge later demand strength (for example, airlines or passenger trains judging demand for special events like Olympic Games or tennis matches), and because it illustrates nicely the experimentation motive for varying prices.

Suppose then an operator has a single seat to fill, and there are two potential travellers. Both have the same valuation for traveling (perfect correlation), and this valuation is uniformly distributed on $[0, 1]$. If the operator charges p to the first traveler, it expects to sell the seat with probability $1 - p$. If the first traveler does not buy, the operator knows the seat is worth less than p to the second. The updated valuation for the second traveler is uniformly distributed on $[0, p]$, and so the optimal price to set, conditional on a first refusal, is $p/2$. The second traveler accepts with probability 1/2, so the expected profit, conditional on a first refusal, is $p/4$. This means the operator's profit problem as a function of the first price set, p, is

$$\max_{p \in [0, 1]} \left\{ (1 - p) p + p\frac{p}{4} \right\}. \tag{22.19}$$

This profit is maximized at $p = 2/3$. If the first traveler refuses, the price is dropped to 1/3. The case of uncorrelated demand, given earlier, has less price dispersion, starting with a lower price (5/8) and ending with a higher one (1/2). With correlated demand, the operator starts with a higher price that includes an experimentation motive to find out more about the second traveler's valuation.

Discriminating with Several Products

When a firm sells several goods with perfectly independent demands, the situation is formally very similar to the one we have just discussed. The main difference is that marginal costs generally differ across products. With several products, there is a possibility of discrimination when different goods are sold at the same price or at prices that are close to each other. As we pointed out in the introduction, it can be quite difficult to determine whether a price difference is discriminatory.

The objective of this subsection is to briefly present some of the prominent examples that are frequently considered to represent price discrimination. In particular, we will discuss spatial discrimination and then look at discrimination over time and tied sales. In all cases that we consider, the client group which might buy one of the goods is clearly identifiable and there is no possibility of personal arbitrage. Using a multi-product offer to discriminate when arbitrage is possible will be studied in the next section. We first develop the optimal pricing strategy for a firm which sells to consumers located at different distances from its production point. We then show how this theory is relevant to a firm which must transport travelers over different distances, and we suggest other applications in transportation.

Suppose as a benchmark that consumers can access a transport service sold at a competitive price, and they can use this service to transport the good from its production point. Using this service, a consumer then pays for each unit of the good, an f.o.b. price set by the firm at its production point plus the transport cost.[29]

Without specific information on individual demand, the firm must charge a uniform tariff. This is the benchmark case of non-discrimination. However, if the firm can take care of delivery itself and if it can circumvent consumers' access to competing delivery services, it can extract more profit even though the delivery point does not reveal information about the demand of the buyers in question.

For illustration, suppose that demand is the same at every point in space. If the firm charges a price p_x to buyers located at a distance x away, the demand is $D(p_x)$ and the consumer surplus is $CS(p_x)$. Transport costs are linear and it costs tx to transport one unit a distance x, with $t > 0$. The firm chooses p_x to maximize

$$CS(p_x) + (1 + \lambda)D(p_x)(p_x - (c + tx)). \tag{22.20}$$

The price chosen will then be similar to that derived earlier, where we now simply use the full marginal cost $c + tx$. It can be shown that as long as the demand is more 'concave'[30] than an exponential function, the rate of increase in the firm's price is less than t per unit distance (see Anderson, 1989). This means that the firm does not pass on all of the transportation costs into the price ('freight absorption'). In other words, the implicit f.o.b. price – the price net of transportation costs – is smaller the farther that buyers are from the production point.

Freight absorption is often used in practice.[31] Tirole (1988) notes that there are good reasons why there should be freight absorption even if demand curves do not satisfy the condition above. First, any pricing policy which over-bills transport costs might provoke arbitrage between consumers, with those who are closer to the factory perhaps buying the good and transporting it themselves, and reselling it to those farther away. Second, buyers far from the production site might also be more likely to be closer to a rival's production site, and this might render their demand more elastic. The firm may consequently be motivated to set a somewhat lower price.[32]

The social benefits from forcing a private firm to set a uniform price are ambiguous. The discriminating firm serves a larger geographic area (which, per se, improves social welfare) but it does so while imposing higher prices on nearby consumers. For linear demand, the social welfare is highest under spatial discrimination when $\lambda = 0$ (see Holahan, 1975), and therefore *a fortiori* is highest when $\lambda > 0$ because the producer surplus is always higher when the firm can discriminate.[33]

Now consider some applications in transportation. Consider first an airline selling long-distance flights between Paris and New York. Customers' points of origin differ: they start out from different regional French airports. Our benchmark is when flights between different regional airports and Paris are sold on a competitive market and are therefore sold at marginal cost. Suppose that the airline can provide exclusive service to Paris, and that the demand for a trip to New York is the same irrespective of the starting point of the travelers (Paris, Bordeaux, Nice. . .), and that this demand is not 'too convex'. The freight absorption principle is manifested by more expensive tickets for tickets who originate farther from Paris (because of the higher cost of service), but price differences are less than the extra cost of serving these customers. In this sense, the more distant customers are subsidized by those closer to Paris.

The analysis also applies to railway pricing, or indeed an urban transportation network. Consider two trips of different length, which therefore involve different costs. Following Phlips' (1983) definition, pricing is discriminatory if the price difference between two trips is not the same as the cost difference. If the demand for the two trips is the same (so that we eliminate any price differences due to demand differences), and if the demand curve is not 'too convex', then optimal prices will be closer than costs. In other words, the price should rise more slowly than the serving costs as a function of distance.

Of course, the analysis of urban transportation prices is much more complex than the sketch presented above. Demand typically depends on the distance traveled and the other transport modes available. Pricing should take congestion into account and so forth, but this simplified framework at least serves to indicate the central role of discriminatory pricing.

There are numerous dimensions other than space over which buyers can be sorted. Time is one obvious example. Airlines often offer lower prices for return trips that include a Saturday night stay. This practice allows them to discriminate between leisure and business trips. Tourists' demand is relatively elastic, whereas business travelers face important timing restrictions. Similarly, prices which differ according to the time and date of departure can allow account to be taken of congestion (which is the reasoning behind peak hour pricing), but it can also be used to discriminate between clients with differing demand elasticities.[34]

Another practice which is often cited as an example of third-degree price discrimination is that of bundling or tying. Sales which combine two goods were recognized by Stigler (1963) to be an efficient means of discriminating. Such sales allow the firm to distinguish buyers interested in both goods from those interested in only one or the other. Package sales, combining transportation plus hotel, allow tourists to pay less for both services than if they were bought individually.

These examples indicate that segmenting the market can be substantially more subtle than just verifying IDs. However, strategies that do not rely on strictly verifiable information might be undone both by arbitrage across individuals or 'within' the individual. The limits that personal arbitrage impose on discriminatory pricing were laid out in the nineteenth century by the French Ponts et Chaussées engineer Jules Dupuit. In his famous article on tolls (1849), he developed an example of price discrimination for a footbridge. He supposed that many workers would like to use the bridge, but that a universal price of 1 centime per user would not suffice to cover construction costs.

In an attempt to impose a special workers' price that would be less than that paid by the rest of the population, Dupuit proposed a discriminatory scheme based on clothing: 'for a crosser with a cap or a smock or jacket, the toll is reduced to 1 c.' (p. 220) instead of 5 c. for the other travelers. However, he also notes that 'it is quite likely that revenues will be reduced because some 5 c. crossers will benefit, by dint of their tenue, from the price reduction that was not meant for them' (p. 220). To staunch this potential arbitrage, he proposed only applying the price reduction at certain times of day (when workers were more likely to be present) or to require that worker present their pay stubs. In the next section, we give a systematic analysis of strategies that allow the firm to prevent personal arbitrage.

PERSONAL ARBITRAGE

Travelers cannot be classed like merchandise by their appearance: they have to be allowed to sort themselves. (Jules Dupuit, 1849)

Discrimination when there is personal arbitrage is effectively an information revelation problem. The firm knows that there is heterogeneity in the willingness to pay among buyers, but it does not have a means of knowing this information directly. In the example of Dupuit's (1849) footbridge, those who are willing to pay only one centime to cross may be relatively poor people who are not workers with a pay stub, or indeed they may be people who do not truly need to cross the bridge and who will not bother if it costs too much.

This problem of information revelation can only be resolved if individual demand varies with price, or if the firm can vary some characteristics of its product, which are differently evaluated by different consumers.

In the example of the footbridge, Dupuit noted that the second possibility could be to price differently according to the time of day. To see how the sale of different quantities can be exploited in the same example, suppose that the workers were sold a coupon, valid for six return trips per week, at a price of 12 c. If the other users only want, at most, one return trip, they will only pay 5 c. per trip rather than buying the ticket tailored for the workers. This type of 'nonlinear pricing' is described in below. Then we consider the use of multi-product offering in the presence of personal arbitrage.

Two-part Pricing with Heterogeneous Customers

As we saw above, a two-part tariff specifies an entry fee A and a marginal price p, at which those who paid the entry fee can get the good. When the firm perfectly knows

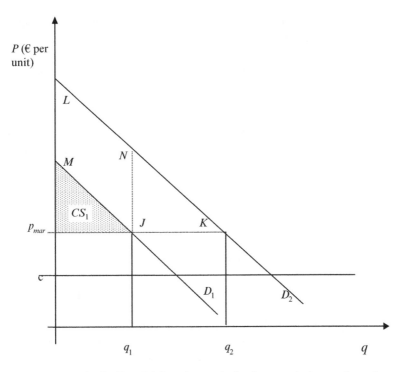

Notes: CS_1: consumer surplus for Type 1 (triangular area in dots between the inverse demand curve D_1 and price P.

Figure 22.3   *Sub-optimality of two-part pricing*

consumer tastes it can use this type of pricing to appropriate the entire consumer surplus, and thus perfectly discriminate. Although, in practice, transportation firms do not have such perfect information, they often use this type of pricing. The SNCF uses different passes for various periods of time. The French Metro (RATP) has the unlimited-ride Orange Card, which has a marginal price of zero. As we shall now see, such a two-part tariff can be useful when the firm does not know the consumers' tastes (see also Oi, 1971).

Suppose there's a fraction α of consumers, corresponding to Type 1 consumers, whose demand at price p is $D_1(p)$ while the rest of the consumers demand $D_2(p)$. Suppose that $D_1(p) < D_2(p)$ for all $p \geq 0$ (the demand curves are shown in Figure 22.3), so that Type 1 consumers are low-demand and Type 2 consumers are high-demand. It follows that consumer surpluses satisfy $CS_1(p) < CS_2(p)$ for all $p \geq 0$.

When the firm has full information it would choose a marginal price $p = c$ and have Type 1 consumers pay an access fee $A_1 = CS_1(c)$, and $A_2 = CS_2(c)$ for the others. The number of trips would be $q_1^* = D_1(c)$ and $q_2^* = D_2(c)$ for consumers of Types 1 and 2, respectively. These are the first-best optimal quantities.[35] Under incomplete information, if the firm offered these two choices, clearly Type 2 consumers would pay the lower entry fee A_1, which would give them access to the same price per trip, and there would thus be personal arbitrage.

One simple solution to circumvent this type of arbitrage is to offer a single two-part tariff. If the firm offered the full-information prices tailored for Type 2 buyers, the consumers with the lower willingness to pay would not buy.

If there are enough Type 1 consumers (if α is large enough), this will not be the best solution. Instead, offering the first-best optimal price tailored for the Type 1 consumers, the firm can put in place an allocation which maximizes total surplus (because marginal price equals marginal cost and both types of buyers are active).

This will be an optimal solution for a public firm when there is no marginal cost of public funds ($\lambda = 0$). If $\lambda > 0$, the firm is also concerned with its profits. Even though the firm can extract the full surplus of Type 1 consumers, it must leave a strictly positive surplus to the others, as we shall now see.

The firm's objective can be split into two parts, the social surplus associated with Type 1 buyers:

$$CS_1(p) + (1 + \lambda)(p - c)D_1(p) + \lambda A \quad \text{(with weight } \alpha\text{)}, \tag{22.21}$$

and the social surplus associated with Type 2 buyers:

$$CS_2(p) + (1 + \lambda)(p - c)D_2(p) + \lambda A \quad \text{(with weight } 1 - \alpha\text{)}. \tag{22.22}$$

Each of these components includes consumer surplus and producer surplus plus the entry fee, which has a value of λ per euro because it is a transfer from consumers to the firm.

First, whatever the marginal price p, it is always desirable to extract the full consumer surplus from Type 1 consumers when $\lambda > 0$. If $A < CS_1(p) < CS_2(p)$, a small increase in the entry fee will have no impact on the quantities consumed and will raise revenues, so the firm is better off. It will therefore choose, as with full information, to set $A = CS_1(p)$, so that consumers with a low willingness to pay are just indifferent between joining and not joining. Nevertheless, in contrast to the solution with full information, the firm now wants to price above marginal cost. Even though the firm would maximize its objective over the Type 1 consumers by choosing $p = c$, this does not maximize social surplus with regard to the Type 2 consumers. The objective can then be written as:

$$CS_2(p) + (1 + \lambda)(p - c)D_2(p) + \lambda CS_1(p), \tag{22.23}$$

where the last term takes into account that an increase in marginal price must be accompanied by a decrease in the entry fee to ensure that Type 1 consumers buy. Evaluating the derivative with respect to p when $p = c$ gives:

$$\lambda(D_2(c) - D_1(c)) > 0. \tag{22.24}$$

The firm can thus improve surplus by increasing the marginal price. As the effect of such an increase on social surplus for Type 1 buyers is negligible (because the derivative at $p = c$ is zero), this price hike is desirable. The optimal marginal price p_{mar} is strictly between marginal cost and the price which maximizes social surplus for Type 2 consumers. This latter price is below the Ramsey–Boiteux price corresponding to demand D_2, because of the negative effect of a higher marginal price on the membership fee.

It is straightforward to show that a fully nonlinear tariff, without the restriction that the second price be linear in quantity, performs better. Figure 22.3 shows that consumers with a high willingness to pay get a surplus (a rent) measured by area *KNLMJ*.

It is possible to reduce this rent without affecting quantities consumed. Suppose that instead of offering a two-part tariff, the firm gives each consumer the option of either the quantity $q_1 = D_1 (p_{mar})$ at entry fee $T_1 = p_{mar}q_1 + CS_1 (p_{mar})$, or else the quantity $q_2 = D_2 (p_{mar})$ at entry fee $T_2 = p_{mar}q_2 + CS_2 (p_{mar})$, plus the area *KNJ*. Type 1 consumers will then prefer the combination (q_1, T_1) to (q_2, T_2). Type 2 consumers would enjoy a surplus of *JNLM* if they chose (q_1, T_1), and they would get at least as much paying T_2 for quantity q_2. The firm then wants to leave the Type 2 consumers with as little rent as possible, that is exactly *JNLM*.

As we shall see, the pricing scheme that we have just described dominates the simple two-part tariff, but it is not generally the optimal tariff. It has a certain number of characteristics of the optimal tariff: Type 1 consumers have zero surplus, and consume less than their first-best optimal quantity (which would be consumed at marginal cost pricing); Type 2 consumers have a strictly positive surplus and are indifferent between the two choices offered. This latter indifference condition is at the heart of the incentive problem which must be solved to find the optimal nonlinear tariff.[36]

Optimal Nonlinear Pricing

Continuing the theme from above, suppose that there is a choice between two quantity-fee combinations (q_1, T_1) and (q_2, T_2). Up until now, we have not considered the problems with personal arbitrage from buyers with weak demand. Taking into account the possibility of such arbitrage can greatly complicate the general analysis, and we shall therefore side-step the issue.[37]

In what follows, because quantities are no longer determined by marginal prices, it will be more useful to write gross surplus as a function of the quantity consumed. To this end, let $V_i (q)$ denote the gross surplus of a buyer of type i consuming quantity q. If personal arbitrage only arises from buyers with high demand, it is clear that there should be no surplus left for consumers with low demand. If their surplus was positive, raising the tariff T_1 would raise revenues without affecting quantities because this would render Package 1 $((q_1; T_1))$ less attractive to Type 2 consumers. This condition for zero surplus for Type 1 consumers can be written as:

$$T_1 = V_1(q_1).$$ (22.25)

On the other hand, a strictly positive surplus must be left to Type 2 buyers, because if the combination (q_1, T_1) is acceptable for Type 1 buyers then the Type 2 buyers would get a strictly positive surplus from this combination. To get them to buy Package 2 $((q_2, T_2))$, they must be enticed with at least as much surplus. However, it is clear that it is not necessary to give them a strictly greater surplus because T_2 can be increased without changing anything else. This indifference condition can be written as:

$$V_2(q_2) - T_2 = V_2(q_1) - T_1,$$ (22.26)

or indeed, using the equality $T_1 = V_1 (q_1)$:

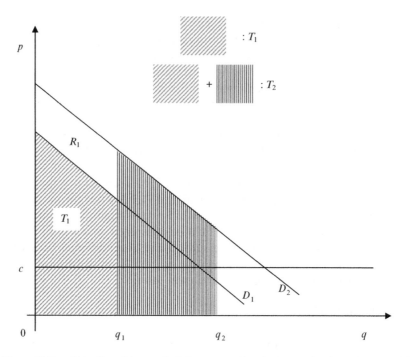

Notes: The tariff T_1, paid by Type 1 buyers, is their gross surplus, the area under demand curve D_1. The informational rent is the area between the two demand curves, from quantity 0 to q_1. The tariff T_2, paid by Type 2 buyers, is their gross surplus minus the informational rent.

Figure 22.4   Tariffs and informational rents

$$T_2 = V_2(q_2) - [V_2(q_1) - V_1(q_1)]. \tag{22.27}$$

The term in brackets is the 'informational rent' which the high demand buyers must be guaranteed under personal arbitrage. If $\lambda > 0$, this rent represents a cost for the firm.

Figure 22.4 illustrates these constraints for arbitrary quantities q_1 and q_2. The informational rent R_1 is greater the higher the quantity consumed by Type 1 buyers. For the choice of q_2, it can be seen from Figure 4 that if $q_2 < q_2^*$, an increase of this quantity will raise social surplus for a Type 2 buyer as well as raising the firm's profits (with the informational rent unchanged) and it is not necessary to change the allocation destined for Type 1 buyers. By a symmetric argument, if $q_2 > q_2^*$, the firm can improve surplus by reducing the quantity addressed to Type 2 buyers.[38] The firm thus chooses to produce the first-best socially optimal quantity (obtained by ignoring the marginal cost of public funds) for buyers whose demand is high. This is also true for $\lambda > 0$. Profits that can be earned by selling to Type 2 buyers depend on social surplus and informational rent. Because the latter only depends on the quantities sold to Type 1 buyers, it is optimal to choose for Type 2 buyers the quantity that maximizes the corresponding social surplus.

If the firm could extract the full surplus of a Type 1 consumer, it would like this consumer to buy $q_1^* = D_1(c)$, because this would extract the maximal surplus. This would

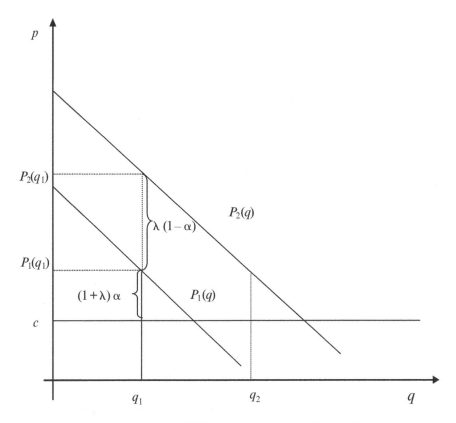

Notes: The vertical distance between c and $P_1(q)$ is proportional to $(1 + \lambda)\alpha$, and the vertical distance between $P_1(q_1)$ and $P_2(q_2)$ is proportional to $\lambda(1 - \mu)$.

Figure 22.5   Optimal nonlinear pricing

also yield the greatest fiscal revenue, which coincides with the social surplus. Because the firm is uncertain about the buyer type, it must take into account the impact the quantity q_1 has on the rent that would accrue were the demand high (as opposed to low).

Taking into account this possibility leads the firm to choose a quantity below the first-best optimal one, q_1^*. At q_1^* the effect of a quantity reduction on social surplus for a Type 1 consumer is negligible, while it allows the surplus to a Type 2 consumer to be reduced. Such a reduction is therefore desirable.

More generally, a decrease of q_1 leads to a lower social surplus associated with Type 1 consumers and a decrease in the informational rents to Type 2 consumers. Figure 22.5 shows that the reduction in social surplus would be $P_1(q_1) - c$, which has a social value of $(1 + \lambda)$ per euro, because this amount is entirely appropriated by the firm. The reduction in informational rent, which from the figure is $P_2(q_1) - P_1(q_1)$, is a transfer from Type 2 consumers to the firm and whose social value per euro is therefore λ. The optimal quantity can thus be seen from the figure: it is the value of q_1 for which the ratio of the vertical distance between the lower demand and marginal cost to the vertical distance between the two demand curves is equal to:

$$\frac{\lambda}{1 + \lambda} \frac{1 - \alpha}{\alpha}. \tag{22.28}$$

Formally, the firm chooses q_1 to maximize:

$$\alpha \left[CS_1 + (1 + \lambda) PS_1\right] - (1 - \alpha)\lambda \left[V_2 (q_1) - V_1 (q_1)\right]$$

$$= \alpha \left[(1 + \lambda) (V_1 (q_1) - cq_1)\right] - (1 - \alpha) \lambda \left[V_2 (q_1) - V_1 (q_1)\right], \tag{22.29}$$

where the last term measures the impact of informational rent on the firm's objective when the buyer is of Type 2 (and a constant term involving $V_2 (q_2)$ is omitted). The first order condition can be written as:

$$V_1' (q_1) = c + \frac{\lambda}{1 + \lambda} \frac{1 - \alpha}{\alpha}[V_2' (q_1) - V_1' (q_1)]. \tag{22.30}$$

To interpret this result and compare it to the earlier pricing formulae, it is useful to rewrite it using the fact that the gross surplus derivative of type i is the price $P_i (q)$, given by the inverse demand curve, which is the demand price at which a consumer of type i would choose to consume q units. We can thus write the formula in terms of mark-ups as:

$$\frac{P_1 (q_1) - c}{P_1(q_1)} = \frac{\lambda}{1 + \lambda} \frac{1 - \alpha}{\alpha} \frac{[P_2(q_1) - P_1(q_1)]}{P_1(q_1)}. \tag{22.31}$$

This formula allows a comparison with uniform Ramsey–Boiteux pricing. This latter pricing induces consumers to buy less than the first-best optimal quantity in order to generate a producer surplus and pricing above marginal cost. The possibility of generating such a surplus depends inversely on the price elasticity of demand: the more elastic demand is, the less feasible it is to raise price without causing too large of a drop in quantity. With nonlinear pricing, decreasing the quantity bought by low-demand consumers has a completely different role. It allows informational rent to high demand consumers to be reduced, while still motivating them to reveal their demand. The distortion is larger when the impact on rent is higher, as measured by $P_2 (q_1) - P_1 (q_1)$, and the relative share of high-demanders is higher, as measured by $1 - \alpha/\alpha$. Because the informational rent is larger as q_1 increases, the high-demanders would prefer the distortion in q_1 to be as small as possible; their welfare is highest when they only constitute a small fraction of total buyers.

Although it is clear that the price per unit will differ between groups of buyers, nothing guarantees that it is decreasing in quantity. In practice, we often see that those who buy more benefit from larger discounts. For example, membership programs or frequent traveler programs allow those who travel more to pay less.

The current analysis does not immediately apply to this type of rebate, in part because we have not explicitly considered the possibility that large buyers could buy up several packages targeted to small buyers (see Alger, 1999, for more on this topic). More generally, the empirical implications of nonlinear pricing merit a deeper study (recent work includes Cohen, 2002; Ivaldi and Martimort, 1994; Leslie, 2003; McManus, 2007).

Multiple Qualities and Discrimination

While there are certain types of nonlinear pricing in transportation, another frequent practice is to offer several classes of service on the same voyage. This practice goes back a long way, and Jules Dupuit gives an extremely perceptive analysis in his 1849 article.

> It is clear that by increasing the number of classes indefinitely, consumers could be made to pay all of the utility that they get from using the railway. However, to do that requires distinguishing among consumers who get different utility from their transportation, and make them voluntarily sort themselves into one or another price category. However, this is a great difficulty, which gives rise to a whole host of measures which are generally quite poorly understood by the public.
>
> Hence, a good many people, on seeing travelers in third class, traveling without a roof over the carriage, on poorly upholstered seats, they denounce the barbarity of the railways. It would cost very little, they say, to put some meters of leather and kilos of horse-hair [on the seats], and it is beyond greed to withhold them.
>
> It is not because of the several thousand francs which they would have to spend to cover the third class wagons or to upholster the benches that a particular railway has uncovered carriages and wooden benches; it would happily sacrifice this for the sake of its popularity.
>
> Its goal is to stop the traveler who can pay for the second class trip from going third class. It hurts the poor not because it wants them to personally suffer, but to scare the rich. The proof is that if today the State were to say to this railroad: here are one hundred thousand francs to improve your carriages, this subsidy would be certainly refused . . . improving the third class carriages could reduce revenues by two million francs and ruin the company.
>
> Thus, it is for the same reason that companies, after being cruel to travelers in third class and miserly for those in second, become prodigious for those in first class. After having refused the poor some necessary comforts, they give the rich what is superfluous.

Walras (1875/1897) had a similar view of the logic which guided the pricing of French railways in the middle of the nineteenth century.

> French railroads ask, respectively, for 10 c. in first class, 7.5 c. in second class, and 5.5 c. in third class; but they put 24 travelers in a first class carriage, 30 in a second class one, and 40 in third class. They also use less comfortable seats, etc. [. . .]
>
> As it happens, the railroads consider, rightly or wrongly, that the average price of 7.66 c., which is close enough to the 7.5 c. which is the second class fare, as being the price of maximal profit; but they do not want to miss the opportunity of getting more from travelers who are prepared to pay more, nor to refuse to get less from travelers who decided not to pay too much.
>
> When people earlier rejoiced at the rule of 1857–1858 that required the companies to put windows in third class, and when today they want heating in winter, and they complain about the harshness of the railroads, they are not understanding the key motivation.
>
> If the third class carriages were comfortable enough that many second class travelers and some of the first class ones would go there, net total product, as we understand it from the theory of monopoly, would fall. That is all there is to it.
>
> The railroads only have third class carriages to avoid missing out on a large number of travelers who, rather than pay the first or second class prices, would have continued to travel in stage coaches.

Following Dupuit and Walras, the choice of the level of comfort in the different seating classes is effectively driven by the desire to make people pay a price corresponding to their willingness to pay, and to avoid personal arbitrage from those from whom the company wants to extract a high fare. Such arbitrage is discouraged by introducing

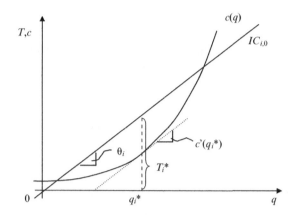

Notes: $IC_{i,0}$ is an indifference curve with slope θ_i going through the origin, and corresponds to zero surplus; $c(q)$ is marginal cost where q stands for quality.

Figure 22.6   Price and quality with perfect discrimination

sufficiently high comfort differences between classes. It is interesting to draw a parallel between the arguments of these authors and our results for nonlinear pricing. We have shown that potential personal arbitrage by high-demanders leads the firm to introduce a difference between the quantities it proposes, a difference which is larger than it would be under perfect discrimination. Dupuit and Walras suggest that railways use a similar logic when they choose the level of comfort. We now show that there is a formal equivalence between these two forms of price discrimination. To show the analogy between discrimination based on different qualities and nonlinear pricing of a homogeneous good, consider the following model due to Mussa and Rosen (1978). We also use an *a* graphical approach that is an alternative to the previous one that used demand curves.

Suppose that there are two types of users, *l* and *h*, differing in their willingness to pay for quality. Assume that their willingness to pay for an extra unit of quality is θ_h and θ_l, respectively, where $\theta_h > \theta_l$. Now let q be the quality level of the service proposed rather than the quantity sold, as it was under nonlinear pricing. The gross surplus of a buyer of type θ_i consuming services of quality q is then given by $V_i(q) = \theta_{iq}$. Each customer only wants one unit of the good, and her willingness to pay is her gross surplus. Her net surplus for a price T is $\theta_{iq} - T$. The marginal cost of service $c(q)$ is increasing and strictly convex.

The combinations of quality q and tariff T that give an equal level of utility to consumer *i* are illustrated in Figure 22.6. These indifference curves are straight lines with slope θ_i (with quality on the horizontal axis and euro price on the vertical). The indifference curve through the origin corresponds to zero surplus and is indicated in the sequel by $IC_{i,0}$. Higher surplus levels correspond to indifference curves farther to the right. The producer surplus for one unit of service (one trip) from quality q sold at tariff T is given by $T - c(q)$. If the firm knew the value of θ_i for each traveler, it could perfectly discriminate and leave no surplus to the buyer. The corresponding producer surplus is $\theta_{iq} - c(q)$, and the firm will therefore choose the quality q_i^* that maximizes this (with social surplus being simply the producer surplus weighted by $1 + \lambda$).

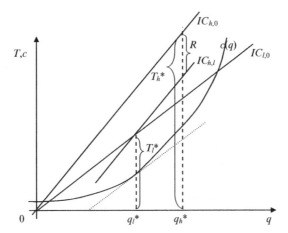

Notes: The informational rent R corresponds to the vertical distance between the indifference curve $IC_{h,0}$ and the indifference curve $IC_{h,1}$.

Figure 22.7   Prices and qualities under individual arbitrage

Figure 22.6 shows the indifference curve for zero surplus and the marginal cost curve as a function of quality. The optimal quality is that which maximizes the distance between the indifference curve and marginal cost, which gives a value q_i^* where the curves have the same slope: formally, $\theta_i = c'(q_i^*)$ (the vertical distance between the two curves is always less than that between the indifference curve and the tangent to marginal cost at q_i^*). With perfect discrimination, the optimal quality will then optimize the willingness to pay for quality with marginal cost of increasing quality.

If the firm does not know the consumers' willingness to pay for quality then, if it were to offer the two first-best optimal qualities, it would necessarily leave some surplus to the high consumer type. Figure 22.7 shows that the combination (q_h^*, T_h^*) is to the left of the high-type user's indifference curve, denoted by $IC_{h,l}$, which goes through (q_l^*, T_l^*), and she therefore prefers this latter combination. In order to motivate her not to choose the low quality, the firm must quote her a price such that she is on the indifference curve $IC_{h,l}$. Just as under nonlinear pricing, it is potential personal arbitrage by the high-demanders which constitutes the constraint for the firm. Again, because the firm is not concerned with arbitrage by the low-demanders, it can extract their full surplus so that the optimal combination will be on the indifference curve $IC_{l,0}$. High-demanders enjoy an informational rent of R, which is measured as the vertical difference between the indifference curve $IC_{h,0}$ and the indifference curve $IC_{h,l}$ (which is the difference between the perfectly discriminatory tariff and what they actually have to pay).

The social surplus associated with high-demanders is then the first-best social surplus. Although this rent does not depend on the high quality, the optimal high quality is q_h^*, as with perfect discrimination. On the other hand, as is seen from Figure 22.7, the firm wants to decrease the low quality below q_l^*. This permits the firm to reduce the informational rent because the indifference curve $IC_{h,l}$ shifts left while, for a small change, the loss of social surplus associated with low-demanders is negligible because q_l^* constitutes its maximum. This model thus confirms Dupuit's (1849) intuition. The comfort in third class is deliberately reduced to dissuade travelers who are ready to pay for higher levels of comfort from traveling at the cheaper fares. Today's economy class air travelers might sympathize. As Tirole (1988, 1993) points out, the comfort offered to the first class travelers actually is not 'superfluous' because it is the level chosen under perfect discrimination; contrary to what Dupuit and Walras thought, it is only by adjusting the lower quality that the firm discourages personal arbitrage. There is therefore a perfect analogy between this model and that of nonlinear pricing, and the results are the same (under reinterpretation). Only passengers whose willingness to pay is high can retain some surplus, and this surplus increases as the fraction of high demanders decreases.

One variant of this model explored by Chander and Leruth (1989), and particularly relevant for transportation, supposes that the quality of comfort class decreases in the number of users as it becomes more congested. The firm then chooses two different prices, with the cheaper class having a lower quality just because it attracts more travelers. The two classes in the Parisian Metro until the 1980s give a striking illustration of this type of strategy.[39] Second class carriages only differed from first class by their color, but fares were lower.[40]

The modern day counterpart to the insights of Dupuit and Walras can be found without much difficulty in air travel. What was true in nineteenth century train carriages sometimes seems to be not very far off from what is found on modern economy class flights. Airlines could scarcely charge such premiums for first and business class travel if economy class were more comfortable.[41]

CONCLUSION

We have focused on discriminatory pricing for a single firm (without rivals) and suggested how this analysis is relevant for transportation. We analyzed a public firm under the assumption that public funds are valued more than consumer surplus, in order to account for inefficiencies in raising tax revenue. Profit maximization arises as a limit case when λ goes to infinity.

This theoretical framework enables us to highlight the similarity between the pricing problem of a public firm and that of a private firm. However, restricting this analysis to monopolies is more restrictive for the private sector. Although several transport modes are effectively monopolies, such as the railways and urban transportation systems, other sectors have several competing carriers, most notably the airlines. We now give a brief review of oligopoly competition.[42] For the discussion that follows, we consider private profit maximizing firms and we let $\lambda = 0$, so that consumer surplus and producer surplus are equally weighted.[43]

There is relatively little work on price discrimination under competition. As regards discrimination without personal arbitrage, standard oligopoly theory fairly quickly delivers some main conclusions. For one good sold to several groups the model most directly comparable with monopoly is Cournot's (1838) framework, where firms choose outputs and price equates aggregate output with the quantity demanded. If each firm has the same marginal costs c_i for serving market i, Lerner's formula becomes:

$$\frac{p_i - c_i}{p_i} = \frac{1}{n_i} \frac{1}{|\eta_i (p_i)|},$$

(22.32)

where n_i is the number of active firms in market i. If firms have different costs, Lerner's formula becomes:

$$\frac{p_i - c^m}{p_i} = \frac{1}{n_i} \frac{1}{|\eta_i\left(p_i\right)|},$$

(22.33)

where

$$c^m = \frac{1}{n_i} \sum_{j=1}^{n_i} c_j$$

(22.34)

is the average cost for serving market i. This formula is directly comparable to the monopoly one. If two groups differ by elasticity of demand, we again find that the price is higher for inelastic demand. However, all prices go to marginal cost when the number of firms becomes large, and competition eliminates price differences. These results can also be applied when firms discriminate with different products, in which case the marginal cost differs from one market to another. A richer framework can be analyzed by supposing that there is also differentiation within each market. One common formulation for demand for differentiated products is founded on discrete choice models, which are described in greater detail in other chapters of this book. One interesting feature of these models is that it is easy to introduce new features, such as quality differences or congestion, into the consumer preferences which are at the heart of the model.[44]

The multinomial logit model is a particularly useful formulation. If prices are the strategic variable, the equilibrium price of firm j in market i is

$$p_{ij} = c_{ij} + \frac{\mu_i}{1 - D_{ij}},$$

(22.35)

where D_{ij} is the equilibrium demand addressed to firm j in market i and depends on prices set by all active firms in market i. Anderson and de Palma (2001) show that this price equilibrium has several intuitive properties. For example, if consumers have a higher tendency to buy the product, then prices will be high and the differences will be large across variants. Furthermore, the more firms there are, or the more similar they are (from the point of view of a group of consumers), the lower prices will be and the more similar they will be across firms.

It can also be understood within this framework why introducing competition in a market can actually lead discriminating firms to exacerbate price differences across different services. Borenstein and Rose (1994) note that following airline deregulation in the United States, price differences increased. The theoretical explanation that they propose is that those travelers who are willing to pay more for a trip (hence, those for whom the reservation value is high) are also those who are the most loyal to a particular airline, which translates to a greater effective heterogeneity between products. When competition is introduced into the marketplace, the difference between the high business class fare and the low economy class fare is amplified by the differential intensity of competition at the two service levels. Competition is more intense for the economy segment.[45] However, more recent work by Gerardi and Shapiro (2007) finds that competition decreases the power of an airline to price discriminate. Price dispersion within the airline industry falls as competition increases, especially on routes where consumers have relatively heterogeneous elasticities of demand. Looking at patterns within different groups of air travelers, Bilotkach (2005) looks at across-airlines' differences in economy class fares for the London–New York market, aimed at different consumer types. He finds that fares targeted to business fliers differ across airlines, while fares targeted to leisure fliers do not.

One issue in the economics of third-degree price discrimination under competition concerns the level of producer surplus when discrimination is not always possible (it could, for example, be illegal). Several authors came to the same conclusion: in contrast to monopoly, it may be that profits are lower when firms can discriminate. Hoover (1948, p. 57) anticipated this result in the context of spatial discrimination.

> The difference between market competition under f.o.b. pricing (with strictly delineated market areas) and under discriminatory delivered pricing is something like the difference between trench warfare and guerrilla warfare. In the former case all the fighting takes place along a definite battle line; in the second case the opposing forces are intermingled over a broad area.

This indicates that the implications of discrimination for profits can be very different, depending on the degree of competition. However, it remains true that welfare falls following the introduction of discrimination if total output does not rise.

In contrast to the analysis of third-degree discrimination, the study of discrimination under personal arbitrage in oligopoly is complicated and there are relatively few general contributions. Notable exceptions include Armstrong and Vickers (2001), Champsaur and Rochet (1989), Ivaldi and Martimort (1994), Rochet and Stole (2001) and Stole (1995). The latter two articles show that if duopolists offer relatively close services, non-linear pricing can lead to two-part tariff with zero profits for each firm (an extension of the Bertrand Paradox). Rochet and Stole (2001) also show that if the services offered are more differentiated, equilibrium pricing resembles the monopoly case.

Theoretical progress on these issues is quite tricky, but it is important to continue to develop the theoretical framework which will allow empirical studies to examine discrimination with personal arbitrage under oligopoly.

ACKNOWLEDGMENTS

We gratefully acknowledge travel funding from the CNRS and NSF under grants INT-9815703 and GA10273, and research funding under grant SES 0452864. We thank Anita Anderson, Alain Béraud, Catherine de Fontenay, Robin Lindsey, André de Palma, Emile Quinet, and Sarah Tulman for their comments and suggestions. We would also like to thank Melbourne Business School and the Autoridade da Concorrencia in Lisbon for their hospitality.

NOTES

1. Price discrimination is also common in other transportation services in addition to rail and air travel. Odlyzko (2004) provides examples from maritime transport, inland waterways and turnpikes, as well as railroads, to argue that price discrimination has been (and is still) prevalent in the development of these sectors.

2. Price discrimination is often also based on time of travel, such as evening or summer tariffs. The simplest analysis assumes that the demands in each period are independent (see also the analysis of peak-load pricing in the Backhaul section below). Gerstner (1986) formulates a peak-load pricing model in which firms account for intertemporal demand shifting.
3. See Clerides (2004) for a definition in which there is no discrimination if the pricing structure is not subject to arbitrage by buyers.
4. For further discussion, see the section on 'Discriminating with Several Products'.
5. In this chapter, we emphasize demand drivers and take marginal cost as constant. The proper attribution of costs is a complex problem in itself.
6. See Leadbelly's 'Rock Island Line'.
7. Nonetheless, McAfee et al. (2006) propose a simple model in which they show that the extent of price discrimination has no theoretical connection to the extent of market power.
8. One other limit on the ability to price discriminate is that firms cannot effectively propose a price menu that is too complex. See Levinson and Odlyzko (2007) for a recent treatment.
9. See Alger (1999) for an analysis of the constraints that are imposed by the potential of arbitrage involving several buyers.
10. For a simple and broader treatment of this subject, see Varian (2000).
11. See Anderson and Engers (2007b) for further discussion of the concept of producer surplus.
12. This quantity is strictly positive and unique if marginal revenue at zero is superior to marginal cost, and if the slope of marginal revenue is always less than that of marginal cost.
13. See Anderson and Engers (2007a) for further discussion of the concept of consumer surplus.
14. Any price below marginal cost causes a deadweight loss because it leads to the sale of some units for which consumers are willing to pay less than the extra social cost that their production would engender.
15. For example, income taxes cause deadweight losses in the labor market.
16. The size of λ has been the topic of several studies. One reasonable estimate for the United States is 0.3 (see Ballard et al., 1985, and Hausman and Poterba, 1987).
17. Consumer surplus at price p is the integral of the demand for prices larger than p.
18. This follows from applying the Implicit Function Theorem to the first order condition to the firm's problem above.
19. A negative lambda might also be applied in a welfare analysis used to evaluate different market outcomes, and where the firms' losses do not contribute to (or need to be financed from) the public purse. Private firms' surplus would usually be weighted (much) less than consumer surplus. For example, a consumer surplus standard, as is arguably used in some antitrust circumstances, would put a weight on producer surplus of zero ($\lambda = -1$).
20. The corresponding aggregate concept simply sums the surpluses over individuals.
21. No further complication is introduced for the preceding analysis when marginal costs are not constant. The optimal quantity, q^*, equates the demand price with marginal cost, and all consumer surplus is extracted. A single (all-or-nothing) tariff equal to gross consumer surplus at this quantity is optimal, and is equivalent to a two-part tariff with a per-unit price equal to the demand price $P(q^*)$ and an entry fee of $A = V(q^*) - P(q^*) q^* (= CS(q^*))$.
22. When marginal costs are not constant, the optimal solution is obtained by equalizing marginal revenues across groups for any given total production level, and then choosing the total quantity which equalizes marginal cost with this common revenue.
23. This discussion assumes that two demands are comparable in the sense that one is more elastic than the other for all prices. It is possible to construct examples for which prices under discrimination are higher or lower than under uniform pricing (see Nahata et al., 1990).
24. This is a special property of linear demand, that marginal revenue corresponding to the sum of demands is equal to the sum of the marginal revenues to the demands for each group.
25. Of course, in the evening, the 'backhaul' is stronger than the 'fronthaul' in the sense that relatively empty trains come into the city and full ones go back out. For the present purposes, we shall identify the stronger demand as the 'fronthaul' even if it happens after the weaker demand (backhaul).
26. See Anderson and Wilson (2008) for a treatment of the backhaul problem when a dominant firm faces a competitive fringe.
27. For references in this area, see Anderson and Schneider (2008), which also contains more analysis of competitive cases. See also Sinsou (1999) for a detailed presentation of the algorithmic methods firms can use for yield and revenue management.
28. The profit associated to the pricing per seat business model is $\pi = (1 - F(p_1)) \{p_1 + p_2(1 - F^2(p_2))\} + F(p_1) \{(1 - F(p_1)) [p_1 + p_2(1 - F(p_2))] + F(p_1)(1 - F(p_1)) p_1\}$. The first term corresponds to the first traveler buying the first (lower-priced) seat, and then one of the other two buys the second seat. The second term corresponds to the first traveler declining the first seat, and then either the second buys it (and the third might buy the second seat), or else only the third might buy the first seat.

29. The term f.o.b. stands for 'free on board' or 'freight on board' and means that the buyer must pay trans-
     portation costs for delivery. In spatial economics, the term f.o.b. price is synonymous with the term 'mill
     price' to indicate the factory price (or the store price).
30. See Anderson and Renault (2003a) for a precise definition of this concept. The condition is equivalent to
     Seade's (1985) condition on the elasticity of inverse demand.
31. Greenhut (1981) presents survey results on spatial pricing by firms.
32. See Lederer and Hurter (1986) for a model of competitive spatial discrimination and Anderson, de Palma,
     and Thisse (1992a, Chapters 8 and 9) for a review of the literature on spatial economics.
33. The case of uniform pricing is a special case of discriminatory pricing. See Greenhut et al. (1987) for other
     developments with monopoly, and Anderson et al. (1989, 1992b) for competition. Quinet (1998) describes
     in detail competition between two airports.
34. There is a large literature on pricing under congestion, following Vickrey's (1969) seminal paper. De
     Palma and Lindsey (2000) treat the problem of two competing toll roads, and de Palma and Lindsey
     (1998) study the role of information acquisition in this context.
35. They are the socially optimal quantities if the fiscal system allows lump-sum redistribution with a zero
     marginal cost of public funds.
36. For further advances on this topic, see Brown and Sibley (1986) and Wilson (1992).
37. It is straightforward to show that the solution we shall describe is not subject to arbitrage by Type 1
     buyers, insofar as it remains the optimal solution when we include an extra constraint to take such arbi-
     trage into account.
38. Recall that the area between marginal cost and demand entails a negative surplus when the latter is below
     the former.
39. Another illustration is that of a toll road with a parallel freeway to the same destination (see de Palma and
     Lindsey, 2000).
40. This system was abolished by Charles Fiterman, Communist Transportation Minister in the first govern-
     ment of the Union of the Left.
41. In practice, the problem faced by the airlines is very complicated because the information that it has about
     passengers is very sparse and evolves over time. See the sub-section on 'Yield Revenue Management'
     above.
42. For a review of the state of the art on price discrimination under oligopoly, see Armstrong and Vickers
     (2001) and Stole (2007).
43. The Competition Authority of the European Union seems to put more weight on consumer surplus.
44. Anderson et al. (1992a) provides background for this model.
45. Borenstein and Rose base their theoretical arguments on Borenstein (1985) and Holmes (1989).

REFERENCES

Alger, I., 1999, Consumer strategies limiting the monopolist's power: multiple and joint purchases. *RAND Journal of Economics*, **30**, 736–757.
Anderson, S.P., 1989, Socially optimal spatial pricing. *Regional Science and Urban Economics*, **19**, 60–86.
Anderson, S.P. and A. de Palma, 2001, Product diversity in asymmetric oligopoly: is the quality of consumer goods too low? *Journal of Industrial Economics*, **49**, 113–135.
Anderson, S.P. and M. Engers, 2007a, Consumer surplus. Article for *International Encyclopedia of the Social Sciences*, 2nd edn. Available at: http://www.gale.cengage.com/iess/content.htm.
Anderson, S.P. and M. Engers, 2007b, Producer surplus. Article for *International Encyclopedia of the Social Sciences*, 2nd edn. Available at: http://www.gale.cengage.com/iess/content.htm.
Anderson, S.P. and R. Renault, 2003a, Efficiency and surplus bounds in Cournot competition. *Journal of Economic Theory*, **113**, 253–264.
Anderson, S.P. and R. Renault, 2003b, Second degree price discrimination à la Pigou. Working Paper, Université de Cergy-Pontoise.
Anderson, S.P. and Y. Schneider, 2008, Price competition with revenue management and costly consumer search. Mimeo, University of Virginia.
Anderson, S.P. and W.W. Wilson, 2008, Spatial competition, pricing, and market power in transportation: a dominant firm model. *Journal of Regional Science*, **48** (2), 367–397.
Anderson, S.P., A. de Palma and J.-F. Thisse, 1989, Spatial price policies reconsidered. *Journal of Industrial Economics*, **38**, 1–18.
Anderson, S.P., A. de Palma and J.-F. Thisse, 1992a, *Discrete Choice Theory of Product Differentiation*. Cambridge, MA: MIT Press.

Anderson, S.P., A. de Palma and J.-F. Thisse, 1992b, Social surplus and profitability under different spatial pricing policies. *Southern Economic Journal*, **58**, 934–949.

Armstrong, M. and J. Vickers, 2001, Competitive price discrimination. *RAND Journal of Economics*, **32**, 579–605.

Ballard, C.L., J.B. Shoven and J. Whalley, 1985, General equilibrium computations of the marginal welfare costs of taxes in the United States. *American Economic Review*, **75**, 128–138.

Bilotkach, V., 2005, Understanding price dispersion in the airline industry: capacity constraints and consumer heterogeneity. In D. Lee, ed., *Advances in Airline Economics*, Vol. 1. Amsterdam: Elsevier, pp. 329–346.

Boîteux, M., 1956, Sur la gestion des monopoles publics astreints à l'équilibre budgétaire. *Econometrica*, **24**, 22–40.

Borenstein, S., 1985, Price discrimination in free entry markets. *RAND Journal of Economics*, **16**, 380–397.

Borenstein, S. and N. Rose, 1994, Competition and price dispersion in the US airline industry. *Journal of Political Economy*, **102**, 653–683.

Brown, S. and D. Sibley, 1986, *The Theory of Public Utility Pricing*. Cambridge: Cambridge University Press.

Champsaur, P. and J.-C. Rochet, 1989, Multiproduct duopolists. *Econometrica*, **57**, 533–557.

Chander, P. and L. Leruth, 1989, The optimal product mix for a monopolist in the presence of congestion effects: a model and some results. *International Journal of Industrial Organization*, **7**, 437–449.

Clerides, S., 2004, Price discrimination with differentiated products: definition and identification. *Economic Inquiry*, **42**, 402–412.

Cohen, A., 2002, Package size and price discrimination in the paper towel market. Working Paper, University of Virginia.

Cournot, A., 1838, *Recherches sur les Principes Mathématiques de la Théorie des Richesses*. Paris: L. Hachette.

De Palma, A. and R. Lindsey, 1998, Information and usage of congestible facilities under different pricing regimes. *The Canadian Journal of Economics*, **31**, 666–692.

De Palma, A. and R. Lindsey, 2000, Private toll roads: competition under various ownership regimes. *The Annals of Regional Science*, **34**, 13–35.

Dupuit, J., 1849, De l'influence des péages sur l'utilité des voies de communication. *Annales des ponts et chaussées*, **17**, 207.

Gerardi, K. and A.H. Shapiro 2007, The effects of competition on price dispersion in the airline industry: a panel analysis. Federal Reserve Bank of Boston Working Paper 07-7.

Gerstner, E., 1986, Peak load pricing in competitive markets. *Economic Inquiry*, **24**, 349–361.

Greenhut, M.L., 1981, Spatial pricing in the United States, West Germany and Japan. *Economica*, **48** (189), 79–86.

Greenhut, M.L., G. Norman and C.-S. Hung, 1987, *The Economics of Imperfect Competition*. Cambridge: Cambridge University Press.

Hausman, J.A. and J. Poterba, 1987, Household behavior and the Tax Reform Act of 1986. *Journal of Economic Perspectives*, **1**, 101–119.

Holahan, W.L., 1975, The welfare effects of spatial price discrimination. *American Economic Review*, **65**, 498–503.

Holmes, T.J., 1989, The effects of third degree price discrimination in oligopoly. *American Economic Review*, **79**, 244–250.

Hoover, E.M., 1937, Spatial price discrimination. *Review of Economic Studies*, **4**, 182–191.

Hoover, E. M., 1948, *The Location of Economic Activities*. New York: McGraw-Hill.

Ivaldi, M. and D. Martimort, 1994, Competition under nonlinear pricing. *Annales d'Economie et de Statistique*, **34**, 71–115.

Laffont, J.-J. and J. Tirole, 1993, *A Theory of Incentives in Procurement and Regulation*. Cambridge, MA: MIT Press.

Lederer, P.J. and A.P. Hurter, 1986, Competition of firms: discriminatory pricing and location. *Econometrica*, **54**, 623–640.

Leslie, P., 2003, Price discrimination in Broadway theatre. *RAND Journal of Economics*, **35**, 520–541.

Levinson, D. and A. Odlyzko, 2007, Too expensive to meter: the influence of transaction costs in transportation and communication. Available at: http://rational.ce.umn.edu.

Lott, J.R. and R.D. Roberts, 1991, A guide to the pitfalls of identifying price discrimination. *Economic Inquiry*, **29**, 14–23.

McAfee, R.P., H.M. Mialon and S.H. Mialon, 2006, Does large price discrimination imply great market power? *Economic Letters*, **3**, 360–367.

McManus, B., 2007, Nonlinear pricing in an oligopoly market: the case of specialty coffee. *RAND Journal of Economics*, **38** (2), 512–532.

Meade, J., 1944, Price and output policy of state enterprise. *Economic Journal*, **54**, 321–328.

Mohring, H., 1976, *Transportation Economics*. Cambridge, MA: Ballinger.

Mougeot, M. and F. Naegelen, 1994, La discrimination par les prix. *Economica*, Paris, France.

Mussa, M. and S. Rosen, 1978, Monopoly and product quality. *Journal of Economic Theory*, **18**, 301–317.

Nahata, B., K. Ostaszewski, and P.K. Sahoo, 1990, Direction of price changes in third-degree price discrimination. *American Economic Review*, **80**, 1254–1258.

Odlyzko, A., 2004, The evolution of price discrimination in transportation and its implications for the internet. *Review of Network Economics*, **3** (3), Article 4.

Oi, W., 1971, A Disneyland dilemma: two-part tariffs for a Mickey Mouse monopoly. *Quarterly Journal of Economics*, **85**, 77–90.

Phlips, L., 1983, *The Economics of Price Discrimination*. Cambridge: Cambridge University Press.

Pigou, A.C., 1938, *The Economics of Welfare*, 4th edn. London: Macmillan and Co.

Quinet, E., 1998, *Principes d'Economie des Transports*. Hanover, Germany: Economica.

Ramsey, F., 1927, A contribution to the theory of taxation. *Economic Journal*, **37**, 47–61.

Rietveld, P., and R. Roson, 2002, Direction dependent prices in public transport: a good idea? The back haul pricing problem for a monopolistic transport firm. *Transportation*, **29**, 397–417.

Rochet, J.-C. and L.A. Stole, 2001, Nonlinear pricing with random participation. *Review of Economic Studies*, **69**, 277–311.

Schmalensee, R., 1981, Output and welfare implications of monopolistic third degree price discrimination. *American Economic Review*, **71**, 242–247.

Seade, J.E., 1985, Profitable cost increases and the shifting of taxation: equilibrium responses of markets in oligopoly. Discussion paper no. 260, University of Warwick.

Sinsou, J.-P., 1999, *Yield at Revenue Management: Optimisation de la Recette dans les Transport de Passagers*. Paris: Les presses de l'institut du transport aerien.

Stigler, G., 1963, A note on block booking. Supreme Court Review, Reprinted in *Organization of Industry*. Chicago, IL: University of Chicago Press.

Stole, L.A., 1995, Nonlinear pricing and oligopoly. *Journal of Economics and Management Studies*, **4**, 529–562.

Stole, L.A., 2007, Price discrimination in competitive environments. In M. Armsbrong and R.H. Porter, eds, *Handbook of Industrial Organization*, Vol. 3. Amsterdam: North-Holland, Chapter 34.

Tirole, J., 1988, *The Theory of Industrial Organization*. Cambridge, MA: MIT Press.

Tirole, J., 1993, *La Théorie de l'Organisation Industrielle*, Vol. 1. Paris: Editions Economica.

Varian, H., 1989, Price discrimination. In R. Schmalensee and R. Willig, eds, *Handbook of Industrial Organization*, Vol. 1. Amsterdam: North-Holland.

Varian, H., 2000, Introduction à la microéconomie. DeBoeuck Université.

Vickrey, W.S., 1969, Congestion theory and transport investment. *American Economic Review*, **59**, 251–261.

Walras, L., 1897, L'Etat et les chemins de fer. Manuscript written 1875. *Revue du Droit Public et de Science Politique*. Mai-juin et juillet-août 1897.

Wilson, R., 1992, *Non-linear Pricing*. Oxford: Oxford University Press.

23 Road congestion pricing
Georgina Santos and Erik Verhoef

CONGESTION PRICING: AN INTRODUCTION

Road pricing has long been viewed as a potentially efficient instrument for dealing with traffic congestion. In 1920, Arthur Pigou used the example of a congested road to explain the economics of external effects, and in particular how a corrective tax can be used to restore efficiency when some goods are not optimally priced at marginal cost. For a congested road, that particular 'good' is other users' travel time (losses), the value of which is not taken into account by individual users when trading off the benefits and costs of making a trip. In this chapter, we will briefly review some of the economic theory of road congestion pricing, as well as some of its practical applications. Indeed, growing traffic congestion around the globe and rapid advances in automated vehicle identification has turned road pricing from a largely academic curiosity to a realistic instrument for modern urban transport policy.

Figure 23.1 gives the standard exposition of Pigou's theory as it appears in practically all modern transport economics textbooks (Pigou himself did not provide a graphical exposition of the problem). It considers a single congested road, with identical users. The horizontal axis represents traffic volume, V, while the vertical axis covers the price dimension. The downward-sloping line d depicts the inverse demand function, the upward sloping curve c is average user cost and mc is marginal social cost. Average cost rises when a higher traffic flow implies a lower speed. Marginal cost exceeds average cost whenever the latter is rising, because the product rule of differentiation implies that $mc \equiv \partial(V \cdot c)/\partial V = c + V \cdot \partial c/\partial V$. The second term is the marginal external cost: the extra cost that an added user causes for all other affected users when entering the road. Quite intuitively, it is the product of volume and the effect of an added user on average (per-user) cost.

Because road users are atomistic price-takers, who consider aggregate travel conditions as independent of their own individual behavior, the free-market equilibrium occurs where the inverse demand d, equal to marginal benefits mb, intersects the average cost c. This is at V^0. Optimal road use, instead, is at the intersection of marginal benefits and marginal – not average – costs; at V^*. Achieving the reduction from V^0 to V^* will produce a net gain in social surplus equal to the shaded area, which is the net result of the implied savings in social cost (the area below mc between V^* and V^0) and the implied loss of benefits (the area below mb between V^* and V^0).

Pigou found that this reduction can be achieved by imposing the optimal road price r^*, which is equal to the marginal external cost ($V \cdot \partial c/\partial V = mc - c$) in the optimum. Because road pricing, unlike many non-economic instruments, not only achieves the optimal volume of traffic (V^*) but also the optimal composition (that is, exactly the trips with the lowest willingness to pay are priced off the road), it is a first-best solution to the problem under consideration. But that does not make it an inherently popular instrument as can

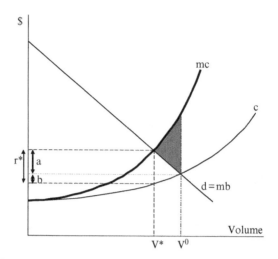

Figure 23.1   The basic economic exposition of road congestion pricing

be seen from Figure 23.1. Before the tax revenues ($V^* \cdot r^*$) are redistributed, not only is the group that remains using the road worse off (the increase in generalized price amounts to *a*), but also the group that is priced off the road (they will have to change behavior, which they preferred not to do before the toll was implemented). All initial users suffer (this could change when heterogeneity in values of time is allowed for as discussed later in the section on the practice of congestion charging). A proper redistribution of toll revenues could of course change this pessimistic conclusion, and the allocation of revenues is consequently often identified as a main instrument to increase social support for road pricing.

The above exposition gives, of course, a very simplified representation of reality. It is nevertheless useful, because it illustrates the basic economic motivation for road pricing in a powerful way. That motivation will not change fundamentally when making the model more complex, for example by extending from a single road to a network, by allowing for heterogeneity of road users, by introducing uncertainty and so forth. Still, introducing such complications usually leads to valuable additional insights into the economics of traffic congestion. We will illustrate this in the next section by considering the dynamics of traffic flows. The next two sections discuss second-best pricing and congestion pricing in practice. The penultimate section addresses the link between theory and practice, and the final section concludes. Throughout the chapter, we will only consider congestion pricing of roads.

CONGESTION PRICING: A DYNAMIC PERSPECTIVE

Traffic congestion in reality is an inherently dynamic phenomenon, with traffic conditions rapidly changing over time and place. A satisfactory modeling of such processes may be a daunting task. But work by Vickrey (1969) and Arnott et al. (1993) demonstrates that it is possible to capture the essence of traffic dynamics in an analytically manageable equilibrium model. They developed what has become known as 'the bottleneck model', arguably the simplest possible dynamic equilibrium model of traffic congestion, which produces results and insights that sometimes contrast sharply with those from the static model discussed above.

The essence of the model is easily explained (for a formal mathematical exposition, see for example Arnott et al., 1993). There is a group of N travellers who wish to arrive at work at the same destination, via the same route, at the same desired arrival time t^*. However, on the way, there is a bottleneck with a limited capacity of s vehicles that can pass per hour. As long as there is no queue upstream of the bottleneck, vehicles can freely pass the bottleneck without any time loss. For convenience, and without loss of generality if there is only one route, we ignore the implied free-flow travel time for such a trip by normalizing it to zero: departure from home, passage of the bottleneck and arrival at work then occur at the same instant. In all other cases, a queue will grow or shrink upstream of the bottleneck, at a rate which is equal to the difference between the departure rate from home and the arrival rate at work, where the latter is equal to the capacity s. Under these assumptions, it is physically impossible for everybody to arrive at work at t^*; instead, the peak will last for N/s hours. Some people will arrive too early, some will arrive too late, and only one individual will arrive exactly at t^*.

Vickrey (1969) introduced the concept of schedule delay costs to characterize the dynamic equilibrium for such a situation. These are the costs associated with arriving before or after the desired arrival time t^*; if such costs did not exist, of course, t^* would not be any more desirable than other arrival times. A dynamic equilibrium is then defined as a situation in which no traveler can reduce his or her travel costs, consisting of travel delay costs plus schedule delay costs, by unilaterally changing the departure time from home. With homogeneous travelers, this means that the sum of travel delay costs and schedule delay costs must be constant over time during the period when arrivals at work occur. Knowing the time pattern of schedule delay cost, it is therefore simple to derive the time pattern of travel delay cost: it has exactly the opposite pattern so that their sum is constant. For example, when schedule delay costs are piecewise linear – as is often assumed, with β denoting the shadow price for an additional hour early and γ for an additional hour late – and a constant value of travel time α applies, travel delay costs must rise linearly over time at a rate β during early arrivals, and drop at a rate γ during late arrivals. For the assumed bottleneck congestion technology, the implied piece-wise linear pattern of travel delays is achieved if the departure rate from home is for drivers arriving before t^* constant and above the capacity s, and for drivers arriving after t^* constant and below s. This relatively simple pattern yields convenient closed-form analytical solutions. Equilibrium cost rises linearly with overall demand N. Aggregate travel delay cost and aggregate schedule delay cost are equal, and therefore each contribute half of the total travel cost. The static model of the previous section would then ignore half of the total cost of congestion.

Travel delay costs are a pure deadweight loss with bottleneck congestion: shortening queues reduces aggregate travel delay cost without raising schedule delay cost. Similarly, there is no benefit in further reducing the departure rate below the bottleneck's capacity once queues are eliminated: this would simply increase schedule delay cost. The optimum is therefore the situation where the departure rate from home is exactly equal to the bottleneck's capacity throughout the peak, so that no queues develop but nevertheless all N users can still exit the bottleneck at the same moments as they did in the original equilibrium. The toll pattern that achieves this should exactly match the time pattern of travel delay cost as it was in the no-toll equilibrium. The toll and schedule delay cost together are then constant over time, implying that travel delay costs will also be constant over time in the dynamic equilibrium (where the sum of these three generalized price components must be constant). Because travel delay costs start at zero (there is no initial queue), they will therefore remain equal to zero: no queue will develop during the peak.

There are various surprises when comparing this toll-supported optimum to the original no-toll equilibrium. We mention three. First, because the outflow from the bottleneck remains the same, we have an optimum in which all individuals still use their cars (there is no need to use public transport or to go car-pooling) and arrive at work at the same time as they did before. However, all except for the very first and very last travelers depart later than they did in the no-toll equilibrium because there is no queuing delay. Contrary to popular beliefs, road pricing (with a time-varying toll) can therefore be effective even if there are no travel alternatives or possibilities to adjust work start times. Second, because tolls replace travel delay costs, the generalized price of travel does not rise, unlike the situation depicted in Figure 23.1. This would mean that social opposition might quickly disappear after the effects of the policy become clear. And third, optimal tolling eliminates all travel delay costs. Each of these three conclusions stands in sharp contrast with the conclusions from the static model.

Space is lacking to discuss various extensions of the bottleneck model (Small and Verhoef, 2007, provide a review). Furthermore, various dynamic congestion functions other than pure bottleneck congestion have been studied, incorporating elements of 'flow congestion' besides queuing at a bottleneck (for example, Chu, 1995). These often do not allow for neat analytical closed-form solutions, as in the bottleneck model. Small and Verhoef (2007, p. 136) compare some of these studies, and conclude that 'the basic bottleneck model overestimates the benefits from optimal tolling, and underestimates the resulting increase in generalized price, by exaggerating the extent to which travel delays can be eliminated without increasing scheduling costs'. The relative size of these biases appears to be smaller for models that, like the bottleneck model, take into account that queuing is typically 'hypercongested' (meaning that the same flow can be achieved at a higher speed and a lower density). The basic bottleneck model therefore produces 'benchmark' results, but these still need not be far from what might be achievable in practice were optimal time-varying tolling to be used.

SECOND-BEST PRICING

Introduction

Pricing schedules such as the ones described above can be considered 'first-best' solutions for two distinct reasons. One is that it is assumed that there are no constraints on the pricing policy. For example, the toll on the example road in the introductory section was optimized to match traffic conditions on that road, implying that there were no restrictions such as, for instance, the road being part of a network on which it is imposed that tolls (perhaps per kilometer) must be equal across links. And the optimal dynamic toll considered above could fluctuate perfectly over time. The second reason is that it is implicitly assumed that there are no other distortions in the entire economy to which the road belongs that would justify interference: prices are equal to marginal costs in all other markets. For example, it is implicitly assumed that the labor market operates perfectly and that there are no distortionary labor taxes in place so that commuting trips are priced efficiently except for congestion. Both assumptions, of course, are quite unrealistic. Road prices that are set so as to maximize social surplus, under conditions where either one or both of these assumptions is violated, are referred to as 'second best'. While first-best pricing is a benchmark that helps understanding the basic economic motivation for implementing congestion pricing, second-best pricing seems (far) more relevant for practical applications, and has received considerable attention over the past decade (Small and Verhoef, 2007, review this literature). In this section, we provide an illustrative analytical example of second-best pricing, and will then proceed with a qualitative discussion of some other relevant cases.

An Analytical Example of Second-best Pricing: Undifferentiated Pricing

It is instructive to present an analytical example of second-best road pricing in some detail. Even though second-best problems come in many variants, the techniques used to solve them are often similar, and discussing one case provides insights that help in understanding and solving other cases. We consider the case where there are two groups of travelers who possibly cause different marginal external costs, for example because they travel at different times of day. Optimality would require the tolls to be different for the two groups, but let us assume that the operator is constrained to set only one toll level r. The question is: at what level should the toll be set? This question was studied for an indeterminate number of groups in Verhoef et al. (1995); here we restrict attention to two groups, A and B.

To find the second-best toll, we recognize that we face a constrained optimization problem and write out the corresponding Lagrangian:

$$\Lambda = \int_0^{V_A} d_A(x)\,dx + \int_0^{V_B} d_B(x)\,dx - V_A \cdot c_A(V_A) - V_B \cdot c_B(V_B)$$

$$+ \lambda_A \cdot (c_A(V_A) + r - d_A(V_A)) + \lambda_B \cdot (c_B(V_B) + r - d_B(V_B)) \qquad (23.1)$$

The first two terms (with integrals) give the benefits for the two groups, as areas under the respective inverse demand functions d; the next two terms give the total cost as the product of volume V and average cost c, and the final two terms are the Lagrangian constraints that indicate that both groups will expand travel up to the point where marginal benefit d equals the generalized price $c + r$. The Lagrangian multipliers λ will reflect, in the second-best optimum, the impact on the optimized objective (social surplus) from a marginal relaxation of the associated constraint. A marginal relaxation of the constraint in this case means a marginal increase in the road price r. Under first-best pricing, the multipliers would therefore be zero; non-zero multipliers reflect that the constraint is binding in the second-best optimum.

The first-order conditions are as follows:

$$\frac{\partial \Lambda}{\partial V_A} = d_A(V_A) - c_A(V_A) - V_A \cdot \frac{\partial c_A(V_A)}{\partial V_A} + \lambda_A \cdot \left(\frac{\partial c_A(V_A)}{\partial V_A} - \frac{\partial d_A(V_A)}{\partial V_A} \right) = 0 \qquad (23.2a)$$

$$\frac{\partial \Lambda}{\partial V_B} = d_B(V_B) - c_B(V_B) - V_B \cdot \frac{\partial c_B(V_B)}{\partial V_B} + \lambda_B \cdot \left(\frac{\partial c_B(V_B)}{\partial V_B} - \frac{\partial d_B(V_B)}{\partial V_B} \right) = 0 \qquad (23.2b)$$

$$\frac{\partial \Lambda}{\partial r} = \lambda_A + \lambda_B = 0 \qquad (23.2c)$$

$$\frac{\partial \Lambda}{\partial \lambda_A} = c_A(V_A) + r - d_A(V_A) = 0 \qquad (23.2d)$$

$$\frac{\partial \Lambda}{\partial \lambda_B} = c_B(V_B) + r - d_B(V_B) = 0 \qquad (23.2e)$$

As might have been anticipated, the first-order conditions are symmetric for groups A and B and substitution of (23.2d) into (23.2a), and (23.2e) into (23.2b), yields the following solution for the Lagrangian multipliers (introducing primes to denote partial derivatives):

$$\lambda_i = \frac{V_i \cdot c_i' - r}{c_i' - d_i'} \quad i = \{A, B\} \qquad (23.3)$$

In accordance with what we just said, these multipliers are zero if r is equal to the marginal external cost $V \cdot c'$, which can – by Equation (23.2c) – be second-best optimal only if this is true simultaneously for both groups.

Equation (23.3) therefore implies that if the marginal external costs are equal between the two groups, and if first-best tolls therefore are not differentiated, the second-best constraint that the tolls be equal is not binding and the first-best optimum is effectively achieved. Otherwise, a group's multiplier increases in absolute value if the toll deviates further from the marginal external cost (the numerator in (23.3)) or if its equilibrium demand is more sensitive with respect to toll changes (d_i' in the denominator is smaller in magnitude). Note in particular that the term $1/(c_i' - d_i')$ equals dV_i/dr. The multiplier therefore indeed gives the overall welfare effect of a marginal increase in toll for the group under consideration, expressed as the wedge between the toll and the marginal external cost multiplied by the change in volume that would arise from a marginal change in the toll. The reader might verify this in a diagram like Figure 23.1 by drawing an equilibrium with an arbitrary toll, determining graphically its welfare effect compared to the no-toll equilibrium, and verifying how this would change following a marginal change in the non-optimal toll.

Equation (23.2c) states that the toll should be set such that a marginal increase produces a welfare gain in the one market that is equal to the welfare loss in the other; a rather intuitive condition. Together with Equation (23.3), it can be solved to find the second-best congestion toll:

$$r_i = \left(\frac{V_A \cdot c_A'}{c_A' - d_A'} + \frac{V_B \cdot c_B'}{c_B' - d_B'} \right) \cdot \left(\frac{1}{c_A' - d_A'} + \frac{1}{c_B' - d_B'} \right)^{-1} \qquad (23.4)$$

The toll is a weighted average of the marginal external costs for the two groups, where a group's weight increases if its sensitivity with respect to marginal toll changes becomes bigger (Verhoef et al., 1995). This matches insights from the literature on optimal taxation (for example, Sandmo, 1975).

Simple as the example may be, it serves to illustrate a number of important lessons from the theory of second-best road pricing. One is that a second-best toll should be set such that welfare losses and gains that arise in different markets, or market segments, from a marginal change in the toll are balanced. The second is that this typically requires the application of toll rules that are more complicated than their first-best counterparts. The risk of making mistakes, either because the correct toll rule is not applied or because not all the necessary information for applying it correctly is available, is bigger than for first-best pricing. Ignoring the second-best nature of the problem, however, and blindly applying first-best toll rules – a policy that is sometimes referred to as 'quasi first-best pricing' (see Small and Verhoef, 2007) – is not an option: it leads to (even?) lower welfare gains from pricing than the gains from second-best pricing, which by definition achieves the highest gains given the constraints that apply. In fact, it may even lead to losses.

Some Other Examples of Second-best Congestion Pricing

As already mentioned, the above example is just one of many possible second-best problems in road pricing. Many studies have recently considered such problems, and space allows us to mention only a few of these (more detailed reviews are given in Lindsey and Verhoef, 2001; and Small and Verhoef, 2007).

One class of second-best problems concerns network interactions, in particular cases where some tolls can be set while not all links in a network, or not all transport modes, are optimally priced. Lévy-Lambert (1968) and Marchand (1968) were the first to study this problem in the context of what is sometimes referred to as the 'classic two-route problem', where one of two parallel links connecting the same origin and destination can be tolled while the other remains untolled. Depending on the demand and cost elasticities, the relative efficiency of second-best tolling in this situation may be disappointingly small due to the congestion spillover on unpriced capacity (see also Liu and McDonald, 1998). Variants of this problem consider private ownership (Verhoef et al., 1996), dynamic bottleneck congestion (Braid, 1996; De Palma and Lindsey 2000), heterogeneity in values of time (Small and Yan, 2001; Verhoef and Small, 2004), larger networks (Sumalee et al., 2005; Verhoef, 2002), and multiple governments (De Borger et al., 2005; Ubbels and Verhoef, 2008).

A second class of problems takes into account pre-existing distortionary taxation on labor markets (for example, Mayeres and Proost, 2001; Parry and Bento, 2001). One of the main lessons that emerge from this literature is that the overall welfare gains of road pricing depend not only on the primary effects of the charge, but also on allocative efficiency impacts from the use of the revenues. For example, lump-sum recycling of revenues, a 'harmless' welfare-neutral measure in a standard partial-equilibrium model, may be seen to harm welfare in a general-equilibrium setting because it discourages labor supply. Conversely, the use of toll revenues to reduce distortionary labor taxes may produce additional benefits.

A third class of problems concerns flat or coarse (step-wise) pricing of a dynamic bottleneck (Arnott et al., 1993). Although the analytics of such problems can be cumbersome, the main conclusion is transparent: efficiency of tolling increases when the allowable time-variability of tolls increases (more steps).

Finally, a related stream of literature has looked on second-best capacity choice in relation to road pricing. The first-best benchmark for this type of problem was derived by Mohring and Harwitz (1962), who showed that under certain technical conditions – in particular neutral scale economies in road construction (constant costs per unit of capacity) and congestion technology (a doubling of capacity and flow leaves the average user cost unaltered) – the revenues from optimal road pricing would be just sufficient to cover the capital cost of capacity supply. Scholars like d'Ouville and McDonald (1990), Wheaton (1978) and Wilson (1983) studied how sub-optimal pricing (including the complete absence of a road price) alters the optimal investment rule for highways. The answer depends on the relative strength of two opposing forces. One is that in absence of pricing, demand will be higher, which would justify a larger capacity. The other is that absent pricing, part of the actual traffic is socially unwarranted 'induced demand', which can partly be discouraged by limiting road capacity. Wilson (1983) concludes that under conditions that he deems 'reasonable', the former of these two forces is stronger, implying that optimal pricing would probably allow us to make smaller road investments.

This concludes our brief review of the literature. We will now turn to actual applications of congestion pricing, and will also discuss the extent to which these applications are indeed designed according to first-best or second-best standards.

CONGESTION CHARGING IN PRACTICE

In this section we describe the congestion pricing schemes that are in operation as of 2008, excluding any past or on-going experiments or future plans. The only exceptions to this are some of the projects described for the United States, which are part of the Value Pricing Pilot program of the Federal Highway Administration in the United States.

Although there have been proposals and, in some cases, trials in the Netherlands, Hong Kong, New York, San Francisco and various towns and cities in the UK, eventually, they have all been abandoned or are still not yet in operation. The reasons have ranged from concern about lack of privacy to equity concerns linked to charge level or public transport provision. Unsurprisingly, there are very few examples of congestion charging in practice. Although the microeconomic theory behind road pricing is sound, public and political acceptability have turned into major barriers to its implementation.

The Norwegian toll rings, very often cited in the road pricing literature, were designed to generate revenues to finance infrastructure. A number of towns in Norway, including Oslo and Bergen, to name the most prominent ones, have tolls, usually surrounding the whole town rather than the city center, with daily charges which never exceed 20 NOK (roughly US$3) for cars and light vehicles. The schemes usually have flat rates throughout the day or during most of the day, but some have differentiated rates according to time of the day. Ramjerdi et al. (2004, Table 1, p. 245), for example, report different tolls in Stavanger for different times of the day (p. 245). The original aim of these toll rings was not to manage traffic demand, and as such the decrease in demand for car travel has typically been low, with estimates varying from zero to 10 percent reduction at most. Similarly there have been no significant changes in private car occupancy rates or demand for public transport (Ramjerdi et al., 2004).

The Road Act and Road Traffic Act in Norway were amended in 2004 in order to enable local authorities to introduce congestion charging if they wish to. The authorities in Bergen and Oslo are currently considering the possibility of managing congestion with some kind of time-varying toll. However, as of 2008, none of the Norwegian toll rings has been turned (legally approved and currently operating) into a demand management tool.

There are also a number of toll highways around the world. Although many have as their only objective revenue generation, some others are designed to relieve congestion. Some examples include the M6 Toll in England, the 407 Express Toll Route (ETR) in Toronto and a number of roads in major Australian cities, such as for example, City Link in Melbourne and the Westlink M7 Toll Road in Sydney.

The M6 Toll in England is a parallel[1] segment to the M6 motorway, which extends 43 km (27 mi). Drivers have the option of using the publicly provided alternative for free or using the toll road. The M6 toll runs from junction 3a on the M6 and rejoins it at junction 11a. Charging is done at toll plazas along the road or at the exit and is not electronic.

The Highway 407 ETR in Toronto extends 108 km (67 mi) from Brock Road in Pickering in the east to the QEW/403 interchange near Hamilton in the west. The 407 ETR charges tolls electronically and is based on distance driven.

The City Link in Melbourne is a toll road in the centre of Melbourne in Australia, which extends 22 km (14 mi), from Tullamarine Freeway to the West Gate Freeway and the West Gate Freeway to the Monash Freeway. The system operates electronically and charges per trip made along the toll segment.

The Westlink M7 Toll Road in Sydney extends 40 km (35 mi), connecting the M2, M4 and M5 motorways. It operates electronically and charges per distance driven.

All these are examples of toll roads where the private sector has stepped in to operate (sometimes also to build) a toll road which provides lower journey times to those who choose the toll road as opposed to the publicly provided alternatives.

We devote the rest of this section to discussing four practical examples of successful implementation of some sort of congestion pricing. The four cases discussed here are the High Occupancy Toll lanes in the United States, since they embody an interesting form of congestion pricing and they have been the major US development for congestion pricing; the Singaporean Area Licensing Scheme and Electronic Road Pricing; the London Congestion Charging Scheme; and the Stockholm congestion tax.

High Occupancy Toll lanes in the United States

High Occupancy Toll (HOT) lanes in the United States are lanes where tolls are applied on low occupancy vehicles wanting to use lanes which are free to use for high occupancy vehicles (HOV). High occupancy is usually defined as vehicles with two or more occupants.

The State Route 91 (SR-91) Express Lanes, which opened in December 1995, were the first practical example of congestion pricing and HOT lanes in the United States (Sullivan and El Harake, 1998). The tolls varied according to a pre-set schedule and by 1998 they had evolved to a highly sophisticated level of variation (Lam and Small, 2001).

Although they were originally privately operated, in January 2003 their operation was taken by the Orange County Transportation Authority (OCTA). The SR-91 Express Lanes extend 16 km (10 mi) between the Orange/Riverside county line and the Costa Mesa Freeway (SR-55) interchange in eastern Anaheim.

OCTA, together with the Riverside County Transportation Commission (RCTC), decides on toll road policies and improvements for the corridor (OCTA, 2008). In July 2003, the OCTA adopted a toll policy for the SR-91 Express Lanes based on the concept of congestion management. Like in the case of Singapore, which is discussed below, tolls are set to optimize traffic flows. In Singapore, traffic is monitored and tolls adjusted every three months. On SR-91 hourly, daily and directional traffic volumes are monitored and tolls increased or decreased accordingly. The highest tolls, which are charged during super-peak hours, are held constant for at least six months once they have been increased (OCTA, 2008).

Tolls apply 24 hours a day, seven days a week, with the lowest one being $1.25 and the highest one, $9.55.[2] There is a discount for cars with three or more occupants, motorcycles, vehicles with disabled person(s) or disabled veteran license plates and zero emission vehicles. For all these travel is free on the SR-91 toll lanes except eastbound Monday to Friday from 4:00 p.m. to 6:00 p.m., when the toll they are charged is half the toll that applies during the hour and day in question. As of 2008, there are over 20 different charges according to day of the week, time of the day and travelling direction (OCTA, 2008).

Being such an innovative policy, the case has been subject to extensive analysis. Studies range from assessment of changes in travel behavior among different socioeconomic groups as a result of the implementation of the express lanes (Li, 2001; Mastako et al., 1998; Sullivan, 2002) to estimates of the values of time and reliability for users of the SR-91 (Lam and Small, 2001; Yan et al., 2002), social benefit–cost analysis for the SR-91 (Sullivan and Burris, 2006) and comparison of the regressive impacts of the SR-91 tolls with those from the Orange County's local option transportation sales tax (Schweitzer and Taylor, 2008).

As of 2008, there are an additional seven HOT lane projects in operation in the United States, which have been partly funded by the Value Pricing Pilot program or by its predecessor, the Congestion Pricing Pilot Program. These are segments of the I-15 in San Diego, California (implemented in 1996), the I-25 in Denver, Colorado (implemented in 2006), the I-394 in Minneapolis, Minnesota (implemented in 2005), the Katy Freeway (I-10) and the US 290 in Houston, Texas (implemented in 1998 and 2000 respectively), the I-15 in Salt Lake City, in Utah (implemented in 2006), and the SR 167 in King County, Seattle, Washington (implemented in 2008). The individual designs vary, and tolls range from 50 cents to $9. In some cases they apply in the morning peak, in others in the afternoon peak, and in others they change in real time with traffic demand. In the latter case, drivers are informed of the toll rate changes through variable message signs located in advance of the entry points. One important advantage of HOT lanes over other pricing systems is that with HOT lanes drivers 'can choose between meeting the vehicle occupancy requirement or paying the toll in order to use the HOV lane' (DeCorla-Souza, 2004, p. 288).

HOT lanes are a clear example of a policy that can never be first-best: not all vehicles on the lane are charged a toll, and unpriced free capacity is available for drivers of low occupancy vehicles who do not wish to pay the toll. This is, however, not to say that the tolls in practice are set according to second-best standards, requiring constrained maximization of social surplus as discussed above. The explicit goal of HOT lanes is to maintain a minimum quality of service on the tolled lanes.

Singapore

In June 1975, the first congestion pricing scheme ever was implemented in Singapore. The system was a paper-based Area Licensing Scheme (ALS). Vehicles had to purchase a license and display it on their windscreen before entering the restricted zone (RZ), although the charge was per day, not per entry, meaning that they could enter and leave the RZ an unlimited number of times during the day. Exemptions included police cars, ambulances, fire engines and public transport buses. Motorcycles, goods vehicles and carpools were initially exempt, but from 1989 onwards they were also required to buy a license (Chin, 2002). No discounts or exemptions were given for residents living inside the RZ, although driving inside the zone without crossing the boundary could be done free of charge. Although it was called Area Licensing Scheme, the system actually operated like a cordon rather than an area licensing. Vehicles were charged on entry (and later exit in the evenings) into the RZ. The hours of charging and the levels of the charges varied throughout the years. They started with the morning peak Monday to Saturday, but later included the inter-peak, from mid-morning till mid-afternoon, and the evening peak (Santos, 2005). Drivers could purchase a whole-day license, which allowed them to drive inside the RZ at any time during the hours of operation of ALS, or a part-day license, which only allowed them to drive during the inter-peak hours on weekdays and the post-peak period on Saturdays.

The system was manually enforced by enforcement officers standing at the boundaries of the RZ, and was thus, prone to error.

The impacts on traffic were drastic. Phang and Toh (1997, p. 99) report that the introduction of ALS increased average speeds from 19 to 36 km (11.8 to 22.4 mi) per hour, exceeding the government target of 20–30 km (12.4–18.6 mi) per hour. According to Willoughby (2000, p. 10), traffic volumes during the morning peak hours fell by 45 percent, well above the expected reduction of 25–30 percent. Car entries were reduced by 70 percent.

This scheme was for many years the only road pricing scheme in the world. It has to be borne in mind that Singapore is a very special case, and as such, replication of the ALS elsewhere would have not been straightforward. Geographically, it is an island city-state, which measures 42 km (26.1 mi) east to west and 23 km (14.3 mi) north to south. It has 3149 km of roads (1955 mi) for a population of about 4.2 million people and 707 000 registered motor vehicles in the year 2002 (Santos et al., 2004). Politically, there is a dominating political party, the People's Action Party, which has won all the elections since 1959. Rising income and a resulting higher demand for private cars in such a small place were not a good combination. Already in the 1970s traffic congestion was seen as a very serious problem, which amongst other things, increased the cost of businesses, and thus, the ALS came to be.

The system was innovative but far from perfect, mainly due to its rudimentary technology (manually enforced paper permits displayed on windscreens).

In June 1995, a paper-based Road Pricing Scheme (RPS), operating in the same way as the ALS, was implemented on an expressway (East Coast Parkway). This was later extended to other expressways. The aim of the RPS was to reduce congestion on the expressways during morning peak times, and to familiarize Singaporeans with both linear passage tolls and road charging outside the CBD (Goh, 2002).

In September 1998, Electronic Road Pricing (ERP) replaced the ALS. Rather than a license to use the RZ, charges apply per-passage. The charging area is divided into central business districts (including the areas previously covered by ALS), where charging applies from 7:30 a.m. to 8:00 p.m., and expressways/outer ring roads, where charging applies from 7:30 to 9:30 a.m., Mondays to Saturdays, except public holidays. The operating hours of all ERP gantries actually end at 1:00 p.m. on the eve of public holidays. Vehicles are charged automatically each time they cross a gantry, on an electronic card, which is inserted in an in-vehicle unit. When the charge cannot be deducted from the card, either because it is not properly inserted or because it does not have sufficient credit, a fine is issued to the vehicle owner.

The only exemptions include emergency vehicles, such as ambulances, fire engines and police cars. ERP rates vary with vehicle type, time of day and location of the gantry. Charges for passenger cars, taxis and light goods vehicles for example vary between S$0.50 and S$3,[3] charges for motorcycles vary between S$0.25 and S$1.50, charges for heavy goods vehicles and light buses vary between S$0.75 and S$4.50, and charges for very heavy goods vehicles and big buses vary between S$1 and S$6. Every three months and during the June and December school holidays the Land Transport Authority assesses traffic speeds where the ERP is in operation and adjusts ERP if and as necessary. Their target speeds are 45 to 65 km per hour on expressways and 20 to 30 km per hour on arterial roads (Land Transport Authority website, 2007).

Also, in February 2003, a graduated ERP rate was introduced in the first five minutes of the time slot with a higher charge in order to discourage motorists from speeding up or slowing down to avoid higher charges (Land Transport Authority website, 2007). Since the graduated rate is introduced in the more expensive band, motorists save some money. For example, where the charge for passenger cars would be S$2 between 8:00 and 8:30 a.m. and S$3 between 8:30 and 9:00 a.m., it is now S$2 between 8:05 and 8:30 a.m., S$2.50 between 8:30 and 8:35 a.m., and S$3 between 8:35 and 8:55 a.m., when it changes to S$2.

The Singaporean ERP is the most fine-tuned road pricing system in the world to date. Since charges vary with vehicle type, time of day and location of the gantry and are only debited per passage, they incorporate a fair degree of differentiation. Although they are not computed on the basis of marginal congestion costs, and are therefore not first-best charges, they are designed to achieve target speeds, and changed when they under- or overshoot these targets. As such, the ERP in Singapore can be considered the most versatile second-best charging scheme to manage traffic demand.

London

The introduction of congestion charging was a central part of Ken Livingstone's manifesto for election to Mayor of London in May 2000. After a number of public consultations, the London Congestion Charging Scheme (LCCS) was implemented in

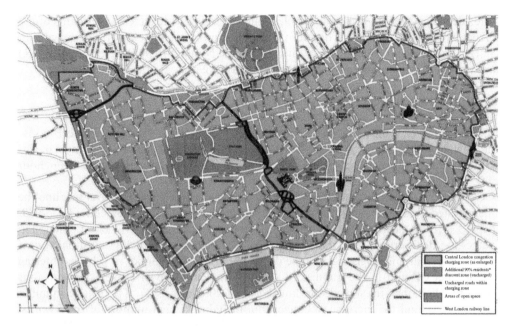

Source: www.cclondon.com

Figure 23.2   Map of the London congestion charging zone

February 2003. All vehicles entering, leaving, driving or parking on a public road inside the Charging Zone (CZ) between 7:00 a.m. and 6:00 p.m.[4] Monday to Friday, excluding public holidays, must pay the congestion charge. This was initially £5,[5] but in July 2005 it was increased to £8 per day. Payment of this charge allows road users to enter and exit the CZ as many times as they wish to and drive inside the CZ as much as they want on that day.

Figure 23.2 shows the limits of the (extended) CZ. The CZ is relatively small. It covers roughly 39 km[2] (15 mi[2]), representing 2.4 percent of the total 1579 km[2] (617 mi[2]) of Greater London. No charge is made for driving on the roads that limit the CZ and there are two free corridors: one north to south along Edgware Road, Park Lane, Grosvenor Place, Bressenden Place and Vauxhall Bridge Road; and another one north-west of the zone, east to west, as the diversion route would have been too long for drivers just wanting to cross that segment of the Westway A40. The dark-coloured roads on Figure 23.2 are all free of charge.

The charging zone is set to shrink. Ken Livingstone's successor, Boris Johnson, who took post in May 2008, announced in November that same year that the western extension would be removed. This is set to happen in January 2011. The CZ will then revert to what it originally was, with an area of 21 km[2], or 1.3 percent of Greater London. The daily charge is likely to be increased to £10.

There are a number of exemptions and discounts, which apply to two-wheelers, emergency vehicles, vehicles used by or for disabled people, buses, taxis and mini-cabs, some military vehicles, alternative fuel vehicles (with stringent emission saving requirements), roadside assistance and recovery vehicles. Finally, vehicles registered to residents of the CZ are entitled to a 90 percent discount when buying at least a week worth of congestion charge. Enforcement is undertaken with Automatic Number Plate Recognition (ANPR) and violators (number plates that use the CZ but have not paid the charge) are fined.

Impacts on traffic, congestion and public transport
Both the number of vehicles with four or more wheels entering the original CZ as well as the number of vehicle-kilometers driven by vehicles with four or more wheels inside the original CZ during charging hours decreased by around 20 percent, with most of this reduction having taken place in the first year of the LCCS and maintained throughout (TfL, 2007, p. 17 and Table 2.4, p. 26; 2008, p. 41).

Congestion, defined as 'the difference between the average network travel rate and the uncongested (free-flow) network travel rate in minutes per vehicle-kilometer' (TfL, 2003, Table 3.1, p. 46), decreased by 30 percent in the first year of the LCCS. This reduction in congestion deteriorated over the period 2005–07, when average delays eventually went back to pre-charging levels, despite the decrease both in the number of vehicles entering the original CZ and in the number of vehicle-kilometers driven by vehicles with four or more wheels having stayed constant between 2003 and 2007. TfL gives a number of reasons behind the increase in congestion, including a high number of road works, particularly in the second half of 2006, as well as during 2007 and into 2008 (TfL, 2007, point 3.2, p. 35 and point 3.10, p. 45), improved bus services, and better environment for pedestrians and cyclists (TfL, 2007, p. 2). In other words, newly recovered network space has been reallocated to users other than charge-paying vehicles. Part of the space is now for the exclusive use of buses, cyclists and pedestrians. TfL (2008, p. 5), however, are keen to point out that the impacts of congestion charging should be 'assessed by looking at the position with and without the scheme, rather than comparing current circumstances with what happened before the scheme was introduced' and that 'comparison of current conditions against a static baseline representing historic conditions is inappropriate'.

The two main modes of public transport in London are buses and underground. The LCCS had impacts on bus use but not on underground use.

The number of bus passengers entering central London increased by 18 percent and 12 percent, respectively, during the first and second years of the LCCS, and have since settled (TfL, 2007, p. 58; 2008, p.86). By the time congestion charging started, bus services had been improved by a combination of more frequent services, new and altered routes, and bigger buses.

Although the number of passengers using the underground decreased during the first year of the LCCS mainly due to the closure of the Central Line for almost three months following a derailment at Chancery Lane station in January (TfL, 2005), there was an increase in the years that followed, although this was not linked to the LCCS but rather, to a background trend of increase in underground use (TfL, 2008, p. 96).

Earmarking of revenues
The Greater London Authority Act 1999 (Acts of Parliament, 1999) requires that net revenues from congestion charging schemes introduced during the first 10 years of the legislation coming into force[6] will be earmarked[7] from their implementation to schemes which are part of the local transport plan. In London, most of these net revenues have

and continue to be allocated to bus network operations. A smaller percentage is allocated to improvement of roads and bridges, road safety, walking and cycling facilities and facilitation of distribution of freight (TfL, 2007, Table 6.3, p. 114).

Heterogeneity of users in London
Congestion charging, by definition, allocates road capacity to those car drivers for whom travelling is most valuable in terms of willingness to pay. In other words, only the car trips which are worth making are the trips that are made under congestion charging. This basic principle rests on heterogeneity, which could refer to various dimensions including the value of the trip, the value of time and reliability, and the value of schedule delays. The issue of users' heterogeneity, which undoubtedly is important in any market allocation, is also crucial in urban transport. Arnott et al. (1994) analyze the welfare effects of an optimal morning peak time-varying toll. Not surprisingly, they find that the toll benefits drivers with high values of time and schedule delay. The vast empirical and theoretical literature on the value of time, value of time distribution, and value of reliability (Calfee and Winston, 1998; Hensher and Goodwin, 2004; Lam and Small, 2001; Mackie et al., 2003; Steimetz and Brownstone, 2005; Wardman, 2001) has identified a number of factors that impact these values. Brownstone and Small (2005) argue that there is substantial heterogeneity in values of time and reliability across the population but it is difficult to isolate its origins.

Notwithstanding that, some widely agreed upon determinants include income and trip purpose. Although the correlations are far from perfect, in general we expect that a higher income leads to a higher value of both working and non-working time; and the more important the trip purpose (work as opposed to shopping, and their corresponding delay penalties) the higher the value of time savings.

London is a very special case because only 10 percent of people entering the charging zone in the morning peak before the LCCS was introduced did so by car (Department for Transport, 2007, Table 1.6).

No stated preference survey has been conducted in London with regards to congestion charging, and no information is held about charge-payers, except for their license plate. Given the lack of data on Londoners' values of time, any conclusions regarding their heterogeneity and any welfare effects from the LCCS can only rest on assumptions. Santos and Bhakar (2006) use data from the Labor Force Survey, provided by the Office of National Statistics, relevant to the periods autumn 2002 and autumn 2003, that detail the mode of travel to work and average incomes of commuters to the City of London that are resident in Greater London. This is the highest-earning group in the UK, as the average income in the City of London is higher than the average income anywhere else in the CZ, and in the country as a whole. Santos and Bhakar (2006) also make the controversial assumption that the value of time is one-and-a-half-times higher in congested conditions (pre-LCCS) in comparison with uncongested (post-LCCS) conditions.[8] They conclude that for a car commuter from Greater London to the City of London the minimum income to benefit from a £5 charge is £1400 per week. This weekly salary of £1400 is roughly equivalent to an annual salary of just under £75000. Given that on average, the richest 10 percent of full-time workers in London earn over £65450 per year (Office for National Statistics 2004, Table 7.7a), it is sensible to expect that quite a number of car commuters would have benefited from the £5 congestion charge.

Using the same methodology, Santos (2008, p. 289) estimates that the minimum weekly salary for a car commuter to benefit from the LCCS with an £8 charge is £2 348, roughly equivalent to an annual salary of £122 000. This obviously reduces the number of drivers who derive net benefits from the LCCS, but it is not possible to determine their number or percentage, given that the finest data on earnings are reported in deciles. It can be asserted however, that the percentage of potential winners is less than 10 percent.

The 90 percent of commuters that used public transport or a non-chargeable mode (such as two-wheelers and taxis) before the LCCS was implemented benefited from charging in the first two years, as travel times were reduced. From the 10 percent that used to enter the CZ by car, 8 percent continued to do so in 2003–05, after charging was introduced. The 2 percent that switched mode may have undergone a reduction in their utilities, caused by the inconvenience of switching mode or cancelling their trips. If the faster and more reliable bus services or the better environment for walking and cycling in the first two years more than compensated any initial decrease in utility the final effect may have been positive. It should be highlighted, however, that all the gains in travel times had been eroded by 2007, which means that public transport users are back to the situation they were in 2002. They do not lose because they do not pay the charge, but they do not benefit either. New public transport users that were priced off when congestion charging started are probably experiencing a loss in utility. As explained above, TfL (2008) argues that 'congestion would be significantly worse in the absence of the scheme' (p. 54), which means that although there are no measurable changes between 2002 and 2008 traffic speeds, there probably would be if the comparison could be done against a 2008-no charge scenario rather than a 2002-no charge one.

This section is not an attempt to conduct a distributional analysis, but rather to show, with a specific example, that heterogeneity across drivers is a fundamental factor in determining the responses to and impacts of congestion charging.

The LCCS may be seen as a second-best scheme in the sense that it is an unsophisticated flat charge, which does not differentiate by vehicle type or time of the day. As far as the time-invariance of the charge, TfL claimed at the time on its website that there was no need to vary the charge because speeds were low throughout the day. TfL (2003, Table 3.3, p. 52) presents the speeds inside the charging zone for 2002, the year before the LCCS was introduced. On average, these were 14.2, 13.5 and 13.7 km per hour for the morning peak, inter-peak and evening peak respectively. Understandably, that was seen as a good enough reason to have only one charge level throughout the day.

Stockholm

The congestion charge in Stockholm has been defined by the government as a tax. It was implemented on 1 August 2007 with the objectives of reducing traffic congestion and emissions. It is a cordon toll system, with a cordon that surrounds the entire Stockholm City, which has a total area of roughly 35.5 km². Like in London, enforcement is undertaken with ANPR, with cameras located at each of the 18 entry and exit points.

Each passage into or out of the area surrounded by the cordon costs SEK 10, 15 or 20 (roughly between US$1 and US$3) depending on the time of the day. The accumulated passages made by any vehicle during a particular day are aggregated and the vehicle owner is liable for either the sum of the charges or SEK 60, whichever is lower.

Exemptions include emergency vehicles, buses, diplomatic cars,[9] motorcycles, foreign-registered vehicles, military vehicles, disabled parking permit holders and vehicles that according to the Swedish Road Administration's vehicle registry, are equipped with technology for running (1) completely or partially on electricity or a gas other than LPG or (2) on a fuel blend that predominantly comprises alcohol (Swedish Road Administration, 2007). In addition to that, vehicles driving on the Essingeleden motorway, part of the European route E4, are also exempt, as it is the main route by-passing central Stockholm with no alternative routes. Finally, since Lidingö island has its only access to the mainland through the congestion tax area, all traffic to and from Lidingö to and from the rest of the Stockholm County is exempt from the tax. The condition for this is that vehicles must pass, within 30 minutes, two separate control points, and at least one of these points is located on Gasverksvägen, Lidingövägen and Norra Hamnvägen.

The congestion tax is paid retroactively. The payment must reach the Swedish Road Administration within 14 days of crossing the cordon. Regular users can set up a direct debit. Other ways of paying include cash or credit card at convenience stores, credit or debit cards on the congestion tax website, or directly to the Road Administration's account (Swedish Road Administration, 2007).

Drivers not paying the tax within 14 days are issued a fine. Eventually, if the vehicle owner continues to refuse to pay, his name is entered in the Enforcement Register (Swedish Road Administration, 2007).

Prior to the introduction of the congestion tax there was a seven month trial period, between January and July 2006 (Eliasson, 2007). A non-binding referendum was held in the City of Stockholm in September 2006, after the trial had finished. About half of the neighboring municipalities also held referendums (Eliasson, 2007). A total of 51 percent in Stockholm voted in favor of the tax,[10] whereas the other municipalities had votes which, when added together, were over 60 percent against the congestion tax (Stockholmsforsoket website, 2007).

Net revenues from the congestion tax are earmarked for new road construction in and around Stockholm. Like in London, a number of transit improvements were introduced before the scheme went ahead. Furthermore, even before the trials took place these improvements had already been undertaken. These included several new bus lines, additional capacity on commuter trains and underground, and more park-and-ride facilities. Kottenhoff and Brundell Freij (2009) conclude that this extra capacity raised the standard and attractiveness of transit in the Stockholm context. They point out that Stockholm had a high initial share of public transport use, which like in the case of London, made the congestion tax more viable. They also stress that a substantial part of the investment funded new direct bus services, which were well received and helped the switch from some private car drivers to transit.

LINK BETWEEN THEORY AND PRACTICE

Two points need to be made about the link between theory and practice. The first one is that although they all seem to be working well, none of the schemes described above were designed or optimized according to first-best or second-best standards. The second one is that there are, as by now the reader has gathered, very few examples of road pricing in the world, and this is probably linked to distributional and acceptability aspects, which have often been identified as the main barrier to widespread implementation (for example, de Palma et al., 2006; Eliasson and Mattsson, 2006; Jones, 1998; Nevin and Abbie, 1993; Santos and Rojey, 2004; Schuitema and Steg, 2008; Small, 1992). Each of these points is discussed below.

Scheme Design

Real-world networks and network users pose constraints on policy formulation and implementation which are in many cases not even known by policy makers. These would be essential to formulate and solve formal (constrained) optimization problems, as explained in the earlier section on second-best pricing.

According to standard partial-equilibrium economic theory, a first-best congestion charge should be set equal to the marginal congestion cost at the efficient level of traffic. None of the charge levels or locations of these schemes were ever determined on the basis of congestion costs, which vary constantly, according to traffic conditions. Nor were they optimized in a second-best fashion to optimally address any relevant constraints.

A number of HOT lanes in the United States and the Singapore ERP have variable pricing, although not set according to marginal congestion cost, but rather, set in line with target speeds or flows. Pursuing this objective could be a form of quasi-first-best pricing (de Palma et al., 2005).

The Stockholm congestion tax has three bands, depending on the time of the day, which makes it a variable pricing scheme to some extent. The LCCS does not entail any variable pricing, except for the charge/no charge variation.

The link between theory and practice is thus a weak one. The reasons why governments have not chosen to follow economic prescriptions on how to set charges can only be speculated upon. These include lack of information to set up the optimization problem in a first-best or second-best setting; and simplicity as an objective, especially when marginal cost pricing, varying in real time, could be confusing to users. The importance of simplicity is emphasized in Levinson and Odlyzko (2008).

It is virtually impossible to compare the charge levels of the different schemes in the United States, Singapore, London and Stockholm to what the first- or second-best charges would be. In order to do so, a full model with information on flows and speeds, vehicle types and origins and destinations would be needed, together with a fair amount of knowledge on the value of time and its distribution, which in turn would vary with mode, trip purpose and income, to name some of the main determinants only.

The schemes in operation are therefore not so much a triumph of economics as of political will, or at most, of political determination somehow inspired by economic ideas.

Distributional and Acceptability Aspects

Jones (1998) notes that the reason why road pricing has never been widely implemented has been the lack of public and political acceptability. He lists a number of public concerns about road pricing. Some of them are:

- Drivers find it difficult to accept the idea that they should be charged for congestion, which is something nobody wants, as opposed to paying for something they wish to acquire.
- Traffic congestion could be relieved by improving public transport or using restraint measures such as pedestrianization or restrictions to access in certain areas.
- Road pricing is a form of taxation and even if revenues were earmarked there would always be fear that the government could change the rules and allocate them to the consolidated fund.
- Road pricing is unfair because those least able to pay the charges will be tolled off.

There are a number of surveys, however, which show that public acceptability increases when the revenues from road pricing are transparently allocated to clear and specific uses in the transport sector.

According to the results of the survey carried out in London by the UK National Economic Development Office (1991), road charges would be acceptable to the majority (70 percent of all groups) if the revenues replaced the revenues of other taxes and/or they were invested on roads or public transport.

Surveys carried out in London between March and August 1999 found that people changed their attitude towards the idea of congestion charging when they were told that revenues would be ring-fenced to transport. A total of 67 percent of the general public thought that road-user charges in central London would be a good idea if net revenues were spent on transport improvements, and the proportion increased to 73 percent when the respondents' spending preferences were introduced (ROCOL, 2000, p. 57).

Schuitema and Steg (2008) also find that the acceptability of road pricing depends on revenue allocation. If car users are compensated for any negative effects, especially through the reduction of other car-related taxes, their acceptability increases, even in the authors' sample of high-income commuters.

Apart from revenue use, other factors affecting acceptability are linked to the users rather than to the scheme itself. Jaensirisak et al. (2005) conduct a stated preference survey in Leeds and London. Although income did not affect the answers, some personal characteristics did seem to have an influence on the degree of acceptability. Road pricing was more acceptable to non-car users and to those who thought pollution and congestion were very serious. This is in line with the results from an attitudinal survey, which was conducted by Accent on behalf of Transport for London, on the question of extending the congestion charging zone in London to the West. Not surprisingly the lowest level of support was from car drivers and the highest from cyclists and those who did not use the western extension during charging hours anyway, followed by those who walked or took public transport (Accent, 2005, pp. 83–84). The responses from the different organizations and businesses, stakeholders and members of the public to the different public consultation exercises simply reflected the way in which the charge and the subsequent modifications would have affected them or the principles for which they stood. Residents of the original charging zone in London were prone to both support the idea of congestion charging but also to ask for a full exemption (not happy enough with a 90 percent discount) and boundary residents were likely to ask for buffer residents' discounts.[11] Business group representatives, freight haulage groups and motoring organizations, amongst others, felt that all vehicles using alternative fuels (including bi/dual fuel and clean diesel) as well as all commercial and delivery vehicles should be entitled to a 100 percent discount, whilst environmental groups felt these vehicles had to pay a higher charge than cars, and disagreed with the exemption granted to two-wheelers. Walking and cycling groups on the other hand, felt the charge was not high enough and the zone should be extended to the whole of Greater London (Accent, 2005).

Gaunt et al. (2007) conducted a survey trying to understand the reasons behind the overwhelming opposition to road pricing in Edinburgh, an idea which was abandoned following the results of the 2005 referendum, where the public voted against the scheme by a ratio of 3:1. Once again, car use was found to be the main determinant of voting behavior, although public transport users as a whole did not support the idea either, as they were not fully convinced that the revenues from the scheme would be used to improve public transport. In addition to that, Ryley and Gjersoe (2006) find that in the case of Edinburgh newspaper coverage did not help, as it was increasingly negative over the time period leading up to the referendum in February 2005.

Although acceptability issues are related to public perception, including perception on revenue use and on how road pricing will affect different groups of road users, the undeniable fact is, as de Palma et al. (2006, p. 161) point out, that road pricing tends to make road users worse off before the allocation of revenues is accounted for. In line with Santos and Rojey (2004), they argue that the welfare impacts can vary by geographical area and that introducing road pricing can (therefore) have distributional effects on the population. Bureau and Glachant (2008) simulate and compare the distributional impacts on commuters of nine toll scenarios for Paris and show that equity effects vary with toll design, also a similar conclusion to that reached by Santos and Rojey (2004).

This last problem embodies a classic political debate: equity versus efficiency. The very nature of a congestion charge means that only those trips worth making are the ones which are going to be made. These trips are often made by individuals with a higher willingness to pay for the trip, and with a relatively high value of time, who coincidentally are individuals on higher incomes.

Eliasson and Mattsson (2006) assess the congestion charging scheme for Stockholm before it was implemented and find that the two most important factors for the net impact of congestion pricing are the initial travel patterns and how revenues are used. They also show that if revenues are used for improving public transport, the congestion charging scheme for Stockholm is progressive rather than regressive. This point is not trivial: tied up with any equity concerns is the use of revenues.

Revenues may be sent to the consolidated fund, used to reduce labor or other distortive taxes, or earmarked for the transport sector. If earmarked for the transport sector, the alternative allocations of road charge revenues vary from investment in infrastructure, to compensation to losers and improvement of public transport, pedestrian and cycling facilities. The way in which the government allocates revenues may change any public and political perceptions, and also ameliorate any perverse distributional impacts.

Small (1983) analyzes the distributional impacts of a peak expressway toll in the San Francisco Bay Area and concludes that if attention is paid to revenue allocation, congestion tolls may be beneficial to many income groups, including lower income groups. He argues that the incidence of tolls should be analyzed only in conjunction with revenue uses. He admits that the low-income driver will be harmed by the imposition of a toll mainly because his time savings will not compensate what he pays. However, the poor as a group can be left better off when revenue allocation is carefully planned. Increasing public transport or reducing regressive local taxes are possible uses that would have this effect.

Goodwin (1989, 1990) suggests that one-third of the revenues should be allocated to each of the following categories: (1) reduction in existing taxes or increase in social expenditure, (2) construction of new roads, improvement of existing ones or improvement in the standards of maintenance of the road infrastructure, (3) improvement in public transport services. He admits that 'a third' is somewhat arbitrary but defends it on the grounds that it is a clear division easy to understand and also represents a good starting point to reach an agreement. Small (1992) proposes a similar program of allocating revenues in thirds and attempting to more than fully compensate the majority who loses and also promote general social goals. His proposal is to allocate one-third of the revenues to each of the following categories: (1) monetary reimbursement to trip makers by funding a program of employee commuting allowances, (2) replacement of motor-vehicle license fees and fuel taxes and/or other taxes, such as VAT or property taxes, (3) new transport services. These types of rules, such as allocating one third to a different and specific use, are arbitrary and would not necessarily ensure support from the voting majority.

Doubtless the authorities empowered to levy congestion charges will readily find a variety of alternative uses for the revenue, each of which may have different impacts on the population and on the motoring public. Judging their distributional equity, their perceived fairness and weighing that against the political difficulty of introducing charges that damage an identifiable section of the population will require political judgment.

CONCLUSION

Road pricing is potentially an efficient instrument to internalize the congestion externality. Since congestion is a dynamic phenomenon and policies are usually constrained by imperfections in other related sectors of the economy and lack of information, the naïve application of first-best prescriptions from textbook models may yield welfare losses rather than gains.

There are very few real world examples of road pricing, with public and political acceptability being the main obstacles to implementation. The most prominent examples, which are in full operation and are working well, are the High Occupancy Toll lanes in the United States, the Singaporean Electronic Road Pricing, the London Congestion Charging Scheme, and the Stockholm congestion tax.

None of these schemes were designed according to first-best or second-best rules. The fact that they are not first-best tolls is appropriate because, as explained in the discussion of second-best pricing, a quasi first-best charge imposed in a second-best situation may easily yield social losses. The fact that they are not second-best either means that they could potentially be redesigned to yield higher benefits. The regulators however have opted for fairly unsophisticated, easy to understand systems, with the most advanced being the Singapore one, and they have chosen to optimize traffic flows or speeds, or simply, to reduce traffic levels.

Although a stricter use of economic principles might have been desirable, the schemes have mostly achieved the objectives they set out to achieve, and can be highlighted as showcases of the feasibility of congestion charging in very different political and institutional settings in the twenty-first century.

ACKNOWLEDGMENTS

Thanks are due to Farideh Ramjerdi for information on the toll rings in Norway, to Jonas Eliasson for information on the Stockholm congestion tax and to Robin Lindsey for extensive comments on an earlier draft. Georgina Santos gratefully acknowledges financial support from the Transport Studies Unit and the Smith School of Enterprise and the Environment at University of Oxford.

NOTES

1. It is not parallel in the strict sense, as it arcs around the north-east of the West Midlands conurbation before re-joining the M6.
2. On the January 2008 toll card, the highest toll was $10.00 on Fridays from 3:00 to 4:00 p.m. It seems that high gas prices and/or the recession have depressed traffic.
3. The exchange rate as of April 2011 is S$1 = US$0.81.
4. The end time was originally 6:30 p.m. but it was brought forward to 6:00 p.m. when the zone was expanded to the west in February 2007.
5. The exchange rate as of April 2011 is GB£1 = US$1.65.
6. This is the period 1999–2009.
7. In the case of the London charge this period would have been 2003–13. However, the clock went back with the extension and the new period is now 2007–17. It is not clear what the earmarking period will be when the extension is removed.
8. There is however some evidence that supports that assumption. MVA et al. (1987, p. 176) estimate that the value of time in congested conditions can be up to 40 percent higher and Wardman (2001, p.125) concludes that it can be 50 percent higher.
9. Under the 1961 Vienna Convention, diplomats are exempt from paying taxes. Staff at the US and German embassies refuse to pay the congestion charge in London, arguing that under the 1961 Vienna Convention, they are exempt from paying taxes. However, the London congestion charge is not a tax but a charge. The Stockholm congestion tax, on the other hand, is a tax.
10. A total of 76.4 percent of eligible voters voted.
11. After more than 3 years, this suggestion was eventually introduced.

REFERENCES

Accent, 2005, Western extension to the Central London congestion charging scheme. Report on Public Consultation and Attitudinal Survey, Final Report prepared for Transport for London, September.

Acts of Parliament, 1999, Greater London Authority Act 1999 c. 29. London, HMSO. Available at: www. hmso.gov.uk/acts/acts1999/19990029.htm

Arnott, R., A. de Palma and R. Lindsey, 1993, A structural model of peak-period congestion: A traffic bottleneck with elastic demand. *American Economic Review*, **83**, 161–179.

Arnott, R., A. de Palma and R. Lindsey, 1994, The welfare effect of congestion tolls with heterogeneous commuters. *Journal of Transport Economics and Policy*, **28** (2), 139–161.

Braid, R.M., 1996, Peak-load pricing of a transportation route with an unpriced substitute. *Journal of Urban Economics*, **40**, 179–197.

Brownstone, D. and K. Small, 2005, Valuing time and reliability: assessing the evidence from road pricing demonstrations. *Transportation Research Part A*, **39** (4), 279–293.

Bureau, B. and M. Glachant, 2008, Distributional effects of road pricing: assessment of nine scenarios for Paris. *Transportation Research Part A*, **42** (7), 994–1007.

Button, K. and E. Verhoef, 1998, *Pricing, Traffic Congestion and the Environment*. Cheltenham, UK: Edward Elgar.

Calfee, J. and C. Winston, 1998, The value of automobile travel time: implications for congestion policy. *Journal of Public Economics*, **69** (1), 83–102.

Chin, A.T.H., 2002, Road pricing: Singapore's experience. Essay prepared for the IMPRINT-EUROPE Thematic Network: 'Implementing Reform on Transport Pricing: Constraints and Solutions: Learning from Best Practice'. Available at: www.imprint-eu.org/public/Papers/IMPRINT3_chin.pdf.

Chu, X., 1995, Endogenous trip scheduling: the Henderson approach reformulated and compared with the Vickrey approach. *Journal of Urban Economics*, **37**, 324–343.

De Borger, B., S. Proost and K. van Dender, 2005, Congestion and tax competition in a parallel network. *European Economic Review*, **49**, 2013–2040.

DeCorla-Souza, P., 2004, Recent US experience: pilot projects. In G. Santos, ed., *Road Pricing: Theory and Evidence*. Oxford: Elsevier, pp. 283–308.

D'Ouville, E.L. and J.F. McDonald, 1990, Optimal road capacity with a suboptimal congestion toll. *Journal of Urban Economics*, **28**, 34–49.

De Palma, A. and R. Lindsey, 2000, Private roads: competition under various ownership regimes. *Annals of Regional Science*, **34**, 13–35.

De Palma, A., M. Kilani and R. Lindsey, 2005, A comparison of second-best and third-best tolling schemes on a road network. *Transportation Research Record*, **1932**, 89–96.

De Palma, A., R. Lindsey and E. Niskanen, 2006, Policy insights from the urban road pricing case studies. *Transport Policy*, **13** (2), 149–161.

Department for Transport, 2007, *Transport Statistics Great Britain*. London: The Stationery Office. Available at: www.dft.gov.uk/pgr/statistics/datatablespublications/.

Eliasson, J., 2007, The Stockholm congestion charging system: a summary of the effects. Paper 1525, 11th World Conference on Transport Research CD-ROM, University of California, Berkeley, June 24–28, 2007.

Eliasson, J. and L. Mattsson, 2006, Equity effects of congestion pricing: quantitative methodology and a case study for Stockholm. *Transportation Research Part A*, **40** (7), 602–620.

Flowerdew, A.D., 1993, *Urban traffic congestion in Europe: road pricing and public transport demand*. Research Report, The Economics Intelligence Unit, London.

Gaunt, M., T. Rye and S. Allen, 2007, Public acceptability of road user charging: the case of Edinburgh and the 2005 Referendum. *Transport Reviews*, **27** (1), 85–102.

Goh, M., 2002, Congestion management and electronic road pricing in Singapore. *Journal of Transport Geography*, **10**, 29–38.

Goodwin, P.B., 1989, The rule of three: a possible solution to the political problem of competing objectives for road pricing. *Traffic Engineering and Control*, **30** (10), 495–497.

Goodwin, P.B., 1990, How to make road pricing popular. *Economic Affairs*, **10**, 6–7.

Hensher, D. and P. Goodwin, 2004, Using values of travel time savings for toll roads: avoiding some common errors. *Transport Policy*, **11** (2), 171–182.

Jaensirisak, S., M. Wardman and A. May, 2005, Explaining variations in public acceptability of road pricing schemes. *Journal of Transport Economics and Policy*, **39**(2), 127–153.

Jones, P., 1998, Urban road pricing: public acceptability and barriers to implementation. In Button and Verhoef, eds, *Pricing, Traffic Congestion and the Environment*. Cheltenham, UK: Edward Elgar, pp. 263–284.

Kottenhoff, K. and K. Brundell Freij (2009), The role of public transport for feasibility and acceptability of congestion charging: the case of Stockholm. *Transportation Research Part A*, **43** (3), 297–305.

Lam, T.C. and K. Small, 2001, The value of time and reliability: measurement from a value pricing experiment. *Transportation Research Part E*, **37** (2–3), 231–251.

Land Transport Authority website, 2007, www.lta.gov.sg/motoring_matters/index_motoring_erp.htm.

Levinson, D. and A. Odlyzko, 2008, Too expensive to meter: the influence of transaction costs in transportation and communication. Paper presented at the Third International Conference on Funding Transportation Infrastructure, Paris, June 19–20.

Lévy-Lambert, H., 1968, Tarification des services à qualité variable: application aux péages de circulation. [Pricing of variable-quality services: application to road tolls]. *Econometrica*, **36**, 564–574.

Li, J., 2001, Explaining high-occupancy-toll lane use. *Transportation Research Part D*, **6** (1), 61–74.

Lindsey, R. and E.T. Verhoef, 2001, Traffic congestion and congestion pricing. In K.J. Button and D.A. Hensher, eds, *Handbook of Transport Systems and Traffic Control*. Amsterdam and New York: Pergamon, pp. 77–105.

Liu, L.N. and J.F. McDonald, 1998, Efficient congestion tolls in the presence of unpriced congestion: a peak and off-peak simulation model. *Journal of Urban Economics*, **44**, 352–366.

Mackie, P., M. Wardman, A. Fowkes, G. Whelan, J. Nellthorp and J. Bates, 2003, Values of travel time savings in the UK: Summary Report, Report to the Department of Transport, Institute for Transport Studies, University of Leeds, Leeds. Available at: www.its.leeds.ac.uk/working/downloads/VOTSummary.pdf.

Marchand, M., 1968, A note on optimal tolls in an imperfect environment. *Econometrica*, **36**, 575–581.

Mastako, K., L. Rillet and E. Sullivan, 1998, Commuter behavior on California State Route 91 after introducing variable-toll express lanes. *Transportation Research Record*, **1649**, 47–54.

Mayeres, I. and S. Proost, 2001, Marginal tax reform, externalities and income distribution. *Journal of Public Economics*, **79**, 343–363.

Mohring, H. and M. Harwitz, 1962, *Highway Benefits: An Analytical Framework*. Evanston, IL: Northwestern University Press.

MVA Consultancy, ITS University of Leeds, and TSU University of Oxford, 1987, *Value of Travel Time Savings*. Newbery, UK: Policy Journals.

National Economic Development Office, 1991, A road user charge: Londoner's views. Report on Survey Findings, Harris/NEDO, London.

Nevin, M. and L. Abbie, 1993, What price roads? Practical issues in the introduction of road user charges in historic cities in the UK. *Transport Policy*, **1** (1), 68–73.

Office for National Statistics, 2004, Regional trends 38: data. Available at: www.statistics.gov.uk/statbase/Product.asp?vlnk=11614&image.x=7&image.y=9.

Orange County Transportation Authority, 2008, 91 express lanes. Available at: www.octa.net/91_express.aspx.

Parry, I.W.H. and A.M. Bento, 2001, Revenue recycling and the welfare effects of congestion pricing. *Scandinavian Journal of Economics*, **103**, 645–671.

Phang, S.Y. and R.S. Toh, 1997, From manual to electronic road congestion pricing: the Singapore experience and experiment. *Transportation Research Part E*, **33** (2), 97–106.

Pigou, A.C., 1920 *The Economics of Welfare*. London: Macmillan.

Ramjerdi, F., H. Minken and K. Østmoe, 2004, Norwegian urban tolls. In G. Santos, ed., *Road Pricing: Theory and Evidence*. Oxford: Elsevier, pp. 237–249.

Ryley, T. and N. Gjersoe, 2006, Newspaper response to the Edinburgh congestion charging proposals. *Transport Policy*, **13** (1), 66–73.

ROCOL Working Group, 2000, *Road Charging Options for London: A Technical Assessment*. London: The Stationery Office. Available at: www.gos.gov.uk/gol/transport/161558/228862/228869/.

Sandmo, A., 1975, Optimal taxation in the presence of externalities. *Swedish Journal of Economics*, **77**, 86–98.

Santos, G., 2005, Urban congestion charging: a comparison between London and Singapore. *Transport Reviews*, **25** (5), 511–534.

Santos, G., 2008, The London experience. In E. Verhoef, M. Bliemer, L. Steg and B. van Wee, eds, *Pricing in Road Transport: A Multi-Disciplinary Perspective*. Cheltenham, UK: Edward Elgar, pp. 273–292.

Santos, G. and J. Bhakar, 2006, The impact of the London congestion charging scheme on the generalised cost of car commuters to the City of London. *Transport Policy*, **13** (1), 22–33.

Santos, G., W. Li and W. Koh, 2004, Transport policies in Singapore. In G. Santos, ed., *Road Pricing: Theory and Evidence*. Oxford: Elsevier, pp. 209–235.

Santos, G. and L. Rojey, 2004, Distributional impacts of road pricing: the truth behind the myth. *Transportation*, **31** (1), 21–42.

Schuitema, G. and L. Steg, 2008, The role of revenue use in the acceptability of transport pricing policies. *Transportation Research Part F*, **11** (3), 221–231.

Schweitzer, L. and B. Taylor, 2008, Just pricing: the distributional effects of congestion pricing and sales taxes. *Transportation*, **35** (6), 797–812.

Small, K.A., 1983, The incidence of congestion tolls on urban highways. *Journal of Urban Economics*, **13** (1), 90–111.

Small, K.A., 1992, Using the revenues from congestion pricing. *Transportation*, **19** (4), 359–381.

Small, K.A. and E.T. Verhoef, 2007, *The Economics of Urban Transportation*. London: Routledge.

Small, K.A. and J. Yan, 2001, The value of 'value pricing' of roads: second-best pricing and product differentiation. *Journal of Urban Economics*, **49**, 310–336.

Steimetz, S. and D. Brownstone, 2005, Estimating commuters' value of time with noisy data: a multiple imputation approach. *Transportation Research Part A*, **39** (4), 279–293.

Stockholmsforsoket website, 2007, www.stockholmsforsoket.se/templates/page.aspx?id=10215 1318.

Sullivan, E., 2002, State route 91 value-prices express lanes: updated observations. *Transportation Research Record*, **1812**, 37–42.

Sullivan, E. and M. Burris, 2006, Benefit-cost analysis of variable pricing projects: SR-91 express lanes. *Journal of Transportation Engineering-ASCE*, **132** (3), 191–198.

Sullivan, E. and J. El Harake, 1998, California Route 91 toll lanes: impacts and other observations. *Transportation Research Record*, **1649**, 55–62.

Sumalee, A., A. May and S. Shepherd, 2005, Comparison of judgmental and optimal road pricing cordons. *Transport Policy*, **12**, 384–390.

Swedish Road Administration, 2007, Congestion tax in Stockholm. Available at: www.vv.se/templates/page3____17154.aspx.

Transport for London (TfL), 2003, Impacts monitoring programme: first annual report. Transport for London, London. Available at: www.tfl.gov.uk/roadusers/congestioncharging/6722.aspx.

Transport for London (TfL), 2005, Congestion charging Central London: impacts monitoring. Third Annual Report. Available at: www.tfl.gov.uk/roadusers/congestioncharging/6722.aspx.

Transport for London (TfL), 2007, Central London congestion charging: impacts monitoring. Fifth Annual Report, London. Available at: www.tfl.gov.uk/roadusers/congestioncharging/6722.aspx

Transport for London (TfL), 2008, Central London congestion charging: impacts monitoring. Sixth Annual Report, London. Available at: www.tfl.gov.uk/roadusers/congestioncharging/6722.aspx.

Ubbels, B. and E.T. Verhoef, 2008, Governmental competition in road charging and capacity choice. *Regional Science and Urban Economics*, **38** (2), 174–190.

US Department of Transportation, Federal Highway Administration, 2008, Value pricing pilot program. Available at: http://ops.fhwa.dot.gov/tolling_pricing/value_pricing/index.htm.

Verhoef, E.T., 2002, Second-best congestion pricing in general static transportation networks with elastic demands. *Regional Science and Urban Economics*, **32**, 281–310.

Verhoef, E.T., P. Nijkamp and P. Rietveld, 1995, Second-best regulation of road transport externalities. *Journal of Transport Economics and Policy*, **29**, 147–167.

Verhoef, E.T., P. Nijkamp and P. Rietveld, 1996, Second-best congestion pricing: the case of an untolled alternative. *Journal of Urban Economics*, **40**, 279–302.

Verhoef, E.T. and K.A. Small, 2004, Product differentiation on roads: constrained congestion pricing with heterogeneous users. *Journal of Transport Economics and Policy*, **38**, 127–156.

Vickrey, W., 1969, Congestion theory and transport investment. *American Economic Review,* **59**, 251–261.

Wardman, M., 2001, A review of British evidence on time and service quality valuations. *Transportation Research Part E*, **37** (2–3), 107–128.

Wheaton, W.C., 1978, Price-induced distortions in urban highway investment. *Bell Journal of Economics*, **9**, 622–632.

Willoughby, C., 2000, Singapore's experience in managing motorization and its relevance to other countries. Discussion Paper TWU-43, TWU Series, The World Bank. Available at: www.worldbank.org/transport/publicat/twu_43.pdf.

Wilson, J.D., 1983, Optimal road capacity in the presence of unpriced congestion. *Journal of Urban Economics*, **13**, 337–357.

Yan, J., K. Small and E. Sullivan, 2002, Choice models of route, occupancy, and time of day with value-prices tolls. *Transportation Research Record*, **1812**, 69–77.

24 The economics of information in transport
Piet Rietveld

INTRODUCTION

Economic analyses of travel behavior are usually based on the assumption that travelers are well-informed about the options they have. In reality the situation may be rather different. Travelers may not know the complete set of alternatives available to them. Another possibility is that travelers are not well-informed about particular features of travel alternatives. Much of the literature focuses on uncertainty on travel times (Chorus, 2007). One possibility is that travelers have biased information on travel times of some alternatives. Another possibility is that the realizations of travel times with transport alternatives are variable due to factors such as incidents or variations in weather conditions. In that case, travelers do not know beforehand what will be the actual travel times of the choices they are considering.

The various cases of incomplete information can be shown to have potentially important implications for the distinct domains of travel behavior such as whether or not to make a trip, modal choice, the timing of a trip or the choice of the route. Lack of information about choice alternatives naturally affects choice probabilities as does biased information about travel times. An example of a systematic gap between perceived and actual travel times is provided by Exel and Rietveld (2009b) who find for a large sample of car travelers that perceptions of public transport travel time exceed objective values by on average 40–50 percent. Analysis of modal choice on the basis of actual behavior (revealed preference) under the assumption that perceived travel times of non-chosen alternatives are equal to objective values would then lead to biased estimates of the underlying utility function.

Variability in the availability and performance of travel alternatives also has important implications for travel behavior. People may dislike uncertainty and this would then affect their choices even when they are well informed on the mean values of the travel alternatives.[1] This leads to issues such as how information provision affects traveler behavior. Further, variability of realizations may induce efforts of information acquisition where costs and benefits of information have to be traded-off. One of the issues is that effects have to be considered at the level of individual travelers and at the system level.

During the last decade, large efforts have been made to increase the availability of information to travelers by means of advanced traveler information systems (ATIS). That ATIS will on average lead to a reduction of travel times is confirmed in a review of the time-saving benefits of the introduction of ATIS on the functioning of road transport systems carried out by Levinson (2003). In a survey of some ten model based studies, the median level of the decrease in overall travel time of all road users is about 7 percent, with some very high outcomes (up to 50 percent), implying that there is substantial variation among studies. Important factors that determine the outcome are the degree of congestion in the network as well as the structure of the network, the specification of incidents in the model and the share of the road users that are equipped with ATIS. From the studies surveyed it appears that as congestion levels increase also the potential gains of ATIS will increase, a point also made by Yang et al. (2003).[2]

In this chapter, I will review some economic aspects of information in transport markets. Main questions addressed are: which factors explain search strategies adopted by travelers facing uncertainty on outcomes of their choices? How do information acquisition strategies determine the use of networks, and what is the resulting demand for information in transport markets? First, I will discuss information acquisition from an economics perspective by characterizing costs and benefits of information, leading to the formulation of optimal strategies to acquire information. This will be done in the context of search strategies leading to sequential information acquisition. I then discuss the broader consequences of information acquisition on the functioning of transport networks. In congested networks, when travelers change their behavior on the basis of information they obtain, this will have consequences not only for their own travel times, but also those of other travelers. This leads to interesting positive (and possibly negative) spillovers having important policy implications. The following section takes the further step of examining within the network model a traveler's choice whether to adopt an ATIS so that the demand function for information can be derived. Some specific themes are then discussed before concluding.

INFORMATION ACQUISITION, A SEARCH THEORETIC PERSPECTIVE[3]

Consider a traveler who lacks information on some travel alternatives. This may be a case of a person who has changed residence and job, and who is considering the best route for his commute, but also the choice between various holiday destinations can be studied by this approach. In the present section, we focus on individual choices and ignore feedbacks on the overall functioning of transport systems (this will be the subject of the following section). Another difference is that in the next section the performance of travel alternatives is inherently uncertain, whereas these uncertainties are ignored here.

There are essentially three strategies available to deal with the lack of information:

1. *Search* for information on the uncertain alternatives and then select the best alternative on which information is available.
2. *Trial and error:* Experience one or more of the uncertain alternatives by selecting them. This provides information on the best alternative to be chosen amongst those tested, in subsequent choice situations.
3. *Skip* uncertain alternatives: choose an alternative in the choice set that is certain.

The *information search* option involves both costs and benefits. Among the costs are the time and cognitive effort needed to get the information. In addition, information may cost money. The *trial and error* option just means that travelers obtain information by trying alternatives;[4] after the search phase they will then adopt the best performing alternative they happened to find. As we will see, the main difference between information search and trial and error lies on the cost side. In the case of search, travelers incur costs in terms of pre-trip efforts, in the case of trial and error the costs relate to the loss in utility from choosing an alternative at random instead of choosing the best known alternative. The *skip* option means that uncertain options are not chosen or explored and that an alternative is chosen that is not plagued by uncertainty, for example 'staying at home'. This option is important because it allows for elastic demand for transport. The extent of elasticity depends on how broadly the choice set is defined: it may include travel alternatives in terms of route, mode, timing or destination. In that case, the lack of information does not lead to a skipped trip, but when an outside alternative such as staying at home is part of the choice set, the information context becomes an important determinant of elastic demand. A traveler who lacks information and incurs high information acquisition costs is likely to forego activities.

Costs and Benefits of Information Search

What factors influence the choice between the three alternatives to deal with uncertainty, and in particular the attractiveness of the information search option? Nelson (1970) sketches a search context where the consumer (traveler) is uncertain about the exact features of alternatives, but he has information on the probability distribution of the utility of the choice options. The consumer then sequentially searches for information about alternatives. Information search involves costs and benefits. When considering a pre-trip context, the costs of information search consist of the time spent on it, the search efforts including the cognitive efforts (Grotenhuis et al., 2007), and the price:

$$MC^s = MC^s(\text{pre} - \text{trip search time, efforts, price}). \tag{24.1}$$

Note, that search efforts are determined among other factors by the user-friendliness of the ATIS or alternative information search channels. Having described the costs of information acquisition we now consider the benefits. As the consumer inspects more alternatives the utility of the best alternative on which information is available will gradually increase. The optimal stopping rule is to continue searching until the marginal cost of information search is equal to the marginal expected return for an additional search (MR) (see Nelson, 1970). The latter is equal to the difference between the expected present value of the utility of the best alternative in a given number of searches (j) minus the expected value of this utility with one search less ($j - 1$):

$$MR_j = E(B_j) - E(B_{j-1}), \tag{24.2}$$

where $E(B_j)$ is the expected present value of the best of j randomly chosen options.[5] In order to be able to determine $E(B_j)$, information is needed on the probability density of all possible alternatives. Expected values of the best alternative can be computed by means of order statistics approaches (Mood et al., 1974).[6]

Costs and Benefits of Trial and Error

Next we consider the strategy of trial and error: just experience an arbitrary chosen travel alternative and observe its utility. The marginal returns of additional alternatives tried is again equal to the marginal returns *MR* defined above. As already indicated above, the difference between information search and trial and error is on the cost side. In the case of search, travelers experience costs in terms of pre-trip efforts, whereas in the case of trial and error the costs relate to the loss in utility from not choosing the best known alternative, but rather trying another alternative in the hope that this one may be even better. Hence the expected marginal costs incurred by trying an additional alternative *j*, MC_j^t, are equal to:

$$MC_j^t = E(B_{j-1}) - u, \tag{24.3}$$

where *u* is the expected benefit, being equal to the mean of the utility density function. Since we assume the distribution of utilities of alternatives to be known, also its mean value *u* is known. Note also that as the number of tested alternatives increases, $E(B_j)$ increases, so that the marginal costs of testing a new travel alternative increase: with each additional trial the gap between $E(B_j)$ and u becomes wider.

In both cases of information search and experience, the optimal number of cases to be considered can be determined once the parameters in terms of time preference, standard deviation and so forth are known. One of the relevant results is that *ceteris paribus* for both strategies, as the frequency of choice increases, the number of alternatives to be inspected increases (Nelson, 1970). Thus, a daily decision like the route choice in the commuting trip is worth a larger number of alternatives to be explored than a trip that is only made once.[7] However, it may well be that trips that are rarely made also involve larger potential costs and benefits. For example, a long distance holiday trip may involve large resources in terms of time and money, leading to high marginal benefits of additional information search.

Reference Alternative: Skipping Uncertain Alternatives

The third choice strategy is to ignore the uncertain alternatives and just stick to the best alternative among the certain ones, including the alternative of not making the trip.

Comparison of Strategies

The choice between the three strategies can be made by comparing the optimal level of the net benefits of the information search strategy (based on the optimal number of alternatives inspected), the optimal outcome of the trial and error strategy, obtained in a similar way, and that of the skip strategy. Figure 24.1 illustrates the choice of information search strategy when there are many alternatives, for example, the joint time and route choice in an urban commuting trip. The expected benefits curve *EB* is applicable for both information acquisition strategies: search and trial and error. The *EB* curve is increasing, but at a decreasing rate: as information is available on more and more alternatives the probability that an additional alternative is found that implies a substantial improvement is becoming smaller and smaller. The trial and error expected cost curve is convex as can be explained by the MC_j^t formula given above: with an increasing number of alternatives already tried, the loss of not using the best known alternative (found in the preceding search) is increasing. In this figure, we assume that information search costs by

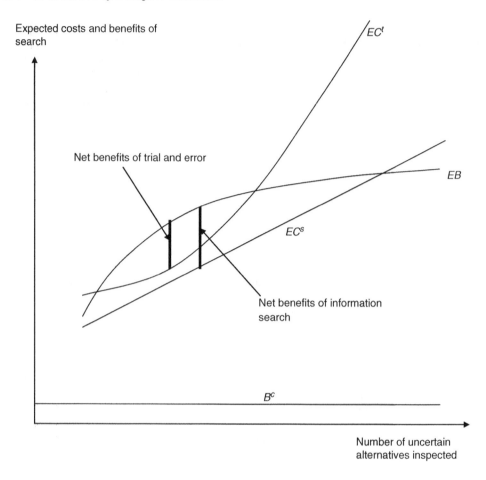

Expected costs and benefits of
search

EC^t

Net benefits of trial and error

EB

EC^s

Net benefits of information
search

B^c

Number of uncertain
alternatives inspected

Notes:
EB: Expected benefits given a set of alternatives inspected
EC^t: Expected costs of trial and error
EC^s: Expected costs of search
B^c: Benefits of choosing best certain alternative

Figure 24.1   Choice of information acquisition strategy

means of ATIS are characterized by a fixed cost to get access to an information system
and a variable cost related to getting information on each alternative. This figure has
been drawn such that ATIS is the optimal strategy: maximum net benefits are obtained
for the information search strategy. Note further that with the given cost structures the
optimal number of alternatives inspected in the search strategy is larger than in the trial
and error strategy. In this example the search strategy dominates the strategy of skipping
uncertain alternatives.

Comparative statics can be applied to Figure 24.1 to analyze the effects of changes
in cost parameters. From a technological viewpoint, it is clear that the introduction of

ATIS has reduced the slope of the information search cost curve. This has two effects: it leads to an increase in the optimal number of alternatives to be inspected, and it increases the probability that information search is indeed the optimal strategy. It brings travelers in their final choice of a travel alternative closer to the best possible one and it reduces the probability that trips are skipped due to uncertainty problems.

Since the search approach implies that travelers trade off the marginal costs and benefits of further search, they will usually stop searching before the whole choice set has been explored. Hence, there is no guarantee that travelers will choose the best alternative. This result coincides with that of bounded rationality and satisficing approaches (Chorus, 2007). The common element of the two is the role played by the cost of information. Note, however, that the background of both approaches is different, since search theory remains entirely within the domain of economics, which is not the case with the other approaches.

A special case occurs when the information acquisition takes place in the context of a trip that is only made once. In such a case the information obtained cannot be used another time, an example being a holiday trip to a certain destination. Then the benefits related to the trip are large, and also variations between alternatives will probably be large. An uninformed trial and error based choice will then by definition lead to a choice with the average utility level within the choice set. In this context marginal costs of information search will probably be low compared with the benefits to be obtained, so that search will be the best strategy. The opposite occurs with a trip where the marginal gains of information are relatively small. For example, it may take a few minutes to get the exact time table of a metro service. There will be a tendency that when frequency is high (say eight trains per hour), the benefits of search leading to shorter waiting time at platforms do not outweigh the search effort on departure times, and travelers tend to go to such metro stops without consulting time tables implying that they arrive randomly at the platforms (Danas, 1980; Tirachini et al., 2008). Fosgerau (2009) gives a thorough analysis of the decision whether or not to plan (search for information) or use the trial and error strategy. In addition to service frequency another relevant factor would be the reliability of a service: when the service is very unreliable, this is another reason to ignore officially published timetables. These examples show that although the choice contexts can be very different (time of departure versus destination choice), the same trade-offs between costs and benefits of information search strategies apply.

Who Benefits from Search?

Of particular interest is the question which types of travelers will be most inclined to make use of ATIS as an information acquisition strategy. Chorus (2007) indicates that in terms of socio-economic features, well educated, high income travelers and professionals are among the most intensive users of ATIS. This is indeed a plausible result in the context of Figure 24.1. The slopes of the *EB*, EC^t and EC^s curves are proportional to the value of time (VOT), implying that the optimal number of searches does not vary with income. But there are two reasons why the search alternative is more likely to be preferred when income increases. First, the fixed part of the EC^s curve will be less than proportional to the value of time, thus leading to a higher probability that with a high

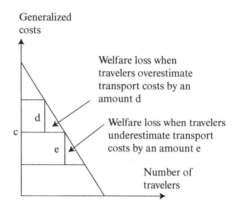

Figure 24.2   Welfare losses due to overestimation or underestimation of transport costs

VOT, search will have the largest positive gap between the *EB* and *EC* curves in Figure 24.1. Second, it improves its performance compared with the outside alternative (B^c does not change).

In Figure 24.2 we present another dimension of the benefits of being informed. We focus on a heterogeneous group of travelers who consider a potential trip to be made only once. The inverse demand curve in Figure 24.2 indicates the variety in the willingness to pay for this trip in terms of generalized costs. Let the actual generalized costs be *c*. Travelers base their decision on their perception of generalized costs. There are clear indications in the literature that travelers have biased and in general inflated estimates of the costs of travel alternatives they do not often choose (see for example Exel and Rietveld (2009a) for car user perceptions of public transport travel times). Consider travelers that overestimate the generalized costs by an amount of *d*. Travelers with willingness to pay between *c* and *c* + *d* then will not make the trip even though they would experience positive net benefits. Applying the rule of half then leads to a welfare loss related to the biased perception as indicated in Figure 24.2.

Underestimation of costs can be treated in a similar way. Suppose travelers underestimate the generalized costs by an amount *e* (see Figure 24.2). Those travelers with willingness to pay between *c* – *e* and *c* who make the trip would regret what they did because they end up with negative net benefits. We conclude that provision of information is beneficial for passengers who have a willingness to pay that is close to the generalized costs, and that have incomplete or biased knowledge on these costs.

On the other hand, passengers with a willingness to pay for the trip that is either much higher or much lower than the actual costs will not benefit from information since their decision will not be affected by it. These findings will be further explored and refined in the next section.

Extensions of Base Sequential Search Model

Transport alternatives have some special features compared with other goods and services delivered that have important implications for information acquisition strategies. These are:

Dependence

Alternative routes are often overlapping for parts of the total routes. This means that information acquisition for one trip will also yield useful information – though incomplete – for alternative routes. This aspect was ignored in the analysis above.[8] Note that it holds for both information acquisition strategies. It means that the choice of additional alternatives to be inspected will be guided by information in related alternatives, implying that fewer alternatives need to be inspected in the choice process.[9]

Variation in the performance of alternatives

Incidents may lead to variability in the performance of a certain travel alternative. In that case the trial and error strategy implies the repeated choice of a certain alternative to acquire information on the distribution of its possible outcomes. This case is addressed by Chancelier et al. (2007) in the context of risk averse drivers who can choose between a route with a fixed outcome and one with an unknown distribution of outcomes. The expected value of the 'random' route is better than that of the 'safe' route. They find that drivers that are close to risk neutral will select the random route and stick to it. The opposite applies to drivers who are strongly risk averse: they are not interested in acquiring information on the distribution of the random route and will stick to the safe one. The most interesting case concerns the middle group that will start the trial and error process by experiencing the random route and then may shift to the safe route depending on the exact degree of risk aversion. A related result will be discussed later in the context of the demand for information.

Discrepancy between official information and actual quality of travel alternatives

The actual duration of trips may be longer than that of the official time table or of free-flow travel time. Information derived from ATIS like travel planners for public transport do not report about this gap, which implies that the trial and error strategy may yield information that is closer to the reality than information search strategy. This would also imply that the benefit curves of trial and error and of information search are no longer identical.

Impacts on performance of alternatives

A third point that deserves further attention is that in the case of congested networks, information search strategies have an impact on the performance of networks. This case is of special interest and will be discussed in the next section.

FEEDBACK EFFECTS OF INFORMATION ON CONGESTION

We now add an ingredient that was missing in the section above: information acquisition has a feedback on congestion levels on roads so that both informed and non-informed road users will be affected. In order to study this case we use a very simple network: a one link network with non-recurrent congestion and elastic demand (for details see Emmerink et al., 1996). After having discussed the results for this simple network, we will discuss more complex networks and other complications. Consider a congested link that can be in two states: high capacity H and low capacity L. Low capacity is the capacity after an incident or a lane closure. We use a static model of congestion. The probability of a low capacity is denoted as p. Pre-trip information is available to a certain group of I (informed) travelers of given size N_I. When the informed travelers prepare for a trip, they know for sure in which of the two states (H versus L) the link will be. Another group of travelers is non-informed (NI). They just know the probability, p, of the low capacity condition. The demand function for transport expresses willingness to pay for the trip, where we assume heterogeneity among road users similar to the case of Figure 24.2. We assume that the Wardrop conditions for network equilibrium will apply (Small and Verhoef, 2007). This means that an informed road user will use the network when private benefits are at least equal to the actual private generalized costs for the prevailing state. An uninformed road user follows a similar strategy, but based on the expected generalized costs.

The above Wardrop approach leads to three equilibrium conditions: two for informed road users and one for non-informed road users. The conditions are interlinked, since the two groups make use of the same network.

The first condition is that in the high capacity case H the marginal road user's willingness to pay within the group of informed road users D_I is equal to the generalized costs C^H he experiences:

$$D_I(Q_I^H) = C^H(Q_I^H + Q_{NI}),\qquad(24.4)$$

where Q_I^H denotes the number of informed travelers that uses the link under the high capacity conditions, and Q_{NI} denotes the non-informed travelers. Clearly, the generalized costs under the high capacity conditions depend on the sum of both informed and non-informed travelers. For the low capacity case L the Wardrop condition for the informed road users can be formulated in a similar way:

$$D_I(Q_I^L) = C^L(Q_I^L + Q_{NI}),\qquad(24.5)$$

Since non-informed road users do not know the actual costs they will experience, they base their decision whether or not to travel on the expected costs, being the mean costs resulting from the high and low capacity costs taking into account the respective probabilities $1 - p$ and p. Hence the Wardrop user equilibrium condition in their case is:

$$D_{NI}(Q_{NI}) = (1 - p).C^H(Q_I^H + Q_{NI}) + p.C^L(Q_I^L + Q_{NI}).\qquad(24.6)$$

When the inverse demand functions D_I and D_{NI} are known, as well as the congestion cost functions C^H and C^L plus their respective probabilities, the resulting equilibrium values Q_I^H, Q_I^L and Q_{NI}, can be derived. Figure 24.3 gives a graphical illustration of the model under the assumption that demand and cost functions are linear.[10]

In the left hand panel, the non-informed road users equate their willingness to pay and expected marginal link travel costs, considering the effects of the behavior of the informed road users on their expected travel costs. They base their decision on the expected number of informed drivers: $E(Q_I) = (1 - p).Q_I^H + p.Q_I^L$. Similarly, in the right hand panel, the equilibrium conditions are given, leading to the number of informed road users that make use of the link under H and L capacity conditions, and where the number of uninformed road

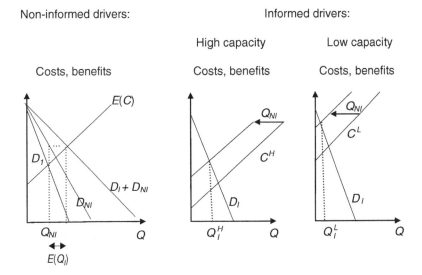

Figure 24.3   Network equilibrium with informed and non-informed road users

users is also accounted for as can be seen from the shift in the cost curve implying higher trip costs related to the volume of uninformed road users using the road.

The impact of the information provision can be determined by comparing the present case with that where there are no uninformed road users. The model results (details can be found in Emmerink et al., 1996) indicate that road use becomes more selective due to the responses of informed road users: under high capacity conditions it increases, while under low capacity conditions it decreases. The balance of the two effects is positive: more travelers will make use of the road. Also, it is interesting to know that the provision of information will lead to an increase of both informed and uninformed travelers. The second result reveals a positive welfare spillover of the information provided to informed travelers. The information provision will induce informed road users not to use the link in the low capacity condition and this means that there is more room for uninformed road users under this condition. Another important result is that while information provision leads to an increase of overall road use, it reduces at the same time the expected link travel costs. This is a strong sign that provision of information is welfare enhancing in this context. It can even be shown that in this context *all* road users benefit from the information provision, no matter whether they belong to the informed or the uninformed group. The degree to which they benefit will vary, however. The benefits of the informed road users tend to be higher than those of the non-informed road users. The nature of the benefits of the non-informed road users is entirely external: they are induced by the behavioral adjustments of the informed road users. For the informed road users, the benefits are highest among those road users that will adjust their driving behavior due to the information provision. Note that this result is similar to the result found above in the context of information provision to correct for wrong cost perceptions.

Finally, we consider the impact of the share of informed road users on the welfare gains. In this model, there is a monotone increasing relationship between the share of

Table 24.1 Combinations of information provision and congestion charging

	Information provision: no	Information provision: yes
Congestion charging: no	1	2
Congestion charging: yes	3	4

informed road users and welfare gains. However, the increase takes place at a decreasing rate, implying that the marginal welfare gains are considerably higher for the first 10 percent of the road users who receive information compared with the last 10 percent. This suggests that where the marginal cost of information provision is positive, the optimum level of information provision is probably not that 100 percent of the road users will have access to it. The point is that there is a possibility that information provision will lead to overreaction of road users, an issue addressed later in this section.

It is important to note that the information provision usually brings the system closer to its optimum, but that the optimum itself cannot be reached. There remains a gap between the user equilibrium with full availability of information and the system optimum. This is illustrated in Table 24.1, where the various combinations of information provision and congestion charging are outlined. In this section we only considered cases 1 and 2. The system optimum (case 4) can be reached via the combination of information provision and congestion charging at its optimal level. Thus, when the aim is to achieve the system optimum, congestion pricing cannot be dropped. In situations where congestion pricing is not feasible, information provision strategies can help in getting closer to the welfare maximum. Note that it matters for the optimal congestion charge whether information is provided. When in this model all drivers are non-informed, the optimal charge would be uniform, independent of whether the high or the low capacity regime applies.[11] When some drivers would be informed, however, the optimal congestion charge would be different in both regimes.

Given the positive externalities that non-informed drivers experience there might be a case for subsidies to stimulate the supply, or use, of information provision. This will be investigated in more detail in the next section.

Broader Review of Literature

The results presented here depend on a number of specific features of the model such as network structure, and specific cost and demand parameters. We will briefly review to what extent results depend on these features. The one-link network structure may be extended to larger networks. Most of the results obtained here will also apply in the context of more general networks. However, the result that *all* road users benefit from information supply does not hold true in more general network structures. In particular, when information supply on a certain link leads to the situation that informed road users would shift to another congested link that is employed by road users with another combination of origin and destination, welfare in the latter group may be negatively affected (Emmerink et al., 1997). Another extension of the model discussed above concerns the inclusion of risk aversion. De Palma and Picard (2005) and de Palma et al. (2011) discuss the case where road users differ in their risk aversion parameter. Equilibrium travel time in the system then depends on the distribution of this parameter. They arrive at a similar result as Emmerink et al. (1997): information provision may be welfare reducing for some road users when it induces changes in travel behavior that aggravate congestion in particular parts of the network.

The result that *aggregate* welfare increases when more road users have access to better information is also found in a paper by Arnott et al. (1996) which addresses a static model of congestion based on the bottleneck model using isoelastic demand and user costs functions. However, there is also a line of literature that underlines that this result does not necessarily hold under more general settings. Schelling (1978) already hinted at the possibility of overreaction to information leading to a decrease in overall system performance when too many actors have access to information. Similar results were found among others by Ben-Akiva et al. (1991) and Emmerink et al. (1995), due to the phenomenon of concentration. These results are obtained in modeling contexts that do not entirely rely on equilibrium contexts with fully rational road users (see also Mahmassani and Liu, 1991).

A major contribution to this theme was provided by Arnott et al. (1999) in a paper based on a dynamic bottleneck model for congestion. Commuters decide on whether and when to depart for work taking into account generalized commuting costs, including queueing costs before passing the bottleneck and scheduling costs related to arriving early or late at work. The uncertainty in the model relates to the capacity of the bottleneck which depends on weather conditions and other factors. Arnott et al. (1999) base their analysis on constant elasticity demand and schedule delay cost functions. They distinguish three information regimes: zero information, perfect information and imperfect information. They show that their earlier result with a static model (Arnott et al., 1996) is not robust: in the dynamic model context it is possible that – in the absence of congestion pricing – a refinement of information from zero information to imperfect information has adverse effects on aggregate welfare.

DEMAND FOR INFORMATION

An important distinction in the benefits of information provision to road users is the one between decision-making benefits and travel-cost benefits. Decision-making benefits accrue to road users that change their behavior based on information provision, by choosing another route, or deciding on whether or not they will travel. Travel-cost benefits accrue to all road users, irrespective of whether the road user is informed himself. It is clear that without decision-making benefits there cannot be travel-cost benefits.[12]

When studying the demand for information, decision making benefits are the key element, since it is decision-making benefits that drive the benefits of information. When we adopt the model of the preceding section several groups of road users can be distinguished according to their benefits of road use (see Table 24.2).

Table 24.2 shows that there are two groups of road users that are affected by information in their decisions: segments 2 and 3. Segment 2 concerns road users that without information would always use the link, whereas when they are provided with information would only use it when it is in its high capacity state.

Segment 3 represents the road users that without information would never use the

Table 24.2   Relationship between trip benefits and demand for information

Road use benefits: Very high (1) to very low (4)	Type of decision as non-informed road user	Type of decision as informed road user	Part of information demand market?
1	Will always use the link	Will always use the link	No
2	Will always use the link	Will only use the link in high capacity state	Yes
3	Will never use the link	Will only use the link in high capacity state	Yes
4	Will never use the link	Will never use the link	No

link, whereas when they are provided with information would only use it in the high-capacity state. Car drivers in segments 1 and 4 would not change their behavior on the basis of information. Hence the potential market for travel information consists of segments 2 and 3 only. Of course, the size of this market for information depends on the parameters of the demand function for transport, the probability of incidents and the parameters of the cost function.

Segments 2 and 3 of the range of travel benefits imply positive decision-making benefits. In these segments there will be a positive demand for information when the price of information – denoted as π – would be zero. For positive values of π the group of road users with a potential interest in trip making would shrink. Let us consider road users in segment 2. When they have information that the L state will prevail, this group of road users will not make the trip, whereas when they are not informed they will still make the trip. When state L prevails, the net benefits of being informed for this group are therefore:

$$C^L(Q) - D(Q).$$ (24.7)

Thus, for the marginal traveler Q^L_{EN} (EN refers to the model feature that demand for information is endogenous) in segment 2 we have

$$p[C^L(Q^L_{EN}) - D(Q^L_{EN})] = \pi.$$ (24.8)

For market segment 3, the decision-making issue for the road users is that with information they will use the link in the high capacity state, whereas without information they will not make the trip. Hence they compare the benefits of the trip with the costs in the high capacity state. The equilibrium condition for travelers in segment 3 therefore reads:

$$(1 - p).[D(Q^H_{EN}) - C^H(Q^H_{EN})] = \pi.$$ (24.9)

Combining these two segments, we find that the total number of road users who are prepared to pay π for information equals $Q^H_{EN}(\pi) - Q^L_{EN}(\pi)$, which can be written as a function of the cost and demand parameters, leading to a downward sloping inverse demand function for transport information. This means that we arrive at an interesting parallel between the demand for transport and the demand for transport information: they share the property that they have the nature of *derived demand* (Quinet and Vickerman, 2004). Just as the demand for transport depends entirely on the parameters of the underlying demand and supply functions for the goods and services to be consumed, the demand for travel information depends entirely on the demand and cost parameters of the underlying transport system. De Palma et al. (2009) enrich this result by incorporating risk aversion as one of the relevant parameters. It is road users with intermediate levels of risk aversion who may benefit most from information provision: road users with low risk aversion will just take the route with the highest variation, and road users with high risk will do the opposite. For the intermediate group, the information is useful to determine which of the routes is best.

An important question concerns the optimal price of information π. The transport market studied here is characterized by negative congestion externalities. When these are not corrected by means of congestion pricing, positive information externalities will occur. The benefits of information acquisition will not only be experienced by the informed road users, but also by the non-informed ones as already shown above. Hence one may expect that standard marginal cost pricing will not lead to a welfare optimum. Indeed, Zhang and Verhoef (2006) find that when externalities prevail the optimal price of information may even be negative, which would provide a case for a subsidy on information provision. Empirical research of Zhang and Levinson (2008) indicates that the maximum willingness to pay for this type of information is rather low (up to $ 1 per trip). One of the reasons for the low valuation is that road users may distrust the accuracy and timeliness of information.

FURTHER ISSUES

In the stylized models discussed above we focused on some essentials for the economics of information on transport. In this section, we briefly discuss a few issues that are important and could lead to refinements in the models mentioned above.

Multiplicity of Information Search Channels

Like in all domains of information acquisition, traffic information can be obtained via various channels. Some of the channels are low-tech and involve information exchange on traffic conditions within social networks, and people directly observing incident queues. Also radio reports play an important role in information acquisition. Other channels involve higher tech components such as route planners that are available for free everywhere on the internet.[13] DRIPs (Dynamic Route Information Panels) are placed at congested places in networks to inform road users on conditions on alternative routes. Automatic route guidance equipment is gradually becoming standard in many countries. Among the current ATIS developments are the provision of dynamic information via automatic route guidance services or cell phones. Since the information from these various sources are close substitutes, the value added to the consumer of *additional* services may be relatively small. In terms of prices, a good number of information channels are just available for free. These include dynamic information obtained via DRIPs and via the radio. As a consequence, the willingness to pay for new ATIS services may be smaller than is sometimes thought (see also Emmerink, 1998). Note also that the rapidly developing use of automatic route guidance equipment in cars has led to relatively low prices to install it, and marginal costs are zero. In this competitive setting, dynamic route information must be of high quality in terms of reliability, customer orientation and timeliness before road users will be prepared to pay for it.

Information Availability and Comfort

The above analyses focus on the use of information in specific choice contexts. One of the outcomes (see Table 24.2) was that depending on one's willingness to pay for a trip to a certain destination, people will be prepared to pay for information in order to avoid making the wrong decisions in terms of trip generation or route choice. There is also another possible view on the demand for information. Travelers may just feel uncomfortable in situations where the consequences of their choices are uncertain (Grotenhuis et al., 2007). They want to know what is going on in the network, even when it would not help them to make better decisions. This means that even travelers who do not experience decision-making benefits as defined in the previous section may have a positive willingness to pay for information. This in turn implies that there is also a market for information provision to improve the general comfort level, possibly in the form of comfort enhancing equipment in vehicles, or subscriptions to services that provide information on incidents, or combinations of both.

Compliance

Compliance is an important theme when studying traffic information systems. Emmerink (1998) and Yin and Yang (2003) indicate that there is a large variation in compliance rates among road users. Many road users just ignore traffic information because they think it may not be sufficiently reliable, it may be outdated, or since they do not want to change their original travel plan and are afraid that changing it may lead to unexpected surprises. They may also ignore information since they expect that this information would lead to an overreaction by other road users so that the available route alternatives would become too crowded. In addition, road users may not entirely trust the traffic information since they are afraid the information is given with the aim of achieving the system optimum (aiming at the maximization of total surplus) implying that their individual interest might be sacrificed for the overall public benefit.

Integration of Transport Modes

Progress in ATIS has been substantial during the last decades, but is has resulted in rather fragmented services. The information provider is usually linked to a particular transport mode such as road, rail or bus. And even within modes, often a certain limitation can be observed in the information provided. For example, information on congestion on national roads is usually not easily connected to information on urban roads. And, within public transport, route planners are sometimes confined to a particular transport company, or a particular mode. This lack of integrated information services on transport networks is a clear manifestation of a lack of integration in a broader sense. These signs are visible both within the public sector where there are strong barriers against horizontal and vertical integration, and the private sector where various companies find it difficult to coordinate their activities. However, there are signs in some countries that gradually the institutional barriers against integration are getting lower. This would be an important step towards truly integrated transport systems (for example, road use by car, parking facilities, train, metro), where clients are not hindered by the lack of integration between such facilities in the making of their travel plans.

Uncertainty on Destination Quality

In the present chapter, we focus on uncertainty about travel costs as a driver in the demand for information. There is of course also another source of uncertainty that is relevant here: uncertainty about the quality of the destination of a trip. This includes uncertainty about destinations in the case of trips purposes such as holiday trips, shopping and various types of recreational visits. Here, too, there is the issue of choosing information acquisition strategies like search versus trial and error. The benefits of visiting trips destinations further away can be analyzed in a way similar to the *EB* curve for transport alternatives sketched in Figure 24.1 (see Rietveld and Woudenberg, 2003). Here we observe the emergence of advanced information services that are provided by individual suppliers to increase their visibility towards customers and information services on the overall supply within a certain market. Similar to what we observed when we examined the search theoretic perspective, this may be expected to lead to shift from trial and error to information search by means of advanced information technologies services, having implications for travel behavior, in particular, destination choice.

CONCLUSION

Incomplete information on travel alternatives leads to travel behavior that is not optimal since travelers will not realize some of the better alternatives. Hence, information acquisition has potential welfare benefits, of course depending on the cost of information. We analyzed the costs and benefits of two main ways of information acquisition: information search – for example by means of ATIS – and trial and error. In the case of search, the costs relate to pre-trip efforts, whereas in the case of trial and error the costs are incurred while making a trip. They relate to the loss in utility from not choosing the best known alternative, but rather trying another alternative in the hope that this one may even be better. Based on the analysis of costs and benefits of both search alternatives, our analysis leads to the conclusion that the share of ATIS as an information acquisition mode will increase, although there will remain situations where trial and error is the better strategy.

The demand for information can be derived as a function of the parameters of demand and costs functions of transport, hence demonstrating the nature of the demand for information as a derived demand. In the case of car use in congested networks, ATIS not only provides benefits to the individual traveler, but also induces feedback on travel times in such a way that non-informed travelers are affected. In most network structures, these effects on other road users are beneficial. For example Levinson (2003) reports some 7 percent as the median decrease in travel times in a series of studies. However, as we have demonstrated, there are cases where the provision of information leads to aggravation of congestion in a particular way, negatively affecting groups of drivers. There might even be situations where provision of information has adverse effects on aggregate welfare. Such adverse effects of information provision can be prevented when congestion pricing is adopted.

We conclude that, although negative welfare effects of information provision cannot be ruled out, in the majority of the cases one may expect information provision to be welfare enhancing, not only for informed travelers, but also for non-informed ones. This would imply the existence of positive externalities in the information market, which makes a case for public supply of such information (such as information panels) or subsidies to users or private providers of information services.

NOTES

1. Also the case of a biased perception of the *variation* in travel times may affect behavior.
2. These results describe general tendencies. In particular cases exceptions may occur. In the third section, which deals with feedback effects of information on congestion we will note that improving information supply does not invariably improve the performance of transport systems.
3. This section bears some relationship with the chapter by Chorus and Timmermans on Personal Intelligent Travel Assistants. The common element of both is the use of utility concepts to compare situations with and without information. The two approaches differ in that Chorus and Timmermans address a one-shot learning context, whereas I consider sequential search strategies. Another difference is that Chorus and Timmermans focus on uncertainty resulting from day-to-day variability in a network, whereas my focus in the present section is on uncertainty resulting from lack of information on travel alternatives that do not necessarily experience day-to-day variations in their quality.
4. Travelers may also adopt search heuristics implying non-arbitrary trials. This will be briefly discussed later in this section.
5. Note that we use an ex-ante perspective here to keep the analysis manageable. $E(B_{j-1})$ represents the expected utility of $j-1$ draws at the start of the information search. Actual information search will lead to realizations B_{j-1} that will be higher or lower than $E(B_{j-1})$, which may have an effect on the length of the search process.
6. In some cases alternatives may not be independent (for example in route choice). This can typically be modeled by nested logit models. In the present context of information acquisition this means getting information on one particular alternative has additional information benefits for related alternatives. This will be shortly discussed at the end of this section.
7. If the trip really is made only once, there is no opportunity to improve on the choice by trial and error as the term is used in the conventional sense. But also in this context it may still be an optimal strategy, as we will see below.
8. Editor's note: The implications of correlations between alternatives are discussed by Walker and Ben-Akiva in their chapter on discrete choice models.
9. Explicit modeling of this would substantially complicate the analysis. The forms of the various functions in Figure 24.1 will not change, but their precise locations certainly will. Note that this issue is related to the theme of search heuristics. Clever search strategies would imply that such interdependences are taken into account in the choice of alternatives to be explored.
10. Linearity of cost functions is needed for graphical illustration. Otherwise the expected cost function shown in the left-hand panel of Figure 24.3 does not solely depend on $E(Q_l)$, but also on the exact values of Q_l^H and Q_l^L.
11. This reasoning is based on the implicit assumption that drivers do not know the day-specific state or day-specific charge for the link before making decisions. If they did know the day-specific charge – but not the day specific state – before making decisions, a differentiated charge would of course make sense.
12. An exception occurs in the case of aversion to uncertainty, discussed in the penultimate section on further issues.
13. Editor's note: See also the chapter by Chorus and Timmermans on Personal Intelligent Travel Assistants.

REFERENCES

Arnott, R., A. de Palma and R. Lindsey, 1996, Information and usage of free-access congestible facilities with stochastic capacity and demand. *International Economic Review*, **37**, 181–203.

Arnott, R., A. de Palma and R. Lindsey, 1999, Information and time-of-usage decisions in the bottleneck model with stochastic capacity and demand. *European Economic Review*, **43**, 525–548.

Ben-Akiva, M., A. de Palma and I. Kaysi, 1992, Dynamic network models and driver information systems. *Transportation Research A*, **25**, 251–266.

Chancelier, J.-P. de, M. Lara and A. de Palma, 2007, Risk aversion, road choice, and the one-armed bandit problem. *Transportation Science*, **41** (1), 1–14.

Chorus, C., 2007, Traveler response to information, Ph.D. Dissertation, Delft University of Technology.

Danas, A., 1980, Arrival of passengers and busses at two London bus stops. *Traffic Engineering and Control*, **21**, 453–478.

de Palma, A. and N. Picard, 2005, Route choice decision and travel time uncertainty. *Transportation Research: A; Policy and Practice*, **39** (4), 295–324.

de Palma, A., R. Lindsey and N. Picard, 2011, Risk aversion, the value of information and traffic equilibrium. *Transportation Science*, forthcoming.

Emmerink, R.H.M. 1998, *Information and Pricing in Road Transportation*. Berlin: Springer.

Emmerink, R.H.M., P. Nijkamp and P. Rietveld, 1995, The potential of information provision in a simulated road transport network with non-recurrent congestion. *Transportation Research C*, **3**, 293–309.

Emmerink, R.H.M., E. Verhoef, P. Nijkamp and P. Rietveld, 1996, Information provision in road transport with elastic demand: a welfare economic approach. *Journal of Transport Economics and Policy*, **30**, 117–136.

Emmerink, R.H.M., E. Verhoef, P. Nijkamp and P. Rietveld, 1997, Information in road networks with multiple origin-destination pairs. *Regional Science and Urban Economics*, **27**, 217–240.

Exel, N.J.A. and P. Rietveld, 2009a, A note on perceptions of public transport travel time and their effect on choice-sets among car drivers. *Journal of Transport and Land Use*, **43** (4), 374–385.

Exel, N.J.A. and P. Rietveld, 2009b, Could you also have made this trip by another mode? An investigation of perceived travel possibilities of car and train passengers. *Transportation Research Part A*, **43** (4), 374–385.

Fosgerau, M., 2009, The marginal social cost of headway for a scheduled service. *Transportation Research B*, forthcoming.

Grotenhuis, J.-W., B. Wiegmans and P. Rietveld, 2007, The desired quality of integrated multimodal travel information in public transport: customer needs for time and effort savings. *Transport Policy*, **14**, 27–38.

Levinson, D., 2003, The value of advanced traveler information systems for route choice. *Transportation Research C*, **11**, 75–87.

Mahmassani, H. and Y.S. Liu, 1991, Dynamics of commuting decision behavior under advanced traveler information systems. *Transportation Research C*, **7**, 91–107.

Mood, A.M., F.A. Graybill and D.C. Boes, 1974, *Introduction to the Theory of Statistics*. New York: McGraw-Hill.

Nelson, P., 1970, Information and consumer behavior. *The Journal of Political Economy*, **78**, 311–329.

Quinet, E. and R. Vickerman, 2004, *Principles of Transport Economics*. Cheltenham, UK: Edward Elgar.

Rietveld, P. and H.E.S. van Woudenberg, 2003, The utility of travelling when destinations are heterogeneous. How much better is the next destination as one travels further? *Journal of Geographical Systems*. **5**, 207–222.

Schelling, T., 1978, *Micromotives and Macrobehavior*. New York: Norton.

Small, K.A., and Verhoef, E.T., 2007, *The Economics of Urban Transportation*. London: Routledge.

Tirachini, A.J., D.A. Hensher and S.R. Jara-Diaz, 2008, Restating modal investment priority with an improved model for public transport analysis. Working paper, Universidad de Chile, Santiago.

Yang, F., F.X. Liu, R.R. He, X. Ban and B. Ran, 2003, Bilevel formulation for optimal traffic-information dissemination. *Transportation Research Record*, **1836**, 21–28.

Yin, Y. and H. Yang, 2003, Simultaneous determination of the equilibrium market penetration and compliance rate of advanced traveler information systems. *Transportation Research A*, **37**, 895–912.

Zhang, L. and D. Levinson, 2008, Determinants of route choice and value of traveler information. *Transportation Research Record*, **2086**, 81–92.

Zhang, R. and E.T. Verhoef, 2006, A monopolistic market for advanced traveller information systems and road use efficiency. *Transportation Research A*, **40**, 424–443.

25 Personal intelligent travel assistants
Caspar G. Chorus and Harry J.P. Timmermans

INTRODUCTION

Recently, rapid technological developments in mobile communications and satellite technology have provided a vision among telecommunication companies, transport agencies, governments and academia of a technological revolution in Advanced Traveler Information Systems towards what can be called a Personal Intelligent Travel Assistant (PITA). Where the term ATIS has been used since the late 1980s to describe a range of travel information systems and services of varying degrees of sophistication, PITA distinguishes itself from the current generation of ATIS in terms of one or more of the following features (Chorus, 2007):

- PITA provides *dynamic* information. That is, based on real-time monitoring of the transportation system and fed into cutting edge models of travel demand and network capacity to predict the state of the network in the near future. As such, PITA is able to provide information that is more reliable than information provided by information systems that use static or historic network data, or use real-time monitoring but fail to translate this data into meaningful predictions of the future state of the transport network.
- PITA provides *personalized, mobile* information. That is, PITA bases the information it provides on an accurate assessment of the traveler's preferences, his or her location in the transport network and the constraints he or she faces (in terms of his or her schedule for the day, but also in terms of, for example, transit season ticket ownership and/or car availability). When deemed necessary, based on an assessment of the state of the transport network in combination with the traveler's personal profile, PITA may decide to provide the traveler with information automatically. Since PITA is mobile (it is, for example, integrated in a traveler's mobile phone), it can assist its users both pre- and in-trip.
- PITA provides *multimodal* information, based on an integrative view of all separate parts of the transport network such as different road networks (highways as well as secondary roads) and a variety of transit options. Given that PITA is mobile, it can also use this information to accommodate interchanges during the trip between these different parts of the multimodal network. As such, PITA facilitates truly 'intermodal' travel choices and helps the traveler integrate the different parts of the transport network efficiently, taking into account the current and predicted multimodal network state.
- PITA provides a range of information *types*. Depending on the situation and the traveler's preferences, PITA may, for example, provide information of type 'assessment' (meaning that one or more of the attributes – such as travel time – of one or more travel alternatives known to the traveler are assessed); type 'advice'

(where the traveler is told what is the best option for his or her current trip); and type 'generation' (meaning that one or more alternatives that were previously unknown to the traveler are disclosed).

It is hoped for (and expected by many, especially policy makers) that the deployment of PITA-like services will lead to a more efficient use of available transport infrastructure by helping travelers make better choices (for example, Commission of the European Communities, 2001, 2007; Department for Transport, 2004; Federal Transit Administration, 2003; Ministry of Transport, Public Works and Water Management, 2002). Particularly, it is expected that information provided through PITA may trigger travelers to adapt their departure time-, route- or mode-choices in ways that lead to a more efficient distribution of mobility across time and space (see Chorus et al., 2006a, for an overview of this literature). For example, the Commission of the European Communities (2001), when discussing the need for an increase in intermodal passenger transport, states that 'the development of intelligent traffic systems to inform passengers of transport conditions should eventually help reduce the time lost on transferring between modes'. Six years later, it mentioned that (multimodal) information is 'one of the critical success factors for mobility in urban networks' (Commission of the European Communities, 2007).

However, investments required for the development and deployment of PITA-services are enormous. These investments involve the gathering of relevant data from the multimodal transport network, synthesizing the data towards meaningful travel information and distributing the information among travelers that are expected to benefit from the information. Given the magnitude of investments needed for the successful development and deployment of PITA-services, and the high expectations concerning the effects of these investments, a clear understanding of the benefits associated with travelers' use of PITA-applications is necessary. First, such understanding may avoid the spending of huge amounts of money and time in suboptimal investments. A second reason for trying to get insight into the value of PITA-information lies in the potential use of these insights as input in models of traveler response to information. Specifically, insights into the value of information may be used to gain understanding of travelers' decisions whether or not to (actively) search for or (passively) pay attention to information provided by PITA-services, and their willingness to pay for such information. In turn, a proper understanding of these issues is a prerequisite for meaningful *ex-ante* assessments of usage levels and effects of PITA-applications.

This chapter provides models of the value of information from PITA-services. We start by providing some historical background of recent developments in the field of travel information provision, ultimately leading to a vision of PITA-services. Then, we provide models of the value of PITA-information. First, a generic concept of information value that is suitable for the analysis of PITA-services is presented. Then, specific formalizations of information value are developed for three types of information that PITA-services are likely to provide: the assessment of known alternatives in terms of their uncertain attributes, the provision of personalized advice and the personalized generation of unknown alternatives. Propositions are formulated that describe how information value is determined by the level of uncertainty contained in the choice situation and the traveler's preferences. For reasons of space limitations, proofs are omitted: these can be obtained from the first author upon request. For simplicity of exposition, we consider singular and binary choice contexts and assume that the information is perceived as perfectly reliable. However, we do discuss how our models can be extended to cover the value of unreliable information and the value of information in multinomial choice sets. We conclude by deriving practical policy implications.

A PERSONAL INTELLIGENT TRAVEL ASSISTANT (PITA): SOME HISTORICAL BACKGROUND

Travel information has been with us for thousands of years, be it in the form of – to name a few – verbal communications between individuals, maps or, more recently, transit timetables. These rather low-tech forms of travel information predominantly served to help people find their way as they traveled towards their destination.

Advanced Traveler Information Services (ATIS)

In the late 1980s, technological advances in the gathering and synthesizing of transportation data and the presentation of information to travelers started to trigger visions of increasing capabilities of travel information services, along with an increasingly important role for such services in traveler decision making (for example, Arnott et al., 1991; Ben-Akiva et al., 1991; Boyce, 1988; Mahmassani and Jayakrishnan, 1991; Polak and Jones, 1993). These visions gradually led to the introduction of the acronym ATIS for Advanced Traveler Information Services (for example, Adler and McNally, 1994; Khattak et al., 1993; Schofer et al., 1993). ATIS started out as systems that, based on observations of the current situation in the transport network in combination with historic data, provided car drivers with travel time estimates, advice or route guidance, and transit riders with up-to-date messages on delays of trains or buses. The information was provided to travelers through radio, variable message signs, telephone services and, starting in the mid-1990s, internet sites.

Over the years, these ATIS-applications became increasingly capable of providing travelers with reliable and relevant information, in times when the negative externalities of passenger transport – in terms of, for example, congestion, inaccessibility of urban areas, safety issues, utilization of fossil resources and environmental pollution – became increasingly relevant.

These two factors in combination (increasing ATIS capabilities and increasing passenger transport externalities) generated substantial interest among transportation academics regarding traveler response to information, or the behavioral aspects of travel information. This interest, which took off in the early 1990s, mainly concerns one of two lines of thought: first, there is a *marketing* point of view (for example, Abdel-Aty, 2001; Abdel-Aty et al., 1996; Khattak et al., 2003; Molin and Chorus, 2004; Molin and Timmermans, 2006; Polydoropoulou et al., 1997), which is predominantly concerned with the potential of ATIS as a business case, either stand alone or as part of an effort to gain or retain customers for some transportation service, for example, urban transit. A second and more dominant line of thought focused on ATIS as a potential tool for Travel Demand Management (TDM). This TDM or *transport policy* point of view (for example, Adler and McNally, 1994; van Berkum and van der Mede, 1993; Chorus et al., 2006a; Emmerink et al., 1995, 1996; Hato et al., 1999; Jou et al., 2005; Kenyon and Lyons, 2003) investigates the high expectations of travel information provision as a means to change traveler behavior in ways that are deemed beneficial to the transport system. Examples of such behavioral changes are a modal shift from car to transit and a more efficient use of the available road capacity due to route and departure time choice adaptations.

Towards a Personal Intelligent Travel Assistant (PITA)

Recently, a second wave of technological developments triggered the idea of a travel information system that is able to pinpoint a traveler's location in the transport network (using a Global Positioning System in combination with Geographical Information Systems), assess transit delays and the level of congestion on a given stretch of road (for example, using transit service data and cell-phone signals in combination with other types of vehicle count data), derive meaningful information from this data given the traveler's personal preferences, and send the information directly to his or her cell-phone or in-vehicle information system. These ideas are currently boosting the development of ATIS towards what has been dubbed Intelligent Travel Information Services (Adler and Blue, 1998), or, more recently, Personal Intelligent Travel Assistants (Chorus, 2007). As elaborated in the introduction, these travel information services are generally envisaged to be able to provide a traveler at anytime, whether on request or automatically, with all the real-time travel information that is relevant to him or her, given his or her place in the multimodal transport network and personal characteristics.

In this chapter, we consider three types of information PITA may provide: (1) information of type 'assessment', involving the assessment of known alternatives in terms of all their uncertain attributes (travel times, costs, seat availability in transit and so forth); (2) information of type 'advice' involving the provision of personalized advice and (3) information of type 'generation', involving the personalized generation of unknown alternatives. Although currently no existing travel information service truly meets the expectations surrounding PITA-services as described in the introduction, it seems plausible to assume that within five years from now, such services will have been successfully implemented. As discussed in the introduction, these developments rely on a proper assessment of the value associated with PITA-information.

VALUE OF INFORMATION FROM A PERSONAL INTELLIGENT TRAVEL ASSISTANT

Before discussing the value of the three particular types of information mentioned above, we first present a general formalization of the notion of information value. In line with a tradition well established in fields such as decision theory (for example, Raiffa and Schlaifer, 1961), (spatial) economics (for example, Weibull, 1978), marketing (for example, Ackerberg, 2003), transportation (for example, de Palma and Picard, 2006) and choice modeling (Chorus and Timmermans, 2008), we conceptualize information value (IV) in terms of the difference between the expected utility[1] of the choice situation that is anticipated after having received the information (EU^+) and that of the current choice situation (EU), minus the costs[2] $(c$, in utils) of the information: $IV = EU^+ - EU - c$.

Crucial here is the definition of EU^+. First, it should be noted that EU^+ depends on the received message M. Although the traveler obviously does not know what message he or she will receive when acquiring the information, he or she may be assumed to have beliefs of what messages are likely to be received. We model these beliefs by perceived probabilities $P(M)$. (See Chorus et al., 2005, for a discussion of how these beliefs relate to the traveler's beliefs concerning the prevailing state of the world and information reliability.) Then, $EU^+(M)$ denotes the expected utility of the anticipated choice situation, as a function of received message M.

Now, the specification of $EU^+(M)$ depends on whether one is willing to assume that the traveler anticipates the acquisition of additional travel information directly upon receiving a message. For example, when considering the acquisition of travel time information for a given car option, the traveler may anticipate that in case a non-favorable message is received concerning car travel time, he or she may go on to acquire travel time information concerning one or more urban transit options. If one wants to cover such anticipations of multiple information acquisitions, the anticipated choice situation directly after having received the information contains travel alternatives as well as information options. However, in line with a more boundedly rational view on decision making, we here assume that the traveler, when considering the acquisition of information, does not explicitly consider acquiring more information directly after having received a message. From this myopic perspective, the choice situation that is anticipated to exist after having acquired a considered bit of information contains travel alternatives alone.

Furthermore, specification of $EU^+(M)$ depends on whether or not a longer-term learning perspective is adopted: information acquisition during the current trip may be of value for future trips as well, for example, in the context of getting to learn a route's mean travel time and travel time variability over time (Chorus et al., 2008b). We focus here on the one-shot learning context: a traveler decides whether or not to acquire information, based only on his expectations of its value for the current trip (the interested reader may find a dynamic perspective, also covering longer-term learning dynamics, in Chancelier et al., 2007). Finally, we focus on information value following from information potential to help the traveler make better choices (that is, choose the alternative that performs best given the current and predicted state of the transport network). Note that apart from this source of information value, risk-averse travelers may additionally value information for its potential to reduce uncertainty as such (for example, de Palma and Picard, 2006). Given our scope, the generic value of acquiring information can be denoted as:

$$IV = \underbrace{\sum_M \underbrace{\left[\max_{j \in C^+(M)} \{ EU_j^+(M) \} \right] \cdot P(M)}_{EU^+(M)}}_{EU^+} - \underbrace{\max_{j \in C} \{ EU_j \}}_{EU} - c \qquad (25.1)$$

Here, EU_j denotes the expected utility of alternative j, $EU_j^+ (M)$ denotes the anticipated expected utility of j after having received a message M, C denotes the current choice set, and $C^+ (M)$ denotes the anticipated choice set after having received message M. Equation (25.1) gives the value of information in utils. Under the assumption that utility is linear in income, and denoting α as the marginal utility of income, $(1/\alpha) \cdot IV$ gives the willingness to pay for information in monetary terms.

The following three sub-sections focus on the types of PITA-information that are the focus of this chapter: the assessment of known alternatives in terms of all uncertain attributes, the provision of personalized advice and the personalized generation of unknown alternatives.[3]

'Assessment': The Value of Acquiring Information Concerning Uncertain Attributes

Consider the situation where a traveler chooses between two travel alternatives (for example, two mode–route–departure time combinations) A and B. The traveler believes that a number of the alternatives' attributes are uncertain: the uncertainty results from day-to-day variability in the transport network (for example, travel time variability) in combination with a possible lack of static knowledge (for example, lack of fare knowledge regarding a transit ride).

Specifically, we assume that the traveler believes that one of $2n + 1$ equiprobable states of the world $s_1 \ldots s_{2n+1}$ may occur, with values of the uncertain attributes of A and B varying between states. Depending on the state of the world, the utility difference (A minus B) associated with the *uncertain attributes* varies between $-n\Delta, \ldots, -\Delta, 0, \Delta, \ldots,$ $n\Delta$ (Δ being a nonnegative number that represents variation in utility associated with the uncertain attributes between two 'adjacent' states of the world). The utility difference (A minus B) in terms of all *certain attributes* is captured in a constant, which from here on we will refer to as an *intrinsic preference* for alternative A. Given these normalizations, the utility of B equals zero for each state of the world, and that of A (relative to B) depends on the state of the world: $V_A (s)$ ranges from $\beta_A - n\Delta$ to $\beta_A + n\Delta$. Depending on the values of β_A and Δ, A is (strongly) preferred over B for some states of the world and vice versa for other states of the world. The traveler maximizes expected utility, which (given that all states are equiprobable) leads to the following expression for the expected utility of the current choice situation:

$$EU = \max\{E(V_A(s)), 0\} = \max\left\{ \sum_{s=s_1}^{s_{2n+1}} \left[\frac{V_A(s)}{2n + 1} \right], 0 \right\} = \max\{\beta_A, 0\} \quad (25.2)$$

Let an information search possibility exist concerning the state of the world s. That is, PITA is able to (faultlessly) assess alternatives A and B in terms of all their uncertain attributes combined, leading to a reliable assessment of the utility of A relative to that of B.

The expected utility of the choice situation that is *anticipated* after having received the information, , can then be formalized as follows: the traveler knows that, given fully reliable information, the probability of receiving particular messages when acquiring information equals her initial perceptions concerning likelihood of occurrence of particular states of the world. As a consequence, given fully reliable information, all $2n + 1$ possible messages concerning A's utility in terms of uncertain attributes, relative to B's, are equiprobable. The traveler also knows that, after having received a message and hence knowing for sure what state of the world will occur, he or she will maximize utility by choosing between A and B. The following equation formalizes this conceptualization of EU^+:

$$EU^+ = \sum_{s=s_1}^{s_{2n+1}} \left[\frac{\max\{V_A(s), 0\}}{2n+1} \right] \tag{25.3}$$

Note that Equation (25.3) differs from (25.2) in the sense that the max-operator enters the summation: the traveler no longer needs to maximize the expected utility of uncertain alternatives, but will be able to maximize the utility of two certain alternatives *after* PITA has informed him or her about the prevailing state of the world. The utilitarian value of information follows from subtracting Equation (25.2) from (25.3):

$$IV = \sum_{s=s_1}^{s_{2n+1}} \left[\frac{\max\{V_A(s), 0\}}{2n+1} \right] - \max\left\{ \sum_{s=s_1}^{s_{2n+1}} \left[\frac{V_A(s)}{2n+1} \right], 0 \right\} \tag{25.4}$$

Intuitively, information value (as defined here) results from a subtle and nuanced interplay between the intrinsic preference for alternative A (β_A), the number of possible states of the world ($2n+1$) and the utility difference between adjacent states of the world (Δ). This intuition can be described as follows: information is valuable for the traveler to the extent that the information is needed to help him or her overcome his or her inability to predict what state of the world will prevail and choose the most valuable alternative. Given fully reliable information, information then is valuable to the extent that the traveler is uncertain with respect to the sign and magnitude of the difference in utility between A and B in the prevailing future state of the world.

When there is only a small intrinsic preference for either of the two alternatives ($|\beta_A|$ is small) or when there is much variation in utility regarding the uncertain attributes of A and B (Δ and/or n is large), this level of uncertainty is relatively high: for some states of the world, A may be much preferred to B and vice versa. However, when the intrinsic preference for one of the two alternatives increases (increasing $|\beta_A|$), or the variation in utility regarding the uncertain attributes decreases (decreasing Δ and/or n), the traveler becomes increasingly knowledgeable concerning the sign and magnitude of the difference in utility between the alternatives in the prevailing future state of the world, without of course knowing what state of the world will prevail. In other words, when increases or Δ and/or n decreases, the traveler knows that there are only few states of the world in which he or she would prefer B over A (or A over B). As a result, information is of limited value. When is large enough (or Δ and/or n are small enough) to ensure that the traveler knows that one of the two alternatives is always preferred to the other one – irrespective of what state of the world will prevail – information loses all of its value. Formally, this reasoning can be put as follows:

Proposition 1:   Given non-zero values for Δ and n, the value of information of type 'assessment' is highest and positive when $\beta_A = 0$; information value decreases, while remaining positive, with increasing levels of as long as $|\beta_A| < n\Delta$. Information value becomes zero when $|\beta_A| \geq n\Delta$.

In sum: information value of type 'assessment' is highest when there is no intrinsic preference for either of the two alternatives, decreases when the absolute value of the traveler's intrinsic preference for one of them increases relative to the values of Δ and n, and becomes zero when the intrinsic preference for one of the alternatives is high enough to ensure that the alternative is always (never) the most valuable one, irrespective of the state of the world.

'Advice': The Value of Being Advised What to do

Consider again the travel choice situation depicted in the above section: a traveler faces a choice between two alternatives A and B and perceives a number of their attributes as uncertain. Instead of discussing the value of predicting the state of the world (assessing the value of all uncertain attributes of A and B), we here focus on the value of being advised by PITA on what alternative to choose. We first consider the situation where PITA provides personalized advice (that is, PITA takes into account the traveler's intrinsic preferences reflected in β_A). Subsequently, to appreciate the added value of personalized advice, we will also formalize the difference in value between personalized advice and not-fully personalized advice (that is, the information service does not take into account β_A when issuing the advice).

The value of personalized advice

Consider the situation where (the traveler knows that) the advice received is personalized. That is, the traveler knows that his or her PITA will base the advice on its beliefs concerning the prevailing state of the world, in combination with its beliefs concerning the traveler's valuation of the utility of uncertain attributes for that state and the sign and magnitude of his or her intrinsic preference for alternative A compared to B. In notation, we assume that (the traveler knows that) PITA faultlessly assesses (1) which of the $2n + 1$ states of the world s will prevail, (2) the utility difference between any two adjacent states of the world, Δ, and (3) the traveler's intrinsic preference, β_A.

To see the implications of the personalized nature of the advice, consider for example a personalized advice to choose alternative A: the traveler knows that PITA will only give the advice when a state of the world will prevail in which the utility of A exceeds that of alternative B. As a consequence, the traveler is aware that PITA may advise him to choose alternative A (B) even if it performs worse than B (A) in terms of uncertain attributes (for example, travel time), as long as the disutility is not too high, and the intrinsic preference for A (B) is high enough.

Importantly, this implies that under the prevailing assumption of fully reliable personalized information (that is, the information is reliable with respect to states of the world as well as associated utilities), the traveler will always comply with received personalized advice. That is, there is no reason for a rational traveler not to comply with a personalized advice – also when the advice is to take the route he or she intrinsically dislikes.

Proposition 2: The value of acquiring a personalized advice from a fully reliable PITA equals the value of having PITA predict what state of the world will prevail (having PITA assess all uncertain attributes of A and B).

This equivalence in terms of information value between personalized advice and assessment of all uncertain attributes of both A and B implies that Proposition 1 also applies to the value of personalized advice. Specifically, the value of personalized advice will be highest when the traveler has no intrinsic preference for either of the two alternatives, and will decrease when the (absolute value of) the intrinsic preference increases, relative to Δ and n.

The intuition behind this equivalence between personalized advice and assessment of all uncertain attributes is as follows: the only difference between information of type 'assessment' and type 'advice' is that the latter type of information involves not only an assessment of what state of the world will prevail, but also combines this assessment with the traveler's preferences to arrive at the selection of the best alternative. As long as (the traveler believes that) PITA is perfectly aware of his or her preferences, the traveler believes that PITA will always select the same alternative as he or she would select him- or herself, given PITA's assessment of the state of the world. As a result, information of types 'assessment' and 'advice' are equivalent in terms of associated benefits. Note that this equivalence does not necessarily apply when so-called 'costs of thinking' (Shugan, 1980) are taken into account: since information of type 'advice' relieves the traveler from the potentially effort-consuming task to combine an assessment of the state of the world with his or her preferences, this type of information might well have an edge over 'assessment' information for some travelers.

Finally, it is interesting to note here that the personalized nature of the advice implies that the actual information content of the advice (concerning what state of the world prevails) in an information-theoretic sense (Shannon, 1948) depends on the relative values of $|\beta_A|$, Δ and n. For example, should the traveler substantially prefer alternative B over A intrinsically (relative to the variation in utility associated with uncertain attributes), then the reception of an advice to choose alternative A provides a signal to the traveler that a state of the world will prevail in which A performs much better than B in terms of uncertain attributes. However, in case the traveler intrinsically prefers A, an advice to choose A provides little information concerning A's and B's uncertain attributes: whether alternative A performs better or (somewhat) worse than B, the condition for providing advice (the utility of A is higher than B in the prevailing state of the world), is met for most states of the world. As a result, in this situation it is difficult for the traveler to infer much information in terms of what state of the world will prevail, from the personalized advice to choose A.

Value-difference between personalized and not-fully personalized advice
Consider now the situation where the traveler knows that advice ignores his or her intrinsic preference for one of the two alternatives (reflected in β_A). However, (the traveler does believe that) the information service faultlessly predicts the prevailing state of the world and faultlessly assesses the utility difference between any two 'adjacent' states of the world (Δ). As a result, we call this type of advice 'not-fully personalized', rather than 'non-personalized'. Intuitively, one would expect that the value of such not-fully personalized advice is less than that of fully personalized advice (that is, advice that does take into account β_A) when the traveler has non-negligible intrinsic preference for one of the two routes.

Proposition 3:   When $0 < |\beta_A| < n\Delta$, the value of acquiring not-fully personalized advice (that is, advice that ignores β_A) is lower than the value of acquiring fully personalized advice. When $|\beta_A|$ is either zero or larger than or equal to $n\Delta$, the value of acquiring not-fully personalized advice equals that of acquiring fully personalized advice.

The intuition behind this proposition can be formulated as follows: when there is no intrinsic preference for either of the two alternatives, intrinsic preferences can be safely ignored by the information service, without loss of information value. When $|\beta_A| \geq n\Delta$, the traveler knows that he or she will always choose A (B), irrespective of what state of the world will occur. Hence, the traveler knows that he or she will ignore any advice, whether or not it is fully personalized: both types of advice are of no value to him or her.

Although, when $0 < |\beta_A| < n\Delta$, the traveler knows that he or she will always comply with personalized advice (see the sub-section above on the value of personalized advice), it depends on the magnitude of $|\beta_A|$ whether or not the traveler knows that he or she will comply with not-fully personalized advice. Assume positive values for β_A for simplicity of argumentation: then, when the traveler's intrinsic preference for A is large,[4] he or she knows that although it is possible that a not-fully personalized advice to take route B may be based on PITA's assessment that one of the few states where the total utility of A is lower than that of B is prevailing, this is not very probable. As a result, the traveler knows that he or she will always choose A and ignore advice. In those cases, not-fully personalized advice has no value to him or her by definition, while personalized advice does have a non-zero value (see Propositions 1 and 2).

When β_A is relatively small, the traveler knows that he or she will comply with advice to choose route B (jut like in the case of personalized advice). However, the traveler also knows that there is a non-zero probability that compliance with this not-fully personalized advice may result in a utility loss: although the advice to choose B is always based on PITA's (correct) assessment that a state of the world prevails in which B performs better than A in terms of its uncertain attributes, this difference may in fact be too small to compensate for the traveler's intrinsic dislike for B. Since the traveler knows that compliance with personalized advice does always result in him or her choosing the optimal route, such personalized advice is of more value to him or her than not-fully personalized advice – even when the traveler knows he or she will comply with the advice.

We conclude by returning briefly to the amount of information (in an information-theoretic sense) that is captured in advice. As discussed above, the amount of information captured in personalized advice depends on the traveler's intrinsic preference for route A. Since not-fully personalized advice does not take into account this intrinsic preference, the amount of information it contains does not depend on the traveler's intrinsic preferences. However, it is important to note that advice to take one of the two routes always contains less value than a message concerning what state of the world PITA thinks will prevail. From a not-fully personalized advice to take route A (B), the traveler may only infer that PITA believes that the advised route performs better than the other one in terms of their uncertain attributes – not how much better. The same holds for personalized advice: although here the amount of information contained in the advice depends on the traveler's preferences, it will at the very best[5] be equally large as the amount contained in a message concerning what state of the world will prevail.

'Generation': The Value of Learning About New Travel Alternatives

Consider now a traveler who finds him- or herself in a situation where he or she has very little knowledge of the local transport network, and knows of no particular feasible mode–route combination that will bring him or her to his or her destination. The traveler knows that he or she may just start the trip by moving in some best guess-direction using a default mode of transport, and try to adjust it underway if necessary. Assume that the traveler believes that the utility he or she will derive from this default option can be written as $U_D = V_D + \varepsilon_D$, where ε_D is a random utility component with mean zero that captures the traveler's uncertainty with respect to the performance of this default option, and V_D is the traveler's best guess concerning the utility of the default option: $E(U_D) = E(V_D + \varepsilon_D) = V_D$.

The traveler believes that there are many available alternatives that are unknown to him or her, which may vary in terms of utility, relative to the 'best guess' utility of the default option. In notation: we normalize the average utility of the default option $(V_D = 0)$, and then write the utility of randomly drawn, available but unknown, alternatives r as $U_r = V + \varepsilon_r$, where V denotes the traveler's perception of the average utility of unknown alternatives, relative to the 'best guess' utility of the default option. The variance of random utility component ε_r reflects the perceived variation in utility across available, but unknown, alternatives relative to that of the default option.

The traveler knows that he or she may ask PITA to generate a travel alternative. Specifically, the traveler knows that PITA contains a database with a random selection of R available alternatives. PITA delivers personalized information, which in this context implies that it is able to rank alternatives in terms of their attractiveness (that is, in terms of U_r) for this particular traveler. As a result, the traveler knows that asking PITA to generate an alternative is equivalent to having the most attractive of R randomly drawn available alternatives added to his or her choice set (which so far was singular and contained only the default option). Given the conceptualizations made so far, the value of asking PITA to generate an alternative can be formalized as follows:

$$IV = EU^+ - EU$$

$$= E(\max\{U_D, \max\{U_1, \ldots, U_r, \ldots, U_R\}\}) - E(U_D)$$

$$= E(\max\{0 + \varepsilon_D, \max\{V + \varepsilon_1, \ldots, V + \varepsilon_r, \ldots, V + \varepsilon_R\}\}) - V_D$$

$$= E(\max\{0 + \varepsilon_D, V + \varepsilon_1, \ldots, V + \varepsilon_r, \ldots, V + \varepsilon_R\}) - 0$$

$$= \int_{\varepsilon_D, \varepsilon_1, \ldots, \varepsilon_R} [\max\{0 + \varepsilon_D, V + \varepsilon_1, \ldots, V + \varepsilon_r, \ldots, V + \varepsilon_R\}] \cdot f(\varepsilon_D, \varepsilon_1, \ldots, \varepsilon_R) d\varepsilon_D \, d\varepsilon_1 \ldots d\varepsilon_R \tag{25.5}$$

Although there are many functional forms to describe the distribution of random utility components $\varepsilon_D, \varepsilon_1, \ldots, \varepsilon_R$, from a computational perspective it is useful to adopt the i.i.d. Extreme Value Type I distribution with variance $\pi^2/6$.[6] This distribution, which has been shown to imply well-known logit probabilities in random utility-based discrete-choice modeling (McFadden, 1974), looks similar to the normal distribution but has slightly fatter tails. When making this distributional assumption, information value as formalized in (25.5) can be rewritten into the following logsum-based formulation:

$$IV = \ln\left(\underbrace{\exp(0) + \exp(V) + \ldots + \exp(V)}_{R \text{ times}}\right) = \ln(1 + R \cdot \exp(V)) \quad (25.6)$$

Proposition 4: The value of personalized information of type 'generation' is an increasing function of both R and V. When V becomes negative, information value remains positive and approaches zero when V approaches $-\infty$.

The more alternatives PITA knows of, and the higher the average utility of available alternatives relative to the 'best guess' utility of the default option, the higher is the value of information. Also when the average utility of available alternatives is perceived to be lower than the 'best guess' utility of the default option, the value of information remains positive. This results from the fact that there is a non-zero probability that the maximum of R randomly drawn alternatives has a utility higher than zero, due to the possibility of a large and positive random utility component for one or more of the available alternatives. In other words, the mere fact that the traveler is uncertain concerning the performance of available alternatives, implies a positive information value.

It is illustrative to compare the value of personalized information with the value of information from a non-personalized information service, that is, one that is unable to rank available alternatives in terms of their attractiveness for the particular traveler. In case of such non-personalized information, the traveler perceives acquiring information as simply making a random draw r from R alternatives. As a result, the expected utility of the information is easily seen to equal:

$$IV = \int_{\varepsilon_D, \varepsilon_r} [\max\{0 + \varepsilon_D, V + \varepsilon_r\}] f(\varepsilon_D, \varepsilon_r) d\varepsilon_D \varepsilon_r$$

$$= \ln(\exp(0) + \exp(V)) = \ln(1 + \exp(V)) \quad (25.7)$$

Proposition 5: The value of non-personalized information of type 'generation' does not depend on R, and is an increasing function of V only. When V becomes negative, information value remains positive. The difference with personalized information of type 'generation' decreases with decreasing levels of R and V, and approaches zero when V approaches $-\infty$ or R equals 1.

The expected utility of non-personalized information then does not depend on the number of alternatives the information service knows of. This is in line with intuition, as knowing more alternatives is not an advantage when the alternative that is ultimately presented to the traveler is drawn randomly. Inspecting Equations (25.6) and (25.7) it is easily seen that the difference in terms of expected utility between personalized information and non-personalized information grows with the number of alternatives PITA knows of, as well as with the average utility of available alternatives. When PITA knows of only one alternative, or when the average utility of unknown alternatives is extremely low, the value of personalized information equals the value of non-personalized information.

MULTINOMIAL CHOICE SETS AND UNRELIABLE INFORMATION

Until now, we have considered information value mainly in the context of binary or singular choice sets (more accurately: sets of known alternatives). Obviously, most actual travel choice situations involve choice sets containing many more known alternatives. Secondly, we have considered situations where the traveler believes that the information service is capable of faultlessly assessing the state of the world. This assumption also seems restrictive when looking at most real-life travel choice situations. In this section, we briefly review how the models presented above may be extended to cover multinomial choice sets and unreliable information, and how the scope adopted until here influences the general applicability of obtained results.

Value of Information in Multinomial Choice Sets

We start with information of type 'assessment': Equations (25.2) to (25.4) may be extended as follows to cover multinomial choice sets: as is the case in the context of binary choice sets, the performance of each alternative in terms of the certain attributes can be modeled by means of a constant with respect to some base alternative. Performance in terms of uncertain attributes – again, relative to the base alternative – differs across states of the world. Note here that the number of relevant states of the world, when the choice set contains k alternatives, equals $(k-1)(2n+1)$. Given these settings, information value can then be modeled using the same principles as were applied earlier: $IV = EU^+ - EU$. The expected utility of the current choice situation (EU) is found by maximizing expected utility over all k alternatives in the choice set. The expected utility of the choice set that is anticipated after having received the information (EU^+) is found by, for each state, selecting the alternative with the highest utility and averaging over the number of states.

Information value of type 'assessment' is highest when the constants of all alternatives equal zero, indicating that the utility of the alternatives fully depends on the uncertain attributes and that each state of the world comes with a different preferred alternative. When there is an alternative whose constant is high enough to be selected in each state of the world, information value becomes zero. However, in contrast with the binary choice situation, information value does not become zero when at least one alternative has a constant that is so low that the alternative is never selected. As long as there remain two or more states that differ in terms of the associated preferred alternative, information value is positive. Since for each state the expected difference between the best performing known alternative and a randomly drawn alternative increases with the number of known alternatives, information value is positively related to the number of known alternatives k, and is therefore higher, *ceteris paribus*, in multinomial than in singular or binary choice sets.

These findings translate to information of type 'advice', since also in multinomial choice sets, the value of fully reliable personalized advice equals that of 'assessment' information. When the advice is not-fully personal (that is, it ignores intrinsic preferences for the k alternatives) information value is lower than in the case of personalized advice, as long as one or more of the intrinsic preferences is non-zero and none of the intrinsic preferences is large enough to make sure that that alternative is always chosen. Note also that in the context of multinomial choice sets, the difference in amount of information between information of types 'assessment' and 'advice' in favor of the latter type increases with k. For large ks, an advice to choose one of the alternatives contains far less information than a $(k - 1)(2n + 1)$-dimensional message concerning what state of the world will prevail.

In the case of information of type 'generation', one may safely assume that the more alternatives someone knows of, the higher will be the utility of the default alternative (the maximum utility alternative of the set of known alternatives). In our notation, one may assume that the value of V (representing the traveler's perception of the average utility of unknown alternatives) is no longer a constant, but is negatively related to k. Since information value has been found to increase with increasing levels of V, more known alternatives means lower value of information of type 'generation'. In addition, it may also be assumed that when k is large, the traveler perceives the probability that PITA generates an alternative that he or she already knows as non-zero. To capture this notion, adaptation of Equations (25.6) and (25.7) is needed. However, it can be seen directly that this notion also supports the conclusion that more known alternatives means lower value of information of type 'generation'.

In sum, the models developed in the previous section can be extended to cover the case of multinomial choice sets, although at the cost of increasing complexity. Intuition and propositions presented in the context of singular and binary choice sets generally appear to hold in the context of multinomial sets. Larger choice sets are expected to lead to higher (lower) information value when considering information types 'assessment' and 'advice' ('generation'). This expectation is supported by an empirical study (Chorus et al., 2007) conducted in a multimodal travel simulator with information provision: travelers acquired more (less) information of types 'assessment' and 'advice' ('generation') when their choice sets became larger.

Value of Unreliable Information

Conceptually, the difference between reliable and unreliable information – in terms of modeling information value – is twofold. First, when information becomes less than fully reliable, it becomes more difficult for the traveler to assess what message he or she will receive when searching for information. Second, when information is unreliable, the traveler cannot be assumed to completely replace any initial perceptions he or she may have with a message. Rather, he or she may be assumed to partially update these initial perceptions, weighing initial knowledge and received information in terms of their relative reliability. Let us look briefly at these differences in relation to the three types of information that we consider.

Concerning information of type 'assessment', the assumption that the traveler believes that each of the equiprobable states of the world is also equally probable to be believed by PITA to prevail, does not hold anymore. PITA may be biased towards incorrectly believing that some states have a higher or lower probability of occurring than others. Also, PITA may believe that a state of the world occurs that the traveler believes is impossible. This unreliability can be modeled by means of a conditional probability table (CPT), where each entry gives the traveler's perceived probability that PITA believes that a given state prevails, conditional on actual occurrence of some (other) state (see Arentze and Timmermans, 2005, for an application of such a CPT in the context of a destination choice model).

Furthermore, the assumption that the traveler completely replaces his initial perceptions concerning what state of the world will occur with received information needs to be replaced by an updating mechanism that allows for the weighing of initial knowledge and information according to their associated perceived reliability. A mechanism that is often used in travel demand models for such an updating process is that of Bayesian learning (for example, Arentze and Timmermans, 2005; Chen and Mahmassani, 2004; Chorus et al., 2006c, 2008b; Jha et al., 1998; Kaysi, 1991; Sun et al., 2005), although a variety of other modeling approaches may be used to this aim as well (for example, Ben-Akiva et al., 1991; Horowitz, 1984; Jotisankasa and Polak, 2006; Viti et al., 2005).

Irrespective of the chosen approach to model information unreliability, each will have as an outcome that the traveler knows that after having received the information, a certain amount of uncertainty remains, leading to a non-zero probability of choosing the 'wrong' route. Since the value of PITA-information of type 'assessment' is clearly linked to its potential to minimize or eliminate this probability, the value of unreliable information will always turn out to be lower than that of fully reliable information (see Chorus et al., 2006b, c, for a numerical illustration of this notion). Finally, note that the traveler may dislike attribute uncertainty per se (apart from the fact that it may cause him or her to choose a sub-optimal alternative). As discussed in the historical background on PITA, this risk aversion is not the topic of this chapter; but note that it clearly results in an additional penalty for information unreliability.

Since the value of advice has been shown to relate in a straightforward way to the value of information of type 'assessment', the above argument appears to hold for the provision of (personalized and not-fully personalized) advice as well: decreasing levels of information reliability imply decreasing levels of the value of information of type 'advice'. Another way to arrive at this conclusion is as follows: the fact that the traveler knows that PITA is unable to faultlessly assess the state of the world limits his or her *ex ante* inclination to comply with advice. A traveler that knows up front that he or she will ignore advice attaches no value to the advice. A traveler that knows that he or she will comply with advice notwithstanding the decrease in reliability knows that the information unreliability will increase the probability that when complying with advice, he or she will choose an alternative that has a lower utility than other known alternatives. As the value of personalized and not-fully personalized advice appears to approach zero when information becomes extremely unreliable, the difference between these two types of advice appears to vanish in the case of extremely unreliable information.

In the context of having a personalized PITA generate a new alternative, a similar line of reasoning holds: when the traveler knows that the information provider is unable to reliably assess the state of the world (in the notation of that sub-section: to reliably assess the utility of unknown alternatives relative to the default option), the value of having PITA generate an unknown alternative decreases. This is due to the fact that an unreliable PITA is unable to perform a reliable ranking of unknown alternatives. As a result, the traveler is no longer sure whether the alternative PITA generates is indeed the best available one. In the context of non-personalized 'generation' information, there is no ranking involved and information unreliability has a smaller impact on information value: only the disutility that risk-averse travelers attach to attribute uncertainty per se results in a penalty for unreliable information.

In sum, the models developed in the previous section can be extended to cover the case of unreliable information, although again at the cost of increasing complexity. This added complexity is larger than that associated with the extension towards multinomial choice sets. We discuss how higher levels of information unreliability induce lower levels of information value, for each of the information types considered. Again, these findings are in line with the empirical study (Chorus et al., 2007) conducted in a multimodal travel simulator with information provision: travelers acquired less information of all types when information became less reliable.

CONCLUSIONS AND PRACTICAL IMPLICATIONS

This chapter presents a vision of a Personal Intelligent Travel Assistant (PITA), an information service that is able to provide a traveler at anytime, whether on request or automatically, with all the real-time travel information that is relevant to him or her, given his or her place in the multimodal transport network and personal preferences. We argue that a good understanding of the value of PITA-information is needed to underpin decisions concerning the large investments needed for the development and deployment of PITA-applications and to gain a proper understanding of their use and effects among travelers. This chapter then provides an attempt to model the value of PITA-information.

First, a generic model of information value is presented, tailored towards the context of myopic expected utility-maximizing decision making and fully reliable information. Then, specific measures of information value are presented for three types of information that PITA-services are likely to provide in the near future: the assessment of known alternatives in terms of all their uncertain attributes (that is, prediction of the state of the world), the provision of personalized advice and the personalized generation of unknown alternatives. These measures can be used to establish the value of information in utilitarian or monetary (willingness to pay) terms, and can also be used to study how information value varies with changes in the level of uncertainty and changes in a traveler's preferences. Relevant propositions are derived for each information type. Although, for reasons of simplicity of presentation, choice situations have been kept simple, involving singular and binary choice sets in the presence of fully reliable information, we discuss how the formalizations presented can be extended towards more complex situations. We conclude this chapter by deriving from the presented models of information value five practical policy implications.

Transit information will not be frequently used by car drivers. Such information therefore only has a small impact on modal split. This implication follows directly from Proposition 1: when one of the available options is strongly preferred over other ones in terms of its certain attributes (what we called the intrinsic preference), relative to the amount of uncertainty contained in the choice situation, information value is low. Car drivers' intrinsic preferences for the car option (based on, for example, 'soft' factors such as status and freedom) lead them to believe – correctly – that no matter the state of the world in terms of travel times and costs (which are the two attributes transit information generally refers to), they will derive more utility from driving their car than from riding transit. This means that they perceive the value of such information to be low. Our models therefore predict that transit information will not be frequently used by car drivers, and that its resulting effect on mode-shares will be low. This contradicts high expectations that policy makers generally have concerning the provision of transit information to car drivers: it is generally believed that such information will correct misperceptions among car drivers concerning the performance of transit alternatives.

Personalized information is likely to achieve relatively high usage levels. This implication needs little additional explanation on top of the discussions presented earlier: the value of personalized information (that is, information that takes into account not only an assessment of the prevailing state of the world, but also an assessment of the traveler's preference structure) is higher than that of otherwise equal forms of non-personalized information. Since the development and deployment of personalized information services is likely to require relatively high levels of investments, it needs to be determined on a case-by-case base whether the expected gains in information value (and hence, expected willingness to pay for the information) warrant the effort to personalize the information service.

Information is used to the extent that its (non-) monetary costs are low. We have shown that information value, irrespective of its type, strongly depends on the level of uncertainty contained in the choice situation, information reliability, the extent to which the information is personalized, and the traveler's preference structure. In many situations, travelers' perceptions of information value may be low or moderate at best. This means that travelers will generally only acquire information when its perceived costs – monetary and non-monetary (effort, attention, time) – are low. Those travel information services and devices that are cheap and easily usable, and provide information in ways that are readable and comprehensible while traveling, are far more likely to be used among travelers than those that do not.

Providing advice may hamper a traveler's ability to learn the characteristics of the transport network. As is argued earlier, advice contains less information, in an information-theoretic sense, than does information of type 'assessment': instead of telling travelers the state of the world, it gives an indirect message (for example, 'given what I believe will be the state of the world, I advise you to take route A'). Confronting travelers with such indirect messages may therefore reduce the learning potential that information provision has. This implication is likely to hold especially in real-life travel choice situations, where a traveler's choice set is likely to contain large numbers of alternatives.

Making information services work well under incident conditions is likely to be cost-effective. Incident conditions are widely known to cause high levels of uncertainty with respect to the attributes (most notably, travel times) of known alternatives, which has been shown earlier to imply a high value of information of type 'assessment' and 'advice'. In addition, when conditions are such that proceeding on the planned route is not a feasible option, the utility of this default option decreases – which has been shown to increase the value of information of type 'generation'. However, travelers are likely to perceive information as particularly unreliable under incident conditions, which may severely decrease perceived information value. Based on this reasoning, it seems worthwhile to invest in information services that are relatively reliable under incident conditions, as these are likely to be of much value to travelers.

As a final note, we feel that the work presented in this chapter strongly suggests that information value, especially the value of relatively advanced, PITA-like information, emerges from the subtle and nuanced interplay between a number of interdependent factors, such as the traveler's preference structure, the level of uncertainty contained in the choice situation, and the type of information. In our view, this implies that willingness to pay for information, and travelers' acquisition of information in general, should best not be conceived as the outcome of a set of linear relations with explanatory variables, notwithstanding the appeal of such an approach in terms of simplicity of analysis. In contrast, we feel that the study of information value, and for that matter, response to information in general, benefits from adopting a more realistic behavioral approach that allows for modeling the subtle relations discussed here.

NOTES

1. Note that, besides the more conventional expected utility-maximization approach to model traveler decision making under uncertainty, recent years have witnessed an increasing interest in alternative frameworks for modeling traveler decision making (Michea and Polak, 2006), for example, based on prospect theory (for example, Avineri and Prashker, 2003), regret theory (for example, Chorus et al., 2006b, 2008a) or satisficing (Chorus et al., 2006c).
2. These costs may involve, in addition to monetary costs, costs of thinking (Shugan, 1980) and attention (Simon, 1978) and opportunity costs of time (for example, Ratchford, 1982). In the remainder of this chapter, we will ignore such information costs.
3. The approach taken here has some similarities to that in the chapter by Piet Rietveld on the economics of information in transport. The two approaches differ in that Rietveld considers sequential search strategies whereas the model here is static.
4. More precisely: when $n + 1/2\Delta < \beta_A < n\Delta$.
5. This is the case when the traveler's intrinsic preference for route A (B) is such that he or she will only choose route B (A) in the extreme state of the world where B's (A's) utility in terms of uncertain attributes is n Δ utils higher than that of A (B). This traveler then knows that when receiving a personalized advice to choose B (A), exactly this extreme state of the world prevails – in which case the advice contains the exact same amount of information as having PITA assess what state of the world will occur.
6. Note that this i.i.d. specification implies that the traveler believes that the level of uncertainty regarding the utility of the default option equals the level of uncertainty regarding the utility of unknown alternatives relative to this default option.

REFERENCES

Abdel-Aty, M.A., 2001, Using ordered probit modeling to study the effect of ATIS on transit ridership. *Transportation Research Part C*, **9** (4), 265–277.

Abdel-Aty, M.A., R. Kitamura, and P.P. Jovanis, 1996, Investigating effect of advanced traveler information on commuter tendency to use transit. *Transportation Research Record*, **1550**, 65–72.

Ackerberg, D.A., 2003, Advertising, learning, and consumer choice in experience good markets: an empirical examination. *International Economic Review*, **44**, 1007–1039.

Adler, J.L. and V.J. Blue, 1998, Toward the design of intelligent travel information systems. *Transportation Research Part C*, **6** (3), 157–172.

Adler, J.L. and M.G. McNally, 1994, In-laboratory experiments to investigate driver behavior under advanced traveler information systems. *Transportation Research Part C*, **2** (2), 149–164.

Arentze, T.A. and H.J.P. Timmermans, 2005, Information gain, novelty seeking and travel: a model of dynamic activity-travel behavior under conditions of uncertainty. *Transportation Research Part A*, **39** (2–3), 125–145.

Arnott, R., A. de Palma, and R. Lindsey, 1991, Does providing information to drivers reduce traffic congestion? *Transportation Research Part A*, **25** (5), 309–318.

Avineri, E. and J.N. Prashker, 2003, Sensitivity to uncertainty: need for a paradigm shift. *Transportation Research Record*, **1854**, 90–98.

Ben-Akiva, M., A. de Palma and I. Kaysi, 1991, Dynamic network models and driver information systems. *Transportation Research Part A*, **25** (5), 251–266.

van Berkum, E.C. and P.H.J. van der Mede, 1993, The impact of traffic information. Joint Ph.D. thesis, Delft University of Technology, Delft.

Boyce, D.E., 1988, Route guidance systems for improving urban travel and location choices. *Transportation Research Part A*, **22** (4), 275–281.

Chancelier, J.-P., M. De Lara and A. de Palma, 2007, Risk aversion, road choice, and the one-armed bandit problem. *Transportation Science*, **41** (1), 1–14.

Chen, R.B. and H.S. Mahmassani, 2004, Travel time perception and learning mechanisms in traffic networks. *Transportation Research Record*, **1894**, 209–221.

Chorus, C.G., T.A. Arentze, E.J.E. Molin and H.J.P. Timmermans, 2005, Value of travel information: a theoretical framework and numerical examples. *Transportation Research Record*, **1926**, 141–152.

Chorus, C.G., E.J.E. Molin and G.P. van Wee, 2006a, Travel information as an instrument to change car-drivers' travel choices: a literature review. *European Journal of Transport and Infrastructure Research*, **6** (4), 335–364.

Chorus, C.G., E.J.E. Molin, G.P. van Wee, T.A. Arentze and H.J.P. Timmermans, 2006b, Responses to transit information among car-drivers: regret-based models and simulations. *Transportation Planning & Technology*, **29** (4), 249–271.

Chorus, C.G., T.A. Arentze, E.J.E. Molin, H.J.P. Timmermans and G.P. van Wee, 2006c, The value of travel information: decision-strategy specific conceptualizations and numerical examples. *Transportation Research Part B*, **40** (6), 504–519.

Chorus, C.G., 2007, Traveler response to information. Ph.D. Thesis, TRAIL Research School, Delft, The Netherlands.

Chorus, C.G., T.A. Arentze and H.J.P. Timmermans, 2007, Information impact on quality of multimodal travel choices: conceptualizations and empirical analyses. *Transportation*, **34** (6), 625-645.

Chorus, C.G., and H.J.P. Timmermans, 2008, Revealing consumer preferences by observing information search. *Journal of Choice Modelling*, **1** (1), 3–25.

Chorus, C.G., T.A. Arentze and H.J.P. Timmermans, 2008a, A random regret minimization model of travel choice. *Transportation Research Part B*, **42** (1), 1–18.

Chorus, C.G., T.A. Arentze and H.J.P. Timmermans, 2008b, A general model of Bayesian travel time learning. Paper presented at the 87th Annual Meeting of the Transportation Research Board, Washington DC.

Commission of the European Communities, 2001, *European Transport Policy for 2020: Time to Decide*. Luxembourg: Commission of the European Communities.

Commission of the European Communities, 2007, Green paper: towards a new culture for urban mobility. Brussels, Belgium.

de Palma, A. and N. Picard, 2006, Equilibria and information provision in risky networks with risk-averse drivers. *Transportation Science*, **40** (4), 393–408.

Department for Transport, 2004, *The Future of Transport: A Network for 2030*. London: Department of Transport.

Emmerink, R.H.M., K.W. Axhausen, P. Nijkamp and P. Rietveld, 1995. Effects of information in road transport networks with recurrent congestion. *Transportation*, **22** (1), 21–53.

Emmerink, R.H.M., P. Nijkamp, P. Rietveld and J.N. van Ommeren, 1996, Variable message signs and radio traffic information: an integrated empirical analysis of drivers' route choice behavior. *Transportation Research Part A*, **30** (2), 135–153.

Federal Transit Administration, 2003, Customer preferences for transit ATIS. Research report nr, FTA-OH-26-7015-2003.1, Washington DC.

Hato, E., M. Taniguchi, Y. Sugie, M. Kuwahara and H. Morita, 1999, Incorporating an information acquisition process into a route choice model with multiple information sources. *Transportation Research Part C*, **7** (2), 109–129.

Horowitz, J.L., 1984, the stability of stochastic equilibrium in a two-link transportation network. *Transportation Research Part B*, **18**, 13–28.

Jha, M., S. Madanat and S. Peeta, 1998, Perception updating and day-to-day travel choice dynamics in traffic networks with information provision. *Transportation Research Part C*, **6**, 189–212.

Jotisankasa, A. and J.W. Polak, 2006, A framework for travel time learning and behavioral adaptation in route and departure time choice. *Transportation Research Record*, **1985**, 231–240.

Jou, R., S. Lam, Y. Liu and K. Chen, 2005, Route switching behavior on freeways with the provision of different types of real-time traffic information. *Transportation Research Part A*, **39** (5), 445–461.

Kaysi, I., 1991, Framework and models for provision of driver information system. Ph.D. thesis, Massachusetts Institute of Technology, Cambridge, MA.

Kenyon, S. and G. Lyons, 2003, The value of integrated multimodal traveler information and its potential contribution to modal change. *Transportation Research Part F*, **6**(1), 1–21.

Khattak, A.J., J.L. Schofer and F.S. Koppelman, 1993, Commuters' enroute diversion and return decisions: analysis and implications for advanced traveler information systems. *Transportation Research Part A*, **27** (2), 101–111.

Khattak, A.J., Y. Yim and L.S. Prokopy, 2003, Willingness to pay for travel information. *Transportation Research Part C*, **11** (2), 137–159.

Mahmassani, H.S. and R. Jayakrishnan, 1991, System performance and user response under real-time information in a congested traffic corridor. *Transportation Research Part A*, **25** (5), 293–307.

McFadden, D., 1974, Conditional logit analysis of qualitative choice-behavior. In P. Zarembka, ed., *Frontiers in Econometrics*. New York: Academic Press, pp. 105–142.

Michea, A. and Polak, J., 2006, Modelling risky choice behavior: evaluating alternatives to expected utility theory. Paper presented at the 11th International Conference on Travel Behavior Research, Kyoto, August 2006.

Ministry of Transport, Public Works and Water Management, 2002, *De markt voor multi-modaal personenvervoer*. Rotterdam, The Netherlands: Rijkswaterstaat (in Dutch).

Molin, E.J.E. and C.G. Chorus, 2004, Willingness to pay for personalized dynamic public transport information services. Paper presented at the 83rd Meeting of the Transportation Research Board, Washington DC.

Molin, E.J.E. and H.J.P. Timmermans, 2006, Traveler expectations and willingness-to-pay for web-enabled public transport information services. *Transportation Research Part C*, **14** (1), 57–67.

Polak, J. and P. Jones, 1993, The acquisition of pre-trip information: a stated preference approach. *Transportation*, **20** (2), 179–198.

Polydoropoulou, A., D.A. Gopinath and M. Ben-Akiva, 1997, Willingness to pay for advanced traveler information systems: Smartraveller case study. *Transportation Research Record*, **1588**, 1–9.

Raiffa, H. and R. Schlaifer, 1961, *Applied Statistical Decision Theory*. Boston, MA: Harvard University Press.

Ratchford, B.T., 1982, Cost-benefit models for explaining consumer choice and information seeking behavior. *Management Science*, **28**, 197–212.

Schofer, J.L., A. Khattak and F.S. Koppelman, 1993, Behavioral issues in the design and evaluation of advanced traveler information systems. *Transportation Research Part C*, **1** (2), 107–117.

Shannon, C.E., 1948, A mathematical theory of communication. *Bell Systems Technical Journal*, **27**, 379–423.

Shugan, S.M., 1980, The cost of thinking. *Journal of Consumer Research*, **7**, 99–111.

Simon, H.A., 1978, Rationality as process and as product of thought. *American Economic Review*, **68** (2), 1–16.

Sun, Z., T.A. Arentze and H.J.P. Timmermans, 2005, Modeling the impact of travel information on activity-travel rescheduling decisions under conditions of travel time uncertainty. *Transportation Research Record*, **1926**, 79-87.

Viti, F., Bogers, E. and Hoogendoorn, S.P., 2005, Day-to-day learning under uncertainty and with information provision: model and data analysis. Paper presented at the 16th International Symposium on Transportation and Traffic Theory, Maryland, USA.

Weibull, J.W., 1978, A search model for microeconomic analysis: with spatial applications. In A. Karlqvist, L. Lundqvist, F. Snickars and J.W. Weibull, eds, *Spatial Interaction Theory and Planning Models*. Amsterdam, The Netherlands: North-Holland Publishing Company.

26 Equity dimensions of transport policies
Alain Trannoy

INTRODUCTION

An introduction is generally devoted to the importance of the subject in order to convince readers to read what follows. I would like to differ from this principle of rhetoric by starting with a provocative observation. In economics, equity dimensions in transportation are far less central to the stage compared to other fields such as education, health, nutrition and housing. Obviously this observation must be taken with a grain of salt since it cannot be totally founded on a fully empirical assessment.[1] Taken at face value, this observation can be depressing when writing a chapter on the role of equity considerations in formulating transport policies. Fortunately, explaining the reasons behind this state of affairs allows one to emphasize the specific and unique role of transport in the well-being of people. In that sense, this observation is fruitful to set up the issue and it leads to the framework that I am adopting to tackle the subject. Before developing this remark, it is important to define what equity means.

A broad definition is sufficient at this stage. Equity considerations are invoked when some normative arguments are laid down about redistribution issues. This extensive definition can be developed in two directions to offer a better understanding of what the two words redistribution and normative mean.

First, redistribution of resources or other determinants of well-being must be a matter of public debate in order for equity concerns to be practically relevant. Redistribution holds a specific property in that it leads to a zero-sum game. It is why many economists following the tradition of Lionel Robbins say that economics has nothing to say about redistribution, restricting the scope of economics to efficiency issues. There is an increase in efficiency when at least someone gains without loss of anyone. On the contrary, in redistribution issues, there is a trade-off between the well-being of individuals composing the society. That said, all conflicts about redistribution are not solved in appealing to equity.

Second, appealing to normative arguments is a prerequisite for the word equity to be worth using. These arguments should apply to more cases than the specific case in discussion. The validity of the argument should also be tested in a situation where the positions of the individuals are reversed. More generally, the reasoning should pass a sort of test of veil of ignorance: ignoring the personal identity but not the personal situation should leave the recommendation derived from the equity rule unchanged. To illustrate, let us take the example of a compulsory purchase of a property by the state to build a new road. The question at stake is how and how much should the owner of the property be compensated. Different answers can be brought to this question which involves many more agents than the unlucky landlord. Indeed, the distribution of well-being among the tax payers or the users of the new road is affected depending on how the compensation is going to be financed, tax or toll. The compensation itself is a zero-sum game between the landlord and the taxpayers or the users of the road. The rule would be an equity rule if the reasoning underlying the compensation will apply to every expropriation arising in the jurisdiction. On the other hand, the compensation will not obey an equity rule if the compensation the landlord obtains depends on his specific power of spoiling the electoral campaign of the incumbent.

After having recalled what equity means in broad terms, I can come back to the claim that equity considerations and particularly equality as an ethical value are invoked less frequently in transportation than in other areas of public intervention such as education, health, housing and nutrition. If it is clear that transportation policies redistribute 'time' and so well-being across the population, it is far from obvious that normative statements are very often used in solving redistribution issues in transportation. Efficiency aspects dominate the fields, at least in the economic literature. I see basically two reasons for this.

First, neither accessibility nor mobility[2] is ever listed among the more pressing needs unless it is required to satisfy a pressing need such as education, nutrition, or health care. The more vital the need is, the more present equality considerations are. Indeed several important authors, and James Tobin (1970) is likely to be the pioneer in the economic literature before John Rawls or Armatya Sen, argue in favor of 'Specific Egalitarianism'. Whatever is thought about a general redistribution policy transferring money from rich to poor, he argues that there are important aspects of well-being where a specific equalizing policy may be good to implement not only for people who will benefit from it but also from a broader social perspective. Interestingly, Tobin does not quote transportation in his list, neither John Rawls in his list of primary goods. Is it just an accident? Let us take for instance the list of ten capabilities proposed by Martha Nussbaum (2000).[3] Good health is mentioned as a prerequisite for the first and second ones ('life' and 'bodily health'). Nutrition and housing are evoked in the second, education in the fourth ('sense, imagination and thought'). The absence of handicap appears in the third ('bodily integrity'), but nowhere are accessibility and mobility mentioned as they are understood by transportation experts. When equality emerges as an important issue for transport, it seems it mainly appears as a means to achieve other more vital goals such as education (school bus), health (ambulance to go to the hospital or the doctor), job search or working (subsidized public transportation).

This reason will be enough to explain why transportation is not a major topic in the equity literature. A more subtle reason may also be mentioned. Spatial mobility supposes freedom to move freely from place to place. In a crude material way, accessibility is associated with the ethical value that challenges equality, liberty.[4] It has many different meanings, but here I refer to the concept of *negative liberty* defined in opposition to positive liberty by Isaiah Berlin (1969). Negative liberty means that no obstacle is put on the road to prevent the individual to pursue his goal. Look at the definition of negative liberty according to Berlin and ask whether the same words could not be employed to express the meaning of accessibility: 'What is the area within which the subject – a person or group of persons – is or should be left to do or be what he is able to do or be, without interference by other persons.' Of course, in transportation, other persons are not very far away and sometimes they badly interfere with you, in particular, in the case of congestion. Congestion is nothing but an obstacle and represents a restriction of your negative liberty of transportation.

Expressed together, the two ideas above are very powerful in explaining why equality is not prominent for transportation. Except in some special cases, accessibility is not viewed as a primary good by philosophers and this statement is even truer for mobility. Without much effort, it is easily thought that mobility is associated with a kind of liberty, the freedom to move quickly. It turns out that freedom is the rival of equality in the theory of justice. I draw a very important consequence from these first observations. Then, except in special circumstances, liberty is likely the dominant value associated with accessibility and mobility. Hence the most natural concept of equity in transportation would be that which puts the concept of freedom at its heart. Do we have a good candidate for this apparently difficult task? Maybe.

As fire and water, it may be thought that liberty and equality are antagonistic values. Equality of opportunity (EOP) is a philosophical theory that tries to associate liberty and, more precisely, the exercise of liberty and equity. *A Theory of Justice* (1971), the monumental work of John Rawls, contains the seeds of the theory and different variants have been proposed since, in a more transparent way, by Richard Arneson (1989), Gerard Cohen (1989), Ronald Dworkin (1981a, b), Marc Fleurbaey (2008), John Roemer (1998) and Armatya Sen (1985). There are differences among these authors and I do not want to dismiss them. Rather than trying to define what the precise meaning of equality of opportunity is for each author, I will use a hybrid one which is enough for my purpose. The requirement of EOP would be that the generalized cost of reaching destinations should be the lowest possible and the more equal. This equality of opportunity will be mainly appraised in terms of accessibility, but it could be supplemented in terms of mobility, involving both the two aspects of a transportation policy, infrastructure and use in an integrated way.

Before offering this global perspective which embraces the two aspects of a transportation policy in a fourth section, I will review more systematically equity dimensions which arise in the two main dimensions of transport policies, transport infrastructure and transport use in the first two sections. I will end by touching upon two steps which are crucial in the process of decision making in transportation, cost–benefit analysis and acceptability. As I argued above, the fact that redistribution is entering in the stage in these two steps does not imply that equity considerations are the matter of discussion. In the first of the last two sections, I will consider whether cost–benefit analysis is really distribution-free as it is generally stated. Some authors (Raux and Souche, 2004, for instance) argue that referring to criteria of justice would overcome some problems of acceptability. Philosophers and economists are well placed to offer a normative solution based on principles of justice to solve acceptability problems. This is clearly useful for the decision maker and the public debate. Nevertheless, in view of the intricacies of the political process, one can doubt that this kind of solution will be adopted in many circumstances. It is a state of affairs which is obviously unfortunate, especially if one views equity principles as laudable attempts to solve conflicts among agents (persons or groups) by resorting to rational thinking and fine principles for humankind. I develop this point of view in the last section.

EQUITY IN THE DESIGN AND COST OF INFRASTRUCTURE

Building transport facilities and using them are the two stages at which equity dimensions can be discussed. In this section, we focus on the former stage and introduce the different issues which command equities consideration. Building a new transport facility requires three agreements: first, the location of the project; second, the funding; and third, the way to compensate the losers whose property has been expropriated. The concepts of fairness that is called for can be spatial justice, that is, the equitable treatment of individuals or groups of people who are located in space. The income dimension does not matter or matters less than in transportation use. The discussion is sometimes posed in terms of groups by referring to people living in the same territory or jurisdiction. The term 'territorial justice' is sometimes used to describe this way of thinking and may seem odd to the economist, at least at first glance. I will come back to this aspect in more detail. But let us just observe that the acceptability of a new project is commonly associated with the mention of some vague principle of territorial justice in the political speeches or in public debate.

Equity Principles in the Design of Infrastructure

The problem at stake is the location of infrastructures such as locations of airports, bus and train stations, and the layout of the network of road, railways or bus lines. Two main points of view come in when discussing the fairness of a new facility. The most immediate is the issue of accessibility. A new facility changes the access to the network. In general, access is improved for a majority of people but it can also be damaged for a substantial minority of people through some severance phenomena. For example, locating an expressway close to a neighborhood may enhance accessibility for the residents when they drive, but impair their accessibility when walking or bicycling. Locating an airport close to a city may enhance accessibility to the air transport mode, but impose noise costs on residents. Residents gain in one dimension, but lose in another. A dynamic point of view can also be adopted. Accessibility to the transportation network is a condition for catching profitable opportunities for business people and job opportunities for workers. In the long run, differences in accessibility transform into differences in growth rates across territories and income levels between individuals. We successively address the equity issues in these two settings.

Equity and accessibility

The issue of access to a network has attracted many distinguished scientists belonging to several fields (geography, operational research, applied mathematics and economics) since the first approach of Weber (1909). Stations, airports and access roads are only a few that come to mind as real examples of facilities affecting access. It is generally assumed that the distribution of agents across space is given. The behavioral response of agents in terms of their choice of where to live is ignored. We relax this assumption in the paragraph below, which is devoted to equity and growth

Transport systems are generally modeled as networks. Networks are composed of vertices or nodes (crossroads, stations, airports, harbors) which are joined together by arcs, edges or links (roads, railways, flights, shipping routes). The nodes serve as access points. Flows occur along the links of the network. Then two broad planning problems can be addressed. They depend on how the location of the population (which is given) is specified. Either it is assumed that the population is already distributed across nodes or the population is located on the entire Euclidian space.

In the former case the allocation problem can be formulated as a Steiner problem (Hwang et al., 1992). The unknown here is the network itself, which is able to connect all the nodes. The problem is to find the network of shortest length, where the length is the sum of the lengths of all links. From an equity point of view, formulating the problem in that manner is specific in the sense that the utility of the access is just given by the length, and I will come back to that point below. The optimal network can have additional vertices to those initially considered to shorten the total length of the network. These new vertices will typically be interconnection stations.

In the latter case, there is a network with at least one link that crosses over the zone occupied by the population. The population cannot initially access the network. Then the planning problem is to find the location of the access facility which minimizes in some sense the generalized transportation cost of the population to the access point, for instance, an airport.

The goal of this chapter is obviously not to review the solutions of these two problems which are complex and, in some sense, specific. It is to offer a better understanding of the equity concepts that have been proposed in the transportation literature and to connect them to the general literature on justice criteria.

A first basic observation is likely useful since it is rarely made among transportation or location economists. It is about what is called the informational basis of the social choice (see Roemer, 1996). What piece of information do we need about the particular situation of every agent involved in the allocation problem to make the equity criterion just meaningful? A specific trade-off between the self-interest of the agents is associated with each equity criterion. One has to accept the use of some common metric to make the situation of the agents comparable.

Let us note that there are some settings where this kind of comparison cannot be accomplished in some objective way. For example, the statement that 'I am particularly bothered by or particularly pleased with President Obakozy' is hardly verifiable unless the brain activation when voting is observed. It explains why the intensity of preferences is not taken into account in voting decisions about representatives. Only ordinal preferences are captured by diverse voting procedures and in those circumstances, the informational basis of social choice is quite poor.

Transportation access provides an example where, in contrast, the situation of every individual can be described by some objective metric. Generally, the distance between the home and the transportation facility serves as a measure of the accessibility to the network (for more complex measures, see Weibull, 1976, 1980). One can use some metric or the journey time by foot, bike or car. Whatever the metric, it is the same for each agent and provides a sound basis to perform objective comparison of well-being across agents. A quite common assumption is the linearity of the utility function with respect to the distance. The disutility is just assumed to be given by the distance. Even if it is very convenient, it is not particularly realistic since costs are generally supposed to be convex. A one hour journey to reach the station is likely to be more than two times as costly than a half-hour journey. So it is more sensible to introduce a convex transformation of the distance to measure the disutility associated to the remoteness from the access point.

The salient point for our purpose is that this convex transformation does not impact the Rawlsian criterion used in location economics known as the minmax. It corresponds to the transportation infrastructure which minimizes the largest loss, that is, the largest distance to the access point. The fundamental two remarks made by social choice theorists such as Sen (1970, 1977) and D'Aspremont and Gevers (1976) are that first the maximin criterion requires the comparison of utility levels of individuals but not of utility differences and, second, that performing the same monotone transformation on utility functions does not change the worst-off individual. Then for the minmax criterion, the choice of the utility representation does not matter. The conclusion is that transportation economists can still live with a linear utility function when applying the minmax criterion.

This conclusion does not hold when we turn our attention to the criterion minisum pioneered by Weber (1909) and which is widely used for example in defining the Steiner tree problem. In terms of information basis to social choice, the requirements are quite the opposite. To make the summation operation meaningful, utility differences across agents involved in the allocation problem should be comparable but we do not need any assumption about utility levels. Here, comes the lack of robustness of this popular criterion. When applying the same monotonic and convex transformation to the distances, we do not keep the same solution. The solution computed for minimizing the sum of the distances to the transport infrastructure will not be the same as the solution computed for minimizing the sum of the squares of the distances. Here the assumption of linearity of utility coupled with the minisum criterion leads to a lack of robustness of the solution.

Morrill and Symons (1977) seem to have been the first to propose some intermediate solution between the minsum criterion which is compatible with a very large degree of inequality and the Rawlsian criterion which corresponds to a infinite degree of inequality aversion. The criterion they propose applies a power transformation with some inequality aversion parameter α larger or equal to 1. With some obvious notations, their criterion reads

$$D^{\alpha}(l) = -\sum_{i=1}^{n} (d_i(x_i, l))^{\alpha}$$

and the criterion corresponds to the minsum for $\alpha = 1$ and converges to the minmax when α goes to infinity. Ironically, the parameter α can also be interpreted as the curvature of the utility loss function. In that case, the above function describes as well the minisum criterion for different parameterization of the utility loss entailed by the journey time to the access point.

Suppose that we stick to the linear utility assumption. It is quite surprising that nobody has thought to use the Nash bargaining solution which requires both comparison of utility levels and differences. The use of the distance as a metric of utility losses would allow such a rich informational setting. Adopting the view point of bargaining seems fairly obvious when the number of players is quite few. For example, there are two relatively small towns competing for a station which enables access to the high speed network which is going to join two main towns. The high speed train will be constructed whether the two small towns reach an agreement or not. The just solution tries to give to each player an advantage with respect to some status quo. The status quo is quite obvious in this context. In case of disagreement, no intermediate station is built and people living in the two small towns have to reach by car or bus one of the two main towns to take the train. The distance to the closest main town provides a measure of severance in case of disagreement. The Nash solution corresponds to a localization of the station that maximizes the product of net advantage in terms of distance across the two cities. That is, if I call s_1 and s_2 the two measures of severance, the location of the infrastructure l has to maximize the quantity

$$N = ((s_1 - d)_1 (x_1, l)) ((s_2 - d)_2 (x_2, l)).$$

Other bargaining solutions may be used as well and there is probably some room for application in the domain of transportation.

Equity and growth

A lot of theoretical work and empirical evidence sheds light on the importance of transportation for endogenous growth (see Aschauer, 1989, and Button, 1998, for a review). The values of estimated output elasticity of public infrastructure investment are quite dispersed from 0.03 to 0.4. These estimations must be taken with a grain of salt for they can be plagued by endogeneity problems. It is quite likely that rich regions and nations develop their transportation network more intensively than poor ones. Reverse causality can occur and the causal effect of transportation infrastructure on growth can only be apprehended by the use of good instruments. However, when addressing equity issues, the question is less about the whole impact of infrastructures on growth measured at the aggregated level than their effect on the disparity of growth rates across regional entities. Even if the national growth rate is enhanced by infrastructures, growth rates of regions crossed over or left out by infrastructures may be affected differently. The focus is really on interregional relationships and equity concepts are designated to operate at the regional level. These equity criteria hinge on the mobility of agents.

In the paragraph devoted to equity and accessibility, the agents have been supposed immobile, which is only true in the very short run. Obviously, in the long run, they are not perfectly mobile meaning that firms and households will move only if the expected utility of the move exceeds the switching costs. The more important these costs are, the less mobile the agents. The expected net benefit of the move is computed over some horizon. When the horizon becomes more remote, the agents turn out to be more mobile. For instance, for quite a long time, aged people have been among the less mobile households. The increase in life expectancy has changed the behavior of retired people who are trying to optimize their location when they stop working.

It is a distinctive feature of economic analysis to emphasize the role of behavioral responses of agents when their environment changes. A transportation network shapes the location of economic activities in the long run (see Banister and Berechman, 2000, for a review). Location theory (see Beckman and Thisse, 1986, for a survey of location choices for production activities) provides partial equilibrium models which analyze the influence of the structure of the transportation network on the location of firms and households. It is well understood by economists, but not necessarily by politicians, that new infrastructure does not necessarily attract activities in regions that the infrastructure crosses over. Firms face a trade-off between return to scales and transportation costs. When serving the local market through local plants, they avoid transportation costs but they do not benefit from economies of scale, whereas it is the opposite when serving the global demand with only one plant. Simulations realized on toy networks (see Peeters et al., 2000) show that a high-speed connection between two towns can favor the location of activities in the larger town if the decrease in transportation costs is sufficiently distinct and scale economies quite large. In the same vein, it is quite well known that the development of the railway network in France in the nineteenth century adopted a radial form around Paris. The intuition that the center of a radial network is the source of a strong agglomeration force is backed by the results of Peeters et al. (1998) regarding the optimal location of a plant with a fixed cost and constant marginal and transportation cost. The radial railway network of France came under attack after World War II when it was realized that one century of development after the starting of the railways network had led to a situation known as 'Paris and the French desert' with virtually no other great city at that time in France (Gravier, 1947).

In return, there is a feedback effect of the economic activity on the shape of the transport system. As the choice of the *minisum* criterion exemplifies, the choice of the transportation network depends on the preexisting location of human activities. So there is clearly the risk of a vicious circle for less dense regions where the weakness of transportation network and activities reinforce themselves through a feedback loop. Contrarily, for rich regions, the case of a virtuous circle is very likely when economies of scale in production and agglomeration externalities are taken into account. The relationship of causality is circular and the process of spatial development is cumulative. The politicians in charge of the development of the less dense regions are aware of this relationship and they are trying to prevent their region from becoming a periphery in the core periphery model.

This political economy snowball effect derived by the interaction of economic and political forces differs from the one described by the new economic geography. This strand of economic literature proposes an integrated way of using general equilibrium models to think about the effect of transport costs on the shape of regional disparities. The important result obtained since Krugman's (1991) landmark article (see for instance the chapter by Lafourcade and Thisse for a review) is that the linkage between the decrease in transports costs and the concentration of economic activity across two regions is not monotonic. An inverse-U shaped curve is generally obtained with two distinct phases. A fall of transport costs goes along with a strengthening of the core when starting from high transport costs. When they are sufficiently low, then a further fall of transport costs goes against concentration and a dissemination of activities across the two regions can take place. Thereby, as Lafourcade and Thisse point out, if the trade-off between economic efficiency and spatial equity in the first stages of the integration process is very likely, the new economic geography suggests that the pursuit of integration can result in a more balanced distribution of activities across regions.

Nevertheless, in developed countries and in the most recent period the link between the development of infrastructure and the fall in transport costs is not completely obvious in view of the result obtained by Combes and Lafourcade (2007). By resorting to the concept of generalized transport cost that combines several distance and time monetary costs, they estimate that the infrastructures and fuel costs contributions account for less than one-tenth of the 38 percent average decline in freight costs that has occurred between 1978 and 1998 in France.

All these considerations argue in favor of complementing the static equity point of view with a dynamic one. The main difficulty is in thinking about equity criteria among regions when coming from the methodological individualism privileged by economists. This view point is iconified by a Bergson–Samuelson social welfare function which aggregates individual utilities. Following methodological individualism, mainstream economists tend to think that discussing welfare at a level other than the individual one is just odd. Social scientists in other fields are not that shy (see for instance Walzer, 1983) and argue that justice can be defined among group of individuals, among communities. For example, appealing to a just peace between Israel and Palestine does not raise objections in principle. Similarly, it seems important to identify in which circumstances it is sensible to raise equity issues about in the development of infrastructures among for instance Landers in Germany, states in the United States or Flanders and Wallonia in Belgium. This does not mean that there is no individual root to these principles of justice defined between communities. It is quite the opposite. The common sense attached to these principles comes from the very fact that they emerge as defending the common interest of many people. If consuming private goods develops the feeling of private interests, consuming public goods as transport infrastructures is associated to public or common interests. As Israeli people share some common interest about peace negotiations, the inhabitants of Bavaria share some common interest in the development of the infrastructure network in Germany. This common interest comes from their relative proximity which makes their need and use of the transportation network quite similar from a broad perspective. Hence, region-based equity concepts do not necessarily violate the methodological individualism. These equity concepts just refer to the common aspect of transportation use of nearby individuals.

However, this link between individual interests and equity criteria defined at the regional community level may be broken in some circumstances. It is relatively easy to imagine a possible conflict between individual and collective values, and more precisely between equity of access and equity in terms of growth. It is going to be the case when equal access in the short run means different growth path in the long run. An individualist criterion supports easy access while a communitarianist criterion may call for a more cautious position. Suppose that there is a relatively poor and mountainous region pinned down between two urbanized regions. If the three regions belong to the same country, it is the interest of the two big regions to set up a high speed connection going straight and crossing over the mountainous region. The interest of the inhabitants of the mountainous region is that some access is built to the line. Suppose that, following an equal access principle between individuals, the request of these inhabitants is satisfied and the station is built. In the short run, politicians and inhabitants may be perfectly happy. But in the long run, plants and firms previously installed in the middle region may move in response to the decrease in transportation costs to one of the two big cities to serve the whole market, thereby leading to high unemployment. In the long run, if wages are not flexible enough to compensate the lack of capital in the region, young will emigrate to one of the big cities and population will decline. In the long run, only farmers will remain. The regional product will shrink in the intermediate region, while it will grow in the two urbanized regions. If this scenario prevails, a trade-off between equity defined in terms of equal access and equity defined in terms of equal regional growth can then appear.

This conflict may be viewed ultimately as a conflict between freedom and identity. On the one hand, the free move of individuals translates into a utility gain if they pay the true social cost of their moves, that is, all externalities like congestion costs are internalized into prices. Nevertheless, it is unclear whether this move can improve both the situation of people who are left behind and those who are joined. There are no general results establishing that free move can lead to efficiency (for economic geography, see Charlot et al., 2006) and the failure to establish Tiebout's conjecture (Calabrese and Romano, 2009). On the other hand, coming back to the above example, the shrinking population in the mountainous region can lead to an identity loss if it has developed a different language, social habits and culture (for bringing identity to economics, see Akerlof and Kranton, 2010). So, in due course the defense of a communitarianist point of view resorts to a different identity of the poor region from the rest of the country. Otherwise, if individuals are perfectly alike all over the country, it is almost an economic nonsense to force some of them to live in worse conditions than others in order to comply with criteria of equity which only then serve as self-justifying the job of local politicians.

Suppose that identity matters. Trannoy (2008)[5] proposes a framework where it seems meaningful to propose equity criteria which can complement efficiency ones when thinking about the development of nationwide or continent-wide transport infrastructure. It is a (modest) attempt to provide explicit welfarist foundations of communitarianist equity criteria linking growth, welfare and migration. Probably, they can be applied to a wider range of allocation problems than pure transport ones and be considered as well for the fairness of regional development policies. Here, we summarize the argument.

Let us think of a situation where some geographical entities as regions or nations with a strong distinct cultural identity have given up their sovereignty to make up a federal state. In particular, they have abandoned their tax power to develop the transport network in an independent way. They also forgo putting any obstacle to free movement of people and firms across the nation territory. It seems common sense that their representatives invoke some stand-alone test when discussing the design of the transportation network. The stand-alone test is extensively used in the literature about cost sharing (see Moulin and Schenker, 1994) but its application is broader. It stems from individual rationality. It corresponds to a situation where every member of a group asks whether it is better to belong to the group or to stand alone. The interest of this basic requirement comes from the fact that it links different notions as individual rationality, equity and strategic considerations. If the stand-alone test is violated, threats of secession must be taken seriously (Alesina and Spolaore, 2005). The stand-alone test can apply to a single region or a coalition of regions. In more broad terms, a transport network project should belong to the core, that is, is should not be blocked by proposals made by any coalitions of players (here regions or nations). A proposal is blocking if with its own resources a coalition of regions can propose to each own member a better allocation, here a better transportation network for the use of its own population.

The fact that the equity criterion should not be purely individualistic dismisses any per-capita value judgment. Imagine a region where only one resident continues to live, while it was very populous in the past. Let us suppose that economists have concluded that the income per capita of this unique resident is similar to that one in the counterfactual situation of sovereign state. The stand-alone test is verified in that very weak sense, but the size of the population and activities settled in the region matters for a communitarianist view point. It does not mean that we can adopt a pure utilitarian view point either since the tyranny of numbers can lead to what the philosopher Parfit (1984) has coined as the 'repugnant conclusion'. Adding up new population with a very tiny level of welfare to the incumbent population is going to increase the Benthamite social welfare function. To avoid such a conclusion, Blackorby et al. (2005) have proposed introducing a critical level, c, such that the social welfare function reads as the sum of discrepancies between individual utility levels U_i and this critical level for the overall population. The critical level is exogenously defined and can correspond to some poverty threshold below which the survival and the dignity of a person is not ensured. It can evolve across time but it is the same for all regions. This parameter has to be chosen by the social decision maker on the basis of opinion and scientific studies.

Thus *critical welfare* in region j at date t with population n_{jt} is defined by:

$$W_{jt} = \sum_{i=1}^{n_{jt}} (U_{ijt} - c_t)$$

(26.1a)

or

$$W_{jt} = n_{jt}(\overline{U_{jt}} - c_t)$$

(26.1b)

where the average utility is defined as

$$\overline{U_{jt}} = \frac{1}{n_{jt}} \sum_{i=1}^{n_{jt}} U_{ijt}.$$

In developed countries, the critical level is surely less than the average utility level. Some reasoning in the following will resort to this feature. The evolution of welfare depends on three elements, the growth of population, average welfare and critical utility. Average welfare growth can be approached by the growth of GDP per capita in first approximation. The growth of population can have several origins, as natural increase or migratory balance. We imagine a situation where the former force is of the same strength in every region to focus on the latter. In the short run at least, economic rationality hinges on migration decisions. Fertility obeys different logic in the short run. In the long run, the natural increase is going down if young emigrate. So we can defend that the driving force of the population evolution is migration.

We first outline an equity criterion directly inspired by the stand-alone requirement. We see the stand-alone test as an additional constraint in an optimal control problem. The welfare defined as in Equation (26.1b) plays the role of a state variable in optimal control. There are as many state variables as regions. The control variable is the transport network. We agree that in reality there are other control variables but, for the problem in hand, we assume that there is only one control variable. The stand-alone equity test is satisfied for region j if the evolution of the transport network as decided at the federal level allows the growth path of the state variable to be as high as it would have been if the region had remained sovereign. As economic geography suggests, the decrease of transport costs induced by the development of the network system can likely violate this rule in the first stage of economic development while it is possible to get a more optimistic conclusion in more mature phases. Admittedly, the process of constructing the counterfactuals one would need to implement this equity criterion would be complex. It would be risky to claim that the counterfactuals are very robust in all circumstances. It may appear that this criterion is too demanding for our current knowledge in regional science and economic geography. Arguably, in most cases, this first criterion cannot lead to an operational rule for decision makers.

We now turn to the formulation of a second equity criterion which can lead to testable implications. The growth of regional critical welfare since the creation of the federal state should be at least as great in the poorest regions as in the richest ones. For two regions, region 1 and 2, the requirement reads

$$\text{If } W_{10} < W_{20}, \text{ then } \frac{W_{1t}}{W_{2t}} \geq \frac{W_{10}}{W_{20}} \text{ for all } t \geq 1 \tag{26.2}$$

The criterion says that the disparity between regional critical welfare should not widen in relative terms. Decomposing the growth of critical welfare for a region j between its population and welfare component is instructive. Let us define $\dot{n}_{jt}$ as the annual growth rate of population due to migration and $\dot{w}_{jt}$ as the annual growth rate of per capita welfare. Then the ratio of critical welfare at two subsequent periods t and $t - 1$ can be written

$$\frac{W_{jt}}{W_{jt-1}} = (1 + \dot{n}_{jt})\left(1 + \frac{\dot{w}_{jt}}{1 - \frac{c}{U_{jt-1}}}\right) \tag{26.3}$$

Then it follows that if two regions grow at the same rate in terms of population and per capita welfare, the poorer region will catch up in terms of the critical welfare criterion.[6] In other words, if the population of the two regions is growing at the same rate, the growth of per capita welfare can be lower in the laggard country for catching up to take place. Assuming that per-capita GDP stands for the measure of average utility,[7] the homothetic growth of the critical welfare entails a weaker requirement in terms of per-capita GDP than that adopted by the European community in shaping its regional policy. Over 80 percent of this regional policy budget is dedicated to convergence objective defined as a catching up of regions whose per-capita GDP falls below 75 percent of the EU average.

In all cases, it is clear that the critical welfare criterion offers a way to outweigh[8] the change of per-capita welfare with respect to the change in population due to migration. For example, if the critical welfare level represents half of the average level of the poor region, which is not an unreasonable statement,[9] then the impact of the growth rate of the per-capita welfare is amplified by a factor of two in that region. Suppose now that the critical welfare level represents one third of the per capita welfare of the rich region, meaning that the poor region has a per-capita welfare of two-thirds of the rich region. Then the impact of the growth rate of the per capita welfare of the rich region is only inflated by 50 percent. Convergence can still be obtained by letting active young people migrate from poor to rich regions. For instance, according to Burda (2009), Eastern Germany has lost more than 1 million inhabitants since the fall of the Berlin Wall. The exodus persists 'since it continues to lose 40–50 000 of its inhabitants each year and most of these are young people who are essential for a sustainable growth in the future'. This shrinking population is taken into account in the critical welfare criterion. Over the same period, a catching up in terms of income levels has occurred with more than half of the per-capita GDP gap between East and West Germany being closed in the past 15 years.

In the particular example of Germany, simple computation shows that the relative gain in per-capita terms is offsetting the migration disequilibrium.

We may summarize all the above discussion by a simple decision rule regarding infrastructure policy. The fair-growth-path view using migration information boils down to the following rule: if the catching up in critical regional welfare holds, then regional and infrastructure policies do not need to be reconsidered. In the opposite case, a case by case study should be undertaken to look at the role of infrastructure policy in the divergent growth path of critical welfares. Then, economists and regional science specialists will be called on to investigate a specific issue by using all available data and models. They may answer in the negative meaning that they are concluding that infrastructure policy is not responsible for the widening gap.

Equity of Cost Sharing of Infrastructure

The problem at hand still involves local, regional or national communities. I imagine a road or a railway which benefits several communities that have to agree on how to share the cost of it. These cost-sharing problems are specific because space represents a physical obstacle that cannot be escaped. If region B is between region A and C, the road and the railway going from A to C has to cross over region B. If region B is populous enough to build a station to let inhabitants of B gain access to use the infrastructure, then the cost sharing problem involves the three regions.

Let us apply the serial cost sharing rule which has received much attention since its introduction by Shenker (1990) and its deep analysis by Moulin and Shenker (1992, 1994). It was originally conceived for problems where n agents request different quantities of a private good, the sum of which is produced by a single facility. With the original serial cost sharing rule, agents are ordered according to their demands, starting from the lowest one, agent 1. The key idea is to decompose the problem in n cost sharing problems. The cost of producing n times the lowest demand is shared equally among all agents. Agent 1 does not support any additional cost. Agent 1 is then left out of the cost sharing game and only $n - 1$ agents remain. We apply the rule of equal share of producing $n - 1$ times the lowest demand from Agent 2, and so on. The game is over when the only remaining agent is that with the highest demand. He solely bears the incremental cost corresponding to the gap of demand with the second highest demand.

This rule can be characterized from two ethical axioms: equal treatment of equals (in terms of demands) and independence of larger demands (a protection of small demanders against larger ones). It satisfies other interesting properties such as the stand alone test and has other characterizations as well. It is therefore natural to investigate its application to the problem of sharing the cost of an infrastructure linking regions or cities. The application has not been deeply investigated (see Fragnelli et al., 2000, for the application of the Shapley value[10]) to infrastructure sharing problems.

I will illustrate the idea through an example. Suppose that there exists four cities ranked on a line indexed 1 to 4. There are three sections of the infrastructure, the first one going from 1 to 2 and so forth with corresponding costs, C_1, C_2, C_3. The problem is then to allocate the cost of these three sections. Consider first the case of four cities of equal size and equal demand whatever the city of departure and destination. The problem is original in that there are two directions of using the railway, from town 1 to town 4 or the

Table 26.1   Traffic in each segment from each city

	Cost of section 1	Cost of section 2	Cost of section 3
City 1	$N_{12} + N_{13} + N_{14}$	$N_{13} + N_{14}$	N_{14}
City 2	N_{21}	$N_{23} + N_{24}$	N_{24}
City 3	N_{31}	$N_{31} + N_{32}$	N_{34}
City 4	N_{41}	$N_{41} + N_{42}$	$N_{41} + N_{42} + N_{43}$

opposite. Thereby we have to apply the serial cost sharing idea to both directions. For the direction 1 to 4, we obtain full bearing of C_1 for city 1, equal sharing of C_2 between 1 and 2, equal sharing of C_3 between cities 1, 2 and 3. For the direction 4 to 1, we get full bearing of C_3 for city 4, equal sharing of C_2 among cities 4 and 3, equal bearing of C_1 among cities 4, 3 and 2. The assumptions translate into equal traffic in each direction, meaning that each direction has to support half of the cost. Adding up we obtain for the shares of the cost and denoting by S_i the shares, one gets:

For city 1: $S_1 = \frac{1}{2}(C_1 + \frac{1}{2}C_2 + \frac{1}{3}C_3) = \frac{1}{2}C_1 + \frac{1}{4}C_2 + \frac{1}{6}C_3$

For city 2: $S_2 = \frac{1}{2}(\frac{1}{2}C_2 + \frac{1}{3}C_3) + \frac{1}{2}(\frac{1}{3}C_1) = \frac{1}{6}C_1 + \frac{1}{4}C_2 + \frac{1}{6}C_3$

For city 3: $S_3 = \frac{1}{2}(\frac{1}{3}C_3) + \frac{1}{2}(\frac{1}{3}C_1 + \frac{1}{2}C_2) = \frac{1}{6}C_1 + \frac{1}{4}C_2 + \frac{1}{6}C_3$

For city 4: $S_4 = \frac{1}{2}(\frac{1}{3}C_1 + \frac{1}{2}C_2 + C_3) = \frac{1}{6}C_1 + \frac{1}{4}C_2 + \frac{1}{2}C_3$

It is clear that these formulas can be extended to generate interesting mathematical regularities with n cities. Let us point out that when the cost of each section is the same, the two remote cities 1 and 4 supports $^{11}/_{36}$ of the costs and the two middle cities $^7/_{36}$ with the serial cost sharing idea. So it is just that the two intermediate cities support a smaller share of the burden than the two polar cities when population and demand is uniformly distributed on the real line. It is so because people living in the polar cities take longer trips on average. Interestingly, the application of the Shapley value gives also equal sharing of the second section in this example and an even more disproportionate of sharing of the two extreme sections. City 1 will bear ¾ of C_1 and the three other cities $^1/_{12}$. The analogue goes for C_3. (See Moulin, 2004, for a discussion of the Shapley value in a similar context.)[11]

The rule has to be adjusted when the cities differ in size. Let us denote the size of the traffic going from city i to city j by N_{ij}. Then the cost of each section should be shared in proportion to the ratio of the traffic originated from the town to the total traffic on the section. Table 26.1 gives the corresponding traffic and allows computation of the shares of the cost of each section for each city. For instance, the share of section 1 for city 1 cost is simply $(N_{12} + N_{13} + N_{14})/(N_{12} + N_{13} + N_{14} + N_{21} + N_{31} + N_{41})$.

It is interesting to investigate whether this rule is consistent with practice. An example is the building of the high speed train between Paris and Strasbourg involving four regions, the Paris region, Alsace and two intermediate regions. It turns out that Alsace is paying the lion's share of the last section (C_3), about 45 percent[12] of the funding coming from the regions, while the three others finance the remaining. We are not far from what the rule predicts in the uniform case, with ½ for city 4.

Equity and the Compensation for Compulsory Acquisition

The building of new infrastructures generally requires compulsory acquisition of land or properties. It is in the power of government to acquire private rights in land without the willing consent of its owner or occupant in order to benefit society. As a direct result of government action, people lose their property. Compensation is to repay them for these losses. It seems well grounded in terms of principles justice, if we refer to Nozick (1974) for which the distribution of property rights is just if brought about by free exchange or gifts among consenting adults. An appropriation by the state is just, as long as it leaves no one worse off. The principle of equivalence is crucial to determining compensation: affected owners and occupants should be neither enriched nor impoverished as a result of the compulsory acquisition. The money paid cannot fully replace what is lost. In some countries, there is legal provision recognizing this in the form of additional compensation to reflect the compulsory nature of the acquisition. In addition, compensation should cover moving costs. In practice, given that the aim of the acquisition is to support growth and welfare, there are strong arguments for compensation to improve the position of those affected whenever possible. There are few issues except the area concerned with the compensation. The market value of real estate may be enhanced by the building of the transportation facility and it should be the majority of cases. It hardly need be observed that the new infrastructure can generate noise nuisance, pollution or severance phenomena for properties alongside which are going to depreciate the value of the real estate. Should it be fair to compensate for the induced loss of wealth? It is a complex matter and I will not treat it. However, the answer is obvious from the point of view of acceptability. The persons who are not compensated for the loss of wealth will try to block or to slow down the project. If the project is worth it for social welfare, it is a pity. Then it is better to appeal to Kaldor–Hicks compensation criterion,[13] which states that a project should be undertaken when people who are made better off with the project could compensate those that are made worse off, in order to reach a Pareto improvement. Kaldor–Hicks is seldom implemented, although infrastructure building provides some means to do so. It is the case, for example, when the project is financed through property tax and the tax base relies upon the fair market value of the property. Compared to the benchmark, the situation before the project, those who benefit from the project will see a rise in taxes, while those who lose from it will see a drop. Henceforth, compensation between the winners and the losers will take place and anything goes. In contrast, if the mechanism has to be designed on an ad-hoc basis, the winners have an interest in blocking it to avoid being taxed and the risks are quite high that the compensation will be given up. The agents concerned by compensation were individuals, a common feature with the next subject which is equity and transport use.

EQUITY AND TRANSPORT USE

I now focus on the use of transport by households and investigate what equity principles may vindicate departing from the efficiency point of view where each user should pay the long run marginal cost (à la Boiteux) integrating congestion costs. The argument has much to say about the vertical dimension of redistribution, that is the distinction between poor and affluent people. In the first part only the income dimension matters and I examine if transfers in kind are optimal in transport. However, the spatial dimension is still important in some respects specifically when considering the question of whether we should compensate commuters.[14] I review the arguments in the second paragraph. Finally, I offer some comments about the usual practice to give some priority to the worst off when congestion is severe. It illustrates the importance of needs, a third dimension which is one of the most popular in any debate on justice (Yaari and Bar Hillel, 1984).

Are Transfers in Kind Optimal in Transport?

There are various examples of transfer in kind or reduced fares, mostly concerning public transportation. Free school bus, free ambulance or cabs (in low-density areas) for old people in poor health going to hospital and free public transportation for unemployed travelling for job search purposes exemplify transport vouchers having a tutelary dimension. Here transportation is just a means to allow people to fulfill specific aims such as primary education, health care or getting a job. Accessibility is becoming a primary good when it helps to fulfill basic needs. Those who benefit from the transfers in kind are persons who are not able to drive because they are too young, too old, too unhealthy or too poor. If the inspiration of specific egalitarianism is clear, it remains to be understood why equity benefit outweighs the efficiency cost traditionally attributed to transfers in kind.

The loss of efficiency described by microeconomics or public economics manuals, even good ones such as Stiglitz (2000), is associated with possibility of substitution. Because public transportation is free, overutilization of public transportation will occur. It will be less costly to give a cheque equal to the *ex-ante* consumption of public transportation. The possibility of substitution is reduced since generally using public transportation is not so pleasant: it may be slow, noisy and very often crowded. Using public transportation is seldom fun. So the loss of efficiency is probably small.

Compensating Commuters, the Pros and Cons

One of the most contentious equity issues is about compensating commuters. A recent debate in French politics illustrates the dilemma: should we give to people who live in a remote village with respect to the center of the city a green cheque for compensating the carbon tax? I here present the pros and cons.

The pros: They live far away to escape non-affordable land prices close to the central business district (CBD). So they are driven out from the city by land prices. It is not their choice and they should be compensated by application of the principle of compensation of EOP. This principle states that people should be compensated for factors for which they cannot be held responsible. (See Fleurbaey, 2008, for an exhaustive presentation of EOP.)

The cons: Living far away is a choice. They could stay closer to the CBD if they diminish their consumption of floor area. They just realize a trade-off between two amenities, be close to the center and space. The application of the principle of natural reward of EOP requires no compensation. This principle says that people should bear the consequences of decisions for which they can be held responsible (Fleurbaey, 2008).

The answer to the question is likely to be different according to the size of the city. For instance, in big cities such as New York, London, Paris, consider the case of a household composed of two adults and two children, where one of the two adults is a worker and the only bread-winner. It is clear that this household cannot rent an apartment on the private market in the center of the city. In contrast, in a small city in the middle of nowhere, the responsibility argument is probably best received. The interested reader can find more on that in Fleurbaey and Trannoy (1998).

Priority Rule and Congestion

It has been argued that poor people suffer more from congestion since they cannot choose their working time. The high-skilled can have more flexible working hours. If the low-skilled have less time-elastic demand than the high-skilled, it will be both more efficient that the Pigouvian tax will hit the high-skilled more than the low-skilled because of the inverse-elasticity rule.[15] It is a case where efficiency and equity go hand in hand as long as public transportation is not available or in short supply.

   Thus far I have presented the maximin as a rule which allows to give priority to the worst off by comparing utility levels of individuals. It is fascinating how many applications of maximin we can find in transportation. Priority to the disabled, pregnant women and elderly in public transportation is an illustration of the local justice of Jon Elster (1992). The comparison of utility levels when all people are standing up reveals who the worst off are. The second observation is that these persons are likely to be less well off when seated down than 'normal' people when standing up. Then, by giving priority to those who are the most deprived of not being seated, the micro-society allocates the scarce resources of seats to the worst off in order to maximize their welfare during transportation. When coming to traffic on roads, priority to ambulances and police forces can be defended on the same grounds. In the case of overbooking, people at the reception desk may try to determine who would be the most deprived by not taking the plane.[16] In the three examples, the bottom line is always to find out who are the neediest persons.

AN INTEGRATED POINT OF VIEW: EQUALITY OF OPPORTUNITY OF ACCESSIBILITY

In the previous two parts, I have focused on a specific aspect of transportation policy. I am trying here to embrace a broader perspective integrating both infrastructure and use. I am sticking to individualistic theories of justice, meaning that individuals are at the center of the stage. The principle of justice I will put forward is the principle of maximum equal freedom for all. Freedom is always at the forefront of any individualistic theory of justice (See Laslier et al., 1997 for a review of the importance of freedom for economic thinking). According to Carter (1999, p. 83) 'Perhaps the most famous example of principle of maximal equal freedom is to be found in the first principle of John Rawls's theory of justice (1971), although the principle gets qualified there so as to refer only to basic liberty [. . .] In contemporary debates among political philosophers this principle is appealed to by both egalitarian and libertarian.' Kolm (2007) considers a possible application of this principle to transport in a footnote.[17] I am following this line and I am going to consider freedom of move as a basic right. The above principle boils down to the following maxim 'Equal and maximal freedom of movement for all' for transport policy.

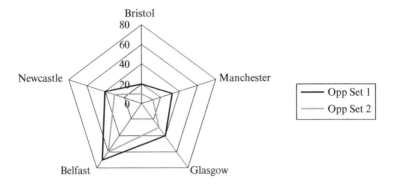

Notes: Axes show the minimum cost in £

Figure 26.1 Accessibility opportunity set for a London resident

In practical terms, it means maximizing the opportunity set of people in terms of reachable destinations by means of transport. Many dimensions matters for spatial mobility: the price of the journey, the travel time, the frequency and so on. This opportunity set is clearly multidimensional. Here we will focus on the price, because it is probably the most sensitive dimension in view of the income inequality. If utility is quasi-linear in income, it is possible to express all other dimensions in money, in such a way that it represents the money-metric loss of utility of the trip. The 'accessibility opportunity set' describes what the minimal budget is to reach every destination, whatever the type of transportation. I have drawn two virtual ones in Figure 26.1 assuming that the individual is living in London. The virtual numbers indicate the minimal budget to reach five important cities in the UK. For the sake of illustration, I draw two opportunity sets, one being inside the other. The smaller the 'spider web' the better, meaning that it is cheaper to reach any destination. The opportunity policy attempts to reduce the size of the spider web as much as possible.

One has to distinguish between the 'accessibility opportunity set' which is common to everybody, at least if transportation authorities do not price discriminate, and the 'individual opportunity set' which depends on the income of the individual. It is a budget set where you can read the maximum number of journeys (an integer) on each axis that an individual can afford, if she devotes all her budget to travel to this specific destination. An example is drawn in Figure 26.2, for a budget of £1000. The larger the set, the better but the second set depends on income distribution which is generally assumed to be given in transportation economics.

For the size of individual opportunity set to be maximized, the transport authorities can only play with the size of the accessibility opportunity set. This set has a public dimension, the transportation network, and a private dimension, the use of her car, or two-wheeled vehicle if any.[18] An EOP transportation policy would obey two rules:

1. Maximize the size and the capacity of the transportation network, with as many points of access as possible. General taxes or taxes on property will be preferable to tolls to cover the cost of infrastructure. Taxes are usually more paid by the rich than

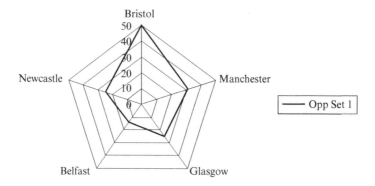

Notes: Axes show the number of journeys that exhaust the budget, given the prices in Figure 26.1.

Figure 26.2   Individual opportunity set for a Londoner with an income of £1000

the poor and this statement is clearly true for property tax. Tolls are uniform and generally do not depend on income, even if there are exceptions.
2. Make the private act of using the network the most affordable possible. Tolls will be only tolerated to internalize congestion costs or other externalities. Gasoline and car prices will be loaded with the lowest taxes, except Pigouvian taxes. Finally, the government should foster competition between suppliers.

You intuitively realize that one of the countries which has likely the transportation policy following the most closely these guidelines is the United States,[19] as least for intercity transportation. I understand that it is a quite provocative stance. I will attempt to bring some argument to sustain this idea. Leave aside the distribution of income, or assume that the per-decile distribution of income is the same in all OECD countries. Then the differences come from the density of infrastructure with respect to the density of the population, the amount of the tolls, the price of the gasoline and the airplane or train ticket, the price of the cars and the intensity of competition.

The United States has a very large network of free highways and airports. For instance the European Union has about 3500 airports while the United States has about 15 000. It is true that airports in the United States play the role of stations in Europe. Gasoline prices are low in the United States when compared with most other Western countries. The United States has the largest system of highways in the world. Toll roads, even if they are present, are concentrated on the east coast which is the densest area (see Zhu et al., 2010). The gas prices in European countries have traditionally been three to four times the price in the United States. Between 10 percent and 15 percent went to pay taxes in the United States. According to Morrison (2005), the deregulation in airfare industry which has taken place since the end of 1970s has been beneficial to consumers with reduced fares. Free entry for foreign competitors in the car market has produced a fall in the share of domestic car makers with no more than 45 percent of market share nowadays.

Notwithstanding, the statement of a US policy following quite closely an EOP policy should be balanced by two observations. First, the statement only holds for intercity transportation (regional scale) and not for commuting where public transportation may be lacking, preventing poor people to move freely to get a job in the urban area. Second, the low price of gas does not internalize local and global environmental externalities. So the current US implementation of the 'Equal and maximal freedom of movement for all' principle for the current generation may limit the freedom of move of the next generations. It will hurt Herbert Spencer (1851) for whom 'every man may claim the fullest liberty to exercise his faculties compatible with the possession of like liberty by every other man'.

Modulo these two caveats, it does not come as a surprise that the United States follows quite closely the EOP policy in transportation, since spatial mobility belongs to the American dream. Spatial mobility is a way to accomplish liberty and freedom is of paramount importance in the United States. Countries do not choose the same field for applying the idea of specific egalitarianism. The United States has a special focus on transportation (private). However European countries give a bigger role of public transportation (buses, metros, railways) in urban areas. It is quite plausible that some European countries succeed more than the United States in implementing an EOP in commuting transportation policy.

It is interesting to have a glance at the specific case of France, which does not seem too much interested in promoting an EOP policy in transportation. France is famous for having developed an efficient high speed train network. It is valuable for high income recipients because they have a high value of time, much less for low income recipients because the price of the TGV ticket is only affordable in off-peak periods. When taking highways, they are paying heavy tolls to private firms and high taxes make the gasoline quite expensive. In addition, the French government, whatever the political party in power, has forbidden as much as possible the entry of contenders in the railways and airline industry to protect the interests of the previous public monopoly. Taxis are rare and thus their availability is unpredictable. All in all, except for urban areas, the comparison is not quite favorable for France. This situation does not seem to worry public opinion. A simple explanation seems that in the French mythology spatial mobility is not valued as it is in the United States.

Finally, EOP will promote a vigorous policy in direction of disabled people for whom the freedom of movement is harshly reduced. Specific facilities to access public transportation are of primary importance when taking seriously the aim of an 'Equal and maximal freedom of movement for all'.

IS COST–BENEFIT ANALYSIS 'DISTRIBUTIONALLY NEUTRAL'?

I treat this issue at the end since it is not specific to transport. Nevertheless, this issue is particularly important in view of the wide use of cost–benefit analysis in transportation analysis (Mackie and Nellthorp, 2000; Willis, 2005).

In a first-best world, where production prices equal to the consumption prices, efficiency and redistribution issues are independent. Then, it will not be necessary to conduct a cost–benefit analysis incorporating the deviation to marginal cost pricing noted in the third part of this chapter. But in a second-best world, this separation of the two spheres cannot be maintained (see Dreze and Stern, 1987).

Cost–benefit analysis is widely used to sort out the best transportation projects (see, for instance, Mackie and Nellthorp, 2000). Cost–benefit analysis can provide an answer to the difficult but specific question in a first-best world: does the project improve the Pareto frontier of the economy at the point on this frontier chosen *ex ante* by the social maker? If there is an improvement, then the aggregate income evaluated at the *ex-ante* prices must increase. This beautiful and useful result should not be overemphasized. There are two important qualifications. The first one is that the project is sufficiently small for not changing the *ex-ante* equilibrium prices. In the case of transportation infrastructure, this assumption is seldom satisfied. It is quite the opposite; it surely affects the land values at least on the neighborhood of the infrastructure. The fact that this change of prices may be neglected in a cost–benefit analysis may be viewed as an empirical question. Nevertheless, this observation is not central to the argument.

The second qualification is that the result does not say that the project will improve the Pareto frontier at any point of the frontier. This point is not always well understood, and sometimes it is thought that cost–benefit analysis does not depend on value judgments about distributional issues. It is clearly incorrect. Let us take a simple example to illustrate the point. Suppose that the project is a highway between the two main cities of a country. Initially, there was a huge income inequality which translates into a low rate of motorization. Consequently, the project was not socially profitable: the criterion of the national income was violated. Suppose now that a political revolution takes place and changes the property rights through lump sum transfers. Now a sufficient proportion of the population can afford the cost of a car. When computing the new demand coming from these new car drivers, it turns out that the intercity highway becomes a good investment. Observe that nothing has changed in the economy except the property rights and induced changes in the aggregate demand and output (more cars and probably fewer luxury goods have been produced). But the changes of the distribution of lump sum incomes are sufficiently strong to change the answer provided by the cost–benefit analysis. Even though the usual cost–benefit analysis relies on the assumption associated to a first-best world, it is not distribution-free.

I would like to make an additional observation. In essence, the cost–benefit analysis is welfarist. It means that goods, bads and services are valued through their influence on the utility of individuals who compose the society. Paternalistic views are excluded. This quite narrow perspective of the goals of the society reflected by cost–benefit analysis is clearly an advantage for getting results. It is obviously a weakness in the social debate where many opinions express some paternalistic views in a form or another. For sure, the main interest of cost–benefit analysis would be lost if one tries to capture too many things in it. It is better that the analysis remains one criterion among many in the social decision making.

I end with an unsettled question which connects subsidized price for equity concerns and CBA. Suppose that some individuals do not pay the marginal cost, so they have a higher demand. Suppose that the project would be socially profitable if we take into account their demand at the subsidized price, but not if we take into account their demand at the marginal cost price. Should we undertake the project?

ACCEPTABILITY AND EQUITY

I conclude with some remarks about the supposed links between acceptability and equity. Acceptability refers to the complex process in modern democratic countries by which a change in transportation facilities or pricing policy is adopted. In countries (Switzerland, and the United States), a referendum or ballot proposition can be organized about the building of a new infrastructure or introducing tolls. In this case, acceptability means that there is a majority of citizens who are voting for the proposal. The study of acceptability merges with that of outcome of majority voting (Cremer et al., 1985; Hansen and Thisse, 1981; Hansen et al., 1986) in planning problems. The outcome may or may not correspond to a fairness solution. There are many cases where majority voting selects an outcome location that corresponds to the location chosen by utilitarianism. For example, it is the case when the network is a tree: there is only a single route between any pair of points located on the network. Then, the majority solution[20] – there does not exist another location on the tree that is preferred by a majority of individuals – coincides with the Weber solution, that is, the location which minimizes the total distance covered by the users who are all located at vertices of the tree. Even in this simple case of a tree, the maximin rule provides a different solution. By the way, it is quite often the case that this outcome of voting generates large inequities vis-à-vis the maximin rule (see the computations of upper bound by Hansen and Thisse, 1981).

In other countries, the way opinions or preferences are aggregated is far more complex and can be described in general terms as a game with four categories of players. Planning authorities are the first of them and have the privilege of playing first in making proposals. Their expertise capacity means that these proposals are backed by cost–benefit analysis or at least by a detailed study of spatial demand and cost structure. In principle, efficiency is likely the dominant value underlying the proposals coming from these authorities. The second player is the general public made of citizens, potential users and taxpayers. In direct democracies, it is very clear how the opinion of these players matter. In representative democracies, it is possible that the process selects an outcome opposed by a majority of citizens. A major change introduced by playing a decision game instead of voting is that an organized minority can block a decision favored by the majority. The public debate enables people to express their intensity of preferences. It is not bad from an equity perspective in itself, since both maximin and utilitarianism are based on comparisons of utilities. The expression of complaint of a utility loss is typically the ingredient that is aggregated through utilitarianism. The public opinion is captured through polls realized about the project or the general mood that politicians can perceive in their close contact with voters in their constituencies. Precisely, the political representatives at the local or regional level are the third type of players. Their reelection for the incumbents may be partly influenced by the realization of transport infrastructure or changing the way to finance them. The last players are the diverse interest groups. (See Guilano, 1992, for a detailed presentation of these groups.) Environmentalists, business interests, real-estate business, landlords whose property values are strongly affected by the building of the facility and farmers are among those who are the most present to defend their view or interest. Their power depends on the political leverage they have on politicians, positively through supporting their campaign or negatively by disrupting their election through vocal criticisms. Then a complex process starts with public information, public debates, proposals and counter-proposals, demonstrations, newspaper articles, media buzz and votes at town or regional council and, in some cases, prosecutions, as for the toll in the Lyon's road tunnel (Raux and Souche, 2004). It is important to emphasize that most of the players of the game and particularly politicians and interest groups act strategically. That is, their behavior depends on how the other players behave. This has the important following consequence: in the public debate, their stated opinion does not necessarily reflect their true opinion. In particular, it is quite likely that the losers have an interest in overemphasizing their losses at the initial stages of the game. What is unknown at the beginning of the game is when the game is over. The acceptability process takes time and then resources. The cost of waiting to obtain an accepted compromise is rarely fully assessed by the players of the game. The end of the game comes when a compromise between the main forces can be reached or when the opponents or the proponents of the project are exhausted. In that sense, it is a kind of equilibrium in the sense that no group or coalition of groups is able to stop the outcome to be implemented.

After having described in general terms the kind of games that are played, it is quite apparent that modeling them is a quite complex task (for an attempt, see Raux and Souche, 2004). The issue I want to address is assessing the importance of equity considerations for the different kinds of players. For sure, the easiest way to stop a project is to say that it is unfair. In truth, diverse interest groups do not hesitate to kill projects by appealing to unfairness considerations. It is a good strategy, if they are opponents to the project. As neuroeconomics has shown, for instance, in the case of the ultimatum game (Sanfey et al. 2003), unfairness induces an emotional shock in the brain. Since everyone has experienced some unfairness in life, claiming unfairness is a way to capture the attention of others. The point is that it is too easy to claim. From a normative point of view, claiming unfairness should start by stating what equity principle should be respected in that matter. As I emphasized in the introduction, an equity principle should have a quite large domain of application and not just be invoked for the problem in hand. The supposed unfairness of the project or its funding should be presented in an articulate way to be accepted as such as a contribution to the debate. It is rarely done and there is room for the planning authorities to intervene in that fairness debate at two stages. First to intervene in the public debate to tell what the received arguments are in terms of fairness. Even if planning authorities are more inclined to discuss efficiency, they are well prepared to think about justice as well, since, by nature, they think in a normative way. It is just a matter of learning concepts at school and in books. For instance, they should be prepared to tell that such argument is inconsistent from a normative point of view since it does not respect the Kantian principle.[21] Second they can intervene in a second stage of the game when the 'efficiency solution' has been rejected and some deep conflict of interest has to be resolved. They should be trained to introduce in the public debate some plan B mixing efficiency and equity arguments that solve the conflict of interests. The equity principle should be related to that used in comparable cases to give more force to the argument in appealing to the force of the rule. The politicians are not likely to support this view since they generally prefer to resort to discretion rather than to rules to avoid tying their hands for future similar decisions. In some cases, they will simply prefer to favor one party closer to their electorate rather than follow a more balanced decision. Another obstacle to pursue in that vein should be mentioned last. Ordinary people would not accept easily that justice matters would, in some sense, be confiscated by experts.

We find again the usual conflict between knowledge and democracy that pervades many policy issues in the modern world.

ACKNOWLEDGEMENTS

I am grateful to André de Palma for his trust, to Robin Lindsey for providing references and a careful reading of a first draft, to Emile Quinet for helpful discussion, constant encouragement and comments, and to Hervé Moulin for a discussion on cost sharing functions. The usual caveat applies.

NOTES

1. For instance, Vickerman (2001, p. 47) states: 'the concept of optimality in transport systems has to bring together these two elements, technical and economic efficiency'. In welfare economics, optimality is not mixed up with efficiency. Optimality underlies the use of some social welfare function which weighs the well-being of individuals and this social welfare function has been maximized.
2. I will use the term 'mobility' to mean travel speed, and 'accessibility' to mean the generalized cost of reaching destinations. When I refer to people who are moving or migrating, I will use the term 'spatial mobility'.
3. See also Nussbaum and Sen (1993).
4. In Ancient Greek, the word for liberty *elcutheria* is formed in opposition to *doulos*, slave. To be free also implies being free to move.
5. See Trannoy (2011) for a shorter version and a corrected proof of the main proposition.
6. The derivative of the right-hand side with respect to W_{j0} is negative, provided that $c/W_{jo} < 1$.
7. See the Stiglitz–Sen–Fitoussi Report (2009) report for proposals to alleviate the deficiencies of per capita GDP as measure of welfare.
8. Since $1 - C/\overline{U}_{jt-1}$ is less than 1.
9. The poverty line is defined as a given percentage of the median income, generally 50 percent or 60 percent.
10. See also Bogomolnaia and Moulin (2010) for references and in-depth discussion of the application of the Shapley value to the minimal cost–spanning problem, that is, to divide the minimal cost of connecting a given set of users to a source.
11. See, in particular, example 5.9, p. 155. I owe the comparison with the Shapley value to Hervé Moulin.
12. From *La Vie du Rail Magazine* No. 3236, 15 September 2010.
13. Despite the fact that the criterion is known to be intransitive.
14. It is also possible to compensate for high asymmetry costs in the same country. For instance, transport by boat from Corsica to mainland France is subsidized. This raises the issues of the relationship between citizenship and accessibility that we do not tackle here. See Dumitru (2011) for a philosophical discussion.
15. The situation differs from the standard Ramsey case which concerns how to raise a given amount of revenue with the least distortion. The rule calls for inelastic demands to be taxed more heavily. Here, the goal is to internalize congestion externalities. it is more efficient to induce travelers with more elastic schedules to retime their trips since rescheduling is less costly for them.
16. This statement need to be qualified. When airlines seek to maximize revenue, which is the case in a deregulated industry, they try to identify travelers who will give up their seats for the least compensation. If every traveler has the same income, those who will be the most deprived by not taking the plane are those who will ask for the most compensation.
17. 'Another classical conception wants to associate to each basic right – which is social liberty for a broad kind of application – material means making it 'real', and wants the resulting freedom to be 'equal for all and maximal' (Rousseau, Condorcet, the 1789 Declaration, Mill, Rawls). Yet, since there is no a priori limit to these associated means (to the size of the cathedral for freedom of cult, of the various means of communication for freedom of expression, of *private planes and airports for freedom to move*, and so forth), this would determine the totality of the allocation of goods, with no rule for choosing among the various goods', Kolm, 2007, p. 11, footnote 20. See also Viegas (2001) for invoking the first principle of justice of Rawls.
18. Here, I am considering the case of individuals in good health. I will consider the case of disabled later on.

19. See Weiner (2005) for information about US transportation policy.
20. This solution is often referred as the Condorcet solution.
21. I refer to the categorical imperative 'Act only according to that maxim whereby you can at the same time will that it should become a universal law.'

REFERENCES

Akerlof G.A. and R.E. Kranton, 2010, *Identity and Economics : How Our Identities Shape Our Work, Wages and Well Being*. Princeton, NJ: Princeton University Press.
Alesina, A. and E. Spolaore, 2005, *The Size of Nations*. Cambridge, MA: MIT press.
Arneson R.J., 1989, Equality and equal opportunity of welfare. *Philosophical Studies*, **56**, 77–93.
Aschauer D.A, 1989, Is public expenditure productive? *Journal of Monetary Economics*, **23**, 177–200.
Banister, D. and J. Berechman, 2000, *Transport Investment and Economic Development*. London: UCL Press.
Beckman, M.-J. and J.-F. Thisse, 1986, The location of production activities. In P. Nijkamp, ed., *Handbook of Regional and Urban Economics*, Vol. 1. Amsterdam: North-Holland, pp. 21–95.
Berlin I., 1969, *Four Essays on Liberty*. Oxford: Oxford University Press.
Blackorby, C., W. Bossert and D. Donaldson, 2005, *Population Issues in Social Choice Theory, Welfare Economics, and Ethics*. Cambridge: Cambridge University Press.
Bogomolnaia, A. and H. Moulin (2010), Sharing a minimal cost spanning tree: beyond the folk solution. *Games and Economic Behavior* **69**, 238–248.
Burda, M., 2009, Half-empty of half-full? East Germany two decades later. Available at: www.VoxEu.org.
Button, K., 1998, Infrastructure investment, endogenous growth and economic convergence. *The Annals of Regional Science*, **32**, 145–162.
Calabrese, S. and R. Romano, 2009, Inefficiencies from metropolitan political and fiscal decentralization: failures of Tiebout competition. Working paper, Carnegie-Mellon N° July.
Carter, I., 1999, *A Measure of Freedom*. Oxford: Oxford University Press.
Charlot, S., C. Gaigne, F. Robert-Nicoud, and J.-F. Thisse, 2006, Agglomeration and welfare: the core-periphery model in the light of Bentham, Kaldor, and Rawls. *Journal of Public Economics*, **90** (1–2), 325–347.
Cohen, G.A., 1989, On the currency of egalitarian justice. *Ethics*, **99**, 906–944.
Combes, P.P. and M. Lafourcade, 2005, Transports costs: measures, determinants and regional disparities implications for France. *Journal of Economic Geography*, **5**, 319–349.
Cremer, H., A.-M. De Kerchove and J.F. Thisse, 1985, An economic theory of public facilities in space. *Mathematical Social Sciences*, **9**, 249–262.
D'Aspremont, C. and L. Gevers, 1977, Equity and the informational basis of collective choice. *Review of Economic Studies*, **44**, 199–209.
Drèze, J.P. and N.H. Stern, 1987, The theory of cost-benefit analysis. In A. Auerbach and M. Feldstein, eds, *Handbook of Public Economics*. North-Holland: Amsterdam.
Dumitru, S., 2011, Migration and equality: should citizenship levy be a tax or a fine? *Ateliers de l'Éthique*, **6**(2), forthcoming.
Dworkin, R., 1981a, What is equality? Part I: equality of welfare. *Philosophy and Public Affairs*, **10**, 185–246.
Dworkin, R., 1981b, What is equality? Part I: equality of resource. *Philosophy and Public Affairs*, **10**, 283–345.
Elster, J., 1992, *Local Justice*. New York: Russell Sage Foundation (in co-publication with Cambridge University Press).
Fleurbaey, M. and A. Trannoy, 1998, La péréquation territoriale en question. *Flux*, **31–32**, 91–98.
Fleurbaey, M., 2008, *Fairness, Responsibility and Welfare*. Oxford: Oxford University Press.
Fragnelli, V., I. García-Jurado, H. Norde, F. Patrone and S. Tijs, 2000, How to share railways infrastructure costs? In F. Patrone, I. García-Jurado and S. Tijs, eds, *Game Practice: Contributions from Applied Game Theory*. Dordrecht, The Netherlands: Kluwer Academic Publishers.
Giuliano, G., 1994, Equity and fairness considerations of congestion pricing. Curbing gridlock, peak-period fees to relieve traffic congestion. Transportation Research Board Special Report 242, Vol. 2, 250–279.
Gravier, J.-F., 1947, *Paris and the French Desert*. Paris: Portulan.
Hansen, P. and Thisse J.-F., 1981, Outcomes of voting and planning : Condorcet, Weber and Rawls locations. *Journal of Public Economics*, **16**, 1–15.
Hansen, P. and J.-F. Thisse, and R. Wendell, 1986, Equivalence of solutions to network location problems. *Mathematics of Operation Research*, **11**, 672–678.
Hwang, F., S. Richard and P. Winter, 1992, *The Steiner Tree Problem*. Amsterdam: North Holland.
Kolm S.-C., 2007, Economic macrojustice: fair optimum income distribution, taxation and transfers. Mimeo.

Krugman, P., 1991, Increasing returns and economic geography. *Journal of Political Economy*, **99** 483–499.

Laslier, J.F., M. Fleurbaey, N. Gravel and A. Trannoy, eds, 1998, *Freedom In Economics: New Perspectives in Normative Analysis*. London: Routledge.

Mackie, P. and J. Nellthorp, 2000, Cost-benefit analysis in transport. In D.A. Hensher and K.J. Button, eds, *Handbook of Transport Modelling*, Vol .1. Oxford: Elsevier Science.

Morrill, R.J. and J. Symons, 1977, Efficiency and equity aspects of optimum location. *Geographical Analysis*, **9**, 215–222.

Morrison, S.A., 2005, Deregulation of US air transportation. In K.J. Button and D.A. Hensher, eds, *Handbook of Transport Strategy, Policy and Institutions*, Vol. 6. Amsterdam: Elsevier, pp. 405–420.

Moulin, H. (2004) *Fair Division and Collective Welfare*. Boston, MA: MIT Press.

Moulin, H. and S. Shenker, 1992, Serial cost sharing. *Econometrica*, **60**, 1009–1037.

Moulin, H. and S. Shenker, 1994, Average cost pricing versus serial cost sharing: an axiomatic comparison. *Journal of Economic Theory*, **64**, 178–201.

Nozick, R., 1974, *Anarchy, State, and Utopia*. New York: Basic Books.

Nussbaum, M., 2000, *Women and Human Development: The Capabilities Approach*. Cambridge: Cambridge University Press.

Nussbaum, M. and A.K. Sen, 1993, *The Quality of Life*. Oxford: Clarendon Press.

Parfit, D., 1984, *Reasons and Persons*. Oxford: Oxford University Press.

Peeters, D., J.-F. Thisse, and I. Thomas. 1998, Transportation networks and the location of human activities. *Geographical Analysis*, **30**, 355–371.

Raux, C. and S. Souche, 2004, The acceptability of urban road pricing: a theoretical analysis applied to experience in Lyon. *Journal of Transport Economics and Policy*, **38** (2), 191–216.

Rawls, J., 1971, *A Theory of Justice*. Cambridge, MA: Harvard University Press.

Roemer, J., 1996, *Theories of Distributive Justice*. Cambridge, MA: Harvard University Press.

Roemer J., 1998, *Equality of opportunity*. Cambridge, MA: Harvard University Press.

Sanfey, A., J. Rilling, J. Aronson, L. Nystrom and J. Cohen, 2003, The neural basis of economic decision-making in the ultimatum game. *Science*, **300** (5626), 1755–1758.

Sen, A.K., 1970, *Collective Choice and Social Welfare*. San Francisco, CA: Holden-Day.

Sen, A.K., 1977, On weights and measures: informational constraints in social welfare analysis. *Econometrica*, **45**, 1539–1572.

Sen A.K., 1985, *Commodities and Capabilities*. Amsterdam: North-Holland.

Shenker, S., 1990, Making greed work in networks: a game-theoretic analysis of gateway service disciplines. Mimeo, Xerox Research Center, Palo Alto.

Spencer, H., 1851, *Social Statics*. London: John Chapman.

Stiglitz–Sen–Fitoussi Report, 2009, Report by the Commission on the Measurement of Economic Performance and Social Progress.

Stiglitz, J., 2000, *Economics of the Public Sector*, 3rd edn. New York: W.W. Norton and Co.

Tobin, J., 1970, On limiting the domain of inequality. *Journal of Law and Economics*, **13**, 263–277.

Trannoy, A., 2007, Equité territoriale, acceptabilité et grandes infrastructures de transport. In J. Maurice and Y. Crozet, eds, *Le calcul économique*. Economica, pp. 402–431.

Trannoy, A, 2011, Equité interrégionale, migrations et grandes infrastructures de transport. In F. Dufaux and P. Philifert, eds, *Justice spatiale et politiques territoriales*, Collection Espace et Justice. Nanterre, France: Presses Universitaires de Paris-Ouest.

Vickerman, R., 2001, The concept of optimal transport systems. In D.A. Hensher, and K.J. Button, eds, *Handbook of Transport Systems and Traffic Control*, Vol. 3. Oxford: Elsevier Science, Chapter 5.

Viegas, J.M., 2001, Making urban road pricing acceptable and effective: searching for quality and equity in urban mobility. *Transport Policy*, **8** (4), 289–294.

Walzer, M., 1983, *Spheres of Justice: A Defense of Pluralism and Equality*. New York: Basic Books.

Weber, A., 1909, *Theory of the Location of Industries*. Translated by C.J. Friedrich, 1929. Chicago, IL: The University of Chicago Press.

Weibull, J.W., 1976, An axiomatic approach to the measurement of accessibility. *Regional Science and Urban Economics*, **6**, 357–379.

Weibull J.W., 1980, On the numerical measurement of accessibility. *Environment and Planning A*, **12**, 53–67.

Weiner. E., 2005, Transportation policy in the USA. In K.J. Button and D.A. Hensher, eds, *Handbook of Transport, Policy and Institutions*, Vol. 6. Amsterdam: Elsevier, pp. 763–777.

Willis, K.G., 2005, Cost-benefit analysis. In K.J. Button and D.A. Hensher, eds, *Handbook of Transport Strategy, Policy and Institutions*, Vol. 6. Amsterdam: Elsevier, pp. 491–506.

Yaari, M. and M. Bar-Hillel, 1984, 'On dividing justly'. *Social Choice and Welfare*, 1–24.

Zhu, Q., F. Qiao, and L. Yu, 2010, Toll roads distribution in the US. *Journal of Systemics, Cybernetics and Informatics*, **8** (4), 76–79.

27 Psychology and rationality in user behavior: the case of scarcity
Jonathan L. Gifford

INTRODUCTION

Scarcity is a common feature of transportation systems, from lack of empty seats on crowded trains, to long queues for takeoff at airport runways, to scarce land available for expanding congested urban highways, to scarce funds available for transportation improvements. Transportation professionals are often called upon to manage this scarcity.

The scarcity problem is relevant in the context of transportation in a variety of ways. First, and most common for policy makers, is the *scarcity of capacity of transportation facilities* at peak periods. Traditionally, many transportation agencies have adhered to a 'predict and provide' philosophy, that is, facility capacity is provided based on a forecasted level of demand, say 20 years into the future. In recent decades, however, such an approach has become problematic for a number of reasons: public opposition to expansion of existing facilities and the construction of new facilities based on concerns about induced demand (see the chapter by Santos and Verhoef in this volume) and impacts on adjacent communities and environmentally sensitive areas. In the face of difficulties expanding or providing new capacity (that is, managing supply), transportation planners have developed techniques for transportation demand management (TDM). While, in theory, correct pricing should be capable of addressing scarcity problems comprehensively, tools such as congestion pricing and optimal pricing are not always available, at least in the short term. As a result, TDM techniques beyond pricing have garnered significant interest among planners and policy makers.

In addition to transportation facilities themselves (for example, highways, roads, railways, and bridges), we must also consider the *scarcity of goods and services* that are complements or substitutes for each category of transportation capacity resource. For instance, the problem of scarce parking (a complementary good to road/passenger car transportation), or scarce transit service (a substitute for passenger car transportation), or scarce fossil fuels, can become very important for travelers and policy makers.

Second, *information* about the availability, choice, related incentives and condition of various transportation facilities and services may also be scarce, especially for certain users (low-income, poorly educated and so forth). A third important resource, which is often overlooked in transportation policy, is the *scarce attention* of the traveler himself. The traveler's attention for making decisions, especially derived decisions such as travel, is a scarce resource, and individuals tend to economize on their cognitive effort.

Previous chapters have addressed the economic tools available for managing scarcity, namely pricing in general and congestion pricing in particular. Previous chapters have also addressed some non-economic tools for managing scarcity, such as driver information and intelligent transportation systems. And finally, the chapter on project appraisal addresses the use of scarce financial resources.

This chapter focuses on non-conventional aspects of managing scarcity in transportation resources. The chapter provides an overview of the relevant theoretical perspectives from the behavioral literature – an interdisciplinary approach including psychology, sociology and economics – and examines how its concepts apply to transportation decisions and transport policy. Next, the chapter briefly touches upon the TDM literature as it relates to the management of scarcity and provides references to standard works on that subject. Finally, the chapter summarizes challenges in assessing the effectiveness of TDM tools, and identifies opportunities for future research.

INFORMATION, ATTENTION AND BEHAVIOR

As noted in the introduction, the scarcity problem is relevant in the context of transportation in a variety of ways, including:

- the scarcity of the *capacity* of transportation facilities and services, their complements, and their substitutes;
- the scarcity of *resources*, financial and material, available for improving and operating transportation facilities and services;
- the scarcity of *information* about the availability and choice of transportation facilities and services; and
- the scarcity of *attention* of the traveler himself for optimizing or improving transportation decisions.

The focus of this chapter is the last two of these, that is, how scarce information and attention affect transportation behavior. It takes as a point of departure that transportation behavior is the result of a problem solving process. Classical economic theory typically assumes that individuals are rational 'utility maximizers' and that their behavior reflects a judgment about what course of action will lead to the greatest utility. Those revealed preferences then are assumed to reflect individual judgments about the number and quality of courses of action available, of quality of information about those courses of action, and the 'cost' (in a generalized sense) of acquiring better information and processing it.

Standard disaggregated transportation modeling relies on this assumption of utility maximization. The predominant theoretical framework of 'random utility maximization' (or RUM) assumes that preferences are randomly distributed (according to known statistical distributions with parameters that can be estimated). RUM assumes that information is complete and free, and that preferences are known completely.

Yet the social sciences have long recognized that utility maximizing behavior is subject to the constraints of an individual's span of attention and inventory of information. In other words, individual rationality is 'bounded' by cognitive capacity. The term 'bounded rationality' was introduced by Herbert Simon in the 1950s in his celebrated book *Administrative Behavior* (Simon, 1955). It refers to the cognitive limitations facing a human decision maker due to the finite amount of attention and knowledge available for considering all existing alternatives and their consequences in solving a particular problem. Decision makers 'satisfice', Simon observed, meaning that they select options that are 'good enough' rather than optimal.

The information available to a decision maker/traveler is *partial* (that is, it does not describe the full universe of actions available and possible reactions to those actions); it is *contaminated* (that is, it typically contains some error); and it is *priced* (that is, obtaining better information requires some expenditure of time, cognitive effort and in some cases monetary outlay) (Traub, 1985).

Simon also made the observation that preferences are dynamic. If individuals find it easy to discover satisfactory alternatives, their aspiration level may rise; if they find it difficult, their aspiration level may fall (Simon, 1955).

The notion that information is imperfect and available only at a price – measured in time, cognitive effort and, sometimes, monetary outlay – has important implications. At some point, individuals take action rather than gather more information about the alternative courses of action available to them. In the extreme case, this may be because the individual concludes that *all* relevant information has been collected and evaluated, or that an imminent threat (or opportunity) requires immediate action. At the opposite extreme, the problem solving process may simply result in doing what's fashionable or taking the first option that presents itself. More commonly, however, individuals must take action on the basis of imperfect information. (For analyses of information acquisition by drivers see the chapters by Rietveld and by Chorus and Timmermans in this volume).

Psychologists generally view behavior and choice as a process of 'environmental adaptation'. In this view, behavior is highly adaptable and context-dependent. People are influenced by the actions of others; they may rely on principles, rules and analogies to make a choice; and the way a problem is presented may affect the decision-making process (called 'framing'). People may simply travel to a certain destination because it is fashionable to go there; some may take a different route if an information stimulus catches their attention, such as advertising of the benefits in terms of reduced congestion. The term 'affect' in psychology refers to emotion or desire. Affective factors in a transportation context, for example, include feelings of power, aggression or fear.

Still a further departure from utility maximization theory is the notion of decision-making 'heuristics', developed by Kahneman and Tversky in one of the most influential papers in behavioral economics (1979). Kahneman won the Nobel Prize in Economics in 2002 for his work critiquing expected utility theory and developing an alternative model called 'prospect theory'. Choices among risky prospects exhibit several pervasive effects that are inconsistent with the basics of utility theory. In particular, people underweight outcomes that are highly likely in comparison with outcomes that are obtained with certainty, even if they yield the same expected utility (the so-called *certainty effect*). In addition, in order to simplify the choice between alternatives, people generally discard components that are shared by all prospects under consideration and focus only on components that distinguish them. This phenomenon, called the *isolation effect*, leads to inconsistent preferences when the same choice is presented in different forms.

Many fields have incorporated the implications of bounded rationality and heuristic bias. The field of psychology has studied the concepts extensively, and many domains of social science have incorporated them, including theories of organizational development, public policy, finance, economics and software design.

IMPLICATIONS FOR TRANSPORTATION BEHAVIOR

In the transportation field, relatively recent studies find that individuals use heuristics in circumstances like habitual traveling, short-distance traveling for shopping purposes (sub-metropolitan) or even in generalized transportation. Affective factors such as the emotional attachment to one's property (the 'endowment effect'), travel for the sake of traveling ('joy riding'), and social motives (social comparison, self-presentation, norms) may contribute to so-called 'wasteful' driving and 'wasteful' commuting (Frost, Linneker and Spence, 1998).

As early as 1987, Mahmassani and Chang proposed modeling transportation patterns, such as departure time, using 'boundedly-rational user equilibrium (BRUE)'. According to their model, BRUE can be attained when all users are satisfied with their travel choices (that is, do not necessarily optimize), meaning that they set an indifference band of tolerable negative outcome (for instance, schedule delay) and make the same travel choice as long as the previous outcome has been within the indifference band. The band reflects travelers' aspiration levels, which can change in the process of learning and interaction with the environment. This means that when BRUE exists, it may not be unique – unlike the equilibrium point in most optimization processes – which would pose dilemmas for flow prediction (Mahmassani and Chang, 1987).

Tversky and Kahneman's prospect theory has been applied in a travel choice context in works by Avineri and Prashker (2004), Bogers et al. (2006), Katsikopoulos et al. (2002), Senbil and Kitamura (2004) and others. For instance, in a route-choice stated-preference experiment, Avineri and Prashker (2004) found evidence of two violations of the expected utility theory: the certainty effect (underweighting of high probabilities in favor of certain travel time outcomes) and inflation of small probabilities.

Habitual travel is seen by many researchers as an example of boundedly rational behavior. The issue of habitual travel and the possibility of inducing change is not fully clarified: some researchers find that travel behavior is neither totally repetitious nor totally variable (Schlich and Axhausen, 2003), some find that habits can be broken (Fujii and Kitamura, 2003), while others find habits more difficult to break (Garvill, Marell and Nordlund, 2003).

Many researchers (Cao and Mokhtarian, 2005; Handy, Weston and Mokhtarian, 2005; Steg, 2005) emphasize the role of affective factors in travel decisions and the difficulty of quantifying and incorporating these factors in travel demand modeling. Such studies find that the choice of travel-related strategies is affected not only by instrumental factors (for example, amount of travel, safety, speed, or cost), but also by attitudes (cognitive, affective and behavioral), as well as social motives (emotions like pleasure, arousal or stress; self-expression of social position and so forth). These findings imply that in many cases policies designed to alleviate congestion may be less effective than expected because such non-instrumental factors are seldom measured and incorporated into demand models.

Non-instrumental factors like mood, emotion and habit may be particularly important for short trips. For example, a recent study of shopping travel behavior used a simple statistical analysis to identify situations where utility maximizing rules are supplemented by simple heuristics and recommended a shift beyond rational choice and metropolitan scale analysis (Burnett, 2006). Short trips are particularly interesting because personal vehicle use in the United States is overwhelmingly local, whether measured in terms of trips or travel. Almost 90 percent of personal vehicle trips are less than 20 miles, comprising 55 percent of all personal vehicle travel (Gifford, 2003).

Non-instrumental factors appear to be important for walking trips as well. Indeed, American architect David Rockwell attempts to 'choreograph' people's movement with the design of the building or public space in which they walk, and his ideas are being utilized in the design of airport terminals (Green, 2006). Many authors, including Golledge (1995) and Passini (1992), have studied the psychological factors related to wayfinding in the context of travel behavior, with a primary focus on *destination choice* and *path selection*. Passini (1992) considers behavioral actions to be linked to wayfinding through a set of subsidiary decisions and subtasks. The complex task of wayfinding is broken down into more manageable subtasks, which are undertaken sequentially, in semi-isolation, while still taking into account the problem as a whole. In Passini's view, those tackling an unfamiliar wayfinding problem do not generally work out a total plan and then execute it. Instead, they have only a global and vague plan at the outset consisting of a few general ideas, and they gradually incorporate new information and deal with unforeseen problems as they occur.

Golledge (1995) contends that the path selection problem has traditionally been ignored or assumed to be the result of minimizing procedures such as selecting the shortest, quickest or least costly path. He develops experiments with route selection to determine relevant criteria when the environment changes and the number of nodes along a path are increased, such as in trip chaining.

McFadden, one of the fathers of the random utility maximization framework and also a winner of the 2000 Nobel Prize in Economics, emphasized the importance of attitude and affective factors in travel behavior in a keynote lecture to the World Conference on Transportation Research in 2007. He suggested that some travel choices might resemble the phenomenon of 'pelotons' in bicycle racing, where a group of cyclists travel together and trade-off as lead cyclist in order to share the extra effort required of the leading edge of the group. In his lecture, McFadden likened changes in travel behavior to a decision to join a peloton, that is, a traveler might be more inclined to adopt a different behavior if other travelers had already taken a step to do so. He suggests that 'understanding the behavior of [peloton] members and the effectiveness of the [peloton] as a collective decision-making group would be useful for understanding . . . how consumers pack together when they drive, ride transit or vote on transportation projects' (2007, p. 273). Bikhchandani, Hirshleifer and Welch (1992) developed a related concept of 'herd' behavior.

In the domain of transportation demand modeling, while the mainstream is still based on the microeconomic utility maximization framework, some aspects of boundedly and non-rational factors have begun to be incorporated in so-called 'activity-based transportation models', which are now becoming operational and are entering the stage of application in transportation planning, such as Albatross by Arentze and Timmermans (2000) or the model by Bhat et al. (2004).

These models use decision heuristics, or a rule-based approach, modeled most frequently as a decision tree. Two basic ideas are central to activity-based travel theory. First, demand for travel is induced by demand for activities. Second, individual travel patterns are subject to various spatial–temporal constraints (Bowman and Ben-Akiva, 2001). In order to model the complexity and multidimensionality of travel behavior, recent research integrates heuristic modeling (that is, decision trees) with rational probabilistic modeling (Bayesian networks) within a sequential rule-based transportation model in the context of Albatross (Janssens et al., 2006). Arentze and Timmermans (2004) develop mental maps as a Bayesian Belief Network and integrate these with activity-based models to simulate an individual's travel choice in space and time.

Taken together, concerns about boundedly and non-rational decision making provide a foundation for exploring non-traditional tools for managing scarcity. These tools are commonly known as 'transportation demand management' or TDM. TDM strategies include pricing strategies, such as parking pricing and congestion charges. They also include tools such as ridesharing (carpooling and vanpooling), flexible work schedules, telework, employee transit subsidies, and high-occupancy vehicle (HOV) and high-occupancy toll (HOT) lanes. For a recent review, see Kuzmyak, Evans and Pratt (2010).

Consideration of boundedly and non-rational factors in travel behavior may enable planners and policy makers to select and implement TDM strategies more effectively. For example, marketing TDM in ways that appeal to travelers' emotions and tastes, or fostering group behavior (that is, pelotons) could enhance the appeal of alternative transportation modes and behaviors. This suggests that marketing and communication may be as important as technical planning and modeling tools in developing effective transportation plans and programs.

CONCLUSIONS

This chapter has examined how psychology and rationality interact with travel behavior in the face of limited cognitive capacity and attention on the part of individual travelers. While limitations on cognitive capacity and attention clearly play a part in travel decisions, conventional random utility maximization models do not adequately account for these factors. Activity-based models that incorporate decision heuristics and Bayesian decision frameworks begin to address these limitations. But much work remains to be done in providing a framework and appropriate tools for developing wise investment and management strategies. Meanwhile, because such non-instrumental factors are seldom measured and incorporated into demand models, policies designed to alleviate congestion or otherwise manage demand may often have impacts that are unexpected and possibly unintended.

ACKNOWLEDGMENTS

The author acknowledges the contributions of graduate research assistants Cristina Checherita, Brian Jacob and Uma Kelekar of the School of Public Policy at George

Mason University, for their contributions to this chapter. Remaining errors are the responsibility of the author.

REFERENCES

Arentze, T.A. and H.J.P. Timmermans, 2000, Albatross: a learning-based transportation oriented simulation system. European Institute of Retailing and Services Studies, Eindhoven, The Netherlands.

Arentze, T.A. and H.J.P. Timmermans, 2004, A learning-based transportation oriented simulation system. *Transportation Research Part B*, **38** (7), 613–633.

Avineri, E. and J. Prashker, 2004, Violations of expected utility theory in route-choice stated preferences: certainty effect and inflation of small probabilities. *Travel Behavior and Values 2004 Transportation Research Record*, **1894**, 222–229.

Bhat, C.R., J. Guo, S. Srinivasan and A. Sivakumar, 2004, Comprehensive econometric microsimulator for daily activity-travel patterns. Electronic Conference Proceedings of the 83rd Annual Meeting of the Transportation Research Board, January 2004, Washington DC.

Bikhchandani, S., D. Hirshleifer and I. Welch, 1992, Theory of fads, fashion, custom, and cultural change as informational cascades. *The Journal of Political Economy*, **100** (5), 992–1026.

Bogers, E.A.I., F. Viti, S.P. Hoogendoom and H.J.V. Zuylen, 2006, Valuation of different types of travel time reliability in route choice: a large scale laboratory experiment. 85th Annual Meeting of the Transportation Research Board, January 2006, Washington DC, TRB 2006 Annual Meeting CD-ROM.

Bowman, J.L. and M.E. Ben-Akiva, 2001, Activity-based disaggregate travel demand model system with activity schedules. *Transportation Research Part A*, **35** (1), 1–28.

Burnett, P., 2006, Choice heuristics, rational choice and situational-related travel demand. 85th Annual Meeting of the Transportation Research Board, January 2006, Washington DC.

Cao, X. and P. Mokhtarian, 2005, How do individuals adapt their personal travel? Objective and subjective influences on the consideration of travel-related strategies for San Francisco Bay Area commuters. *Transport Policy*, **12** (4), 291–302.

Frost, M., B. Linneker and N. Spence, 1998, Excess or wasteful commuting in a selection of British cities. *Transportation Research Part A*, **32** (7), 529–538.

Fujii, S. and R. Kitamura, 2003, What does a one-month free bus ticket do to habitual travelers? An experimental analysis of habit and attitude change. *Transportation*, **30**, 81–95.

Garvill, J., A. Marell and A. Nordlund, 2003, Effects of increased awareness on choice of travel mode. *Transportation*, **30** (1), 63–79.

Gifford, J.L., 2003, *Flexible Urban Transportation*. Oxford: Elsevier Sciences.

Golledge, R.G., 1995, Path selection and route preference in human navigation: a progress report. *Spatial Information Theory Lecture Notes in Computer Science*, **988**, 207–222.

Green, J., 2006, Passengers may now pirouette to Gate 3. *The New York Times*.

Handy, S., L. Weston and P.L. Mokhtarian, 2005, Driving by choice or necessity? *Transportation Research Part A*, **39** (2–3), 183–203.

Janssens, D., G. Wets, T. Brijs, K. Vanhoof, T. Arentze and H. Timmermans, 2006, Integrating Bayesian networks and decision trees in a sequential rule-based transportation model. *European Journal of Operational Research*, **175** (1), 16–34.

Kahneman, D. and A. Tversky, 1979, Prospect theory: an analysis of decision under risk. *Econometrica*, **47**, 263–292.

Katsikopoulos, K.V., D.L. Fisher, Y. Duse-Anthony and S.A. Duffy, 2002, Risk attitude reversals in drivers' route choice when range of travel time is provided. *Human Factors*, **44** (3), 466–473.

Kuzmyak, J.R., J.E. Evans, IV and R.H. Pratt, 2010, Employer and institutional TDM strategies. Traveler Response to Transportation System Changes, Transit Cooperative Research Program, report 95, Washington DC., Transportation Research Board.

Mahmassani, H.S. and G.L. Chang, 1987, On boundedly rational user equilibrium in transportation systems. *Transportation Science*, **21** (2), 89–99.

McFadden, D., 2007, The behavioral science of transportation. *Transport Policy*, **14**, 269–274.

Passini, R., 1992, *Wayfinding in Architecture*. New York: Van Nostrand Reinhold.

Schlich, R. and K.W. Axhausen, 2003, Habitual travel behaviour: evidence from a six-week travel diary. *Transportation*, **30**, 81–95.

Senbil, M. and R. Kitamura, 2004, Reference points in commuter departure time choice: a prospect theoretic test of alternative decision frames. *Journal of Intelligent Transportation Systems*, **8** (1), 19–31.

Simon, H.A., 1955, A behavioral model of rational choice. *Quarterly Journal of Economics*, **69**, 99–118.

Steg, L., 2005, Car use: lust and must. Instrumental, symbolic and affective motives for car use. *Transportation Research Part A: Policy and Practice*, **39** (2–3), 147–162.

Traub, J.F., 1985, Complexity of approximately solved problems. *Journal of Complexity*, **1** (1), 3–10.

PART V

COMPETITION AND REGULATION

28 Competition, regulation and public service obligations
Marco Ponti

INTRODUCTION: THE CONCEPTUAL BACKGROUND

The traditional 'social choice' approach states that public intervention is needed in the presence of social goals and/or of market failures. Historically this intervention has assumed the form known as 'command and control', that is, direct public production or, more frequently, by means of 'public agencies'. Within this model, the public actor (the 'principal') is assumed in fact to be both benevolent and all-knowing. Therefore he will be perfectly able both to obtain from his 'agents' (the above-mentioned public agencies in charge of providing the service) efficient results, and to succeed in targeting welfare maximization. But the assumption of benevolent and all-knowing public principals and agencies is clearly unrealistic, and considering these public principals as 'humans', and not angels, in the line of the 'public choice' school, is much more realistic.[1] Among the many facts that prove this orientation, are the performances of the public agencies which have in general deteriorated over time, due to mechanisms of 'capture', that is, the influence of the interests of the agency on the decision maker, of 'rent seeking', that is, the tendency of the agency to reduce its effort, and of 'informative rents', that is, the possibility of the agency to manipulate the relevant information in its favour (see Buchanan, 1969). The State has difficulties in simultaneously meeting welfare and efficiency objectives. It faces problems in getting productive efficiency: the minimization of labor costs is an all-important factor of efficiency, while welfare objectives are in general connected with enhancing employment and labor conditions. But also managerial skills are compensated and motivated by more by profit than by simple 'good governance', that is the best possible outcome of public management.

Nevertheless, state intervention is needed not only in order to reach 'autonomous' welfare goals, but also when the market fails to deliver productive or allocative efficiency.

These facts have motivated both the concept and the practical policy of public intervention, which is how to choose between several types of public service procurement: 'command and control' (defined as the direct intervention of the public sector), 'regulation' (defined as an indirect public intervention, aimed to reach welfare goals by setting rules incentivating efficiency-oriented actors) and 'market competition' (defined as non-intervention). These categories can be seen within a 'subsidiarity'[2] context: command and control is to be employed whenever regulation fails to deliver, and regulation is to be employed whenever market competition fails to deliver.

REASONS FOR PUBLIC INTERVENTIONS

Within the transport sector, there is a wide range of situations in which intervention is needed. These situations are well known: the main ones are natural monopolies; others are externalities both within its standard definition, like those related to the environment, and in the form of 'club' externalities, like congestion, where only the participants are affected; others are information asymmetries (related mainly to safety issues, that is, the insufficient perception of risk); finally there are other 'special' transport failures, like the 'Mohring effect' (Mohring, 1972) for public transport[3] or the existence of large scale and/or space economies, high information costs (that may generate demand volatility). Also income redistribution can in some way be included in the scope of state intervention, and even if it cannot be defined as a 'market failure', it can be a legitimate public objective. Furthermore, public service obligations (PSO), that can be defined as the mandatory provision of services with characteristics of continuity, universality and equality for all the users, do have a distributional content, to an extent which will be explored latter. Which service is in need of public intervention, and which one can be left open for competition, depends both on the political objectives and on the 'technical' evaluation of the efficiency of the relevant market mechanism. Those two points indicate the choice between command and control, regulation and market competition.

The role of technical evaluation is limited to a well-defined subset of public objectives. *Productive* efficiency (or cost minimization) is the main one, given that in this area the public 'principal' faces severe conflicts of interests. A second set of objectives is related to natural monopolies and other market failures of the same kind (problems of efficient tariffs and access rules and so forth) that generate mainly *allocative* problems (that is, losses of welfare).

Other public objectives cannot be kept strictly at a technical evaluation level (that is, measured in terms of social surplus losses or gains), since their nature remains mainly political: distributive and environmental issues.

But even in these cases, a regulatory attitude looks more effective than direct state intervention. For example, if a country, or a region, decides that local public transport has to be provided free of charge, this is a perfectly acceptable choice. Probably less so if these services are produced via command and control practices, and not via competitive tendering, given the generally higher costs connected with the former practice (Segal, 1998; Shapiro and Willig, 1990).

In the case of an opposite political choice, if a free-market provision of collective transport generates unstable results (that is, wide and inefficient variations of supply), or 'dominant' (quasi-monopolistic) firms not justified by economies of scale, a proper regulation is again needed, although this does not generally call for a return to command and control practices.

Environmental issues are in theory *allocative* failures as social surplus is not maximized due to 'excessive' consumption, since some users generate costs higher than their utility. Nevertheless, the same concept of externality implies a relevant *distributive* content as some actors, even those with high utility, damage other actors without due compensation. Furthermore, the uncertainties linked to the measurement of the related economic costs leave a wide scope for political judgement.

But also in this case, the tools needed to reach environmental improvements have to be

Table 28.1   The subsidiarity chain in transport policy action

Policies	Main areas of intervention	Examples/Current issues
Liberalization and market competition	• Transport services in general	• Long distance rail and bus services • Air and maritime services
Regulation	• Infrastructure operation/ building • Unstable/non existing markets of services • Efficient charging and access rules	• Public–private partnership in infrastructures • Demsetz competition for local transport services • Competitive tendering for concessions • Slot allocation
Command–Control and Planning (direct public action)	• Infrastructure design and location • Environmental and social values • Land use/transport policies	• European Common Transport Policy, TEN, *etc.* • Kyoto standards • Urban sprawl containment

efficient, that is, able to minimize the social costs involved in every environmental policy. And a regulatory approach appears more efficient – emphasizing, as it does, 'vouchers' and tariff techniques rather than following the 'traditional' approach of imposing constraints and prohibitions.

While the scope for public decision remains very large within the transport sector, the scope for command and control practices (as an alternative to public regulation as defined above) seems to be shrinking, at least in theory.

This trend can be checked through time: more competition/regulation is present now than in the past 50 years, even if not in a linear form (for example, at the end of the nineteenth century there was not much competition, but more private operators than at present, especially in railways and local transport). Across space, a similar tendency can be seen at work, especially in the two emerging large economies, China and India, evolving clearly from a pure command and control context to a more market-oriented one.

The various scopes of the three identified policies – command and control/traditional planning, regulation, and market competition/liberalization – will now be analyzed more in detail, focusing on their pertinence areas and on examples of implementation, according to the general lines summarized in Table 28.1.

THE SCOPE OF COMMAND AND CONTROL IN THE TRANSPORT SECTOR

Important issues within transport policies remain to be addressed through some form of command and control with planning instruments, even accepting the increasing role of regulation. The connections between land use, infrastructure planning and landscape control are the main areas where a more direct public role has to remain dominant.

Low-density land use has been increasingly generated by mass motorization, via the enhanced accessibility of low-cost residential and commercial areas (see Litman, 2002; Maffi and Ponti, 2002). Low-density land use nevertheless makes public transport provision very costly, public transport is generally subsidized, and more so in the case where its full cost becomes unaffordable by many users.

Therefore several external costs seem embedded in low density, unplanned land use: public transport subsidies[4] and environmental and other external costs: costs of congestion, accidents and road damage, of a more transport-intensive pattern of settlements (where individual transport becomes dominant). In theory, getting rid of any subsidy to public transport, and at the same time internalising all the transport externalities of road transport will solve the problem without any explicit planning activity. But this scenario is rather unrealistic, least to say that since this issue is also related with landscape values, that cannot be reasonably priced[5] especially where land is scarce and/or has special historic or naturalistic values.

Regulation can well intervene here in optimizing the construction and management process of infrastructures (public financing, concessionaire regimes and so forth). Regulation activity is called to play its role in a later stage, after the planning process. Distribution-related issues and PSOs are also addressed mainly within the field of explicit public intervention, that is, they seem to have a definite planning content.

THE SCOPE OF MARKET COMPETITION AND LIBERALIZATION

Within the subsidiarity approach suggested above, market competition has to be promoted as far as evidence of its failures emerges. Setting aside infrastructure operations, where only regulated or 'Demsetz' competition is possible (Demsetz, 1968), within transport services the different modes offer a quite diverse picture.

Within the dominant land transport mode, road haulage is basically open to competition, and no major problem exists, thanks to very limited economies of scale and entry barriers that characterize this mode. The same pressure of competition and the social weakness of the operators (sometimes small self-employers) generates problems of law-enforcement, that have to be improved, and even stricter environmental and safety standards are possible, but a re-regulation of this market seems out of question.

Remaining within the road mode, long-to-medium distance bus services are urgently in need of real liberalization, at least in continental Europe. Long-to-medium distance buses compete with rail services for low-income demand, and these services do not have any real impact on the environment, nor any need of subsidies, in contrast to the rail and local bus services. Their development is impeded by regulations protecting the rail activity. Both the users and the taxpayers are severely damaged by this defence of the (public) rail services: the users, given the limits often imposed on the bus system when it competes with rail services, and the taxpayers, given the fiscal burden generated by rail subsidies. This is a very effective example of 'non-benevolent princes', given the social characteristic of the patronage of these services. The situation, nevertheless, is now slowly improving.

Local public transport is quite a different case. Here, the British experience (see Banister, 1997; Fawkner, 1999) seems illuminating. Full liberalization has generated problems of unstable markets, followed by spatial quasi-monopolies: they are contestable more within the economics textbooks than in practical terms. The users have been damaged, as the quality of service has deteriorated. Here theory supports these practical results: Mohring effects (see Ponti, 1997), network effects and other types of market failures apparently are working together with some characteristics of the demand (related to information, the long-term effects of the decisions on residential location and on car ownership, and so forth) in generating severe problems.

On the opposite side, regulated Demsetz competition has delivered good results across the board, for instance in the UK (see, for the well-known London case, Transport for London, 2007). Moreover, since regulated competition, in terms of competitive tendering, can fully guarantee *any* social objective (even free transport, if so decided), the widespread European resistance to the opening of this type of market is another example of 'non-benevolent princes', captured by the interests of the suppliers of the service. In due time, even some form of full liberalization may well be introduced, subsidizing the low-income users instead of the suppliers (this approach has been proposed in the UK), and carefully checking the above-mentioned and ever possible undesirable consequences (Mohring and network effects, and other market failures).

A far more uncertain picture comes from the rail sector. Here, even within the services, environmental externalities are limited, but both economies of scale and sunk costs are present, together with the above-mentioned other problems (Mohring effects and such like). Furthermore, rail services have strong interlinks with infrastructure operations, generating large transaction and severance costs, in case of vertical disintegration.

There exists very little experience in liberalization of rail services. The British case has been very peculiar in its form, and anyway not very successful, mainly due to severe mistakes in regulating the infrastructure (see also the subsection below entitled 'Privatization of the assets'). On top of this, there is little overall experience of free access of rail services over a given track network (other than a partial case in the United States).

The European liberalization process has been up to now restricted to limited entries within the freight sector over a time span of more than 15 years. Nevertheless, the reason for this slow pace is far from technical in nature: liberalization has been opposed with large success by the incumbent public companies, with the European single states (their owners) protecting and helping this opposition.

The main problems here are two-fold: the degree to which separating the services from the infrastructure can generate high transaction costs (see Gomez-Ibànez, 2003), and the possible economies of scale in rail services. The existence of the first problem is evident: for a subway line, the separation of infrastructure from services has little economic sense. The rolling stock here is an essential asset, barely divisible from the infrastructure, and lacking any secondary market. So, where does the threshold lie? Possibly in presence of complex networks, where long-distance passenger services are operated together with freight and local services, separation is advisable. In the case of isolated networks, or networks with limited demand, separation seems a dubious choice, and a sound public regulation of a monopoly can well substitute open-access strategies.

Economies of scale are certainly present in rail services (rolling stock procurement in large quantities and maintenance are strong examples). But here any real experience of a free market is lacking with the exception of the United States, but the American situation is very complex, with state regulation sometimes overlapping federal regulation, and many forms of private and public operators for both the infrastructure and the services. In this case, a well-defined dynamic policy can be suggested. Let the market decide whether economies of scale play a dominant role. Let public regulation be focused on breaking all the possible entry barriers (technical, financial, informative and so forth), even helping the implementation of a secondary market for rolling stock (see the British 'Roscoes'). If a dominant company emerges thanks to its long-range lower costs, all the better for the users; the regulator has only to avoid abuses of dominant positions (that is, the setting of a 'Microsoft-on-wheels'). Given the actual role of the dominant inefficient public companies, it is for sure a long way to go before a dominant rail company, based purely on its competitive merits, will emerge.

Leaving the surface transport sector, the situation looks similar within the air sector. Notwithstanding widespread declarations of liberalized markets, the sector is highly protected and self-protecting.[6] The slot regime is based on 'grandfather's rights', so that the most lucrative routes are plied only by incumbent companies, and the intercontinental services are in general not open to external competition. Cross-subsidies in these cases are a natural behaviour of the operators, and so the other markets are affected too (see Doganis, 2001).

The argument that large companies sometimes are suffering (even before September 11), while low-cost new entrants are prospering, and therefore that competition is in fact at work, does not seem convincing at all. When large national companies are suffering, it is first from high costs, low productivity and unsound fare policies; the only new development is that the States involved are surely less ready now to subsidize them, and in Europe there are growing constraints on doing so.

The low-cost companies are operating from minor airports and cannot attack the high-yield routes. Yet these companies are growing *notwithstanding* the present barriers and, thanks to their inexpensive fares are attracting low income travellers and, more recently, also budget-conscious business travellers.

A completely different structure of the entire air sector will probably emerge from a real liberalization of this market, if the agreement reached on the North Atlantic services is followed by other long-distance markets (that is, Europe–Asia and so forth). Little can be said of something never experienced before.

Even in this sector economies of scale and economies of network size may play a relevant role. There are also some doubts of another type of market failure that may emerge, in the form of an empty core market (see Tucci, 2002), with the consequent need of some form of public regulation.

But first of all, a real competitive market has to be promoted, getting rid of the national champion concept, that has nothing to do with efficiency and the protection of users. Only after this attempt, if problems of instability or incomplete markets persist, can public regulatory intervention be properly aimed (fossil fuels are not taxed at all in this sector, and are considered very polluting since they are burned in the upper atmosphere, where their emissions include frozen steam, considered a further greenhouse factor).

Sea shipping may be a case of an unstable liberalized market, already operating for many years.[7] The wide fluctuations of demand, supply and prices may have generated some inefficient outcomes under the shape of unstable markets (especially overcapacity), but on balance the overall benefits of this competitive setting seem to make public intervention not advisable, if not in order to protect the environment. Also, in this sector fossil fuels are not taxed.

THE SCOPE OF PUBLIC REGULATION

The Issues

As we have seen, public regulation has to simulate the market pressures toward efficiency, where market competition cannot work properly or where a specific social policy has been chosen such as PSOs. The former is the case of natural monopolies, that is, transport infrastructures, the latter of public transport services, which are often provided as legal monopolies, though in general they are not natural monopolies.

Let us first note that club or co-operative solutions of this problem[8] can work only in theory: transport infrastructures are in fact not only natural monopolies, but also legal monopolies, in the sense that land use, of which they are a relevant building brick, is planned (under a command and control type of public intervention, as we have seen above). Nevertheless, infrastructures operations and physical construction can be efficiently regulated, that is, left to efficiency-oriented actors (basically private ones under competitive conditions).

This is already so for the pure construction activities, regulated by competitive tendering, as well as construction combined with operations, that is, project financing practices, which deserve an in-depth analysis, as we will see later.

Designing a proper regulatory regime for infrastructures is a highly complex task, with many aspects still to be tested and even not fully understood. Furthermore, the resistance of the political actors (Ponti, 2001) to a shift from a command and control regime to regulation practices seems especially strong (yet another proof of the capture mechanisms so well defined within the already mentioned public choice approach).

The Main Regulatory Policies for Infrastructures and Public Transport Services

There exists a wide range of regulatory policies; the main ones are summarized here (Figure 28.1) in order of their degree of innovative content, that is, in inverse order of their distance from the command and control policies which are frequently the status quo. This also can be seen as a kind of subsidiarity chain.

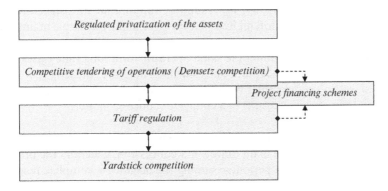

Figure 28.1   The subsidiarity chain in transport infrastructure regulation

This chain is somewhat different and more complex than the one proposed by Gomez-Ibanez (2003) in his book on the general subject of infrastructure regulation, since purely private contracts, mentioned in that text as one of the main categories of regulation, are rare within the transport sector, while other issues look far more relevant.

Privatization of the assets
This is the radical British model for every public utility sector. The implicit risk of jeopardizing public interest seems nevertheless quite high, given the option value embedded in this choice, that is basically non-reversible (since a public buy-back or expropriation is a rather unlikely possibility). Capture risks remain paramount, given both the length of the public–private relationship involved (practically eternal), and the power held by a (generally) large private monopolist, so created by a public decision.

In railways, the British experience has shown severe problems both in information control during the privatization phase (see Nuti, 1997), (apparently, the real future costs of maintenance were underestimated on purpose by the public seller, in order to get a more favourable price), and in the subsequent regulatory policy. The core issue is that a *private* natural monopoly is contestable as a property (others may buy it), but keeps too much power against its public regulator. Hence this is a policy that again assumes a 'benevolent, all-knowing prince'. Periodic tenders for concessions appear to be a far less demanding strategy, since the market pressure itself, and the transparency involved in the tendering process helps a more multi-faceted control of the results.

For airport infrastructures (again mainly a British experience) the problems seem less severe, even if questions remain on the possible impact on future land use and localization choices in the long run, that are mainly of public nature.

Competitive tendering of concessions (Demsetz competition) of infrastructure operations
We have already mentioned the advantages of this tool for transport services, when full-fledged competition is deemed not advisable. For infrastructure operations, the experience is still quite limited, but in theory it looks like a balanced policy, limiting the risks of capture linked with very long public–private relationships. For some type of infrastructure nevertheless, the length of the concession has to be fine-tuned, based on the technical sophistication of the involved operations, and the consequent need for sufficient learning time for the new-entrant company. For example, rail and air infrastructures may well need longer concessions than toll highways (that have mainly a simple maintenance and toll collection content).

It is quite obvious that retaining the same operator for a long time raises the risks of information asymmetries and capture phenomena. Therefore, the length of concessions can be limited, setting proper rules both for the incumbents and for the new entrants in case the re-tendering process results in a change of concessionaire.

Building and operating concessions (project financing)
When a new investment is the main object of a concession, generally the practice in use sets a very lengthy concession period, assuming the need for a complete recovery of the invested capital.

This practice has the well-known advantage of joining the responsibility of construction, operation and maintenance, with the consequent overall optimisation of the entire system. But we have already seen the risks of long concessions (see also Ponti and Gervasoni, 1996).

Furthermore, long concessions for infrastructures are generally accounted for by the need of amortization of long-life investments. But this is a highly questionable argument for transport infrastructures: these assets (essentially civil works) have a practically *infinite* life, and therefore there is no physical amortization at play, only financial amortization, and sound contractual constraints on maintenance standards and obligations seem a sufficient controlling tool. The rationale for linking the assumed physical amortization with the financial amortization is weak. Therefore this approach has to be considered with prudence, given also its capability of disguising public expenditures for private ones, via too generous risk guarantees in favour of the private investors, that transform in fact those investments into risk-free sovereign loans. This was the case for the high speed rail lines in Italy, but many other projects have similar contents, not easy to immediately identify, given also the ever-present possibility of reopening negotiations in the long run, and far from a competitive context and the related transparency.

This is another element that suggests a prudent attitude toward project financing strategies: the old-fashioned competitive tendering of construction contracts, followed by a sound periodic tendering of concessions for operations and maintenance, may often be a more prudent choice, where even the charges to the users can be kept under better control.

Tariff regulation

Tariff regulation is required basically in two cases: (1) dealing with transport services, when there are distributive, congestion or environmental issues to be taken into account; (2) dealing with infrastructures, when productive efficiency has to be reached without competitive tendering, that is, when the provider of the service is assumed unchangeable, an extreme case of which is privatization of the main assets. Price-capping is the main technical tool in those cases. Of course, there are possible mixed or overlapping situations; that is, cases where social issues are present together with efficiency issues.

We deal in some more detail with the issues related to tariff regulation both within the transport services and within infrastructures (see below).

Yardstick competition

This strategy (also known as 'tournament') is admittedly a form of simulated market, but it is by far the most conservative policy among the ones considered here, and remains quite close to command and control practices.

The regulator limits himself to compare the results of different public companies in the same field (for example, airports or railways), setting 'prizes' and 'punishments' in accordance to their performances. So far, so good. But in practice this strategy has limited impacts, since it is not able to change the basic capture mechanisms that generate the need of regulation in first place.

Some Technical Examples of Regulatory Issues Within the Transport Infrastructure Sector

Congestion charges and access rationing

Congestion implies a general and inefficient mismatching of demand and supply of transport infrastructure (access rationing concerns basically the same issue, implying insufficient capacity for infrastructures where traffic is regulated for technical reasons). Two main problems can be underlined here. The first one is related to project financing.

The rationale of construction costs of a natural monopoly being charged to the users have to be related with some form of congestion charge, otherwise this charging generates a well-known welfare 'deadweight loss'. In turn, congestion charges are assumed to be by definition efficient, and therefore the related revenues may efficiently (and equitably, see the club externality problem) be used for financing the infrastructure costs.[9] But infrastructures suffer from indivisibilities, so in general they are under-utilized at the beginning of their technical life, and excessively congested toward the end. Nevertheless financial needs go the opposite way: they are maximal at the beginning and thereafter tend to decline.

A second issue related to congestion is the (highly questionable) difference between the road mode and the controlled access modes, that is, railways, airports and ports. Congestion on roads has to be regulated via social surplus-maximizing charges, that exclude the less willing-to-pay traffic. It is assumed that, since congestion is non-existing (or minimal) within the controlled access modes, for them no congestion charging is needed. This would be true *if and only if* the excess demand in these modes is excluded by the traffic controller with a surplus-maximizing rationale, that is, via tariffs selecting the users with highest willingness to pay for the scarce services provided. But this is in general not the case: access to railways and airports capacity (slots) is controlled basically by grandfather's rights or similar inefficient criteria.

Auctioning the capacity, or setting a rationing access tariff, are the only two possible surplus-maximizing practices (exactly coincident with a road pricing approach). These two alternative practices differ in turn only from a distributive point of view (the first one skims all the social surplus from the users in favor of the operator of the infrastructure, while the second one leaves part of it to the users).

The minimal efficient dimension issue

The minimal efficient dimension is a kind of preliminary issue in regulating network infrastructures. The efficient dimension of a regulated firm must be such as this firm is large enough to exhaust economies of scale; but it must be the minimal one, in order to reduce the market power of this firm against the regulator, again due to capture risks. In transport this applies to toll highways and rail tracks; it can be considered a problem of 'horizontal unbundling', as compared with the 'vertical unbundling' issue dominant in non-transport sectors. The issue arises because for these networks there is no market mechanism to determine their efficient operational dimensions (that is, the level of breaking up of the network).

So the issue at stake here is a problem of balancing the possible economies of scale against excessive power. This excessive power in turn also may well have a negative impact on the proper working of a Demsetz market of concessions, and not only on the regulator.

Toll highway networks have very limited economies of scale, related only to the dimension of the maintenance centres. Therefore it is reasonable to split up the concessions in sub-sets of few hundred kilometers each.[10] (Electronic toll collection has become highly automated, and vehicles can be charged without impeding traffic flow.)

Concessions are now generally based on a set of toll links, or on a single link to be built and operated, and so forth. But the traffic structure within dense areas (that is, in the European context) is mainly short-distance, and the demand for mobility is served by the entire local network, of which the toll links are just a component, and not always the largest one in terms of capacity.

Within this picture, a toll level that is aimed only at cost recovery or at *productive* efficiency (via an incentivating mechanism), is far from optimal in terms of *allocative* efficiency. Congestion and environmental externalities determine an optimal allocation of traffic flows that is far from the one induced by cost-recovery tolls (if not under extremely restrictive conditions, as the assumptions of the Mohring–Harwitz self-financing scheme). And if one considers also the possible economies of scale concerning maintenance activities and minor investments, an *area-based concession scheme* looks a much more sensible strategy.

Furthermore, an area-based concession may well include other critical components: for example, the management of traffic information for emergencies (as in the case of major accidents), and even ancillary activities like parking facilities and public transport prioritization (streetlights, separate lanes and so forth). Also, schemes for shifting the number of available road lanes from one direction to another in peak periods (that is, reversible lanes) can become a component of a package of activities that conceives the road system of an area as an integrated service or utility.

These packages have obviously to be committed under competitive tendering, and the duration of the concession can be kept limited, in the order of less than ten years, limiting the capture risks involved in longer concessions (see Newbury, 1998).

For rail networks, the picture is even more complicated, due to the fact that even the experience of sub-national concession of infrastructures is very limited. Nevertheless, it is extremely unlikely that economies of scale coincide exactly with national borders (see Preston et al., 1999), that is that the historical conditions that determine the present dimension of the national networks have some economic sensible basis.

The Japanese experience tends to show that minimal efficient dimensions are probably more near a regional scale (for large countries at least), depending on the number of long distance lines that have to be cut in separating the networks (generally few, compared to the local lines that remain within the same region; Japan Railway and Transport Review, 1994).

Also in this case, there is a long way to go, at least in Europe, where a strong nationalistic rationale continues to dominate over economic efficiency.

Financial issues

The established rule of setting a proper rate of return for regulated companies is based in general on the calculation of the WACC (Weighted Average Cost of Capital) index. This index is needed to remunerate properly the invested capital, especially, but not only, when investments are financed through the tariffs in an explicit way, and not left within the price-cap mechanism (see the following section). There are then two issues: estimating the invested capital and assessing the proper WACC.

The correct evaluation of invested capital (also known as RAB, Regulatory Asset Base) within a concession regime is a high controversial issue. In the first place, its magnitude has to be kept to a minimum: productive efficiency requires, for capital not less than for labor, that the resources employed are only the necessary and efficient ones.

But often a conflict of interests exists within the public sector: in selling a concession, or in privatizing an existing one, the state may be willing to maximize its revenues, and doing so may permit or even promote a RAB far larger than the minimum technically needed in order to operate the infrastructure efficiently. This capital can be really of limited amount if the physical assets are kept public, see below.

Furthermore, the actual price at which the concession is sold can be far higher than the 'book value' of capital required: its price may well represent the discounted value of future expected profits. In turn, if the 'sale value' is in some way included within the RAB instead of the book value, there is a risk of a spiralling and self-induced increase of the values of the entire concession system, given the fact that a 'normal' level of profit on capital is guaranteed via the tariff mechanism. Also this second over-evaluation problem may generate a conflict of interests within the public administration, if short-term revenue maximization prevails on efficiency and on the defence of users from undue rents.

In turn, the definition of a proper WACC requires special attention: it is necessary to take into account the specific level of risk of every regulated sector. For example, within transport infrastructures, if the commercial risk is taken away from the concessionaire by the public regulator, the WACC has to be lowered in consequence.

Furthermore, it is advisable to define a target leverage level, in order to avoid opportunistic composition of capital from the concessionaires (that is, to set the allocation of capital between debt and equity only in order to maximize its remuneration through the regulated tariffs, and not following normal financial optimization rules[11]). Finally, concessionaires that are floated (that is, which value is left to the judgement of the stock market) deserves a special attention from the regulator, that must be extremely transparent and prudent in all its regulatory actions, especially as far as the 'X' parameter of the price-cap formula is concerned.[12]

Also, the inflation index within the price cap formula has to be handled with care: there is a tendency to set it on the basis of the expected inflation rate rather than the actual rate. But this is an improper tool for addressing efficiency: inflation is an exogenous factor for the regulated company, and efficiency goals have to be addressed by adjusting the X parameter, which is designed to increase efficiency within the price cap formula (see the following point).

Further price-cap problems: patterns and levels of efficient costs
The price-cap mechanism, although by far the best known tariff-regulation tool available for infrastructure concessions, faces several problems, of which a few are summarised here: a first one is related to which type of risk should be left to the regulated companies. In transport infrastructures, it seems reasonable to leave to them only (or almost only) the industrial risks, and not the commercial ones (that is, those related to the level of demand).

The basic rationale for this sectoral advice is linked to the exogenous nature of demand variations on transport infrastructures: these variations basically depend on the overall economic growth of the country and from national and regional transport policies (competing infrastructures and their tariffs, gasoline prices, liberalization of services and so forth). In fact, if a company faces a risk that is outside its control, it has to behave on the safe side, maximizing the relevant prices. It is the same rational that allows to the regulated company a full recovery of inflation (within the price-cap formula).

A second problem is related to the efficiency parameter, that is in general included in the price-cap formula. Its definition requires an accurate benchmarking, even if efficient costs can be known mostly through a learning by doing process.

Within concessions of transport infrastructures, this is far from easy, giving the absolute dominance of monopolistic, inefficient examples from which the relevant data have to be derived. Even the speed at which efficiency has to be obtained (implicit in the X value), has to be estimated taking into account the specific constraints faced by each sector (labor contracts, and so forth).

Obviously the starting base, set usually each five years (the 'regulatory lag'), when the price-cap is recalculated, are the costs[13] incurred at that moment by the concessionaire, and not its revenues. The reason is that the objective of the mechanism is to make the users pay for efficient costs, and only for them, allowing for an incentivizing factor, that is linked to the possible extra profits gained in each five-year period by the concessionaire, thanks to its efficiency. This periodic re-adjustment of the tariff is known as the 'claw-back' procedure.[14]

The regulation of investments

Price-caps, or competitive tendering, in theory automatically guarantee the financial efficiency of the investments: only the ones capable of generating net profits will be implemented by the regulated company.

The problem here, as we have already seen, is that by far the largest part of the transport investments in infrastructures are *not* profitable in financial terms, and are generally decided by the public actors for a set of social objectives. As far as this decision remains outside the autonomy of the concessionaire, it is perfectly correct then to finance the investments via a public source of revenue. This source can be both direct transfers, or an increase of tariffs on the whole network.

Transfers are generally dominant for railways (and ports), while higher tariffs are used for highways. Airport investments are in general self-financed, with some cases of state or local subsidy for the smaller ones.

But guaranteeing the funds for investments to a profit-oriented concessionaire or agency, generates the Averch–Johnson (1962) phenomenon, that is, the pressure to maximize the level of guaranteed investments. In this way, in fact, given a normal level of risk and a corresponding normal level of profits, the *total amount* of profits of the regulated company is also maximized. Therefore, special care has to be given to the evaluation of the social benefits of the (proposed) investments, to their design standard, and to their costs, even if a competitive tendering is made mandatory (that is not always the case, and anyway it is subject to information asymmetries on the side of the regulator).

All considered, *large* investments in the transport sector may well be kept within a command and control frame, especially if the benefits of project financing schemes are not fully guaranteed. This may well be the case for toll highways, that present low technical complexity: as we have seen, the potential efficiency gains of integrated construction and operations seem limited, and a different, more sensible strategy can be recommended.

The regulation of safety and quality
It is well known that a monopolist regulated on the tariff (and access rules) side, has to be regulated also on the quality side, since there are no longer present specific incentives motivating quality (and sometime safety) improvements, as generally in the case of market pressures. The problem here is technically quite complex (also demand elasticity can be a factor, as well as the information level of the different players, specially on safety issues), in contrast to which, price regulation is, at least in conceptual terms, a more straightforward issue.

Quality and safety of transport services provided by transport infrastructures require not only specific experiences and benchmarking, but need also a direct and active role of the users, that are the main stakeholders, and generally, those who pay for the services (the 'residual claimants').

There is up to now little experience on the possible involvement of these subjects in the regulatory process, and there is a strong urgency to develop such experience. Setting abstract quality standards is useful, but certainly not sufficient. Furthermore, it remains open the question of objective measurements of safety and quality, in order to limit the potential costs of litigation, in case of disagreement between the regulator (and the stakeholders) and the regulated companies.

Finally, the proper balance between mandatory standards and well-designed incentives is another problem that deserves special consideration in quality regulation, while for safety, the standard has to remain obviously the dominant policy.

The problem of the 'number of tills'
The issue of the 'number of tills' deals with the sub sectors of an activity (that is, complementary services, like restaurants, ticket offices, parking, gasoline stations and so forth), that have to be regulated (or subsidized) separately. This issue is well known within airport regulation, but it is present also in railways and highway infrastructures (the main difference is that a proper regulatory experience is almost absent in the latter cases).

The core of the problem is to determine how complex the regulatory action should be. There are in fact trade-offs: a fine-tuned regulation may be in theory more efficient, but it is less transparent and leaves less scope to the regulated companies to develop general strategies of optimisation. Let's start with toll highway concessions. A dual-till is already present in some form, when infrastructure investments are decided and financed on top of the regulation of tariffs related to operations .

If tariff regulation takes into account also congestion and environmental issues, we can speak of a 'triple till', that is, three different tools of public intervention.

For airports, the dominant theoretical approach is known as 'dual till': tariffs are price-capped on the *air* side (landing fees, *etc.*), while on the *land* side (commercial activities, parking, and so forth), the possible monopolistic rents are skimmed via specific royalties, since it is technically almost impossible to regulate every single price of the services in offer.

In case of periodic competitive tendering of airport concessions, since the overall expected rate of return determines the royalty offered by the competitors, its effect is similar to the one of a single till approach.

The single-till approach, used, for example, in the regulation of London airports, limits price-capping on the air-side. But this generates a distorted price signal: since the price-cap periodically eliminates rents from the overall revenues, even if applied on the air-side only, the tariffs on the air-side tend to decline sharply as the rents on the land-side rise. Therefore, the more traffic (that is, congestion) an airport develops, the lower its air-side tariffs become, which is clearly inefficient in allocating the relevant traffic.

Within the rail sector, state intervention is generally of the triple till type (that is, on investments, on infrastructure operations and on services).The trade-offs involved here are especially evident. Given the complexity of the sector, this triple-till approach risks to render opaque the public objectives embedded in the sector. What is the final cost for the public purse of the entire system?

Furthermore, it is possible to reduce the number of tills to two: the subsidies given to the rail services may well include those that in the triple till case are earmarked for the infrastructure operations. The only remaining advantage of the triple till is its effect on competition in rail services: given the high entry barriers existing in the sector, low track-use tariffs (that is, priced at marginal costs) are definitely more pro-competition (without the need for explicit subsidies to the service operators which are not easy to muster within a competitive environment).

These examples can be extended to other infrastructures as well (ports, for example), since the core issues are basically the same.

IMPACT OF PROPER REGULATION ON OVERALL TRANSPORT POLICY

Efficiency

As we have seen, the main goal of regulation is an increase of efficiency. In case of monopolistic public operators, these efficiency gains can be both allocative and productive.

Within the mainstream theory, in the case of private monopolistic operators, only allocative efficiency (and equity, by the way) is in play, since productive efficiency is supposedly incentivized by the profit-maximization objective of the private actor. But recent elaborations (see Coco and De Vincenti, 2008) have demonstrated, quite convincingly, that – even for private operators – the implicit efforts[15] needed to obtain productive efficiency are really maximized only within a properly regulated contest. For example, higher-than-market wages can guarantee the support of the trade unions in case of public policies aimed at liberalizing a specific sector, and this is not a minor goal for a private monopolist.

Lower costs and prices in turn permit an easier social acceptance of other public actions: for example, in the road transport sector, efficient charges for congestion or for internalizing external costs will be implemented with less opposition if other infrastructure costs are lowered by efficient operations. Similar results are valid also for other, more explicit social objectives: for example, given limited public resources for local passenger transport, lower production costs induced by competitive tendering can definitely permit extended services or lower fares as an alternative.

Innovation

Regulation simulates, as we have described, market pressure on efficiency. But a simulated market pressure in turn can generate a powerful incentive also on technical and managerial innovation.

The slow pace of railway management innovation in Europe is strongly linked to insufficient incentives: public companies cannot go bankrupt, and wages and salaries are paid also on century-old practices and technologies, that are unable to follow the evolution of the demand. French railways are a remarkable exception, at least in terms of technical innovation, but the public costs involved in this innovation have been, and still are, quite large, and with shaky overall industrial results (exports, ailing rolling stock production).

In the case of 'flag' airline companies, the lack of any efficiency-oriented regulation has proven in the past very disruptive (even if here probably the proper regulation will be quite near full liberalization). What has been the cumulative social opportunity cost of scores of years without low-cost alternatives (that is, managerial innovation) that emerged only when a (still partial) liberalization has been permitted?

Concerning infrastructures, given the limited experience of incentivizing regulation in this field, probably the potential of technical innovation in this sector remains still largely untapped (see also the outlines of innovative, area oriented road concessions proposed later).

Finally, proper regulation practices can reduce critical entry barriers in several sectors. Unbundling rail infrastructures from operations may be an effective example, since it reduces substantially the market power of the incumbent rail service companies. But similar situations are present within the port and airport systems as well. First, unbundling of port and airport operations may reduce the market power of the concessionaire, and, second, traditional (even if less formal) alliances among dominant operators and infrastructures can be broken by a proper regulation of the latter.

Investments

The preceding text has presented, with some elaborations, a position in favor of a rather traditional, planning-oriented attitude on large investments, given the risks generated by the extreme distance of these economic activities from the conditions required for efficient functioning of competitive markets. Nevertheless, sound regulatory practices can create benefit also in this area. An example is the reduction of overinvestments ('gold plating') in airports. Too expensive airports (and the examples are plenty) are an additional barrier to the entry of low cost operators, that in fact tend to choose secondary, 'no frills' airports; the main hope here is that the reduced willingness to subsidize (as shown earlier) large flag carriers (that actually pay for the top-grade airports) will generate spontaneous pressures to reduce airport costs across the board, curbing unnecessary luxury-oriented investments. But similar situations are present also in some railways infrastructures, where less than essential investments abound.

PUBLIC SERVICE OBLIGATIONS AND INCOME DISTRIBUTION

PSO and Vertical Equity (Income Differences)

Even if the implicit goals of public service obligations (PSO)[16] is and income distribution are related, they are not totally coincident; anyhow they are political goals that will gain in consistency if treated within a single context.

In general, PSO are intended to supply the entire population with a service in a non-discriminating way. This obligation concerns also private, non subsidized services: airlines or restaurants cannot deny provision of their services to anyone paying for it. This is a weak regulation, in general, since the providers have a definite interest in selling their services to the largest possible population, and discrimination by race or dress is actually disappearing.

The objectives of these impositions have first a distributive content (allowing people unable to pay for the costs they generate, to have a service); they have also a wider social aim, to provide a general social message, for some basic service, of non-discrimination, not even by income , as would be in the case of revenue-based individual subsidies.

Universal access is one virtue of PSO. Another is simplicity of implementation (tariffs equal for everyone and sometimes everywhere).

But the main negative aspects are large:

- First of all, the distributive effectiveness. Since everyone is subsidized, the net economic resources going to low-income users are severely reduced for a given amount of public expenditure.
- Second, subsidizing the rich from the public purse seems highly questionable in terms of equity (this case is frequent in transport, given the dominance of public services going to central areas, and given the fact that land rent in general captures a relevant share of the benefits of low fares, especially in rail transport).
- Third, the deadweight surplus loss related to subsidized consumption is larger if more people are consuming that good or service, and more so if they have an elastic demand such as people who can choose an alternative transport mode.

PSO and Horizontal Equity

A second issue is that of horizontal equity, in the sense that *ceteris paribus* (for example, the same level of income), all the citizens are entitled to the same level of social benefits.

This issue contributes to many conceptual difficulties related with PSO. Why do some areas have subsidized transport services and others not, or far less so? In transport, this problem is very relevant indeed because of the substantial spatial differences. Are isolated residences always entitled to subsidized transport? And what if they become in time mainly holiday houses? Furthermore, given the economies of scale of public transport, dispersed demand requires usually a far higher per capita subsidy than the demand in dense corridors, where also the external benefits are in general higher, making the subsidy of dense demand far more efficient (assuming equal the distributive effect).

A special link emerges here between horizontal and vertical equity: it is quite obvious that in any location provided with a subsidized transport service (or infrastructure), part of the benefit of the subsidy is captured by land rent (that location has a higher value than another without such service). Two distributive problems emerge. The first, as we have seen, is of vertical equity (land owners tend to be richer than the average transport user) and the second is of horizontal equity. Furthermore, providing subsidized transport to low-density areas gives a wrong price signal in terms of location choices: urban sprawl can be actually accelerated if subsidized public transport is felt as guaranteed to any location.

An argument in favor of PSO is often related to the need to protect local cultures, avoiding excessive urbanization, preserving traditional ways of life in agricultural areas or in islands and so forth. Sometimes this argument is related with vertical equity, since isolated/agricultural areas also present lower average incomes. But even in this case, as we will see, more selective and efficiency-oriented policies than PSO can be recommended.

PSO and Special Social Groups (Disadvantaged People)

Elderly or disabled people may be entitled, if so decided, to subsidies and/or with special technical aid devices. Furthermore, since the average age in the more developed countries is rapidly growing, these technical aspects tend to receive wide public support.

The only possible issue here is again one of income distribution: helping only the disabled or elderly passengers that are poor allows for far higher level of intervention for them, for a given amount of public funds available. As a practical example, this issue concerns the trade-off between providing taxi services for the disabled poor, or a (possibly) far more expensive universal service of wheelchair-capable buses, assuming that the disabled rich may well pay for the taxi services themselves.

PSO and Positive Externalities

In general, as we have seen, PSO are aimed at providing universal services, that is, have a social-oriented content (vertical and horizontal equity). But some efficiency issue can also be at play, in case of market failures generating underconsumption of public transport. This is the case of the Mohring effect (positive externalities due to increase frequency of services) and of the network effect (additional users of a network add new possible destinations for other users), that can in fact be seen as positive consumption externalities.

These phenomena may indeed justify subsidies insofar as marginal cost pricing calls for fares below average cost. Anyhow, the order of magnitude of the related subsidies seems small if compared to the ones associated with social goals, at least in the case of dense traffic routes.[17] Furthermore, PSO, given its implicit cross subsidization content, does not look the more favorable technical solution for this issue.

PSO and Problems of Political Decision Making

The outline that has been provided for both the PSO policy and more in general for objectives not related with economic efficiency, like income distribution, assumes a traditional context of decision makers as 'benevolent, all-knowing (elected) princes'.

More realistic assumptions lead to a symmetric more realistic picture of the decision process, especially in this field, where political consensus plays a dominant role.

The basic tenet of the public choice approach is related to the main real objective of the decision makers, that is re-election. Special interest groups tend to be effective both in organizing votes and in protesting against unfavorable policies, while the majority, the taxpayers and so forth tend to perceive the benefits and the costs of any policy in far less readable terms, and/or only in the long run.

The mechanism by which special interests dominate the general interest is known as capture, as we have seen. In turn, capture can happen in more than one way: the lobbying activity of private actors is able to influence the decision maker (this is the traditional way) or, in case of public actors, the decision maker himself willingly promotes special interests in order to be re-elected, given the voting power that we have described.

This is especially true if the percentage of the entitled electors who choose to vote tends to decrease, as is happening in many developed countries.

The mechanism is also self-sustaining in another way, known as 'log-rolling': an issue in favor of a special interest is also backed by the politicians patronizing a different issue, under the agreement that in turn the favor will be returned.

The examples of this generation mechanism of PSO in transport are straightforward: if a district or a social group will be entitled to PSO, or subsidies, even if the rationale looks weak and the costs high, then often others will follow suit. Nobody in fact will oppose the initiative, expecting in turn to get the same electoral benefits.

The Implementation of PSO Within a Regulatory Context

General aspects

First of all, it has to be kept in mind that PSO have an implicit subsidy content: a service obligation is really such only if it generates costs to the operator higher than the corresponding revenues. Here the issue at stake is related far more to equity than to efficiency, while efficiency is the main goal of regulation. Therefore, the decision process may engage different actors. Efficiency, in fact, tends to be delegated to technical, independent bodies (the regulatory authorities), while equity maintains a high political content, and must remain within the political sphere, being the expression of the elector's will of a more or less egalitarian society (by definition, nobody can be against efficiency per se).

This conceptual separation leads to the opportunity of a corresponding practical separation: distributive goals, in terms of well-defined standards, must be given to the regulator by the political body, since the overlapping and contradictions of multiple objectives is seen as one of the main causes of the state failure in managing directly public utilities (that is, via command and control practices).

Direct subsidies versus cross subsidies

A PSO (since it generates losses for the operators) can be compensated directly by the state (or by a local administration), or indirectly by cross-subsidization among services. The direct approach has both positive and negative aspects. The positive aspect is that the social opportunity cost of imposing a PSO is made explicit and transparent, and therefore can become object of public debate. The negative aspect is some complexity and the up-front cost for the public purse.

Cross-subsidies mean that the services operating at a loss have to be paid for by the ones generating profits, within a bundled context that allows for this equilibrium.

Cross-subsidization is a simple and widely-used solution, but as a general approach it presents several severe drawbacks.

- There is a major problem of horizontal equity: why do the users of certain services (for example, the ones in a dense area), have to pay with their tariffs for the users in another (that is, low-density) area? If sustaining these services is a perfectly legitimate goal of a region, the entire region (that is, the taxpayers) have to pay for that goal.
- There is a problem of transparency of the social goals, that tend to become hidden beneath cross-subsidization. Even the real opportunity cost of the policy becomes blurry: who can say exactly the cost of keeping a certain service? If that cost is made explicit, it may well emerge that a different technical solution is more effective or less expensive (for example, substituting a train service with a bus service).
- Even in the case of a cross-subsidized set of services appointed via competitive tendering (Demsetz competition, see the following point), the information rent of the operator seems much larger than in the case of direct subsidies, especially in the medium-long run, where the social issues initially involved may change.
- Last, but certainly not least, is the issue of competition. In several cases, the choice of cross-subsidizing some services (instead of a direct subsidy), becomes a strong argument against competition. The reasoning looks naïve, but its use is widespread: it is remarked that a private or a new entrant in a competitive process, will dismiss the non-profitable services, operating in terms of cherry picking. The success of this argument (that cannot have any room in case of direct subsidies) with the political body seems simple: the captured decision makers are only happy to have a reason to avoid competition, that tends to cut off the exchange of favors that we have seen being the main base of the capture mechanism.

An obvious argument in favor of cross subsidization is related to complexity (transaction, or severance, or Coase costs): under certain technical dimensions (that is, services in certain hours in the same city, or feeder lines and so forth) it becomes impractical to subsidize directly such services or to set a specific competitive bidding for them.

Demsetz competition as a possible implementing tool

Let us assume that a political decision has been taken in favour of PSO for a set of services that cannot be paid directly by the users (for reasons of demand density, or income, or both). Let us also assume that this happens within a regulatory context, that is where there are strong efficiency objectives. The subsidized services can be appointed, for a limited period, to a monopolist, in competitive tendering process (Demsetz competition), in order to minimize the cost of subsidy (after having properly set the quality and the tariff required). At the limit, this can be done also for free services, if so decided.

The competition can be easily extended to the technical solution (a mode against another one). Also, the issue of the emerging cost for the public purse of the subsidy (as compared to a cross-subsidized scheme) is easily answered. In fact, if it is also decided that the users of the profitable services have to pay for the unprofitable ones, it is sufficient to use the royalties deriving by a similar procedure for appointing these services (and, besides, by definition these royalties will be maximized by competitive tendering). Without sacrificing any social goal, transparency will also gain from this process, since the opportunity and political costs both of subsidizing some services, and of charging the users of some other ones more than the cost they generate, will become explicit.

PSO in a dynamic perspective

The need to regulate some economic activity may change with the evolution of the relevant markets (more entering operators, or the rise of a dominant one), and/or the technology (ending in this way some condition of natural monopoly, or adding new ones, like in information-related sectors). The same is even more true for PSO. In this sense, PSO can be different both in space and time. Still more obviously, these decisions can, and do, vary in time, with the evolution of the social needs and priorities.

The main issue that seems to emerge here is the quality of public and political debate, at the different administrative level and involving the relevant stakeholders. In turn, this quality depends on the level of information available. And since one of the tools of the regulatory approach to public services is the disclosure of the correct information, generally hidden within a command and control approach, every implementation procedure of PSO has to focus on the proper level of public information on which it is based, and that can be generated over time, and with appropriate instruments.

CONCLUDING REMARKS

Public regulation of transport services and infrastructures is a high complex task, and basically still in its infancy. Command and control practices dominate even when they are no longer needed. The liberalization process in turn is slowed down by extended "capture" phenomena.

A first point has to be underlined, as demonstrated: regulated (Demsetz) competition does not conflict with social objectives. Even free transport can (and must) be provided within a competitive context.

The main tenet of the problem is the following: direct intervention (command and control), regulation, and market competition have to be considered within a subsidiarity approach. Why does this approach make explicit a definite hierarchy of strategies? Because the traditional assumption known as social choice, of a 'benevolent, all-knowing prince' is no longer acceptable, even if the perfectly egoistic prince embedded in the public choice scenario is also too extreme. A balanced attitude has to stay on the safe side: if you can, do not assume the prince as necessarily benevolent and fully informed.

Nevertheless, public regulation and market competition are not so far apart as is commonly considered. The market is not the absence of rules and constraints, quite the contrary: it has been built as a complex set of rules and laws, that have needed a couple of centuries to be properly set, and are under continuous evolution, as social values (and the technology of the sector) evolve.[18]

There is a large ideological difference between liberal values and pure laissez-faire.

Furthermore, public regulation itself is not a purely technical issue: in reality, embedded in regulation choices are different visions of economic democracy and of social priorities.

As we have underlined at the beginning, the transport sector is quite peculiar in this sense: it is full of market failures, and involves very critical values and social objectives (freedom of movement, the environment, safety and security, and so forth). The stronger the drive to liberalization, the more the (necessary) public intervention has to be attentive and up-dated; in other words, the more 'market' we want, the better 'state' we need. Nothing is really spontaneous in market competition: it is a political construction, and much work remains to be done within the transport sector.

NOTES

1. This has to be noted, not only within the radical context of a 'public choice' setting, where the public 'principal' is presented as a standard *homo oeconomicus*, maximizing egoistic objectives. Even within a more relaxed setting, where the mix of egoistic and altruistic objectives may be varied, and *ex-ante* basically unknown, imprudence argues against assuming a pure 'benevolent, all-knowing prince' hypothesis.
2. A term of dominant use within the European Commission policy papers.
3. The Mohring effect comes from the fact that additional users of public transport generate an increase of its frequency, and this in turn benefits other users, without the additional users perceiving these 'external' benefits.
4. Subsidies are non-perceived costs, and in this sense can be seen as externalities.
5. Think of the price of a Tuscany 'renaissance' landscape, menaced by a dozen high rise condominiums. Infrastructure planning has similar problems: on top of the all-important landscape issues, here the natural and legal monopoly phenomena are also present, as are present regional development objectives. Moreover, for setting priorities and, therefore, supporting planners in taking into account efficiency objectives, the traditional cost–benefit analysis can provide an important support.
6. Editor note: *cf.* chapter 'Competition and Regulation in Air Transport' in this *Handbook*.
7. Editor note: *cf.* chapter Competition and Regulation in maritime transport in this *Handbook*.
8. An extreme market-oriented vision, roads can be provided by free associations of builders and users, without any public intervention.
9. Provided that the conditions of the Mohring–Harwitz theorem hold; otherwise, the revenues will be greater or lower than capacity costs.
10. If market power and network economies are considered, different conclusions can be reached (see Fayard 2005), but the real regulatory power has always to be taken into account in deciding the dimensions of the regulated firms, in order to avoid unbalanced situations.
11. The composition of capital of a company is generally dictated, in a competitive context, by the prevailing risk and relative costs. Since the calculation the cost of capital (WACC) by the regulator is based on fixed rules, known by the regulated company, the composition chosen can become conditioned by these rules, and not by the market of capitals.
12. The price cap formula in general terms is the following: $Ti = T i\text{-}1 \, (CPI\text{-}X + Q)$, where Ti is the tariff at a given year i, CPI is the Consumer Price Index, X is the yearly reduction of costs to be achieved, and Q is a quality factor, that can be either negative or positive.
13. WACC included as 'normal profit'.
14. Without the claw-back mechanism, extra-profits obtained due to efficiency gains and so forth within a regulatory period, will last forever, while in a competitive context they are limited in time.
15. Efforts are in fact a form of cost, even in practical terms.
16. PSO imposed on firms in terms of tariffs, or location of routes and stops, or frequency (that is, generating costs above the corresponding revenues) are no longer permitted by the European rules, except with a consensual agreement (service contracts).
17. See Ponti (1997). But this issue is controversial, see also Parry and Small (2007). Furthermore, in any case of economies of scale there exist this type of positive consumption externalities; for example, even air services are supposed to be subsidized following too strictly this principle.
18. A good example comes from the former Soviet Union: the destruction of the State has generated a highly distorted economic structure (organised crime, and so forth). In that country, the task of reconstructing proper market rules looks much more challenging than the destructive phase.

REFERENCES

Averch, H. and Johnson L., 1962, Behaviour of the firm under regulatory constraint. *American Economic Review*, **52**, 1052–1069.
Banister, D., 1997, Bus deregulation in the UK. In J. McConville ed., *Transport Regulation Matters*. London: Pinter, pp. 31–54.
Buchanan, J.M., 1969, *Cost and Choice: An Enquiry in Economic Theory*. Chicago, IL: Markham.
Coco, G. and C. De Vincenti, 2008, Optimal price-cap reviews. *Utilities Policy*, **16**, 238–244.
Demsetz, H., 1968, Why regulate utilities. *Journal of Law and Economics*, **11**, 55–66.
Doganis, R., 2001, *The Airline Business in the 21st Century*. London and New York: Routledge.
Fawkner, J., 1999, *Buses in Great Britain, Privatisation, Deregulation and Competition*. London: London Transport.
Fayard, A., 2005, Analysis of highway concession in Europe. In G. Ragazzi-Werner Rothengatter, ed., *Procurement and Financing of Motorways in Europe*. Amsterdam: Elsevier, pp. 15–28.
Gomez-Ibànez, J., 2003, *Regulating Infrastructures. Monopoly, Contracts and Discretion*. Cambridge, MA: Harvard University Press.
Japan Railway and Transport Review, 1994, *Domestic Transport in Japan Present and Future*. Japan Railway and Transport Review, 1 March, pp. 2–4.
Litman T., 2010, Land use impacts on transport. Available at: http://www.vtpi.org/tdm/tdm20.htm.
Maffii S. and Ponti M., 2002, *Pianificazione dei trasporti e del territorio: effetti attesi ed effetti perversi*. Milan, Italy: Ricerchetrasporti.
Mohring H., 1972, Optimization and scale economies in urban bus transportation. *American Economic Review*, **62** (4), 591–604.
Newbery, D.M., 1998, *Fair and Efficient Pricing and the Finance of the Roads*. University of Cambridge.
Nuti F., 1997, *Il caso britannico*. In Nomisma, *Liberalizzazione e Privatizzazione Nelle Ferrovie Europee*. Florence, Italy: Vallecchi.
Parry, I. and K.A. Small, 2007, Should urban transit subsidies be reduced? Paper presented at the 54th Annual North American Meetings of the Regional Science Association International, 2007, Savannah, Georgia.
Ponti, M., 1997, Le esternalità di consumo nei trasporti collettivi. *Economia e Politica Industriale*, **96**, Franco Angeli.
Ponti, M., (2001), The European transport policy in a 'public choice' perspective. 9th World Conference on Transport Research, Seoul.
Ponti, M. and A. Gervasoni, 1996, Il finanziamento delle infrastrutture. *Ricerca Economica e Trasporto*, Federtrasporto – Centro Studi.
Preston, J., A. Root, and D. Van de Velde, 1999, *Railway Reform and the Role of Competition: The Experience of Six Countries*. London: Ashgate.
Segal, I.R., 1998, Monopoly and soft budget constraint. *Rand Journal of Economics*, **29**, 596–609.
Shapiro, C. and R. Willig, 1990, Economic rationales for the scope of privatisation. In E.N. Suleiman and J. Waterbury, eds, *The Political Economy of Private Sector and Privatization*. Boulder, CO: Westview Press.
Transport for London (2007), Central London congestion charging impacts monitoring. Fifth Annual Report, Transport for London, London.
Tucci, G., 2001, Ricerca di stabilità dell'equilibrio di lungo periodo nell'industria del trasporto aereo internazionale. 42° Corso Internazionale I.S.T.I.E.E.- Nuova regolazione dei trasporti: principi e strumenti, Università di Trieste.

29 The theory of incentives applied to the transport sector

Elisabetta Iossa and David Martimort

INTRODUCTION

Efficient transport infrastructure is crucial to economic development. Improvements in transport networks enhance competitiveness and boost economic growth by raising the marginal product of labor and capital and thus the overall efficiency of the productive mix (see, for example, Aschauer, 1989). Furthermore, as firms tend to locate in areas offering wider access to supply and demand markets, transport infrastructures enhance some locations attractiveness towards new productive settlements which result in self-reinforcing growth mechanisms (see Messina, 2008).

But how should transport infrastructure be procured and financed? Substantial institutional changes have taken place in the European Public Transport scene over the past 20 years. The use of contracting has been spreading over all transport sectors and greater risk transfer to private operators has been achieved. At the same time, competitive tendering practices have gradually been implemented to replace direct awarding of contractual rights and a number of municipal operators have been privatized.

The spread of public-private partnerships (hereafter abbreviated as PPPs) is a significant part of this trend. Under a PPP, a public authority (local or central government or a government agency) enters a long-term contractual arrangement with a private supplier (or a consortium of private suppliers) for the delivery of some services. The supplier takes responsibility for building infrastructure, financing the investment and then managing and maintaining the assets. At the end of the contract, assets are transferred to the government under terms agreed to in the contract. Payments to the contractor can either come from the users of the service or from the government in the form of shadow tolls.

In Europe, transport infrastructures, such as the oldest highways and rail networks, have traditionally been built on the basis of public funding, whether regional, national or community originated. Most of the road or rail projects currently underway also follow this pattern. After a few French private highways (Cofirute, AREA, ACOBA), the PPP approach was pioneered in the UK by the Private Finance Initiative (PFI) in 1992 (Grout, 1997). The first transport project was the Isle of Skye bridge, connecting the Isle of Sky to the mainland. PPPs have since been used for a number of urban transportation projects and for some of the biggest infrastructure projects and isolated links (tunnels bridges) throughout Europe, such as the Eurotunnel and London Underground. Private involvement in highways construction and management has also increased substantially in recent years following sector reforms in France, Italy and Spain and the PPP approach is now being adopted to build transport infrastructure also in Eastern European countries (Kappeler and Nemoz, 2010). In the United States, PPPs in the transport sector were developed in the 1970s for inner-city infrastructure (Rosenau, 2000) and are currently used for projects involving highways and road transportation (CBO, 2007). In Australia, New South Wales was the early adopter, opening the way for a series of toll roads in the 1990s.

Developing countries witnessed a dramatic increase in how the private sector was involved in building and funding infrastructure activities over the last 20 years. Since the 1990s, the private sector has invested 180 billion USD in transport infrastructure and by 2006 a total of 1000 private projects had been initiated. Latin America accounts for 40 percent of all transactions. By (sub)sectors, the majority are road projects, followed by the railroad sector. In terms of the size of investment, the road and railroad sectors amount to 47 percent and 20 percent of private participation experiences in developing countries, respectively (Estache et al., 2009). According to the Private Participation in Infrastructure Project (PPIAF) Database, transport was the sector with the fastest growth of projects with private participation in 2005–06 worldwide. The investment doubled in 2005 and rose another 30 percent in 2006, to almost US$30 billion. Substantially higher investments were undertaken in airports, railways and seaports, though investment in roads declined. The most common type of project was concession, followed by greenfield projects.

Observers give different explanations to governments' support for PPPs. First, the private finance aspect of PPPs has permitted the public sector to finance the construction of infrastructure 'off the balance sheet', overcoming constraints on public spending set by the Maastricht Treaty (IPPR, 2001).[1] Second, some governments have supported PPPs in an attempt to increase the participation of the private sector in the provision of public services, allegedly believing that private operators would secure efficiency gains. Whilst empirical evidence has shown that private firms are often more efficient than state ones, many instances also exist where the opposite holds.[2] Other commentators, and generally academics, argue that PPPs have the potential to generate substantial efficiency gains compared to more traditional forms of procurement, but this potential is sector specific and sometimes also project-specific.

In the transport sector, the empirical evidence on the performance of PPP is mixed. On the one hand, as reported by the EC White Paper (2001), private financing of infrastructure has so far received little attention in Europe from private investors, especially cross-border infrastructures on which profits, often low, are by no means certain. Furthermore, traffic/revenue forecasts have often been overoptimistic, leading to costly renegotiation, and numerous instances where projects have been abandoned or taken in house (Guasch, 2004). Opportunistic renegotiations lead by the private operators were pervasive in Latin America's highway projects in the 1980s for example. More recently, in the concession to design, finance, build, operate and transfer the 43-km M1–M15 motorway in Hungary, for example, many commercial vehicles kept using an alternative untolled road. This lead to a debt default by the private partner and to both the concession and debt obligations being taken over by the public-sector party (European Commission, 2004). In the UK, the controversial London Underground PPP project saw one of the three contractors filing for bankruptcy leaving taxpayers to pay the bill and the service taken in house. The Eurotunnel Project suffered a long history of cost overruns. In Australia, some big projects failed, such as the Cross City Tunnel which went into receivership in December 2006 owing AU-$570m (Private Finance Journal, September 2008). On the other hand, the 'Partnership Victoria projects' initiative is considered to be a success, thanks to well-designed incentives, robust legislation and contracts where outputs were generally well specified (Leruth, 2009). The 13-km long, high-level Confederation Bridge between New Brunswick and Prince Edward Island was one of the first Canadian procurements to use a private sector consortium to build and operate a facility through a long-term contract and also proved to be a success story (Conference Board of Canada, 2008). Overall, practitioners and academics agree that it is difficult to find conclusive evidence on the performance of PPPs in the transport sector.

In this chapter, we provide a theoretical framework to identify circumstances in which the main characteristics of PPP arrangements are suitable to provide incentives for the private providers in the transport sector. For this purpose we characterize PPPs in transport by four main features: (1) tasks bundling, (2) high risk transfer, (3) long-term contracting and (4) private finance.[3]

1. Task bundling. A PPP typically involves the bundling of the design, building, finance, and operation of the project, which are contracted out to a consortium of private firms that is responsible for all aspects of services.
2. Risk transfer. Compared to traditional procurement, a PPP contract involves a greater transfer of risk (for example, construction risk and operational risk) and responsibility to the contractor.
3. Long-term contracting. A PPP contract is a long-term contract lasting typically 20 to 35 years.
4. Private finance is a substantial feature of the contract.

To capture these features, we present a simple model of procurement in a multitask environment where the agent not only manages existing assets necessary to provide the service but also may design, build and finance these assets.

We already know from the seminal work on privatization by Sappington and Stigliz (1987), but also from more basic results in the Theory of Incentives (see the textbook treatment in Laffont and Martimort, 2002) that a good understanding of the cost of delegating a task or service to the private sector can only be obtained in a world where this task delegation is impeded with agency costs. Those agency costs are often due to the non-observability of the efforts undertaken on the delegated tasks: the case of moral hazard. Intuitively, when any effort that could improve the returns on the delegated task is non-observable, providing enough incentives to the private sector for completing that task requires to let him enjoy more of the returns. Such delegation is costless when the firm is risk neutral. Indeed, the principal can 'sell' the activity to the delegatee for a fixed fee equal to its expected return. However, such delegation is definitively more costly when the firm is risk-averse and those returns are uncertain since the contract should provide insurance to the firm. This trade-off between incentives and insurance is the key source of agency costs. Optimal contracts in such an environment are intermediate between fixed-price contracts that have good incentive properties and cost-plus contracts that provide insurance. Of course, these lessons are more intricate as the environment gets more complex like in a PPP context. Analyzing such complex delegation patterns through the lenses of the Theory of Incentives is the perspective we took in Iossa and Martimort (2008). In the present chapter, we apply this methodology to discuss contractual and incentive issues for PPPs in the transport sector.

The basic model is described in the next section. In the following section, we use it to show how bundling of project phases into a single contract can be optimal to induce contractors to look at the long-term performances of the asset and to invest in asset quality. Further, we show that bundling goes hand in hand with more risk transfer to the contractor, which provides a rationale for both bundling and risk transfer to be key features of PPP arrangements.

Then, we focus on the choice of contract length for financially free-standing projects where users' fees represent all of the contractor's revenue. We show that relying only on private finance can lead to distortions in the choice of the length of the contract, which result in reduced incentives for the contractor to invest in infrastructure quality.

The following section studies the dynamics of PPP contracts. We start by analyzing the trade-off between investment and maintenance and the impact this has on risk allocation over time. When the public authority has a strong commitment power, we show that the optimal long-term contract entails increasing incentives over time to foster the renewal of investment. Cost-plus contracts arise in early periods whereas fixed-price agreements are expected close to the end of the contract.

In the penultimate section, we extend the analysis of the dynamics of PPP contracts to the case where commitment is limited, governance is weak and political risk makes renegotiation likely. This allows us to discuss the effect of institutional quality on the performance of PPPs. In particular, we show that the risk of regulatory opportunism raises the potential benefit of cost-plus contracts.

The final section summarizes our conclusions.

THE BASIC MODEL

A government or public entity (referred to as G) relies on a private firm or consortium (referred to as F) to provide the transportation services for society. Production of the service requires a multi-stage project involving not only building but also managing the transport infrastructure. Payments to the contractor come from users of the service. So, for example, for highways the contract charges a toll to users (as in Italy or France). For airports, the contractor receives a landing fee from airlines and a rental charge from lessees (say airport shops). For railways, the contractor charges train operating companies for access to the rail network and passengers pay train operating companies for the service.[4]

Demand for the service is stochastic and influenced not only by the quality of the infrastructure but also by the effort exerted by F when providing the service. So, for example, the benefit enjoyed by users of motorways depends on the route safety and thus on the quality of the highway as well as on maintenance effort. In railways, transport demand depends on the quality and comfort of trains, on service reliability, on-the train services, the efficiency of the ticketing system and so on. Major risks affect transport projects at operating stage which include technology, traffic/revenue risks; interest rate and foreign exchange risks; *force majeure* risks. Even when there is a reasonable level of confidence in forecasts, demand can be dramatically affected by competition from other modes or facilities, changing user needs and macroeconomic conditions. In toll roads projects, for example, uncertainty often comes from the availability of alternative untolled roads and from the conditions affecting the wider network, such as economic activity levels or tourism demand.

We capture the above features by assuming that users have an inelastic demand for the service up to some price level p_0 which is given by:

$$D(p) = \begin{cases} d_0 + da + e + \eta & \text{if } p \leq p_0 \\ 0 & p > p_0. \end{cases}$$

where a is the effort in infrastructure quality, whilst e is the effort in service quality. The marginal benefits of the agents' efforts are positive, in particular $d \geq 0$ and $d_0 \geq 0$ denotes some base level of demand that is obtained even without any effort. These quality efforts have disutility counted in monetary terms of $a^2/2$, $e^2/2$, respectively, with no (dis-) economies of scope between efforts. Exogenous demand risk is captured by the random variable η which is normally distributed with zero mean and variance σ^2.

The firm's expected revenue is therefore:

$$E_\eta(R) = p_0 E_\eta (\max\{d_0 + da + e + \eta, 0\}) \approx p_0(d_0 + da + e),$$

where the approximation above holds when σ^2 is small enough compared to the base level of demand d_0.

For simplicity, we assume away any incentive problem on the cost side and assume zero marginal costs of providing the services.

Delegation of services to the private sector takes place in a moral hazard environment so that both a and e are nonverifiable. We focus on moral hazard as the sole source of incentive problems as this fits well with the observation made by Bajari and Tadelis (2001) that, in many procurement contexts, the buyer and the seller face the same uncertainty on costs and demand conditions. Unless stated otherwise, only the realized demand D is observable and can be used *ex ante* at the time G and F contract together.

In practice many aspects of service quality in transport concessions are observable and verifiable by third parties. This is the case, for example, of train punctuality and rail crash rates in rail concessions, travel time variability in bus concessions and asphalt quality, congestion levels or mortality rates in highway concessions. For these aspects of quality, the PPP contract should specify quality targets and then use bonuses and penalties to incentivize the contractor to invest so as to meet these targets. This is indeed what we observed, for example, in the PPP contracts for London Underground. The payment regime specified a monthly charge, set during the procurement, that covered maintenance, renewal and upgrading of the infrastructure. The charge would then be adjusted up or down, depending on the performance achieved by the contractors relative to the baseline set in the contract. The various areas of performance were: (1) *capability*, a measure of the capacity of the infrastructure, capturing the average journey time; (2) *availability*, a measure of the reliability of rolling stock, signalling, track, and station-based equipment; (3) *ambience,* a measure of the quality of the environment for passengers, including the condition and cleanliness of trains and stations and the provision of passenger information.

In settings where the investment in quality is contractible, adequate penalties for noncompliance can suffice to ensure that contractual obligations are met. But when the investment is noncontractible, a moral hazard problem arises. This problem could be studied within our framework by simply reinterpreting D as a quality indicator and by considering an incentive payment linked to quality levels.

Keeping here our focus on noncontractible quality, we assume that the risk-neutral government G maximizes an expected social welfare function, defined as the social benefit of the service net of its costs and of the payment made to F.[5] The firm F also maximizes expected profit but it is risk-averse with constant absolute degree of risk-aversion $r > 0$. The assumption of risk-neutrality for G fits well the case where the transport project is small relatively to the share of the overall budget or even the unique project under a transport agency's responsibility.[6] The assumption of risk-aversion for F captures the fact that a PPP project might represent a large share of this firm's activities so that the firm can hardly be viewed as being fully diversified.

Benchmark

Suppose that efforts are observable and contractible. G can run a competitive auction to attract potential service providers. G has all bargaining power *ex ante* and chooses a fee for the service provider that makes him just indifferent between producing the service or getting his outside option normalized at zero. At the first-best, F is fully insured by G and thus bears no risk. The contract forces F to choose the first-best efforts defined as:

$$(a^{FB}, e^{FB}) = \arg\max_{(a, e)} p_0(d_0 + da + e) - \frac{a^2}{2} - \frac{e^2}{2} = (dp_0, p_0). \tag{29.1}$$

The first-best quality-enhancing effort a^{FB} trades off the marginal social value of that effort, given by its impact on revenues (dp_0), with its marginal cost (a). The service quality effort e^{FB} trades off the marginal benefit of increasing revenues (p_0) with its marginal monetary disutility (e). The offered contract is then defined as a pair (a^{FB}, e^{FB}), and a reward such that the firm's expected profit is zero. The observability of a and e allows contracts to be based on them. Under those conditions, welfare is maximized. The case where a and e are not observable is dealt with in the next section.

THE BENEFITS OF BUNDLING

The main feature of a PPP is the bundling of various phases of contracting. In a typical PPP, design (D), building (B), finance (F) and operation (O) of the project (this is the so-called 'DBFO model') are contracted out to a consortium of private firms. This consortium generally includes a construction company and a facility-management company and it is responsible for all aspects of the service.[7] So for example, a PPP contract may provide for the contractor to construct, finance, manage and maintain a highway section, a tram line, a light rail, an underground line or a bridge. The contractor recoups his initial investment either through user charges or through a direct payment from the government (or any of its agencies) or through a combination of both. In this section, we study the effect of bundling on the contractor's incentives to make nonverifiable investment in infrastructure quality and effort in service quality, which increases the demand for the service.

Unbundling

Under traditional contracting, G approaches first a builder and then a separate operator. The operator receives a revenue-sharing rule $t(R)$. We follow Holmström and Milgrom (1991) and restrict the analysis to linear rules of the form $t(R) = \alpha + \beta R$. The fee α is a fixed payment to the firm (or subsidy) paid upfront. The coefficient β is meant for the share of those profits which are left to the firm; the share $1 - \beta$ being kept by the government. So, in a payment mechanism solely based on user charges, the contractor receives its revenues directly through charges on the end users of the infrastructure facility and bears all demand risk. This corresponds to the case $\alpha = 0$ and $\beta = 1$. Instead, with a payment mechanism based on availability, the government rewards the contractor for making the service available but the payment is independent of the actual service usage. This corresponds to the case where $\alpha > 0$ and $\beta = 0$ so that the contractor's reward is fixed and the government retains all demand risk. The other cases fall between these two extreme options.

To simplify presentation and fit with the empirical evidence for transport, we rule out the theoretical possibility that the builder obtains an incentive payment that depends on the realized demand D, and assume instead, that he receives a fixed payment.[8]

Since his fixed payment cannot reward the quality enhancing effort put into the design of the project, the builder does not exert any effort:

$$a_u = 0. \tag{29.2}$$

Turning now to the operator who is willing to maximize the certainty equivalent of his expected utility given the builder's own effort, his incentives constraint can be written as:

$$e = \arg\max_{\tilde{e}} \alpha + \beta p_0 (d_0 + \tilde{e}) - \frac{\tilde{e}^2}{2} - \frac{r\sigma^2\beta^2 p_0^2}{2} = \beta p_0. \tag{29.3}$$

Increasing β raises demand-enhancing effort, but as more operational risk is then transferred to F the risk-premium $r\sigma^2\beta^2 p_0^2/2$ increases too. Assuming that G has all the bargaining power *ex ante* with both the builder and the operator, he can extract all their rent and just leave them indifferent between providing the service and getting their outside opportunities normalized at zero. In particular, the fee a is just set to cover the risk-premium that must be paid to have the risk-averse operator bearing some operational risk as requested for incentive reasons.

Finally, G just maximizes social welfare taking into account the incentive constraints (29.2) and (29.3) and the total benefit and cost of effort, including the risk-premium. This yields the following expression of G's problem:

$$\max_{e} p_0 (d_0 + e) - \frac{e^2}{2} - \frac{r\sigma^2\beta^2 p_0^2}{2} \text{ subject to (29.3)}.$$

This gives the following expression of the second-best effort and marginal reward:

$$e_u^{SB} = \beta^{SB} p_0 = \frac{p_0}{1 + r\sigma^2}. \tag{29.4}$$

We observe that $\beta^{SB} \in (0, 1)$ which captures the fact that the risk-averse firm only receives a fraction of the overall profit for insurance reasons and undersupplies effort below its first-best value. Finally, the fixed-payment α^{SB} is determined so that the firm breaks even in expectation.

Because providing incentives requires the agent to bear more risk and this is socially costly, the second-best effort is less than its first-best level. As it is standard with this linear-CARA model, an increase in demand risk (making σ^2 larger) also means that the trade-off between insurance and incentives is tilted towards low-powered incentives.[9] For further references, note that social welfare under unbundling can be written as:

$$W_u^{SB} = p_0 d_0 + \frac{p_0^2}{2(1 + r\sigma^2)}. \tag{29.5}$$

From this characterization of the incentive constraint, we get:

Result 1   *The optimal payment mechanism comes closer to be based on user charges only when risk-aversion and demand risk are small (high-powered incentives). The payment mechanism moves towards being based on availability only when risk-aversion and demand uncertainty are large (low-powered incentives).*

Transferring demand risk to the contractor gives him incentives to boost demand and raise consumer surplus but it costs the government in terms of a higher risk-premium. The optimal payment mechanism trades off incentives and insurance. This is in line with the well-known fact that, in operation contracts for urban public transport, the lower the demand risk (the better demand can be forecasted), the closer the contract is to a fixed-price contract. Further, both the power of the incentive scheme β and investment a^{SB} rise with d. That is, for PPPs in transport, when demand levels is significantly affected by the contractor's action (thus d is high), demand risk should be borne mainly by the contractor. Otherwise, it should be borne mainly by the government. As reported by the Conference Board of Canada (2008), in the Confederation Bridge project the bulk of project risks were transferred to the consortium, who placed a \$200m performance bond and a letter of credit for \$73 million in the event that performance defaults exceed \$200m. The project is reported a success.[10]

Bundling

Under bundling both the building of the infrastructure and the operational phase are in the hands of a consortium which chooses both a and e to maximize

$$(e, a) = \arg \max_{(\tilde{e}, \tilde{a})} \alpha + \beta p_0 (d_0 + d\tilde{a} + \tilde{e}) - \frac{\tilde{a}^2}{2} - \frac{\tilde{e}^2}{2} - \frac{r\sigma^2 \beta^2 p_0^2}{2}.$$

Taking into account the additional non-negativity constraint $a \geq 0$, we obtain the following incentive constraints:

$$e = \beta p_0; \text{ and } a = \beta p_0 d = de \tag{29.6}$$

Note, in particular, that the effort e follows the same formula as in the case of unbundling. This is no longer the case for a which changes thanks to the positive externality that is internalized under bundling.

A consortium internalizes somewhat the impact of building a high quality infrastructure because it increases its revenues. Moving towards more risk transfer also raises incentives on infrastructure quality; an objective which cannot be directly achieved by the public authority since that quality is hardly contractible.

Finally, taking into account how the firm chooses investment in infrastructure quality and effort, G solves the following problem:

$$\max_{(a,\, e)} p_0(d_0 + da + e) - \frac{a^2}{2} - \frac{e^2}{2} - \frac{r\sigma^2\beta^2 p_0^2}{2} \text{ subject to} \tag{29.6}.$$

which gives the following equilibrium levels of effort

$$e_b^{SB} = \frac{p_0(1 + d^2)}{1 + d^2 + r\sigma^2} \text{ and } a_b^{SB} = \frac{p_0 d(1 + d^2)}{1 + d^2 + r\sigma^2},$$

The level of welfare under bundling is given by

$$W_b^{SB} = p_0 d_0 + \frac{p_0^2(1 + d^2)}{2(1 + d^2 + r\sigma^2)}.$$

Result 2   *Bundling strictly dominates unbundling:* $W_b^{SB} > W_u^{SB}$. *The welfare gain from bundling increases with the magnitude of the externality d:*

$$\frac{\partial}{\partial d}(W_b^{SB} - W_u^{SB}) > 0.$$

With bundling there is a positive infrastructure quality-enhancing effort and an increase in cost-reducing effort. PPP projects are associated with higher powered incentives and more operational risk being transferred to the private sector:

$$e_b^{SB} = \beta_u^{SB} p_0 = e_u^{SB}; a_b^{SB} = \beta_b^{SB} p_0 d > a_u^{SB}$$

Bundling induces the agent to internalize the effect of his quality-enhancing investment a on the share of revenues that he bears at the operational stage. This unambiguously raises welfare, and the stronger the effect of infrastructure quality on revenues, d, the greater the benefit of bundling. Furthermore, bundling shifts more risk to F and brings the additional benefit of increasing its incentives to invest in asset quality. Thus, moving from traditional procurement to PPP changes revenue-sharing rules: bundling and risk transfer go hand-in-hand under PPP whereas unbundling and less risk sharing contracts are more likely under traditional procurement. This rationalizes existing evidence that PPP projects are characterized by more risk transfer and thus greater risk-premia than traditional procurement.

BOX 29.1 BUNDLING OR UNBUNDLING?

MAIN RESULTS:

- The optimal payment mechanism comes closer to be based on user charges only when risk-aversion and demand risk are small (high-powered incentives).
- The payment mechanism moves towards being based on availability only when risk-aversion and demand uncertainty are large (low-powered incentives).
- Bundling strictly dominates unbundling: it generates greater infrastructure quality-enhancing effort and more cost-reducing effort.
- The welfare gain from bundling is greater the stronger the effect of infrastructure quality on service demand.
- PPP projects are associated with higher powered incentives and more operational risk being transferred to the private sector:

Main Hypotheses: Demand depends on contractor's effort on quality of infrastructure and on quality of operation; it is a random variable. Hidden efforts on quality of infrastructure and on operations; the contractor is risk-averse and faces demand risk.

Literature

Two strands of the literature on PPPs have emphasized the multitask nature of the procurement problem when building and managing assets are at stake. Hart (2003) built on Hart et al. (1997) provided a model where the sole source of incentives is ownership. A builder can perform two kinds of investment (productive and unproductive) which may both reduce operating costs, although only the productive investment also raises the benefit of providing the service. Under traditional procurement, the builder cannot internalize the impact of his effort either on benefits or on costs and, as a result, implements too little of the productive investment but the right amount of the unproductive one. Under PPP, the builder internalizes partly the impact of his productive investment whereas he also exerts too much of the unproductive one. Turning to the case where ownership concerns a public good and still using the property rights approach, Besley and Ghatak (2001) showed that ownership should lie in the hands of that player with the highest valuation for the public good, explaining thereby that non-governmental organizations may be given property rights. Finally, Francesconi and Muthoo (2006) considered the case of impure public goods and, in a model where each party may have control rights on a subset of decisions, showed that shared authority can be optimal in case the parties' investments are comparable.

Bennett and Iossa (2006a) studied the desirability of bundling project phases and of giving ownership to the investor. In their model innovations are non-contractible *ex ante* but verifiable *ex post*. Ownership of the asset gives control right to the owner to decide whether to implement quality enhancing or cost-reducing innovation proposed by the investor. It is shown that the hold-up problem is less severe under PPP, compared with traditional procurement, when there is a positive externality between the building and managing stages. With a negative externality the opposite can hold. Further public ownership acts as a commitment for the government to renegotiate and share with the investor the surplus from the implementation of the innovation. Private ownership is, however, optimal for generic facilities with high residual value.

Martimort and Pouyet (2008) built a model where both the quality of the infrastructure and operating costs are contractible. Agency costs are lower under a PPP when there is a positive externality between building and managing assets compared with traditional procurement. Granting ownership is an imperfect way of aligning incentives but, to a large extent, the important issue is not who owns the asset but instead whether tasks are bundled or not. That insight is developed in various extensions of their basic model allowing for risk-sharing as a motive for forming consortia, or political economy. In this respect, a common theme of their model and ours is that PPP comes with higher powered incentives which are prone to collusion and capture of public officials. When those institutional costs are taken into account, relying on PPP becomes less attractive.

Finally, in Iossa and Martimort (2008), we build upon the above two models and provide a unified framework, with elements of both complete contracting and property rights, which highlights the positive effects of bundling in the presence of a positive externality and the negative ones in the presence of a negative externality.

Applications

Our results suggest that PPPs are likely to deliver efficiency gains when bundling has the potential to yield significant demand increase and when risk is effectively transferred to the private operator. A report commissioned by the Treasury Taskforce (Arthur Andersen and Enterprise LSE, 2000) estimated saving on a sample of PFI projects equal to 17 percent, compared to traditional procurement.[11] Evidence of successful PPP projects in transport also exists. For example, the TransMilenio bus transport project developed in 2000 in Bogotá achieved significant improvements in the efficiency, safety and environmental impact of the system. The $90m PPP contract for the Washington DC metro led to 600 percent increase in property values in the affected areas. The 30 year contract for Colombo port in Sri Lanka saw the construction of three container berths and one passenger berth whilst the port remained operational throughout; the throughput increased by 350 percent from 2000 to 2004.[12] In the seven years following its privatization, the PPP operator for the Italian motorway network reported a fall by about 50 percent in mortality rates and an increase in the usage of electronic toll payment system of 227 percent.[13]

However, evidence of PPP failure are also recorded. Costs have escalated to record levels for the Channel Tunnel Rail link, the PPP operator for London Underground has gone bust and many PPP transport projects have failed to raise the interest of investors. Whilst warning against lack of comprehensive dataset, Blanc-Brude et al. (2006) studied a sample of road projects financed by the EIB between 1990 and 2005 in all EU-15 countries plus Norway. They found that *ex ante* construction costs (that is, costs before construction actually starts) are some 20 percent higher for PPP roads than for traditionally procured roads. The data does not reveal the actual (*ex post*) cost of the projects and thus whether risk transfer under PPP was effective in containing cost overruns.

In practice, PPPs are often employed out of a need for governments to use private finance for financing infrastructure. In Iossa and Martimort (2008), we showed that a potential benefit of private finance stems from the possibility that lenders bring in the expertise of outside financiers in evaluating risks. Outside financiers can condition how much repayment they request from the firm on the extra information they have on the contractor's effort. As the financial contract is made under a better information structure, the extra round of contracting with financiers has more benefits in terms of improved incentives than costs in terms of modified risk-sharing. In this respect, bundling the task of looking for outside finance (be it through outside equity or debt) and operating assets can improve on the more traditional mode of procurement where the cost of investment is paid through taxation and investment is not backed up by such level of expertise within the public sphere.

CONTRACT LENGTH

In this section, we focus on a cost of private finance that comes from the absence of a powerful means to provide incentives: government transfers. We consider the case of financially free-standing projects, where there are no direct subsidies from the government to the firm. The firm must then cover its initial investment I from the revenues it generates from charging user fees over the length T of the contract. After date T, the PPP goes back under public ownership and the access toll is set at zero. In this setting, we analyse the determinants of the optimal contract duration when project revenues only come from charging users. For this purpose we assume that the shocks on the level of demand are drawn once for all whereas the cost of effort in infrastructure quality is sunk and borne once for all beforehand. For simplicity, we disregard effort in service quality.

With these assumptions in mind, intertemporal income smoothing for the firm leads to rewrite the firm's discounted stream of certainty-equivalent payoffs when choosing effort a and making the investment I as:

$$E_\eta\left(u\left(-I - \frac{a^2}{2} + \int_0^T p_0(d_0 + da + \eta)exp(-\rho t)dt\right)\right)$$

$$= u\left(-I - \frac{a^2}{2} + (1 - exp(-\rho T))p_0(d_0 + da) - \frac{r\sigma^2}{2}(1 - exp(-\rho T))^2 p_0^2\right)$$

where ρ is the interest rate in the economy.

This immediately leads to the following moral hazard constraint:

$$a = (1 - exp(-\rho T))dp_0. \tag{29.7}$$

When government transfers cannot be used to provide incentives, higher investment in infrastructure quality can be induced either by raising the tariffs charged to users for the service, p_0, or by increasing the length of the contract, T. The longer the duration of the contract T, the greater the firm's investment since its benefits accrue over a longer period. Note that the term $1 - exp(-\rho T)$ plays the same role as β in Equation (29.3) above. Instead of directly sharing the revenue with the firm in each period, the government lets the firm enjoy all revenue but for a finite duration.

With no subsidies, however, the duration of the contract may have to serve also another purpose, namely that of ensuring that the revenues from the project over the whole duration of the contract are sufficient to cover the initial investment undertaken by the firm, that is:

$$(1 - exp(-\rho T))p_0(d_0 + da) - \frac{a^2}{2} - \frac{r\sigma^2}{2}(1 - exp(-\rho T))^2 p_0^2 \geq I. \qquad (29.8)$$

Consider the case (1) where the investment constraint (29.8) is slack, that is, expected revenues over the duration of the contract are enough to cover the up-front investment. The second-best effort level that maximizes expected welfare is then easily obtained as:

$$a^{SB} = \frac{dp_0}{1 + r\sigma^2} = dp_0(1 - exp(-\rho T^{SB})). \qquad (29.9)$$

From which, we derive the optimal unconstrained length of the franchise as:

$$T^{SB} = \frac{1}{\rho}\ln\left[1 + \frac{1}{r\sigma^2}\right]. \qquad (29.10)$$

Thus, when the budget constraint is slack (at $a = a^{SB}$), the length of the contract is chosen for the sole purpose to create incentives for investment in infrastructure quality. We then obtain:

Result 3   *Assume that the investment constraint is slack. Franchise lengths are shorter when discount rates are lower, in more uncertain environments or when risk-aversion is greater.*

As longer contracts are also riskier – future demand is more difficult to forecast – both higher demand risk and a greater degree of risk-aversion call for reducing the incentive power and for more insurance which is obtained by reducing the length of the contract. Thus in situations where demand volumes are volatile and difficult to forecast, the optimal contract duration is shorter than in sectors where demand is stable and predictable. An example in order is the case of motorways where franchises can be allowed before or after completion. The model predicts that, in the latter, franchise lengths should be shorter to take into account a greater uncertainty on future demand. Instead PPP contracts for the renovation of small transport networks (rather than construction of new ones), often entail little initial investment. When the state of the existing network is known, risk is low and the length of the contract can be set sufficiently long so as to boost quality investment.

Things change in case (2) where the budget constraint is binding (at $a = a^{SB}$). Now the length of the contract must be chosen so as to guarantee that the stream of expected revenues coming from user charges is sufficient to cover the firm's investment as well as the risk-premium. Franchise length is then given by (29.8) where the inequality is now replaced by an equality. In big transport projects for new infrastructures, or in PPP contracts for renewal of transport networks that suffered from years of underinvestment (for example, London Underground) when in public hands, finance constraints are generally binding.

To see the effect of a binding budget constraint, suppose that T^{SB} is such that (29.8) does not hold. The length of the contract has to be modified to ensure that the firm breaks even, that is, that the stream of future revenues is sufficient to cover the initial investment. We get:

Result 4   *Assume that the investment constraint is binding. Franchise lengths are shorter in more uncertain environments, when risk aversion is greater, when consumers' willingness to pay is greater (p_0 greater), when investment is lower (I lower).*

These results have implications for the renegotiation of franchise contracts near bankruptcy. One should expect those renegotiations to increase the length of the contracts to secure investment. This is indeed what we observe in practice, one famous example being the Channel Tunnel; also Guasch (2004) reports numerous instances where contract length was extended when demand fell short of the forecasted level and the operator encountered financial difficulties.

The above result highlights a cost of private finance, namely, the distortions in incentives that results from the need to modify contract length away from the level that ensures optimal incentives.

BOX 29.2   CONTRACT LENGTH

MAIN RESULTS:

- Higher investment in infrastructure quality can be induced either by raising the tariffs charged to users for the service or by expanding contract length,
- Optimal franchise length depends on the size of the investment cost compared to the expected project revenues.
- When the investment cost is high compared to the expected project revenues, there is an additional cost of private finance, namely the distortion in incentives that results from the need to increase contract length to achieve budget balance.
- Optimal franchise lengths are shorter when discount rates are lower, in more uncertain environments, when risk-aversion is greater, and when investment is lower.

Main Hypotheses: Same hypotheses as in Box 29.1. The project is financially free-standing, meaning that investment cost should be covered by project revenues.

Engel et al. (2001) also endogenize contract length in a setting where there is no moral hazard. The procedure they suggest is the Least Present Value Revenue (LPVR). The idea is to award a contract to the firm bidding the lowest LPVR and the contract ends when the LPVR is received. The tariff and the rate of discount (fixed or variable) are generally agreed at bidding stage or set in advance by G. If demand and tariffs adversely affect revenues, the concession runs for additional years until LPVR is secured. Since the firm is still residual claimant on cost saving, it provides incentives to operate at optimal costs because any gains are fully captured by F. LPVR should be used when F cannot influence demand and in which objective quality standards can be set, measured, and enforced: for example, roads or landing strips in airports.

Although a common wisdom is that contract length should be related to the life cycle of the investments sunk by the firm, what is the optimal contract length of a concession contract is an issue relatively unexplored by the economic literature. One exception is Ellman (2006) who emphasizes that the long-term nature of PPP contracts favors incentives by the government but it has a cost in terms of reduced flexibility. He showed that a longer contract length helps to protect the contractor from his investment being expropriated by the government but it reduces the incentives of the government to discover new service innovations since changes are costly to renegotiate. In Iossa and Martimort (2008), we also study the trade-off between incentives and flexibility though our focus is on investment by the firm in cost-reducing effort.

CONTRACTUAL DYNAMICS: THE TRADE-OFF BETWEEN INVESTMENT AND MAINTENANCE

PPP projects are typically long-term projects which might cover 20 to 35 years. Over a long-lasting project where the quality of durable assets and infrastructures may significantly depreciate, an important issue concerns the extent to which contractors are willing to invest to improve the stock of existing infrastructure in the long-run or whether they prefer to choose management strategies that keep costs low in the short-run.

To analyse the trade-off between investment and maintenance, we now assume that the firm gets a basic stock of infrastructure to provide public service on G's behalf at date $t = 1$. Improving this stock requires some extra investment which costs $a^2/2$ today but this pays off tomorrow in terms of increasing demand by an amount da. Another strategy would be to avoid incurring any initial investment and then increasing demand with more service quality.

Profits in each period are respectively given by:

$$\pi_1 = p_0(d_0 + e_1 + \eta_1) - \frac{a^2}{2} \text{ and } \pi_2 = p_0(d_0 + da + e_2 + \eta_2)$$

where the demand uncertainty η_i ($i = 1, 2$) is normally distributed with zero mean and variance σ^2, and e_i is effort in service quality undertaken at date i. The demand shocks are assumed to be independent in the two periods. This assumes no cumulative effects due for instance to demand growth. Investing increases accounting costs in the short-run but, because of a positive externality between design and operation, increases demand by da with $d > 0$. Implicit in our formulation is the fact that the cost of investment is not observable to *G* meaning that it is (at least partly) aggregated with other costs, noticeably the first-period operating costs, in the firm's book. For simplicity, there is no discounting. We will also assume that the investment in infrastructure has some extra social benefit *ba* that accrues to *G* (this can be viewed as the residual value of the infrastructure at the end of the franchise). Assuming that investment is verifiable, its first-best level satisfies therefore:

$$a^{FB} = p_0 d + b.$$

Let us turn now to the case where the investment *a* is non-verifiable and must be induced by *G* through adequate incentives. Denote $t_i(\pi_i) = \alpha_i + \beta_i p_i$ the profit-sharing rule used at date *i*.[14] Let us first consider the case where *G* can commit himself to such a two-period contract $\{t_1(\pi_1), t_2(\pi_2)\}$.

Still assuming a quadratic disutility of maintenance effort in each period, the firm chooses its whole array of actions (a^*, e_1^*, e_2^*) to maximize its long-run expected payoff:

$$(a^*, e_1^*, e_2^*) = \arg\max_{(a, e_1, e_2)} \sum_{i=1}^{2}\left(\alpha_i + \beta_i p_0(d_0 + e_i) - \frac{e_i^2}{2}\right) - \beta_1\frac{a^2}{2} + \beta_2 dp_0 a.$$

This leads to the following incentive constraints:

$$e_1 = \beta_1 p_0, \quad e_2 = \beta_2 p_0, \text{ and } \beta_2 dp_0 = \beta_1 a. \tag{29.11}$$

An interesting benchmark is obtained when *G* offers the stationary contract with slope β_u^{SB}, that is, the contract that would be optimal in the absence of any concern on the renewal of the infrastructure. This contract induces a stationary effort $e_1 = e_2 = \beta_u^{SB}p_0$ and an investment level, namely $a = dp_0$, which is privately but not socially optimal if $b > 0$. There is too little investment in renewing infrastructure with such stationary contract. Raising this investment requires modifying the intertemporal pattern of incentives.

Result 5 *Assuming full commitment, the optimal long-term contract entails higher powered incentives towards the end of the contract than at the beginning and an inefficient level of investment:*

$$e_1^{SB} < e_u^{SB} < e_2^{SB}, \text{ and } a^{SB} < a^{FB}.$$

The intuition behind this proposition can be understood as follows. By offering low-powered incentive contracts in the earlier periods and high-powered contracts towards the end of the relationship, *G* makes *F* bear less of the costs and enjoy most of the benefits associated to its non-verifiable investment. This boosts the firm's incentives to undertake the non-verifiable investment. Still, this is not enough to align the private incentives to invest with the socially optimal ones and underinvestment follows.[15]

A shift towards higher-powered incentives is observed in practice for highways where price regulation generally evolves from cost plus to price cap (see, for example, the case of Italian and French highways). Urban public transport contracts also exhibit such pattern with a systematic move towards fixed price contracts.

BOX 29.3   CONTRACTUAL DYNAMICS: TRADE -OFF
          BETWEEN INVESTMENT AND MAINTENANCE

MAIN RESULTS:

- To motivate early costly investment in infrastructure quality, the optimal long-term contract calls for low-powered incentives in the earlier periods of the contract and high-powered incentives towards the end of the relationship.
- Thus, the optimal long-term contract entails greater profit shares left to the firm towards the end of the contract than at the beginning.
- Risk transfer to the contractor increases over time.

Main Hypotheses: in a two-period framework, the contractor makes unobservable infrastructure-improving investment in the first period, which enhances second period's quality and service demand. The government can fully commit to a long-term contract.

Literature

The literature on intertemporal incentive problems under moral hazard is huge. Most of it assumes separability between the benefits and costs of working on a project in different periods, thus stressing the role of history dependent contracts to smooth incentives.[16]

Laffont and Tirole (1993, Chapter 8) proposed an adverse selection model with repeated auctions of incentive contracts which shares many features of our model, most noticeably the shift towards higher powered incentives over time. An incumbent firm invests in period 1 but, because of contract renewal, may lose the benefits of its investment if it is not granted the new contract for date 2. They particularly focused on the necessary bias towards the incumbent as an incentive tool to secure investment and show that this bias matters all the more that investment is not easily transferable. A major result of their analysis is also that incentives to invest are fostered with incentive schemes which are higher powered over time. Our pure moral hazard model can be viewed as providing a simplified version of the same insight.

Dewatripont and Legros (2005) argue that *ex-ante* competition between potential consortia may limit the extent of cost overruns and that introducing a third-party (typically outside shareholders or creditors) in a PPP contract may improve monitoring which limits cost overruns as well.

The systematic move towards fixed-price contracts over time is also studied in Gagnepain et al. (2009) in the case of urban transportation. They give another rationale for such patterns of increasing subsidies based on the idea that those short-term contracts are renewed on the basis of earlier information on cost performances. Subsidies which are renegotiation-proof exhibit such patterns. Finally, this trend is observed in practice also because of a tendency towards more price cap regulation and less monitoring by governments to reduce red-tape.

THE ROLE OF THE INSTITUTIONAL FRAMEWORK: REGULATORY AND POLITICAL RISKS

A critical issue in PPPs is whether the public authority will face its responsibilities over the rules on prices, public obligations and so on that are specified in the contracts and that influence the value of the transaction. Private financing of big transport infrastructure makes investors especially vulnerable to opportunistic governments. First, the investment is largely sunk and may require a long period to be recouped; the assets cannot be moved elsewhere, if at all, except at great cost. Second, transport projects often provide services that are essential to consumers, making choices related to tariffs levels highly politically sensitive.[17] Significant political tension for example characterized the procurement process in the London Underground PPPs. Particularly strong was the opposition of the newly elected Mayor of London who initiated several legal challenges to the PPPs during the procurement process.

Governments generally agree to compensate investors for political risks, although in practice justifications for government actions are used to delay or prevent such payments. Thus, private investors generally assume the risks associated with dispute resolution and the ability to obtain compensation should the government violate the concession agreement.[18]

In Latin America and Caribbean countries various episodes were observed where, once the investment was made, the government (possibly a different one) retreated on its promises, satisfying users' demands to reduce tariffs or appropriating the investor's profits. Instances have also been recorded where the government passed legislation to nullify contractual clauses (see Guash et al., 2007). Political risk has also played a crucial role in Central and Eastern Europe. A major obstacle to the PPP policy in Hungary has been the frequent change in political attitudes towards PPPs and user tolls (see Brench et al., 2005), as since 1990 each change in government resulted in a different attitude and a different institutional framework for PPPs. At a more general level, Hammami et al. (2006) find that private participation (in the form of PPP, privatization or traditional procurement) is more prevalent in countries with less corruption and with an effective rule of law.

Regulatory risk discourages potential investors and raises the cost of capital and the risk-premium (higher tariffs, or smaller transfer price) paid for PPPs. The political controversy that surrounded the £16 billion London Underground project of 2002–03 made lenders nervous so that 85 percent of the debt had to be guaranteed by the public sector at a fairly late stage in the procurement process. The consequences for taxpayers were badly felt following the failure of one of the contractors. Guasch and Spiller (1999) estimate that the cost of regulatory risk ranges from 2 to 6 percent points to be added to the cost of capital depending on country and sector. An increase of 5 points in the cost of capital to account for the regulatory risk leads to a reduction of the offered transfer fee or sale price of about 35 percent or equivalently it requires a compensatory increase in tariffs of about 20 percent.

Some observers have argued that a weak governance may go hand in hand with lack of training: In Latin American countries, governments often did not receive instruments adequate to their mandate (Guash et al., 2006). To improve governance, a number of countries have created dedicated PPP units – centers of expertise – to manage the contract with the private contractor.[19] These include for example the Central PPP Policy

Unit in the Department of Finance in Ireland, the Unita' Tecnica della Finanza di Progetto in Italy and Partnership UK in the UK.

In the remainder of this section, we briefly consider the scope and consequences of regulatory opportunism. The non-stationary path of incentives described in Result 5 is of course highly dependent on G's ability to commit to increase subsidies in the second period to reward F's initial investment. We assume now that such commitment power is absent and that renegotiation takes place at date 2 with G still having all bargaining power at that stage and extracting, through an adequate fee, all surplus that F could withdraw from renegotiation.

When date 2 comes along, F's investment a^0 is sunk and the second period profit-sharing rule is renegotiated to reach the optimal trade-off between maintenance effort and insurance that would arise in a static context, that is, conditionally on the investment level a^0 which was previously sunk. This yields the standard expressions for the second period maintenance effort and the slope of the renegotiated incentive scheme:

$$\beta_2^0 = \frac{1}{1 + r\sigma^2}.$$

Under limited commitment, G can still adjust the second-period fixed-fee to extract all surplus of the firm given his expectation over the investment level a^0 at this date and, of course, expectations are correct in equilibrium.

Anticipating the slope of date 2 incentive scheme and knowing also the slope of the first-period incentive scheme, F chooses his investment so that

$$\beta_u^{SB} dp_0 = \beta_1 a. \tag{29.12}$$

With an opportunistic principal, welfare is lower than with full commitment. Moreover, the second-period contract entails lower powered incentives than under full commitment because the second-period incarnation of G does not take into account the impact of the contract he offers on the firm's incentives to invest at date 1. Since $e_2^0 = e_u^{SB} < e_2^{SB}$, Equation (29.12) implies that the firm enjoys less of the benefits of investment. To maintain incentives for investment, the firm's reward must be less contingent on the realized profits in period 1. This makes first-period incentives even further low powered.

Result 6   *With an opportunistic principal, investment is lower and profit-sharing rules are even more tilted towards full insurance in both periods than under full commitment:*

$$e_1^0 < e_1^{SB}, \quad e_2^0 < e_2^{SB} \text{ and } a^0 < a^{SB}.$$

Literature

The model above considers a renegotiation led by the government with the possibility of breaking an initial agreement. In a sense, the intertemporal incentive scheme is thus closer to a sequence of short-term contracts. In a two-period principal-agent model with

---

BOX 29.4   ROLE OF INSTITUTIONAL FRAMEWORK: REGULATORY AND POLITICAL RISKS

MAIN RESULTS:

- Private financing of big transport infrastructure makes investors especially vulnerable to opportunistic governments.
- With opportunistic governments, the welfare gain from bundling is reduced.
- Regulatory risk raises the cost of capital and the risk-premium.
- With an opportunistic government, investment is lower and incentives are even less high-powered in both periods than under full commitment.

Main Hypotheses: in the framework of a two period analysis, the contractor makes unobservable infrastructure-improving investment in the first period, which enhances second period's quality and service demand. The government can fully commit to a long-term contract.

---

short-term contracting and pure adverse selection, Laffont and Tirole (1993, Chapter 9) formalized the so-called 'ratchet effect'. This effect refers to the possibility that an agent with a high performance today will tomorrow face a more demanding incentive scheme, an intertemporal pattern of incentives similar to the one highlighted above. The ratchet effect leads to much pooling in the first period as the agent becomes reluctant to convey favorable information early in the relationship. In our model the emphasis is on moral hazard, and the corresponding pattern of incentives induces the agent to invest less in early periods. In the context of PPP contracts, this effect partially nullifies the benefits of bundling and suggests that PPPs should be preferred in stable institutional environments.

Closer to the previous analysis, but still in a pure adverse selection framework, Aubert and Laffont (2002) analysed the mechanism through which a government can affect future contracting by distorting regulatory requirements to take into account possible political changes and subsequent contract renegotiation. Assuming that the current contract binds all future governments, imperfect commitment yields two main distortions. First, the initial government will delay the payment of the information rent to the second period, thereby free-riding on the cost of producing a higher quantity and leaving higher rents. Second, the degree of information revelation in the first period will be strategically determined to affect the beliefs of the new government.[20]

CONCLUSIONS

The use of PPPs in transport is widespread. Notwithstanding the policy relevance, still little theoretical and empirical work exists. In this chapter, we have reviewed and unified in a common and flexible framework the existing literature on PPPs that is relevant for transport economics in an attempt to fill this gap from the point of view of incentives.

Our analysis has pointed out that the bundling of project phases that characterizes PPPs provides incentives to the private contractor to take into account the costs of long-term project, from building to maintenance and operation. When the externality across project stages is positive, this improves incentives and, through appropriate risk transfer, yields better infrastructure and service quality. Thus our analysis suggests that PPPs are more beneficial when a better quality of the infrastructure can significantly impact on benefits at the operational stage and when demand for the service is stable and easy to forecast. This points to the suitability of PPPs in the transport sector, where infrastructure quality is key and short-term demand is relatively stable.

We have seen that in a PPP contract, although this is not specific to PPPs, the contractor can be incentivized through the allocation of demand risk and the choice of contract length. In sectors such as transport, where users pay for the service and demand levels are affected by the contractor's effort, demand risk is optimally transferred to the contractor. Contract length should be longer for transport modes where demand risk is lower and where the capital investment is greater, as in the rail industry as opposed to maritime transport. Financially free-standing projects can bring the additional cost that contract length must be increased to allow the firm to recoup its initial investment, which results in excessive risk transfer. Thus, welfare under PPPs is higher when service quality is verifiable, demand risk is low or the firm can diversify risk, and when there are government contributions or the initial capital investment is low.

Bundling of project phases and long-term contracting allow PPPs arrangements to provide efficient long-term incentives and to optimize the trade-off between investment and insurance along the life of the project. This helps to incentivize the contractor but it requires institutions with strong commitment power. As the risk of regulatory opportunism increases, the case for PPPs is weaker.

An important issue that has been left out of the analysis is related to the procurement process for PPPs. Most PPP or PFI contracts are too complex to use the open or restricted procedure. In most PPPs, the contracting authority is unable to determine the technical specifications and the appropriate price level in advance. Therefore, until now the negotiated procedure has been the preferred solution for procuring PPP or PFI contracts. Current experience shows, however, that the procurement process for PPPs has been costly and time consuming. Albeit with differences between sectors, it has been estimated that PPP tendering periods last an average of 34 months (NAO, 2007) and that procurement costs can reach 5–10 percent of the capital cost of a project (Yescombe, 2007).[21] Recently however the European Commission introduced the Competitive Dialogues, a new procedure for PPPs contracts (EU Directive 2004/18/EC).

ACKNOWLEDGMENTS

We wish to thank Emile Quinet and Robin Lindsey who invited us to contribute this chapter and provided extensive comments on a first version that improved exposition. We also wish to thank Antonio Estache for helpful suggestions.

NOTES

1. The Eurostat made a decision (news release 18/2004) on the accounting of PPPs to ensure homogeneity across member states and limit accounting tricks made to comply with the rules of the Stability and Growth Pact.
2. For a survey of empirical studies on privatization and contracting out, see Megginson and Netter (2001).
3. See chapter by Estache et al. in this volume for a more in-depth discussion of the main features of PPP in transport.
4. We do not explicitly model here the case where the contractor receives a shadow toll from the government (as for highways in the UK) but the analysis easily extends to that case, assuming that demand is verifiable and can be contracted upon.
5. This assumption simplifies presentation and stresses that the fact that the risk premium necessary to induce the firm's participation has the highest possible cost. Having a redistributive objective with a weight less than one for the firm's profit in the government's objective function or introducing a positive cost of public funds would also give us the same insights at the cost of an increased complexity in the modeling. Note also that our model can easily accommodate the possibility of externalities – be they positive on employment say, or negative on environment – and include them into the net social value of the firm's activity.
6. In the case of a large country's government, the deadweight loss in the cost of taxation (say the cost of taxation is convex) may as well introduce a behavior towards risk for the government if the project represents a large share of the budget. See Lewis and Sappington (1995) and Martimort and Sand-Zantman (2007) who analyze the consequences of having risk-averse local governments for contract design. Often, the basic insight of those models is that risk-aversion on the principal's side reduces incentive distortions.
7. Variations of the DBFO contract include Design–Build–Operate (DBO), Build–Operate–Transfer (BOT), Build–Own–Operate–Transfer (BOOT), Build–Lease–Operate–Transfer (BLOT) and so forth.
8. The justification for this assumption is twofold. First, G may have a limited ability to commit to future rewards for the builder and be unable to delay payment for the delivery of the infrastructure. Second, there might be the possibility of collusion between G and the operator to exaggerate the contribution of the operator to cost-reducing activities and underestimate that of the builder.
9. So far, our analysis has assumed away any cost of public funds. Suppose that any transfers from and payments to the government are weighted by a factor $1 + \lambda$ where λ is the positive cost of public funds. Then, the objective function is essentially the same as above if the social benefit of the project becomes $(b_0 + b_a)/(1 + \lambda)$. Intuitively, counting more any extra euro given to the firms and raised through taxation, is equivalent to reducing the social value of the project. As a result, since e_u^{SB} given by (29.4) does not depend on the social benefit of the project (and any externality that may be incorporated into it), the power of incentives under unbundling remains unchanged as the cost of public funds becomes positive. The benefits of bundling tasks that we will highlight below will be de facto reduced but remain still positive. A second by-product of this discussion is that the issue of whether or not to bundle tasks is independent of whether public funds are costly or not.
10. However, it was argued that too much risk was transferred to the contractor, given its limited control over the demand for the service.
11. However, Pollock and Vickers (2000) question the Andersen report and argue that once outliers are excluded from the calculations the average saving is 6 percent.
12. See the case studies and reports of the National Council for Public Private Partnerships (NCPPP), on http://www.ncppp.org/aboutus/index.shtml.
13. See www.autostrade.it.
14. For simplicity we rule out here the possibility that contract $t_2(\pi_2)$ depends on the first period realization of demand.
15. In Iossa and Martimort (2008), we discuss how our results would change if we allowed for history-dependent contracts in the spirit of Rogerson (1985). We also discuss the possibility of learning about costs of growing demand over time or of investment depreciating over time.
16. See Laffont and Martimort (2002, Chapter 8) and the references therein.
17. A number of political motives have been proposed to explain the interests of the public-sector party itself in reneging PPP contracts. The government may increase its chances to be re-elected by expanding spending or by promoting investment in public works that create jobs and boost economic activity (Guasch, 2004). By reneging, the government may also circumvent the opposition's scrutiny and reap the political benefits resulting from higher present spending, for example, a higher probability of being re-elected (Engel et al., 2006).
18. The focus of this section is on how the lack of commitment can lead to opportunism by governments, which exploit the sunk nature of the firm's investment. Another, equally important, source of weak

commitment refers to contract renegotiation that favors the firm. Gagnepain et al. (2009) estimate a structural principal-agent model of contract renegotiation in the French urban transport sector and show that subsidies paid to operators increase over time during the duration of the contract, suggesting lack of commitment by public authorities.

19.   For a study of delegated contracting in PPPs, see, for example, Bennett and Iossa (2006b). For a discussion on the role of a PPP Unit, see Rachwalski and Ross (2008).

20.   Other kinds of political risks have been considered in the literature. For instance, Che and Qian (1998) use the property rights approach to show that relinquishing firms' ownership to local governments may help in a context with insecure property rights where a national government may expropriate owners.

21.   These transaction costs are also to a large extent independent of the size of a project, which suffices to make PPP unsuitable for low capital value projects. HM Treasury (2006) in the UK currently considers PFI projects for less than £20m as poor value for money.

REFERENCES

Arthur Andersen and Enterprise LSE, 2000, Value for money drivers in the private finance initiative. London: The Treasury Taskforce.

Aschauer, D.A., 1989, Is public expenditure productive? *Journal of Monetary Economics*, **23**, 177–200.

Aubert, C. and J.J. Laffont, 2002, Political renegotiation of regulatory contracts. Mimeo IDEI, Toulouse.

Bajari, P. and S. Tadelis, 2001, Incentives versus transaction costs: a theory of procurement contracts. *RAND Journal of Economics*, **32**, 387–407.

Bennett, J. and E. Iossa, 2006a, Building and managing facilities for public services. *Journal of Public Economics*, **90**, 2143–2160.

Bennett, J. and E. Iossa, 2006b, Delegation of contracting in the private provision of public services. *Review of Industrial Organization*, **29**, 75–92, Special Issue on Public–Private Partnerships.

Besley, T. and M. Ghatak, 2001, Government versus private ownership of public goods. *Quarterly Journal of Economics*, **116**, 1343–1372.

Blanc-Brude, F., H. Goldsmith and T. Välilä, 2006, Ex ante construction costs in the European road sector: a comparison of public–private partnerships and traditional public procurement. European Investment Bank, Economic and Financial Reports 2006/01.

Brench, A., T. Beckers, M. Heinrich and C. von Hirschhausen, 2005, Public-private partnerships in new EU Member Countries of Central and Eastern Europe. European Investment Bank, Vol 10, no. 2.

CBO, Congressional Budget Office, 2007, Trends in public spending on transportation and water infrastructure, 1956 to 2004. Congressional Budget Office, Pub. No. 2880.

Che, J. and Y. Qian, 1998, Insecure property rights and government ownership of firms. *Quarterly Journal of Economics*, **113**, 467–496.

Conference Board of Canada, 2008, Steering a tricky course effective public–private partnerships for the provision of transportation infrastructure and services. The Conference Board of Canada, Canada.

Dewatripont, M. and P. Legros, 2005, PPPs: contract design and risk transfer. *European Investment Bank Papers*, **10**, 120–141.

Ellman, M., 2006, The optimal length of contracts with application to outsourcing. Discussion paper, Universitat Pompeu Fabra.

Engel, E., R. Fisher and A. Galetovic, 2001, Least present value of revenue auctions and highway franchising. *Journal of Political Economy*, **105**, 993–1020.

Engel, E., R. Fisher and A. Galetovic, 2006, Renegotiation without holdup: anticipating spending in infrastructure concessions. Cowles Foundation Discussion Paper 1567.

Estache, A., J.L. Guash, A. Imi and L. Trujillo, 2009, Multidimensionality and renegotiation: evidence from transport-sector public–private-partnership transactions in Latin America. *Review of Industrial Organization*, **35**, 41–71.

European Commission (EC), 2001, European transport policy for 2010: time to decide. White Paper. Brussels, European Commission COM (2001/370).

European Commission (EC), 2004, *Resource Book on PPP Case Studies*. Brussels: Directorate General Regional Policy.

Francesconi, M. and A. Muthoo, 2006, Control rights in complex partnerships. Mimeo.

Gagnepain, P., M. Ivaldi and D. Martimort, 2009, The cost of contract renegotiation: evidence from the local public sector. Discussion papers, Toulouse School of Economics.

Grout, P., 1997, The economics of the private finance initiative. *Oxford Review of Economic Policy*, **13**, 53–66.

Guasch, J.L., 2004, Granting and renegotiating infrastructure concessions: doing it right. WBI Development Studies, World Bank.

Guasch, J.L. and P. Spiller, 1999, *Managing the Regulatory Process: Design, Concepts, Issues and the Latin America and Caribbean Story*. Washington DC: World Bank.

Guasch, J.L., J.J. Laffont and S. Straub, 2007, Concessions of infrastructure in Latin America: government-led renegotiations. *Journal of Applied Econometrics*, **22** (7), 1267–1294.

Hammami, M., J.F. Ruhashyankiko and E.B. Yehoue, 2006, Determinants of public–private partnerships in infrastructure. Working Paper No 06/99, International Monetary Fund.

Hart, O., 2003, Incomplete contracts and public ownership: remarks and an application to public–private partnerships. *Economic Journal*, **119**, 69–76.

Hart, O., A. Shleifer and R. Vishny, 1997, The proper scope of government: theory and an application to prisons. *Quarterly Journal of Economics*, **112**, 1119–1158.

HM Treasury, 2006, *Strenghtening Long-Term Partnerships*. London: HM Treasury.

Holmström, B. and P. Milgrom, 1991, Multi-task principal-agent analyses: incentive contracts, asset ownership and job design. *Journal of Law, Economics and Organization*, Special Issue, 24–52.

Institute for Public Policy Research (IPPR), 2001, *Building Better Partnerships*. London: Institute for Public Policy Research.

Iossa, E. and D. Martimort, 2008, The simple micro-economics of public private partnerships. Mimeo, Toulouse School of Economics.

Kappeler, A. and M. Nemoz, 2010, Public private partnerships in Europe: before and during the recent financial crisis. Economic and Financial report 2010/04, European Investment Bank.

Laffont, J.J. and D. Martimort, 2002, *The Theory of Incentives: The Principal-Agent Model*. Princeton, NJ: Princeton University Press.

Laffont, J.J. and J. Tirole, 1993, *A Theory of Incentives in Procurement and Regulation*. Cambridge, MA: MIT Press.

Leruth, L., 2009, Public–private cooperation in infrastructure development: a principal-agent story of contingent liabilities, fiscal risks, and other (un)pleasant surprises. *Networks and Spatial Economics*, Special Issue.

Lewis, T. and D. Sappington, 1995, Optimal capital structure in agency relationships. *RAND Journal of Economics*, **26**, 343–361.

Martimort, D. and J. Pouyet, 2008, Build it not: normative and positive theories of public–private partnerships. *International Journal of Industrial Organization*, Special Issue on PPPs, **26**, 393–411.

Martimort, D. and W. Sand-Zantman, 2007, Signalling and the design of delegated management contracts for public utilities. *Rand Journal of Economics*, **37**, 763–782.

Megginson, W. and J. Netter, 2001, From state to market: a survey of empirical studies on privatization. *Journal of Economic Literature*, **39**, 321–389.

Messina, G., 2008, Time is money: measuring transport infrastructures from the new economic geography perspective. Research Department, Bank of Italy.

National Audit Office (NAO), 2007, *Improving the PFI Tendering Process*. London: National Audit Office, HC149.

Pollock, A. and N. Vickers, 2000, Private pie in the sky. *Public Finance*, **14–20**, 22–23.

Rachwalski, M.D. and T.W. Ross, 2008, Running a government's P3 program: centralized agency or line departments? Mimeo, University of British Columbia.

Rogerson, W., 1985, Repeated Moral Hazard. *Econometrica*, **53**, 69–76.

Rosenau, P.V., ed., 2000, *Public-Private Policy Partnerships*. Cambridge, MA: MIT Press.

Sappington, D. and J. Stiglitz, 1987, Privatization, Information and Incentives, *Journal of Policy Analysis and Management*, **6**, 567–582.

Yescombe, E., 2007, *Public Private Partnerships: Principles of Policy and Finance*, Elsevier.

30 Public–private partnerships in transport
Antonio Estache, Ellis Juan and Lourdes Trujillo

INTRODUCTION

The twenty-first century has started with significant ideological changes involving an increasing popular rejection of a strong role for the private sector in the management and financing of public services. This change is most obvious in developing countries but is not a minor phenomenon elsewhere, most obviously in Continental Europe and to some extent in the UK. Yet despite these changes, despite the high profile contract renegotiations in Latin America and Africa and despite the recurring debate on the matter within the EU, public–private partnerships (PPP) continue to be on the agenda of many politicians in both developed and developing countries.[1]

For many governments, the main motivation is the need to reduce the fiscal costs of the transport sector. The concern to cut unit costs is often also present, but less obviously so. It has usually been more present in Anglo-Saxon countries but increasingly so in other countries as well as indicated by the EU experience. The conviction that private operators are likely to be able to deliver services more efficiently is indeed often also a key driver of the continued effort to get into PPPs.

Whatever the driving forces behind PPPs, they are expected to deliver infrastructure or services at reasonable cost and with attention to social aspects. They also increasingly involve the government making explicit comparisons with public funded and managed alternatives. Even when public sector borrowing costs will be lower, other factors are considered. These include the opportunity cost of public funds and foreign exchange, the efficiency and expertise the private sector might bring to the project and the availability of international liquidity to support specific project types which lend themselves well to some type of securitization.

To some extent, this continued enthusiasm may be counterintuitive in view of recurring international financial and liquidity crises over the last 10–20 years. These crises should have reduced the interest in project finance to finance new toll roads, new airports, new ports and new railways in emerging markets. Although after the financial crises in East Asia, Russia, Mexico, Brazil and Argentina during the 1990s, project financing systematically slowed down, it has also systematically recovered. This is because new sources of money continued to appear until the crisis that hit the financial markets at the end of the first decade of the twenty-first century. From pension assets to emerging bond markets to new types of bank debt, liquidity was not lacking. In 2006, just a year before the crisis hit, private capital flows to emerging markets reached a peak of US\$ 623 billion.[2] Even if credit to some actors may have been tighter, the global financial markets continued to be liquid and investors were still looking for predictable sources of revenue which most transport infrastructures are potentially capable of providing. Spreads over the returns from safe bonds demanded to finance specific infrastructure projects increased to hedge against increased credit risk after each crisis, including the last one, and as a result increased de-leveraging, but the market has not disappeared and is unlikely to do so as the recent evidence reviewed below shows. The market has been slowed maybe, but is hanging in there and continues to attract the interest of governments, investors and infrastructure operators.

This does not mean that changes will not take place. Although the long term trend has favored the continued growth of PPPs, and is likely to continue doing so, some things changed in the way the public sector associates with the private sector. Every crisis teaches the dealmakers something new about how to improve risk management. Every crisis also reveals an impressive creativity by these dealmakers who learn from the mistakes of the past. In the process, the nature of the deals evolves, as do their size and the level and types of leveraging. New types of financial instruments and contractual arrangements to ease PPP in transport continue to be developed.

Some things do not change, however. For instance, transport infrastructure where the end-user is represented by corporate or commercial clients continues to tend to be less risky given their greater capacity to pay tariffs and charges (that is, airports, ports, cargo railways and so forth). Conversely, transport infrastructure where the end-user is represented by consumers continues to tend to have more affordability issues and therefore higher risks (that is, urban transport, toll roads, and so forth). But some of the predictable factors are more problematic. First, forecasts of revenues, traffic and economic activity continue to be overoptimistic, so that 'best case' scenarios often continue to be 'sold' as 'base case' scenarios, helping to justify the investment decisions.[3] Second, the lack of attention to project evaluation continues to support a willingness to use ever-larger amounts of debt in project capital structures. Long-term projects continue to be undertaken which use short-term debt, buoyed by confidence that when the debt matured, it will simply be 'rolled over' on equivalent (or better) terms. Floating-rate debts are still common, further increasing interest rate risk. Projects that generated local currency revenues continue to be financed in international markets, even if lenders and borrowers know that exchange rates in emerging markets are increasingly unpredictable. Third, governments continue to get into deals with risk allocations they do not recognize simply because they ignore the potential consequences of renegotiation. This may explain why some of the highest renegotiation rates are observed in the transport sector (see Guasch, 2004).

This chapter summarizes the evidence on the evolution of transport PPPs and in the process provides a primer on the associated policy issues. To do so, the next section offers a brief overview of the evolution of the role of the private sector in transport infrastructure. The following one discusses the central role of project finance in the implementation of PPP policies. Then a section covers the main debate on risk allocation in the design of PPPs. Another addresses the main residual roles for the public sector in transport, with an emphasis on the regulatory debates surrounding the adoption of PPPs. The last section concludes.

THE RISE OF PRIVATE PARTICIPATION IN TRANSPORT

The rise of PPPs in transport has its roots in broader worldwide privatization initiatives during the 1990s. While the catalyst may have been the dramatic changes introduced by the Thatcher administration in the UK, the bulk of the transactions actually took place

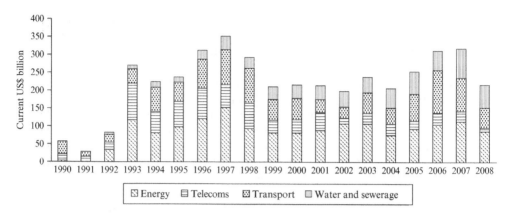

Figure 30.1   Investment commitments in infrastructure projects with private participation in developing countries by sectors, 1990–2008

in developing countries. Figure 30.1 provides a snapshot of the dramatic increase in the involvement of the private sector in the development and funding of public facilities and services across infrastructure activities during from 1990 to 2008, when the crisis hurt all investments across sectors. It shows that transport benefited from a relatively small share of the private commitments to the sector (about 15 percent of the US$ 1600 billion or so committed over that period to all infrastructure sectors). It is also a relatively small share of the investment needs of the sector since the commitments made for this 15-year period represent very roughly the investment needed in 1 year in transport in the developing world.

While the amounts do not represent a huge share of the investment needs of the sector, they are very significant. On average, these deals represent about US$ 10 billion annually in the developing world alone and about twice as much when developed countries are considered. This is around 55 projects a year across transport sub-sectors in developing countries alone. There is no strictly comparable data for developed countries but most estimates turn around 20 large projects a year on average over the last 20 years, with a growing number of projects in the last 5 years or so before the 2008 crisis.

The distribution of projects across sectors and regions is also of interest. About two-thirds of the projects are in roads, about a fifth in rail, around 12 percent in airports and less than 7 percent in ports. The average project size also varies significantly across sectors ranging from about US$ 100 million in ports to about US$ 300 million in rail. The average project in roads and airports is roughly around US$ 180 million.

At the regional level, Europe captures about a third of the projects, Asia/Oceania and North America capture about a quarter each and Latin America about a fifth. Africa and the Middle East do not seem to attract many transport PPPs. Within developing countries, about half of the projects during the last 15 years or so were signed in Latin America and about a quarter in East Asia. The largest projects tend to be in East Asia with an average project size of about US$ 250 million, followed by Latin America with projects of about US$ 190 million on average. In the other regions the average projects are less than US$ 80 million.

There are many forms of private participation in transport, including:

- *Greenfield projects such as Build, Operate, Transfer (BOT) projects,* where the private sector has the primary responsibility for financing, developing and operating the facility for a fixed period of time, which should be sufficient to both repay debt and provide the required return on investment. At the end of the concession, assets are transferred to the government under terms agreed to in the contract. Perhaps the most familiar form of participation in transport infrastructure, this has been employed in many different variations.[4] There are alternative versions of these contracts such as *Build, Own and Operate (BOO)*, where the private sector obtains the ownership and control of the facilities, with no transfer to the public sector.
- *Concessions,* where the private sector receives the mandate to operate and expand an existing network and in the process is asked to take on most of the commercial risks associated with the business. Often these contracts are done as joint ventures, in which the public and private sectors share responsibility for financing and operation of public facilities; often also, these contracts include a greenfield project subcontract which covers the additional investment obligations to be delivered under the concession contract.
- *The contracting out of services,* where the private sector is contracted to provide services on behalf of the government for compensation, either in terms of a share of revenue, profit, or payments from the government. In general, contracting out does not involve financing risk, although it may involve revenue risk.

Concession contracts, followed by greenfield projects tended to dominate the large scale PPPs over the 20 years or so prior to the crisis. They represented over 70 percent of all contracts signed in developing countries in the sector. Divestitures are much less common than in energy or in telecoms for instance but they do take place in all sectors; in particular airports – a sector for which management contracts are also relatively more common than in the other transport subsectors. The 2007–08 crisis has introduced a lot of uncertainty of the direction of the market across infrastructure and transport is no exception. According the World Bank Private Participation in Infrastructure most recent data updates, activity in transport declined in 2008. There was a pronounced decline in the number of projects – a 40 percent decline from the level in 2007 and a 53 percent drop from that in 2006. An interesting fact is the increased in average size of transport projects since the crisis. The average project size grew from US$ 150 million in 2004 to US$ 410 million in 2008, while the median rose from US$ 57 million to US$ 230 million.

THE CENTRAL ROLE OF PROJECT FINANCE IN TRANSPORT PPPS

While it is quite common to grant private operators the responsibility for the delivery of services in specific cities and regions, or at the country level, the investment components of these responsibilities are often subject to specific contractual forms. These specific forms of the contracts supporting the investments are driven by the ability to pull together financing schemes around the specific investment project. Project finance is indeed typically used in those sectors that require large capital expenditures, that have long-lived assets, and that require long periods to amortize investment costs and generate required rates of return for both creditors and equity holders.

Project finance is generally used to describe financings in which the lenders look to the cash flows of an investment project for repayment, without recourse to either equity sponsors or the public sector to make up any shortfall. The sponsor usually tries to structure the project so that the gross assets and liabilities of the project are kept off the sponsor's balance sheet.[5]

In the end, the deals are financed from a wide range of very different potential sources, each with different positions, stakes, and incentives that influence the project outcomes. Some of these sources may only be available at different stages in the life cycle of the project. These sources include equity, mezzanine finance, commercial lending, bond finance, project leasing, development finance institutions, export credits, finance or guarantees provided by bilateral export credit agencies and derivative products, including securitization.[6]

This is roughly how a deal is put together in practice. In general, the private operator is granted a concession by the government to design, build and/or operate transport services or infrastructure for a specified period. This concessionaire typically is responsible for raising the finances required to carry out the project. At the end of the concession period, the facilities and their operation may be transferred to the host government, depending on the nature of the contract. The concessionaire will typically form a Special Purpose Vehicle (SPV), in which a project or a set of projects are treated as a separate entity from the sponsors. Funds are then borrowed solely based on the project's or project package's cash flows and the equity in the SPV itself.[7] This independence allows the project package to be separated from the equity investors' balance sheet; therefore it is frequently referred to as 'off-balance sheet financing'.[8]

The financing structure has a number of recurring characteristics. For instance, bank debt is the primary debt funding source, and sponsor equity is committed – and sometimes paid up-front – prior to the provision of any debt finance. In general, the cash flows of the project's package are the principal basis for returns for both debt and equity investors, and the project's assets are the principal collateral for any borrowings. It is important to note that payments to equity holders are subordinate to operating costs and debt service obligations. Once the project is operational, lenders have no or very limited recourse to the credit of the project's owners (either sponsor equity or government in the case of BOT projects). Overall, the transaction heavily relies on contractual commitments between the project participants, which is why the regulatory and supervision capacity of governments is so crucial to the success of these transactions.

The difficulties encountered in emerging markets in the 1990s and the well-publicized problems experienced by some transport infrastructure projects have forced both the private and public sectors to expand the idea of project financing. While the ultimate goal may be to arrange project borrowings which will provide a minimal expected rate of return to sponsor equity, and at the same time be quite undemanding for the sponsor or the government, such a goal has proven almost impossible to accomplish, except in a few extraordinary situations.

The advantages of project finance vary across participants in the transactions.

Promoters of project finance (sponsors and investment bankers) prefer project finance because it has allowed them to undertake projects without exhausting their ability to borrow for traditional projects, and without increasing debt ratios (or at least those that are calculated based on reported financial statements). Project finance structures can be used by companies to limit their financial risk to a project to the amount of their equity investment.[9] In addition, if the project itself has particularly strong and secure cash flows, project finance may allow more debt to be employed in the financing mix, since creditors do not have to worry about project cash flows being siphoned off for other corporate uses.

Project finance may provide stronger incentives for careful project evaluation and risk assessment. Since the project's cash flows are keys to obtaining financing, such projects should undergo careful technical and economic review and sensitivity analysis. This may lead to clarification of the nature and magnitude of project risks and what causes them. Having a detailed, objective assessment of project risks and potential may not only enable risks to be allocated to the appropriate parties, but in some cases, the project analysis itself may reveal ways to change the project to reduce the overall level of risks or to improve their allocation. For example, demand analysis of a toll road may show opportunities to delay expansion until certain traffic levels trigger new investments in capacity.

But project finance also has some disadvantages. It is more complex than traditional corporate or public financing, typically involving many more parties and resulting in significantly higher transaction costs. The complexity of project finance deals also makes them very expensive. The due diligence process conducted by lenders, legal counsel and other technical experts results in higher development costs, with higher fees and interest margins than what is typically charged. It is not unusual for a project finance transaction to cost twice as much as straight debt or equity finance. Total costs may reach 7 to 10 percent of total project value. When acting as a financial advisor to a project, investment banks will typically charge high monthly fees, plus all expenses. They also typically receive a success fee if the project reaches financial closure, which can range from 0.0025 to 1.0 percent of total project value.

Negotiations on various aspects of the project are usually protracted and may be quite contentious. This is especially true for transport projects, which typically are politically sensitive, have high visibility and retain strong public interest and participation. Getting parties with diverse interests to agree on the nature and magnitude of risks is very hard, let alone getting them to agree on who should bear these risks. The documentation associated with project financing is almost always complex and lengthy.

Even after the financing is closed, the project will usually be subject to closer monitoring by all parties. Because lenders primarily rely on revenue flows to repay their loans, the degree of lender supervision of the management and operation of the project will most likely be greater than for an ordinary corporate loan. Likewise, public officials need an ongoing program to monitor contract compliance and potential exposure to any guarantees that have been provided, as well as regulatory oversight when deemed necessary. Project financing makes this monitoring particularly complex. In the initial stages, sponsors are likely to fund their equity contribution either internally or from on-balance sheet borrowings. Governments need to be careful to monitor the sources of this initial investment. In some cases, while the project equity appeared sound, the additional borrowing by the sponsor's parent company so weakened the overall company that bankruptcy of the parent impaired the ability to undertake the specific project obligations. In sum, monitoring risk is not only an issue at the beginning of a PPP, it is an issue throughout the duration of the contract.

RISK AT THE CENTER OF TRANSPORT PPPS

The identification and management of risks is at the core of the design of any PPP. This is particularly obvious in the context of the project finance dimensions of the PPP because of the non-recourse or limited recourse nature of project debt and the limited contractual undertakings of the project owner. Since each project faces a different set of risks, it is always best to try to identify them at the outset and allocate them to the appropriate parties. This is why one of the first tasks that public officials should address is to understand the distribution of risks to which each party is committed. In many renegotiations or regulatory disputes, the ultimate responsibility and resolution will be based on the assignments spelled out in the contract.

The experience of the last 10–15 years suggests that risks are actually very real! Various studies have shown the extent to which things often do not happen the way they were planned. According to Guasch (2004), about 75 percent of the transport contracts in Latin America were renegotiated. Flyvbjerg and his various co-authors (2003, 2005) have managed to document that the problem is just as important in developed economies. They show that risks should be a concern at all stages of the process.

For new projects, they start at the construction phase where the major risks are delays in completion and the commencement of project cash flows; cost overruns with an increase in the capital needed to complete construction; and the insolvency or lack of experience of contractors or key suppliers. Construction costs may exceed estimates for many reasons, including inaccurate engineering and design, escalation in material and labor costs, delays in project start-up or even changes in the design specification. Cost overruns typically are handled through a fixed-price and fixed-term contract, with incentives for completion and for meeting pre-specified investment goals. Other alternatives include provision for additional equity infusions by the sponsor or standby agreements for additional debt financing. It is always sensible for developers to establish an escrow or contingency fund to cover such overruns. Delays in project completion can result in an increase in total costs through higher capitalized interest charges. It also may affect the scheduled flow of project revenues necessary for debt service costs and operating and maintenance expenses.

In developing countries, in addition, there is also the risk of unavailability of equipment or materials for construction or operation. This is especially true with respect to rolling stock, or for specialized equipment such as gantry cranes or loading bridges used in ports or airports. Transit bottlenecks, tariffs, foreign currency fluctuations and other factors can cause a significant increase in costs. Moreover, there are also the risks that the main contractors and key subcontractors lack the experience, reputation (needed to engage in an effective fine tuning of the contract – that is, in its interactions with subcontractors), financial, technical or human resources to be capable of completing the project in timely fashion on budget. This risk is best addressed through tough pre-qualification of bidders (if sponsors are also contractors); through certification and monitoring if unrelated parties are used; and by ongoing financial oversight of the contracting companies themselves, to make sure that poor results from other projects or from weak balance sheets do not spill over into the specific project of interest.

Transport projects can also have a substantial environmental impact. Such projects frequently attract strong opposition from community and environmental groups over issues of pollution, congestion, neglect of public transport and visual impact. Similarly, land acquisition can be a protracted process with the potential for extensive legal delays, particularly in developing countries.[10] In general, the public sector often ends up taking on the responsibility for most of these risks since often it is easier for the public sector to take the responsibility for acquiring the rights-of-way, paying for them and contributing them to the project. Project sponsors often try to ensure that the government bears the risk of providing all necessary land within a given time frame or be liable for damages. Furthermore, the cost of land acquisition can become a major factor where land values have risen rapidly or are subject to speculative activity over which the project developer has no control. In these cases, agreement on some form of cost ceiling may be necessary in the concession contract. In some cases, a special government body may be charged with implementing the land acquisition process. Generally, the host government should ensure that required licenses and permits be obtainable without unreasonable delay or expense.

Risks are also very present at the operating phase. The major risks for transport projects in these stages relate to technology; traffic/revenue risk; regulatory and legal changes; interest rate and foreign exchange risks; *force majeure* risk; and political risk. PPP designers cannot ignore new technologies since they can either significantly improve the profitability of a project or adversely affect any project that uses obsolete technology. For example, the use of automatic toll collection technology reduces collection costs and the scope for graft. Another example is technological improvements in customs processing, so that border crossings on major arterial toll roads can be traversed more quickly, saving time for users and making the road more valuable.

Unlike project financing in other sectors, take-or-pay or fixed-price contracts are typically not available in transport, so that demand risk is a major issue in virtually all projects. Even when there is a reasonable level of confidence in forecasts, demand can be dramatically affected by competition from other modes or facilities, changing usage patterns, and macroeconomic conditions. These interrelated issues, over which the project sponsor often has little or no control, are very difficult to predict and represent a major risk to financing. In particular, forecasting during the early years can be quite subjective. To the extent that these risks are driven by economic conditions, there is a potential role for the government to play in risk-sharing, either through traffic or revenue guarantees or other forms of support. (These are discussed in more detail below.)

But demand uncertainty must be viewed realistically. Over-optimism in traffic projections is common for privatization teams focusing on convincing private operators of the value of their business and for potential operators who want to get the deal, convinced that they can renegotiate almost anything once they have taken over the business.[11] To see this, take the case of toll roads. Traffic volumes are very sensitive to income and economic growth and the failure to recognize this may be one of the main reasons why so many toll road projects have failed or ended in bitter renegotiations. Motorization and vehicle-kilometers traveled tend to increase faster than income levels. This high income elasticity, especially for leisure trips, makes toll roads especially sensitive to macro-economic conditions. For roads that serve export activities, exchange rate changes can dramatically affect trade, leading to major changes in demand patterns.

Many toll road projects in the last decade have dramatically overestimated traffic levels for a wide range of reasons. In some of the Mexican road concessions, traffic volumes were only one-fifth forecast levels.[12] In Hungary, the M1 motorway attracted only 50 percent of expected volume in its first year of operation. The Dulles Greenway, outside of Washington, initially only attracted one-third of its expected daily volume. Even after a toll reduction of 40 percent, the Greenway still was only able to achieve two-thirds of its originally forecast volume. Note that some of these demand risks can be hedged against through contracts with flexible duration as proposed by Engel et al. (2001).

Similar issues have been raised in the context of traffic forecasts for railways. In the railways context, it has not been uncommon for forecasters to underestimate the risks associated with unfair competition by the trucking industry as was the case in Argentina or Brazil during the 1990s reform. Some of the Argentinean concessions ended up with negative cash flows, partially a consequence of the loss of traffic to truckers willing to price below cost to recover some of the traffic lost as a result of initial improvements in rail traffic credited to the restructuring of the sector.

Financial risk is the risk that cash flows might be insufficient to cover debt service and then to pay an adequate return on sponsor equity. Financing constraints, especially the lack of long-term debt capital, are a significant hindrance to toll road development. Since the advent of financial crises in emerging markets, few projects are able to generate returns on investment sufficient to attract private capital. This suggests that until macro-economic risk premiums decline and traffic growth is more established, only a limited set of projects will be undertaken without substantial government support. The financial crises will force many programs to slow down and force debt restructuring of many of the existing concessions. There is a need to promote more secure financing structures to reduce the risk of potential bailouts.

In theory, financial risk is best borne by the private sector, but in transport projects there is likely to be substantial government risk sharing either through revenue or debt guarantees, or participation by state or multilateral development institutions. There also may be cash grants or other financial contributions that serve to improve the project rate of return on private finance. Passenger transport tariffs tend to be very politically sensitive and governments are often more willing to grant subsidies to finance costs than to aim at full cost recovery as they more often do with freight transport.[13]

The recurring financial crises of the last 15 years have shown that currency risks need to be taken seriously. The main currency risk is driven by the impact on the value of the business of fluctuations in the exchange rate. In addition, the toll concession can be subject to a convertibility risk which refers to the possibility that the operator may not be allowed to exchange local for foreign currency. These are major issues for some projects, where revenues are commonly in local currency and adjustments for inflation and exchange rates may lag or encounter political opposition. Projects can reduce this risk by tapping domestic capital markets where possible. Most projects attempt to mitigate exchange risk by provisions for indexing to inflation, although in practice the magnitude of exchange volatility has made such requirements difficult to enforce.

There is also increasing evidence that PPP designers need to anticipate more carefully *force majeure* issues. This refers to risks beyond the control of either the public or private partner, such as floods or earthquakes, which impair the project's ability to earn revenues. While some private insurance is becoming available for catastrophic risks, the public sector generally is faced with the need to restructure the project should such disasters occur. This may take the form of extending the concession term or providing additional financial support. The rule is that remedies in the event of *force majeure* risks should be stated in the contracts; for example cash compensation or an extension of the concession term equal to the length of the disturbance.

In addition to these business-related risks, there are risks associated with the interactions with the public sector. The main risks in this category are regulatory, legal and political risks. Regulatory risk stems from the weak implementation of regulatory commitments built into concession contracts but also in laws or other legal instruments relevant to the value of the transaction. The question asked is whether the regulator will exercise its authority and responsibilities over prices, public obligations, competition rules and similar rules that are specified in the contracts and that influence the value of the business. The solution is to try to make sure that regulators have rules to follow and that they are independent enough to be able to enforce them.

But even if regulatory rules are clear enough, they are only as effective as the regulators can be. The best designed regulatory environment is useless if the regulator is not independent or fair. This risk is more common than it appears and pressures on regulators are a major source of concern which investors reflect in their required rate of return. In 1999, a major factor in the restructuring of Mexico's toll road program was the pressure on regulators to cut tolls. In Thailand, a similar concern resulted in decision by the government to cut by 50 percent a toll level it had committed to in a BOT contract. Similar examples could be provided for a large number of countries in more recent years. The outcome is generally that the government ended up taking over the facility.

The range of problems that can arise is quite wide. For instance, non-compete clauses have been at the center of well publicized tensions in the sector. One case is the SR-91 High Occupancy Toll lanes facility in Orange County, CA, where a non-competition clause prevented construction of new capacity in the congested travel corridor and led to a public takeover in 2003. Another is the Northern Boulevard Périphérique toll road in Lyon.[14] The contract with the private operator stipulated that capacity on a free parallel alternative be reduced in order to assure sufficient traffic on the toll road. But in the face of strong public opposition capacity of the alternative was restored, the toll was reduced and the concession was cancelled (see Reux and Souche, 2004).

PPPs typically cover periods of ten years or more. The relevant legal and regulatory environment is likely to change substantially over that period. The rules dealing with the financial consequences of these changes between government, users and operators are critical and yet often forgotten. The rules must cover the possibility of adaptation of the contract terms during the tenure of the project financing.

Political risk concerns government actions that affect the ability to generate earnings. These could include actions terminating the concession; imposition of taxes or regulations that severely reduce the value to investors; restrictions on the ability to collect or raise tariffs as specified in the concession agreement; and precluding contract disputes to be resolved in reasonable ways. Governments generally agree to compensate investors for political risks, although in practice justifications for government actions may be cited to delay or prevent such payments. Thus, private investors generally assume the risks associated with dispute resolution and the ability to obtain compensation should the government violate the concession agreement. The issue of meeting financial obligations while disputes are resolved may be achieved through a requirement of debt service reserves, escrow or standby financing.[15]

The credibility of the government to uphold contractual obligations and the willingness and ability to provide compensation for political risks are key issues for project finance. Issue of delays or denials of tariff increases have made many prospective parties wary of entering into new projects. This is especially true for foreign capital, which is perceived as especially vulnerable to political risks. Some of the more risky emerging markets may require support from multilateral or bilateral financial institutions to reduce this risk exposure. In addition, political risk insurance may also help manage issues of inconvertibility, transfer and confiscation.

The project finance component of PPPs involves many participants, each with important roles to play. They include the government, the constructors, the operators/ concessionaires, the lending commercial banks and the very heterogeneous groups of other lenders which include national and regional development banks, bilateral agencies, export credit agencies, and development finance institutions.

The allocation of risks among all these actors is thus clearly an essential dimension of the design of PPPs. One of the long-standing tenets of project finance has been that the project participant who controls or is best able to manage the risks should bear them. While true in principle, reality often fails to live up to the goal. Risk allocation is complex and difficult, and for all practical purposes it is a negotiated process. For example, governments are responsible for changes in the law, yet the risk and consequences of such changes are often shifted to the private sector. Or, the central bank may have the greatest responsibility for inflation and interest rate outcomes, yet in reality it is often the project developers, creditors, and equity providers who end up bearing the interest rate risk. There are numerous other risks that do not necessarily end up being borne by the party best able to manage them. More often, it is the best and most experienced negotiator that ends up bearing the least amount of risk.

Also, the level and type of risk encountered may change over time. The 1998 Asian crisis increased perceived risk levels enough to increase the required rate of return to levels unachievable for most projects. On the other hand, governments may fall prey to a 'fear–greed cycle', in which governments become afraid of program failure and thus offer increasingly better terms. Alternatively, prospective concessionaires who worry that they will get left out bid unrealistically. Subsequently, the element of greed takes over in which governments may fail to live up to commitments and the private sector seeks ways to privatize gains and socialize the project's risks.

Successful PPPs have been characterized by a broad level of risk-sharing between the public and private sectors. Generally, the private sector is better at managing commercial risks and responsibilities such as those associated with construction, operation, and financing. In contrast, transport projects most likely depend on public participation in areas such as acquisition of right-of-way, political risk and, in some cases, traffic and revenue risk. PPPs have worked best when experienced, well-capitalized firms have enough discretion over design and confidence in pricing policy to accept construction and some degree of traffic risk, while the government assumes the risks that it controls and gives consideration to financial support or guarantees if traffic levels in the early years are insufficient.

Ultimately, the market seems to be adjusting in the kind of contracts it is writing. Athias and Saussier (2007) highlight the fact that the contracting parties try to sign not only complete rigid contracts in order to avoid renegotiations but also flexible contracts in order to adapt contractual framework to unanticipated contingencies and to create incentives for cooperative behavior. In the case of toll roads, this gives rise to multiple toll adjustment provisions and to a tradeoff between rigid and flexible contracts at the design stage. In an econometric assessment of 71 contracts, they find that the standard view that a rigid contract is to be preferred as soon as specific assets are high, may be true only if other conditions concerning poor adaptation of costs, renegotiation costs and the probability of seeing the contract enforced are met.

THE ROLE OF THE PUBLIC SECTOR IN PPPS

Besides the contractual partnership with the private operator, there are two main ways in which the government continues to be involved in the activities covered by the PPP. The first is the provision of *ex-ante* guarantees and ex-post guarantees which consist of financial contributions to offset the consequences of undesirable unexpected events which have resulted in a renegotiation of the contract. The second is the regulation of the sector, which generally includes the monitoring of commitments made by all parties through the contract.

Guarantees

Governments may have to provide guarantees for a wide range of reasons as suggested in the recent book by Irwin (2007). When unexpected events arise and a contract undergoes renegotiation, governments need to come up with a mix of government actions that ensures that an acceptable financial return can be generated. This means that the rate of return of the PPP has to cover its cost of capital.[16] These actions may include some redesign of the financing schemes to include guarantees but also of the project design, including its duration as suggested by Engel et al. (2001).

A variety of mechanisms can be used to support private financing *ex ante* by facilitating the closure of the financing aspects of the PPP. These range from revenue enhancements to equity guarantees. Equity guarantees give the private operator the option to be bought out by the government at a price that guarantees a minimum return on equity. Although the liability is contingent, the government in effect assumes project risk and corresponding private sector incentives to contain costs and promote demand by maintaining high quality are reduced. A debt guarantee is an equivalent instrument to protect the lenders. It ensures that the government will pay any shortfall related to principal and interest payments. The government may also guarantee any refinancing that is scheduled. It creates significant government exposure and reduces private sector incentives, although it may decrease the cost or increase the amount of debt available to the project. Governments can also provide subordinated loans which can fill a gap in the financing structure between senior debt and equity. From the government's perspective, they also have the attractive feature that they can be repaid with a return if the PPP is successful. There are also a number of interventions which reduce the risks associated with demand. A minimum traffic or revenue guarantee, in which the government compensates the concessionaire if traffic or revenue falls below a minimum threshold, is a relatively common form of support for toll roads and more rarely so in railways, airport or ports.[17] This guarantee can often help facilitate the access of the operator to the financial market.[18] The main alternative to this guarantee to protect against demand risk is to allow the contract to have a variable duration. The contract ends when the cumulative demand has reached the level stipulated in the bidding documents. *Ex post*, this can also be achieved through contract extensions. These types of financial support involve limited public sector risk, but also do little to support or enhance private financing. First, a government can extend the concession term if revenues fall below a certain amount. Second, a government can restrict competition or allow the development of ancillary services by the concessionaire.

For developing countries, the main risk may be the exchange rate risk. With an exchange rate guarantee, the government agrees to compensate the concessionaire for increases in financing costs due to exchange rate effects on foreign financing. Exchange rate guarantees expose the government to significant risk, as well as increasing the incentive to utilize foreign capital. This can be an important challenge of highly leveraged transactions in foreign currency.

In addition to these instruments, which are typically discussed and assessed and negotiated before the contracts are signed, there is a series of instruments government often use as part of the renegotiation of contracts. These include grants or subsidies which ideally should be identified *ex ante* but which are more common as part of contract restructuring, at least in the transport sector. In Argentina, this subsidy took the form of a forgiveness of accumulated payments due to the government for the right to operate the concession. In general, these grants or subsidies have no provision for repayment. A common approach to commit to subsidies *ex ante* in some OECD countries is the provision of subsidies through shadow tolls. Under a shadow toll, the government contributes a specific payment per vehicle to the concessionaire. Because they are paid over time, they may be less of a burden on the public budget. The drawback of shadow tolls, though, is that they may not provide investors with much protection from revenue risks. In addition, the payment of shadow tolls over time creates a credit risk for concessionaires. Another potential disadvantage is that users do not pay tolls and therefore are not faced with any congestion, road damage, emissions or other externalities they impose. These inefficiencies can be reduced in a number of ways, such as a declining payment schedule as volumes increase or a maximum traffic level beyond which shadow tolls are not paid. Output-based aid (OBA) is another example of subsidy driven PPP. In this case, it is a mechanism for providing explicit performance-based subsidies to support the delivery of basic services where policy concerns – such as limited affordability for some consumers, a desire to capture positive externalities or the infeasibility of imposing direct user fees – justify public funding to complement or replace user fees.

Institutional Roles of Government in PPPs

While these financing dimensions of the additional role of government in PPPs are quite essential, they are relatively simple in relation to regulation and monitoring responsibilities, the second main role of the public sector in PPPs. Normally it is the government that perceives the need for an infrastructure project and determines whether it is suitable for PPPs. In some countries, special units are prepared to package and prepare the PPPs on behalf of the government (Dutz et al., 2006). The specifics, of course, will depend partly on the political and economic situation facing the country, as well as the characteristics of the project itself. It might be necessary to enact specific legislation, or even to change the constitution, to enable the financing to proceed. (Many national constitutions prohibit private ownership or control of essential public facilities.) In addition, since PPPs are critically dependent on contractual obligations between many parties to the deal, it might be necessary to enact legislation specific to the project or sector. It also may require the clarification of laws relating to the recognition and enforcement of contractual obligations and security rights, or the laws relating to nationalization, expropriation and arbitration. The regulatory regime within which the project is to function should also be clearly defined.

Maybe the most underestimated institutional dimension around PPP transactions is the setup of the institutional capacity to monitor the contract. The standard suggestion is to create an independent regulator who will monitor the commitments made by all parties to the PPP and is accountable to all these parties, including the users, for the effectiveness with which it delivers this regulatory function. This academic recommendation has not been overwhelmingly endorsed in the transport sector. While independent regulatory institutions are quite a common match for PPP arrangements in utilities services such as electricity, telecommunications or water services, they are not as common for the transport sector. Indeed, few countries have created a transport regulator that monitors all PPPs across subsectors. Most are in Latin America and even then, in most cases, land transport and waterborne transport are generally handled by different agencies.

In most cases, the PPPs are regulated by a public sector agency specialized in a specific sector. Road Agencies supervise both public and private roads and often have a responsibility to monitor transactions associated with secondary roads. Ports, airports or railways PPPs are generally controlled by a specialized agency. Ports authorities generally enjoy that mandate for ports, but are generally assigned a single or a set of ports. They are responsible for the management of the PPPs in the port under their mandate. In countries with multiple ports, a national agency often supervises all the local port authorities and, in some instances, may manage the award of the concessions in each port even though their monitoring is assigned to the local port authorities. Similar arrangements are observed for airports. A single authority is generally responsible for the award of airport concessions, but in countries with multiple airports, local supervision of compliance with the contractual commitments is not uncommon. Rail is simpler. Concessions are generally regional and in most country, they cover the whole country. The most common institutional arrangement in that case is a single regulator for all rail concessions. In large countries with significant passenger and in particular suburban transport as in Argentina or Brazil for instance, the passenger and freight rail services are unbundled and the management and key PPP decisions of passenger rail services are often assigned to the cities or municipalities served by these suburban operators.[19]

The main advantage of a national model of regulation of all transport infrastructures is that it ensures consistency in the handling of transport sub-sectors and infrastructures across the country. It also allows the countries with limited human capital to do the most with the scarce skills available. The main disadvantage is that the government loses sometimes much needed flexibility to deal with sector or regional specificities. There is no clear best practice benchmark. For the road sector, after a number of failed attempts, road agencies are starting to deliver in terms of maintenance as well as in terms of investment choice and implementation. The port sector is starting to realize it needs to look for a new model as the nature of the business is changing (Estache and Trujillo, 2007). The main challenge for the airport sector has been the difficulties encountered in addressing jointly military and civilian needs in airports. It is still adjusting to the fast growing traffic and it is likely that this sector will have to rethink its model as well once the market has settled. Overall, an unbundled model also creates some problems in terms of the coordination of the subsectors' policies. One of the reasons why so many countries have a hard time supporting effectively the development of effective multi-modalism is the atomization of the policy design and regulation of transport activities in the assignment of government responsibilities. The main solution to this coordination problem is to rely on a competition agency to address any concern of inconsistent regulatory decisions. This option is however precluded to many countries that do not have a competition agency or the necessary skills in those agencies.

CONCLUDING COMMENTS

Recurrent developments in emerging financial markets and the recent credit crisis catalyzed by the US mortgage crisis have so far not dramatically changed the appetite for transport infrastructure projects. Transport infrastructure projects that have significant commercial risk will face however higher interest rates, with debt premia for political, currency, regulatory, and sectoral risks. They will also face lower equity contributions with some actors unwilling to put more than 5–10 percent of equity in the PPP, in particular in developing countries (see Correia et al., 2006). The substitution of construction equity for portfolio equity will not suffice. Depending on the particular project, rates of LIBOR – London Interbank Offered Rate – plus 6 to 10 percent should not be unexpected.[20] In addition, widely used performance indicators such as Debt Service Cover Ratios have been adjusted, so that previous standards such as coverage of 1.5 times interest payments now are commonly 2.0 times or even higher. As a result, there will be increasing pressure for governments either to become involved as equity holders in these projects or to provide guarantees.

PPP efforts in transport, in particular in developing countries, are shifting from new projects to the privatization, rehabilitation and expansion of existing facilities. What investors are looking for is now clearer. They are keen on an established track record of the facilities to lower perceived risks – and the record of successful PPPs in the port and airport sectors are generating a collective sense of record for these sectors. They are also keen on knowing more about the associated revenue stream from the outset, particularly when they need to cover capacity additions. They have become really key elements in transport PPPs since they drive not only the net present value of the deals and their rate of return, but also the availability of cash in the short term. Efforts to bundle transport projects into PPP 'packages' for both revenue diversification and to obtain cash flows have also increased over time as obvious ways of minimizing or spreading the risks.

Another major change that seems to be taking place is that transport PPPs appear to be in the hands of an increasingly concentrated number of actors, including operators, sponsors, bankers and investors. About 15 to 20 project players have emerged at the aggregate level and even less within each subsector. This group is characterized by large size and large capacity to invest; (relatively) low cost of capital with deep access to financial markets; sophisticated development skills; and strong financial support from their parent companies. It is also an increasingly multinational club with a global presence in competitive and non-competitive transactions. While local investors and others may participate in specific niches, these major organizations have become quite effective at setting the acceptable standards and de facto practices in transport project finance.

As the key actors are increasingly well known, and as transport policy and regulatory institutions start to be able to deliver on their mandates, PPPs will become more effective policy tools in developing countries. The road to success has been – and still is – long, simply because governments and their policy advisers have somehow been slow to learn from mistakes. There are enough success stories to be confident about the future of PPPs as an instrument of transport policy. The hopes should however be limited to those activities for which PPP can help (ports, airports and high traffic roads for investment). For some countries with high commercial, institutional or political risks, PPPs are not going to be the optimal option for many of their transport needs. For all the others, ignoring them would be just as bad a policy decision.

NOTES

1. To our knowledge, there is no single definition of PPP. It covers a wide range of transactions where the private sector is assigned some responsibility, including investment. It ranges from management contracts with no investment obligations to concessions contracts with significant investment obligations in addition to operational and management obligations. In general, these contracts allow the private operators to collect money directly from the users. Increasingly, there are also many examples in which the government commits to cover the costs of financing the operations or investment. The Public Finance Initiative (PFI) in the UK includes many examples of such contracts which imply an explicit payment by the public sector. Note, however, that renegotiations of contracts with the private sector often have the same outcome since governments end up subsidizing the operations which were supposed to be self-financed when the contracts were signed. A useful encompassing overview of the issues is provided in Yescombe (2007) and a stimulating much shorter discussion is offered by Brown (2005). For a provocative discussion of the differences in viewpoint between academics and practitioners on PPPs, see Grimsey and Lewis (2005).
2. World Bank: Global Financial Markets.
3. See Flyvbjerg et al. (2003, 2005) or Trujillo et al. (2002) for detailed discussion of the strategic motivations explaining recurring optimism in traffic forecast.
4. These include Build–Own–Operate–Transfer (BOOT), Build–Lease–Transfer (BLT), Build–Transfer–Operate (BTO), Design–Build–Finance–Operate (DBFO) and Design–Construct–Manage–Finance (DCMF).
5. For a discussion of examples in the airport sector, see Juan (1995). For an example of how this is formalized in a financial model of the port sector, see the description of the financial model used for the financing of a container port terminal discussed in the World Bank Port Reform Toolkit (2007) http://www.ppiaf. org/documents/toolkits/Portoolkit/Toolkit/reference/Financial percent20Model/manual_f.pdf.
6. Equity is generally the lowest ranking form of capital because the claims of the equity investors will rank behind all creditors. On the positive side, the equity holders gain disproportionately if the project performs better than expected. Different forms of investment other than straight equity might be considered as 'pseudo-equity'. For example, in the UK, project sponsors will commonly consider lending debt to the Special Purpose Vehicle (explained later in the text) that is subordinated to all other borrowings. This might be considered as an alternative to additional equity, and is normally based on tax considerations

and standing in bankruptcy should the concession fail. Mezzanine finance falls somewhere between senior debt and equity. Examples include subordinated debt and preference shares. Payments are made to these investors only after senior debt is serviced and will only be made if certain conditions are satisfied, such as minimum coverage ratios or investment requirements related to the performance of the project. The risks taken by mezzanine providers are greater than those of senior creditors, and so required returns will be higher (but lower than those required by traditional equity investors). Mezzanine capital might be provided by certain investment trusts, mutual funds, or insurance companies.

7.   As the SPV is usually only a legal construct, it needs to ensure that it performs its obligations under the concession agreement by sub-contracting those obligations to third parties. The principal parties usually are the construction contractor and the operator of project facilities. It is common for one or both of these parties to be part of the sponsor consortium, or an affiliate of the sponsors. Since there are usually multiple sponsors, the relationship between them is clearly defined and usually set out in a shareholders' agreement. The SPV might have other equity investors, such as development finance institutions or the government. The SPV is capitalized by the sponsors in agreed proportions, normally on the terms set out in an agreement that deals not only with the sponsors' initial capital investments but also with any further obligations with respect to future contribution obligations. In addition, rules are established with respect to how the SPV is to be administered, how it is to be financed, how sponsors share profits and how, if at all, sponsors may transfer or sell their shareholdings or interests in the SPV.

8.   Note that the commercial banks that generally lend directly to the SPV tend to have a very significant control over the SPV. On the one hand, they are expected to finance the project on a non-recourse or a limited recourse basis, emphasizing project revenues as the primary source of repayment of interest and principal. It is in return for agreeing to finance the project on such a basis that the banks are likely to require the ability to exercise a considerable degree of control over the SPV and its activities, and to have 'step-in rights' should any one of a large number of triggering default events occur.

9.   The non-recourse nature of the debt in a project financing may change during the life of the project. For example, debt may be structured to provide recourse to the project sponsor only during the construction and commissioning phases.

10.   For example, land assembly was a major factor in delays in the construction of the Bangkok elevated highway.

11.   See Trujillo et al. (2002) for a longer discussion of the strategic behavior in transport bids.

12.   The importance of the elasticity of demand to the tolls and its political consequences were strongly underestimated simply because an alternative free routing was assumed to take care of any inability to pay high tolls for some of the potential road users and political unhappiness. In this case, elasticity mattered a lot more to traffic volume than sometimes anticipated by politicians and project designers. Elasticities have been found to depend on many factors (trip purpose, trip frequency, journey length and section length, average speed and percentage of heavy trucks on toll-free alternatives). In this respect the experience of developing countries may be different from the experience of OECD countries where elasticities are typically lower during peak periods and usually small in magnitude; see Burris (2003) or Matas and Raymond (2003).

13.   In many countries, often developed, infrastructure subsidies are also quite common for ports and rail.

14.   In this specific case the problem was more a bad design of the initial contract.

15.   These political risks are starting to be documented quite well empirically. For instance, Athias and Saussier (2007) find that contracts signed with left-leaning public authorities, rather than with right-leaning public authorities, appear to be more likely rigid. This seems to corroborate the conjecture that private concessionaires have a better reputation among right wing public authorities.

16.   See Alexander et al. (2001) for a discussion of the cost of capital in the transport sector.

17.   Note that in some countries such as Chile, for instance, minimum income guarantees to protect the operator are introduced jointly with revenue sharing schemes which allow the government to share – 30–50 percent – into extra profits (that is, revenue generating a return in excess of 15 percent) when traffic is consistently above forecast.

18.   If government's share 'downside risk' with the private sector through guarantees, they should also consider seeking instruments that allow profit on the 'upside'. One way to do this is by a revenue-sharing arrangement in which the government receives a portion of revenues above a minimum traffic threshold.

19.   Editor note: see the chapter on rail regulation by Chris Nash for a discussion of the experience with a rail track authority in the UK.

20.   The LIBOR is the average rate at which some large banks lend to other banks without any asset commitments.

REFERENCES

Alexander, I., A. Estache and A. Oliveri, 2001, A few things transport regulators should know about risk and the cost of capital. *Utilities Policy*, **9**, 1–13.

Athias, L. and S. Saussier, 2007, Contractual flexibility or rigidity for public private partnerships? Theory and evidence from infrastructure concession contracts. Mimeo, ATOM, Paris.

Brown, C., 2005, Financing transport infrastructure: for whom the road tolls. *Australian Economic Review*, **38** (4), 431–438.

Burris, M.W., 2003, The toll-price component of travel demand elasticity. *International Journal of Transport Economics*, **30** (1), 45–59.

Correia, L., A. Estache and S. Jarvela, 2006, Is debt replacing equity in regulated privatized infrastructure in developing countries? *Utilities Policy*, **14** (2), 90–102.

Dutz, M., C. Harris, I. Dhingra and C. Shugart, 2006, PPP unites, what are they, and what do they do, public policy for the private sector. Policy Note no. 311, September.

Engel, E., R.D. Fischer and A. Galetovic, 2001, Least-present-value-of-revenue auctions and highway franchising. *Journal of Political Economy*, **109**, 993–1020.

Estache, A. and L. Trujillo, 2007, Transport cost levels, productivity and efficiency measures: some theory and main policy uses. OECD-ECMT Round Table 132.

Flyvbjerg, B., N. Bruzelius and W. Rothengatter, 2003, *Megaprojects and Risk: An Anatomy of Ambition*. Cambridge: Cambridge University Press.

Flyvbjerg, B., M. Skamris Holm and S.L. Buhl., 2005, How (in)accurate are demand forecasts in public works projects? The case of transportation. *Journal of the American Planning Association*, **71** (2), 131–146.

Grimsey, D. and M. Lewis, 2005, Are public private partnerships value for money? Evaluating alternative approaches and comparing academic and practitioners views. *Accounting Forum*, **29**, 345–378.

Guasch, J.L., 2004, *Granting and Renegotiating Infrastructure Concessions: Doing It Right*. Washington DC: The World Bank.

Irwin, T.C., 2007, Government Guarantees: *Allocating and valuing risk in privately financed infrastructure projects, directions in development*. Washington DC: The World Bank.

Juan, E., 1995, Airport infrastructure: the emerging role of the private sector: recent experiences based on ten case studies. CFS Discussion Paper Series 115, World Bank, Cofinancing and Financial Advisory Services Department, Washington DC.

Matas, A. and J.-L. Raymond, 2003, Demand elasticity on tolled motorways. *Journal of Transportation and Statistics*, **6** (2/3), 91–108.

Raux, C. and S. Souche, 2004, The acceptability of urban road pricing: a theoretical analysis applied to experience in Lyon. *Journal of Transport Economics and Policy*, **38** (2), 191–216.

Trujillo, L., E. Quinet and A. Estache, 2002, Dealing with demand forecasting games in transport privatization. *Transport Policy*, **9** (4), 325–333.

World Bank, 2007, *Global Financial Markets*. Washington DC: The World Bank.

World Bank, 2007, *Port Reform Toolkit*. Washington DC: The World Bank.

Yescombe, E.R., 2007, Public–Private Partnerships: Principles of Policy and Finance. New York: Elsevier.

31 Parking economics
Richard Arnott

INTRODUCTION

For many years, transport economists slighted parking, treating it simply as a fixed cost added on to the end of a trip. That has been changing. Not only is there a growing literature on the economics of parking, but also urban transport economists are coming to recognize parking as an essential element of the urban transportation problem and urban economists to realize its importance as a land use.

In a world without distortions, the economics of parking would be rather straightforward, following basic economic principles. But there are many distortions associated with parking or related to it. Most shopping center parking and employer-provided parking is free, and most curbside (on-street) parking is underpriced. The demand for personal parking is derived from the demand for auto travel, and urban auto travel is generally underpriced due to the absence of congestion pricing. Parking garages and parking lots are discretely spaced. The friction of space then confers market power on private suppliers, which they exploit by pricing above marginal cost. The price differential between on- and off-street parking induces cruising for curbside parking, which contributes to traffic congestion. As a result of these and other distortions, parking policy is very much an exercise in the theory of the second best.

Almost all parking policy is local. Since most local governments lack the resources and expertise for systematic data collection and internal policy analysis, most parking studies are done at the neighborhood level by consulting firms, based on accepted but often economically flawed planning practice. Local policies are typically based on consultants' recommendations (for example, City of Riverside Redevelopment Agency, 2002) as filtered through local politics. This decentralized, incremental and poorly documented policy process probably ensures that local parking needs are attended to reasonably well, but may result in parking policy that is highly inefficient at the aggregate level. Good economic policy analysis should be based on empirical studies firmly grounded in microeconomic theory. Unfortunately, because there has been so little systematic collection of data on parking and parking policy,[1] this chapter's policy analysis will be based primarily on a priori reasoning.

Transportation scientists and engineers, as well as urban planners, have, of course, devoted considerable attention to modeling parking and parking search (Young, 2000, which provides a solid review of the state of the art a decade ago; Benenson and Martens, 2008; Benenson, Martens, and Birfir, 2008; Bonsall and Palmer, 2002; and Lam et al., 2006) and to parking policy and management, from the design, location and regulation of downtown parking garages and surface parking lots (Alroth, 1999; Chrest et al., 2004; de Cerreño, 2002; Litman, 2005, 2008; Urban Land Institute and International Council of Shopping Centers, 2003; Urban Land Institute and National Parking Association, 2005), to the choices of how much curbside to allocate to parking in different neighborhoods, what meter rates and time limits to apply to curbside parking and how best to enforce them, and what information to provide drivers to assist them in their search for parking, to green parking policy (EPA, 2006). While this literature demonstrates engineering expertise and common sense, with some exceptions economic analysis is conspicuous by its absence. This chapter will complement this literature by considering parking from an economic perspective.

Parking may be on street or off street. On-street parking is often referred to as curbside parking. There are two broad classes of off-street parking, parking lots or surface lots, and parking garages/structures.

The chapter starts by presenting some empirical regularities related to parking, with the aim of conveying the importance of parking as an economic problem. Next is a section applying the received microeconomic theory of transportation, in the spirit of Mohring's *Transportation Economics* (1976) and Quinet and Vickerman's *Principles of Transport Economics* (2004), to the economics of parking, the first part developing the first-best theory, in the short run and then in the long run, and the second part illustrating how the theory can be extended for second-best analysis. This is followed by a discussion of selected issues in parking policy from an economic perspective – curbside parking, a soft downtown parking freeze and minimum parking requirements – to give a flavor of the issues involved, and then touches on others facets of parking policy.

SOME EMPIRICAL REGULARITIES RELATED TO PARKING

Empirical regularities regarding parking in the United States are hard to come by since few cities and no metropolitan areas collect parking data on a systematic basis. What data are collected are poorly documented, making cross-city comparisons difficult.[2] Estimates of the number of parking spaces per car range between three and six. With 110 million households, a car ownership rate of 2.0 per household, 300 square feet per parking space (including access space), and four parking spaces per vehicle, close to 10 000 square miles of space are allocated to parking in the United States. Since the bulk of parking is on ground, the land area allocated to parking in the United States must exceed 8000 square miles, an area larger than the state of Massachusetts. A more economically relevant figure would be the proportion of US land value devoted to parking, but no one has attempted to estimate this.

Parking, as an economic problem, is particularly important in the downtowns of major metropolitan areas. Unfortunately, since the definition of downtown/central business district (CBD) varies considerably across cities, cross-city comparisons are problematic. Also, for a particular city, different databases often use different geographic definitions and apply to different years. To avoid these difficulties, we report consistent statistics for one city and one downtown area.[3]

The City of San Francisco[4] has a land area of 47.4 square miles, a resident population of about 750 000 and an estimated daytime population of 950 000. The number of registered vehicles is about 475 000, of which 382 000 are cars and 64 000 are trucks, with 28.5 percent of households owning no vehicle. The City has 1088 miles of streets, with a paved area of 7.0 square miles, and 7200 intersections. The journey-to-work modal shares are:

drive alone 40.5 percent, carpool 7.7 percent, public transportation 30.3 percent, bicycle 2.3 percent, walk 9.6 percent, work at home 7.6 percent, and other 2.1 percent. There are 602 000 parking spaces, including 320 000 on-street parking spaces, of which about 25 000 are metered, 67 000 off-street parking spaces downtown, of which 15 000 are city-owned, and 215 000 off-street parking spaces elsewhere in the city. Parking meter rates vary from $1.50 to $3.00/hr. The average first-hour, 12-hour and monthly-unreserved off-street CBD parking rates are $9.25, $30.75 and $339. Parking garage construction costs average $45 000 per space. Annual meter revenue is $30 million and parking fine revenue is $90 million. About 90 000 resident parking permits are issued, generating about $6 million in revenue.

A couple of back-of-the-envelope calculations will prove insightful. With 475000 registered vehicles and 602000 parking spaces, there are only 1.27 parking spaces per registered vehicle, which appears too low.[5] Even the conservative estimate of 602000 parking spaces implies that the ratio of parking area to land area is 0.14 and, excluding off-street parking spaces downtown, that the ratio of parking land area to land area is 0.12. Also, taking the length of a curbside parking stall as 24 feet, on-street parking has a total length of almost 1500 miles, which, accounting for intersections, implies curbside parking on both sides of the street almost everywhere in the city; and taking the width of a curbside parking stall as 8 feet, the area occupied by curbside parking is 2.2 square miles, almost one-third of the paved area of the city.

The density of off-street parking is considerably higher in the downtown core than in the rest of the metropolitan area. Parking in Boston (2001) reports that in 1997/8, in Downtown Boston, there were 160 000 employees per square mile and 29 000 parking spaces per square mile. With 300 square feet per parking space, this implies a ratio of parking floor area to land area of 0.31. This parking density can obviously not be sustained with on-street parking alone. In fact, in the Financial District, 87 percent of parking spaces are off-street. The above figures for the City of San Francisco and Downtown Boston point to the obvious but important fact that garage parking is concentrated in areas of high employment density, especially CBDs.

No one, to our knowledge, has attempted to estimate the social costs of parking for the nation as a whole. However, the above data permit educated guesses of the social cost of the space used in parking for the City of San Francisco. Suppose that the mean monthly parking rental rate for the City is $200, a conservative estimate. With 602 000 parking spaces and 750 000 residents, this implies a mean annual parking rent per resident of almost $2000. Since Class A office space is about $40/ft^2-yr in downtown San Francisco, and since the bulk of that is for land, the annual shadow rent of a premium CBD parking space likely exceeds $10 000.

Much parking policy is based on parking planning standards. Litman (2008) provides an excellent review and discussion of these standards. A common form of parking standard is minimum parking requirements, which specify the minimum number of parking spaces that must be provided by different land uses. Information on the design and costing of parking garages is provided in Chrest et al. (2004), and Urban Land Institute and National Parking Association (2005).

PARKING ECONOMICS AS AN APPLICATION OF TRANSPORT MICROECONOMIC THEORY

There is a well-developed body of microeconomic theory, both algebraic and geometric, dealing with congestible facilities, of which transportation facilities are a particular application. See Arnott and Kraus (2003), Mohring (1976), Quinet and Vickerman (2004, especially chapter 7), and Small and Verhoef (2007, Sections 3.3 and 3.4). This section starts by applying the first-best theory to the economics of parking, and then moves on to the messier but more policy-relevant second-best theory.

To develop the theory, we work with a toy model. Consider a static economy consisting of two islands joined by a causeway. The economy's residents are located on island 1, and a shopping center and its parking lot on island 2. All travel is for shopping. To simplify, no time on a shopping trip is actually spent shopping. The demand for trips is a function of the full price of a shopping trip: $n = n(P)$. The full price of a trip is the sum of travel cost and parking cost. Both the causeway and the parking lot are congestible. Specifically, the time for a return trip along the causeway is $f(n,k)$, where k is the capacity of the causeway, and the time it takes to find a parking spot and walk from the parking spot to the shopping center and back is $g(n,K)$, where K is the capacity of the parking lot. Where ρ is the value of time (which is assumed to be the same for different transportation activities), τ is the congestion toll per round trip, and μ is the parking fee per unit time, the full price of a trip is

$$P = \rho f(n, k) + \tau + (\rho + \mu)g(n, K), \tag{31.1}$$

comprising the cost of travel time, the congestion toll and the money and time cost of parking.

First-best Theory

We start by considering the short run, in which the capacity of the road and the parking lot are fixed.

Short-run analysis
Turn to Figure 31.1; *uc* denotes user cost, *msc* marginal social cost, *ce* congestion externality cost, and subscripts t, p, and Σ denote travel, parking and trip (the sum of travel and parking), respectively. Each panel displays user cost and marginal social cost as a function of the number of trips. The middle panel applies to travel cost, the bottom panel to parking cost, and the top panel to trip cost. Since total travel cost per unit time is ρnf, the marginal social travel cost of a trip is $\rho(f + nf_n)$, where ρnf_n is the travel congestion externality cost – the external cost of an extra trip due to the increase in travel time it causes. Similarly, the marginal social parking cost of a trip is $\rho(g + ng_n)$, where ρng_n is the parking congestion externality cost – the external cost of an extra trip due to the increase in parking time it causes. Trip user cost is obtained by vertically summing travel user cost and parking user cost, and marginal social trip cost by vertically summing the marginal social travel cost and marginal social parking cost.

Figure 31.2 plots the trip user cost, the marginal social trip cost and the trip demand

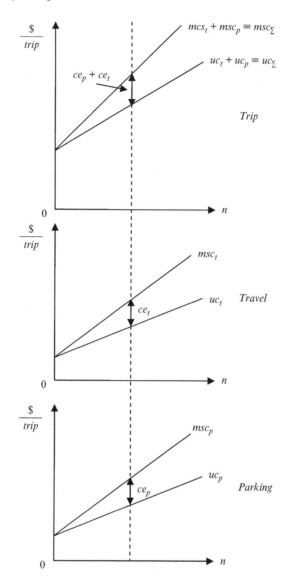

Figure 31.1   Trip, travel and parking user cost, marginal social cost and congestion externality cost curves

curve. Note that the demand is for trips, and that both the demand for travel and the demand for parking are derived from the demand for trips. Since the inverse demand curve is the marginal willingness-to-pay or marginal social trip benefit curve, the social optimum corresponds to the point of intersection of the marginal social trip cost and trip demand curves. The social optimum can be decentralized by charging a congestion toll equal to the travel congestion externality cost, evaluated at the optimal number of trips, $\tau^* = \rho[nf_n]^*$, and a parking fee per unit time equal to parking congestion externality cost,

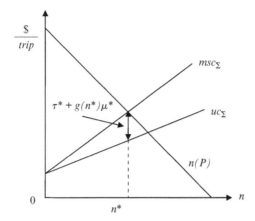

Figure 31.2   The first-best, short-run optimum and its decentralization

divided by the length of time parked, $\mu^* = \rho[ng_n/g]^*$. The essential point is that the short-run optimum can be decentralized by setting trip price equal to short-run marginal social trip cost. This can be done by setting the travel price equal to short-run marginal social travel cost (which is achieved by setting the congestion toll equal to the travel congestion externality cost) and the parking payment equal to short-run marginal social parking cost (which is achieved by setting the parking fee equal to the parking congestion externality cost per unit time parked).

Long-run analysis
The long-run analysis of a congestible facility treats capacity as variable. Here the capacities of both the causeway and the parking lot are treated as variable. Turn to Figure 31.3. *LRMC, LRAC* and *SRAC* denote long-run marginal cost, long-run average cost, and short-run average cost, respectively; otherwise, the notation is the same as in Figures 31.1 and 31.2. Short-run average parking cost equals average fixed parking cost (the cost of the parking lot, including the land) plus parking user cost. Draw in the short-run average parking cost curves for each level of parking lot capacity. Then draw in the long-run average parking cost curve as the lower envelope of the short-run average parking cost curves, as well as the corresponding long-run marginal parking cost curve. Obtain the long-run average and marginal travel cost curves in the same way. Then add the long-run average travel cost curve and the long-run average parking cost curve vertically to obtain the long-run average trip cost curve. Do the same to obtain the long-run marginal trip cost curve. The upper panel of the figure displays the long-run optimum, which is characterized by the point of intersection of the trip demand curve (the marginal social trip benefit curve) and the marginal social trip cost curve. Given the optimal number of trips, n^*, the optimal parking capacity, K^*, can be determined from the short-run average parking cost curve tangent to the corresponding long-run curve at n^*, as shown in the lower panel of the figure; optimal causeway capacity is determined analogously.

One of the central issues in the first-best, long-run analysis of a congestible facility is the extent to which the congestible facility should be self-financing. The central

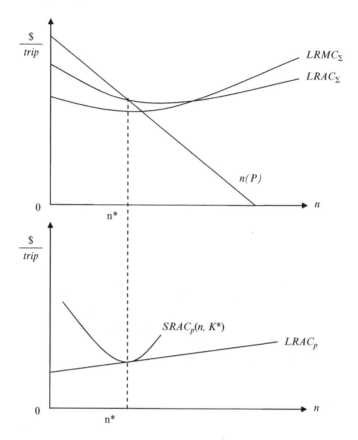

Figure 31.3   The first-best, long-run optimum

result, known as the Self-Financing Theorem, is that, when there are constant long-run average costs, the revenue obtained from the optimal fee raises just the right amount of revenue to finance optimal capacity – the congestible facility breaks even. When there are decreasing long-run average costs, a deficit arises, and when there are increasing long-run average costs, a surplus occurs. Here there are two congestible facilities, the causeway and the parking lot. Theory and empirical work (reviewed in Small and Verhoef, 2007) suggest that a single road exhibits decreasing long-run average travel cost but that a road network exhibits more or less constant average cost because the space allocated to intersections increases more than proportionally to capacity. No work has been done on estimating whether long-run parking average cost is increasing or decreasing in n, but a priori reasoning suggests that either may occur: holding fixed garage size, doubling the density of garage users and the number of parking garages reduces average walking distance but increases land costs.[6]

The first-best analysis of parking does differ somewhat from the conventional first-best analysis of a congestible facility since the demand is for car trips rather than parking per se and since the user cost for a trip is obtained through the vertical summation of the user cost curves for travel and parking. But the basic insights from the first-best analysis of congestible facilities carry through: it is efficient for parking to be priced at short-run marginal social cost; parking capacity should be determined such that the marginal social benefit of capacity equals the marginal social cost; and the extent to which parking should be self financing depends on the homogeneity properties of the long-run cost function.

The above discussion assumed trip demand to be stationary. But, in fact, of course trip demand varies systematically over the day and by day of the week. Though treating non-stationarity considerably complicates the analysis, the basic insights carry through. There are three general approaches to treating non-stationarity. The first is to divide time into periods, such as peak and off peak, and to apply the analysis separately for each time period (allowing for cross-price effects in demand). The weakness of this approach is that it fails to treat the history-dependent nature of congestion. The second is to employ Vickrey's bottleneck model (Vickrey, 1969), which treats congestion as a queue behind a bottleneck of fixed flow capacity. The third is to employ a more sophisticated, history-dependent treatment of congestion.

Second-best Theory

First-best theory deals with the efficient allocation of resources, as well as the decentralization of efficient allocations, when the only constraints are resource (or scarcity) and technological constraints. The theory of the second best deals with the efficient allocation of resources, as well as decentralization of efficient allocations, in the presence of unalterable 'distortions', where the word distortions is used broadly to describe deviations from the Arrow–Debreu model of competitive general equilibrium and include such diverse economic elements as asymmetries in information, product differentiation, transaction costs and incomplete markets (see, for example, Salanié, 2000). Put alternatively, the theory of the second best deals with the efficient allocation of resources when there are constraints in addition to scarcity and technological constraints.

This chapter will illustrate application of the theory of the second best to several aspects of the economics of parking. Consider first the model presented in the previous subsection, and suppose that, for whatever reason, a congestion toll cannot be applied to auto travel. The second best in this case is simply to set the parking payment equal to the first-best parking payment plus the first-best congestion toll. Trip price as a function of flow is then the same as in the first best, and the short- and long-run first-best allocations can be achieved. This result derives from the simplicity of the model.

Ordinarily, the second best entails a trade-off between distortions. To illustrate this, modify the model so that there are two roads leading to the shopping center, denoted by subscripts. The first road exhibits flow congestion, as in the model above, but the second is uncongestible. The efficient allocation can then be decentralized by applying the first-best congestion tolls to both roads: $\tau_1^* > 0$ and $\tau_2^* = 0$ (since there is no congestion on the second road). Now suppose that a congestion toll cannot be applied to auto travel. The first-best allocation can still be achieved by adding τ_1^* to the first-best parking payment for those who travel on the first road but charging those who travel on the second road only the first-best parking payment. However, this policy requires the parking authority to distinguish whether an individual traveled to the shopping center using the first or the second road, which is generally not possible. If the parking payment must be independent of the road taken to the shopping center, then we have a proper

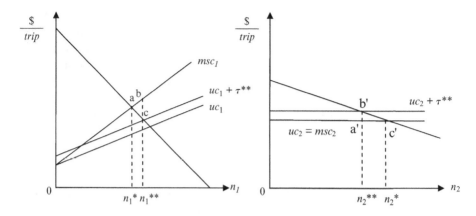

Figure 31.4   Second-best optimal parking fee

second-best problem, with a trade-off between distortions. If the parking payment is set equal to τ_1* plus the first-best parking payment, the full price faced by road 1 travelers will be correct, but the full price faced by road 2 travelers will be too high, resulting in too few road 2 trips. If the parking payment is set equal to the first-best parking payment, the full price faced by road 2 travelers will be correct, but the full price faced by road 1 travelers will be too low, resulting in too many road 1 trips. Since welfare losses are 'areas', rising with the square of the size of a distortion, it is typically the case that 'two smaller distortions are better than one larger one'. In this case, the second-best optimum entails setting the parking payment somewhere in between the first-best parking payment and the first-best parking payment plus τ_1*. Specifically, the parking payment, τ** should be set such that a small increase in the parking payment has zero marginal deadweight loss – where the increase in deadweight loss from reducing road 2 trips equals the decrease in deadweight loss from reducing road 1 trips. These results are displayed in Figure 31.4. The deadweight loss triangle for the former distortion is labeled a'b'c' in the right-hand panel of Figure 31.4; that for the latter distortion is labeled abc in the left-hand panel.

The analysis of second-best capacity is typically more difficult than that of second-best pricing. Return to the example of the previous paragraph, which concerned second-best pricing taking capacities as fixed. How should the road capacities and parking capacity be adjusted away from their first-best levels to reduce the distortion deriving from the inability to apply a congestion toll to road 1? Assume that the parking fee is set at its first-best level. As a point of reference, start with the first-best capacity levels. There are too many trips on road 1. Should the transportation authority respond by increasing or decreasing road 1 capacity? There are two opposing effects. On one hand, since road 1 capacity is set at its first-best level and since there are too many trips, road 1 is more congested than in the first-best allocation. If the number of trips were held fixed, it would be second-best efficient to expand road 1. On the other hand, expanding road 1 lowers the congestion on the road and hence the full trip price for road 1 travelers, which induces an increase in the number of road 1 trips, so that the number of road 1 trips becomes even more excessive. A complete analysis is complicated, with the results depending on second-order properties of the demand function and the congestion functions. But

Wilson (1983) argues that with realistic parameter values second-best capacity exceeds first-best capacity.

We shall present further applications of the theory of the second best in the next section, where we discuss issues in parking policy.

Review of the Literature on the Economics of Parking

This brief review aims to convey the current state of the literature and its evolution, and is far from exhaustive. The literature on the economics of parking is in its infancy and, due to absence of data, is almost entirely theoretical. The early work on the economics of parking argued that parking, like any other commodity, should be priced at its social opportunity cost (Roth, 1965; Vickrey, 1954). Over the next quarter century, parking was largely ignored by economists, in modal choice studies being treated simply as a fixed cost added to an auto trip. Donald Shoup has done much to stimulate recent interest in the subject. In the 1990s he championed cashing out employer-provided parking and over the last decade cashing out shopping center and curbside parking. His extensive research and policy advocacy on the subject is synthesized in Shoup (2005).

Four noteworthy papers were written on the economics of parking during the 1990s. All treated some second-best issues. Glazer and Niskanen (1992) pointed out possible perverse effects from per-unit-time curbside fees when auto congestion is unpriced and parking duration a choice variable; Arnott et al. (1992) extended the Vickrey bottleneck model to analyse the temporal-spatial equilibrium of curbside parking when all drivers have a common destination (interpretable as the CBD) and desired arrival time in both first-best and second-best scenarios; Verhoef et al. (1995) discussed the use of parking fees and parking regulations as a substitute for road pricing; and Arnott and Rowse (1999) focused on cruising for parking in steady state when parking spots are 'unsaturated' – less than fully occupied – providing the first example in the context of parking of multiple equilibria.[7]

Over the last decade, the literature has been adding realistic complications to models of parking. Calthrop (2001) considered the market power exercised by individual parking garages, due to the friction of space. Arnott et al. (2005) incorporated the effect of cars cruising for parking on traffic congestion, and investigated the optimal amount of curbside to allocate to parking, which trades off increased traffic congestion (including cruising for parking) against the cost of additional garage parking. Arnott and Rowse (2009b) considered the use of curbside parking time limits to reduce the excess demand for underpriced curbside parking. An obvious next step in the direction of realism is to include mass transit.

Anderson and de Palma (2004, 2007) pursued another line of development that focuses on spatial differentiation, modifying a reduced-form version of Arnott et al. (1992) to incorporate cruising for parking on lateral side streets. Anderson and de Palma (2004) started by considering the situation where parking is unpriced and therefore a common property resource, and showed that equilibrium entails overuse close to the CBD and underuse further away. They then showed that the cruising-for-parking externality can be internalized through monopolistically competitive[8] pricing by parking operators, each of whom controls the parking on a particular side street. This suggests that a private parking operator efficiently internalizes the congestion internal to her parking facility, analogous to a result in club theory (Scotchmer, 1985). Anderson and de Palma (2007) extended Anderson and de Palma (2004) to treat the allocation of land between residences and parking, essentially incorporating parking and cruising for parking into the monocentric city model.

The modeling of parking in traffic microsimulators on real networks is becoming increasingly sophisticated. Integration of such models with economic models that account for individual decision making vis-à-vis parking and travel should result in a powerful tool for parking policy analysis.

Litman (2005, 2006, and 2008) provides excellent overviews of the parking planning literatures from an economic perspective.

SELECTED ISSUES IN PARKING POLICY

As noted in the introduction, parking policy is an important facet of urban transportation policy, especially in downtown areas, and can also have important impacts on urban land use. In this section, we discuss three issues in urban parking policy, to give a taste of the economics involved – curbside parking policy, a soft freeze on downtown parking and minimum parking requirements – and then touch on some other issues.

Curbside Parking Policy

Curbside parking is a scarce economic resource. The first-best economics of curbside parking is straightforward. In the short run, where the amount of curbside allocated to parking is fixed, not necessarily at the optimal level, it is efficient to price curbside parking at that level which clears the market. Two difficulties would be encountered in applying this rule in practice. The first is that the prices would vary continuously over space and over the day, and in response to stochastic variations in demand. The second is that spatial search for a parking space needs to be considered. Vickrey (1954) advocated responsive pricing with a target vacancy rate, and Shoup (2005) coarser pricing to achieve an average vacancy rate over the busy period of the day. In the long run, the efficient amount of curbside to allocate to parking is that for which the marginal social benefit of a curbside parking space equals the marginal social cost. The marginal social benefit of a curbside parking space equals the reduction in aggregate parking costs; the marginal social cost equals the increase in aggregate travel time costs due to less road space being available for traffic circulation.

The second-best economics of curbside parking are considerably more complicated. There are potentially many distortions that curbside parking policy can be used to mitigate. The most obvious is the underpricing of urban auto travel. But there may also be important distortions in the urban land market, perhaps the most important of which in the context of parking policy is minimum parking requirements, which shall be discussed below. In addition, because of the friction of space, off-street parking operators exercise market power, which will also be discussed below. Also, curbside parking policy may itself be constrained by political considerations.

Arnott and Rowse (2009a) consider one scenario with inelastic demand for downtown travel (so that the underpricing of urban auto travel generates no deadweight loss), only auto travel (so that there is no modal choice distortion), and curbside and garage parking. The distortion they consider is the underpricing of curbside parking; garage parking is priced at marginal cost. The stock of cars cruising for parking adjusts to equalize the full prices of curbside and garage parking.[9] The expected time to find a curbside parking space depends on the ratio of the stock of cars cruising for parking to the turnover rate of curbside parking spaces. Holding fixed the price differential between curbside and garage parking, a doubling of curbside parking spaces would then result in a doubling of the stock of cars cruising for parking, which would worsen traffic congestion. Since the marginal social cost of a curbside parking space includes the increase in congestion it induces, the second-best amount of curbside parking falls short of the first-best level. This argument is weakened to the extent that curbside parking limits are effective in reducing cruising for parking (Arnott and Rowse, 2009b).

The industrial organization of private off-street parking operators has received little study. Calthrop (2001) models a monopoly parking operator; Anderson and de Palma (2004) assumes monopolistic competition; and Arnott and Rowse (2009a) treats Bertrand spatial competition but ignores capacity constraints, which likely significantly impacts the form of equilibrium. Empirical work on the topic is virtually non-existent. Info-Sage (2003) lists parking garage fee schedules in Boston as a function of time parked. The typical fee schedule has a fixed component plus a component that is concave in parking duration. Since it is difficult to justify on the basis of cost, this shape of fee schedule suggests price discrimination, but provides little insight into industry structure. In France, VINCI has a virtual monopoly on public (but contracted out) garage parking. The exercise of market power by private parking operators is potentially important for parking policy. For example, the fee differential between on- and off-street parking affects the stock of cars cruising for parking, while the pricing of off-street parking above marginal cost increases full trip price, which offsets the underpricing of urban auto congestion. Also, the taxation and regulation of private parking operators are potentially important aspects of parking policy, but have been given scant attention in the literature.

An important issue that the literature has rather overlooked (but see Glazer and Niskanen, 1992) is how the curbside parking fee schedule should vary with parking duration. The first-best curbside parking fee schedule would contain a fixed component corresponding to the congestion caused by entering and leaving a parking space, and a component linear in parking duration corresponding to the opportunity cost of the curbside parking space. When traffic congestion is unpriced and all parking is curbside, the second-best curbside parking fee schedule would add to the fixed component an amount equal to the average external congestion cost for the trip of marginal curbside parkers. When there is unpriced congestion and both curbside and off-street parking, the second-best curbside parking fee schedule should be set taking into account the market power exercised by private off-street parking operators. In practice, curbside parking fees are proportional to time parked, subject to curbside parking time limits, but today's technology readily allows more sophisticated pricing.

A Soft Downtown Parking Freeze

A recent policy trend, in the downtown areas of both European and North American cities, is to introduce a soft parking freeze, which freezes the amount of off-street parking for existing buildings, including parking garages, and imposes ceilings on the amount of parking that may be constructed for new buildings.[10] Boston, New York and San Francisco have had such a policy in effect for many years. The second-best argument justifying this policy runs as follows: Urban auto travel is underpriced, which distorts modal choice away from public transit and towards the car. Restricting the amount of parking downtown increases the price of urban auto travel, mitigating the distortion. The argument would be sound if the underpricing of urban auto travel were the only distortion. But there are at least three other potentially important distortions. The first is the underpricing of curbside parking. Reducing the amount of off-street parking causes its price to rise, increasing the price differential between curbside and off-street parking and therefore the number of cars cruising for parking. The second is the exercise of market power by off-street parking operators. The resulting overpricing of parking (recall that the stock of cars cruising for parking adjusts to equalize the full prices of curbside and off-street parking) discourages urban auto travel but increases the congestion caused by cars cruising for parking. The third is the subsidization of off-street parking by employers and merchants (parking validation).

The point is not that a soft downtown parking freeze is misguided, but that its wisdom is difficult to ascertain, requiring sophisticated quantitative second-best analysis. Furthermore, because cities differ from one another quantitatively, a policy that works in one city may not work in another. The accuracy of policy forecasts based on aggregative simulation models of downtown parking, with parameters customized to individual cities, remains to be seen. A recent line of development, which should prove very useful in city-specific analysis of parking policies, is the extension of microscopic traffic simulation models to treat parking.[11]

Minimum Parking Requirements and the Subsidization of Parking

Minimum parking requirements are local regulations, based on planning practice, that specify the minimum amount of parking that must be provided by a land user. They vary by land use, and may be based on the number of employees (for commercial and industrial land use), number of apartments or hotel rooms, square footage (for retail stores and perhaps apartment buildings) and so forth (see, for example, City of Boston, 2001). In the United States and Europe, until recently, they were applied in almost all cities. Most central cities applied them originally in the 1950s, with the aim of stemming the decline of the downtown core by reducing traffic congestion, and their adoption quickly spread to the smaller and suburban cities (Jakle and Sculle, 2004).

Shoup (2005) has been spearheading opposition to minimum parking requirements in the United States. The argument against them goes broadly as follows: Minimum parking requirements have resulted in a vast over-supply of off-street parking, whose long-run social costs have entailed more than the wasted space. Minimum parking requirements have essentially mandated free or at least heavily subsidized off-street (including shopping center and employer-provided[12]) parking, which has distorted modal choice towards the car. Combined with the many other subsidies to auto travel in the 1950s and 1960s, the policy encouraged low-density suburban sprawl, which contributed to the decline in mass transit. Furthermore, the free parking provided by suburban shopping centers has contributed to the decline of downtown commercial districts. In response, downtown parking has been underpriced too, through low meter rates and parking validation programs. The excess demand for curbside parking has generated considerable cruising for parking, which has exacerbated downtown traffic congestion, further encouraging suburbanites to shop at the mall rather than downtown. In response to this revisionism, many US cities, including Boston, New York and San Francisco, as well as some European cities, including Zurich, replaced minimum with maximum parking requirements on new buildings.

Economists have yet to study minimum parking requirements. Shoup's argument may be on the mark. But there is probably more to the story. Why were minimum parking requirements introduced in the first place, if not in response to some perceived market failure?[13] Perhaps minimum parking requirements were a sound, second-best response to underpriced urban auto congestion,[14] or restrained the exercise of the market power conferred on private parking providers by the friction of space. Minimum parking requirements did not mandate that parking be provided free. Why then have most suburban shopping centers provided parking free rather than pricing it?[15] And why have employers in the United States at least provided free or heavily subsidized parking but not provided a comparable commuting subsidy to their employees who walk to work or take mass transit? Many pricing anomalies can be explained as some form of price discrimination. Is that the case here?

Other Aspects of Parking Policy

Standardized zoning regulations affect the siting and density of garage parking, and planning codes determine the engineering and design standards applied in their construction. But there appears to be little consistency across cities in other aspects of economic policy with respect to parking garages. In some cities, almost all garage parking is public; in others it is almost all private. Private garage parking fees are regulated in Manhattan, but not in most other cities. Most cities tax private parking garages through the property tax, and some apply supplementary taxes on gross revenue or parking spaces. Wisely applied, parking garage policy can substantially reduce the distortions associated with parking garages' exercise of market power deriving from the friction of space. While not well documented, casual observation indicates that cities everywhere are moving in the direction of 'cashing out' (charging for) curbside parking that was previously provided free.

Four other types of off-street parking are important. The first is surface parking at shopping centers. The second is surface parking on a site with a built structure on it, other than a shopping center, such as hospital parking, hotel parking and off-street residential parking. This parking may or may not be restricted to the structure's occupants and their visitors/customers. If it is so restricted, there may or may not be a charge for its use; if it is not so restricted, parkers not associated with the land use are invariably charged. Often such parking is underutilized because of restrictions on its use. The third type of off-street parking is on vacant lots awaiting development or redevelopment. The fourth type, which is more prevalent in Europe than in North America, is surface or garage parking next to mass transit stations, 'park-and-ride' facilities aimed at encouraging mixed-mode commuting.

Freight delivery adds considerably to congestion in downtown areas. Large trucks ensnarl traffic, particularly when traveling in rush hour on secondary streets, and delivery vans often double park when making deliveries. Cities differ widely in their policies with respect to freight deliveries. Policies include restricting the size of truck allowed in the downtown area and the times at which freight deliveries can be made.

Most cities in the United States, and some in Europe, have resident parking policies, which restrict parking on a neighborhood's residential streets to residents' cars with a permit to park in that neighborhood. Resident parking policies effectively increase parking capacity for neighborhood residents at the expense of non-residents.

A relatively recent innovation has been the development of parking information systems that provide real-time information on parking availability. It may only be a few years before auto-parking guidance and information systems become as commonplace as today's auto-navigation systems. They have the potential to significantly reduce the costs of parking search and the congestion caused by cars cruising for parking.

Parking enforcement is an integral component of a city's parking program. At what rate should parking fines be set? How much should be spent on enforcement? And what enforcement technology should be applied? The literature on the economics of tax evasion is relevant here (see Sandmo, 2004, for a review). Cities are moving to increasingly sophisticated curbside parking charging and enforcement systems.

Parking fees and fines may contribute significantly to local government revenue; in the San Francisco data given earlier, parking meter and fine revenue was almost $200 per resident. Furthermore, when curbside parking is saturated and where it substitutes for garage parking, curbside meter revenue is an ideal source of government revenue. Raising the meter rate simply converts cruising-for-parking time costs dollar for dollar into tax revenue, with no burden, and has the added benefit of reducing traffic congestion (Arnott and Rowse, 2009a).

Litman (2008) provides an excellent review and synthesis of the current state of the art with respect to parking policy.

Little attention has been given to the political economy of parking policy. From one perspective, there are political constraints on policy optimization; from another, parking policy is the outcome of political competition between competing interest groups. Since parking policy is local and since local voters are residents, local politics is no doubt central to resident parking policy. And, without the lobbying done by downtown merchant associations, it is hard to explain how low curbside meter rates are in most downtown areas.

CONCLUSION

Parking and parking policy have been unjustly neglected by transportation economists. Since the cost of parking is an important component of the cost of auto trips with a downtown destination, parking policy can be effective in reducing the downtown auto modal share. Parking contributes significantly to downtown traffic congestion, through the curbside allocated to parking, and through the congestion caused by cars entering and leaving parking and cruising for parking and by parked delivery vans; parking policy can reduce downtown traffic congestion. Parking is also a major land use in downtown areas; parking policy can improve the efficiency of land use. Just as bad parking policy can seriously undermine the quality of life downtown, so can good parking policy sharply improve it.

The major reason parking and parking policy have been overlooked by transport economists is that almost all parking policy is local. Local governments muddle through, applying planning standards and adjusting them in response to neighborhood concerns. Few cities have done a parking inventory, even fewer keep it updated, and fewer still have the resources to collect the data and to hire the consultants needed to simulate parking policies, or the expertise to develop coherent parking policies. There are good grounds for optimism, however. The parking modules in traffic network simulation models have improved sharply in recent years, and it should not be long before their use is routine. Furthermore, since there is increased acceptance of pricing policies within the transportation planning community, the next generation of parking modules should take into account the responsiveness of individual travel and parking behavior to parking prices. Big city transportation planning departments will be the first to adopt such models, and will use them to rationalize their parking policies. Parking best practice, based on their experience, will then filter down to smaller cities.

These technological improvements notwithstanding, economists still have an essential role to play in the formulation of parking policy. They are needed to ensure that the welfare economics of policy evaluation is done correctly, that individual travel and parking decision making, as well as strategic interaction between players in parking games, are modeled soundly, and that an appropriate vocabulary is developed for discussing the effects of parking policy. They also have an advocacy role in arguing for pricing policies to supplement or replace the cumbrous regulatory schemes that planners are inclined to impose.

ACKNOWLEDGMENTS

I would like to thank James Yang for excellent research assistance, the editors for very helpful comments on an earlier draft, and Kay Axhausen and Tilmann Rave for providing information on parking policy in Zurich and Munich.

NOTES

1. Some of the major cities have well thought out and well documented parking policies. See, for example, Boston Transportation Department (2001) for Boston and d'Amato (2006) for Los Angeles. There are also national and trans-national parking associations that attempt to establish and document best practice; see, for example, European Commission (2001).
2. Jakle and Sculle (2004) provide an enjoyable, well-written and informative history of parking and parking policy in the US from a planning perspective that is sprinkled with facts and figures.
3. d'Amato (2006) documents parking policy in Los Angeles.
4. The data in this paragraph are obtained from The San Francisco Transportation Fact Sheet, October 2008, and Parking in America (NPA, 2008).
5. The Fact Sheet does not provide definitions or information on data collection. The number of parking spaces in the remainder of the city is likely underestimated.
6. By the Envelope Theorem, if parking capacity is provided at minimum cost, the marginal cost of increasing parking capacity is the same however capacity is increased. Thus, it would be equally valid to consider

the conceptual exercise of doubling the density of garage users and the height of each parking garage, holding fixed the number of garages.

7. The multiplicity of equilibria in this context is analogous to that found in the context of traffic flow; see Walters (1961) and the literature that has evolved from it. Gridlock is an extreme example of a Pareto inferior equilibrium. Since trip time is infinite the entry rate is zero, and since there is gridlock the exit rate is zero too.

8. In these and most other models in the parking economics literature, transport costs cause parking (and land) at different locations to be imperfect substitutes and hence differentiated products.

9. Consider the effects of raising the curbside parking fee on the assumption that doing so does not alter the equilibrium price of garage parking. Since the full price of curbside parking is therefore unchanged, cruising-for-parking costs are converted dollar-for-dollar into parking revenue. Furthermore, traffic congestion is reduced, benefiting all drivers. Thus, the extra parking revenue is raised with a negative burden!

10. A hard parking freeze in contrast simply freezes the total number of parking spaces at the level when the freeze was implemented.

11. Two such programs, VISSIM and TransModeler, include sophisticated parking modules that accommodate curbside, off-street and illegal (including double) parking, with exit from and entry to both curbside and garage parking, as well as cruising for parking, contributing to traffic congestion. They can also be customized to include an outer loop that allows for individuals' economic responses to changes in parking policy.

12. Small and Verhoef (2007) make the informed guess that US urban commuters pay for at most 2.5 percent of their workplace parking costs.

13. Jakle and Sculle (2004) provide a well-documented history of downtown parking in the United States. Up until World War II, off-street, non-residential parking was provided almost exclusively by the private sector, in garages and parking lots. There was a general perception that the market provided inadequate parking close to the downtown core, and that the congestion caused by cars cruising for parking was contributing to the decline of the downtown commercial district. It was also felt that downtown parking needed to be regulated and rationalized.

14. Theory indicates that, unless demand is sufficiently elastic, second-best capacity of an underpriced congestible facility is higher than first-best capacity (Wilson, 1983).

15. One explanation is that the transactions costs associated with pricing shopping center parking would exceed the shopping center owners' benefits from doing so; another is that the minimum parking requirements are so excessive that shopping center owners view the parking they provide as a fixed cost; yet another is that shopping center owners may not charge for parking for similar reasons that restaurateurs do not charge for a table rent.

REFERENCES

Alroth, W., 1999, Parking and terminals. In *Transportation Engineering Handbook*, 5th edn. Washington DC: Institute of Transportation Engineers.

Anderson, S. and A. de Palma., 2004, The economics of pricing parking. *Journal of Urban Economics*, **55**, 1–20.

Anderson, S. and de Palma., A., 2007, Parking in the city. *Papers in Regional Science*, **86**, 621–632.

Arnott, R., A. de Palma and R. Lindsey, 1992, A temporal and spatial equilibrium analysis of commuter parking. *Journal of Public Economics*, **45**, 301–335.

Arnott, R. and M. Kraus., 2003, Principles of transportation economics. In R.W. Hall, ed., *Handbook of Transportation Science*, 2nd edn. Berlin: Springer, pp. 689–726.

Arnott, R., T. Rave and R. Schöb, 2005, Some downtown parking arithmetic. *Alleviating Urban Traffic Congestion*, Cambridge, MA: MIT Press, Chapter 2.

Arnott, R. and J. Rowse, 1999, Modeling parking. *Journal of Urban Economics*, **45**, 97–124.

Arnott, R. and J. Rowse, 2009a, Downtown parking in auto city. *Regional Science and Urban Economics*, **39**, 1–14.

Arnott, R. and J. Rowse, 2009b, Curbside parking time limits. Mimeo.

Benenson, I. and K. Martens, 2008, From modeling parking search to establishing urban parking policy. *Künstliche Intelligenz*, 3/2008, 8–13.

Benenson, I., K. Martens and S. Birfir, 2008, PARKAGENT: An agent-based model of the parking in the city. *Computers, Environment and Urban Systems*, **32**, 431–439.

Bonsall, P. and I. Palmer, 2002, Modeling drivers' car parking behavior using data from a traffic choice simulator. *Transportation Science*, **12**, 321–347.

Boston Transportation Department, 2001, Parking in Boston: Access Boston 2000–2010.

Calthrop, E., 2001, Essays in Urban Transport Economics, Ph.D. Thesis, University of Leuven, Leuven, Belgium.

Chrest, A., M. Smith, S. Bhuyan, D. Monahan and M. Iqbal, 2004, *Parking Structures: Planning, Design, Construction, Maintenance and Repair*, 3rd edn. Boston, MA: Kluwer.

City of Boston, 2001, Guidelines by the Boston Transportation Department for use by the Zoning Board of Appeal, 5, parking ratios. Mimeo.

City of Riverside Redevelopment Agency, 2002, Comprehensive downtown parking study. Mimeo, Wilbur Smith Associates.

d'Amato, A. 2006, Organizational and operational review of parking at the City of Los Angeles Department of Transportation. LA Department of Transportation Parking Report.

de Cerreño, A., 2002, The dynamics of on-street parking in large central cities. NYU Rudin Center for Transportation Policy and Management.

Environmental Protection Agency (EPA), 2006, Parking spaces/community places: finding the balance through smart growth solutions. EPA 231-K-06-001, Washington DC.

European Commission, 2001, Parking policy measures and their effects on mobility and the economy. Available at: http://cordis.europa.eu/cost-transport/src/cost-342.htm.

Glazer, A. and E. Niskanen, 1992, Parking fees and congestion. *Regional Science and Urban Economics*, **22**, 123–132.

Info-Sage Inc., 2003, Guide to Boston parking.

Jakle, J. and K. Sculle, 2004, *Lots of Parking: Land Use in a Car Culture*, Charlottesville VA: University of Virginia Press.

Lam, W., Z. Li, H. Huang and S. Wong, 2006, Modeling time-dependent travel choice problems in road networks with multiple user classes and multiple parking facilities. *Transportation Research B*, **40**, 368–395.

Litman, T., 2005, Transportation cost and benefit analysis. 5.4. Parking. Victoria Transport Policy Institute. Available at: www.vtpi.org.

Litman, T., 2006, Parking taxes, evaluating options and impacts. Victoria Transport Policy Institute. Available at: www.vtpi.org/parking_tax.pdf.

Litman, T. 2008. Parking management: strategies, evaluation, and planning. Victoria Transport Policy Institute. Available at: www.vtpi.org/park_man.pdf.

Mohring, H., 1976, *Transportation Economics*. Cambridge, MA: Ballinger.

National Parking Association (NPA), 2008, Parking in America. The National Parking Association's first annual review of parking rates in the United States and Canada.

Quinet, E. and R. Vickerman, 2004, *Principles of Transport Economics*. Cheltenham, UK: Edward Elgar.

Roth, G., 1965, *Paying for Parking*. London: Institute for Economic Affairs.

Salanié, B., 2000, *The Microeconomics of Market Failures*. Cambridge, MA: MIT Press.

San Francisco Municipal Transportation Agency (SFMTA), 2008, San Francisco Transportation Fact Sheet.

Sandmo, A., 2004, The theory of tax evasion: a retrospective view. Discussion paper 2004, 31, Norwegian School of Economics.

Scotchmer, S., 1985, Profit maximizing clubs. *Journal of Public Economics*, **27**, 25–45.

Shoup, D., 2005, *The High Cost of Free Parking*. Chicago, IL: American Planning Association, Planners Press.

Small, K. and E. Verhoef, 2007, *The Economics of Urban Transportation*. Abingdon, England: Routledge.

Urban Land Institute and the International Council of Shopping Centers, 2003, *Parking Requirements for Shopping Centers*. Washington DC: Urban Land Institute.

Urban Land Institute and National Parking Association, 2005, *The Dimensions of Parking*. 4th edn. Washington DC: Urban Land Institute.

Verhoef, E., P. Nijkamp and P. Rietveld, 1995, The economics of regulatory parking policies: the (im)possibilities of parking policies in traffic regulation. *Transportation Research Part A*, **29**, 141–156.

Vickrey, W., 1954, The economizing of curb parking space. *Traffic Engineering*, November, 62–67. Reprinted in *Journal of Urban Economics*, **36**, 1994, 42–65.

Vickrey, W., 1969, Congestion theory and transport investment. *American Economic Review Papers and Proceedings*, **53**, 452–465.

Walters, A., 1961, The theory and measurement of private and social cost of highway congestion. *Econometrica*, **29**, 676–699.

Wardman, M., 2001, A review of British evidence on time and service quality valuations. *Transportation Research Part E*, **37**, 107–128.

Wilson, J., 1983, Optimal road capacity in the presence of unpriced congestion. *Journal of Urban Economics*, **13**, 337–357.

Young, W., 2000, Modeling parking. In D.A. Hensher and K.J. Button, eds, *Handbook of Transport Modeling*. Amsterdam: Elsevier, pp. 409–420.

32 The industrial organization of competition in local bus services

Philippe Gagnepain, Marc Ivaldi and
Catherine Muller-Vibes

INTRODUCTION

In most countries, local transport services by bus, which are a major component of regional passenger transportation systems, are subject to the scrutiny of policy makers for at least two contextual reasons. First, while the passenger transport services have always been highly regulated, the public transportation policy is now experiencing deregulation and/or privatization in an industry where urban transport companies are heterogeneous in their ownership status, which can be public or private, as well as in the diversity of transport modes they offer (bus, train, underground and tramway). Second, while the modal share of bus transport services has been declining for several decades in most developed economies, the growing environmental concern raises the calls for promoting urban mass transit (as opposed to private car).

This chapter is aimed at deepening our understanding of the functioning of competition in the local bus transportation industry and to evaluate its effectiveness. It provides an overview of the competitive constraints that are at work in the industry as discussed in the economic literature, and sketches empirical tests to check whether the intuitions provided by the economists are in line with the reality of the industry. To address these various issues, the first three sections of this text survey the economic literature on bus competition, emphasizing the case of UK which is used as a benchmark. We suggest that earlier contributions, proposed in the late 1980s, (that is, just after the deregulation of the industry) are very often based on unrealistic assumptions, mainly chosen because the authors lack of a sufficient perspective on the effects of deregulation. Hence, we focus on the most recent literature, which we attempt to survey as completely as possible. The objective is to draw the main conclusions or results which are shared by the analysts or researchers on how this economic activity functions. In the last section, we propose some methods to empirically test these main predictions of the economic literature.

The analysis is summarized as follows. The first section reviews what it is empirically known about the technological features and the economic performance of bus operators.[1] The following one focuses on the analysis of demand for urban transport services. Then a section analyses the competition in local bus service industry, leading to the conclusion that operators do not compete in prices but mainly in frequency. The last section concludes.

COST AND PRODUCTION ANALYSIS

The cost and production analysis addresses three main issues. First it is aimed at measuring economies of scale, economies of density and economies of scope which are key structural elements to describe in economic terms the technology behind an industry. Second, it should provide a measure of the level of *technical efficiency* to evaluate the performance of firms. Finally, it discusses the definitions for the output variables. In the literature, either supply indicators (for example, vehicle-kilometers or seat-kilometers), demand-related output measures (for example, passenger-kilometers or the number of passengers) or multidimensional output definitions are used (see De Borger and Kerstens, 2006, for a discussion on the choice of output measures).

Technological Characteristics

Let us first review some characteristics of the technology for bus transport services, such as returns to scale, economies of density and economies of scope. It is a common result that bus companies experience increasing returns to scale (see Farsi et al. 2006, 2007; Filippini and Prioni, 2003). More specifically, it seems that smaller firms benefit from increasing returns to scale, as opposed to larger firms which exhibit constant or even decreasing returns (see Kerstens, 1999; Matas and Raymond, 1998; Viton, 1997). For the British bus industry, Cowie and Asenova (1999) estimate that small companies of fewer than 200 buses experience some economies of scale. They also find that the size of such returns varies with the company type whether it is public limited, private limited, or municipal. Sakano and Obeng (1995) find increasing returns to scale for the US urban transit industry. Overall, a significant number of empirical studies are in line with a U-shaped average cost function exhibiting increasing returns to scale for the smaller operators, which become constant and finally decreasing as companies' size increases.

In most empirical studies, economies of density are frequently found regarding the bus companies' technology. As already pointed out, the distinction between economies of density and economies of scale is very important in industries that provide their services over a network. In these cases, the firm size is more closely related to the size of the network than to the output provided over that network. For this reason it is important to distinguish cost changes that occur because of output changes only and cost changes that occur because of a proportional network and output change. Among studies which estimate that bus companies fail to operate at an efficient density are Farsi et al. (2006) and Filippini and Prioni (2003) on the Swiss market, Matas and Raymond (1998) for Spain and Shaw-Er et al. (2005) for Taiwan. It appears that bus operators could obtain cost-saving benefits by extending their output scale.

Some articles have focused on the multi-modal side of the industry and have asked whether a bundling of operations from different urban transport modes (bus, train, metro, for instance) is preferable to a separated configuration. They converge to the conclusion that economies of scope are significant in the industry, and that their results are in favor of integrated multi-modal operators. Farsi et al. (2007) conducted a study in Switzerland and found increasing returns to scale in almost all outputs. They consider that these returns, combined with cost complementarities, can be considered as a suggestive evidence for natural monopoly. Viton (1993) also finds positive economies of scope and concludes that together with the nature of economies of scale, they support the formation of larger multi-modal systems in the San Francisco Bay Area.

Efficiency

The recent literature on performance of operators of local bus services shows that there still exists a substantial level of inefficiency in this industry. However, huge differences exist over time and across countries. Cowie and Asenova (1999) find a high degree of inefficiency in the British bus industry which they interpret as an indicator of wasteful competition. However, Cowie (2002) estimates that the average efficiency has improved in the UK, suggesting that mergers may have allowed existing group companies to operate closer to the optimal level of output. Heseltine and Silcock (1990) find for the British operators that the main total unit cost reduction was achieved by productivity improvements. Working on a sample of Spanish cities, Garcia-Sanchez (2009) finds that a majority of municipalities are technically inefficient, mainly due to scale inefficiency. This is a similar result to Kerstens (1999) who indicates that inadequacies in scale are the major source of poor performance in her sample of French urban transport service operators. Some studies though are more optimistic in their measurements of efficiency, in particular, in the UK. Viton (1997) finds that 80 percent of bus systems are efficient in the United States. Wunsch (1996) who compares 178 European urban transport companies claims that two British firms, in the cities of Manchester and Sheffield, are among the first on his list in terms of technical performance. However, he takes into account only dominant bus companies and he admits that his result depends crucially on data quality. Most studies underline the dispersion in the efficiency measures they obtain within the same country or area (see De Borger and Kerstens, 2006; Kerstens, 1999. The exception is Salas, 1998, who finds that, in Sweden, the levels of efficiency are very similar among companies).

Private / Public Ownership

Contrary to a common argument, there is substantial evidence in the literature that private bus companies do not operate more efficiently than public companies. Ownership type does not seem to be a crucial determinant in the firms' performance, as shown in Odeck and Sunde (2001) and Garcia-Sanchez (2009) for the Norwegian market and Viton (1997) who shows that US public and private systems share the same distribution of technical efficiency. Fazioli et al. (1993) found no relation between technical efficiency and ownership among a sample of Italian urban transit firms precisely because of the absence of effective competition for both public and private operators and strong regulation. Filippini and Prioni (2003) underline that the results in their study on a Swiss sample depend on the specification of output and network variables. However, although we can assert there is no strong evidence of a higher efficiency for private firms, some studies do find that they perform better. Cowie and Asenova (1999) find privately owned firms are not more technically efficient, although they exhibit a considerable level of managerial efficiency. They find that values of increasing returns to scale for small companies not only vary with the ownership type (public/private) but also with the actual form of private ownership. Relevance of ownership as a determinant for performance is also found in Kerstens (1996) and De Rus and Nombela (1997) for the French and Spanish market, respectively. At this point, the literature is considered inconclusive regarding the impact of ownership type on efficiency.

Subsidies

There is some evidence that subsidies are associated with an increase of operating costs. In particular, Kerstens (1996) corroborates this assertion when analyzing a sample of French urban transit companies. Sakano and Obeng (1995) examine US transit systems and report that subsidies lead to excess use of labor relative to capital and excess use of fuel relative to capital and labor.

Incentive Contracts

Several recent studies have revealed the positive effects of incentive contracts on technical efficiency. In Kerstens (1996), empirical findings confirm the importance of appropriate incentives in contracting for monopoly. Risk-sharing agreements seem to stimulate the performance of organizations. These results for French operators are confirmed by Gagnepain and Ivaldi (2002a) who develop a method which should help to clarify the choice of regulation in the urban transport industry. They conclude that cost-plus contracts are dominated by any type of second-best contract. These results are in line with those of Roy and Yvrande-Billon (2007) who find that operators under cost-plus contracts exhibit a higher level of technical inefficiency than operators under fixed-price agreements. De Borger and Kerstens (2006) survey other European studies which exhibit that high-powered incentive contracts improve efficiency.

Competitive Tendering

The available evidence suggests that competitive tendering may improve performance. These results are exhibited by Hensher and Wallis (2005) who review the international successes and failures of competitive tendering from ten developed countries. De Borger and Kerstens (2006) in their survey give a more detailed description of the effects of competitive tendering.

Methodologies / Discrepancies

It is important to bear in mind that all these performance analyses differ in several aspects. First, there exist several approaches to estimate efficiency on the basis of observed data. Efficiency, as measured by a deviation from the unobserved cost or production frontier, can be estimated by means of parametric and non-parametric methods aimed at determining the production or cost frontiers. On the one hand, parametric methods require the specification of a functional form for the frontier, a popular one being the flexible translog cost function. On the other hand, non-parametric approaches do not need to specify a functional form; they construct the frontier by enveloping the data on inputs and outputs by piecewise linear hyperplanes, as proposed by the extensively used data envelopment analysis (DEA) method. Both methodological strands have advantages and weaknesses, related to the presence (or not) of measurement errors or the requirement to specify functional forms. Detailed descriptions and discussions of parametric and non-parametric methodologies are presented in Lovell (1993) and Brons et al. (2005), respectively.

A second source of differences in the measurement of efficiency comes from the definition of the output variable. A significant number of studies conclude that operators' performances differ substantially depending on the output specification considered. Supply indicators (for example, vehicle-kilometers or seat-kilometers) or demand-related output measures (for example, passenger-kilometers or the number of passengers) have been used.

A third crucial aspect in the model specification for measuring efficiency is that models should account for relevant measures of service and network characteristics. Bus-transit services have been recognized as very heterogeneous across countries and even cities. This is confirmed by Brons et al. (2005) and De Borger and Kerstens (2006) who find significant and consistent effects of the type of database, region and output measurement method.

Fourth, some authors underline the need to decompose the measures of efficiency into their components (allocative and technical). For example, Viton (1997) suggests that the result of similar efficiency distributions between private and public firms might hide the fact that private systems would be more allocatively efficient. Also, according to him, the distinction between managerial and organizational efficiency seems relevant in this industry, particularly in measuring the impact of ownership type on efficiency. This conclusion is confirmed by Cowie and Asenova (1999) (see also Gagnepain and Ivaldi, 2002b).

Further Research

Although the literature on measuring efficiency in the urban transport industry is extensive, some aspects still have to be investigated more thoroughly. An international comparison on the effects of deregulation and competition on efficiency would be of high interest. Also, only a few studies take into account the presence of other transport modes on the market. Indeed, the presence of economies of scope and the call for limiting private car traffic to the benefit of urban modes because of environmental policies make this multi-output aspect of the industry particularly relevant. Further analysis of the decomposition of efficiency into its several components to better understand the effects of ownership and deregulation on efficiency seems to be a next step in the research agenda.

DEMAND ANALYSIS

In this section, we review the values of bus demand elasticities found in the literature. We discuss different types of elasticities. First, we look at the own price elasticities. Note that the own price elasticity of the demand that a firm faces is always more elastic than the aggregate elasticity of market demand. This is because there are fewer substitutes for a product at the market level than at the firm level. An example would be the substitution between competing bus services on a market as opposed to substitution between different transport modes on this market. Second, we present the measures of cross-price elasticities of demand which evaluate the substitution patterns between competitors (transport modes or services). For example, the cross-price elasticity from bus to car tells us the percentage increase in car demand following a one percent increase is bus fare. In the bus-transit industry competition can come from other bus operators, as well as other transport modes (train, metro, car and so forth). Finally, we report the values of income and service quality elasticities found in the literature.

Own Price Elasticities

It is a common result in the literature that the demand for bus-transit is not elastic in the short run. Most studies on bus-transit own-price elasticities agree on a value of -0.4 and this result is summarized in four surveys on urban demand by Balcombe et al. (2004), Dargay and Hanly (1999), Goodwin (1992) and Oum et al. (1992).

These studies emphasize that authors now agree on the necessity to consider dynamic changes in these own-price elasticities. All studies allowing elasticities to vary over time, that is to say, allowing demand to adjust to changes in price in the long-run, have agreed that demand in the long run is more elastic than demand in the short run. The role of dynamics in urban transport demand is the objective of the survey conducted by Goodwin (1992) who estimates that long-run elasticities range between 1.5 to 3 times higher than short-run elasticities. He concludes that a time-dependent specification for the demand is preferred. In the literature (Balcombe et al., 2004; Goodwin, 1992) the long-term response should be expected in a period of 5 to 20 years according to the authors. Only Matas (2004) for the Spanish market finds that 95 percent of the effects are realized within 3 years. As shown in the literature, the values for long-term own-price demand elasticities vary from -0.4 to -1.3. However, values significantly greater than 1 are rare in the literature. Among the articles displaying the highest values are Gilbert and Jalilian (1991); Dargay and Hanly (1999) and Romilly (2001) on the British market. On the other hand, a study conducted by Deb and Filippini (2010) on the Indian market leads to relatively small values of long-run elasticities, which the authors interpret as the effect of the low level of development in India and the fact that public transport is still a necessity there.

The fact that long-term elasticities are higher than short-term elasticities has the following implications. First, the full behavioral response to fare changes cannot be properly identified by means of unlagged time-series models. Demand models estimated on cross-section data can only reveal long-run price elasticities. Second, in this industry, the range of responses open to people is larger in the long run. Car ownership decisions require time to be implemented. It is well known that this dynamic aspect of demand is an important consideration in implementing policy strategies.

Another important finding of the literature on own-price elasticities for bus-service demand is that the estimated measures vary with the type of ticket purchased by customers. The common result is that demand for a single ticket is more elastic than demand for a travel pass. Instead of building a price index to analyse the impact of a change in this price on demand, some authors have disaggregated these effects with respect to the different categories of tickets available to the customers. De Rus (1990) estimates fare disaggregated elasticities for bus-transit in Spanish cities and finds that data disaggregated by ticket fare provides a deeper understanding of demand responses. As he finds that price sensitivity decreases as we move from single tickets to the travel pass, he concludes that an aggregate approach fails to allow explicitly for shifts in demand between ticket types and that the role of cross-effects between ticket types is key for the pricing policy. These results are in line with other studies on aggregate data, such as Tegnér and Holmberg (1998) on the Swedish market, and on micro data as in Hensher (1998) and Taplin et al. (1999). However, these last two analyses report smaller values for the elasticities. Matas (2004) in a more recent article with aggregate data on the Spanish market confirms these previous results and concludes that there is scope for a more efficient non-uniform pricing policy with positive effects on demand while minimizing the negative effects on revenue.

Cross-price Elasticities / Substitution Effects

A change in fare for a transport mode can lead a customer to switch to another competitor, within the range of all available urban transport modes available (private car, train, bus, metro or others). These substitution effects between travel modes are important when analysing competition and we present here the main literature findings on these measures.

The common result in the literature is that these substitution effects between modes are of a small magnitude in the short run. However, some authors consider that these findings, combined with higher long-run own-price elasticity for car and bus use, make modal shifts more feasible than often assumed (Goodwin, 1992). Hensher (1998) who distinguishes between fare classes finds that, in the Sydney metropolitan area, the largest cross-elasticity between private car and train travel pass is 0.335 in the event of an increase in the price of car utilization. He also finds that there are more changes between modes for a given fare class than between fare classes within modes. The strongest cross-mode substitution for a given fare class (excluding car) occurs between train and bus single tickets with cross-elasticities of 0.067 and 0.057 for train-to-bus and bus-to-train respectively. Taplin et al. (1999) who aim at improving the methodology presented in Hensher (1998) estimate that the most significant differences observed between the two approaches are a large decrease in the elasticity of demand for car with respect to the price of a ticket for a single trip called Bus Single (from 0.066 to 0.018), and a large increase in Bus Single with respect to car cost (from 0.116 to 0.212). Matas (2004) looks at cross-price elasticities between ticket types and between transport modes. According to his results, bus users are sensitive to both bus and underground prices and quality, whereas underground users are only sensitive to underground characteristics. However, he also concludes that there is not enough information to understand the impact on modal shifts from car to public transport. Dargay and Hanly (1999) observe that the cross-elasticity between bus patronage and motoring costs appears to be negligible in the short run and about 0.3 to 0.4 in the long run. According to them there is some price substitution between bus and car use, although comparatively small. Balcombe et al. (2004) find that, in urban areas outside London, public transport use is sensitive to car costs but car use is much less dependent on public transport costs. Oum et al. (1996) in a study of the Dutch urban market estimate that the relative price of private car must rise significantly to induce a significant number of car drivers to switch to public transport modes.

Trip Purpose / Peak and Off-peak Demand

Fare elasticity is different for different journey purposes. Trips made to go to work or to school are considered as peak demand, whereas trips for leisure or shopping are much more flexible in the time of the day and correspond to an off-peak demand. One would expect fare elasticity to be higher for off-peak demand than for peak demand where customers do not have much choice but to travel. In their review of the literature, Balcombe et al. (2004) observe that the mean off-peak elasticity for buses (precisely, –0.5) is at least twice the peak elasticity (that is, –0.2). This is in line with the World Bank report by Oum et al. (1990) and a literature review by Fowkes et al. (1993). Ivaldi and Viauroux (1999) also find significant differences in urban trip purposes.

Income Elasticities and Car Ownership Effect

Dargay and Hanly (1999) observe that, in the UK, the income elasticity of demand for bus services, which includes car ownership effects, is negative in the long run. This is in line with the literature and suggests that bus transport is an inferior good (see Balcombe et al. 2004; Bresson et al., 2003.) The negative long-run elasticity reflects the effect of income through its positive effect on car ownership and use, and the negative effect of the latter on bus patronage. They estimate that income elasticity ranges between -0.5 to -1 in the long run. However, as car ownership approaches saturation the income elasticity can be expected to become less negative. Romilly (2001) finds a positive value of 0.61 for his long-term income elasticity, suggesting that the economic growth has outweighed the inferior good aspect of the service. Matas (2004) also finds a positive value for the income elasticity (precisely, 0.15) in Spanish cities. He explains the difference with Dargay and Hanly (1999) by the higher population density of Spanish cities, which makes them better suited to public transport use than to car use.

Service Elasticities

Regarding service elasticities, Matas (2004) estimates a service elasticity of 0.24, although he explains that, in aggregate studies, a very crude proxy for the quality of service is used, and it is difficult to give an adequate interpretation of the estimated elasticities. Quality is defined in different ways in different studies and this complicates comparisons of their estimated elasticities which range between 0 and 1. De Rus (1990) finds a high coefficient of variation between the different cities. According to Deb and Filippini (2010) and as expected from the literature, service quality is the most significant policy variable as it has the largest impact on travel demand. Bresson et al. (2003) show that, in France and in the UK, fare and service elasticities are of a similar magnitude (although opposite in sign), so that an increase in fares combined with an equivalent increase in service (vehicle kilometers) would have only marginal effects on patronage.

Methodologies / Discrepancies

Several approaches are used in the literature to compute reliable measures for urban transport demand elasticities. There is common agreement that variances in values for the different elasticities are influenced by several factors, both related to methodological aspects and to features of the industry. In particular, Nijkamp and Pepping (1998) have carried out a comparative analysis of elasticity values of transport demand resulting from 12 studies in various countries. Their analysis indicates that the difference between aggregate (macro-) and disaggregate (micro-) models, as well as with other assumptions, explain the variance in the values of elasticities across studies. They also find that the country involved, the number of competitive modes, and the type of data collected are important factors in accounting for the level of elasticities. These conclusions confirm the findings of Oum et al. (1992) who survey the elements that impact the estimation of demand elasticities in different studies. Oum et al. emphasize the need to take into account intermodal competition because, otherwise, own-price and cross-price elasticities are biased given that they ignore some of the competing services. They also underline that different functional forms can result in widely different elasticity estimates, even with the same set of data. Note that models also differ with the choice of the definition of the dependent variable (whether one considers journeys or passengers-kilometers) and the way fares are aggregated into a price index. They observe that results differ according to the area or country under analysis, which have their own features (in particular for their urban-transit services). This is why they highlight the fact that disaggregated data would lead to a wide range of elasticities as they would reflect unique market conditions. Dargay and Hanly (2002) find a considerable variation in the fare elasticity across counties, ranging from 0 to -3 in the long run. Bresson et al. (2003) in their comparative study between France and the UK confirm the relevance of taking into account countries' heterogeneity. The study by Dargay and Hanly (1999) corroborates the findings of Nijkamp and Pepping (1998) and Oum et al. (1992). First, they find a large variance of elasticities across counties in the UK; second, they conclude that estimated elasticities from different studies are not directly comparable. More precisely, they assess it is inappropriate to apply the value of an estimated elasticity for different circumstances or to average the values of elasticities from different studies.

Further Research

The preceding review of the literature on urban public transport demand highlights some areas for improvement in the methodologies adopted so far. First, models for disaggregated data have rarely been estimated and they would constitute a considerable enhancement in urban public transport demand studies. They would allow us to capture the specific effects of the markets under scrutiny, such as different ticket fares, trip purposes and customer categories. An aggregate elasticity hides these specific effects. Second, more structure could be applied to the models and the interaction between supply and demand could be taken into consideration. Third, the literature suggests that a comprehensive representation of the market is important as we observe significant differences in characteristics across cities. Competition from other modes should be taken into account to avoid bias in the measures of elasticities. Fourth, functional forms have to be chosen carefully as they can lead to very different results, even applied to the same dataset. Econometric testing of different model alternatives would be a useful part of the research agenda.

COMPETITION ANALYSIS

Entry

As a general rule, a firm enters the market only if it can earn positive profits. When entry happens on a significant scale, an incumbent firm is expected to react. In the early deregulation period, the literature focusing on bus competition suggested that entry may be a relevant issue and has shed light on several cases of entry in local markets. Entry usually occurs on the periphery of the incumbent's main market area, particularly if the incumbent has a local reputation.[2] Some smaller operators have attempted to enter on a small scale hoping not to invoke a response from the incumbent firm. The literature suggests however that entry strategies have been unsuccessful in most cases (see Preston, 1988, for an early analysis. Note that the literature does not provide any further evidence of successful entry in the 1990s or the 2000s.)

To explain why entry was unsuccessful in the early deregulation period and why it was scarce in the years following deregulation, an important argument is that the industry is not perfectly contestable. As an indication that the industry is not contestable, we list as a first step the usual conditions which guarantee that a market is perfectly contestable. As a second step, we discuss why these conditions seem not to be met in the bus transportation industry.

According to Banister (1997), Baumol (1987) and Shepherd (1984), a perfectly contestable market requires the following conditions:

- Entry is free;
- Entry is perfectly reversible, that is, sunk costs are zero;
- The incumbent and the entrant have access to the same technology;
- The incumbent and the entrant have equal access to all customers in the market, that is, consumers are not loyal to the incumbent's products; the services of the incumbent and the entrant are easily accessible (for instance, bus terminals can be used by all operators);
- There is an active second hand market for capital assets (for example, the entrant has access to 'cheap' buses for its rolling stock);
- The regulator imposes time lags to prevent sudden changes in prices or withdrawal of services by the incumbent firm. This means that 'hit and run' strategies, where the entrant enters the market over a short period and enjoys high prices, can be implemented.

In a contestable market, any attempt by incumbent firms to earn excessive profits would be unsuccessful. Furthermore, even if there is just one firm offering the service, this firm would be engaged in average cost pricing and have zero profits. If positive profits were obtained, competitors would enter the market and undercut the incumbent's prices and profits. Hence, the important idea is that the mere *threat* of entry forces the incumbent not to behave as a monopoly despite the intrinsic properties of the market which enable it to do so.

The economic literature is unanimous in stating that the local bus transportation industry is not perfectly contestable. In the very first years of deregulation, Beesley

(1990), Button (1988), Evans (1991) and Preston (1988) suggest that many factors prevent the markets from being contestable:

- Existence of barriers to entry: the access to bus stations and the use of travel cards have acted as barriers to entry; the incumbent may have more convenient terminal positions; entrants may not obtain access to bus stations; information points may be manned solely by the incumbent firm's staff and entrant firms may be located at the least attractive stands in the bus station; other practices include the blocking of a rival's bus, occupying a stand or using couriers to persuade customers to use one company's buses in preference to another. Barriers to entry may have been underestimated at the moment of deregulating the market.
- Existence of sunk costs: trained staff (managerial, administrative and platform) is costly. An entrant finds it difficult to hit and run if its employees are not highly qualified.[3]
- Practices which raise rivals' costs: operators may withhold surplus buses from the second hand market, hoping that the price of old buses would increase as their availability decreased, hence making entry to the local market more difficult.
- Economies of experience, economies of scale, economies of density, and economies of scope: the incumbent may have a larger network than the entrant and may therefore be able to offer more attractive area-wide tickets than the entrants; the incumbent may be better known.
- Incumbents can reduce prices very quickly (usually within 24 hours).

During the 1990s, these initial intuitions were confirmed. Evans (1990, 1991) insists on the fact that the incumbents can change their prices immediately in response to entry, since operators are allowed to change fares without notice. As a result, incumbents can enjoy super-normal profits on high density routes. Moreover, the 'experience' input is essential to explain the tactical advantage of the incumbent firm, given that it is usually better informed about different aspects of providing the service. Beesley (1990) claims that barriers to entry are numerous. For instance, garage locations and other property rights play a key role since they directly affect the likelihood that local markets can be opened to competition. The law may itself impede entry: for instance, entrants are required to remain at least six weeks in the market; sub-contracting to drivers is restricted.

Banister (1997) contributes to this view of the industry when he states that the characteristics of the industry and the strategic actions of the incumbent both impede the local transport market from being contestable. In addition to the previous factors, Banister proposes the following characteristics:

- The need to replace the ageing bus fleet, which requires greater capital investment than the smaller companies are able to obtain or willing to risk;
- The fear of competitive disadvantage of the smaller operators against the larger operators is significant in the bus industry;
- Large and small companies do not have access to finance on equal terms. Incumbents tend to have weaker risks of bankruptcy than entrants because they have a larger size and have a bigger purse. The incumbent may own routes else-

where, which earn high profits that can be used to cross-subsidize less competitive routes.

At the same time, Banister sheds light on the possible actions to be taken by the incumbent to reduce the arrival of entrants. These actions are:

- Build up consumer loyalty;
- Establish a reputation for toughness by maintaining a presence in the market;
- Reorganize the network so that economies of scale and density can be obtained;
- Maintain ownership of fixed assets such as terminal, booking and maintenance facilities.

Banister thus concludes unambiguously that

> the theory of contestable markets does not apply to the bus industry. In 1985 it may have been attractive to accept the contestability arguments, but this does not seem to be true anymore ten years after, since the size of operations seems important. The role of the small operators is reduced to competing through the tendering process for the socially necessary services.

After 2000, the initial propositions listed above, on why the industry is not contestable, are corroborated and new claims are made on this issue. First, De Borger and Kerstens (2006) suggest that the rolling stock capital of entering firms has the characteristics of a sunk cost. More importantly, the incumbent's strategic actions impede entry:

- Incumbents can easily cut prices and adjust schedules;
- The incumbent operates the fixed facilities (a central bus station for instance) available that are crucial to exploit network economies (interconnections between different lines or sets of lines), given that the demand structure is characterized by complementarities between lines.

Second, Langridge and Sealey (2000) emphasize the idea of the economies of experience enjoyed by the incumbent. They note for instance that the confederation of Passenger Transport in the UK (the major lobbyist for bus operators, see http://www.cpt-uk.org/) believes that the incumbent operator always has an advantage over the entrant though knowledge and experience, resources (staff), infrastructure and reputation.

New strategic behaviors are emphasized as well. Some of them are related to the idea of combining competitive services and subsidized concessions allocated to operators though competitive tendering. In particular, Langridge and Sealey (2000) note that entrants could minimize barriers related to lower knowledge and experience by entering from a contiguous market in which they had already gained some knowledge and experience and/or entering a local bus market on a small scale, which could be achieved by obtaining contracts with the local authority.[4] At the same time, many incumbents are eager to enter into the new quality partnerships with local authorities, even if this entails supporting high costs of investment in new vehicles and related infrastructure. This suggests that they are looking for long term partnerships through the creation of local monopolies.

Finally, as suggested by Van der Veer (2002), under entry threats, the incumbent may run more buses and increase the frequency of the service (compared to a situation where it is protected from entry) to avoid leaving profitable gaps. Wang and Yang (2005) corroborate these findings; they suggest that deterrence through an increase of the service level is a dominant strategy for an incumbent under various market conditions, which in turn explains the high levels of service in many industries. Accommodation occurs mostly on routes where demand is high. Blockaded entry occurs on routes where demand is low.

Competition in Price or Frequency

Early theoretical models on bus competition have usually been based on strong assumptions which were in most cases unrealistic:

- All operators face the same costs;
- All operators and passengers have complete information about services and fares;
- Operators have information about demand;
- Each passenger has a preferred departure time and is indifferent between immediate backwards and forward rescheduling;
- Traffic conditions are such that journey times are the same throughout the day;
- Departure times and fares of other operators are fixed.

(See Evans, 1987, and Preston, 1988, for a survey.)

Moreover, it has been suggested that service quality matters and is therefore a key factor in bus competition. (See Bly and Oldfield, 1986; Dodgson and Katsoulacos, 1988; Dodgson et al., 1992, 1993; Glaister, 1985, 1986.[5]) In particular, minibuses have been considered as relevant actors in theoretical frameworks with quality differentiation, where competition can be implemented on a horizontal perspective where firms compete in fixed time schedules and prices. Regular buses were thought of as cheap and slow services, while minibuses were associated with lower travel time and higher prices.

These different assumptions have been, to various degrees, criticized later on. The most important criticisms have been related to the assumptions of quality differences and price competition. Preston (1988) suggests that consumers have difficulties in perceiving quality differences. Moreover consumers' loyalty to a particular firm seems to be unrealistic: Users usually board the first bus that arrives. A model's outcome of two firms offering distinct qualities of service and charging different fares has not been as common as might be expected.[6] Such a model of competition would probably be more relevant in explaining inter-modal competition.

Thus, it seems to have been accepted that competition has tended to take the form of service wars with fares matching. Passengers board the first bus that arrives, hence making frequency the key factor for competition. Competition in fares has been mainly restricted to branded ticketing such as system passes, return ticketing, multi-rider tickets or discount vouchers; branded ticketing is thus seen as a tool for operators to increase the consumer's incentives to be loyal to one specific company – it is an attempt by operators to develop strategic barriers to entry (see Fernández and Muñoz, 2007).

Later on, many authors, such as Van Reeven and Janssen (2006) and Wang and Yang (2005) have confirmed these early intuitions. Price competition (and therefore price reduction) is not particularly prevalent in the bus industry.[7] Operators have limited scope for meaningful product differentiation that could make consumers loyal.

However, on long distance services such as intercity bus services, consumers' loyalty and price competition (through higher services quality) are more relevant. In this case, quality matters, and ticket prices constitute an important fraction of the generalized price paid by consumers. Hence, product differentiation on long-distance routes makes entrants resistant to pricing and scheduling responses of incumbent operators. Scheduling competition is more stable in this case.

Random Schedules

The previous section suggests that competition mostly takes the form of frequency wars. Analysts then go a step further when they explain that the arrival time of a bus at a stop is random.

Ellis and Silva (1998), Gomez-Lobo (2007), Oldale (1998) and Van Reeven and Janssen (2006) all agree on the fact that the incentives for price competition are smaller than what was expected, even if more than one operator is present on a local transport market. Two main reasons explain this result. First, users do not particularly care for quality difference, and second, they incur a cost if they want to shop around for the lowest priced bus. Contrary to Evans (1987), which assumes that operators' services are scheduled, these authors consider some degree of uncertainty surrounding arrival times at bus stops. In their model, users arrive at a stop and will wait for the arrival of the next bus. An important assumption is that the distribution of passengers across time is uniform, that is, there are no masses of passengers clustered around departure points. The optimal reaction of the bus operators consists then of randomizing arrival schedules at the bus stop, and setting the highest possible prices.

Given that consumers do not differentiate between one bus company from another, random frequencies have to be expected for the following reasons. Some buses may bunch together or some may be alone at a given position in time and space. In the first case, each operator has an incentive to drive just in front of the others. Thus, a profile where each bus is alone in a position cannot be an equilibrium either, since buses have an incentive to fall back and drive just in front of the next bus that is following behind. These techniques are known as head running and leapfrogging.[8] Hence, randomizing the arrival at a bus stop is the best strategy for each operator competing on the same route, and this forces the rivals to guess the arrival time of their competitors. A striking example is the case of Manchester in the UK, where the first two years of deregulation were characterized by services changing between 1500 to 2000 times annually. Bus companies cannot credibly provide timetable information. In these conditions, competition does not guarantee low prices.

A RESEARCH AGENDA

The economic literature proposes a number of arguments as to why bus competition might be limited in liberalized industries. Several reasons could explain such a situation. First, the technology used in the industry favors large and experienced operators and therefore impedes the entry of new competitors on an equivalent scale. Second, the fact that the transportation service occurs on short distances restricts the incentives of the consumers to look for the cheapest operator and/or the company offering the highest quality standards. Price competition is therefore likely to be very limited, even on routes where more than one operator is present. Note that, where there is no regulation providing incentives to bus companies to comply with the time schedules, there is no guarantee of a proper coordination of consumers at bus stops, which again limits the scope for competition.

As pointed out above, most of the contributions drawn from the economic literature are theoretically derived, although based on experts' knowledge and experience. Although these theoretical arguments are intuitive and convincing, they often wait to be empirically validated. There are potential avenues of investigation.

First, one should test the contestability of the market. It is well known that, if a technology exhibits increasing returns to scale, then the associated industry is highly concentrated or is operated by a single firm. In this case, the presence of too many production units prevents the efficient size of the industry being reached, which could be socially costly. Without entering into the details of this theory, this result invites us to evaluate the level of economies of scale and scope, which is usually performed by means of the estimation of cost functions. To do so, one can use data at the depot or firm level. Now, the question of the adequate level of disaggregation to measure output in a network industry is still open and subject to research. However, if estimating firms' cost functions is crucial to characterize the economic fundamentals of the bus industry, recall that such an exercise is not immune from other constraints that the firms are facing, such as the regulatory conditions. For instance, the local regulators may impose different quality targets, or the driving conditions may vary from one urban network to another, and this may explain cost differences across local areas.

Second, another set of evidence supporting the non-constestability of the bus industry can be achieved though the detection of predatory pricing. Following Motta (2004), predatory pricing implies that the incumbent sets low prices for a period and sacrifices short-run profits, so that the entrant believes that positive profits cannot be obtained. When the entrant leaves the market, the incumbent then increases prices and reaches high profits again, which in the long run outweigh possible losses incurred by foreclosing entry. Note that observing that entry occurs is not enough to conclude that the market is competitive or that there are no predatory practices. To properly detect predation, prices should be compared to marginal and average costs. Following Motta, a test of predation could be implemented as follows. First, from the estimated cost function, we can evaluate total and marginal costs. Second, actual prices must be compare to these estimated costs: (1) If the price is above total average costs, then the presumption is that the firms are not taking predatory actions; (2) if the price is below total average costs but above marginal costs, then predation should not be presumed, but the burden of proof is on the side of the competition authority; (3) If the price is below marginal costs, then there is a case for predation. Again note however that these tests should not be applied without taking into account the regulatory and competition constraints. Indeed regulation of prices and services or competition from other transport modes could clearly affect the pricing strategies of bus companies.

Third, one should test the theoretical prediction that, companies do not compete on prices at the route level in the short run. There are at least two ways to test this assertion. There is a direct approach that consists of estimating a structural model of the industry that comprises a demand function and a pricing equation. This approach could be implemented using models specified along the line of the econometrics of differentiated products markets (see Davis and Garces, 2010, for a presentation of these models). There is also an indirect approach that is easier to carry out. It is indirect in the sense that it tests a necessary condition not a sufficient condition, namely that the number of firms on the market has no effect on the price level. This approach relies on the structure–conduct–performance paradigm which states that the structure of a market determines the operators' pricing conduct and therefore their profitability. The ability to obtain significant profits is inversely related to the number of firms and/or their market share, and thus is positively correlated with concentration. If operators do not compete on price, as suggested by the economic literature, a non-significant *long-lasting* relationship between the price and the variable measuring the degree of presence of firms on the market should be obtained. Note that one should similarly test for the impact of the market structure on frequencies.

The research agenda is thus particularly rich. It is also urgent as the effectiveness of competition in the bus industry becomes a crucial issue in many countries over the world.

ACKNOWLEDGMENTS

This chapter is drawn from a report commissioned by the Competition Commission and published at http://www.competition-commission.org.uk/inquiries/ref2010/localbus/pdf/ 100929_Review_of_economic_literature.pdf. We would like to thank Robin Finer and his team at the Competition Commission for their helpful insights and remarks. The views expressed in the paper, and any remaining errors, are solely ours.

NOTES

1. Note that De Borger and Kerstens (2006), Brons et al. (2005) and Berechman (1993) have surveyed the literature on technical efficiency for bus transit.
2. Note moreover that, during this period, several factors have favored entry; these factors are: the management of the entrant firm has personal knowledge of the area chosen for entry; or the entrant may have hired former employees of the incumbent firm. Beesley (1990) notes that the population density and the incumbent's initial market power are other factors, which influence positively the likelihood of entry.
3. Highly skilled employees are so important in the production process that it is not uncommon to observe bus operators attempting to recruit a rival's staff by offering higher wages and better work conditions.
4. They also shed light on the fact that, if the incumbent is unsuccessful in the tendering process, it may attempt to provide subsequently a commercial service in order to force the withdrawal of the rival of the tendered service.
5. See also Nash (1985), for a discussion of Glaister's assumptions. A more recent contribution on differences in service quality is Yang et al. (2001).
6. Note that, currently, there are a number of low cost/'no frills' bus companies in towns across the UK that compete with higher quality offerings by the larger operators. (for example, Whippet bus in Cambridge).
7. Recently, price competition models have been proposed by various authors. See, for instance, Zhou et al. (2005). Their model is, however, more relevant to describing bus operators' habits in developing countries, such as China and other Asian countries, or modernized cities with high-density population, such as Hong Kong and Singapore.

8. Other older "bad habits" of bus operators are discussed in Forster and Golay (1986). They entail "hanging back" (the buses go slowly so as to pick up as much traffic as possible), "missing out a bus stop" (if the driver decides that there are too few passengers to stop for), "turning" (a nearly empty bus turns around before the end of the route and go back in the opposite direction), or "overtaking".

REFERENCES

Balcombe, R., R. Mackett, N. Paulley, J. Preston, J. Shires, H. Titheridge, M. Wardman and P. White, 2004, The demand for public transport: a practical guide. Report TRL 593, Transport Research Laboratory.

Banister, D., 1997, Bus deregulation in the UK. In J. McConville, ed., *Transport Regulation Matters*. London: Pinter, pp. 31–53.

Baumol, W.J., 1987, Natural monopoly and contestable market analysis. In A. Gillie, L. Levacic and G. Thompson, eds, *Politics and Economic Policy*. London: Hodder and Stoughton, pp. 229–243.

Beesley, M.E., 1990, Collusion, predation and merger in the UK bus industry. *Journal of Transport Economics and Policy*, **24**, 295–310.

Berechman, J., 1993, *Public transit economics and deregulation policy*. Amsterdam: North-Holland.

Bly, P.H. and R.H. Oldfield, 1986, Competition Between minibuses and regular bus services. *Journal of Transport Economics and Policy*, **20** (1,) 47–68.

Bresson, G., J. Dargay et al., 2003, The main determinants of the demand for public transport: a comparative analysis of England and France using shrinkage estimators. *Transportation Research Part A*, **37** (7), 605–627.

Brons, M., P. Nijkamp, E. Pels and P. Rietveld, 2005, Efficiency of urban public transit: a meta analysis. *Transportation*, **32**, 1–21.

Button, K.J., 1988, Contestability in the UK bus industry, experience goods and economies of experience. In J.S. Dodgson and N. Topham, eds, *Bus Deregulation and Privatization: An International Perspective*. Aldershot, UK: Avebury and Brookfield, 1988.

Cerasi, V., B. Chizzolini and M. Ivaldi, 2010, The impact of mergers on the degree of competition in the banking industry. CEPR Working Paper.

Cowie, J., 2002, Acquisition, efficiency and scale economies, an analysis of the British bus industry. *Transport Reviews*, **22** (2), 147–157.

Cowie, J. and D. Asenova, 1999, Organisation form, scale effects and efficiency in the British bus industry. *Transportation*, **26**, 231–248.

Dargay, J. and M. Hanly, 1999, Bus fare elasticities. Report to the UK Department of the Environment, Transport and the Regions. London, ESRC Transport Studies Unit, University College London, 132.25.

Dargay, J. and M. Hanly, 2002, The demand for local bus services in England. *Journal of Transport Economics and Policy*, **36** (1), 73–91.

Davis, P. and E. Garces, 2010, *Quantitative Techniques for Competition and Antitrust Analysis*. Princeton, NJ: Princeton University Press.

Deb, K. and M. Filippini, 2010, Public bus transport demand elasticities in India. Quaderni della facoltà di Scienze economiche dell'Università di Lugano, number 1002.

De Borger, B. and K. Kerstens, 2006, The performance of bus-transit operators. Working Paper.

De Rus, G. and G. Nombela, 1997, Privatisation of urban bus services in Spain. *Journal of Transport Economics and Policy*, **31**, 115–129.

De Rus, G., 1990 Public transport demand elasticities in Spain. *Journal of Transport Economics and Policy*, **24** (2), 189–201.

Dodgson, J.S. and Y. Katsoulacos, 1988, Quality competition in bus services. Some welfare implications of bus deregulation. *Journal of Transport Economics and Policy*, **22** (3), 263–281.

Dodgson, J.S., Y. Katsoulacos and C.R. Newton, 1992, A modelling framework for the empirical analysis of predatory behaviour in the bus services industry. *Regional Science and Urban Economics*, **22**, 51–70.

Dodgson, J.S., Y. Katsoulacos and C.R. Newton, 1993, Application of the economic modelling approach to the investigation of predation. *Journal of Transport Economics and Policy*, **27** (2), 153–168.

Ellis, J. and E.C.D. Silva, 1998, British bus deregulation: competition and demand coordination. *Journal of Urban Economics*, **43**, 336–361.

Evans, A., 1990, Competition and the structure of local bus markets. *Journal of Transport Economics and Policy*, **24**, 255–281.

Evans, A., 1987, A theoretical comparison of competition with other economic regimes for bus services. *Journal of Transport Economics and Policy*, **21** (1), 7–36.

Evans, A.W., 1991, Are urban bus services natural monopolies? *Transportation*, **18**, 131–150.

Farsi, M., A. Fetz, and M. Filippini, 2007, Economies of scale and scope in local public transportation. *Journal of Transport Economics and Policy*, **41**, 345–361.

Farsi, M., M. Filippini and M. Kuenzle, 2006, Cost efficiency in regional bus companies: an application of new stochastic frontier models. *Journal of Transport Economics and Policy*, **40** (1), 95–118.

Fazioli, R., M. Filippini and P. Prioni, 1993, Cost-structure and efficiency of local public transport: the case of Emilia Romagna bus companies. *International Journal of Transport Economics*, **20** (3), 305–324.

Fernández, J.E. and J.C. Muñoz, 2007, Privatization and deregulation of urban bus services: an analysis of fare evolution mechanisms. *Journal of Transport Economics and Policy*, **41**, 25–49.

Filippini, M. and P. Prioni, 2003, The influence of ownership on the cost of bus service provision in Switzerland: an empirical illustration, *Applied Economics*, **35** (6) 683–90.

Foster, C. and J. Golay, 1986, Some curious old practices and their relevance to equilibrium in bus competition. *Journal of Transport Economics and Policy*, **20**, 191–216.

Fowkes, A.S., N. Sherwood and C.N. Nash, 1993, Segmentation of the travel market in London and estimates of elasticities and value of travel time. ITS Working Paper 345, University of Leeds.

Gagnepain, P. and M. Ivaldi, 2002a, Incentive regulatory policies: the case of public transit systems in France. *Rand Journal of Economics*, **33** (4), 605–629.

Gagnepain, P. and M. Ivaldi, 2002b, Stochastic frontiers and asymmetric information models. *Journal of Productivity Analysis*, **18** (2), 145–159.

Garcia-Sanchez, I.M., 2009, Technical and scale efficiency in Spanish urban transport: estimating with data envelopment analysis. *Advances in Operations Research*, Vol. 2009, Article ID 721279.

Gilbert, C.L. and H. Jalilian, 1991, The demand for travelcards on London regional transport. *Journal of Transport Economics and Policy*, **25** (1), 3–29.

Glaister, S., 1985, Competition on an urban bus route. *Journal of Transport Economics and Policy*, **19**, 65–81.

Glaister, S., 1986, Bus deregulation, competition and vehicle size. *Journal of Transport Economics and Policy*, **20** (2), 217–244.

Gomez-Lobo, A., 2007, Why competition does not work in urban bus markets: some new wheels for some old ideas. *Journal of Transport Economics and Policy*, **41**, 283–308.

Goodwin, P.B., 1992, A review of new demand elasticities with special reference to short and long run effects of price changes. *Journal of Transport Economics and Policy*, **26** (2), 155–186.

Hensher, D.A., 1998, Establishing a fare elasticity regime for urban passenger transport. *Journal of Transport Economics and Policy*, **32** (2), 221–246.

Hensher, D.A. and I.P. Wallis, 2005, Competitive tendering as a contracting mechanism for subsidising transport: the bus experience, *Journal of Transport Economics and Policy*, **39**, 295–321.

Heseltine, P.M. and D.T. Silcock, 1990, The effects of bus deregulation on costs. *Journal of Transport Economics and Policy*, **24**, 239–254.

Ivaldi, M. and C. Viauroux, 1999, A parsimonious approach to multidimensional choice models of urban transport. Mimeo IDEI.

Kerstens, K., 1996, Technical efficiency measurement and explanation of French urban transit companies. *Transportation Research Part A*, **30** (6), 431–452.

Kerstens K., 1999, Decomposing technical efficiency and effectiveness of French urban transport. *Annales d'Economie et de Statistique*, **54**, 129–155.

Langridge, R. and R. Sealey, 2000, Contestability in the UK bus industry? The National Bus Company, and the Tilling Mark II effect. *Transport Policy*, **7**, 105–115.

Lovell, C.A.K., 1993, Production frontiers and productive efficiency. In H. Fried, C.A.K. Lovell and S.S. Schmidt, eds, *The Measurement of Productive Efficiency: Techniques and Applications*. Oxford: Oxford University Press.

Matas, A., 2004, Demand and revenue implications of an integrated public transport policy: the case of Madrid. *Transport Reviews*, **24** (2), 195–217.

Matas, A. and J.L. Raymond, 1998, Technical characteristics and efficiency of urban bus companies. *Transportation*, **25**, 243–263.

Motta, M., 2004, *Competition Policy, Theory and Practice*. Cambridge: Cambridge University Press.

Nash, C.A., 1985, Competition on an urban bus route: a comment. *Journal of Transport Economics and Policy*, **19**, 313–319.

Nijkamp, P. and G. Pepping, 1998, Meta-analysis for explaining the variance in public transport demand elasticities in Europe. *Journal of Transportation and Statistics*, **1** (1), 1–14.

Odeck J. and O. Sunde, 2001, The relative efficiency of public and private bus companies? APRES 2001.

Oldale, A., 1998, Local bus deregulation and timetable inability. LSE working paper, no. EI/21.

Oum, T.H., H.P.C. van Ooststroom, and J.H. Yoon, 1996, The structure of travel demands in the Netherlands: an application to predict modal shares under the sustainable development goals. *International Journal of Transport Economics*, **23** (1), 31–62.

Oum, T.H., W.G. Waters and J.S. Yong, 1990, A survey of recent estimates of price elasticities of demand for transport. World Bank Working Paper, WPS 359.

Oum, T.H., W. G., Waters and J.S. Yong, 1992, Concepts of price elasticities of transport demand and recent empirical estimates. *Journal of Transport Economics and Policy*, **26** (2), 139–154.

Preston, J., 1988, Regulation, competition and market structure: a literature review of the stage bus industry. Working paper no. 267, University of Leeds.

Romilly, P., 2001, Subsidy and local bus service deregulation in Britain: a re-evaluation. *Journal of Transport Economics and Policy,* **35** (2), 161–193.

Roy, W. and A. Yvrande-Billon, 2007, Contractual practices and technical efficiency: the case of urban public transport in France. *Journal of Transport Economics and Policy*, **41** (2), 257–282.

Sakano, R. and K. Obeng, 1995, Re-examination of inefficiencies in urban transit systems: a stochastic frontier approach. *Logistics and Transportation Review*, **31**, 377–392.

Salas O., 1998, Technical efficiency during deregulation of the urban bus system in Sweden. Working Papers in Economics No 4.

Shaw-Er, J., W. Chiang and Y.-W. Chen, 2005, Cost structure and technological change of local public transport: the Kaohsiung city bus case. *Applied Economics*, **37** (12), 1399–1410.

Shepherd, W.G., 1984, Contestability versus competition. *The American Economic Review*, **74**, 572–587.

Taplin, J.H.E., D.A. Hensher and B. Smith, 1999, Preserving the symmetry of estimated commuter travel elasticities. *Transportation Research Part B*, **33**, 215–232.

Tegnér, G. and I. Holmberg, 1998, Public transport demand analysis: a non-linear time-series model for Stockholm region. Transportation Planning Methods, Volume I, European Transport Conference, Proceedings of Seminar Dvol. P423, 277–290.

Van der Veer, J.P., 2002, Entry deterrence and quality provision in the local bus market. *Transport Reviews*, **22**, 247–265.

Van Reeven, P. and M.C.W. Janssen, 2006, Stable service patterns in scheduled transport competition. *Journal of Transport Economics and Policy*, **40**, 135–160.

Viton, P. A., 1993, How big should transit be? Evidence on the benefits of reorganization from the San Francisco Area. *Transportation*, **20**, 35–57.

Viton P.A., 1997, Technical efficiency in multi-mode bus transit: a production frontier analysis. *Transportation Research Part B*, **31** (1), 23–39.

Wang, J.Y.T. and H. Yang, 2005, A game theoretic analysis of competition in a deregulated bus market. *Transportation Research Part E*, **41**, 329–355.

Wunsch, P., 1996, Cost and productivity of major urban transit systems in Europe: an exploratory analysis. *Journal of Transport Economics and Policy*, **30**, 171–186.

Yang, H., H.Y. Kong and Q. Meng, 2001, Value of time distributions and competitive bus services. *Transportation Research Part E*, **37**, 411–424.

Zhou, J., W.H.K. Lam and B.G. Heydecker, 2005, The generalized Nash equilibrium model for oligopolistic transit market with elastic demand. *Transportation Research Part B*, **39**, 479–563.

33 Competition and regulation in rail transport
Chris Nash

INTRODUCTION

The railway revolution of the nineteenth century saw railways established as the dominant mode of transport, in many countries built by private profit-seeking companies.
Even after the rise of motorized road transport after World War I robbed them of this
dominance, railways have remained very important in countries with large volumes of
freight moving very long distance, such as North America, Russia, India and China and
in countries with large amounts of medium-distance passenger transport in Europe and
Japan. Railways also play a key role in commuter transport in large cities worldwide.
However with the growth of road transport competition came serious financial problems
for the railways, and a need to reconsider how they were provided.

For more than a hundred years, it was assumed throughout most of the world that
railways were natural monopolies and that they needed tight regulation to make them
perform in the public interest. It is true that in some countries, most notably the United
States, there was a policy of maintaining competition between parallel privately owned
railroads offering a choice of railroad between all major points, but this did not stop
the United States from implementing tight control on freight rates and on decisions to
abandon track (Winston, 2006). In most other countries, railways were regulated, and by
the end of the 1940s they were largely government owned.

In the United States, legislation in 1970 separated loss-making long-distance passenger
services into a government-owned company operating over the tracks of the freight companies. In 1980, as part of a general trend towards deregulation, the Staggers Act greatly
reduced regulatory control over rates and abandonments, in the belief that competition
from other modes and between alternative sources of supply was enough to prevent the
abuse of monopoly power in most cases (Winston, 2006). There was no attempt to introduce more intramodal competition in the rail sector as part of this reform and indeed
continued mergers reduced the degree to which even two competitors survived between
all major points. Nor was there any suggestion of separating infrastructure from operations, or for the most part of providing mandatory access to the infrastructure of one
operator for other operators.

Attempts to introduce increased competition within the rail network were pioneered
in Europe in the 1990s, and followed the standard network industry argument that the
natural monopoly element of a public utility was the infrastructure (Vickers and Yarrow,
1988); by separating this from operations it would be possible to have competing operators running over the same track. Thus in many European countries infrastructure is
now in the hands of a completely different organization from operations, there is now
complete open access to the infrastructure for new entrants in the freight sector within
the European Union, and international passenger services including cabotage provided
that they do not threaten the financial stability of domestic services operated under

public service obligations; consideration is being given to completely opening up the domestic passenger market to competition as well. The one country to have followed this vertical separation model elsewhere is Australia, at least regarding the interstate network, although Russia is moving in the same direction. This model has hardly led to a reduction in regulation, however, with a new requirement for all European Union members to have a regulatory body independent of the infrastructure manager.

In the meantime, by the 1990s, the disastrous economic position of many railways in Latin America led to the development of another model in which long vertically integrated concessions were offered by means of competitive tendering for discrete parts of the network.(Thompson, 2003). This is a way of introducing competition for the market rather than competition in the market. It is an approach which has been much used for passenger services in Europe, Australia and North America, although often with separation of infrastructure and operations. In some other countries, privatization was pursued without other restructuring, so in New Zealand a single vertically integrated railway was privatized with no requirement to offer access to other operators; in Japan, in 1987 the national rail network was split into a set of regional vertically integrated passenger companies, and the shares of the more profitable ones sold to the private sector, with a government-owned freight company operating over their tracks. By contrast, despite extensive debates, the major railways of India and China remain largely on the traditional vertically integrated state-owned model.

Thus, we now have a wide variety of organizational and regulatory structures for the rail industry, which should provide good evidence on what approaches to competition and regulation work best and in what circumstances. The following sections will explore these different approaches in more detail. First, we discuss the literature on railway cost functions and what it can tell us about the implications for costs of the various approaches. We then consider research on the specific issues of vertical separation, open access competition for freight and passenger traffic, franchising for freight and passenger traffic and regulation and infrastructure charges, before reaching our conclusions.

THE IMPLICATIONS OF ALTERNATIVE APPROACHES FOR COSTS

An important starting point for the consideration of these alternative approaches is the literature on estimation of rail cost functions. Rail cost functions generally relate costs to output of passenger services, output of freight services and route kilometers operated. The measures of output may be train kilometers or passenger and freight tonne kilometers; given that particularly for passenger traffic, both commercial and social considerations dictate operation of a frequency of service higher than would minimize costs, there is an argument for the former. Obviously, further disaggregation would be desirable; bulk freight trains and container trains have different costs, as do long distance, commuter and regional passenger trains.

If an equal proportionate increase in all outputs and route kilometers leads to the same proportionate increase in costs, then the railway is said to experience constant returns to scale. If an equal proportionate increase in all outputs holding route kilometers constant leads to the same proportionate increase in costs, then it is said to have constant returns to density. If splitting the production of passenger and freight outputs and of infrastructure into two or more companies (that is separating infrastructure from operations, separating freight and passenger operations or separating all three) leads to increased costs, the railway is said to experience economies of scope.

Thus, the key questions about alternative approaches to rail organization in terms of rail costs are what will be the impact on costs of:

- Having parallel vertically integrated railways serving the same routes – will there be loss of economies of density?
- Separating infrastructure from operations – will there be loss of economies of scope between the two, and are there transactions costs from having the two in separate hands?
- Separating freight from passenger operations – will there be loss of economies of scope here?

Extensive research on the estimation of cost functions for vertically integrated US railroads (Caves et al., 1987; Keeler 1974) has clearly established that railways are subject to major economies of traffic density, or in other words doubling the amount of traffic over a given route leads to a less than doubling of costs. This means that any attempt to introduce competition by having parallel companies serving the same routes is likely to have a cost penalty if each has its own infrastructure. These economies of density clearly result from the fact that higher density traffic leads to better utilization of indivisible infrastructure (a single track railway already has substantial capacity; widening it to two tracks segregated by direction of traffic can increase capacity four fold, and a four track route also segregated by speed achieves a more than proportionate increase again). If this were the sole source of economies of traffic density then having competing operators over the same track would not lead to a loss of such economies. However, there is evidence that economies of traffic density actually apply to train operations as well, since where density is higher it is possible to operate longer better loaded trains and through trains to a greater number of destinations (Grimm and Harris, 1983). Thus having competing operators over the same infrastructure is likely to incur some cost penalties. By contrast, these same studies find no evidence of economies of scale, suggesting that – at least in American conditions – there is no cost penalty to having a number of regionally separated vertically integrated rail companies as then existed. However, in a study of European railways prior to the separation of infrastructure and operations, Preston (1996) found 'U' shaped cost curves in which economies of density gave way to diseconomies for the most densely trafficked European railways, whilst economies of scale did exist for the smaller European systems. The optimal size of a vertically integrated rail system in European circumstances appeared to be roughly that of Norway, with 37 m train kilometer per annum on 4000 km of track. A later study by Smith et al. (2009) found that, after vertical separation, British passenger train franchisees – with 20–25 companies operating in total some 120 m train km per annum over 17000 km of track – displayed slight economies of scale but again strong economies of density, suggesting that having competing passenger companies operating over the same track would be an expensive solution.

A number of studies have also found costs involved in separating infrastructure from

Table 33.1   Approaches to railway organization

Geographical area	Nature of traffic	Solution
America	Freight dominated	Vertically integrated freight railways Separate passenger operator.
Europe	Mixed	Vertical separation with open access freight competitors Franchised passenger services
Japan	Passenger dominated	Vertically integrated regional passenger operators, separated freight
India, China	Very heavy passenger and freight traffic	Vertically integrated railways providing both passenger and freight services

operations resulting from a loss of economies of scope (for example, Bitzan, 2003). Moreover there also appear to be economies of scope from having the some operator providing different types of freight service (Ivaldi and McCullough, 2001); although Cantos (2001) finds statistically insignificant evidence of diseconomies of scope between freight and passenger operations for European railways, this may simply reflect the effects of congestion on shared infrastructure, which is not avoided by placing these operations in separate companies.

This might suggest that the most appropriate form of competition to introduce into the rail sector is to offer franchises for a single vertically integrated company. Any reform that leads away from having a single vertically integrated monopolist appears to involve some cost disadvantages. But breaking up such monopolies may have advantages as well. On track competition may be seen as having a greater impact on quality of service and technical and dynamic efficiency than an occasional franchise competition. Passenger services very often involve government intervention into service and pricing decisions to a degree not found in freight, together with the provision of subsidies, suggesting that competition for a franchise will work, when on track competition may not. There is an argument from a marketing point of view that the passenger and freight markets are totally separate and need separate approaches, and also that freight services get more priority when in the hands of a separate organization not subject to the political pressure that often accompanies passenger services. Moreover freight flows are often very different geographically and require different management configurations than passenger traffic.

Thus, it is not surprising that different geographical circumstances lead to different solutions (Table 33.1). In a passenger dominated railway, there may be strong advantages in having regional or route based vertically integrated passenger franchises, with most traffic contained within the franchise, but the very different pattern of freight flows may suggest a separate freight operator operating over the tracks of the passenger companies. In a freight-dominated railway, the argument is the reverse. Where passenger and freight are both important, and there is a fear that placing the infrastructure with one may disadvantage the other, there is an argument for complete separation on the European model. But where traffic is very dense, the interaction between the different types of traffic and the infrastructure manager is particularly complex, and it may be unsurprising that in these cases movement away from a single vertically integrated operator is cautious (Wu and Nash, 2000).

It seems that very different solutions are best for different circumstances. But this does not necessarily imply that what we currently have is in all cases optimal. For instance, whilst vertically integrated freight operators might make sense for North America, one may certainly ask whether there would be benefits in America from on-track competition for freight, and whether this has worked in Australia, where with a somewhat similar traffic mix it has been implemented. Would the Japanese approach of vertically integrated regional passenger companies work better in Europe than that actually taken, at least away from the main freight corridors where passenger traffic dominates? Or would Japan have done better to introduce more competition by competitive tendering for passenger franchises?

The aim of the rest of this chapter is to examine the extent to which the evidence enables questions like these to be answered.

VERTICAL SEPARATION

The massive increases in infrastructure costs in Britain which followed the bankruptcy of Railtrack are often quoted as arguments against separation of infrastructure from operations, but a number of other factors appear to have been involved here, including weak regulation, mismanagement by Railtrack of its maintenance contracts and an inherited backlog of renewals (Nash et al., 2005). Complete separation in some other countries, such as Sweden, appears to have worked much better (Nilsson, 2002a). More formal econometric evidence on the impact of vertical separation is limited and inconsistent. Not surprisingly, there is clear evidence that the level of infrastructure investment affects both passenger and freight train operating costs (Cantos, 2001) although what is surprising is that whilst it appears to reduce freight train operating costs it increases those for passenger. So it is obvious that any vertical separation will have to provide incentives or regulation to ensure adequate infrastructure investment. Reference has already been made to US studies showing that vertical separation raises costs (for example, Bitzan, op. cit.), but these take evidence solely from vertically integrated freight railways and ask what would happen to train operating costs if infrastructure spending were reduced to zero and vice versa, rather than what would happen if infrastructure spending were in the hands of another organization. Three studies have attempted to examine the evidence of European railways post privatization; whilst Friebel et al. (2003) find no clear conclusion, both the others (Growitsch and Wetzel, 2009; Rivera-Trujillo, 2004) find that vertical separation raises costs, although in the latter case the result is very variable from one country to another.

The most obvious explanation for this lies in the transactions costs involved (Merkert, 2007). Following Williamson (1985), Merkert postulates that high transactions costs arise from asset specificity, complexity and uncertainty in the relationship between infrastructure managers and train operators. Given the long-term nature of railway assets, it is likely that infrastructure managers and train operating companies will require long-run contracts, setting out procedures for the interaction of the two and with penalty clauses for poor performance, which in turn need to be monitored and disputes as to the causes of poor performance resolved. Bouf et al. (2005) argue that the main areas in which conflicts between infrastructure managers and train operators may occur are the following:

- Network changes, where investment plans have to be agreed and their cost shared amongst the interested parties (given the existence of joint costs, this leaves scope for attempts at free riding by different train operating companies);
- Access and timetable establishment (where different operators may be competing for the same paths; a particular source of dispute here seems to be the planning of track maintenance and renewals, where complete line closures are the most efficient approach for the infrastructure manager but very disruptive for operators);
- Delays and disruption (which may be caused by faults on the part of the infrastructure manager or one of the train operators; given their daily occurrence, monitoring and agreement on responsibility is necessarily expensive).

However, Merkert (2009) finds that, whilst transactions costs are higher in vertically separated systems, the increase is a small proportion (less than 1 percent) of total costs. Thus, the explanation for substantial economies of scope between infrastructure and operations must lie elsewhere, for instance, in better alignment of incentives and increased pressure on the costs of the infrastructure manager. If we wish to introduce competition, whether on track or by franchising, there is an argument for some form of vertical separation. In the case of on-track competition, it is clear that if one of the train operators is also responsible for infrastructure, it will have an incentive to favor its own services, both in planning and in real-time operations. The key question then is whether an independent regulator can fully overcome this problem. In the case of franchises, the argument for separation is less strong, particularly where a geographical split of franchises into relatively self-contained networks is possible. But in a complex network, with services to a wide variety of destinations sharing tracks over part of the route, it will be inevitable that vertically integrated franchises will run over each others tracks, unless the network is franchised as a single entity, in which case it may be difficult to maintain a number of competing bidders, as the losers would have no chance of participating in the market until the time came for refranchising. Obviously growth of an international franchising market reduces this problem.

European Union legislation initially just required accounting separation, with non-discriminatory infrastructure charges and slot allocation. However, there were many complaints that the timetabling process and other requirements regarding safety certification of vehicles, driver training and so forth were used by vertically integrated companies (House of Lords, 2005). Thus further legislation was introduced requiring at least that infrastructure charges and slot allocation should be the responsibility of a body not engaged in train operation, that appeal should be available to a regulator independent of the infrastructure manager, and that specified harmonized procedures should be followed regarding safety certification. Nevertheless, there remains a suspicion that the most effective way of ensuring non-discriminatory access is by complete separation of infrastructure from operations.

Different degrees of separation are also to be found (Nash, 2008). In some European countries (for example, Germany, Austria, Italy), infrastructure and operations remain separate subsidiaries of the same holding company (with disputes between them, investment plans and so forth handled at the holding company level), whilst in others (for example, Sweden, the Netherlands, Britain) they are completely separate organizations. Most remarkable is the case of France, where there is a completely separate state-owned infrastructure manager (RFF) but it contracts all operations, maintenance and renewal work back to the dominant state owned operator, SNCF (thus permitting close integration of infrastructure and train operations at the day-to-day level). Obviously both these approaches may afford economies of scope but may also give the opportunity for discrimination. It has been suggested in Britain that infrastructure may be leased to the franchisee, as happens in Latin America; with the change of government in 2010, an experiment with this approach on a franchise well segregated from the rest of the network has been suggested. In India, the first small move towards permitting new entry has come via allowing new container operators to provide their own terminals and wagons and run their own trains, but they must not only pay for track access but also hire drivers and locomotives from Indian Railways (Singh, 2007). All these arrangements try to reduce the costs of separation, but at the expense of opportunity and motivation for discrimination to favor the integrated operator. Of course, continued links between the infrastructure manager and the dominant operator only reduce transactions costs where there is a dominant operator, so the argument for such an approach is that there can be sufficient competition to force the operator to behave efficiently, whilst the dominant operator retains perhaps 90 percent of the market as in Germany (Kirchner, 2005).

OPEN ACCESS COMPETITION FOR FREIGHT AND PASSENGER TRAFFIC

Although access to each others' tracks may be offered as part of a freely negotiated commercial contract between two operators, and mandated access for other freight operators has been a condition of allowing merger in some US cases, as well as some freight franchises in Latin America, in general, experience of open access for freight operators has been confined to Europe and Australia. In Europe, open access was first introduced for certain categories of international rail freight under Directive 91/440 in 1991; it was extended to all international rail freight within the European Union in 2006 and to all freight in 2007.

In some countries, complete freight open access was granted long before it was a Europe-wide requirement and appears quite successful; for instance, in Britain, where the existing operators were privatized as two companies, several other companies have entered and the share of the market of the dominant operator is steadily falling. In the Netherlands, Germany and Sweden, there are also a number of new operators. In general, the new operators appear to be either rail freight customers (Direct Rail Services, Rail4Chem) or owned by existing major operators in other countries (the major competing consortia operating through the Alps). In most of these cases there is clear evidence of improved performance, with rising rail market share (Copenhagen Economics, 2004). That there has not been more new entry appears to be partly due to continued stifling of competition by governments hostile to it and partly because of a general lack of profitable opportunities. Elsewhere, in Australia, open access for freight operators appears to have been a success in the long-distance general merchandise market, where some distribution companies run their own trains leading to a much greater rail freight market share (Bureau of Transport and Regional Economics, 2007).

Thinking back to the US evidence on economies of traffic density (Grimm and Harris, 1983), as well as its generally poor profitability, it is not surprising that there has been no entrant into operating network freight services handling single wagons, and it has been argued that loss of more profitable traffic with which this shares costs may lead to the abandonment of single wagonload traffic in Europe (as has already happened in some countries) to the overall detriment of rail freight market share (McKinsey, 2005).

By contrast, there is no current legal requirement in Europe to allow open access for passenger operators. Outside Europe, there are a number of cases (for example, Iran, Malaysia, Vietnam) where new operators have been invited to join public-private partnerships, usually to offer particular services to the tourist industry, but this is to exploit marketing skills and access private capital rather than to introduce competition. In Russia, there are some examples of open access competition mainly where the state railway could not afford to invest in rolling stock to exploit certain market opportunities, although new entrants are required to hire locomotives and drivers from the state company (Dementiev, 2007). Within Europe, even though a few countries (notably Germany, but also, subject to regulatory approval, Britain) offer opportunities for open access entry to the passenger market, actual entry has been negligible. Again, this is not really surprising given the lack of profitability of many services (90 percent of European passenger services are operated under some sort of a public service obligation; CER, 2005), the lack of capacity particularly at peak times and around the major cities and the advantages of a network operator that can exploit economies of scale and marketing advantages such as though ticketing from anywhere to anywhere in the network (although a regulator can make this a requirement for all operators, as in Britain). Moreover research has suggested that, by cream skimming – duplicating the most popular services, whilst reducing train loads and losing economies of density – open-access entry in the passenger market may have undesirable outcomes (Preston et al., 1999) unless it is regulated to ensure it only occurs when in the public interest. On the other hand, there is evidence that by leading to better services and lower prices, a limited amount of open access competition has provided net benefits in Britain (Griffiths, 2009).

Thus whilst on-track competition has enjoyed some success for bulk flows of commodities, including containers, there is limited evidence and less reason to suppose it would work either for network freight or, in general, for passenger operations.

FRANCHISING FOR FREIGHT AND PASSENGER TRAFFIC

The idea of franchising natural monopolies by means of competitive tender is to secure services the state wishes to see continue at the maximum profit to the state or for the minimum subsidy (Demsetz, 1968, originally suggested a competition to see who would supply at the lowest price to the public). The idea is that the competition promotes innovation in terms of services and cost control by selecting the operator with the best bid, and thus incentivizes all bidders to be efficient. Since they are committed to paying a certain premium or surviving on a certain subsidy, the incentive to improve performance and reduce costs remains throughout the life of the franchise, although it may be weaker in the later years when any initiatives will have less time to repay themselves. Thus the need for regulation is minimized, compared with outright privatization, and the ability for the government to influence future patterns of fares and services preserved.

The process of privatizing entire national rail systems through concessions really started in Argentina in 1989, and over the following years spread throughout South America and also to a number of African countries (Thompson, 2003). The general pattern in South America was of 30-year concessions for integrated freight railways (although varying from 20 years in Chile to 50 years in Mexico), with separate much shorter franchises for (mainly suburban) passenger services. The freight franchises involved payment of a premium to the government as well as commitments to investment, but commercial freedom to the operator in terms of services and charges; the passenger franchises involved commitment to minimum service levels and maximum fares. Generally, in the years before concessioning the rail systems had been performing very poorly, with declining traffic and productivity, increasing losses and deteriorating assets. This was reversed by the process of franchising, and a major improvement in performance in all these dimensions was achieved, but problems emerged in terms of the ability of the parties to comply with the terms of the franchises, particularly in Argentina where there were both cases where concessionaires were unable to meet their commitments regarding investment and where governments were unable to provide the level of subsidy to which they were committed (Kogan, 2006). This immediately reveals one of the dilemmas of franchising. A long franchise is desirable if the franchisee is to be responsible for maintenance and investment in the infrastructure, provision of rolling stock and for commercial development of the services, as otherwise they may have inadequate incentive to invest in long-term developments. However, not only do long franchises give the incumbent a monopoly for a considerable period of time, but also they invariably raise the issue of renegotiation, as external developments in terms particularly of the state of the economy may change both what the franchisee can afford to pay or to spend in investment, and what the government can afford to buy. The Argentinean government could have terminated the franchises and begun the process of competitive tendering again, but it saw this as an expensive and risky process. So it preferred renegotiation, despite the risk that the lack of competition may leave the incumbent in a strong position to seek favourable terms, whilst by signalling a willingness to renegotiate, the message may be given that the best strategy is for bidders to win with unrealistic bids which they can then renegotiate.

Franchising within Europe began with Sweden, where in the reforms of 1988 the regions were made responsible for subsidising regional services and could choose to go out to competitive tender. But these franchises were much more on the basis of a short term (2–5 years) contracts to provide specific services at specific fares for which they were reimbursed on a gross cost basis; as already mentioned, infrastructure was completely separated and they simply paid for track access, whilst rolling stock was leased from the franchising authority, so train operating companies did not need to make any significant investment and therefore short term contracts were not a problem. Later all subsidized services were made subject to competitive tender; long-distance services being franchised by the national government but on a net cost basis. In general, the Swedish approach to franchising has been successful, achieving better quality services at lower cost (typically

20 percent has been quoted as the saving), although there have been some problems, in terms of allegations of predatory bids both from the incumbent and from a major new entrant, and in terms of successful bidders who then found themselves unable to operate the required services (for instance, because of a shortage of drivers) or who found the franchise unprofitable and became bankrupt (Alexandersson and Hulten, 2005). Broadly, this approach to franchising has also been used for some regional services in Germany (Lehmann, 1999), Denmark and the Netherlands, with similar outcomes. By contrast with this gradual approach, in 1993 the decision was taken that all passenger services in Britain, whether profitable or not, would be franchised by means of competitive tendering. Unlike elsewhere in Europe, the incumbent was not allowed to bid, but its operations were divided into a set of 25 train operating companies and the winner of a franchise competition simply took control of the company with its existing staff. Rolling stock was placed in the hands of separate leasing companies, so that train operating companies would again need to make little investment. However, the leasing companies themselves bore the residual value risk, and this made them reluctant to invest without a longer term lease; alternatively they might do so but charge more for a short-term lease to cover the risk. The eventual outcome was that, in many cases, the government provided guarantees that successor franchisees would lease the same stock.

Initially, franchises were let for 7 years (more in a few cases where heavy investment was required) for which period they would need to provide at least minimum levels of service and some fares were regulated. Initially, the franchisees enjoyed healthy growth of traffic and cost reductions, although those in the regional sector, whose bids were predicated more on substantial cost reductions than on revenue growth, became financially unsound. After a change of government in 1997, ambitious plans for rail investment were brought forward, on the basis of much longer franchises in which the train operating companies would be involved in infrastructure investment alongside financial and construction partners through special purpose vehicles. Bidders were essentially invited to come up with innovative proposals, for expanding capacity and improving services. However, the process of awarding franchises for such widely varying long-term bids was complex. In the meantime, following the fatal accident at Hatfield in October 2000, which was due to faulty track, and the subsequent bankruptcy of Railtrack, rapid cost increases on both infrastructure and operations made this strategy unaffordable and a return was made to 7-year franchises with very tight specification of service levels. By this time, more than half of all franchises had been renegotiated or placed on a management contract; as well as due to financial problems, this occurred where there was a wish to achieve comparable refranchising dates between different franchises to redraw the boundaries between them. There is some evidence that the placing of so many franchises on short-term negotiated franchises or annually negotiated management contracts weakened cost control and contributed to the rapid growth in train operating costs, although other factors, including competition between companies for a limited pool of skilled staff, including drivers, appear also to be factors (Smith et al., 2009). Refranchising is now well advanced in Britain, but there is concern that many of the new set of bids may be unrealistic in their ambitious forecasts for revenue growth and one, that serving the important East Coast Main Line, has failed twice for this reason in the last few years.

In Britain (as in Sweden and Germany), franchising was associated with a strong growth in traffic, although the evidence is that this was mainly due to other factors, such as strong economic growth, rising costs of motoring and increased road congestion over the period in question (Wardman, 2006). The problem was the failure to achieve a sustained reduction in costs. A number of other countries, including Australia – the case of Melbourne (Mees, 2007) – and Portugal – the trans Tagus services – have experienced similar problems of unrealistic winning bids being renegotiated early in their lives. Clearly, these experiences suggest that there are difficulties, particularly with long franchises. Short gross cost contracts in which the operator bears relatively little risk appear to work better, although whilst these are appropriate for regional and commuter services, it is doubtful whether this is an appropriate way to procure commercial services, since most of the decisions remain with the government rather than the operator. For longer franchises, it appears that a combination of risk sharing, clear break points and carefully defined terms and conditions for renegotiation might overcome the difficulties, but there is insufficient experience yet to reach a firm conclusion to this effect.

REGULATION AND INFRASTRUCTURE CHARGES

We have commented above that for a hundred years railways were seen as monopolies that needed regulation, and also – rather remarkably – that in 1980 the United States largely removed this regulation without other measures to increase competition. Even more remarkably, that measure was an enormous success. In the 20 years following deregulation, both unit operating costs and freight rates fell by almost two-thirds, and whilst this had a variety of causes including changes in traffic mix, it is estimated that deregulation alone caused freight rates to fall by more than 20 percent (Winston, 2006). The explanation seems to be partly the form of the regulation, which required railways to adhere to published tariffs calculated according to prescribed rules, preventing negotiation with individual carriers and requiring cross subsidization between customers and commodities. When it was removed, railways were able to price differentiate, covering their fixed costs from more profitable traffics whilst attracting all traffic that would pay its marginal cost and offering discounts for measures that reduced costs such as full train loads, or the use of larger wagons. It should not be assumed that all forms of regulation would have the same adverse consequences.

In Japan, privatization has been accompanied by continued fares regulation, using the fact that the former state railway was broken up into six different companies, plus the existence of many longer standing private railways, to implement a very interesting approach based on benchmarking to determine whether cost increases used to justify increased prices are reasonable (Mizutani, 1997).

Within Europe, there has also been a long-term trend to remove regulation of freight charges; where passenger charges are still regulated, this is for reasons of social policy, and railways are compensated for loss of revenue by the state. A whole series of studies (for example, Oum and Yu, 1994) has established that in the period before the major European reforms, those railways with greater autonomy and lower subsidies were the most efficient in terms of cost and productivity. However, as commented above, one feature of the reform of European railways has been the requirement to introduce a regulator even where one did not previously exist. In part this is simply because of the recognition that the infrastructure manager remains a monopoly supplier to the train operating companies, but also because of the need to secure non discriminatory access in cases where the infrastructure manager is still involved in train operations. Thus it is infrastructure charges and access conditions, rather than charges to end users, that are now regulated in Europe.

A consequence of separation of infrastructure from operations is that infrastructure charges become a key factor in influencing the behavior of both train operating companies and infrastructure managers. Ideally, train operating companies would be incentivized to make the best use of existing capacity by paying for their actual use of the system at short-run marginal social cost, whilst infrastructure managers would be incentivized to provide enhancements to the infrastructure by being rewarded for the improvements they bring about. There are difficulties in achieving these two aims. First, marginal social cost is not easy to measure. Econometric work in a number of countries suggests that marginal maintenance and renewal costs are around 20 percent of average costs per gross tonne kilometer (Wheat and Smith, 2008), whilst it is necessary to rely on engineering formulae to identify the relative impact per gross tonne kilometre of different designs of rolling stock. Marginal cost must include the costs of congestion (additional trains adding to the risk of delay to other trains on the network; Gibson et al., 2002) and scarcity (the fact that when all slots are filled train operators can only gain additional slots by taking them from someone else, Nash et al., 2004).

But charges based on short-run marginal social cost reward the infrastructure manager for keeping capacity scarce rather than for enhancing the infrastructure. A performance regime with penalties for unreliability may provide some incentive for enhancement, but correct incentives to both the train-operating company (or franchising authority) seeking the enhanced facilities and to the infrastructure manager would seem to require investment costs to be paid by those requiring the investment. This may be feasible as part of a two-part tariff, with the fixed part reflecting the avoidable cost of the capacity ordered by the train operator under a long-term contract and the variable part the short-run marginal social cost of capacity use. But whilst this is fully consistent with a franchising approach in which whoever wins the franchise pays the same fixed cost, it is not consistent with non-discriminatory on track competition as different operators will face different charges. The ideal solution in which any new entrant compensates the train operator which paid for the infrastructure for loss of contribution towards fixed costs (Baumol, 1983) is also difficult in terms of the information requirements this places on the regulator.

Scarcity charges are also problematic. Ideally charges would reflect the opportunity cost of use of the capacity in its next best use. However, as Quinet (2003) points out, such charges could only be estimated if the best use of the infrastructure has already been determined, and therefore their use is no different from 'command and control' type decisions on how to use capacity. They will only achieve an optimal outcome if taxes and subsidies are present to reflect costs and benefits not falling on the train operator, including benefits to passengers, and reductions in external cost from diverting traffic from road or air. On the other hand, the revenue from simply diverting traffic from an existing operator will not form part of the social benefit of allocating a slot to a particular use if the result is merely duplication of service. A revenue sharing arrangement in which the new entrant compensates the existing operator for any loss of revenue therefore appears desirable.

Economists often advocate auctioning to ensure scarce resources go to those who value them most. But auctioning could be very complex to administer, given the different amounts of capacity different trains require at different points of the network, and the fact that the willingness to pay of the train operator will depend on what other slots they, and their competitors, are allocated. Nilsson (2002b) puts forward a scheme which he believes to be feasible, in which operators bid for the set of slots they wish for, but also indicate by how much their bid would change if they were allocated a slot earlier or later than they desire. An optimization program would then be used to design the best timetable, and operators given a chance to revise their bids having seen the actual allocation. There is no experience of such a system in practice yet, however, although this type of iteration – without money bids – is inevitably the way in which timetables are designed when a number of operators have conflicting demands for capacity. Nilsson notes that this process will only work when the competition is between operators serving different types of traffic for the reasons noted above.

Given all these conflicting aims and complications, it is not surprising that a wide variety of actual structures and levels of rail access charges have emerged, ranging from charges based purely on marginal wear-and-tear cost to multipart tariffs and charges based on fully allocated cost (Nash, 2005). These differences partly reflect different circumstances – for instance, tight budget constraints make pure short-run marginal cost pricing impossible, spare capacity makes scarcity and congestion charges unnecessary – and partly different philosophies in terms of the extent to which rail infrastructure is seen as a social or commercial issue. Whilst clearly governments short of money may regard subsidizing rail infrastructure as a low priority, there is evidence that high infrastructure charges greatly in excess of marginal cost can lead to significant loss of social benefits (ECMT, 2003). Moreover the scope for price differentiation according to elasticities of demand for a rail infrastructure manager is limited – whilst obviously they can differentiate between intercity and regional passenger, bulk freight and container trains, they cannot distinguish between the freight commodities or passenger journey purposes which are carried by a particular type of train. There is also evidence that in some countries, notably in Central Europe, there is an attempt to earn high surpluses on freight infrastructure charges in order to support large passenger networks for which the government cannot afford to pay (CER, 2005).

CONCLUSIONS

In this chapter, we have reviewed experience to date with deregulation and the introduction of competition into railways. We have seen that a variety of approaches has been taken, ranging from simple deregulation of the freight railways of North America, through privatization of vertically integrated passenger railways in Japan and vertically integrated long-term freight franchises in South America to the complete separation of infrastructure and operations and introduction of on-track competition and passenger franchises in Europe and Australia. Whilst it is hard to reach firm conclusions on what works best in what circumstances given the limited evidence, some generalizations are in order.

There seems good reason to suppose that separation of infrastructure from operations generates cost and complexity. Thus, if competition from other modes, or between different suppliers at alternative locations, is adequate to enforce efficiency then the case for such separation is weak. This is most likely to be the situation in highly competitive freight markets, with appropriate pricing of other modes to reflect externalities and where rail systems are privatized, so there is no government involvement. Once governments are directly involved in financing rail infrastructure or operations, then there is a case for competitive tendering to ensure the best value from use of the facilities in question, although we have seen that such an approach has not been without problems, particularly where franchises are long and inaccurate forecasts or changed circumstances have led to renegotiation. Nevertheless, franchising by means of competitive tender has led to improved performance of the rail system in most cases where it has been implemented.

In a franchising system, the government is likely to remain ultimate owner of the infrastructure, but this can be leased to the main operator. There seem to be good commercial and operational reasons for separating passenger and freight operations in such a system, with the minority operators having access to the infrastructure controlled by the majority one.

It is where it is desired to promote on-track competition in the freight market on dense networks shared with heavy passenger traffic that the case for complete separation of infrastructure from operations is strongest. There is good evidence that on-track competition works for bulk freight and container traffic, but whether the same benefits can be achieved by strong regulation without complete separation remains unclear.

Given the widely differing circumstances in different parts of the world, it is thus unlikely that there is a single best solution. The deregulation of private freight operators in North America has been very successful, but hardly forms a model for countries where passenger traffic is very important, particularly where much of this is social rather than commercial. The privatization in Japan appears to have worked well, but similarly does not provide a solution where governments wish to be heavily involved in specifying passenger services and fares, and where subsidies are required, as this leaves them in the hands of monopoly operators. In these circumstances, some form of franchising seems essential. Typically, it does appear that most railway reforms have at least had some beneficial effects. But the evidence is that all reforms are a compromise between introducing competition and minimizing transactions costs and loss of economies of scale, density and scope; it is likely that different solutions work best in different circumstances, but we are a long way short of being able to provide definitive evidence on what works best in what circumstance in terms of competition and regulation of railways.

REFERENCES

Alexandersson, G. and S. Hulten, 2005, Sweden. In *Reforming Europe's Railways: An Assessment of Progress*, 39-56, Brussels: Community of European Railways and Infrastructure Managers, pp. 39–56.

Baumol, W. J., 1983, Some subtle pricing issues in railroad regulation. *International Journal of Transport Economics*, **10** (1–2), 341–355.

Bitzan, J., 2003, Railroad costs and competition. *Journal of Transport Economics and Policy*, **37** (2), 201–225.

Bouf, D., Y. Crozet and J. Lévêque, 2005, Vertical separation, disputes resolution and competition in the railways industry. Presented at the 9th Conference on Competition and Ownership in Land Transport, Lisbon.

Bureau of Transport and Regional Economics Information, 2007, Australian rail freight performance indicators. Paper 59, Canberra.

Cantos, P., 2001, Vertical relationships for the European railway industry. *Transport Policy*, **8** (2), 77–83.

Caves, D.W., L.R. Christensen, M. Tretheway and R.J. Windle, 1987, Network effects and the measurement of returns to scale and density for US railroads. In A. F. Daugherty, ed., *Analytical Studies in Transport Economics*. Cambridge: Cambridge University Press, pp. 97–120.

Community of European Railways and Infrastructure Managers (CER), 2005, *Public Service Rail Transport in the EU: An Overview*. Brussels: CER.

Copenhagen Economics, 2004, Marketing opening in network industries. Final Report, DG Internal Market, European Commission, Brussels.

Dementiev, A., 2007, Vertical divestiture as a competitive strategy: the case of railway passenger transport reform in Russia. Paper presented at the 10th International Conference on Competition and Ownership in Land Passenger Transport, Hamilton Island, Australia.

Demsetz, H., 1968, Why regulate utilities? *Journal of Law and Economics*, **11**, 55–66.

European Conference of Ministers of Transport (ECMT), 2003, *Reforming Transport Taxes*. Paris: ECMT.

Friebel, G., M. Ivaldi and C. Vibes, 2003, Railway (de)regulation: a European efficiency comparison. IDEI report no. 3 on passenger rail transport, University of Toulouse.

Gibson, S., G. Cooper and B. Ball, 2002, Capacity charges on the UK rail network. *Journal of Transport Economics and Policy*, **36** (2), 341–354.

Griffiths, T., 2009, On rail competition: the impact of open access entry on the Great Britain rail market. Paper presented at the International Conference on Competition and Ownership in Land Passenger Transport, Delft, September 2009.

Grimm, C.M. and R.G. Harris, 1983, Structural economics of the US rail freight industry: concepts, evidence and mergers. *Transportation Research Part l*, **17A** (4A), 271–281.

Growitsch, C. and H. Wetzel, 2009, Testing for economies of scope in European railways: an efficiency analysis. *Journal of Transport Economics and Policy*, **43** (1), 1–24.

House of Lords, 2005, Liberalising rail freight movement in the EU. European Union Committee, 4th Report, 2004-5.

Ivaldi, M. and G.J. McCullough, 2001, Density and integration effects on Class 1 US freight railroads. *Journal of Regulatory Economics*, **19**, 161–182.

Keeler, T.A., 1974, Railroad costs, returns to scale and excess capacity. *Review of Economics and Statistics*, **56**, 201–208.

Kirchner, C., 2005, Germany. In *Reforming Europe's Railways: An Assessment of Progress*. Brussels: Community of European Railways and Infrastructure Managers.

Kogan, J., 2006, Latin America: competition for concessions. In J. Gomez-Ibanez and G. de Rus, eds, *Competition in the Railway Industry*. Cheltenham, UK: Edward Elgar.

Lehmann, C., 1999, Germany. In D. van de Welde, ed., *Changing Trains, Railway Reform and Competition: The Experience of Six Countries*. Aldershot, UK: Ashgate.

McKinsey and Co., 2005, *The Future of Rail Freight in Europe*. Brussels: CER.

Mees, P., 2007, Franchising and performance based contracts: lessons from public transport in Melbourne. Paper presented at the 10th International Conference on Competition and Ownership in Land Passenger Transport, Hamilton Island Australia.

Merkert, R., 2007, A transaction cost perspective on the organization of European railways. Paper presented at the World Conference on Transport Research, University of California, Berkeley, June.

Merkert, R., 2009, The measurement of transaction costs in railways. Ph.D. Thesis, University of Leeds.

Mizutani, F., 1997, Empirical analysis of yardstick competition in the Japanese railway industry. *International Journal of Transport Economics*, **24** (3), 367–392.

Nash, C., S. Coulthard and B. Matthews, 2004, Rail track charges in Great Britain: the issue of charging for capacity. *Transport Policy*, **11** (4), 315–328.

Nash, C., 2005, Rail infrastructure charges in Europe. *Journal of Transport Economics and Policy*, **39** (3), 259–278.

Nash, C.A., A. Smith and B. Matthews, 2005, Great Britain. In *Reforming Europe's Railways: An Assessment of Progress*. Brussels: Community of European Railways and Infrastructure Managers.

Nash, C.A., 2008, Passenger railway reform in the last 20 years: European experience. *Research in Transportation Economics*, **22** (1), 61–70.

Nilsson, J.E., 2002a, Restructuring Sweden's railways: the unintentional deregulation. *Swedish Economic Policy Review*, **9** (2), 229–254.

Nilsson, J.-E., 2002b, Towards a welfare enhancing process to manage railway infrastructure access. *Transportation Research Part A*, **36** (5), 419–436.

Oum, T.H. and C. Yu, 1994, Economic efficiency of railways and implications for public policy: a comparative study of the OECD countries railways. *Journal of Transport Economics and Policy*, **28** (2), 121–138.

Preston, J., 1996, The economics of British Rail privatisation: an assessment. *Transport Reviews*, **16** (1), 1–21.

Preston, J., G. Whelan and M. Wardman, 1999, An analysis of the potential for on-track competition in the British passenger rail industry. *Journal of Transport Economics and Policy*, **33** (1), 77–94.

Quinet, E., 2003, Short term adjustments in rail activity: the limited role of infrastructure charges. *Transport Policy*, **10** (1), 73–80.

Rivera-Trujillo, C., 2004, Measuring the productivity and efficiency of railways (an international comparison). Ph.D. Thesis, University of Leeds.

Singh, M., 2007, Competition in rail freight transport: the case of Indian railways. Paper presented at the World Conference on Transport Research, University of California, Berkeley, June.

Smith, A.S.J., C.A. Nash and P.E. Wheat, 2009, Passenger rail franchising in Britain: has it been a success? *International Journal of Transport Economics*, **36** (1), 33–62.

Smith, A.S.J., P.E. Wheat and C.A. Nash, 2009, Exploring the effects of passenger rail franchising in Britain: evidence from the first two rounds of franchising (1997–2008). Paper presented at the 11th International Conference on Competition and Ownership in Land Passenger Transport, Delft.

Thompson, L., 2003, Changing railway structure and ownership: is anything working? *Transport Reviews*, **23** (3), 311–355.

Vickers, J. and G. Yarrow, 1988, *Privatisation: An Economic Analysis*. Cambridge MA: MIT Press.

Wardman, M., 2006, Demand for rail travel and the effects of external factors. *Transportation Research Part E*, **42** (3), 129–148.

Wheat, P. and A. Smith, 2008, Assessing the marginal infrastructure maintenance wear and tear costs for Britain's railway network. *Journal of Transport Economics and Policy*, **42** (t2), 189–224.

Williamson, O.E., 1985, *The Economic Institutions of Capitalism*. New York: The Free Press.

Winston, C., 2006, The US: private and deregulated. In J. Gomez-Ibanez and G. de Rus, eds, *Competition in the Railway Industry*. Cheltenham, UK: Edward Elgar, pp. 135–152.

Wu, J.H. and C. Nash, 2000, Railway reform in China. *Transport Reviews*, **20** (1), 25–48.

34 Airport governance and regulation: three decades
of aviation system reform
David Gillen

INTRODUCTION

This chapter examines the evolution of airport governance and regulation over the last 30 years and assesses the case for privatization.[1] In this period the aviation system has been subject to significant change in the delivery and organization of air services but much less so in the organization and delivery of infrastructure services. Today, airports in developed economies are run as modern businesses, or at least in a commercial-like way. There has been a transition from positioning airports as public utilities to being multi-product firms delivering airside services to a range of airlines, and terminal retail and access services to passengers, plus additional ancillary services to other parts of the aviation supply chain.

Interestingly, the study of airport performance and price setting under differing governance structures has only recently attracted the interest of economists. A large part of the reason was that until the late 1990s, with the exception of the UK, airports were owned by some level of government that treated them as a public utility and in many cases used them as a device for some broader policy initiative. The fact that airports seemed to cover their costs, and needed government support for investment, provided some evidence that airports had not, and presumably would not, use any market power. The issues that had previously occupied economic analysts were not pricing and market power, but rather congestion pricing to allocate scarce capacity, undertaking benefit–cost studies to assess proposed capacity investments and developing strategies to mitigate noise externalities. There was little questioning of whether airports were operating in an institutional setting which gave them the incentive to produce and price efficiently. Nor was there a close economic assessment of airport performance including runway pricing, runway investment and gate (facility) utilization. It was presumed that publicly and locally owned airports would keep prices close to costs, set price structures efficiently, provide the range of services that users were willing to pay for, and keep costs to a minimum. Subsequent analysis dispelled these myths (see Armstrong et al., 1994; Morrison and Winston, 2008; Starkie and Yarrow, 2008).[2]

Over the last two decades network industries have faced reform and restructuring. Telecommunications, electricity, water and transportation, have seen extensive change in most OECD countries. There has been privatization or corporatization of public enterprises, and associated with this incentive regulation has been introduced. In the United States, this has occurred in all except the airport sector. There has been a widespread attempt to alter the institutional framework in which utility and transport industries operate. These industries face stronger incentives to perform efficiently, and where they possess some market power, the use of this is constrained to minimize damage to incentives to perform efficiently. Evidence in the aviation sector from most countries which have embarked on programs of reform suggests that performance overall has improved significantly (see Gillen and Niemeier, 2008; Hooper et al., 2000; Parker, 1999; Starkie and Yarrow, 2008).

In the majority of developed countries around the world, airport ownership, governance and regulation have undergone significant change. Governments have pursued new airport policies, sometimes in conjunction with aviation system reform as in the EU. The shift that occurred across many countries had several common sources. Air traffic was growing at rapid rates and airports needed to invest in capacity. There was a general rethinking of the role government should play in the economy, and airports were considered a place where the private sector could legitimately provide the needed service and investment. The deregulated airline sector was showing significant improvements in productivity and product innovation and many argued that this could be and should be extended to the airport sector. There was a newfound recognition of the relationship between ownership structure, governance and economic performance.

Market forces operate irrespective of the institutions created by society, but the effects of institutions in shaping the oversight, management and performance of firms is a key issue. So it is with governance and oversight in the airport sector. The institutional setting, which is generally ignored in investigating governance evolution, is important in affecting corporate governance and the strategic behaviour of firms. Institutions which establish formal rules and facilitate the development of informal rules act to constrain economic agents' behavior and can incentivize them in differing ways. This occurs because institutions can affect the payoffs for various economic activities. The institutional framework can embody two types of incentives: formal (property rights under a set of laws) and informal such as reputation. Under the institutional setting we want agents within the organization engaged in carrying out productive activities such as innovation and not unproductive activities such as rent-seeking.

In aviation, a good example of the impact of institutions on airport governance is market liberalization and, in particular, international bilaterals. Those markets which have more open sky agreements, rather than restrictive bilaterals, change the distribution of power between airports and airlines and in part define the competitive market for airport services. The UK has a liberal market system, and has opted for greater airport privatization, whereas Germany is more of a co-ordinated market system and it has opted for semi-privatization with regulation.[3]

In this chapter, I examine the evolution of airport governance and the various forms it has taken. I also examine airport regulation and assess whether it is needed and what form might be preferable if it is deemed necessary. The first section examines the types of governance structures that have evolved in different countries. In the second section, I discuss the types of airport regulation that exist and their weaknesses. I also examine the question of whether airports can operate competitively and whether there is a need (or desire) for regulation. The next section considers whether privatization is desirable and the factors which contribute to successful privatization. A concluding section closes the chapter.

AIRPORT GOVERNANCE: AN EVOLUTION[4]

The forces of reform have, for several reasons, been slow to deal with airports. The move to private ownership has been slower than in other industries. In many cases, governments have opted for partial rather than full privatization. In North America, even though there is a long tradition of privately owned utilities and transport industries, there has been a reluctance to move away from public or local ownership of airports. Canada, for example, chose the 'not-for-profit' governance model rather than privatization. The move towards full privatization has been strongest in the UK and later Australia and New Zealand, both countries which formerly relied on the UK model of public enterprise, and which followed the UK with extensive privatization programs. In continental Europe there has been a preference for partial privatization, with the public sector remaining with majority ownership in many cases.

If one differentiates between the degree and mode of the shift of airports out of public ownership, there are at least seven possible ownership/governance structures:

- Government owned/operated (United States, Spain, Singapore, Finland, Sweden)
- Government owned, privately operated[5] (United States (via contracts), Chile, Hamilton –Canada)
- Independent not-for-profit corporations (Canada)
- Fully private for-profit via IPO (Initial Public Offering) with stock widely held (originally BAA – the British Airport Authority)
- Fully private for-profit via trade sale with share ownership tightly held (Australia, New Zealand)
- Partially private for-profit with private controlling interest (Denmark, Austria, Switzerland)
- Partially private for-profit with government controlling interest (Hamburg, France, China, Kansai – Japan)

Government Owned/Operated Airports

The general goal of government-owned and operated airports is to focus on the primary function of the airport and to suppress other sources of commercial value. Often, government-run airports have non-commercial objectives that have included the protection of national carriers or promotion of economic activities and development, with less of a long-term focus with respect to infrastructure investments. For such airports, investments are likely to compete with other government priorities and often there is an observed lack of consistency between aviation policy and the efficient use of airport assets. Airports can also be used for economic and development objectives; many regional airports would fit this class even in places in Europe.

Government Owned, Privately Operated

In the United States, (almost all) airports are government owned (locally) but effectively privately operated, with a high degree of contracting out.[6] US airports benefit from Federal grants and interest-free bonds when investment is required, yet they typically exhibit a lack of investment in aeronautical infrastructure, albeit in many cases due to local land use restrictions, zoning laws and political pressure from vocal interest groups. US airports also exhibit some airline participation in the ownership of terminal buildings. The top 50 airports in the United States show a significant interest in developing non-aeronautical commercial value, but beyond this there is a high degree of variability across airports (reflecting local government willingness to extend airport operations beyond the primary function).

The US model, particularly of port authorities, has become deep-rooted because of long-term leases signed between airports and airlines giving them in many cases exclusive control of entire terminals or concourses and the right to approve or veto capital spending plans.[7] This type of arrangement made the 'signatory airlines' joint ventures with the airport. For taking this risk, the incumbent airlines were able to control airport expansion and to some degree the ability of competitors to enter some markets.

Independent Not-for-profit Corporations

This structure is the current regime in Canada, arising from a gradual devolution from government operation that began in the mid-1990s. Canadian airport authorities operate their airports under a 60-year lease agreement (which is extendable) after which time, the land and assets revert to the federal government. As not-for-profit entities, Canadian airports have not been subject to direct regulation (of aeronautical charges). There has been a significant amount of infrastructure investment at Canadian airports over the last ten years. However, the types and levels of investment have been subject to some debate concerning the possibility of 'gold plating': extravagant or unnecessary investment that leads to higher charges for airlines and passengers. Canadian airports exhibit varying degrees of focus on complementary non-aviation activities but all of the larger airports utilize passenger facility charges (usually bundled into airfare prices) to help finance investments.[8] An ongoing issue in Canada is the payment of 'ground rent' by airports to the Federal government, which under the current regime amounts to 12 percent of gross revenues for any airport with annual revenues over $250m Cdn. Airports and airlines have argued that the form and level of rent payments had led to inflated aeronautical charges. The Canadian model of airport governance has not been duplicated anywhere else in the world.

Fully Private for-profit via IPO

Fully privatized airports have shown both a strong market orientation and a strong customer focus. BAA is the oldest example of airport privatization implemented via an IPO.[9] BAA, which includes the London airports (Heathrow (LHR), Gatwick (LGW) and Stansted (STN)) plus three airports in Scotland, has exhibited a strong orientation towards complementary retail business and non-complementary business on and off airport land. This is perhaps explained in part by the form of price regulation applied to these airports: a 'single till' price cap, under which revenue from all sources (aeronautical and non-aeronautical) is used in deciding how much aeronautical prices can increase. This has led to low (non-market) aeronautical prices at LHR. It has also led to a reduction in service quality and an underinvestment in some assets, mostly terminals.

While these airports have shown a willingness to develop markets and make strategic investments, there is also evidence that links between management and the government have remained strong and that political decision making plays a direct role in augmenting private commercial interests (for example, the private demand for an additional runway at LHR and the public decision to instead support an additional runway at STN). A recent competition commission report has recommended the divestiture of the three London airports into separate entities, and on September 17, 2008, Ferrovial announced that Gatwick would be put up for sale.[10]

Fully Private for-profit via Trade Sale

In Australia airports under federal ownership were corporatized in the 1980s, which meant that the airports had a more commercial focus, were expected to achieve cost recovery as a group, (though there were cross subsidies from large to smaller airports) and their accounts were publicly available. Smaller airports were owned either by the federal or local governments, and in the 1980s the federal government transferred ownership of smaller airports to local governments.

Airports in Australia were privatized beginning in 1996–97. Brisbane, Melbourne and Perth were privatized first. Sydney airport was privatized in 2002. Airports have been sold to private interests via trade sales in which investment consortia bid to purchase the airports. These consortia typically have included airport management companies and/or infrastructure investment companies (along with pension funds). In Australia, airports were sold under a lease agreement of 50 years plus an automatic extension of 49 years, after which the airports revert to the federal government. Like UK airports, Australian airports have exhibited a strong market focus, but unlike their UK counterparts Australian investors seem to have taken a more long-term investment perspective immediately following the sale and have, according to some, a more unified strategic view of how the airport should develop.

The main three New Zealand airports, Auckland, Wellington and Christchurch, were corporatized in the late 1980s. New Zealand followed a similar model to Australia but governments did have some share ownership; government shareholdings in Auckland and Wellington were sold in part in the late 1990s and the airports now have majority private ownership, with only Auckland being publicly listed. Christchurch remains owned by the local government. After an attempt by the Ontario Teachers Pension Fund to purchase majority ownership in 2008, the New Zealand Government placed restrictions on who could purchase shares and the amount any one shareholder could hold.

Partially Private for-profit with Government Controlling Interest

Athens, Rome and Hamburg are all examples of airports that are for-profit entities where private investors are limited to a minority interest; others include Belfast, Brussels, Budapest, Copenhagen, Dusseldorf and Frankfurt and airports in Argentina, Chile, Colombia and Mexico. Interestingly, the existence of a for-profit (commercial) objective and minority private interest has in general been viewed by the stakeholders as enough to cause a fundamental change in management attitude and orientation towards developing commercial value. It appears that even though government remains the majority shareholder, these airports are able to make decisions and develop strategies that a government-run airport would not. This includes air route development and retail development. (For example, Hamburg Airport reported 20 new routes in 2007 and will open a 7000 m^2 retail plaza in 2008. It has also had a significant increase in the number of carriers serving the airport including low cost and charter carriers.) In some cases, such airports have pursued strategic investments with carriers and have sought to maximize the relative contribution of non-aviation revenues. The degree and intrusiveness of government intervention via regulation and oversight remains a potential issue.

Partially Private for-profit with Private Controlling Interest

Copenhagen Airport is an example of an airport that has become a for-profit company with the majority share held by a single private investor (Macquarie Airports). This form of governance has, like those airports with minority private ownership, been successful in bringing a more entrepreneurial and commercial orientation to airport operations and strategy. One potential effect of this form of privatization is the possibility of raising more private capital (investors willing to pay more for a controlling interest) and also the possibility of a more coherent long-term investment orientation. For 'hands-on' investors like Macquarie Airports, majority ownership appears to be a minimum condition for their involvement, however there may be little de facto difference between minority and majority ownership. The reason for this is that governments through regulation and oversight can exert significant influence and constraint on the development of commercial value, whether or not there is a majority ownership.[11] Consequently, in the realm of partial privatization a lot may depend on jurisdiction-dependent government regulations, oversight, larger objectives and transparency in airport management–government relations.

AIRPORT REGULATION: OPTIONS AND EXPERIENCE FROM VARIOUS COUNTRIES

An airport has two obvious sides to its business: the airside market (passenger airlines and cargo companies as direct customers, and fixed base operators as tenants) and the non-airside market (enplaning and deplaning passengers as direct customers, retail businesses as tenants, and landside tenants). Each side gives rise to a multitude of outputs with peak and off-peak periods in both markets. However, revenues are generally bundled as airside (monies from fees and charges to airlines for runway, apron and terminal use) and non-aviation (monies from retail and commercial activity including land leases).

The perception that airports are monopolies and will exploit their monopoly power has figured into the regulation of charges that airports can levy. This includes charges for airside activities such as landing and passenger terminal fees but also fees for non-aviation activities.[12] The form that this regulation has taken varies from country to country.[13] Essentially there are four types of price regulation: *Single-till price regulation* takes the form of a price-cap applied to all revenues deriving from the airport on all commercial activities. Price regulation is by way of a price-cap using the RPI-X formula and the regulatory review periods vary between three to five years.[14] With single till price regulation, carriers share part of the airports' commercial revenues by paying lower aeronautical charges. *Dual-till price regulation* separates aeronautical functions from non-aeronautical ones. The regulator determines the level of allowed average aeronautical charges by considering aeronautical revenues and costs only. Consequently, the corresponding asset base includes aeronautical assets only. *Rate-of-return* regulation benchmarks the profitability of regulated activities to the average obtained from reference airports or businesses. It sets an allowed return on a defined asset base. *Price monitoring* is currently implemented in Australia and New Zealand. The regulators use a trigger or 'grim strategy' regulation where a light-handed form of regulation is used until the subject firm sets prices or earns profits or reduces quality beyond some point, and thus triggers a long-term commitment to intruding regulation (see note 25 for a description of potential changes in New Zealand).

The essence of the debate of single versus dual till is the impact it has on airport economic efficiency. The relative merits of dual versus single till essentially rest on two issues. First, do airports have (and exercise) market power in both aviation and non-aviation sectors, and second what represents a 'fair' distribution of the rents? There is significant debate regarding the first question.

The major argument for not including non-aviation revenues under a single till is that they result in perverse incentives when airports are capacity constrained and they may create costs when airports have lots of capacity. When airports are capacity constrained and a single till is in place, as more revenue is made on the non-aeronautical side, aeronautical charges must be lowered to remain under the price cap. Thus, in the presence of congestion, prices are reduced when economic efficiency dictates that they should be raised. If profit-maximizing airports are not capacity constrained, they have every incentive to stimulate demand (and revenue) via lower prices on the aeronautical side. Thus, in the non-constrained case, single till price-cap regulation is not necessary. Indeed, in the United States, airports voluntarily enter into contracts with airlines to share rents if the signatory airlines agree to share the risks of costs exceeding revenues. There is no regulation requiring this type of agreement. There is the often-cited condition that US airports should not make profits, but that is not the case. Airports must use any revenues in excess of expenses to improve the airport; these funds cannot be diverted to non-airport use.

At an airport without capacity constraints, the incentive is for the airport to lower charges on the airside, due to demand complementarities with non-airside business.[15] Even here the airlines obtain the rents since they do not pass the lower airside fees on to passengers in the form of lower prices, unless the market is highly competitive. This airside pricing is efficient because the marginal cost associated with excess capacity is likely to be below average cost and consequently the efficient outcome is to promote the use of airside capital. Therefore, non-airside rents are used to promote more efficient use of airside capacity. If there are demand side complementarities, the airport would set fees on the airside such that the marginal revenue from an additional operation, which would include both airside and non-airside revenue, is equal to marginal cost. In other words they would fully internalize the externality.

While the comparison of single and dual till forms of price-cap regulation favors dual till, there is a strong argument to be made for no price-cap regulation. This is because the implementation of a single regulatory regime will have divergent efficiency and distributional effects across the system given the heterogeneous characteristics (congestion, location-based market power, degree of airline competition) of airports.

In addition, there are two cost-side effects of regulation. First, the determination of allowed capital investment in the rate base distorts incentives for capital, as airports will strategically engage in over-investment. Second, once the regulatory rule is in place, airports have an incentive to minimize costs if the target allowable revenue level is reached. Thus, we would expect over investment in some infrastructure (gold plating) in order to influence the price-cap and then reductions in operation costs (lowering of service quality) in order to maximize realized profits. In the case of larger national airports in the Canadian system, the airport authorities are formally treated as 'not-for-profit' entities under the corporation act, so that any profits must be reinvested. The resulting incentive structure therefore exacerbates the gold plating problem.

Finally, what is not often considered in the debate on airport regulation is that airports can directly contribute to the degree of airline competition through pricing and capital investment decisions. Therefore policy makers should not only consider the welfare effects of airport regulation in relation to airports and their customers, but also the associated welfare effects on airline competition that result from airport pricing and investment decisions under the various regulatory regimes; for a full discussion of this issue see Zhang and Zhang (2006) and Basso and Zhang (2007).

Aside from efficiency considerations, distributional concerns remain as to which parties will capture the rents arising from geographic location and scarcity of supply.[16] Location rents are essential to allocate limited space efficiently (Starkie and Yarrow, 2008). Currently, at capacity constrained airports, airlines holding property rights to peak-demand slots capture all the rents that could be shared with or allocated to the airport. Under a single till price-cap, where the tendency is for aeronautical charges to fall, airlines will actually obtain some of the airport's location rents as well. The airlines might argue that they are responsible for generating the non-airside rents and therefore are as deserving of them as the airport. But it is the airport that undertakes the investments and contracts and therefore takes the risk.

Airport Regulation in the United States

US airport regulation is essentially a cost-of-service form of regulation. This type of regulation is relatively intrusive as the regulator must approve every price change and, in some cases, service decision. While the United States has no formal regulator, airports must justify with the carriers and their political masters that airport fees are cost based. One could also argue that those airports that still adhere to the principles of residual financing behave as if they operate under a single till form of price-cap regulation.[17] The important difference in the United States is that sharing of revenues is voluntary, albeit under governance that requires break-even; the airports are required to set aeronautical fees so as to collect revenues that reflect the costs of providing the service. Thus individual prices are indirectly regulated in the sense that the aggregate of revenues cannot exceed costs. This however does not imply cost minimization.

The US form of indirect regulation provides for neither static nor dynamic efficiency. Static efficiency is not achieved since fees reflect accounting rather than economic costs. Any excess demands are rationed through a quantity method such as flow control whereby either flights within a given time or distance from the constrained airport are not allowed to depart until a slot is available for them or arriving aircraft are stacked up waiting their turn to land. Dynamic efficiency refers to innovation in both improved processes and product development. It also ensures that the incumbent airlines appropriate the majority of rents at capacity constrained airports due to slot ownership and fare premiums. Dynamic efficiency is frustrated since there are no price signals that reveal the value of added capacity. Any excess demand reflects a failure to price scarce resources appropriately and the rent due to slots accrues to the carriers that hold the slots. They show up in the form of hub premiums.

In 2008, the US Transportation Secretary announced a proposal for a new way to manage congestion at New York's LaGuardia Airport.[18] The facility was capped from 1968 to 1999, but the cap was eliminated by Congress for all high density airports (the others were Kennedy, O'Hare, Newark and Washington National – now Reagan National) in the early 2000s.

The US Department of Transport (US DOT) is proposing two market-based options that would require a limited number of flights operated by the airlines in a given day, known as slots, to be made available through an auction process. Under the first option, all air carriers would be given up to 20 slots a day for the ten year life of the rule. Over the next five years, 8 percent of the additional slots currently used by an airline would be available to any carrier via an auction. An additional 2 percent of the slots would be retired to help cut the substantial delays at the airport; with record delays being set in 2007. Under this proposal, proceeds from the auction would be invested in new congestion and capacity initiatives in the New York region.

The second option also gives airlines access to up to 20 slots a day for a ten year period. Beyond those flights, 20 percent of the slots currently used by the airlines would be made available over the next five years to all airlines through an auction. Under this option, the carriers would retain the net proceeds of the auction. Almost immediately upon the announcement every interest group came out against the proposal: airlines, the Port Authority, the Air Transport Association, and foreign airline associations. The prospect of privatizing US airports is examined later in the chapter.

Airport Regulation in the EU

In the EU, rate-of-return or price-cap regulation is the norm. The best examples are the UK (which regulates the BAA), France, Denmark and Ireland. With rate-of-return regulation (ROR) the key questions are first what constitutes a 'fair' return on capital invested and second, what capital invested should be included in the 'allowed rate base'?[19] This form of regulation is very time-intensive and generally involves lengthy regulatory hearings. As Tretheway (2001) points out, ROR regulation tends to be complex, unresponsive and expensive to administer.

Price cap regulation, by far the dominant form of regulation in the UK, on the other hand was introduced precisely to overcome the problems associated with rate-of-return regulation. It was designed to lower the overall costs of regulation and to provide the incentives for firms to act in a way that improves economic welfare. Given the information asymmetry between the regulator and the regulated firm, one of the key objectives is to incentivize the firm to reveal its true costs by allowing the firm to keep efficiency gains within the price control period. The next period's prices are adjusted for inflation and the X-factor.[20]

Pure and hybrid price caps differ in the way in which the X in the price cap formula is set. A pure price cap sets X without reference to the costs of the regulated airport but may set it with reference to a broad airport benchmarked cost, while hybrid price caps set the X with reference to a regulated cost base. Hybrid price caps provide fewer incentives for cost reductions. For European airports none of the regulators have developed a pure price capping system. The price caps at Aéroports de Paris (ADP), Copenhagen and Dublin are based on costs.[21]

At some EU airports, predominantly in Germany, we also observe revenue-sharing agreements which often relate the level of charges to the passenger growth over a certain period. The model is that the airline and the airport agree that airside charges will be reduced if the rate of passenger growth is achieved or maintained at some agreed upon level. These so-called sliding scales can be combined with price cap regulation as in the case of Hamburg (Gillen and Niemeier, 2008) and Vienna.[22] At Frankfurt airport, for example, both parties agreed that with a projected passenger growth rate of 4 percent, average charges could be increased by 2 percent since 4 percent was deemed to be below the desired target. In the case of a higher growth rate, airlines participate with a 33 percent share in additional revenues. With lower growth rates the airport cannot fully compensate revenue losses through higher charges. Only 33 percent of the loss can be compensated. The agreement results in a sliding scale of airport charges that is related to passenger growth.

Recent New Directions for Airport Regulation in the EU

A proposal on airport charges was approved by the European Parliament on October 23, 2008, and sent to the European Council. It was approved on February 11, 2009. The objective of the Directive is to establish a general framework setting common principles for the levying of airport charges.[23] The Directive imposes new obligations on many airports regarding transparency, consultation, non-discrimination, and arbitration, and it opens up a new avenue for airlines to pursue their grievances. This move by the EU sustains its view that airports have market power and will use it. This continental European view differs from what we see in Australia, New Zealand and even the United States.[24]

Airport Regulation in Australia and New Zealand

Australia and New Zealand have what has been termed 'light-handed' regulation, something unique to these two countries. The major airports in both countries have been privatized since the mid-1990s with the exception of Sydney which was privatized in 2002. With this change in ownership and governance, formal regulation was put in place in Australia and airports were subjected to a price cap of the RPI-X form. These caps were in place for five years, at which time there would be a review (Forsyth, 2002). It was expected that price caps would probably be continued. The caps were set by the government and they were administered by the Australian Competition and Consumer Commission (ACCC). In both Australia and New Zealand, it was a dual till system.

In 2001, the Australian Productivity Commission released a report which recommended the end of price cap regulation for all airports. This move was stimulated in part by the tight control of prices under the price cap while the airline industry faced turmoil. The result was a poor financial performance for airports. Price cap regulation seemed to be workable in strong economic conditions but was not flexible with economic down-turns and weak airline performance. In 2002, the government announced that it would replace regulation with monitoring for seven major capital city airports, and would not regulate or monitor other airports, a move from formal dual till price cap regulation to 'light-handed' regulation. This regulatory form places no immediate constraints on aero-nautical charges but monitors prices with a view to 'taking action' if prices are judged to be too high. After its first five years in operation, price monitoring was reviewed in 2007 and renewed for another five years (with some adjustments). Local/municipal relations (land development) and the valuation of airport land and assets (for determining aero-nautical charges) have been issues under this system.[25]

New Zealand did not formally regulate its airports after privatization, though it did provide for a review of airport pricing behavior with the threat of more explicit regulation should this behavior be unacceptable. The New Zealand approach involved a general provision set out in legislation to enable a review of pricing in industries such as airports. This review could be initiated by the Minister at any time. In 1998, a review of pricing at Auckland, Christchurch and Wellington airports was initiated. The Commerce Commission undertook the review and recommended price regulation of Auckland airport (NZ Commerce Commission, 2002).

A Commerce Act review was undertaken in 2007. The government recommended that Auckland, Wellington and Christchurch (all international airports) be subject to much more stringent, hands-on, price monitoring and even regulation and that it be adminis-tered by the New Zealand Commerce Commission. These recommendations have not yet been introduced with legislative changes.[26]

Forsyth (2006) provides an assessment of the light handed regulatory approach. He notes that it works reasonably well, with prices somewhat above what might be the case under tight regulation but well below monopoly levels. Also, airports seem to be relatively cost efficient, probably because increasing profits from increased efficiency is unlikely to draw the ire of 'light-handed' regulators. In effect the regulator seems willing to allow airports that are efficient to keep some of the gains obtained from being cost efficient. A heavy handed regulator might have reduced prices so all the cost efficiency gains were passed on to the airline. There are problems with investment incentives as well as with the 'process' of light-handed regulation because it does not provide guidelines by which to judge or sanction the performance of the airports. Forsyth (2006) stresses that cost-based guidelines would result in inefficient cost plus regulation. Better to establish first the objectives of regulation and then set in place a set of guidelines that provide incentives for efficiency.

Other Airport Regulatory Models

Canada's lack of formal airport regulation stems from the form of governance that resulted when the Federal government devolved the airports beginning in the mid-1990s. The Federal government did not want airports to be privatized, mostly because of the lack of worldwide experience with the fully privatized airport model at that time. It was also concerned that the use of revenue bonds by airports to invest in capacity can have a deleterious impact on downstream airline competition. The reason is that airlines provide the bond guarantees and this in turn gives the airlines some power over capacity investment. The Canadian government chose a not-for-profit model which seemed to address all of the concerns the government had in adopting the new airports policy.[27] The policy was evolutionary in starting with four airports (Vancouver, Edmonton, Calgary and Montreal) and subsequently including the remaining Tier 1 airports; Tier 1 airports are those included in the National Airport System.[28]

Fees and charges under the airport authority legislation were not regulated or subject to review. Airport authorities were free to set charges where they wanted and could impose different types of charges as they wished. Because they were established as non-share capital entities they could not go to the capital market for funds for investments. Therefore, all airport authorities levy an airport improvement fee (AIF) as a source of funds for capital investments. The nature of the Canadian model led to a lack of price regulation; first, the not-for-profit model meant all monies must be reinvested and second the lack of access to the broader capital market to fund needed investments meant there was a need for the AIF. Any constraints on the airports' ability to set these fees as needed could potentially jeopardize investments in capacity.

There is relatively little work which has assessed airport regulation in China. A recent study by Zhang and Yuen (2007) indicates that seven airports in China have been privatized and are listed on the Chinese stock exchange. These airports include Xiamen, Shanghai, Shenzhen, Beijing, Hainan and Guangzhou – in which Shanghai International Airport Ltd holds both Hongqiao and Pudong airports. They point out that the fundamental role of the IPOs was to improve airport efficiency, not necessarily to raise capital. Market discipline was to be introduced. The evidence was that cost efficiency was low. The economic performance of airports in China is challenged from two opposing forces. Growth in the aviation sector is larger than any other aviation market in the world and more capacity is needed quickly. Therefore cost efficiency is not a priority. On the other hand, the ownership and governance structure of airports are being shifted to more local control, and although the state has influence, local concerns for efficiency place pressure on the airport.

AIRPORT AND MARKET POWER; THE EVOLVING AIRPORT BUSINESS

There is the emerging view that the airport business has evolved from its public utility beginnings and that now the institutional and market settings are changing to limit the airport's market power and its incentive to abuse that power.[29]

A number of factors influence an airport's ability to set airside prices. Airports are constrained by intermodal competition. A good example of air-rail competition, in a large airport context, is the impact on the demand for flights between London and Paris with the completion of the Chunnel connecting the UK with continental Europe; with the introduction of high speed trains the number of direct flights offered between London and Paris was reduced by almost 50 percent.[30] For smaller airports, there is greater access provided by well-developed roadway systems and in the case of Europe, rail systems.

Therefore, passengers can easily access alternative airports. A good example is the drain of passengers from Schiphol Airport in Amsterdam to airports in Belgium and western Germany via rail when the Dutch government placed an environmental tax on passenger tickets for Schiphol. Manchester Airport in the UK has grown significantly with high quality road access. Airports in North America can have a number of substitutes which are accessible via freeways. Vancouver Airport in British Columbia and Seattle Tacoma Airport in Washington state are one example; Toronto, Canada and Buffalo, New York, are another example. Also short haul flights are competing with autos particularly when there are three or four in the travelling party.

In the case of larger airports, the number of flights an airport can attract depends on both the airport's attractiveness as a point of departure/arrival and on its usefulness as a hub for connecting passengers. In the former case, an airport's bargaining power with airlines derives from its geographic proximity to 'non-connecting' passengers and the degree to which it competes with other airports for those passengers. In the absence of competition airlines are faced with the choice of using the airport or ignoring that segment of the passenger market. However, the airport may still be constrained in its pricing to the extent that non-hub airports prefer the services of several rival airlines rather than be dominated by one or two.[31] The airport managers prefer to have competing sources of airside business to protect against the risk of a carrier failing or facing a bilateral monopoly. This provides downward pressure on airside prices, particularly in countries such as Canada, Australia and New Zealand where the domestic carriers are discount or charter airlines with low margins that compete with dominant and previously government-owned carriers.

Domestic liberalization had a significant impact on reducing the market power of airports. With the deregulation of air services a number of things occurred. First, airlines were able to move between markets, build networks and have airports bid for their services. A second aspect is the way in which services are now delivered. In a regulated environment in which airports were viewed as public utilities, airports had a set of posted prices generally based on aircraft weight for landing charges. Airports assumed the risk of traffic loss and airlines paid posted prices with no long-term contracts. However, airline deregulation has brought about a significant change and shift in risk. Airlines are now more footloose as the low cost carriers can easily move from one airport to another and legacy carriers also can establish bases at some non-hub airports. Airports now have an incentive to negotiate long term contracts with carriers and engage in incentive pricing (see Starkie and Yarrow, 2008, for a discussion).[32] Such contracts specify charges, service quality (turn around times, advertising, co-investments) and length of the contract. The average charge paid by larger and/or base carriers will be less than the posted price; Starkie (2009) reports two such contracts in the UK that have this characteristic. Furthermore, airports with their lumpy capital now have an incentive to have airlines establish a base and to develop a route. Thus competition between airports is not simply about spatial adjacency but also exists across wide geographic markets as airports bid for airline base investments.

There are numerous examples of airline market power at airports; American Airlines shut down its hub at San Jose, Air Canada withdrew 20 percent capacity from Vancouver airport when it obtained new longer haul aircraft and realigned its network. BA abandoned its second hub at Gatwick, easyJet withdrew from Dortmund and Ryanair reduced capacity at Stansted and withdrew service from several continental European airports. Airports are characterized by sunk capital, airlines are capital with wings. Airports have every incentive to negotiate contracts with downstream users.

A significant change was the commercialization of the airport industry. There was greater emphasis to pursue a more commercial focus even among government-owned airports. This led to a more business like approach, a change in mindset and the development of non-aviation revenues. These changes underlined the dependency of retail revenues on passenger volumes, creating a symbiotic relationship between airlines and airports.

The market power of airports has been further reduced by greater liberalization of international air travel, changes to airline ownership restrictions and negotiations of open skies agreements. There is more scope for airlines to choose destinations other than those previously designated in bilateral agreements. There is greater market entry with rights of establishment; Virgin America and Virgin Blue in Australia being good examples. Airports are being asked to respond to the new services and demands of the airline business models as well as to the dynamics of the market. They are responding as they bid for airlines.

CONCLUSIONS

Whether an airport is government run, a not-for-profit organization or a for-profit corporation, it is subject to market forces that define commercial value and competition along with (private and social) economic costs and benefits. These costs and benefits will change depending on the set of institutions in place and the governance structure. Governance, regulation and oversight by government agencies augment, or perhaps impede, free-market forces by placing constraints on the actions and decisions of airports and providing a particular set of incentives; incentives which move managers in one direction rather than another. The resulting economic impact of governance and regulatory institutions is therefore defined by the interaction of the underlying market forces with the implemented (as distinct from 'intended') constraints imposed and the behavioural responses of relevant decision-makers (airport management, airlines and passengers) to the incentives that are actually created.

The actual ownership and regulatory environments of airports across the world represent compromises between conflicting objectives; efficiency has been one of the main motivations for change, but only to an extent. The very different approaches to the airport problem adopted across different countries possibly reflects different views on the best ways to pursue efficiency objectives, but it also reflects the different non-efficiency objectives which governments are pursuing in their airport policies. Some governments are more eager to maximize revenues on privatization than others, some are more focused on promoting and protecting competition in aviation markets, some are more willing to become involved in detailed economic regulation than others and some take the view that the threat of regulation will be sufficient to discipline pricing behavior.

The economic regulation of airports across the world ranges from tight rate-of-return regulation to liberalized light-handed implicit regulation. As markets grow, there is an expectation that more governments will shift policies to favor light-handed regulation with privatization. The exception is the EU where airlines faced with increasing competition in many markets and international liberalization successfully lobbied Brussels to introduce a common EU airport fee regulation. It is highly unlikely the United States will shift its governance model anytime soon. Canada may move to privatization with some form of regulation or oversight. China will in the near to medium term continue to rely on public ownership but with a greater emphasis on commercialization.

Privatization is motivated by a desire to improve allocative, productive and dynamic efficiency. Allocative efficiency refers to prices being close to incremental costs; there is mixed evidence whether it has improved under privatization but certainly it is no worse than with government ownership where distortions arise from the pursuit of non-economic objectives. Productive efficiency has improved with privatization and lower costs. Given the rapid growth in the aviation sector in the last two decades and the improvements in customer service and service quality, the airport experience for customers has been welfare improving under the shift in governance structure. With privatization what we have seen is a discernible improvement in innovation and the development of aviation products to satisfy the demands of a dynamic marketplace. In my view, dynamic efficiency has not been given enough attention in the debate regarding preferred governance structures and whether to regulate. As an example, efficient prices for congestion are more likely to be introduced in a privatized regime than with public ownership or regulation.

Should airports be regulated? Our examination of airports in Australia, New Zealand, North America and Europe reveals differing views across jurisdictions. Continental Europe seems to have maintained a position that airports have market power, at least on the airside, and therefore must be regulated.[33] Those predisposed to regulation should recognize the trade-off between imperfect regulation at airports, and the economic effects of the exercise of market power and the potential (or actual) distortion that specific industry regulation can introduce. The adverse effects of market power need to be quite substantial to justify formal regulation. Market economies outperform regulated economies generally because no one has enough information or foresight to understand the changing environment, so the market's seemingly messy processes of experimentation and correction yield better results than a regulator's analysis; financial markets perhaps excepted.

Airline deregulation has been the single most important factor in affecting the balance of power between airports and airlines. It has fundamentally changed the way airlines and airports do business, largely because it has led to the introduction of new airline business models, new demands on airports and the need to compete for air services. The deregulation of airports is needed to improve the returns from airline deregulation. Countries that maintain restrictive international air service agreements and maintain foreign ownership limits, or fail to put in place rights of establishment, preserve barriers to entry. In some cases, such barriers convey market power to the carrier since airports cannot bid for services from other carriers. On the other hand the carriers are not able to easily switch between airports. In the case of secondary airports, such as spokes in a hub-and-spoke system, airports will have less market power regardless of regulatory regime because they depend on the carrier to provide access to a hub. With liberalization and open skies agreements, airports can bid for airline services and airlines are free to choose which airport best serves their needs and business model.

Some, including many airlines, take the view that airports are essential facilities and therefore should be tightly regulated. A proper application of the doctrine of essential facilities should recognize the prominence of dynamic over static efficiency in promoting consumer welfare. Regulators and airlines may be averse to recognizing these tradeoffs because – unlike with severely distorted prices – the welfare losses from foregone innovation may be unobservable to the regulators' constituencies. Moreover, an emphasis on dynamic efficiency requires the short-term regulator to take the 'long view' – fostering the competitive process rather than emulating the competitive outcome.

ACKNOWLEDGMENTS

I owe an intellectual debt to Peter Forsyth, Hans-Martin Niemeier, David Starkie and Michael Tretheway for educating me over the years about airport economics and regulation. This chapter draws on joint work with Peter Forsyth and Hans-Martin Niemeier (Ashgate 2007) and Peter Forsyth et al., (Ashgate, 2004). I am grateful to the editors in particular Robin Lindsey as well as Michael Tretheway for comments on an earlier version.

NOTES

1. The focus is on the economic regulation of airports rather than safety or environmental regulation.
2. While publicly owned firms did not charge prices well above costs (and indeed, often allowed revenues to fall short of total costs), they did not necessarily produce at minimum cost, and often did not supply what the users were willing to pay for.
3. Another interesting difference is that Germany is based on a civil law tradition whereas the UK is based on a common law tradition.
4. This section draws on material in Gillen and Morrison (2008).
5. Some US airports have multiple contracts for services that are in effect privately run.
6. Midway Airport is the only US airport that is being privatized and is regarded as an important experiment that may shape future US airport governance. Some analysts have predicted that isolated privatization cannot succeed in the US as individual private airports must pay full market rates for their capital while their government-owned competitors do not.
7. Examples of port authorities include New York & New Jersey, Seattle and Boston.
8. This is a direct consequence of the way the airport authorities legislation is structured and restricts access to certain types of capital.
9. BAA is currently majority owned by Ferrovial of Spain.
10. See UK Competition Commission (2008).
11. That being said, Macquarie Airports has divested all airports in which they held minority shares.
12. Airside fees would include landing, terminal, security and emergency/policing fees. Commercial fees are those negotiated for concession and lease agreements.
13. In the debate on how to regulate airports, three features are important: the complementarity between airside and non-airside activity, the degree to which airports are congested (capacity constrained) and the level of competition in the industry (or at the airport if it is a hub). With regard to the complementarity issue Starkie (2001) argues that the effect of increased airside movements on passenger volumes and non-airside revenues has a strong effect on airport pricing incentives. Capacity constraints influence the consequences for different price structures and just as importantly, the ability of the airport to cover its capital expenses.
14. In the RPI-X formula RPI is the retail price index and 'X' is the limiting offset. The value of X is determined by the regulator based on a range of criteria including, for example, whether the industry is high or low productivity, the performance of the firm in the previous regulated period and whether the regulator wishes to incentivize the firm to reduce costs.

15. Czerny (2006) argues that single till is superior to dual till under a welfare-maximizing metric. However his model assumes a monopoly airport for all revenue streams and for flight activity.
16. Note that these are not monopoly rents arising from market power per se.
17. Residual financing means that at the end of the fiscal year if revenues are less than costs the signatory airlines using the airport are responsible for covering the difference.
18. See US Department of Transportation (2008), Announcement of LaGuardia Congestion Rule (http://www.dot.gov/affairs/dot5308.htm).
19. Liquidity ratio, risk and economic conditions are considered in setting the allowed rate of return.
20. 'X' depends on how the regulator assesses the trade-offs under its objectives given the cost and demand climate in which the firm operates. A high positive X-factor (that is, RPI-X, resulting in lower real prices) might indicate that the firm revealed substantial cost savings in the past or it may indicate that the regulator sees considerable scope for further efficiency improvements during the next control period. A high negative X-factor (that is, RPI + X, enabling a real price increase) is an indicator that the regulator might be placing more emphasis on the firm's planned investments and the firm facing rising incremental costs.
21. Most important, price cap regulation does not regulate the charging structure according to arbitrary cost allocations based on historic costs.
22. At two German airports, Frankfurt and Düsseldorf, the revenue sharing agreements are the result of Memorandum of Understanding between the airports and its users. This agreement was legalized as a public contract between the airport and regulator (Klenk, 2004). In case of disagreement the charges would be fixed according to cost based regulations.
23. These principles are to be transposed into national law by each EU Member State within 24 months of the Directive's entry into force.
24. Airport regulation in the UK is treated differently than in continental Europe primarily because most airports have been fully privatized and have not been regulated; the exception of course being BAA airports. However the new EU Directive includes UK airports, as well as continental EU airports.
25. Australian airports have been highly entrepreneurial. Similar to the privatized UK airports they have focused on developing non-aviation revenues including non-complementary investments on airport land factory retail outlets, shopping malls and, in one case, a brick factory!
26. Under the new rules, airports (Auckland, Wellington and Christchurch) would be subject to an enhanced disclosure regime, which would include information on how their charges are set based on stipulated input methodologies (how costs should be calculated) developed by the Commerce Commission. The Commerce Commission would monitor the way airports are setting charges against non-binding pricing principles and, if it finds stricter controls are needed, it would be able to recommend that further regulatory measures be imposed.
27. The concerns which shaped the new airports policy included the need to reinvest in infrastructure without drawing on federal government funds, avoiding full privatization and allowing airports to meet the needs of people and industry in their particular region.
28. The NAS includes airports in all national, provincial and territorial capitals, as well as airports with annual traffic of 200 000 passengers or more.
29. See Starkie (2009).
30. This result was perhaps due to two related factors; the value of slots at LHR which could be reallocated to now more valuable routes and the encouragement of slot trading by the slot coordinator at LHR.
31. Spoke airports generally prefer to be serviced through two competing hubs, or with direct and indirect (through a hub) service.
32. The agreement between Frankfurt Airport and Lufthansa that set landing charges based on passenger growth is a good example.
33. Germany is a good example of such a view despite the fact that every resident is within one hour's travel time of an airport.

REFERENCES

Armstrong, M., S. Cowan and J. Vickers, 1994, *Regulatory Reform: Economic Analysis and British Experience*. Cambridge, MA: MIT Press.
Basso, L. and A. Zhang, 2007, Congestible facility rivalry in vertical structures. *Journal of Urban Economics*, **61** (2), 218–237.
Czerny, A., 2006, Price-cap regulation of airports: single-till versus dual-till. *Journal of Regulatory Economics*, **30**, 85–97.

Forsyth, P., 2002, Privatization and regulation of Australian and New Zealand airports. Paper presented at the Fourth Hamburg Aviation Conference: Hamburg, Germany.

Forsyth, P., 2006, Airport policy in Australia and New Zealand: privatization, light handed regulation and performance. Paper presented at the Workshop on Comparative Political Economy and Infrastructure Performance: The Case of Airports, Madrid September 2006.

Forsyth, P., D. Gillen, A. Knorr, O. Mayer, H.-M. Niemeier and D. Starkie, eds, 2004, *The Economic Regulation of Airports: Recent Developments in Australia, North America and Europe.* Aldershot, UK: Ashgate Publishers.

Gillen, D. and H.-M. Niemeier, 2008, Comparative political economy of airport infrastructure in the European Union: evolution of privatization, regulation and slot reform. In C. Winston and G. de Rus, eds, *Aviation Infrastructure Performance: A Study in Comparative Political Economy.* Washington DC: Brookings Institute, pp. 36–63.

Gillen, D. and W. Morrison, 2008, Airport governance and regulation in the 21st century. Mimeo, Centre for Transportation Studies, University of British Columbia.

Hooper, P., R. Cain and S. White, 2000, The privatization of Australia's airports. *Transportation Research Part E*, **36**, 181–204.

Klenk, M., 2004, New approaches to airline/airport relations: the charges framework for Frankfurt Airport. In P. Forsyth, D. Gillen, A. Knorr, O. Mayer, H.-M. Niemeier and D. Starkie, eds, *The Economic Regulation of Airports.* German Aviation Research Society Series. Aldershot, UK: Ashgate Publishers, pp. 125–140.

Morrison, S. and C. Winston, 2008, Delayed! US aviation infrastructure policy at the crossroads. In C. Winston and G. de Rus, eds, *Aviation Infrastructure Performance: A Study in Comparative Political Economy.* Washington DC: Brookings Institution, Chapter 5.

New Zealand Commerce Commission, 2002, Final Report. Part IV Inquiry into airfield services at Auckland, Wellington and Christchurch International Airports, August.

Parker, D., 1999, The Performance of BAA before and after privatization. *Journal of Transport Economics and Policy*, **33** (2), 133–145.

Starkie, D., 2001, Reforming UK airport regulation. *Journal of Transport Economics and Policy*, **35** , 119–135.

Starkie, D., 2009, Changes in the airline–airport relationship: implications for regulation. Paper presented at the 12th Hamburg Aviation Conference, Hamburg, February 12, 2009.

Starkie, D. and G. Yarrow, 2008, The single-till approach to the price regulation of airports. In D. Starkie, ed., *Aviation Markets: Studies in Competition and Regulatory Reform.* Aldershot, UK: Ashgate Publishing Company, pp. 123–131.

Tretheway, M., 2001, Airport ownership, management and price regulation. Report to the Canadian Transportation Act Review Committee, April.

UK Competition Commission, 2008, BAA airports market investigation: provisional findings report. Available at: http://www.competition-commission.org.uk/inquiries/ref2007/airports/provisional_findings.htm.

US Department of Transportation, 2008, Announcement of LaGuardia congestion rule. Available at: http://www.dot.gov/affairs/dot5308.htm.

Zhang, A. and A. Yuen, 2007, Airport policy and performance in mainland China and Hong Kong. In C. Winston and G. de Rus, eds, *Aviation Infrastructure Performance: A Study in Comparative Political Economy.* Washington DC: Brookings Institute, 125–140.

Zhang, A. and Y. Zhang, 2006, Airport capacity and congestion when carriers have market power. *Journal of Urban Economics*, **60** (2), 229–247.

35 Competition and regulation in air transport
Anming Zhang, Yimin Zhang and Joseph A. Clougherty

INTRODUCTION

The world airline industry has received a great deal of attention from scholars in a number of different disciplines: economics, management, political science and so on. The sustained interest in this industry is due in part to its fundamental importance as a contributor to exchange, development and economic growth. Furthermore, the airline industry was at the forefront of public policy reforms with respect to liberalization of regulatory policies: namely, the bellwether deregulation of US domestic markets in 1978 (Derthick and Quirk, 1985). Until 1978, the US airline industry was regulated by the Civil Aeronautics Board (CAB). Through the experiences of unregulated intrastate airlines in California and Texas – which offered lower fares than comparable regulated services between states – and a few chartered international airlines, the deregulation of market entry commenced in 1978 with the passage of the 'Airline Deregulation Act' (Levine, 1987). Fare pricing was fully liberalized in 1982, and the CAB itself was abolished in 1984.

Following US deregulation there has been a worldwide move away from government regulation towards liberalization of air services and 'open skies'. The unleashing of airline competition has led to a number of strategic actions being taken by airlines in a liberalized competitive environment, including mergers and consolidation, competition over frequency and scheduling, hub-and-spoke network formation, and international alliance agreements. In this chapter, we provide a review of the research that aims to understand the rationales – and welfare implications – behind these various strategic actions that were ultimately set in motion by enhanced competitive forces.

One might ask how the present review is different from earlier reviews: where Borenstein (1992), Evans and Kessides (1993), Morrison and Winston (1995) and Tretheway and Kincaid (2005) focused on the US domestic market; and where Button et al. (1998) focused on the EU market. In order to add value and not duplicate effort, this review departs from previous reviews in a few respects: by employing game theoretic analysis in the review; by more fully considering the international – not just domestic and regional – dimensions to air transport competition; and by focusing on more recent developments (for example, the international implications of airline consolidation, competition over frequency and scheduling, airline network competition, strategic alliances, air cargo and the airport–airline relationship).

In order to support these aims, the chapter is organized as follows. The next section considers the airline consolidation phenomenon. This is followed by a reflection on how airline competition manifests in terms of price, frequency/scheduling and network competition. Consideration then turns to the international regulatory regime for air transport and the resulting rationale for international strategic alliances. The next section identifies the salient features of the air cargo sector and the implications these features have for policy reform. The penultimate section considers the emerging scholarship that integrates airports and air passenger markets into a unified analysis. The final section contains concluding remarks.

AIRLINE MERGERS AND CONSOLIDATION

While airlines responded in a number of different fashions (hub-and-spoke network, frequency/scheduling competition, frequent flyer programs, price discrimination, yield management, optimal contracts for inputs and so on) to enhanced competitive pressures in the post-1978 liberalized environment, one particular practice – consolidation in search of network economies – particularly surprised scholars and industry observers. Pre-deregulation studies indicated that the airline industry was characterized by constant returns to scale (Caves, 1962; Douglas and Miller, 1974; Keeler, 1978; White 1979); hence, scholars assumed that a liberalized airline industry would approach the perfectly competitive ideal.[1]

In the post-deregulation era, airline consolidation took three principal forms: domestic airline mergers (for example, the series of mergers that led to Canadian Airlines); integration of domestic and international airline routes (for example, Qantas becoming a domestic carrier and not just an international carrier); and international strategic alliances (for example, Lufthansa's participation in Star Alliance). In particular, domestic airline mergers have been found to involve substantial network economies (Brueckner and Spiller, 1991, 1994; Brueckner et al., 1992). These economies are founded in part on the presence of substantial density economies (fixed costs on a route are quite high, but the marginal cost of an additional passenger is quite low).[2] The same principle applies to integration of domestic and international routes (Clougherty, 2002, 2006; Dresner, 1994; Oum et al., 1993); and international strategic alliances (Brueckner, 2001; Zhang and Zhang, 2006a).

The spate of domestic airline mergers in the late 1980s and early 1990s generated a great deal of public policy concern and scholarly interest. In particular, the TWA/Ozark and Northwest/Republic pairings in the US market elicited substantial scrutiny – in fact the US Department of Justice unsuccessfully advised the US Department of Transportation to block these mergers. Furthermore, domestic consolidation occurred in many nations: for example, British Airways acquired British Caledonian and Air France purchased Air Inter. The high profile nature of domestic airline mergers led to a substantial amount of scholarship considering the welfare implications of these mergers with the literature splitting along the familiar market-power/efficiency-gains lines. The efficiency-gains camp (Brueckner et al., 1992; Brueckner and Spiller, 1991, 1994; Levine, 1987) observed that consolidation allowed the exploitation of hub-and-spoke networks and economies of traffic density which generated substantial consumer benefits in markets served by hubs (for example, pairings between east and west coast cities in the United States) and compensated for market-power effects. While the market-power camp stressed the ability of airlines to raise fares for markets into and out of hub cities (Borenstein, 1989, 1991; Werden et al., 1991) and via multi-market competition (Evans and Kessides, 1994; Kim and Singal, 1993).

Some scholars have moved beyond strictly considering the domestic efficiency and market-power effects of domestic merger activity to include the importance of international effects. Oum et al. (1993) first raised the point that international strategic effects should be considered when evaluating the welfare implications of domestic merger activity. The significant economies generated by domestic consolidation suggest that home-nation airlines may reap additional profits in imperfectly competitive international markets, and home-nation consumers in international markets may also experience lower prices due to efficiencies. In supportive empirical work, Dresner (1994) found that airline hub size increased the number of international passengers out of the hub. Furthermore, Clougherty (2002, 2006) found that the matching of extensive domestic networks with international routes and the completion of domestic mergers both substantially increase the market shares of airlines in imperfectly competitive international markets. Accordingly, the phenomenon of the integration of domestic and international routes appears to be driven by the obvious joint-economies of production involved with providing both domestic and international air transport service. In short, the competitive position of airlines in international markets appears to be improved when extensive domestic networks are matched up with international services.

A third strategic action taken by airlines in the deregulated market environment involves the proliferation of international strategic alliances. While this form of airline consolidation will be explored in more detail later, it bears reiterating that network economies are fundamental to explaining all three forms of airline consolidation. First, domestic airline mergers increased airline network size by allowing airlines to further increase the scale of their domestic hub-and-spoke systems. Second, the integration of international and domestic routes increased airline network size by allowing international routes to be integrated into domestic hub-and-spoke systems. Third, international strategic alliances allow hub-and-spoke networks to expand globally into foreign markets that might otherwise be impossible to integrate into an airline's operation.

AIRLINE COMPETITION

Airline competition unleashed by deregulation takes the form of both price and non-price competition, and of network competition.

Price Competition

A consequence of airline consolidation is that the 'effective' number of firms has actually fallen, and most routes are served by only one, two or three airlines. This suggests that small numbers oligopoly is the dominant market structure in the industry. A natural question then is: how competitive are these oligopoly airline routes? The answer to this question depends on how oligopolistic airlines compete with each other. Airline competition may be modeled with certain simple oligopoly models: the Cournot model and the Bertrand model. In general, which model is 'correct' for an industry depends in large part on its production technology. In Cournot competition, firms commit to quantities, and prices then adjust to clear the market, implying the industry is flexible in price adjustments, even in the short run. On the other hand, in Bertrand competition, capacity is unlimited or easily adjusted in the short run. In reality, some industries behave like Bertrand and others Cournot.

Brander and Zhang (1990) investigate the degree of competitiveness on 33 duopoly routes out of Chicago. These routes were dominated by American Airlines and United Airlines for which Chicago is a major hub.[3] Brander and Zhang test the competitiveness of these duopoly airline markets by estimating the market conduct parameter. They use route-specific data on each airline's fare, market share, marginal cost, and elasticity of demand for the third quarter of 1985 to estimate 'conduct parameters'.[4] The estimates provide strong support for Cournot behavior. The conclusions of the base case are robust to variations in the elasticity of demand and cost specification. Brander and Zhang (1990, p. 580) conclude: 'In our sample of United Airlines and American Airlines duopoly routes, we found strong evidence against the cartel hypothesis and against the highly competitive Bertrand hypothesis. Cournot behavior falls within what we take to be the plausible range for this set of markets, taking into account the various errors and approximations that underlie our reasoning.'

The above analysis of pricing decisions in an oligopoly has focused on maximizing profit in a *single period*. If airlines undertake repeated interactions, it seems natural that they will use contingent strategies, in which the price (or quantity) chosen in any period depends on the actions that have occurred in previous periods. By introducing uncertainty about changes in market conditions, Green and Porter (1984) and Porter (1983) develop a theory of oligopoly that can explain price wars. In their theory, firms cannot tell with certainty whether a fall in their own profits has been caused by a rival's deviation from the implicit collusive output, or by worsened market conditions. Brander and Zhang (1993) examine the dynamic interaction between United Airlines and American Airlines on a set of duopoly routes out of Chicago. They test both the constant behavior models and the two Green–Porter price war models. The constant behavior models are all rejected, whereas the price-war models can both describe the data although the Cournot-based version is preferred.

Frequency/Scheduling Competition

The above analysis focused mainly on price competition (where quantity/capacity competition indirectly affects realized prices). Yet, airline competition can also revolve around non-price aspects, especially quality of service attributes, which influences consumers' choice between airlines. These include scheduling (if an airline offers its flights at popular times, it will attract patrons), safety record, in-flight amenities, frequent flyer programs, on-time performance, as well as schedule delay time and flight frequency. The last point, schedule delay time and flight frequency, is found to be a very important factor influencing both the industry demand and firm-specific demand. Schedule delay time refers to the time between a passenger's desired departure and the actual departure. According to Douglas and Miller (1974), the schedule delay associated with a carrier may be decomposed into 'frequency delay' and 'stochastic delay'. The former refers to the difference between one's desired departure time and the closest *scheduled* departure by the airline, whereas the latter is the delay caused by excess demand for one's preferred flight(s). Both delays depend largely on the carrier's flight frequency.

Most studies on airline schedule decisions take a spatial approach. In the typical spatial model, consumers have a distribution of desired departure (or arrival) times, and airlines set flight schedules taking into account the preferences of consumers. Airline pricing decisions are also related to their scheduling decisions given that the consumer's total travel costs include both ticket price and schedule delay. The most general form of such a model would assume consumers' desired departure (arrival) time to be distributed along a line (representing the time of day when airports are in operation) or over a closed circle (assuming the airport is open for round-the-clock operation). Then scheduling decisions would involve airlines optimally choosing location (flight times) as well as the number of locations (frequencies) on the line or over the circle. As this problem is techni- cally unmanageable for multiple airlines, simplifying assumptions must be imposed to yield analytical or numerical results.

Brueckner and Zhang (2001) consider scheduling and fare decisions by a monopoly carrier and study how network structure affects these decisions. In their model, there are three cities (A, B and H) with symmetric demand for travel between the individual city pairs (AB, AH and BH). For each city-pair market, consumers' desired arrival times are uniformly distributed over a circle representing a 24-hour clock with a density D and the monopoly airline spaces its arrival times equally around the circle. The 'market area' for each flight is determined as follows:

$$\delta - p - \alpha|t_a - t^*| - \beta h \geq 0, \text{ or } \alpha|t_a - t^*| \leq \delta - p - \beta h \tag{35.1}$$

where δ is benefit per trip to the passenger, p is the ticket price, α is disutility per hour of schedule delay, t_a is scheduled arrival time, t^* is desired arrival time, β is disutility per hour of travel time and h is travel time between any two cities. This leads to the follow- ing expression for demand per flight, given the uniform distribution of t^* with density D:

$$\frac{2D}{\alpha}(\delta - p - \beta h). \tag{35.2}$$

As the number of passengers per flight cannot exceed the number of potential passen- gers, the actual demand per flight must satisfy

$$q = \min\left\{\frac{2D}{\alpha}(\delta - p - \beta h), \frac{D}{f}\right\} \tag{35.3}$$

where f is the frequency of flights.

With a fixed cost per flight c, the monopoly airline's problem can be formulated as:

$$\max 3(fpq - fc) \tag{35.4}$$

for the fully connected (FC) network and

$$\max 2fpq + fPQ - 2fc \tag{35.5}$$

for the hub-and-spoke (HS) network where city-pair markets AH and BH are serviced with direct flights but passengers in the AB market must travel via city H, the hub. P and Q are the price and demand per flight for the AB market.

Based on this model, Brueckner and Zhang (2001) conclude that the airline will provide excessive flight frequency relative to the social optimum in both network structures. While flight frequency is higher in the HS network than in the FC network, some passengers who would take a trip in the FC network may not do so under the HS network. It is also found that the monopoly airline's choice of network type exhibits an inefficient bias toward the HS network.

Brueckner and Zhang (2001) assume somewhat unrealistically that each flight has only a fixed cost with no variable cost and that the capacity per flight is unlimited. Yet, Brueckner (2004) sets a more general cost structure with each flight entailing a fixed cost as well as a variable cost per seat. Furthermore, the number of seats per flight is used as a choice variable for the airline to capture the well-known economies from operating larger aircraft. On the demand side, a passenger will undertake travel when

$$B \geq p + G + \delta T/4f \tag{35.6}$$

where B is travel benefits (consumer specific with a uniform distribution), p is airfare, G is the cost of actual travel time, and $\delta T/4f$ is the average schedule-delay cost. (T denotes the number of available hours for arrival, and f denotes flight frequency, so the time interval between flights is T/f, and the average time to the nearest flight is $T/4f$. δ is passengers' per-hour schedule delay cost.)

While still considering a monopoly airline, Brueckner (2004) concludes that switching from an FC to an HS network leads to increases in both flight frequency and aircraft size, thus stimulating local traffic in and out of the hub. In addition, HS networks are shown to be preferred by the airline when travel demand is low, when flights are expensive to operate, and when passengers place a high value on flight frequency but are not excessively inconvenienced by the extra travel time required for a connecting trip. The welfare analysis shows that the flight frequency, traffic volume and aircraft size chosen by the monopolist are all inefficiently low under both network types. Moreover, in the most plausible case, the monopolist's network choice exhibits an inefficient bias toward the HS network.

While the model in Brueckner (2004) captures simplistically nearly all the key elements of an airline's scheduling problem, one important factor is missing: competition from other carriers. As incorporating competition in general would make the airline scheduling problem analytically unmanageable, Lindsey and Tomaszewska (1999) assume that the frequency is fixed and determined exogenously, and so the competing airlines' scheduling decisions only involve setting the flight times and the interrelated fare decision. Alternatively, Schipper et al. (2003, 2007) assume that the flights are evenly spaced around a circle, thus removing flight timing as a decision variable, and focusing instead on the frequency decision.

Brueckner and Flores-Fillol (2007) tackle the problem from another angle, circumventing the complexities of the spatial approach by assuming that consumers care about overall flight frequency rather than the departure times of individual flights. In their model, consumers make travel decisions based on 'travel benefit – airfare – schedule delay cost' with a schedule delay cost equal to $\delta T/4f$. With two duopoly airlines providing competing services, the travel benefit for an individual consumer has two components: b, equal to the gain from travel, and a, the airline brand-loyalty which gives additional utility from using airline 1 relative to travel on airline 2. It is assumed that *a* varies across consumers with a uniform distribution over the range [−α/2, α/2]. Thus, a consumer will prefer airline 1 to airline 2 when

$$b + a - p_1 - \delta T/4f_1 > b - p_2 - \delta T/4f_2. \tag{35.7}$$

Airlines' profits are formulated as

$$\pi_i = p_i q_i - f_i(\theta + \tau s_i) \tag{35.8}$$

where θ is the fixed cost per flight, τ is the variable cost per seat, and *s* is the size of aircraft (number of seats per flight) which is endogenously determined by the relationship *q* = *fs*.

Based on this model, Brueckner and Flores-Fillol (2007) generate a number of useful comparative-static predictions, while welfare analysis shows that equilibrium flight frequencies tend to be inefficiently low. Brueckner and Flores-Fillol (2007) also point out that this approach to schedule competition may be applied to other issues in the airline industry. For example, Heimer and Shy (2006) use this type of model to study airline alliances, and Brueckner and Girvin (2008) use a version of the model to study the effect of airport noise regulation on flight frequency and aircraft 'quietness' in a competitive setting. Furthermore, the approach can be used in other transportation settings where scheduling matters, such as intercity train travel, or with any type of cargo market, where frequency of service is often a shipper's concern.

Hub-and-spoke Network and Network Competition

The emergence and prevalence of hub-and-spoke networks is one of the most surprising developments in the deregulated airline industry. The formation of a hub-and-spoke network (hubbing) can affect both demand and costs. The effect of hubbing on costs has been well researched in the literature (for example, Hendricks et al., 1995, 1999). Costs can go down due to higher traffic densities in HS operations than in FC operations, but these cost savings might be offset by the circuitous routings sometimes involved in hub operations.

Hubbing can also affect demand (which then affects profits via revenue), starting with its effect on passenger travel time and schedule delay time. One of the most important trade-offs in an airline operation is that between frequent air service with a one-stop hub connection and infrequent but point-to-point (non-stop) service. More specifically, as compared to non-stop flights, an HS network increases the average passenger's travel time because of the need for extra connecting time at the hub and the circuitous routing of the passenger's trip. It can, on the other hand, reduce the passenger's schedule delay time (discussed above) owing to the increased frequency of service on each route. The total effect on travel time is thus the difference between the time penalties (extra ascent/descent, connect time, extra cruise time) and the reduction in scheduled wait time. In addition, it allows the airline to serve many more city-pair routes when new spokes are added.

Oum et al. (1995) formalize the airline industry's wide-held view that airlines form hub-and-spoke networks as a strategic response to competitors rather than to simply save costs.[5] Oum et al. consider a three-city network serviced by two competing airlines. The airlines are denoted by A and B and the three cities are denoted by H, I, J with city-pair markets IH, JH, IJ indexed by 1, 2 and 3, respectively. Travel demand by the passengers is based on the full-price ρ which consists of ticket price p and schedule delay cost g: $\rho = p + g$. In this approach, g is modeled as a function of traffic volume: $g = g(x)$. As frequency generally increases with volume and schedule delay decreases with frequency, g is assumed to be monotonically decreasing in x.

For a linear (FC) network, the profit functions for the two carriers are

$$\pi^{FC} = \sum_{k=1}^{3} x_k \rho_k - \sum_{k=1}^{3} x_k g_k(x_k) - \sum_{k=1}^{3} c_k(x_k) \tag{35.9}$$

when passengers in the three city-pair markets are carried by direct flights with cost c_k for the airlines. For a hub-and-spoke (HS) network when city H serves as the hub, passengers in market 3 (city pair IJ) must take connecting flights in IH and HJ (market 1 and 2), and so the profit function for the airlines are

$$\pi^{HS} = \sum_{k=1}^{3} x_k \rho_k - \sum_{k=1}^{2} (x_k + x_3) g_k(x_k + x_3) - \sum_{k=1}^{2} c_k(x_k + x_3). \tag{35.10}$$

In this setting, marginal profits in different markets are independent for a FC network, but interrelated for a HS network:

$$\frac{\partial^2 \pi^{FC}}{\partial x_k \partial x_j} = 0, \, k \neq j, \tag{35.11}$$

$$\frac{\partial^2 \pi^{HS}}{\partial x_k \partial x_3} > 0, \, k = 1, \, 2. \tag{35.12}$$

The above inequality indicates the demand complementarity between local traffic and connecting traffic in an HS network. This network effect can arise owing to either returns to scale on the production side or network service quality on the demand side. Specifically, if increased traffic volume allows the airline to raise the load factor of any scheduled flight, then declining unit costs from greater aircraft seat utilization would contribute to increased marginal profits. Alternatively, if increased traffic volume allows the airline to increase flight frequency, then improved convenience will raise passengers' willingness to pay, thereby leading to higher marginal profits. The production side complementarities had been widely recognized in the literature, while Oum et al. emphasize that even if there are no scale economies, network complementarity can still arise because of demand considerations.

To explore the effects of the network complementarity on airlines' competitive strategy, Oum et al. (1995) set up a two-stage network game for the duopoly airlines. In the first stage, airlines make their network decisions, either using an FC or an HS network. Then, in the second stage, given networks in place, the airlines make their output decisions. The network structure is indicated by a variable θ ($\theta = 0$ for FC and $\theta = 1$ for HS). After solving the second stage problem and substituting the optimal solution, the first stage decisions of the two airlines can be formulated as a game of network structure:

$$\text{Airline } A: \quad \max_{\theta^A} \pi^A(\theta^A, \theta^B)$$

$$\text{Airline } B: \quad \max_{\theta^B} \pi^B(\theta^A, \theta^B).$$

Then, Oum et al. established that

$$\pi^A(1, \theta^B) > \pi^A(0, \theta^B), \quad \theta^B = 0, 1$$

$$\pi^B(\theta^A, 1) > \pi^B(\theta^A, 0), \quad \theta^A = 0, 1. \tag{35.13}$$

The above results show that hubbing can be used as both an offensive and a defensive strategy in airline network rivalry. Hubbing improves an airline's profit, compared with an FC network, when the rival chooses a FC network; and hubbing also defends an airline when the rival engages in hubbing. In effect, under the specified conditions, hubbing is the airline's dominant strategy. Nevertheless, in the duopoly setting, airlines are not necessarily better off if they both choose an HS network as opposed to an FC network. In other words, hubbing being a dominant strategy does not rule out the possibility that

$$\pi^A(1, 1) < \pi^A(0, 0), \quad \pi^B(1, 1) < \pi^B(0, 0), \tag{35.14}$$

especially if hubbing requires an additional investment at the hub airport or passengers in the connecting market place a premium on direct flight patterns. Indeed, it is possible to construct a numerical example so that all of the above inequalities hold true as shown in Oum et al. (1995), thus demonstrating a classic Prisoners' Dilemma. Furthermore, if the network decision is not taken simultaneously by the two airlines, then hubbing may have another strategic effect – entry deterrence. This happens if the following conditions are satisfied:

1. As a monopoly, airline A's profit is higher with an FC network than with an HS network due to the additional investment required in the hub airport:

$$\pi^A(0|\text{no entry from B}) > \pi^A(1|\text{no entry from B}) \tag{35.15}$$

2. Prisoners' Dilemma in a duopoly is so strong that:

$$\pi^B(0, 0) > 0 > \pi^B(1, 1) \tag{35.16}$$

3. Airline A is better off with hubbing in a monopoly than with non-hubbing in a duopoly:

$$\pi^A(1|\text{no entry from B}) > \pi^A(0, 0). \tag{35.17}$$

This case implies that a possible entry by a rival will be pre-empted if, and only if, the incumbent chooses an HS network. In fact, hubbing in this case does not offer any cost or revenue advantage; its use is purely strategic.

In conclusion, the prevalence of HS networks after airline deregulation can be explained by cost advantages in production (economies of density) or revenue advantages through demand (network complementarity). Moreover, when there is neither cost nor revenue advantage, the threat of potential entry alone can give rise to an HS network as opposed to an FC network.

Yield Management

Yield management is the process of understanding, anticipating and reacting to consumer behavior in order to maximize revenue. Airlines monitor through the use of specialized software how quickly their seats are being reserved, and offer discounts when it appears that seats will otherwise be vacant. The airline uses a complex fare structure, which identifies several types of passengers, such as business and leisure. For each fare class, airline planners estimate the demand and assign a fare. They then maximize revenue by allocating seats for each fare class subject to the capacities of the aircraft assigned to the flights. In particular, by offering early booking with discount-fare seats, an airline is able to gain revenue from seats that may otherwise fly empty. On the other hand, early booking with discount seats may result in insufficient seats being left (protected) for full-fare passengers who may book at a later time, thereby losing revenue from the full-fare segment of the demand that has higher yield than the discount segment.

Littlewood (1972) proposed a seat inventory control rule, known as *Littlewood's rule*, that discount-fare bookings should be accepted as long as their revenue value exceeds the expected revenue of future full-fare bookings. After Littlewood's contribution, significant progress has been made on the subject of seat inventory allocation – especially on optimal protection level since the late 1980s. For recent literature surveys on yield management and pricing, see Bitran and Caldentey (2003) and Elmaghraby and Keskinocak (2003).

Most studies in the literature were concerned with operational decisions of a seat-allocation problem that is intrinsically *internal* to airlines, although most markets (routes) are served by two or more airlines. A small but growing literature has been developing that introduces competition into the seat-allocation problem. For example, Li et al. (2008) introduce differential costs into the airline strategic rivalry model (previous studies have either abstracted away costs or assumed that costs are symmetric among competing firms). This is necessary because cost asymmetry plays a critical role in the determination of airlines' seat allocation and pricing strategies. Using a game theoretical approach to study competing airlines' seat allocation problem, Li et al. derived necessary conditions that assure the existence of a pure-strategy Nash equilibrium. They also examine both competition and cooperation (collusion) equilibria, as the issue of collusion has become increasingly relevant in the era of strategic alliances among carriers with different cost structures. They further demonstrate that rivalry over seat-allocation between carriers may lead to the classic Prisoners' Dilemma,[6] an important finding as it helps shed light on how airlines may compete in a repetitive environment. Finally, they obtain some new insights into optimal decision-making with respect to seat allocation among flights under collusion.

While the effect of competition on yield management has started to attract formal analysis, the effects of yield management on competition and on regulation have received little attention. This remains as an important area for further research.

INTERNATIONAL AIR TRANSPORT AND STRATEGIC ALLIANCES

International Regulatory Regime

Unlike many other industries, air transportation is regulated internationally. Ever since the Chicago Convention was negotiated in 1944, virtually all commercial aspects of international air transportation have been governed by bilateral air services agreements (ASAs) which are negotiated by the relevant national governments. ASAs are based on the principle of reciprocity within a single industry – that is, an 'equal and fair exchange' of air transport rights between countries with, possibly, different market size, geographical characteristics and economic interests, and with airlines of different strength. Some ASAs go so far as to pool revenues between carriers. Thus, ASAs quite consciously reject the logic of comparative advantage as the basis for international trade in airline services. In one sense, this bilateral system was an interesting solution to a competition issue, because countries at that time (1944) feared unilateral application of monopoly power by a trading partner; the bilateral system, nevertheless, introduced another set of competition problems by constraining entry, thus leading to oligopolistic international markets (Warren and Findlay, 1998).[7]

Following the precedent of the first US–UK bilateral agreement in 1946 ('Bermuda I'), ASAs generally specify services (passenger, cargo) and routes to be operated between the two countries, and stipulate fare-setting mechanisms. They usually specify the airlines with the right to fly on each route and determine the capacity that can be provided by each of those designated airlines. At British insistence, the US–UK agreement was renegotiated in 1977 ('Bermuda II') with significantly more restrictive terms.

However, more recent renegotiations of ASAs, beginning with the US–Netherlands agreement of 1992, have definitely moved in the direction of greater liberalization. In 1995, for example, the United States and Canada implemented an 'open skies' agreement, which provided Canadian carriers with unlimited freedom to fly from any point in Canada to any point in the United States. On the other hand, US carriers had their flight frequencies to the three largest Canadian cities (Toronto, Montreal and Vancouver) constrained for three years, but otherwise were free to serve routes with frequencies of their choice. After the three-year 'grace period', there was complete freedom of entry and operations by any US or Canadian carriers involving all trans-border airline routes between the two countries. Complete pricing freedom by the carriers was provided subject to the usual provisions concerning the abuse of dominant position and unreasonable discrimination.

Although these more liberal ASAs are referred to generically as 'open skies' agreements (OSAs), it is important to note that this is a misleading label, since these agreements generally exclude third-country airlines, prohibit cabotage and so on; thus, OSAs still fall well short of establishing completely free trade in airline services.[8] Despite these limitations, however, the OSAs have certainly increased competition on many international routes, to the clear benefit of consumers and shippers.

Domestic Regulation, Domestic Deregulation and International Dimensions

As noted in the Introduction, the deregulation of US domestic airline service markets represented a significant event, as the regulation of the US industry under the CAB severely curtailed the competitive behavior of US airlines and significantly affected the nature of airline competition. In particular, the freedom to set prices and quantities, and to enter and exit markets was restricted during the regulated era. The lack of scope for market-based competition led airlines to express their competitive instincts in different venues. For instance, Douglas and Miller (1974) show how price and entry regulation distort the market equilibrium for quality attributes and thus introduce additional inefficiency through excess quality competition that led to even higher prices. The example of American Airlines – recognized in the regulated era for its ability to lobby for political favors, and recognized in the deregulated era as a leading innovator with its adoption of hub-and-spoke networks and frequent-flyer-programs – also illustrates how regulation channeled competitive instincts into perverse (from a social welfare perspective) manifestations.

Furthermore, entry regulation made it difficult for airlines to create optimal domestic network structures, as which routes they could operate in was determined by regulatory fiat. Regulation of US airlines also placed restrictions on the integration of domestic route structures with international route structures. The traditional US international carriers (PanAm and TWA) were not allowed to significantly expand their domestic networks, as this was the domain for the traditional US domestic carriers (for example, American and United Airlines). For instance, Morrison and Winston (2000) note that the integration of domestic and international routes was a primary motivation behind the US domestic airline consolidation noted earlier.

Accordingly, economists universally agreed that domestic airline deregulation would improve consumer welfare. It is true that the degree of enthusiasm for deregulation has waned since 1978; yet, nearly all economists still agree that deregulation has generally resulted in lower prices for the traveling public. Bailey et al. (1985) and Morrison and Winston (1986) provide relatively complete analyses of the early effects of deregulation that confirm the substantial welfare gains and increases in effective competition.

Since the United States deregulated its airline industry in 1978, there has been substantial domestic liberalization of the airline industry in many countries. US deregulation influenced Canadian aviation policy almost immediately, as the 'New Canadian Air Policy' – a step in loosening Canadian airline regulation – was unveiled in early 1984. By January 1, 1988, the industry was fully deregulated,[9] and a period of intense competition and industry consolidation had begun (Iacobucci et al., 2006).

Inspired by the US domestic deregulation experience, the European Union was active in deregulating its internal market through a sequence of three packages for liberalization and integration (Button et al., 1998). The first package began in 1988 with the mandate to open up the existing structure, followed by Package 2 (in 1990) with the liberalization of the intra-EU international market, and then by Package 3 (in 1993) with an open European air transport market. Package 3 contained gradual introduction of cabotage within the EU, starting with 'tag-end cabotage'.[10] In April 1997, the EU created a single aviation market similar to the US domestic market: that is, any EU-registered carrier has the right to operate flights between or within any of the 'then' 15 EU member countries, as well as in Norway and Iceland. National ownership rules have been replaced by EU ownership criteria, and airlines have been given freedom to set fares, with safeguards against predatory pricing through EU competition policy rules. So far, these changes do not apply to extra-EU agreements.

Significant progress in domestic airline deregulation and competition has also been made in the Asia–Pacific region (see Huenemann and Zhang, 2005, for a review). Consider, for example, the three Northeast Asian countries – China, Japan and Korea. In Korea, Asiana Airlines, a trunk carrier, was allowed to enter the industry in 1988 to compete against the incumbent monopoly Korean Air. Major recent developments include the liberalization of fare setting for domestic routes in August 1999, and the signing of an open-skies agreement with the United States a year earlier. In Japan, two low-cost carriers entered the domestic market in 1998; although limited in scope, these were the first independent entries since the 1960s. The passage in Japan of the new 'Civil Aeronautics Law' in 1999 represents a significant deregulatory step, as it substantially liberalized the operating license system, fare approval system and other regulatory provisions. The liberalization also allowed airlines to set various fares beginning in the year 2000. Finally, the Chinese market has shifted from a monopoly to a more competitive market structure (Zhang, 1998). Furthermore, China's international aviation policy appears to shift away from the previous conservative approach, which was motivated primarily by carrier protection, to a proactive one that views aviation primarily as a facilitator of national trade, foreign direct investment, tourism and economic development. This is evidenced by, among others, the bold move in the newly signed Sino–US ASAs and the granting of a large number of fifth-freedom rights for air cargo and, to a lesser extent, for passenger service (Zhang and Chen, 2003). As argued by Zhang and Chen, the liberalization efforts have contributed not only to a more competitive market place, but also to the industry's dramatic growth. In 2007, China (excluding Hong Kong, Macau and Taiwan) ranked second in the world (behind the United States) in both passenger-kilometers and freight ton-kilometers, in comparison to its 33rd place in passenger-kilometers and 35th in ton-kilometers in 1980 (ICAO, 1981, 2008).

As already noted, enhanced domestic competition could be considered a hindrance to the competitiveness of national carriers in international markets since large domestic networks (enabled by high domestic concentration and reduced competition) potentially yield supply-side and demand-side benefits for airlines competing in international markets. Yet, on the other hand, domestic competition might also involve positive effects with respect to the international competitiveness of national airlines. Clougherty and Zhang (2009) identify three paths via which domestic rivalry (domestic competition) might influence international performance on the part of airlines. First, when there is an equivalence between the number of domestic and international competitors (that is, every domestic airline also serves international markets) then increasing the number of domestic competitors also increases the number of international competitors representing the nation. Accordingly, a strategic effect results as having multiple national competitors in world markets will enhance exports. Second, a 'joint-economies of production' effect derives from the impact of domestic rivalry and entry on the size of an incumbent firm's domestic operation, since domestic operation size affects international performance in the airline industry (Clougherty, 2002, 2006). Third, domestic rivalry may also pressure firms to improve product quality and/or productivity, thus enhancing the competitiveness of home-nation airlines in international markets.

It is the 'enhanced-performance of competitors' effect – what might be referred to as a pure rivalry effect – that Clougherty and Zhang (2009) pay particular attention to in their theoretical setup where they are able to model in a simple fashion the dynamic that domestic rivalry requires firms to innovate and improve. Moreover, Clougherty and Zhang empirically test for the impact of domestic rivalry on airline performance while abstracting away from the number-of-competitors effect and holding constant any joint-economies of production effect. They find enhanced domestic competition to increase the market shares of airlines in international markets. In short, an additional rationale behind domestic deregulation and competition could well be the promotion of domestic carriers' competitiveness in international markets. Accordingly, the dramatic growth in domestic competition due to low cost carriers (LCCs) – for example, Southwest Airlines in the US, Ryan Air in Europe and Air Asia in Asia – may significantly impact international competitive outcomes.

Furthermore, LCCs have displaced significant market share from full service airlines (FSAs). Using a very different business model, LCCs are driving conversion of some FSAs to LCCs or modifying the FSA business model to be more LCC-like. As a consequence, one of the most important aspects of today's airline industry is that of competition between FSAs and low cost carriers, and to a lesser extent (but gaining in importance), that of competition between LCCs. While significant effort has been extended to the empirical analysis of LCC impact – see, for example, Tretheway and Kincaid (2005) for a literature review on the effect of LCCs on air fares – analytical work is relatively rare and is, we believe, called for.

Strategic Alliances

A major implication of the existing international regulatory regime for airlines is that they are constrained from directly serving domestic markets in a foreign country. This constraint has led, in large part, to yet another 'surprising' development in the deregulated airline industry: the emergence and prevalence of international strategic alliances. Since the early 1990s, airlines have made active efforts to form airline alliances. While merger activities have slowed down since 2000 (though the recent Delta/Northwest merger may be a harbinger of a new round of domestic consolidation), strategic alliances are increasingly used by airlines. The result of this activity is that the three major global alliance groups – namely, Star Alliance, Oneworld and SkyTeam – now account for about 60 percent of the world market.[11]

Apart from the regulatory restrictions on access to foreign markets and the foreign ownership limitations in most countries, a number of reasons exist as to why airlines from different countries form strategic alliances, including expansion of seamless service networks, traffic feeding between partners, cost efficiency, quality improvement and various marketing advantages (for example, frequent flyer programs). Alliance carriers may also attempt to gain market power through cooperative pricing. In 1992, the US government began granting immunity from antitrust investigation to selective alliances. Generally this privilege has been tied to a country's willingness to sign an open-skies agreement with the United States. For example, in 1992, the KLM–Northwest alliance was the first to receive immunity: this privilege followed the Netherlands being the first country to sign an open-skies agreement with the United States. As such, antitrust immunity allows the alliance carriers to practice cooperative pricing without being subject to US antitrust law. These carriers may also have a competitive advantage over their competitors as a result.

Zhang and Zhang (2006a) investigate the issue of strategic alliances and alliance rivalry – where each alliance member maximizes its own profit and some share of its partner's profit – in the context of both within-alliance and cross-alliance interactions. They focus on the strategic motives of an alliance and on how a strategic advantage is conferred. Their second objective is to investigate whether strategic alliances should be viewed as causes for anti-competitive concerns.

Considering a complementary alliance in which two airlines link up their complementary networks, Zhang and Zhang find that such an alliance confers a strategic advantage by allowing the partners to credibly commit to greater output levels, owing to both within-alliance complementarities and cross-alliance substitutabilities. Even if an alliance creates a negative direct effect on profit, it might be pursued, either because it is a dominant strategy in alliance rivalry or because it would deter entry. Although rivalry between different alliances can sometimes lead to a Prisoners' Dilemma for firms, it tends to improve economic welfare because it would, owing to the strategic effect, result in greater output levels than would be found in the absence of the rivalry. This price effect of a complementary alliance is consistent with the finding of earlier work (for example, Brueckner, 2001) using different models. On the other hand, an alliance can arise due purely to the threat of entry; such an alliance may reduce welfare. Note that these results parallel with those of network competition, as discussed earlier.

The competition between strategic alliances is modeled à la Cournot fashion in Zhang and Zhang (2006a). Using a Bertrand competition approach, Bilotkach (2005) investigates the price effects of a complementary alliance – namely, codesharing – on both 'connecting' and local passengers. He points out that codesharing allows the partners to price discriminate the local passengers from the connecting passengers. Building on this insight, Czerny (2009) demonstrates the point in a more general setting with an n-city network. He shows that, whilst the price for connecting passengers falls following codesharing, the fares for local passengers rise; as a result, consumer surplus falls if the latter dominates the former. This welfare result runs against the existing wisdom on complementary alliances, and might have an important policy implication.

COMPETITION IN AIR CARGO AND POLICY IMPLICATIONS

In discussing airline competition and regulation, much attention has inevitably been focused on passenger transportation. This is understandable given, historically, the passenger orientation of air transportation. However, there has been growing interest in the liberalization of air cargo services for the last several years. The interest arises due not only to the push by shippers and traders, and by major freighter carriers – especially air express operators – but also in large part due to the fast growth of the cargo sector. Air transportation is a major lubricant for trade and carries nearly 40 percent of world trade by value – although carrying less than 2 percent by weight (Ammah-Tagoe, 2004).

For the last two decades, airfreight volume has grown at between 1.5 and 2 times the growth rate of worldwide GDP, and has grown faster than air passenger volume. For instance, the US market – which is by far the world's largest air cargo market – grew at a real annual rate of 5.1 percent between 1993 and 2002, which is higher than the US GDP growth (Ammah-Tagoe, 2004). Further, the revenue freight ton-miles increased from one-third of the revenue passenger ton-miles in 1982 to one-half in 2003. In many developing and emerging economies (where airfreight could be vital for exports and often for domestic shipments in the face of poor road conditions), the growth rate of air cargo is typically 50 percent greater than the passenger market (Caves and Gosling, 1999). Finally, there has been dramatic growth in international air cargo. This can be seen from the US market: among different types of cargo, international freight has the highest growth rate. Further, from 1993 to 2002, the US airfreight tonnage grew at 46 percent and the ton-miles grew at 63 percent (Ammah-Tagoe, 2004), thus suggesting that more air cargo is enplaned with longer international journeys.

As a result, the airplane, whose primary role used to be that of transporting people, has gradually expanded into that of transporting cargo. Initially, cargoes were carried mainly in the belly space of the passenger aircraft (or the back section of 'combi' aircraft). Although dedicated cargo fleets were developed over the years, joint passenger–cargo production has remained, especially for international air cargo. For instance, about half of airfreight is currently carried in passenger aircraft in the Asia–Pacific region. As a consequence, both the network and flight scheduling are dictated both by passenger needs and passenger flows. Yet, air passengers and air cargo have different needs and preferences. Air passengers generally prefer flying directly to their destination (non-stop) wherever possible, as compared to flying with stops and connections. If a transfer is needed, they prefer waiting time at the connecting airport to be as short as possible. They also prefer an attractive airport environment, rich in dimensions, or endowed with facilities to enable them to work fluently and/or shop casually, thus making the waiting time as productive and enjoyable as possible. Moreover, passengers want a daytime flight rather than a late-night/early-morning flight. On the other hand, cargo is relatively indifferent to such preferences and sometimes may even have an opposite preference to that of the passenger (for example, in some markets, airfreight generally needs to move late-night/early-morning). Whether it travels direct or connects (hubs) through one or more airports, is of lesser consequence than for passengers. Cargo is also less sensitive to transfer flight synchronization, and to airport terminal services. By contrast, cargo is sensitive to other salient factors, including whether a change of aircraft is required, whether pallets need to be broken down and rebuilt, and the cost of transshipment handling.

Furthermore, airfreight flows tend to be unbalanced or 'uni-directional': much more flows from Asia to the United States than from the United States to Asia (the traditional 'back-haul' problem). By contrast, air passenger travel is much more balanced: passengers tend to make a two-way journey, from home to destination and back again. As a consequence, all-cargo carriers sometimes design their networks with 'big circle' routes, while passenger carriers tend to fly east–west or north–south along the same linear route linking two cities. Cargo also tends to move from manufacturing to distribution centers, or from production to consumption centers, whilst passengers tend to travel to and from centers of commerce, production and leisure.

As a result of the cargo-passenger differences, all-cargo carriers often have different routing needs and operational priorities than passenger carriers. It is mainly for this reason that all-cargo carriers, which include air-express integrators, argue that separate all-cargo air traffic rights need to be negotiated in a quite distinct manner to that of the air traffic rights negotiated in bilateral ASAs on behalf of passenger carriers. In particular, the bi-directional nature of passenger traffic suggests that it is more natural for countries to negotiate passenger traffic rights on a reciprocal basis than to negotiate cargo traffic rights on a reciprocal basis.

The above analysis shows a stronger rationale for *multilateral* airfreight liberalization – the optimal air cargo routing is circular rather than bilateral – than for *multilateral* passenger liberalization, thereby requiring the fifth/seventh-freedoms that allow cargo to go through third countries and to set up regional air cargo hubs. Internationally, 'GATS 2000' once again raises the issue of how – and to what extent – the air transport industry should be dealt with in the WTO.[12] Various possibilities to expand the scope of the services in the GATS Annex have been advanced by governments, international organizations and various trade associations during the past few years. One prominent proposal is to include some services involving traffic rights, specifically all-cargo services and express delivery services, under the Annex.

Since substantial liberalization in the air passenger sector is not likely to occur in the near future, the debate on this proposal has centered on whether the air cargo rights should be separated from the air passenger rights, and be liberalized first through the multilateral services liberalization program of the GATS. Yet, air cargo may be carried in the belly compartment of a passenger aircraft, or in a freighter aircraft configured exclusively for that use. In the United States, the passenger and cargo businesses are largely separated in the sense that they are conducted by different firms, with the air cargo market being dominated by dedicated air express carriers (integrators). The shares of cargo in total revenue range from 1.4 percent (America West) to 7.7 percent (Northwest) for the nine major US passenger airlines, with an average of 4 percent. These shares are considerably lower than the shares of their Asian counterparts (Zhang and Zhang, 2002). More importantly, the nature of the air transport industry in Asia has led to the widespread use of wide-bodied jets on dense routes, with correspondingly greater capacity for large amounts of freight being carried as belly-hold traffic. As a consequence, Asian passenger airlines intensively compete for general air cargo business, which is in sharp contrast to the pattern developed in the US market. In the United States, most passenger carriers use narrow-bodied aircraft for their domestic operations, which puts severe limitations on their capacity to carry cargo.

As a consequence, opening traffic rights for cargo may result in differential impacts on the US and Asian carriers, and separating airfreight rights from passenger rights in air services negotiations might be fraught with difficulty because of the distinctive inter-linkage of passenger and air cargo businesses in Asia and other regions. In effect, whilst it appears that some of the US carriers backed the proposal, most Asian airlines found it difficult to accept. For this reason IATA, the inter-airline or trade association that represents the interests of worldwide airlines, has yet to develop an industry perspective on the proposal (Zhang and Zhang, 2002).

The situation in Europe is something in-between: the cargo revenue shares of major European airlines are greater than the shares of their US counterparts; but, the

European market is also different from the Asian market, though for a slightly different reason. As noted in Button (2003), there were significant amounts of belly-hold cargo in the European market during the regulatory reform period, yet it was not a significant part of overall freight movement in the EU as trucking and, to a lesser extent, rail were viable alternative transport modes. More recently, the shifts in supply – owing largely to the emergence of low-cost carriers – have led to less belly-hold traffic as major carriers seek faster turn-around times in order to attract and retain passenger flows.

The above analysis suggests that liberalizing airfreight rights through the GATS multilateral process may be difficult given that too many airlines with different aircraft mixes are involved. As such, air cargo may have a better chance of being liberalized on a bilateral or regional basis. For instance, Korea agreed to open the air-cargo market with 27 countries (in contrast to 17 passenger OSAs). Furthermore, of over 85 bilateral OSAs that have been concluded since 1992, about 50 also grant the fifth-freedom right for all-cargo services, whereas only four agreements grant this right for passenger services.

Moreover, it appears that air passenger transport services are gradually separating from cargo services. In an effort to cater more to the needs of cargo, some medium-to-large size airlines have begun to develop their dedicated cargo fleet and networks. While carriers like British Airways and some US carriers only use belly-holds in aircraft scheduled around passenger operations – generally taking only the higher valued cargo – many large Asian and European carriers (including Korean Air, Cathay Pacific Airways, Lufthansa and Air France) operate a fleet of dedicated freighters to supplement their belly-cargo capacity. These airlines could thus coordinate the cargo operations through a combination of passenger (belly space) and cargo flights, as well as associated passenger and cargo networks. Separating cargo from passenger services will have a significant impact on policy and air cargo market liberalization, as it will then be easier to liberalize cargo markets. One of the most difficult, but crucial, issues in the negotiation of air services agreements is that the negotiation of cargo rights may not be easily separated from the negotiation of passenger rights in those circumstances where cargo and passenger services are jointly produced (Zhang and Zhang, 2002). Yet the foreseen segregation of cargo and passenger operations is in line with the liberalization trend and policy developments in the international aviation market – that is, the effort to put air cargo under the GATS.[13]

EFFECT OF AIRPORT POLICY AND AIRLINE PERFORMANCE

The previous sections have reviewed the airline research focusing on the strategic actions taken by airlines in the post-1978 liberalized competitive environment. As the network properties of airlines became well understood (and the limits reached – for example, the de-emphasis on networks represented by low-cost carriers Southwest, Ryanair, Easyjet, JetBlue, WestJet, Air Asia and so on[14]), researchers recently turned their attention to the airport–airline relationship and related implications. As a transportation infrastructure facility, airports reach final consumers (passengers) both directly – via passenger terminals – and indirectly through air carriers (runways, cargo terminals and so on). For the latter, an airport is an input provider to the downstream firms (airlines) that compete with each other in the air travel market.

Investigation of this vertical structure may involve an integration of the airline and airport research themes, which, despite a natural link between airport and airline services, have yet to be substantially integrated. This is changing however. A strand of recent research has explored the implications of airline market structure for the airport's charge, capacity investment and financing (for example, Basso 2008; Brueckner, 2002, 2005; Pels and Verhoef, 2004; Zhang and Zhang, 2006b; see Basso and Zhang, 2007 for a comprehensive literature review). It is found that if the number of air carriers serving the airport is sufficiently large and hence the airlines are atomistic, then the traditional results on congestion pricing, investment and financing derived from transportation infrastructures such as roads are applicable to the airport case. On the other hand, if the number of air carriers is one (monopoly) or small (oligopoly) then the airlines are not atomistic and the traditional results need to be adjusted. As argued by Brueckner (2002) and others, airlines at major congested hub airports are not usually atomistic and hence are not usually price-takers.

While the above strand of literature addresses the issue of how airlines shape the way airports operate, it does not consider the impact of airports on airline performance. Airlines began to note the crucial role airports played with respect to cost competitiveness. The fee that airlines pay to airports – usually including landing/take-off, aircraft parking and terminal charges – amounts to 2 percent to 7 percent of overall airline costs, and the impact of such airport charges on airlines depends on several factors including an airport's regulatory environment. Since the late 1980s, there have been significant regulatory changes for airports in many countries.[15] Many airports in Europe, Australia, New Zealand and Asia have been, or are in the process of being, privatized. In addition, even for public (government-owned) airports, there is a trend of corporatization and commercialization. In Canada, airports recently devolved from direct federal control to become autonomous entities, and major airports – though still government owned – are now managed by private not-for-profit corporations. As a result, public airports have been under growing pressure to be more financially self-sufficient and less reliant on government support. In the United States, the Wendell H. Ford Aviation Investment and Reform Act for the Twenty-First Century (AIR 21) was legislated in 2000; the act stated that beginning in fiscal year 2001, no federal grant would be made to fund an airport unless the airport submitted a written competition plan. The competition plan must include information on the availability of airport gates and related facilities, leasing and sub-leasing arrangements, gate-use requirements, gate-assignment policy and whether the airport intends to build or acquire gates that would be used as common facilities (Ciliberto and Williams, 2010). In particular, the FAA is against airport practices to give exclusive or preferential facility usage to particular airlines and believes that this restricted airport access harms airline competition.

Using data from those airport competition plans, Ciliberto and Williams (2010) investigate the role of limited access to airport facilities ('airport barriers') as a determinant of air fares, and more specifically of the 'hub premium', in the US airline industry. Controlling for both the demand-side (product differentiation) and supply-side (market power) factors, they find the unconditional premium on the medium fare is 12.5 percent for tickets out of a hub and 6.8 percent for tickets into a hub. After controlling for the markup airlines can charge because they offer a differentiated product, the hub premium is 8 percent for tickets out of a hub and 6.4 percent for tickets into a hub. These results conform to Borenstein (1989), as he finds carriers dominating both ends of a route (50 percent of departures) to charge median and high-end prices 6 percent greater than do airlines with a small presence at both airports. The hub premiums are completely explained away once product differentiation (mainly, a larger network at an airport) and airport barriers are controlled for. The airport barriers that are key determinants of the hub premium are exclusive access to – and dominance of – gates at the market endpoint airports as well as sub-leasing terms and restrictions. Finally, Ciliberto and Williams propose that if airports enforce stricter sub-leasing terms between airlines (set a maximum limit of 15 percent on gate sub-leasing charges), median fares across all markets in their sample would fall by about 6 percent.

More generally, the regulatory, corporate governance and competitive atmosphere surrounding airports also conceivably lead to tangible performance and efficiency effects concerning airport services. These in turn represent important inputs that affect airlines on both the demand- and supply-sides. For instance, an airport that faces a nearby competitor airport might well charge lower landing fees than a similar airport in a virtual monopoly position; and lower landing fees would in turn affect the competition amongst airlines. Furthermore, the performance atmosphere surrounding airports might encourage large-scale investments in hub structures by airlines – structures which of course translate into altered competitive outcomes in the markets for airline services. This line of research would combine both the airline and airport research themes; in particular, it would involve theoretical and empirical investigations of the relationship between the degree of airport competition and airline competitiveness.

CONCLUSIONS

Our review of the research on competition and regulation in air transport was mindful of previous work in this vein and thus attempted to take a different tack in considering the body of knowledge on this issue. First, we attempted to not only review work using game theoretic analysis of airline competition issues but also to employ such methods in the review itself. Second, we attempted to more fully consider the international dimensions to air transport competition: for example, the international implications of domestic airline consolidation, deregulations outside of the United States and EU, and developments in China and other nations. Third, we also focused on more recent developments in airline competition – as competitive rivalry now manifests over such diverse realms as frequency-and-scheduling, networks, strategic alliances, air cargo, and the airport–airline relationship.

In considering the work analyzing airline consolidation, we identified the three principal forms of consolidation: domestic airline mergers, the integration of domestic with international routes and international strategic alliances. We also considered how deregulation unleashed market forces that led to airlines competing over prices, frequency-and-scheduling and networks. In particular, hub-and-spoke networks – as opposed to fully connected networks – are often a dominant strategy for airline rivalry and for entry deterrence, irrespective of the supply and demand side advantages that networks yield.

We also reviewed developments in the regulatory regime for air transport: the international regulatory regime and the domestic deregulation phenomenon. With regard to domestic deregulation, we surveyed developments in Asia, Europe and North America. And with regard to the international regulatory regime, 'open skies' treaties are noted to have substantially enhanced international competition, but to still involve a number of exclusions with regard to competitive activity. Further, we consider the scope for strategic alliances as driven both by limitations in the regulatory environment and by other rationales.

Air cargo represents an oft neglected area of air transport, as passenger transport has often taken precedence both in terms of policy and scholarship. Yet air cargo has substantially grown over the past decades and its relative importance with respect to passenger transport has accordingly increased. A crucial distinguishing feature of air cargo transport is the need for more multilateral routing structures that the system of bilateral agreements finds difficult to accommodate. While some efforts have been made to separate cargo from passenger transport and then bring cargo regulation to the WTO level, the prevalence of wide-bodied aircraft in Asia (where cargo and passengers are entwined) represents a significant impediment to this policy breakthrough.

Another area of research that has been neglected until recently is the need to consider airports and airline-service in an integrated manner. Economists interested in aviation issues first focused on the properties of airline service competition, but after extensively researching these issues many scholars moved their focus to the realm of airports. Yet, only a relatively small strand of literature has attempted to consider a potential two-way relationship between airline market structure and airport decisions over charges, investment and financing. Fully considering the vertical nature of airline-services and airports appears then to be a fruitful area of future research.

We end this review with the observation that the latter two issues – air cargo and the integration of airlines and airports – will likely receive a great deal of scholarly (as well as public policy) interest in the coming years. It is these areas of air transport regulation and competition that we currently know the least about. Hence, future reviews of regulatory and competition issues will have much to say on these topics.

ACKNOWLEDGMENTS

We would like to thank Robin Lindsey, Emile Quinet and Mike Tretheway for helpful comments. Financial support from the Social Science and Humanities Research Council of Canada (SSHRC) is gratefully acknowledged.

NOTES

1. In addition, researchers have argued that the contestability hypothesis may apply to the deregulated airline market (Baumol et al., 1982). The hypothesis contends that firms do not have market power if entry and exit to these markets is costless, even if they are the only service provider. In such a market, the threat of potential entrants – who enter a market as soon as profit opportunities arise – prevents excessive prices.
2. Caves et al. (1984) distinguish between the *economies of traffic density* and the *economies of firm size*. Under the latter, output is expanded by adding points to the network; whereas under the former, output

expands by increasing service within a given network. They found that roughly constant returns to firm or network size exist for rather broad ranges of airline traffic, but that sizeable economies of traffic density seem to exist up to fairly large volumes of traffic. Studies by Gillen et al. (1986) and Brueckner and Spiller (1994) also found evidence of strong density economies.

3.   Hence, the paper confines itself to cases in which full service network carriers compete with each other. We discuss the issue further in concluding remarks.

4.   Brander and Zhang use existing estimates in the literature to determine the elasticity of demand and estimate marginal costs. They assume that marginal cost per passenger is constant and the same for each airline per route, but is decreasing in flight distance. Fischer and Kamerschen (2003) consider a more general specification of costs.

5.   Zhang (1996) further argues that competing airlines would, for strategic reason, choose different airports to hub and thus form separate HS networks.

6.   Each airline's dominant/non-cooperative strategy is to over-protect its full-fare seats in order to gain a strategic advantage over its rival. Accordingly, each airline unilaterally has an incentive to engage in strategic seat allocation control (supported by a sophisticated computer reservation system); but if both airlines seek to gain such an advantage, then both will be worse off than if they forgo this advantage by cooperating in their choice of full-fare seat protection.

7.   In discussing the exchange of rights for air services between nations, a vocabulary has emerged that is referred to as *the nine freedoms of the air*. The first five freedoms are specified in the Chicago documents (the Chicago Convention itself and the complementary International Air Services Transit Agreement) while the others have been articulated subsequently. Aviation issues of international interest are discussed under the aegis of the International Civil Aviation Organization (ICAO), an inter-governmental agency that was also a product of the Chicago negotiations. Another important organization, the International Air Transport Association (IATA), whose members are airlines not governments, dates from 1919.

8.   There are a few exceptions including the EU's single air transport market (see below) and the Single Aviation Market Agreement (SAM) signed by Australia and New Zealand in 1996, which permit the airlines of each country full cabotage rights in the other countries.

9.   The northern region of Canada remained partially regulated however.

10.   Of the nine freedoms of the air (see note 4), the eighth and ninth freedoms refer to the right to provide air services between points within a single foreign country ('cabotage'), either as a continuation of a flight from the home country or with a separate aircraft. The former is the eighth freedom and is sometimes also referred to as 'tag-end cabotage', whereas the latter is the ninth freedom.

11.   The same trend has recently appeared in the US domestic market. Over the past few years, virtually all of the US hub-and-spoke carriers have entered into broad codesharing partnerships, including the United/US Airways alliance that began in January 2003, and the three-way alliance between Northwest, Continental and Delta initiated in June 2003. For analysis of US domestic airline alliances, see for example Bamberger et al. (2004), Clougherty (2000) and Ito and Lee (2007).

12.   'GATS 2000' refers to the new round of multilateral negotiations on services trade under the General Agreement on Trade in Services (GATS), mandated to start in 2000.

13.   Furthermore, it is important to note that many of the air cargo decisions today are actually driven by a few global forwarders who collectively purchase up to 50 percent of total cargo lift. As a consequence, factoring forwarders' behavior may be critical to fully understand the economic and policy issues regarding air cargo. Cross-border issues are also very important for air cargo due to the conflicts between national security and just-in-time intermodal operations.

14.   This trend seems counterintuitive inasmuch as low-cost carriers (LCCs) cater generally to passengers with lower values of time who put less emphasis on quick, direct, flights. There are several reasons why LCCs prefer point-to-point networks over hub-and-spoke (HS) networks: (1) LCCs have generally been the entrants over the last two decades, and the fixed costs of entering with a point-to-point network are much lower than an HS network, as setting up a hub entails substantial fixed costs and suitable hub airports are in short supply. (2) In order to save airport charges, avoid congestion and avoid head-to-head competition with full-service airlines, LCCs prefer use of secondary airports, which are cheaper than central airports but less conducive to hub operations. (3) The point-to-point operation facilitates fast turnaround time at airports and thereby improves aircraft utilization, a main feature of LCC business model. (4) The lower frequencies of service involved with point-to-point networks, as compared to HS networks, match with the lower values of schedule delay LCC customers typically exhibit (direct flights do involve less time in travel, but LCC direct flights are often at inconvenient times during the day and come at lower frequencies during the day). That said, it should be pointed out that some LCCs have begun to experiment with HS networks (Southwest hubs 20 percent of its passengers now); hence, we may begin to see networks being increasingly employed by LCCs in the future.

15.   Airport governance and regulation is reviewed at length in the chapter by David Gillen.

REFERENCES

Ammah-Tagoe, F., 2004, Freight shipments in America. Washington DC: Bureau of Transportation Statistics, US Department of Transportation.

Bailey, E.E., D.R. Graham and D.P. Kaplan, 1985, *Deregulating the Airlines*. Cambridge, MA: MIT Press.

Bamberger, G.E., D.W. Carlton and L.R. Neumann, 2004, An empirical investigation of the competitive effects of domestic airline alliances. *Journal of Law and Economics*, **47** (1), 195–222.

Basso, L.J., 2008, Airport deregulation: effects on pricing and capacity. *International Journal of Industrial Organization*, **61**, 218–237.

Basso, L.J. and A. Zhang, 2007, An interpretative survey of analytical models of airport pricing. In D. Lee, ed., *Advances in Airline Economics*, Vol. 2. Amsterdam: Elsevier, pp. 89–124.

Baumol, W.J., J.C. Panzar and R.D. Willig, 1982, *Contestable Markets and the Theory of Industry Structure*. San Diego, CA: Harcourt Brade Javanovic.

Bilotkach, V., 2005, Price competition between international airline alliances. *Journal of Transport Economics and Policy*, **39** (2), 167–189.

Bitran, G. and R. Caldentey, 2003, An overview of pricing models for revenue management. *Manufacturing & Service Operations Management*, **5**, 203–229.

Borenstein, S., 1989, Hubs and high fares: dominance and market power in the US airline industry. *Rand Journal of Economics*, **20** (3), 344–365.

Borenstein, S., 1991, The dominant-firm advantage in multiproduct industries: evidence from the US airlines. *Quarterly Journal of Economics*, **106** (4), 1237–1266.

Borenstein, S., 1992, The evolution of US airline competition. *Journal of Economic Perspectives*, **6**, 45–73.

Brander, J.A. and A. Zhang, 1990, Market conduct in the airline industry: an empirical investigation. *RAND Journal of Economics*, **21** (4), 567–583.

Brander, J.A. and A. Zhang, 1993, Dynamic oligopoly behaviour in the airline industry. *International Journal of Industrial Organization*, **11**, 407–435.

Brueckner, J.K., 2001, The economics of international codesharing: an analysis of airline alliances. *International Journal of Industrial Organization*, **19**, 1475–1498.

Brueckner, J.K., 2002, Airport congestion when carriers have market power. *American Economic Review*, **92**, 1357–1375.

Brueckner, J.K., 2004, Network structure and airline scheduling. *Journal of Industrial Economics*, **52**, 291–312.

Brueckner, J.K., 2005, Internalization of airport congestion: a network analysis. *International Journal of Industrial Organization*, **23**, 599–614.

Brueckner, J.K., N. Dyer and P.T. Spiller, 1992, Fare determination in airline hub and spoke networks. *Rand Journal of Economics*, **23** (3), 309–333.

Brueckner, J.K. and R. Flores-Fillol, 2007, Airline schedule competition. *Review of Industrial Organization*, **30**, 161–177.

Brueckner, J.K. and R. Girvin, 2008, Airport noise regulation, airline service quality, and social welfare. *Transportation Research Part B*, **42**, 19–37.

Brueckner, J.K. and P.T. Spiller, 1991, Competition and mergers in airline networks. *International Journal of Industrial Organization*, **9**, 323–342.

Brueckner, J.K. and P.T. Spiller, 1994, Economies of traffic density in the deregulated airline industry. *Journal of Law and Economics*, **37**, 379–415.

Brueckner, J.K. and Y. Zhang, 2001, A model of scheduling in airline networks: how a hub-and-spoke system affects flight frequency, fares and welfare. *Journal of Transport Economics and Policy*, **35**, 195–222.

Button, K.J., 2003, Implementation process of the European Community's air transport market and the common air transport policy. In L.-J. Cho and Y.H. Kim, eds, *Building an Integrated Transport Market for China, Japan and Korea: Building a Regional Coordinating Institution*. Honolulu: The EWC/KOTI, pp. 3–56.

Button, K.J., K. Haynes and R. Stough, 1998, *Flying into the Future: Air Transport Policy in the European Union*. Cheltenham, UK: Edward Elgar.

Caves, D.W., L.R. Christensen and M.W. Tretheway, 1984, Economies of density versus economies of scale: why trunk and local service airline costs differ. *Rand Journal of Economics*, **15**, 471–489.

Caves, R.E., 1962, *Air Transport and Its Regulators: An Industry Study*. Cambridge, MA: Harvard University Press.

Caves, R.E. and G.D. Gosling, 1999, *Strategic Airport Planning*. Amsterdam: Pergamon.

Ciliberto, F. and J.W. Williams, 2010, Limited access to airport facilities and market power in the airline industry. *Journal of Law and Economics*, **53** (3), 467–495.

Clougherty, J.A., 2000, US domestic airline alliances: does the national welfare impact turn on strategic international gains? *Contemporary Economic Policy*, **18** (3), 304–314.

Clougherty, J.A., 2002, US domestic airline mergers: the neglected international determinants. *International Journal of Industrial Organization*, **20**, 557–576.

Clougherty, J.A., 2006, The international drivers of domestic airline mergers in twenty nations: integrating industrial organization and international business. *Managerial and Decision Economics*, **27**, 75–93.

Clougherty, J.A. and A. Zhang, 2009, Domestic rivalry and export performance: theory and evidence from international airline markets. *Canadian Journal of Economics*, **42**, 440–468.

Czerny, A.I., 2009, Code-sharing, price discrimination and welfare losses. *Journal of Transport Economics and Policy*, **43**, 193–212.

Derthick, M. and P.J. Quirk, 1985, *The Politics of Deregulation*. Washington DC: The Brookings Institution.

Douglas, G.W. and J.C. Miller III, 1974, Quality competition, industry equilibrium, and efficiency in the price-constrained airline market. *American Economic Review*, **64** (4), 657–669.

Dresner, M., 1994, Hubbing effects on the Canada–US transborder air market. *Logistics and Transportation Review*, **30** (3), 211–221.

Elmaghraby, W. and P. Keskinocak, 2003, Dynamic pricing in the presence of inventory considerations: research overview, current practices, and future directions. *Management Science*, **49**, 1287–1309.

Evans, W.N. and I.N. Kessides, 1993, Structure, conduct and performance in the deregulated airline industry. *Southern Economic Journal*, **59** (3), 450–467.

Evans, W.N. and I.N. Kessides, 1994, Living by the 'golden rule': multimarket contact in the US airline industry. *Quarterly Journal of Economics*, **109** (2), 341–366.

Fischer, T. and D.R. Kamerschen, 2003, Price-cost margins in the US airline industry using a conjectural variation approach. *Journal of Transport Economics and Policy*, **37** (2), 227–259.

Gillen, D.W., T.H. Oum and M.W. Tretheway, 1986, *Airline Cost and Performance*. Vancouver, BC: Centre for Transportation Studies, University of British Columbia.

Green, E.J. and R.H. Porter, 1984, Noncooperative collusion under imperfect price information. *Econometrica*, **52** (1), 87–100.

Heimer, O. and O. Shy, 2006, Code-sharing agreements, frequency of flights, and profits under parallel operations. In D. Lee, ed., *Advances in Airline Economics*, Vol. 1. Amsterdam: Elsevier, pp. 163–181.

Hendricks, K., M. Piccione and G. Tan, 1995, The economics of hubs: the case of monopoly. *Review of Economic Studies*, **62**, 83–99.

Hendricks, K., M. Piccione and G. Tan, 1999, Equilibria in networks. *Econometrica*, **67**, 1407–1434.

Huenemann, R. and A. Zhang, 2005, Issues in competition policy for the airline industry in APEC economies. In E. Medalla, ed., *Competition Policy in the New Millenium*. London: Routledge, pp. 145–169.

Iacobucci, E., M. Trebilcock and R. Winter, 2006, The Canadian experience with deregulation. *University of Toronto Law Journal*, **56**, 1–74.

ICAO, 1981, 2008, *Annual Report: The State of International Civil Aviation*. Annual issues. Montreal, Canada: International Civil Aviation Organization.

Ito, H. and D. Lee, 2007, Domestic codesharing, alliances and airfares in the US airline industry. *Journal of Law and Economics*, **11** (2), 89–97.

Keeler, T.E., 1978, Domestic trunk airline regulation: an economic evaluation. In *Study on Federal Regulation*, S. Doc. 96-14, 96 Cong. 1 sess. Washington DC: US Government Printing Office.

Kim, E.H. and V. Singal, 1993, Mergers and market power: evidence from the airline industry. *American Economic Review*, **83** (3), 549–569.

Levine, M.E., 1987, Airline competition in deregulated markets: theory, firm strategies and public policy. *Yale Journal on Regulation*, **4**, 283–344.

Li, M.Z.F., A. Zhang and Y. Zhang, 2008, Airline seat allocation competition. *International Transactions in Operational Research*, **15**, 439–459.

Lindsey, R. and E. Tomaszewska, 1999, Schedule competition, fare competition and predation in a duopoly airline market. In T. Oum and B. Bowen, eds, *Proceedings of the Air Transport Research Group (ATRG) Sessions at the 8th Triennial World Conference on Transportation Research*. Omaha, NE: Institute of Aviation, University of Nebraska at Omaha.

Littlewood, K., 1972, Forecasting and control of passenger bookings. *AGIFORS Symposium Proceedings*, **12**, 95–117.

Morrison, S.A. and C. Winston, 1986, *The Economic Effects of Airline Deregulation*. Washington DC: Brookings Institution Press.

Morrison, S.A. and C. Winston, 1995, *The Evolution of the Airline Industry*. Washington DC: Brookings Institution Press.

Morrison, S.A. and C. Winston, 2000, The remaining role for government policy in the deregulated airline industry. In S. Peltzman and C. Winston, eds, *Deregulation of Network Industries: What's Next?* Washington DC: Brookings Institution Press, pp. 1–40.

Oum, T.H., A.J. Taylor and A. Zhang, 1993, Strategic policy in globalizing airline networks. *Transportation Journal*, **32**, 14–30.

Oum, T.H., A. Zhang and Y. Zhang, 1995, Airline network rivalry. *Canadian Journal of Economics*, **28**, 836–857.

Pels, E. and E.T. Verhoef, 2004, The economics of airport congestion pricing. *Journal of Urban Economics*, **55**, 257–277.

Porter, R.H., 1983, Optimal cartel trigger-price strategies. *Journal of Economic Theory*, **29**, 313–338.

Schipper, Y., P. Nijkamp and P. Rietveld, 2003, Airline deregulation and external costs: a welfare analysis. *Transportation Research Part B*, **37**, 699–718.

Schipper, Y., P. Nijkamp and P. Rietveld, 2007, Deregulation and welfare in airline markets: an analysis of frequency equilibria. *European Journal of Operations Research*, **178**, 194–206.

Tretheway, M.W. and I.S. Kincaid, 2005, The effect of market structure on airline prices: a review of empirical results. *Journal of Air Law and Commerce*, **70**, 467–498.

Warren, T. and C. Findlay, 1998, Competition policy and international trade in air transport and telecommunications services. *World Economy*, **21**, 445–456.

Werden, G.J., A.S. Joskow and R.L. Johnson, 1991, The effects of mergers on price and output: two case studies from the airline industry. *Managerial and Decision Economics*, **12**, 341–352.

White, L.J., 1979, Economies of scale and the question of 'natural monopoly' in the airline industry. *Journal of Air Law and Commerce*, **44**, 545–73.

Zhang, A., 1996, An analysis of fortress hubs in airline networks. *Journal of Transport Economics and Policy*, **30**, 293–308.

Zhang, A., 1998, Industrial reform and air transport development in China. *Journal of Air Transport Management*, **4**, 155–164.

Zhang, A. and H. Chen, 2003, Evolution of China's air transport development and policy towards international liberalization. *Transportation Journal*, **42**, 31–49.

Zhang, A. and Y. Zhang, 2002, A model of air cargo liberalization: passenger vs. all cargo carriers. *Transportation Research Part E*, **38**, 175–192.

Zhang, A. and Y. Zhang, 2006a, Rivalry between strategic alliances. *International Journal of Industrial Organization*, **24**, 287–301.

Zhang, A. and Y. Zhang, 2006b, Airport capacity and congestion when carriers have market power. *Journal of Urban Economics*, **60**, 229–247.

36 Competition and regulation in seaports
Hilde Meersman, Eddy Van de Voorde and
Thierry Vanelslander

INTRODUCTION

Port competition, especially at the level of freight handling, has become an important topic in transport economics. This is due not only to the enormous volumes of freight involved, but also to derived effects, including in relation to employment and investments. Port competition unfolds at various levels. Within a given country, ports may compete for freight flows as well as for investment in additional infrastructure. Within a port cluster, they may vie for the same hinterland. And between port ranges, there is growing competition for investments and traffic.[1] Port competition is a fascinating and complex phenomenon, not in the least because of the international nature of the goods-handling groups involved.

In general, competition is good for society resulting in lower prices, more output and better services. However, in the presence of economies of scale and scope, production by a single firm will lead to lower average costs than production by many, smaller companies. This natural monopoly can result in an abuse of market power because the monopolist can realize additional profits by raising the price and reducing the output. To avoid this abuse of market power, the regulator can intervene by designing mechanisms which will prevent the monopolist taking advantage of his dominance.

Regulation makes sense in the case of market failure, when there is a natural monopoly, and when it can improve sector performance. This implies that the consumer surplus will go up, production will be more cost-efficient, the range of services offered will be wider, prices will reflect the equilibrium between supply and demand, quality will improve, the rate of innovation will go up and so forth. As a consequence, it might become easier to attract capital to the sector and boost investments.

The port sector has, as many utility industries, been subject to a wave of privatization and deregulation with consequences for competition within as well as outside the sector. At the same time, the sector has to face increased cooperation and merger activities driven by the search for scale economies and control over the logistics chain. The resulting concentration may result in abuses of market power, hampering and counteracting the advantages of the deregulation process. Due to the complex and highly dynamic nature of the port sector and the diversity of the players involved in port activities, understanding and safeguarding port competition is a difficult task. Therefore, this contribution starts with the definition of a seaport, port activities, port players and port competition. The next part focuses on two major forces which impact the port sector: changes in organisational structures of the ports as a consequence of privatization and deregulation, and the striving of shipping companies for control over the logistics chain. Finally, a number of evolutions which will impact the port competition game in the near future are presented.

DEFINITION OF PORT COMPETITION

To understand the nature of competition in the port sector, it is necessary to start with a correct definition of a port. This will help to delimit the different types of port activities and their relevant markets.

The focus in this contribution is on large seaports that are characterised by three important elements:

- the maritime aspect, that is, location on the shore and/or the capacity to handle ocean-going vessels;
- the goods-handling function;
- the distribution function, including hinterland connections.

A port's maritime accessibility depends not just on its proximity to the sea, but also, primarily even, on its capacity to handle ocean-going vessels. Most seaports may be categorized as such merely on the basis of the location criterion. Some, like the port of Antwerp, are located further inland but are nevertheless accessible to sea-going ships, so that they too may be regarded as 'seaports'. In addition, there are inland ports which are not accessible to sea-going vessels, but which nevertheless fulfil an important function in accommodating goods flows.[2] The distinction between seaports and inland ports is however becoming increasingly blurred, due to the deployment of feeder vessels, short-sea shipping services, estuary shipping services and the like.

Definitions of a seaport used to stress the goods-handling aspect. The definition proposed by Flere (1967, p. 3) is a case in point: 'A port exists to provide terminal facilities and services for ships, and transfer facilities and services for waterborne goods and/or passengers'. This formulation suggests that one of the principal functions of a seaport is the transfer of freight from ship to land or onto other vessels. This aspect also comes to the fore in the functional models from that period. Jansson and Shneerson (1982), for example, distinguish between the functions represented in Figure 36.1. The emphasis is clearly on the approach and mooring of the vessel and on subsequent loading and

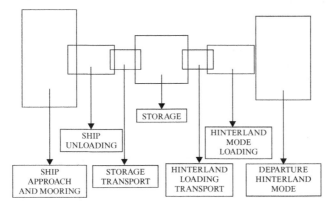

Source: *Based on Jansson and Shneerson, 1982*

Figure 36.1   Principal activities in a seaport according to Jansson and Shneerson

Table 36.1   The world's largest ports in 2002 and 2007

	2002		2007	
Port	Cargo turnover (million metric tonnes)	Port		Cargo turnover (million metric tonnes)
Singapore	335.2	Shanghai		561.4
Rotterdam	321.9	Singapore		483.6
Shanghai	238.6	Ningbo-Zhoushan		471.6
South Louisiana	196.4	Rotterdam		401.1
Hong Kong	192.5	Guangzhou		341.3
Houston	161.2	Tianjin		309.4
Chiba	158.9	Qingdao		265.0
Nagoya	158.0	Qinhuangdao		246.0
Gwangyang	153.4	Hong Kong		245.4
Ningbo	150.0	Busan		243.5

Source: AAPA, 2009.

unloading. Table 36.1 compares the largest seaports in the world in 2002 and 2007 based on the goods-handling function. Quite noticeable is the sharp increase in volume handled in all ports and the strong growth achieved in Asian ports in particular.

However, some ports are more than a place for freight transfer between vessel and quay or from one vessel onto another. In the definition proposed by Branch (1986, p. 1), the connections with the hinterland and the distribution function are also emphasised:

> A sea port has been defined as a terminal and an area within which ships are loaded with and/ or discharged of cargo, and includes the usual places where ships wait for their turn or are ordered or obliged to wait for their turn, no matter the distance from that area. Usually, it has an interface with other forms of transport and in so doing provides connecting services.

In fact, loading and unloading operations in seaports are an entirely derived effect of those ports' inherent mercantile function. In the course of the 1950s, many seaports acquired an additional function besides trade and freight handling. Due to agglomeration effects (primarily economies of scale, localization benefits and urbanization benefits), ports came to be seen as excellent locations for certain industrial activities. In this manner, they developed into important links, not just in the trade and transport chains, but also in industrial chains. The significance of the industrial function also comes to the fore in the seaport definition formulated by the EC Working Party on Seaports from 1975, particularly in the latter part:

> A seaport is understood to be a ground and water surface, featuring superstructures and cranery, which primarily enable receiving sea vessels, unloading and loading them, freight storage, receipt and expedition of those commodities using land transport modes, and which also allow enterprise activities, which are in line with sea transport.

Modern seaports are important nodes in the logistics chain and therefore the focus has shifted to so-called value-added activities (Figure 36.2), an indication that the perception

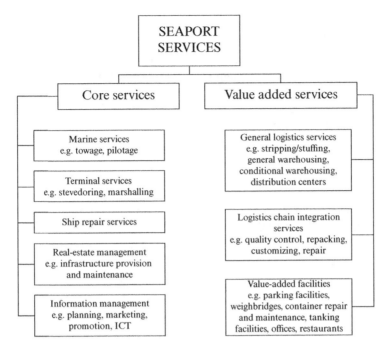

Source: Based on World Bank, 2001.

Figure 36.2   Principal roles of seaports according to the World Bank

of seaports is becoming more and more complex. This has led to the involvement of a large amount of actors which interact in a variety of ways and for whom the coordination of their activities is crucial to guarantee a smooth and efficient flow of goods and documents. The key players are the shippers, the shipping lines, the intermediaries such as agents and forwarders, the terminal operating companies and the hinterland transport providers.

In Figures 36.3 and 36.4, an attempt is made to structure the various market players within a port (marked with boxes) and to show who provides services to who (marked with arrows). This structure is applied from two entirely different perspectives.

Figure 36.3 takes a commodity flow approach. The shipper engages an agent and/ or forwarder in order to get his goods loaded onto the vessel of a shipping company. Shipping companies call on stevedores or terminal operators for throughput and storage. Dotted lines indicate that certain parties can be skipped or are incorporated in another chain company. Figure 36.3 confirms that shipping companies in particular rely on services provided by third parties (for example, pilots, towage services, ship repairers, provisioning, waste reception facilities and bunkers).

In the second case (Figure 36.4), the port authority occupies a central position. A port authority can roughly divide the other market players into two groups: the port users and the service providers. Among the port users are, first and foremost, the shipping companies. Other port users are shippers and industrial companies that are located within the port perimeter and have taken a concession on land. The service providers are

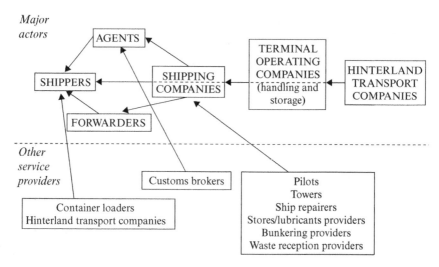

Figure 36.3   Subprocesses of cargo throughput, commodity flow point of view

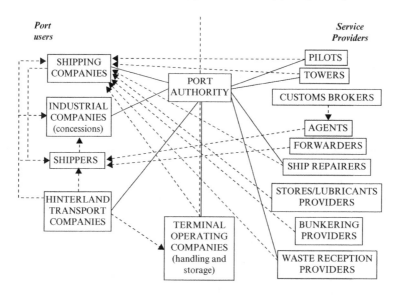

Figure 36.4   Subprocesses of cargo throughput, port authority point of view

a heterogeneous group that includes pilotage and towage services, agents, forwarders, ship repairers, suppliers of food and spare parts, waste reception facilities and bunkering firms. Special cases are the stevedores, who are increasingly evolving towards terminal operating companies. They provide services (transhipment, storage, stripping, stuffing and so forth) to shipping companies and shippers for which they receive payment. At the same time, they pay the port authorities for a concession. Links with the port authority in terms of concession or permissions to operate are marked with full lines, whereas dotted arrows mark links between parties without port authority involvement.

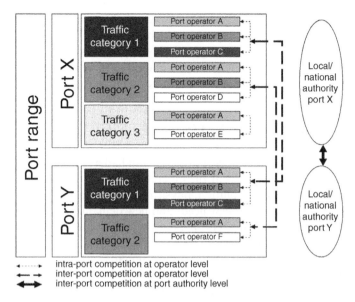

intra-port competition at operator level
inter-port competition at operator level
inter-port competition at port authority level

Source: Based on *Van de Voorde and Winkelmans (2002, p.12)*.

Figure 36.5   Different levels of port competition within a port range

Both figures illustrate how the large number of parties involved in port activities, each of which has its own objectives, gives rise to a strong heterogeneity, both within the port and between ports. The major challenge is to organize this complex playing field such that the market forces can guarantee an unhindered flow of goods through the logistics chain in the most efficient way. The multi-product multi-actor character of the modern ports requires a dynamic view on port competition.

Traditionally, port competition is regarded as competition between and within ports. Verhoeff (1981) considers four levels which result in different potential markets for different types of port services:

- competition between port undertakings focuses on activities of specific service providers in a port such as towing, stevedoring, warehousing and so forth;
- competition between ports for traffic in a certain range;
- competition between port clusters which are groups of ports in each other's vicinity with common geographical characteristics;
- competition between port ranges which group ports located along the same coastline or with a large common hinterland.

Van de Voorde and Winkelmans (2002) consider three levels or types of port competition, which are illustrated in Figure 36.5.

The first level is the intra-port competition at operator level between operators within a given port with regard to a specific traffic category. The inter-port competition at operator level occurs between operators from different ports mainly within the same range and serving more or less the same hinterland. And finally, there is the inter-port competition at port authority level focusing on the utility mission of seaports. There is an additional, higher level of port competition, which is the one of the logistics chains. Ports will try to become a node in the most successful logistics chains and take advantage of the cost effectiveness of this chain to increase their market share and improve their economic impact. It is especially at this level that modern port competition plays.

PORT ORGANIZATION AND PORT EFFICIENCY

Over the past decades, evolution in port privatization had as its main target to stimulate competition and improve efficiency at the different levels. All ports have, in the course of time, undergone a profound evolution, physically and in terms of organization. These changes have come in response to new needs and new demands from customers, that is, shipping companies and terminal operators, but also as a consequence of a more general privatization and deregulation wave.

The involvement of national or regional governments in the port sector has a long tradition and has always been justified by strategic, social and/or economic interests. Strategically countries are eager to control their gateways to the rest of the world. Historically, ports played a crucial role in the defence, safety and development of a region. They were indispensable for the conquest and exploration of new regions and were links to large trading areas. Even today, ports are crucial for the development of a region as is illustrated clearly by the situation of the landlocked developing countries. Their lack of territorial access to the sea and high transit costs continue to impose serious constraints on their overall socioeconomic development.

From an economic point of view, port regulation was mainly justified by the argument that the port industry had the characteristics of a natural monopoly with large sunk infrastructure costs and economies of scale. However, following the evolution of other utility industries, the possibility of unbundling port services increases competition in the port industry and changes the role of the regulator.

The major concern is the coordination of all the privatized port activities in such a way that the goods move smoothly from the ship to the hinterland and vice versa. This can materialize by a better organizational structure which will improve the efficiency of the port and by the control of different stages of the logistics chain. The latter often materialises by forms of cooperation between shipping companies, stevedores, port authorities and logistics services providers, impacting the market structure and the competition game.

The main dimensions for distinguishing between port organizational types are the degree of decisional and financial independence on the one hand and the degree of involvement of the port authority in the commercial management and day-to-day operations on the other (Bichou and Gray, 2005; Op de Beeck, 1999, pp. 35–48). Decisional and financial independence of the seaport authority institution are a function of the degree of public involvement, which corresponds to the institutional setting in which the port is embedded. Op de Beeck (1999, pp. 11–23 and 50–73) considers a number of alternatives for each of the two dimensions which are represented in Figure 36.6.

With respect to decisional and financial independence, five port organizational types are distinguished:

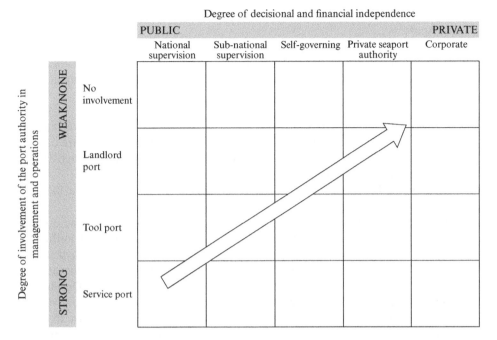

Source: *Based on Op de Beeck (1999, pp. 11–23 and 50–73).*

Figure 36.6   Seaport organization matrix

- Seaports under direct national jurisdiction are incorporated into a national government department. The seaport is often used as an instrument to generate a more general national policy objective. Profits are not necessarily reinvested in port infra- and superstructure but can be retained to cross-subsidise other public sectors. Losses will be borne by the government.
- Seaports under sub-national jurisdiction are fully dependent on a lower-level government which can be at a state, provincial or local level.
- In self-governing public seaports, the port authorities have some power to regulate, control and improve the seaport's operations, development and financial undertakings. Their independence from the public authorities is reflected in the fact that the seaport commissioners and director are appointed rather than elected. In order for it to be 'autonomous', the seaport authority should at least be able to regulate labor in the port.
- Shares are found in corporate seaports which allow limited liability and easy transfer of ownership. Shares can be owned by the government and/or the private sector. Major goals of corporate seaports are of a commercial nature, although in the case of a government corporation socio-economic interests can also impact the management and decision process.
- Fully privately owned and operated non-corporate seaports are totally independent from any public government. They are subordinate to laws on private enterprises. They often are a subsidiary of an industrial undertaking. Such a

seaport may also be part of a company exploiting a complementary mode of transport.

With respect to the degree of involvement of the port authority in the commercial management and day-to-day operations of a port, especially in the cargo-handling activities, four port organizational types are distinguished:

- A service port owns and operates all the port assets, infrastructure as well as superstructure and is traditionally fully public. The port authority takes care of all the operations, although it is frequently the case that the cargo handling activities are managed and organized by a separate public entity.
- A tool port also owns the port infrastructure and superstructure, but the actual cargo handling is executed by private cargo-handling companies
- In a landlord port there is no intervention of the port authorities in the organization and management of the cargo-handling operations. The port authority is responsible for the infrastructure and acts as a regulator. The infrastructure is leased to private companies or industries which will provide and maintain the necessary superstructure. The lease can take different forms (Asian Development Bank, 2000, p. 20). A land lease grants the concessionary the right to use and operate a port area on payment of a fixed amount. In the case of a lease to operate and manage, the management and operation of a seaport site, its equipment and administration are transferred to a management company, against a share of cargo-handling charges. A lease to build makes the lessee financially responsible for all infra- and superstructure improvements and constructions, transferring these to the lessor, usually the port authority, upon termination of the lease contract, but allowing the lessee to earn a toll on facilities constructed.
- In a fully privatized port there is no direct government interference, although there can be an official port regulator to control monopolistic behavior.

From the late 1980s on there was a wave of port reforms towards a larger involvement of the private sector in the financing and management of ports and port operations. In Figure 36.6 this means a movement away from the bottom left corner in the direction of the upper right-hand corner. This evolution is illustrated by Figure 36.7 which gives the evolution of the share of different corporate and ownership structures for 97 of the major world container ports between 1991 and 2004 (Cheon et al., 2009). The authors use a slightly different classification, but this has no impact on the general tendency towards less government involvement.

Suykens and Van de Voorde (1998, p. 254) summarize a number of socioeconomic and technological pressures which induced governments to introduce organizational change to seaports. Society in general, and therefore also transportation as a derived economic activity, has been tending towards less public involvement in operational matters. This trend was strengthened by, for example, European transport policy, which aimed at eliminating state aid that distorts competition, including in the domain of transportation. Technological changes partly imposed by the rise of a global economy, forced container-handling activities to increase productivity in order to remain competitive.

Specific reasons for a shift away from predominant public involvement in container-

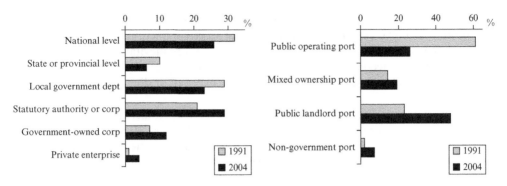

Source: *Based on Cheon et al. (2009).*

Figure 36.7 *Corporate and ownership structure of major world container ports, 1991–2004*

handling operations are that public port operators were usually barely cost-effective, that they relied on old technologies, responded hardly at all to customer requirements, provided only limited services, offered limited capacity and exhibited little labour discipline (Asian Development Bank, 2000). The ultimate goal of this deregulation wave was to stimulate competition in order to improve the productivity and efficiency in the port sector.

In a survey of empirical work on efficiency measurement in the port industry Gonzalez and Trujillo (2007, p. 28) come to the conclusion that 'there is no agreement on whether shifting from a public to a private property system improves efficiency. . . However, the evidence shows that changes in regulation, introduced by port reforms, have had positive effects on all activities and countries analyzed.'

Although a lot of the empirical work takes into account the multi-product nature of port activity, the links with the logistics chain are generally neglected. A port can be highly cost-effective in the cargo-handling from ship to quay, but can lose all its advantages when the hinterland connections are poor.

COOPERATION, MERGERS AND CONCENTRATION

As ports are links in logistics chains, it does not always make sense to consider the productivity of a terminal or port as an isolated entity. Resolving a pressure point in one link may simply transfer the problem to another. In this manner, productivity improvement in one section of the logistics process can actually increase cost elsewhere (Valleri and Van de Voorde, 1996, p. 127). Increasing the capacity of vessels, for example, will spread the cost of sailing over more containers, but at the same time it requires a greater processing capacity and thus the deployment of more substantial means at the terminal. Otherwise, the bottleneck will simply be shifted from the maritime route to the port and hinterland section of the transport chain.

The various port actors usually manage one or several links in the logistics process. The fact that goods-handlers, shipping companies and port authorities tend to hold different views on productivity is due to the specific inputs and outputs in their part of that process. However, it is not always possible to ascertain unequivocally for each actor what precisely their input and output status is, as there are inevitably company-specific factors to take into account. A terminal operator, for example, may service several shipping companies. Conversely, a shipping company may call at different terminals in the same port.

Shipping companies are large, strategically important customers of seaports. On the one hand they attract traffic and industrial activity to the port, while on the other they are attracted by such industrial activity. There have been also substantial scale increases on the part of shipping companies in recent times. Economies of scale have been achieved internally by operating larger vessels, and externally through horizontal cooperation and/or mergers and takeovers. Additionally, shipping companies have set their sights on terminal operators and inland transport services, as operations are increasingly approached from the perspective of complex logistics chains, whereby each link must contribute to the constant optimisation of the entire chain. This has altered the competitive balance in the market, as shipping companies have gained in power through their overall control of logistics chains.

In the case where a shipping company, through vertical integration, has gained control of the container terminal where its vessels are loaded and unloaded, that company will, of course, find it relatively easy to determine in which links of the chain the greatest cost savings may be achieved by distributing resources differently so that the productivity level of the different links is modified. What is then required is for the various links to be geared to one another in such a way that productivity gains are maximized in links where the greatest cost reduction is achieved. This way, the shipping company is able to increase the productivity of the chain as a whole. In the case where a shipping company has not achieved vertical control, the impact of each action depends on the prevailing relationship between shipping lines and terminal operators.

Within the ports themselves, there has been an important structural evolution: traditional stevedoring firms are increasingly developing into more complex terminal operating companies, as a lack of working capital induces mergers, takeovers and externally funded expansion projects. External capital is sometimes also provided by shipping companies. Port authorities, for their part, initially chose to watch rather passively from the sideline as this evolution unfolded but are getting more actively involved in the cooperation and concentration evolution.

Quite enlightening in this respect is the work of Heaver et al. (2001), in which the various forms of cooperation and concentration in the maritime sector are examined. The observed configuration still exists today, with some parties engaging more actively than others in the search for partnerships. Table 36.2 provides an overview of the various forms of cooperation that characterize the sector and in which shipping companies, terminal operators and port authorities can be involved. The diagonal blocks are mainly forms of horizontal cooperation, whereas the off-diagonal blocks contain forms of vertical cooperation.

The reasons for respectively horizontal cooperation and vertical cooperation are often quite different. In the case of horizontal cooperation, the companies' optimal shape depends on the benefits of scale and scope. These are present for as long as large-scale production and service provision results in economies. Such scale and scope effects

Table 36.2   Strategic cooperation in the maritime sector (with examples)

Market players	Shipping companies	Stevedores	Port authorities	Hinterland transport operators
Shipping companies	* Vessel sharing agreements (e.g. Maersk Line and CMA-CGM on its WestMed service as from March 2009) * Joint-ventures (e.g. Alhmark Lines and Svenska Orient Linien under the name SOL Alhmark Lines AB to run a multipurpose operation between Sweden/Finland and Western Mediterranean ports) * Consortia (e.g. North Europe-South Africa SAECS consortium, comprising of vessel operators Deutsche Afrika-Linien (DAL), Maersk Line, MOL and Safmarine) * Alliances (e.g. Grand Alliance: Hapag Lloyd, NYK and OOCL) * Mergers/acquistions (e.g. Qatar Shipping Company and Qatar Navigation as announced May 2009) * Conferences (e.g. ESPMC-WITASS Conference: Container Cargo Lines, CMA CGM, CSAV, Hapag-Lloyd, Hamburg Süd and 'K' Line, liquidated October 2008)			
Stevedores	* Joint-ventures (e.g. CHKY Alliance carriers (Coscon, Hanjin, 'K' Line, Yang Ming) and ECT (Hutchison) at Rotterdam Euromax from September 2008) * Dedicated terminals (e.g. MSC in Bremerhaven) * Share (e.g. Tangier Med Gate: 50% Eurogate Tanger (itself 20% CoMaNav, 40% Contship Italia, 40% Eurogate) and 20% CMA CGM, 10% CMA CGM subsidiary CoMaNav, as well as 20% MSC from May 2008) * Consortia (e.g. Pacific International Lines (PIL) and Container and Terminal Services (CTS) at Chittagong Container Terminal (CCT) from July 2008)	* Mergers/acquisitions (e.g. MSC 51% from NYK Ceres Terminals in New Orleans Terminals) * Joint-venture (e.g. National Container Company (NCC, 80%) and Eurogate (20%) at Baltic Container Terminal, open 2009)		

833

Table 36.2 (continued)

Market players	Shipping companies	Stevedores	Port authorities	Hinterland transport operators
Port authorities	Concessions for dedicated terminals (e.g. APM Terminals at Lazaro Cardenas from 2008).	* Concessions (e.g. Antwerp Deurganckdock by PSA and DP World since 2004) * Joint-ventures (e.g. Odessa Port Authority and Hamburg Port Consultants at Odessa)	Alliances (e.g. Port of Rotterdam and Humber Trade Zone since 2004)	
Hinterland transport operators	CMA-CGM operating its rail arm CMA-CGM Rail, operating block trains from various ports	DP World owning the Germersheim inland rail and barge teminal	Port of Rotterdam being shareholder in Betuweline operator Keyrail	SNCF buying over road operator Geodis

Source: Own processing of data from various shipping companies, stevedores and port authorities; based on Heaver et al. (2001).

Table 36.3   *Top 8 global terminal operators: financial results and market share (2007)*

	Turnover	EBITDA	Throughput	
	million USD	million USD	TEU[a]	share
HPH	4864	1649	66.3	14
PSA	3009	1462	58.9	12
DP World	2731	1100	43.3	9
APM Terminals	2519	404	31.4	6
HHLA	1857	597	7.2	1
ICTSI	361	118	3	1
APL Terminals	609	113	4.5	1
Cosco Pacific	51	29	39.8	8
World total			485	

Notes: [a] TEU figures based on capital shares.

Source: Containerisation International.

are instrumental to companies' merger and diversification strategies. They also affect pricing, entry and exit behavior, and whether or not a long-term sustainability of the competitive advantage is feasible.

The question arises whether recent horizontal mergers in the maritime and port industry have confirmed the existence of economies of scale and scope. The past decade saw two evolutions: on the one hand, shipping companies have become ever larger through mergers, takeovers and organic growth, which has led to greater concentration; on the other, there has been closer cooperation through strategic alliances. In both cases, the purpose was clearly to benefit optimally from economies of scale and scope within the boundaries set by antitrust legislation.

Table 36.3 shows that in the terminal operating business, merging groups have been more successful in increasing market share and obtaining good financial results. The top company in 2007, HPH, realised a market share of 14 percent with a worldwide throughput of more than 66 million TEU,[3] on a total throughput by all operators of 485 million TEU. The top eight companies together represent 52 percent of the worldwide market. However, the picture is mixed depending on the company considered. It is striking that HPH has obtained a turnover which is relatively a lot higher than that of PSA, whereas its throughput is not that different. The difference in EBITDA is even smaller. A similar difference between turnover and EBITDA balance can be found between DP World and APM Terminals.

In the case of vertical cooperation, the central question is how the vertical chain can be organized in the most efficient way. As Table 36.2 clearly demonstrates, the maritime and port industry is characterized by a variety of forms of vertical cooperation and integration, ranging from controlled market transactions to full vertical integration. The impact of vertical integration on competition has been the subject of much industrial economic research, and it presents a constant challenge to the regulating authorities. As far as the maritime and port industry is concerned, insights into the objectives and outcomes of horizontal and vertical cooperation are still rather limited. There is a need for further

Table 36.4   *Overview of fleet sizes and vessels ordered on May 30, 2008, and October 09,*
             2009

Owner	Operational fleet				Orders			
	Ships		TEU		Ships		TEU	
	30/5/08	9/10/09	30/5/08	9/10/09	30/5/08	9/10/09	30/5/08	9/10/09
Maersk Line	550	538	2006	2028	71	66	325	357
MSC	396	403	1289	1508	54	49	578	590
CMA CGM	392	358	936	1026	76	59	631	499
Evergreen	179	156	628	575	10	0	109	0
APL	127	138	428	547	33	20	234	143
Hapag-Lloyd	139	115	505	468	14	14	123	123
Coscon	146	144	454	466	73	56	528	425
China Shipping	133	140	421	461	34	16	234	144
NYK	121	109	410	414	38	18	213	107
Hanjin	87	92	365	411	40	30	315	270

Source: DynaLiners.

empirical research into, among other things, the existence of economies of scale and scope.

FUTURE MARKET POWER AND COMPETITION IN THE PORT SECTOR

In order to understand how port competition may evolve further, greater insight is required into the maritime context as a whole. In which direction will the maritime sector move in the foreseeable future? Which position should port authorities adopt? Will players presently acting within the port perimeter, such as terminal operating companies, be able to survive independently? These are crucially important questions to the sector and its players, yet all are shrouded in uncertainty. Moreover, the market is not static, but extremely dynamic. One may therefore reasonably assume that each market player will try to anticipate on likely strategic moves by other players.

Shipping Companies: Further Reorganization, Mergers and Scale Increases?

Thus far, there has been a strong integration movement mainly in the container business. Yet, precisely in this dynamic sub-sector, that one can make a peculiar observation: despite the fact that shipping companies have been complaining for some time about relatively low freight rates due to overcapacity, they continue to invest steadily in additional capacity. Table 36.4 provides an overview for May 2008 of the operational fleets of and vessel orders placed by the leading shipping companies.

The underlying strategy of these shipping companies is clear to see: in response to already low freight rates, they are attempting to deploy additional capacity at a lower operational cost per slot. Moreover, they consider a mixed fleet as a means of spreading risks. Additional cost control can be achieved through mergers and takeovers, and the entailed capacity reduction. Strategic and financial considerations by the holdings that control the shipping companies will keep capacity further in check, through strategic alliances, new partnerships, the rerouting of vessels. These evolutions may/will result in shifts in terms of direct port calls, which will in turn affect the volume of freight to be carried to and from the hinterland. On the other hand, it is perfectly conceivable that a port may compensate largely or even wholly for a drop in direct port calls through additional (maritime) feeder services.

This evolution will have important consequences for the rest of the maritime logistics chain, including ports and their hinterland services. In the short to medium term, the pressure of such reorganizations will result in a profound reshuffle of services offered. New alliances will be formed, leading to further mergers and takeovers. On the side of the shipping companies, the market will stabilize, though there will of course be fewer players following the inevitable rationalization and concentration drive.[4]

In the very short run, overcapacity mainly due to falling demand as a consequence of for instance an economic and/or financial crisis, leads to the cancellation or slowdown of orderings where contractually possible, and to modified sailing schemes. In the cases where none of these are possible, for whatever contractual reason, shipping companies keep on operating their regular sailing schemes at a loss if they have enough back-up cash. But for none of the companies, such situation is sustainable in the longer run.

The further increases in vessel sizes may also have a profound impact in the longer-run evolution. Whether there will be a further evolution towards ships of 10 000 to 12 000 TEU, or even up to Malaccamax-sized vessels of 18 000 TEU will depend on the context, but certainly there is no denying that the new generation of Maersk vessels, with a capacity of over 13 500 TEU, represent another step in that direction. The question arises how far one can/should go in order to achieve economies of scale and scope. For example, in the deployment of 8000-plus TEU vessels, the number of calls is restricted to main ports handling large volumes and serving as 'hubs'. When the additional handling costs in the hub-and-spoke system become too large, one may reasonably assume that it will then become interesting for non-main-ports to attract smaller ships, for example, in the order of 1500 to 2000 TEU, offering direct origin-to-destination services. However, as Hopman and Nienhuis (2009) indicate one should anticipate on further developments in the field of automated throughput, in combination with the introduction of tracking and tracing of containers. If throughput is fully automated, the capital costs increase, while the operational costs become negligible. Larger volumes will result in a lower average cost which will be an incentive for organizing hub-and-spoke port systems involving increasingly large vessels.

The present state of science suggests that increasing vessel size will lead to a different cost function, among other things because of the necessity of a second engine. Moreover, shipping companies have had some unpleasant experiences with scale increases in tanker shipping, including the imposition of higher port dues. The expectation is therefore that they will not allow themselves to become captured by a port where port authorities are all too aware that the shipowners' price elasticity is extremely low. Finally, economies of scale realised at sea may be lost through higher terminal and hinterland transportation costs due to the greater freight volumes involved.

Table 36.5   Recent and planned expansion of container capacity in the Hamburg – Le Havre range

Port	Terminal	Free capacity / Planned increases
Amsterdam	no structurally idle capacity, no specific plans	
Antwerpen	Deurganckdok terminals	2009: 4 000 000 TEU idle
	Saeftinghedok terminals?	2015? 7 000 000 TEU additional
Bremen	CT 4	2009: 1 900 000 TEU idle
Hamburg	Eurogate Container Terminal Hamburg CTH	2010: 1 900 000 TEU additional
	HHLA Container Terminal Burchardkai CTB	2010: 2 400 000 TEU additional
	HHLA Container Terminal Altenwerder CTA	2010: 600 000 TEU additional
	HHLA Container Terminal Tollerort GmbH CTT	2010: 1 050 000 TEU additional
Le Havre	Port 2000	Phase 2: 2 quay walls in a tidal terminal (2008–2009), 500 000 TEU increase
		Phase 3: 6 quay walls in a tidal terminal (?), 500 000 TEU increase
Rotterdam	EUROMAX terminal	2009: 2 300 000 TEU
	Maasvlakte 2	2014: 17 000 000 TEU
Vlissingen	Westerschelde Container Terminal	2 000 000 TEU, no specified date
Wilhelmshaven	Jadeweserport	2009: 2 900 000 TEU additional
Zeebrugge	no structurally idle capacity, no concrete plans	

Source: Based on data from various port authorities.

Additional Capacity and Scale Increases at Landside

The economic benefits shipping companies seek through far-reaching scale increases and the corresponding cost reduction must not be wasted through bottlenecks on the quay, in the terminal or during connecting in-land transport. Port authorities and terminal handling companies are well aware of this and try to maintain sufficient available capacity.

Many Northern European ports intend to further expand in the short to medium term, albeit almost entirely in terms of container throughput capacity. Table 36.5 provides an overview of these expansion plans. It is not always clear whether the capacity expansion is motivated to relieve congestion, to cope with increasing demand, and/or to pre-empt expansion by competing ports. The result is quite predictable: any substantial growth in capacity will further aggravate the overcapacity in the global market and at certain European terminals, where operational quays are already lying idle.[5]

Besides these plans for additional capacity, there is also the issue of the organization of freight handling at terminals. Here, too, there is a concentration movement, inspired in part by the growing need for investment capital, which the original owners are often no longer able to supply themselves. This concentration movement has also created a buffer against any attempt at vertical integration on the initiative of the shipping companies.

Obviously, the prospect of even further concentration among terminal operators poses an economic threat to shipping companies, as reduced competition may lead to lower productivity growth, longer vessel-handling times and, perhaps most importantly of all, higher handling rates. The latter evolution is primarily a consequence of the fact that shipping companies no longer have a choice among any number of rival terminal operators, but are increasingly dependent upon large players who operate in different locations and are therefore able to negotiate longer-term package deals for services in those different ports. This way, the focus of port competition is gradually shifting from the level of individual port authorities to that of terminal operators, that is, large groups that are able to offer regional networks of services.

Shipping companies will not be prepared to continue to undergo this evolution. As their relative market power is at stake, it seems logical that they should put greater effort into acquiring so-called dedicated terminals, be it under joint ventures with locally active terminal operators or otherwise. This needs not be detrimental to the port authorities' cause, as it will at least make shipping companies less footloose, in the sense that a long-term relationship is forged that makes them less likely to relocate (Heaver et al., 2001). In the short term, such dedicated terminals may however lead to lower utilization rates of available capacity.

Scale increases and expanding ports have also consequences for the hinterland connections. Especially in densely populated areas where the hinterland traffic interacts with other freight and passenger traffic, the scale advantages generated at the maritime side might get fully lost due to congested or inappropriate hinterland connections. As a consequence a port with good and reliable hinterland connections will have a strong competitive advantage.

A New Role for the Regulator and the Port Authorities?

The involvement of port authorities in commercial activities within the logistics chain is declining. Consequently, the market power of those port authorities and, as the case may be, the public authorities that control them is also decreasing.[6] In other words, managerial control over the maritime logistics chain now lies only partly with the ports and the undertakings located in those ports.

According to Estache and Trujillo (2009), the question is not so much whether the port authorities will survive, but rather how views on the management of ports will develop. There are, after all, various new reasons why port authorities may continue to play a role, even if it may be a very different one from today's. They will certainly continue to play an important facilitating role, including in relation to infrastructure and intermodal integration, and perhaps also in respect of superstructure.

In the current negotiation game between shipping companies and terminal operators, those same port authorities do, however, hold a strong trump card: they have the power to grant concessions and to determine their duration. Once a long-term concession has been awarded, they lose much of their market power, though. It has, for example, hitherto proven very hard to penalize concession holders who fail to achieve the objectives of their business plan. Consequently, there is an economic incentive for port authorities to award long-term concessions (for example, 30 years), but in conjunction with mandatory interim objectives agreed upon beforehand with the concession holder.[7]

Otherwise, the negotiating strength of port authorities has become quite limited, certainly when compared to that of the major shipping companies, who often join forces in strategic alliances, and terminal operators, among whom the past decade has seen a concentration trend towards a limited number of global players. If port authorities wish to enhance their market power, they must proceed proactively and cooperate intensely to attain common or parallel goals. This may be achieved through cross participation in one another's capital. From that moment, every tonne or TEU that is loaded or unloaded generates profit for each participating port authority. Ruinous competition between port authorities can thus be avoided. Moreover, the negotiating strength of those port authorities will be significantly enhanced, not only because cooperation implies that they are effectively a larger player, but also because it will be much harder for shipping companies and terminal operators to play port authorities off against one another. Furthermore, such cooperation would undoubtedly result in less excess capacity.

However, the concentration waves in the port and shipping sector and the reduced power of the port authorities bring with it the danger of limited competition which requires still the intervention of a regulator. Economists generally distinguish between economic and social regulation. The former is the control of prices, service quality, and entry conditions in specific sectors. The latter is the regulation of risks to health, safety, and the environment.

The role of the regulator in the port sector is clearly summarised in the Port Reform Toolkit of the World Bank (2001, pp.267–8): 'Ensuring the efficient and competitive functioning of a port in a context of limited or weak competition is the purpose of economic regulation of ports'. Although this is a clear formulation, in practice the story is more complicated due to the different levels at which competition plays in the port sector. Each level may require a specific regulatory mechanism. The competition between terminal operating companies within a port plays mainly at the level of the concession policy which has to be fair, transparent and open towards all the companies. Once the concession is granted and when there is for instance only one single terminal operating company, there should be control mechanisms to avoid the abuse of market power of the natural monopolists. Traditionally the economic regulatory mechanisms are designed to reduce, remove or compensate for barriers to entry, to regulate tariffs and prices, and to guarantee a good quality of service.

Europe has a relatively long tradition of public regulation and intervention in seaports. Nevertheless, it is surprising that the Treaty of Rome, establishing the European Economic Community, makes no mention of seaports. However, according to a subsequent judgment by the European Court of Justice (April 4, 1974) in a dispute between the European Commission and the French government, the general stipulations of the Treaty are applicable to maritime transport. Consequently, many port-related issues (for example, rules of competition, subsidising) may be approached from the perspective of these general stipulations. With the 1992 reform of the Treaty, with a view to the creation of the European single market, it was stipulated that maritime transport was subject to the terms of the Treaty.

In addition, seaport policy is also a function of industrial policy. Whatever the European Commission decides in that field has direct consequences for port policy (for example, energy policy, agricultural policy, social policy, taxation, transport policy, maritime policy). In recent time, the European Commission has devoted much closer attention to transport in general and seaports in particular. On December, 10, 1997, the European Commission published a 'Green Paper on Seaports and Maritime Infrastructure'. The purpose was to launch a debate on seaports and their efficiency, their integration into multimodal networks and the rules of competition that should apply.

In early 2001, the European Commission issued a draft guideline concerning access to the market of port services. The purpose was to ensure the right to free entrepreneurship in the port services sector, in accordance with the basic treaties of the European Union. However, in November 2003, the European Parliament rejected the proposed compromise. In 2004, an amended guideline was put forward that strove to regulate goods-handling, towage, pilotage, mooring and unmooring. But again, the proposal was rejected. No subsequent, explicit action was taken, apart from a wide-ranging stakeholder consultation, six workshops which the Commission held and a communication from the Commission (Commission of the European Communities, 2007) which gives an overview of planned initiatives and which seeks to promote greater dialogue between all stakeholders.

CONCLUSION

The port sector has been subject to a wave of privatization, deregulation and re-organization with consequences for competition within as well as outside the sector. In recent years, it had to face increased cooperation and merger activities driven by the search for scale economies and control over the logistics chain.

The largest players, that is, the shipping companies, drive competition and they benefit maximally from evolutions in global trade. Within the shipping sector, there has been a spectacular scale increase and a far-reaching concentration movement. A similar concentration trend exists among terminal operating companies, where one can witness the entry of foreign capital in what were originally local or national companies. This implies greater market power for terminal operators because shipping companies now face global terminal operators who are operating in origin as well as destination ports.

Next to horizontal integration, a trend of vertical cooperation and merger activity is clearly present. Shipping companies are participating strongly in port-related activities in various ways, ranging from contractual agreements to full integration. The resulting concentration may entail abuses of market power, which may hamper and counteract the advantages of the deregulation process. As shipping companies and terminal operating companies continue to grow in size, the relative market power of port authorities is declining. Their remaining tools are the provision of freight-handling capacity, the concession policy and the port dues. However, they can take a more active position in the concentration movement by joining forces in strategic alliances of their own.

The concentration waves in the port and shipping sector and the reduced power of the port authorities bring with it the danger of limited competition which requires still the intervention of a regulator to reduce, remove or compensate for barriers to entry, to regulate tariffs and prices where necessary, and to guarantee a good quality of service.

NOTES

1. The hinterland of a port consists of the areas from which cargo originates, as well as the areas where cargo moving through the port is destined. A port cluster groups ports in each other's vicinity with common geographical characteristics. A port range is a group of ports located along the same coastline or with a large common hinterland.
2. Among the largest European inland ports are Duisburg (110 million tons in 2007), Paris (22 million tons), Liège (21.2 million tons) and Cologne (11.1 mn tons).
3. TEU is the abbreviation for 'twenty-foot equivalent unit'. A standard forty-foot ($40 \times 8 \times 8$ feet) container equals two TEU (each $20 \times 8 \times 8$ feet).
4. As far as the forming of alliances is concerned, there is a certain parallel to be drawn with the air transport industry. The main difference lies in the fact that, in the airline business, all major carriers belong to alliances and only the smaller companies have stayed on the sidelines, while in the maritime sector, some of the large companies have not joined an alliance (see for example MSC and CMA-CGM).
5. Typical examples are Amsterdam, Cagliari, Zeebrugge and Sines.
6. The question of where market power actually resides cannot be answered unequivocally, as the situation varies from port to port. In the case of such mainports as Rotterdam and Antwerp, it is already the case that terminals are given in concession, albeit mostly under a joint venture between a shipping company and a terminal operator. From this, we draw the following conclusions:

   a. The shipping companies and terminal operators involved appear to adhere to the saying 'If you can't beat them, join them'. Rather than engaging in an all-consuming competitive struggle, they prefer to collaborate. The immediate effect is, however, a new decline in the relative power of port and public authorities;
   b. Revenues from a dedicated terminal may be higher, but now they need to be divided. In the case of a 50/50 terminal, the operator must, unlike in the past, give up 50 percent of profits to the shipping company. On the other hand, terminal operators thus acquire greater certainty that freight flows will be retained or may even increase in the future

7. The proposed strategy is in any case purer than that previously applied by some port authorities in an effort to enhance their competitive position. A case in point was the move by the port authority of Rotterdam in 1999 to acquire a 35 percent stake in terminal operator ECT. Such action, be it temporary or on a more permanent basis, raises the specter of conflict of interest, not in the least because the port authority continues to hold power of decision when it comes to the granting of concessions.

REFERENCES

American Association of Port Authorities (AAPA), 2009, Port news. *Advisory*, **34** (10), www.aapa-ports.org/members/advisory/html/2000/advisory34-10.htm.

Asian Development Bank, 2000, *Developing Best Practices for Promoting Private Sector Investment in Infrastructure: Ports*. Manila, Philippines: Asian Development Bank. Available at: www.adb.org/Documents/Books/Developing_Best_Practices/Ports/default.asp.

Bichou, K. and R. Gray, 2005, A critical review of conventional terminology for classifying seaports. *Transportation Research Part A*, **39**, 75–92.

Branch, A.E., 1986, *Elements of Port Operation and Management*. London: Chapman and Hall Ltd.

Cheon, S., D. Dowall and D.-W. Song, 2009, Evaluating impacts of institutional reforms on port efficiency changes: Ownership, corporate structure, and total factor productivity changes of world container ports, *Transportation Research Part E*, doi:10.1016/j.tre.2009.04.001.

Commission of the European Communities, 2007, Communication on a European Ports Policy. Communication from the Commission. Available at: http://ec.europa.eu/transport/logistics/freight_logistics_action_plan/doc/ports/2007_com_ports_en.pdf.

Coppens, F., F. Lagneaux, H. Meersman, N. Sellekaerts, E. Van de Voorde, G. Van Gastel, T. Vanelslander, A. Verhetsel, 2007, Economic impact of port activity: a disaggregate analysis. The case of Antwerp. Working paper document no. 10. Brussels: NBB.

Estache, A. and L. Trujillo, 2009, Global economic changes and the future of port authorities. In H. Meersman, E. Van de Voorde and T. Vanelslander, eds, *Future Challenges for the Port and Shipping Sector*. London: Informa, pp.69–87.

Flere, W.A., 1967, *Port Economics*. London: The Dock & Harbour Authority.

Gonzalez, M.M. and L. Trujillo, 2007, Efficiency measurement in the port industry: a survey of the empirical evidence. Department of Economics Discussion Paper Series No. 07/08, City University, London.

Heaver, T., H. Meersman and E. Van de Voorde, 2001, Co-operation and competition in international container transport: strategies for ports. *Maritime Policy and Management*, **28** (3), 293–306.

Hopman, H. and U. Nienhuis, 2009, The future of ships and shipbuilding: a look into the crystal ball. In H. Meersman, E. Van de Voorde and T. Vanelslander, eds, *Future Challenges for the Port and Shipping Sector*. London: Informa, pp. 27–52.

Jansson, J.O. and D. Shneerson, 1982, *Port Economics*. Cambridge, MA: MIT Press.

Op de Beeck, R., 1999, *Port Operation and Governance Systems: a Comparative Approach*. International Course in Port Management and Harbour Administration. Antwerp, Belgium: Antwerp Port Engineering and Consulting (APEC).

Suykens, F. and E. Van de Voorde, 1998, A quarter of a century of port management in Europe: objectives and tools. *Maritime Policy and Management*, **25** (3), 251–261.

Valleri, M. and E. Van de Voorde, 1996, Port productivity: what do we know about it? In M. Valleri, ed., *L'industria portuale: per uno sviluppo sostenibile dei porti*. Bari: Cacucci.

Van de Voorde, E. and W. Winkelmans, 2002, A general introduction to port competition and management. In E. A. Huybrechts, eds, *Port Competitiveness*. Antwerp, Belgium: Ed. de Boeck.

Verhoeff, J.M., 1981, Zeehavenconcurrentie: overheidsproductie van havendiensten, in Verhoeff, J.M., ed., *Vervoers- en haveneconomie: tussen actie en abstractie Leiden*. Schiedam, The Netherlands: Stenfert Kroese, pp. 181–202.

World Bank, 2001, *Port Reform Toolkit: Module 3: Alternative Port Management Structures and Ownership Models*. Available at: http://rru.worldbank.org/logandopen.aspx?DocumentID=868&URL=http://rru.worldbank.org/Toolkits/Documents/Ports/mod3.pdf

37 Competition and regulation in maritime transport
Mary R. Brooks

INTRODUCTION

Shipping has been an international business since the days of the Phoenician traders, and a truly global industry since the advent of the flag of convenience (FOC, for example, Panama and Liberia) during the Prohibition era in the United States. Inputs to shipping businesses are purchased from the most cost-effective source; mobility of assets and the ability to source labor (seafarers) and capital equipment (ships, containers) from the most advantageous seller also mark shipping as a long-established global business. The industry, likely the first to fully exploit tax havens and multi-level holding company arrangements, provides an interesting window through which those interested in firm behavior, competition and regulation may look at strategies taken by maritime transport companies in response to globalization and the role regulation plays in shaping those strategies.

While there are many sectors to the industry, it is generally conceded that the majority of shipping activities can be categorized into two main groups – the tramp market and the liner market. These sectors are secondary markets derived from the demand for traded goods, and are discussed in more detail later in the chapter. Figure 37.1 illustrates the nature of the maritime transport market supply and demand. The industry thus has three major players: those who carry the cargo (the right hand circle), those who supply the cargo (the left hand circle) and those that provide supports or inputs to these two so that the transport service may take place. The demand for shipping from cargo interests may be direct from the cargo owner (as defined in a contract of sale of goods) or may take place via (an) agent(s) contracting for carriage on behalf of the cargo owner, such as a third party (called 3PL in the US), a freight forwarder or a non-vessel operating common carrier (NVOC). Hence, the demand side of the market in Figure 37.1 is composed of direct purchasers and those who do so via an agent, both of which may also be in the supply business. The supply side is similarly composed of different types of actors; carriers may supply either tramp or liner services or both to the cargo interests. While there is limited interplay between carriers offering liner and tramp shipping, cargo interests may supply their own transport, hence the overlap between the cargo and carrier circles. The supply of both tramp (unscheduled carriage) and liner (scheduled common carriage) shipping is highly competitive and global in nature; this supply will be discussed in more detail later. Support services face tertiary demand, derived from the demand for shipping. All operate within an environment of multilateral, national and local or regional regulation.

This chapter examines the market for shipping services, excluding the land interface of maritime transport as that is covered in the chapter by Meersman, Van de Voorde and Vanelslander in this volume. This chapter focuses on the market for maritime transport services. What is said about the market for ships is generally true of the market for the

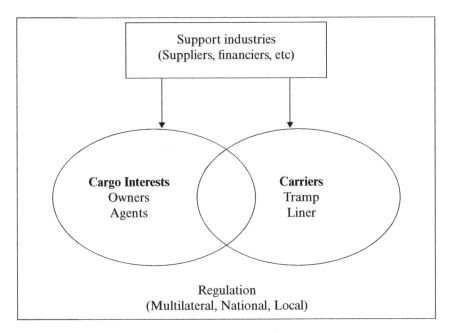

Figure 37.1   Conceptual framework of the maritime transport market (a traditional view)

sale and purchase of specialty ships as well, but these do not tend to be chartered under the same terms and conditions. Cruise and ferry vessels do not exist in the large numbers seen in the tanker, dry bulk and containership markets, and so the markets for specialty ships are less competitive than the three largest. This chapter also does not discuss the transport of LNG (Liquid Natural Gas) as it too is a niche market. The chapter begins with a review of the scholarly perspectives about the nature of these markets, before focusing in specifically on the nature of tanker and dry bulk markets (called tramp markets), followed by a discussion of their regulation. It then moves to examine the liner market, followed by a discussion of its regulation. The tramp market reflects a relatively laissez-faire situation with limited regulation from a competition perspective. On the other hand, competition authorities heavily regulated the liner market; the reasons for this very different approach to competition regulation are explored. Conclusions about each type of market (tramp or liner) are made within the section on its regulation. These are two very different market structures and so there really are no common conclusions to be drawn. A summary table comparing them is presented in the course of the chapter.

SCHOLARLY PERSPECTIVES ON THE MARKETS FOR SHIPPING SERVICES

There are two primary bodies of literature on firm behavior of relevance to a discussion on regulation and firm behavior – the industrial organization (IO) paradigm and resource-based strategic management theory. Neither has adequately accounted for the discrepancies among jurisdictions in public policies and resulting government regulation and enforcement on the behavior of global firms. Because of the potential for significant disharmony across regulatory jurisdictions, both of these literatures need to more fully incorporate these impacts.

In the IO paradigm (Scherer, 1970), the basic conditions of supply and demand influence the market structure, which affects conduct – the combined actions of the firms in the market. In turn, conduct influences the performance of the market with feedback to market structure as well as the supply and demand conditions. According to Caves (1980), in any firm, the top managers' perceptions of market structure and the particular firm's strengths and weaknesses determine that firm's choice of strategy and, subsequently, its choice of organizational structure. Galbraith and Kazanjian (1978) explained future changes in strategy as follows: if a firm adapts to a changing market environment by adopting a new strategy, but retains its existing structure, the mismatch will lead to a decline in performance. It is this decline that will provoke the firm to develop a new structure compatible with its new strategy, resulting in improved performance due to strategic fit.

Regulation (government policies) is a determinant of market structure and thus affects the conduct of firms in the market. In Rugman and Verbeke's (2000) assessment of the environmental strategies of six multinationals, they concluded that regulation is a sixth force to be added to Porter's (1980) five forces model, its impact being of direct significance to the firm's strategy development. Both liner and tramp firms respond not only to changing market conditions, but also to those that arise from new regulatory policies and enforcement, or new opportunities that emerge from the absence of regulation. A shipping company's choice of strategy, and therefore organizational structure, is due not only to its ability to take strategic or opportunistic advantage of existing market conditions but also to do so in an environment of minimal or no regulation, depending on its flag of registry and its ports of call.

Resource-based strategic management theorists (for example, Barney, 1986; Hamel and Heene, 1994) argued that a critical step in developing sustainable competitive advantage for the firm lies in matching the firm's resources (or addressable resources held by alliance partners) to market opportunities in the environment. Firms choose strategies that most completely exploit their unique assets and capabilities. The concept of addressable resources provides a partial explanation for the widespread adoption of strategic alliances as a growth path for liner companies (Brooks, 2000). Anti-competitive liner regulation directly impacts the range of market opportunities available to liner firms, restricting options to those business activities that will not jeopardize their antitrust immunity. As the terms of that immunity vary by jurisdiction, strategic responses can be expected to differ. When anti-trust immunity is lifted in Europe on 18 October 2008,[1] new strategic responses can be expected.

On the other hand, in tramp shipping the addressable resources, afforded by global access to low-cost inputs made available by poor flag state enforcement of regulation, can hardly be considered to provide sustainable competitive advantage to the carrier. All operators in the market that choose to operate under a flag of convenience can easily acquire these same low-cost inputs. This means that the only unique internal asset a tramp operator may have is its managerial skill in making the opportunistic best use of non-unique resources. As a result, most vessel operators in the market follow similar strategies, the most profitable being those blessed with solid managerial and financial skills.

The two literatures present complementary perspectives. The IO paradigm, if regulation (government conduct) is added as a sixth force, provides a more complete explanation for firm behavior. When considered within the context of the advantage-seeking behavior (for example, the matching of resources to opportunities) proposed by the resource-based strategic management literature, the combination provides a holistic view of firm behavior. Regulation directly influences firm behavior and reacts to the behavior it produces. The relationship is direct and a continuous loop.

THE TANKER AND DRY BULK MARKETS

The tramp market services the transport needs of both dry and liquid bulk products. Based on demand in ton-miles, the tanker trade (both crude and oil products) is the most important trade in ocean shipping, accounting for 39.5 percent of the ton-miles demanded in 1985, growing to 40.3 percent in 2005 (Figure 37.2). Iron ore, coal and grain – the key dry bulk cargoes – account for an additional 27.7 percent in 2005 (down from 31.8 percent in 1985). All other cargo, including both container and general cargo, does not appear to be as important as the bulks, accounting for only 29.5 percent of demand in 2005, up from 28.7 percent in 1970 (UNCTAD, 1987, 2007).

The tramp operator carries cargo for its owners or, via charter-party, for others who contract for its services. For the most part, cargo is carried for one cargo owner at a time. In this part of the market, the carrier chases the cargo; trade imbalances are

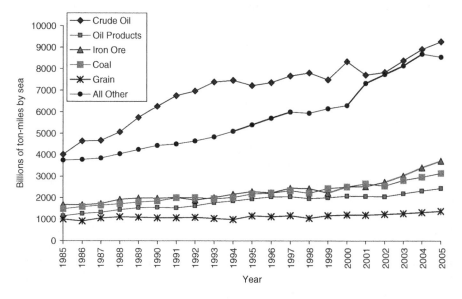

Source: Created with data from UNCTAD (2007), *Review of Maritime Transport 2006,* Geneva: United Nations Conference on Trade and Development, and prior years.

Figure 37.2   World seaborne trade

accommodated by sailing in ballast to the nearest port having cargo seeking a ship or by stowing the vessel with any available cargo for a new destination. A vessel's future deployment may bear little resemblance to its current one. When the owner, or his agent or ship manager, knows that the vessel will soon be back on the market looking for cargo to carry, the owner's ship broker will begin the process of finding a new cargo owner (or his agent), making known vessel characteristics, and depending on the type of business desired, other information that would be needed to make a decision. The Baltic Exchange is one market where this type of contracting arrangement may be made. The tanker owner may seek to 'spot' charter his vessel to carry crude for a single voyage from, say, the Gulf of Arabia to North Europe (seeking a dirty rate for the voyage, expressed in the Worldscale index, not unlike interest rates are often quoted as a percentage over LIBOR, the London Interbank Offered Rate), *or* he may choose to charter his vessel for a period of time, known as a time charter and priced in US dollars per deadweight ton of the vessel per day, *or* he may choose to charter the vessel as a hull – without crew, fuel, insurance and the like (known as a bareboat charter). Bareboat charters are priced in US dollars per deadweight ton of the vessel per day. The tanker owner entering the charter market may always trade in the spot market, the time market or in some judicious combination of the two; he may be an oil company with spare capacity or an opportunistic vessel owner speculating in the market or an owner merely biding time until the vessel is sold to another operator or for scrap.

Because not all trade routes can physically handle the largest of ships, economies of scale in tanker and dry bulk shipping have already been achieved. The upper limit of tanker size was reached in 1980 with the lengthening of the Ultra Large Crude Carrier, *Seawise Giant*, to 564 739 dwt. A similar phenomenon occurred in dry bulk shipping; port depth and transit passages became the limiting factors in the development of economies of scale (Brooks, 2003). Economies of traffic density were considered as likely exhausted in the tanker market by Talley et al. (1986).

While freight rates in differing vessel size and charter type segments may move somewhat in concert, charter rates are highly volatile, unstable and difficult to predict. Glen (2007) concluded that modern analysis of bulk shipping markets has moved away from the structural modeling of the market as undertaken by Beenstock and Vergottis (1989a, 1989b, 1993) towards efforts that focus on modeling its volatility and the use of derivatives to manage risk, for example Kavussanos and Visivikis (2006). As noted by Marlow and Gardner (1980) and Wright (1991), the tramp market with its unrestricted competition is very close to a perfectly competitive market as defined by neoclassical economics.[2] This has yielded a ripe playground for econometric modelers and financial scholars, and there is no shortage of academic literature examining charter rates, ship prices and the like.

However, the market is not quite perfectly competitive. Lags in information exchange can occur; for example, the charterer's agent may need to seek confirmation that the complete deal – vessel class,[3] quality, capabilities, and availability – is acceptable to his principal, while the ship broker may need to confirm that the intended use, trade route and rate, if outside his authorized range, are acceptable to his principal. Furthermore, the strategic choice of the ship owner to play in spot (voyage) charter, time charter or follow a combination strategy alters the number of vessels available in a particular market at that point in time. Both of these in combination make some room for oppor-

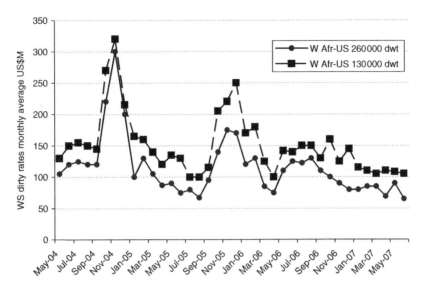

Notes: These are the monthly average spot market rates (the dirty rate at Worldscale), with the route held constant (West Africa–United States), for two different sizes of vessel (a 130 000 dwt tanker and a 260 000 dwt tanker).

Source: Lloyd's Shipping Economist, (2004–2007), Tanker and dry bulk statistics. *Lloyd's Shipping Economist.* 26 (8)–29 (8), monthly, various pages.

Figure 37.3   Tanker voyage charter rates (130 000 versus 260 000 dwt)

tunistic arbitrage in the market prices for vessel charters. Add to this the complexity of the owner who is also playing in the sale and purchase market, or deciding if it is time to lay up or scrap his vessel, and the 'game' becomes highly unpredictable.

There exists not only the opportunity for arbitrage between period (time) and voyage charter rates for vessels of similar size by the astute buyer, but also the occasional opportunity for arbitrage between vessels of different sizes in either voyage or time markets. To illustrate, Figure 37.3 plots the Worldscale (WS)[4] average monthly prices reported for two different vessel sizes on a single route in the spot (voyage) market. These freight rates reflect the variance in the prices paid and the economies of scale offered by the larger vessel per ton of crude; the figure illustrates that, while the rates tend to move generally in concert, there are some months when the gap is very large (as in December 2006) or very small (as in November 2004) and others when it does not move in the same direction at all (for example, November 2005). (The dirty rates, rates for the carriage of crude oil as opposed to refined, are a monthly average and so the volatility of day-to-day fluctuations has been smoothed to some extent.) Figure 37.4 illustrates a similar pattern in the time charter market (the charter price being set for a period of time rather than for a single voyage). Here, the time charter rates are indexed to make comparison easier, but they reflect different vessel characteristics and therefore somewhat different uses and deployment. (An Aframax tanker is about 105 000 dwt while the VLCC [Very Large Crude Carrier] is in the vicinity of 280 000–300 000 dwt in size.) The data illustrate that vessel charter rates in terms of dollars per day do not always move synchronously, but

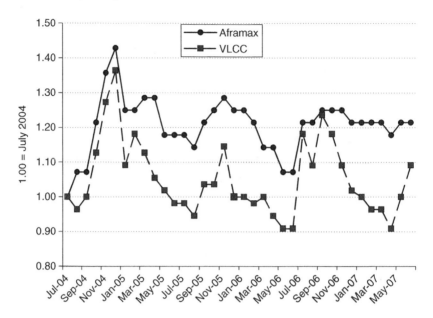

Notes: Indexed comparison of Aframax and VLCC Time Charter rates (12 month rate in US$ per day) with 1.00 = July 2004.

Source: Lloyd's Shipping Economist, (2004–2007), Tanker and dry bulk statistics. *Lloyd's Shipping Economist.* 26 (8)–29 (8), monthly, various pages.

Figure 37.4   Tanker time charter rates (Aframax versus VLCC)

reflect the characteristics of demand at a point in time and do offer the charterer that has flexibility in his contracting requirements some measure of opportunity for arbitrage in the market (and also the opportunity for ship brokers to engage in activity similar to traders in a spot market).

A similar pattern can be seen in the dry bulk market, where Figure 37.5 compares the voyage and time charter rates for a three-year period and holding the vessel size constant. While free market competition characteristics may result in price-taking behavior, tanker and dry bulk supply are not substitutable given the nature of the products carried; the markets have quite different characteristics, as tanker markets have a core supply owned by the cargo interest (the major oil companies) while dry bulk does not. Beenstock and Vergottis (1993) concluded that spillover effects between tramp and dry bulk sectors, arising from their common input of shipyard production, were relatively weak.

Like the charter market, the second-hand market for all vessels is purely competitive and unregulated, except for those practices all businesses must meet under the national legislation of the country in which the business is incorporated. Discipline is imposed to some extent on the buyer–seller relationship by the need to have the vessel financed, classed and insured. Self-regulation is the core principle in practice.

To recap, there are a number of factors that contribute to the volatility of freight rates in the tramp market. Capital costs are high and sunk, and only so much adjustment to supply can be achieved through slow steaming, placing vessels in lay-up or by scrapping

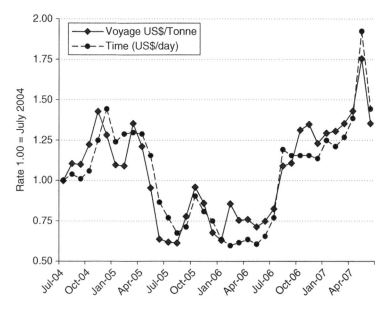

Notes: Indexed comparison of voyage and time charter rates (12 month rate in US$ per day) with 1.00 = July 2004 for a Capesize vessel of approximately 150 000 dwt.

Source: Lloyd's Shipping Economist, (2004–2007), Tanker and dry bulk statistics. *Lloyd's Shipping Economist.* 26 (8)–29 (8), monthly, various pages.

Figure 37.5   Dry bulk charter rates July 2004–July 2007

early. Furthermore, because many of the oil majors own their own vessels to meet core demand requirements, the tanker spot market must absorb much of the fluctuation in short-term demand. Some contribution to revenue stability for both tanker and dry bulk ship-owners is available by hedging charter rates through the Baltic International Freight Futures Exchange (BIFFEX) in London. As the capacity supplied to the market adjusts much more slowly than demand, there is enormous pressure on ship-owners to cut costs and corners.

The industry in the 1990s reflected such a race to the bottom.[5] Tamvakis and Thanopoulou (2000) found that dry bulk vessel charterers at that time were unwilling to pay a premium for quality vessels. This, coupled with the decline in overall freight rates evident in the second half of the 1990s, did not bode well for capital reinvestment, supporting the earlier conclusion by Peters (1993) that freight rates, by merely covering operating expenses, leave little contribution for vessel replacement or fleet expansion. There was an absence of incentive to invest in vessels, let alone quality vessels. The result was a distinct trend towards older vessels, with the average age of vessels moving well beyond half their economic life of 20 years. In 1985, the average age of a ship was a little more than 11 years (UNCTAD, 1987); by 1998 it was 14.8 years, with tankers averaging 15.0 years and container ships averaging a more respectable 11.0 years (UNCTAD, 2000). This was of significant concern to regulators in the mid-1990s, because age was found to be a critical factor in the structural failure of dry bulk carriers (BTCE, 1994),

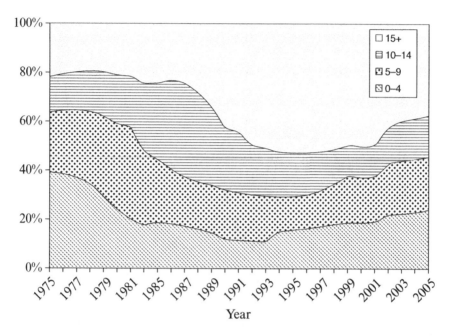

Source: Created with data from UNCTAD (various years), *Review of Maritime Transport 2006,* Geneva:
United Nations Conference on Trade and Development.

Figure 37.6   Age of vessels

and in marine pollution. In recent years, improvements in the fortunes of all shipping
sectors resulting from higher energy and commodity prices, as well as economic expansion in the past few years, have reversed this decline (Figure 37.6).

One way for a ship-owner to cut costs is to register his vessels under a flag offered by
an open registry country.[6] The deteriorated tanker market situation in the 1990s was
blamed on the existence of these flags of convenience and the widespread use of tax
havens for shipping income. Panama and Liberia dominated as registries of choice for
the tanker and dry bulk fleets, but they were not alone in providing a shelter for those
seeking commercial advantage. The majority of the largest ship-owners opted for regis-
tration under a foreign flag, looking for the locale with the lowest level of government
interference and the best fiscal arrangements. Flagging under one's home flag resulted
when the home government offered owners preferential access to cargo (as is the case
with the US Military Sealift Program) or a generous FOC-like tax and labor regulatory environment. The rise of second registers, like the Norwegian International Ship
Register, meant that the market players were not only free to buy inputs at global prices,
but could do so from the comfort of a developed country base of operations or via a ship
management company that could operate offshore.

The key economic features of the tramp market are summarized in Table 37.1, and
are implicated in the regulatory response by government through its establishment of
conditions applicable to ships registered under its flag, and through the government's
adoption and implementation of multilateral regulation via multilateral agencies.

Table 37.1   Key economic features of shipping industry sectors

Feature	Tramp	Liner
Goods carried	Bulk cargoes	Mostly containers; some breakbulk
Product/service sold	Voyage, time or bareboat charter	Traditionally: space on a scheduled service; More recently: logistics, terminal services, value-add activities
Market structure	Open entry and exit; numerous operators	Conference (closed entry in all but the United States) alongside non-conference operators (open entry); numerous operators but top ten account for about 60 percent of market
Buyer–seller relationship and pricing	Charter contract negotiated in a competitive and free market; price is volatile with arbitrage possibilities between market segments	Cargo interests share the vessel with many others; price-fixing is common between conference members but on some routes confidential service contracts are the norm.
	Cargo usually carried using a waybill as a contract of carriage	Contract of carriage may be waybill or bill of lading.
Availability of economies of scale	Limits of vessel size have been reached.	Limits of vessel size have not been reached.
	One-ship companies are common as an instrument to minimize corporate liability.	One-ship companies are less common as scheduled service makes avoidance of liability difficult.
Key drivers of firm behavior	Return on capital employed; resultant cost-cutting to be competitive; opportunities provided by regulatory gaps	Return on capital employed is better in terminal operations and logistics services, and so diversification is becoming more common; top global cargo owners provide a desired core business; until anti-trust immunity is removed, there remain opportunities to engage in co-operative or collusive activities

TRAMP REGULATION

All shipping must conform to the regulations imposed by the state of the flag the ship flies. The International Maritime Organization (IMO), a UN organization, has the mandate to deal with technical issues in the industry and has taken a lead role in dealing with ship safety by strengthening the obligations incumbent upon signatory flag states. Its key achievements have been the passage of a number of conventions that form the core of ship safety and security regulation today. Throughout the 1990s, the IMO's regulatory focus was on issues of vessel safety and marine pollution, while since 2001 it has turned its attention to security and air emissions.

Catastrophic accidents have plagued the tramp industry, but many have led to much-needed legislation. The sinking of the *Titanic*, for example, ultimately led to the *Safety of Life at Sea Convention, 1914,* while the development of modern collision regulations were attributed to the 1917 collision of the *Mont Blanc* and *Imo* in Halifax Harbor, a catastrophe resulting in the largest man-made explosion prior to the atomic bomb, and severe damage to 60 percent of the city. The 1989 *Exxon Valdez* grounding was not the world's largest tanker spill; in fact, it was only 13 percent the size of the 1979 *Atlantic Empress* spill off Tobago. However, because the *Exxon Valdez* spill happened in the United States, and in waters with vibrant tourism and fishing industries, the ensuing outrage precipitated the passage of the US *Oil Pollution Act of 1990,* which holds tanker operators *in US waters* fully liable for the environmental damage they may cause.

The grounding of the *Amoco Cadiz* off the Brittany coast of France in 1978 was the catalyst for MARPOL 78,[7] and it accelerated acceptance of a key regulatory principle – port state control (PSC). Under PSC, port states can manage their coastal waters nationally by enforcing provisions of conventions to which the flag state is not a party *if* the port state is a contracting party and the instrument is in force. This realignment of regulation shifted control for marine pollution and seafarer rights regulatory enforcement to port state governments, thereby diminishing the ability of a carrier to avoid liability through the use of flags of convenience.

Throughout the 1990s, port states grew increasingly concerned that unfettered competition within the tanker and bulk markets was encouraging a race to the bottom that was not in the public interest of the port state. Investigations in Canada (Public Review Panel, 1990), Australia (House of Representatives, 1992) and Europe (Donaldson, 1994) all concluded that, while human error is a critical factor in vessel accidents, flag state regulation failed to eradicate the compounding factor of substandard shipping. They also concluded that many flag states and ship-owners do not discharge their responsibilities adequately. PSC provided a means of dealing with the problem, and, throughout the 1990s, PSC organizations grew in membership and number – from three in 1994 to eight in 2000. Today, most major flags and maritime nations now participate in PSC groups. While it appears that the United States is the only major flag and maritime nation not participating in PSC activities, this is not the case. The United States has consistently preferred to undertake its own PSC agenda (Cuttler, 1995) including a public reporting system and an inspection program that systematically targets owners as well as vessels. The regulatory focus, in the wake of continuing incidents like the 2002 sinking of the *Prestige*, remains firmly fixed on maritime safety (Urrutia, 2006).[8]

More recently, the multilateral regulatory focus has moved to vessel security (with the passage of the *International Ship and Port Facility Security Code of 2002,* known as the ISPS Code) and air pollution from ships, but these changes have been directed at all parts of the market, not just the tramp market.

Most governments have been pleased that the market for tramp shipping has been a freely competitive one, with prices set by the market. However, they have been concerned that such freedom has been accompanied by a race for the bottom in terms of vessel quality and age, raising the prospect of greater risk of marine pollution, air pollution from vessel emissions, and lower vessel security. The mere existence of multilateral regulation, adoptable at each country's option, brought insufficient pressure to bear on vessel owner behavior in the 1990s. In spite of port state control initiatives, the number

Table 37.2   Key regulatory features of shipping industry sectors

Feature	Tramp	Liner
Vessel Regulation	By flag state; by some port states on entering vessels Regulation focuses on safety and security of the vessel, seafarer safety and protection of national waters from pollution.	
Price Regulation	None	Conferences have antitrust immunity for price-fixing at the national level; competition is regulated nationally.
Cargo Regulation	Generally related to hazardous materials	Generally related to hazardous materials; security inspections on containers before loading for US ports
Enforcement	By flag state; by some port states on entering vessels but with restrictions. (The enforcement capability is entrenched in Article 218 of the UN *Convention on the Law of the Sea*.)	
Key International Regulatory Concerns	Safety and security	Anti-competitive behaviour; security

of countries opting out of International Labor Organization Convention (No. 147) concerning *Minimum Standards in Merchant Ships* provided evidence that existence of the legislation is insufficient. Bloor et al. (2006) and Sampson and Bloor (2007) noted that the smart regulatory framework provided by port state control has proven to be more effective as businesses in this industry operate beyond the constraints imposed by flag governments. On the other hand, the recent success of the ISPS Code illustrates that, if the US market requires a vessel to comply with international regulation in order to gain access to the opportunities arising from high US consumer demand, such access serves as a strong incentive to comply with the regulation. The takeaway from this discussion is that actions by the most powerful trading nations, if taken in concert, can offset damaging opportunistic behavior that is not in the larger public interest.

To conclude, the key regulatory features of the tramp market are summarized in Table 37.2. The next section will examine the liner market, providing a critical contrast between the two. While the tramp sector's market structure was described before and separately from regulation, the regulation of the liner market is very much dependent upon assumptions about the liner firm's pricing strategy; because of this complexity, the liner market and its regulation are discussed in chronological sequence rather than conceptually.

THE LINER MARKET, PRICE-MAKING AND REGULATION

Over the 1990s, the rate of growth in merchandise trade outstripped the rate of growth in world GDP and commodity output (WTO, 2000) and after a recession in the early 2000s, growth continued to reflect this pattern. From 1990 to 1998, the demand for seaborne trade in ton-miles grew by 25 per cent (UNCTAD, 2000); over the same period, world exports in billions of US dollars grew by 57 percent (International Monetary Fund,

2000). The additional growth was largely in higher value goods – component parts, semi-finished and finished goods – carried in containers. While not dominant in terms of ton-miles demanded, as seen in Figure 37.2, the liner sector's value to trade in transport services has been speculated to exceed that of the tramp sector, both tanker and dry bulk combined.

Reliable liner shipping enables manufacturers to buy components from many sources, consolidate them in a less expensive location for assembly and ship the final product to a third or subsequent location to be sold. Components may be moved numerous times in the process of getting a product to retail. There is greater interest on the part of developing countries to add value at the source of the raw material chain (for economic development purposes) and a continuing desire by developed country manufacturers to locate assembly where labor is cheap. The combination of low cost transportation, inexpensive global telecommunications, and a financial system that is highly efficient in moving funds to pay for the process has resulted in the phenomenal growth seen in the past decade for container shipping, the most important of the liner sub-sectors.

Relative to the tramp industry, there has been less concern in the liner sector about substandard shipping. Because liner vessels maintain a consistent service schedule, they call the same ports on a regular basis; they also operate in a market where some buyers are prepared to pay more for premium services. Hence, ship-owners tend to gravitate towards quality in operations. A scheduled service also enables the liner operator to hire crews on long term contracts or salary, not a traditional practice in tramp shipping. Flags of convenience have lost some of their dominance to those flags with a combination of tax advantages and better disclosure practices; while the two largest flags used in container shipping are Panama and Liberia (both flags of convenience), the third largest is Germany, with the United Kingdom, the United States and Denmark close behind (UNCTAD, 2007). Furthermore, the value of the cargo carried drives the carrier to exercise greater diligence in maintaining seaworthiness.

Unlike tramp shipping, where scale economies from larger vessels have already been achieved, the true upper limits of liner vessel size have not yet been reached. Until 1988, the largest container vessels were about 4500 TEU,[9] constrained by the dimensions of the Panama Canal. Once American President Lines decided that this was an artificial limitation, the industry's reticence to buy larger 'post-Panamax' vessels vanished, but a Malacca-max vessel (a vessel as large as can be handled by the Malacca Straits) has yet to be built.[10] The near future is not likely to see such a vessel built, as the market softened in 2007, and there is considerable excess capacity coming on stream in 2008 and 2009.

Like tramp shipping, liner shipping is also capital-intensive. The adjustment of supply to demand is extremely difficult because the market demands regular, weekly, fixed-day sailing schedules. Containerization caught on in the 1950s and 1960s in response to extremely low profitability in the general cargo market (Gardner, 1985), and the benefit that containerization improved asset utilization for ship owner and cargo owner alike. Unlike tramp shipping where the carrier chases cargo, the liner operator commits to serving a route and particular terminals to assure the cargo owner of continuing, regular supply of predictable sailings. With directional imbalances and cyclical and seasonal variations, liner supply must be maintained to service peak or near-peak demand; the resultant reserve capacity tempts firms in non-peak periods to engage in discount pricing (OECD, 2002), but lower rates, because of relative inelasticity, do not result in

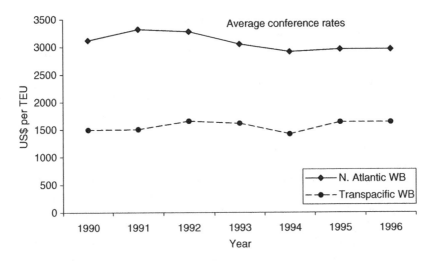

Source: UNCTAD (1996, p. 61).

Figure 37.7 Liner conference indices (Pre-US Deregulation)

significantly more demand. Fearing price instability, regulators agreed throughout the twentieth century that price-fixing should be granted anti-trust immunity. This resulted in considerable price stability in the years prior to the passage of the US *Ocean Shipping Reform Act of 1998*, as reflected in Figure 37.7.

In contrast to the tramp market, companies in the liner market offer scheduled services to third party logistics suppliers and cargo owners who purchase only the space necessary. The traditional practice was to price the service according to a tariff based on the commodity carried; as a result of this price discrimination, Zerby and Conlon (1978, Table 5, p. 42) illustrated that the supply of capacity served those cargo owners with lower value cargoes better than they would have been served under a simpler 'freight all kinds' (or uniform) freight rate. Early studies of conference pricing, including Deakin and Seward (1973), Heaver (1973) and Schneerson (1976), convinced regulatory authorities that price discrimination, and the anti-trust immunity that allowed it to happen effectively, were in the best interests of the purchasers of the service.

In the United States, conferences were granted antitrust immunity by the *Shipping Act, 1916*. It followed the British lead, established after a Royal Commission in 1909 (United Kingdom, 1909). By the 1980s, reform of conference regulation began in the United States and Canada in an effort to introduce a more competitive climate. The United States passed *The Shipping Act of 1984*, allowing for such pro-competitive practices as independent action within the conference framework; Canada followed suit with its own version in 1987. This reform agenda was fraught with debate. ACCOS (1992), Clyde and Reitzes (1995), Davies (1986), Kreis (1990), Part X Review Panel (1993), Pirrong (1992) and Sjöstrom (1989), are but a few of the hundreds of studies in the field. Game-theoretic analysis (including the theory of the core, for example, Pirrong, 1992, and Sjöstrom, 1989 and the theory of contestable markets (for example, Davies, 1986) failed to be embraced in the studies and reports by regulators (including Commission of the European Communities, 1999; Federal Maritime Commission, 1989a). There was no consensus on the appropriateness of anti-trust immunity for conference pricing nor on whether such immunity delivered the price stability sought by cargo owners with long-term trade deals to be serviced.

A second wave of reform began in the 1990s, as the European Union began implementation of its liberalization of internal maritime transport (Brooks and Button, 1992) and ultimately provided a block exemption for alliance (consortia) activity among liner companies (Brooks, 2000). The ability of carriers to price discriminate, as a group within the conference or individually outside the system, became much more finely tuned as information systems improved. By the early 1990s, liner carriers were actively price discriminating, not just on the traditional basis of commodity (and its inherent value), direction, weight and the need for refrigeration, but also by customer type, with those booking their own shipments getting a significant discount (Brooks and Button, 1996).[11] Also through this period, consolidation within liner shipping was rampant; the top 20 carriers by capacity on offer reported by *Containerisation International* controlled 38.8 percent of TEU capacity in 1990 (Fossey, 1990) and 52.9 percent by 1998 (Brooks, 2000). Six mergers took place from January 1996 to August 1997 and 15 takeovers between March 1995 and November 1997 (Fossey, 1998). Furthermore, the block exemption granted alliances spurred the formation of global alliances during this period, and a profound restructuring of the industry occurred in advance of the next wave of reform (Brooks, 2000), originating in the United States with the passage of the *Ocean Shipping Reform Act of 1998 (OSRA)*.

Under *OSRA*, American firms were freed to negotiate carriage arrangements as confidential service contracts covering multiple voyages (and possibly routes). The combination of this ability and the increasing growth in non-conference operations led to the situation today where ocean freight rates in the liner market are more stable for most (the largest companies negotiating term service contracts, which account for 80–90 percent of US traffic) and less stable for some (the smaller shipper without clout or those with discretionary or occasional shipments). Rates may now be more volatile, or unstable if you wish, because the routes under review have more non-conference alternatives (as conferences continue to lose players and market share on most routes[12]). The increasing presence of discussion agreements and door-to-door rates, where either is allowed,[13] further mask the truth about rate stability.[14]

The principle of 'common carriage' (that which is in short supply must be distributed equitably) has a long history in US transport regulation. However, the *Shipping Act of 1984* breached this principle by allowing service contracts, and *OSRA* abandoned its remaining vestiges in favor of less transparency and greater private contracting when it eliminated the requirement for carriers to match service contract terms for 'similarly situated' shippers (a protection mechanism for smaller shippers with reduced power in dealing with carriers[15]). The increased volatility in liner rates is obvious when Figure 37.8 is compared with Figure 37.7. The Figure 37.8 data show a range in the index for the 21 months as having a maximum of 46.5 in August of 2006, a minimum of 33.2 in December of 2006, thereby exhibiting a variability of 28 percent over the four months of the peak (pre-Christmas) shipping season in 2006. A cargo owner looking for stability must now negotiate it, and most do.

By the turn of the millennium, global carriers contemplated more than alliances as a

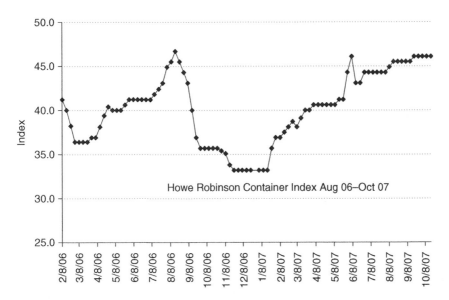

Note: Weekly data for 3300 TEU gearless 55 000 dwt 24 knots

Source: http://www.carstenrehder.de/marketreports.htm, citing Lloydslist.com data, accessed during October 2007. Data used with the permission of *Lloyd's List* (Informa).

Figure 37.8 Recent conference rates

means of competing successfully, with investments in dedicated container terminals and the development of logistics subsidiaries emerging as two new strategic responses. This diversification led to competition between global supply chains (Robinson, 2005). By 2003–2004, only three of the top ten liner operators were not classified by Notteboom and Merckx (2006) as highly developed freight integrators, a path they noted as one leading to greater profitability. According to UNCTAD (2007, p. 64), the liner industry continued its march to consolidate, with the top 20 carriers controlling 71 percent of the capacity by mid-September 2005. However, when Fusillo (2006) analysed the concentration of the industry using the Herfindahl index by trade lane, he uncovered declining concentration on a route-by-route basis in major US trade lanes. He concluded that barriers to mobility had dropped with alliances, supporting his earlier findings that liner supply was less fixed than before (Fusillo, 2004). This may go some way towards explaining why Lam et al. (2007) found that the mergers and acquisitions of 1998–2002, and the concentration of slot capacity on the transpacific route, were not accompanied by better financial performance for carriers. The market has simply become more dynamic and less predictable.

Given this market structure, and in the context of the regulation of the industry noted in Table 37.2, liner firm behavior has been largely positive, with companies adequately meeting growing world trade requirements. However, the injection of excess vessel capacity anticipated in 2008 and 2009 should have a dampening effect on prices and on the growth of the total fleet. In the short to medium term, because of the anticipated change in anti-trust immunity (discussed shortly), liner pricing, for those not engaging in confidential service contracting, is likely to become even more volatile rather than less. Prices will certainly be less transparent. On the other hand, liner regulation in Europe did not allow the conference to present a door-to-door price to the buyer, and the new regime is likely to see more service bundling. Carriers may now decide to go head-to-head against the services of a freight consolidator who quotes the cargo owner a door-to-door price. The freight forwarder or third party logistics supplier already provides a check on the power of the largest carriers. What is clear is that the largest shippers and third party logistics suppliers will get price stability via contracting.

Looking forward, what will the removal of anti-trust immunity mean for pricing and rate stability in the industry? In the run-up to the reversal of European Commission policy on anti-trust immunity, Haralambides et al. (2002) evaluated the issue of rate stability. While they argued that rates were lower but more volatile, the truth is that they could not really assess the issue because only a small share of the traffic travels on published tariffs, and this share continues to get smaller every year. The previous discussion argues that prices will be more volatile for that part of the market not using confidential service contract. The dampening factor on volatility could be the availability of pricing, capacity and demand information.

Therefore, pricing in the future could look more like pricing in the tramp market, unless a constructive agreement is made on what information may be exchanged between carriers. In a letter dated 6 August 2004, the European Liner Affairs Association (ELAA) proposed a radical change in its philosophy with respect to the way that price stability could be achieved, by achieving rate transparency via a third party information exchange system. This was a radical departure from conference carriers' long-standing and adversarial relationship with Europe's DG IV (Competition). Marlow and Nair (2006) provide an excellent summary of the debate leading up to the ELAA proposal for an information exchange system to support the industry in the period following removal of anti-trust immunity.

As noted by Benacchio et al. (2007), conference activity also declined in Europe accounting for only 40 percent of external trade by value from the EU25; they concluded that conferences do not appear to be indispensable to ensuring liner services that are both stable in price and adequate in capacity. They argued that the purpose of the tariff is to serve as a reference point for the negotiation of all other rates within and outside the conference system. The information exchange proposed by the ELAA could provide that reference; the key question then is what the information exchange will look like. In the summer of 2006, the ELAA proposed that a third-party aggregate the monthly data (in TEUs both dry and reefer (refrigerated container) by trade lane) supplied by carriers, with an 8–12 week lag in publication (Leach, 2006) The European Union (2007) response was much less specific; its September 2007 *Guidelines* about what may (or may not) be included in maritime transport co-operation agreements were quite general:

- Technical agreements on the implementation of environmental standards will be allowed (Para. 35), as will be exchanges of information necessary to the joint operation of vessels in alliances (Para. 38).
- Any information that removes uncertainty about the operation of the market so that competition may be restricted will not be allowed in the information exchange (Para. 41).

- Revelation of information that will indicate likely future conduct by liner operators will not be allowed (Para. 43).

The Commission is concerned that the exchange of information by carriers will reveal their intentions and reduce market uncertainty thereby reducing the intensity of competition. Paras. 50–58 of the *Guidelines* detail what types of information the Commission views as problematic; they include commercially sensitive information such as prices, capacity and costs, the nature of that information (individual versus aggregated), the age of the data (how recent it is), and the frequency of exchange. Para. 57 indicates that 'a price index based on appropriately aggregated data is unlikely to infringe on Article 81(1) of the Treaty, provided that the level of aggregation is such that the information cannot be disaggregated so as to allow undertakings directly or indirectly to identify the competitive strategies of their competitors.' The discussion on what the information exchange will look like in October 2008 is still a considerable way from reaching a conclusion.

On the American side of the Atlantic Ocean, the necessity of a conference exemption in the United States is certainly in question. The US Antitrust Modernization Commission (2007, p. 352) has concluded that anti-trust immunity should be removed, as 'there does not appear to be anything unique about ocean carriers that would merit holding them to a lesser standard [than other kinds of businesses]'. This has come as no surprise; the trade press predicted the burial of liner shipping in the anti-trust immunity details a year earlier (Edmonson, 2006).

The changes in liner shipping regulation, the use of sophisticated information management systems by buyers of liner services, the development of integrated supply chain operators, and the gradual reform of the industry have all been pro-competitive in nature. The liner shipping industry remains the only one with anti-trust immunity in the developed world, and that is about to disappear in Europe. When that happens, its continued existence in the United States and Canada will be irrelevant as it takes two ends of a trade route to grant it for it to be effective. Fusillo's (2006) prediction that the removal of the block exemption for conferences will be accompanied by supra-normal pricing as a result of increasing concentration and oligopoly pricing will be tested. Whether the information exchange improves stability will also be a fertile ground for future research in this industry.

CONCLUSIONS

Assessment of the link between firm strategy formulation (and implementation) and the firm's regulatory environment is a complex task. Liner regulation, with its substantial international variation in the treatment of anti-competitive activities, confers a different set of strategic advantages on liner firms from those awarded by the absence of enforcement or international regulatory consistency on tramp firms, for example.

Strategy and structure decisions are not merely influenced by managerial perception of market structure, but are driven by managerial perception of the regulatory environment and the opportunities it offers (Brooks, 2000). Regulation (or its absence or international disharmony) and each firm's strategic response form a continuous loop, each prompting the other to respond. This chapter has argued that pro-competitive regulation in both the tramp and the liner sectors have profoundly influenced managerial conduct.

The need for an interventionist role for government in the allocation of resources has diminished. As markets have liberalized, resources have been allocated more efficiently through market mechanisms. The role of the state in developing human resources and commercial infrastructure grows ever more important to the state's prosperity (Dunning, 1997); a single nation's competitiveness now rests on its ability to supply location-bound assets to attract or retain firm-specific mobile assets. Location-bound assets unfortunately have not been a feature of the shipping industry (the exception being terminal investment and sales offices), and to retain the critical foreign exchange income a shipping registry provides, governments in developing countries have been quite prepared to offer not only tax and labor advantages, but also lax enforcement of flag state obligations.

These developing countries' responses raise the bar for developed country regulators who are increasingly being called to ensure a safe and secure industry, one that addresses environmental sustainability. Regulators respond to undesirable firm behavior by imposing constraints, ranging from prescriptive commercial practices to regulations satisfying a political agenda. There is a fine balance between allowing the market to respond to greater transport demand arising from trade growth, and encouraging substandard shipping or anti-competitive behavior to emerge. Because both liner and tramp sectors have different economic drivers, market structures and ship-owner concerns, and because regulators have provided special conditions for the industry, shipping companies have taken divergent paths in their responses to regulatory discrepancies.

In tramp shipping, the theory predicts that strategies will be similar and purely opportunistic. The dominant strategy being followed is attempted cost leadership (Porter, 1980); revenue enhancement is difficult, if not precluded, by the price-taking nature of this commodity-like market. The deleterious impact of the strategy on vessel maintenance is recognized by management, resulting in a multitude of one-ship companies; this structural device isolates the owner's environmental liability and, for some, avoids owner disclosure. The current regulatory environment has a direct impact by encouraging this commonly used strategy–structure combination. Only recently, as noted by Bloor et al. (2006), has smart regulation of the type seen in port state control provided disincentives for the most blatant abuses.

In liner companies, a wide spectrum of firm responses to government regulatory conduct has developed, including strategic alliances and related diversification. The key strategic decisions for a liner firm are (1) to engage (or not) in a conference and/or a discussion agreement (about to disappear); (2) to deliver the service alone or within a consortium (alliance); (3) to grow the business organically, by joint venture or via merger (or acquisition); and (4) to diversify the business activities by investing further along the supply chain. Each of these paths has the potential for anti-competitive behavior. Because regulators have not agreed on a common multilateral approach, the result is litigation, and the application of national regulation on a subject of multi-country jurisdiction. The jurisdictional seesaw between regulators in the United States and Europe is once more about to tip. Over time this seesaw has been progressively more pro-competitive, and, when the anti-trust immunity is removed, the nature of the information exchange allowed will determine if it has tipped for the last time. In any event, this latest plan of action will render US anti-trust immunity irrelevant, and thereby effecting the recommendations of the Anti-trust Modernization Commission by default.

In sum, firm behavior in shipping companies has been directly impacted by regulatory climate – changes, enforcement of changes, or absence of regulation – albeit in different ways in different sectors. Regulatory response is prompted by a combination of that behavior and the pressure exerted on regulators by stakeholders – the general public, industry associations, and so on. Neither the IO paradigm nor the resource-based management literature adequately account for the direct impact of regulation on firm strategy–structure decisions.

Are there lessons for other industries? Shipping, which globalized earlier in the twentieth century than most industries, illustrates the challenges that accompany globalization benefits. Global firms will respond to any economic downturn by following a strategy based on the exploitation of regulatory gaps. Operating and strategic decisions made by firms are responsive to the opportunities posed and limitations imposed by the applicable regulatory framework. The globalization of industry requires multilateral mechanisms for greater harmonization of regulation applicable to industry; unilateral litigation is not preferable to multilateral consensus on appropriate regulation and enforcement.

In the modern global trading environment, the nature of competition has changed. While tramp operators have long operated in a freely competitive market, liner companies have, through gradual regulatory reform, moved in that direction. While earlier studies focused on the need for conferences to maintain price stability, and later studies (for example, Brooks, 2000) showed that alliances offered the benefits of lower costs and slot-sharing, the modern liner company has moved into a new competitive environment. Today, the services of ocean liners are complemented by port and landside operations so that competition takes place between supply chains and not solely on the ocean leg.

POSTSCRIPT

The data used in this chapter to illustrate the principles of maritime transport economics was current as of 2008. Since the writing of this chapter, the impact of the global economic crisis has become apparent, but is not yet fully appreciated. The crisis was quickly felt in the industry; softening transport market conditions in the first half of 2008 developed into serious market disequilibrium in the latter half of 2008. The question, therefore, is: what is new since these conclusions were written and do these events change the conclusions above?

There have been three significant change–response 'factors' since 2008.

First, the global economic crisis resulted in a fall of the Baltic Dry index – the index of freight rates for the movement of dry bulk cargoes – by about 90 percent over six months in 2008, and ship charter rates for bulk carriers at the end of 2008 were running 70 percent less than the rate for the same period the previous year. It was reported in London that some liner operators were carrying containers port-to-port for zero dollars just to retain customers. While there has been improvement in volumes and rates since the end of 2008, a repeat of low liner rates was rumored in August of 2010 as additional vessel capacity continued to be delivered by shipyards. As a result of the global economic crisis, and the high profile bankruptcies of some carriers, one Greek bulk owner saw the situation as an opportunity to diversify into liner shipping, and many ship owners that had been good stewards of their resources in prior years saw opportunities for acquiring cheap assets. Slow-steaming became an industry-wide response, for economic rather than environmental reasons. For ship owners, interest continued in exploiting regulatory gaps for profit but governments were loath to address regulatory issues given the fragility of many national economies and other national economic priorities. Looking forward, governments' responses to address regulatory gaps in this industry are unlikely to be found for as long as financial industry and economic health issues remain.

Second, the European Commission removal of anti-trust immunity for liner conferences came to pass and yet there has been no observable change in liner pricing strategies at the trade lane level. Tariff structures have remained as is, even in lanes where there are blatant discriminatory practices. It appears that governments lack the willpower to take on the anti-competitive pricing practices where they continue, again because they have higher economic priorities elsewhere.

Third, in the intervening period, citizen interest in environmental regulation, particularly of greenhouse gas (GHG) emissions, has grown considerably. The pressure on governments to agree to multilateral environmental regulations affecting the shipping industry was insufficient to negotiate change of a significant nature at the Copenhagen meeting. In the run-up to Copenhagen, both airline and shipping industries were pressuring for industry-led global solutions to be developed. The airline industry succeeded in getting consensus on a way forward, while the shipping industry failed to deliver its GHG plan. While multilateral progress to change regulation has failed, local and regional governments have bowed to citizen pressure in some locales and implemented stringent policies against the industry, California and New York states being good examples. Such a piecemeal regulatory response is likely to trigger long-run regulatory disharmony that ship owners will exploit.

Do these factors change the overall conclusions above? The events of the past two years have shown that the industry and its market players will continue to seek opportunities in downturns as can be expected in a globalized market; it has also shown that governments lack the political will to address regulatory gaps in tough economic times. The industry fallout from the unwillingness of governments to respond strategically has shown that regulators have lost their balance on the tightrope between the maritime transport market and citizen forces seeking change.

NOTES

1. Council Regulation (EC) 1419/2006 of 25 September 2006 repeals Council Regulation (EEC) 4056/86 rules for the application of Articles 85 and 86 of the Treaty of Rome, granting liner conferences a block exemption with respect to the fixing of rates and other conditions of carriage within the conference system. This repeal takes effect as of 18 October 2008, and is in effect regardless of what other jurisdictions may 'explicitly or tacitly' allow with respect to rate-fixing by conferences or discussion agreements.
2. Marlow and Gardner (1980) concluded that the benefits of the competitive nature of the industry accrued to the cargo-importing nation, thus arguing against market intervention by nations supplying shipping services in this market. That is, if the market is efficient, all rents will accrue to importers, and an intervention by government acting to secure advantages for exporters will be a wasteful effort at redistribution of the rents.
3. A classification society sets and maintains standards for vessel construction, and it will initially examine

the drawings of a vessel to be built to ensure that it meets 'class' standards. The society chosen by the ship owner will periodically survey the vessel and evaluate whether these standards have been maintained over time. The class of the vessel not only determines its insurance premium, but it acts as a signal of the quality of the vessel to a potential purchaser or charterer.

4. Worldscale (WS) is an index that allows comparison of freight rates for tanker routes of various sizes. The WS rate for a particular route represents a voyage charter rate for a hypothetical 75 000 dwt tanker for a particular route with WS 100 representing 100 percent of the break-even cost for such a tanker on a particular route. WS Rates are published in US$ per ton of crude oil for the voyage. Therefore if the price is listed for an alternate vessel size on the route is WS75 or WS125, it is 75 percent or 125 percent, respectively, of the annual published WS index for the route.

5. Once could take this literally, in the sense that unsafe vessels may end up on the bottom of the ocean. Here, it is meant as a race to the lowest quality.

6. Tolofari et al. (1986) found that open registries offer lower costs than traditional registries on all components of service supply.

7. The *Protocol of 1978* modified the *International Convention for the Prevention of Pollution from Ships, 1973*, becoming known as MARPOL 1978.

8. This particular incident underscored regulatory gaps in the minds of Europeans as it has been argued that the Spanish government's decisions in the handling of the stricken tanker caused the damage to be more severe than might otherwise have occurred.

9. A TEU is a twenty-foot equivalent unit or the capacity of carrying a unit of cargo $20' \times 8' \times 8'$ in dimension.

10. Economies of scale in container ship size are greater the longer the route. Technically, there are no constraints on the construction of a 15 000 TEU container ship; the reality of its commercial deployment, however, depends upon the trade route, the cargo-handling capabilities of ports on the route, and port draft. See Cullinane and Khanna (1999) for an excellent discussion on this issue.

11. Almost all liner rate research (and conclusions about what was paid) has been based on published tariffs, with the sole exception of this study of invoices (as opposed to tariffs) from a cooperative carrier. What is published (in a tariff) is not necessarily paid. Brooks and Button (1996) demonstrated that a carrier can and does quote prices that differ by type of shipper (shipper, freight forwarder or consignee), found that shippers enjoyed a 'markedly lower rate' than either freight forwarders or consignees. They also concluded that occasionally shippers pay more than the published tariff (the reason why would be a matter for speculation)!

12. There were 71 conference agreements on file in the United States as of 30 September 1988 (FMC, 1989b); prior to the implementation of OSRA, that number had dropped and by June of 2001, there were only 19 on file with the Federal Maritime Commission (FMC, 2001). When the Commission (FMC, 2001, p. 18) compared calendar years 1998 and 2000, they noted that conference service contracts fell from 596 to 3 for TACA, and from 125 to 7 for the US Australasia Agreement. Of the 1000 services contracts they surveyed, fully 98 percent were individual service contracts as opposed to multi-carrier conference service contracts. The majority of conference agreements on file within a year of implementation of *OSRA* were in the Latin American trades (FMC, 2000) as conferences came to be replaced by discussion agreements. Not only did the number of conferences decrease, but the number of members in one also deteriorated. Using the Trans-Atlantic Conference Agreement to illustrate, there were 17 members in the mid-1990s and by the beginning of 2001, only seven remained (TACA, 2001).

13. These are not allowed in Europe.

14. The European Union *White Paper* (European Union, 2004, para. 17) concluded that discussion agreements could be worse than conferences as they could 'eliminate effective external competition to conferences'.

15. Reitzes and Sheran (2002) predicted, based on their assessment of the magnitude of change following OSRA (noted *supra*, note 9), that OSRA reform would encourage liner companies to differentiate their services in ways of value to shippers, thereby diminishing the need for conferences and hastening the demise of anti-trust immunity.

REFERENCES

ACCOS, 1992, Report of the Advisory Commission on Conferences in Ocean Shipping. Washington DC, April.

Barney, J.B., 1986, Types of competition and the theory of strategy: toward an integrative framework. *Academy of Management Review*, **11** (4), 791–800.

Beenstock, M. and A. Vergottis, 1989a, An econometric model of the world market for dry cargo freight and shipping. *Applied Economics*, **21** (3), 339–356.

Beenstock, M. and A. Vergottis, 1989b, An econometric model of the world tanker market. *Journal of Transport Economics and Policy*, **23**, 263–280.

Beenstock, M. and A. Vergottis, 1993, The interdependence between the dry cargo and tanker markets. *Logistics and Transportation Review*, **29** (1), 3–38.

Benacchio, M., C. Ferrari and E. Musso, 2007, The liner shipping industry and EU competition rules. *Transport Policy*, **14** (1), 1–10.

Bloor, M., R. Darra, Y. Gilinskiy and T. Horlick-Jones, 2006, Unicorn among the cedars: on the possibility of effective 'smart regulation' of the globalized shipping industry. *Social & Legal Studies*, **15** (4), 534–551.

Brooks, M.R., 2000, *Sea Change in Liner Shipping: Regulation and Managerial Decision-Making in a Global Industry*. Oxford: Pergamon Press.

Brooks, M.R., 2003, Water transport systems and port developments. In *Transportation Planning and Engineering in Encyclopedia of Life Support Systems (EOLSS)*. Oxford: EOLSS Publishers. Available at: http://www.eolss.net.

Brooks, M.R. and K.J. Button, 1992, Shipping within the framework of a Single European Market. *Transport Reviews*, **12** (3), 237–251.

Brooks, M.R. and K.J. Button, 1996, The determinants of shipping rates: a North Atlantic case study. *Transport Logistics*, **1** (1), 21–30.

Bureau of Transport and Communications Economics (BTCE), 1994, *Structural Failure of Large Bulk Ships*. Canberra: Australian Government Publishing Service.

Caves, R.E., 1980, Industrial organization, corporate strategy and structure. *Journal of Economic Literature*, **18**, 64–92.

Clyde, P.S. and J.D. Reitzes, 1995, *The Effectiveness of Collusion Under Anti-Trust Immunity: The Case of Liner Shipping Conferences*. Washington: Federal Trade Commission.

Commission of the European Communities, 1999, Commission Decision of 16 September 1998 relating to a proceeding pursuant to Articles 85 and 86 of the EC Treaty (Case No. IV/35.134: Trans-Atlantic Conference Agreement). Official Journal of the Commission of the European Communities, L 95, 1.

Cullinane, K. and M. Khanna, 1999, Economies of scale in large container ships. *Journal of Transport Economics and Policy*, **33**, 185–208.

Cuttler, M., 1995, Incentives for reducing oil pollution from ships: the case for enhanced port state control. *Georgetown International Environmental Law Review*, **8**, 175–205.

Davies, J.E., 1986, Competition, contestability and the liner shipping industry. *Journal of Transport Economics and Policy*, **20** (3), 299–312.

Deakin, B.M. with T. Seward, 1973, *Shipping Conferences: A Study of Their Origins, Development and Economic Practices*. Cambridge: Cambridge University Press.

Donaldson, Lord of Lymington, 1994, *Safer Ships, Cleaner Seas*. London: Her Majesty's Stationery Office.

Dunning, J., 1997, *Alliance Capitalism and Global Business*. New York: Routledge.

Edmonson, R.G., 2006, Will Congress revisit OSRA. *The Journal of Commerce*, **30**, 17.

European Union, 2004, White Paper on the review of Regulation 4056/86, applying the EC competition rules to maritime transport (COM (2004) 675). Brussels, October. Available at: http://eur-lex.europa.eu/LexUriServ/site/en/com/2004/com2004_0675en01.pdf.

European Union, 2007, Guidelines on the application of Article 81 of the EC Treaty to maritime transport services. Draft, *Official Journal of the European Union*, 14 September 2007, C 215, 3–15.

Federal Maritime Commission, 1989a, *An Analysis of the Maritime Industry and the Effects of the 1984 Shipping Act*. Washington DC: Federal Maritime Commission.

Federal Maritime Commission, 1989b, 27th Annual Report for fiscal year 1988, Washington DC: Federal Maritime Commission.

Federal Maritime Commission, 2000, The Ocean Shipping Reform Act: an interim status report. Washington DC, June. Available at: http://www.fmc.gov/images/pages/OSRA_INTERIM_STATUS_REPORT.pdf.

Federal Maritime Commission, 2001, The impact of the Ocean Shipping Reform Act of 1998. September. Available at: http://www.fmc.gov/images/pages/OSRA_Study.pdf.

Fossey, J., 1990, Top 20 carriers consolidate. *Containerisation International*, June, 46–51.

Fossey, J., 1998, Winds of change. *Containerisation International*, February, 35–38.

Fusillo, M., 2004, Is liner shipping supply fixed? *Maritime Economics & Logistics*, **6** (3), 220.

Fusillo, M., 2006, Some notes on structure and stability in liner shipping. *Maritime Policy and Management*, **33** (5), 463–476.

Galbraith, J.R. and R.K. Kazanjian, 1978, *Strategy Implementation: Structure, Systems and Process*, 2nd edn. St. Paul, MN: West Publishing Company.

Gardner, B., 1985, The container revolution and its effects on the structure of traditional UK liner shipping companies. *Maritime Policy and Management*, **12** (3), 431–446.

Glen, D., 2007, Modelling of dry bulk and tanker markets. *Maritime Policy and Management*, 33 (5), 195–208.
Hamel, G. and A. Heene, 1994, *Competence-Based Competition*. New York: Wiley.
Harambides, H., A. Veenstra, M. Fusillo, W. Sjostrom and U. Hautau, 2002, Final Report for the European Commission. Rotterdam: Erasmus University, 12 November.
Heaver, T.D., 1973, The structure of liner conference rates. *Journal of Industrial Economics*, 21 (3), 257–265.
House of Representatives Standing Committee on Transport, Communication and Infrastructure, 1992, *Ships of Shame: Inquiry into Ship Safety*. Canberra: Australian Government Publishing Service.
International Monetary Fund, 2000, *International Financial Statistics Yearbook 1999*. Washington DC: International Monetary Fund.
Kavussanos, M. and I. Visivikis, 2006, Shipping freight derivatives: a survey of recent evidence. *Maritime Policy and Management*, 33 (3), 233–255.
Kreis, H.W.R., 1990, European Community competition policy and international shipping. *Fordham International Law Journal*, 13, 41–45.
Lam, J.S.L., W.Y. Yap and K. Cullinane, 2007, Conduct, structure and performance on the major liner shipping routes. *Maritime Policy and Management*, 34 (4), 359–382.
Leach, P.T., 2006, Conferring on conferences, *The Journal of Commerce*, 3, 24–25.
Lloyd's Shipping Economist, 2004–2007, Tanker and dry bulk statistics. *Lloyd's Shipping Economist*, 26 (8)–29 (8), monthly, various pages.
Marlow, P. and R. Nair, 2006, Liner shipping and information exchange: a European perspective. *Marine Policy*, 30 (6), 681–688.
Marlow, P. B. and B. Gardner, 1980, Some thoughts on the dry bulk shipping sector. *Journal of Industrial Economics*, 29 (1), 71–84.
Notteboom, T., and F. Merckx, 2006, Freight integration in liner shipping: a strategy serving global production networks. Growth and Change, 37 (4), 550–569.
Organisation for Economic Co-operation and Development (OECD), 2002, Competition policy in liner shipping. Final Report, Paris: Organisation for Economic Co-operation and Development, 16 April.
Part X Review Panel, 1993, *Liner Shipping Cargoes and Conferences*. Canberra: Australian Government Publishing Service.
Peters, H., 1993, *The Maritime Transport Crisis*. Washington DC: The World Bank.
Pirrong, S.C., 1992, An application of core theory to the analysis of ocean shipping markets. *Journal of Law and Economics*, 35, 89–131.
Porter, M.E., 1980, *Competitive Strategy: Techniques for Analyzing Industries and Competitors*. New York: Free Press.
Public Review Panel on Tanker Safety and Marine Spills Response Capability, 1990, *Protecting Our Waters*. Ottawa: Supply and Services.
Reitzes, J.D. and K.L. Sheran, 2002, Rolling seas in liner shipping. *Review of Industrial Organization*, 20, 51–59.
Robinson, R., 2005, Liner shipping strategy, network structuring and competitive advantage: a chain systems approach. In K. Cull *Shipping Economics: Research in Transportation Economics*. Vol. 12. Amsterdam: Elsevier, pp. 247–289.
Rugman, A. and A. Verbeke, 2000, Six cases of corporate strategic responses to environmental regulation. *European Management Journal*, 18 (4), 377–385.
Sampson, H. and M. Bloor, 2007, When Jack gets out of the box: the problems of regulating a global industry. *Sociology*, 41 (3), 551–569.
Scherer, F.M., 1970, *Industrial Market Structure and Economic Performance*. Chicago, IL: Rand McNally.
Schneerson, D., 1976, The structure of liner freight rates. *Journal of Transport Economics and Policy*, 10, 52–67.
Sjöstrom, W., 1989, Collusion in ocean shipping: a test of monopoly and empty core models. *Journal of Political Economy*, 97 (5), 1160–1179.
TACA, 2001, Submission of the Trans-Atlantic Conference Agreement in the matter of OECD. Discussion Paper on Regulatory Reform in International Maritime Transport. Available at: http://www.oecd.org/dataoecd/4/19/1823853.pdf.
Talley, W.K., V.B. Agarwal and J.W. Breakfield, 1986, Economies of density of ocean tanker ships. *Journal of Transport Economics and Policy*, 20 (1), 91–100.
Tamvakis, M.N. and H.A. Thanopoulou, 2000, Does quality pay? The case of the dry bulk market. *Transportation Research Part E: Logistics and Transportation Review*, 36 (4), 297–307.
Tolofari, S.R., K.J. Button and D.E. Pitfield, 1986, Shipping costs and the controversy over open registry. *The Journal of Industrial Economics*, 34 (4), 409–427.
UNCTAD, 1987, *Review of Maritime Transport 1986*. New York: United Nations.
UNCTAD, 1996, *Review of Maritime Transport 1995*. New York: United Nations.
UNCTAD, 2000, *Review of Maritime Transport 1999*. New York: United Nations.
UNCTAD, 2007, *Review of Maritime Transport 2006*. New York: United Nations.

United Kingdom Royal Commission, 1909, Report of the Royal Commission on Shipping Rings, Cd. 4668.

Urrutia, B., 2006, The EU regulatory action in the shipping sector: a historical perspective. *Maritime Economics & Logistics*, **8** (2), 202.

US Antitrust Modernization Commission, 2007, Report and recommendations. Washington, DC: Antitrust Modernization Commission. Available at: http://www.amc.gov.

World Trade Organization (WTO), 2000, Annual Report 2000. Geneva: World Trade Organization.

Wright, G., 1991, Freight rates in the tramp shipping market. *International Journal of Transport Economics*, **18**(1), 47–54.

Zerby, J.A. and R.M. Conlon, 1978, An analysis of capacity utilization in liner shipping. *Journal of Transport Economics and Policy*, **12** (1), 27–46.

Name index

Subject index